CODIFICATION OF INTERNATIONAL STANDARDS ON AUDITING AND INTERNATIONAL AUDITING PRACTICE STATEMENTS (ISAs) (ABBREVIATED)

AUDITING
An International Approach
FOURTH EDITION

Wally J. Smieliauskas, Ph.D., C.P.A., C.F.E.
Joseph L. Rotman School of Management
University of Toronto

Kathryn Bewley, Ph.D., C.A.
York University

McGraw-Hill
Ryerson

Toronto   Montréal   Boston   Burr Ridge, IL   Dubuque, IA   Madison, WI
New York   San Francisco   St. Louis   Bangkok   Bogotá   Caracas
Kuala Lumpur   Lisbon   London   Madrid   Mexico City   Milan
New Delhi   Seoul   Singapore   Sydney   Taipei

McGraw-Hill Ryerson

Auditing
An International Approach
Fourth Edition

ISBN-13: 978-0-07-095169-3
ISBN-10: 0-07-095169-1

1 2 3 4 5 6 7 8 9 10 TCP 0 9 8 7

Printed and bound in Canada

EDITORIAL DIRECTOR: Joanna Cotton
SPONSORING EDITOR: Rhondda McNabb
DEVELOPMENTAL EDITORS: Hope Miller/Marcia Luke
MARKETING MANAGER: Joy Armitage Taylor
SENIOR EDITORIAL ASSOCIATE: Christine Lomas
COPY EDITOR: Shirley Corriveau
PRODUCTION COORDINATOR: Zonia Strynatka
COVER DESIGN: Dianna Little
COVER IMAGE CREDIT: © ImageState/Almay
PAGE LAYOUT: Bookman Typesetting
PRINTER: Transcontinental Printing Group

National Library of Canada Cataloguing in Publication

Smieliauskas, Wally

    Auditing / Wally J. Smieliauskas, Kathryn Bewley. — 4th Canadian ed.

Includes index.

Second Canadian ed. written by Jack C. Robertson, Wally J. Smieliauskas

ISBN-13: 978-0-07-095169-3
ISBN-10: 0-07-095169-1

    1. Auditing—Textbooks.   I. Bewley, Kathryn, 1955-   II. Title.

HF5667.S567 2006   657'.45   C2006-904928-9

W. J. Smieliauskas dedicates this book to
Fabrice and Adrian

Kathryn Bewley dedicates this book to
her husband

About the Authors

Wally J. Smieliauskas is a professor of accounting at the University of Toronto, where he has been a member of the faculty since 1979. In 1987 he served as chair of the CAAA's Expectation Gap Task Force, which made a submission to the MacDonald Commission. Also in 1987, he co-chaired the CAAA conference that had as invited speaker Nobel laureate Herbert Simon.

Professor Smieliauskas is a certified public accountant and has worked in industry and public accounting. He spent his 1986–87 sabbatical year with the firm of Deloitte & Touche.

Professor Smieliauskas is a member of the American Institute of Certified Public Accountants, the Canadian Academic Accounting Association, and the Association of Fraud Examiners.

Professor Smieliauskas's research and writing interests include auditing and the role of accounting in society. He has published numerous articles on educational and technical topics in such journals as *Accounting Review, Contemporary Accounting Research, Journal of Accounting Research, Journal of Accounting Literature,* and *Auditing: A Journal of Practice and Theory.* In 1999, the Canadian Academic Accounting Association published his research monograph entitled "A Framework for Assurance Evidence and Its Role in Accounting." This monograph has been extensively cited and quoted in the International Federation of Accountants *Issues Paper on the Foundations of Assurance Principles* published in April 2003.

At the University of Toronto, Professor Smieliauskas developed the first degree-credit introductory auditing course (in 1981) and the first advanced auditing course (in 1990). In 1988 he was the first director of the MBA Co-op Program in Professional Accounting, a position he held until 1993. The program is designed to facilitate the entry of undergraduates from various fields into the profession, and to provide a broader management education as well as specialized training in accounting, auditing, and tax topics. It has evolved to become the Master of Management & Professional Accounting (MMPA) program now offered through the University of Toronto's Mississauga campus.

Kathryn Bewley has been a professor of accounting and auditing at York University since 1991. As well, she is a member of the Institute of Chartered Accountants of Ontario. Professor Bewley began her career in auditing with Clarkson Gordon in Toronto.

Professor Bewley has her PhD from the University of Waterloo. Her main research focus is on the impact of regulations, including auditing standards, on the information companies report and how people use that information, with a particular interest in environmental reporting. Her work has been published in several professional and academic journals.

Brief Contents

Contents

PART II

BASIC AUDITING CONCEPTS AND TECHNIQUES

Chapter 10   Audit Sampling   370

PART III

AUDIT APPLICATIONS

Chapter 11   Revenues, Receivables, and Receipts Process   423

Chapter 12   Purchases, Payables, and Payments Process   469

Chapter 13   Production and Payroll Process   510

PART IV

OTHER PROFESSIONAL SERVICES

Preface to the Fourth Edition

This is the first edition co-authored with Kate Bewley and we are sure that readers will notice the substantial improvements that have ensued. Although Kate has been involved in earlier editions, the dynamics this time have totally changed. Kate has replaced retired co-author Jack Robertson, Professor Emeritus, University of Texas at Austin. Jack has left us with a strong foundation on which to build an auditing text for the 21st century. Kate has greatly facilitated the evolution of what started as a Canadian adaptation of an American audit text into a uniquely Canadian text with an international orientation. We are confident that our approach is well suited to meeting the needs of professional accountants in an age of international convergence of audit standards. Welcome aboard, Kate!

In this our fourth edition, we have updated the myriad of professional developments that have taken place in the post-Enron environment. These include the creation of the public accountability boards and their monitoring activities, and increasing emphasis on corporate governance, internal controls, risk-based auditing, independence, and quality controls. In this edition, we summarize these developments through mid-2006, offering our perspective on their significance. We refer to this dramatically altered corporate landscape as the "post-Enron audit environment." In this new environment, we see not only radical changes in audit standards and the regulatory environment, but also significantly revised expectations of the auditor's role in corporate governance and capital markets. This environment is characterized by more risks for auditors and their clients than ever before, as well as more restrictions on non-audit services for audit clients.

Fraud, corporate governance, independence risk, the role of audit committees, global convergence of audit and accounting standards and information technology have all become more prominent since the third edition; consequently, all these issues have been updated for the fourth edition. As in past editions, we continue to provide thorough coverage of auditing at the conceptual and procedural levels. Overall, we hope that students come away with a well-rounded and forward-looking learning experience in the field of auditing.

WHAT'S NEW IN THE FOURTH EDITION

This fourth edition has a number of compelling features designed with students in mind. Each concept has been carefully developed/revised to facilitate the ease and enjoyment of your auditing learning experience. The following is a list of these integral features:

- extensive *CICA Handbook* changes through mid-2006 that incorporate a risk-based approach to auditing
- updated referencing to International Standards on Auditing (ISAs) and their convergence with Canadian auditing standards

These include:

- understanding the audit client's business, its operating environment, and risks
- assessing the risk of material misstatement in the financial statements on an assertion-by-assertion basis
- developing auditing objectives and gathering evidence with auditing procedures
- making judgements about the fair presentation of financial statement assertions
- a significant reorganization of topics, placing professional ethical and legal responsibilities at the beginning of the text, and integrating strategic systems auditing (SSA) and information technology (IT) throughout

- an innovative introduction of critical-thinking concepts integrating ethical, accounting, as well as auditing theory to help structure professional audit decision making and analysis in financial reporting
- a pioneering chapter on fraud awareness, of which fraud detection procedures are integrated in the rest of the text
- strategic systems auditing, seen in previous editions, is now used throughout the text to help explain business risk and risk-based auditing
- information systems and information technology topics integrated with the coverage of internal control and control evaluation in audit planning
- comprehensive coverage of the assurance engagement concept as it applies now to internal auditing, audits of internal control, as well as to external and public sector auditing
- website appendices on the more technical aspects of statistical sampling in auditing, corporate governance, critical thinking, integrating auditing, accounting, and ethical reasoning
- various updated anecdotes, asides, and "casettes" (short cases) that all enrich the text material
- several new critical-thinking and Internet assignment questions complement the preceding changes

KEY FEATURES

International Auditing

This edition continues the incorporation of international auditing standards. Since the last edition, the rigour and acceptability of International Standards on Auditing (ISAs) as issued by the International Federation of Accountants (IFAC) continues to grow. At the time of writing, Canadian auditing standards are in the process of harmonizing coverage with the ISAs, and thus are becoming very similar. This edition provides *CICA Handbook* Assurance section references and the corresponding ISA references whenever these exist. References to U.S. auditing standards, issued by the PCAOB for public companies and the AICPA for non-public companies, are included when these are important in the Canadian environment. This brings students to the leading edge of auditing and responds to the increasing focus on international auditing and accounting standards in the real world of business management.

CICA Handbook Assurance Recommendation Updates: Risk-based Auditing

The major change in *CICA Handbook* Assurance Recommendations since the last edition is the introduction of *CICA Handbook*, sections 5141 and 5143, requiring a risk-based approach to auditing. Related changes to other CICA Assurance Recommendations have also been incorporated. All these changes bring the CICA Assurance Recommendations closer to international auditing standards. This edition includes these newly issued standards as enacted to mid-2006, taking the view that they incorporate best practices formally into the professional standards. In particular, the new risk-based approach builds on the idea of the strategic systems approach to auditing, developed in the 1990s, that the auditor needs to understand the client's business as management runs it in order to conduct an effective audit. By formally placing these business risk assessment requirements into the standards, the CICA has linked these requirements more clearly to the generally accepted auditing standards (GAAS), which outline the required procedures and judgements supporting the auditor's opinion on whether the financial statements are materially misstated.

Fraud Auditing

This text was the first to contain full-chapter coverage of fraud awareness auditing, a crucial topic in the new millennium. With the rapid global growth in white-collar crime, especially that of fraudulent financial reporting, auditors have had to take more responsibility for fraud detection, particularly in the area of premature revenue recognition. The basic purpose of the fraud chapter (Chapter 17) is to create awareness of, and sensitivity to, the signs of potential errors, irregularities, frauds, and corruption. The chapter contains some unique insights on extended auditing and investigation procedures. In addition, fraud coverage is integrated throughout the text, consistent with the increased need for auditors to detect fraud.

Post-Enron Environment

As previously mentioned, a most compelling change to this new edition is the incorporation of a post-Enron perspective throughout the text. This perspective includes the changes to the auditing standards, the regulatory environment, and society's expectations, as well as an analysis of the significance of these changes. Specific post-Enron topics include: increased monitoring of the profession by accountability boards such as CPAB, increased emphasis on good corporate governance, the increased importance of audit committees, independence guidance, fraud risk assessments, the risk-based audit approach, and increased liability due to statutory law.

Critical Thinking

The pioneering coverage of logical argumentation in auditing has been expanded to the broader concept of critical thinking. Such an expanded approach to a more formalized skepticism incorporates assessments of the character of individuals with whom the auditor deals, the language used in the reasoning, as well as the logic of the reasoning. Such an approach to skepticism and ethical reasoning is increasingly important in detecting fraudulent financial reporting. Critical thinking provides an improved framework for tackling issues that require integration of ethical, accounting, as well as audit reasoning. Critical-thinking concepts are first introduced in Chapter 2, and then are found integrated throughout the text where appropriate, as well as in new critical-thinking discussion questions.

Learning Aids

Each chapter and section in *Auditing: An International Approach* contains a number of pedagogical features that both enhance and support the learning experience. They include the following:

- **Learning Objectives.** Each chapter opens with a new presentation of pertinent learning objectives for the following chapter material. These are repeated as marginal notes throughout the chapters. In addition, all Exercises and Problems and Discussion Cases are cross-referenced to their corresponding Learning Objectives to assist student learning.
- **Professional Standards References.** Each chapter references the relevant professional standards for the chapter topics.
- **Anecdotes and Asides.** Illustrative anecdotes and asides are found throughout the text and have been updated considerably with this new edition. Some are located within the chapter text, while others stand alone (in boxes) to add realism and interest for students. The result is a real-world flavour to the treatment of auditing.
- **Exhibits.** To assist in the learning process, we have included several more exhibits in this edition to visually illustrate teaching concepts.
- **Icons for Critical Thinking, Fraud/Ethics, International Standards, and Internet Assignments.** For quick and easy identification purposes, we have included these icons to flag the text material dealing with these major issues.

Casettes

The "casettes" are a feature, unique to this text, which are presented as short stories structured to reveal error, irregularity, or fraud in an account. An *audit approach* follows, which describes an audit objective, desirable controls, and tests of control procedures and audit of balance procedures that can result in discovering the situation. The casettes occur in the "applications" chapters (Chapters 11–14), and also in Chapter 17.

The purpose of the casettes is to enliven the study of auditing. They replace the typical lengthy exposition of auditing fundamentals with illustrative situations based on real events. There are 23 casettes with auditing approaches in the applications chapters. Another 20 casettes are in the end-of-chapter discussion case sections. The case stories are told in these and the students' assignment is to write the audit approach sections.

Key Terms

Throughout the text, key terms are highlighted in boldface print. An alphabetical key terms reference list with definitions is in the back of the text.

Kingston Case

The Kingston Company case is a practice case, which appears on the Online Learning Centre for this text (**www.mcgrawhill.ca/college/smieliauskas**), and accompanies this fourth edition. The company description starts in Chapter 6 and continues through to Chapter 15. Assignments related to the Kingston case connect many of the technical topics in a logical sequence of auditing engagement activities. However, there are numerous exercises, problems, and discussion cases at the end of each chapter that are unrelated to the Kingston Company. To enhance clarity, the case material is integrated throughout the text.

ORGANIZATION
. . . .

Part I—Introduction to Auditing and Public Practice

Part I consists of five chapters covering the basic orientation to auditing as a profession. Chapter 1 introduces the concept of auditing and the role of the public accounting profession. Chapter 2 introduces generally accepted auditing standards, assurance standards, and quality control standards, providing an overview of the audit process. Chapter 3 covers audit reports, including audits of internal control over financial reporting. Chapter 4 discusses professional ethics including a technical appendix on critical thinking. Chapter 5 covers professional legal responsibilities, including technical appendices on the effects of recent legislation and an introduction to basic corporate governance concepts as it affects the auditor.

PART II—Basic Auditing Concepts and Techniques

Part II is organized to present financial statement auditing from the business risk perspective. Chapter 6 starts this off with a discussion of how auditors obtain an understanding of the client's business, its environment, and its risks, and how this knowledge is used to assess the risk that the financial statements are materially misstated. It explains the link from the business strategy to its business processes and the related accounting cycles that create the financial statements, and describes management's assertions contained in the financial statements. Chapter 7 expands on the business understanding by giving an overview of information systems and information technology used in business to capture and report financial information, and the controls used by management to reduce risks of materially misstating this information. Chapter 8 presents the fundamental concepts and tools that are used in planning the audit fieldwork, including materiality, audit risk, evidence-gathering procedures, audit programs, and working paper documentation. Chapter 9 elaborates on internal control consideration in an audit engagement, describing control risk assessment and control testing.

The topics presented in Chapters 6 to 9 provide a basis for developing an appropriate overall strategy for the audit, the detailed audit plan, and specific programs used to perform the audit. Chapter 10 covers the pervasive concept of audit testing, how testing is affected by the audit risk model, and how representative testing can be implemented using the most simple formulas and tables from statistical sampling. An extensive appendix to Chapter 10 provides more details on the technical aspects of statistical sampling, and is located in the Online Learning Centre.

Part III—Audit Applications

Part III contains four chapters that address performing the work set out in a detailed audit plan for the main business processes that will need to be managed in every organization, and a fifth chapter that wraps it all up with audit completion considerations. The processes covered are as follows: the Revenues, Receivables, and Receipts Process (Chapter 11); the Purchases, Payables, and Payments Process (Chapter 12); the Production and Payroll Processes (Chapter 13); and the Finance and Investment Process (Chapter 14). Each of these chapters provides an overview of the transactions, balances, and risks of misstatement in the business process, the relevant controls, and auditing procedures. Short casettes are used to illustrate the application of concepts and techniques in practice, and examples of audit programs are provided to demonstrate the kinds of audit procedures that can be used. Each of these chapters also provides an overview of the balance sheet approach as a basis for the overall analysis of the financial statements. Chapter 15 presents various activities involved in completing the audit work such as the audit of the revenue and expense accounts, overall analytical review, lawyer's letters, management representation letters, subsequent events, and adjustments to the financial statements.

Part IV—Other Professional Services and Responsibilities

The three chapters in Part IV (Chapters 16 to 18) can stand alone or be integrated with the preceding chapters. Chapter 16 deals with other assurance and some non-assurance services offered by public accounting firms. Chapter 17 covers fraud awareness auditing in more detail. It gives students a better understanding of the mindset and specialized procedures needed to more effectively detect frauds. This chapter has benefited from our association with the Association of Certified Fraud Examiners. Chapter 18 introduces students to the standards, methodology, and reports of internal auditors and public sector auditors. Note that Part IV and the advanced material of earlier chapters (often located on the Online Learning Centre) can be used to develop the core topics for advanced auditing courses, if preferred.

PROFESSIONAL STANDARDS

. . . .

This text contains numerous references to authoritative statements on auditing standards and to standards governing other areas of practice. Even so, the text tries to avoid the mere repetition of passages from the standards, concentrating instead on explaining their substance and operational meaning in the context of making auditing decisions. Instructors and students may wish to supplement the text with current editions of pronouncements published by the International Federation of Accountants (IFAC), the Canadian Institute of Chartered Accountants (CICA), the Certified General Accountants Association of Canada (CGA-Canada), and the Institute of Internal Auditors (IIA).

SUPPLEMENTS

Several additional resources for introductory auditing courses are available for instructors and students:

CaseWare IDEA Software—Student Version: If practical, hands-on exposure to CaseWare IDEA is important to your course objectives, there is now the option to package a student version of CaseWare IDEA. Integrating the use of this software with the 4th edition of the text, student exercises requiring the use of CaseWare IDEA have been developed. These are integrated with the text's Kingston Company case and are available on the Online Learning Centre.

Instructors' Resource CD: The instructor support materials available on the Instructors' Resource CD include:

- *Instructors' Resource Guide*—The Instructor's Resource Guide includes a description of the Kingston Company case and a set of syllabi for organizing topical coverage. Each chapter contains suggested answers for all the review checkpoints, multiple-choice questions, Kingston Case assignments, exercises and problems, and discussion cases. Blank forms for some homework assignments can be removed and copied for the students. (Note: Also available as a downloadable from the Instructors area of the Online Learning Centre)
- *Computerized Test Bank*—The Computerized Test Bank contains numerous multiple choice, short-answer, and essay questions.
- *Microsoft® PowerPoint® Slides*—The PowerPoint® Slides offer a summary of chapter concepts for lecture purposes. (Note: Also available as a downloadable from the Instructors' area of the Online Learning Centre)

Online Learning Centre—(www.mcgrawhill.ca/college/smieliauskas): The Online Learning Centre serves as an extension of the text, providing supplements, additional content, and regularly updated material for students and instructors. The Information Centre includes such material as the text Preface, Table of Contents, and a sample chapter. The Student Edition contains an interactive student component with additional chapter questions, true/false questions, Internet exercises, and the Kingston case material and questions. New to the fourth edition are also exercises, integrated with the Kingston case, which require the use of CaseWare IDEA.

*i*Learning Sales Specialist

Your Integrated Learning Sales Specialist is a McGraw-Hill Ryerson representative who has the experience, product knowledge, training, and support to help you assess and integrate any of the following products, technology, and services into your course for optimum teaching and learning performance. Whether it's helping your students improve their grades, or putting your entire course online, your *i*Learning Sales Specialist is there to help you do it. Contact your local *i*Learning Sales Specialist today to learn how to maximize all of McGraw-Hill Ryerson's resources!

*i*Learning Services Program

McGraw-Hill Ryerson offers a unique *i*Learning Services package designed for Canadian faculty. Our mission is to equip providers of higher education with superior tools and resources required for excellence in teaching. For additional information visit http://www.mcgrawhill.ca/highereducation/iservices.

ACKNOWLEDGEMENTS
· · · · · · · · · · · ·

The International Federation of Accountants (IFAC), the Certified General Accountants Association of Canada (CGA-Canada), and the Canadian Institute of Chartered Accountants (CICA) have generously given permission for liberal quotations from official pronouncements and other publications, all of which lend authoritative sources to the text. In addition, several publishing houses, professional associations and accounting firms have granted permission to quote and extract from their copyrighted material. Their co-operation is much appreciated because a great amount of significant auditing thought exists in this wide variety of sources.

We are also very grateful to the staff at McGraw-Hill Ryerson who provided their support, management skills, and ideas—especially our developmental editor, Hope Miller, whose hard work and attention to detail kept us on track and transformed what we wrote into a book.

A special acknowledgement is due Joseph T. Wells, former chairman of the Association of Certified Fraud Examiners. He created the Certified Fraud Examiner (CFE) designation. Mr. Wells is a well-known authority in the field of fraud examination education and his entrepreneurial spirit has captured the interest of fraud examination professionals throughout North America.

Special acknowledgement is also due to Steven E. Salterio of Queen's University. Steven contributed greatly to the strategic systems approach to auditing used in this text.

This text could not have been completed without the co-operation and input of our many auditing students over the years. Special thanks go to Enola Stoyle for material that was adapted in various forms in this text.

We are grateful to many people involved in the auditing profession in various roles who generously shared their time and ideas with us over the years as the new materials for the book took shape in our minds and on paper, including Jean Bédard, Janne Chung, Susan McCracken, Steve Fortin, Geneviève Turcotte, John Carchrae, James Sylph Alan Willis, Robert Langford, Andre de Haan, Joy Keenan, Sylvia Smith, Dianne Hillier, Jan Munro, Greg Shields, and Karen Duggan.

We would like to acknowledge our appreciation for the great academics and practitioners, who influenced us in various ways as we developed this text, including Ron Gage, Al Rosen, Randy Keller, Don Cockburn, Dagmar Rinne, Morley Lemon, Ingrid Splettstoesser-Hogeterp, Don Leslie, Larry Yarmolinsky, Bill Scott, Efrim Boritz, Joel Amernic, Donna Losell, Ulrich Menzefricke, Russell Craig, Kevin Lam, Yoshihide Toba, Takatoshi Hayashi, Ping Zhang, Hung Chan, Len Brooks, Manfred Schneider, and Irene Wiecek. Also, we have been inspired often by Rod Anderson's 1984 text, *The External Audit*, which set out a logical conceptual framework for auditing still stands the test of time.

And lastly, our sincere thanks go out to all the reviewers for their careful review and many detailed and candid comments that were extremely useful in revising this new edition: Christopher Batch of Wilfrid Laurier University, Ralph Cecere of McGill University, Peggy Coady of Memorial University, Vincent Durant of St. Lawrence College, Brian and Laura Friedrich of CGA-Canada, Concetta Gillard of Athabasca University, W. E. Gough of Centennial College, Tom Kozloski of Wilfrid Laurier University, Shirley Lamarre of CGA-Canada, Donna Losell of University of Toronto, Brad MacDonald of the Saskatchewan Institute of Applied Science and Technology, Christine Maher of Conestoga College, Stuart Munro of Sheridan College, Jagdish Pathak of University of Windsor, Louis W. Petro of University of Windsor, Rand Rowlands of George Brown College, Stephen Spector of Simon Fraser University, and Joan Wallwork of Kwantlen University College.

Wally Smieliauskas and Kate Bewley
June 2006

PART I
Introduction to Auditing, Public Practice, and Professional Responsibilities

CHAPTER
1

Professional Practice

Chapter 1 gives you an introduction to professional accounting practice. Other accounting courses helped you learn the principles and methods of accounting, but here you will begin to study the ways and means of practising accounting and auditing outside the classroom.

LEARNING OBJECTIVES

After completing this chapter, you will be able to:

1. Explain the importance of auditing.

2. Distinguish auditing from accounting.

3. Explain the role of auditing in information risk reduction.

4. Describe the current audit environment, including regulatory oversight.

5. Describe the other major types of audits and auditors.

6. Outline how public accountants (PAs) are regulated.

7. Provide an overview of international auditing.

8. Research websites on accounting and auditing activities of PA organizations. (Appendix 1A)

9* Chronicle the historical development of auditing standards, including the criticisms and responses of the profession. (Appendix 1B)

10* Describe alternative theories of the role of auditing in society. (Appendix 1C)

* Learning objectives marked with an asterisk (*) and their corresponding topics are considered advanced material. *Note:* Appendices 1B and 1C are located on the text Online Learning Centre.

INTRODUCTION: THE COMING OF AGE OF THE AUDIT SOCIETY

LEARNING OBJECTIVE

1 Explain the importance of auditing.

Auditing is a field of study that has received considerable media attention lately. In fact, in the business press, audit-related issues are mentioned daily. Headlines such as "Auditors: The Leash Gets Shorter," "The Betrayed Investor," "Dirty Rotten Numbers," and "Accounting in Crisis" indicate that the attention has not been all positive. This attention arises from the fact auditing is critical to the proper functioning of capital markets. And, when audits are perceived to fail, capital markets can fail as well. Without effective audits modern capitalist societies cannot fulfill their role of being the most efficient economic systems resulting in the highest living standards. An example of an effective auditor follows:

AN EXAMPLE OF AN EFFECTIVE AUDITOR

Molex incorporated is a $2.2 billion electronics manufacturer headquartered in Chicago. In late 2004 Molex's auditor, Deloitte and Touche, complained that CEO J. Joseph King and his chief financial officer had not disclosed that they allowed a bookkeeping error worth 1% of net income into the audited results. When the auditor demanded on Nov. 13 that King be removed from office, the board initially stood behind the CEO with a unanimous vote.

Then Deloitte did something unexpected: It quit. Two weeks later the firm wrote a blistering and detailed account of the affair for public disclosure at the SEC. That virtually assured that no auditor would work for Molex again as long as King was in charge. Within 10 days the directors had eaten crow: They ousted King, promised to hire a new director with financial expertise for their audit committee, and agreed to take training classes in proper financial reporting.

Source: "The Boss on the Sidelines," *Business Week*, April 25, 2005, p. 94.

The preceding example illustrates effective auditors in the new business environment of the early twenty-first century. The role of audits is so critical to advanced capitalism that some refer to such societies as **audit societies**. Audit societies are those in which there is extensive monitoring of economic (and other politically important) activities to help assure that capital markets are efficient. Audit societies also include those in which auditors monitor the effectiveness and efficiency of government. For example, the Gomery commission inquiry (www.gomery.ca) that caused a political uproar in Canada in 2005 began as a result of an audit investigation of questionable sponsorship payments that resulted in "no value" for taxpayer money spent. As a result of these and similar developments, auditing is increasingly recognized as part of a broader process of social control. This expanding role of auditing is at the heart of the audit society concept.[1]

But what exactly is auditing? Simply put, **auditing** is the verification of information by someone other than the one preparing the information. Since there are many types of information, there can be many types of audits. Most of this text focuses on audits of financial statement information or *financial statement auditing* for short. Before describing auditing in more detail, we will try to make financial statement auditing more intuitive with a simple illustration.

A Simple Illustration of the Importance of Auditing

Assume you have always wanted to run your own business, say, a Thai food restaurant. After some searching, you find an owner who wants to retire and is willing to sell his busy

---

[1] M.P. Power, *The Audit Society* (New York: Oxford University Press, 1997).

restaurant in a choice location of a major metropolitan area for $3 million. One of the first things you ask yourself is whether the business is worth the $3 million asking price. How do you do that?

One thing you can do is find out the price of similar properties—comparison shopping. But ultimately, you must decide on the value of this particular business. This is when accounting information can be useful. Accounting helps answer such questions as: What is the business's net worth (assets – liabilities)? What is its profitability?

Let's say the owner of the restaurant claims annual profit of $600,000. First you would want to reach an agreement on how the profit is calculated. Should it be on a cash basis? Before tax? After tax? Calculated under generally accepted accounting principles? These are the possible criteria you would use in measuring the profitability (earnings) of the business.

Once you decide on the criteria for measurement you need to use a decision rule with your measurement. Businesses are frequently valued on some multiple of earnings. For example, if you are willing to pay five times current earnings (properly calculated using your agreed criteria) and the current owner reports $600,000 earnings annually, then you would be willing to pay five times $600,000 or $3 million for the business. So you need accounting information to establish that $600,000 is the current earnings number.

But the owner prepares the accounting records. How do you know that they are accurate? There may be errors because the owner has not kept good records. Or, worse, the owner has a conflict of interest and may inflate earnings in order to get a higher price for the business than it is really worth. In other words, you are concerned with the risk of overpayment of your investment.

For example, if the earnings are only $500,000 then the most the business is worth to you is five times $500,000 or $2.5 million rather than the $3 million asking price. There is always the risk that the owner, in this case also the preparer of the financial information, is overstating earnings so that he will be paid more than his business is worth.

In order to reduce this risk, what can you do? Hire an auditor! To minimize these risks you want assurance that the $600,000 figure reported by the current owner is accurate.

The auditor can help you by verifying the earnings are as the owner asserts. The earnings can be on whatever basis you agree to, usually **generally accepted accounting principles (GAAP)**. The auditor can be used to independently and competently verify the earnings so that you will have more confidence (more assurance) on the numbers you are basing your decision on. The auditor increases the reliability or reduces the risk of the information you are using in your decision making. For example, if the auditor verifies that earnings are really $400,000, then you would be unwilling to pay more than five times $400,000 or $2 million for the restaurant. The difference between the original asking price ($3 million) and what you should actually pay ($2 million) is an illustration of the value of the audit— in this case $1 million. Therefore, if the audit fee is under $1 million you would be better off having an audit. We hope that this simplified example enables you to see the potential value of auditing in investment decision making.

In general, as long as the audit fee is less than expected savings (expected value of audited information) in reducing uncertainty about earnings and value, you should consider hiring an auditor to do the verification work. This example also illustrates how auditing provides more general social services. The restaurant owner can retire getting a fair price for his business, and you can achieve your dream of owning a restaurant and being your own boss. This is accomplished by using a fair exchange price based on reliable (accurate, trustworthy) information.

The transaction entries that you learn in your accounting courses are part of the raw data auditors deal with. The summarization of all the transactions over a period is achieved through the financial statements. So when auditors verify the reliability of this information, they reduce the risk associated with the financial statements, frequently referred to as **information risk**.

Now, imagine this illustration extended to all investors contemplating even a partial ownership of a business, for example, investors in the stock market, and you will have some idea of how auditing can facilitate efficient economic activities by reducing financial information risk. And, when auditors fail to do a proper job of verification (that is, fail to reduce information risk), the type of headlines noted at the beginning of this section can result.

Note that when you make an investment you agree to enter into a contract to purchase from another party. Let us call you, the investor, the first party and the seller, the second party. Notice, however, that there is a third party, the auditor. The auditor is a third independent party hired to verify the information provided by the second party. Why is the auditor hired? Basically, an auditor is hired because you, the first party, do not trust the information provided by the second party. You feel the information risk is too high; therefore, you hire the third-party auditor to provide independent verification of the information provided by the second party. We refer to this relationship throughout the text as **three-party accountability**. In an audit society this three-party accountability is so institutionalized that regulators require certain second parties to pay for the audit. In particular, companies whose shares are traded on regulated stock exchanges (public companies) are required to hire an independent auditor to audit the annual financial statements. The accountability is still three party because the purpose of the audit is to reduce information risk for the first party, but the public company second party pays the audit fee.

Three-party accountability is illustrated in Exhibit 1–1. It is represented as a triangle because there are three parties: the auditor of the financial information, management that prepares the financial information, and the users of the financial information. One reason the triangle reflects an **accountability relationship** is that management is accountable to the users; however, the users do not trust management sufficiently to rely on their financial statements. To reduce these doubts, the users demand that the financial statements be verified by a competent, independent third party—the auditor. Thus, the auditor is also accountable to the user to properly verify the financial information. This three-party accountability is an important distinguishing feature of auditing and pertains to many engagements. Exhibit 1–1 indicates how three-party accountability applies to Molex and the Thai restaurant examples given previously.

Three-party accountability is important because it distinguishes the type of services that only auditors can provide from other services, such as tax work and business advisory services, that anyone can provide. We will clarify this important concept throughout the rest of the text, especially Chapters 2 and 16. For now, think of it as reducing the information risk on information created by the second party, the preparer of the information. Reducing information risk is synonymous with improving the credibility of, or providing assurance on, information produced by the second party.

EXHIBIT   1–1   THREE PARTIES INVOLVED IN AN AUDITING ENGAGEMENT
(THREE-PARTY ACCOUNTABILITY)

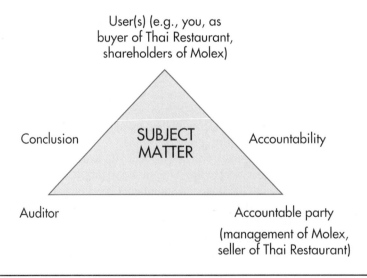

We hope you found the preceding illustrations useful. Next, we further clarify the roles of accounting and auditing in the financial reporting environment.

USER DEMAND FOR RELIABLE INFORMATION

Accounting

LEARNING OBJECTIVE
2 Distinguish *auditing* from *accounting.*

The following three underlying conditions affect demand by users for accounting information:

1. **Complexity.** A company's transactions can be numerous and complicated. Users of financial information are not trained to collect and compile it themselves. They need the services of professional accountants.
2. **Remoteness.** Users of financial information are usually separated from a company's accounting records by distance and time, as well as by lack of expertise. They need to employ full-time professional accountants to do the work they cannot do for themselves.
3. **Consequences.** Financial decisions are important to the state of investors' and other users' wealth. Decisions can involve large dollar amounts and massive efforts. The consequences are so important that good information, obtained through the financial reports prepared by accountants, is an absolute necessity.

Accounting is the process of recording, classifying and summarizing into financial statements a company's transactions that create assets, liabilities, equities, revenues and expenses. It is the means of satisfying users' demands for financial information that arise from the forces of complexity, remoteness and consequences. The function of **financial reporting** is to provide statements of financial position (balance sheets), statements of results of operations (income statements), cash flow statements and accompanying disclosure notes (footnotes) to outside decision makers who have no internal source of information like the management of the company has. A company's accountants are the producers of such financial reports. In short, accounting tries to record and summarize economic reality for the benefit of economic decision makers (the users).

Due to advances in **information technology (IT)**, the form in which accounting records are stored has changed dramatically over the past few decades. Although these changes have affected the form and logic of audit evidence, the basic role of verification for users and their decision-making needs has not changed.

The goal of generally accepted accounting principles (GAAP), which you studied in your financial accounting courses, is to yield financial statements that represent as faithfully as possible the economic conditions and performance of a company. This is why GAAP is the most common criteria used in preparing financial statements. However, as illustrated in the introduction, auditors are independent financial reporting external experts that are frequently asked to verify that these goals are met by the preparers of financial statements.

**R E V I E W
CHECKPOINTS**   1.1   Explain how the auditor can help you in your investment decision making.

More on Auditing

Financial decision makers usually obtain their accounting information from companies that want to obtain loans or sell stock. This source of information creates a potential **conflict of interest**, which is a condition that creates society's demand for audit services. Users need more than just information; they need reliable error-free information. Preparers and issuers (directors, managers, accountants and others employed in a business) might benefit by giving false, misleading or overly optimistic information. The potential conflict has become real

PART I   Introduction to Auditing, Public Practice, and Professional Responsibilities

enough to create a natural scepticism on the part of users. Thus, they depend on professional auditors to serve as objective intermediaries who will lend some credibility to financial information. This "lending of credibility" is also known as **providing assurance**, and external auditing of financial statements is described as an **assurance engagement**.

Auditing does not include the function of financial report production. That function is performed by a company's accountants under the direction of its management. Auditors obtain evidence that enables them to determine whether the information in the financial statements is reliable. Auditors then report to the users that the information is reliable by expressing an opinion that the company's presentation of financial position, results of operations and cash flows statement are in accordance with GAAP, or some other disclosed basis of accounting. This opinion is the assurance provided by the assurance function, as it relates to the traditional financial statements. Assurance always requires three-party accountability, as discussed previously.

When the auditor is external to and independent of the party preparing the financial information, the term **external auditor** is often used. Auditors must be independent of the production of the information that is audited in order to achieve three-party accountability. External auditors are separate firms that can provide a range of services to outside parties in addition to external audits. Because of this broader range of activities, external auditing firms are also frequently referred to as "public accounting firms."

External auditors work for clients. A **client** is the person (company, board of directors, agency or some other person or group) who retains the auditor and pays the fee. In financial audits the client and the auditee usually are the same economic entity. The **auditee** is the actual designation of the company or other entity whose financial statements are being audited. Occasionally the client and the auditee are different. For example, if Conglomerate Corporation hires and pays the auditors to audit Newtek Company in connection with a proposed acquisition, Conglomerate is the client and Newtek is the auditee.

As explained previously, reliable financial information helps make capital markets efficient and helps people understand the consequences of a wide variety of economic decisions. External auditors practising the assurance function are not, however, the only auditors at work in the economy. Bank examiners, Canada Revenue Agency auditors, provincial regulatory agency auditors (e.g., auditors with a province's Commissioner of Insurance), internal auditors employed by a company, and the office of the Auditor General of Canada all practise auditing in one form or another.

- -

REVIEW CHECKPOINTS

1.2   What is auditing? What condition creates demand for audits of financial reports?

1.3   What is the difference between a client and an auditee? What are the three parties in three-party accountability?

1.4   What is the difference between auditing and accounting?

1.5   What conditions create demand for financial reports, and who produces financial reports for external users?

- -

DEFINITIONS OF AUDITING
- - - - - - - - - - - -

Definitions of Auditing

In 1971, the American Accounting Association (AAA) Committee on Basic Auditing Concepts prepared a comprehensive definition of auditing as follows:

> Auditing is a systematic process of objectively obtaining and evaluating evidence regarding assertions about economic actions and events to ascertain the degree of correspondence between the assertions and established criteria and communicating the results to interested users.

This definition contains several ideas important in a wide variety of audit practices. The first and most important concept is the perception of auditing as a systematic process that is purposeful, logical and based on the discipline of a structured approach to decision making. Auditing is not haphazard, unplanned or unstructured.

The audit process, according to this definition, involves obtaining and evaluating evidence that consists of all the influences that ultimately guide auditors' decisions, and relates to assertions about economic actions and events. When beginning an audit engagement, an external auditor is given financial statements and other disclosures by management and thus obtains management's assertions about economic actions and events (assets, liabilities, revenue, expense). Evidence is then acquired that either substantiates or contradicts these management assertions.

External auditors generally begin work with explicit representations from management—assertions of financial statement numbers and information disclosed in footnotes. Other auditors, however, are typically not so well provided with explicit representations. An internal auditor, for example, may be assigned to "evaluate the cost effectiveness of the company's policy to lease, rather than to purchase, heavy equipment." A governmental auditor may be assigned to determine, for example, whether goals of creating an environmental protection agency have been met by the agency's activities. Often times, these latter two types of auditors must develop the explicit standards of performance for themselves. This latter type of engagement is called **direct reporting**.

The purpose of obtaining and evaluating evidence is to ascertain the degree of correspondence between the assertions and established criteria. Auditors will ultimately communicate their findings to interested users. To communicate in an efficient and understandable manner, there must be a common basis for measuring and describing financial information. Such a basis constitutes the established criteria essential for effective communication.

Established criteria may be found in a variety of sources. For external auditors, governmental auditors and Canada Revenue Agency inspectors, the criteria largely consist of the GAAP. Canada Revenue Agency inspectors also rely heavily on criteria specified in federal tax acts. Government auditors may rely on criteria established in legislation or regulatory agency rules. Bank examiners and provincial insurance board auditors look to definitions and rules of law. Internal and governmental auditors rely extensively on financial and managerial models of efficiency and economy, as well as on generally accepted accounting principles. All auditors rely to some extent on the elusive criteria of general truth and fairness.

Exhibit 1–2 on the next page depicts an overview of financial statement auditing.

Audit Objective and the Auditor's Report

The American Accounting Association definition is sufficiently broad and general to encompass external, internal and governmental auditing. Although the Canadian Institute of Chartered Accountants (CICA) has not defined auditing, its Assurance Handbook Recommendation, "Audit of Financial Statements—An Introduction," in section 5090 sets forth the main objective of a financial audit as follows:

> The objective of the audit of financial statements is to express an opinion whether the financial statements present fairly, in all material respects, the financial position, results of operation and cash flows in accordance with generally accepted accounting principles, or in special circumstances another appropriate disclosed basis of accounting. Such an opinion is not an assurance as to the future viability of an entity nor an opinion as to the efficiency or effectiveness with which its operations, including internal control, have been conducted. . . . In the performance of an audit of financial statements, the auditor complies with generally accepted auditing standards (GAAS), which (as set out in paragraph 5100.02) relate to the auditor's qualifications, the performance of the audit and the preparation of his or her report.[2]

---

[2] The Auditing Recommendations of the *CICA Handbook* are authoritative CICA pronouncements on auditing theory and practice.

EXHIBIT 1-2   OVERVIEW OF FINANCIAL STATEMENT AUDITING

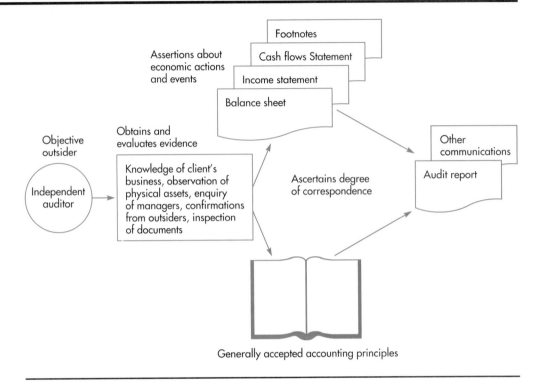

The CICA statement of objective restricts auditing interest to external auditors' audit of the traditional financial statements and their footnotes. However, as the needs of users change, new audit objectives and reports are created to meet new needs. Thus, the *CICA Handbook* also offers guidance on such divergent topics as reporting on control procedures at service organizations, on matters related to solvency, and on examination of a financial forecast in a prospectus. A set of evolving "assurance standards" (presented in Chapter 2) may provide a framework to govern a wide range of assurance services.

The expression of the auditor's opinion on financial statements is found in the last paragraph of the audit report. A standard report is shown in Exhibit 1–3. (Chapter 3 explains this and other audit reports in more detail.)

EXHIBIT 1-3   AUDITOR'S REPORT

To the Shareholders of.....................

I have audited the balance sheet of .... as at ...., 20......, and the statements of income, retained earnings and cash flows for the year then ended. These financial statements are the responsibility of the company's management. My responsibility is to express an opinion on these financial statements based on my audit.

I conducted my audit in accordance with Canadian generally accepted auditing standards. Those standards require that I plan and perform an audit to obtain reasonable assurance whether the financial statements are free of material misstatement. An audit includes examining, on a test basis, evidence supporting the amounts and disclosures in the financial statements. An audit also includes assessing the accounting principles used and significant estimates made by management, as well as evaluating the overall financial statement presentation.

In my opinion, these financial statements present fairly, in all material respects, the financial position of the company as at ...., 20......, and the results of its operations and the changes in its cash flows for the year then ended in accordance with Canadian generally accepted accounting principles.

City

Date

(signed)...

Chartered Accountants

Source: *CICA Handbook*, paragraph 5400.22.

A Definition of Auditing Relating to "Risk Reduction"

LEARNING OBJECTIVE

3 Explain the role of auditing in information risk reduction.

Although it is sometimes difficult to distinguish between a definition and a theory, most statements of theory begin with a definition. A theoretical viewpoint currently gaining popularity is that auditing is a "risk-reduction activity." The definition that supports this view is: Auditing is a process of reducing (to a socially acceptable level) the information risk to users of financial statements.

Economic activity takes place in an atmosphere of **business risk**. Business risks result from significant conditions, events, circumstances or actions that could adversely affect the entity's ability to achieve its objectives and execute its strategies.[3] Auditors do not directly influence a company's business risk, but they are responsible for proper disclosure of these risks in the financial statements. As the complexity of the business world grows, auditors are finding that they must increasingly focus their efforts in understanding the client's business risks. This understanding is necessary if the increased business complexity is to be properly reflected in the financial statements.

Information risk refers to the failure of the financial statements to appropriately reflect the economic substance of business activities, including business risks and uncertainties. In particular, information risk from the auditor's perspective is the risk (probability) that the financial statements distributed by a company will be materially false and misleading. **Materiality**, as used in auditing, has the same meaning as it does in your accounting courses. Basically, a material misstatement is one that would affect user decision making.

Financial analysts and investors depend on financial reports for making stock purchase and sale decisions. Creditors (suppliers, banks and so on) use them to decide whether to give trade credit and bank loans. Labour organizations use financial reports to help determine a company's ability to pay wages. Government agencies and Parliament use them in preparing analyses of the economy and in making laws concerning taxes, subsidies and the like. These various users cannot take it upon themselves to determine whether financial reports are reliable and, therefore, low on the information-risk scale. The users do not have the expertise, resources, or time to enter thousands of companies to satisfy themselves about the veracity of financial reports; thus, they hire independent auditors to perform the assurance function and reduce the information risk. Auditors assume the social role of attesting to published financial information, thereby offering users the valuable service of assurance that the information risk is low. This role of auditors has been institutionalized through laws and regulations.

This risk-reduction definition may appear very general. As your study of auditing continues, you will find that auditors perform many tasks whose primary objective is to reduce the risk of giving an inappropriate opinion on financial statements. Auditors are careful to work for trustworthy clients, to gather and analyze evidence about the data in financial statements and to take steps to ensure that audit personnel report properly on the financial statements when adverse information is known. Subsequent chapters of this text will have more to say about various information risk-reduction activities.

R E V I E W
C H E C K P O I N T S

1.6   What would you answer if asked by an anthropology major: "What do auditors do?"

1.7   What is the essence of the risk-reduction definition of auditing?

[3] www.camagazine.com.

THE CURRENT ENVIRONMENT OF AUDITING

. . . .

LEARNING OBJECTIVE
4 Describe the current audit environment, includ-
ing regulatory oversight.

The audit environment has undergone profound changes as a result of spectacular corporate failures in North America such as Enron and WorldCom in 2002. This section briefly summarizes these changes. Later chapters explain the audit significance of these changes in more detail. Appendix 1B on the text website provides a brief overview of the history of the profession leading up to these changes.

As a result of these and other corporate scandals, the integrity of North American capital markets is being questioned all over the world. WorldCom's failure was the last straw, prompting the passage of the most drastic legislation to affect the accounting profession since 1933.

The Sarbanes-Oxley Act

On July 30, 2002, President Bush signed the U.S.'s *Sarbanes-Oxley Act (SOX)* into law. This legislation had been progressing through Congress since the fall of Enron. The WorldCom failure catalyzed the legislative process and guaranteed quick passage and approval by President Bush. The SOX created a five-member **Public Company Accounting Oversight Board (PCAOB)** with the authority to tighten quality control of audit practices and report on the results of inspections of audit firm practices. The full ramifications of SOX will become known only as the SEC and PCAOB begin implementing this legislation. But the following are key features:

- increased penalties for corporate wrongdoers
- more timely and extensive financial disclosures
- new options of recourse for aggrieved shareholders

SOX and the financial disasters that preceded it have had a huge impact on corporate governance and the regulation of accounting and auditing around the world. For example, in Canada, the CICA has recently helped organize the creation of its own **Canadian Public Accountability Board (CPAB)** to oversee the auditors of public companies. The CPAB also tightens quality control of audit practice and report on inspections of audit firm practices. In addition, several of Canada's largest pension and mutual funds banded together in 2002 to form the **Canadian Coalition for Good Governance**. This organization, which controls $400 billion in assets, is monitoring executives, audit committees, auditors, and boards of directors in corporate Canada for compliance with what they consider good corporate governance and financial reporting practices. However, in Canada, for the time being at least, the profession continues to be self-regulating. Under SOX in the U.S., the profession will be much more constrained under the PCAOB.

The PCAOB's composition was finalized in April 2003. Its first actions included the following: (1) conducting an inspection of the Big Four accounting firms, (2) creating a registry system for PA firms, (3) conducting a review of existing audit standards, and most importantly, (4) taking on the task of setting future audit standards in the U.S. The last action is noteworthy in that it represents the first time in the American profession's history that auditing standards will not be set by its professional institute, the AICPA. The corporate failures, such as Enron and WorldCom in 2002, the fall of Arthur Andersen, and the resulting passage of SOX dramatically changed the corporate environment. We refer to this changed world as the **post-Enron world**. These actions by the PCAOB reflect the dramatically increased regulation of the profession in the post-Enron world.

In the post-Enron world, auditors of public companies are increasingly finding that their work is being second-guessed by regulators. The Canadian, U.S., and other accountability boards around the world will likely make this second-guessing of professional judgement a permanent fixture of the audit environment.

The post-Enron world is a more complicated one for auditors and the profession. However, auditing will likely become more important to accounting firms and to society. As the post-Enron world unfolds, the implications for the profession will become clearer. The specific effects that were evident in 2006 are included in this text.

Until 2002, the accounting profession was largely self-regulating around the world. By **self-regulation** we mean the profession established the rules that governed audit practice and monitored compliance with these rules. This trust in a self-regulatory audit profession changed with the corporate scandals of 2002/2003 along with the perceived failure of the profession to detect these problems. The crucial role of auditing in well-functioning capitalist societies had been made clear as never before.

But this increased attention came at a price: it was no longer considered acceptable to limit monitoring of the profession to the professionals themselves because it had become painfully obvious how the profession's perceived failures impacted extensively on the markets. The markets hit multi-year lows at the height of the corporate scandals on 2002, just about when WorldCom declared its bankruptcy and prompted the speedy passage of the SOX legislation in the U.S. SOX basically provides more external monitoring and control of the profession. External monitoring includes groups representing more of the broader public interest, as well as the government. The mix of monitors depends on the country. Since most of the corporate failures that prompted the changes took place in the U.S., America has tended to lead in promoting new ways of providing oversight of auditors, and the instrument of their change mechanism is SOX. The influence of SOX has spread throughout the world and in much broader areas of corporate activities as we will see shortly.

SOX has broad corporate consequences. We begin with a quick overview of its main impact on auditors.

- public management certification for financial reporting
- a new audit report on the new internal control statements made by management
- closer regulation of the profession, including regular monitoring of its activities
- greater responsibilities assigned to client audit committees
- increasing importance of the role of the internal auditor

Internal control statements are statements about the reliability of the system or process that creates the financial statements.[4] We will discuss the evolving concept of internal control in much greater detail throughout the rest of this text.

Perhaps the most important result of SOX has been the increased monitoring of the profession and its many consequences for the auditor. The influence of SOX in Canada has led to the creation of accountability boards. These boards have quite different authorities and responsibilities than their American counterparts because of differences in the legal systems and political institutions between the two countries.

In the U.S., the PCAOB has nation-wide legislative backing for its monitoring and enforcement activities. PCAOB has final authority on auditing standards, ethical, independence standards, and quality control criteria that will be used to monitor the profession. Monitoring reports are made available to the public at www.pcaob.org/inspection.

In Canada, the CPAB does *not* have legislative backing. This means that if an accounting firm claims legal privilege of client confidentiality, the CPAB cannot review those client documents. This restriction has put a constraint on the CPAB's monitoring activities. Also, the CPAB is directly funded by the audit firms and some have questioned its independence of the profession. In contrast, the PCAOB is directly funded by the SEC. Finally, the CPAB uses the profession's auditing, ethics, independence, and quality control standards in performing its monitoring. However, like the PCAOB, the CPAB issues reports on its monitoring that are made public at www.cpab-ccrc.org.

---

[4] We deviate from official terminology by always referring to "reports" as auditor-prepared and "statements" as management-prepared communications.

The first two elements of SOX relate to increased management responsibility for financial reporting and required external audit of the internal control statement prepared by management. Management certification of financial reporting means that management must state in writing that it is not aware of any factual errors or omissions of facts that would make the financial and internal control statements misleading. These elements are best summarized as attempts to strengthen the system of corporate governance generally. Corporate governance principles are covered in Appendix 5A. Audit committees and internal auditing are also covered in more detail later.

REVIEW CHECKPOINTS

1.8   What is meant by self-regulation? How is self-regulation for the profession being affected in the post-Enron environment?

1.9   What are the differences between Canadian and U.S. accountability boards?

OTHER KINDS OF AUDITS AND AUDITORS

LEARNING OBJECTIVE

5 Describe the other major types of audits and auditors.

The AAA, CICA, and the risk-reduction definitions apply to the financial audit practice of independent external auditors who practise auditing in public accounting firms. The word *audit*, however, is used in other contexts to describe broader kinds of work.

The variety of audit work performed by different kinds of auditors causes some problems with terminology. Hereafter in this text, "independent auditor," "external auditor," "chartered accountant (CA)," "certified general accountant (CGA)" and "public accountant (PA)" will refer to people doing audit work with public accounting firms. In the governmental and internal contexts following, auditors are identified as governmental auditors, operational auditors, and internal auditors. While many of these auditors are chartered accountants or certified general accountants, the initials *PA, CA* and *CGA* in this text will refer to auditors in public practice. (Internal and governmental audit work is covered in more detail in Chapter 18.) We will use the neutral term *PA* as much as possible in this text.

Internal and Operational Auditing

The Institute of Internal Auditors (IIA) defined **internal auditing** and stated its objective as follows:

> Internal auditing is an independent, objective assurance and consulting activity designed to add value and improve an organization's operations. It helps an organization accomplish its objectives by bringing a systematic, disciplined approach to evaluate and improve the effectiveness of risk management, control, and governance processes.[5]

Internal auditing is practised by auditors employed by an organization, such as a bank, hospital, city government or industrial company. Some internal auditing activity is known as **operational auditing**. Operational auditing (also known as **performance auditing** and **management auditing**) refers to the study of business operations for the purpose of making recommendations about the economic and efficient use of resources, effective achievement of business objectives and compliance with company policies. The goal of operational auditing is to help managers discharge their management responsibilities and improve profitability.

Internal and operational auditors also perform audits of financial reports for internal use, much as external auditors audit financial statements distributed to outside users. Thus, some internal auditing work is similar to the auditing described elsewhere in this text. In addition, the expanded-scope services provided by internal auditors include: (1) reviews of control systems that ensure compliance with company policies, plans, procedures and with laws and regulations; (2) appraisals of the economy and efficiency of operations; and (3) reviews of

---

[5] www.theiia.org

effectiveness in achieving program results in comparison to pre-established objectives and goals.

Operational auditing is included in the definition of internal auditing cited previously. In a similar context a PA may consider operational auditing performed by independent PA firms as a distinct type of management consulting service whose goal is to help a client improve the use of its capabilities and resources to achieve its objectives. So, internal auditors consider operational auditing integral to internal auditing, and external auditors define it as a type of management consulting service offered by public accounting firms. It is important to distinguish between consulting and external auditing. Only PAs are allowed to perform external audits whereas anyone can legally provide consulting services. This is further clarified in Chapters 2 and 16.

Internal auditors need to be independent of the line managers in an organization, much like the external auditors need to be independent of the company management. Independence helps internal auditors be objective. They can make recommendations for correction of poor business decisions and practices, and they can praise good decisions and practices. If they were responsible for making the decisions or carrying out the practices themselves, they could hardly be credible in the eyes of upper-management officers to whom they report. Consequently, the ideal organizational arrangement is to have internal auditors with no other responsibilities than to audit and to report to a high level in the organization, such as a financial vice president and the audit committee of the board of directors. This arrangement is a type of internal independence that enhances the appraisal function (internal audit) within a company. In the SOX world, internal auditor reporting to independent audit committees is increasingly viewed as indispensable for good corporate governance.

Public Sector (Governmental) Auditing

The Office of the Auditor General of Canada (OAG) is an accounting, auditing and investigating agency of Parliament, headed by the Auditor General. In one sense, OAG auditors are the highest level of internal auditors for the federal government as a whole. Many provinces have audit agencies similar to the OAG. These provincial auditors answer to provincial legislatures and perform the same types of work described under governmental auditing following. In another sense, the OAG and similar provincial auditors are really external auditors with respect to government agencies they audit because they are organizationally independent.

Many government agencies have their own internal auditors and inspectors: for example, most federal ministries (e.g., Department of National Defence or Canada Revenue Agency) and provincial agencies (education, welfare, controller). Well-managed local governments (cities, regions, townships) also have internal audit staffs. Government activities at all levels of government is frequently referred to as the public sector.

Internal and public sector auditors have much in common. The OAG shares with internal auditors the same elements of expanded-scope services. The OAG, however, emphasizes the accountability of public officials for the efficient, economical and effective use of public funds and other resources. The CICA sets accounting and auditing standards for all public sector audit engagements including the federal, provincial and local levels of government.

In the public sector you can see the audit function applied to financial reports and a compliance audit function applied with respect to laws and regulations. All government organizations, programs, activities and functions were created by law and are surrounded by regulations that govern the things they can and cannot do. For example, in some provinces there are serious problems of health card abuse and fraud by ineligible persons. A hospital cannot simply provide free services to anyone because there are regulations about eligibility of tourists and visitors from other countries. A compliance audit of such a service involves a study of the hospital's procedures and performance in determining eligibility and treatment of patients. Nationwide, such programs involve millions of people and billions of taxpayers' dollars.

Also, in the public sector you see **value-for-money (VFM) audits**, a category that includes economy, efficiency and effectiveness audits. Government is always concerned

SOME EXAMPLES OF RECOMMENDATIONS BASED ON VALUE-FOR-MONEY AUDITS CONDUCTED BY THE ONTARIO PROVINCIAL AUDITOR

HEALTH CARE: Stronger efforts needed to control undesirable patterns of practice by health care providers.

INSURANCE: Cost effectiveness of Ontario Insurance Commission monitoring activities was considered adequate.

EDUCATION: Need to improve procedures for availability of programs to exceptional children.

YOUNG OFFENDERS: Suggested improvements to documentation before releasing young offenders.

CRIMINAL LAW: Several recommendations made for better utilization of courtroom and judicial resources.

Source: 1994 Annual Report by the Office of the Provincial Auditor of Ontario, Table of Contents. Reproduced with permission of the Office of the Auditor General of Ontario (formerly the Office of the Provincial Auditor of Ontario) © Queen's Printer for Ontario, 1995.

about accountability for taxpayers' resources, and value-for-money audits are a means of seeking to improve accountability for the efficient and economical use of resources and the achievement of program goals. Value-for-money audits, like internal auditors' operational audits, involve studies of the management of government organizations, programs, activities and functions.

Comprehensive governmental auditing is auditing that goes beyond an audit of financial reports and compliance with laws and regulations to include economy and efficiency and effectiveness audits. The public sector standard on the elements of comprehensive auditing is similar to the internal auditors' view. (These elaborations are presented in Chapter 18.)

The audit of a governmental organization, program, activity, or function may involve financial auditing, compliance auditing, or VFM auditing, or all of them (a comprehensive audit). Public sector standards do not require all engagements to include all types of audits. The scope of the work is supposed to be determined by the needs of those who use the audit results.

Regulatory Auditors

For the sake of clarity, other kinds of auditors deserve separate mention. You probably are aware of tax auditors employed by the Canada Revenue Agency. These auditors take the "economic assertions" of taxable income made by taxpayers in their tax returns and audit these returns to determine their correspondence with the standards found in the *Income Tax Act*. They also audit for fraud and tax evasion. Their reports can either clear a taxpayer's return or claim that additional taxes are due.

Federal and provincial bank examiners audit banks, trust companies and other financial institutions for evidence of solvency and compliance with banking and other related laws and regulations. In 1985 these examiners as well as external auditors made news as a result of the failures of two Alberta banks—the first Canadian bank failures in over 60 years.

Fraud Auditing and Forensic Accounting

Many people think that the main responsibility of a PA is to detect fraud in financial reporting. This is not the case! According to auditing standards, auditors are not required to perform mandatory investigative procedures to find all fraud. Instead, the PA needs to be skeptical and have a questioning mind so as to be ready for the possibility that management is dishonest. The PA needs to assess fraud risk by looking for fraud risk factors. Some firms are beginning to screen clients before any wrongdoing is even suspected. The screening is done by specialist auditors who may do sensitive interviews or review unusual transactions or suspicious circumstances. In a normal audit the procedures are diagnostic not investigative. We will make this distinction clearer later in the text.

Fraud auditing is a special in-depth investigation of suspected fraud done by those with specialized training and often involving a specialist auditor. It is a separate engagement done, for example, on behalf of the audit committee. Fraud auditing is a proactive approach to detect financial statement frauds using accounting records and information, analytical relations, and an awareness of fraud perpetration and concealment.

Fraud auditing and forensic accounting are huge growth areas for PA firms in the post-Enron world. The main reason for this is that white collar crime is one of the fastest growth areas in crime, and police and regulators need the expertise of auditors to carry out these investigations. But there are also other factors and these distinguish fraud auditing from forensic accounting. Forensic accounting is the broader term. **Forensic accounting** includes fraud auditing and uses accounting and/or auditing skills in investigations involving legal issues. The legal issues may be criminal (fraud) or civil. Examples of civil legal disputes include insurance claims for losses of various types, and valuation of spousal business assets in a divorce proceeding.

Fraud is an intentional attempt to deceive someone (victim) so that another party (the fraudster) can gain at the expense of the victim. Fraud falls under the criminal code and includes deception based on manipulation of accounting records and financial statements.

There are two specialist designations available for investigative engagements. One is a specialist designation for CAs referred to as CA-IFA for investigative and forensic accounting. See the website at www.rotman.utoronto.ca/difa for details.

There is also an older association of certified fraud examiners (CFEs) providing training for an internationally recognized designation that does not require any other accounting designation. See its website at www.cfenet.com for details.

Some people feel all PAs should take more responsibility to detect fraud, especially financial statement fraud, and that this may be the main reason for the existence of the profession. Appendix 1C on the Online Learning Centre discusses this increasingly influential view in more detail. Chapter 17 also gives more details on forensic accounting and fraud auditing.

. . . .

REVIEW CHECKPOINTS

1.10   Distinguish between forensic accounting and fraud auditing.

1.11   What is fraud?

1.12   What is operational auditing? How does the CICA view operational auditing?

1.13   What are the elements of comprehensive auditing?

1.14   What is compliance auditing?

1.15   Name some other types of auditors in addition to external, internal and governmental auditors.

1.16   Are financial statement audits intended to find fraud?

. . . .

PUBLIC ACCOUNTING
. . . .

The Accounting Profession

There are professional accounting associations at the national and international levels. For example, in Canada, there is the Canadian Institute of Chartered Accountants (CICA), the Certified General Accountants Association of Canada (CGA-Canada), and CMA Canada. Internationally, there is the International Federation of Accountants (IFAC), and in the U.S., the American Institute of Certified Public Accountants (AICPA), whose members are referred to as Certified Public Accountants or CPAs.

Even within a single country, however, there are a number of professional associations representing accountants. Within Canada, for example, there are the provincial Institutes of Chartered Accountants (the chartered accountants organization in Quebec is called Order of Chartered Accountants of Quebec), there are the Certified General Accountants Associations, the Societies of Management Accountants, and the Institute of Internal Auditors. Each of these organizations has developed its own professional designation as follows: the Chartered Accountants (CAs), Certified General Accountants (CGAs), Certified Management Accountants (CMAs), Certified Internal Auditors (CIAs) and Certified Fraud Examiners (CFEs). The requirements for obtaining these various designations vary greatly, so it is best to consult your provincial organization or local chapter for the details. A listing of websites with education and certification requirements is provided in Appendix 1A at the end of this chapter.

Generally, the distinguishing features of these various designations are as follows: CAs have traditionally been oriented to providing auditing and related public accounting services for large companies, CMAs have been oriented primarily to providing private management and internal accounting services, CIAs are oriented primarily to provide private internal audit services to larger organizations, and CGAs aim to provide all types of services. In virtually all provinces, CGAs can be public accountants like CAs, but tend to service smaller audit clients. There is considerable overlap among all these accounting professionals. They all provide accounting, tax and management advisory work, with CAs and CGAs primarily providing these services to the public and CMAs and CIAs providing these services to their full-time employer companies.

Recently, CGAs and CMAs have obtained public practice rights throughout Canada. It is therefore more appropriate to talk about public accountants as PAs instead of CAs in a text about external auditing. Although we will use the more generic term PA throughout the text, many of our illustrations will be based on standards set by the CICA. The reason for this is that the CICA's standards are given legal standing in the courts through the various Federal and Provincial Corporation Acts, and through various regulatory policy statements. In addition, when CGAs and CMAs practise public accounting, their guides refer to the use of the *CICA Handbook* standards in the performance of public accounting services.

Public Accounting Firms

Many people think of public accounting in terms of the "big" accounting firms. As of 2006, there are four big firms (called the "Big Four"): Ernst & Young, Deloitte & Touche, KPMG, and PricewaterhouseCoopers. Notwithstanding this perception, public accounting is practised in hundreds of practice units ranging in size from sole proprietorships (individuals who "hang out a shingle") to international firms employing thousands of professionals. Many students look on public accounting as the place to begin a career: for three to ten years they gain intimate knowledge of many different business enterprises; they then select the industry segment in which to pursue their interests. Public accounting experience provides an excellent background to almost any business career.

Public accountants do business in a competitive environment. They perform audit services in the public interest, yet they also need to make a living doing this. Hence, they have a profit motive like other professionals. This duality—profit and professional responsibility—creates tensions between the need to perform quality services and the desire to make a profit. As a result of increased litigation against the profession in the 1990s, the profession lobbied for legislation making it harder to sue professional accounting firms. Such legislation was passed in 1995 in the U.S., and its passage allowed public accounting firms to take on the **limited liability partnership (LLP)** form of organization, which will be covered in Chapter 5. The LLP form of organization is now commonplace in Canada and around the world.

The U.S. and Canada went through an economic boom in the second half of the 1990s. This was also a time of unprecedented growth in non-audit services for the public accounting firms. However, by the late 1990s, this rapid growth had led to concerns about the independence of audit services provided by accounting firms that also engaged in extensive, possibly conflicting, non-audit services for the same client. Many blame this lack of independence as the primary cause of the profession's problems in the post-Enron world.

Public accounting as a whole is a major employer of PAs performing assurance services, tax services and consulting services. Exhibit 1–4 shows a typical organization of a PA firm, although PA firms do differ in their organization. Some have other departments than those shown, such as small-business advisory and compensation consulting departments. Others have different names for their staff and management positions. The exhibit shows the most typical organizational structure for a larger PA firm.

In Exhibit 1–4 you see the various staffing levels within a PA firm. You will most likely start work as a staff accountant on graduation. Staff accountant is the usual entry level into the profession and involves carrying out work under the supervision of more senior people. Keep in mind that auditors need to verify virtually everything the client claims in financial reporting. This includes such mundane things as verifying the correct addition and extensions of financial data and reconciling physical amounts with recorded amounts. How does a user know that the balance sheet balances? Someone needs to verify the seemingly obvious and that someone is the auditor. Staff accountants tend to work on tedious details, but look positively on this experience as it is a form of apprenticeship. In most firms the responsibility increases quickly once you demonstrate you can be relied upon to do the work assigned to you.

Depending on the firm there may be several levels of staff accountants. Individuals who have just passed the professional exams are usually the most senior staff accountants and are ready to be promoted to manager.

Managers are usually those who have passed the professional exams, have at least two years' experience, and have demonstrated good leadership skills. This means having good people management skills both with clients and staff accountants. Technical skills alone are usually not sufficient to be a manager. The ability to expand the firm's practice becomes increasingly important. Being able to get along comfortably with client personnel is a high priority because without good interpersonal skills it is difficult to get the information an auditor needs. These personal dynamics are very important the higher up you work in a PA firm. Keep this context in mind as you read the description of various procedures in subsequent chapters. Managers supervise most of the details of the audit engagement as explained throughout this text. They are the backbone of the audit at the technical level. Managers normally have three to ten years' experience at a firm.

EXHIBIT 1–4   TYPICAL ORGANIZATION OF A PA FIRM

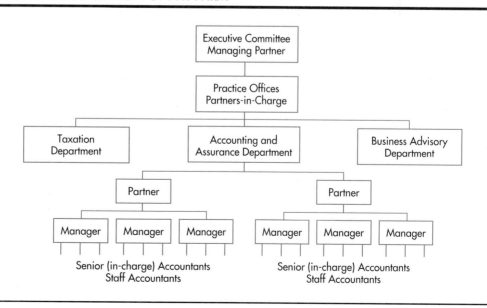

Partners, working closely with managers, take overall responsibility for the audit and lead meetings with client management and its audit committee. Partners have usually had at least ten years' experience and are the only permanent employees in a PA firm. About 5 percent of those with a PA designation become a partner. The rest go into industry or other PA firms. For more information on these positions, career opportunities, and the latest salary trends for PAs in North America, see the following websites: www.mcintyre-smith.com or www.roberthalffinance.com.

Assurance Services

Audits of traditional financial statements are the most frequent type of assurance services for public companies and for most large and medium nonpublic companies. Auditing amounts to around 50 percent of the business of most PA firms—a percentage that has been fluctuating dramatically over the past three decades. Most of this text is about the audit of traditional financial statements.

Accounting and review services are the "nonaudit" or other services, performed frequently for medium and small businesses and not-for-profit organizations. A great deal of nonaudit work is done by small public accounting practice units. PAs can be associated with clients' financial statements without giving the standard audit report. They can perform compilations, which consist of writing up the financial statements from a client's books and records, without performing any evidence-gathering work. They can perform reviews, a service in which some evidence-gathering work is performed, but which is lesser in scope than an audit. (Compilation and review standards are explained in more detail in Chapter 16.)

Assurance services are also performed on information in presentations other than traditional financial statements. Since assurance is the lending of credibility by an independent party (assurer, auditor) to the representations made by one person or organization to another, demand for numerous kinds of PA organizations has arisen. Public accountants have provided assurance to vote counts (e.g., Academy Awards), to the dollar amount of prizes claimed to have been given in lottery advertisements, to investment performance statistics, and to characteristics claims for computer software programs. These nontraditional services are governed by professional standards.

In this text we reference three sets of professional standards: Canadian, international, and, to a lesser extent, American. These standards influence one another and, increasingly, there is a tendency for these standards to converge. For example, the CICA's Assurance and Auditing Standards Board's first strategy is to influence international standards by providing commentary on exposure drafts of new international standards. Once a new international standard is adopted, the CICA issues a Canadian exposure draft incorporating unique Canadian circumstances requiring any modification of the international standard before being incorporated in the CICA standards. Other countries follow a similar process. The overall trend is convergence to a common set of standards.

This convergence is one of the defining characteristics of the post-Enron world, thus it is becoming more important to be aware of the similarities, as well as the differences, among the standards. Henceforth, any reference to "*CICA Handbook*, section" or "section" is intended to refer to the *CICA Handbook*. International standards reference IFAC's auditing handbook which recommends **international standards on auditing (ISAs)**. American PCAOB standards are referenced to its **Auditing Standards** (ASs).

Taxation Services

Local, provincial, national and international tax laws are often called accountant and lawyer full-employment acts. The laws are complex, and PAs perform services of tax planning and tax return preparation in the areas of income, sales, property and other taxation. A large proportion of the practice in small accounting firms is tax practice. Tax laws change frequently, and tax practitioners must spend considerable time in continuing education and self-study to keep current with them.

Consulting Services

All accounting firms handle a great deal of consulting. Consulting and management advisory services are the great "open end" of public accounting practice, placing accountants in direct competition with the non-PA consulting firms. The field is virtually unlimited, and a list of consulting activities could not possibly do justice to all of them. Indeed, accounting firms have created consulting units with professionals from other fields—lawyers, actuaries, engineers and advertising executives, to name a few. Until Enron, many of the large accounting firms had tried to become "one-stop shopping centres" for clients' auditing, taxation and business advice needs. However, as a result of the chilling effect of the SOX many of these consulting activities for audit clients have now been greatly restricted.

Nevertheless, consulting work for nonaudit clients continues and may even expand to new nonconflicting areas such as eldercare, where the PAs provide a package of services for the elderly ranging from assurance services to consulting, bill paying, and financial planning. In large PA firms the consulting department is quite often independent from the auditing and accounting department, performing engagements that do not directly interact with the audits performed by other professionals. PA firms are greatly restricted in the types of consulting or business advisory services they can provide to audit clients, but there are no such restrictions for nonaudit clients. In contrast, the OAG has on staff an equally wide range of expertise, but all its combined expertise goes into the audits and studies performed for Parliament. The OAG does not distinguish audits from consulting work, instead marshalling all its abilities to study the wide range of social, agricultural, defence, engineering and personnel activities it gets charged to investigate.

REGULATION OF PUBLIC ACCOUNTING

. . . .

LEARNING OBJECTIVE
6 Outline how public accountants (PAs) are regulated.

Regulation of public accounting in Canada, as with most professional groups, is a provincial matter. Most provinces have laws—public accountancy acts—that specify who can be allowed to practise public accounting in the province. For example, until late 2002, Ontario's *Public Accounting Act* licensed only CAs to perform audits and reviews. However, as part of the post-Enron reform process, this legislation was amended in December of that year to also allow CGAs and CMAs to perform these functions. These reforms were linked to the creation of the new Accountability Board, which provides oversight for all PAs in the province. Similar regulatory reforms have taken place throughout the rest of Canada.

The general trend in provincial public accountancy legislation in recent years has been to open up public accounting to CGAs and CMAs, as well as CAs. There is a desire to increase accessibility of public accounting services at a reasonable cost while maintaining standards. The concern is to protect the public interest, particularly that of vulnerable third parties. This is done primarily through quality control standards and the CPAB monitoring that has been implemented in recent years. These are further explained in Chapter 2.

In addition to the system of regulation outlined previously, there are other factors that have great influence on the profession. These include the legal system in which the profession operates (discussed in Chapter 5) and regulators that have an impact on practising auditors. These regulators include, at the federal level, the Superintendent of Financial Institutions, who has the prime responsibility for regulating the financial services industry falling under the jurisdiction of the *Federal Bank Act*. At the provincial level there are the securities commissions, which are charged with the responsibility of investor protection and with ensuring the fairness and efficiency of the capital markets in a province. There are securities commissions in every province and territory. Due to the division of powers between the provinces and the federal government, there is no national-level securities commission in Canada comparable to the SEC in the United States.

The Ontario Securities Commission (OSC) has responsibility for the biggest and most developed capital markets in Canada. It will be used as an illustration of the impact a regulator can have on public accounting. The OSC has three principal activities in ensuring the orderly functioning of capital markets within its jurisdiction, such as the Toronto Stock Exchange:

1. registering persons trading in securities and commodity futures contracts
2. reviewing and clearing of prospectuses
3. enforcing the *Securities Act* and *Commodity Futures Act*

Activities 2 and 3 have the most impact on public accountants. **Prospectuses** are information, usually including financial information, about a firm that accompanies any new issuance of shares in a regulated securities market. The staff of the OSC includes the chief accountant and a chief forensic accountant who work under the director of enforcement. The Office of the Chief Accountant is responsible for the formulation of financial reporting policy and for monitoring the application of accounting principles and auditing standards by report issuers and their auditors. Financial statements are reviewed on a selective basis, and up to one-quarter of companies reviewed receive comment letters relating to inadequacies in their financial reports. The companies' auditors are also informed of problems noted. If the financial reporting problems are severe enough, the Enforcement Branch is notified. In 2001 the OSC found revenue recognition to be a significant problem area for high-tech firms.

An example of an Enforcement Branch action affecting an auditor follows:

OSC COMMISSIONERS CONTINUE MANAGEMENT CEASE TRADE ORDER AGAINST NORTEL INSIDERS, MAY 31, 2004

TORONTO—Following a hearing held today, a panel of Ontario Securities Commission (OSC) Commissioners has made a final order under paragraph 2 of subsection 127(1) of the *Securities Act* that all trading by certain directors, officers and insiders of Nortel Networks Corporation and Nortel Networks Limited in securities of Nortel Networks Corporation and Nortel Networks Limited cease until two full business days following the receipt by the Commission of all filings, including financial statements, the corporations are required to make pursuant to Ontario securities law. This order continues the temporary order made by the Director on May 17, 2004.

Source: www.osc.gov.on.ca/About/NewsReleases/2004/nr_20040528_osc-nortel-cont-cease-trade.jsp

---

This OSC action followed the launching of investigations in April 2004 by the SEC and OSC of Nortel's accounting. Nortel, one of Canada's premiere high-tech companies in the telecommunications industry had to restate its financial results for quarterly periods going back through 2003, 2002 and 2001. Subsequently, the restated 2003 results reduced earnings by 41 percent. Nortel's stock price had gone from a high of $124 in July 2000 to the $4 range in January 2005. The earlier 2003 earnings triggered millions of dollars of bonus payments to management. In January 2005, 12 of the senior executives agreed to return $10.4 million of these bonuses. However, Nortel is still seeking repayment of 2003 bonuses from managers who had been fired in April 2004.

An independent review by Nortel's audit committee concluded that the corporate culture encouraged financial manipulation with weak internal controls. In January 2005, the board of directors went through a major reorganization with half the board members leaving. In addition, a high-profile ethics watchdog and compliance officer was hired to help change the corporate culture. The saga is still ongoing with lawsuits and investigations continuing. This example illustrates why good corporate governance principles need to be followed. (Corporate governance principles are explored in more detail in Appendix 5A.)

The OSC also monitors auditing and accounting standards-setting of the CICA, and provides input on emerging issues and commentary on proposed standards. In addition, since 1989 the OSC has issued Staff Accounting Communiqués (SACs), which are intended to explain the OSC staff's views on specific reporting issues. Although the SACs have no official OSC approval, OSC staff are likely to challenge any treatment that is inconsistent with an SAC. In recent years the OSC, by publishing the results of its monitoring program, filing complaints to provincial disciplinary committees and through its representation on CICA standard-setting boards, has made a significant, ongoing impact on the profession.

However, there are other regulators that affect the profession. For example, the Canadian Investor Protection Fund, which is sponsored by the Toronto and the Montreal stock exchanges, the Canadian Venture Exchange and the Toronto Futures Exchange, as well as by the Investment Dealers Association of Canada, is a trust established to protect customers in the event of the financial failure of a member firm (any member of a sponsoring organization, and some American bond dealers that trade in Canada). In recent years Fund staff have taken a more active supervisory role. The Fund oversees regular, monthly, quarterly and annual reporting, periodic surprise visits to the offices of a member firm and at least one surprise financial questionnaire a year. The Fund can fine and set sanctions if a member firm violates capital, reporting or other requirements. The Fund develops policy statements that address standards for internal control within member firms. Auditors must be aware of these standards when auditing member firms. Internal control reports are discussed in more detail in Chapter 3.

Another regulator that affects Canadian auditors whose client firms have dealings with U.S. securities markets is the **Securities and Exchange Commission (SEC)**. In recent years many Canadian companies have gone to American and other international markets to raise cash through **initial public offerings (IPOs)**. Many Canadian companies are finding it cheaper to raise money on public markets in other countries, because if they do so in Canada they need to file regulatory documents in each province. This increases the cost of financing in Canada. The Canadian Department of Finance has for a number of years explored the idea of creating a national securities regulator (like the SEC in the U.S.), or some national coordinator of provincial securities commissions, to improve the quality and competitiveness of Canadian securities markets.[6] The impact of the SEC on auditors is discussed in Appendix 1B.

The most important recent development in the regulation of the Canadian accounting profession is the creation of the Canadian Public Accountability Board on July 17, 2002. The Board is intended to represent the public interest by being dominated by non-CAs as members (seven of the eleven Board members are to be non-CAs). The Board monitors audit practice and conducts annual inspections of accounting firms to assess their ability to protect the public interest. The Board has the power to impose sanctions on any auditor that fails to protect the public interest. It is viewed as the first in a series of major structural reforms to protect the integrity of Canada's financial accounting systems. Other steps include the CICA's evolving standard for auditor independence, and the creation of boards at the provincial level to oversee the professional conduct and peer review systems.

Finally, there are regulators such as provincial ministries of the environment and natural resources, which have an indirect impact on the profession through restrictions they place on client activities that the clients themselves may need to disclose as part of the client's business risk.

It is clear from this brief review that the profession is facing an increasingly complex regulatory environment and that auditors must be sensitized to regulatory concerns in order to do a proper audit. Auditors also need to be concerned with meeting the demands of regulators in different countries. A part of the solution is to use common worldwide standards to the extent feasible.

· ·

REVIEW CHECKPOINTS

1.17   Identify several types of professional accountants and their organizations.

1.18   What are some examples of assurance services rendered on representations other than traditional financial statements?

1.19   What are the three major areas of public accounting services?

1.20   Locate Nortel's audit committee report on the Internet. Is the OSC or the SEC website more user-friendly for investors?

· ·

[6] A. Freeman and K. Hawlett, "Keep IPO's at Home: Martin." *The Globe and Mail*, March 8, 1996, B1.

INTERNATIONAL AUDITING

LEARNING OBJECTIVE
7 Provide an overview of international auditing.

Many of the large public accounting firms are worldwide organizations that have grown rapidly in the last few decades paralleling the increased economic integration of their global clientele. Developments such as the North American Free Trade Agreement (NAFTA), the evolution of the European Economic Union and other free trade zones, and the pervasive effects of technological change are all contributing to increased global harmonization of auditing and accounting standards. For these reasons the **International Federation of Accountants (IFAC)**, created in 1977, mirrors the activities at an international level what national institutes have been doing domestically. In particular, IFAC publishes its own handbook on auditing standards that recommends international standards on auditing (ISAs). ISAs cover such issues as basic principles of auditing, auditor's reports, professional independence, reliance on other auditors abroad and professional qualifications.

The issue is when ISAs will achieve worldwide acceptance. On April 1, 2002, the **International Auditing and Assurance Standards Board** was created with resources commensurate with its responsibilities. The board now has probably the largest group of technical audit standard-setting support staff in the world, thereby making future ISAs more rigorous. Within five years ISAs will likely be the dominant standards.

The CICA's policy is to adopt ISAs as is unless Canadian conditions require a different standard, and to keep existing practice until the CICA adopts a new ISA. Generally, the remaining significant differences between the *CICA Handbook* and the ISAs are that the ISAs tend to focus more on (1) financial information instead of financial statements, (2) procedures rather than broader standards, (3) rules of professional conduct (something not covered in the *CICA Handbook*), (4) engagement letters, (5) reliance on other auditors, and (6) special purpose auditor reports. Convergence, or **international harmonization**, as it is frequently called, is a key focus of Canadian and U.S. standard setters in the post-Enron world. High-priority projects include going-concern, fraud, and the audit risk model. These topics are covered later in the text.

The CGAs have published their own GAAP guide, which, in addition to the *CICA Handbook*, references U.S. and international standards and notes key differences between the Canadian requirements and those of the IFAC and the United States.

As the world becomes more interdependent, many concepts and terms used in other countries will become increasingly accepted in Canadian practice. Indeed, many large firms already use manuals and training materials reflecting international practice. This text makes use of those terms and concepts and does not restrict itself to those currently used in the *CICA Handbook*.

REVIEW CHECKPOINT   1.21   Find the *IFAC Handbook* on the IFAC website.

SUMMARY

This chapter began by illustrating and defining auditing, distinguishing it from accounting. The practice of public accounting is rooted in the history of auditing. The accounting profession has been undergoing radical changes since the bankruptcy of Enron in December 2001. These changes are being accompanied by broad corporate governance and regulatory reforms.

Auditing is practised in numerous forms by various practice units including PA firms, the Canada Revenue Agency, the OAG, internal audit departments in companies and several other types of regulatory auditors. Fraud examiners, many of whom are internal auditors and inspectors, have found a niche in auditing-related activities.

Many auditors aspire to become CGAs, CAs, CPAs, CIAs, CFEs, or CMAs; this involves passing rigorous examinations, obtaining practical experience and maintaining competence through continuing professional education. Each of these groups has a large professional organization that governs the professional standards and quality of practice of its members.

This chapter has given you a broad overview of auditing. Being aware of the "bigger picture"of the context of auditing is increasingly important for effective auditing. It is also important for more structured skepticism or critical thinking that auditors are expected to exercise in order to meet changing public expectations of auditors, especially those related to fraud detection.

We end this introduction with a brief overview of what you can expect from this text. Part I, consisting of the first five chapters, introduces you to the most fundamental concepts you will need to consider as an auditor. Part II introduces you to evidence-based concepts, refining the important concept of internal control. In Part III, you will learn to apply the concepts studied thus far to the various accounts in the financial statements. This part concludes with the opinion to support the audit report and reflects an evaluation of financial statements as a whole. Part IV covers other assurance engagements and specialized types of auditors and auditing.

When you begin a study of auditing, you may be eager to attack the nitty-gritty of doing financial statement audit work. Although this text will enable you to learn about auditing, instructors are seldom able to duplicate a practice environment in a classroom setting. You may feel frustrated about knowing "how to do it." This frustration is natural because auditing is done in the field under pressure of time limits and in the surroundings of client personnel, paperwork, and accounting information systems. This text can provide a foundation and framework for understanding auditing, but nothing can substitute for the first few months of work when the classroom study comes alive in the field.

Refer to the text Online Learning Centre for Appendices 1B and 1C.

MULTIPLE-CHOICE QUESTIONS FOR PRACTICE AND REVIEW

1.22 When people speak of the assurance function, they are referring to the work of auditors in:
a. Lending credibility to a client's financial statements.
b. Detecting fraud and embezzlement in a company.
c. Lending credibility to an auditee's financial statements.
d. Performing a program results audit in a government agency.

1.23 Company A hired Sampson & Delila, CAs, to audit the financial statements of Company B and deliver the audit report to Megabank. Which is the client?
a. Megabank.
b. Sampson & Delila.
c. Company A.
d. Company B.

1.24 According to the CICA, the objective of an audit of financial statements is:
a. An expression of opinion on the fairness with which they present financial position, results of operations and cash flows in conformity with generally accepted accounting principles.
b. An expression of opinion on the fairness with which they present financial position, results of operations and cash flows in conformity with accounting standards promulgated by the Financial Accounting Standards Board.
c. An expression of opinion on the fairness with which they present financial position, result of operations and cash flows in conformity with accounting standards promulgated by the CICA Accounting Standards Committee.
d. To obtain systematic and objective evidence about financial assertions and report the results to interested users.

1.25 Bankers who are processing loan applications from companies seeking large loans will probably ask for financial statements audited by an independent PA because:
a. Financial statements are too complex for them to analyze themselves.
b. They are too far away from company headquarters to perform accounting and auditing themselves.
c. The consequences of making a bad loan are very undesirable.
d. They generally see a potential conflict of interest between company managers who want to get loans and their needs for reliable financial statements.

1.26 Operational audits of a company's efficiency and economy of managing projects and of the results of programs are conducted by whom?
  a. Management advisory services departments of PA firms in public practice.
  b. The company's internal auditors.
  c. Governmental auditors employed by the federal government.
  d. All of the above.

1.27 Independent auditors of financial statements perform audits that reduce and control:
  a. The business risks faced by investors.
  b. The information risk faced by investors.
  c. The complexity of financial statements.
  d. Quality reviews performed by other PA firms.

1.28 The primary objective of compliance auditing is to:
  a. Give an opinion on financial statements.
  b. Develop a basis for a report on internal control.
  c. Perform a study of effective and efficient use of resources.
  d. Determine whether auditee personnel are following laws, rules, regulations and policies.

EXERCISES AND PROBLEMS

1.29 **Controller as Auditor.** The chairman of the board of
LO.2 Hughes Corporation proposed that the board hire as controller a PA who had been the manager on the corporation's audit performed by a firm of independent accountants. The chairman thought that hiring this person would make the annual audit unnecessary and would consequently result in saving the professional fee paid to the auditors. The chairman proposed to give this new controller a full staff to conduct such investigations of accounting and operating data as necessary. Evaluate this proposal.

1.30 **Controller as Auditor.** Put yourself in the position of
LO.2 the person hired as controller in the above situation. Suppose the chairman of the board moves to discontinue the annual audit because Hughes Corporation now has your services on a full-time basis. You are invited to express your views to the board. Explain how you would discuss the nature of your job as controller and your views on the discontinuance of the annual audit.

1.31 **Logic and Method.** Identify four major factors affect-
LO.3 ing information risk that make the need for independent audits important in today's business world. Give two examples for each of the factors.

1.32 **Logic and Method.** Auditors must have a thorough
LO.3 knowledge of generally accepted accounting principles (GAAP) if they are to properly perform an audit of the financial statements of a company. Explain why this is so. Use capital leases as an example of the need for this knowledge.

1.33 **Operational Auditing.** Bigdeal Corporation manufac-
LO.5 tures paper and paper products and is trying to decide whether to purchase and merge Smalltek Company. Smalltek has developed a process for manufacturing boxes that can replace other containers that use fluorocarbons for expelling a liquid product. The price may be as high as $45 million. Bigdeal prefers to buy Smalltek and integrate its products, while leaving the Smalltek management in charge of day-to-day operations. A major consideration is the efficiency and effectiveness of the Smalltek management. Bigdeal wants to obtain a report on the operational efficiency and effectiveness of the Smalltek sales, production and research and development departments.

Required:
Who can Bigdeal engage to produce this operational audit report? Several possibilities exist. Are there any particular advantages or disadvantages in choosing among them?

1.34 **Auditor as Guarantor.** Your neighbour invited you to
LO.1 lunch yesterday. Sure enough, it was no "free lunch" because he wanted to discuss the annual report of the Dodge Corporation. He owns Dodge shares and just received the annual report. He says: "Pricewaterhouse prepared the audited financial statements and gave an unqualified opinion, so my investment must be safe."

Required:
What misconceptions does your neighbour seem to have about the auditor's role with respect to Dodge Corporation?

1.35 **Identification of Audits and Auditors.** Audits may be
LO.5 characterized as (a) financial statement audits, (b) compliance audits—audits of compliance with control policies and procedures and with laws and regulations, (c) economy and efficiency audits and (d) program results audits. The work can be done by independent (external) auditors, internal auditors or governmental auditors. Below is a list of the purposes or products of various audit engagements:
1. Render a public report on the assumptions and compilation of a revenue forecast by a sports stadium/ racetrack complex.
2. Determine the fair presentation in conformity with GAAP of an advertising agency's financial statements.
3. Report on how better care and disposal of vehicles confiscated by drug enforcement agents could save money and benefit law enforcement.
4. Determine costs of municipal garbage pickup services compared to comparable service subcontracted to a private business.
5. Audit tax shelter partnership financing terms.

6. Study a private aircraft manufacturer's test pilot performance in reporting on the results of test flights.
7. Conduct periodic examination of a bank for solvency.
8. Evaluate the promptness of materials inspection in a manufacturer's receiving department.

Required:
Prepare a three-column schedule showing: (1) Each of the engagements listed above; (2) the type of audit (financial statement, compliance, economy and efficiency, or program results); and (3) the kind of auditors you would expect to be involved.

1.36 Analysis and Judgement. As part of your regular year-
LO.3 end audit of a publicly held client, you must estimate the probability of success of its proposed new product line. The client has experienced financial difficulty during the last few years and—in your judgement—a successful introduction of the new product line is necessary for the client to remain a going concern.

There are five steps, all of which are necessary for successful introduction of the product: (1) successful labour negotiations between the construction firms contracted to build the necessary addition to the present plant and the building trades unions; (2) successful defence of patent rights; (3) product approval by the Health Branch; (4) successful negotiation of a long-term raw material contract with a foreign supplier; and (5) successful conclusion of distribution contract talks with a large national retail distributor.

In view of the circumstances, you contact experts, who have provided your audit firm with reliable estimates in the past. The labour relations expert estimates that there is an 80 percent chance of successfully concluding labour negotiations before the strike deadline. Legal counsel advises that there is a 90 percent chance of successfully defending patent rights. The expert on Health Branch product approvals estimates a 95 percent chance of approval. The experts in the remaining two areas estimate the probability of successfully resolving (*a*) the raw materials contract and (*b*) the distribution contract talks to be 90 percent in each case. Assume these estimates are reliable.

Required:
What is your assessment of the probability of successful product introduction? (Hint: You can assume the five steps are independent of each other.)

1.37 What do you think management certification of finan-
LO.4 cial statements means? Has management's responsibility changed since the inception of SOX? Why do we need auditors if management "certifies" its financial statements? Discuss in class.

APPENDIX 1A

HOW TO BECOME A PA IN CANADA

Professional Accounting Designations Available in Canada

Following is a list of Canadian professional accounting designations as discussed in the chapter. The designations are organized by primary orientation. As noted in the text, there can be considerable overlap. Refer to these websites for additional guidance on how to obtain each designation or certification.

Public Accounting

Chartered Accountant (CA): www.cica.ca
Certified General Accountant (CGA): www.cga-canada.org

Internal Auditing

Certified Internal Auditor (CIA): www.theiia.org

Management Accounting

Certified Management Accountant (CMA): www.cma-canada.org

Forensic Accounting and Fraud Auditing

Certified Fraud Examiner (CFE): www.cfenet.com

Other Specialist Designations

The CICA now allows a variety of specializations within public accounting because some CAs will choose to become specialists because of a personal interest, experience, and expertise in particular area of work. The CICA recognizes specialty designations in investigative and forensic accounting, business valuation, information systems audit and control, and insolvency and restructuring. Specialist designations require academic and work experience. The academic requirement is normally met by taking designated program courses offered through universities, mostly through distance learning. Once the academic and other requirements are met, a CA is allowed to identify the specialty along with the CA designation. For example, a CA-IFA stands for a CA specializing in investigative and forensic accounting.

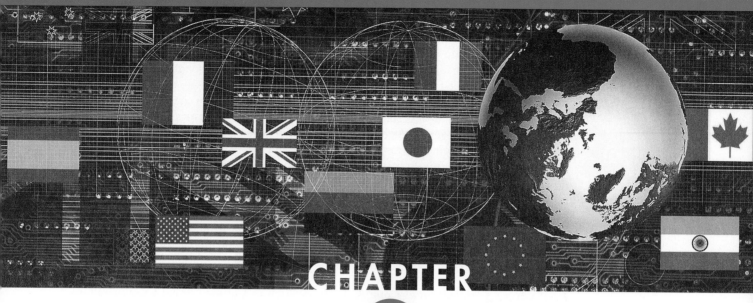

CHAPTER

2

Audit, Assurance, and Quality Control Standards

Chapter 2 explains three sets of interrelated practice standards for audit services offered by PAs: audit, assurance and quality control standards.

LEARNING OBJECTIVES

After completing this chapter, you will be able to:

1. List the various practice standards for internal, governmental and independent auditors, identifying their sources.

2. Determine whether the eight CICA generally accepted auditing standards (GAAS) were followed in specific fact situations

3. Interpret the standard unqualified audit report.

4. Summarize the audit process.

5. Outline the characteristics of professional skepticism and critical thinking.

6. Explain the importance of general assurance standards, using examples of assurance matters.

7. Explain how requirements of quality control standards are monitored for PA firms.

PRACTICE STANDARDS

LEARNING OBJECTIVE

1 List the various practice standards for internal, governmental, and independent auditors, identifying their sources.

Practice standards are general guides for the quality of professional work. The North American accounting and auditing profession has many sets of standards, depending upon which sets are included or excluded in a particular count. This chapter deals directly with three sets: assurance standards, as suggested by various sections of the *CICA Handbook*; generally accepted auditing standards, issued by the CICA Assurance and Auditing Standards Board; and quality control standards as reflected in firm peer reviews, and in provincial Institutes' practice inspection manuals and the CICA's *Guide for Developing Quality Control Systems in Public Accounting*. As stated in Chapter 1, several accountability boards have been created in different countries in the post-Enron world. These boards, especially the PCAOB, will likely introduce new standards in auditing and quality control to complement existing standards developed by the profession.

Other chapters in this text explain other sets of standards. Chapter 4 covers the Rules of Professional Conduct. The CICA Recommendations for Compilation and Review Services are explained in Chapter 16. The CICA's public sector audit standards and the internal audit standards (Institute of Internal Auditors) are in Chapter 18. *Professional Standards and Practices for Certified Fraud Examiners* (Association of Certified Fraud Examiners) are found in Appendix 17B.

Another set of auditing standards is known as the International Standards of Auditing (ISA), issued by the International Auditing and Assurance Standards Board (IAASB). In the international community, accountants and regulators have a great interest in convergence or **harmonization**—that is, making the standards co-ordinated, if not uniform, throughout the world. The ISAs are a first step in this direction. They are cited in this text along with the Canadian generally accepted auditing standards. Some differences exist, however. The *CICA Handbook* has summaries of the points on which the ISAs differ from Canadian generally accepted auditing standards in section 5101. Also, CGA-Canada has prepared a guide relating CICA standards to ISA and U.S. standards.

You will find very few references to the accounting recommendations in this text. The CICA issues accounting standards but this text concentrates on auditing and the practice of accounting, not on the accounting rules themselves. An overview of generally accepted auditing standards is provided in the next section.

GENERALLY ACCEPTED AUDITING STANDARDS (GAAS)

LEARNING OBJECTIVE

2 Determine whether the eight CICA generally accepted auditing standards (GAAS) were followed in specific fact situations

The CICA's generally accepted auditing standards or GAAS were first written as a short statement of eight standards. Since 1975, these eight have been augmented by additional explanations and requirements in the Assurance Recommendations of the *CICA Handbook*, section 5100. The eight basic standards are shown in Exhibit 2–1, classified as the general standard, examination standards and reporting standards.

The Assurance Recommendations of the *CICA Handbook* are issued from time to time in a numbered series. Officially they are considered "interpretations" of the eight basic standards, but, for all practical purposes, they are also GAAS. Any auditor who does not follow *Handbook* directives can be judged to have performed a deficient audit.

The auditing standards literature also includes a series of guidelines. Although officially considered less authoritative and less binding than the recommendations, auditors still must justify any departures from them. For the most part, the guidelines give technical help.

The *IFAC Handbook*, which was first discussed in Chapter 1, has nothing comparable to *CICA Handbook*, section 5100. Instead of general standards, IFAC's International Standards on Auditing (ISAs) tend to be more detailed, but these detailed standards address the issues summarized by the general standards. IFAC also issues **International Audit Practice Statements (IAPSs)**, which like the CICA's **Audit Guidelines (AUGs)**, are intended to provide more practical assistance in implementing the standards. Throughout this text we will list any ISAs or IAPSs relevant to a particular topic along with their corresponding *Handbook* sections and AUGs. Currently, the *CICA Handbook* is generally more comprehensive than the *IFAC Handbook*.

Auditing standards are quite different from auditing procedures. Auditing procedures are the particular and specialized actions auditors take to obtain evidence in a specific audit engagement. **Auditing standards** are audit quality recommendations that remain the same over time and for all audits. Audit procedures may vary, depending on the complexity of an accounting system (whether manual or computerized), the type of company, and other situation-specific factors. These differences explain why audit reports refer to an audit "conducted in accordance with generally accepted auditing standards," rather than "in accordance with auditing procedures." As such, considerable judgement is required to apply audit procedures in specific situations.

GAAS General Standard

The general standard of GAAS (as shown in Exhibit 2–1) relates to the personal integrity and professional qualifications of auditors as covered in paragraph 5100.02 of the *CICA Handbook*.

Competence

The first general standard requires competence—adequate technical training and proficiency—as an auditor. This competence starts with education in accounting, because auditors hold themselves out as experts in accounting standards and financial reporting. It continues with on-the-job training in developing and applying professional judgement in

---

EXHIBIT 2-1   GENERALLY ACCEPTED AUDITING STANDARDS

Generally Accepted Auditing Standards are as follows:

General standard

The examination should be performed and the report prepared by a person or persons having *adequate technical training* and *proficiency in auditing*, with *due care* and with an *objective state of mind*.

Examination standards

1. The auditor should plan and perform the audit to reduce audit risk to an acceptably low level that is consistent with the objective of an audit. The auditor should plan the nature, timing and extent of direction and supervision of engagement team members and review of their work.
2. The auditor should obtain an understanding of the entity and its enviroment, including internal control, sufficient to identify and assess the risks of material misstatement of the financial statements whether due to fraud and error, and sufficient to design and perform further audit procedures.
3. The auditor should obtain sufficient appropriate audit evidence to be able to draw reasonable conclusions on which to base the audit opinion.

Reporting standards

1. The report should *identify the financial statements* and distinguish between the *responsibilities of management* and the *responsibilities of the auditor*.
2. The report should describe *the scope* of the auditor's examination.
3. The report should contain either an expression of *opinion on the financial statements* or an assertion that an opinion cannot be expressed. In the latter case, the reason therefor should be stated.
4. Where an opinion is expressed, it should indicate whether the financial statements *present fairly, in all material respects*, the financial position, results of operations and changes in financial position in accordance with an appropriate disclosed basis of accounting, which except in special circumstances should be Canadian generally accepted accounting principles. . . .The report should provide adequate explanation with respect to any reservation contained in such opinion.

Note: Emphasis has been added by the authors in the form of *italics*.
Source: *CICA Handbook*, section 5100.

real-world audit situations. This stage gives practice in performing the assurance function, in which auditors learn to (1) recognize the underlying assertions being made by the management of a company in each element (account) in the financial statements, (2) decide which evidence is relevant for supporting or refuting the truth of the assertions, (3) select and perform procedures for obtaining the evidence, and (4) evaluate the evidence and decide whether the management assertions correspond to reality and GAAP. Auditors must be thoughtfully prepared to encounter a wide range of judgement on the part of management accountants, varying from true objective judgement to the occasional extreme of deliberate misstatement.

Objectivity

The general standard also requires an objective state of mind. In this sense, objectivity is a matter of intellectual honesty and impartiality. Auditors are expected to be unbiased and impartial with respect to the financial statements and other information they audit. They are expected to be fair not only to the companies and executives who issue financial information, but also to the outside persons who use it. This type of objectivity in assurance services is achieved through the maintenance of professional independence. There are two aspects of independence: independence in fact and independence in appearance. Independence in fact is a mental attitude that is essential for an objective state of mind. Independence in appearance is another matter and is addressed in more detail in the Rules of Professional Conduct (Chapter 4). The appearance of independence—avoiding financial and managerial relationships with clients—is important because appearances are all the public users of audit reports can see. They cannot see inside auditors' heads to detect the "mental attitude." Independence must be zealously guarded because the general public will grant social recognition of professional status to auditors only as long as they are perceived to be independent.

Some critics of the public accounting profession say the fact that auditors are paid by their clients is an undesirable arrangement. They argue that it is impossible to be independent from the party paying the fee. Accountants have generally not taken such criticism seriously because the alternative would be some form of public government control of accounting fees, and very few PAs want government involvement. What is unique about auditors is that, although a company pays the auditor, the auditors' real clients are the third-party users of financial statements. The auditor therefore needs to differentiate responsibilities to the company from responsibilities to third parties. Addressing such ethical conflicts in a competent manner is part of what makes public accounting a profession. (See Chapter 4 for more details.)

The notion of individual independence is more specific in the conduct of each audit engagement. In essence, an individual auditor must not subordinate his or her judgement to others and must stay away from influences that might bias judgement. In more specific terms, auditors must preserve their independence in the "Three Aspects" presented in the following box.

Due Professional Care

The exercise of due professional care requires observance of the general standard and the field work standards. Auditors must be competent and independent; they must plan and supervise the audit, understand the auditee's control structure and obtain sufficient competent evidence if they are to be properly careful. Their training should include computer auditing techniques because of the importance and pervasiveness of computers in the business world.

Due care in an audit is best understood in the context of the prudent auditor. The idea of a prudent professional practitioner is present in other social science theories—for example, the "economic person" of economic theory and the "reasonable person" in law. Mautz and Sharaf summarized the qualities of the prudent auditor:

> A prudent practitioner [auditor] is assumed to have a knowledge of the philosophy and practice of auditing, to have the degree of training, experience, and skill common to the average

independent auditor, to have the ability to recognize indications of irregularities, and to keep abreast of developments in the perpetration and detection of irregularities. Due audit care requires the auditor to acquaint himself with the company under examination, the accounting and financial problems of the company . . . to be responsive to unusual events and unfamiliar circumstances, to persist until he has eliminated from his own mind any reasonable doubts he may have about the existence of material irregularities, and to exercise caution in instructing his assistants and reviewing their work.[1]

THREE ASPECTS OF PRACTICAL INDEPENDENCE

PROGRAMMING INDEPENDENCE

Auditors must remain free from interference by client managers who try to restrict, specify or modify the procedures auditors want to perform, including any attempt to assign personnel or otherwise control the audit work. Occasionally, client managers try to limit the number of auditors permitted in a location.

INVESTIGATIVE INDEPENDENCE

Auditors must have free access to books, records, correspondence and other evidence. They must have the co-operation of management without any attempt to interpret or screen evidence. Sometimes, client managers refuse auditors' requests for access to necessary information.

REPORTING INDEPENDENCE

Auditors must not let any feelings of loyalty to the client or auditee interfere with their obligation to report fully and fairly. Neither should the client management be allowed to overrule auditors' judgements on the appropriate content of an audit report. Disciplinary actions have been taken against auditors who go to a client management conference with a preliminary estimate for a financial adjustment and emerge after agreeing with management to a smaller adjustment.

LESSONS AUDITORS IGNORE AT THEIR OWN RISK

Litigation is an exacting and uncompromising teacher, but it provides auditors with some hard and useful lessons. The tuition is the high cost of malpractice insurance, legal fees, adverse court decisions, embarrassing publicity and stress.

- There is no substitute for knowledge of the client's business.
- There is no substitute for effective, ongoing, substantial supervision of the work of people assigned to the engagement.
- The partner-in-charge of the engagement must constantly emphasize the importance of integrity, objectivity and professional skepticism in carrying out the audit.

Source: W.D. Hall and A.J. Renner, "Lessons That Auditors Ignore at Their Own Risk," *Journal of Accountancy*, July 1988, pp. 50–58.

*All material from the *Journal of Accountancy* appearing in this text is reprinted with permission by the American Institute of Certified Public Accountants, Inc. Opinions of the authors are their own and do not necessarily reflect policies of the AICPA.

[1] R. Mautz and H. Sharaf, *The Philosophy of Auditing* (American Accounting Association, 1961) p. 140.

Due professional care is a matter of what auditors do and how well they do it. A determination of proper care must be reached on the basis of all facts and circumstances in a particular case. When an audit firm's work becomes the subject of a lawsuit, the question of due audit care is frequently at issue (as you will see in the law cases in Chapter 5).

· ·

REVIEW
CHECKPOINTS

2.1   What is the difference between auditing standards and auditing procedures?

2.2   By what standard would a judge determine the quality of due professional care? Explain.

2.3   What are the three specific aspects of independence that an auditor should carefully guard in the course of a financial statement audit?

· ·

GAAS Examination Standards

The three examination standards set forth general quality criteria for conducting an audit. Auditors cannot effectively satisfy the general standard requiring due professional care if they have not also satisfied the standards of field work.

Planning and Supervision

Section 5150 of the *Handbook* contains several lists of considerations for planning and supervising an audit. They are all concerned with (1) preparing an audit program and supervising the audit work, (2) obtaining knowledge of the client's business, and (3) dealing with differences of opinion among the audit firm's own personnel.

A written audit program is desirable. An **audit program** is a list of the audit procedures the auditors need to perform to produce the evidence needed for good audit decisions. The procedures in an audit program should be stated in enough detail to instruct the assistants about the work to be done. (You will see detailed audit programs later in this text.)

An understanding of the client's business is an absolute necessity. An auditor must be able to understand the events, transactions and practices characteristic of the business and of the management that may have a significant effect on the financial statements. This knowledge helps auditors identify areas for special attention (the places where errors, irregularities or frauds might exist), evaluate the reasonableness of accounting estimates made by management, evaluate management's representations and answers to enquiries and make judgements about the appropriateness of accounting principles choices, covered in section 5141.

Where does an auditor get this understanding of a business? By being there; by working in other companies in the same industry; by conducting interviews with management and other client personnel; by reading extensively—CICA accounting and audit guides, the *CGA-Canada Public Practice Manual*, industry publications, other companies' financial statements, business periodicals and textbooks; by getting a thorough familiarization presentation by the partner-in-charge of the audit before beginning the engagement; and by being observant and letting on-the-job experience sink into long-term memory. Auditors are increasingly structuring their understanding of the client's business through use of knowledge acquisition frameworks from strategic management. These strategic management frameworks (covered in more detail in Chapter 6) provide a structured approach to gaining deep knowledge of the client's business and industry.

There is no guarantee that all the auditors on an audit team will always agree among themselves on audit decisions, which range from inclusion or omission of procedures to conclusions about the fair presentation of an account or the financial statements as a whole. When differences of opinion arise, audit personnel should consult with one another and with experts in the firm to try to resolve the disagreement. If resolution is not achieved, the audit firm should have procedures to allow an audit team member to document the disagreement and to dissociate himself or herself from the matter. Particularly in a situation where there are disagreements, the basis for the final audit decision on the matter should be documented in the working papers for later reference.

Timing is important for audit planning. To have time to plan an audit, auditors should be engaged before the client's fiscal year-end. The more advance notice auditors can have, the better the service they are able to provide. An early appointment benefits both auditor and client. The audit team may be able to perform part of the audit at an **interim date**—a date some weeks or months before the fiscal year-end—and thereby make the rest of the audit work more efficient. At an interim date, auditors can perform preliminary analytical procedures, do a preliminary assessment of internal control risk, test the controls and audit some account balances. Advance knowledge of problems can enable auditors to alter the audit program as necessary so that year-end work (performed on and after the fiscal year-end date) can be more efficient. Advance planning for the observation of physical inventory and for the confirmation of accounts receivable is particularly important.

Too Late

FastTrak Corporation got mad at its auditor because the partner in charge of the engagement would not agree to let management use operating lease accounting treatment for some heavy equipment whose leases met the criteria for capitalization. FastTrak fired the auditors 10 weeks after the company's balance sheet date, then started contacting other audit firms to restart the audit. However, the audit report was due at the OSC in six weeks. Every other audit firm contacted by FastTrak refused the audit because it could not be planned and performed properly on such short notice with such a tight deadline.

Internal Control Assessment

The second examination standard requires an understanding of the client's internal control. Internal control consists of a company's control environment, accounting system and control procedures. The existence of a satisfactory internal control system reduces the probability of errors and irregularities in the accounts. This in turn provides the foundation for the work auditors do in an assessment of control risk. Control risk is the probability that a material misstatement (error or irregularity) could occur and not be prevented or detected on a timely basis by the company's internal control structure policies and procedures as discussed in section 5220.

Internal control may be defined simply as a system's capability to prevent or detect material data processing errors or fraud and provide for their correction on a timely basis. Auditors need to know enough about the client's control system to assess the control risk.

The primary purpose of control risk assessment is to help the auditors develop the audit program, which specifies the nature, timing and extent of the audit procedures for gathering evidence about the account balances that will go into the financial statements. The second field work standard presumes two necessary relationships: (*a*) good internal control reduces the control risk, and an auditor thus has a reasonable basis for minimizing the extent of subsequent audit procedures; (*b*) conversely, poor internal control produces greater control risk, and an auditor must increase the extent of subsequent audit procedures. If auditors were to assume no relationship between the quality of controls and the accuracy of output, then an assessment of control risk would be pointless. Audit efficiency would be lost in many cases. (Chapters 7 and 9 explain the work involved in control risk assessment.)

Sufficient, Appropriate Evidential Matter

Evidence is the heart of assurance function work for audits of financial statements and for assurance to nonfinancial information. The third examination standard requires auditors to obtain enough evidence to justify the decision about an opinion on financial statements. **Evidence** is all the influences upon the minds of auditors that ultimately guide their decisions. Evidence includes the underlying accounting data and all available corroborating

---

CONTROL LAPSE CONTRIBUTES TO DUPLICATE PAYMENTS

All Points Trucking processed insurance claims on damages to shipments in transit on its trucks, paying them in a self-insurance plan. After payment, the claims documents were not marked "paid." Later, the same documents were processed again for duplicate payments to customers, who kicked back 50 percent to a dishonest All Points employee. The auditors learned that the documents were not marked "paid," concluded that the specific control risk of duplicate payments was high, extended their procedures to include a search for duplicate payments in the damage expense account, found them, and traced the problem to the dishonest employee. Embezzlements of $35,000 per year were stopped.

---

information as discussed in section 5300. Appropriate evidence—evidence that is reliable and relevant—may be quantitative or qualitative; it may be objective or subjective; it may be absolutely compelling to a decision or it may only be mildly persuasive. The audit team's task is to collect and evaluate sufficient appropriate evidence to afford a reasonable and logical basis for audit decisions.

The standard refers to "sufficient," rather than "absolute," evidence. Auditors do not audit all of a company's transactions and events. They audit data samples and make audit decisions by inference, in most cases.

The standard takes a broad brush to procedures for gathering evidence—inspection, observation, enquiry and confirmation. This is not a complete enumeration of evidence-gathering procedures. (Chapter 8 contains a more thorough explanation of audit objectives and procedures.)

REVIEW CHECKPOINTS

2.4 What three elements of planning and supervision are considered essential in audit practice?

2.5 Why does the timing of an auditor's appointment matter in the conduct of a financial statement audit?

2.6 Why does an auditor obtain an understanding of the internal control system?

2.7 Define audit evidence.

GAAS REPORTING STANDARDS

LEARNING OBJECTIVE
3 Interpret the standard unqualified audit report.

The ultimate objective of independent auditors—the report on the audit—is guided by the four GAAS reporting standards. These four deal with GAAP, auditor and management responsibilities, adequate disclosure, and report content. Auditing standards dictate the use of a "standard report." (The standard unqualified audit report is shown in Exhibit 2–2, and you should review it in relation to the discussion that follows.)

"Unqualified," in the name of the report, means "good" in the sense that the auditors are not calling attention to anything wrong with the audit work or the financial statements. "Qualified" means "bad" in the sense that the financial statements contain a departure from GAAP or the scope of the audit work was limited. (You will study "qualified" audit reports in Chapter 3.) All standard **unqualified reports** contain these features:

1. **Title.** The title should refer to the auditor, thus indicating that the report is based on an audit examination and not some other types of engagement.

EXHIBIT 2-2   AUDITOR'S REPORT

To the Shareholders of ....

I have audited the balance sheet of .... as at ...., 20.........., and the statements of income, retained earnings and cash flow for the year then ended. These financial statements are the responsibility of the company's management. My responsibility is to express an opinion on these financial statements based on my audit.

I conducted my audit in accordance with Canadian generally accepted auditing standards. Those standards require that I plan and perform an audit to obtain reasonable assurance whether the financial statements are free of material misstatement. An audit includes examining, on a test basis, evidence supporting the amounts and disclosure in the financial statements. An audit also includes assessing the accounting principles used and significant estimates made by management, as well as evaluating the overall financial statement presentation.

In my opinion, these financial statements present fairly, in all material respects, the financial position of the company as at ...., 20.........., and the results of its operations and the cash flows for the year then ended in accordance with Canadian generally accepted accounting principles.

City   (signed) ....

Date   Chartered Accountant

Source: *CICA Handbook*, paragraph 5400.262.

2. **Address.** The report shall be addressed to the client, which occasionally may be different from the auditee.

3. **Notice of audit.** A sentence should identify the financial statements and declare that they were audited. This appears in the introductory paragraph.

4. **Responsibilities.** The report should state management's responsibility for the financial statements and the auditor's responsibility for the audit report. These statements are also in the introductory paragraph.

5. **Description of the audit.** The second paragraph (scope paragraph) should declare that the audit was conducted in accordance with generally accepted auditing standards and describe the principal characteristics of an audit.

6. **Opinion.** The report should contain an opinion (opinion paragraph) regarding conformity with generally accepted accounting principles.

7. **Signature.** The auditor should sign the report, manually or otherwise.

8. **Date.** The report should be dated with the date when all significant field work was completed.

Generally Accepted Accounting Principles (GAAP)

The fourth reporting standard refers to GAAP, which is used in most circumstances. In the audit report, this standard is shown to be met with the opinion sentence in the opinion paragraph: "In our opinion, the financial statements . . . present fairly in all material respects the financial position . . . and the results of operations and cash flows . . . in accordance with Canadian generally accepted accounting principles." In this opinion sentence, auditors make a statement of fact about their belief (opinion). Auditors are the professional experts, so users of financial statements rely upon the audit opinion.

However, determining the appropriate GAAP in a company's circumstances is not always an easy matter. Students often think of *CICA Handbook Recommendations* on accounting standards as the complete body of GAAP. Not so. GAAP consists of all the accounting methods and procedures that have substantial authoritative support. The *CICA Handbook* is only one source of such support, albeit the highest and most powerful. It is widely recognized that "the meaning of 'present fairly in accordance with GAAP' in the audit report" sets forth a hierarchy of authoritative support for various sources of GAAP.

Handbook Recommendations cover many accounting issues and problems. When the *Handbook* covers an issue, its standards are considered generally compelling. However, the *Handbook* has not covered all conceivable accounting matters. When a conclusion about GAAP cannot be found in *Handbook Recommendations,* auditors usually go down a hierarchy to find the next highest source of support for a client's accounting solution to a financial reporting problem. Reference can be made to positions on accounting matters by the affected provincial Securities Commission or to international standards. Reference can also be made to other countries' authoritative pronouncements such as the U.S.'s Financial Accounting Standards Board (FASB) announcements, industry audit and accounting guides, consensus positions of the CICA's Emerging Issues Committee, and other accounting literature.

The unqualified opinion sentence contains these implicit messages: (*a*) the accounting principles in the financial statements have general acceptance (authoritative support); (*b*) the accounting principles used by the company are appropriate in the circumstances; (*c*) the financial statements and notes are informative of matters that may affect their use, understanding and interpretation (full disclosure accounting principle); (*d*) the classification and summarization in the financial statements is neither too detailed nor too condensed for users; and (*e*) the financial statements are accurate within practical materiality limits, covered in section 5142 or ISA 320. This last feature refers to materiality and accuracy. Auditors and users do not expect financial account balances to be absolutely accurate to the penny. Accounting is too complicated, and too many estimates are used in financial statements to expect absolute accuracy. After all, many financial reports use numbers rounded to the thousands, even millions, of dollars! Everyone agrees that financial figures are "fair" as long as they are not "materially" misstated—that is, misstated by enough to make a difference in users' decisions. (Chapter 8 explains "materiality" in more detail.) All of these issues involve what is called professional judgement. Professional judgement can be defined very generally as "making a decision using professional standards and other criteria while maintaining professional ethics responsibilities." The preceding issues are examples of the need to exercise professional judgement in applying GAAP. (Chapter 4 covers auditors' professional ethics responsibilities.)

Consistency

The fourth reporting standard calls for explicit reporting in accordance with GAAP except in special circumstances. Prior to 1991, all audit reports contained a sentence confirming that GAAP had been "consistently applied" when no changes in the application of accounting principles had been made. This sentence referred to a company's use of the same accounting procedures and methods from year to year. However, an official pronouncement, section 1506, governs the accounting and disclosure of a company's change of accounting principles.

In 1991 the fourth reporting standard was changed to allow the audit report to be silent (that is, implicit) about consistency when no accounting changes had been made or any changes that were made were properly disclosed in the financial statements.

Adequate Disclosure

The fourth reporting standard also has a second implicit report element. The standard requires auditors to use professional judgement to decide whether the financial statements and related disclosures contain all the important accounting information users need for their decisions. Disclosure of information not specified completely in sources of authoritative support may be necessary. Auditors may need to deal with a rare and unusual fact situation that nobody has encountered before. Using this standard, auditors have latitude for determining what is important and what is not. Likewise, users of financial statements also have the right to claim that certain information is necessary for adequate disclosure. In fact, many lawsuits are brought forward on the issue that certain necessary information was not disclosed, and auditors must show reasons for lack of disclosure.

When auditors believe that some information is necessary for adequate disclosure, yet the company refuses to disclose it, a departure from GAAP exists. A "qualified opinion" is usually written, and the reason for the departure (missing disclosure) is described in the audit report. Sometimes the missing disclosure is added to the audit report itself.

Report Content

The third reporting standard states the requirements concerning an opinion. There are two elements in the first sentence:

1. The report shall contain either an expression of opinion on the financial statements or an assertion that an opinion cannot be expressed.

The first sentence divides opinion statements into two classes: (*a*) opinions on statements taken as a whole (i.e., unqualified, adverse and qualified opinions) and (*b*) the denial of opinion. An **adverse opinion** is the opposite of an unqualified opinion. It states that the financial statements are not in accordance with GAAP. A **denial of opinion** is an auditor's declaration that no opinion is given. The standard applies to financial statements as a whole, that is, the standard applies equally to a set of financial statements and footnotes and to each individual financial statement and footnote. The second sentence adds the requirement to explain why an opinion cannot be expressed:

2. In the latter case, the reasons therefore should be stated.

Combining reporting standards three and four, an explanation is required whenever there is a report reservation. Thus, when the adverse opinion, qualified opinion or denial of opinion is rendered, all the substantive reasons for doing so must be explained. An additional paragraph is generally used for such an explanation.

The first two reporting standards relate to auditor responsibilities and the need to identify the financial statements covered by the opinion. Every time PAs (even when acting as accountants associated with unaudited financial statements) are associated by name or by action with financial statements, they must report on their work and responsibility. The character of the work is usually described by the standard reference to an audit in accordance with generally accepted auditing standards. But if an audit has been restricted in some way or if the statements are simply unaudited, the auditor must say so.

The "degree of responsibility" is indicated by the form of the opinion. Auditors take full responsibility for their opinion about conformity with GAAP when they give either an unqualified or an adverse opinion. They take no responsibility whatsoever when they give a denial of opinion. They take responsibility when they give the qualified opinions for all matters except those stated as the reasons for the qualification. (Qualified and adverse opinions and denials of opinion are discussed more fully in Chapter 3.) These are part of the association rules that cover information the PA is "associated with." The association rules will be covered in Chapter 16 after you have been introduced to other types of PA engagements.

REVIEW CHECKPOINTS

2.8   What are the eight important features of a standard unqualified audit report?

2.9   Identify various authoritative support for GAAP with an indication of their ranking.

2.10 Do auditors take any responsibility for clients' choices of accounting principles?

2.11 What four kinds of audit opinion statements are identified in this chapter? What is the message of each one?

2.12 What messages are usually implicit in a standard audit report?

OVERVIEW OF THE AUDIT PROCESS
. . . .

LEARNING OBJECTIVE

④ Summarize the audit process.

In this section we give an overview of the audit process and the organization of the subsequent chapters as it relates to this process. The audit process is outlined in Exhibit 2–3.

1. Decide Whether to Accept or Retain the Client

An increasingly important decision is whether to do an audit in the first place. About half of all PA firms in Canada who did audits before the creation of the CPAB have decided to stop performing audits because they did not feel it was worthwhile to be monitored by the CPAB, or adhere to the new quality control standards. The consequences of quitting on a client can be severe in the SOX world, where the departing auditor must report publicly to the SEC within 24 hours why he/she is leaving. Other PA firms can quickly learn under this system what they are getting into. Recall the example from Chapter 1 where a $2 billion electronics manufacturer was forced to replace their CEO, and the board had to promise to take training classes in proper financial reporting and hire a new financially literate director for the audit committee before they could find a replacement auditor! This illustrates that auditors have much more leverage under SOX than previously.

Several issues need to be considered in accepting an engagement. Why is the audit requested? What are the client's expectations? Perhaps the client does not need an audit? Answering such questions helps manage expectations on both sides so as to reduce the number of problems later on. The Chapter 1 Molex example lists some dramatic changes in expectations with a new auditor.

An important issue for a first audit engagement is obtaining the client's permission to contact the predecessor auditor. Rules of professional conduct require getting such permission. The predecessor auditor has unique insights and knowledge that a successor auditor would find invaluable in gaining an understanding of the new client. On the other hand, failure to obtain such permission from the client is a warning sign to the new auditor that the client may have something to hide or is too risky. Increasingly, PA firms are paying more

---

E X H I B I T   2 - 3   OVERVIEW OF THE AUDIT PROCESS

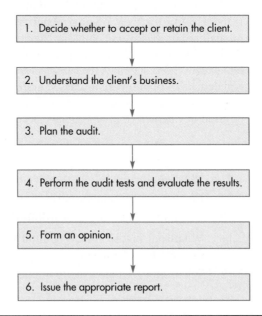

1. Decide whether to accept or retain the client.

2. Understand the client's business.

3. Plan the audit.

4. Perform the audit tests and evaluate the results.

5. Form an opinion.

6. Issue the appropriate report.

attention to the risks all clients bring with an engagement. If those risks prove to be too high, the PA firm will decline the engagement. If the PA firm turns down an engagement with a long existing client, this is sometimes referred to as *firing the client*. As seen with the demise of Arthur Andersen, firms should not keep risky clients, no matter how lucrative their fees. Fortunately, the recent improvements in corporate governance have reduced these risks for auditors.

Auditors also need to assess if they are independent of the client. This is a key consideration in quality control standards for audits. Factors to consider that affect the auditors independence with respect to an audit client include having any significant financial interest in the client, or performing incompatible other services for the client that puts the auditor in the position of auditing his own work. The general principle of independence rules is to avoid actual and perceived conflicts of interest with the users of financial statements. As you will see, independence and conflict-of-interest rules can become quite technical, but all of these need to be resolved before accepting the audit engagement.

A final major issue to consider before accepting an engagement is competency. Does the auditor have the business and industry expertise to carry out the audit effectively? Does the auditor have enough resources in the available time to perform an effective audit. Does the auditor have enough staff to take on the client and realistically meet reporting deadlines? Large clients tend to be audited by larger PA firms because they already have resources in place, offices and staff where the client has significant activities. There are definite economies of scale that come into play for global audit clients. For example, in auditing a large airline auditors not only need to be available to examine widely dispersed operations, but also to give specialized expertise required to meet local safety regulations. Safety regulations may require extensive technical monitoring reports, and a control system is needed to perform the necessary inspections and filing of timely reports to local regulators. Failure to do this can cause the airline to be shut down. To be effective in assuring proper disclosure of these risks and uncertainties in financial reporting the auditor needs to have the necessary expertise and resources. There are more factors to consider in accepting or retaining an engagement.

In the post-SOX environment an early decision needs to be made on whether the internal controls are providing sufficiently reliable data. A review of prior year's audit working papers can be very valuable. But auditors are increasingly interested in the client's capacity to maintain good controls since now they need to take more responsibility for them. For new clients, auditors ask for evidence that the underlying accounting records reconcile to the general ledger and that ending balances flow to the financial statements. Auditors also frequently ask for copies of prior-year financial statements and all adjusting journal entries as part of the process of initially assessing the client's internal control capabilities.

Finally, the auditor needs to consider the riskiness of accepting the client. This includes the likelihood of being sued and any other adverse effects of taking on the client. Some auditors are more risk averse than others; therefore, this is, in large part, a decision based on risk preferences. These issues are summarized in the following box:

ISSUES TO CONSIDER WHEN DECIDING TO ACCEPT OR RETAIN THE CLIENT

1. Why is the client requesting an audit?
2. Will the client allow you to contact the predecessor auditor, if applicable?
3. Is the auditor independent for this engagement?
4. Is the auditor competent for this engagement?

If the auditor decides to accept the client, the auditor should document the understanding with the client about the expectations and limitations of the audit engagement.

2. Understand the Client's Business

The auditor next needs to obtain a better understanding of the client's overall control environment and related risks, along with a better understanding of the client's business for the period under audit. At this point, the auditor performs preliminary analytical procedures to gain a better understanding. This consists of enquiries of management and analysis of the relationships of financial data for the period under audit. Preliminary analytical procedures help identify unusual (more risky) areas that the auditor may want to target for more detailed audit work. Enquiries can also be made with outsiders that deal with the client such as bankers, lawyers, outside analysts and business associations to help assess the overall reputation of the client.

Use of industry, client, and competitor websites and Internet searches are proving to be powerful tools in gaining an understanding of the client. Web logs ("blogs") include public comments about any topic including comments from customers, rivals employees, and even management (see GM's Vice-Chairman Bob Lutz's FastLaneBlog). This is a free and growing source of very current information on just about any topic. Blogs are estimated to be the fastest growing part of the Internet. Blogs tend to be linked by topic so fairly soon they may provide invaluable information to auditors on clients. The caution is that the information is frequently biased, anecdotal, speculative and unreliable. Although unreliable on their own, blogs, when combined with other information, can be useful in identifying company risks and potential financial statement disclosures.

An important new development is assigning forensic accountants on regular audit teams to screen for fraud risks. The forensic specialists talk to management and audit committees, especially when there are concerns about internal controls or information from whistle-blowers. Audit standards no longer allow auditors to assume that management is honest (as was done until 2003). The auditor must assess the risk of management fraud and if it is too high (the auditor will rarely be certain that there is no risk), she may need to call in the forensic specialists.

Auditors must assess a number of risks and keep reassessing them throughout the engagement as more evidence is gathered. (Chapters 7 and 8 cover assessment of risks in auditing in more detail.)

3. Plan the Audit

Assess Materiality

With sufficient understanding of the client and user needs, the auditor can further plan for the audit. The most basic planning decision is establishing the materiality level. That is, the auditor needs to identify the acceptable amount of misstatements. This is determined by the amount of misstatement that would affect user decisions. Clearly a one penny overstatement in office supplies is not going to affect any user's decision. But there must be a level at which it should make a difference—think back to the restaurant illustration at the beginning of Chapter 1. What amount of misstatement would be important to you?

Auditors need to make this assessment on every audit. Materiality is also discussed in your financial accounting courses. This is the same materiality used in planning the audit. You may wonder why not just set materiality equal to zero? The short answer is that would be too costly and because of the need to use estimates, impossible to do on a timely basis. You would have to wait until everything is realized before issuing financial statements. So, an auditor, and users, must settle for something greater than zero. How much greater depends on user needs and other circumstances—part of the context of the engagement covered in Chapter 1.

There are qualitative and quantitative aspects to materiality assessment. Examples of qualitative aspects include whether a misstatement will result in a change in an earnings trend, a change from a loss to a positive income, or a breach of a bond covenant. An intentional misstatement is much more serious than a random or unintentional one. An example of quantitative materiality is some rule of thumb based on a fixed percentage. In the restaurant example, a quantitative example is to use 5 percent of reported earnings.

The assessment of materiality has a pervasive impact on the audit so it is a key judgement made in audit planning. The engagement partner normally makes this decision near the beginning of the engagement. The materiality judgement and its consequences are further discussed in Chapters 3 and 8.

Assess Audit Risk

After identifying the materiality level, the auditor needs to assess the acceptable risk of material misstatement in the financial statements after the audit. This risk is called **audit risk**. The acceptable level of audit risk is determined by the auditor based on the consequences of the auditor failing to detect material misstatements. Important consequences include client dissatisfaction, possible lawsuits, and auditor loss of reputation. Arthur Andersen failed primarily due to its lost reputation when prosecuted for Enron and its clients left in droves. In fact, the whole profession's reputation was tarnished and it is now living with the consequences via the CPAB, SOX, and other regulatory fallout.

The auditor takes these risks into account by planning an appropriate level of audit risk for the engagement. This assessment is based on the auditor's tolerance for risk—the higher the tolerance the higher the planned audit risk. PA firms normally provide guidance for audit risk as a matter of firm policy because all partners feel the consequences of this decision. As with materiality it is not normally possible to reduce the risk to zero; therefore the auditor must decide on a maximum acceptable level for the audit engagement. This maximum level is referred to as **planned audit risk** (or "audit risk" for short). Like materiality, the audit risk has a pervasive impact on audit planning and that is why it is important to identify the risk level early in the planning process. Generally, as materiality or audit risk levels are increased the less evidence the auditor needs to gather. If either is decreased the auditor must do more work.

Make Preliminary Assessment of Inherent and Control Risk

In planning the audit, audit risk can be viewed as consisting of several components, with two important ones being inherent risk and control risk. **Inherent risk** is the risk of material misstatements before considering the effects of controls. **Control risk** is the risks that the internal controls will fail to detect and correct the material misstatements that do occur. Many auditors combine the evaluation of inherent and control risks because they feel this simplifies audit planning. For example, good controls, i.e., control risk is low, might have a deterrent effect on inherent risk so that inherent risks are lower when controls are strong (control risk is low).

Inherent and control risks are not set by the auditor at some planned level like audit risk is. Inherent and control risks are part of the client characteristics, part of the context of the audit. There is nothing the auditor can do to change these risks during the audit. The auditor's responsibilities are to assess them for audit planning purposes and to report on fairness of presentation of the client's internal control statement. Auditors consider both of these responsibilities in planning the audit.

Decide on Audit Strategy

For the audit of financial statements, the level of inherent and control risks can greatly influence the remainder of the audit strategy. The biggest impact is on the mix of testing of controls and testing of account balance procedures. The timing of the audit work can also be greatly affected. When auditors put more reliance on tests of controls, the audit work can be spread more evenly over the period under audit. When auditors do not put as much reliance on controls, most of the audit work is concentrated in the period immediately following the balance sheet date. More details on audit strategies are provided in Parts II and III of this text.

There can be considerable overlap between testing of controls as part of the audit of financial statements and testing of controls as part of the audit of internal control statements. The major difference is that in the audit of internal control statements the focus is on design of internal controls at a point in time, whereas in financial statement audits the focus of testing is on the performance of the system of control over a particular period—the same period of time as covered by the financial statements. Another way to characterize the difference is that control statements require more extensive tests of the design of the system whereas financial statement audits focus on testing the operations, assuming the design is good. (For more details, see Part II of the text.) These planning issues are summarized in the following box.

PLANNING THE AUDIT

1. Establish materiality.
2. Identify acceptable audit risk.
3. Make preliminary assessment of inherent and control risks.
4. Decide on audit strategy.

---

4. Perform the Audit Tests and Evaluate the Results

There are three broad categories of audit testing:

1. tests of internal control
2. substantive tests using analytical procedures
3. other substantive tests

The easiest way to distinguish between control testing (item 1) and substantive testing (items 2 and 3) is that control tests are indirect tests of the dollar accuracy of the financial statement amounts whereas substantive tests are direct tests of the accuracy of the financial statement numbers. At the planning stage, the broad mix of these categories of procedures is decided and the resulting strategies either concentrate most of the audit work in the months after the balance sheet date (called the balance sheet approach or substantive approach) or spread the audit work over a much longer period that includes the months well before the balance sheet date (called the income statement approach or combined approach). Audit staffing problems can be considerably reduced when the audit work can be spread over a longer period, but the combined approaches tend to be more complex and limited to the larger clients.

Regardless of the strategy, the auditor must collect sufficient appropriate evidence to support the audit opinion. The objective is the same—what varies among the strategies is the efficiency with which the audit can be conducted. The effectiveness of an audit should not be influenced by the type of strategy followed in carrying out the audit.

PERFORM THE AUDIT TESTS AND EVALUATE THE RESULTS

- Tests of controls:
  (a) for verifying control risk assessment below maximum
  (b) for issuing an opinion on management's report on internal controls
- Analytical procedures as substantive tests
- Other substantive procedures

---

5. Form an Opinion

At the end of the audit, after all the evidence has been gathered, the auditor should be able to reach a conclusion about the fairness of the presentation of the financial statements and the internal control statement. If not, he must be willing to state that he cannot reach an opinion.

6. Issue the Appropriate Report

The audit report is the most important part of the audit process because it is the only part that is visible to the public and thus determines the auditor reputation. In other words the audit report is the visible product of the audit. If the report did not reflect the auditor's true belief, it would be a fraudulent document and the auditor herself would be guilty of committing fraud. The SEC is on record as making such accusations against some of the major accounting firms. Hence, it is extremely important that the auditor's belief be accurately reflected in the report.

This explains why auditor independence and integrity can be even more important than auditor technical competence. If users are to accept the audit report at face value, then users need to have confidence that it reflects the auditor's true beliefs. The truthfulness of the audit report should be unimpeded by the fact that conflicts of interest can arise when the auditor is paid by the client to verify its performance. The Rules of Professional Conduct and Professional Ethics help assure that this is the case.

There are three major types of reports issued by the auditor: (1) the auditors report on the financial statements, (2) the auditors report on the internal control statement prepared by management and (3) the auditors' reports which are restricted to management and the audit committee. The first two reports are public. The third is a byproduct of the audit indicating how client's operations can be improved. The first two reports are explained in Chapter 3 and the third in Chapter 15. Most of this text deals with evidence gathering for the first report, which is the traditional audit report.

. . . .

R E V I E W   2.13   What factors should the auditor consider in accepting a client?
CHECKPOINTS   2.14   What are the auditor' responsibilities in detecting?

. . . .

PROFESSIONAL SKEPTICISM AND CRITICAL THINKING
. . . .

LEARNING OBJECTIVE
5 Outline the characteristics of professional skepticism and critical thinking.

"Professional skepticism" is a buzz phrase that appears frequently in auditing literature and speech. **Professional skepticism** is an auditor's tendency not to believe management assertions, a tendency to ask management to "prove it" (with evidence). Professional skepticism is inherent in applying due care in accordance with the general standards. The business environment that has seen errors and fraud in financial reports dictates this basic aspect of professional skepticism: "A potential conflict of interest always exists between the auditor and the management of the enterprise under audit."

Holding a belief that a potential conflict of interest always exists causes auditors to perform procedures to search for errors and frauds that would have a material effect on financial statements. This requirement tends to make audits more extensive and more expensive. The extra work is not needed in the vast majority of audits where no errors, irregularities or frauds exist. Nevertheless, auditors have had to react in all audits to the misdeeds perpetrated by a few people.

Even so, auditors must be careful when exercising professional skepticism and when holding a belief regarding a potential conflict of interest. Once an audit is under way and procedures that are designed to search for errors and frauds have been performed and none have been found, the audit team must be willing to accept the apparent fact there is no evidence that the potential conflict is a real one. Overtones of suspicion can be dispelled by evidence.

Still, due audit care requires professional skepticism on the part of auditors—a disposition to question all material assertions made by management whether oral, written or incorporated in the accounting records. However, this attitude of skepticism must be balanced with an open mind about the integrity of management. Auditors should neither blindly assume that every management is dishonest nor thoughtlessly assume management to be perfectly honest. The key lies in auditors' objectivity and in the audit attitude towards gathering the evidence necessary to reach reasonable and supportable audit decisions.

Professional skepticism is part of an older disciplined and more general approach to thinking called **critical thinking**. With the development of the broader assurance engagement concept discussed in the next section, there is a growing need for auditors to be aware of critical thinking. Critical thinking considers how, when *and whom* management is trying to persuade in making its assertions. A framework for critical thinking is introduced in Appendix 4B, after discussion of professional ethics in Chapter 4, which is also part of critical thinking. As auditors take more responsibility to detect fraud, an attitude of professional skepticism becomes increasingly important to the profession. Audits are part of the category of engagements called assurance, which is the topic of the next section.

REVIEW CHECKPOINTS

2.15   Why should auditors act as though there is always a potential conflict of interest between the auditor and the management of the enterprise under audit?

2.16   Can the auditor detect deception without being skeptical? Explain.

ASSURANCE STANDARDS

LEARNING OBJECTIVE

6 Explain the importance of general assurance standards, using examples of assurance matters.

In March 1997, the CICA issued section 5025, "Standards for Assurance Engagements." The significance of this standard, the first of its kind in the world, arises from the fact that it is intended to provide an umbrella framework for all existing and future audit-type engagements. This means the standard is intended to provide a framework for auditing and related engagements for a large variety of subject matters besides financial statement audits. Over time this framework will influence the future evolution of the rest of the *Handbook*. Its importance therefore cannot be overemphasized.

An *assurance engagement* is defined in paragraphs 5025.03–.04 as follows:

> An engagement where, pursuant to an accountability relationship between two or more parties, a practitioner is engaged to issue a written communication expressing a conclusion concerning a subject matter for which the accountable party is responsible. An *accountability relationship* is a prerequisite for an assurance engagement. An *accountability relationship* exists when one party (the "accountable party") is answerable to and/or is responsible to another party (the "user") for a subject matter or voluntarily chooses to report to another party on a subject matter. The accountability relationship may arise either as a result of an agreement or legislation, or because a user can be expected to have an interest in how the accountable party has discharged its responsibility for a subject matter.

The assurance standard does not supersede exisiting audit and review standards, but it is influencing future changes to more specific standards. The assurance framework is designed to provide guidance for expanding assurance service to new "subject matters" not currently covered in the *Handbook*. The general relationships are given in Exhibit 2–4.

EXHIBIT   2–4   UNIVERSE OF PA ENGAGEMENTS

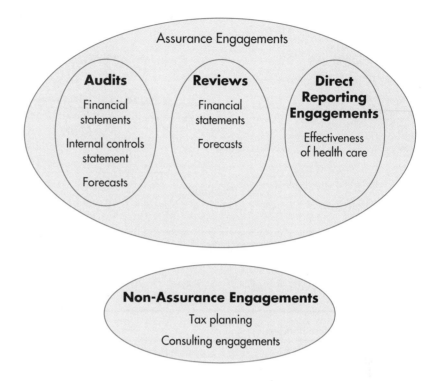

An assertion is a statement about some relevant aspect of a subject matter—for example, that a building exists as of a certain point in time. The assurance standards in section 5025 are quite broad in that they can be applied to assertions that are unwritten and only implied (called **direct reporting engagements**) as well as to written assertions (called **attestation engagements**). *Handbook* paragraphs 5025.05–.06 state:

> In an attest engagement the practitioner's conclusion will be on a written assertion prepared by the accountable party. The assertion evaluates, using suitable criteria, the subject matter for which the accountable party is responsible. In a direct reporting engagement, the practitioner's conclusion will evaluate directly using suitable criteria, the subject matter for which the accountable party is responsible. . . . In these standards, the accountable party is referred to as management. Depending on a circumstance, the user could include a variety of stakeholders such as shareholders, creditors, customers, the board of directors, the audit committee, legislators or regulators. The practitioner is the person who has overall responsibility for the assurance engagement.

These relationships are illustrated in Exhibit 2–5 following. For example, the practitioner of paragraph 5025.06 in a financial statement assurance engagement has traditionally been referred to as an **external auditor**. Since most of this text deals with financial statement audits, we will continue using the traditional terminology for much of the text. After we have become familiarized with other assurance services in Chapter 16, we will explain the assurance standards in more detail. Here, in this chapter, we focus on existing auditing standards and provide an overall comparison between GAAS and the newer assurance standard.

The assurance standard was written long after GAAS for financial statement audits. In Exhibit 2–6 you can see the ideas borrowed from the existing GAAS.

EXHIBIT   2-5   THREE PARTIES INVOLVED IN AN ASSURANCE ENGAGEMENT (THREE-PARTY ACCOUNTABILITY)

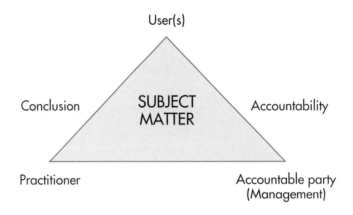

Source: *CICA Handbook*, paragraph 5025.07.

EXHIBIT   2-6   COMPARISON OF ASSURANCE AND AUDIT STANDARDS
(The numbers are in the sequence of the more familiar and specific GAAS)

Assurance Standards	Auditing Standards
1. The practitioner should seek management's acknowledgment of responsibility for the subject matter as it relates to the objective of the engagement. If the practitioner does not obtain management's acknowledgment, the practitioner should: (a) obtain other evidence that an accountability relationship exists, such as a reference to legislation or a regulation; (b) consider how the lack of management's acknowledgment might affect his or her work and conclusion; and (c) disclose in his or her report that acknowledgment of responsibility has not been obtained. The assurance engagement should be performed with due care and with an objective state of mind. The practitioner and any other persons performing the assurance engagement should have adequate proficiency in such engagements. The practitioner and any other persons performing the assurance engagement should collectively possess adequate knowledge of the subject matter. In addition, when a specialist is involved, the practitioner should consider whether the practitioner's involvement in the engagement and knowledge of the subject matter elements involving the specialist is sufficient to enable the practitioner to discharge his or her responsibilities.	1. The examination should be performed and the report prepared by a person or persons having adequate technical training and proficiency in auditing, with due care and with an objective state of mind.
2. The work should be adequately planned and the practitioner should ensure that any other persons performing the assurance engagement are properly supervised.	2. The work should be adequately planned and properly executed using sufficient knowledge of the entity's business as a basis. If assistants are employed they should be properly supervised.
	3. A sufficient understanding of internal control should be obtained to plan the audit. When control risk is assessed below maximum, sufficient appropriate audit evidence should be obtained through tests of controls to support the assessment.
4. The practitioner should consider the concept of significance and the relevant components of engagement risk when planning and performing the assurance engagement. Sufficient appropriate evidence should be obtained to provide the practitioner with a reasonable basis to support the conclusion expressed in his or her report.	4. Sufficient appropriate audit evidence should be obtained, by such means as inspection, observations, enquiry, confirmation, computation and analysis, to afford a reasonable basis to support the content of the report.

EXHIBIT 2-6   COMPARISON OF ASSURANCE AND AUDIT STANDARDS (continued)

Assurance Standards	Auditing Standards

5,6,7,8. As a minimum the practitioner's report should:

   (a) identify to whom the report is directed;

   (b) describe the objective of the engagement and the entity or portion thereof, the subject matter and the time period covered by the engagement;

   (c) in an attest report, identify management's assertion;

   (d) describe the responsibilities of management and the practitioner;

   (e) identify the applicable standards in accordance with which the engagement was conducted;

   (f) identify the criteria against which the subject matter was evaluated;

   (g) state a conclusion that conveys the level of assurance being provided and/or any reservation the practitioner may have;

   (h) state the date of the report;

   (i) identify the name of the practitioner (or firm); and

   (j) identify the place of issue.

5. The report should identify the financial statements and distinguish between the responsibilities of management and the responsibilities of the auditor.

6. The report should describe the scope of the auditor's examination.

7. The reservation should be expressed in the form of a qualification of conclusion or a denial of conclusion when the practitioner is unable to obtain sufficient appropriate evidence to evaluate one or more aspects of the subject matter's conformity with the criteria.

When the practitioner:

   (a) in a direct reporting engagement, concludes that the subject matter does not conform with criteria; or

   (b) in an attest engagement, concludes that the assertion prepared by management does not present fairly the criteria used or the conformity of the subject matter with the criteria or essential information has not been presented or has been presented in an inappropriate manner,

he or she should express a reservation in the form of a qualification of conclusion or an adverse conclusion.

7. The report should contain either an expression of opinion on the financial statements or an assertion that an opinion cannot be expressed. In the latter case, the reasons therefor should be stated.

8. A reservation should be expressed when the practitioner:

   (a) is unable to obtain sufficient appropriate evidence to evaluate one or more aspects of the subject matter's conformity with the criteria;

   (b) in a direct reporting engagement, concludes that the subject matter does not conform with the criteria; or

   (c) in an attest engagement concludes that (i) the assertion prepared by management does not present fairly the criteria used, (ii) the assertion prepared by management does not present fairly the subject matter's conformity with the criteria, or (iii) essential information has not been presented or has been presented in an inappropriate manner.

A reservation should provide an explanation of the matter giving rise to the reservation and, if reasonably determinable, its effect on the subject matter.

A. Before undertaking an assurance engagement, the practitioner should have a reasonable basis for believing the engagement can be completed in accordance with the standards in this *Section*.

B. The practitioner should identify or develop criteria that are suitable for evaluating the subject matter.

When generally accepted criteria consistent with the objective of the engagement exist, the practitioner should use them in forming his or her conclusion except when and only when, the intended users of practitioner's report are

8. Where an opinion is expressed, it should indicate whether the financial statements present fairly, in all material respects, the financial position, results of operations and changes in financial position in accordance with an appropriate disclosed basis of accounting, which except in special circumstances should be generally accepted accounting principles. The report should provide adequate explanation with respect to any reservation contained in such opinion.

EXHIBIT 2-6   COMPARISON OF ASSURANCE AND AUDIT STANDARDS (continued)

Assurance Standards	Auditing Standards
an identifiable limited group of users and he or she is satisfied such users agree their needs are met by using criteria other than generally accepted criteria. In such cases, the practitioner's report should not include a reservation with respect to generally accepted criteria but should include a caution that the report is intended only for the use of the intended users.	
In no circumstances should the practitioner perform the engagement using criteria which, in his or her judgement, would result in a report that would be misleading to intended users.	
C. The practitioner should document matters that in his or her professional judgement are important in providing evidence to support the conclusion expressed in his or her report.	

A, B, C, designates section 5025 standards that are not directly comparable to a GAAS standard.

The major differences lie in the areas of practitioner competence, internal control and reporting. With respect to practitioner competence, GAAS presume knowledge of accounting and require training and proficiency as an auditor (meaning an auditor of financial statements, since that was the only kind of assurance engagement being performed when the GAAS were written). On the other hand, the assurance standards are more general, requiring training and proficiency in assurance engagements and knowledge of the "subject matter of the engagement." The assurance service refers to the ability to recognize the information being asserted, to determine the evidence relevant to the assertions, and to make decisions about the correspondence of the information asserted with suitable criteria. The "knowledge of the subject matter" is not confined to accounting and financial assertions because assurance engagements may cover a wide variety of information. Note, however, that the first assurance standard does not allow auditors to provide assurance on assertions beyond their level of competence, for example, adherence to complex legal contracts.

The assurance standards, unlike GAAS, have no requirement regarding an understanding of the internal control structure for an information system. Considerations of internal control are implicit in the task of obtaining sufficient evidence for financial statement audits. However, some kinds of assured information may not have an underlying information control system in the same sense as a financial accounting and reporting system.

Reporting is different because assurance engagements on nonfinancial information do not depend upon generally accepted accounting principles. These are the only criteria for financial statement audits. The assurance standards speak of "evaluation against suitable criteria" and "accordance with generally accepted criteria" and they leave the door open for assurance engagements on a wide variety of informational assertions. An illustration of how far assurance engagements can go is provided in the *Wall Street Journal* article excerpt given in the first box on the next page.

The assurance standards shown in Exhibit 2–6 provide guidance and a broad framework for a wide variety of assurance engagements PAs can perform in public practice.

Many people appreciate the value of auditors' assurance to historical financial statements, and they have found other representations for PAs to assure, as illustrated in the second box on the next page.

An important new type of assurance engagement required by SOX is the audit of internal control statements prepare by management. Like audits of financial statements these internal control audits verify the accuracy of management's internal control statement. The fundamental difference is the subject matter.

A main objective in developing the assurance standards is to provide a general framework for, and set reasonable boundaries around, the assurance services offered by public accountants. Whether these standards actually "set boundaries" remains to be seen. After all, before the assurance standards were published, PAs were using the GAAS audit standards as a point of departure for other assurance engagements. New assurance opportunities must now use the assurance standards as the point of departure.

FORE!

Wilson Sporting Goods Company is using PAs to prove that amateur golfers can hit Wilson's Ultra golf ball farther than they can hit competitors' golf balls. Wilson says the PAs certify that Wilson's Ultra outdistances its competitors by an average of 5.7 yards per drive.

Competitors aren't impressed by Wilson's accountants. "I can walk off a golf ball's distance as well as any accountant," says Harry Groome, an accountant executive with Ayer, Inc., the ad agency for the Maxfli gold balls made by Dunlop Slazenger Corporation. "Using a PA is an odd way to measure a golf drive."

Marlene Baddeloo, a manager for the Chicago office of Coopers & Lybrand, which oversees the golf-ball competitions sponsored by Wilson, agrees "that anyone could pace off a golf driving range to see how far a ball goes." But she says Coopers staffers since last May have checked that Wilson employees haven't doctored the results at more than 30 driving ranges. "We also make sure the amateurs participating aren't affiliated with Wilson or its competitors and haven't been paid to participate," she adds.

The use of accountants may upset Wilson's competitors, but it sure makes the accountants happy. "Our personnel love . . . {to} wear shorts and spend the day out in the air," says Ms. Baddeloo. "I get a lot of volunteers."

Source: Lee Burton, "After This, CPAs May Take Over Instant-Replay Duties for Football." *The Wall Street Journal* July 19, 1991, p. B1. This work is protected by copyright and it is being used with the permission of *Access Copyright*. Any alteration of its content or further copying in any form whatsoever is strictly prohibited.

EXAMPLES OF ASSURANCE ENGAGEMENTS

- Insurance claims data.
- Labour data for union contract negotiation.
- Newspaper and magazine audience and circulation data.
- Integrity and security of a computer network.
- Investment performance statistics.
- GST and real estate tax bases.
- Political contributions and expenditures.
- Financial feasibility of a rapid transit system.
- Cost justification for a utility rate increase.
- Regulator's questionnaire on business ethics and conduct.

Source: Courtesy of Alan Winters.

A special framework in the *IFAC Handbook* covers the international standards for assurance engagements. It was issued in 2005 and was heavily influenced by the *CICA Handbook*, section 5025. Assurance standards are explained in more detail in Chapter 16.

2.17   What are the major differences between assurance standards and GAAS?

2.18   Define assurance engagements.

2.19   What is the theoretical essence of an assurance service?

2.20   What is the purpose served by assurance standards?

QUALITY CONTROL STANDARDS

LEARNING OBJECTIVE

7 Explain how requirements of quality control
standards are monitored
for PA firms.

Generally accepted auditing standards must be observed in each audit engagement conducted by a PA firm. Thus, each PA firm needs to observe GAAS in conducting its entire
audit practice. While GAAS relate to the conduct of each audit engagement, quality control
standards govern the quality of a PA firm's audit practice as a whole. Quality control can be
defined as actions taken by a public accounting firm to evaluate compliance with professional standards. And a "system of quality control" is designed to provide reasonable assurance of conforming with professional standards. Professional standards include GAAS as
covered in the *CICA Handbook*, as well as provincial Rules of Conduct.

Elements of Quality Control

The International Federation of Accountants (IFAC) has identified four basic elements of
quality control. These are listed and explained briefly in Exhibit 2–7. In contrast, the AICPA
has identified nine basic elements of quality control. These are as follows: (1) Independence, (2) Assigning personnel to engagements, (3) Consultation, (5) Supervision,
(5) Hiring, (6) Professional development, (7) Advancement, (8) Acceptance and continuation of engagements, and (9) Inspection. These may be further refined by the PCAOB. The
PCAOB has not yet moved on quality control standard setting, but plans to do so in the next
few years.

   Both the 1978 Adams Report (the *Report of the Special Committee to Examine the Role
of the Auditor*) and the 1988 Macdonald Commission Report (*Report of the Commission to
Study the Public's Expectations of Audits*) recommended the development of quality control standards to guide PA firms. More recently several regulatory agencies have taken initiatives to discipline substandard performance of professional staff in PA firms and criticized
the individual-level focus of the provincial disciplinary process. In response provincial institutes are amending their bylaws to bring firms, as well as individuals, within the disciplinary process. This expanded disciplinary process will require new guidelines for evaluating
systems of quality control. Increasing litigation is also putting pressure on firms to develop

EXHIBIT   2–7   ELEMENTS OF QUALITY CONTROL

1. Quality control policies and procedures should be implemented at both the level of the audit firm and
   on individual audits.
2. The audit firm should implement quality control policies and procedures designed to insure that all
   audits are conducted in accordance with ISAs or relevant national standards of practices.
3. The firm's general quality control policies and procedures should be communicated to its personnel in a
   manner that provides reasonable assurance that the policies and procedures are understood and
   implemented.
4. The auditor should implement those quality control procedures which are, in the context of the policies
   and procedures of the firm, appropriate to the individual audit. In particular, delegated work should be
   properly directed, supervised and reviewed.

Source: ISA 220. "This text is an extract from International Standard of Auditing 220 of the International Auditing and Assurance
Standards Board, published by the International Federation of Accountants (IFAC) in February 2006 and is used with permission."

good systems of quality control so that they can demonstrate compliance with professional standards and thus minimize the loss from litigation. Recently, the International Federation of Accountants has issued a policy statement proposing that member bodies provide more guidance on quality control systems. In its *Handbook*, the CICA has issued a framework of quality control standards for firms in performing assurance engagements. This framework is not considered part of assurance recommendations. The framework is listed in the box below. A CICA study entitled "Guide for Developing Quality Control Systems in Public Accounting" proposes detailed guidance based on five key components or areas: clients, personnel, engagement procedures, practice administration and a quality control review program.

Exhibit 2–8 illustrates the implementation of a quality control systems as proposed by the CICA study using the five key components as a framework. The study proposes that the areas of clients (including independence from the clients) and engagement procedures be given top priority when implementing a system in stages. The right-hand columns in Exhibit 2–8 reflect a suggested priority in setting up a firmwide quality control system. Note in Exhibit 2–8 that the five key components or quality control areas have been subdivided into a series of refined elements that allow firms to better articulate all the different aspects of quality control. The Exhibit 2–8 framework is not a standard at the current time, but indicates where Canadian more detailed guidance may be headed. Note that this framework can be extended to include tax and management advisory services, and one controversy is the extent to which these other services should also be considered in the quality control system.

However quality control standards evolve, firms can use these or similar criteria in developing their policies and procedures for quality control, and the related documentation. When a peer review or quality review is conducted, the reviewers "audit" the PA firm's statement of policies and procedures designed to ensure compliance with the elements of Exhibits 2–7 and 2–8 or similar criteria. These statements of policy and procedures may vary in length and complexity, depending on the size of the PA firm and the regulatory system affecting them. (Students who wish to know these policies and procedures in detail when interviewing for a job should ask for a copy of the firm's "quality control document.")

Accountability Boards Quality Control

As noted in Chapter 1, accountability boards have been created in the U.S. and Canada to help preserve the integrity of the financial reporting system. With respect to the monitoring of quality control of audit practice, these boards will be introducing new rules, most of which are geared to improving auditor independence. These rules include five-year rotations

---

.005 • *The firm's system of quality control should include policies and procedures addressing each of the following elements:*

(a) *leadership responsibilities for quality within the firm;*

(b) *ethical requirements;*

(c) *acceptance and continuance of client relationships and specific assurance engagements;*

(d) *human resources;*

(e) *engagement performance; and*

(f) *monitoring.*

The quality control policies and procedures should be documented and communicated to the firm's personnel. [DEC. 2005]

Source: The CICA Virtual Professional Library 2004

EXHIBIT 2-8   IMPLEMENTING A QUALITY CONTROL SYSTEM

Quality Control Area/Elements	First Priority	Second Priority
A. Clients (refer to Chapter 5)		
1. Independence and Objectivity	✔	
2. Prohibited Investments	✔	
3. Conflicts of Interest	✔	
4. Confidentiality	✔	
5. Acceptance and Continuance	✔	
6. New Client Proposals	✔	✔
B. Personnel (refer to Chapter 6)		
1. Hiring		✔
2. Assignment		✔
3. Performance Evaluation		✔
4. Advancement		✔
5. Continuing Professional Education	✔	
6. Restriction of Professional Staff Activities	✔	
C. Engagement Procedures (refer to Chapter 7)		
1. Engagement Letters	✔	
2. Planning and Execution	✔	
3. Documentation	✔	
4. Supervision and Review	✔	
5. Resolution of Differences of Opinion		✔
6. Consultation with Peers		✔
7. Independent Review	✔	
8. Management Letters	✔	
D. Practice Administration (refer to Chapter 8)		
1. Use of Firm Name		✔
2. Access to Client Files	✔	
3. Security of Confidential Information	✔	
4. Retention of Files		✔
5. Software Usage and Security		✔
6. Technical Reference Materials	✔	
7. Litigation and Professional Conduct		✔
8. Advertising and Promotion		✔
9. Solicitation of Clients	✔	
E. Quality Control Review Program (refer to Chapter 9)		
1. Internal Review		✔
2. Monitoring Client Services		✔
3. Monitoring Quality Control		✔
4. Premerger Review		✔
Total Elements	17	16

*Same as Exhibit 4–2 in CICA's *Guide for Developing Quality Control Systems in Public Accounting*, p. 35.

of partners, and strict limits on consulting services that have the potential to create conflicts of interest with the auditing role. Such prohibited consulting services include: valuation services, legal services, information technology systems design, and internal audits for clients with more than $50 million in assets. In addition, the U.S. Board will study the requirements of audit firm rotation, and the potential conflict created when audit firms' personnel leave to work for clients. These are primarily issues of professional ethics and are outlined in more detail in Chapter 4.

In monitoring PA firm quality control practices, the boards would need to consider implementation controls to prevent these conflicts. The quality control elements listed in Exhibits 2–7 and 2–8 are examples of criteria that could be used to implement the monitoring. In future, the accountability boards may issue their own standards for accounting firms' quality controls, including: monitoring of ethics and independence, internal and external consulting on audit issues, audit supervision, hiring, development and advancement of audit personnel, client acceptance and continuance, and internal inspections.

The PCAOB has indicated that it will actively set future auditing independence and quality control standards. In contrast, the CPAB has indicated they will let the profession decide on these standards.

Monitoring of Quality Control: Practice Inspection, Peer Reviews and Quality Inspections

Practice inspection, peer reviews and quality inspections are "audits of the auditors." **Practice inspection** is the name given to the system of reviewing and evaluating practice units' audit files and other documentation by an independent external party. The main objective of practice inspection is to evaluate conformity of members' work with the *CICA Handbook* and professional, ethical principles and rules of conduct (covered in Chapter 4). The practice unit can be an individual or an entire office, in which case the individual members of the office are evaluated relative to their level of responsibility. Provincial institutes' practice inspection programs apply to all members and consist of several steps:

1. selection of practice unit for inspection (a practice unit can be a PA firm, an office of a firm or a sole practitioner)
2. completion of practice inspection questionnaires gathering general information about the practice and quality control systems of the practice unit
3. assignment of inspector
4. inspection of a sample of engagement files
5. report of inspection—each report focuses on an individual in a practice units
6. follow-up review
7. a report to the professional conduct committee if necessary[2]

There are some minor variations among provincial practice inspection programs relating to types of engagements reviewed and the way the inspection reports are prepared. The overall focus is on an individual member's performance, and the orientation is more educational than disciplinary in character, although serious deficiencies of professional practice could lead to a complaint with a professional conduct committee. This is further explained in Chapter 4. Practice inspections are a useful complement to a firm's system of quality control. Their success is reflected in the fact that many countries have followed this Canadian model, including Ireland, Norway, China and Australia.

Peer reviews are a practice inspection, usually done as a special engagement by another audit firm. A firm's peer review usually is done by another PA firm engaged by the firm reviewed. The reviewers issue a report giving conclusions about the firm's compliance with quality control standards and making recommendations about ways to improve the audit practice.

Quality inspections are an examination and evaluation of the quality of the overall practice. They are thus aimed more at the firm level rather than at individuals. A quality inspection involves an extensive study of a firm's quality control document, including interviews with audit personnel and selection of audit engagements for detailed study of the quality of work and of adherence to GAAS and quality control standards.

A quality inspection has the same objective as a peer review, but is less extensive. Quality inspections usually are requested by the smaller PA firms. The new accountability boards have taken on the primary job of regulating inspections of firms' audit operations to ensure compliance with the various quality control criteria outlined in the preceding section.

Their inspection inspection reports can be found at their websites: www.cpab-ccrc.org for the CPAB and www.pcaobus.org for the PCAOB inspection reports, respectively.

---

[2] CICA, *Guide for Developing Quality Control Systems in Public Accounting* (CICA, 1993), p. 17.

The first CPAB report dealt with the first inspections of the Big Four firms in Canada (issued October 6, 2004). The most common problems were the lack of documentation (work was said to have been done, but there was no documentation of it) and independence violations. But the CPAB indicated that these problems did not represent negligent work. However, there are definite expectations of improvement in future inspections.

SEC Practice Section members are also required to report to the SEC any litigation against the firm or its personnel alleging audit deficiencies involving public companies or regulated financial institutions. The SEC obtains lawsuit documents related to the litigation, but it does not attempt to try the case. The SEC's goal is to determine whether the litigation has any bearing on quality control deficiencies in the public accounting firm. In Canada sometimes a regulator such as the OSC will ask that a PA firm or individual be reviewed by a provincial institute reviewer. In the future, this will more likely involve the Public Accountability Board. This is usually in response to a complaint made to the regulator, but it sometimes arises from regular monitoring of annual reports and filings submitted to the regulator.

The extent of work involved in practice inspections, peer reviews or quality inspections is greatly influenced by the quality of documentation concerning the quality control system. Generally, if the quality control documentation is good and the reviewer can rely on extensive internal monitoring of quality control, less work is required than if documentation is poor and the reviewer must rely more on her own detailed inspection of files.

REVIEW CHECKPOINTS

2.21 Consider the following quality control policy, identifying the quality control element to which it relates: "Designate individuals as specialists to serve as authoritative sources; provide procedures for resolving differences of opinion between audit personnel and specialists."

2.22 What is the practice inspection, and what roles does it play in the quality control self-regulation of the profession?

2.23 Compare the quality inspection reports of CPAB and PCAOB. Do the PA firms in the U.S. and Canada have similar quality control problems?

2.24 What is the meaning of quality control as it relates to a PA firm?

SUMMARY

The assurance standards are the general framework for applying "assurance engagements" to a wide range of subjects. They are the quality guides for general assurance work. Theoretically, they could serve as quality guides for independent audits of financial statements. However, they were created long after GAAS for audits of financial statements, and therefore GAAS remains the predominant framework for most engagements.

Financial statement auditors are most concerned with the eight GAAS standards because they are the direct guides for the quality of everyday audit practice. The general standard sets requirements for auditors' competence, objectivity and due professional care. The three examination standards set requirements for planning and supervising each audit, obtaining an understanding of the client's internal controls and obtaining sufficient appropriate evidence to serve as a basis for an audit report. The four reporting standards cover requirements for GAAP, auditor and management responsibilities, adequate disclosure and report content.

These GAAS have been widely copied. When you study Chapter 18, on public sector and internal auditing, you will see that the CICA and internal audit standards incorporate all the GAAS and many elements of assurance concepts. All auditors have some common ground in generally accepted auditing standards.

In all matters relating to financial statement audits, auditors are advised to have a sense of professional skepticism. This attitude is reflected in a "prove it with evidence" response to management representations, to answers to enquiries and to financial statement assertions themselves. Critical thinking is a broader idea covered in Chapter 4 that considers not only the evidence, but also whether management representations themselves are useful. Critical thinking considers how and when management is trying to persuade users.

While assurance standards and GAAS govern the quality of work on each individual engagement, the quality control elements guide a PA firm's audit practice as a whole. Quality control is the foundation of the self-regulatory system of peer review, practice inspection and quality inspection. The nine elements of independence, assigning personnel, consultation, supervision, hiring, professional development, advancement, acceptance and continuance of clients, and inspection are usually the objects of a firm's policies and procedures for assuring that GAAS are followed faithfully in all aspects of the firm's practice.

As an auditor, you must have a thorough understanding of these practice standards, especially GAAS. All practical problems can be approached by beginning with a consideration of the practice standards in question. Auditing standards do not exist in a vacuum. They are put to work in numerous practical applications. Practical applications of the standards will be shown in subsequent chapters on audit program planning, execution of auditing procedures, gathering evidence and auditing decisions.

MULTIPLE-CHOICE QUESTIONS FOR PRACTICE AND REVIEW

Check the website, www.mcgrawhill.ca/college/robertson, for additional end-of-chapter material.

2.25 It is always a good idea for auditors to begin an audit with the professional skepticism characterized by the assumption that:
  a. A potential conflict of interest always exists between the auditor and the management of the enterprise under audit.
  b. In audits of financial statements, the auditor acts exclusively in the capacity of an auditor.
  c. The professional status of the independent auditor imposes commensurate professional obligations.
  d. Financial statements and financial data are verifiable.

2.26 When Client Company prohibits auditors from visiting selected branch offices of the business, this is an example of interference with:
  a. Reporting independence.
  b. Investigative independence.
  c. Auditors' training and proficiency.
  d. Audit planning and supervision.

2.27 After the auditors learned of Client Company's failure to record an expense for obsolete inventory, they agreed to a small adjustment to the financial statements because the Client president told them the company would violate its debt agreements if the full amount were recorded. This is an example of a lack of:
  a. Auditors' training and proficiency.
  b. Planning and supervision.
  c. Audit investigative independence.
  d. Audit reporting independence.

2.28 The primary purpose for obtaining an understanding of the company's internal controls in a financial statement audit is:
  a. To determine the nature, timing and extent of auditing procedures to be performed.
  b. To make consulting suggestions to the management.
  c. To obtain direct sufficient appropriate evidential matter to afford a reasonable basis for an opinion on the financial statements.
  d. To determine whether the company has changed any accounting principles.

2.29 Auditors' activities about which of these generally accepted auditing standards are not affected by the auditee's utilization of a computerized accounting system?
  a. The audit report shall state whether the financial statements are presented in accordance with GAAP.
  b. The work is to be adequately planned and assistants, if any, are to be properly supervised.
  c. Sufficient appropriate evidential matter is to be obtained . . . to afford a reasonable basis for an opinion regarding the financial statements under audit.
  d. The audit is to be performed by a person or persons having adequate technical training and proficiency as an auditor.

2.30 Which of the following is not found in the standard unqualified audit report on financial statements?
  a. An identification of the financial statements that were audited.
  b. A general description of an audit.
  c. An opinion that the financial statements present financial position in conformity with GAAP.
  d. An emphasis paragraph commenting on the effect of economic conditions on the company.

2.31 The assurance standards do not contain a requirement that auditors obtain:

a. Adequate knowledge in the subject matter of the assertions being examined.

b. An understanding of the auditee's internal control structure.

c. Sufficient evidence for the conclusions expressed in an attestation report.

d. Independence in mental attitude.

2.32 Auditor Jones is studying a company's accounting treatment of a series of complicated transactions in exotic financial instruments. She should look for the highest level of authoritative support for proper accounting in:

a. Provincial Securities Commission Staff Position Statements.

b. CICA industry audit and accounting guides.

c. CICA recommendations in the *Handbook*.

d. Emerging Issues Committee Consensus Statements.

2.33 Which of the following is not an example of a quality control procedure likely to be used by a public accounting firm to meet its professional responsibilities to clients?

a. Completion of independence questionnaires by all partners and employees.

b. Review and approval of audit plan by the partner in charge of the engagement just prior to signing the auditor's report.

c. Evaluating professional staff after the conclusion of each engagement.

d. Evaluating the integrity of management for each new audit client.

2.34 Which of the following concepts is not included in the wording of the auditor's standard report?

a. Management's responsibility for the financial statements.

b. Auditor's responsibility to assess significant estimates made by management.

c. Extent of auditor's reliance on the client's internal controls.

d. Examination of evidence on a test basis.

2.35 Which of the following is not mandatory when performing an audit in accordance with Generally Accepted Auditing Standards?

a. Proper supervision of assistants.

b. Efficient performance of audit procedures.

c. Understanding the client's system of internal controls.

d. Adequate planning of work to be performed.

EXERCISES AND PROBLEMS

2.36 **Audit Independence and Planning.** You are meeting
LO.4 with executives of Cooper Cosmetics Corporation to arrange your firm's engagement to audit the corporation's financial statements for the year ending December 31. One executive suggests the audit work be divided among three staff members. One person would examine asset accounts, a second would examine liability accounts and the third would examine income and expense accounts to minimize audit time, avoid duplication of staff effort and curtail interference with company operations.

Advertising is the corporation's largest expense, and the advertising manager suggests that a staff member of your firm, whose uncle owns the advertising agency that handles the corporation's advertising, be assigned to examine the Advertising Expense account. The staff member has a thorough knowledge of the rather complex contact between Cooper Cosmetics and the advertising agency.

Required:

a. To what extent should a PA follow the client's suggestions for the conduct of an audit? Discuss.

b. List and discuss the reasons why audit work should not be assigned solely according to asset, liability and income and expense categories.

c. Should the staff member of your PA firm whose uncle owns the advertising agency be assigned to examine advertising costs? Discuss.

2.37 **Examination Standards.** You have accepted the en-
LO.2 gagement of auditing the financial statements of the C. Reis Company, a small manufacturing firm that has been your client for several years. Because you were busy writing the report for another engagement, you sent a staff accountant to begin the audit, with the suggestion that she start with the accounts receivable. Using the prior year's working papers as a guide, the auditor prepared a trial balance of the accounts, aged them, prepared and mailed positive confirmation requests, examined underlying support for charges and credits, and performed other work she considered necessary to obtain evidence about the validity and collectibility of the receivables. At the conclusion of her work, you reviewed the working papers she prepared and found she had carefully followed the prior year's working papers.

Required:

The opinion rendered by a PA states that the audit was made in accordance with generally accepted auditing standards.

List the three generally accepted standards of field work. Relate them to the above illustration by indicating how they were fulfilled or, if appropriate, how they were not fulfilled.

(ICAO adapted)

2.38 **Time of Appointment and Planning.** Your public
LO.4 accounting practice is located in a town of 15,000

population. Your work, conducted by you and two assistants, consists of compiling clients' monthly statements and preparing income tax returns for individuals from cash data and partnership returns from books and records. You have a few corporate clients; however, service to them is limited to preparation of income tax returns and assistance in year-end closings where bookkeeping is deficient.

One of your corporate clients is a retail hardware store. Your work for this client has been limited to preparing the corporation income tax return from a trial balance submitted by the bookkeeper.

On December 26 you receive from the president of the corporation a letter containing the following request:

> We have made arrangements with the First National Bank to borrow $500,000 to finance the purchase of a complete line of appliances. The bank has asked us to furnish our auditor's certified statement as of December 31, which is the closing date of our accounting year. The trial balance of the general ledger should be ready by January 10, which should allow ample time to prepare your report for submission to the bank by January 20. In view of the importance of this certified report to our financing program, we trust you will arrange to comply with the foregoing schedule.

Required:

From a theoretical viewpoint, discuss the difficulties that are caused by such a short-notice audit request.

(AICPA adapted)

2.39 **Reporting Standards.** PA Musgrave and his associates
LO.3 audited the financial statements of North Company, a computer equipment retailer. Musgrave conducted the audit in accordance with the general and field work standards of generally accepted auditing standards and therefore wrote a standard audit description in his audit report. Then he received an emergency call to fill in as a substitute tenor in his barbershop quartet.

No one else was in the office that Saturday afternoon, so he handed you the complete financial statements and footnotes and said: "Make sure it's OK to write an unqualified opinion on these statements. The working papers are on the table. I'll check with you on Monday morning."

Required:

In general terms, what must you determine in order to write an unqualified opinion paragraph for Musgrave's signature?

2.40 **GAAS in a Computer Environment.** The Lovett Cor-
LO.2 poration uses an IBM mainframe computer system with peripheral optical reader and high-speed laser printer equipment. Transaction information is initially recorded on paper documents (e.g., sales invoices) and then read by optical equipment that produces a magnetic disk containing the data. These data file disks are processed by a computer program, and printed listings, journals and general ledger balances are produced on the high-speed printer equipment.

Required:

Explain how the audit standard requiring "adequate technical training and proficiency" is important for satisfying the general and field work standards in the audit of Lovett Corporation's financial statements.

2.41 **Audit Report Language.** The standard unqualified re-
LO.3 port contains several important sentences and phrases. Give an explanation of why each of the following phrases is used instead of the alternative language indicated.
  1. Address: "To the Board of Directors and Stockholders" instead of "To Whom It May Concern."
  2. "We have audited the balance sheet of Anycompany as of December 31, 1997, and the related statements of income, retained earnings and cash flows for the year then ended" instead of "We have audited the attached financial statements."
  3. "We conducted our audit in accordance with generally accepted auditing standards" instead of "Our audit was conducted with due audit care appropriate in the circumstances."
  4. "In our opinion, the financial statements referred to above present fairly . . . in conformity with generally accepted accounting principles" instead of "The financial statements are true and correct."

2.42 **Public Oversight of the Accountancy Profession.** The
LO.7 Canadian Public Accountability Board (CPAB) and the Public Company Accounting Oversight Board (PCAOB) in the U.S. will provide oversight for public accountants who audit public companies. What are the objectives of these boards? What factors should these boards consider in assessing public accountants' work?

2.43 **Scope of an Audit, Requirement for Specialist Ex-
LO.4 pertise.** Consider the following two situations.
  a. The auditor discovers during the audit that the client company has entered a complex legal contract that involves transferring assets to another company if that company performs certain future services by obtaining supplies from a foreign country. The auditor is unable to establish whether the contract imposes any financial liability or has any other financial impact on the client company.
  b. The auditor learns that the client company is required to comply with environmental standards that require it to monitor various emissions using complex scientific techniques. The amounts of the financial penalties that can be imposed by the government are determined by the nature and extent of noncompliance with these scientific standards.

Required:

Contrast these two situations in terms of the auditor's responsibility to perform audit procedures and issue a report. Include a recommendation on which form of report would be issued in each case, based on your analysis.

2.44 **Assurance Engagements, General Assurance
LO.4 Standards.** A radio advertisement for a new software

management product included the following statement: "According to ITR, Knovel's new software product will pay back in three months."

ITR is an information technology (IT) research firm that is hired by various companies in the IT industry to provide reports on IT usage and sales in the IT market. As soon as ITR's president heard the ad on his car radio, he immediately phoned Knovel and told them to stop using the ad.

Required:
Discuss whether ITR's statement is the result of an assurance engagement. Consider the parties involved, the subject matter, the accountability relationships, the nature of the report and any other relevant aspects of the situation. Why do you think ITR's president wanted the ad stopped?

2.45   Fair Presentation in Accordance with GAAP. The
LO.3   fourth reporting standard of GAAS states that the auditor's opinion on the financial statements should indicate whether they present fairly the financial position, results of operations and changes in financial position in accordance with GAAP. The CICA *Handbook Recommendations* are an important source of GAAP. However, the *Recommendations* may allow for different interpretations and choices in how they are applied, or they may be silent.

Required:
a. How does the auditor assess whether financial statements are in accordance with GAAP when a conclusion on GAAP is not found in the CICA *Handbook Recommendations*? Give an example of an accounting issue that may not be covered in the *Recommendations*.
b. How does the auditor assess whether financial statements are in accordance with GAAP when the CICA *Handbook Recommendations* allow for different accounting methods to be acceptable? Give an example of an accounting issue for which alternate acceptable accounting treatments are provided in the *Recommendations*.

2.46   Missing Disclosure Described in Auditor's Report.
LO.3   Bunting Technology Corporation is a large public company that manufactures the IXQ, a telecommunications component that speeds up Internet transmission over fibre optic cable. Subsequent to its current year end, but before the audited financial statements are issued, a competitor of Bunting launches a new product that increases transmission speed one hundred times more than Bunting's IXQ and sells for one-tenth of the price. Bunting has approximately 11 months of inventory of the IXQ in inventory, based on the current year's sales levels.

Bunting's auditors, Ditesmoi & Quail (DQ), have determined that this subsequent event warrants a writedown of Bunting's year end inventory to reflect technological obsolescence. Given that the IXQ is Bunting's main product, the writedown will be highly material. DQ argues that this development will result in a permanent change in Bunting's future earnings potential and cash flows, and it would be misleading users if it is not included in the current year financial statements.

Bunting's management refuses to record the inventory writedown, arguing that the event occurred after the year end and therefore does not relate to the current year's results. Also, since the competitor's product is brand new, management argues that there is significant uncertainty about whether it will perform as well as the competitor claims in actual use. Thus, it is premature to assume it will have an impact on IXQ sales, and it is impossible to estimate a dollar amount of the impact. Management is also concerned that by publicly reporting information about the competing product in Bunting's annual report, DQ will jeopardize several large sales contracts that Bunting is currently negotiating and this may lower sales even more than if the information were withheld.

DQ issues a qualified audit report that spells out its estimate of the material impact of the technological obsolescence on Bunting's assets, net income and retained earnings.

Required:
Discuss the issues raised by DQ's decision to issue a qualified report in this situation. Consider the impact of DQ's audit report qualification on Bunting, on users of the audited financial statements, and on DQ as Bunting's auditor.

2.47   Auditor's "Professional Scepticism." Auditors are re-
LO.5   quired to have "professional scepticism" but an auditor must also rely on management representations in order to complete the audit. Discuss the inherent conflicts in these two requirements and how they may be resolved.

2.48   Assurance Engagement Other than Audit or Review.
LO.6   During 2002 and 2003, United Nations weapon inspectors entered Iraq to search for "weapons of mass destruction." These include chemical, biological and nuclear weapons. It has been reported that these weapons and equipment for manufacturing them may be concealed in public buildings such as schools, hospitals or apartment buildings.

Required:
Identify the subject matter and design an approach for assessing risks and probabilities of weapons existing, and for implementing the inspection. Use basic audit definitions and approaches from financial statement auditing. For example, compare the weapons inspectors' objectives to the approach to looking for a material understatement of a financial statement liability.

2.49   On the Internet, check the
LO.7   most recent CPAB report.

CHAPTER

3

Reports on Audited Financial Statements and Audited Internal Control Statements

This chapter covers the most frequent variations in audit reports. Management has primary responsibility for the fair presentation of financial statements in conformity with generally accepted accounting principles. Auditors have primary responsibility for their own audit reports of the financial statements. You must know the standard unqualified report as a starting place because this chapter explains reasons for changing the standard language when auditors cannot give a "clean opinion."

LEARNING OBJECTIVES

After completing this chapter, you will be able to:

1 Determine whether a PA is associated with financial statements.

2 Describe the three levels of assurance.

3 Compare and contrast the scope and opinion paragraphs in a standard unqualified audit report.

4 For a given set of accounting facts and audit circumstances, analyze a qualified, adverse, and denial audit report.

5* Write an unqualified audit report, containing additional explanation or modified wording for specific issues allowed by GAAS.

6 Compare and contrast the opinions in a financial statement audit versus an internal control audit.

7 Explain why auditors have standards for reporting on the "application of accounting principles."

8 Determine the effects of materiality on audit report choices.

9* Write an audit report in which the principal auditor refers to the work of another auditor. (Appendix 3A)

10* Write the required modifications to the audit report when prior-year comparative financial statements are changed. (Appendix 3A)

11* Identify the type of audit report issued when an audit engagement is limited. (Appendix 3A)

12* Explain auditors' reporting responsibilities with respect to "other information" and supplementary (including pro forma) information. (Appendix 3A)

13* Describe the reporting requirements involved in auditors' association with summarized financial information. (Appendix 3A)

* Learning objectives marked with an asterisk (*) and their corresponding topics are considered advanced material. *Note:* Appendix 3A is located on the text Online Learning Centre.

ASSOCIATION WITH FINANCIAL STATEMENTS

LEARNING OBJECTIVE

1 Determine whether a PA is associated with financial statements.

Auditing standards require a report to be rendered in all cases where a PA's name is **associated with financial statements**. As a PA, you are associated with financial statements when (1) you have consented to the use of your name in connection with the statements; or (2) you have prepared or performed some other services with respect to the statements, even if your name is not used in any written report, covered in *Handbook,* paragraph 5020.04.

The concept of association is far-reaching. PAs are associated with financial statements and must render reports even in such cases as these: (1) financial statements are merely reproduced on an accountant's letterhead, (2) financial statements are produced by the accountant's computer as part of a bookkeeping service, and (3) a document containing financial statements merely identifies an accountant as the public accountant or auditor for the company. The reason a report is required is that most users of financial statements assume that an audit has been conducted and that "everything is OK" whenever an independent accountant is known to be involved with financial statements. Consequently, an obligation exists to inform the users about the nature of the work performed, if any, and the conclusions the PA has made about the financial statements. This is summarized in more detail on the text Online Learning Centre.

The next section outlines the various levels of assurance that are possible in PA engagements. We then discuss in detail the audit reports that result from an audit of financial statements—the main type of auditing covered in this chapter and text. We end the chapter, however, with a discussion of the audit report that arises from the audit of management's internal control statement. This relatively new report was prompted by SOX and the post-Enron environment that led to SOX.

REVIEW CHECKPOINT

3.1   Why should PAs issue a report whenever they are associated with financial statements?

LEVELS OF ASSURANCE

· · · · · · · · · · · ·

In practice, accountants and auditors can render three types of conclusions (known as **levels of assurance**) about financial statements. The highest level is considered to be the audit assurance exemplified by the standard unqualified report (sometimes known as the **clean opinion**). Its opinion sentence reads: "In our opinion, the accompanying financial statements present fairly, in all material respects." This opinion sentence is sometimes called **positive assurance** because it is a forthright and factual statement of the PA's opinion based on an audit. Positive assurance is also frequently referred to as **reasonable** or **high assurance** in the *Handbook*. ISA 100 also refers to audit assurance as high assurance.

The middle level is known as **moderate** or **negative assurance**. A negative assurance conclusion is typical in the review report of unaudited financial statements, thus: "Based on my review, nothing has come to my attention that causes me to believe that these financial statements are not, in all material respects, in accordance with Canadian generally accepted accounting principles" per paragraph 8200.42 of the *Handbook*. This conclusion is called negative because it uses the backdoor phrase "nothing has come to my attention" to give assurance about conformity with GAAP. Auditing standards prohibit the use of negative assurance in reports on audited financial statements because it is considered too weak a conclusion for the audit effort involved, covered in section 5400.15. However, negative assurance is permitted in reviews of unaudited financial statements, in letters to underwriters, and in reviews of interim financial information. (More details about review reports on unaudited financial statements are found in Chapter 16.)

The lowest level of assurance is a **no assurance** engagement. The most common examples are compilation engagements, which can be considered a form of specified procedures engagements. Compilation engagements are not considered to be assurance engagements because the practitioner is not required to audit, review, or otherwise attempt to verify the accuracy or completeness of the information provided by management. The practitioner is, therefore, not expressing a conclusion on the reliability of the statements compiled. The auditor's involvement in compiling the financial statements is presumed, however, to add accounting credibility to the financial statements even though there is no supporting evidence or audit assurance provided. For example, accounting credibility includes the use of correct account titles and format of the financial statements without verifying the accuracy of the underlying accounting records. (More details about compilation reports on unaudited financial statements are in Chapter 16).

The levels of assurance are depicted in Exhibit 3–1. It should be noted that audit, review and compilation engagements are intended to provide the specified assurance levels given in Exhibit 3–1. As we will see when discussing the denial of opinion, under some conditions not even an audit engagement can provide much assurance.

EXHIBIT 3–1 LEVELS OF ASSURANCE

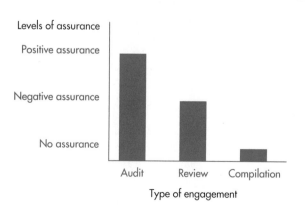

. . . .

REVIEW
CHECKPOINTS

3.2   What is the most important distinction between an auditor's opinion on financial statements and other PA communications?

3.3   What is negative assurance? When is negative assurance permitted?

3.4   What is the difference between assurance and accounting credibility?

. . . .

STANDARD UNQUALIFIED REPORT AND VARIATIONS

. . . .

LEARNING OBJECTIVE

3 Compare and contrast the scope and opinion paragraphs in a standard unqualified audit report.

In this section we cover the various audit reports on management's financial statements. There are two broad categories: the standard unqualified report and various report reservations. We start with the standard unqualified report.

The standard unqualified report contains three basic segments: (1) the introductory paragraph, (2) the scope paragraph and (3) the opinion paragraph. An example is given in Exhibit 3–2. The technical details of this report were introduced in Chapter 2. The ISA equivalent report is given in Appendix 3B, and is quite similar other than the exceptions noted in this chapter.

Meaning of the Introductory, Scope, and Opinion Paragraphs

Many users understand the audit report by counting the paragraphs! Crude as this may seem, it makes some sense because the three standard paragraphs are supposed to convey the same messages for all audits. The first place most analysts look at in the client's annual report is the audit report. The reason is that any major problems in using the financial statements should be identified there.

Introductory Paragraph

The introductory paragraph declares that an audit has been conducted and identifies the financial statements. These identifications are important because the opinion paragraph at the end is an opinion on these financial statements. If one or more of the basic financial statements is not identified in the introductory paragraph, the opinion paragraph likewise should

---

EXHIBIT   3-2   AUDITOR'S REPORT

To the Shareholders of ....

I have audited the balance sheet of .... as at ...., 20.........., and the statements of income, retained earnings and cash flows for the year then ended. These financial statements are the responsibility of the company's management. My responsibility is to express an opinion on these financial statements based on my audit.

I conducted my audit in accordance with Canadian generally accepted auditing standards. Those standards require that I plan and perform an audit to obtain reasonable assurance whether the financial statements are free of material misstatement. An audit includes examining, on a test basis, evidence supporting the amounts and disclosure in the financial statements. An audit also includes assessing the accounting principles used and significant estimates made by management, as well as evaluating the overall financial statement presentation.

In my opinion, these financial statements present fairly, in all material respects, the financial position of the company as at ...., 20.........., and the results of its operations and the cash flows for the year then ended in accordance with Canadian generally accepted accounting principles.

City   (signed) ....

Date   Chartered Accountant

Source: *CICA Handbook*, paragraph 5400.22.

not offer any opinion on it (them). The introductory paragraph also gives notice of management's responsibility for the financial statements and the auditors' responsibility for the audit report, as covered in *Handbook* paragraph 5400.08 or ISA 700.

Scope Paragraph

Auditors must render a fair presentation of their own work, as well as an opinion on the financial statements. The scope paragraph is the auditor's report of the character of the work in the audit. This portion of the report is vitally important for disclosure of the quality and extent of the audit itself.

The sentence "I conducted my audit in accordance with Canadian generally accepted auditing standards" refers primarily to the general and examination standards. Its message is that (1) the auditors were trained and proficient, (2) the auditors were independent, (3) due professional care was exercised, (4) the work was planned and supervised, (5) a sufficient understanding of the internal control structure was obtained, and (6) sufficient appropriate evidential matter was obtained. To the extent that one or more of these general and field work standards is not actually satisfied during an audit, the scope paragraph must be qualified. A qualification in this paragraph means the addition of words explaining exactly which standard was not satisfied. Such qualifications may be caused by lack of sufficient appropriate evidence, such as restrictions on procedures imposed by the client, as outlined in section 5510 or ISA 700. In practice, auditors always change the standard opinion paragraph language when the scope paragraph is qualified.

The scope paragraph contains general descriptions of the audit work in addition to the reference to generally accepted auditing standards. It makes special mention of the auditors' assessment of the choice of accounting principles and the evaluation of the overall financial statement presentation. The scope paragraph also lists any conditions that prevented the auditor from getting sufficient appropriate evidence. Such conditions can indicate areas of improvement in the client's system of recordkeeping.

Opinion Paragraph

Users of audited financial statements are generally most interested in the opinion paragraph, which is actually one long sentence. This sentence contains the auditors' conclusions about the financial statements. It is the public manifestation of the private audit decision process.

The third and fourth reporting standards are incorporated in the opinion sentence:

1. The standard report states that the financial statements are presented in accordance with generally accepted accounting principles.
2. The standard report, by its silence, regards the financial statement disclosures as reasonably adequate.
3. The standard report contains an expression of opinion regarding the financial statements.
4. An "overall opinion" is expressed in the standard report, so no reasons for not doing so need to be stated.
5. The scope paragraph gives the "clear-cut indication of the character of the audit examination," and the degree of responsibility is unqualified positive assurance.

With regard to the fourth reporting standard, other examples later in this chapter will show how auditors assert that an opinion cannot be expressed (denial of opinion) and how audit responsibility can be limited (qualified opinion).

When reading the reporting standards, you should understand the term "financial statements" to include not only the traditional balance sheet, income statement and cash flow statement, but also all the footnote disclosures and additional information (e.g., earnings per share calculations) that are integral elements of the basic financial presentation required by GAAP. The first and fourth standards are explicit in the standard report. The second and third standards are effectively on an implicit reporting basis—that is, the report comments on consistency only when accounting principles have been changed *and* disclosures are considered inadequate. The adequacy of disclosures may be judged by GAAP requirements, but auditors also must be sensitive to the information needs of investors, creditors and other users when considering the need to disclose information that is not explicitly required by GAAP. Disgruntled investors often use the "lack of informative disclosure" criterion as a basis for lawsuits.

Reservation in the Audit Report

Subsequent sections of this chapter explain the major variations on the standard report. These are referred to as **reservations** in the auditor's report. There are two basic reasons for giving a report other than the standard unqualified audit report.

When the financial statements contain a departure from GAAP, including inadequate disclosure, the auditors must choose between a qualified opinion and an adverse opinion. The choice depends on the materiality (significance) and pervasiveness of the effect of the GAAP departure. This is frequently referred to as an **accounting deficiency reservation**.

When there is a scope limitation (extent of audit work has been limited), and the auditors have not been able to obtain sufficient appropriate evidence on a particular account balance or disclosure, the auditors must choose between a qualified opinion and a denial of opinion. The choice depends on the materiality of the matter for which evidence is not sufficient. Scope limitation reservations are also frequently referred to as **audit deficiency reservations**.

R E V I E W
C H E C K P O I N T S

3.5   Think about the standard unqualified introductory and scope paragraphs: (*a*) What do they identify as the objects of the audit? (*b*) What is meant by this sentence: "We conducted our audit in accordance with Canadian generally accepted auditing standards"?

3.6   What are the major reasons for departures from the standard unqualified report?

AUDIT REPORT RESERVATIONS

LEARNING OBJECTIVE
4 For a given set of accounting facts and audit circumstances, analyze a qualified, adverse, and denial audit report.

Audit reports other than the standard unqualified audit report are called audit report reservations. The most common report reservations are called **qualified reports** because they contain an opinion paragraph that does not give the positive assurance that everything in the financial statements is in conformity with GAAP. There are two basic types of qualified reports: GAAP departure reports and scope limitation reports.

GAAP Departure Reports

A company's management can decide to present financial statements containing an accounting treatment or disclosure that is not in conformity with GAAP. The reasons are varied. Management may not wish to capitalize leases and show the related debt, may calculate earnings per share incorrectly, may not accrue unbilled revenue at the end of a period, may make unreasonable accounting estimates or may be reluctant to disclose all the known details of a contingency. Whatever the reason, the fact is a departure from GAAP. Now the auditor must decide the type of opinion to render.

If the departure is immaterial or insignificant, it can be treated as if it did not exist. The audit opinion can be unqualified. What is considered immaterial under the circumstances is a matter of the auditor's professional judgement. Critical thinking can help structure this decision.

If in the auditor's judgement the departure is material enough to potentially affect users' decisions based on the financial statements, the opinion must be qualified. In this case, the qualification takes the "except-for" language form. The opinion sentence begins: "In my opinion, except for the [nature of the GAAP departure explained in the report], the financial statements present fairly, in all material respects . . . in accordance with generally accepted accounting principles." This except-for form of GAAP departure qualification isolates a particular departure, but says that the financial statements are otherwise in conformity with GAAP. The nature of the GAAP departure can be explained in a separate paragraph (called the reservation paragraph) in the audit report between the scope paragraph and the opinion paragraph, as covered by *Handbook* paragraph 5510.28.

In the except-for qualified report, the introductory and scope paragraphs are the same as the standard unqualified report. They are not changed. After all, the audit has been performed without limitation, and the auditors have sufficient appropriate evidence about the financial statements, including the GAAP departure.

GAAP-departure report examples are hard to find in published financial statements. Most published statements come under the jurisdiction of the provincial securities commissions, which require public companies to file financial statements in conformity with GAAP without any departures. Exhibit 3–3 shows a GAAP departure due to a failure to record depreciation.

However, if the GAAP departure is (1) much more than material or "so significant that they overshadow the financial statements," or (2) pervasive, affecting numerous accounts and financial statement relationships, an adverse opinion should be given (we will refer to these possibilities as **super-materiality**). An adverse opinion is exactly the opposite of the unqualified opinion. In this type of opinion, auditors say the financial statements do not

---

EXHIBIT   3-3

Departure from generally accepted accounting principles—no depreciation recorded.
When the auditor has determined that a qualification is the type of reservation required, the following wording may be appropriate.

AUDITOR'S REPORT

To the Shareholders of ....

I have audited the balance sheet of .... as at ...., 20.........., and the statements of income, retained earnings and cash flows for the year then ended. These financial statements are the responsibility of the company's management. My responsibility is to express an opinion of these financial statements based on my audit.

I conducted my audit in accordance with Canadian generally accepted auditing standards. Those standards require that I plan and perform an audit to obtain reasonable assurance whether the financial statements are free of material misstatement. An audit includes examining, on a test basis, evidence supporting the amounts and disclosures in the financial statements. An audit also includes assessing the accounting principles used and significant estimates made by management, as well as evaluating the overall financial statement presentation.

Note .... describes the depreciation policy with respect to the company's manufacturing plants and equipment. The note also indicates that the company is not depreciating its head office building, which it acquired 5 years ago, on the grounds that it is not a producing asset and is maintaining its value as a potential rental or resale property. In this respect the financial statements are not in accordance with generally accepted accounting principles. The estimated useful life of similar buildings is usually considered to be between 30 and 40 years. If depreciation had been provided on the basis of an estimated useful life of, say, 35 years, depreciation for the current year would have been increased by $.......... (20..........$..........), net income after taxes would have been decreased by $..........(20..........$..........), accumulated depreciation would have been increased by $..........(20..........$..........) and the balance of deferred income taxes and the closing balance of retained earnings would have been reduced by $..........(20..........$..........) and $..........(20..........$..........) respectively.

In my opinion, except for the effects of the failure to record depreciation as described in the preceding paragraph, these financial statements present fairly, in all material respects, the financial position of the company as at ...., 20.........., and the results of its operations and the cash flows for the year then ended in accordance with Canadian generally accepted accounting principles.

(signed).....................................

(CHARTERED ACCOUNTANT)

Source: *CICA Handbook*, section 5510.A, Example A.

present the financial position, results of operations and changes in financial position in conformity with generally accepted accounting principles. The introductory and scope paragraphs should not be qualified because, in order to decide to use the adverse opinion, the audit team must possess all evidence necessary to reach the decision. When this opinion is given, all the substantive reasons must be disclosed in the report in the reservation paragraph(s), as covered by *Handbook* paragraph 5510.28.

Because of the securities commission requirements, adverse opinions are hard to find. The example in Exhibit 3–4 is an adverse opinion due to a disagreement between the auditor and management on the carrying value of a long-term investment. The departure from GAAP is considered to be super-material, or well in excess of what would be considered material for an "except for" qualification.

As a practical matter, auditors generally require more evidence to support an adverse opinion than to support an unqualified opinion. Perhaps this phenomenon can be attributed to auditors' reluctance to be bearers of bad news. However, audit standards are quite clear that if an auditor has a basis for an adverse opinion, the uncomfortable position cannot be relieved by giving a denial of opinion. Consider GAAP departure reports as those situations where the auditor knows the true state of affairs—there is or there is not an accounting deficiency. The next section will outline those situations where the deficiency is due to the auditor not knowing the true state of affairs. These are situations where there are limitations on the scope of the auditors' work.

EXHIBIT   3-4   ADVERSE REPORT

Departure from generally accepted accounting principles—disagreement on carrying value of a long-term investment. When the auditor has determined that an adverse opinion is the type of reservation required, the following wording may be appropriate. (For an adverse opinion, "present fairly" in the opinion paragraph, need not be modified with the phrase "in all material respects")

AUDITOR'S REPORT

To the Shareholders of ....

I have audited the balance sheet of .... as at ...., 20.........., and the statements of income, retained earnings and cash flows for the year then ended. These financial statements are the responsibility of the company's management. My responsibility is to express an opinion of these financial statements based on my audit.

I conducted my audit in accordance with Canadian generally accepted auditing standards. Those standards require that I plan and perform an audit to obtain reasonable assurance whether the financial statements are free of material misstatement. An audit includes examining, on a test basis, evidence supporting the amounts and disclosures in the financial statements. An audit also includes assessing the accounting principles used and significant estimates made by management, as well as evaluating the overall financial statement presentation.

The company's investment in X Company Ltd., its only asset, which is carried at a cost of $10,000,000, has declined in value to an amount of $5,850,000. The loss in the value of this investment, in my opinion, is other than a temporary decline and in such circumstances, generally accepted accounting principles require that the investment be written down to recognize the loss. If this decline in value had been recognized, the investment, net income for the year and retained earnings would have been reduced by $4,150,000.

In my opinion, because the write-down has not been made for the significant decline in value of the investment described in the preceding paragraph, these financial statements do not present fairly the financial position of the company as at ...., 20.......... and the results of its operations and the cash flows for the year then ended in accordance with Canadian generally accepted accounting principles.

(signed).......................................
CHARTERED ACCOUNTANT

Date

City

Source: *CICA Handbook*, section 5510.A, Example H.

**REVIEW
CHECKPOINTS**

3.7   With reference to evidence, what extent of evidence is required as a basis for the unqualified opinion? for an adverse opinion? for an opinion qualified for GAAP departure?

3.8   What effect does the materiality of a GAAP departure have on the auditors' reporting decision?

Scope Limitation Reports

Auditors are in the most comfortable position when they have all the evidence needed to make a report decision, whether the opinion is to be unqualified, adverse or qualified for a GAAP departure. However, two kinds of situations can create **scope limitations**, which are conditions where the auditors are unable to obtain sufficient appropriate evidence. They are (1) management's deliberate refusal to let auditors perform some procedures and (2) circumstances, such as late appointment of auditor, in which some procedures cannot be performed.

If management's refusal or the circumstances affect the audit in a minor, immaterial way, or if sufficient appropriate evidence can be obtained by other means, the audit can be considered to be unaffected, and the report can be unqualified as if the limitation had never occurred.

Management's deliberate refusal to give access to documents or decide to otherwise limit the application of audit procedures is the most serious condition. It casts doubt on management's integrity. (Why does management refuse access or limit the work?) In most such cases, excluding ones in which the limitation clearly relates to financial matters already known to be immaterial, the audit report is qualified or an opinion is denied, depending upon the materiality of the financial items affected.

Exhibit 3–5 shows two reports that illustrate the auditors' alternatives. The illustrated failure to take physical counts of inventory might have been a deliberate management action, or it might have resulted from other circumstances (such as the company not anticipating the need for an audit and appointing the auditor after the latest year-end).

In Panel A the opinion is qualified, using the except-for language form. Here the lack of evidence is considered material but not "super-material" to overwhelm the meaning of a qualified audit opinion and the usefulness of the unaffected parts of the financial statements. The proper qualification phrase is: "In our opinion, except for the effects of adjustments, if any, as might have been determined to be necessary had we been able to examine evidence regarding the inventories, the financial statements present fairly, in all material respects, . . . in conformity with generally accepted accounting principles." This report "carves out" the inventory from the audit reporting responsibility, taking no audit responsibility for this part of the financial statements.

Notice that the introductory paragraph in Panel A is the same as for an unqualified report. However, the scope paragraph is qualified because the audit was not completed entirely in accordance with generally accepted auditing standards. Specifically, sufficient appropriate evidence about the inventories was not obtained. Whenever the scope paragraph is qualified for an important omission of audit work, the opinion paragraph should also be qualified.

In Panel B the situation is considered fatal to the audit opinion. The inventories are too large and too important in this case to say "except for adjustments, if any." The audit report then must be a denial of opinion. In the U.S. and in international standards such as ISA 700 a denial of opinion is referred to as a **disclaimer of opinion**.

It is important to remember that scope limitation reservations arise only when it is not possible to obtain compensating assurance from alternative audit procedures. If, for example, in Panel A and Panel B the auditor had been able to satisfy himself through alternative procedures that the inventory was materially accurate, then an unqualified opinion could have been issued for both panels. Thus, scope limitation reports are issued only if in the auditor's judgement there are insufficient alternative procedures to compensate for the restriction.

EXHIBIT 3-5A   SCOPE LIMITATION REPORTS

PANEL A: QUALIFIED OPINION

Scope limitation – the auditor is appointed during the year and is unable to observe the inventory count at the beginning of the year. (It is assumed that the prior year's figures were unaudited and that the auditor was able to satisfy himself of herself with respect to all other aspects of inventories and all other opening figures.) When the auditor has determined that a qualification is the type of reservation required, the following wording may be appropriate:

AUDITOR'S REPORT

To the Shareholders of ....

I have audited the balance sheet of .... as at ...., 20.... and the statements of income, retained earnings and cash flows for the year then ended. These financial statements are the responsibility of the company's management. My responsibility is to express an opinion on these financial statements based on my audit.

Except as explained in the following paragraph, I conducted my audit in accordance with Canadian generally accepted auditing standards. Those standards require that I plan and perform an audit to obtain reasonable assurance whether the financial statements are free of material misstatement. An audit includes examining, on a test basis, evidence supporting the amounts and disclosures in the financial statements. An audit also includes assessing the accounting principles used and significant estimates made by management, as well as evaluating the overall financial statement presentation.

Because I was appointed auditor of the company during the current year, I was not able to observe the counting of physical inventories at the beginning of the year nor satisfy myself concerning those inventory quantities by alternative means. Since opening inventories enter into the determination of the results of operations and cash flows, I was unable to determine whether adjustments to cost of sales, income taxes, net income for the year, opening retained earnings and cash provided from operations might be necessary.

In my opinion, except for the effect of adjustments, if any, which I might have determined to be necessary had I been able to examine opening inventory quantities, as described in the preceding paragraph, the statements of income, retained earnings and cash flows present fairly, in all material respects, the results of operations and cash flows of the company for the year ended ...., 20.... in accordance with Canadian generally accepted accounting principles. Further, in my opinion, the balance sheet presents fairly, in all material respects, the financial position of the company as at ...., 20.... in accordance with Canadian generally accepted accounting principles.

(signed) ....

CHARTERED ACCOUNTANT

City

Date

Source: *CICA Handbook*, section 5510A, Example J.

To summarize, we can view audit reservations as arising from two types of circumstances: audit deficiencies or scope limitations, and accounting deficiencies resulting from a GAAP departure. Audit deficiencies can result in either a qualification or denial of opinion, depending on the significance of the scope limitation. In an audit deficient reservation, both the scope and opinion paragraphs are affected. When there is an audit deficiency, the auditor does not have enough evidence or does not know the true state of affairs.

An accounting deficiency, on the other hand, can result in either a qualification or adverse opinion, depending on the significance of the GAAP departure. In an accounting deficiency reservation, only the opinion paragraph is affected.

It should be stressed that both the auditor and clients work to avoid a report reservation. There may be much discussion and negotiation between the auditor and client management to avoid a report reservation. This negotiation is discussed in more detail in Chapter 15 after we have considered the available evidence at the end of the engagement.

To reach a conclusion about an accounting deficiency the auditor must have sufficient appropriate evidence to support the conclusion. The auditor is in a position to know the true state of affairs.

EXHIBIT   3–5B   SCOPE LIMITATION REPORTS

PANEL B: DENIAL OF OPINION

Scope limitation – the physical inventory count was not observed by the auditor and there are serious deficiencies in the accounting records and in the system of internal control over inventory. When the auditor has determined that a denial of opinion is the type of reservation required, the following wording may be appropriate. (For a denial of opinion, "presented fairly" in the opinion paragraph need not be modified with the phrase "in all material respects.")

AUDITOR'S REPORT

To the Shareholders of ....

I have audited the consolidated balance sheet of .... as at ...., 20.... and the consolidated statements of income, retained earnings and cash flows for the year then ended. These financial statements are the responsibility of the company's management. My responsibility is to express an opinion on these financial statements based on my audit.

Except as explained in the following paragraph, I conducted my audit in accordance with Canadian generally accepted auditing standards. Those standards require that I plan and perform an audit to obtain reasonable assurance whether the financial statements are free of material misstatement. An audit includes examining, on a test basis, evidence supporting the amounts and disclosures in the financial statements. An audit also includes assessing the accounting principles used and significant estimates made by management, as well as evaluating the overall financial statement presentation.

I was not appointed auditor until after (year-end date) and thus did not observe the taking of physical inventories at either the beginning of the year or the end of the year and was not able to satisfy myself concerning inventory quantities by alternative means. Also, my examination indicated serious deficiencies in internal control over inventory. As a consequence, I was unable to satisfy myself that all revenues and expenditures of the company had been recorded nor was I able to satisfy myself that the recorded transactions were proper. As a result, I was unable to determine whether adjustments were required in respect of recorded or unrecorded assets, recorded or unrecorded liabilities and the components making up the statements of income, retained earnings and cash flows.

In view of the possible material effects on the financial statements of the matters described in the preceding paragraph, I am unable to express an opinion whether these financial statements are presented fairly in accordance with Canadian generally accepted accounting principles.

(signed) ....

CHARTERED ACCOUNTANT

City

Date

Source: *CICA Handbook*, section 5510A, Example M.

OTHER RESPONSIBILITIES WITH A DENIAL

A denial of opinion because of severe scope limitation or because of association with unaudited financial statements carries some additional reporting responsibilities. In addition to the denial, these rules should be followed:

- If the PA should learn that the statements are not in conformity with generally accepted accounting principles (including adequate disclosures), the departures should be explained in the denial.
- If prior years' unaudited statements are presented, the denial should cover them as well as the current-year statement.

Exhibit 3–6 summarizes the discussion as an audit decision process to either some type of reservation (routes to far right column) or an unqualified opinion (route to far left column). Make sure you understand the reasoning summarized in this exhibit.

EXHIBIT 3-6   AUDIT REPORT DECISION PROCESS

Unqualified Opinion	Type of Deficiency	Level of Misstatement	Report Reservation
	Is there a scope restriction?	YES → Can the restriction lead to GAAS failure to detect pervasive material misstatement	YES Denial
	NO	NO Can the restriction lead to GAAS failure to detect material misstatement	YES Qualified based on scope restriction (assuming there are no known GAAP deficiencies)
	NO		
	Is there GAAP deficiency?	YES Does the GAAP deficiency lead to pervasive material misstatement?	YES Adverse opinion
		NO Does the GAAP deficiency lead to material misstatement?	YES Qualification based on accounting deficiency
Unqualified Opinion	NO		

REVIEW
CHECKPOINTS

3.9   What are the differences between a report qualified for a scope limitation and a standard unqualified report?

3.10 What are the differences between a report in which the opinion is denied because of scope limitation and a standard unqualified report?

3.11 For which opinions does the auditor know about the client's situation? Explain.

Effects of Lack of Independence

Independence is the foundation of the audit function. When independence is lacking, an audit in accordance with generally accepted auditing standards is impossible. When the auditors lack independence they should resign or not accept an audit engagement by the Rules of Professional Conduct (discussed in Chapter 4). An audit is not simply the application of tools, techniques and procedures of auditing; it is also the independence in mental attitude of the auditors. This idea is reflected in the general standard and in CICA provincial Codes of Professional Conduct, an example of which is Rule 204, titled "Independence."

204.1 [Independence In] Assurance and Specified Auditing Procedures Engagements

A member or firm who engages or participates in an engagement:
   (a)   to issue a written communication under the terms of an assurance engagement; or

(b)   to issue a report on the results of applying specified auditing procedures;
shall be and remain independent such that the member, firm and members of the firm shall be and remain free of any influence, interest or relationship which, in respect of the engagement, impairs the professional judgement or objectivity of the member, firm or a member of the firm or which, in the view of a reasonable observer, would impair the professional judgement or objectivity of the member, firm or a member of the firm.

This rule applies to the auditors of financial statements. The criteria for determining independence are discussed in Chapter 4.

REVIEW CHECKPOINTS

3.12   If an auditor is not independent with respect to a public company client, what should she do?

3.13   Why is independence important for auditors?

UNQUALIFIED OPINION WITH EXPLANATION OR MODIFICATION

LEARNING OBJECTIVE

5 Write an unqualified audit report, containing additional explanation or modified wording for specific issues allowed by GAAS.

Several circumstances may permit an unqualified opinion paragraph, but they raise the need to consider additional information and additional paragraphs to the standard report. Four such situations are covered in this section.

- **Consistency.** Effects of various changes in accounting and the appropriate disclosure.
- **Emphasis paragraph(s).** Additional explanatory paragraphs that "emphasize a matter" of importance.
- **Uncertainty.** Paragraph that draws attention to accounting and disclosure for contingencies.
- **Going Concern.** Paragraph that draws attention to problems of being able to continue as a going concern.

Consistency

There is no longer a need to make reference to consistency even when there are changes in accounting principles as long as the changes are properly disclosed in the financial statements, covered by paragraph 5400.19.

Other changes that do not require consistency references in the audit report are the following: (1) changes in accounting estimates, (2) error corrections that do not involve a change in accounting principles, (3) changes in the classification or aggregation of financial statement amounts, (4) changes in the format or basis of the statement of cash flows (e.g., from a balancing format to a net change format), and (5) changes in the subsidiaries included in consolidated financial statements as a result of forming a new subsidiary, buying another company, spinning off or liquidating a subsidiary or selling a subsidiary. However, failure to disclose any of these changes could amount to a GAAP departure and could present a different reason for qualifying the opinion.

When evaluating a change in accounting principle, auditors must be satisfied that management's justification for the change is reasonable. In the United States there is an additional requirement that the change be to a "preferable" principle. The U.S. standard "Accounting Changes" states:

The presumption that an entity should not change an accounting principle may be overcome only if the enterprise justifies the use of an alternative acceptable accounting principle on the basis that it is preferable.

A change from accelerated depreciation to straight-line "to increase profits" may be preferable from management's viewpoint, but such a reason is not reasonable justification for most auditors. If the U.S. auditors cannot agree that a change in accounting principle is preferable, then an opinion qualification based on a departure from GAAP is appropriate. In the United States the SEC requires auditors to submit a letter stating whether the change is to a preferable principle—one that provides a better measure of business operations.)

Emphasis Paragraph(s)

Sometimes auditors opt to add additional information in the audit report. This type of addition to the audit report is known as the **emphasis of a matter** paragraph. Beyond the standard unqualified report wording, auditors have one avenue for enriching the information content in an audit report. They can add one or more paragraphs to emphasize a matter they believe readers should consider important or useful. An emphasis paragraph can be added when the auditor intends to write an unqualified opinion paragraph. Indeed, the matter emphasized is not supposed to be mentioned in the standard unqualified opinion sentence.

Currently there are some limits on the content of an emphasis paragraph. For example *Handbook*, paragraph 5510.49 specifically prohibits reference to contingencies on going concern issues if they are already properly disclosed in the financial statements. In addition, the *Handbook* specifically mentions that the following information may be provided in a final paragraph: information required by statute, covered in paragraph 5701.03; unaudited comparative figures, paragraph 5701.10; and comparative figures reported on by other auditors, paragraph 5701.11. However, since the time section 5701 was issued, several new issues have evolved that expands the content of an emphasis paragraph. These issues include foreign reporting requirements, use of another appropriate disclosed basis of accounting besides GAAP, and going-concern issues. An example of additional comments attached to but distinct from the auditor's report, relating to Canadian GAAP and foreign reporting requirements, is shown in Exhibit 3–7.

Uncertainty

Previously in this chapter, you studied scope limitations in which management or circumstances prevented the auditors from obtaining sufficient appropriate evidence about a part of the financial statements. A different type of problem arises when client uncertainties exist. We will refer to these as accounting uncertainties because they do not arise from scope restrictions. Instead they are related to accounting measurement uncertainties. A good example of an accounting uncertainty is an accounting contingency, which is defined in *Handbook*, paragraph 3290.02:

> A contingency is . . . an existing condition, or situation, involving uncertainty as to possible gain ("gain contingency") or loss ("loss contingency") to an enterprise that will ultimately be resolved when one or more future events occur or fail to occur. Resolution of the uncertainty may confirm the acquisition of an asset or the reduction of a liability or the loss or impairment of an asset or the incurrence of a liability.

EXHIBIT   3–7   EXAMPLE OF ADDITIONAL COMMENTS PARAGRAPH

**Comments by Auditor for U.S. Readers
on Canada–International Reporting Difference**

International reporting standards for auditors require the addition of an explanatory paragraph when the financial statements are affected by conditions and events that cast substantial doubt on the company's ability to continue as a going concern, such as those described in Note .... to the financial statements. My report to the shareholders dated ...., 20.......... is expressed in accordance with Canadian reporting standards which do not permit a reference to such events and conditions in the auditor's report when these are adequately disclosed in the financial statements.

City

Date

(signed) ....

CHARTERED ACCOUNTANT

Source: *CICA Handbook*, AUG 21.

Section 3290 sets forth accounting and disclosure standards for contingencies. One of the most common contingencies involves the uncertain outcome of litigation pending against the company. Accounting uncertainties include not only lawsuits, but also such things as the value of fixed assets held for sale (e.g., a whole plant or warehouse facility) and the status of assets involved in foreign expropriations.

Auditors may perform procedures in accordance with generally accepted auditing standards, yet the uncertainty and lack of evidence may persist. The problem is that it is impossible to obtain audit "evidence" about the future. The concept of audit evidence includes information knowable at the time a reporting decision is made and does not include predictions about future resolution of uncertainties. Consequently, auditors should not change (modify or qualify) the introductory, scope or opinion paragraphs of the standard unqualified report when contingencies and uncertainties exist. When the audit has been performed in accordance with generally accepted auditing standards, and the auditor has done all the things possible in the circumstances, no alteration of these standard paragraphs is necessary as long as the uncertainty has been properly disclosed.

When significant uncertainties about future events exist about such matters as tax deficiency assessments, contract disputes, recoverability of asset costs, lawsuits and other important contingencies, they should be explained clearly and completely in footnotes to the financial statements. These disclosures are as much a part of management's responsibility as the balance sheet, income statement and cash flow statement. *Handbook*, paragraph 5510.46 advises that:

> when a contingency is accounted for and disclosed in accordance with Canadian GAAP it is not appropriate to draw attention to the contingency by expressing a reservation of opinion or by mentioning it in a separate paragraph following the auditor's standard report.

Under international and U.S. audit standards, however, the auditor may decide to add a paragraph to the report as a "red flag" drawing attention to the uncertainty, per ISA 701, paragraph 8.

Uncertainty situations may cause audit reports to be qualified for departures from GAAP, if (1) management's disclosure of the uncertainty is inadequate, (2) management uses inappropriate accounting principles to account for the uncertainty, and (3) management makes unreasonable accounting estimates in connection with the effects of the uncertainty. The audit report also may be qualified because of a scope limitation regarding available evidence about an uncertainty.

"SUBJECT-TO" OPINIONS PRIOR TO 1980

From the early 1960s until 1980, auditors gave "subject-to" opinions for accounting uncertainty situations. The opinion sentence was qualified with these words: "In our opinion, subject to the effects of such adjustments, if any, as might have been determined had the outcome of the uncertainty discussed in the preceding paragraph been known..." The explanatory paragraph was placed before the opinion paragraph, and the opinion was considered qualified. You may see this form of "subject to" opinion when you use reports issued in 1980 and earlier. However, the audit standards were changed in 1980, and now (1) the "subject to" wording is prohibited, (2) the explanatory paragraph is no longer used, and (3) the opinion sentence itself is unqualified.

Going Concern

Generally accepted accounting principles are based on the going-concern concept, which means the entity is expected to continue in operation and meet its obligations as they become due, without substantial disposition of assets outside the ordinary course of business, restructuring of debt, externally forced revisions of its operations (e.g., a bank reorganization forced by the Superintendent of Financial Institutions) or similar actions. Hence, an opinion that financial statements are in conformity with GAAP means that continued existence may be presumed for a "reasonable time" not to exceed one year beyond the date of the financial statements.[1] This one-year time horizon was reiterated in the CICA's Exposure Draft on going-concern issues, released in March 1996.

Dealing with questions of going concern, or lack thereof, is difficult because auditors are forced to evaluate matters of financial analysis, business strategy and financial forecasting. Most managements are unwilling to give up and close their businesses without strong attempts to survive. Sometimes, survival optimism prevails until the creditors force bankruptcy proceedings and liquidation. Auditors are generally reluctant to puncture any balloons of optimism. Managers and auditors both view news of financial troubles in an audit report (an attention-directing paragraph or a disclaimer based on going-concern doubt) as a "self-fulfilling prophecy" that causes bankruptcy. However fallacious this view might be, it still prevails and inhibits auditors' consideration of going-concern questions.

Auditors are responsible for determining whether there is a significant doubt about a company's ability to continue as a going concern. No careful auditor should ignore signs of financial difficulty and operate entirely on the assumption that the company is a going concern. Financial difficulties, labour problems, loss of key personnel, litigation and other such things may be important signals. Likewise, elements of financial flexibility (salability of assets, lines of credit, debt extension, dividend elimination) may be available as survival strategies. (In U.S. auditing standards, these elements of financial flexibility and management strategy are known as **mitigating factors** that may reduce the financial difficulties.)

Accounting and finance research efforts have produced several bankruptcy prediction models. These models use publicly available financial information to classify companies into "fail" and "nonfail" categories. At least one auditing firm uses such a model as an analytical review tool. Auditing standards, however, make no mention of research models, specifying instead many company-specific considerations and elements of internal information for analysis. (One bankruptcy prediction model is described briefly in the appendix to Chapter 8 of this text.)

Auditor's responsibilities for the going-concern assumption are currently the same as for contingencies, per paragraph 5510.53. However, the CICA Research Study, "The Going Concern Assumption," gives recommendations leaning toward U.S. practice except that it quantifies key threshold probabilities whereas U.S. standards do not. The key audit recommendations of the CICA's going-concern study are as follows:

1. Require auditors on every audit to perform procedures to provide reasonable assurance about the validity of the "going-concern" assumption.
2. Evaluate results of procedures performed.
3. If significant (20–50 percent probability) or substantial doubts (50 percent or greater probability) are raised, assess management's plans to address these matters, considering if they can be effectively implemented. (Note: The very existence of such plans should call "going concern" into question.)
4. Expand the auditor's reporting responsibilities when doubt about the validity of the "going-concern" assumption becomes substantial. Include an explanatory paragraph even if doubt is adequately disclosed in the notes.
5. Issue an adverse opinion where substantial doubt exists and disclosure is inadequate.
6. Issue an adverse opinion if virtually certain, and GAAP no longer applies.

According to this study, five types of audit reports may be used when going-concern problems exist. The first is a standard report with no additional explanatory paragraphs as long as doubts are significant or less and properly disclosed in the notes to the financial statements. The second is a standard report with an unqualified opinion paragraph and an additional explanatory paragraph(s) to direct attention to management's disclosures about the problems. This second type of standard report would be used when there are substantial doubts and the company has properly disclosed these problems in the notes.

---

[1] *The Going-Concern Assumption*, CICA Research Report (CICA, 1991).

The third type of report is an adverse opinion that arises from failure to disclose substantial doubts, or when it is virtually certain that the company will fail to continue as a going concern, and GAAP no longer applies.

A fourth type of report is a qualification for a GAAP departure if the auditor believes the company's disclosures about financial difficulties and going-concern problems are inadequate. Such a report is shown in Exhibit 3–8. The fifth type of report is a report qualified for a scope limitation if evidence that does exist or did exist is not made available to the auditors, leading to the "except for adjustments, if any" type of qualified opinion explained earlier in this chapter. These different reports arise from the refined classification scheme reflected by the going-concern study recommendations.

So what is current GAAS regarding going concern? The current *Handbook* recommendation that applies is paragraph 5510.53, which effectively states that if there is a "going-concern" problem, an unqualified opinion is given as long as the problem is adequately disclosed. If the facts are not adequately disclosed, the auditor should issue a reservation of the audit opinion. An illustration of an "except for" qualification reservation is shown in Exhibit 3–8.

There are Auditing (issued September 1995) and Accounting (issued March 1996) Exposure Drafts related to going concern. The Accounting Exposure Draft uses a significant doubt concept similar to that described above from the CICA Research Study. However, the Auditing Exposure Draft uses the term "factors that cast doubt" on the entity's ability to

---

EXHIBIT   3–8   A QUALIFIED REPORT EXPLAINING GOING-CONCERN PROBLEMS

Departure from generally accepted accounting principles—inadequate disclosure of matters affecting the company's ability to continue as a going concern. When the auditor has determined that a qualification is the type of reservation required, the following wording may be appropriate.

AUDITOR'S REPORT

To the Shareholders of ....

I have audited the balance sheet of .... as at ...., 20-1 and the statements of income, retained earnings and cash flows for the year then ended. These financial statements are the responsibility of the company's management. My responsibility is to express an opinion on these financial statements based on my audit.

I conducted my audit in accordance with generally accepted auditing standards. Those standards require that I plan and perform an audit to obtain reasonable assurance whether the financial statements are free of material misstatement. An audit includes examining, on a test basis, evidence supporting the amounts and disclosures in the financial statements. An audit also includes assessing the accounting principles used and significant estimates made by management, as well as evaluating the overall financial statement presentation.

The accompanying financial statements, in my opinion, do not draw attention explicitly to doubts concerning the company's ability to realize its assets and discharge its liabilities in the normal course of business. These doubts arise because it is uncertain whether the company will be able to refinance long-term debt in the amount of $................... due on ...., 20-2 in view of the existence of recurring operating losses in the past five years and the deficiency in working capital of $................... as at ...., 20-1. If refinancing cannot be arranged, it is not known whether the company can sell its hotel property for an amount sufficient to realize its carrying value of $................... and to generate adequate funds to repay this debt.

In my opinion, except for the omission of the disclosure described in the preceding paragraph, these financial statements present fairly, in all material respects, the financial position of the company as at ...., 20-1 and the results of its operations and its cashflows for the year then ended in accordance with generally accepted accounting principles.

(signed) ....
CHARTERED ACCOUNTANT

Date

City

Source: *CICA Handbook*, section 5510.A, Example F.

continue as a going concern. It is not clear whether "cast doubt" is comparable to "significant doubt," and perhaps this will be clarified in the final standards.

One thing that is clear in the current standards is that contingencies related to going concern that are appropriately disclosed in the financial statements are specifically prohibited as a subject matter for an emphasis paragraph, covered in *Handbook,* paragraphs 5510.49 and 5510.52. Whether this will continue to be the case depends on the final form of the Going-Concern Standards in the post-Enron environment. ISA 570, paragraph .33 requires an emphasis-of-matter paragraph that highlights the existence of a significant doubt regarding the going-concern assumption. The CICA is currently in the process of developing accounting and auditing guidelines on going concerns. It will likely be similar to ISA 570.

REVIEW CHECKPOINTS

3.14   Check the CICA's website at www.cica.ca for the status of their going-concern projects. A recent CICA study shows that only 46 percent of companies that failed had any indication of going-concern problems in the previously audited financial statements.[2] Do you think this is acceptable? Discuss in class.

AUDIT REPORTS ON INTERNAL CONTROL STATEMENTS

LEARNING OBJECTIVE

6 Compare and contrast the opinions in a financial statement audit versus an internal control audit.

As explained in the first two chapters, the SOX Act in the U.S. and increasing interest in corporate governance have caused a new statement to be added to the audited financial statements, the internal controls statement (or "Reporting on Internal Control Over Financial Reporting" as it is officially called). To fully appreciate the meaning of the internal controls statement you will need to study more about the concept of internal controls in later chapters. Most of you have not studied internal controls before, unlike the traditional financial statements which are covered in your accounting courses.

Internal control can have varying meanings depending on the criteria used. However, for purposes of the internal control statement required by the CICA standard entitled "Reporting on Internal Control Over Financial Reporting," internal controls are limited to internal controls over financial reporting. This is consistent with U.S. requirements.

These requirements are mainly concerned with accounting controls. That is, controls related to the accuracy of accounting recordkeeping and safeguarding of assets. This distinction is covered in more detail in Chapter 9.

An example of an internal control statement by management follows in Exhibit 3–9.

Under CICA proposed rules the auditor verifies the accuracy of the internal controls statement for public companies just like he verifies the accuracy of financial statements. In fact, the proposed standards require that the audit of financial statements and the audit of the internal control statement be part of the same engagement. This is primarily because of synergies between these two types of audits that arise from the close link between accounting controls and accuracy of the financial statements.

In its *Handbook* section Ballot Draft (Appendix A, Example A), the CICA recommends the wording of a separate audit report on management's internal control statement, shown in Exhibit 3–10.

Note that in Exhibit 3–10 there are six paragraphs instead of the three associated with the unqualified report of the audit of financial statements. The first is like the introductory paragraph of the audit of financial statements (regular audit). This paragraph identifies the statement covered and the responsibilities of the auditor and management.

The second paragraph is a new paragraph that defines the internal controls covered by management's statement.

---

[2] See Alison Arnot, "Reporting a Going Concern," *CGA Magazine,* July–August 2004, pp. 26–31.

EXHIBIT 3-9   REPORT OF MANAGEMENT

REPORT OF MANAGEMENT
Big Corporation and Subsidiary Companies

Management's Report on Internal Control Over Financial Reporting

Management is responsible for establishing and maintaining adequate internal control over financial reporting of the company. Internal control over financial reporting is a process designed to provide reasonable assurance regarding the reliability of financial reporting and the preparation of financial statements for external purposes in accordance with accounting principles generally accepted in Canada.

The company's internal control over financial reporting includes those policies and procedures that (i) pertain to the maintenance of records that, in reasonable detail, accurately and fairly reflect the transactions and dispositions of the assets of the company; (ii) provide reasonable assurance that transactions are recorded as necessary to permit preparation of financial statements in accordance with accounting principles generally accepted in Canada, and that receipts and expenditures of the company are being made only in accordance with authorizations of management and directors of the company; and (iii) provide reasonable assurance regarding prevention or timely detection of unauthorized acquisition, use, or disposition of the company's assets that could have a material effect on the financial statements.

Because of its inherent limitations, internal control over financial reporting may not prevent or detect misstatements. Also, projections of any evaluation of effectiveness to future periods are subject to the risk that controls may become inadequate because of changes in conditions, or that the degree of compliance with the policies or procedures may deteriorate.

Management conducted an evaluation of the effectiveness of internal control over financial reporting based on the framework in Internal Control – Integrated Framework issued by the Committee of Sponsoring Organizations of the Treadway Commission. Based on this evaluation, management concluded that the company's internal control over financial reporting was effective as of December 31, 200X. Management's assessment of the effectiveness of the company's internal control over financial reporting as of December 31, 200X has been audited by BigFour LLP, an independent registered public accounting firm, as stated in their report which is included herein.

Chief Executive Officer   Chief Financial Officer
March 17, 200X +1   March 17, 200X +1

The third paragraph is like the scope paragraph in a regular report explaining the character of the auditor's examination. Note that the engagement requires providing reasonable (high) assurance on the effectiveness of internal control.

Before we get to the opinion paragraph, we discuss the last two paragraphs. The fifth paragraph is the inherent limitations paragraph indicating that there is a risk that controls will not guarantee the financial statements are free of material misstatements. There is an added caution that the current evaluation of controls will not necessarily apply to the future. There is nothing comparable in the regular report. The sixth paragraph indicates that the audit is done in conjunction with the financial statement audit.

The fourth paragraph expresses the opinion. Note the need to reference conformity with established criteria as the basis of the opinion, the reference to materiality, and a "fairly stated" management's assessment. The reference to management's assessment makes clear that management has made its assertion explicit in a written statement, Exhibit 3–9—what we are calling management's internal control statement. This publicly stated written assertion is what makes the engagement an attestation engagement. An **attestation engagement** is an assurance engagement in which the management assertions are explicitly made public in written statements. However, note that the auditor also provides a second opinion in this paragraph. This second opinion is a direct reporting opinion on internal controls and is intended to complement the first opinion.

If management were to conclude its internal controls were weak in its internal control statement, then the attest opinion could give an unqualified opinion on the fairness of management's internal control statement. However, given that the controls themselves are weak, the direct reporting opinion could be adverse. The significance of this dual nature of opinion is illustrated in Chapter 16.

EXHIBIT 3-10   AUDITOR'S REPORT

AUDITOR'S REPORT
To the Shareholders of W Company Ltd.

I have audited the effectiveness of W Company Ltd.'s internal control over financial reporting as at December 31, 20X3, in accordance with [the suitable control criteria, for example, "criteria established in Internal Control—Integrated Framework issued by the Committee of Sponsoring Organizations of the Treadway Commission (COSO)], and management's assessment thereof included in the accompanying [title of management's report]. W Company Ltd.'s management is responsible for maintaining effective internal control over financial reporting and for its assessment of the effectiveness of internal control over financial reporting. My responsibility is to express an opinion on management's assessment and an opinion on the effectiveness of the company's internal control over financial reporting based on my audit.

A company's internal control over financial reporting is a process designed to provide reasonable assurance regarding the reliability of financial reporting and the preparation of financial statements for external purposes in accordance with generally accepted accounting principles. A company's internal control over financial reporting includes those policies and procedures that (1) pertain to the maintenance of records that, in reasonable detail, accurately and fairly reflect the transactions and dispositions of the assets of the company; (2) provide reasonable assurance that transactions are recorded as necessary to permit preparation of financial statements in accordance with generally accepted accounting principles, and that receipts and expenditures of the company are being made only in accordance with authorizations of management and directors of the company; and (3) provide reasonable assurance regarding prevention or timely detection of unauthorized acquisition, use or disposition of the company's assets that could have a material effect on the financial statements.

I conducted my audit of the effectiveness of W Company Ltd.'s internal control over financial reporting, and management's assessment thereof, in accordance with the standards established by the Canadian Institute of Chartered Accountants (CICA) for audits of internal control over financial reporting. Those standards require that I plan and perform the audit to obtain reasonable assurance about whether effective internal control over financial reporting was maintained in all material respects. My audit included obtaining an understanding of internal control over financial reporting, evaluating management's assessment, testing and evaluating the design and operating effectiveness of internal control over financial reporting, and performing such other procedures as I considered necessary in the circumstances. I believe that my audit provides a reasonable basis for my opinion.

In my opinion, management's assessment that W Company Ltd. maintained effective internal control over financial reporting as at December 31, 20X3, is fairly stated, in all material respects, in accordance with [the suitable control criteria, for example, "criteria established in Internal Control—Integrated Framework issued by the Committee of Sponsoring Organizations of the Treadway Commission (COSO)"]. Also, in my opinion, W Company Ltd. maintained, in all material respects, effective internal control over financial reporting as at December 31, 20X3, in accordance with [the suitable control criteria used for assessing and reporting on the effectiveness of internal control over financial reporting].

Because of its inherent limitations, internal control over financial reporting may not prevent or detect misstatements. Also, projections of any evaluation of effectiveness to future periods are subject to the risk that controls may become inadequate because of changes in conditions, or that the degree of compliance with the policies or procedures may deteriorate.

I have also audited, in accordance with Canadian generally accepted auditing standards, the [financial statements] of W Company Ltd. and my report dated [date of specified report, which should be the same as the date of the report on the effectiveness of internal control over financial reporting] expressed [nature of opinion].

[City]   (signed) ....

[Date]   CHARTERED ACCOUNTANT

Source: "Ballot Draft of Reporting on Internal Controls Over Financial Reporting," Example A, www.cica.ca.

The fourth paragraph also specifies that the opinions are on the state of controls at a specific point in time ("as at"). This point in time should be the same as the balance sheet date. This is indicated in the sixth paragraph. The standard also requires that the auditor who does the financial statement audit also does the audit of internal control over financial reporting. The term **audit of internal control over financial reporting** is used to refer to both the attest and the direct reporting audits of internal control. This standard is intended to meet the requirements of the Canadian Securities Administrators (CSA). Under current CSA rules, international control statements are required for public companies, but the audits of these statements are optional.

REPORTING ON THE APPLICATION OF ACCOUNTING PRINCIPLES

LEARNING OBJECTIVE
7 Explain why auditors have standards for reporting on the application of accounting principles.

The subject of "reporting on the application of accounting principles" touches a sensitive nerve in the public accounting profession. It arose from clients' shopping for an auditor who would agree to give an unqualified audit report on a questionable accounting treatment. "Shopping" often involved auditor-client disagreements, after which the client said: "If you won't agree with my accounting treatment, then I'll find an auditor who will." These disagreements often involved early revenue recognition and unwarranted expense or loss deferral. A few cases of misleading financial statements occurred after shopping resulted in clients' switching to more agreeable auditors. However, the practice is not entirely undesirable, because "second opinions" on complex accounting matters often benefit from consultation with other PAs.

Handbook, section 7600 established procedures for dealing with requests for consultation from parties other than an auditor's own clients. These parties can include other companies (nonclients who are shopping), lawyers, investment bankers and perhaps other people. Section 7600 is applicable in these situations:

- when preparing a written report or giving oral advice on specific transactions, either completed or proposed
- when preparing a written report or giving oral advice on the type of audit opinion that might be rendered on specific financial statements
- when preparing a written report on hypothetical transactions

The standard does not apply to conclusions about accounting principles offered in connection with litigation support engagements or expert witness work, nor does it apply to advice given to another PA in public practice. It also does not apply to an accounting firm's expressions of positions in newsletters, articles, speeches, lectures, and the like, provided that the positions do not give advice on a specific transaction or apply to a specific company.

The basic requirements are to consider the circumstances of the request for advice, its purpose and the intended use of the report of the advice; to obtain an understanding of the form and substance of the transaction in question; to review applicable GAAP; to consult with other professionals if necessary; and to perform research to determine the existence of creditable analogies and precedents (e.g., find the authoritative support). When the request for advice comes from a business that already has another auditor, the consulting PA should consult with the other auditor to learn all the facts and circumstances.

Written reports are required and should include these elements:

- description of the nature of the engagement and a statement that it was performed in accordance with standards for such engagements
- statement of relevant facts and assumptions, and the sources of information
- statement of the advice—the conclusion about appropriate accounting principles or the type of audit report, including reasons for the conclusions, if appropriate
- statement that a company's management is responsible for proper accounting treatments, in consultation with its own auditors
- statement that any differences in facts, circumstances or assumptions might change the conclusions

The purpose of the section 7600 standards is to impose some discipline on the process of shopping/consultation and to make it more difficult for companies to seek out a "willing" auditor.

. . . .

R E V I E W
CHECKPOINTS

3.15   Compare and contrast audit reports on financial versus internal control statements. Why are they different?

3.16   Why might "opinion shopping" be suspect? beneficial?

. . . .

SUMMARY

. . . .

LEARNING OBJECTIVE

8 Determine the effects of materiality on audit report choices.

This chapter began with setting forth the requirement that auditors must report whenever they are "associated with" financial statements. This report can take different forms in different circumstances—audit assurance, negative assurance and no assurance. These levels of assurance are further explained in terms of (1) reports qualified for (*a*) scope limitations, and (*b*) departures from GAAP; (2) adverse reports resulting from GAAP departures; and (3) denials of opinion resulting from lack of independence and lack of sufficient appropriate evidence.

Throughout this chapter's explanation of the auditors' choices of reports, the materiality dimension played an important role. When an auditor makes decisions about the audit report, immaterial or unimportant information can be ignored and treated as if it did not exist. However, when inaccuracies, departures from GAAP, accounting changes and uncertainties have a large enough financial impact, the standard audit report must be changed. In practice, when an auditor decides a matter is material enough to make a difference, a further distinction must be made between misstatements not too much greater than material (which we call "materiality") and "super-materiality." Materiality means that the item in question is important and needs to be disclosed or that the opinion needs to be qualified for it. The information cannot simply be ignored. Super-materiality means that the item in question is important and has a pervasive impact on the reporting decision. The biggest distinction between the two materialities is the number of users affected by the potential misstatements: super-materiality affects many more users than does materiality. In the post-Enron environment, the amount of misstatement that is considered acceptable has been reduced in many audits so that both materialities have also been reduced. As you will see, this effectively increases the amount of audit work in the engagement.

Auditing standards refer to several basic circumstances that cause departures from the standard unqualified audit report. These circumstances are shown in Exhibit 3–11 in relation to the influence of materiality. You can see that each report is qualified when the situation involves materiality, but becomes a disclaimer or an adverse report when the situation

EXHIBIT 3–11   INFLUENCE OF MATERIALITY ON AUDIT REPORTS

Circumstances for Departure from Standard Report	Required Type of Report	
	Materiality	Super-Materiality
Departure from GAAP	Qualified "except for": Separate paragraph discloses reasons and effects.*	Adverse Opinion: Separate paragraph discloses reasons and effects.
Limitation on scope (lack of evidence)	Qualified Opinion: Refers to possible effects on financials.	Denial of Opinion: Separate paragraph explains limitations.
Uncertainty	Unqualified Opinion**	Unqualified Opinion**

*Where the departure is necessary to make the financials not misleading, an unqualified opinion is issued with an explanation of the circumstances.
**Unless there is a failure to properly disclose the uncertainty.

involves super-materiality. The exception is the lack of independence issue, where materiality does not make a difference.

Audit reports can also be modified and expanded with additional paragraphs. Such additions to the audit report arise from the need for an "emphasis of a matter" paragraph. The final topic in the chapter is "shopping" for accounting principles and auditors. Standards exist to raise the public perception that auditors are careful about competing with each other on the basis of professional opinions.

REVIEW CHECKPOINTS

3.17   Explain the effect of materiality or super-materiality on an auditor report when the client uses an accounting method that departs from generally accepted accounting principles.

3.18   Explain the effect of super-materiality on an auditor report when there is a scope limitation.

3.19   Explain the effect of super-materiality on an auditor report when there is a material uncertainty associated with the financial statements.

3.20   Identify the levels of assurance associated with auditor reports.

3.21   Under what conditions would an auditor use an "emphasis of a matter" paragraph?

MULTIPLE-CHOICE QUESTIONS FOR PRACTICE AND REVIEW

3.22   A PA developed a system for clients to enter transaction data by remote terminal into the PA's computer. The PA's system processes the data and prints monthly financial statements. When delivered to the clients, these financial statements should include:

a. A standard unqualified audit report.

b. An adverse audit report.

c. A report containing a description of the character of the examination and the degree of responsibility the PA is taking.

d. A description of the remote terminal system and of the controls for ensuring accurate data processing.

3.23   According to the CICA, what is the objective of an audit of financial statements?

a. An expression of opinion on the fairness with which they present financial position, results of operations and cash flows in conformity with GAAP.

b. An expression of opinion on the fairness with which they present financial position, results of operations and cash flows in conformity with FASB.

c. An expression of opinion on the fairness with which they present financial position, results of operations and cash flows in conformity with GAAS.

d. To obtain systematic and objective evidence about financial assertions and report the results to interested users.

3.24   Some of the GAAS reporting standards require certain statements in all audit reports ("explicit") and others require statements only under certain conditions ("implicit" basis). Which of the following combinations correctly describes these features of the reporting standards?

Standards	(a)	(b)	(c)	(d)
1. GAAP	Explicit	Explicit	Implicit	Implicit
2. Consistency	Implicit	Explicit	Explicit	Implicit
3. Disclosure	Implicit	Implicit	Explicit	Explicit
4. Report	Explicit	Explicit	Implicit	Implicit

3.25   A PA finds that the client has not capitalized a material amount of leases in the financial statements. When considering the materiality of this departure from GAAP, the PA's reporting options are:

a. Unqualified opinion or denial of opinion.

b. Unqualified opinion or qualified opinion.

c. Emphasis paragraph with unqualified opinion or an adverse opinion.

d. Qualified opinion or adverse opinion.

3.26   An auditor has found that the client is suffering financial difficulty and that the going-concern status is seriously in doubt. Even though the client has placed good disclosures in the financial statements, the PA must choose between the following audit report alternatives:

a. Unqualified report with a going-concern explanatory paragraph or denial of opinion.

b. Denial of opinion.

c. Qualified opinion or adverse opinion.

d. Standard unqualified report.

3.27   A company accomplished an early extinguishment of debt, and the auditors believe that recognition of a huge loss distorts the financial statements and causes them to be misleading. The auditors' reporting choices are:

a. Explain the situation and give an adverse opinion.

b. Explain the situation and give a denial of opinion.

c. Explain the situation and give an unqualified opinion, relying on Rules of Professional Conduct to not be associated with misleading financial statements.

d. Give the standard unqualified audit report.

3.28 Which of these situations would require an auditor to insert an explanatory paragraph about consistency in an unqualified audit report?

a. Client changed its estimated allowance for uncollectible accounts receivable.

b. Client corrected a prior mistake in accounting for interest capitalization.

c. Client sold one of its subsidiaries and consolidated six this year compared to seven last year.

d. None of the above.

3.29 Phil became the new auditor for Royal Corporation, succeeding Liz, who audited the financial statements last year. Phil needs to report on Royal's comparative financial statements and should write in his report an explanation about another auditor having audited the prior year:

a. Only if Liz's opinion last year was qualified.

b. Describing the prior audit and the opinion but not naming Liz as the predecessor auditor.

c. Describing the audit but not revealing the type of opinion Liz gave.

d. Describing the audit and the opinion and naming Liz as the predecessor auditor.

3.30 When other independent auditors are involved in the current audit on parts of the client's business, the principal auditor can write an audit report that:

a. Mentions the other auditor, describes the extent of the other auditor's work and gives an unqualified opinion.

b. Does not mention the other auditor and gives an unqualified opinion in a standard unqualified report.

c. Places primary responsibility for the audit report on the other auditors.

d. Names the other auditors, describes their work and presents only the principal auditor's report.

3.31 An "emphasis of a matter" paragraph inserted in an audit report causes the report to be characterized as:

a. Unqualified opinion report.

b. Divided responsibility.

c. Adverse opinion report.

d. Denial of opinion.

3.32 When will an auditor express an opinion containing the phrase "except for"?

a. When the client refuses to provide for a probable income tax liability that is very material, or super-material.

b. When there is a high degree of uncertainty associated with the client company's future.

c. When he or she did not perform procedures sufficient to form an opinion on the valuation of accounts receivable which are material.

d. When the auditor is basing his or her opinion in part on work done by another auditor.

EXERCISES AND PROBLEMS

3.33   **Association with Financial Statements.** For each of
LO.1   the situations described below, state whether the PA is or is not associated with the financial statements. What is the consequence of being associated with financial statements?

a. PA audits financial statements and his or her name is in the corporate annual report containing them.

b. PA prepares the financial statements in the partnership tax return.

c. PA uses the computer to process client-submitted data and delivers financial statement output.

d. PA uses the computer to process client-submitted data and delivers a general ledger printout.

e. PA lets client copy client-prepared financial statements on the PA's letterhead.

f. Client issues quarterly financial statements and mentions PA's review procedures but does not list PA's name in the document.

g. PA renders consulting advice about the system to prepare interim financial statements but does not review the statements prior to their release.

3.34   **Reports and the Effect of Materiality.** The concept of
LO.8   materiality is important to PAs in audits of financial statements and expressions of opinion on these statements. How will materiality influence an auditor's reporting decision in the following circumstances?

a. The client prohibits confirmation of accounts receivable, and sufficient appropriate evidence cannot be obtained using alternative procedures.

b. The client is a gas and electric utility company that follows the practice of recognizing revenue when it is billed to customers. At the end of the year, amounts earned but not yet billed are not recorded in the accounts or reported in the financial statements.

c. The client leases buildings for its chain of transmission repair shops under terms that qualify as capital leases. These leases are not capitalized as leased property assets and lease obligations.

d. The client company has lost a lawsuit. The case is on appeal in an attempt to reduce the amount of damages awarded to the plaintiffs.

3.35   **Scope Limitation, Auditor Independence.** Crow Cor-
LO.4   poration, a public company, has set up a number of limited partnerships to pursue some risky development projects. The limited partnerships borrow money from various financial institutions to support the development projects, and Crow guarantees these loans. Crow's interest in each limited partnership is set at a level just

below the percentage that would require the partnerships, and their debts, to be included in Crow's consolidated financial statements. These percentages are set out specifically in the professional accounting recommendations that form the basis of GAAP for the purpose of Crow's financial reporting.

Zilch Zulch, LLP (ZZ) has been the auditor of Crow since its incorporation thirty years ago. The current CFO of Crow was formerly an audit partner in ZZ and was in charge of the Crow audit for five years before Crow hired her as its CFO. Because of her familiarity with ZZ's approach to setting materiality for its audits, the CFO was able to suggest the amount of a loan that could be guaranteed in each limited partnership without being material. If an individual loan was material, it would need to be disclosed as a contingency in Crow's consolidated financial statements even if the partnership was not required to be consolidated. Approximately 1,000 limited partnerships were set up, since a large sum of money was required to fund Crow's development activities. Because of the way the limited partnerships were structured, none of them was consolidated and no disclosure of Crow's loan guarantees to the partnerships was disclosed in Crow's 2000 financial statements, despite the fact that in total they exceeded the reported long-term debt and shareholders' equity of Crow.

Zero Mustbe, the audit partner in charge of the audit of Crow's 2000 consolidated financial statements, was somewhat puzzled as to why there were so many limited partnerships, since only one development project was being undertaken. However, he was assured by Crow's CFO that the structure was appropriate and in accordance with GAAP because, in her words, "It was all set up by financial engineers with PhDs in ZZ's consulting group. These people know all about GAAP and are much smarter that you are, Zero, so there is nothing to be concerned about."

As a result of his audit work, Zero provided a clean audit opinion on Crow's 2000 consolidated financial statements. During 2001, adverse events resulted in Crow being unable to meet its obligations under the loan guarantees and it went bankrupt.

Required:

Comment on the adequacy of Zero's audit, the independence and scope issues raised, and the appropriateness of issuing a clean audit report in this scenario.

3.36   **Negative and Positive Assurance and Users' Needs.**
LO.2   Ellen Eagle is a banker in a small town. Her customers, Dave and Dot Dauber, are the owners of a franchised candy store in town. They have an opportunity to buy a second franchised store in a nearby town, and are requesting that Ellen increase their bank loan from $300,000 to $2,000,000 to finance this acquisition. The Daubers are two of Ellen's best customers and have always made their loan payments on time during the ten years they have been customers of her bank. Currently, Ellen is requiring the Daubers to provide annual financial statements with a review report of a PA. To approve the requested loan increase, the bank's head office will require them to provide audited annual financial statements.

Required:

Distinguish between a review report and an audit report. Why would the bank require an audit instead of a review in this case? Do you think the bank's policy is reasonable?

3.37   **Arguments with Auditors.** Officers of the company do
LO.4   not want to disclose information about the product liability lawsuit filed by a customer asking $500,000 in damages. They believe the suit is frivolous and without merit. Outside counsel is more cautious. The auditors insist upon disclosure. Angered, the Kingston Company chairman of the board threatens to sue the auditors if a standard unqualified report is not issued within three days.

Required:

Explain the issues raised in the preceding situation. What actions do you recommend to the company's auditor?

3.38   **Errors in a Comparative Report with Change from**
LO.10   **Prior Year (Appendix 3A).** The following audit report was drafted by an assistant at the completion of the audit of Cramdon, Inc., on March 1, 2005. The partner in charge of the engagement has decided the opinion on the 2004 financial statements should be modified only with reference to the change in the method of computing sales. Also, due to a litigation uncertainty, an uncertainty paragraph was included in the audit report on the 2003 financial statements, which are included for comparative purposes. The 2003 audit report (same audit firm) was dated March 5, 2004, and on October 15, 2004, the litigation was resolved in favour of Cramdon, Inc.

Auditor's Report
To the Board of Directors
of Cramdon, Inc.:
We have audited the accompanying financial statements of Cramdon, Inc., as of December 31, 2004 and 2003. These financial statements are the responsibility of the Company's Management. Our responsibility is to express an opinion on these financial statements based on our audits.

We conducted our audits in accordance with generally accepted auditing standards. Those standards require that we plan and perform the audit to obtain reasonable assurance about whether the financial statements are free of material misstatement. An audit includes examining, on a test basis, evidence supporting the amounts and disclosures in the financial statements. An audit also includes assessing the accounting principles used and significant estimates made by management, as well as evaluating the overall financial statement presentation. We believe that our audit provides a reasonable basis for our opinion.

As discussed in Note 7 to the financial statements, our previous report on the 2003 financial statements contained an explanatory paragraph regarding a particular litigation uncertainty. Due to our lawyer's meritorious defence in this litigation, our current report on these financial statements does not include such an explanatory paragraph.

In our opinion, based on the preceding, the financial statements referred to above present fairly, in all material respects, the financial position of Cramdon, Inc., as of December 31, 2004, and the results of its operations and its cash flows for the period then ended in conformity with generally accepted accounting principles consistently applied, except for the changes in the method of computing sales as described in Note 14 to the financial statements.

/s/ PA Firm
March 5, 2005

Required:
Identify the deficiencies and errors in the draft report and write an explanation of the reasons they are errors and deficiencies. Do not rewrite the report.

3.39 **Negative and Positive Assurance and Users' Needs.**
L0.2 One of your neighbours, Hans House, is a minority shareholder of Grackle Corporation, a private company. Grackle is also the company that employs Hans. Recently Hans and the other Grackle Corporation shareholders were asked to approve a resolution that would waive the requirement for the company to have its financial statements audited. The company has been audited in past years, but would have a review instead of an audit if the resolution is passed unanimously by the shareholders. Hans knows that you are an advanced accounting student and has asked for your advice on whether he should vote for or against the audit waiver.

Required:
List the factors that Hans should consider in making this decision. What fact situations would support voting for the audit waiver, and what fact situations would indicate he should vote against the waiver?

3.40 **Distinguishing Forms of Assurance.** Explain the dif-
L0.2 ference between "negative assurance" and an "adverse opinion."

3.41 **GAAS General Standard, Audit Scope.** Give three ex-
L0.4 amples of fact situations in which the General Standards of GAAS are not met. For each example, explain the impact of the violation on the scope of the audit and the audit report.

3.42 **GAAS Examination Standard, Audit Scope.** Give one
L0.4 example of a fact situation in which each of the three Examination Standards of GAAS are not met. For each example explain the impact of the violation on the scope of the audit and the audit report.

3.43 **Audit Opinion on Financial Statements.** The unqual-
L0.3 ified audit opinion states that the financial statements ". . . present fairly . . . in accordance with Canadian generally accepted accounting principles."

Required:
a. Explain, from the perspective of the auditing profession, reasons why the auditor's opinion on fair presentation of financial statements is given in reference to Canadian generally accepted accounting principles.

b. Explain, from the perspective of financial statement users, the contrasting view that the auditor's responsibility to assess the fair presentation goes beyond a literal interpretation of whether the statements meet the requirements of Canadian GAAP.

c. Which position, part (a) or part (b), do you agree with? Why?

3.44 **Audit Scope Limitations—Auditor Appointed Late**
L0.4 a. What alternate procedures can an auditor perform to determine whether the inventory balance is not materially misstated when he or she is appointed in the middle of the year and did not observe the inventory count at the end of the prior year?

b. What alternate procedures can an auditor perform to determine whether the inventory balance is not materially misstated when he or she was appointed after the year end under audit and was not able to observe the count of the either the opening or the ending inventory?

c. What are the reporting implications if alternate procedures can be performed and provide sufficient audit evidence in situations (a) and (b) above?

d. What are the reporting implications if alternate procedures cannot be used to satisfy audit evidence requirements in situations (a) and (b) above?

3.45 **Audit Scope Limitations—Client Imposed**
L0.4 a. What alternate procedures can an auditor perform to determine whether the accounts receivable balance is not materially misstated when client management will not permit audit confirmations to be used?

b. What are the reporting implications if alternate procedures can be performed and provide sufficient audit evidence in situation (a)?

c. What are the reporting implications if alternate procedures cannot be used to satisfy audit evidence requirements in situation (a)?

3.46 **Reporting on Contingencies.** Describe the current re-
L0.5 quirements of Canadian GAAS for reporting for contingencies and uncertainties. Identify the pros and cons of the current approach, contrasting these with the pros and cons of the "subject to" opinions that were used in Canada prior to 1980.

3.47 **Reporting Going-Concern Uncertainties.** Current
L0.5 Canadian GAAS do not permit the auditor to refer to a going-concern uncertainty in the audit report when the uncertainty is properly disclosed in the financial statement notes.

Required:
a. Describe the strengths and weaknesses of this approach, taking into consideration the perspectives of the company, its financial statement users and its auditor.

b. Identify one or more alternative reporting methods that may be more beneficial to financial statement users.

c. You have been invited to comment to the Canadian assurance standards-setting board on its current audit reporting standards. What comment would you make to the standard setters on the issue of audit reporting when there is substantial doubt about a company's ability to continue as a going concern?

3.48 **Going-Concern Assumption—One Year Limitation.**
LO.5 For the purpose of assessing the going-concern assumption it is presumed that the auditor will consider whether the company will continue in existence for a "reasonable time" that does not exceed one year beyond the date of the financial statements. Give reasons that auditors are not required to consider the entity's ability to continue as a going concern for a period longer than one year. In your opinion, is this one year limitation reasonable? Explain and evaluate possible alternate approaches to support your opinion.

3.49 **Standard-Setting Research.** Investigate the history
LO.5 and current status of the CICA Exposure Draft on the Going-Concern assumption that was originally issued in 1996. Use the CICA website, *CA Magazine* and other professional publications to conduct this research. Explain how the due process involved in setting Canadian auditing standards is illustrated by the history of this Exposure Draft.

3.50 **Going-Concern Issue.** PA is the auditor of Jayhawk
LO.5 Inc. Jayhawk's revenues and profitability have decreased in each of the past three years and as of this year end, 2003, its retained earnings will fall into a deficit balance. Jayhawk's long-term debt comes due in 2004 and its management is currently renegotiating the repayment date and terms with its bondholders. According to PA's discussions with management, the renegotiation is not going well and there is a significant risk that the bondholders will put Jayhawk into receivership and liquidate its assets. Jawhawk's CFO has provided draft 2003 financial statements to PA that are prepared in accordance with GAAP.

Required:
a. Discuss the audit reporting implications of the preceding situation.
b. Assume the long-term debt repayment date was not until 2005. Would your response differ?

3.51 **Going-Concern Audit Reporting.** *CICA Handbook,*
LO.5 paragraph 5510.53 provides guidance for audit reporting when there is a going concern problem.

Required:
a. Critique the audit reporting required by paragraph 5510.53 from the perspective of a financial statement user who owns shares of the auditee company.
b. Assume the role of the company's auditor. How would you respond to the criticisms raised in (a)?

3.52 **Report on the Application of Accounting Principles.**
LO.7 *CICA Handbook*, section 7600 sets out procedures relating to requests for advice from a PA from parties other than the PA's audit clients.

Required:
a. What are the purposes of section 7600?

b. Describe the requirements of section 7600 and explain how effective they are in achieving the purposes described in part (a).

3.53 **Report on the Application of Accounting Principles.**
LO.7 Kite Corporation's auditor, PA1, formed the opinion that Kite should accrue for estimated future costs to clean up an environmental problem on one of Kite's properties in its 2003 financial statements. Kite requested a second opinion from PA2 on this issue. PA2 gave an opinion that the estimated liability amount is contingent on various future events that are highly uncertain, such as changes in environmental regulations and environmental cleanup technologies. Thus it is a contingency that is too uncertain to accrue and, in accordance with GAAP, it should only be disclosed. Kite's management sides with the opinion of PA2 because it prevents the company from reporting a loss, allows Kite's management to receive bonuses for 2003, and in their view it is a more appropriate application of GAAP.

Required:
a. Assume that Kite is a public company and PA1 and PA2 are Big Four audit firms. What public perception of auditors may arise if disputes on the application of GAAP can be resolved by the public company obtaining an opinion from another auditor?
b. Take the role of PA1. What issues arise by Kite taking this action in your dispute over the accrual of the contingent liability?
c. Take the role of PA2. What considerations should you make before issuing your opinion?
d. Take the role of one of Kite's Directors. What issues arise by Kite's management taking this action in resolving its dispute with PA1 over the accrual of the contingent liability?

3.54 **Audit Evidence from Specialists.** Lark Limited reports
LO.9 a material balance of deferred development costs in its current financial statements. The cost relates to the development of a mobile robot that can be used to monitor temperature, humidity and security in large warehouses. Lark's auditor obtained an engineers' report to support the technological feasibility of the robotics project and a market research consultant's report to determine the selling prices and volumes likely to be achieved over the first ten years that the product is marketed.

Required:
Explain the nature of audit evidence obtained in this case. How would this audit evidence affect the auditor's report. Compare the use of these specialists' reports in the audit to using the reports of other auditors.

3.55 Find Nortel's 2004 annual report on its website or SEC
LO.4 filings, and review the audit reports for 2001–2004. In light of Nortel's history (as indicated in Chapter 1), do you think these reports are appropriate? Discuss.

3.56 Explain how an auditor can issue an
LO.6 unqualified and adverse opinion on internal controls in the same engagement.

Note: Appendix 3A is located on the text Online Learning Centre.

APPENDIX 3B

. . . .

THE INDEPENDENT AUDITOR'S REPORT ON A COMPLETE SET OF GENERAL PURPOSE FINANCIAL STATEMENTS
(ISA 700 (Revised), December 2004, pp.14–15)

Report on the Financial Statements
We have audited the accompanying financial statements of ABC Company, which comprise the balance sheet as at December 31, 20X1, and the income statement, statement of changes in equity, and cash flow statement for the year then ended, and a summary of significant accounting policies and other explanatory notes.

Management's Responsibility for the Financial Statements
Management is responsible for the preparation and fair presentation of these financial statements in accordance with International Financial Reporting Standards. This responsibility includes: designing, implementing and maintaining internal control relevant to the preparation and fair presentation of financial statements that are free from material misstatement, whether due to fraud or error; selecting and applying appropriate accounting policies; and making accounting estimates that are reasonable in the circumstances.

Auditor's Responsibility
Our responsibility is to express an opinion on these financial statements based on our audit. We conducted our audit in accordance with International Standards on Auditing. Those standards require that we comply with ethical requirements and plan and perform the audit to obtain reasonable assurance whether the financial statements are free from material misstatement.

An audit involves performing procedures to obtain audit evidence about the amounts and disclosures in the financial statements. The procedures selected depend on the auditor's judgment, including the assessment of the risks of material misstatement of the financial statements, whether due to fraud or error. In making those risk assessments, the auditor considers internal control relevant to the entity's preparation and fair presentation of the financial statements in order to design audit procedures that are appropriate in the circumstances, but not for the purpose of expressing an opinion on the effectiveness of the entity's internal control. An audit also includes evaluating the appropriateness of accounting policies used and the reasonableness of accounting estimates made by management, as well as evaluating the overall presentation of financial statements.

We believe that the audit evidence we have obtained is sufficient and appropriate to provide a basis for our audit opinion.

Opinion
In our opinion, the financial statements give a true and fair view of (or 'present fairly, in all material respects,') *the financial position of ABC Company as of December 31, 20X1, and of its financial performance and its cash flows for the year then ended in accordance with International Financial Reporting Standards.*

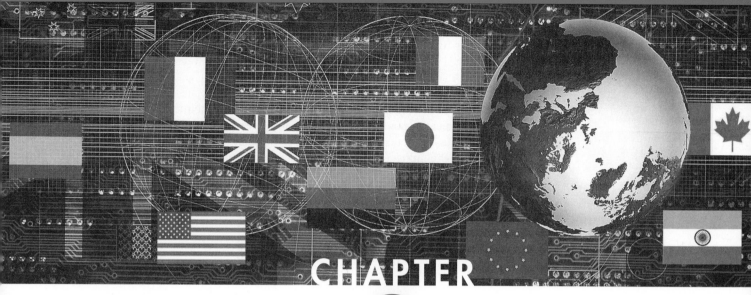

CHAPTER

4

Professional Ethics and Auditor Responsibilities

This chapter highlights the regulation of auditors and PAs. As you will see, regulation and discipline depend on published codes of ethics and effective enforcement practices.

LEARNING OBJECTIVE

① Explain the increasing importance of critical thinking and ethical decision making in professional judgement.

As part of a privileged profession, auditors are responsible to society. This responsibility can be divided into three categories: moral responsibilities, professional responsibilities and legal responsibilities. Morality deals with character and "doing the right thing." What is right is determined largely by social norms. Thus, auditors have a responsibility to conform to social norms. However, social norms are changing and a study of ethics may be helpful in preparing for lifelong adaptation. Auditors' **moral responsibilities** can be summarized as "a public accountant should be upright, not kept upright." Ethics relates to proper conduct in one's life. A study of ethics helps the auditor develop a set of principles by which to live.

The more formal ethical responsibilities auditors have are referred to here as **professional responsibilities**. Professional responsibilities (or **professional ethics**) are the rules and principles for the proper conduct of an auditor in her professional work. Professional ethics are necessary for a number of reasons: to obtain the respect and confidence of the public, to distinguish the professional from the general public, to achieve order within the profession, and to provide a means of self-policing the profession. These professional responsibilities (as distinguished from more general moral responsibilities that everyone should adhere to) are largely captured in the professional ethics for accountants and auditors, which is the topic of this chapter.

Legal responsibilities are covered in the next chapter (Chapter 5).

General Ethics

A pervasive sense of proper ethical conduct is critical for professional accountants. Two aspects of ethics operate in the professional environment—general ethics (the spirit) and professional ethics (the rules). Mautz and Sharaf have contributed the following thoughts to the linkage between general and professional ethics:

> The theory of ethics has been a subject of interest to philosophers since the beginnings of recorded thought. Because philosophers are concerned with the good of all mankind, their discussions have been concerned with what we may call general ethics rather than the ethics of small groups such as the members of a given profession. We cannot look, therefore, to their philosophical theories for direct solutions to our special problems. Nevertheless, their work with general ethics is of primary importance to the development of an appropriate concept in any special field. *Ethical behaviour in auditing or in any other activity is no more than a special application of the general notion of ethical conduct devised by philosophers for men generally. Ethical conduct in auditing draws its justification and basic nature from the general theory of ethics. Thus, we are well advised to give some attention to the ideas and reasoning of some of the great philosophers on this subject.* [Emphasis added][1]

Overview

What is ethics? Wheelwright defined ethics as "that branch of philosophy which is the systematic study of reflective choice, of the standards of right and wrong by which it is to be guided, and of the goods toward which it may ultimately be directed."[2] In this definition, you can detect three key elements: (1) ethics involves questions requiring reflective choice (decision problems); (2) ethics involves guides of right and wrong (moral principles); and (3) ethics is concerned with the consequences of decisions.

What is an ethical problem? A problem exists when you must make a choice among alternative actions, and the right choice is not absolutely clear. An ethical problem may be described as one in which the choice of alternative actions affects the well-being of other persons.

What is ethical behaviour? There are two standard philosophical answers to this question: (1) ethical behaviour is that which produces the greatest good, and (2) ethical behaviour is that which conforms to moral rules and principles. The most difficult problem situations arise when two or more rules conflict or when a rule and the criterion of "greatest good" conflict. Some examples are given later in this chapter to illustrate these difficulties.

[1] R.K. Mautz and H.A. Sharaf, *The Philosophy of Auditing* (American Accounting Association, 1991).
[2] Philip Wheelwright, *A Critical Introduction to Ethics*, 3rd ed. (Indianapolis, Ind.: Odyssey Press, 1959).

Why does an individual or group need a code of ethical conduct? While it has been said that a person should be upright and not be kept upright, a code serves as a useful reference and benchmark for individuals. A code specifies the criteria for conduct of a profession. Thus, codes of professional ethics are able to provide some direct solutions that may not be available in general ethics theories. Furthermore, an individual is better able to know what the profession expects. From the profession's viewpoint, a code is a public declaration of principled conduct and a means of facilitating enforcement of standards of conduct. Practical enforcement and profession-wide internal discipline would be impossible if members were not first put on notice of the standards.

A Variety of Roles

The role of decision maker does not fully describe a professional person's entire ethical obligation. Each person acts not only as an individual but also as a member of a profession and a member of society. Hence, accountants and auditors are also spectators (observing the decisions of colleagues), advisers (counselling with co-workers), instructors (teaching accounting students or new employees on the job), judges (serving on disciplinary committees of provincial associations), and critics (commenting on the ethical decisions of others). All of these roles are important in the practice of professional ethics.

An Ethical Decision Process

Your primary goal, in considering general ethics, is to arrive at a set of acceptable methods for making ethical decisions. Consequently, you must understand the general principles of ethics in order to grasp the behaviour directed by rules of professional conduct.

In the previous definition of ethics, one of the key elements was reflective choice. This involves an important sequence of events beginning with the recognition of a decision problem. Collection of evidence, in the ethics context, refers to thinking about rules of behaviour and outcomes of alternative actions. The process ends with analyzing the situation and taking an action. Ethical decision problems almost always involve projecting yourself into the future to live with your decisions. Professional ethical decisions usually turn on these questions: "What written and unwritten rules govern my behaviour?" and "What are the possible consequences of my choices?" Principles of ethics can help you think about these two questions in real situations.

To Tell or Not to Tell?

In your work as an auditor, you discover that the cashier, who has custody over the petty cash fund, has forged several payment records in order to cover innocent mistakes and to make the fund balance each month when it is replenished. Your investigation reveals that the amount involved during the year is $240. The cashier is a woman, age 55, and the president of the company is a man who can tolerate no mistakes, intentional or otherwise, in the accounting records. In fact, he is unyielding in this respect. He asks you about the results of your audit. Not doubting that the cashier would be fired if the forgeries were known, should you remain silent and thus not tell the truth?

Philosophical Principles in Ethics

We could dispense with the following discussion of ethical theories if we were willing to accept a simple rule: "Let conscience be your guide." Such a rule is appealing because it calls on an individual's own judgement, which may be based on wisdom, insight, adherence to custom or an authoritative code. However, it might also be based on self-interest, caprice, immaturity, ignorance, stubbornness, or misunderstanding.

In a similar manner, reliance on the opinions of others or on the weight of opinion of a particular social group is not always enough. Another person or a group of persons may perpetuate a custom or habit that is wrong (e.g., smoking). To adhere blindly to custom or to group habits is to abdicate individual responsibility. Titus and Keeton summarized this point succinctly: "Each person capable of making moral decisions is responsible for making his own decisions. The ultimate locus of moral responsibility is in the individual."[3] Thus, the function of ethical principles is not only to provide a simple and sure rule, but also to provide some guidelines for taking individual decisions and actions. The box presented previously ("To Tell or Not to Tell?") and the one that follows demonstrate some ethical problems that, for most people, would present difficult choices. Consider them in light of the ethical principles discussed in the following box.

CONFLICTING DUTIES

As a result of your fine reputation as a public accountant, you were invited to become a director of a local bank and were pleased to accept the position. While serving on the board for a year, you learned that a bank director is under a duty to use care and prudence in administering the affairs of the bank, and that failure to do so in such a way that the bank suffers for a financial loss means that the director(s) may be held liable for damages. This month, in the course of an audit, you discover a seriously weakened financial position in a client who has a large loan from your bank. Prompt disclosure to the other bank directors would minimize the bank's loss, but, since the audit report cannot be completed for another three weeks, such disclosure would amount to divulging confidential information gained in the course of an audit engagement (prohibited by confidentiality principles). You can remain silent and honour confidentiality principles (and fail to honour your duty as a bank director), or you can speak up to the other directors (thus violating confidentiality principles). Which shall it be?

There are a number of ethical theories, which can be subdivided into two types: monistic and pluralistic. **Monistic theories** assume that universal principles apply regardless of the specific facts. **Pluralistic theories**, on the other hand, assume that there are no universal principles and that the best approach is to use the principles that are most relevant in a particular case.

There are a number of monistic theories. The most important are deontological (or duty-based) theories dominated by the ideas of Immanuel Kant, and utilitarianism. **Deontological (Kantian) ethics** assumes that there are universal principles (**imperatives**) such as the biblical ten commandments that must always be followed regardless of the consequences. Kant maintained that motive and duty alone define a moral act, not the consequences of the act.

The general objection to the imperative principle is the belief that so-called universal rules always turn out to have exceptions. The general response to this objection is that if the rule is stated properly to include the exceptional cases, then the principle is still valid. The problem with this response, however, is that human experience is complicated, and extremely complex universal rules would have to be constructed to try to cover all possible cases.[4]

[3] Harold H. Titus, and Morris Keeton, *Ethics for Today*, 4th ed. (New York: American Book-Stratford Press, 1966), p. 131.

[4] Several rules of professional conduct to be discussed shortly are explicitly phrased to provide exceptions to the general rules (for example, rules 210 and 204 of the ICAO Rules of Professional Conduct). Imperative rules also seem to generate borderline cases, so the ethics divisions of PA professional bodies issue interpretations and rulings to explain the applicability of the rules.

Another major problem with duty-based ethics is that duties can conflict; one then needs to sort out which duty is most important. This may depend on the specific context. The professional rules of conduct have been greatly influenced by duty-based Kantian ethics. The rules can be viewed as duties of professional accountants. We also have the problem of potential conflict of professional rules, most notably the rule of confidentiality and the rule of not being associated with misleading information. These rules are discussed in more detail later in the chapter.

Utilitarianism relies on the principle of utility, which says that when we have a choice between alternative actions or choices, we pick the one that results in the best consequences (that is, has the highest utility). **Consequentialism** suffers from the opposite problem of duty-based ethics: it says that achieving the greatest good for the greatest number is all that matters. But what if a minority were to suffer as a result? And we ignore their rights?

These problems in monistic theories illustrate that they are not sufficient by themselves to handle the complexities of most real-life ethical problems, including those of practical, professional ethics. Nevertheless, they can be important principles to use when providing reasons for a claim or decision. For example, standard economic theory is based on utilitarianism. This theory is the one used in cost-benefit analysis that you may be familiar with from your management accounting courses. However, exclusive reliance on one principle can lead to problems. The cost-benefit analysis approach was used by many PA firms in the 1990s when they decided to put more emphasis on further developing the management consulting side of their practices rather than auditing. In some cases, auditing was viewed as a "loss leader" to use as a tool for creating more lucrative consulting practices. At the time the big PA firms were also the largest consulting firms in the world.[5] The resulting increase in consulting revenues was so large that the appearance of independence was affected. In fact, in the case of Arthur Andersen overreliance on consulting lead to its eventual demise. This focus on utilitarian primacy has thus caused the profession a great deal of grief. With the passage of SOX and other reforms the pendulum now seems to be swinging the other way—the focus on quality control may in part be viewed as putting more emphasis on the duties of auditors toward investors.

To better prepare you to deal with the ethical and other issues of professional judgement in the current post-Enron audit environment, it is useful to have a framework to provide more structure to your thinking. We refer to this as the **critical-thinking framework**. The framework consists of principles, concepts and their application. Ethics is an important concept within the framework. A brief description of the framework follows, with more detail provided in Appendix 4A on the text Online Learning Centre.

It is important to be aware of various principles of critical thinking, which we briefly summarize in the following box.

PRINCIPLES OF CRITICAL THINKING

E 1. Critical thinking has a purpose that leads somewhere, has implications and consequences, settles a question or solves a problem.

E 2. Critical thinking requires an enquiring mind that identifies an important issue or controversy, considers the goals in light of the many perspectives possible on the issue and decides on the best goal in the circumstances. Critical thinking identifies the claims that need to be justified to achieve a goal.

E 3. Critical thinking is used to persuade someone (including yourself) to accept a claim. Of course others may try to persuade you to accept another claim. You and

---

[5] For a good review of the history of the profession during this period, see Arthur R. Wyatt, "Accounting Professionalism— They Just Don't Get it!," *Accounting Horizons*, March 2004, pp. 45–54.

others are aware you may have these conflicting claims. You try to resolve this conflict in a co-operative way through the critical-thinking process, in which you and others are open minded and receptive to being persuaded by good reasoning.

4. Critical thinking is based on reasoning using argumentation. Argumentation is the process of supporting or justifying a claim related to resolving a controversy or issue. Critical thinking is the essence of being objective.

E 5. Critical thinking is expressed through and shaped by language, which can be used to develop concepts and ideas.

E 6. Critical thinking requires being aware of the power of language, its ability to manipulate and the importance of specific words chosen to persuade. The words chosen reflect value judgements and have emotional content, which is communicated to the listener. This is part of the persuasion process.

E 7. Critical thinking requires making important assumptions and reasons explicit so that they are open to scrutiny by others. This is the best path to truth and knowledge and these are the ultimate goals of a questioning mind.

Critical thinking involves use of principles which should be actively considered in analyzing a controversy or issue facing the auditor (such as a disagreement with management on a financial reporting issue). The principles having a dominant ethical component are marked with an "E." As you can see all of the principles, other than the strict logical ones, have an important ethical component. In particular, note the importance of a questioning mind. It represents a mental attitude that incorporates the rest of the critical thinking principles. It should be clear that scepticism is a key part of critical thinking through the questioning mind concept. Thus, critical thinking takes traditional audit virtues, extending them to a more holistic approach to judgement.

What distinguishes ethical reasoning from all other types of reasoning is that ethics needs to consider the perspective of others. This consideration includes the consequences of one's decision on others and the ability to imagine how others will feel about these consequences. This ability to imagine is frequently referred to as **moral imagination**. This need for more imagination, along with ethical principles such as utilitarianism and Kantian imperatives, is what distinguishes moral reasoning from all others. For example, moral imagination is necessary to anticipate the incentives that would act as indicators of fraud. Moral imagination is also necessary to understand user needs in financial reporting. Had the CEO at Molex (the company described at the beginning of Chapter 1) used his moral imagination, he may not have been fired. The same is true of the former CEO of Boeing Corp. discussed in Appendix 4A.

Auditors cannot simply rely on standard setters' moral imaginations to anticipate all possible situations. Every engagement has its own unique features; consequently, auditors must tailor their moral imaginations to the specific circumstances of a particular engagement. It is part of being a professional rather than just a technician following standards and rules of conduct mechanically. For this reason it may not be sufficient to merely follow GAAP and GAAS and rules of conduct on an engagement.

Principle 4 reflects the role of logic in critical thinking and the need for logical justification. Logic essentially means identifying proper reasons to support a claim or conclusion. Logic is the study of the link between reasons and a conclusion. We want that link to be strong on an audit engagement. But we also want a second condition to be met before we can say that an audit conclusion is justified by the reasons given. That condition is that the reasons are true or substantially true. If both these conditions are satisfied, then we can say that our conclusion is justified by the reasons. The term "sound reasoning" is also used when our conclusions are justified this way. Sound reasoning is the essence of being objective on an issue.

Whereas logic is concerned with the link between reasons and conclusion, the truthfulness of reasons is determined by the field of studies that are the source of the reasons (e.g., accounting and auditing theory). The persuasiveness of reasons is also greatly influenced by the choice of words used in stating the reasons. A critical thinker must be concerned that language is used to clarify, not cloud or bias the reasoning. For example, use of the words "present fairly" is part of an effort by the auditor to persuade the user of the acceptability of the audited financial statements.

Professional judgement in auditing is essentially critical thinking on accounting issues and the evidence related to the issues. The process can be summarized in the steps shown in Exhibit 4–1. The critical thinking framework can be used for deciding when an audit conclusion is sufficiently justified. When this reasoning is documented in an audit, there is no basis for questioning the sufficiency of audit documentation. For a more complete discussion of this critical thinking framework, along with illustrations of its application, see Appendix 4A.

This brief review of the principles of ethics and critical thinking provides some background on the way people approach difficult decision problems. The greatest task is to take general ethical principles and apply them to a real decision. Applying them through codes of professional conduct is a challenge. Appendix 4A provides more discussion and background to help meet this challenge.

The rest of this chapter is devoted to the more practical rules of professional conduct, related concepts and principles, and their application in relevant situations. However, these professional rules and principles rely for their justification on the various ethical theories discussed in this section, especially duty-based theories.

EXHIBIT   4–1   A FRAMEWORK OF CRITICAL THINKING PRINCIPLES ACHIEVING A GOAL WITH AN ENQUIRING MIND

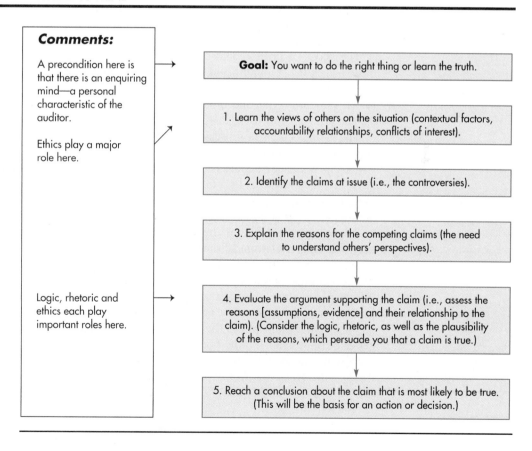

REVIEW
CHECKPOINTS

4.1   What roles must a professional accountant be prepared to occupy in regard to ethical decision problems?

4.2   When might the rule "Let conscience be your guide" not be a sufficient basis for your personal ethical decisions? for your professional ethical decisions?

4.3   Assume that you accept the following ethical rule: "Failure to tell the whole truth is wrong." In the illustrations about (*a*) your position as a bank director and (*b*) your knowledge of the cashier's forgeries, what would this rule require you to do? Why is an unalterable rule like this classed as an element of duty-based ethical theory?

4.4   How does utilitarian ethics differ from duty-based ethics?

4.5   Why are simplified monastic theories of ethics not sufficient for professional decision making?

4.6   Why is critical thinking becoming more important in the post-Enron environment?

4.7   How does professional ethics relate to critical thinking?

RULES OF PROFESSIONAL CONDUCT AND CODE OF ETHICS

LEARNING OBJECTIVE

2 Analyze whether a PA's conduct conforms to provincial Rules of Professional Conduct.

All the Canadian PA bodies (CAs, CGAs, CMAs) and IFAC have their own rules of professional conduct for their members and students, either provincially or nationally. Generally, these rules are published as a part of the member's *Handbook,* which identifies the various activities and regulations of the PA institute or association, including a section on professional conduct. Codes of conduct need to develop a balance between detailed rules and more general principles. The codes also need to be practical; as a result, they tend to have similar frameworks, as indicated in the box on the next page.

The codes of professional conduct are usually organized hierarchically, with general principles at the beginning and increasing detail and specifics as one goes from the rules to specific interpretations of the rules. The general principles are sometimes referred to as "ideal standards" and the more specific rules and related interpretations as "minimum standards."

The various codes of professional conduct are meant to apply to all members subject to certain exceptions for students and members not in public practice. Generally, for CAs and CMAs the issuance of codes is the responsibility of provincial institutes or societies. CGAs have a national code set by CGA-Canada; however, provincial CGA associations may add modifications to the national code. Recently, the CA provincial institutes have substantially harmonized their codes so that the CA code can be viewed as more of a national one.

An example of a code is the ICAO *Member's Handbook,* which identifies the various activities and regulations of the Ontario Institute, including a section on professional conduct. The professional conduct section is divided into three parts: a Foreword, the Rules of Professional Conduct, and the Interpretation of the Rules. Many people consider the Foreword the most important part of the professional conduct regulations[6] because it contains a set of principles that are intended to provide guidance in the absence of specific rules. In particular, unlike the rules that many people think of as "thou shalt nots"—a series of rules against—the Foreword sets out the broad principles providing guidance in the absence of specific rules. The Foreword is must reading for CA members and students because the *Members' Handbook specifically advises members that all the rules that follow "are to be read in the light of the Foreword to the rules."* In this sense, the forward is

---

[6] K. Gunning, "Required Reading," *CA Magazine,* November 1992, pp. 38–40.

analogous to the conceptual framework of accounting, e.g., section 1000 of the *CICA Handbook*, and the rules themselves are like the recommendations in the *CICA Handbook*.

The Foreword has clearly defined sections. The first section sets out the purpose of the rules, which is to guide the profession in serving the public. The second section reviews the key characteristics that mark a profession and a professional, concluding that "chartered accountancy is a profession."

The third section identifies the six "fundamental statements of accepted conduct" around which all the rules are centred. These six principles can be summarized as follows:

1. The member should act to maintain the profession's reputation.

2. The member should use due care and maintain his or her professional competence.

3. The member should maintain independence in the appearance as well as the fact of independence of his or her professional judgement.

4. The member should preserve client confidentiality.

5. The member should base his or her reputation on professional excellence—in particular, advertising should inform, not solicit.

6. The member should show professional courtesy to other members at all times.

These principles can be interpreted as ideals to which every professional aspires. The rules themselves are more specific because they are intended as guides to action and to be enforceable. However, adherence to the rules represents only a minimum acceptable or floor level of performance for CAs. On the other hand, because they are more detailed, the rules allow the implementation of a code through the use of concrete benchmarks against which a member's performance can be compared.

EXAMPLE OF A FRAMEWORK FOR A CODE OF CONDUCT FOR PROFESSIONAL ACCOUNTANTS

- Introduction and purpose
- Fundamental principles and standards
- General rules
- Specific rules
- Discipline
- Interpretations of rules

From *Professional Ethics in Accounting*, 1st edition by BROOKS. © 1995. Reprinted with permission of South-Western, a division of Thompson Learning: www.thompsonrights.com. Fax 800-730-2215.

The Foreword singles out for further discussion several of the principles that require additional guidance: (*a*) sustaining professional competence (related to principle 2 above), (*b*) avoiding conflicts of interest in respect of a client's affairs (related to principle 3), and (*c*) practice development based on professional excellence rather than self-promotion (related to principle 5). It will be evident from the space devoted to the rules themselves that these particular principles seem to require the most detailed guidance for members. However, as the Foreword makes clear, in a world where ethical decision-making is becoming more complex yet indispensable for maintaining the public interest, the absence of specific rules makes the principle that much more important. As a result, some writers have concluded that the six principles should be given much more prominence, and used more frequently.[7]

---

[7] Ibid.

After the Foreword come the Rules of Conduct themselves. The ICAO Council also publishes "Council Interpretations of (Rules of Conduct)," which are detailed explanations of specific rules necessary to help members understand particular applications. Anyone who departs from Council interpretations has the burden of justifying that departure in any disciplinary hearing.

The CMAs have a similar set of provincial rules for each provincial society. For example, the Society of Management Accountants of Ontario (SMAO) *Handbook on Ethics* contains predominantly general principles of ethics; the more detailed rules and interpretations are covered in the remainder. Where CMAs have the right to perform assurance engagements, the rules require that they comply with local legislation.

The CGAs have a national code of conduct that provides the basic framework for the provincial association rules. The CGA code consists of a preamble that explains why a code is necessary and who is affected; a statement of ethical principles; Rules of Conduct, with guidance concerning their application to certain specific situations; and, finally, a set of definitions of terms used throughout the CGA code.

The IFAC includes a code of ethics for PAs as part of their standards. IFAC avoids preparing detailed rules or interpretations because such details will be influenced by national laws and culture. However, IFAC does develop a general framework which it feels can serve as a base for a particular country's national ethical guidelines. This framework consists of identifying the overall obligation to serve the public interest, the objectives, the fundamental principles and a code. The objectives consist of the following: credibility, professionalism, quality of services and confidence. The fundamental IFAC ethical principles are integrity, objectivity, professional competence and due care, confidentiality, professional behaviour and technical standards. The code part of IFAC's ethics section is divided into three parts: Part A applying to all PAs, Part B applying to PAs in public practice and Part C applying primarily to PAs in industry.

There is much similarity in the concepts of all professional codes, which are reviewed in the next section, along with the related rules.

Rules of Professional Conduct

The Rules of Professional Conduct derive their authority from the bylaws of the various PA professional bodies (or those professional bodies that strive to be recognized as PAs).

Members of the professional bodies (CAs, CGAs, CMAs) are held responsible for compliance with the rules by all persons associated with them in public practice, including employees and partners. In addition, members may not permit other people to carry out on their behalf acts which are prohibited by the rules.

The various PA institutes and associations have several detailed rules of conduct. They have much in common and we cannot list all of them. So, we pick one for illustration purposes only. The rules used by the Institute of Chartered Accountants of Ontario (ICAO) are used as an example in the box on page 97. Unless otherwise specified, when we reference Rules or Codes of Conduct in this chapter, we refer to appropriate sections of institute's or association's professional accounting ethics.

In terms of the critical thinking framework, these rules can be viewed as important reasons for taking (or not taking) a particular action. Specifically, the rules follow the logic of Kantian imperatives or duties. Although there is also an element of utilitarianism as indicated in the discussion following.

An outline of typical rules and their topics is presented next. An authority on professional ethics, Len Brooks at the University of Toronto, has identified certain principles in codes of conduct that apply to all professional accountants. See the box on page 98.

The rest of this chapter discusses ethical and critical-thinking principles, and related rules in more detail. However, you should refer to the appropriate *Member's Handbooks* for CAs, CGAs, or CMAs for more extensive guidance on rules related to these professional groups.

THE INSTITUTE OF CHARTERED ACCOUNTANTS OF ONTARIO (ICAO)

RULES OF PROFESSIONAL CONDUCT

TABLE OF CONTENTS

Fundamental Principles in Codes of Conduct for Professional Accountants

Members should:

- at all times maintain the good reputation of the profession and its ability to serve the public interest

- perform with:
  - integrity
  - objectivity
  - independence
  - professional competence
  - due care
  - confidentiality

- not be associated with any misleading information or misrepresentation

From *Professional Ethics in Accounting*, 1st edition by BROOKS. © 1995. Reprinted with permission of South-Western, a division of Thompson Learning: www.thompsonrights.com. Fax 800-730-2215.

Serving the Public Interest

The single most important principle is that accountants must serve the public interest; they can only do so if the profession maintains a good reputation at all times. The remaining principles all serve to support this first principle. "The phrase 'at all times' is significant because the public will view any serious transgression of a professional accountant, including those outside business or professional activity, as a black mark against the profession as a whole. Consequently, if a professional accountant is convicted of a minimal offense or fraud, his or her certification is usually revoked."[8]

The most important way to serve the public interest is to competently fulfill the role the public expects of the professional. This role is succinctly captured by Rule 205, which prohibits the PA from being associated with false or misleading information. As stated in the auditor's report, the role of the auditor is to express an opinion based on the audit, while the responsibility of management is to prepare the financial statements. In fulfilling his or her responsibility, the auditor reduces the risk of the financial statements being false or misleading to an appropriately low level. This concept has been captured throughout most of this text through the use of such terms as "present fairly," "in all material respects," "audit risk," "materiality," and "risk of material misstatements."

If the audit fails to detect a material misstatement, then the audit fails. This was dramatically illustrated by the rapid demise of Arthur Andersen as a result of the failure of their Enron audit. The profession is now particularly sensitized to the importance of not being associated with misleading information. And Rule 205 now probably represents the most important rule over all others. This is particularly true in light of responsibilities placed on auditors by SOX and the CPAB, as discussed in Chapter 1.

Integrity

Integrity is the duty to be honest and conscientious in performing professional services. Integrity relates to the basic character of the professional—a PA must "be upright not kept upright." Without the integrity of its members, the profession cannot maintain its good reputation and serve the public interest.

[8] L. J. Brooks, *Professional Ethics for Accountants* (Minneapolis/St. Paul: West Publishing, 1995), p. 120.

INDEPENDENCE AND OBJECTIVITY

• • • • • • • • • • •

Independence and objectivity are closely related terms. Independence rule 204.1 was introduced to you in Chapter 3. The rather fine distinction is based mainly on the fact that independence is the term given to objectivity in the special case of assurance engagements, and that independence is a way of achieving objectivity.

The term "independence" is also used in the *Canadian Business Corporations Act*, in some provincial corporations acts, and in various professional Rules of Conduct. The key Canadian legislation requires that the auditor be "independent"—presumably, the fact of independence must be determined by the courts.

The *Canadian Business Corporations Act*, section 161, defines independence as a key qualification of an auditor, as indicated in the following box:

---

161. **(1)** **Qualification of auditor.**—Subject to subsection (5), a person is disqualified from being an auditor of a corporation if he is not independent of the corporation, any of its affiliates or the directors or officers of any such corporation or its affiliates.

(2) **Independence.**—For the purpose of this section,
  (a) independence is a question of fact; and
  (b) a person is deemed not to be independent if he or his business partner
    (I) is a business partner, a director, an officer or an employee of the corporation or any of its affiliates, or a business partner of any director, officer or employee of any such corporation or any of its affiliates;
    (II) beneficially owns or controls, directly or indirectly, a material interest in the securities of the corporation or any of its affiliates, or
    (III) has been a receiver-manager, liquidator or trustee in bankruptcy of the corporation or any of its affiliates within two years of his proposed appointment as auditor of the corporation.

(3) **Duty to resign.**—An auditor who becomes disqualified under this section shall, subject to subsection (5), resign forthwith after becoming aware of his disqualification.

Source: Canadian Business Corporations Act, section 161.1.

The term "independence" is internationally recognized. For example, the International Federation of Accountants Technical Standard on Ethics, section 8, specifies that "professional accountants in public practice when undertaking a reporting assignment should be independent in fact and appearance." Similar wording is used in the SMAO's Code of Conduct with respect to the need for independence on assurance engagements.

Clearly, independence is an important concept for PAs. For this reason we discuss both independence and objectivity. However, since the focus of this text is on audits, our focus will be on independence.

The CICA, IFAC, and CGA-Canada all have an independence standard of framework based on five threats or risks to independence as follows:

1. self-review threat, which occurs when a PA provides assurance on his or her own work
2. self-interest threat, which occurs, for example, when a PA could benefit from a financial interest in a client
3. advocacy threat, which occurs when a PA promotes a client's position or opinion
4. familiarity threat, which occurs when a PA becomes too sympathetic to a client's interests

5. intimidation threat, which occurs when a PA is deterred from acting objectively by actual or perceived threats from a client

Under all the independence standards, the PA must identify and evaluate the significance of any independence threat. If threats are other than clearly insignificant, the PA must apply safeguards to eliminate the threats or take action to reduce them to a level that would pose no real or perceived compromise. If no safeguards are adequate to preserve independence, the PA must eliminate the activity, interest, or relationship that is creating the threat, or refuse to perform or continue the particular engagement.[9]

We will refer to the need to control these independence threats as the **independence principle**. Such principles can be very useful in assisting sound auditor ethical reasoning by helping to structure the reasoning process. As noted in Chapter 2, independence issues continue to be a problem for even the largest firms according to the CPAB's 2004 monitoring report.[10]

The Canadian legislation referred to previously requires independence for financial statement audit services. However, review services in connection with unaudited financial statements, engagements to report on prospective financial statements (forecasts and projections), other assurance services and engagements to express opinions on representations other than financial statements (e.g., reports on internal control) all require independence. In this regard you should be aware of the definition of "public practice." A member is considered to be in the public practice of accounting if (1) he or she "holds out to be a PA," that is, lets it be known publicly that the member is a PA, and (2) offers to perform for clients the types of services rendered by other public accountants. The latter part of the definition is very broad because PAs perform a wide range of accounting, audit, taxation and consulting services.[11] The result of this definition is that most PAs who seek to obtain clients from the general public are in the practice of public accounting. For example, the PAs who work for H&R Block, the tax preparation corporation, are in public practice if they let themselves be known as PAs.

The concept of independence is critical to the public accounting profession. Since the purpose of independent financial auditing is to lend credibility to financial statements, auditors must in fact be impartial and unbiased with respect to both the client management and the client entity itself.

Auditors must not only be independent in fact, but also independent to outside decision makers who rely on their assurance services. Independence, in fact, is a mental condition and is difficult to demonstrate by physical or visual means. Thus, some appearances of lacking independence may be prohibited in specific interpretations of the independence principle. Note how awareness of other perspectives is crucial to correctly assess the various independence risks. The rest of the critical thinking framework is also useful for deciding if the independence risks are appropriately low for a specific situation. Thus, critical thinking and the independence principle have a great deal of overlap. This should not be surprising as independence risks are but one category of specific points at issue on a particular engagement.

The period of the prohibited activities depends on the circumstances. A member may divest a prohibited financial interest before the first work on a new client begins, after which it is improper to reinvest when the engagement will continue for future years. Direct or indirect financial interests are allowed up to the point of materiality (with reference to the PA's wealth). This provision permits members to hold mutual fund shares and have some limited business transactions with clients so long as the investments do not reach material proportions.

---

[9] As modified, *CA Magazine*, October 2002, p. 51.

[10] www.cpab_ccrc.org for the latest reports.

[11] The CICA's definition of public accountant in its *Terminology for Accountants*, 4th ed. (1992), is as follows: "1. The performance of services for clients, the purpose of which is to add credibility to financial information that may be relied upon by interested parties. 2. The performance of independent professional accounting and related services for clients. 3. Any service so defined by a particular statute or authority."

As noted previously, SOX in the U.S. is having a global influence in determining which threats to independence are against the public interest. The currently prohibited activities seem to focus on the self-review threat. Other threats will likely be identified as the SEC and PCAOB establish regulations required by the Act. Historically, earlier standards and rules of professional conduct focused on self-interest and intimidation threats through rules on financial interests and rules related to conflicts of interest. These more detailed rules are reviewed next.

Permitted Loans

Generally, the Codes or Rules of Conduct allow home mortgages, immaterial loans, and secured loans all made under a client's normal lending procedures, terms and requirements, if the client is a bank or other financial institution.

Independence is also not considered impaired by a member obtaining these kinds of personal loans from assurance service clients: (*a*) auto loans and leases collateralized by the automobile, (*b*) insurance policy loans based on policy surrender value, (*c*) loans collateralized by cash deposits at the same financial institution, and (*d*) credit card balances and cash advances equivalent to other customers of the client in the normal course of business. Thus, an individual involved in the audit of a bank can have an auto loan at the bank, borrow money secured by cash in a certificate of deposit, and have the bank's credit card. For insurance company clients, the PA can borrow against the cash surrender value of a life insurance policy. However, the loans should have the same terms as granted to other customers of the institution in the normal course of business. Potentially, these kinds of permitted loans could be abused in spirit, as apparently happened in the United States. The key ethical judgement is understanding "the normal course of business" and, more basically, the types of loans that could lead to at least the perception of impairment of auditor independence.

The Codes of Conduct collectively prohibit activities that amount to the ability to make decisions for the client or to act as management, broadly defined. The appearance of independence is impaired if such a connection existed at any time during the period covered by the financial statements, regardless of whether the association was terminated prior to the beginning of the audit work. The presumption is that members cannot be independent and objective when attesting to decisions in which they took part or with which they appeared to be connected.

In terms of ethical principles, these rules may be justified on a utilitarian theory basis as far as direct financial interests are concerned. The logic is something like this: The greatest good is created by making a situation free of any suspicious circumstances, no matter how innocent they may be in truth. The goodwill of public reliance and respect is greater than the PA's sacrifice of the opportunity to invest in securities of clients or participate in their management.

Other Issues Related to the Independence Principle

In addition to the issues previously discussed, there are other rules relevant to the independence principle, now briefly described.

Honorary Positions in Nonprofit Organizations

Ordinarily, independence is impaired if a PA serves on an organization's board of directors. However, members can be honorary directors of such organizations as charity hospitals, fund drives, symphony orchestra societies and other nonprofit organizations so long as (1) the position is purely honorary, (2) the PA is identified as an honorary director on letterheads and other literature, (3) the only form of participation is the use of the PA's name, and (4) the PA does not vote with the board or participate in management functions. When all these criteria are satisfied, the PA/board member can perform assurance services because the appearances of independence will have been preserved.

Retired Partners

Independence problems do not end when partners retire, resign or otherwise leave an accounting firm. A former partner can cause independence to be impaired in some circumstances in connection with her association with a client of the former firm. However, the problems are solved and independence is not impaired if (1) the person's retirement benefits are fixed, (2) the person is no longer active in the accounting firm (sometimes even retired partners remain "active"), and (3) the former partner is not held out to be associated with the accounting firm by a reasonable observer. Regulators may have stricter rules relating to former partners.

Accounting and Other Services

If a PA performs the bookkeeping and makes accounting decisions for a company and the management of the company does not know enough about the financial statements to take primary responsibility for them, the PA cannot be considered independent for assurance services. The problem in this situation relates to the appearance of the PA having both prepared the financial statements or other data and given an audit report or other assurance on his own work. The PA can perform the bookkeeping and counsel the client management about the accounting principles choices, but in the final analysis, the management must be able to say, "These are our financial statements (or other data); we made the choices of accounting principles; we take primary responsibility for them." Again, regulators may have stricter rules relating to such bookkeeping services.

SOX prohibits the following services for auditors of publicly traded companies: internal audit services for the client, financial-information-system design and implementation, and even tax services. All of these services must be preapproved by the client's audit committee and disclosed to regulators.

Rotation of Partners and Second Partner Review

CPAB and SOX require rotation of the lead audit partner and/or concurring review partner (but not the audit firm) every five years. The five-year period includes time spent providing professional services as a non-partner (for example, manager) and includes years before 2002. The intent of the rule is to prevent auditors from becoming too complacent and not sufficiently sceptical with the client relationship.

A second partner review is now mandated by both CPAB and SOX.

Actual or Threatened Litigation

Independence can be threatened by appearances of a PA trying to serve her own best interests. This condition can arise when a PA and a client move into an adversary relationship and away from the co-operative relationship needed in an assurance engagement. PAs are considered not independent when (1) company management threatens or actually starts a lawsuit against the PA alleging deficiencies in audit or other assurance work and (2) the PA threatens or starts litigation against the company management alleging fraud or deceit. Such cases may be rare, but auditors can find out a way out of such difficult audit situations by ending the assurance engagement. Essentially the PA–client relationship ends, and the litigation begins a new relationship.

Investor or Investee Relationships

In this context "investor" and "investee" have the same meaning as in the accounting rules about accounting for investments on the equity method, covered in *Handbook* section 3050. The *investor* is the party that has significant influence over a business, and the *investee* is the business in which the investor has the significant influence.

When the PA's client is the investor, a PA's direct or material indirect financial interest in a nonclient investee impairs the PA's independence. The reasoning for the basic rule is that the client investor, through its ability to influence a nonclient investee, can increase or decrease the PA's financial stake in the investee by an amount material to the PA, and, therefore, the PA may not appear to be independent. The exception is: If the nonclient investee is immaterial to the investor, independence is not considered impaired when the PA's financial interest in a nonclient investee is immaterial in relation to the PA's wealth.

When a PA has an investment in a nonclient investor: (a) independence with respect to a client investee that is material in the financial statements of the investor is impaired when the PA has any direct or material indirect financial interest in the nonclient investor; (b) independence with respect to a client investee that is not material in the financial statements of the investor is not impaired, even if the PA's investment is material to the PA, as long as the PA does not have significant influence over the actions of the nonclient investor; but (c) independence with respect to a client investee that is not material in the financial statements of the investor is impaired when the PA has a large enough investment to give the PA a significant influence over the actions of the nonclient investor, which then can influence (manage) affairs of the client investee. The reasoning underlying the independence impairment conclusions in these relationships is that the PA occupies a position similar to being a member of management of the client investee.

Effect of Family Relationships

The Codes of Conduct and all the interpretations apply to "members," but you should not confuse being a member of a professional accounting institute, society or association with the use of the word *member* in the rule. For purposes of independence, the terms *member* and *member's firm* generally include:

- all partners in the accounting firm
- all professional employees participating in the engagement, including audit, tax and management consulting personnel
- all other manager-level employees located in a firm office that does a significant part of the audit
- any PA firm person formerly employed by or connected with the audit client in a managerial capacity unless the person (a) is disassociated from the client and (b) does not participate in the engagement
- any PA firm professional (e.g., partner, manager, staff) who is associated with the client in a managerial capacity and is located in an office of the PA firm that does a significant part of the engagement

The term "member" excludes "students" registered under the bylaws of the professional body. However, the Codes of Conduct generally apply to students as well as members.

This enumeration permits (a) financial relationships by manager-level personnel located in offices not involved in the audit; (b) financial relationships by staff in offices not involved in the audit and in an office involved in the audit as long as they are not on the engagement itself; (c) former managerial relationships by partners, managers and staff, provided they are now disassociated from the client and do not participate in the engagement; and (d) current managerial relationships by managers and staff, provided they do not participate in the engagement and are located in an office that does not do a significant part of the engagement. All this is rather complicated, but the bottom line is that it is rare for any partners/shareholders in the firm to be able to have any of the financial or managerial relationships. It is possible for managers and staff to have such relationships, provided they are far removed from the actual work on the audit engagement.

Financial interests of spouses and dependent persons (whether related or not) and some financial interests of close relatives are attributed to the member. (Close relatives include nondependent children, stepchildren, brothers, sisters, parents, grandparents, parents-in-law and the spouses of each of these.) Thus, for example, independence would be impaired if (a) a spouse or dependent grandfather of a member had a direct financial interest in an audit client or (b) a member on an engagement knew about a material financial interest of a nondependent daughter or brother in a client.

Employment relations of spouses, dependent persons and close relatives can be attributed to a member. Positions that can exercise significant influences over the operating, financial or accounting policies of the client are attributed to the member and impair independence.

Positions that are "audit sensitive" (e.g., cashier, internal auditor, accounting supervisor, purchasing agent, inventory warehouse supervisor) are attributed to the member and impair independence. However, such employment poses no problem when it cannot influence the audit work (e.g., secretarial, nonfinancial) or is not audit-sensitive.

The Code of Conduct rules are the minimum criteria relating to independence. PA firms can make more limiting rules. The anecdote in the next box shows some rules given to PA firm job applicants by a Big Four accounting firm.

IF EMPLOYED BY "ANONYMOUS FIRM," I UNDERSTAND THAT:

Professional staff members of the firm, their spouses and dependents are prohibited from owning or controlling investments in any of our clients and certain related non-clients, and I will be required to dispose of any such investments before commencing employment with the firm.

I will be prohibited from disclosing nonpublic information regarding clients or other entities to anyone, other than for firm business, or using it for any personal purpose.

I will be expected to devote my energies to the firm to the fullest extent possible and refrain from other business interests that might require significant time or that could be considered a conflict of interest.

Neither an offer of employment nor employment itself carries with it a guarantee of tenure of employment, and my employment, compensation and benefits can be terminated, with or without cause or notice, at any time at the option of the firm or myself.

Analysis

Generally, the Rules of Professional Conduct and corporation acts legislation imply a fine distinction between independence and integrity and objectivity. The spirit of the rules is that integrity and objectivity are required in connection with all professional services, and, in addition, independence is required for assurance services. In this context integrity and objectivity are the larger concepts, and "independence" is a special condition largely defined by the matters of appearance specified in the codes or their interpretations. Conflicts of interest, as for example cited in ICAO Rule 204, refers to the need to avoid having business interests in which the accountant's personal financial relationships or the accountant's relationships with other clients might tempt the accountant to fail to serve the best interests of a client or the public that uses the results of the engagement.

The issue of independence gained much more prominence on January 6, 2000, when the SEC made public a report of thousands of violations, by one of the Big Four firms, of rules requiring PAs to remain independent from companies they audit. This occurred despite earlier concerns about independence. In the U.S., these concerns resulted in a new private sector body, the Independence Standards Board, created in May 1997. The Board issued its first standard in 1999 requiring auditors to confirm their independence annually to audit committees. Other items on the Board's agenda included an official definition of independence and a conceptual framework on independence. This Board was disbanded and replaced in 2002 by the PCAOB created under SOX. This new Board has even more demanding objectives and became fully operational in April 2003. It is clear that maintenance of independence is a continuing and growing concern within the profession.

Phrases such as "shall not knowingly misrepresent facts" and "[shall not] subordinate his or her judgement to others" emphasize conditions people ordinarily identify with the concepts of integrity and objectivity. PAs who know about a client's lies in a tax return, false journal entries, material misrepresentations in financial statements and the like have violated both the spirit and the letter of the Rules of Conduct. However, in tax practice, a PA can act as an advocate to resolve doubt in favour of a taxpayer-client as long as the tax treatment has a reasonable or justifiable basis.

Professional Competence and Due Care

The professional competence and due care principles of the Codes of Conduct can be summarized as follows:

A. *Professional competence.* Undertake only those professional services that the member or the member's firm can reasonably expect to be completed with professional competence.

B. *Due professional care.* Exercise due professional care in the performance of professional services.

C. *Planning and supervision.* Adequately plan and supervise the performance of professional services.

D. *Sufficient relevant data.* Obtain sufficient relevant data to afford a reasonable basis for conclusions or recommendations in relation to any professional services performed.

Analysis

The professional competence and due care principles are a comprehensive statement of general standards that PAs are expected to observe in all areas of practice. These are the principles that enforce the various series of professional standards. For example, there is usually a specific rule relating to compliance with professional standards.

Compliance with Professional Standards

A member engaged in the practice of public accounting shall perform his professional services in accordance with generally accepted standards of practice of the profession, from Rule 206 of ICAO.

Analysis

This rule may be viewed as an extension and refinement of the due care principle. It implies adherence to duly promulgated technical standards in all areas of professional service. These areas include review and compilation (unaudited financial statements), consulting, tax and "other" professional services. The practical effect of this rule is to make noncompliance with all technical standards subject to disciplinary proceedings. Thus, failure to follow auditing standards, accounting and review standards, and assurance, compilation and professional conduct standards is a violation of this rule.

Accounting Principles   The compliance rule requires adherence to official pronouncements of accounting principles, with an important exception relating to unusual circumstances where adherence would create misleading statements. The rule itself concedes that unusual circumstances may exist; it permits PAs to decide for themselves the applicability of official pronouncements and places on them the burden of an ethical decision. The rule is not strictly imperative because it allows PAs to exercise a utilitarian calculation for special circumstances. The compliance rule requires adherence to official pronouncements unless such adherence would be misleading. The consequences of misleading statements to outside decision makers would be financial harm, so presumably the greater good would be realized by explaining a departure.

As a result of the November 1997 Supreme Court of Canada ruling in *Kripps* v. *Touche Ross,* this compliance rule is likely to become more influential in the future. This is further discussed in Chapter 5.

Confidentiality

The general principle of confidentiality is as follows:

> A member in public practice shall not disclose any confidential information without the specific consent of the client.

This principle shall not be construed (1) to relieve a member of his or her professional obligations[12] to comply with a validly issued and enforceable subpoena or summons, (2) to prohibit a member's compliance with applicable laws and government regulations, (3) to prohibit review of a member's professional practice under *Member's Handbook* bylaws, or (4) to preclude a member from initiating a complaint with or responding to any enquiry made by the ethics division or trial board or a duly constituted investigative or disciplinary body of the members' professional group (CAs, CMAs, or CGAs).

Members of any of the bodies identified in (4) above and members involved with professional practice reviews identified in (3) above shall not use to their own advantage or disclose any member's confidential client information that comes to their attention in carrying out those activities. This prohibition shall not restrict members' exchange of information in connection with the investigative or disciplinary proceedings described in (4) above or the professional practice reviews described in (3) above.

Confidential information is information that should not be disclosed to outside parties unless demanded by a court or an administrative body having subpoena or summons power. Privileged information, on the other hand, is information that cannot even be demanded by a court. Common law privilege exists for husband–wife, attorney–client and physician–patient relationships. In all the recognized privilege relationships, the professional person is obligated to observe the privilege, which can be waived only by the client, patient or penitent. (These persons are said to be the holders of the privilege.) ICAO Council Interpretation 210.1, paragraph 1 states:

> The duty to keep a client's affairs confidential should not be confused with the legal concept of privilege. The duty of confidentiality precludes the member from disclosing a client's affairs without the knowledge or consent of the client. However, this duty does not excuse a member from obeying an order of a court of competent jurisdiction requiring the member to disclose the information.

> A court will determine whether or not a member should maintain the confidentiality of client information depending on the facts of each case.

PAs and clients have attempted to establish privilege for tax file workpapers so as to shield them from Canada Revenue Agency summons demands (tax file workpapers contain accountants' analyses of "soft spots" and potential tax liability for arguable tax positions), but have so far been unsuccessful. As noted in Chapter 2, privilege has been invoked by a number of PA firms when the CPAB attempted to gain access to audit files as part of its monitoring of quality control practices.

The rules of privileged and confidential communication are based on the belief that they facilitate a free flow of information between parties to the relationship. The nature of accounting services makes it necessary for the PA to have access to information about salaries, products, contracts, merger or divestment plans, tax matters and other data required for the best possible professional work. Managers would be less likely to reveal such information if they could not trust the PA to keep it confidential. If PAs were to reveal such information, the resultant reduction of the information flow might be undesirable, so no PAs should break the confidentiality rule without a good reason.

Difficult problems arise over auditors' obligations to "blow the whistle" on clients' shady or illegal practices. Generally, the codes indicate that confidentiality in such cases can be overridden by reason of obtaining or following legal advice. If a client refuses to accept an

---

[12] C. Chazen, R.L. Miller, and K.I. Solomon, "When the Rules Say: See Your Lawyer," *Journal of Accountancy*, January 1981, p. 70.

audit report that has been modified because of inability to obtain sufficient appropriate evidence about a suspected illegal act, failure to account for or disclose properly a material amount connected with an illegal act or inability to estimate amounts involved in an illegal act, the audit firm should withdraw from the engagement and give the reasons in writing to the board of directors. In such an extreme case, the withdrawal amounts to whistle-blowing, but the action results from the client's decision not to disclose the information. For all practical purposes, information is not considered confidential if disclosure of it is necessary to make financial statements not misleading.

Auditors are not, in general, legally obligated to blow the whistle on clients. However, circumstances may exist where auditors are legally justified in making disclosures to a regulatory agency or a third party. Such circumstances include: (1) when a client has intentionally and without authorization associated or involved a PA in its misleading conduct, (2) when a client has distributed misleading draft financial statements prepared by a PA for internal use only, (3) when a client prepares and distributes in an annual report or prospectus misleading information for which the PA has not assumed any responsibility, or (4) when a client falls under the requirements of Bill C-22 (anti-money laundering legislation). PAs and other professionals need to report cash transactions of $10,000 or more, which the PA helped facilitate and which appear to be suspicious, to the Financial Analysis and Reports Centre (www.fintrac.gc.ca). Failure to do so can result in a fine of up to $2 million and five years in prison for facilitating criminal activities.

PAs should not view the rules on confidential information as a licence or excuse for inaction where action may be appropriate to right a wrongful act committed or about to be committed by a client. In some cases auditors' inaction may be viewed as part of a conspiracy or willingness to be an accessory to a wrong. Such situations are dangerous and potentially damaging. A useful initial course of action is to consult with a lawyer about possible legal pitfalls of both whistle-blowing and silence. Then, decide for yourself.

Contingency Fees and Service Without Fees

ICAO Rule 215 states, "A member engaged in the practice of public accounting or a related function shall not offer or agree to perform a professional service for a fee payable only where there is a specified determination or result of the service . . . A member engaged in the practice of public accounting or a related function shall not represent that he or she performs any professional service without fee except services of a charitable, benevolent or similar nature . . ."

For a fee to be considered a contingency fee, two characteristics need to be met:

1. its terms must be contracted for before any services are performed

2. the amount paid for the performance must be directly affected by the results obtained

Generally, if one of these characteristics is not present, the fee is not a contingency fee and therefore does not violate the ICAO's Rule 215,[13] or similar rules by other accounting bodies, such as the CGA-Canada's Rule 508. Fees are not contingent if they are fixed by a court or other public authority or, in tax matters, determined as a result of the finding of judicial proceedings or the findings of government agencies; nor are fees contingent when they are based on the complexity or time required for the work. The current Rule 215 is quite restrictive, conflicting with some statutes such as the *Federal Bankruptcy Act* and *Provincial Trustee Acts*, which allow fees based on the results of the PA's work. Because of these conflicts with statutory law, some have called for modifications of the rules to apply to assurance engagements only.[14]

Rule 215 prohibits contingent fees in assurance engagements where users of financial information may be relying on the PA's work. Acceptance of contingent fee arrangements,

---

[13] C. Schultz, "When Talk Turns to Contingency Fees," *CA Magazine*, May 1988, p. 29.
[14] Ibid. p. 33.

during the period in which the member or the member's firm is engaged to perform any type of assurance engagement, is considered an impairment of independence.

Fee Quotation

ICAO Rule 214 states that "a member shall not quote a fee for any professional services unless requested to do so by a client or prospective client, and no quote shall be made until adequate information has been obtained about the assignment." It is thus against Rule 214 to quote a fee "over the phone" or quote a fixed charge for all audits. There is extensive anecdotal evidence that particularly during economic downturns some firms practise "low balling" or charging a fee that is below cost in order to obtain an engagement. Low balling would appear to be in violation of at least the spirit of Rule 214 since presumably the need for the information about the assignment is to ensure that an adequate audit is done in which the costs are recovered (no service should be provided for free unless for charitable purposes). The real concern is that auditors may cut back on audit procedures to the point of reducing the quality of audits.[15]

Discreditable Acts

CGA-Canada's Rule 101 states that "a member shall not permit the member's firm name or the member's name to be used with, participate in or knowingly provide services to any practice, pronouncement, or act which would be of a nature to discredit the profession." Generally, we will refer to this and related rules as **discreditable act rules**.

Analysis of Discreditable Act Rules

The discreditable act rules may be called the moral clauses of the Codes, but they are only occasionally the basis for disciplinary action. Penalties usually are invoked automatically under the bylaws, which provide for expulsion of members found by a court to have committed any fraud, filed false tax returns or been convicted of any criminal offence; or found by the Disciplinary Committee to have been guilty of an act discreditable to the profession. Discreditable acts can include (*a*) withholding a client's books and records when the client has requested their return; (*b*) practising employment discrimination in hiring, promotion or salary practices on the basis of race, colour, religion, sex, or national origin; (*c*) failing to follow government audit standards and guides in governmental audits when the client or the government agency expects such standards to be followed; and (*d*) making, or permitting others to make, false and misleading entries in records and financial statements. An extreme example of an actual discreditable act is given in the box following.

EXTREME EXAMPLE OF A DISCREDITABLE ACT

The Enforcement Committee found that Respondent drew a gun from his desk drawer during a dispute with a client in his office in contravention of Section 501.41 [discreditable acts prohibition] of the [Texas] Rules of Professional Conduct. Respondent agreed to accept a private reprimand to be printed . . . in the Texas State Board Report.

Source: Texas State Board Report (February 1986).

Advertising and Other Forms of Solicitation

The rules relating to solicitation state that a member shall not seek to obtain clients by advertising or other forms of solicitation in a manner that is false, misleading, or deceptive. Solicitation through coercion, overreaching, or harassing conduct is prohibited.

[15] M.C. Carscallen, "Fee Completion Hurts Integrity of Accounting Services," *The Bottom Line,* April 1991, p. 20.

Analysis

The Rules permit advertising with only a few limitations. The current rules apply only to PAs practising public accounting and relate to their efforts to obtain clients. Basic guidelines about advertising include the following:

- Advertising may not create false or unjustified expectations of favourable results.
- Advertising may not imply the ability to influence any court, tribunal, regulatory agency or similar body or official.
- Advertising may not contain a fee estimate when the PA knows it is likely to be substantially increased, unless the client is notified.
- Advertising may not contain any representation that is likely to cause a reasonable person to misunderstand or be deceived, or that contravenes professional good taste.

Advertising consists of messages designed to attract business that are broadcast widely (e.g., through print, radio, television, billboards, and pop-up ads on various websites) to an undifferentiated audience. The guidelines basically prohibit false, misleading and deceptive messages.

Solicitation, on the other hand, generally refers to direct contact (e.g., in person, e-mail, telephone) with a specific potential client. In regard to solicitation, the rules basically prohibit extreme bad behaviour that tends to bring disrepute on the profession.

The advertising rule has undergone many changes over the last three decades. Long ago, all advertising by PAs was prohibited. Then, institutional-type advertising on behalf of PAs in general was permitted. Then, in 1979, in response to the Charter of Rights guarantee to members, the ICAO approved advertising "in good taste," with limitations on style, type size, and the like. The other professional bodies followed suit.

Most PAs carry out only modest advertising efforts, and many do no advertising at all. According to a recent article, advertising so far has been precisely targeted—for example, at chief financial officers of wholesalers in the food industry. Firms have generally used local, rather than national, advertising. The biggest problem in advertising so far is that members may make claims they are unable to substantiate.

Firms rarely obtain new clients through advertising, but it can be effective in generating business in the form of new services for existing clients or from referrals. Overall, other than some isolated examples of creative advertising by some firms, the profession has not pursued advertising aggressively. Nevertheless, it is likely PAs will advertise more in the

THE ART OF ADVERTISING

In 1987, three charges were brought against "a partner of Ernst & Whinney" in Ontario under subsections (c), (a) and (d). The discipline committee found the member "not guilty" on the first charge, but "guilty" on the second and third. Both guilty charges concerned a 1985 ad he had placed in *The Globe and Mail* which stated, in part, "Canada's Fastest Growing Firm of Business Advisors Announces Its Newest Partners."

The committee found the ad misleading in two ways. First, "accountants do not have a monopoly on the term 'business advisors.'" Second, the claim was made on the basis of statistics that were "accurate as they relate to the participating chartered accountant firms [but] without disclosure of the necessary parameters or basis for the statement, it is misleading."

The member received a written reprimand, was assessed court costs of $6,000, and was fined $5,000.

Source: Tim Falconer, *CA Magazine*, October 1993, p. 46.

future.[16] This seems to be especially true as websites by PA firms continue to proliferate (see Chapter 8).

Public practice is generally marked by decorum and a sense of good taste. However, there are exceptions, and they tend to get much attention—most of it disapproving, from other PAs and the public in general. The danger in bad advertising is that the advertiser may develop an image as a professional huckster, which may backfire on efforts to build a practice.

Communications Between Predecessors and Successors

In the case of audits, successor auditors are required to make certain enquiries of predecessor auditors when a new client is obtained, e.g., Rule 302 of Professional Conduct of ICAO. Rule 302 and similar rules of other accounting bodies in fact apply to all public accounting engagements, including compilation and review work.

Interpretation to Rule 302 gives advice to PAs when communicating with the predecessor. First, the successor PA should ask the new client to notify the predecessor (incumbent) PA of the proposed change by the client. The successor should then enquire of the predecessor "whether there are any circumstances that should be taken in account which might influence the potential successors' decision whether to accept the appointment," per Interpretation 302. Normally, the successor should await the reply of the predecessor before commencing work for the new client. The interpretation also requires that the predecessor reply promptly to the successor's queries. When enquiries are made, the successor must obtain the client's permission for the predecessor to disclose confidential information. When confidentiality is in doubt, legal advice should be obtained. An important issue is how much effort the predecessor should make in supplying information to the successor. The interpretation suggests a minimum of discussing with the successor "reasonable information about the work being assumed" and then gives advice on what constitutes "reasonable."

In addition to the rules of professional conduct, PAs should be aware of any federal and provincial legislation, including securities legislation, regulating changes in professional appointments.

Commissions and Referral Fees

A. Prohibited Commissions
A member in public practice shall not for a commission recommend or refer to a client any product or service, or for a commission recommend or refer any product or service to be supplied by a client, or receive a commission, when the member or the member's firm also performs for that client public accounting.

This prohibition applies during the period in which the member is engaged to perform public accounting services and the period covered by any historical financial statements involved in such services.

B. Permitted Commission
A member in public practice is not prohibited by this rule in receiving a commission from the sale or purchase of an accounting practice.

Analysis
A **commission** is generally defined as a percentage fee charged for professional services in connection with executing a transaction or performing some other business activity. Examples are insurance sales commissions, real estate sales commissions, and securities sales commissions. The rules treat such fees as an impairment of independence when received from assurance engagement clients, just like ICAO's Rule 215 treats contingent fees.

[16] T. Falconer, "The Art of Advertising," *CA Magazine*, October 1993, pp. 43–46.

However, many PAs perform financial planning for businesses and individuals, and they have seen commissions for insurance, securities, mergers and acquisitions, and other transactions go to other professionals. They want some of this action. The rules permit such commissions, provided the engagement does not involve assurance services.

Most of the commission fee activity takes place in connection with personal financial planning services. PAs often recommend insurance and investments to individuals and families. When the rule change was under consideration, critics pointed out that commission agents (e.g., insurance salespersons, securities brokers) cannot always be trusted to have the best interests of the client in mind when their own compensation depends in large part on clients' buying the product that produces commissions for themselves. These critics bemoaned the demise of the only advisers, PAs, who could not take commissions. They made the point that "fee-only" planning advisers, who do not work on commission, were more likely to have the best interests of the client in mind, directing them to investment professionals who handle a wide range of alternatives. In light of these matters, some PAs make it a point to provide financial planning services on a fee-only basis. This is also the position of the newly organized Financial Planners Standards Council of Canada, which is dedicated to maintaining a licensing system for certified financial planners (CFPs) in Canada. This organization is sponsored by the CICA, CGA-Canada, and SMAC, among other associations.

The rules also include fee arrangements related to commissions. Referral fees are (*a*) fees a PA receives for recommending another PA's services and (*b*) fees a PA pays to obtain a client. Such fees may or may not be based on a percentage of the amount of any transaction. Referral involves the practice of sending business to another PA and paying other PAs or outside agencies for drumming up business. These activities are banned by the Rules of Conduct on the basis that they impair the principle of objectivity. The sole exception is sale or purchase of an accounting practice, covered in Rule 216.

Form of Organization and Name

General Rule Relating to Form of PA Organization
Each practice office shall be under the personal charge of a member who is a public accountant.

General Rule Relating to Name of PA Organization
A member shall not practise public accounting under a firm name that is misleading. Names of one or more past owners may be included in the firm name of a successor organization.

Analysis
The rules allow members to practise in any form of organization permitted by provincial laws and regulations—proprietorships, partnerships, professional corporations, limited liability partnerships, limited liability corporations and ordinary corporations. Most provincial accountancy laws prohibit the general corporate form of organization for PAs; however, there has been a recent push for the limited liability partnership form of organization due to increased legal risks. Under the limited liability partnership (LLP) form of organization, most partners do not have their personal assets at risk. The only partners with personal assets at risk are those involved in the litigated engagement; the rest of the partners risk only their investment in the partnership. In the traditional form of partnership, all partners' personal assets are at risk. Thus, the limited liability partnership is a great improvement at a time of increased litigation. Many PA firms are now LLPs.

In 1992 the AICPA approved a move to permit PAs to practise in limited liability corporations and ordinary corporations like other businesses. This has led to non-PA firms such as American Express owning PA firms.

PAs have been beset by lawsuits for damages in which they and their insurers are the only persons left with any money (e.g., in cases of business failure), and multimillion-dollar damages have been awarded to plaintiffs against them. In the proprietorship, partnership and

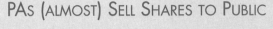

PAs (ALMOST) SELL SHARES TO PUBLIC

Nearman & Lents, a Florida PA firm, formed a corporation named Financial Standards Group, Inc., and filed a registration statement with the Securities and Exchange Commission to sell shares to the public. The accounting firm wanted to "go national on a large scale, and . . . raise $3 million or $4 million capital."

The registration became effective, and some shares were actually sold. However, Nearman & Lents withdrew the offering and gave the money back to the purchasers. Florida regulators had raised questions about the company practising public accounting without a license with non-PA ownership, which was prohibited. Financial Standards Group did not become the first publicly held PA firm.

The venture met resistance. Accounting traditionalists and lawyers who specialize in suing accountants for misconduct have generally frowned on letting accountants avail themselves of the limited legal liability provided by a corporation. Regulators have also discouraged accounting firms from issuing shares to outsiders for fear that outside equity partners might taint a firm's ability to judge [audit] a client's books impartially.

Source: New York Times, June 14, 1990 and SEC.

professional corporation forms of business, all the business and personal assets of PAs are exposed to loss to such plaintiffs. Many PAs think the tort liability litigation process has gotten out of hand, and so they seek some protection through new forms of organization. See the preceding box for some consequences that can arise from an attempt at innovative forms of PA firm organization.

The Canadian Rules of Conduct effectively block persons who are not PAs from being owners. This rule section creates problems for tax and management consulting services personnel who are not PAs. They cannot be admitted to full partnership or become shareholders without causing the other owners who are PAs to be in violation of the rule. Thus, an accounting firm may employ non-PAs who are high on the organization chart, but these persons may not be unrestricted partners or shareholders under current rules.

Rules of Conduct and Ethical Principles

Specific rules in the Rules of Conduct may not necessarily be classified under one of the ethics principles. Decisions based on a rule may involve various elements of different ethical theories. The rules have the form of duties or imperatives because that is the nature of a code of conduct. However, elements of other theories seem to be apparent in the underlying rationale for most of the rules. If this perception is accurate, then pluralistic theories may be used by auditors in difficult decision problems where adherence to a rule would produce an undesirable result. Appendix 4A discusses other factors to consider in audit decision making and justification.

REVIEW CHECKPOINTS

4.8   What ethical responsibilities do members of the provincial associations/institutes have for acts of nonmembers who are under their supervision (e.g., recent university graduates who are not yet PAs)?

4.9   Is an incorporated accounting practice substantially different from an accounting practice organized in the form of a partnership? In the form of a limited liability partnership?

4.10   Define the term contingency fee, explaining how such fees apply to PAs. Do you feel a change is necessary to rules for contingency fees in Canada?

4.11   Do auditors need to report suspicious activities to the police? Explain.

REGULATION AND QUALITY CONTROL

LEARNING OBJECTIVE

4 Outline the types of penalties that various provincial associations and government agencies can impose on PAs when enforcing rules of professional conduct.

As a PA, you will be expected to observe rules of conduct published in several codes of ethics. If you are a PA and have a client who is a public company, you will be subject to the following:

Examples of Rules of Conduct	Applicable to:
Members' Handbook ICAO, CGA-Canada's Code of Ethical Principles and Rules of Conduct	Persons licensed by province to practise accounting or, if no licence required in province, persons belonging to provincial institutes, societies or organizations
Business Corporations Acts, Securities Acts at federal and provincial levels and CGA requirements	PAs (usually PAs performing public accounting services) within the various jurisdictions
U.S. Securities and Exchange Commission and PCAOB	Persons who practise before the SEC as accountants and auditors for SEC-registered companies (including auditors of many large Canadian corporations)

If you are an internal auditor, you will be expected to observe the rules of conduct of the Institute of Internal Auditors. As a management accountant, you will be expected to observe the Society of Management Accountants' standards of ethical conduct for management accountants. Certified fraud examiners are expected to observe the Association of Certified Fraud Examiners' Code of Ethics.

Regulation and professional ethics go hand in hand. Codes of ethics provide the underlying authority for regulation. Quality control practices and disciplinary proceedings provide the mechanisms of self-regulation. **Self-regulation** refers to quality control reviews and disciplinary actions conducted by fellow PAs—professional peers. Elements of PAs self-regulation have been explained in terms of the quality control standards (Chapter 2).

Self-Regulatory Discipline

Accounting firms, as well as individuals, are subject to the Rules of Professional Conduct of the institutes, associations, or societies only if they choose to join these organizations. But as a practical matter, anyone wishing to practise public accounting finds that the added

FRAUD EXAMINER EXPELLED FOR FRAUD

Curtis C was expelled by the board of regents at its regular meeting on August 4, 1991. Mr. C, formerly an internal auditor employed by the City of S, was a member from February 1989 until his expulsion. He was the subject of an investigation by the trial board for falsifying information.

Mr. C wrongfully represented himself as a certified internal auditor, when in fact he did not hold the CIA designation. Such conduct is in violation of Article 1.A.4 of the CFE Code of Professional Ethics.

L. Jackson Shockey, CFE, CPA, CISA, chairman of the board of regents, said: "We are saddened that a member has been expelled for such conduct. However, in order to maintain the integrity of the CFE program, the trial board vigorously investigates violations of the Code of Professional Ethics. When appropriate, the board of regents will not hesitate to take necessary action."

Source: Reprinted with permission from the September, 1991, issue of CFE News, a publication of the Association of Certified Fraud Examiners, Inc., in Austin, TX © 1991.

credibility of belonging to a professional group greatly improves the chances of establishing a successful practice. Thus, enforcing the Rules of Conduct is an important means of regulating the profession. Regulators can suspend a member's activities on certain exchanges; the professional bodies can initiate other disciplinary proceedings.

An Illustration of Self-Regulation: A Provincial Institute's Disciplinary Process

A provincial institutes' bylaws and rules of professional conduct in the *Member's Handbook* provide the basis for self-regulation. The institutes have a duty to investigate all written complaints received about their members and students, as well as information from the media that may indicate professional misconduct. The Professional Conduct Committee, which represents a broad cross-section of the membership, investigates the complaints and decides whether further action is necessary. The committee considers the respondents' reply and all relevant data in making its decision.

Three general conclusions are possible:

1. The member did not breach the rules and the process is ended.
2. The member did or may have breached the rules, but the infraction is not serious enough to prosecute before the discipline committee; the respondent is informally admonished in writing or at a committee meeting.
3. Charges are laid and the matter is brought up before the discipline committee where a process similar to a civil trial procedure is followed. The discipline committee can reach a decision of not guilty or guilty. There is also an appeal process, which is headed by yet another committee, the Appeal Committee.

In a guilty verdict the penalties can include any one or more of the following:

- the member or student be reprimanded
- the member or student be suspended from the institute
- the student be struck off the register of students
- the member be expelled from membership in the institute
- the member satisfactorily completes a professional development course(s) and/or an examination(s) and/or engage an adviser or tutor
- the member complete a period of supervised practice
- the member be reinvestigated by the professional conduct committee
- the member or student be charged costs and/or fined
- the member or student be disciplined in such other way as the committee may determine
- the decision and order(s) be publicized along with the member's or student's name

The penalties listed previously cover a range of severity. In many cases a discipline committee can admonish or suspend a PA and require additional **continuing professional education (CPE)** to be undertaken. The goal is to help the PA attain an appropriate level of professional competence and awareness. Although intended as a constructive resolution, the CPE requirement is similar to "serving time." Persons who fail to satisfy CPE conditions will find themselves charged with "actions detrimental to the profession," for violations of rules such as CGA-Canada's Rule 606 or ICAO's Rule 201, and expelled as "second offenders."

The expulsion penalty, while severe, does not prevent a PA from continuing to practise accounting. Membership in a professional group, while beneficial, is not required. However, a PA must have a valid licence in order to practise public accounting in certain provinces. CGAs are subject to disciplinary action for any offence that constitutes a breach of professional conduct. This disciplinary action is brought on by the member's association or professional corporation, or, if the action is outside these groups, by the board of directors of CGA-Canada, per Rule 602.1.

Public Regulation Discipline

Provincial institutes of chartered accountants, provincial associations of CGAs, and provincial societies of CMAs are self-governing agencies. Depending on the province's *Public Accounting Act*, they issue licences to practise accounting in their jurisdictions or certificates indicating they have met the standards to be a PA. Most provinces require a licence or certification procedure to use the designation *CA* or *Chartered Accountant*, and some limit the assurance (audit) function to licenceholders. Most provinces do not regulate work in areas of management consulting, tax practice or bookkeeping services.

Provincial institutes, associations and societies have rules of conduct and disciplinary processes as outlined above. Through the disciplinary process, the provincial institutes, associations and societies can admonish a licenceholder; but, more importantly, they can suspend or revoke the licence to practise in some provinces. Suspension and revocation are severe penalties because a person no longer can use the PA title and cannot sign audit reports. When candidates have successfully passed the PA examination or fulfilled other requirements and are ready to become PAs, some provincial institutes administer an ethics examination or an ethics course intended to familiarize new PAs with the rules of professional conduct.

This traditional self-regulatory system is now being supplemented by CPAB, established in 2002. (Recall that the CPAB is a national body that reviews public company audits and the auditors' quality control systems.) This new system doubles the amount spent nationally on practice inspection. A review of the first report was provided in Chapter 2 and is publicly available on CPAB's website at www.cpab-ccrc.org. The comparable PCAOB's quality inspection report of U.S. PA firms can also be found at its website www.pcaobus.org.

The goal of both accountability boards is to act as a preventive control to problems of audits of public companies in both countries. The initial round of inspections focused on compliance with quality control standards, similar to practice inspections and peer review discussed in Chapter 2. In addition the first round of inspections put the spotlight on the four largest PA firms with the largest clients. Future inspections, however, will be extended to many more PA firms and will increasingly stress the quality of the audit output. This will be done by analyzing the results of specific engagements. Thus, there will be increased stress on monitoring questionable accounting practices allowed by the auditor and the effect on the external audit of problems on the independence and competence of the client's internal audit function.

The results of the monitoring will be made public. In addition, all auditors will be subject to disciplinary actions by the accountability boards, including restricting the ability to perform audits of public companies. Further disciplinary action may be taken by the PA institutes or associations. CPAB is hoping that its inspection process of PA firms will be acceptable to PCAOB.

In Canada, the profession will continue to set auditing, independence and quality control standards whereas in the U.S. the PCAOB has taken over this role for public company audits.

Exhibit 4–2 summarizes the new disciplinary system in Canada arising from the creation of CPAB. The **AASOC** and **ASSOC** stand for the **Auditing and Assurance Oversight Council** and the **Accounting Standards Oversight Council**, respectively. **PICA** stands for **Provincial Institutes of Chartered Accountants** (or other relevant professional accounting body). The exhibit illustrates that standard setting (right side of exhibit) is separate from the monitoring of audit process (left side of exhibit). As noted, this is not the case in the U.S. Note also that the CPAB can report PA firms to a professional body, which can then subject the firm to a provincial institute/association disciplinary process, as described previously.

As noted in Chapter 2, the provincial securities commissions sometimes file complaints with the Professional Conduct Committees of the provincial institutes or associations. In addition, some securities commissions, notably the OSC, have been assertive in not accepting financial statements that they consider at odds with GAAP. The OSC now issues staff accounting communiqués (SACs) in which it highlights major problem areas. Any company attempting to use the disfavoured technique may find that its financial statements are unacceptable to the OSC even though there is no reservation in the auditor's report.

EXHIBIT   4-2   PUBLIC OVERSIGHT MODEL (CANADA)

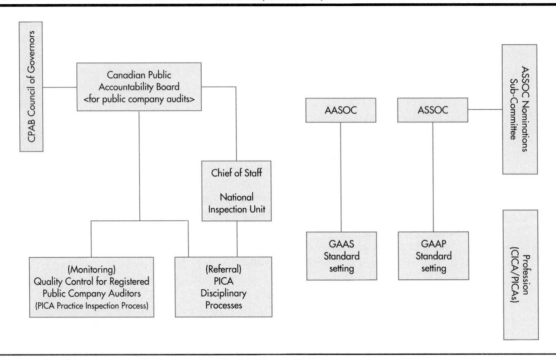

Source: "Busy Year Ahead for Oversight Council," *The Bottom Line*, March 2003, page 21.

The OSC is going even further. "It has a plan to increase its supervision of auditors and other financial advisers and to gain the power to take disciplinary action against them." Although these proposals have yet to be enacted, the OSC already exerts some control over firms via out-of-court settlements, as indicated in the box below.

The SEC also conducts public regulation disciplinary actions. Its authority comes from its rules of practice, one of which, Rule 2(e) provides that the SEC can deny, temporarily or permanently, the privilege of practice before the SEC to any person found (1) not to possess the requisite qualifications to represent others, or (2) to be lacking in character or integrity or to have engaged in unethical or improper professional conduct, or (3) to have willfully violated any provision of the federal securities laws or their rules and regulations. When conducting a "Rule 2(e) proceeding," the SEC acts in a quasijudicial role as an administrative agency.

The SEC penalty bars an accountant from signing any documents filed by an SEC-registered company. The penalty effectively stops the accountant's SEC practice. In a few severe cases, Rule 2(e) proceedings have resulted in settlements barring not only the individual accountant but also the accounting firm or certain of its practice offices from accepting new SEC clients for a period.

PREVENTIVE MEDICINE

"For example, in response to problems arising from the audit of National Business Systems, Inc., the OSC agreed that the partner in charge of that audit would not act as the senior or second partner in charge of the audit of a public company for a year. It was also agreed that procedures and systems would be reviewed by an auditor from another firm and that the results would be resubmitted to the OSC. Moreover, arrangement was made to have the Toronto office inspected by a partner from outside Canada to ensure professional standards were met. The firm agreed to pay $70,000 to cover OSC expenses."

Source: J. Bedard, and L. LeBlanc, *CA Magazine*, November 1991, p. 42.

The OSC and other Canadian regulators have been pushing to have similar disciplinary powers within their jurisdictions. Clearly, if the self-regulating process of the institutes is not sufficient to deter bad practices, regulators are willing to step in. In 1991 members of the ICAO approved a proposal giving the institute the power to subject firms to disciplinary action. In 2002 the Ontario legislature passed legislation that not only opened up public practice rights to CGAs and CMAs but also increased the penalties for auditors associated with misleading reporting.

In the next chapter we will see how in reaction to a recent Supreme Court of Canada ruling in *Hercules* v. *Ernst & Young*, there are renewed calls in the Canadian press for new securities laws that will hold auditors firmly liable for any negligence in financial statements. Other recent regulatory developments include greater independence and enforcement powers for Ontario and Quebec securities commissions, and increased harmonization procedures between the Alberta and British Columbia commissions. These structural changes in the regulatory climate are likely to increase regulatory disciplinary actions against PAs in the future.

The Canada Revenue Agency can also discipline PAs as a matter of public regulation. The Canada Revenue Agency can suspend or disbar from practice before it any PA shown to be incompetent or disreputable or who has refused to comply with tax rules and regulations. The Canada Revenue Agency can also levy monetary fines for improper practices. The Revenue Ministry has made public its willingness to prosecute those accountants it suspects of "deliberate attempt to defraud the federal treasury."[17]

According to a study by Brooks and Fortunato, most disciplinary actions by the ICAO stem from violating the standards affecting the public interest (200 level).[18] Over a roughly three-year period (1988–90), most violations involved just four rules:

Rule 201: Good Reputation of Profession representing
20 percent of all violations   36 violations
Rule 202: Integrity and Due Care representing 16 percent
of all violations   29 violations
Rule 205: False and Misleading Representations representing
11 percent of all violations   20 violations
Rule 206: Expressing an Opinion Without Complying with
GAAS representing 12 percent of all violations   21 violations

EXAMPLE OF PUBLIC DISCIPLINARY NOTICE

Member Found Guilty of Breaching Rule of Professional Conduct 215
Re: Contingent Fees
A member has been found guilty of a charge of professional misconduct, laid by the professional conduct committee, under Rule of Professional Conduct 215, of agreeing to render professional services for a fee contingent on the results.

It was ordered that the member:
• be reprimanded in writing by the chairman of the hearing
• be assessed costs of $1,500 to be paid within a specified time
• that the decision and order be published in Check Mark

It was determined that the publication of the member's name was not necessary in the circumstances, as there was no evidence of any intent to breach the rules of professional conduct or moral turpitude on the part of the member, and that this was a matter of first instance.

[17] J. Middleniss, "Too Many Accountants Guilty of Fraud, Liberals Vow Crackdown on Shady Advisers," *The Bottom Line*, March 1994, p. 1.
[18] L. Brooks, and V. Fortunato, "Disciplines at the ICAO," *CA Magazine*, May 1991, p. 45.

This same study also found that "all but one of the ICAO convictions we examined resulted in disclosure of the convicted member's names, and 95 percent resulted in levying the costs of hearing on that person. Of those convicted 78 percent were reprimanded, of which 44 percent were also suspended; 17 percent of the total convicted were expelled from the profession." The average fine levied for these cases was $5,695.[19]

REVIEW CHECKPOINTS

4.12   What options does the Canada Revenue Agency have to discipline PAs?

4.13   What organizations and agencies have Rules of Conduct you must observe when practising public accounting? internal auditing? management accounting? fraud examination?

4.14   What penalties can be imposed by provincial institutes on CAs in their "self-regulation" of ethics code violators?

4.15   What penalties can be imposed by the CPAB on PAs who violate rules of conduct?

CONSEQUENCES OF UNETHICAL/ILLEGAL ACTS

Ethics is serious business. Several sectors of professional and public life exist under general clouds of suspicion. Even though many practitioners of accounting, business management, finance, journalism, law, medicine, and politics conduct themselves in an exemplary fashion, some people hold generally unfavourable perceptions of them. PAs used to rank near the top of trustworthy professions. But in the post-Enron environment since 2002 one could argue they were closer to the bottom end of the scale (see Chapter 1). This is a major problem because without the public's confidence, the accounting profession cannot meet the public interest.

However, conforming to rules of behaviour is not always easy because of potential conflicts in the rules. The most troublesome area lies in the potential conflict between rules related to confidentiality on the one hand, and the prohibition against association with misleading information on the other. Whenever there is a conflict of interest situation for the auditor, there is a potential to create a threat to the auditor's independent state of mind. Brooks[20] identified the following deficiencies in professional Codes of Conduct:

- No or insufficient prioritization is put forward to resolve conflicting interests.

- Consultation on ethical matters is encouraged for some members, but is inhibited for others.

- A fair reporting/hearing process is not indicated, so members are uncertain whether to come forward.

- Protection is not offered to a whistle-blower.

- Sanctions are often unclear, and their applicability is not defined.

- Resolution mechanisms for conflicts between professionals and firms, or employers, or employing corporations are not put forward.

According to an article by Sandra Rubin,[21] the latest round of mergers among the accounting firms is making these deficiencies even more critical to the integrity of the financial reporting system. The problem is the perception of increased conflict of interest and the fact that the merged firms will be so big that no single nation (or national body) will be able to regulate them. The role of the **International Organization of Securities Commissions (IOSCO)** will likely increase the future regulation of the huge international PA firms.

[19] Ibid, pp. 42–43.
[20] L.J. Brook, Professional Ethics for Accountants (Minneapolis/St. Paul: West Publishing Company: 1995), p. 126.
[21] Sandra Rubin, *Financial Post*, November 13, 1997.

SUMMARY

This chapter began with considerations of moral philosophy, explained the provincial Rules of Professional Conduct and ended with the agencies and organizations that enforce the rules governing PAs' behaviour.

Professional ethics for PAs is not simply a matter covered by a few rules in a formal Rule of Professional Conduct. Concepts of proper professional conduct permeate all areas of practice. Ethics and its accompanying disciplinary potential are the foundation for PAs' self-regulatory efforts.

Your knowledge of philosophical principles in ethics will help you make decisions about the provincial Rules of Professional Conduct. This structured approach to thoughtful decisions is important not only when you are employed in public accounting but also when you work in government, industry and education. The ethics rules may appear to be restrictive, but they are intended for the benefit of the public as well as for the discipline of PAs.

PAs must be careful in all areas of practice. Regulators' views on ethics rules may differ in several aspects from the provincial institute views. As an accountant, you must not lose sight of the nonaccountants' perspective. No matter how complex or technical a decision may be, a simplified view of it always tends to cut away the details of special technical issues to get directly to the heart of the matter. A sense of professionalism coupled with a sensitivity to the impact of decisions on other people is invaluable in the practice of accounting and auditing.

Finally, it should be noted that there is a strong link between codes of conduct and GAAS. In fact, codes of conduct can be viewed as a means of fufilling auditor responsibilities for GAAS and assurance standards. For example, the first GAAS standard, which relates to the personal attributes of the auditor (see Chapter 2), closely corresponds to the ethical principles of integrity, objectivity, independence, professional competence and due care discussed previously. The dominance of ethical issues over accounting or auditing techniques is increasingly being recognized throughout the profession. Most audit failures appear to be attributable to poor professional judgement, at least in hindsight, that arise from improper consideration of conflicts of interest on various disclosure and measurement issues.[22]

MULTIPLE-CHOICE QUESTIONS FOR PRACTICE AND REVIEW

4.16 Auditors are interested in having independence in appearance because:
 a. They want to impress the public with their independence in fact.
 b. They want the public at large to have confidence in the profession.
 c. They need to comply with the standards of field work of GAAS.
 d. Audits should be planned and assistants, if any, need to be properly supervised.

4.17 If a PA says she always follows the rule that requires adherence to CICA pronouncements in order to give a standard unqualified audit report, she is following a philosophy characterized by:
 a. The imperative principle in ethics.
 b. The utilitarian principle in ethics.
 c. The generalization principle in ethics.
 d. Reliance on one's inner conscience.

4.18 Which of the following "committees" have been authorized to discipline members in violation of the rules of professional conduct?
 a. CICA Committee on Professional Ethics.
 b. Appeals Committee.
 c. Discipline Committee.
 d. Professional Conduct Committee.

[22] Ibid, p. 69; also see S. Gunz and J. McCutcheon, "Some Unresolved Ethical Issues in Auditing," *Journal of Business Ethics,* 1991.

4.19 Which of the following bodies does not have any power to punish individual members for violations of the Rules of Professional Conduct?
a. CICA.
b. Canada Revenue Agency.
c. OSC.
d. ICAO.

4.20 Phil Greb has a thriving practice in which he assists lawyers in preparing litigation dealing with accounting and auditing matters. Phil is "practising public accounting" if he:
a. Uses his CA designation on his letterhead and business card.
b. Is in partnership with another PA.
c. Practises in a limited partnership with other PAs.
d. Never lets his clients know that he is a PA.

4.21 The ICAO should remove its general prohibition against PAs taking commissions and contingent fees because:
a. CAs prefer more price competition to less.
b. Commissions and contingent fees enhance audit independence.
c. The Charter of Rights will force the change anyway.
d. Objectivity is not always necessary in accounting and auditing services.

4.22 PA Smith is the auditor of Ajax Corporation. Her audit independence will not be considered impaired if she:
a. Owns a $1,000 worth of Ajax shares.
b. Has a husband who owns $2,000 worth of Ajax shares.
c. Has a sister who is the financial vice president of Ajax.
d. Owns $1,000 worth of the shares of Pericles Corporation, which is controlled by Ajax as a result of Ajax's ownership of 40 percent of Pericles's shares, and Pericles contributes 3 percent of the total assets and income in Ajax's financial statements.

4.23 When a client's financial statements contain a material departure from a *CICA Handbook* Accounting Recommendation and the PA believes that disclosure is necessary to make the statements not misleading:
a. The PA must qualify the audit report for a departure from GAAP.
b. The PA can explain why the departure is necessary, and then give an unqualified opinion paragraph in the audit report.
c. The PA must give an adverse audit report.
d. The PA can give the standard unqualified audit report with an unqualified opinion paragraph.

4.24 Which of the following would not be considered confidential information obtained in the course of an engagement for which the client's consent would be needed for disclosure?
a. Information about whether a consulting client has paid the PA's fees on time.
b. The actuarial assumptions used by a tax client in calculating pension expense.
c. Management's strategic plan for next year's labour negotiations.
d. Information about material contingent liabilities relevant for audited financial statements.

4.25 Which of the following would probably not be considered an "act discreditable to the profession":
a. Numerous moving traffic violations.
b. Failing to file the PA's own tax return.
c. Filing a fraudulent tax return for a client in a severe financial difficulty.
d. Refusing to hire Asian Canadians in an accounting practice.

4.26 The U.S. Securities and Exchange Commission would consider an audit firm's independence not impaired when:
a. A partner completed the client's audit in January, retired from the firm in March, and became a member of the former client's board of directors in August.
b. A partner who had been in charge of the firm's national audit co-ordination office retired in May 2000, and became a member of the board of directors of one of the firm's clients in August 2002.
c. A partner in the firm has a father-in-law who is the warehouse supervisor for an audit client.
d. The audit firm helped the client perform data processing for three months during the current year in connection with preparing financial statements to be filed with the SEC.

4.27 A PA's legal licence to practise public accounting can be revoked by:
a. The CICA.
b. Provincial Institute of PAs.
c. Auditing Standards Board.
d. Provincial securities commissions.

4.28 A PA's independence would not be considered impaired if he had:
a. Owned common shares of the audit client but sold them before the company became a client.
b. Sold short the common shares of an audit client while working on the audit engagement.
c. Served as the company's treasurer for six months during the year covered by the audit but resigned before the company became a client.
d. Performed the bookkeeping and financial statement preparation for the company, which had no accounting personnel, and the president had no understanding of accounting principles.

4.29 When a PA knows that a tax client has skimmed cash receipts and not reported the income in the federal income tax return but signs the return as a PA who prepared the return, the PA has violated which Rule of Professional Conduct?
a. Confidential Client Information.
b. Integrity and Objectivity.
c. Independence.
d. Accounting Principles.

EXERCISES AND PROBLEMS

· ·

4.30   Independence, Integrity and Objectivity Cases.

LO.3   Knowledge of the rules of conduct and related interpretations on independence, integrity and objectivity will help you respond to the following cases. For each case, state whether the action or situation shows violation of the Rules of Professional Conduct, explain why and cite the relevant rule or interpretation.

a. PA R. Stout performs the audit of the local symphony society. Because of her good work, she was elected an honorary member of the board of directors.

b. N. Wolfe, a retired partner of your PA firm, has just been appointed to the board of directors of Palmer Corporation, your firm's client. Wolfe is also an ex officio member of your firm's income tax advisory committee, which meets monthly to discuss income tax problems of the partnership's clients, some of which are competitors of Palmer Corporation. The partnership pays Wolfe $100 for each committee meeting attended and a monthly retirement benefit, fixed by a retirement plan policy, of $1,000.

(AICPA adapted)

c. PA Archie Goodwin performs significant day-to-day bookkeeping services for Harper Corporation and supervises the work of the one part-time bookkeeper employed by Marvin Harper. This year, Marvin wants to engage PA Goodwin to perform an audit.

d. PA Fritz's wife owns 20 percent of the common shares of Botacel Company, which wants Fritz to perform the audit for the calendar year ended December 31, 2007.

e. Fritz's wife gave her shares to their 10-year-old daughter on July 1, 2007.

f. Fritz's daughter, acting through an appropriate custodian, sold the shares to her grandfather on August 1, 2007. His purchase, as an accommodation, took one-half of his retirement savings.

g. Fritz's father managed to sell the shares on August 15 to his brother, who lives in Brazil. The brother fled there 20 years ago and has not returned.

h. Clyde Brenner is a manager in the Regina office of a large national PA firm. His wife, Bonnie, is assistant controller in ATC Corporation, a client of the firm whose audit is performed by the New York office. Bonnie and Clyde live in Rhode Island and commute to their respective workplaces.

i. Clyde Brenner just received word that he has been admitted to the partnership.

j. The Rockhard Trust Company, a client of your firm, privately told your local managing partner that a block of funds would be set aside for home loans for qualified new employees. Rockhard's president is well aware that your firm experiences some difficulty hiring good people in the midsize but growing community and is willing to do what he can to help

while mortgage money is so tight. Several new assistant accountants obtained home loans under this arrangement.

4.31   Independence, Integrity and Objectivity Cases.

LO.3   Knowledge of the rules of conduct, interpretations thereof, and related rulings on independence, integrity and objectivity will help you respond to the following cases. For each case, state whether the action or situation shows violation of the Rules of Professional Conduct, explain why, and cite the relevant rule or interpretation.

a. Your client, Contrary Corporation, is very upset over the fact that your audit last year failed to detect an $800,000 inventory overstatement caused by employee theft and falsification of the records. The board discussed the matter and authorized its lawyers to explore the possibility of a lawsuit for damages.

b. Contrary Corporation filed a lawsuit alleging negligent audit work, seeking $1 million in damages.

c. In response to the lawsuit by Contrary, you decided to start litigation against certain officers of the company, alleging management fraud and deceit. You are asking for a damages judgement of $500,000.

d. The Allright Insurance company paid Contrary Corporation $700,000 under fidelity bonds covering the employees involved in the inventory theft. Both you and Contrary Corporation have dropped your lawsuits. However, under subrogation rights, Allright has sued your audit firm for damages on the grounds of negligent performance of the audit.

e. Colt & Associates, PAs, audit Gore Company. Ms. Colt and Bill Gore (president) found a limited real estate partnership deal that looked too good to pass up. Colt purchased limited partnership interests amounting to 23 percent of all such interests, and Gore personally purchased 31 percent. Unrelated investors held the remaining 46 percent. Colt and Gore congratulate themselves on the opportunity and agree to be passive investors with respect to the partnership.

f. A group of dissident shareholders filed a class-action lawsuit against both you and your client, Amalgamated, Inc., for $30 million. They allege there was a conspiracy to present misleading financial statements in connection with a recent merger.

g. PA Anderson, a partner in the firm of Anderson, Olds & Watershed, (a professional accounting corporation), owns 25 percent of the common shares of Dove Corporation (not a client of AO&W). This year Dove purchased a 32 percent interest in Tale Company and is accounting for the investment using the equity method of accounting. The investment amounts to 11 percent of Dove's consolidated net assets. Tale Company has been an audit client of AO&W for 12 years.

h. Durkin & Panzer, PAs, regularly perform the audit of the North Country Bank, and the firm is preparing for the audit of the financial statements for the year ended December 31, 2007.

i. Two directors of the North Country Bank became partners in D&P, PAs, on July 1, 2007, resigning their directorship on that date. They will not participate in the audit.

j. During 2007, the former controller of the North Country Bank, now a partner of D&P, was frequently called on for assistance regarding loan approvals and the bank's minimum chequing account policy. In addition, he conducted a computer feasibility study for North Country.

(AICPA adapted)

k. The Cather Corporation is indebted to a PA for unpaid fees and has offered to give the PA unsecured interest-bearing notes. Alternatively, Cather Corporation offered to give two shares of its common stock, after which 10,002 shares would be outstanding.

(AICPA adapted)

l. Johnny Keems is not yet a PA but is doing quite well in this first employment with a large PA firm. He's been on the job two years and has become a "heavy junior." If he passes the PA exam in September, he will be promoted to senior accountant. This month, during the audit or Row Lumber Company, Johnny told the controller about how he is remodelling an old house. The controller likes Johnny and had a load of needed materials delivered to the house, billing Johnny at a 70 percent discount—a savings over the normal cash discount of about $300. Johnny paid the bill and was happy to have the materials, which he otherwise would not have been able to afford on his meager salary.

m. PA Lily Rowan inherited $1 million from her grandfather, $100,000 of which was the value of shares in the North Country Bank. Lily practises accounting in Hamilton, and several of her audit clients have loans from the bank.

n. Groaner Corporation is in financial difficulty. You are about to sign the report on the current audit when your firm's office manager informs you that the audit fee for last year has not yet been paid.

o. Your audit client, Glow Company, is opening a plant in a distant city. Glow's president asks that your firm's office in that city recruit and hire a new plant controller and a cost accountant.

4.32 General and Technical Rule Cases. Knowledge of the
LO.2 rules of conduct, interpretations thereof and resolutions of Council related to general and technical standards will help you respond to the following cases. For each case, state whether the action or situation shows violation of the ICAO Rules of Professional Conduct, explain why, and cite the relevant rule or interpretation.

a. PA P. Stebbins helped Price Corporation prepare a cash flow forecast of hospital operations. The forecast was presented by Stebbins at a city council hearing for approval under the city's health services ordinance. Stebbins's report, which accompanied the forecast, consisted entirely of a full description of the sources of information used and the major assumptions made but did not include a disclaimer on the achievability of the forecast.

b. Kim Philby of Philby & Burgess, PAs, received a telephone call from his friend John, who is financial vice president of U.K. Auto Parts. U.K. distributes parts over a wide area and does about $40 million in business a year. U.K. is not a client but is audited by Anderson, Olds & Watershed CAs, a venerable firm in the city. Kim has been hoping that John would switch auditors. Today John wants to get Kim's opinion about accounting for lease capitalizations related to a particularly complicated agreement with franchise dealers. Kim makes notes and promises to call John tomorrow.

c. PA Maclean gave a standard unqualified audit report on the financial statements of Anglo Korp. The annual report document did not contain supplementary oil and gas reserve information required by the *Handbook*.

d. Saul Panzer is a former university football player. Saul is a PA who works for Aggregate Corporation, which owns controlling interests in 42 other corporations. Theodolinda Bonner, president of Aggregate, has assigned Saul the task of performing audits of these corporations and submitting audit opinions directly to her for later presentation to the board of directors.

e. PA Blunt audits the Huber Hope Company. Huber's controller, also a PA, has conducted his own audit of Little Hope, Inc., Huber's single subsidiary, which amounts to 10 percent of the total assets, revenue and income of the consolidated entity. Blunt has written an audit report that carefully explains reliance on "part of examination made by other independent auditors," with added language to explain the controller's role.

4.33 Responsibilities to Clients' Cases. Knowledge of the
LO.2 rules of conduct and interpretations thereof on confidential client information and contingent fees will help you respond to the following cases. For each case, state whether the action or situation shows violation of the ICAO Rules of Professional Conduct, explain why and cite the relevant rule or interpretation.

a. PA Sally Colt has discovered a way to eliminate most of the boring work of processing routine accounts receivable confirmations by contracting with the Cohen Mail Service. After the auditor has prepared the confirmations, Cohen will stuff them in envelopes, mail them, receive the return replies, open the replies and return them to Sally.

b. Cadentoe Corporation, without consulting its PA, has changed its accounting so that it is not in conformity with generally accepted accounting principles. During the regular audit engagement, the PA

CHAPTER 4 Professional Ethics and Auditor Responsibilities

discovers that the statements based on the accounts are so grossly misleading that they might be considered fraudulent. PA Cramer resigns from the engagement after a heated argument. Cramer knows that the statements will be given to John Cairncross, his friend at the Last National Bank, and knows that John is not a very astute reader of complicated financial statements. Two days later, Cairncross calls Cramer and asks some general questions about Cadentoe's statements and remarks favourably on the very thing that is misrepresented. Cramer corrects the erroneous analysis, and Cairncross is very much surprised.

c. A PA who had reached retirement age arranged for the sale of his practice to another public accountant. Their agreement called for the transfer of all working papers and business correspondence to the accountant purchasing the practice.

d. Martha Jacoby, PA, withdrew from the audit of Harvard Company after discovering irregularities in Harvard's income tax returns. One week later, Ms. Jacoby was telephoned by Jake Henry, PA, who explained that he had just been retained by Harvard Company to replace Ms. Jacoby. Mr. Henry asked Ms. Jacoby why she withdrew from the Harvard engagement. She told him.

e. Amos Fiddle, PA, prepared an uncontested claim for a tax refund on Faddle Corporation's amended tax return. The fee for the service was 30 percent of the amount that the Canada Revenue Agency rules to be a proper refund. The claim was for $300,000.

f. After Faddle had won a $200,000 refund and Fiddle collected the $60,000 fee, Jeremy Faddle, the president, invited Amos Fiddle to be the auditor for Faddle Corporation.

4.34 **Other Responsibilities and Practices Cases.** Knowl-
LO.2 edge of the rules of conduct and interpretations thereof regarding various other responsibilities and practices will help you respond to the following cases. For each case, state whether the action or situation shows violation or potential for violation of the ICAO Rules of Professional Conduct, explain why, and cite the relevant rule or interpretation.

a. PA R. Stout completed a review of the unaudited financial statements of Wolfe Gifts. Ms. Wolfe was very displeased with the report. An argument ensued, and she told Stout never to darken her door again. Two days later, she telephoned Stout and demanded he return (1) Wolfe's cash disbursement journal, (2) Stout's working paper schedule of adjusting journal entries, (3) Stout's inventory analysis working papers, and (4) all other working papers prepared by Stout. Since Wolfe had not yet paid her bill, Stout replied that provincial law gave him a lien on all the records and that he would return them as soon as she had paid his fee.

b. The PA firm of Durkin & Panzer had received promissory notes in payment of the Henshaw Hacksaw company tax return preparation fee. Six months after the notes were due, PA Durkin notified Dave Henshaw that the notes had been turned over to the North Country Bank for collection.

c. PA Panzer has been invited to conduct a course in effective tax planning for the City Chamber of Commerce. The C. of C. president said a brochure would be mailed to members giving the name of Panzer's firm, his educational background and degrees held, professional society affiliations, and testimonials from participants in the course held last year comparing his excellent performance with that of other PAs who have offered competing courses in the city.

d. PA Philby is a member of the provincial bar. Her practice is a combination of law and accounting, and she is heavily involved in estate planning engagements. Her letterhead gives the affiliations: Member, Provincial Bar of —, and Member, CICA.

e. The PA firm of Burgess & Maclean has made a deal with Cairncross & Company, a firm of management consulting specialists, for mutual business advantage. B&M agreed to recommend Cairncross to clients who need management consulting services. Cairncross agreed to recommend B&M to clients who need improvements in their accounting systems. During the year both firms would keep records of fees obtained by these mutual referrals. At the end of the year, Cairncross and B&M would settle the net differences based on a referral rate of 5 percent of fees.

f. Sturm & Drang, PAs, conduct an aggressive, growing practice in Middle City. The firm pays 20 percent of first-year fees to any staff member (below partner) who brings in a new client.

g. Jack Robinson and Archie Robertson (both PAs) are not partners, but they have the same office, the same employees, and a joint bank account, and they work together on audits. A letterhead they use shows both their names and the description "Members, ICAO."

h. PA Dewey retired from the two-person firm of Dewey & Cheatham. One year later, D&C merged practices with Howe & Company, to form a regional firm under the name of Dewey, Cheatham & Howe Company.

i. Fritz Brenner, PA, died and widow Brenner inherited the interest he had in the PA firm of Brenner & Horstmann, P.C. Can widow Brenner share in the partnership as a passive investment? She is not a PA.

4.35 **Rules of Professional Conduct**
LO.2 *Required:*
For each of the following completely independent situations, describe the rules of professional conduct that are relevant. Have they been violated? Support your conclusion.

Situation A
Randi Woode, PA, was working on the year-end audit of her client, Pads N' Pens (PNP). PNP is an office stationery retailer with a July 31 year-end. She was having difficulty completing the audit because some accounting

records for the months of April and May had been destroyed in a fire.

She told the owner-manager of PNP, Joe Smith, that she might have to qualify her audit report because of her inability to substantiate some of the balances on the financial statements. Joe pointed out that he had been her client for eight years and that she knew him to be honest and trustworthy. He also said a qualified report would harm his negotiations with the bank for additional loans. After considering PNP's need for additional financing, as well as their long-standing relationship, Randi agreed to issue an unqualified report.

Situation B

Lori Wilkes is an audit senior with a large PA firm in Toronto. She has learned that one of her largest clients, Superior Motors Ltd. (SML), is planning to acquire Steelco Inc. SML is Canada's largest automobile manufacturer, and Steelco is one of SML's biggest steel suppliers. Lori is confident that SML's acquisition of Steelco will reduce SML's costs dramatically, and that as a result, SML's share price will rise. She has, therefore, encouraged her boyfriend, Tom, to buy some shares while being careful not to divulge the real reasons behind her recommendation.

Situation C

After obtaining his PA designation, Larry Wilde decided to set up his own public accounting practice. He reasoned that naming his practice "Quality Chartered Accountancy Services" would best attract new clients.

(ICAO adapted)

4.36 **Rules of Professional Conduct.** In mid-May, Aileen
LO.2 Macdonald, PA, received a phone call from one of her largest clients, a manufacturer. The client wanted to know more details about the impact that the GST would have on his 2001 operations and financial statements. When Aileen and the client had discussed the results of the 1999 audit last February, part of their conversation had dealt with the tax. Aileen had indicated that she would be sending a newsletter about the tax by July 1.

Since February there had been more changes to the legislation, which Aileen and her partners hadn't had time to absorb. However, Aileen had registered for the annual June provincial conference, where she would attend the four technical sessions on the GST. She planned to ask questions about her client's situation during the question-and-answer periods that followed each session.

Aileen explained to the client that she would have more information within a month and would contact him then. At that time, she will ask the client for names of firms that might be interested in receiving her newsletter.

Required:

Which rules of professional conduct are relevant to the above situation? Discuss the rules with which Aileen Macdonald is in compliance as well as those she may have violated.

(ICAO adapted)

Discussion Cases

· ·

4.37 **General Ethics.** Is there any moral difference between
LO.1 a disapproved action in which you are caught and the same action that never becomes known to anyone else? Do many persons in business and professional society make a distinction between these two circumstances? If you respond that you do (or do not) perceive a difference while persons in business and professional society do not (or do), then how do you explain the differences in attitudes?

4.38 **Ethics Decision Problem.** You are treasurer of a
LO.1 church. A member approaches you with the following proposition: "I will donate shares to the church on December 31, if, on January 1, you will sell them back to me. All you will need to do is convey the certificate with your signature to me in return for my cheque, which will be for the asking price of the shares quoted that day without reduction for commissions."

The member's objective, of course, is to obtain the income tax deduction as of December 31, but he wants to maintain his ownership interest. The policy of the church board is not to hold any shares but to sell shares within a reasonably short time.

Consider:

a. Should the treasurer accommodate the member? Would you if you were treasurer?

b. Would your considerations and conclusions be any different if:
1. The church were financially secure and the gift were small in amount?
2. The church were financially secure and the gift were large?
3. The church would be in deficit position for the year were it not for the gift?

4.39 **Competition and Audit Proposals.** Accounting firms
LO.2 are often asked to present "proposals" to companies' boards of directors. These "proposals" are comprehensive booklets, accompanied by oral presentations, telling about the firm's personnel, technology, special qualifications and expertise in hope of convincing the board to award the work to the firm.

Dena has a new job as staff assistant to Michael, chairman of the board of Granof Grain company. The company has a policy of engaging new auditors every seven years. The board will hear oral proposals from

12 accounting firms. This is the second day of the three-day meeting. Dena's job is to help evaluate the proposals. Yesterday, the proposal by Anderson, Olds & Watershed was clearly the best.

Then Dena sees Michael's staff chief, a brash go-getter, slip a copy of the AOW written proposal into an envelope. He tells Dena to take it to a friend who works for Hunt and Hunt, a PA firm scheduled to make its presentation tomorrow. He says: "I told him we'd let him glance at the best proposal." Michael is absent from the meeting and will not return for two hours.

What should Dena do? What should PA Hunt do if he receives the AOW proposal, assuming he has time to modify the Hunt and Hunt proposal before tomorrow's presentation?

4.40 **Engagement Timekeeping Records.** A time budget is
LO.2 always prepared for audit engagements. Numbers of hours are estimated for various segments of the work—for example, internal control evaluation, cash, inventory, report review and the like. Audit supervisors expect the work segments to be completed "within budget," and staff accountants' performance is evaluated in part on ability to perform audit work efficiently within budget.

Sarah is an audit manager who has worked hard to get promoted. She hopes to become a partner in two or three years. Finishing audits on time weighs heavily on her performance evaluation. She assigned the cash audit work to Craig, who has worked for the firm for 10 months. Craig hopes to get a promotion and salary raise this year. Twenty hours were budgeted for the cash work. Craig is efficient, but it took 30 hours to finish because the company had added seven new bank accounts. Craig was worried about his performance evaluation, so he recorded 20 hours for the cash work and put the other 10 hours under the internal control evaluation budget.

What do you think about Craig's resolution of his problem? Was his action a form of lying? What would you think of his action if the internal control evaluation work was presented "under budget" because it was not yet complete, and another assistant was assigned to finish that work segment later?

4.41 **Audit Overtime.** All accountants' performance evalua-
LO.2 tions are based in part on their ability to do audit work efficiently and within the time budget planned for the engagement. New staff accountants, in particular, usually have some early difficulty learning speedy work habits, which demand that no time be wasted.

Elizabeth started work for Anderson, Olds & Watershed in September. After attending the staff training school, she was assigned to the Rising Sun Company audit. Her first work assignment was to complete the extensive recalculation of the inventory compilation, using the audit test counts and audited unit prices for several hundred inventory items. Her time budget for the work was six hours. She started at 4 p.m. and was not finished when everyone left the office at 6 p.m. Not wanting to stay downtown alone, she took all the necessary working papers home. She resumed work at 8 p.m. and

finished at 3 a.m. The next day, she returned to the Rising Sun offices, put the completed working papers in the file, and recorded six hours in the time budget/actual schedule. Her supervisor was pleased, especially about her diligence in taking the work home.

What do you think about Elizabeth's diligence and her understatement of the time she took to finish the work? What would you think of the case if she had received help at home from her husband? What would you think of the case if she had been unable to finish and had left the work at home for her husband to finish while he took off a day from his job interviews?

4.42 **Form of Practice, Technical Standards and Confi-**
LO.2 **dentiality.** Knowledge of the rules of conduct and interpretations thereof will help you respond to this case problem.

Gilbert and Bradley formed a corporation called Financial Services, Inc. Each took 50 percent of the authorized common shares. Gilbert is a PA and a member of the provincial institute. Bradley is a CPCU (Chartered Property Casualty Underwriter). The corporation performs auditing and tax services under Gilbert's direction and insurance services under Bradley's supervision. The opening of the corporation's office was announced in a full-page advertisement in the local newspaper.

One of the corporation's first audit clients was the Grandtime Company. Grandtime had total assets of $600,000 and total liabilities of $270,000. In the course of the audit, Gilbert found that Grandtime's building with a book value of $240,000 was pledged as a security for a 10-year term note in the amount of $200,000. The client's statement did not mention that the building was pledged as security for the 10-year term note. However, as the failure to disclose the lien did not affect either the value of the assets or the amount of the liabilities, and the audit was satisfactory in all other respects, Gilbert rendered an unqualified opinion on Grandtime's financial statements. About two months after the date of his opinion, Gilbert learned that an insurance company was planning to loan Grandtime $150,000 in the form of a first-mortgage note on the building. Realizing the insurance company was unaware of the existing lien on the building, Gilbert had Bradley notify the insurance company of the fact that Grandtime's building was pledged as security for the term note.

Shortly after the events described above, Gilbert was charged with several violations of professional ethics.

Required:
Identify and discuss the Rules of Professional Conduct violated by Gilbert and the nature of the violations.

(AICPA adapted)

4.43 **Rules of Professional Conduct.** You and Laura Cooper
LO.2 are the two partners of a PA firm in Ottawa. After your two-week Caribbean vacation, you return to the office to discover that your secretary is busily preparing to mail some brochures. You have never seen the brochures

before and your secretary explains that Laura had them printed during your absence. The brochures are colourful and glossy and the name of your firm is boldly displayed on the front cover. You pick up a brochure and notice that it describes your firm as "the PA firm where clients always come first." On the last page of the brochure, readers are advised that new audit clients will not be charged a fee for any management consulting services provided in the first full year.

You ask Laura about the brochures, and she tells you that she had them specially designed and printed to increase the firm's profile and competitiveness. She believes that mailing these brochures to all the top companies in Ottawa will not only increase the firm's client base but will also help it develop a high-quality image by getting a reputation for obtaining the "best clients." Furthermore, she plans to contact all recipients of the brochure in a few weeks to arrange a "follow-up" meeting to discuss their accounting and auditing needs.

Required:

Describe which rules of professional conduct may have been violated and indicate your professional responsibilities and course of action.

(ICAO adapted)

4.44 Conflict of Clients' Interests. Jon Williams, PA, has
LO.3 found himself in the middle of the real-life soap opera "Taxing Days of Our Lives."

The cast of characters:
Oneway Corporation is Jon's audit and tax client. The three directors are the officers and also the only three shareholders, each owning exactly one-third of the shares.

President Jack founded the company and is now nearing retirement. As an individual, he is also Jon's tax client. Vice president Jill manages the day-to-day operations. She has been instrumental in enlarging the business and its profits. Jill's individual tax work is done by PA Phil.

Treasurer Bill has been a long-term, loyal employee and has been responsible for many innovative financial transactions and reports of great benefit to the business. He is Jon's close personal friend and also an individual tax client.

The conflict:
President Jack discussed with PA Jon the tax consequences to him as an individual of selling his one-third interest in Oneway Corporation to vice president Jill. Later, meeting with Bill to discuss his individual tax problems, Jon learns that Bill fears that Jack and Jill will make a deal, put him in a minority position and force him out of the company. Bill says: "Jon, we have been friends a long time. Please keep me informed about Jack's plans, even rumours. My interest in Oneway Corporation represents my life savings and my resources for the kids' university. Remember, you're little Otto's godfather."

Thinking back, Jon realized that vice president Jill has always been rather hostile. Chances are that Phil would get the Oneway engagement if Jill acquires Jack's shares and controls the corporation. Nevertheless, Bill will probably suffer a great deal if he cannot learn about Jack's plans, and Jon's unwillingness to keep him informed will probably ruin their close friendship.

Later, on a dark and stormy night:

Jon ponders the problem. "Oneway Corporation is my client, but a corporation is a fiction. Only a form. The shareholders personify the real entity, so they are collectively my clients, and I can transmit information among them as though they were one person. Right? On the other hand, Jack and Bill engage me for individual tax work, and information about one's personal affairs is really no business of the other. What to do? What to do?

Required:
Give Jon advice about alternative actions, considering the constraints of the ICAO's Rules of Conduct.

4.45 Independence, Management Responsibility for
LO.3 Financial Statements. PA has been engaged by Pinto Inc. for several years. His work involves compiling the monthly financial reports for Pinto's management and providing advice to Pinto's president on cost controls, taxes and other financial reporting matters. PA has also performed a review engagement on the annual GAAP financial statements that are provided to the company's shareholders and its banker. As Pinto's business was growing rapidly, two years ago it hired a full-time CFO to handle the expanding accounting and reporting requirements. The CFO is a former banker who was laid off by the bank and was recommended for the job by Pinto's COO, an old school friend, even though he had never previously worked as a CFO. Over the two years that CFO has held the position, he has sought advice from PA on many accounting, tax and reporting issues.

At first, PA thought the CFO was learning the job by asking all these questions. However, after two years the PA began to realize that the CFO was merely implementing whatever PA suggested, without questioning it. When PA insisted that the CFO complete various accounting and tax analyses for the current-year financial statements on his own, the CFO stalled at first and then finally admitted that he couldn't do the analyses. PA needed to work over the weekend to provide the required information so the company could file its tax returns and payroll tax information forms on time. As a result of these events, PA has become concerned that Pinto's management does not know enough about its own financial statements to take primary responsibility for them.

Just prior to the current year-end, the Pinto shareholders met to approve the appointment of PA as the company's independent accountant for another year. Pinto has three shareholders who each own 30 percent of the common shares, while 20 current and former employees own the remaining 10 percent. At this meeting, some of the shareholders expressed concern about the financial management at Pinto, and demanded that PA be engaged to audit the company's financial statements rather than just doing a review.

Required:

Discuss the professional issues raised in the above case. Assess whether or not PA should accept the audit engagement, and recommend an appropriate course of action for PA.

4.46 **CGA Code of Ethics.** The issue of ethical conduct is

LO.1 becoming more and more important in the professional practice of PAs.

Required:

a. Identify the sequence of steps that have been proposed for an auditor to follow in attempting to resolve an ethical dilemma.

b. What are the two broad aims of the CGA Code of Ethical Principles and Rules of Professional Conduct?

c. Briefly describe the three mechanisms by which the CGA Code of Ethical Principles and Rules of Professional Conduct work.

(CGA-Canada adapted)

4.47 **Independence.** You are an audit manager with the firm

LO.3 of Wu, Potter and McKinley, PAs. You and Ray St. Claire, a manager with another PA firm, are having a discussion about auditor independence. Ray says, "On the one hand, the public seems to be demanding more and more assurance from us about more and more aspects of a client's operations, but to maintain our practice in today's environment we have to be competitive to be able to attract new clients."

Required:

a. Identify and briefly explain the competitive practice on the part of auditors to which Ray is referring.

b. Why is this perceived as a threat to auditor independence and the quality of audits?

c. With reference to parts *a.* and *b.*, what could a client do, at least in theory, to take advantage of this situation? What is the reason this strategy might not work?

d. What does the CGA-Canada Code of Ethics say about this issue?

(CGA-Canada adapted)

4.48 **Audit Proposals.** Smith and Mulberry (S&M) were

LO.2 asked by Behometh Ltd. to submit a proposal for its audit. This involved a 30-minute presentation to the board of directors and a written submission. The submission included a fixed fee quote for the first two years, a detailed outline of the proposed audit strategy, and a list of the qualifications of the audit team to be assigned. Five other PA firms were invited to bid on the engagement. S&M put in a "lowball" bid because the partners saw this as a golden opportunity to get exposure in this industry.

Several weeks later, Edgar Brown, chairman of the board, telephoned Mike Mulberry, congratulating him on being awarded the audit. The conversation went as follows:

Edgar: I'm pleased to offer you the engagement, Mike, and I want you to know you weren't the lowest bid. What really impressed us was your attitude and promise to give us personal attention. It's so refreshing to find an auditor who openly states there needs to be a completely harmonious relationship between auditor and client.

Mike: We're really pleased to be your auditors, Edgar. We were a little apprehensive about not having any experience in your industry.

Edgar: Well Mike, since you did indicate you would hire someone experienced to oversee the engagement, I really see no problem. I certainly support your idea of Stan Biggs, since he knows the industry inside out. We're a little sorry to lose him. He had only been with us two years since obtaining his PA and was a fine controller.

Mike: Yes, his knowledge of your operations should allow us to complete the audit in the minimal time.

Edgar: There is one favour you can do us right away, Mike. We would like to start a national ad campaign that depicts our auditor slashing prices to the bone on our products. We would like you to be the auditor in that ad.

Mike: Acting's not really my strong suit, Edgar, but I'm sure we can accommodate you on that.

Edgar: By the way Mike, to show how much we value our auditors, I want to give you a key to the executive washroom, a special pass that allows you to park in restricted zones and a letter that will give you folks an additional 25 percent off our employee store prices.

Mike: Thanks very much, Edgar.

(ICAO adapted)

The following week Mike went out to review the working papers of the predecessor auditors. He was shocked at the poor quality of work evident in these files. However, given the rule against criticism of fellow members, he believed it would be inappropriate to mention this to Behometh.

The audit went very smoothly. In fact, with Biggs in charge, S&M even managed to turn a profit on the job.

Several months later some information came to light, which Mike was not sure if he should worry about. Although Biggs had severed all employment ties with Behometh prior to joining S&M, apparently he still retained 1,000 shares of voting stock in the company.

Required:

Discuss the ethical issues in this case.

(ICAO adapted)

4.49 **Rules of Professional Conduct.** The Canada Revenue

LO.2 Agency was recently granted the power to impose new "preparer penalties" on individuals who have received payment for preparing a tax return in which the taxpayer is found to have understated its taxes payable. Tax preparers are liable for penalties of up to $100,000 if the CRA finds that the preparer was aware that the taypayer was under-reporting its taxes payable. Formerly, only the taxpayer could be penalized.

Required:
Given that the rules of conduct for professional accountants already prohibit PAs from being associated with false or misleading information and require them to conduct themselves with integrity, why do you think these preparer penalties were considered necessary by federal law makers?

4.50 **Contingency Fees.** PA provides assurance on a forecast
LO.2 income statement included in a the prospectus for a public offering of shares of Mustang Inc. PA's engagement letter with Mustang states that the fee for the assurance report will be 10 percent of the proceeds of the share issue.

Required:
Discuss the appropriateness of this fee arrangement in light of the rules of professional conduct.

4.51 **Forms of Public Accountants' Organizations.** Three
LO.2 forms of organization for public accountants are unlimited liability partnership, limited liability partnership or limited liability professional corporation.

Required:
What are the pros and cons of each form from the perspective of public accountants in these firms and from the perspective of users of public accountants' assurance reports? In particular, consider the implications of these different organizational forms for public accountants' incentives to perform their functions with due care and with objectivity.

4.52 **Public Accounting as a Career.** A and B, two 40-some-
LO.2 thing PAs, are raising a few glasses at the local pub to celebrate their 15 years in partnership, and are taking the opportunity to reflect over their choice of career.

A: All in all, I think public accounting has been a good career choice for me. I've been able to do very challenging, analytical work. I've had the opportunity to be very helpful to many business owners and have seen a number of my clients become millionaires—and I

think I can give some of the credit for that to the good financial advice I gave them, especially in those really tough times when they didn't know how they were going to cover the next payroll! And I think my assurance reports added value to financial reports and were helpful to the people using them, even if I didn't even know specifically who those people were a lot of the time. But at the same time, it's been really hard work and long hours, and I probably could have made more money with less effort if I had become a lawyer or a doctor.

B: I think you are probably right about that. Sometimes I think being a public accountant is like taking some kind of "vow of poverty." Our clients get rich, but we are only allowed to charge by the hour because otherwise, say if we took shares in our client's companies instead of fees or took a percentage of the tax savings we identify for them, we would lose our appearance of independence. To me the big irony of being a public accountant is that our duty is to serve the public, and so we need to stay independent of the clients we report on, but the public doesn't pay us—our clients do! If we are going to make a living at this we need to maximize our profitability and yet it seems the rules of professional conduct are designed to prevent us from ever making a lot of money at this!

Required:
Discuss the views of the two PAs, that public accountants' duty to the public and operating a profit-oriented business are incompatible. Do you agree? Generate some possible solutions that would resolve the dilemma they see. Evaluate the solutions you have generated in terms of their effectiveness and practicality, given the context in which public accounting is practised and the public needs that it fills. Which of your possible solutions do you think would be the most practical and effective?

4.53 Use the critical-thinking framework to explain
LO.2 why serving the public interest should be the most important principle for PAs.

4.54 Explain how the independence principle can be
LO.3 derived from the critical-thinking framework.

CHAPTER

5

Legal Liability and Corporate Governance Issues

In this chapter we will focus on the legal responsibilities of auditors, as dictated by the courts. This chapter will help you understand PAs' legal liability for professional work, and the role of corporate governance in creating this liability.

LEARNING OBJECTIVES

After completing this chapter, you will be able to:

1 List some examples of potential civil and criminal litigation facing PAs.

2 Outline the various types of common law liability for PAs, citing specific case precedents.

3 Outline the various types of statutory law liability for PAs.

4* Explain how SOX has influenced corporate governance. (Appendix 5A)

5* Recognize U.S. SEC (statutory) law liability issues. (Appendix 5B)

* Learning objectives marked with an asterisk (*) and their corresponding topics are considered advanced material. *Note:* Appendices 5A and 5B are located on the text Online Learning Centre.

THE LEGAL ENVIRONMENT

· · · · · · · · · · · ·

LEARNING OBJECTIVE

1 List some examples of potential civil and criminal litigation facing PAs.

Most of this chapter is devoted to legal liability under common law, which is because this is the main source of auditor liability in the past. However, we also introduce you to the increasingly important liability arising from law established by legislation or (statutory law). SOX is an example of statutory law. This U.S. law is proving to be very influential in shaping legislation in Canada and around the world in the post-Enron environment. We saw this through some of the effects of SOX discussed in Chapter 1. In Canada, we also do not have anything like the Securities and Exchange Commission (SEC) Acts that were passed in the U.S. in the 1930s. But we are getting there as discussed in this chapter.

In addition to the statutory law discussed in the previous paragraph, there is legislation prohibiting money laundering and payment of bribes. Under this legislation, PAs also have responsibilities to disclose such activities once they are aware of them. These responsibilities are also covered in this chapter and in Appendices 5A and 5B (which are located on the text Online Learning Centre). Appendix 5A considers this legislation within the broader context of corporate governance principles.

Corporate governance concepts help clarify auditor responsibilities through various parts of the client organization. Appendix 5A thus provides a good start to your study of audit evidence gathering in Part II of this text.

The chapter ends with Appendix 5B (also on the Online Learning Centre), which introduces you to the SEC Acts and some influential court cases, both of which affect affect auditor liability. We will review the U.S. experience because it is useful for providing some perspective on the likely future impact of recent Canadian securities legislation.

Legal liability has been increasing for all professionals, not just PAs. "Tort reform" has been a hot topic in the business and popular press. Record-setting damages have been awarded and professional liability insurance premiums have increased dramatically, and in some cases insurance is difficult to obtain. The problems affect everyone, from manufacturers to rock concert promoters. PAs are likewise affected. In the 1990s, payments for litigation were over four times greater than in the 1980s. Payments in the U.S. now run into the billions. Twenty-seven medium-sized accounting firms formed their own offshore captive insurance company in Bermuda to get adequate liability insurance.

PAs are potentially liable for monetary damages and even subject to criminal penalties (e.g., under SEC rules), including fines and jail terms, for failure to perform professional services properly. They can be sued by clients, clients' creditors, investors and the government. Exposure to large lawsuit claims is possible through class actions permitted under federal rules of court procedure in Canada and the United States. In a class action suit, a relatively small number of aggrieved plaintiffs with small individual claims can bring suit for large damages in the name of an extended class. After a bankruptcy, for example, 40 bondholders who lost $40,000 might decide to sue, and they can sue on behalf of the entire class of bondholders for all their alleged losses (say $40 million). In some jurisdictions, lawyers will take such suits on a contingency fee basis (a percentage of the judgement, if any). The size of the claim and the zeal of the lawyers make the class action suit a serious matter. In the United States, class action suits have become such a problem that they threaten the existence of many firms. Arthur Andersen and some regional firms have already been forced into bankruptcy as a result of such litigation.

Lawsuit Causes and Frequency

One study of law cases showed that accountants' and auditors' legal troubles arose from five major types of errors. In 129 cases, 334 errors were found, classified as follows: (1) 33 percent involved misinterpretation of accounting principles, (2) 15 percent involved misinterpretation of auditing standards, (3) 29 percent involved faulty implementation of auditing procedures, (4) 13 percent involved client fraud, and (5) 7 percent involved fraud by the auditor.[1] These data suggest that accountants and auditors are exposed to liability for failure to report known departures from accounting principles, for failure to conduct audits properly, for failure to detect management fraud and for actually being parties to frauds. Threat of lawsuits has also affected how PAs conduct their work in consulting services and tax practice. Lest you believe that audit practice bears all the liability, be aware that about 60 percent of civil damage suits arise from tax practice disputes. However, lawsuits related to audits tend to be "high cost" resulting in much higher claims.[2]

All litigation is serious and results in expenses for defence, but not all cases result in payments for damage. In fact, about 40 percent of the lawsuits in the 1960–85 period were dismissed or settled with no payment by the accounting firm. Another 30 percent were settled by payment of approximately $1 million or less. This leaves about 30 percent of the cases where the auditors paid significant damage awards. All these data relate to lawsuits over audit services, to the exclusion of lawsuits about nonaudit services and other matters.[3]

Audit Responsibilities

Many users of audit reports expect auditors to detect fraud, theft and illegal acts, and to report them publicly. Auditors take responsibility for detecting material misstatements in financial statements; however, they are very cautious about taking responsibility for detecting all manner of fraud, and are especially cautious about accepting a public reporting responsibility. Fraud and misleading financial statements loom large among the concerns of financial statement users. They are afraid of information risk due to intentional misstatements, and they want it to be reduced, even eliminated. Some of their expectations are very high, and for this reason an expectation gap often exists between the diligence users expect and the diligence auditors are able to accept.

The audit responsibility for detection of fraud in financial statements is a complex topic, as seen in Chapters 7 and 17. Auditors take some responsibility but not as much as many users expect. For example, see *Handbook,* sections 5135 and 5136. This disparity leads to lawsuits, even when auditors have performed well.

· ·

R E V I E W   5.1   What are class action lawsuits, and why should auditors be concerned about them?
C H E C K P O I N T S   5.2   What are some causes of auditors' involvement in lawsuits as defendants?

5.3   What proportion of lawsuits against accountants relate to tax practice?

· ·

The next parts of this chapter cover PAs' legal liabilities under common law and statutory law. The principle of *stare decisis* or "to stand by a previous decision" is an important principle of common law. The practical problem in many cases, however, is whether the facts in a given case are similar enough to a precedent-setting one. Rarely are the facts exactly the same. Common law is all the cases and precedents that govern judges' decisions in previous lawsuits. Common law is "common knowledge," in the sense that judges tend to follow the collective wisdom of past cases decided by themselves and other judges. Common law is not enacted in statutes by a legislature. In contrast, statutory law is all the prohibitions enacted by a legislature—for example, the *Canada Business Corporation Act* and related provincial Corporation Acts.

---

[1] St. Pierre, K., and J. Anderson, "An Analysis of Audit Failures Based on Documented Legal Cases," *Journal of Accounting, Auditing, and Finance,* Spring 1982, pp. 236–37.

[2] S. Andersen and J. Wolfe, "A Perspective on Audit Malpractice Claims", *Journal of Accountancy,* September 2002, p. 59.

[3] Zoe-Vonna Palmrose, "An Analysis of Auditor Litigation and Audit Service Quality," *Accounting Review,* January 1988, pp. 55–73.

In the post-Enron environment, the world of PA legal liability has turned topsy-turvy. Until Enron, the major source of liability was under common law, but Enron changed all that. On June 19, 2002, Arthur Andersen was successfully prosecuted by the U.S. Justice Department for obstruction of justice regarding the Enron audit. The fatal damage to Andersen, however, seems to have been caused by the SEC, which charged Arthur Andersen with securities fraud two years previously over its audit of Waste Management Company. Andersen ultimately paid a $7 million fine in June 2001. It should be noted that when the SEC prosecutes, it is under statutory law. This set the stage for Arthur Andersen's rapid loss of reputation when the Enron audit problems surfaced six months later. Andersen had already lost most of its big clients by the time of its conviction, which was overturned by the U.S. Supreme Court in 2005, and the accounting world was shocked and dazed by the speed of its disintegration. Andersen's fall served as a warning of what could happen to even the largest and most respected of accounting firms when they lost the public's trust. In fact, the entire profession's reputation was tainted by the Enron/Andersen affair.

Since Enron, the SEC appears to have become much more aggressive in imposing statutory legal liability. For example, on January 29, 2003, the SEC sued one of the Big Four firms for securities fraud, alleging that it let Xerox Corp. inflate pretax earnings by over $3 billion from 1997 to 2000. In April 2002, Xerox agreed to a record $10 million penalty to settle SEC charges that they inflated revenue and earnings during this period. By this point Xerox had also dropped the PA firm as its auditor. After an investigation, the SEC made its first fraud case against a major accounting firm since Enron's collapse. The SEC alleged that, "Instead of putting a stop to Xerox's fraudulent conduct, the PA firm defendants themselves engaged in fraud by falsely representing to the public that they had applied professional auditing standards to their review of Xerox's accounting." The PA firm vigorously and publicly defended its work, but the case illustrates that statutory law may become a bigger threat to the profession than common law liability, especially if reputational effects are taken into consideration.

It should be noted that under SEC law, the concept of securities fraud puts a greater burden of proof on the defendant PA as outlined in Exhibit 5B-1 of Appendix 5B than is generally the case for fraud defendants as discussed in this chapter. In addition, the SEC doctrine of "fraud on the market," discussed later in this chapter, further increases PA liability to broader classes of potential plaintiffs.

In Ontario, Bill 198 was passed December 9, 2002, giving the Ontario Securities Commission potentially greater power in setting rules for appointing auditors than even SOX. These events suggest that statutory law liability may in the future present a far greater threat to the profession than common law liability. This was also indicated in Appendix 1B, which noted that some influential public officials already feel self-regulation of the profession has proven to be a failure.

However, there are few precedents to go by other than those already outlined. So, other than noting the potential changes in future liability in this introduction, this chapter focuses on the more traditional sources of auditors' legal liability.

LIABILITY UNDER COMMON LAW

LEARNING OBJECTIVE
2 Outline the various types of common law liability for PAs, citing specific case precedents.

Legal liabilities of PAs may arise from lawsuits brought on the basis of the law of contracts or as tort actions for negligence. Breach of contract is a claim that accounting or auditing services were not performed in the manner agreed. This basis is most characteristic of lawsuits involving public accountants and their clients. Tort actions cover the civil complaints (e.g., fraud, deceit and injury), and such actions are normally initiated by users of financial statements.

Tort refers to a private or civil wrong or injury. The rule of the law of torts is to compensate victims for harm suffered from the activities of others. The problem for tort law is to identify those actions which create a right to compensation. In doing so the law takes into account the fault or blame of the defendant (breach of duty) and whether the defendant's conduct could be considered the cause of the harm (causation). Both breach of a duty to the plaintiff and causation must be established in order for the defendant to be found liable for damages. However, the burden of proof for tort actions varies depending on social policy. For example, under "no fault" schemes the burden of compensation is spread widely to all automobile owners.[4]

Suits for civil damages under common law usually result when someone suffers a financial loss after relying on financial statements later found to be materially misleading. In the popular press, such unfortunate events are called audit failures. However, a distinction should be made between a business failure and an audit failure. A business failure is a bankruptcy or other serious financial difficulty experienced by an auditor's client. Business failures arise from many kinds of adverse economic events. An audit failure is an auditor's faulty performance, a failure to conduct an audit in accordance with GAAS with the result that misleading financial statements get published.

Characteristics of Common Law Actions

When an injured party considers herself damaged by a PA and brings a lawsuit, she generally asserts all possible causes of action, including breach of contract, tort, deceit, fraud or whatever else may be relevant to the claim.

Burden of Proof on the Plaintiff

Actions brought under common law place most of the burdens of affirmative proof on the plaintiff, who must prove (1) that he or she was damaged or suffered a loss, (2) the necessary privity or beneficiary relationship, (3) that the financial statements were materially misleading or that the accountant's advice was faulty, (4) that he or she relied on the statements or advice, (5) that they were the direct cause of the loss, and (6) that the accountant was negligent, grossly negligent, deceitful or otherwise responsible for damages. Appendix 5B reviews the U.S. Securities Acts, a type of U.S. statutory law that regulates the PA profession. There you will find that some of the U.S. statutes shift some of these burdens of affirmative proof to the PA.

Clients may bring a lawsuit for breach of contract. The relationship of direct involvement between parties to a contract is known as *privity*. When privity exists, a plaintiff usually need only show that the defendant accountant was negligent. (Ordinary negligence—a lack of reasonable care in the performance of professional accounting tasks—is usually meant when the word *negligence* stands alone.) If negligence is proved, the accountant may be liable, provided the client has not been involved in some sort of contributory negligence in the dispute—that is, that it can be shown that the client contributed to his own harm.

Smith v. London Assurance Corp. (1905)

This was the first North American case involving an auditor. The auditor sued for an unpaid fee, and the company counterclaimed for a large sum that had been embezzled by one of its employees, which they claimed would not have occurred except for the auditor's breach of contract. The evidence indicated that the auditors indeed failed to audit cash accounts at one branch office as stipulated in an engagement contract. The court recognized the auditors as skilled professionals and held them liable for embezzlement losses that could have been prevented by nonnegligent performance under the contract.

Fifty years ago, it was very difficult for parties, other than contracting clients, to succeed in lawsuits against auditors. Other parties not in privity had no cause of action for breach of contract. However, the court opinion in the case known as *Ultramares* expressed the view that, if negligence were so great as to constitute gross negligence—lack of minimum care in performing professional duties, indicating reckless disregard for duty and responsibility —grounds might exist for concluding that the accountant had engaged in constructive fraud.

[4] J.E. Smyth, D.A. Soberman, and A.J. Easson, *The Law and Business Administration in Canada*, 7th ed. (1995), pp. 76–79.

Actual fraud is characterized as an intentional act designed to deceive, mislead or injure the rights of another person.

Ultramares Corporation v. Touche (1931)

The *Ultramares* decision stated criteria for an auditor's liability to third parties for deceit (a tort action). In order to prove deceit, (1) a false representation must be shown, (2) the tort-feasor must possess scienter—either knowledge of falsity or insufficient basis of information, (3) intent to induce action in reliance must be shown, (4) the damaged party must show justifiable reliance on the false representation, and (5) there must have been a resulting damage. The court held that an accountant could be liable when he did not have sufficient information (audit evidence) to lead to a sincere or genuine belief. In other words, an audit report is deceitful when the auditor purports to speak from knowledge when he has none. The court also wrote that the degree of negligence might be so gross, however, as to amount to a constructive fraud. Then the auditor could be liable in tort to a third-party beneficiary.

Another important result of the *Ultramares* case was that the accountants were not liable to third parties for ordinary negligence. This had two ramifications for public accountants: (1) auditors were not liable to third parties under common law for the next 35 years and (2) this decision had a major impact on the U.S. Congress and influenced its passage of the SEC Acts of 1933 and 1934, creating a statutory responsibility to third parties where none existed under common law (see Appendix 5B).

Most auditor legal responsibilities arise from the law of negligence, which is the part of the common law known as the law of torts. Negligence is the failure to perform a duty with the requisite standard care (due care). The standard relates to one's public calling or profession.

Under the common law of torts for negligence (which is based on fault theory and causation as discussed previously), all of the following four elements of negligence must be established by the plaintiff if he is to successfully sue the auditor.

I. Four Elements of Negligence

1. There must be a legal duty of care to the plaintiff.
2. There must be a breach in that duty (e.g., failure to follow GAAS and GAAP).
3. There must be proof that damage resulted (otherwise the plaintiff is limited to the amount of audit fee).
4. There must be a reasonably proximate connection between the breach of duty and the resulting damage (e.g., losses must occur subsequent to firm's audit).

The auditor's defence is to demonstrate that at least one of the preceding elements is missing. The auditor may also use a contributory negligence argument that the plaintiff contributed to his own loss by, for example, not correcting internal control weaknesses. However, the contributory negligence defence applies only to parties having a contractual relationship with the auditor. Just to keep things straight, the auditor is the first party, the contractual client (who hires the auditor for the audit engagement and thus has privity of contract with the auditor) is the second party, and other audited financial statement users are third parties.

II. Due Care to Whom?

A key issue in establishing liability against auditors is to whom do they owe a duty of care? The contractual client (the second party to the contract) is owed a duty of care due to privity of contract. The client is the organization that appoints the auditor, a corporation, a proprietorship or a partnership. The engagement letter is critical in specifying the contractual obligation, particularly for nonaudit engagements. This explains the importance of having the engagement letter in the first place—it is the basis for establishing the liability of the auditor to second parties.

Under the *Foss* v. *Harbottle* (1842) principle, financial stakeholders cannot sue for losses suffered simply because the corporation in which they hold the stake has suffered losses. This is the flipside of the protection that the stakeholder gets from suits by the corporation's creditors. Just as a creditor cannot sue the corporation's owners, the owners cannot sue on behalf of the corporation. The corporation itself, as a "legal person," has to claim any damages. In the case of auditors, the owners are not viewed as having privity of contract with the auditors; only the corporation has privity of contract. Thus, shareholders can take action only as third parties, and then they must establish damages separate from that to the corporation. It turns out that the difficulty of establishing this latter point has greatly limited legal liability to Canadian accountants from shareholders (even though the audit report is addressed to the shareholders).

The most important source of liability to auditors, however, is from third parties. This relates to a principle of common law that got transplanted from third-party liability for acts causing injury or physical damage (*Heaven* v. *Pender*, 1883). Until recently, courts were unwilling to compensate for pure economic losses—that is, where there was no physical injury or damage to a plaintiff's person or property. However, that situation has changed dramatically. The *Ultramares* v. *Touche* case (1931) confirmed that there is no third-party liability for financial losses caused by ordinary auditor negligence. Only if the auditor had committed the fraud or constructive fraud (gross negligence) could the auditor be held liable to third parties.

The leading case for extending tort law to cover pure economic loss is *Hedley Byrne* v. *Heller and Partners*, which is described in the following box:

HEDLEY BYRNE & CO. LTD. v. Heller & Partners Ltd. [1964] A.C. 562 (H.L.)

In *Hedley Byrne,* the National Provincial Bank telephoned and wrote to Heller & Partners on behalf of Hedley Byrne to find out whether Easipower Ltd., a customer of Heller & Partners, was of sound financial position and thus a company with which Hedley Byrne would want to do business. Heller & Partners, disclaiming all responsibility to both enquiries by National Provincial Bank, said Easipower Ltd. was of sound financial shape. Hedley Byrne, in reliance on those statements, entered into a contract with Easipower Ltd., which subsequently thereafter sought liquidation.

The House of Lords, in deciding that Heller & Partners Ltd. would have been liable except for the disclaimer, established the modern role governing liability for professional advisers whose negligence gives rise to economic loss. A professional adviser has an implied duty of care in making an oral or written statement to another person whom he or she knows or should know will rely on it in making a decision with economic consequences.

Source: From *Professional Ethics in Accounting*, 1st edition by BROOKS. © 1995. Reprinted with permission of South-Western, a division of Thompson Learning: www.thompsonrights.com. Fax 800-730-2215.

Another reason that *Hedley Byrne* v. *Heller* is so important to the public accounting profession is that it established the precedent of third-party liability for (ordinary) negligence to "reasonably foreseeable third-parties." These third parties would include eventually, as a result of subsequent cases, present shareholders and lenders, as well as limited classes of prospective shareholders and prospective lenders.

This precedent-setting decision was upheld by the Supreme Court of Canada in *Haig* v. *Bamford* (1976). The Supreme Court concluded that auditors owe a duty to third parties of which they have "actual knowledge of the limited class that will use and rely on the statements." The details of this are given in the following box:

HAIG v. Bamford et. al. (1976) 72 D.L.R. (3d) 68

In *Haig,* the Saskatchewan Development Corporation agreed to advance a $20,000 loan to a financially troubled company in part based on the conditional production of satisfactory audited financial statements. The company engaged Bamford's accountants to prepare the statements. The accountant knew that the statements would be used by Saskatchewan Development Corporation. Relying on the accountant's information, Saskatchewan Development Corporation advanced $20,000 to the company. Later investigation disclosed that a $28,000 prepayment on two uncompleted contracts had been treated as if the contracts had been completed, thereby showing a profit instead of a loss, and the accountants failed to spot the error. The court held that where an accountant has negligently prepared financial statements and a third party relies on them to his or her detriment, a duty of care in an action for negligent misstatement will arise in the following circumstances: the accountant knows that it will be shown to a member of a limited class of which the plaintiff is a member and which the accountant actually knows will use and rely on the statement; the statements have been prepared primarily for guidance of that limited class and in respect of a specific class of transactions for the very purpose for which the plaintiff did in fact rely on them; the fact that the accountant did not know the identity of the plaintiff is not material as long as the accountant was aware that the person for whose immediate benefit they were prepared intended to supply the statements to members of the very limited class of which the plaintiff is a member.

Source: From *Professional Ethics in Accounting,* 1st edition by BROOKS. © 1995. Reprinted with permission of South-Western, a division of Thompson Learning: www.thompsonrights.com. Fax 800-730-2215.

The contemporary *Toromont* v. *Thorne* case (1975) also upheld the *Hedley Byrne* precedent, as it applied to Canada, of liability to known third parties (in this case a prospective investor, Toromont). Auditor's liability in Canada was further extended to prospective investors (reasonably foreseeable third parties) in *Dupuis* v. *Pan American Mines* (1979), the details of which are given in the following box:

DUPUIS v. Pan American Mines

On June 15, 1971, a draft prospectus pertaining to Pan American Mines Ltd. and its wholly owned subsidiary, Central Mining Corporation, was filed with the Quebec Securities Commission. Included in the prospectus was a consolidated balance sheet of Pan Am and its subsidiary, which had been audited by the accounting firm of Thorne, Gunn, Helliwell & Christenson, and on which Thorne, Gunn had expressed an unqualified opinion. On June 16, 1971, the securities commission authorized trading in Pan Am shares and distribution of the prospectus. Pan Am was then listed on the Canadian Stock Exchange, but in November 1971 trading in the shares was suspended, and in February 1972 Pan Am was delisted.

The plaintiff, Albert Dupuis, brought an action claiming that he had suffered a loss on shares of Pan Am purchased between the time the shares were listed and the time trading was suspended. His action was based on the alleged falsity of some of the information contained in the prospectus, including the auditors' report and the notes to the consolidated financial statement.

The judges' decision was worded in part as follows: "When an auditor prepares a balance sheet which he knows is going to be inserted in a company prospectus offering stock for sale, *I believe he has a duty to make sure that the contents of that balance sheet are accurate* so that prospective investors will not be led into error by it" (emphasis added).

In conclusion, the judge gave the plaintiff judgement against Thorne, Gunn for $89,266.91, with interest from October 15, 1971, and costs.

Source: H. Rowan, "Legal Cases," *CA Magazine,* August 1979, pp. 36–39. Reproduced by permission from *CA Magazine,* published by the Canadian Institute of Chartered Accountants, Toronto, Canada.

CAPARO INDUSTRIES PLC. v. Dickman et al. [1991] 2. W.L.R. 358 (H.L.)

Caparo, in its takeover of Fidelity plc, had Touche Ross & Co. audit the financial statements of Fidelity. Caparo later alleged that its purchase of shares and subsequent takeover were made in reliance on the accounts, which they claimed were misleading and inaccurate in that they showed a pre-tax profit of £1.3 million instead of a loss of £400,000. Caparo sued Touche Ross for negligence, maintaining that Touche Ross owed them a duty of care as shareholders and potential investors with respect to the audit and certification of the accounts.

The House of Lords decided that Touche Ross owed no duty of care to Caparo either as a potential investor before it was registered or as a shareholder thereafter, for the following reasons:

While there is no general principle that will determine the existence and scope of a duty of care in all cases, in order for a duty of care to arise, there must be: the harm said to result from the breach of duty must have been reasonably foreseeable; there must be a relationship of sufficient "proximity" between the party said to owe the duty and the party to whom it is said to be owed; and the situation must be one in which, on policy grounds, the court considers it fair, just and reasonable that the law should impose a duty of a given scope on the part of one party for the benefit of the other.

Source: From *Professional Ethics in Accounting,* 1st edition by BROOKS. © 1995. Reprinted with permission of South-Western, a division of Thompson Learning: www.thompsonrights.com. Fax 800-730-2215.

In summary, through 1979, Canadian courts had gradually widened auditor's liability under common law to include limited classes of third parties.

The recent *Caparo Industries Plc.* v. *Dickman* case (1991) in the United Kingdom, however, has the potential to reverse this increasing liability to third parties, since it limits liability to those third parties of which auditors have knowledge.[5]

A related Canadian case is given in the following box:

FLANDERS v. Mitha

In August 1992 Justice Holmes of the B.C. Supreme Court ruled in *Flanders* v. *Mitha* (1992) that "disgruntled investors sueing a BC accounting firm Buckett & Sharpley for negligently preparing a housing co-op's financial statements must show that they actually relied on those statements when making their investment decision." During the court proceedings none of the plaintiffs was found to have actually relied on the financial statements in purchasing an apartment. They either relied on the realtor or had made the purchase decision prior to requesting and receiving the financial statements from the realtor. *Flanders* v. *Mitha* (1992) thus limits the auditor's liability when his or her work is used by a client to solicit investments from the public.

---

[5] M. Paskell-Mede, "Duty of Care Revisited," *CA Magazine,* December 1993, pp. 34–35.

The interesting questions are whether the Canadian courts will continue to take this narrow approach (some other recent British Columbia decisions suggest so), and whether regulatory agencies, such as the Ontario Securities Commission (OSC), will succeed in convincing legislatures to make companies, their directors and auditors legally responsible to shareholders under revised securities acts for all misleading documents (as in the United States). Currently, Canadian auditors' legal liability to third parties follows largely from common law. (The four elements of negligence were in *Toromont* v. *Thorne et al.* [1975], in which the auditors were found negligent, but the plaintiffs could not prove that they suffered losses as a result.) Nevertheless, some articles in the 1990s financial press made it clear that litigation against auditors in Canada was reaching alarming proportions. There are currently several major lawsuits against PAs outstanding in Canada. It will take years to resolve them.

In summary, the current status of auditor third-party legal liability under common law appears to be as follows: The courts have attempted to strike a fair balance between reliable information for users of financial statements and unreasonable risk to the auditor. This balance has resulted in Canadian auditors currently being liable for negligent error to limited classes of third parties. Third parties are often classified in the following categories:

(*a*) known third parties

(*b*) reasonably foreseeable third parties

(*c*) all third parties relying on financial statements

The trend in litigation suggests the courts will most likely draw the line between categories (*b*) and (*c*) for purposes of deciding to whom auditors owe a duty of care under common law.

Fraudulent misrepresentation is a basis for liability in tort (established in *Haig* v. *Bamford*), so parties not in privity with the accountant may have causes of action when negligence is gross enough to amount to constructive fraud. These other parties include primary beneficiaries, actual foreseen and limited classes of persons, and all other injured parties.

State Street Trust Co. v. Ernst (1938)

Accountants, however, may be liable to third parties, even without deliberate or active fraud. A representation certified as true to the knowledge of the accountants when knowledge there is none, a reckless misstatement or an opinion based on grounds so flimsy as to lead to the conclusion that there was no genuine belief in its truth, are all sufficient upon which to base liability. A refusal to see the obvious, a failure to investigate the doubtful, if sufficiently gross, may furnish evidence leading to an inference of fraud so as to impose liability for losses suffered by those who rely on the balance sheet. In other words, heedlessness and reckless disregard of consequences may take the place of deliberate intention. In this connection we are to bear in mind the principle already stated, that negligence or blindness, even when not equivalent to fraud, it nonetheless evidence to sustain an inference of fraud. At least, this is so if the negligence is gross.

Primary beneficiaries are third parties for whose primary benefit the audit or other accounting service is performed. Such a beneficiary will be identified to, or reasonably forseeable by, the accountant prior to or during the engagement, and the accountant will know that her work will influence the primary beneficiary's decisions. For example, an audit firm may be informed that the report is needed for a bank loan application at the North Land Bank in the Kingston Company case (located on the Online Learning Centre). Many cases indicate that proof of ordinary negligence may be sufficient to make accountants liable for damages to primary beneficiaries.

CIT Financial Corp. v. Glover (1955)

Auditors are liable to third parties for ordinary negligence if their reports are for the primary benefit of the third party. Thus, the privity criterion may not serve as a defense when third-party beneficiaries are known.

PAs may also be liable to foreseeable beneficiaries—creditors, investors or potential investors who rely on accountants' work. If the PA is reasonably able to foresee a limited class of potential users of his or her work (e.g., local banks, regular suppliers), liability may be imposed for ordinary negligence. This, however, is an uncertain area, and liability in a particular case depends entirely on the unique facts and circumstances. Beneficiaries of these types and all other injured parties may recover damages if they are able to show that a PA was grossly negligent and perpetrated a constructive fraud.

Rusch Factors, Inc. v. Levin (1968)

With respect to the plaintiff's negligence theory, this case held that an accountant should be liable in negligence for careless financial misrepresentations relied upon by actually foreseen and limited classes of persons. According to the plaintiff's complaint in the case, the defendant knew that his certification was to be used for, and had as its very aim and purpose, the reliance of potential financiers of the Rhode Island corporation.

Rosenblum, Inc. v. Adler (1983)

Giant Stores Corporation acquired the retail catalog showroom business owned by Rosenblum, giving stock in exchange for the business. Fifteen months after the acquisition, Giant Stores declared bankruptcy. Its financial statements had been audited and had received unqualified opinions on several prior years. These financial statements turned out to be misstated because Giant Stores had manipulated its books.

In finding for the plaintiffs on certain motions, the New Jersey Supreme Court held that Independent auditors have a duty of care to all persons whom the auditor should reasonably foresee as recipients of the statements from the company for proper business purposes, provided that the recipients rely on those financial statements . . . It is well recognized that audited financial statements are made for the use of third parties who have no direct relationship with the auditor . . . Auditors have responsibility not only to the client who pays the fee but also to investors, creditors and others who rely on the audited financial statements.

[The case went back to the trial court for further proceedings.]

Defences of the Accountant

The defendant accountant in a common law action presents evidence to mitigate or refute the plaintiff's claims and evidence. For example, the accountant might offer evidence that the plaintiff was not in privity or not foreseen, that the financial statements were not misleading or that the plaintiff contributed to the negligence. The primary defence against a negligence claim is to offer evidence that the audit had been conducted in accordance with GAAS with due professional care.

Some courts hold plaintiffs to a strict privity criterion to have a standing in court. In New York courts, the general rule is that these conditions must be met: (1) the accountants must have been aware that the financial reports were to be used for a particular purpose, (2) the accountants must have known that a particular third party was going to rely on the reports, and (3) some action by the accountants must link them with the third party and must demonstrate that the accountants knew of the reliance on the reports. In response to these conditions, some users of financial statements have invented a request for a **reliance letter**. Users have requested accountants to sign letters saying that they have been notified that a particular recipient of the financial statements and audit report intends to rely upon them for particular purposes.

The AICPA has warned accountants to be careful when signing such letters so that they do not become an automatic proof of users' actual reliance.

In several Canadian cases the auditors successfully argued that clients should not have relied on the financial statements to make their investment decision.[6] A good example is when banks claim that they have been mislead by the financial statements. A key issue in

---

6 Auditing in Crisis," *The Bottom Line*, March 1990.

this instance is the fourth element of negligence: Did the banks' losses follow from the auditor's breach of duty with regard to auditing the financial statements? Paskell-Mede notes that "the courts carefully review the degree of reliance plaintiff bankers have on misleading financial statements. Banks usually have available to them not only their customers' financial statements but a great deal of other information as well. Their decision to continue a loan is very often based on considerations quite apart from any reliance they may place on the opinion of the customer's auditors. In these circumstances the auditors ought not to be found liable—or at least not entirely—for the bank's losses." In general, "it's refreshing to see a court carefully reviewing the degree of reliance plaintiff bankers place on misleading financial statements."[7]

Liability in Compilation and Review Services

You may find it easy to think about common law liability in connection with audited financial statements. Do not forget, however, that PAs also render compilation and review services and are associated with unaudited financial information (see Chapter 16). People expect PAs to perform these services in accordance with professional standards, and courts can impose liability for accounting work judged to be substandard. PAs have been assessed damages for work on such statements, as shown in *1136 Tenants' Corporation* v. *Max Rothenberg & Co.* Approximately 11 percent of losses in the AICPA professional liability insurance plan involve compilation and review engagements relating to unaudited financial statements.

1136 Tenants' Corporation v. *Max Rothenberg & Co.* (1967)

> Despite defendant's claims to the contrary, the court found that he was engaged to audit and not merely write up plaintiff's books and records. The accountant had, in fact, performed some limited auditing procedures including preparation of a worksheet entitled "Missing Invoices 1/1/63–12/31/63." These were items claimed to have been paid but were not. The court held that, even if accountants were hired only for write-up work, they had a duty to inform plaintiffs of any circumstances that gave reason to believe that a fraud had occurred (e.g., the record of "missing invoices"). The plaintiffs recovered damages of about $237,000.

One significant risk is that the client may fail to understand the nature of the service being given. Accountants should use a meeting and an engagement letter to explain clearly that a compilation service ("write-up") involves little or no investigative work, and that it is lesser in scope than a review service. Similarly, a review service should be explained in terms of being less extensive than a full audit service. Clear understandings at the outset can enable accountants and clients to avoid later disagreements.

Yet even with these understandings, public accountants cannot merely accept client-supplied information that appears to be unusual or misleading. A court has held that a PA's preparation of some erroneous and misleading journal entries without sufficient support was enough to trigger common law liability for negligence, even though the PA was not associated with any final financial statements. CICA and ISA standards for compilations require PAs to obtain additional information if client-supplied accounting data are incorrect, incomplete or otherwise unsatisfactory. Courts may hold PAs liable for failure to obtain additional information in such circumstances.

When financial statements are reviewed, PAs' reports state: "Based on my review, nothing has come to my attention that causes me to believe that these financial statements are not, in all material respects in accordance with generally accepted accounting principles" (*Handbook,* paragraph 8200.42 and ISA 910 Appendix 3). Courts can look to the facts of a case and rule on whether the review was performed properly. Generally, the same four elements of negligence must be met for review engagements as for audit engagements. The only difference is that "due care" in review engagements should follow the standards for

---

[7] H. Rowan, "Are Banks Looking to Pin the Blame?" *CA Magazine,* June 1988.

review engagements rather than the standards for audits. Generally, it would appear that third-party liability continues to flow to the same classes of persons who would be relying on the financial statements.[8] Some courts might decide a PA's review was substandard if necessary adjustments or "material modifications" should have been discovered. These risks tend to induce more work by PAs beyond superficial enquiry procedures.

A 1987 New York case, however, may create an attitude more favourable for PAs' review work on unaudited financial statements. In 1985 William Iselin & Company sued the Mann Judd Landau (MJL) accounting firm, claiming damages for having relied on financial statements reviewed by MJL. Iselin had used the financial statements of customers for its factoring–financing business. A customer had gone bankrupt and Iselin's loans became worthless. A New York appeals court dismissed the case, saying that third parties (Iselin) cannot rely on reviewed financial statements as they can on audited financial statements to assure themselves that a company is financially healthy. The court observed that MJL expressed no opinion on the reviewed financial statements. Iselin's lawyer was reported to have observed: "Accountants and their clients will find that reviews are useless, since no one can rely on them."

. . . .

REVIEW
CHECKPOINTS

5.4   What must be proved by the plaintiff in a common law action seeking recovery of damages from an independent auditor of financial statements? What must the defendant accountant do in such a court action?

5.5   What legal theory is derived from the *Ultramares* decision? Can auditors rely on the *Ultramares* decision today?

5.6   Define and explain *privity*, *primary beneficiary* and *foreseeable beneficiary* in terms of the degree of negligence on the part of a PA that would trigger the PA's liability.

5.7   What proportion of lawsuits against PAs relate to compilation and review (unaudited financial statements) practice?

. . . .

III. Due Care: Its Meaning

A key aspect to the second element of negligence is the meaning of due care. What is it that the auditor must be breaching? Due professional care implies the careful application of all the standards of the profession (GAAS, GAAP) and observance of all the rules of professional conduct. The courts have interpreted due care to be that of a reasonably prudent practitioner; neither the extremes of the highest possible standards nor the lowest acceptable or minimum standards would be considered due care. This suggests that looking at Rules of Professional Conduct or the *Handbook* may not always be sufficient in the courts' view because these would be viewed as minimal standards. In fact, over the years the courts have helped shape audit practice by their interpretation of due care. For example, the concept of testing (less than 100 percent examination of the accounts) was first accepted as reasonable by the precedent-setting decision in *London vs. General Bank* (1895). This case was also the first to acknowledge that there is some limit on the auditor's responsibility for the detection of fraud and the *duty* to take increased care in the presence of suspicious circumstances. This case influenced the development of later professional announcements and hundreds of subsequent cases (e.g., *1136 Tennants* [1967]). However, the general legal standard is that an auditor is "a watchdog not a bloodhound" (in re *Kingston Cotton Mill Company [1896]*). This means that it is reasonable for auditors to assume management's honesty as a working hypothesis as long as the auditor can provide documented reasons for this assumption. Nonetheless, auditors need to be alert to factors (evidence) that conflict with this hypothesis. If there is such evidence, auditors must take additional precautions under the due care requirement, as discussed in Chapters 9 and 17.

---

[8] "The Jury's Still Out on Review Engagement Liability," *CA Magazine*, June 1988.

Another example of the courts' influence in setting auditing standards (and therefore influencing due care provisions) is the requirement that the auditor corroborate management assertions with her own evidence. The auditor cannot just rely on management's words; she must justify reliance through checking, testing and other audit procedures. This practice following from the third examination standard has been shaped by decisions in many court cases, such as *Continental Vending* (1969) and the Canadian *Toromont* v. *Thorne* (1975).

An obvious example of court influence in determining what constitutes auditor due care is *McKesson Robbins* (1939) (discussed in Appendix 5A). This can be viewed as ultimately influencing the creation of *Handbook,* section 6030, ISA 501 and similar sections in U.S. standards. In that case, the auditor failed to observe inventory or confirm receivables. It should thus be evident that the due care provision of negligence has significantly shaped and probably will continue to influence the development of audit standards. One impact of the *Continental Vending* case, discussed in Appendix 5A, is that the courts did not accept the auditor's defence that the auditor was following GAAP (i.e., the auditor was able to establish that the footnote in the financial statement was in accordance with GAAP); instead, the courts expected the auditor to use some higher standard of fairness in deciding on proper disclosure. This has led to much greater diligence on the part of standard setters when disclosing various types of information.

A sense of urgency on this issue of fairness has been introduced to Canadian courts, as indicated in the following box:

ACCOUNTING PROFESSION HAS A DUTY TO SHAREHOLDERS

Before buying shares in a company, investors usually rely on an important safeguard—the auditor's opinion of its financial statements. And that opinion usually declares that the statements are both "presented fairly" and are "in accordance with generally accepted accounting principles (GAAP)." For decades, though, auditors have tried to duck legal liability to the investors they serve. Auditors appear to want what doesn't exist: authority without responsibility.

This spring two Canadian lawsuits promise to clarify the trust that investors can place in auditors. One case, *Stephen Kripps et al.* v. *Touche Ross* (now Deloitte Touche) *et al.,* emerged from the B.C. Court of Appeal last month. In 1985, Kripps et al. relied on the audited financial statements of a mortgage company to buy $1.9 million of its debentures. The company went into receivership and the investors lost $2.7 million including interest. The investors sued the auditor, lost in a lower court, and won at appeal.

A 2-to-1 appeal court majority ruled that "Touche had actual knowledge that a simple application of GAAP would . . . lead to financial statements that could not be said to have fairly represented the financial position" of the company. "Auditors cannot hide behind [the formula] 'according to GAAP' " the court declared, "if the auditors know . . . that the financial statements are misleading." It ruled against Touche. The court's point is correct—GAAP is too loose a standard to be a sufficient safeguard by itself. That's why the financial statements must also be "presented fairly," to use the actual language of the auditor's opinion. Despite the ruling's validity, some accountants want the Canadian Institute of Chartered Accountants (CICA) to support an appeal by Touche to the Supreme Court.

Postscript: On November 6, 1997, the Supreme Court of Canada denied Deloitte & Touche's right to appeal the negligence ruling against it by the B.C. Court of Appeal. The *Kripps* v. *Touche Ross* decision thus may make it easier for investors to sue Canadian auditors in the future. The other case referred to in the above editorial is discussed at the end of this chapter.

Source: The Financial Post, "Accounting Profession Has a Duty to Shareholders," *The Financial Post*, May 20, 1997. Sun Media Corp.

IV. Other Elements of Negligence

The two other elements of negligence have also proven to be material issues in various court cases. The third element requires that some damage must occur to the third party—otherwise, it is limited to recovering the audit fee only. This was the situation in *Toromont* v. *Thorne*.

The last element of negligence requires that there be a causal link between the breach of duty and the resulting damage. Thus, for example, if losses occur before the time of the audit, or if it can be proven in some other way that the plaintiff did not rely on the audited information to any significant degree, the lawsuit will fail.

Perhaps at this point it is useful to note the relationship between joint and several liability and the fourth element of evidence. In Canada and the United States we have **joint and several liability**, meaning any of several defendants that have caused part of the damages are liable to the plaintiffs for the entire amount of damages. This system was set up to protect plaintiffs from having to sue several different parties to recover the full amount of damages. Under joint and several liability, the courts can force the defendant with the "deepest pockets" to pay all the damages even though he may have contributed, say, only 1 percent to the losses. It is, of course, then up to the defendant auditor to recover from the other defendants its share of the losses. If the other defendants are in bankruptcy, however, this can leave the auditor with all the losses.

The following box, from a *National Post* article, indicates the problems that joint and several liability can cause in Canada.

OUTDATED LIABILITY LAWS HARMING ECONOMY: ICAO

TRANSACTIONS 'JUST DON'T GET DONE' AS AUDITORS TURN AWAY BUSINESS

Canada's antiquated liability laws are badly hurting the economy, according to the country's largest accounting body, which is spearheading demands for liability reform.

The Institute of Chartered Accountants of Ontario—with 35,000 members—said the laws lag behind those in other parts of the world and the failure to make crucial reforms could force an exodus of investment to more attractive jurisdictions.

The ICAO estimates the amount of litigation against the big accounting firms has increased by more than 300% since 1988. The cost of liability insurance for auditors is as much as three times higher than it was in 2001, and the number of firms offering audit services in Canada has dropped by 50% in the past two years, from 400 to just over 200.

Brian Hunt, president and chief executive officer of the ICAO, said failure to fully reform the laws could result in a worst-case scenario where individuals and business ask, "Why would I do business in Canada, when I could get more protection south of the border?"

A recent ICAO survey of more than 500 small- and mid-sized accounting firms in Ontario showed that almost three-quarters of the firms surveyed say they have faced a moderate to significant increase in professional liability costs over the past five years. Two-thirds also said liability-related issues are

deterring them from taking on client engagements.

Joel Cohen, executive audit partner at mid-tier Canadian accounting firm RSM Richter LLP, said the current regime also restricts access to the capital markets, even for well-governed companies operating in stable industries, because audit firms are unwilling to take on the risk of providing accounting and auditing services.

"We are at a competitive disadvantage," Mr. Cohen said.

Mr. Cohen said the current liability environment has forced RSM Richter to turn down engagements on five or six transactions in the past six months alone. He said it is doubtful the companies involved will find an audit firm in Canada willing to help them.

"We are limiting liability anyway by limiting access to our service," he said.

In one case, RSM Richter needed to enlist another department auditor for a client of its firm. But, Mr. Cohen said, no one was willing to take on the risk, even though the client was a "solid company, making profits, where the business was not risky."

Canada's liability laws "inhibit the completion of transactions. They just don't get done," he added.

Len Crispino, president and chief executive officer of the Ontario Chamber of Commerce, said he has heard anecdotal evidence among his members to support the accountants' position. "It's becoming tougher and tougher to get an accounting firm," he said, "and, in a sense, we all lose."

The key issue is Canada's "joint-and-several" liability laws, which mean an auditor who is only 1% to blame for a corporate bankruptcy can be forced to pay out 100% of the costs associated with any litigation.

Mr. Cohen said the main problem with Canada's joint-and-several liability laws is that they make the risks of providing audit and accounting services "unquantifiable."

That is not the same in other countries. In Australia, legislators recently enacted laws to cap the amount of liability that audit firms could be forced to suffer. In the United States, federal legislators introduced a form of proportionate liability—the costs of losing in litigation are proportionate to the attributed blame—as far back as 1995, and 39 states have eliminated or significantly amended their joint-and-several liability laws. The U.K. and the European Union have also indicated plans to move away from joint-and-several liability.

The Ontario government has recognized the issue and has passed legislation to put some limits on professional liability. However, joint-and-several liability continues to apply in many cases, including civil suits involving audited documents such as prospectuses, take-over bid circulars and issuer bid circulars, which are generally considered higher risk.

The ICAO is pushing for further changes to fully eliminate joint-and-several liability, Mr. Hunt said. He said he expects resistance from the legal community and from shareholder activists who might perceive reform as something that only favours the big accounting firms. But, he said, these groups do not understand the magnitude of the problem.

Mr. Hunt said not only would the number of firms offering audit services in Canada continue to decline, but there could be a drain of qualified and experienced accountants to countries where the risks of performing audits is much lower. He said this will all add up to audit costs that will be higher in Canada than in other countries.

One sign of the increased risks, Mr. Cohen said, is the cost of professional indemnity insurance for audit firms, which tripled in Canada between 2001 and 2004.

The big accounting firms are also feeling the pinch of rising costs due to Canada's liability regime, said Lou Pagnutti, chairman and chief executive officer for Canada at big four accounting firm Ernst & Young LLP. Since the collapse of Arthur Andersen, the big accounting firms are finding it increasingly difficult to obtain professional indemnity insurance in Canada, he said. "Even if you can get it", he said, "the premiums have increased." Premiums here for the big firms have risen by as much as 30% to 40% a year, forcing them to arrange expensive self-insurance, Mr. Pagnutti said. "Absent liability reform", he said, "there will be further cost increases."

Source: Duncan Mavin, "Outdated liability laws harming economy: ICAO: Transactions 'just don't get done' as auditors turn away business," *The National Post*, Wednesday, June 29, 2005, p. FP7. Material reprinted with the express permission of: "National Post Company," a CanWest Partnership.

A recent development in the profession in light of these potential legal liabilities has been the creation of **limited liability partnerships (LLPs)**. In 1998, Ontario was the first province to enact legislation allowing the use of the LLP form of organization, followed by Alberta in 1999. LLPs limit the legal liability of most partners only to the assets of the LLP. With the traditional partnership form of organization, the partners themselves are liable for all debts and liabilities incurred by their firm. In an LLP, the negligent partner is still liable to the extent of her own personal assets. The personal assets of nonnegligent partners, however, are not threatened in the LLP form of organization. Thus the LLP form of organization can generally reduce the risk to partners of legal liability. However, the LLP form of organization did not prevent the demise of Arthur Andersen and so there are now obvious limits to its benefits. In particular, the LLP form may have less impact under a system where the primary source of legal liability is from statutory law via a high profile regulator that can affect the LLP's reputation in the marketplace—a system that looks increasingly likely in the post-Enron environment.

Auditor's Liability When Auditor Is Associated with Misleading Financial Information

If the courts conclude that the auditor is associated with misleading financial statements, even if such statements are in conformity with GAAP, they may conclude that the auditors are fraudulently negligent. If auditors are found guilty of a fraudulent misrepresentation, then there are no limits on third-party liability. In U.S. courts the concept of gross negligence–constructive fraud has been used to expand auditor liability to larger classes of third parties. This is done not only through U.S. common law but also in statutory law via the U.S. Securities Acts. As a result, there have been several cases in the United States in which auditors have been found guilty of fraud when they otherwise would have been found to be only negligent (see, e.g., *Continental Vending* in Appendix 5A).

Interestingly, the Ontario Securities Commission appears to be interested in increasing auditors' legal responsibility to shareholders by revising the Securities Acts in Ontario. This may be a way of expanding auditor liability to wider classes of third parties in Ontario (e.g., see subsequent discussion of "Auditing in Crisis"). This, combined with the increasing influence of the Charter of Rights and Freedoms legislation on the courts, may make the Canadian legal environment more comparable to that of the United States in the near future. In addition, class action legislation has recently been approved in Quebec (1979), Ontario (1993) and British Columbia (1995). Contingency fees are another issue being considered by the Ontario Law Society; implementing them would also make the Ontario environment more comparable to that of the United States. Thus, many of the problems of high litigation rates and insurance premiums and costly court decisions may soon be imported to at least parts of the Canadian legal environment. Recent requirements to expand auditor responsibilities for detecting money-laundering schemes will further add to the liabilities burden.

AUDITOR'S LIABILITY UNDER STATUTORY LAW

LEARNING OBJECTIVE

3 Outline the various types of statutory law liability for PAs.

A great deal of liability for American auditors arises from statutory law under the SEC. These SEC laws give the SEC the legal right to decide what is GAAP. There is nothing comparable in Canadian legislation, yet increasingly the OSC and Quebec regulators are seeking more enforcement power over professionals such as PAs operating in the capital markets. We will discuss the latest developments at the end of the chapter.

What is unique about Canadian statutory law is the *Canada Business Corporation Act* (CBCA) and related provincial corporation acts.

The highlights of the CBCA are as follows (to be covered in more detail in your business law course):

1. The CBCA identifies conditions under which the auditor is not considered independent in Section 161.

2. It identifies conditions of appointing and retiring the auditor in sections 162 and 163.

3. It identifies the auditor's rights and responsibilities in section 168:

    (*a*) to attend shareholder meetings

    (*b*) to provide a written statement of reasons for a resignation

    (*c*) to make an audit examination unimpeded and gain access to data the auditor considers necessary

4. The CBCA identifies the financial statements subject to audit, and specifies that the financial statements must be in conformity with the *CICA Handbook*. (Note that this represents a stark contrast with U.S. securities law, which allows the SEC to decide what is GAAP. The important point is that the ultimate authority in the United States is the SEC, whereas here in Canada the ultimate authority on accounting issues is the CICA via the *Handbook*. This gives *Handbook* standards much higher legal status than comparable standards in the United States.)

5. Until 1994 the CBCA applied to all companies incorporated under the act, having revenues in excess of $10 million or assets greater than $5 million. Under amendments to the CBCA made in 1994, privately held companies are no longer required to have their financial statements audited or disclosed. The *Ontario Business*

Corporations Act requires audits only for companies having $100 million of either assets or revenues; other provincial corporations acts vary in their reporting requirements.

In December 1995 the American accounting profession was successful in having the U.S. Congress pass (over President Clinton's veto) the *Private Securities Litigation Reform Act*, which changes auditor liability under SEC section 10b (discussed in Appendix 5B). There are three objectives to the Act. First, it is intended to "discourage abusive claims of investors' losses due to fraudulent misstatements or omissions by issuers of securities" (and professionals associated with the misstatements or omissions, such as auditors). Second, the Act provides more protection against securities fraud. Third, the Act increases the flow of forward-looking financial information." The Act meets these objectives by imposing specific pleading requirements; by reducing the effectiveness of discovery in coercing settlements; by mandating sanctions for frivolous claims; by giving the plaintiff class far more control of class actions; by providing for proportionate liability except in cases of knowing fraud; by creating a safe harbour for forward-looking information; and by codifying auditor's responsibilities to search for and disclose fraud.[9]

For the purposes of this chapter, the most important feature of the Act concerns the reform of "joint and several liability," which under SEC law now only applies to auditors who knowingly commit a violation of the security law. "A defendant (auditor) whose conduct is less culpable is liable only for a percentage of the total damages corresponding to the percentage of responsibility allocated to the defendant (auditor) by the jury . . . Thus, for example, if a PA firm is found 10 percent responsible for an injury and insolvent corporate management is allocated 90 percent, the PA firm no longer will have to make up all of the management's share (as long as the PA firm did not engage in knowing fraud)."[10]

The CBCA was amended in 2001 to change the liability associated with financial statement misrepresentations from one of joint and several liability to a modified proportionate liability regime. Auditors in Canada are now liable under the CBCA to that which corresponds to their degree of responsibility for the loss (**proportionate liability**). However, the proportionate liability is modified in that if other defendants in the lawsuit are unable to pay, the auditor is then liable for additional payments capped at 50 percent of his original liability under the proportionate system. For example, if the auditor is found to be liable to pay 20 percent of the damages incurred by the user under the proportionate system, then under the modified proportionate system, the maximum liability is 20 percent plus 50 percent of 20 percent or 30 percent. Under some conditions the courts can revert to the joint and several liability where the auditor may be required to pay up to 100 percent of the damages.[11]

Post-Enron provincial legislation in Canada under the leadership of the **Canadian Securities Administrators (CSA)** is creating a whole new set of auditor liabilities. These liabilities were in response to decreased liabilities resulting from the *Hercules* case discussed in the following box, which took away most third-party liability under common law.

The *Hercules* and *Kripps* cases illustrate that common law decisions can sometimes conflict, just as they did for the confidentiality rules explained in Chapter 4. The *Hercules* case along with post-Enron developments prompted Ontario to pass its Bill 198 in December 2002. Bill 198 is similar to SEC laws discussed in Appendix 5B. The CSA is promoting passage of similar legislation throughout Canada's provinces in an effort to demonstrate that Canadian regulators are as concerned in preserving the integrity of their capital markets as the SEC is in the U.S. The legislation referred to at the end of the *Hercules* box is Bill 198. The intent of Bill 198 (and other similar legislation) is to make it easier for investors to recover damages from accountants, directors and others associated with misleading financial reporting.

[9] A.R. Andrews, and G. Simonette Jr., "Tort Reform Revolution," *Journal of Accountancy*, September 1996, p. 54.
[10] Ibid., p. 50.
[11] See M. Paskell-Mede, "Fair shares," *CA Magazine*, November 2001, pp. 31–32.

Auditors Not Legally Liable to Investors, Top Court Rules

An auditor who signs a company's financial statements has no legal liability to shareholders or investors.

That's the thrust of a ruling by the Supreme Court of Canada brought down Thursday in the case of *Hercules Managements Ltd. et al.* v. *Ernst & Young et al.*

The court's concern, observers say, is to protect auditors from unlimited liability to thousands of investors who may use the audit opinion for many different purposes.

The annual financial statement is now a joke, says Al Rosen, a professor of accounting at York University in Toronto and a partner in Rosen & Vettese Ltd., forensic accountants.

"Public accountants may think this is a wonderful win for them," Rosen added. "But in the long run I see this as a disaster. Who really needs an audit of financial statements that is not useful for investor decision-making?"

The court's ruling was applauded by Michael Rayner, president of the Canadian Institute of Chartered Accountants. "The decision leaves the profession in a legal environment in which it can maximize its contribution to the capital markets," Rayner said yesterday.

The court has "tried to provide a reasonable amount of liability for auditors," he added.

"We believe the responsibility of auditors is important . . . and there are still significant redresses available through the courts for auditors who are engaged in a situation where there is clear negligence on their part."

The effect of the court's ruling could be short-lived. Brenda Eprile, executive director of the Ontario Securities Commission—Canada's leading securities regulator—says provincial regulators are working on a legal framework that will re-establish the legal liability of auditors to investors.

Hercules Managements was the 80 percent shareholder of Manitoba-based Northguard Acceptance Ltd., which lent money on mortgages in the 1970s and early 1980s. Ernest & Young was the auditor.

In 1984, Northguard went into receivership. Hercules sued Ernst & Young, alleging negligence.

The action was dismissed by the Manitoba Court of Queen's Bench, and by the Manitoba Appeal Court. It was heard by the Supreme Court on December 6. The Canadian Institute of Chartered Accountants gained status with the court to argue in favor of protecting auditors from liability.

The court's ruling does not declare whether Ernst & Young was negligent.

On the issue of liability, the court said audited financial reports only call for "a duty of care" by the auditors when they are used "as a guide for the shareholders, as a group, in supervising or overseeing management."

For this reason, there appears to be no direct liability to the shareholders for any reduction in value of their equity, jointly or individually.

"The law in Canada in respect of the responsibility of auditors is basically consistent with the United Kingdom, the United States and many other countries," Rayner said.

"I feel that I have been run over by a truck," said Mark Schulman, of the Winnipeg law firm of Schulman and Schulman, who acted for Hercules.

He points out that one motions judge, three judges of the court of appeal and seven judges in the Supreme Court all ruled against Hercules, and thoroughly entrenched the principle of no general auditor liability.

Eprile pointed out that auditors are already liable, under securities acts to investors, in the narrow case when the audited financial statements appear in a prospectus.

"We are recommending that we amend our securities legislation . . . to call for liability in the [entire] secondary market," she said.

That would mean that the public company, the auditor, the directors and possibly the underwriters would be liable for any negligent disclosure when investors buy a company's shares through a stock exchange.

The legislation has been drafted, Eprile said. It would be uniform across Canada and may take a year or two to get through provincial legislatures, she said.

Source: Philip Mathias, "Auditors Not Legally Liable to Investors, Top Court Rules," *The Financial Post*, May 24, 1997, p. 3. Sun Media Corp.

This legislation creates a statutory law civil liability for PAs and others accused of misleading the public. The legislation could allow class action lawsuits against PAs, placing the burden of proof on the defendant PA that a drop in the client's share price was due to a financial statement misrepresentation (the "fraud on the market" theory used by the SEC in the

U.S.). In other words, once a misrepresentation has been identified, it is up to the auditor to show that any losses suffered by investors were not due to the misrepresentation. The plaintiff would not have the burden of proving negligence by the PA. However, the proposed legislation could put caps on the PA's liability, as well as use the proportionate rather than the joint and several liability rule. Moreover, these limitations on liability would not apply if the PA knowingly deceived the market.[12]

Although Bill 198 was passed in December 2002, it was not proclaimed (put into force) until late 2004 and went into effect December 2005. The article below discusses the significance of this legislation.

These legislative initiatives seem to be inspired by U.S. statutory law covered in Appendix 5B. It should be noted that PAs in Canada already have similar liabilities for initial public offerings of securities. The new legislation extends the liability to subsequent financial statements of companies already listed on the TSE. But such an extension would expose the Canadian PA to far more potential legal liability than is currently the case.

LAW TO MAKE IT EASIER FOR INVESTORS TO SUE

MORE GROUNDS FOR SUITS

So you lost money on a stock and want to sue the company for misleading statements.

What's already a common practice in the United States is coming to Canada. Canadian public companies are readying themselves for broad new legislation that will greatly increase investors' ability to file civil lawsuits against them.

The new civil liability legislation will come out by the end of the year and substantially widens the type of disclosure investors can use as a basis for litigation.

This means that false or misleading information in press releases and financial statements will soon be fair game. It can even extend to public oral statements, such as conference calls or speeches, made by authorized company representatives. Currently, investor lawsuits are limited to information in a prospectus.

This new addition to the *Ontario Securities Act* was actually introduced by the provincial government in late 2004. But the clock is now ticking for companies to get their disclosure models in order, since it comes into effect Dec. 31. . . .

"This may constitute the biggest change to Canadian securities law in the last 25 years," according to a report by law firm Borden Ladner Gervais LLP.

One of the most significant parts of the new law is how plaintiffs will no longer have to prove they relied on the misrepresentation when investing in a company. For example, under the current legislation, an investor would have to say "I bought this stock reliant on XX amount of earnings, and it turns out they were really XXX . . . I relied on this information and I can prove it," said Paul Findlay, a lawyer at Borden Ladner who co-wrote the report.

This was a significant stumbling block to class-action suits in Ontario, since they typically involve groups of shareholders and it was pretty much impossible to prove that each investor had looked at and relied on the information in question, he added.

With this impediment removed, there's little doubt there will be an increase in securities class-action lawsuits in the province. Plus, it could make it more attractive for shareholders to file suits against cross-listed Canadian companies here, Mr. Findlay said. In the past, these actions have often taken place in the United States, which already has some provisions for materially false and misleading information in continuous disclosure.

Source: Lori McLeod, "Law to make it easier for investors to sue: More grounds for suits," *The National Post*, Friday, November 15, 2005, p. FP12. Material reprinted with the express permission of: "National Post Company," a CanWest Partnership.

---

[12] See M. Paskell-Mede, *CA Magazine*, June/July, 2003, pp. 34–36 for more details.

OTHER ISSUES

1. Fiduciary Duty of Accountants

According to an article by G. McLennan, a unique feature of Canadian common law that may precipitate a litigation crisis here is the expanding concept of fiduciary duty as it applies to accountants. An accountant may be a fiduciary in many different situations, including when he or she acts as a trustee, receiver, auditor or simply an adviser to a peculiarly vulnerable client. Accountants may also be liable for simply assisting someone who is a fiduciary to another, although this would only be the case where a PA knows the fiduciary relationship and knows it is being dishonestly breached.

Allegations of a breach of fiduciary duty have become increasingly common in lawsuits against accountants in Canada. If a court concludes that an accountant is a fiduciary, he or she may be held responsible for damages, even though (1) the PA's conduct did not cause the damage, (2) the plaintiff failed to take reasonable steps to mitigate those damages, or (3) the plaintiff was partially at fault or other third parties contributed to the damages suffered. Thus, common defences to a negligence action, such as contributory negligence, remoteness of damages, failure to mitigate and no duty of care, do not apply to an action in breach of fiduciary duty.

Literally, fiduciary means "trust-like," but the term has been used in so many contexts in the courts that it is applied as if it related to, among other things, all breaches of duty by accountants.

The closest thing to legal definition is that set forth in the Supreme Court of Canada decision concerning *LAC Minerals* v. *Corona Resources*. In *LAC Minerals* the court stated there were three factors to consider when determining if a fiduciary duty exists:

1. The fiduciary has scope for the exercise of some discretion or power.
2. The fiduciary can unilaterally exercise that power or discretion so as to affect the beneficiary's legal or practical interests.
3. The beneficiary is peculiarly vulnerable to or at the mercy of the fiduciary who is holding the discretion or power.

Case law provides illustrations when such a duty exists; the article by M. Paskell-Mede reviews several of these cases. Generally, when an accountant acts as a receiver/manager or trustee in insolvency situations, he or she owes a fiduciary duty to creditors of an insolvent corporation. Where an accountant has an established relationship with one lender, it may be that it is a breach of fiduciary duty to also act as a trustee or receiver of the insolvent borrower. Accountants that act as financial advisers or tax advisers also have a fiduciary duty. Accountants that have successfully defended themselves in lawsuits involving breach of fiduciary duty have done so by showing that either factors 1 or 3 in the definition were not present.[13]

2. Confidentiality Versus Misleading Financial Statements

In Chapter 4 we noted that there may be a potential conflict between rules dealing with confidentiality and rules dealing with association with misleading financial statements. There is a conflict between similar rules in the U.S. code that has been the focus of two court cases there: *Consolidata Services* v. *Alexander Grant* (1981) and *Fund of Funds* v. *Arthur Andersen* (1982). In *Consolidata*, the courts ruled that auditors should have preserved confidentiality, and in *Fund of Funds*, the courts ruled that the confidential information should have been used to prevent misleading reports. The inconsistent legal results from these two

---

[13] G. McLennan, "Trust Not," *CA Magazine* (June-July, 1993), pp. 40–43 and M. Paskell-Mede, "Adviser Relationships," *CA Magazine*, May 1995, pp. 27–32.

cases illustrate that the rules can be just as difficult to resolve for the courts as they are for practising auditors. In both cases, however, it was the auditors who lost—and paid. (The court awarded damages to Fund of Fund's shareholders in the amount of $80 million, the largest judgement ever made against a public accounting firm until that time.)

3. Legal Liability Implications for Auditor Practice

As a result of the increasingly litigious climate, auditors ought to

(*a*) be wary of what kind of clients are accepted

(*b*) know (thoroughly) the client's business (KNOB)

(*c*) perform quality audits:

   (*i*) use qualified personnel, properly trained and supervised, and motivated

   (*ii*) obtain sufficient evidence (including proper elicitation of oral evidence and documentation of client's oral evidence)

   (*iii*) prepare good working papers

   (*iv*) obtain engagement and representation letters

The increased litigation has also caused improvements in audit working paper files through:

(*a*) use of forceful management letters that are "unambiguous and couched in terms of alarm with respect to problematic internal controls or sloppy bookkeeping

(*b*) use of detailed memos in the working papers describing the conversation with the client and accompanied by a follow-up letter to the client

(*c*) use of a letter to the client or note to the file documenting discussions to reduce audit fees or changing to a review engagement"[14]

Legal Liability for Failure to Disclose Illegal Acts

Handbook, section 5136, "Misstatements—illegal acts," provides expanded guidance on detecting and disclosing illegal acts or possibly illegal acts. One of the objectives of this *Handbook* section is to reduce the auditor's exposure to legal liability. It does this (1) by reducing the risk that GAAS will be misinterpreted by auditors and the courts; (2) by establishing recommendations for the auditors to follow, such as that of obtaining written representation from management about illegal acts, that reduce the likelihood of an audit failing to detect a material misstatement arising from the consequences of an illegal act; and (3) by providing a defence for the auditor if he or she fails to detect a material misstatement despite conducting the audit in accordance with the standards.[15]

Illegal acts is another area where potential ethical and legal conflicts may now be expected to grow. According to an article by M. Paskell-Mede, the whistle-blowing responsibility of the auditor to third parties may be expected to grow even in the absence of a regulator since plaintiffs are raising the issues of association more frequently in lawsuits. It is Paskell-Mede's impression that plaintiffs whose lawyers recognize that their case is weak—as a result of inability to demonstrate either actual reliance on the financial statements or that a direct duty of care was owed with respect to those statements—are now compensating for this weakness by presenting the claim as one based on association. In such instances, the plaintiff's lawyer will argue that their client relied on the auditor's reputation. However, the courts so far have upheld the obligation for auditors to maintain client confidentiality. For example, in *Transamerica Financial Corporation, Canada* v. *Dunwoody & Company,* the judge decided that client confidentiality overrode whistle-blowing to a third-party plaintiff, especially since the plaintiff was already aware of irregularities at the client. For

---

[14] M. Paskell-Mede, "So Sue Me," *CA Magazine,* February 1991, pp. 36–38.
[15] V. Murusalu, "Drawing the Line," *CA Magazine,* January/February 1995, pp. 68–69.

Paskell-Mede, this is evidence that the courts are becoming more careful about assigning blame to auditors—that they are becoming more sophisticated in analyzing the causal connection between the illegal misrepresentation and damages.[16]

Is There an Auditor Liability Crisis in Canada?

Some people argue that there is no auditor's legal liability crisis in Canada. M. Paskell-Mede takes this position and gives a review of the differences between the American and Canadian legal systems concerning auditors' legal liability. In the United States, pending suits against auditors total about US$20 billion. There is a definite crisis there. Do we have a problem of the same magnitude in Canada?

The author does not think so and identifies some important differences:

1. Jury trials are common in the United States for civil cases but "virtually extinct" for auditor liability suits in Canada. American juries tend to be more sympathetic to plaintiffs and swayed by factors other than the evidence. Judges are less influenced by the drama of the courtroom setting, and tend to be better experienced and better trained in dealing with commercial disputes.

2. Punitive damages are not available in Canada for mere negligence. Moreover, any damages awarded are only a fraction of the compensatory damages assessed (instead of the multiples used in the United States).

3. In Canada the unsuccessful party must pay up to 50 to 60 percent of the legal fees of the opposing side and possible other costs (e.g., 1 percent of the amount claimed). This tends to discourage frivolous suits.

4. Class actions (a few suing on behalf of many) are much rarer in Canada because of the belief here that each plaintiff may rely on the accountant's work differently. This is changing, however, with more provinces allowing class actions, as noted earlier.

5. The U.S. national regulator, the SEC (nothing comparable in Canada), uses the "fraud on the market" theory, which assumes that the entire market for shares is affected by misrepresentations. This greatly increases the liability exposure of auditors of publicly traded companies.

"Faced with these differences it seems safe to assume that Canadian accountants will not face lawsuits of the same magnitude and frequency as those experienced by U.S. accountants, assuming no fundamental changes to our legal systems. On the other hand, lawsuits in Canada are getting larger and some CA firms may soon exceed their insurance limits and be forced into bankruptcy. Thus it may simply be a matter of time before we, too, face a liability crisis."[17]

Others argue that the profession has been facing a liability crisis since the 1980s. In a series of articles entitled "Auditing in Crisis" in the March 1990 issue of the *Financial Post*, the following points were made:

A vicious cycle had started by 1990 in that due to severe competition (partly caused by the many mergers in the 1980s) audit fees had been lowered, resulting in lower-quality audits. This, combined with more aggressive reporting, resulted in more problem audits, which in turn increased lawsuits. Plaintiffs also were increasingly of the type that can litigate indefinitely (financial institutions, government agencies). This came at a time of increased policing of accounting firms by regulators such as the OSC. As a result, the total number of lawsuits increased dramatically starting in the 1980s. For example, there were 18 major lawsuits initiated between 1985 and 1990. Compare this to a total of 9 between 1917 and 1984. In addition to the increased lawsuits, the damage awards per lawsuit have increased dramatically. This, combined with an exponential growth in lawsuits in the United States, has greatly increased North American professional liability insurance premiums (premiums have risen by 10 percent per year).

[16] M. Paskell-Mede, "Tales of Sherwood Forest," *CA Magazine*, August 1994, pp. 47–48.
[17] M. Paskell-Mede, "What Liability Crisis," *CA Magazine*, May 1994, pp. 42–43.

The series of articles also provides much anecdotal evidence that there are sometimes serious problems in many auditor–client relationships. For example, according to a vice president of finance of a major Canadian company, "it's very easy for management to browbeat an auditor at any time in the audit," and "anything goes unless there is a rule to the contrary (in the *Handbook*)."

To combat these problems, key recommendations developed in an article by M.F. Murray were that the auditors report to a company's audit committee, that standard setters should reduce the number of accounting alternatives in GAAP, that auditors need more guidance on how to report on a company's ability to continue and that auditors need to better document high-risk clients and be ready to take immediate defensive measures. Some firms now even "fire" their troublesome clients. Some warning signs of potentially troublesome clients include financial or organizational difficulty, involvement in suspicious transactions, uncooperativeness, fee pressures, refusal to sign engagement and representation letters, and frequent involvement in litigation.

Before accepting clients, PAs should ask why clients are changing accountants, visit the client's business, meet their accounting and tax personnel and check their references. A useful client acceptance checklist could be used that documents whether a client should be accepted for an engagement. This form should be prepared before the engagement letter is submitted. If this screening does not result in rejection of an existing or prospective client, it may also be used to identify engagements that require extra precautions, such as very precise engagement letters and advance collection of fees.[18] In the post-Enron environment, these recommendations have become standard practice and will likely be mandatory once the various new accountability boards and newly empowered regulators develop their own tightened requirements.

SUMMARY

Litigation against accountants has virtually exploded in the United States and to a lesser extent in Canada. Damage claims of hundreds of millions of dollars have been paid by PA firms and their insurers. Insurance is expensive and hard to obtain. The SEC has sued two of the five largest accounting firms for securities fraud within the last two years. One of these firms, Arthur Andersen, paid fines of $7 million and later was convicted of "obstructing justice" and forced into bankruptcy. Accountants are not alone in this rash of litigation, which affects manufacturers, architects, doctors and people in many other walks of life. The professional accounting organizations have joined with other interest groups pushing for "tort reform" of various types (e.g., limitation of damages, identification of liability) in an effort to stem the tide. Other effects of this climate take the form of changing the nature of organizations in which public accountants practice (such as to LLPs).

Accountants' liability to clients and third parties under common law has expanded. Fifty years ago, a strict privity doctrine required other parties to be in a contract with and known to the accountant before they could sue for damages based on negligence.

Of course, if an accountant was grossly negligent in such a way that his or her actions amounted to constructive fraud, liability exists as it would for anyone who committed a fraud. Over the years the privity doctrine was modified in many jurisdictions, leading to liability for ordinary negligence to primary beneficiaries (known users) of the accountants' work product, then to liability based on ordinary negligence to foreseen and foreseeable beneficiaries (users not so easily known). While the general movement has been to expand accountants' liability for ordinary negligence, some jurisdictions have held closer to the privity doctrine of the past. The treatment can vary from province to province. The *Kripps* v. *Touche Ross* case discussed in this chapter has also called into question the sufficiency of conformity with GAAP defense in Canada, but it is unclear what alternative standards auditors will be held to. Future court cases will likely clarify this issue.

[18] M.F. Murray, "When a Client Is a Liability," *Journal of Accountancy*, September 1992, pp. 54–58.

Accountants' liability under statutory law is also growing rapidly, especially the potentially wide influence of Ontario's Bill 198 on other Canadian provinces, the changes in the CBCA and Bill C-22, which can label accountants as "racketeers." Regulatory laws in the United States greatly changed the obligations of public accountants. Canadian PAs whose clients obtain financing from the United States may be affected by these laws, and these laws also have had an influence on Canadian laws such as Bill 198.

Under common law a plaintiff suing an accountant had to bring all the proof of the accountant's negligence to the court and convince the judge or jury. In the case of a public offering of securities registered in a registration statement filed under a *U.S. Securities Act* or Ontario's Bill 198, the plaintiff only needs to show evidence of a loss and that the financial statements were materially misleading. Case rested. Then, the accountant shoulders the burden of proof of showing that the audit was performed properly or that the loss resulted from some other cause. The burden of proof has thus shifted from the plaintiff to the defendant. The securities acts also impose criminal penalties in some cases. As indicated throughout the chapter, many commentators feel that the profession is in the midst of a liability crisis that imposes major changes in auditor responsibilities.

Appendix 5A explains Bill C-22 and other statutory laws affecting accountants and corporate governance. This appendix also reviews detailed discussion of internal controls in subsequent chapters.

Appendix 5B reviews U.S. statutory law in some detail because many court cases setting legal precedents for accountants were launched as a result of these statutory laws.

Both appendices are located on the Online Learning Centre.

MULTIPLE-CHOICE QUESTIONS FOR PRACTICE AND REVIEW

5.8   Under the Foreign Corrupt Practices Act of 1977:
   a. Companies must refrain from bribing foreign politicians for commercial advantage.
   b. Independent auditors must audit all elements of a company's internal control system.
   c. Companies must establish control systems to keep books, records and accounts properly.
   d. Independent auditors must establish control systems to keep books, records and accounts properly.

5.9   The management accountants employed by Robbins, Inc., wrongfully charged executives' personal expences to the overhead on a government contract. Their activities can be characterized as:
   a. Errors in the application of accounting principles.
   b. Irregularities of the type of independent auditors should plan an audit to detect.
   c. Irregularities of the type independent auditors have no responsibility to plan an audit to detect.
   d. Illegal acts of a type independent auditors should be aware might occur in government contract business.

5.10   Which of these laws does the U.S. Securities and Exchange Commission not administer?
   a. Securities Act of 1933.
   b. Securities and Exchange Act of 1934.
   c. Racketeer Influenced and Corrupt Organization Act.
   d. Foreign Corrupt Practices Act of 1977.

5.11   Good Gold Company sold $20 million of preferred shares. The company should have registered the offering under the Securities Act of 1933 if it were sold to:
   a. 150 accredited investors.
   b. One insurance company.
   c. 30 investors all resident in one state.
   d. Diverse customers of a brokerage firm.

5.12   When a company registers a security offering under the Securities Act of 1933, the law provides an investor with:
   a. An SEC guarantee that the information in the registration statement is true.
   b. Insurance against loss from the investment.
   c. Financial information about the company audited by independent PAs.
   d. Inside information about the company's trade secrets.

5.13   A group of investors sued Anderson, Olds & Watershed, PAs, for alleged damages suffered when the company in which they held common shares went bankrupt. In order to avoid liability under the common law, AOW must prove which of the following?
   a. The investors actually suffered a loss.
   b. The investors relied on the financial statements audited by AOW.
   c. The investors' loss was a direct result of their reliance on the audited financial statements.
   d. The audit was conducted in accordance with generally accepted auditing standards and with due professional care.

5.14 The Securities and Exchange Commission document that governs accounting in financial statements filed with the SEC is:
   a. Regulation D.
   b. Form 8-K.
   c. Form S-18.
   d. Regulation S-X.

5.15 Able Corporation plans to sell $10 million common shares to investors. The company can do so without filing an S-1 registration statement under the Securities Act (1933) if Able sells the shares:
   a. To an investment banker who then sells them to investors in its national retail network.
   b. To no more than 75 investors solicited at random.
   c. Only to accredited investors.
   d. Only to 35 accredited investors and an unlimited number of unaccredited investors.

5.16 A "public company" subject to the periodic reporting requirements of the Exchange Act (1934) must file an annual report with the SEC known as the:
   a. Form 10-K.
   b. Form 10-Q.
   c. Form 8-K.
   d. Form S-3.

5.17 When investors sue auditors for damages under Section 11 of the Securities Act (1933), they must allege and prove:
   a. Scienter on the part of the auditor.
   b. That the audited financial statements were materially misleading.
   c. That they relied on the misleading audited financial statements.
   d. That their reliance on the misleading financial statements was the direct cause of their loss.

EXERCISES AND PROBLEMS

5.18 **Responsibility for Errors and Irregularities.** Huffman & Whitman, a large regional PA firm, was engaged
L0.2 by the Ritter Tire Wholesale Company to audit its financial statements for the year ended January 31. Huffman & Whitman had a busy audit engagement schedule from December 31 through April 1, and they decided to audit Ritter's purchase vouchers and related cash disbursements on a sample basis. They instructed staff accountants to select a random sample of 130 purchase transactions and gave directions about the important deviations, including missing receiving reports. Boyd, the assistant in charge, completed the working papers, properly documenting the fact that 13 of the purchases in the sample had been recorded and paid without the receiving report (required by stated internal control procedures) being included in the file of supporting documents. Whitman, the partner in direct charge of the audit, showed the findings to Lock, Ritter's chief accountant. Lock appeared surprised but promised that the missing receiving reports would be inserted into the files before the audit was over. Whitman was satisfied, noted in the workpapers that the problem was solved, and did not say anything to Huffman about it.

Unfortunately, H&W did not discover the fact that Lock was involved in a fraudulent scheme in which he diverted shipments to a warehouse leased in his name and sent the invoices to Ritter for payment. He then sold the tires for his own profit. Internal auditors discovered the scheme during a study of slow-moving inventory items. Ritter's inventory was overstated by about $500,000 (20 percent)—the amount Lock had diverted.

Required:
   a. With regard to the 13 missing receiving reports, does a material weakness in internal control exist? If so,

does Huffman & Whitman have any further audit responsibility? Explain.
   b. Was the audit conducted in a negligent manner?

5.19 **Responsibility for Errors and Irregularities.** Herbert
L0.2 McCoy is the president of McCoy Forging Corporation. For the past several years, Donovan & Company, PAs, has done the company's compilation and some other accounting and tax work. McCoy decided to have an audit. Moreover, McCoy had recently received a disturbing anonymous letter that stated: "Beware, you have a viper in your nest. The money is literally disappearing before your very eyes! Signed: A friend." He told no one about the letter.

McCoy Forging engaged Donovan & Company, PAs, to render an opinion on the financial statements for the year ended June 30, 2003. McCoy told Donovan he wanted to verify that the financial statements were "accurate and proper." He did not mention the anonymous letter. The usual engagement letter providing for an audit in accordance with generally accepted auditing standards (GAAS) was drafted by Donovan & Company and signed by both parties.

The audit was performed in accordance with GAAS. The audit did not reveal a clever defalcation plan. Harper, the assistant treasurer, was siphoning off substantial amounts of McCoy Forging's money. The defalcations occurred both before and after the audit. Harper's embezzlement was discovered by McCoy's new internal auditor in October 2003, after Donovan had delivered the audit report. Although the scheme was fairly sophisticated, it could have been detected if Donovan & Company had performed additional procedures. McCoy Forging demands reimbursement from Donovan for the entire amount of the embezzlement, some $40,000 of which occurred before the audit and $65,000 after. Donovan has denied any liability and refuses to pay.

Required:

Discuss Donovan's responsibility in this situation. Do you think McCoy Forging would prevail in whole or in part in a lawsuit against Donovan under common law? Explain your conclusions.

(AICPA adapted)

5.20 **Common Law Liability Exposure.** A PA firm was en-
LO.2 gaged to examine the financial statements of Martin Manufacturing Corporation for the year ending December 31. Martin needed cash to continue its operations and agreed to sell its common share investment in a subsidiary through a private placement. The buyers insisted that the proceeds be placed in escrow because of the possibility of a major contingent tax liability that might result from a pending government claim against Martin's subsidiary. The payment in escrow was completed in late November. The president of Martin told the audit partner that the proceeds from the sale of the subsidiary's common shares, held in escrow, should be shown on the balance sheet as an unrestricted current account receivable. The president was of the opinion that the government's claim was groundless and that Martin needed an "uncluttered" balance sheet and a "clean" auditor's opinion to obtain additional working capital from lenders. The audit partner agreed with the president and issued an unqualified opinion on the Martin financial statements, which did not refer to the contingent liability and did not properly describe the escrow arrangement.

The government's claim proved to be valid, and, pursuant to the agreement with the buyers, the purchase price of the subsidiary was reduced by $450,000. This adverse development forced Martin into bankruptcy. The PA firm is being sued for deceit (fraud) by several of Martin's unpaid creditors who extended credit in reliance on the PA firm's unqualified opinion on Martin's financial statements.

Required:

a. What deceit (fraud) do you believe the creditors are claiming?
b. Is the lack of privity between the PA firm and the creditors important in this case?
c. Do you believe the PA firm is liable to the creditors? Explain.

(AICPA adapted)

5.21 **Common Law Liability Exposure.** Risk Capital Lim-
LO.2 ited, an Alberta corporation, was considering the purchase of a substantial amount of treasury shares held by Sunshine Corporation, a closely held corporation. Initial discussions with the Sunshine Corporation began late in 2002.

Wilson and Wyatt, Sunshine's accountants, regularly prepared quarterly and annual unaudited financial statements. The most recently prepared financial statements were for the year ended September 30, 2002.

On November 15, 2002, after extensive negotiations, Risk Capital agreed to purchase 100,000 shares of no par, class A capital shares of Sunshine at $12.50 per share. However, Risk Capital insisted on audited statements for calendar year 2002. The contract that was made available to Wilson and Wyatt specifically provided:

Risk Capital shall have the right to rescind the purchase of said shares if the audited financial statements of Sunshine for the calendar year 2002 show a material adverse change in the financial condition of the corporation.

The audited financial statements furnished to Sunshine by Wilson and Wyatt showed no such material adverse change. Risk Capital relied on the audited statements and purchased the treasury shares of Sunshine. It was subsequently discovered that, as of the balance sheet date, the audited statements were incorrect and that in fact there had been a material adverse change in the financial condition of the corporation. Sunshine is insolvent, and Risk Capital will lose virtually its entire investment.

Risk Capital seeks recovery against Wilson and Wyatt.

Required:

Assuming that only ordinary negligence is proved, will Risk Capital prevail:
a. Under the *Ultramares* decision?
b. Under the *Rusch Factors* decision?

5.22 **Common Law Liability Exposure.** Smith, PA, is the
LO.2 auditor for Juniper Manufacturing Corporation, a privately owned company that has a June 30 fiscal year. Juniper arranged for a substantial bank loan, which was dependent on the bank receiving, by September 30, audited financial statements showing a current ratio of at least 2 to 1. On September 25, just before the audit report was to be issued, Smith received an anonymous letter on Juniper's stationery indicating that a five-year lease by Juniper, as lessee, of a factory building that was accounted for in the financial statements as an operating lease was in fact a capital lease. The letter stated that there was a secret written agreement with the lessor modifying the lease and creating a capital lease.

Smith confronted the president of Juniper, who admitted that a secret agreement existed but said it was necessary to treat the lease as an operating lease to meet the current ratio requirement of the pending loan and that nobody would ever discover the secret agreement with the lessor. The president said that, if Smith did not issue his report by September 30, Juniper would sue Smith for substantial damages that would result from not getting the loan. Under this pressure and because the working papers contained a copy of the five-year lease agreement supporting the operating lease treatment, Smith issued his report with an unqualified opinion on September 29. In spite of the fact that the loan was received, Juniper went bankrupt. The bank is suing Smith to recover its losses on the loan and the lessor is suing Smith to recover uncollected rents.

Required:
Answer the following, setting forth reasons for any conclusions stated:
a. Is Smith liable to the bank?
b. Is Smith liable to the lessor?
c. Was Smith independent?

(AICPA adapted)

5.23 **Common Law Liability Exposure.** Farr and Madison,
LO.2 PAs, audited Glamour, Inc. Their audit was deficient in several respects:
1. Farr and Madison failed to audit properly certain receivables, which later proved to be fictitious.
2. With respect to other receivables, although they made a cursory check, they did not detect many accounts that were long overdue and obviously uncollectible.
3. No physical inventory was taken of the securities claimed to be in Glamour's possession, which in fact had been sold. Both the securities and cash received from the sales were listed on the balance sheet as assets.

There is no indication that Farr and Madison actually believed the financial statements were false. Subsequent creditors, not known to Farr and Madison, are now suing based on the deficiencies in the audit described above. Farr and Madison moved to dismiss the lawsuit against it on the basis that the firm did not have actual knowledge of falsity and therefore did not commit fraud.

Required:
May the creditors recover without demonstrating that Farr and Madison had actual knowledge of falsity? Explain.

5.24 **Liability in a Review Engagement.** Mason and Dil-
LO.2 worth, PAs, were the accountants for Hotshot Company, a closely held corporation owned by 30 residents of the area. M&D had been previously engaged by Hotshot to perform some compilation and tax work. Bubba Crass, Hotshot's president and holder of 15 percent of the shares, said he needed something more than these services. He told Mason, the partner in charge, that he wanted financial statements for internal use, primarily for management purposes, but also to obtain short-term loans from financial institutions. Mason recommended a "review" of the financial statements. Mason did not prepare an engagement letter.

During the review work, Mason had some reservations about the financial statements. Mason told Dilworth at various times he was "uneasy about certain figures and conclusions," but that he would "take Crass's word about the validity of certain entries since the review was primarily for internal use in any event and was not an audit." M&D did not discover a material act of fraud committed by Crass. The fraud would have been detected had Mason not relied so much on the unsupported statements made by Crass concerning the validity of the entries about which he had felt so uneasy.

Required:
a. What potential liability might M&D have to Hotshot Company and other shareholders?
b. What potential liability might M&D have to financial institutions that used the financial statements in connection with making loans to Hotshot Company?

(AICPA adapted)

5.25 **Regulation D Exemption.** One of your firm's clients,
LO.3 Fancy Fashions, Inc., is a highly successful, rapidly ex-
and panding company. It is owned predominantly by the
LO.5 Munster family and key corporate officials. Although additional funds would be available on a short-term basis from its bankers, this would only represent a temporary solution of the company's need for capital to finance its expansion plans. In addition, the interest rates being charged are not appealing. Therefore, John Munster, Fancy's chairman of the board, in consultation with the other shareholders, has decided to explore the possibility of raising additional equity capital of approximately $15 million to $16 million. This will be Fancy's first public offering to investors, other than the Munster family and the key management personnel.

At a meeting of Fancy's major shareholders, its lawyers and a PA from your firm spoke about the advantages and disadvantages of "going public" and registering a share offering in the United States. One of the shareholders suggested that Regulation D under the Securities Act of 1933 might be a preferable alternative.

Required:
a. Assume Fancy makes a public offering for $16 million and, as a result, more than 1,000 persons own shares of the company. What are the implications with respect to the Securities Exchange Act of 1934?
b. What federal civil and criminal liabilities may apply in the event that Fancy sells the securities without registration and a registration exemption is not available?
c. Discuss the exemption applicable to offerings under Regulation D, in terms of two kinds of investors, and how many of each can participate.

(AICPA adapted)

5.26 **Applicability of Securities Act and Exchange Act.**
LO.3 1. The partnership of Zelsch & Company, PAs, has
and been engaged to audit the financial statements of
LO.5 Snake Oil, Inc., in connection with filing an S-1 registration statement under the Securities Act (1933). Discuss the following two statements made by the senior partner of Zelsch & Company.
   a. "The partnership is assuming a much greater liability exposure in this engagement than exists under common law."
   b. "If our examination is not fraudulent, we can avoid any liability claims that might arise."
2. Xavier, Francis & Paul is a growing, medium-sized partnership of PAs located in the Midwest. One of

the firm's major clients is considering offering its shares to the public. This will be the firm's first client to go public. State whether the following are true or false. Explain each.

  a. The firm should thoroughly familiarize itself with the securities acts, Regulation S-X, and Regulation S-K.
  b. If the client is unincorporated, the Securities Act (1933) will not apply.
  c. If the client is going to be listed on an organized exchange, the Exchange Act (1934) will not apply.
  d. The Securities Act (1933) imposes an additional potential liability on firms such as Xavier, Francis & Paul.
  e. So long as the company engages in exclusively intrastate business, the federal securities laws will not apply.

5.27 Section 11 of Securities Act (1933) Liability Exposure.
LO.3 and LO.5
The Chriswell Corporation decided to raise additional long-term capital by issuing $20 million of 12 percent subordinated debentures to the public. May, Clark & Company, PAs, the company's auditors, were engaged to examine the June 30, 1993, financial statements, which were included in the bond registration statement.

May, Clark & Company completed its examination and submitted an unqualified auditor's report dated July 15, 1993. The registration statement was filed and became effective on September 1, 1993. On August 15 one of the partners of May, Clark & Company called on Chriswell Corporation and had lunch with the financial vice president and the controller. He questioned both officials on the company's operations since June 30 and enquired whether there had been any material changes in the company's financial position since that date. Both officers assured him that everything had proceeded normally and that the financial condition of the company had not changed materially.

Unfortunately, the officers' representation was not true. On July 30 a substantial debtor of the company failed to pay the $400,000 due on its account receivable and indicated to Chriswell that it would probably be forced into bankruptcy. This receivable was shown as a collateralized loan on the June 30 financial statements. It was secured by shares of the debtor corporation, which had a value in excess of the loan at the time the financial statements were prepared but was virtually worthless at the effective date of the registration statement. This $400,000 account receivable was material to the financial condition of Chriswell Corporation, and the market price of the subordinated debentures decreased by nearly 50 percent after the foregoing facts were disclosed.

The debenture holders of Chriswell are seeking recovery of their loss against all parties connected with the debenture registration.

Required:
Is May, Clark & Company liable to the Chriswell debenture holders under Section 11 of the Securities Act

(1933)? Explain. (Hint: Review the *BarChris* case in Chapter 5.)

(AICPA adapted)

5.28 Rule 10b-5 Liability Exposure under the Exchange Act (1934).
LO.3 and LO.5
Gordon & Groton, PAs, were the auditors of Bank & Company, a brokerage firm and member of a national stock exchange. G&G examined and reported on the financial statements of Bank, which were filed with the Securities and Exchange Commission.

Several of Bank's customers were swindled by a fraudulent scheme perpetrated by Bank's president, who owned 90 percent of the voting shares of the company. The facts establish that Gordon & Groton were negligent in the conduct of the audit but neither participated in the fraudulent scheme nor knew of its existence.

The customers are suing G&G under the antifraud provisions of Section 10(b) and Rule 10b-5 of the *Exchange Act* (1934) for aiding and abetting the fraudulent scheme of the president. The customers' suit for fraud is predicated exclusively on the negligence of G&G in failing to conduct a proper audit, thereby failing to discover the fraudulent scheme.

Required:
Answer the following, setting forth reasons for any conclusions stated:
  a. What is the probable outcome of the lawsuit?
  b. What might be the result if plaintiffs had sued under a common law theory of negligence? Explain.

(AICPA adapted)

5.29 Foreign Corrupt Practices Act.
LO.3 and LO.4
Major Manufacturing Company is a large diversified international corporation whose shares trade on the New York Stock Exchange. The U.S. Department of Justice and the SEC have investigated the Global Oil Well Equipment Company, a subsidiary of Major. The agencies allege that Global has engaged in activities clearly in violation of the *Foreign Corrupt Practices Act*.

Tobias (Global president), Wilton (vice president), and Clark (regional manager of operations in Nogoland) have conspired to make payments to influential members of Nogoland's Parliament in order to influence legislation in Global's favour. The agencies allege that Tobias, Wilton and Clark met secretly in Geneva and decided to give inducements to Mr. Rock, the Speaker of Nogoland's Parliament. They made a $750,000 loan to Mr. Rock's manufacturing business at a 2 percent interest rate. They gave a $10,000 diamond to Mrs. Rock as a memento of the Rock's wedding anniversary. They paid Jeremy Rock's tuition to medical school. These expenditures were classified as investments, commissions and promotion expenses in the Global financial statements. Their nature and purpose were not otherwise disclosed.

Required:
  a. What provisions of the FCPA have apparently been violated by these actions by Global and its officers?
  b. What penalties might be assessed on the corporation, if convicted? on Tobias, Wilton and Clark?

(AICPA adapted)

5.30 Management Fraud Probability Assessment. This is
LO.3 an exercise designed to reveal some facts of reasoning
and and decision making. The "fraud involvement test" is
LO.5 fictional.

A team of accountants and psychologists has developed a procedure to test for the existence of management involvement in fraudulent activities. The procedure consists of developing a personality profile of key managers and relating this profile to a master profile compiled from interviews conducted by clinical psychologists with a substantial number of individuals who have admitted to perpetrating material frauds. If the manager's profile is sufficiently similar to the master profile, the test signals "fraud." If there is not sufficient similarity, the test signals "no fraud." In the last 18 months, the procedure has been tested extensively in the field by a national public accounting firm and it has found the following:

- If a key manager has been involved in a material fraud, the test procedure indicates "fraud" 8 times out of 10.
- If a key manager has not been involved in a material fraud, the test will nonetheless indicate "fraud" 20 times out of 100.
- The evidence indicates that about 10 key managers in 100 have been involved in material fraud.

Based on these results, what is your assessment of the probability that a key manager who receives a "fraud" test signal is actually involved in fraudulent activities?

5.31 Audit Report and Legal Liabilities. The auditor's re-
LO.2 port below was drafted by Smith, a staff accountant at
the firm of Wong & Wilson, PAs, at the completion of
the audit of the financial statements of PPC Ltd., a publicly held company, for the year ended March 31, 2003.
The report was submitted to the engagement partner,
who reviewed the audit working papers and properly
concluded that an unqualified opinion should be issued.
In drafting the report, Smith considered the following:

- During the fiscal year, PPC changed its amortization method for capital assets. The engagement partner concurred with this change in accounting principles and its justification, and Smith included an explanatory paragraph in the auditor's report.
- The 2003 statements are affected by an uncertainty concerning a lawsuit, the outcome of which cannot presently be estimated. Smith has included an explanatory paragraph in the auditor's report.
- The financial statements for the year ended March 31, 2002 are to be presented for comparative purposes. Wong & Wilson had previously audited these statements and expressed an unqualified opinion.

The report which Smith drafted appears below:

Independent Auditor's Report
To the Board of Directors of PPC Ltd.:
We have audited the accompanying balance sheet of
PPC Ltd., as of March 31, 2003 and 2002, and statements of income and retained earnings for the year then

ended. These financial statements are the responsibility
of the company's management.

We conducted our audits in accordance with generally accepted auditing standards. Those standards require that we plan and perform the audit to obtain reasonable assurance about whether the financial statements are fairly presented. An audit includes examining, on a test basis, evidence supporting the amounts and disclosures in the financial statements. An audit also includes assessing significant estimates made by management, as well as evaluating the overall financial statement presentation. We believe that our audits provide a basis for determining whether any material modifications should be made to the accompanying financial statements.

As discussed in Note X to the financial statements, the company changed its method of computing amortization in fiscal 2003.

In our opinion, except for the accounting change, with which we concur, the financial statements referred to above present fairly, in all material respects, the financial position of PPC Ltd. as of March 31, 2003, and the results of its operations for the year then ended in conformity with generally accepted accounting principles.

As discussed in Note Y to the financial statements, the company is a defendant in a lawsuit alleging infringement of certain copyrights. The company has filed a counteraction, and preliminary hearings on both actions are in progress. Accordingly, any provision for liability is subject to adjudication of this matter.
Wong & Wilson, PAs
May 5, 2003

Required:
Identify the deficiencies in the order in which they appear in the auditor's report as drafted by Smith. Do not redraft the report.

(CGA-Canada adapted)

5.32 Liability for Auditor Negligence. You have been called
LO.2 to testify as an expert witness in a negligence action
brought against another public accounting firm, Muss,
Tache & Co. (Muss). Briefly, the facts of the case are:

- Muss's client is insolvent.
- A major cause of the insolvency was overvaluation of the net assets of a wholly owned subsidiary, which led to its failure.
- The subsidiary was audited by another PA firm, Able & Co. (Able).
- The primary auditor (Muss) accepted the work of Able without examination of either the subsidiary's accounting records or Able's working papers.
- The action was initiated by the bank that was the primary creditor.
- Muss's defence hinged on these factors:
  (a) There was no need to examine the other auditor's working papers, since the other firm was in good standing with the Institute.
  (b) Since the subsidiary constituted only 12 percent of consolidated net income, it was not material anyway.

Required:

a. Discuss whether or not the bank will be successful in its suit for damages, with reference to the factors the court would consider in arriving at its decision.

b. If Muss, Tache & Co. had made an internal quality control review several weeks after the issue of the audit report and the review indicated that Muss should have performed some work on the subsidiary, what action should Muss, Tache & Co. have taken at the time? Assume that the review had occurred before Muss's client's insolvency became known and before that bank's negligence action was initiated.

c. Discuss the factors that Muss, Tache & Co. should have considered when determining the materiality for this engagement.

(ICAO adapted)

5.33 **Liability in a Prospectus Engagement.** Alex P. Keaton
LO.2 Jr. has just returned to the office after an exhausting "busy season." His partner, Malory Dowell, called Alex into her office.

"Alex, I have good news and bad news. First the good news! I've just returned from Expansion Exploration Ltd. and they are going public to help finance their Arctic activities. Therefore, you finally get a chance to work on a prospectus engagement! The bad news is that they want to have the prospectus and the underwriting agreement signed by next Friday, the 31st of March.

"Fortunately, we have been their auditors for the past five years, so we won't have any problems there. Also, I'm quite certain that all five years have had "clean" opinions.

"They have provided me with a copy of their interim financial statements for the five months ended February 28, 1999. As you may recall, their last year-end was September 30, 1998.

"What I would like you to do now, is to provide me with a memo for our planning file briefly outlining what our involvement is to be on this prospectus and describing what communications we are going to have to provide to the securities commission as a result of this involvement."

Required:

a. Assume the role of Alex P. Keaton Jr. and prepare the memo requested by Malory Dowell.

b. Indicate the parties to whom it could be shown that the auditors owe a legal duty of care in this particular situation, and discuss the implications.

(ICAO adapted)

5.34 **Litigation Resulting from Bankruptcy of Client.** A
LO.2 bank that lent considerable funds to a "high-flying" and, until its recent bankruptcy, highly successful real estate development company has hired your firm to investigate the company's long-time auditors, a medium-sized PA firm. The bank has claimed that the financial statements did not fairly represent the company's financial position. The senior partner in your firm in charge of the investigation has been provided with full access to the complete working papers of the initial auditor in order to complete the investigation. If the matter ultimately goes to court, the case will likely be very high in profile and will likely receive significant media coverage.

The senior partner in your firm has assigned you, a manager with considerable auditing experience, to assist him in evaluating the auditors' quality of work and actions.

Required:

a. Outline what you would do to help your senior partner prepare for the investigation. You should give details of those items he should consider in his preparation as well as the guidelines that would be used to develop an opinion as to the appropriateness of the auditors' actions.

b. On what basis (bases) will the court decide the auditors' liability in this situation?

(ICAO adapted)

5.35 **Money Laundering, Auditor Responsibilities.** PA is
LO.3 the audit intermediate on the current year's audit of Blu-
and root Inc., a publicly traded sugar importer and refiner.
LO.4 During the audit of Bluroot's cash records and bank account reconciliations, PA notes numerous instances where a large dollar amount was deposited into one of the company's bank accounts and then an identical amount was transferred out, usually same or the next day. PA presents a list of these "unusual transactions" to the company treasurer for further explanation. The treasurer, who is very busy, takes the list and says she will get back to PA as soon as possible. Several hours later, the treasurer tosses the list on PA's desk and says, somewhat impatiently, "I don't know why you wasted expensive audit time making up this list. All of these transactions offset, so there is no net effect on our cash balance. Most of them relate to intercompany transfers with our many foreign subsidiary companies, for cash management purposes. As you note, we have 12 bank accounts with four different banks in order to facilitate cash transfers with our subsidiaries. Also, some of these are probably just bank errors that the bank discovered and subsequently corrected. That happens quite frequently because of the complexity of our banking arrangements. For your audit purposes, all you need to record in your audit file is that the transactions offset and all our intercompany balances agree at year-end. What happens between year-ends is of no significance to your audit! So please get on with completing the necessary audit tests and stop wasting your time and our money!"

PA is upset by this response. Of particular concern is that several of the sugar-cane producing countries where Bluroot has subsidiaries are listed on list of "Non Cooperating Countries and Territories" issued by the OECD's Financial Action Task Force on Money Laundering, a topic that PA covered in a recent staff training course. And, in other audit tests of the management travel expenses, PA noticed that the treasurer and two of her assistants traveled to these countries on numerous occasions during the year.

PA records all of the details of this investigation in the audit working papers, and discusses the situation with the audit manager the following morning. The audit manager says she will take PA's concerns to the audit partner and also with the PA firm's forensic audit specialists. Several months later, PA learns that the RCMP has undertaken a confidential investigation of Bluroot's financial transactions under suspicion of illegal money laundering activities and PA is asked to answer some questions by the officers investigating the case.

Required:

a. Evaluate the actions of PA and other members of the PA firm in the above case in dealing with the possible illegal acts that they discovered during their audit. What actions and procedures did PA take that uncovered this situation? What different actions might PA have taken that would have allowed the potential money laundering to go undetected?

b. What are the difficulties that can arise for an auditor in "whistle-blowing" as illustrated in the above case? Can you identify other difficulties that might arise when an auditor suspects illegal acts at a client, more generally?

5.36   Use the critical-thinking framework to help resolve the confidentiality versus misleading financial statements conflict discussed in this chapter.

PART II
Basic Auting Concepts and Techniques

CHAPTER
6

Understanding the Client's Business and Risks

In Chapter 6, you will begin your quest to understand your client's business and accompanying risks. Here you will study the activities, concepts, and tools seen in a typical audit engagement.

LEARNING OBJECTIVES

After completing this chapter, you will be able to:

1 Describe the activities PAs undertake before a financial statement audit engagement.

2 Explain why auditors need knowledge of the client's business, its environment, and the client's risks at the start of a financial statement audit.

3 Explain how auditors gain understanding of business risk through strategic analysis and business process analysis.

4 Summarize how changes in information systems, information technology, and e-commerce can affect business risks and processes.

5 Illustrate how the auditor's business risk analysis is used to make a preliminary assessment of the risk that the financial statements are materially misstated.

6 Identify the procedures and sources of information auditors can use to obtain knowledge of a client's business and industry.

7 Outline the relationships among business processes, accounting processes, accounting cycles, and management's general purpose financial statements.

8 Describe the five principal management assertions in financial statements and their application in establishing audit objectives.

9* Describe strategic systems approaches to understanding business risk.

* Learning objectives marked with an asterisk (*) and their corresponding topics are considered advanced material.

The chapters in Part II of this text explain the activities, concepts, and tools used in the planning stage of audit field work. The goal in Part II is to help you obtain knowledge about these activities, concepts, and tools, understand their significance, and be able to explain how they apply in the context of planning a financial statement audit. In practice, experienced auditors use the concepts and tools as they perform their field-work activities, but for your study purposes, this text presents these topics in a linear fashion, as set out in the Learning Objectives at the start of each chapter.

AN OVERVIEW OF THE AUDIT ENGAGEMENT

For organizational purposes, topics related to planning the audit engagement are covered in Part II and topics related to audit field work are explained in Part III.

Chapter 6 starts off with the pre-engagement arrangements made as the PA takes on the role of independent auditor, and then outlines the activities involved in developing an understanding of the client's business and its environment. This knowledge is applied to assess the business risk, which is analyzed in terms of the client's strategy and business processes. The chapter explains how this analysis helps the auditor to understand the business performance that management communicates to stakeholders in its financial statements, and to assess the risk of there being material misstatements in these financial statements. The business and accounting processes that generate financial statements, and the form and content of management's financial statements are then outlined. Finally, the chapter presents the concept of management assertions, explaining how these are used to establish audit objectives.

Looking ahead, the remaining chapters in Part II take you through the audit planning process, which involves applying your knowledge and understanding to create a preliminary audit plan. Chapter 7 (Information Systems, Technology and Internal Controls) expands on the knowledge you need to plan the audit by describing the systems and control activities used to capture, summarize and present reliable financial information. Understanding the systems and controls helps auditors to decide the key areas to audit. Chapter 8 (Audit Planning: Concepts and Tools) explains preliminary analysis, materiality, risk and evidence and explains the fundamental concepts and tools that auditors use to develop an audit program. This program identifies the procedures needed to provide the evidence to support the audit opinion. Chapter 9 (Internal Control Evaluation and Testing) expands on the understanding required to evaluate and test controls, and Chapter 10 (Audit Sampling) presents techniques used in audit testing. Finally, we look at how the auditor integrates business understanding with the key auditing concepts in the preliminary audit plan to create an overall strategy for obtaining evidence to support the audit opinion. Refer to the following overview, which depicts all of the audit planning topics covered in Part II.

In Part III, the text moves on to explain the actual audit work, and requires you to apply the concepts and tools in specific accounting processes in the client's business. You will learn how auditors gather evidence from different components of the client' systems and processes by testing controls and balances and performing other analytical procedures, and how new knowledge learned by doing audit procedures is used to refine the preliminary plan. Part III of the text will also explain how auditors synthesize all their knowledge and evidence to form an opinion on whether the financial statements are fairly presented in accordance with GAAP based on their audit findings. The critical activities of documenting the audit planning, the evidence gathered and basis of the opinion at the conclusion of the audit field work, will also be discussed in Part III. Experience shows us that the most important part of learning how to audit happens on the job. After working through Parts II and III of the text, you should be ready to join an audit team out in the field and fully appreciate the tasks you will be trained to do under the supervision of more experienced auditors.

**OVERVIEW OF AUDITING PLANNING
ACTIVITIES, CONCEPTS AND TOOLS IN PART II**

TIMING: (approx.)	PRE-ENGAGEMENT	INTERIM AUDIT (BEFORE YEAR END)	YEAR-END AUDIT (AT AND AFTER YEAR-END)
AUDIT PLANNING ACTIVITIES Chapter 6 and Chapter 7	Pre-engagement arrangements	Understand client's business, environment and risks. Understand client's information systems, technology and internal controls.	Obtain management's financial statements. Analyze the business and its performance. Assess risks of financial statement mis-statements.
AUDIT PLANNING TOOLS Chapter 8	Materiality decisions → Preliminary analysis → Audit risk model → Audit programs → Audit working papers		
AUDIT PLANNING CONCEPTS Chapter 6–10	Business risk Inherent risk Management assertions and audit objectives	Control risk and control objectives Sufficient appropriate audit evidence	Audit procedures Audit approach

PRE-ENGAGEMENT ARRANGEMENTS

· · · · · · · · · · ·

Auditors undertake several activities before beginning any audit work on a client's financial statements. In general, these can be called the **pre-audit risk management activities**. Auditors try to reduce risk by carefully managing the engagement. Risk in an audit engagement generally refers to the probability that something will go wrong that could lead to the financial statements being misstated. The flip side of risk management is quality management, which was explained in Chapter 2 under the heading of "Quality Control Standards." The topics covered next can best be understood in the context of risk management and quality management.

Client Selection and Retention

An important element of a public accounting firm's quality control policies and procedures is a system for deciding to accept a new client and, on a continuing basis, deciding whether to resign from audit engagements. Public accounting firms are not obligated to accept undesirable clients, nor are they obligated to continue with audit clients when relationships deteriorate or when the management comes under a cloud of suspicion. For example, an auditor may think twice about accepting an engagement with management that has a poor business reputation or where an assumption of management integrity cannot be made.

Client acceptance and retention policies and procedures include (1) obtaining and reviewing financial information about the prospective client—annual reports, interim statements, registration statements, annual information forms and reports to regulatory agencies; (2) enquiring of the prospective client's banker, legal counsel, underwriter or other persons who do business with the company for information about the company and its management; (3) evaluating the public accounting firm's and individual auditors' independence with regard to the prospective client; (4) communicating with the predecessor auditor, if any, for information on the integrity of management, on disagreements with management about accounting principles, auditing procedures or similar matters, and on the reasons for a change of auditors; (5) considering whether the engagement would require special attention or involve unusual risks; and (6) considering the need for special skills (e.g., IT auditing or specialized industry knowledge).

Decisions to continue auditing a client are similar to acceptance decisions, except that the public accounting firm will have more first-hand experience with the company. Retention reviews are done annually and take into account any major events, such as changes in management, directors, ownership, legal counsel, financial condition, litigation status, nature of the client's business, scope of the audit engagement or any change that could affect the auditors' independence. In general, conditions that would have caused an accounting firm to reject a prospective client may develop and lead to a decision to discontinue the engagement. For example, a client company may expand and diversify on an international scale to such an extent that a small public accounting firm may not have the competence to continue the audit. It is not unusual to see newspaper stories, like the one following, about firms dropping clients after directors or officers admit to falsification of financial statements or to theft and misuse of corporate assets.

SEMI-TECH AUDITOR QUITS OVER "LACK OF TRUST"

The Toronto Stock Exchange suspended all trading in Semi-Tech Corp. yesterday, even as it emerged the firm's former auditors had served notice in late 1997 that they were quitting over a "breakdown of trust" with the Toronto holding company and Singer, its principal subsidiary.

Neither the investing public nor regulators have been told why Ernst & Young was replaced.

The fact surfaced only after the two companies fled into U.S. bankruptcy protection this month—revealing a patchwork of questionable acquisitions, unusual deals and a history of related-company transactions that appear to lack many of the usual controls.

Court documents filed in the United States and Canada show the unraveling of the international empire stitched together by Hong Kong businessman James Ting has been years in the making—and the change of auditors was a key trouble sign.

Minutes of a meeting of Semi-Tech's audit committee in November, 1997, show the company was warned by Robert Long of Ernst & Young that the auditors were "unhappy" with financial reporting and wanted out.

"Mr. Long confirmed Ernst & Young would not conduct the Singer audit and they wished to be replaced as auditors of Semi-Tech Corp. and Singer," the minutes say.

"The reason given was a breakdown of trust between these entities and Ernst & Young," the minutes say.

"He said their replacement should be speedy or they would have to act on their own. He said that the stated reason for the change in auditors should be a breakdown in the relationship with Ernst & Young."

Singer had a stock market value of about $663-million (US) at the time, while Semi-Tech was valued at about $88-million.

Shares in the two firms—once the darlings of investors from New York to Hong Kong—have been trading for pennies in recent days in both New York and Toronto. In addition, Deloitte & Touche, the replacement auditor, has now suspended all work on Singer's 1998 financials pending an investigation of a troubling Russian transaction.

Source: Sandra Rubin, "Semi-tech Auditor Quit over 'Lack of Trust'," *The Financial Post,* Friday, September 24, 1999, page C1/FRONT. Material reprinted with the express permission of: "National Post Company," a CanWest partnership.

Communication Between Predecessor and Successor Auditors

When companies change auditors, the former auditor is called the predecessor, and the new auditor the successor. Experience has shown that clients have fired their auditors because of arguments about the scope of the audit or the acceptability of accounting principles. Sometimes these arguments involve auditors' access to necessary evidence, questions of early revenue recognition or disputes over deferral of expenses and losses. Often, however, a change in business ownership or a concern over fees is the reason for a change.

The rules of professional conduct of the provincial institutes or associations require a successor auditor to initiate contact with, and attempt to obtain basic information directly from, the predecessor. The reason for this is that the former auditor knows a great deal about the client and can give the new auditor information that will be useful in (1) deciding whether to accept the new client and become the successor auditor, and (2) planning the audit. The rules of professional conduct require the predecessor auditor to respond promptly to communications from the successor.

It is common practice for the successor auditor to explain the situation and the rules to the client, asking the client to give consent to the predecessor to speak to the successor and allow the successor to review the audit files. The client's consent will determine the amount of client information that is conveyed to the successor. Note that the audit files belong to the auditor, not the client, but confidentiality must be respected even after the auditor–client relationship ends. If the client refuses to give this consent, the successor auditor should be wary. This would raise serious concerns about the integrity of the new client's management and the successor may decide it is too risky to accept this new client.

With consent, the predecessor auditor can speak freely. It is not unusual to have a cordial change of auditors and see the successor conduct interviews with the predecessor auditor's staff and obtain copies of the predecessor auditor's working papers. This exchange greatly facilitates the successor's first-time audit.

A change of auditors could cause the successor auditor's report to be modified from the standard form. It is important to note that the predecessor–successor situation is not the same "using the work and reports of other independent auditors" topic explained in Appendix 3A. That situation involved the engagement of two or more audit firms auditing the financial statements for the same year. The predecessor–successor situation arises in the topic of "reporting on comparative statements" (Appendix 3A). In this case the successor auditor may be reporting on the current year, but the client may present the prior-year financial statements audited by the predecessor. The successor's report should disclose this fact in a separate paragraph of the auditor's report following the opinion paragraph or in the notes to the financial statements.[1]

[1] *CICA Handbook,* paragraph 5701.11.

Engagement Letters

When a new audit client is accepted, the auditor must obtain an **engagement letter** (Exhibit 6–1). Effective August 2005, Canadian standards require that the auditor and client management establish a mutual understanding of, and agreement on, the terms of the audit engagement. The agreement is documented in writing to reduce the risk that either the auditor or the entity may misinterpret the needs or expectations of the other party. The agreement should cover the objective, scope and limitations of the audit and the respective responsibilities of the auditor and management.

For continuing clients, the auditor confirms the terms of the engagement in writing on an annual basis, taking into account whether there are any new circumstances that would require the terms of the engagement to be revised, such as a significant change in the nature or size of the entity's business.

The engagement letter also sets forth an agreement about the fee to be charged. Normally fees are based on the time required to perform the services. Such time estimates require some familiarity with the accounting system.

The engagement letter is, in effect, the audit contract. It may contain special requests and assignments to be undertaken by the auditors, or it may be a standard letter stating that an audit of financial statements will be performed in accordance with generally accepted auditing standards. An engagement letter can help in avoiding legal liability for claims that the auditors did not perform the work promised. For example, agreeing on a completion date in advance can reduce disappointments later in the engagement. Also, there may be changes in fees and services from year to year that should be communicated clearly in an engagement letter.

The appendix to *CICA Handbook,* section 5110 provides a generic template for an engagement letter. Each letter needs to be adapted to the specific circumstances of the client organization and the audit. As an example, an engagement letter for the audit of a privately held real estate development company is illustrated in Exhibit 6–1.

EXHIBIT   6–1   EXAMPLE OF AN ENGAGEMENT LETTER

November 6, 2006

Ms. Harriet Liu, President
Real Estate Development Limited
600 Paree Street
Richmond, B.C.

Dear Harriet:

This letter will confirm the terms of engagement covering my audit of the financial statements of Real Estate Development Limited for its fiscal year ending December 31, 2006.

Objective, scope and limitations
My statutory function as auditor of Real Estate Development Limited is to report to the shareholders by expressing an opinion on Real Estate Development Limited's annual financial statements. I will conduct my audit in accordance with Canadian generally accepted auditing standards and will issue an audit report.

An auditor conducting an audit with Canadian generally accepted auditing standards obtains reasonable assurance that the financial statements taken as a whole are free of material misstatement, whether caused by fraud or error. It is important to recognize that an auditor cannot obtain absolute assurance that material misstatements in the financial statements will be detected because of:

(a)   factors such as use of judgment, and the use of testing of the data underlying the financial statements;
(b)   inherent limitations of internal control; and
(c)   the fact that much of the audit evidence available to the auditor is persuasive rather than conclusive in nature.

Furthermore, because of the nature of fraud, including attempts at concealment through collusion and forgery, an audit designed and executed in accordance with Canadian generally accepted auditing standards may not detect a material fraud. Further, while effective internal control reduces the likelihood that misstatements will occur and remain undetected, it does not eliminate that possibility. For these reasons, we cannot guarantee that fraud, error and illegal acts, if present, will be detected when conducting an audit in accordance with Canadian generally accepted auditing standards.

Unless unanticipated difficulties are encountered, at the conclusion of my audit, I will submit to you a report containing my opinion on the financial statements. If during the course of my work it appears for any reason that I will not be in a position to render an unqualified opinion on the financial statements, I will discuss this with you.

EXHIBIT   6-1   Continued

My responsibilities

I will perform the audit in accordance with Canadian generally accepted auditing standards. These standards require that I plan and perform the audit to obtain reasonable assurance about whether the financial statements present fairly, in all material respects, the financial position, results of operations and cash flows in accordance with Canadian generally accepted accounting principles. Accordingly, I will plan and perform my audit to provide reasonable, but not absolute, assurance of detecting fraud and errors that have a material effect on the financial statements taken as a whole, including illegal acts whose consequences have a material effect on the financial statements.

One of the underlying principles of the profession is a duty of confidentiality with respect to client affairs. Accordingly, except for information that is in or enters the public domain, I will not provide any third party with confidential information concerning the affairs of Real Estate Development Limited without Real Estate Development Limited's prior consent, unless required to do so by legal authority, or the rules of professional conduct/code of ethics of the provincial Public Accountancy Council.

I will communicate in writing to you the relationships between me and Real Estate Development Limited (including its two related entities, Shopping Mall Joint Venture and Retirement Home Joint Venture) that, in my professional judgment, may reasonably be thought to bear on my independence. Further, I will confirm my independence with respect to Real Estate Development Limited.

The objective of my audit is to obtain reasonable assurance that the financial statements are free of material misstatement. However, if I identify any of the following matters, they will be communicated to you:

(a)   misstatements, resulting from error, other than trivial errors;
(b)   fraud or any information obtained that indicates that a fraud may exist;
(c)   any evidence obtained that indicates that an illegal or possibly illegal act, other than one considered inconsequential, has occurred;
(d)   significant weaknesses in the design or implementation of internal control to prevent and detect fraud or error; and
(e)   related party transactions identified by me that are not in the normal course of operations and that involve significant judgments made by management concerning measurement or disclosure.

The matters communicated will be those that I identify during the course of my audit. Audits do not usually identify all matters that may be of interest to management in discharging its responsibilities. The type and significance of the matter to be communicated will determine the level of management to which the communication is directed.

I will consider Real Estate Development Limited's internal control to identify types of potential misstatements, consider factors that affect the risks of material misstatement, and design the nature, timing and extent of further audit procedures. This consideration will not be sufficient to enable me to render a separate opinion on the effectiveness of internal control over financial reporting.

My understanding of the intended purposes of the financial statements is to report to the Real Estate Development Limited shareholders and to satisfy the requirements of Real Estate Development Limited's credit agreement with the Regal Bank of British Columbia.

Management's responsibilities

Management is responsible for:

Financial statements
(a)   the preparation and fair presentation of Real Estate Development Limited's financial statements in accordance with Canadian generally accepted accounting principles;
(b)   acknowledging that, for the differential reporting options that have been used to present the financial statements,:
      (i)   Real Estate Development Limited meets the criteria for using such reporting options;
      (ii)   You have obtained consent from each shareholder, including those not otherwise entitled to vote with respect to the preparation of financial statements using the following differential reporting options:
             • Preferred shares issued in tax planning arrangements that would otherwise be presented as liabilities will be presented as equity.
             • The fair value of financial assets and liabilities will be disclosed only for those financial assets and liabilities, both recognized and unrecognized, for which fair value is readily obtainable.
      (iii) such consent has not been withdrawn;

Completeness of information
(c)   providing me with and making available complete financial records and related data, and copies of all minutes of meetings of shareholders, directors and committees of directors;
(d)   providing me with information relating to any known or probable instances of non-compliance with legislative or regulatory requirements, including financial reporting requirements;
(e)   providing me with information relating to any illegal or possibly illegal acts, and all facts related thereto;
(f)   providing me with information regarding all related parties and related party transactions;

Fraud and error
(g)   the design and implementation of internal control to prevent and detect fraud and error;
(h)   an assessment of the risk that the financial statements may be materially misstated as a result of fraud;
(i)   providing me with information relating to fraud or suspected fraud affecting the entity involving:
      (i)   management;
      (ii)   employees who have significant roles in internal control; or
      (iii) others, where the fraud could have a non-trivial effect on the financial statements;
(j)   providing me with information relating to any allegations of fraud or suspected fraud affecting the entity's financial statements communicated by employees, former employees, regulators or others;
(k)   communicating its belief that the effects of any uncorrected financial statement misstatements aggregated during the audit are immaterial, both individually and in the aggregate, to the financial statements taken as a whole;

Recognition, measurement and disclosure
(l)   providing me with its assessment of the reasonableness of significant assumptions underlying fair value measurements and disclosures in the financial statements;
(m)   providing me with any plans or intentions that may affect the carrying value or classification of assets or liabilities;

EXHIBIT 6-1   Continued

(n) providing me with information relating to the measurement and disclosure of transactions with related parties;

(o) providing me with an assessment of all areas of measurement uncertainty known to management that are required to be disclosed in accordance with Canadian generally accepted accounting principles;

(p) providing me with information relating to claims and possible claims, whether or not they have been discussed with Real Estate Development Limited's legal counsel;

(q) providing me with information relating to other liabilities and contingent gains or losses, including those associated with guarantees, whether written or oral, under which Real Estate Development Limited is contingently liable;

(r) providing me with information on whether Real Estate Development Limited has satisfactory title to assets, liens or encumbrances on assets exist, or assets are pledged as collateral;

(s) providing me with information relating to compliance with aspects of contractual agreements that may affect the financial statements;

(t) providing me with information concerning subsequent events; and

Written confirmation of significant representations

(u) providing me with written confirmation of significant representations provided to me during the engagement on matters that are:

(i) directly related to items that are material, either individually or in the aggregate, to the financial statements;

(ii) not directly related to items that are material to the financial statements but are significant, either individually or in the aggregate, to the engagement; and

(iii) relevant to your judgments or estimates that are material, either individually or in the aggregate, to the financial statements.

Other matters

I will ask that your personnel, to the extent possible, prepare various schedules and analyses, and make various invoices and other documents available to me. This assistance will facilitate my work and minimize your audit costs.

As part of my services, I may also submit to you a memorandum containing any suggestions for improvement of existing systems of internal control, accounting policies and procedures and other related matters which come to my attention during the course of my work.

I ask that my name be used only with my consent and that any information to which I have attached a communication be issued with that communication unless otherwise agreed to by me.

In addition to the audit services referred to above, I will prepare your federal and provincial income tax returns and other special reports as required. Management will provide the information necessary to complete these returns / reports and will file them with the appropriate authorities on a timely basis.

I will also be pleased to provide additional services upon request, in areas such as income tax planning, and GST and PST advice.

My charges to the company for my services will be made at my regular rates plus out-of-pocket expenses. Bills will be rendered on a regular basis with payment to be made upon presentation.

The above terms of my engagement will be effective from year to year until amended or terminated in writing. If you have any questions about the contents of this letter, please raise them with me. If the services outlined are in accordance with your requirements and if the above terms are acceptable to you, please sign the copy of this letter in the space provided and return it to me. I appreciate the opportunity to be of service to your company.

Yours very truly,

....
Kelley K. Randu, PUBLIC ACCOUNTANT

The services and terms set out are as agreed.
Real Estate Development Limited

Per: ....
                   Harriet Liu   [date]

Source: *CICA Handbook*, section 5110, appendix.

Staff Assignment

When a new client is obtained, most accounting firms assign a full-service team to the new client. For larger clients, this team usually consists of the audit engagement partner (the person with final responsibility for the audit); the audit manager; one or more senior audit staff members; staff assistants or PA students; information technology or industry specialists (if needed); a tax partner; and a second audit partner. For smaller clients the team may consist of only one or two people, the partner and a staff assistant, especially if the public accounting firm itself is small.

Firm policy may require that a second audit partner review the work of the audit team. This partner is supposed to have a detached professional point of view because he or she is not directly responsible for keeping the client happy.[2]

---

[2] A second audit partner is required for audits of financial statements filed with the U.S. Securities and Exchange Commission. On SEC engagements, the audit engagement partner is required to rotate to other clients so that he or she does not remain in charge of the same client for so many years that his or her independence could become impaired by overfamiliarity.

Time Budget

The partner and manager in charge of the audit prepare a plan for the timing of the work and set the number of hours that each segment of the audit is expected to take. This time budget is based on last year's performance for continuing clients, taking into account any changes in the client's business. In a first-time audit, the budget may be based on a predecessor auditor's experience or on general experience with similar companies. A simple time budget follows.

	Audit Time Budget (hours)	
	Interim	Year-End
Knowledge of the business	15	
Internal audit familiarization	10	
Assessment of control risk	30	10
Audit program planning	25	
Related parties investigation	5	15
Client conferences	10	18
Cash	10	15
Accounts receivable	15	5
Inventory	35	20
Accounts payable	5	35
Other accounts		10
Representation letters		10
Financial statement review		25
Report preparation		12
Total	160	175

This time budget is illustrative only and not complete. Real-time budgets are much more detailed. Some specify the expected time by level of staff person on the team (partner, manager, in-charge accountant, staff assistant, specialists). The illustration shows time at interim and at year-end.

Interim audit work refers to procedures performed several weeks or months before the balance sheet date. The exact timing of the interim depends on the circumstances in a particular audit. Some factors to consider include: when enough transaction data will be available to make it efficient for the auditor to visit to perform procedures; when client reconciliations or count procedures are performed and available for audit purposes; when client staff has time to accommodate the auditors and assist with the audit procedures, and other practical issues.

Year-end audit work refers to procedures performed shortly before and after the balance sheet date. Audit firms typically spread the workload out during the year by scheduling interim audit work so that they will have enough time and people available when many audit clients have year-ends on the same date (December 31 is common). For many audit firms, the audit "busy season" runs from October through June of the following year. The interim work can consist of both internal control risk assessment work and audit of balances as they exist at the early date[3] or examination of documents or electronic information that are only available for a certain time during the year and not retained.[4]

Everyone who works on the audit reports the time taken to perform procedures for each segment of the audit. These time reports are recorded by budget categories for the purposes of (1) compiling a record for billing the client, (2) evaluating the efficiency of the audit team members, and (3) compiling a record for planning the next audit. Time budgets may create job pressures if staff members feel pressure to "meet the budget." Beginning auditors often experience frustration as they learn how to do audit work efficiently, and may be tempted to

---

[3] These parts of the audit work are described in *CICA Handbook*, paragraphs 5141.069, .086, .090, .101.
[4] As discussed in *CICA Handbook*, paragraph 5300.28.

understate the actual time they spent when reporting their chargeable hours. Since these time records will be used to budget future audits, not enough time may be allowed for in next year's audit if staff understate the time they needed to do the required work. Firms can alleviate time pressures by building learning time into budgets for less experienced staff.

REVIEW CHECKPOINTS

6.1   What sources of information can a PA use in connection with deciding whether to accept a new audit client?

6.2   Why does a successor auditor need to obtain the client's consent for a predecessor auditor to give information about the former audit client?

6.3   What benefits are obtained by having an engagement letter?

6.4   What persons and skills are normally assigned to a "full-service" audit team?

6.5   What is interim audit work? year-end audit work?

UNDERSTANDING THE CLIENT'S BUSINESS, ITS ENVIRONMENT AND RISKS

LEARNING OBJECTIVE

2 Explain why auditors need knowledge of the client's business, its environment and the client's risks at the start of a financial statement audit.

Understanding the client's business and its operating environment is very important in an audit as it helps to assess the risk of the financial statements. Therefore, auditing standards explain the sources of information about the client entity and its environment, including its internal control, and the risk assessment procedures that the auditor is required to perform to obtain the understanding of the client.[5]

The standards also require a discussion among the engagement team about the susceptibility of the client's financial statements to material misstatement. Based on this shared understanding, the audit team can identify what can go wrong at the financial statement level.[6] The risk assessment at the financial statement level considers classes of transactions, account balances, and disclosures in the financial statements. The auditor also assesses risks at the assertion level (assertions are discussed later in this chapter). The standards further require the auditor to determine the significance and likelihood of the risks. This chapter will focus on understanding the client's business and its environment and risks, and the assertions contained in its financial statements. Chapter 7 will cover understanding the information systems and internal controls that produce the financial statements.

The auditor's objective in obtaining an understanding of the client's business and risks is to design an effective audit program that addresses all the significant risks of financial statement misstatements. An audit program is a list of the audit procedures believed necessary to obtain sufficient, appropriate evidence that will serve as the basis for the audit report. *CICA Handbook* 5145.04 requires the auditor to "prepare audit documentation that provides the support for the representations in the auditor's report."[7] A mental program "in my head" is not sufficient. Audit programs are explained more fully in Chapters 8, 9, and 10.

In order to design the audit, auditors must understand the broad economic environment in which the client operates, including such things as the effects of national economic policies (e.g., price regulations and import/export restrictions), the geographic location and its economy (e.g., Alberta's predominantly resource-based economy, or Ontario's manufacturing-based economy), and developments in taxation and regulatory areas (e.g., deregulation in agriculture and air transport, approval processes in the drug and chemical industries). For example, when the Canadian dollar increases relative to the U.S. dollar, many Canadian firms that rely on exports to the United States are negatively affected because this economic event makes their products more expensive and thus less competitive in the U.S. market.

---

[5] *CICA Handbook* 5141 is harmonized with ISA 315, both standards provide similar recommendations and guidance on understanding the entity, its business environment, and its internal control. This text explains audits of business entities, but the concepts, tools, and procedures also apply to audits of other types of entities such as schools, hospitals, charitable organizations, etc.

[6] *CICA Handbook* 5141.14 to .19.

[7] The audit documentation must show that the auditor complied with GAAS; support the auditor's conclusions for every relevant financial statement assertion; and demonstrate that the underlying accounting records agree with the financial statements.

Industry characteristics also affect business risks. There is a great deal of difference in the production and marketing activities of banks, insurance companies, mutual funds, supermarkets, hotels, oil and gas, agriculture, manufacturing and so forth. No auditors are experts in all these businesses. Audit firms typically have people who are expert in one or two industries and rely on them to manage audits in those industries. Indeed, some PA firms have a reputation for having many audit clients in a particular industry, while other PA firms have a larger presence in other industries.

An example of industry-related risk is presented in the following box. It shows how, despite an international trade agreement that many softwood businesses based their strategies on, many forestry businesses were negatively affected when their trading partners began collecting duties that were not provided for in the agreement. This is a risk faced by businesses in industries that depend on foreign sales. Auditors need to be aware of such risk to understand the business performance and how it affects the financial statements. For example, the unexpectedly high duties could put some companies into financial distress if profits fall sharply and additional financing needs arise that cannot be met. Alternately, if a forestry company audit client's financial statements indicate growth in profitability while this heavy duty was being imposed, this goes against expectations and needs to be investigated carefully. It may suggest a misstatement.

Greater knowledge of business is required than in the past because auditors are increasingly expected to use integrative reasoning in reaching their conclusions. Accounting is supposed to reflect the economic substance of transactions and this usually requires asking the right business questions of management. Effective questioning requires strong understanding of the client's business, its environment, and risks.

B.C. SOFTWOOD LUMBER INDUSTRY IN CRISIS

From May 22, 2002 to Dec 20, 2004 most Canadian softwood lumber exported to the U.S. was subject to a combined countervailing and anti-dumping duty of 27%, collected by U.S. Customs. As of December 20, 2004, the duty has been reduced to 20%. Committees of the North American Free Trade Agreement (NAFTA) and World Trade Organization (WTO) both ruled in 2005 that these duties are not justified, but U.S. Customs continued to collect them.

The Canadian defence involved federal and provincial governments and the forest industry. The federal government has the overall responsibility for co-ordinating national activities related to the countervailing duty, while provincial governments have the lead in addressing the allegations that relate to provincial programs. The forest industry has the lead in the anti-dumping duty case.

In a poll of its members taken in June 2003, the Canadian Federation of Independent Businesses found that 70% of BC's small forestry businesses reported being significantly or somewhat harmed by the lumber dispute. The graph below shows the magnitude of the duties paid by the industry.

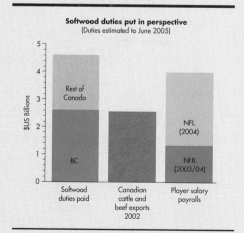

SOFTWOOD LUMBER DUTIES COMPARISON

Softwood duties put in perspective
(Duties estimated to June 2005)

Sources:
www.for.gov.bc.ca/HET/Softwood/ (accessed October 2005).
Softwood lumber export duties: BC Stats estimate.
Cattle and beef exports: Industry Canada's Strategis website (data from Statistics Canada converted to U.S. dollars)
Player salary payrolls: *USA Today*.
Note: NHL payroll excludes incentives and salaries of players appearing in fewer than 30 games; NFL payroll may not include short-term and practice squad players.

The following box illustrates of the kinds of risks a high-technology business faces. Intellectual property rights and patent infringements create a risk that the liabilities are understated in the financial statements. In this case, the company faces significant risks related to developing and patenting its technology, and to being aware of other similar patents that are in place. Management needs a process to manage these risks, and auditors need to assess whether these risks and liabilities have been reported fully in the financial statements.

TECH COMPANY MAY NEED FURTHER $550-MILLION TO SETTLE BLACKBERRY PATENT INFRINGEMENT CLAIM

Research In Motion Ltd. may have to pay $550-million (U.S.) more than it has set aside to settle claims that its BlackBerry e-mail device infringes another company's patents.

Liability for infringement could reach $1-billion, said ThinkEquity analyst Pablo Perez-Fernandez. RIM has reserved only $450-million to cover damages for infringement and licensing fees until the patents run out in 2012. The $1-billion estimate followed the refusal on Oct. 7 by a U.S. appeals court to overturn an August jury finding of infringement of the patents, which are owned by a closely held company, NTP Inc.

RIM faces a court order halting BlackBerry service in the United States if it can't get the verdict thrown out. More than 70 percent of the company's $1.35-billion in annual revenue comes from the United States. It has $2.5-billion in cash, marketable securities, short- and long-term investments and the money set aside for the litigation, Mr. Perez-Fernandez said.

"They can come up with a billion if they have to," said Mr. Perez-Fernandez, who rates the Waterloo, Ont.-based company's shares "sell" and does not own them. "When the $450-million settlement was announced, it was clear it was a discount."

Investors are likely to accept a higher settlement price if it means an end to the litigation, analysts said. A payment of more than $450-million would be "positively received by RIM investors," said Mike Abramsky, an RBC Dominion Securities analyst in Toronto, in an Oct. 10 note to clients. Mr. Abramsky has a "sector perform" rating on the shares. "Every $200-million additionally paid to NTP equates to only $1 a share."

RIM's U.S. shares have fallen 19 percent since the company announced an impasse in the settlement June 9 and are down 22.3 per cent this year.

In June, RIM co-chief executive officer James Balsillie said his company has "backup technology" to work around the patented inventions in dispute if it can't come to an agreement with NTP. The company will do what it takes to continue selling BlackBerrys, which are now owned by more than three million people, Mr. Balsillie said.

In the meantime, the U.S. Patent and Trademark Office is reviewing the NTP patents to see if they should have been issued. A decision against NTP would end the litigation in favour of RIM.

REVIEW CHECKPOINTS

6.6   Why does the auditor need a good understanding of the client's business and its environment?

6.7   How do changes in the economic environment affect a business's risks?

6.8   How do changes in the industry environment affect a business's risks?

6.9   What specific risks exist in high-tech companies?

BUSINESS RISK APPROACH TO AUDITING

· · · · · · · · · · · ·

LEARNING OBJECTIVE

3 Explain how auditors gain understanding of business risk through strategic analysis and business process analysis.

Business risk can be defined as an event or action that will adversely affect an organization's ability to achieve its business objectives and execute its strategies. For example, the development of the PC and its word-processing capabilities reduced dramatically the market for electric typewriters thereby threatening the business objectives of many firms in the typewriter business. More recently, the capability for people to download music and movie files over the Internet severely challenged business models of the music and movie industries and their methods of making profits.

The financial statement auditor seeks to understand management's risk assessment process. This is management's process for identifying business risks that could affect financial reporting objectives and for deciding on actions to address and minimize these risks. Understanding management's risk assessment process helps to assess the risk that the financial statements could be materially misstated. Auditing standards emphasize the auditors need to understand business risk, e.g., *CICA Handbook*, section 5141 and ISA 315.

This process is described as the **entity's risk assessment process** as follows:

> During the audit, the auditor may identify risks of material misstatement that management failed to identify. In such cases, the auditor considers whether there was an underlying risk of a kind that should have been identified by the entity's risk assessment process, and if so, why that process failed to do so and whether the process is appropriate to its circumstances. If, as a result, the auditor judges that there is a material weakness in the entity's risk assessment process, the auditor communicates to the audit committee or equivalent.[8]

In this text we will refer to this requirement for the auditor to the understand the client's business risks and strategy as the **business risk approach**.

In obtaining an understanding of business risks, auditors can make use of a mental model and system thinking. A mental model "consists of organized knowledge, integrated data about the patterns and cues, and rules for linking knowledge and cues."[9] Mental models are used throughout the audit and updated continuously for new information. Systems thinking involves viewing the organization in a complex web of relationships between the client and relevant features of the client's external environment. In systems thinking the auditor considers not only cause and effect relationships that affect the client's business but also how random shocks, such as the previous softwood lumber duties example, can change its dynamics. This allows the auditor to get a deep understanding of the business risks facing the client organization and their potential consequences. The next part of this section explains a systems-thinking based methodology for analyzing business risk.

Business risk analysis is a process auditors can use to learn about the risks the business faces, management's strategy for addressing those risks to meet organization goals, and the business processes it uses to implement the strategy. There are two parts of business analysis: strategic analysis and business process analysis. At the end of the business risk analysis the auditor should be able to answer the following questions:

1. What is the client's strategy?
2. Is it sustainable?
3. What are the business risks/threats to the client?
4. What business processes, information systems and internal controls does the client use to manage those risks?
5. What are the gaps or weaknesses in the client's risk management approach?
6. Do those gaps affect the financial statements?

Answers to these questions allow the auditor to identify significant risks that could result in material misstatements. In particular, the answer to question 4 requires an in-depth

---

[8] *CICA Handbook*, paragraph 5141.078.
[9] Tim Bell and Ira Solomon, *Cases in Strategic-Systems Auditing* (KPMG and University of Illinois, 2002).

evaluation of the design of internal controls and how effectively they have been implemented during the audit period. For your study purposes, information systems and internal control will be covered more fully later in Chapter 7.

Strategic Analysis

The audit team begins the strategic analysis by gaining an understanding from senior client management (for example, the chief executive officer or chief operating officer) about the business objectives, key strategies employed to achieve those objectives and risks that threaten achievement of those objectives. In for-profit entities, objectives are normally some combination of profitability and growth. Other entities might have much more complex objectives: for example, an inner city health clinic's goals may revolve around providing medical services to immigrant populations that are underserved by the traditional means of medical service delivery.

Strategies involve the way the organization establishes systems and processes to achieve the business objectives at a more detailed implementation level. Common strategies include being an industry cost leader (i.e., having the lowest costs), or differentiating your products from those of your competitors (i.e., finding some element of the product that a large subset of purchasers value and delivering it to them).

The following box illustrates the risks faced by a company that enjoys market leadership from selling the most popular hand-held e-mail devices. Competitors are constantly in the wings looking for ways to take away some of Blackberry's market share. Notice that the company in this example is the same one we looked at previously as an example of the risks of patent infringement litigation. The same company can face a variety of different risks from different aspects of its strategy, so auditors must take a broad view of the business environment to identify all important risks that may exist. The more successful the company, the more complex and varied its risks may be.

NOKIA'S KEYBOARD PHONE LATEST THREAT TO BLACKBERRY

Nokia Corp. joined the ranks of would-be BlackBerry killers yesterday, unveiling its first keyboard phone with a similar look and feel of the e-mail device made by Research In Motion Inc. The Finland-based company's Nokia E61, due out in the first quarter of 2006, follows the introduction of non-clamshell devices from Hewlett-Packard Co. and Motorola Inc. that also feature a typewriter keypad for thumb tapping. The look and feel was first popularized by the BlackBerry from RIM and then also by Treo from Palm Inc. This one, however, would be the first based on Symbian, the most widely used operating system for advanced wireless phones in most markets outside the U.S.

Source: "Nokia's Keyboard Phone Latest Threat to Blackberry," *The Globe and Mail*, October 13, 2005, p. B17. Used with permission of The Associated Press. Copyright © 1995. All rights reserved.

The strategic analysis is the beginning of the auditor's development of an understanding of management's process for identifying business risks relevant to financial reporting objectives and how management makes decisions about what actions to take to address those risks. The business risk approach requires the auditor to enquire about business risks that management has identified and consider whether they may result in material misstatement.

In smaller businesses where management may not have a formal risk assessment process, the auditor should discuss with management how risks to the business are identified by management and how they are addressed.

Business Process Analysis

Management tries to minimize business risks by designing well thought-out business processes. Business processes can be defined as a structured set of activities within the entity that are designed to produce a specific output in accordance with the business strategy. Examples include customer relations management in a consumer products distribution firm, processing income tax returns in the Canada Revenue Agency's operations, or patent searches and registration processes in a technology development company. If the business process produces value-added output in the way that the strategy intended it to do, it is more likely that the business will achieve its objectives and not fall prey to the various risks.

The business process view of the firm has become an important perspective in management in recent years. The interest in business processes arises from the realization that a firm's success ultimately depends on how well its management can execute the main aspects of its strategy, such as cost leadership, differentiation, or focus. (See Appendix 6A for details of types of strategies.) Business processes are a structured set of activities within the organization that are designed to produce a specific output in accordance with the business strategy. Exhibit 6-2 shows examples of some typical business processes for an airline company and a manufacturing company.

The theory underlying the business process view has its roots in value chain analysis, as shown in Exhibit 6-3. The exhibit describes value chains. It shows how business processes cross boundaries between the traditional functional areas in organizations, such as sales, marketing, manufacturing and research and development, and group employees from different functional specialties to complete a piece of work. This business process based

---

EXHIBIT   6-2   EXAMPLES OF BUSINESS PROCESSES IN A PASSENGER AIRLINE COMPANY

- Market and sell services.
  1. Develop a marketing plan.
  2. Form and continue alliances with other airlines.
  3. Establish positive customer contact.
- Provide transportation services.
- Acquire, maintain and manage assets.
- Manage safety and risk.

EXAMPLES OF BUSINESS PROCESSES IN A MANUFACTURING COMPANY

Production Processes
- Production planning
  1. Schedule production.
  2. Order materials.
- Manufacturing
  1. Assemble product.
  2. Test product.
  3. Record costs of materials, labour and overhead used.
- Shipping
  1. Ship product ordered.
  2. Record inventory used.

Order Fulfilment Process
- Process sales orders
  1. Receive the order.
  2. Enter the order.
  3. Clear the order once shipped.
- Account for the sale
  1. Credit checking and approval.
  2. Generate invoice upon shipment.
  3. Post sales journal entry.

E X H I B I T   6 - 3   VALUE CHAIN ANALYSIS

Value chain analysis is described as "a framework for analyzing the contribution of individual activities in a business to the overall level of customer value the firm produces, and ultimately to the firm's financial performance."* The diagram shows the traditional, functional way of viewing business in vertical columns (e.g., research and development, or "R & D"). Value chain analysts claim that these functional areas are not the source of the firm's competitive advantage. It is how the firm organizes these functions to accomplish the activities of the business that determines whether a strategy is successfully implemented. The diagram shows processes (e.g., "add and keep customers") as cutting horizontally across the various functional areas. The processes are action oriented in keeping with the idea of finding what activities cause the customer to value the products or services delivered by a business.

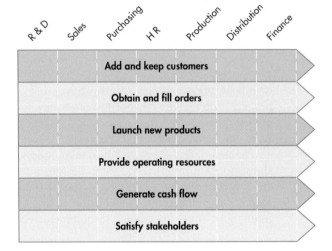

Value Chains and Traditional Business Functions

---

* Michael Porter, *Competitive Advantage: Creating and Sustaining Superior Performance* (New York: Free Press, 1985).

management approach has been facilitated by the development of powerful information systems that can integrate enterprise-wide resource and accounting information. These systems are often called **enterprise resource planning systems (ERPS)**.

The business process view also highlights the fact that business organizations differ in terms of the kinds of activities they perform and the technology they use. Some organizations use mainly routine tasks that can easily be reduced to simple formal rules that require little judgement (e.g., inventory ordering in a grocery business). These types of tasks can easily be programmed, and these organization are more likely to be run hierarchically. In contrast, organizations in which activities tend to be nonroutine and judgemental (e.g., an engineering firm designing specifications for office towers) would have complex, important functions in their operation that could not be programmed, and would tend to be run less hierarchically.

You can think of business processes as the unique ways in which organizations co-ordinate work, information and knowledge to produce a value-added product or service. Information systems can help organizations to achieve efficiencies by automating parts of their business processes, but automating requires careful analysis and planning. If more complex systems are used to strengthen the wrong process of business model, the business can become more efficient at doing things that it should not be doing. As a result the business's strategy will not be achieved and it will become vulnerable to competitors that have a better model. The most important strategic decisions involve understanding what business processes need improvement and how information systems can improve them, not simply buying the latest information technology.[10]

---

[10] Adapted from K. Laudon and J. Laudon, *Management Information Systems*, sixth edition (New Jersey: Prentice Hall, 2000).

The business process analysis continues to deepen the auditor's understanding that began in the strategic analysis. This additional depth of understanding should allow the auditor to identify risk areas that may affect the amounts and relations among the numbers recorded in the accounting system and the financial statements. The process analysis may also suggest disclosures that should be present in the notes to the financial statements. Business risks and audit risk assessment are discussed in more detail in Chapter 8 in the context of the audit risk model and developing the audit program, and in Chapter 9 in the context of evaluating and testing the internal controls.

R E V I E W
C H E C K P O I N T S

6.10   Explain the business risk approach to the audit. What is its purpose?

6.11   What are the two parts that make up business analysis? What is the goal of business analysis?

6.12   How does understanding the business's strategy help the auditor to assess business risk?

6.13   What is a business process?

6.14   How do business processes relate to strategy and business risk?

6.15   Give an example of one business risk that affects the airline industry, and one that affects a manufacturing business.

6.16   How do organizational differences relate to strategies and business processes?

EFFECTS OF INFORMATION TECHNOLOGY AND E-COMMERCE ON BUSINESS RISK

LEARNING OBJECTIVE

4 Summarize how changes in information systems, information technology, and e-commerce can affect business risks and processes.

Analyzing the effects of IT and e-commerce in the entity's business strategy is also an important component of the business risk analysis. As a business becomes more involved with e-commerce, and as its information systems become more integrated and complex, it will change its business processes and introduce new business risks that could affect the financial statements. Making enquiries of managers responsible for the entity's e-commerce activities, such as the chief information officer or equivalent, may be useful to gather the necessary knowledge.

E-commerce activities may be complementary to an entity's traditional business, such as an on-line order entry system run over the Internet, or it may represent a new line of business, such as when the firm uses its website to both sell and deliver digital products via the

---

INDUSTRIES THAT ARE BEING TRANSFORMED BY E-COMMERCE

(a) computer software
(b) financial services
(c) travel services
(d) books and magazines
(e) recorded music and movies
(f) advertising
(g) news media
(h) education

In addition, many other industries, in all business sectors, have been significantly affected by e-commerce.

Source: Adapted from *CICA Handbok,* Assurance Guideline AuG-32.

Internet. In an industry significantly affected by e-commerce, such as those in the preceding box, business risks that can affect the financial statements may be greater.

In understanding management's strategy and risk assessment process for e-commerce the auditor would consider factors such as:

- alignment of e-commerce activities with the entity's overall business strategy

- sources of revenue for the entity and how these are changing (for example, whether the entity will be acting as a principal or agent for goods or services sold)

- management's evaluation of how e-commerce affects the earnings of the entity and its financial requirements

- the extent to which management has identified e-commerce opportunities and risks in a documented strategy that is supported by appropriate controls, or whether e-commerce is subject to ad hoc development responding to opportunities and risks as they arise

- management's commitment to relevant codes of best practice or Web-seal programs

- information security issues arising from the firm's website, which can provide an access point to the entity's financial records. The security infrastructure and related controls can be expected to be more extensive where the website is used for transacting with business partners, or where systems are highly integrated. Information systems and technology are covered in more detail Chapter 7.

REVIEW CHECKPOINTS

6.17   How do risks of IT and e-commerce affect the risks of financial statement misstatements?

6.18   What are the implications of a business using e-commerce on its business analysis?

BUSINESS RISK AND THE RISK OF MATERIAL MISSTATEMENT

LEARNING OBJECTIVE

5 Illustrate how the auditor's business risk analysis is used to make a preliminary assessment of the risk that the financial statements are materially misstated.

The objective of a financial statement audit is to render an opinion on whether the financial statements, taken as a whole, are materially in accordance with generally accepted accounting standards. The term "materially" refers to the concept of "materiality." This concept is explained further in Chapter 8, but for our purposes it refers to a misstatement that is significant enough to affect an important decision that someone might make based on using the financial statement information. That is, a misstatement is material if it could lead someone to make a poor decision and suffer a loss from it, when they probably would have made a good decision if they used information that was not misstated. The auditor learns about management's understanding of business and process risks, independently assesses the business risk and management's risk assessment process to determine the risk that the financial statement could be materially misstated. This section describes a process the auditor can use to make this risk assessment.

The auditor knows that management has to take certain risks to achieve rewards in the marketplace. Those are the risks management accepts from being in business. Other risks, however, can be managed in any of four ways:

- avoided by not performing those business activities that would cause the risk to occur

- reduced to an acceptable level via management controls embedded in business processes

- tolerated on a cost/benefit basis

- transferred to another party via a contract (e.g., insurance)

After understanding the business risks, the auditor needs to consider which risks are high. The auditor considers two factors in this analysis, the likelihood of the risk occurrence and the magnitude of the risk. Each risk is qualitatively judged according to a three-point scale on likelihood of occurrence ("unlikely," "possible" or "probable") and magnitude of risk ("insignificant," "moderate" and "significant.") When considered together these two assessments result in classifying a risk as "low," "medium" or "high."

Exhibit 6-4 shows a graphical representation of the assessment process. For example, the business risk represented by point A indicates a risk that is probable to occur and if it did occur it would have a significant effect. Therefore, the auditor would classify the risk at point A as a high risk. The business risk represented by point E indicates a business risk that is unlikely to occur and if it did occur it would be insignificant in size. Hence, the auditor would classify this risk as low.

Most business risks are managed through well-designed business processes although some fall into the accepted or transferred category. The auditor considers any of the risks that threaten to prevent the entity from carrying out the process effectively. The auditor then identifies the controls that management has in place to ensure efficient and effective functioning of the key business processes. Here, "controls" can be broadly defined as, for example, "those elements of an organization (including its resources, systems, processes, culture, structure and tasks) that, taken together, support people in the achievement of the organization's objectives."[11] See Exhibit 6-5 for examples of management controls.

One way the auditor can consider these management controls is by determining if the key performance indicators employed by management are effective at controlling the process and whether management is actually using these controls. At this point the auditor makes a preliminary assessment of whether management controls are appropriate for producing reliable financial statements. Controls are explained further in Chapters 7, 8, 9 and 10 because they are a pervasive consideration in all stages of planning and performing the audit.

EXHIBIT   6-4   INITIAL RISK ASSESSMENT

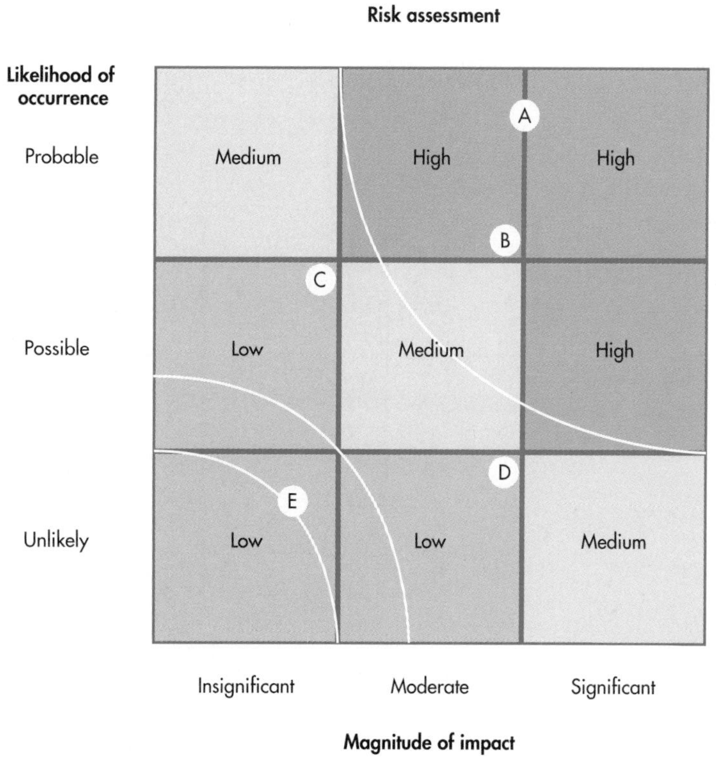

---

[11] CICA Criteria of Control Committee.

EXHIBIT   6–5   EXAMPLES OF MANAGEMENT CONTROLS

- Budget systems
- Forecasting systems
- Physical measures of process performance (e.g., defect rates)
- Quality enhancement programs
- Performance indicators (both financial and nonfinancial)
- Process monitoring activities
- Traditional accounting internal controls

After considering the management controls, the auditor evaluates the results that effective functioning of controls have on the original risk analysis. Exhibit 6-6 shows the auditor reassessing business risk after examining and testing the management controls. The business risk referred to as point C has been moved by the auditor from an overall risk judgement of near medium to well into the low category. The auditor has reclassified the business risk referred to as point A from being a clearly high risk to a medium-to-high risk. Note, however, that controls did not reduce the risks associated with point B. All the risks that are not moved into the low category by management controls are significant risks and need to be subject to further audit work. These residual risk categories effectively represent categories for which the control risks are high. In other words, the controls fail to reduce the risks that the financial statements do not portray the actual business performance.

EXHIBIT   6–6   RISK ASSESSMENT AFTER CONSIDERING MANAGEMENT CONTROLS

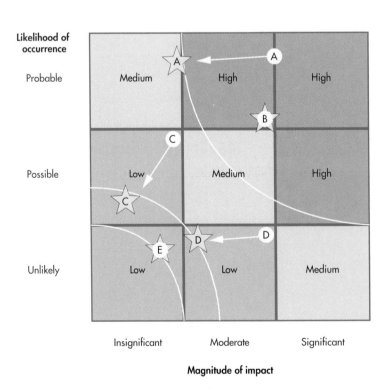

R E V I E W
C H E C K P O I N T S

6.19   How can business risks be managed?

6.20   What is the relationship between business risks and business processes?

6.21   What are some examples of management controls? What are the purposes of management controls?

6.22   Why does the auditor consider the controls management has in place over business processes?

6.23   How does business analysis relate to the auditor's goal of assessing the risk that the financial statements are materially misstated?

BUSINESS INFORMATION SOURCES AND METHODS

LEARNING OBJECTIVE

6 Identify the procedures and sources of information auditors can use to obtain knowledge of a client's business and industry.

The following is a list of methods auditors can use to obtain knowledge of the client's business, its industry and its environment. The methods indicate the wide variety of information sources auditors have available for gaining an understanding of the client's business.

Enquiry, Including Prior Working Papers

For continuing audits, information about the client is available in the documentation from the previous years' audits, such as permanent file documents and in prior audit working papers (documentation is covered in Chapter 8). Personnel who worked on the audit in prior years are available to convey their understanding of the business.

Enquiry and interviews with the company's management, directors and audit committee can bring auditors up to date on changes in the business and the industry. Such interviews with client personnel have the multiple purposes of building personal working relationships (which includes observations about the co-operation and integrity of client managers), obtaining general understanding and probing, with discretion, for problem areas in the financial statements.

One important aspect of the enquiry-based familiarization is obtaining an understanding of the client's information system and related business processes that are relevant in producing financial reports. The system and processes also indicate the client's method of communicating the roles and responsibilities of the employees involved in internal control over financial reporting. The audit team needs to obtain an understanding of the information system, which consists of infrastructure (physical and hardware components), software, people, procedures, and data. Many information systems make extensive use of information technology (IT). Infrastructure and software will be absent, or have less significance, in systems that are exclusively or primarily manual. This understanding helps the auditor to determine the use of IT versus manual procedures in recording significant accounting transactions, the complexity of the information system, its organization, and the availability of data and system documentation that may be needed to perform the audit procedures. Information systems and IT are discussed more in detail in Chapter 7.

Enquiry also provides an understanding of the needs of the users of the client's financial statements. Part of this is obtained when assessing whether to accept the engagement, but an important part is also obtained at this enquiry stage. The information obtained from enquiries of management, when combined with analysis of management's draft financial statements (covered later in this chapter), helps the auditor to assess what is significant to users. The materiality concept is a way of quantifying significance to users. Materiality is covered in Chapter 8.

Observation

At the same time that enquiries and interviews take place, the audit team can take a tour of the company's physical facilities. This is the time to look around for activities and things that should be reflected in the accounting records. For example, an auditor might notice a jumbled pile of materials and parts in the warehouse and make a mental note to check how these items are valued in the inventory account balance. The tour is the time to see company personnel doing their normal day-to-day tasks. Later, the auditors will meet these same people in more directed evidence-gathering circumstances.

Study

CICA and AICPA industry accounting and auditing guides are sources of explanations of the typical transactions and accounts used by various kinds of businesses and not-for-profit organizations. They were written by accountants for accountants. In addition, most industries have specialized trade magazines and journals. You may not choose to read *Canadian Grocer* for pleasure, but magazines of this special type are valuable for learning and maintaining industry expertise. Specific information about public companies can be found in registration statements and annual report filings with the provincial securities commissions.

General business magazines and newspapers often contribute insights about an industry, a company and individual corporate officers. Many are available, including *Canadian Business*, *Report on Business Magazine*, *Business Week*, *Forbes*, *Harvard Business Review*, *Barron's*, *The Wall Street Journal*, and the business sections of newspapers such as *The Globe and Mail* and the *National Post*. Practising auditors typically read several of these regularly. A selection of other public information sources is shown in the following box.

SOURCES OF BUSINESS AND INDUSTRY INFORMATION

General Information
Statistics Canada (including economic forecasts)
D & B Principal International Businesses
Standard & Poor's Register of Corporations, Directors and Executives
CICA Industry Guides, Audit Risk Alerts
Value Line Investment Survey
Moody's manuals (various industries)
CFO Magazine
Standard & Poor's Corporation Records
Analysts' reports
D & B Key Business Ratios
Firm libraries, universities, dissertations on specialized industry topics

Communications Media
Canadian Journal of Communication
Broadcasting-Cablecasting Yearbook (annual)
Advertising Age (twice weekly)
Broadcasting (weekly)
Publishers Weekly (weekly)
Variety (weekly)
Client websites, trade associations, conferences

The Internet is an increasingly important information source for auditors. Clients post financial statements and other information on their websites. Industry information and information on comparable companies can be obtained on the Internet. This information allows the auditor to improve his knowledge of the business and design more effective analytical procedures. Search engines like Google are an efficient tool for finding relevant websites. For larger clients, analyst and credit rating coverage can prove to be invaluable sources of information. Many of the articles in the business press are based on changes in credit ratings or in analyst recommendations concerning specific companies and industries. Brokerage firms' websites provide lists of companies followed by their analysis. There are also investor websites, such as Motley Fool (www.fool.com), that can provide valuable clues of potential problems in a client's (or potential client) business. Be aware, however, that Internet information may not always come from reliable sources, use it with caution. A minimum knowledge of the client and its industry is necessary to properly interpret such information.

Other Aspects of Understanding the Business

The general study of a business previously discussed can lead to some specific areas for further investigation and planning, some of which are explored following.

First-Time Audits

A first audit requires more work than a repeat engagement. If an existing company has been operating for a while, but has never been audited, the additional work includes an audit of the beginning balances in the balance sheet accounts. In other words, the starting place for the audited accounting must be established with reliable account balances. Such accounts as inventory, fixed assets and intangible assets affect the current-year income and cash flow statements. This work may involve going back to audit several years' transactions that make up the permanent account balances.

Internal Auditors

Audit efficiency can be realized by working in tandem with internal auditors. Independent auditors should understand a company's internal audit activities as they relate to the internal control system. Internal auditors can also assist by performing parts of the audit under the supervision of the independent audit team. External auditors' co-operation with internal auditors is explained in more detail in Chapter 18.

Analysis

The auditors' own analysis of the client's financial statements can contribute a significant understanding of the business and how it has operated for the period covered by the financial statements. Analytical procedures (e.g., ratio and comparison analyses) applied at the beginning of the audit can point out specific areas of audit risk. These applications are explained in more detail in Chapter 8.

Specialists

Auditors are not expected to be experts in all fields of knowledge that may contribute information to the financial statements. The understanding of the business can indicate the need to employ specialists on the audit. Specialists are persons skilled in fields other than accounting and auditing, such as actuaries, appraisers, legal counsel, engineers, chemists and geologists. Specialists are not members of the audit team but their expertise is required to obtain the understanding and evidence needed to audit a particular business. When specialists are engaged, auditors must ensure they have appropriate professional qualifications and good reputations. A specialist should be unrelated to the company under audit, if possible. Auditors must obtain an understanding of the specialist's methods and assumptions. The auditor also must verify all significant information that the specialist's conclusions are based on if the specialist's work will be a significant piece of evidence used to form the audit opinion.[12]

R E V I E W
C H E C K P O I N T S

6.24   What are some of the methods and sources of information the auditor can use to understand a client's business?

6.25   When does an auditor need to use the work of a specialist?

[12] *CICA Handbook*, section 5049.

MANAGEMENT'S FINANCIAL STATEMENTS

LEARNING OBJECTIVE

7 Outline the relationships among business processes, accounting processes, accounting cycles, and management's general purpose financial statements.

Two points need to be made about the financial statements: (1) the management of the company is responsible for preparing them, thus they contain management's assertions about economic actions and events; and (2) the numbers in them are produced by the company's control system, which includes the accounting system, and can be found in the company's trial balance. The relationship between the trial balance and the financial statements is shown in Exhibit 6-7, and the relationship between the financial statements and the assertions is illustrated in Exhibit 6-8.[13] (These exhibits use the trial balance of the Kingston Company, which is the subject of the case study located on the Online Learning Centre.)

EXHIBIT   6-7   KINGSTON COMPANY TRIAL BALANCE, DECEMBER 31, 20X2

Revenue process	Purchasing process	Production process	Financing process		Debit	Credit
X	X	X	X	Cash	484,000	
X				Accounts receivable	400,000	
X				Allowance for doubtful accounts		30,000
X				Sales		8,500,000
X				Sales returns	400,000	
X				Bad debt expense	50,000	
	X	X		Inventory	1,940,000	
	X			Capital assets	4,000,000	
	X			Accum amortization		1,800,000
	X			Accounts payable		600,000
	X			Accrued expenses		10,000
	X			General expense	1,955,000	
		X		Cost of goods sold	5,265,000	
		X		Amortization expense	300,000	
			X	Bank loans		750,000
			X	Long-term notes		400,000
			X	Accured interest		40,000
			X	Share capital		2,000,000
			X	Retained earnings		900,000
			X	Dividends declared	0	
			X	Interest expense	40,000	
			X	Income tax expense	196,000	
					15,030,000	15,030,000

The illustrative Kingston trial balance is short and simple. Real companies have more complex trial balances with hundreds of accounts. To simplify the audit plan, auditors typically view the business as having a fairly standard set of business processes that have a set of accounts and an **accounting process** related to them. An accounting process can also be viewed as a subcomponent of a business process. Four simplified accounting processes are used in this illustration: (1) revenue process; (2) purchasing process; (3) production process; and (4) financing process. Briefly, Process 1 deals with accounting for the sales activities of the firm, Process 2 deals with accounting for purchasing, Process 3 deals with accounting

---

[13] In Exhibit 6-7 and thereafter, the term *amortization* is the general term for allocating capital asset costs over the years' benefited in accordance with *CICA Handbook*, section 3061. Historically and internationally, specialized names for amortization have evolved in practice. Depreciation is amortization when applied to tangible capital assets, such as machinery and buildings, while the term depletion tends to be used for natural resources. In practice, amortization tends to be used in the more restricted sense of applying to intangible assets and premium or discount on long-term debt. Consistent with the *CICA Handbook*, however, we treat all these allocations as specialized names for amortization.

for manufacturing and inventory costing and Process 4 deals with the accounting for all the financing activities of the firm.

Another way to think of an accounting process is as a *cycle*. A cycle reflects a set of accounts that go together in an accounting system and record transaction information from the same business process. The routine transactions arising from a business process tend to run through the same accounting process over and over, like a cycle. These routine, everyday transactions are recorded by the client's accountants using the journal entries that always use the same set of accounts. Using the revenue process as an example, the idea of the cycle organization is to group together accounts related to one another by the transactions that normally affect them all. This cycle starts with a sale to a customer along with the recording of an account receivable, which is later collected in cash or

EXHIBIT 6-8   KINGSTON COMPANY UNAUDITED FINANCIAL STATEMENTS

BALANCE SHEET

Cash	$ 484,000	Accounts payable	$ 600,000
Accounts receivable	370,000	Accrued expenses	10,000
Inventory	1,940,000	Accrued interest	40,000
Current Assets	$2,794,000	Current Liabilities	$ 630,000
Capital assets (gross)	$4,000,000	Long-term debt	$1,150,000
Accum amortization	(1,800,000)		
		Share capital	$2,000,000
Captial assets (net)	$2,000,000	Retained earnings	1,194,000
		Total Liabilities	
Total Assets	$4,994,000	and Shareholder Equity	$4,994,000

STATEMENT OF INCOME

Sales (net)	$8,100,000
Cost of goods sold	5,265,000
Gross Profit	$2,835,000
General expenses	$2,005,000
Amortization expense	300,000
Interest expense	40,000
Operating Income Before Taxes	$ 490,000
Income Tax Expense	196,000
Net Income	$ 294,000

CASH FLOWS

Operations:	
Net Income	$ 294,000
Amortization	300,000
Decrease in Accounts Receivable	90,000
Increase in Inventory	(440,000)
Increase in Accounts Payable	150,000
Decrease in Accrued Expenses	(40,000)
Decrease in Accrued Interest	(20,000)
Cash Flow from Operations	$ 334,000
Investing Activities:	
Purchase Captial Assets	$ (1,000,000)
Financing Activities:	
Bank Loan	$ 750,000
Repay Notes Payable	(200,000)
Financing Activities	$550,000
Increase (Decrease) in Cash	$ (114,000)
Beginning Balance	600,000
Ending Balance	$ 484,000

NOTES TO FINANCIAL STATEMENTS
1. Accounting Policies
2. Inventories
3. Plant and Equipment
4. Long-term Debt
5. Stock Options
6. Income Taxes
7. Contingencies
Etc.

provided in an allowance for doubtful accounts. The typical journal entries used in this cycle are:

dr   Accounts Receivable
    cr   Sales Revenue
To record sales made on account.

dr   Cash
    cr   Accounts Receivable
To record collection of receivables.

dr   Bad Debt Expense
    cr   Allowance for Bad Debts
To provide for accounts receivable that are likely to be uncollectible.

dr   Allowance for Bad Debts
    cr   Accounts Receivable
To write off uncollectible accounts receivable previously provided for.

Auditors find it easier to audit related accounts with a co-ordinated set of procedures instead of attacking each account as if it existed alone because much of audit knowledge can be gained from the fact that predictable relationships should exist among these accounts. For example, if sales decrease but accounts receivables increase, this could be a warning sign that a business is getting into financial difficulties. Also, the audit evidence that is available for one component of the cycle often also contains information for other components, e.g., recording collection of a receivable involves recording the invoice information, as well as the information about the cash collected.

In Exhibit 6-7, the Kingston accounts are rearranged into an order not normally seen in a trial balance. This is done to illustrate the idea of the processes/cycles. You can see that some accounts are in more than one cycle. For example, the cash account is represented in all the cycles, because: (*a*) cash receipts are involved in cash sales and collections of accounts receivable (revenue process), (*b*) cash receipts arise from issuing shares and loan proceeds (finance process), (*c*) cash disbursements are involved in buying inventory and capital assets and paying for expenses purchases process), and (*d*) cash disbursements are involved in paying wages and overhead expenses (production process).

When placed in the financial statements, the accounts and their descriptive titles make the assertions that are the focal points of audit procedures. Exhibit 6-8 carries the accounts forward to the financial statements. Exhibit 6-9 illustrates the relationships among business

EXHIBIT   6-9   RELATIONSHIPS AMONG BUSINESS PROCESSES, ACCOUNTING CYCLES AND FINANCIAL STATEMENTS

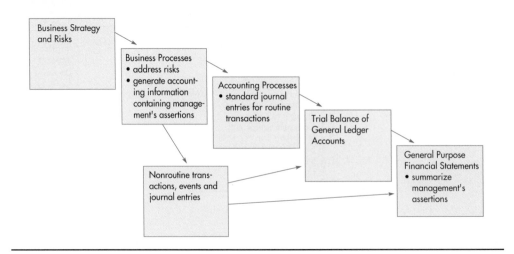

processes, accounting cycles and the financial statements. These process/cycles are covered in more detail in Chapters 11 through 14.

· ·

REVIEW
CHECKPOINTS

6.26   What are four of the major "accounting processes"? What accounts can be identified with each?

6.27   Why is the cash account involved in more than one accounting process/cycle?

6.28   Why do auditors tend to find it easier to look at accounting processes and cycles rather than individual trial balance accounts?

· ·

MANAGEMENT FINANCIAL STATEMENT ASSERTIONS AND AUDIT OBJECTIVES

· · · · · · · · · · · ·

LEARNING OBJECTIVE

8 Describe the five principal management assertions in financial statements, and their application in establishing audit objectives.

As you study this section, keep in mind this scheme of things:

- Management's accounting system produces a trial balance.
- Management arranges the trial balance in financial statements and thereby makes certain assertions about the financial statements.
- Auditors take these assertions as focal points for the audit work.
- The practical audit objectives are to obtain and evaluate evidence about the assertions made by management in financial statements. We will start with five principal assertions that are very broadly defined, but that are mutually exclusive and collectively exhaustive descriptions of the claims contained in management's financial statements:

    1. Existence
    2. Completeness
    3. Ownership
    4. Valuation
    5. Presentation

Exhibit 6-10 following illustrates the five principal assertions in some detail with relation to the inventory in the balance sheet.

Various alternate sets of assertions have been developed and used in audit practice to provide finer definitions and/or to be easier to relate to financial statement information and auditing procedures. However, all versions of describing the set of assertions can be reduced to the five preceding principal assertions. For example, *CICA Handbook*, section 5300 and ISA 500 classify assertions in the form of a framework the auditor should use to identify and assess the risks of material misstatement at the financial statement and assertion levels, to guide the design and performance of further audit procedures. The assertions as set out in *CICA Handbook*, section 5300 are shown in the box on the next page. These five principal assertions are described in more detail now in the context of their audit objectives and procedures.

Existence

The audit objective related to existence is to establish with evidence that assets, liabilities and equities actually exist and that revenue and expense transactions actually occurred. Occurrence is the existence assertion for transactions. An error relating to the existence assertion occurs when an account balance is overstated. Thus, auditors will count cash and inventory, confirm receivables and payables and perform other procedures to obtain evidence related to their specific objectives of determining whether cash, inventory, receivables, insurance in force and other assets actually exist. Beginning students must be careful at this

EXHIBIT 6-10   MANAGEMENT ASSERTIONS ABOUT INVENTORY

Balance Sheet

Cash	$ 484,000		Accounts payable	$ 600,000
Accounts receivable	370,000		Accrued expenses	10,000
Inventory	1,940,000		Accrued interest	40,000
Current assets	2,794,000		Current liabilities	650,00
Capital assets	4,000,000		Long-term debt	1,150,000
Accum. amortization	(1,800,000)		Share capital	2,000,000
Capital assets (net)	2,200,000		Retained earnings	1,194,000
Total assets	$ 4,994,000		Total liabilities and shareholders' equity	$ 4,994,000

Existence
Inventory in the balance sheet physically exists.

Valuation
Inventory is properly stated at cost.
Inventory listings are accurately included in the inventory accounts.
Valuation is reduced, where appropriate, to market lower than cost.

Completeness
Inventory quantities include all items on hand, in transit, and stored at outside locations.

Ownership
The company has legal title or similar rights of ownership to the inventory.
Inventory excludes items billed to customers or owned by others.

Presentation and Ownership
Inventory is held for sale or use in the ordinary course of business.
Inventory is properly classified as a current asset.
Major inventory categories and their valuation bases are adequately disclosed in notes.
Pledge or assignment of inventory as collateral is appropriately disclosed in notes.

ASSERTIONS FOR CLASSES OF TRANSACTIONS, ACCOUNT BALANCES, AND PRESENTATION AND DISCLOSURE

Assertions used by the auditor fall into the following categories:

(a) assertions about classes of transactions and events for the period under audit:
   (i)   occurrence—transactions and events that have been recorded have occurred and pertain to the entity;
   (ii) completeness—all transactions and events that should have been recorded have been recorded;
   (iii) accuracy—amounts and other data relating to recorded transactions and events have been recorded appropriately;
   (iv) cut-off—transactions and events have been recorded in the correct accounting period; and
   (v)   classification—transactions and events have been recorded in the proper accounts;

(b) assertions about account balances at the period end:
   (i)   existence—assets, liabilities and equity interests exist;
   (ii) rights and obligations—the entity holds or controls the rights to assets, and liabilities are the obligations of the entity;

(iii) completeness—all assets, liabilities and equity interests that should have been recorded have been recorded; and

(iv) valuation and allocation—assets, liabilities and equity interests are included in the financial statements at appropriate amounts and any resulting valuation or allocation adjustments are appropriately recorded; and

(c) assertions about presentation and disclosure:

(i) occurrence and rights and obligations—disclosed events, transactions and other matters have occurred and pertain to the entity;

(ii) completeness—all disclosures that should have been included in the financial statements have been included;

(iii) classification and understandability—financial information is appropriately presented and described, and disclosures are clearly expressed; and

(iv) accuracy and valuation—financial and other information are disclosed fairly and at appropriate amounts.

The auditor may use the assertions as described above or may express them differently provided all aspects described above have been covered. For example, the auditor may choose to combine the assertions about transactions and events with the assertions about account balances. As another example, there may not be a separate assertion related to cut-off of transactions and events when the occurrence and completeness assertions include appropriate consideration of recording transactions in the correct accounting period.

Source: *CICA Handbook*, section 5300.21.

point, however, because finding evidence of existence alone generally proves little about the other four assertions.

Completeness

The objective related to completeness is to establish with evidence that all transactions and accounts that should be presented in the financial reports are included. A completeness error exists when the account balance is understated. Thus, auditors' specific objectives include obtaining evidence to determine whether, for example, all the inventory on hand is included, all the inventory consigned out is included, all the notes payable are reported and so forth. Auditing this assertion means auditing what is not there, so verifying this assertion creates special difficulties for the auditor. A verbal or written management representation saying that all transactions are included in the accounts is not considered a sufficient basis for deciding whether the completeness assertion is true. To obtain persuasive evidence about completeness auditors usually need to gather corroborating evidence from several different sources.

Cutoff

A special aspect of existence and completeness is **cutoff**. Proper cutoff means accounting for all transactions that occurred during a period and neither postponing some recordings to the next period nor accelerating next period transactions into the current-year accounts. Since cutoff errors result in accounts being overstated or understated they can be related to either the existence or the completeness assertions.

Simple cutoff errors can occur in the revenue accounting process when late December sales invoices are recorded for goods not actually shipped until January or when cash receipts are recorded through the end of the week (e.g., Friday, January 4) and the last batch for the year should have been processed on December 31. They can happen in the purchases process when there is a failure to record accruals for expenses incurred but not yet paid, thus understating both expenses and liabilities. A failure to record purchases of materials not yet received, and therefore not included in the ending inventory, results in understating both inventory and accounts payable.

In a financial statement audit, the cutoff date usually refers to the client's year-end balance sheet date; however, a "cutoff" can be required at other times, for example when one accounting system is converted to a new system during the year.

Ownership (or Rights and Obligations)

The objective related to ownership is to establish with evidence that amounts reported as assets of the company represent its property rights and that the amounts reported as liabilities represent its obligations. In plainer terms the objective is to obtain evidence about ownership and "owership." You should be careful about ownership, however, because the idea includes assets (rights) for which a company does not actually hold title. For example, an auditor will have a specific objective of obtaining evidence about the amounts capitalized for leased property. Likewise, the "owership" idea includes accounting liabilities that a company may not yet be legally obligated to pay. For example, specific objectives would include obtaining evidence about the obligations under a capitalized lease or the estimated liability for product guarantees.

Valuation

The objective related to valuation or allocation is to determine whether proper values have been assigned to assets, liabilities, equities, revenue and expense. Valuation can involve the measurement assumption used (historic cost, fair value, present value) or the method of allocating joint costs. Auditors obtain evidence about specific valuations by reconciling bank accounts, comparing vendors' invoices to inventory prices, obtaining lower-of-cost-or-market data, evaluating collectibility of receivables and so forth. Many valuation and allocation decisions amount to decisions about the proper application of GAAP.

Presentation (and Disclosure)

Auditors also must determine whether accounting principles are properly selected and applied, whether financial information is presented in accordance with the underlying economic reality, whether disclosures are adequate, and whether any GAAP that apply have been followed. This objective relates to financial statement presentation and disclosures. Specific objectives include proper current and long-term balance sheet classification, and footnote disclosure of accounting policies. The presentation and disclosure objective is the meeting place for accounting principles and audit reporting standards.

Compliance

Although not normally listed as a separate assertion, compliance with laws and regulations is very important for a business, and disclosure of known noncompliance is sometimes necessary for presentation of financial statements in conformity with generally accepted accounting principles. The compliance assurance can be expected to continue to increase in importance as auditors' requirements to assess compliance with codes of conduct and to attest to effectiveness of control procedures as new laws and regulations are brought into force to improve governance and accountability (in response to corporate scandals). Auditors gather evidence about specific objectives related to financial laws and regulations, such as provincial securities acts, tax withholding regulations, minimum wage laws, wage and price guidelines, credit allocation regulations, income tax laws, and specialized industry regulations. Compliance with legal terms of the company's private contracts (e.g., merger agreements and bond indentures) is also important for financial statement presentations. The importance of this assertion has also been elevated through the issuance of section 5136 of the *CICA Handbook*, "Misstatements—Illegal Acts," which provides additional guidance on dealing with this assertion. When the sole purpose of an engagement is to audit compliance with various laws, regulations or rules, the engagement is called a **compliance audit**. This type of engagement is discussed in Chapter 16.

Compliance with laws and regulations is also a required characteristic of governmental audits, such as those by the Auditor General and provincial auditors. It is generally an objective for internal auditors with respect to managerial policies. Compliance auditing is a major topic in Chapter 18 (Internal and Governmental Auditing).

Assertions and Audit Procedures

Financial statement assertions are important because they are the fundamental management claims that are to be audited. They are the focal points for all audit procedures. When audit procedures are specified, you should be able to relate the evidence produced by each procedure to one or more specific objectives tailored to specific assertions. The way to begin planning when you have a list of audit procedures (for example, from last year's audit) is to ask:

- "What are the assertions management is making by reporting this financial information?"
- "Which assertion(s) does this procedure produce evidence about?"
- "Does the list of procedures (the audit program) cover all the assertions?"

The extent to which a particular procedure is used, however, will be determined by qualitative factors, the cost of the procedure, the risks associated with each assertion and materiality. Risk and materiality are covered in Chapter 8.

You can simplify the five major assertions by thinking of them as existence, completeness, ownership, valuation and presentation. Just do not forget that each of them has additional aspects, depending on the financial items you are auditing and the audit evidence available concerning these items.

REVIEW
CHECKPOINTS

6.29   Briefly explain the five principal assertions that can be made about assets and liabilities and auditors' objectives related to each.

6.30   How do financial statement assertions relate to audit procedures?

6.31   Why is the completeness assertion particularly challenging to obtain audit evidence about?

6.32   Why should auditors think about a compliance assertion that is not listed in the auditing standards about assertions?

6.33   How are assertions used in audit planning?

STRATEGIC SYSTEMS APPROACHES TO BUSINESS ANALYSIS

LEARNING OBJECTIVE
9 Describe strategic systems approaches to understanding business risk.

This section expands on the business analysis techniques explained earlier in this chapter. The 1990s saw a trend to develop new audit approaches that apply a technical knowledge of the theory of organizational strategy to evaluate a client's competitive position and its effect on the client's business risk. These new developments have been referred to as the **strategic systems approach** to auditing or **SSA** audits. An SSA audit can be characterized as a top-down approach that starts with an understanding of corporate strategy and the business as a whole to determine the effects on the financial statements. A key innovation in the SSA audit was the requirement for the auditor to try to understand the business as management runs it, but with an objective point of view. In contrast, the traditional financial statement audit tended to focus on a bottom-up approach, gathering evidence on individual transactions and aggregating them to the financial statement level.

The strategic systems approach is an application of systems thinking, as discussed earlier in the chapter. The audit team obtains an understanding of management's strategy by interviewing the senior managers and the managers of the various business units in the organization. The auditors learn about the business objectives (e.g. cost leadership, differentiation, market share) and the strategies management has in place to meet those objectives. Appendix 6A provides an introduction to frameworks used for strategic analysis. The appendix covers two commonly used approaches: an environment-centred approach (PEST analysis) and the firm's position in the industry (Porter's Five Forces model). Appendix 6A also describes three examples of generic strategies that firms often pursue. There are other frameworks for performing strategic analysis, such as product life cycle analysis and SWOT (Strength, Weaknesses, Opportunities and Threats) analysis. Many auditing students complete a course in strategic management that will cover all of these and more in detail.

Through discussions among the audit team members, auditors can assess whether the strategy is guiding the whole operation. For example, is top management's strategy for increasing customer satisfaction with their retail shopping experience reflected in the actions of store level management when they are deciding staffing plans? The auditor also enquires as to what the lower levels of management perceive as the risks that might threaten the successful implementation of the business strategies. These audit procedures, enquiry and team discussions deepen the audit team's knowledge of how the strategies are implemented and whether there are gaps between what top management says is the strategy and what business unit managers are attempting to carry out.

Once the auditor has a sound understanding of management's objectives, strategies and risks, she needs to assess the completeness of management's analysis. In particular the auditor considers whether management has identified all of the risks that might have a material effect on the business. If management's analysis is found to be incomplete, additional discussions with senior management are undertaken and depending on the outcome of such discussions, this situation would be taken into account in the auditor's assessment of business and audit risks.

Every business that is audited will have a number of processes as part of a set of activities that it carries out in creating value for its customers. The auditor, via interviews with various operating managers, defines what processes exist in a particular client. Auditors are aided in this task with generic process models that outline typical business processes found in clients in a particular industry. The auditor should choose only those processes that are key to the business and then within each process choose key subprocesses to examine in detail since it is not cost-effective to audit all processes. The choice of key processes can be made by considering the following factors:

- *Strategic relevance.* How vital is the process to the strategy and objectives of the client? The more vital the process, the more likely it will be considered key.
- *Inherent business risk.* This risk is the likelihood of a business risk occurring, ignoring the effects of the client's control environment (as explained following). The more likely the process is to contain business risks as identified in the strategic analysis, the more likely the process will be considered "key." Some factors that might be taken into account in determining the level of inherent business risk are as follows:
  - complexity of the process
  - management judgement needed in the process
  - likelihood the process will generate nonroutine transactions
  - extent of management judgement over these nonroutine transactions
- *Control environment.* This aspect reflects the auditor's assessment of the overall attitude, awareness and commitment of management concerning the importance of control and its emphasis within the entity. The types of factors considered include:
  - management philosophy and operating style
  - organizational structure

- management control systems
- systems development controls
- personnel policies

The auditor would subjectively weigh each of the three factors (strategic relevance, inherent business risk and control environment) in selecting which processes are key business processes for a particular client.

For each of the key business processes, the auditor would learn, via interviews with management, the following:

- process objectives (the roles the process plays in achieving the entity's business objectives)
- process activities
- classes of accounting transactions and systems employed
- process risks
- process controls (those management controls that the deal with the identified process risks)

The identification of key business process then guides the auditor's evaluation of management's process controls and how likely they are to have prevented material misstatement in the financial statements. This understanding and risk assessment is the starting point for designing further audit procedures that are targeted at the most significant risks. Important aspects of the SSA audit relating to understanding the business and its risks have now been incorporated into auditing standards such as *CICA Handbook*, section 5141 and ISA 315.

· ·

REVIEW   6.34   What is an SSA audit and how does it differ from a more traditional audit approach?

CHECKPOINTS   6.35   How does an auditor learn about management's strategy?

6.36   How are key business processes identified? How does the auditor's understanding of key business processes affect risk assessment?

· ·

SUMMARY
· ·

This chapter covered two major topics. The first was a set of activities auditors undertake when beginning an audit engagement. These pre-engagement activities start with the work of deciding whether to accept a new client and become its auditor and, on an annual basis, deciding whether to continue as auditor for existing clients. Public accounting firms are not obligated to provide audits to every organization that asks for one, and they regularly exercise discretion about the organizations with which they wish to associate. The investigation may involve the co-operative task of communicating with the former (predecessor) auditor of the organization. Once a client is accepted, the pre-engagement work continues with the preparation of an engagement letter, and the assignment of partners, managers, and staff to the job, and the preparation of a time budget for the audit.

We also covered the important process of obtaining an understanding of the client's business, its environment, and risks. The auditor's analysis of the client's strategy and how it addresses its business risks were reviewed. We then looked at how the auditor uses the results of analyzing the business and its risks to assess the likelihood that the financial statements could be materially misstated. Methods and sources of information were explained. The last part of the activities topic was a brief explanation of the financial statements, the business processes that generate transactions and accounting data, and the grouping of accounts into cycles for purposes of organizing the audit.

The second topic related to the basic practical concepts involved in performing audits. The financial statements were explained in terms of the primary assertions management makes in them, and these assertions were identified as the focal points of the auditors' procedural evidence-gathering work. Finally, expanded coverage of strategic systems approaches to auditing was provided.

As a summary, Exhibit 6-11 illustrates the components of the financial reporting process that were explained in this chapter. The client's business and its environment generate the activities that are captured, monitored and controlled by the information systems, which include manual and automated processes. The information systems are based on a financial reporting framework. This usually includes generally accepted accounting principles and internal control elements.

Information systems and internal controls will be covered in more detail in Chapter 7. These information systems provide input into the accounting journals and ledgers from which the company's general purpose financial statements and other financial disclosures (such as Management's Discussion and Analysis) are created. The assertions management makes in these financial statements are the subject matter of the audit. Chapters 8 and 9 will cover the concepts, tools, and procedures that auditors use to perform a financial statement audit and form an audit opinion.

EXHIBIT   6-11   THE FINANCIAL REPORTING PROCESS IN AN AUDIT CLIENT COMPANY

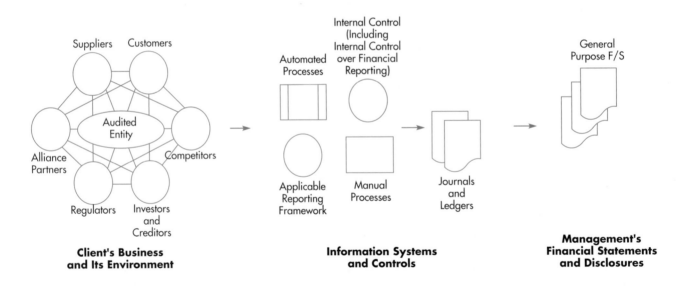

Source: Timothy B. Bell, Mark E. Peecher and Ira Solomon, *The 21st Century Public Company Audit* (KPMG International, 2005), p. 4.

MULTIPLE-CHOICE QUESTIONS FOR PRACTICE AND REVIEW

6.37 An audit engagement letter should normally include the following matter of agreement between the auditor and the client:
  a. Schedules and analyses to be prepared by the client's employees.

  b. Methods of statistical sampling the auditor will use.
  c. Specification of litigation in progress against the client.
  d. Client representations about availability of all minutes of meetings of the board of directors.

6.38 When a successor auditor initiates communications with a predecessor auditor, the successor should expect:
  a. To take responsibility for obtaining the client's consent for the predecessor to give information about prior audits.
  b. To conduct interviews with the partner and manager in charge of the predecessor audit firm's engagement.
  c. To obtain copies of some or all of the predecessor auditor's working papers.
  d. All of the above.

6.39 Generally accepted auditing standards require that auditors prepare and use:
  a. A written engagement letter for new audits.
  b. A written engagement letter for continuing audit clients.
  c. A written audit program.
  d. All of the above.

6.40 The revenue process of a company generally includes these accounts:
  a. Inventory, accounts payable and general expenses.
  b. Inventory, general expenses and payroll.
  c. Cash, accounts receivable and sales.
  d. Cash, notes payable and capital stock.

6.41 Understanding the client's business environment is important to the auditor because:
  a. it helps distinguish interim audit work from year-end audit work.
  b. management's draft financial statements contain assertions about the business environment.
  c. it helps the auditor to assess the risks that the financial statement contain misstatements.
  d. it eliminates the need for the auditor to understand the client's internal controls.

6.42 Business risk is related to business strategy because:
  a. auditors assess business risk so they can provide their clients with a business strategy.
  b. business risks are events or actions that cause changes in technology.
  c. managers frequently change their businesses risks in response to changes in the business strategy.
  d. business risks are events or actions that will have a negative effect on the audit client's ability to achieve its strategic objectives.

6.43 Information technology changes affect business risk when:
  a. they result in a need to change business processes.
  b. they involve entering e-commerce activities.
  c. when systems become more integrated and complex.
  d. all of the above.

6.44 The auditor assesses a business risk as high when:
  a. it is unlikely and moderate.
  b. it is likely and significant.
  c. it is possible and insignificant.
  d. it is likely and insignificant.

6.45 Which of the following is not likely to be an important source of information the auditor can use to understand a client's business :
  a. geologist's reports on mineral reserves.
  b. internal auditors.
  c. retail sales statistics.
  d. Monday night football scores.

6.46 Management's general purpose financial statements:
  a. are the responsibility of the auditor.
  b. include only non-routine transactions.
  c. make assertions that are the focal point of audit procedures.
  d. can rarely be reconciled to the client's trial balance.

6.47 The cash account is included in more than one accounting process/cycle because:
  a. all the business processes involve either receiving or paying out cash at some point.
  b. cash is the most difficult asset to control.
  c. cash is the easiest asset to steal.
  d. cash can be either an asset or a liability.

6.48 If the XYZ company reports a $355,000 balance of accounts receivable, the existence assertion means:
  a. there are no accounts receivable by XYZ that have not been included in the balance.
  b. all the amounts making up the $355,000 balance will be collected in full, in cash.
  c. all the amounts included in the $355,000 balance represent valid sales on account that are still outstanding and due to the company.
  d. the receivables have not been sold to another company.

EXERCISES AND PROBLEMS

6.49 **Communications Between Predecessor and Successor Auditors.** Assume that your client was audited last
LO.1   year by PA Diggs. Your client was generally pleased with the services provided by Diggs, but he thinks the audit work was too detailed and interfered excessively with normal office routines. You have asked your client to inform Diggs of the decision to change auditors, but he does not wish to do so.

Required:

List and discuss the steps you should follow with regard to dealing with a predecessor auditor and a new client before accepting the engagement. (Hint: Use the independence rules of conduct for a complete response to this requirement.)

6.50 **Audit Planning.** Walter Wolf was pleased. He had been
LO.8   with the firm of Riding, Hood & Co. less that a year-

and-a-half since graduation from university and had received excellent performance reviews on every engagement. Now he was being given "in charge" responsibility on an audit. It was a small client, but it felt good to have the firm show such confidence in him. He planned to show that the firm had made the right decision.

Walter thought back to some of the advice his seniors had given him. Two comments in particular stood out as key steps to a successful audit:

- Careful attention to planning the audit pays dividends. Time spent on audit planning is never wasted.
- Avoid being a mechanical auditor by focusing on management's assertions embodied in the financial statements and the related audit objectives when planning audit tests.

Required:

a. Develop a list of tasks that Walter should perform in planning this audit engagement, before any audit testing begins.
b. *Handbook,* section 5300 lists management assertions embodied in financial statements. List and briefly describe the associated audit objectives that relate to these assertions.

(ICAO adapted)

Classes of Transactions	General Ledger Accounts
Cash receipts	Cash
Cash disbursements	Accounts receivable
Credit sales	Allowance for doubtful accounts
Sales returns and allowances	
Purchases on credit	Inventory
Purchase returns	Capital assets
Uncollectible account write-offs	Accounts payable
	Long-term debt
	Sales revenue
	Investment income
	Expenses

6.51 Understand the Business—Transactions and Ac-
LO.7 counts. In the table above, the left column names several "classes of transactions." The right column names several general ledger accounts.

Required:
Identify the general ledger accounts that are affected by each class of transactions.

Approach:
Match the classes of transactions with the general ledger accounts where their debits and credits are usually entered.

6.52 Financial Assertions and Audit Objectives. You were
LO.6 engaged to examine the financial statements of Kingston Company for the year ended December 31.

Assume that on November 1, Kingston borrowed $500,000 from North Country Bank to finance plant expansion. The long-term note agreement provided for the annual payment of principal and interest over five years. The existing plant was pledged as security for the loan.

Due to the unexpected difficulties in acquiring the building site, the plant expansion did not begin on time. To make use of the borrowed funds, management decided to invest in stocks and bonds, and on November 16 the $500,000 was invested in securities.

Required:
What are the audit objectives for the audit of the investments in securities at December 31?

Approach:
Develop specific assertions related to securities (assets) based on the five general assertions.

6.53 Assertions. In the assertions listed in *CICA Handbook,*
LO.8 paragraph 5300.21 (see text box on pages 188–189) cross reference each to the five principal assertions. Why are these different terms used to describe assertions in different audit guidance materials?

6.54 Specialists' Work as Audit Evidence. What additional
LO.2 work does an auditor need to perform if a specialist's report is being used as audit evidence to form an audit opinion?

6.55 Business Processes, Different Industries. What busi-
LO.7 ness processes would be related to each of the four accounting processes in the following businesses?
a. a bicycle manufacturing business.
b. an architect firm.
c. a retail grocery store.

DISCUSSION CASES

6.56 Client Selection. You are a PA in a regional accounting
LO.1 firm that has 10 offices in three provinces. Mr. Shine has approached you with a request for an audit. He is president of Hitech Software and Games, Inc., a five-year-old company that has recently grown to $40 million in sales and $20 million in total assets. Mr. Shine is think-

ing about going public with a $17 million issue of common shares, of which $10 million would be a secondary issue of shares he holds. You are very happy about this opportunity because you know Mr. Shine is the new president of the Symphony Society board and has made quite a civic impression since he came to your medium-size city seven years ago. Hitech is one of the growing employers in the city.

Required:

a. Discuss the sources of information and the types of enquiries you and the firm's partners can make in connection with accepting Hitech as a new client.

b. Does the profession require any investigation of prospective clients?

c. Suppose Mr. Shine has also told you that 10 years ago his closely held hamburger franchise business went bankrupt, and upon investigation you learn from its former auditors (your own firm) that Shine played "fast and loose" with franchise-fee income recognition rules and presented such difficulties that your office in another city resigned from the audit (before the bankruptcy). Do you think the partner in charge of the audit practice should accept Hitech as a new client?

6.57 **Predecessor and Successor Auditors.** The president of
LO.1 Allpurpose Loan Company had a genuine dislike for external auditors. Almost any conflict generated a towering rage. Consequently, the company changed auditors often.

Wells & Ratley, PAs, was recently hired to audit the 20x3 financial statements. The W&R firm succeeded the firm of Canby & Company, which had obtained the audit after Albrecht & Hubbard had been fired. A&H audited the 20x2 financial statements and rendered a report that contained an additional paragraph explaining an uncertainty about Allpurpose Loan Company's loan loss reserve. Goodbye A&H! The president then hired Canby & Company to audit the 20x3 financial statements, and Art Canby started the work. But before the audit could be completed, Canby was fired, and W&R was hired to complete the audit. Canby & Company did not issue an audit report because the audit was not finished.

Required:

Does the Wells & Ratley firm need to initiate communications with Canby & Company? with Albrecht & Hubbard? with both? Explain your response in terms of the purposes of communications between predecessor and successor auditors.

6.58 **Risk of Misstatement in Various Accounts.** Based on
LO.5 information you have available in Chapter 6:

a. Which accounts may be most susceptible to overstatement? to understatement?

b. Why do you think a company might permit asset accounts to be understated?

c. Why do you think a company might permit liability accounts to be overstated?

d. Which direction of misstatement is most likely: income overstatement or income understatement?

6.59 **Assertions, Critical Thinking.** How does the
LO.8 study of assertions relate to the critical-thinking framework discussed in Chapter 4?

6.60 **Comprehensive Business Risk Analyses:**
LO.3 **Sleeman Breweries Ltd**[14]

Introduction

In 1984 John Sleeman began to build a brewing company whose goal was to dominate the craft brewing market in Canada by producing excellent ales and lagers. John began by acquiring the trademark symbol of the beaver on the maple leaf, and then he obtained the exclusive rights to distribute a unique bottle. John wanted his first product, based on an old family recipe, to be a traditional ale called "Sleeman Cream Ale." He incorporated the company under the name of The Sleeman Brewing and Malting Company Limited.

In 1988, a credit crunch came for the fledgling company when a significant creditor suddenly began to feel uneasy about the prospects for repayment based primarily on sales of Sleeman Cream Ale. John looked to the United States for a partner and found that partner in the Stroh Brewing Company who purchased shares in Sleeman. Along with the financial support and expertise of the company came the enthusiasm, energy and determination of Doug Berchtold, currently COO of Sleeman, a seasoned veteran from the senior financial ranks of Stroh.

John, Doug and all the management and employees worked very hard in 1989 and subsequent years, adding new products and increasing brewing capacity. Additional ales and lagers were added incrementally and the company grew in market share and volume. In 1995 it repurchased all the shares that Stroh had acquired. In 1996 after a reverse takeover of Okanagan Spring Brewery, Sleeman became a publicly traded company on the Toronto Stock Exchange, listed under the trading symbol, ALE.

The introduction of Honey Brown Lager in 1997 proved far more successful than anyone had hoped. It nearly doubled their market share and caused Sleeman to break ground on a new brewhouse expansion of 300,000 hectolitres (hl) (90 million bottles), bringing their total capacity in Guelph to 500,000 hl. Honey Brown Lager appealed to an increasing number of female consumers looking for an alternative to the traditional beer products. It has significantly stimulated the growth of Sleeman and has actually led to the expansion of the overall craft market size through a modest contraction of the traditional beer and ale market. Throughout the period 1988 to 1999 Sleeman had expanded by the introduction of its own products and the acquisition of smaller craft brewers either by purchase of shares or assets. Sleeman is now the largest craft brewer in Canada and is larger than the next four smaller craft brewers combined.

[14] Copyright © 1999, University of Waterloo. This case was prepared as a basis for instructional purposes rather than to illustrate either effective or ineffective handling of a particular situation.

Today's Beer Industry

Ontario is the largest consumer of beer and ale in Canada (in 1996, Statistics Canada reports that Ontarians consumed 7.6 million hl, compared to the total Canadian consumption of 20.3 million hl). In the province of Ontario, the provincial government creates a barrier for entry into the market through the operation of the Brewers Retail and the LCBO retail stores as the only two distribution outlets for beer and ale products. Brewers Retail (BRI) is owned by Labatt (43 percent), Molson (54 percent) and Sleeman (3 percent). These three companies form the "Shareholders." The LCBO is owned entirely by the province.

BRI requires every producer to distribute their products to each individual retail outlet from which they want to sell, or pay BRI a transfer fee for doing so. The shareholders of BRI (including Sleeman) have the critical mass necessary to avoid most transfer fees while most other breweries must pay the $15/hl charge. In addition, Brewers Retail collects and sorts bottle returns. The average bottle is used twenty times before it is crushed and recycled. Molson and Labatt receive the traditional brown bottle back. As Sleeman uses its own distinctive bottles, they are returned to them via Brewers Retail. If a new entrant uses its own distinctive bottle, these bottle returns are either sorted for a fee by BRI or crushed and recycled without being returned. It is usually too costly for a new entrant to use anything but the traditional brown bottle, almost guaranteeing that its product is indistinguishable from Molson's and Labatt's products.

The current economic factors of low inflation, low interest rates, good GNP growth rates and stable raw material costs have created a stable business environment for the beer and ale industry in general. The reason the overall market is changing has much more to do with social and cultural factors than economic ones. The population demographics in the three key areas of Ontario, Quebec and the Western provinces of Alberta and British Columbia are changing. The baby boomers are getting older, and older people do not drink as much beer as their younger counterparts. The boomers have more money than any previous generation and they use it in different ways. Today, consumers will spend more money on a product if it is perceived to either be fashionable or increase the quality of life.

One of the biggest differences in the market is the adoption of a healthier lifestyle in which drinking to excess is discouraged. This approach is reinforced by the adoption by the government of stringent anti-drink and driving legislation and enforcement. Also, the ability to motivate people to drink alcohol in general is closely monitored by the government and the main advertising message that is allowed is one of socially responsible drinking. All these factors together have created an environment where the traditional beer market is shrinking and the craft market is expanding. The craft beer and ale market has managed to take advantage of the change in demographics to reinforce the image that it is distinctly different than the traditional beer and ale market in Canada.

In addition to increased laws over drinking and driving, government also uses the brewing industry to collect additional tax revenues. Through a policy of aggressive taxation at the retail level, the government benefits from substantial revenues and provides no special subsidies or other tax relief for the industry.

There is little new in the way of technology in the beer and ale industry. The process has changed very little in several hundred years. The ingredients are one of the primary factors that make one product distinct from another. The physical process of combining, heating and fermenting the mixture changes from one company to another and this also changes the texture and the flavor of one product over another. The shelf life of a bottle is established by brewers to be ninety days, so in all provinces in Canada, most beer and ale that is over ninety days is pulled from the shelves and discarded. This rule has more to do with chemistry than any other factor: beer and ale begin to degenerate in chemical composition after that time.

The next largest factor after chemistry that differentiates one beer or ale from another is advertising and image. This is where the craft industry has been able to make the largest inroads on the traditional beer industry. Craft brewers require higher gross margins due to lower volumes and higher unit overhead costs, and fortunately the baby boomers are willing to pay the higher per bottle price that keeps the craft brewers in business.

The price for craft market products has an upper limit and a lower limit set in the market place. The upper limit is the price of imported beer and ale. These imported products are perceived to be premium products, some of the more common ones are Heineken and Guinness. They are priced higher due to a combination of freight, higher tariff duties and a higher price that reflects their global image. The craft industry has quality products, but these products are not perceived by the purchasing public at this time as providing the necessary "badging" to command a price greater than the premium imports.

The domestic beer industry giants, Labatt and Molson, set the lower limit on prices. They set a price for beer that is the same within a defined geopolitical region, such as the Maritimes, Ontario, Quebec and Western Canada. Frequently, but not always, that price is the same throughout Canada. The price of domestic beer is increasing at a faster rate than the premium imports are increasing, thus decreasing the price spread between the two. This "price squeeze" has caused the craft industry to put more emphasis on image and less emphasis on price as the price spread declines.

The consumer has little, if any, ability to affect price. The most that a consumer can do if one product becomes too expensive is to switch to a lower-priced product. The bargaining power of suppliers is also almost non-existent. The ingredients for beer and ale can be found in plentiful supply in almost every region in Canada. As a result of these market forces, Canadian craft beer producers' ability to satisfy gross margin requirements through price increases is declining. This trend has accelerated the consolidation of small brewers to increase volumes. Sleeman now has a presence either through direct production or distribution in every province of Canada. As a craft beer producer, its products occupy a market and price niche above the traditional beer market and below the premium imports.

Sleeman's Strategy

It is Sleeman's intention to remain the premier craft brewer in Canada and to be identified by consumers as the first alternative to traditional beer and ale consumption. Some of the key differences between the craft industry and the beer industry are described briefly in the table below, along with the relative position of Sleeman.

Although its marketing image is that of a family-owned craft brewer it shares characteristics of both industries. This places it in the delicate position of balancing the image of the craft brewer while approaching the size of the traditional brewers. It accomplishes this by acquiring small regional brewers and optimizing their production, marketing and distribution, while leaving the unique market attributes of the brewery intact. This approach created a collective of small regional craft brewers. The method most often used to improve profits after an acquisition is to perform clerical, data entry, production, distribution and sales at the local level, and consolidate the senior management from sales, marketing, finance and procurement processes at the Guelph location. This requires strong internal controls at the local levels since all data are input at the local level. Sleeman relies on good controls to reduce its administrative presence at the acquired company and to ensure that the acquired companies conform to Sleeman's policies and procedures. Sleeman has used this approach very successfully in the past and expects to use it in all future acquisitions.

As the number of acquisitions has increased, so has

Sleeman's confidence in its ability to predict earnings based on past and projected sales and earnings. The asset base of the companies it acquires is typical of the craft industry. The land and buildings are generally from five to fifty years of age, and in some cases the family may have owned the land for more than fifty years. Each of the acquisitions is specifically chosen to complement the existing product line on either a regional or national basis. Sleeman seeks to acquire only those companies that can add value to its existing product portfolio. It has historically sought companies with premium products that are well defined to a particular region or province. Many of the acquisitions are not in a growth stage when Sleeman makes the acquisition since inappropriately qualified senior management often stifles the potential growth. Sleeman uses its expertise to further develop and market the regional brands, thus adding value to its own brands.

Sleeman also makes certain that the acquired products do not simply reduce the sales of the existing Sleeman product line. The new products must be capable of sustaining their own sales growth once Sleeman takes over, but not by stealing market from other Sleeman products. Many small companies attempt product diversification, but the company resources and their markets are too small to support the diversification endeavour. Frequently, a rationalization of the existing product lines within the acquired company takes place once Sleeman gains control. Sleeman will reduce the number of products the acquired company sells and concentrate only on those products that have the most potential. This sometimes results in Sleeman shedding one or more of its own products if it feels that the newly acquired product will increase overall sales. Thus Sleeman constantly renews itself with each new product or acquisition.

Another strategic issue that Sleeman looks at closely is the ability to expand to new markets. The Canadian market is saturated and although the craft brewers can take from the existing beer market, even that market is only so large. The two most obvious markets that Sleeman would like to expand to are Europe and the United States. The extent to which the target has a market

SUMMARY OF BEER AND ALE INDUSTRY IN CANADA

Industry	Annual Volumes (hectolitres; hl)	Number of Products	Distribution of Product	Annual Sales Dollars (000s)	Ownership
Craft	Under 100,000	Less than six	Local or regional	$50–$10,000	Private; closely held
Sleeman	600,000	More than ten	Local, regional or national	$75,000	Public; closely held
Traditional	Over 5,000,000	More than ten	National	Over $300,000	Public; widely held

image in either the U.S. or Europe enhances its likelihood of selection within the Sleeman family.

Additional Current Issues

John reviewed the 1998 financial statements; they were the best of any year that the company had been in business. The three-year audited comparative financial statements (Exhibit 6.60-1) showed the success that had been achieved by concentrating on the core lines of ale and lager. Their next product launch was not to take place until the late spring of 2000, but preliminary market research showed that it had the potential to double the size of the overall craft industry market. This increase was at the expense of the large breweries like Molson and Labatt since the overall consumption of the beer industry had actually declined over the last few years. It meant that even with the introduction of competitors' products in the next two or three years, Sleeman could potentially capture a full twelve to fifteen percent of the total market of the entire beer, ale and lager industry. The cost to Labatt and Molson would be significant and would lead to the very real threat of intense price and marketing retaliation from each of them. John doubted that Sleeman could survive if both of the two industry giants decided to wage a full-scale price and advertising war against Sleeman.

John questioned the market research for the new product and had gone so far as to engage another marketing firm to verify the original test results. Although the second firm never saw the results of the original firm's research, and the test subjects and the testing methods were not the same, the results were quite similar.

Sleeman had expanded in the 1990s as fast as its infrastructure would allow. John pondered the ramifications of expanding to one million hectolitres at the Guelph plant. This was the minimum size it needed to go to if the market predictions were as accurate as they appeared to be. The initial product launch of new product would take almost 250,000 hectolitres, and their existing 1999 production of 450,000 hectolitres at the Guelph plant would take a significant portion of the existing capacity. Sleeman had just finished putting the final touches on the new brewhouse and that was to have kept it free from production bottlenecks for the next three to five years. There was even a suggestion from Allan Brash, vice president of operations, that Sleeman consider taking advantage of the economies of scale and expand by two million hectolitres. That would put it at almost half the capacity of either Labatt or Molson.

During the current year, Sleeman's former partner, Stroh Brewing Company, sold its brewing interests to Pabst Brewing. Pabst was now looking for a Canadian partner to continue the business of importing the Stroh family of brands into Canada. Based on Stroh's former relationship with Sleeman, Pabst approached Sleeman. John was now considering whether to enter this relationship which would mainly involve importing beer from the U.S. but also some additional production of certain Stroh brands in Canada. The Stroh products primarily appeal to a very price-conscious customer who would not normally purchase Sleeman's high-quality craft brews.

What would the public think about a premium craft brewer as an importer/brewer of a price-oriented brand? Would the public perceive Sleeman as a craft brewer if it expanded its capacity to over two million hectolitres for its own high-quality craft products? Even at one million it was in a transitional world between all its traditional competitors and the two industry giants in Canada. Labatt was owned by Interbrew, one of the largest brewers in the world, whose head office is in central Europe, and who has a worldwide capacity of 50 million hectolitres. Sleeman did not intend to compete with Interbrew, and John was concerned what the effect might be if Sleeman was perceived as a serious threat to Labatt.

Required:

Based on your understanding of the strategic systems approach to auditing, answer the following questions.
a. What are Sleeman's key business objectives? Why are these objectives being pursued?
b. What is Sleeman's strategy for achieving its objectives? What are the key factors that have shaped the current degree of success or failure of this strategy? Does Sleeman's strategy appear to be working?
c. What are the key threats (business risks) to the sustainability of Sleeman's strategy?
d. What are Sleeman's core products and services?
e. Who are Sleeman's customers?
f. Within which markets does Sleeman's operate?
g. What are the key business processes at Sleeman?
h. Analysis of a key business process begins with defining its objectives or, in other words, explaining management's vision for how the process contributes to the overall business objectives. What are the process objectives for Sleeman's mergers and acquisitions management process? What risks threaten Sleeman's achievement of mergers and acquisition process objectives? How might those risks effect Sleeman's financial statements?
i. Identify some critical success factors (CSFs) for the mergers and acquisitions process. Speculate about what key performance indicators (KPIs) Sleeman's might use to control its mergers and acquisitions process.
j. Focus on the new product development and marketing process. The process objective is to ensure that end consumers view Sleeman's brands as a high-quality alternative to mass-produced beers. Assume you as the auditor have identified as a process risk that brand image will suffer if it becomes widely known that Sleeman produces low cost/low quality Pabst beer, as well as its Sleeman's premium brands, in the same plant. How will you, as an auditor, address this risk in carrying out your audit?

EXHIBIT 6.60-1   SLEEMAN BREWERIES LTD.

Audited Balance Sheets
December 26, 1998, December 27, 1997, and December 28, 1996
All dollar amounts are in thousands

	1998	1997	1996
Assets			
Current:			
Accounts Receivable	$ 10,299	$10,342	$ 6,643
Inventories, WIP & Finished Goods	4,789	3,435	3,466
Bottle Deposits	7,183	5,032	4,149
Prepaid Expenses	1,303	473	717
Total Current Assets	$ 23,574	$19,282	$14,975
Property, Plant & Equipment	41,865	33,365	28,356
Long-term Investments	3,308	4,631	4,006
Deferred Income Taxes	566	–	–
Intangible Assets	36,342	13,980	14,631
Total Assets	$105,655	$71,258	$61,968
LIABILITIES AND SHAREHOLDERS' EQUITY			
Current:			
Bank Indebtedness	$ 2,547	$281	$ 3,733
Accounts Payable & Accrued	17,483	14,029	9,032
Current Portion of LTD	4,745	3,821	2,655
Total Current Liabilities	$ 24,775	$18,131	$15,420
Long-term Debt Obligations	29,465	19,156	17,389
Deferred Income Taxes	–	1,510	969
	$ 54,240	$38,797	$33,778
Shareholders' Equity:			
Share Capital	38,310	26,110	25,670
Retained Earnings	13,105	6,351	2,520
Total Equity	$ 51,415	$32,461	$28,190
Total Liabilities and Equity	$105,655	$71,258	$61,968

SLEEMAN BREWERIES LTD.

Audited Income Statements and Statements of Retained Earnings
Years ended December 26, 1998, December 27, 1997 and December 28, 1996
Dollar amounts are in thousands, except per share data

	1998	1997	1996
Net Revenue	$ 76,023	$54,061	$39,217
Cost of Goods Sold	34,575	26,080	19,737
Gross Margin	$ 41,448	$27,981	$19,480
Selling, General & Administrative Expense	26,302	18,663	13,897
Earnings before: Interest, Income Taxes, Depreciation and Amortization	$ 15,146	$ 9,318	$ 5,583
Depreciation & Amortization Expense	3,697	3,135	2,335
Interest Expense	2,112	1,442	1,441
Earnings before Income Taxes	$ 9,337	$ 4,741	$ 1,807
Income Taxes	2,582	911	325
Net Earnings	$ 6,755	$ 3,830	$ 1,482
Retained Earnings, Beginning of Year	6,350	2,520	1,038
Retained Earnings, End of Year	$ 13,105	$ 6,350	$ 2,520
Earnings per share—Basic	$0.44	$0.29	$0.14
Earnings per share—Fully Diluted	$0.43	$0.28	$0.14

6.61 **Business Understanding, Risk Analysis.** Assume you
LO.2 have recently been assigned to the audit team working
LO.3 on the financial statement audit of Loblaw Companies
Limited[15] ("Loblaw"). As a member of the team you are
now in the process of gaining an understanding of the
client's business, environment and risks.

From the *2004 Loblaw Annual Report* you have
learned the following about this business and its strategy:

Loblaw is Canada's largest food distributor and a
leading provider of general merchandise products and
services. Loblaw is committed to providing Canadians
with a one-stop destination in meeting their food and
everyday household needs. This goal is pursued through
a portfolio of store formats across the country.

It operates across Canada under various operating
banners (including Atlantic SaveEasy, Atlantic Superstore, Extra Foods, Fortinos, Loblaws, Lucky Dollar
Foods, Maxi, Maxi & Cie., No Frills, Provigo, The Real
Canadian Superstore, The Real Canadian Wholesale
Club, Shop Easy Foods, SuperValu, Valu-mart, Your Independent Grocer, Zehrs Markets, Cash & Carry and
other banners). These banners are set up as 658 corpo-
rate-owned stores, 400 franchised stores, and 519 associated stores. The store network is supported by 32
warehouse facilities located across Canada. Some
130,000 full-time and part-time employees execute its
business strategy in more than 1,000 corporate and franchised stores from coast to coast. This makes Loblaw
one of Canada's largest private sector employers.

Loblaw is known for the quality, innovation and
value of its food offering. It also offers Canada's
strongest control label program, including the unique
President's Choice and *no name* brands.

While food remains at the heart of its offering,
Loblaw stores provide a wide, growing range of general
merchandise products and services. In addition, *President's Choice Financial* services offer core banking, a
popular MasterCard ®, auto and home insurance plus
the *PC Points* loyalty program.

Loblaw seeks to achieve its business objectives
through stable, sustainable and long-term growth. It
seeks to provide superior returns to its shareholders
through a combination of dividends and share price
appreciation. Its willingness to assume prudent operating risks is equaled by its commitment to the maintenance of a strong balance sheet position.

In executing its strategies, Loblaw allocates the resources needed to invest in and expand its existing markets. It also maintains an active product development
program.

Loblaw is highly selective in its consideration of acquisitions and other business opportunities. Given the
competitive nature of its industry, Loblaw also strives to
make its operating environment as stable and as cost
effective as possible. It works to ensure that its technology systems and logistics enhance the efficiency of its
operations.

It strives to contribute to the communities it serves
and to exercise responsible corporate citizenship.

Required:

a. Based on the preceding information, list the industry,
   regulatory and other external factors that are relevant
   in understanding Loblaw's business and its environment. Use the risk factors outlined in Appendix 6B
   as a guide. (Optional: Extend your research by
   reviewing Loblaw's full *Annual Report* (available at
   www.sedar.com) and other Internet research sites,
   and identify additional relevant information to assess
   the risks.)

b. Link the risk factors you identified in part (*a*) to the
   risks in Loblaw's operations. Link these operating
   risks to risks of Loblaw's financial statements being
   materially misstated.

c. Outline Loblaw's strategy and describe, in general
   terms, the business processes you expect to find the
   company using to achieve its strategy.

d. While reading through the business section of the
   newspaper, you also came across following article on
   Loblaw's third-quarter results for 2005. What strategic risks are illustrated in the results being described
   in the article? Speculate on what strategic errors
   and/or business process deficiencies at Loblaw have
   contributed to these "woes." What impact do you
   expect these events to have on Loblaw's financial
   results for 2005?

LOBLAW TO STAY COURSE DESPITE WOES, PROFIT SLUMP

Despite a third quarter plagued by supply-chain
glitches, higher-than-expected restructuring costs
and a 25.6-per-cent profit slump, Loblaw Cos. Ltd.
will stick to its current retooling strategy, the grocery chain said yesterday.

Canada's largest supermarket operator reported
its summer-quarter profit fell to $192-million, or
70 cents a share from $258-million or 94 cents, a
year ago.

That missed analyst expectations of $1 per
share even though the company had previously
warned its restructuring—including an overhaul of
supply chains, systems and offices—would cause
short-lived profit fluctuations.

---

[15] *Loblaw Companies Limited 2004 Annual Report.*

"We're the first to admit that the execution of both the restructuring of supply chain and the adoption of a common-systems platform has taken longer and been more disruptive than planned," president John Lederer said.

"These disruptions have affected our performance in the short term. We're not happy about it. We're in the process of resolving it and we'll be a much stronger company as a result."

Additionally, a new third-party-operated general merchandise warehouse and distribution centre for Eastern Canada failed to reach "planned operating efficiency or capacity."

Loblaw said sales increased 6.4 per cent from a year earlier, to $8.7-billion from $8.1-billion, with all regions showing growth. However, sales at stores open a year or more were flat, adversely affected by the supply-chain mishaps with the general merchandise and health and beauty care departments bearing the greatest brunt.

Loblaw said this cut profit by $20-million, while restructuring and other charges caused a drag of $17-million. There was also a $40-million charge relating to an audit and proposed assessment by the Canada Revenue Agency examining GST charged on certain products.

Source: Rita Trichur, "Loblaw to Stay Course Despite Woes, Profit Slump," *Canadian Press*, November 11, 2005, p. B5.

6.62 LO.2 LO.3 LO.5 **Business Understanding, Retail Industry.** The newspaper article following discusses strategic issues related to two large Canadian retailers: HBC and Winners. Based on the information provided (and, optionally, other Internet research you may wish to do), identify the strategies being followed in these two businesses. Apply the strategic systems approach outlined in the chapter, as follows:

a. Explain management's objectives, strategies and risks in the two businesses. What similarities and differences did you notice?

b. In your opinion, did the managers in both businesses fully analyze the risks involved and take action to address them? Support your opinions with facts from the article (and your additional research, if any).

c. Do you think it is possible that any of the risks you have identified might have a material effect on the businesses? If so, what financial implications might these risks have, and could they affect the financial statements?

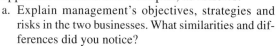

"COST-CONSCIOUS STRATEGY SCORES WINNER FOR HBC"

Hudson's Bay Co., in the midst of an unfriendly takeover battle, appears to be having success in at least one area: its push to woo the value-conscious shopper. Indeed, the efforts may even be hurting a key competitor.

Winners, the discounter known for big-box stores and brand-name goods at lower prices, has experienced a drop in same-store sales at outlets open a year or more—an indication that the business is suffering. And some observers say it may be getting a bit more difficult for Winners to find quality goods from suppliers.

Why? Because a few years ago, HBC chief executive officer George Heller decided to take aim at Winners' thriving "off-price" business. He wanted to ensure that his regular suppliers provided HBC with the same type of low-priced, end-of-season and excess goods that have made Winners such a destination.

"They've choked off the supply a little bit to Winners," says David Howell, president of consul-

tancy Associate Marketing International. "It's probably one of the smarter things that George has done. It's a good strategy and it seems to be working."

HBC, which owns the Bay, Zellers and Home Outfitters, has increased its selection of the so-called off-price products—everything from jackets to housewares—and marketed them heavily through flyers and in-store signs as "power buys." It opened special in-store boutiques called Style Outlets for discount items and, last year, began opening separate Designer Depot outlets similar to Winners stores.

In the midst of the push, late last month, HBC became the target of a $1.1-billion hostile takeover bid from U.S. financier and HBC shareholder Jerry Zucker, who is unhappy with the company's performance and says he can run it better.

Despite HBC's struggles, its off-price strategy stands out as a rare glimmer of hope. Executives didn't like to see their vendors supplying their stores with full-price products under well-known labels and then selling those very items—perhaps a little later in the season—to Winners at a fraction of the price.

"There's such a big appetite in the Canadian marketplace for off-price product and it's so underserviced," says Marc Chouinard, chief operating officer at HBC. "It's not surprising that this strategy is giving us what we want."

Sherry Lang, vice-president of investor relations at TJX Cos., the large U.S.-based parent of Winners, rejects any suggestion of overly tough competition with HBC for supplies. "Winners has enormous clout in sourcing globally," she says.

Rather, Winners' difficulties began in the last half of 2004 when its buyers purchased too much inventory too far in advance of the season, she says. It was forced to mark down prices heavily after other retailers began to do so, she says.

The weak results continued into the first half of 2005 as Winners' merchants attempted to correct the situation, she says. They purchased less inventory, and lowered all pricing at the stores, although she wouldn't say to what extent.

The results this year are soft, as well, because they are being compared to an "exceptionally" strong first half of last year, she adds.

Last week, TJX reported that October same-store sales at its Canadian division, which also includes HomeSense, fell 5 per cent and in the third quarter 4 per cent.

Ms. Lang says Winners' latest sales were short of expectations and hurt by unseasonably warm fall weather. She says the outlook is better for the remainder of the year.

Robert Johnston, a vice-president at Mr. Zucker's U.S. company, says Mr. Zucker is pleased that HBC is making inroads in its off-price strategy. But it took too long to get it off the ground, he says, adding Mr. Zucker would accelerate the off-price program if he took over HBC.

And while TJX has faltered of late, it has been vastly more successful over the past few years in its financial performance, compared with that of HBC, he adds.

Winners and sister off-price chain HomeSense still enjoy a comfortable lead in the category, generating more than $1.3-billion (U.S.) in annual sales.

HBC has about $250-million (Canadian) of annual "power buy" sales today, and aims to double that over the next three years, Mr. Chouinard says.

Kingston Case questions related to Chapter 6 are on the Online Learning Centre that accompanies this text.

APPENDIX 6A

FRAMEWORKS FOR STRATEGIC ANALYSIS

. . . .

This appendix covers two frameworks that are often used for strategic analysis, an environment-centred approach (PEST analysis) and the firm's position in the industry (Porter's Five Forces model). It then outlines three generic strategies based on the Porter model as an illustration of business strategies.

PEST analysis

PEST refers to four contextual categories that form the environment in which a firm operates:

- political-legal factors
- economic factors
- social factors
- technological factors

Overall, the PEST analysis should be a "broad brush." The factors that are considered in a PEST analysis may include:

1. **Political factors:** (*a*) government stability, (*b*) taxation policy, (*c*) government spending, (*d*) government relations with other countries, (*e*) industrial policy (e.g., towards privatization, regulation and nationalization).

   Legal factors: (*a*) employment law, (b) monopolies and mergers legislation, (*c*) environmental protection laws, (*d*) foreign trade regulations.

2. **Economic factors:** (*a*) inflation, (*b*) employment, (*c*) disposable income, (*d*) business cycles, (*e*) interest rates, (*f*) GNP growth rates, (*g*) exchange rates, (*h*) energy and basic raw materials prices.

3. **Social and cultural factors:** (*a*) population demographics, (*b*) income distribution, (*c*) levels of education, (*d*) lifestyle changes, (*e*) attitudes to work and leisure, (*f*) consumerism, (*g*) social mobility.

4. **Technological factors:** (*a*) new discoveries/developments in our own or related (e.g., supplier) industry, (*b*) speed of technology transfer (diffusion), (*c*) government spending on research, (*d*) rates of obsolescence.

The PEST analysis addresses the "big picture" in which a firm operates. It provides the context in which to perform a more detailed industry level analysis.

Porter's Five Forces Model

In order to understand the client's position in the industry, Porter's Five Forces Model aids in understanding the competitive pressures at work on the firm.[1] The intensity of these pressures as a whole will determine relative industry profitability and greatly influence relative firm profit potential. Exhibit 6A-1 shows the relationship among the five forces.

- **Threat of new entrants** is largely determined by such factors as: economies of scale, proprietary product differences, brand identity, buyer switching costs, capital requirements, access to distribution, absolute cost advantages, government policy, and new entrants' fear of retaliation.

- **Bargaining power of buyers** is largely determined by two factors: bargaining leverage and price sensitivity. Bargaining leverage is mainly determined by buyer concentration

[1] For more details see Chapter 1 of M. Porter, *Competitive Advantage* (Free Press, 1985).

versus firm concentration, buyer volume, buyer switching costs relative to firm switching costs, buyer information, and the ability of firm to backward integrate. Price sensitivity is largely governed by price of component versus total purchases needed to make product, product differences, brand identity, impact of component on quality/performance, and buyer profits.

- **Threat of substitutes** is mostly determined by relative price performance of substitute products, buyer switching costs, and buyer propensity to substitute.
- **Bargaining power of suppliers** is mainly determined by differentiation of inputs, switching costs of suppliers and firms in the industry, presence of substitute inputs, supplier concentration, importance of volume to supplier, cost relative to total purchases in the industry, and threat of forward integration of supplier versus backward integration of firms in the industry.
- **Intensity of competitor rivalry** is largely determined by industry growth, intermittent overcapacity, fixed costs/value added, product differences, branch identity, switching costs, concentration and balance, informational complexity, diversity of competitors, and exit barriers from industry.

Upon completing this analysis, the auditor has the information necessary to understand the firm's strategy and position in the industry.

Three Generic Strategies

A Canadian teaching at Harvard University, Michael Porter, developed a framework for analyzing strategies in his book *Competitive Strategy*. There, he outlined what he called three generic strategies: cost leadership, differentiation, and the application of both of those strategies to a narrow part of the industry, which he denoted as a "focus" strategy.

Cost Leadership
This is perhaps the easiest strategy to understand. The firm tries to become the lowest-cost producer in the industry while producing products/services with all the necessary features the buyer wants. This allows the firm to charge at or near industry average prices and, combined with its low costs, results in above-normal profits. If the cost leader does not have all the features normally required by buyers, then the cost leader's profits may be eroded significantly as it must make price concessions to make up for the lack of features. So while costs are the focus of this strategy, the firm must still pay attention to all the features that a buyer wishes the product to have.

EXHIBIT   6A-1   PORTER'S FIVE FORCES

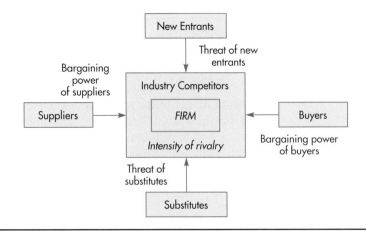

Differentiation

In this strategy the firm attempts to be unique in its industry along some dimension(s) that are widely valued by buyers. That is, the product or service has some unique feature for which the buyer is willing to pay a price premium. Of course this does not mean that cost is not important, as the cost of the unique feature must be less than the price premium to result in above-average profits. Further, all other costs combined need to be at or below industry average to have above-average profits. While a differentiation strategy focuses on unique features that appeal to a broad variety of buyers, costs must still be carefully managed.

Focus

Both cost leadership and differentiation are applied to the products or services for the industry. A focuser is different, in that it attempts to optimize its product or service for a narrow segment of the industry. The focus can either be on cost leadership or on differentiation. The segments focused on must have unique needs that cannot readily be satisfied by broad-based competitors.

Porter argues that if you are not following one of these three generic strategies, in the long run you will be "caught in the middle" as competitors who are following one of the three strategies take away your profitable customers. In other words, careful implementation of one of these three strategies, taking into account the industry environment and the firm's resources, results in obtaining a sustainable competitive advantage.

Each of these generic strategies has risks associated with it, as outlined in the following table:

Risks of Cost Leadership	Risks of Differentiation	Risks of Focus
Cost leadership is not sustained because: • Competitors imitate. • Technology changes. • Other bases for cost leadership erode.	Differentiation is not sustained because: • Competitors imitate. • Bases for differentiation become less important to buyers.	Competitors imitate: The target segment becomes unattractive as demand disappears or the basis of segmentation disappears.
Features that must be present in the product or service change and the cost leader does not make the changes.	The cost of the differentiated feature rises above the price premium or other costs rise relative to industry average.	Broadly targeted competitors overwhelm the segment: • The segment differences with other segments narrow. • The advantages of a broad line increase.
Cost focusers achieve even lower costs in each segment they service, leaving no room for a broad-based cost leader.	Differentiation focusers achieve even greater differentiation in segments, leaving no room for a broad-based differentiator.	New focusers subsegment the industry even further.

APPENDIX 6B BUSINESS RISK FACTORS

. . . .

Business risks that the auditor considers when assessing of the risk of material financial statement misstatement include the following:

UNDERSTANDING THE ENTITY AND ITS ENVIRONMENT, INCLUDING ITS INTERNAL CONTROL

Industry, regulatory and other external factors, including the applicable financial reporting framework

Industry conditions
(a) The market and competition, including demand, capacity, and price competition
(b) Cyclical or seasonal activity
(c) Product technology relating to the entity's products
(d) Energy supply and cost

Regulatory environment
(a) Accounting principles and industry-specific practices
(b) Regulatory framework for a regulated industry
(c) Legislation and regulation that significantly affect the entity's operations
  (i) Regulatory requirements
  (ii) Direct supervisory activities
(d) Taxation (corporate and other)
(e) Government policies currently affecting the conduct of the entity's business
  (i) Monetary, including foreign exchange controls
  (ii) Fiscal
  (iii) Financial incentives (e.g., government aid programs)
  (iv) Tariffs, trade restrictions
(f) Environmental requirements affecting the industry and the entity's business

Other external factors currently affecting the entity's business
(a) General level of economic activity (e.g., recession, growth)
(b) Interest rates and availability of financing
(c) Inflation, currency revaluation

Nature of the entity

Business operations
(a) Nature of the business
  (i) Profit-oriented (e.g., financial or other services, manufacturer, wholesaler, importer, exporter)
  (ii) Government (e.g., federal, provincial, territorial, local)
  (iii) Government organization (e.g., department/ministry, Crown corporation, fund, agency)
  (iv) Not-for-profit organization (e.g., an entity established for social, educational, religious, health or philanthropic purposes)
(b) Nature of revenue sources (e.g., manufacturer, wholesaler, banking, insurance or other financial services, import/export trading, utility, transportation, technology products and services)
(c) Products or services and markets (e.g., major customers and contracts, terms of payment, profit margins, market share, competitors, exports, pricing policies, reputation of products, warranties, order book, trends, marketing strategy and objectives, manufacturing processes)
(d) Conduct of operations (e.g., stages and methods of production, business segments, delivery of products and services, details of declining or expanding operations)
(e) Alliances, joint ventures, and outsourcing activities
(f) Involvement in electronic commerce, including Internet sales and marketing activities
(g) Geographic dispersion and industry segmentation
(h) Location of production facilities, warehouses, and offices
(i) Key customers
(j) Important suppliers of goods and services (e.g., long-term contracts, stability of supply, terms of payment, imports, methods of delivery such as "just-in-time")
(k) Employment (e.g., by location, supply, wage levels, union contracts, pension and other post-employment benefits, stock option or incentive bonus

arrangements, and government regulation related to employment matters)

(l)   Research and development activities and expenditures

(m)   Transactions with related parties

(n)   Nature of expenditures including programs and activities of not-for-profit and government entities

Investments

(a)   Acquisitions, mergers or disposals of business activities (planned or recently executed)

(b)   Investments and dispositions of securities and loans

(c)   Capital investment activities, including investments in plant and equipment and technology, and any recent or planned changes

(d)   Investments in non-consolidated entities, including partnerships, joint ventures and special-purpose entities

Financing

(a)   Group structure — major subsidiaries and associated entities, including consolidated and non-consolidated structures

(b)   Debt structure, including covenants, restrictions, guarantees, and off-balance sheet financing arrangements

(c)   Leasing of property, plant or equipment for use in the business

(d)   Beneficial owners (local, foreign, business reputation and experience)

(e)   Related parties

(f)   Use of derivative financial instruments

(g)   Form of ownership (e.g., private company, public company, partnership, joint venture, government-owned or controlled, member-owned)

Financial reporting

(a)   Accounting principles and industry-specific practices

(b)   Revenue recognition practices

(c)   Accounting for fair values

(d)   Inventories (e.g., locations, quantities)

(e)   Foreign currency assets, liabilities and transactions

(f)   Industry-specific significant categories (e.g., loans and investments for banks, accounts receivable and inventory for manufacturers, research and development for pharmaceuticals)

(g)   Accounting for unusual or complex transactions including those in controversial or emerging areas (e.g., accounting for stock-based compensation)

(h)   Financial statement presentation and disclosure

Objectives and strategies and related business risks

(a)   Existence of objectives (e.g., how the entity addresses industry, regulatory and other external factors) relating to, for example, the following:

(i)   Industry developments (e.g., a potential related business risk might be that the entity does not have the personnel or expertise to deal with the changes in the industry)

(ii)   New products and services (e.g., a potential related business risk might be that there is increased product liability)

(iii)   Expansion of the business (e.g., a potential related business risk might be that the demand has not been accurately estimated)

(iv)   New accounting requirements (e.g., a potential related business risk might be incomplete or improper implementation, or increased costs)

(v)   Regulatory requirements (e.g., a potential related business risk might be that there is increased legal exposure)

(vi)   Current and prospective financing requirements (e.g., a potential related business risk might be the loss of financing due to the entity's inability to meet requirements)

(vii)   Use of IT (e.g., a potential related business risk might be that systems and processes are incompatible)

(b)   Effects of implementing a strategy, particularly any effects that will lead to new accounting requirements (e.g., a potential related business risk might be incomplete or improper implementation)

Measurement and review of the entity's financial performance

(a)   Key ratios and operating statistics

(b)   Key performance indicators

(c)   Employee performance measures and incentive compensation policies

(d)   Trends

(e)   Use of forecasts, budgets and variance analysis

(f)   Analyst reports and credit rating reports

(g)   Competitor analysis

(h)   Period-on-period financial performance (revenue growth, profitability, leverage)

Internal control components

(a)   the control environment;

(b)   the entity's risk assessment process;

(c)   the information system, including the related business processes, relevant to financial reporting, and communication;

(d)   control activities; and

(e)   monitoring of controls.

Source: *CICA Handbook*, paragraphs 5141.020–.043 and Appendices A and B.

CHAPTER

7

Information Systems, Technology, and Internal Controls

Chapter 7 provides an overview of information systems and the information technology (IT) used in them. This chapter will also introduce control aspects of information systems by describing the internal controls that management includes within its information systems. Knowledge of systems and controls is needed to assess risk and design effective audit procedures.

LEARNING OBJECTIVES

After completing this chapter, you will be able to:

1 Describe the elements of an information system.

2 Describe the basic components of internal control: the control environment; management's risk assessment process; information systems and communication; control activities; and monitoring.

3 Understand how a company's control environment, information systems and its general and application control activities are related to the risk that its financial statements are misstated.

*4 Highlight the characteristics and control risks in simple LAN-based computer systems.

*5 Highlight the characteristics and control risks in personal computer-based information systems.

*6 Describe the effects of e-business on auditing (Appendix 7A).

*7 Ensure the security of credit card payments using SSL and SET protocols (Appendix 7B).

* Learning objectives marked with an asterisk (*) and their corresponding topics are considered advanced material. *Note:* Appendices 7A and 7B are located on the text Online Learning Centre.

Understanding Information Systems and Technology

LEARNING OBJECTIVE

① Describe the elements of an information system.

Once the auditor has gained an understanding of the client's business, strategy, business risks and business processes, his next step is to learn about the client's information system. The basic components and functions of an information system are provided in the following box.

What Is an Information System?

An **information system** can be defined technically as a set of interrelated components that collect (or retrieve), process, store and distribute information to support decision making and control in an organization. In addition to supporting decision making, co-ordination and control, information systems may also help managers and workers analyze problems, visualize complex subjects and create new products.

Information systems contain information about significant people, places and things within the organization or in the environment surrounding it. By **information** we mean data that have been shaped into a form that is meaningful and useful to human beings. **Data**, in contrast, are streams of raw facts representing events occurring in organizations or the physical environment before they have been organized and arranged into a form that people can understand and use.

The figure below shows the components and functions of an information system. An information system contains information about an organization and its surrounding environment. Three basic activities—input, processing and output—produce the information organizations need. Feedback is output returned to appropriate people or activities in the organization to evaluate and refine the input.

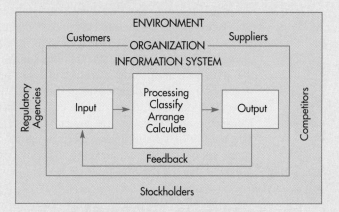

Source: Kenneth C. Laudon and Jane P. Laudon, *Management Information Systems*, ninth edition, © 2006, pp. 13, 15, 17. Adapted by permission of Pearson Education, Inc., Upper Saddle River, NJ.

Information systems consist of infrastructure (physical and hardware components), software, people, procedures and data. Many information systems are highly automated, making extensive use of **information technology (IT)**. Information systems may also have some manual components. Systems that are primarily manual will have little or no hardware and software.

Information Systems and Business Processes

The information system will be related to all of the key business processes. The important aspects of the information system for the auditor to understand are how it relates to financial reporting, and how it is used to communicate information within the organization. In organizations with **enterprise resource planning (ERP) systems**, the information inputs and outputs from many or all the business processes will be processed in an integrated manner, so the accounting component of the information system will be closely related to many other functional areas such as sales, inventory, human resources, cash management, etc. The business process view described in Chapter 6 provides logical links between information generated in various processes and the accounting component of the information system.

The auditor needs to gain an understanding of how the client's information system is used in its financial reporting process and identify the risk associated with IT use. As shown in the following box, the functions of the information system can be directly related to the assertions and audit objectives that guide the auditor in planning procedures to obtain audit evidence.

INFORMATION SYSTEM FUNCTIONS AND FINANCIAL STATEMENT ASSERTIONS

An information system includes methods and records that:

(a) identify and record all valid transactions;
(b) describe on a timely basis the transactions in sufficient detail to permit proper classification of transactions for financial reporting;
(c) measure the value of transactions in a manner that permits recording their proper monetary value in the financial statements;
(d) determine the time period in which transactions occurred to permit recording of transactions in the proper accounting period; and
(e) present properly the transactions and related disclosures in the financial statements.

Transactions may be initiated manually or automatically by programmed procedures. Recording includes identifying and capturing the relevant information for transactions or events. Processing includes functions such as edit and validation, calculation, measurement, valuation, summarization and reconciliation, whether performed by automated or manual procedures. Reporting relates to the preparation of financial reports as well as other information, in electronic or printed format, that the entity uses in measuring and reviewing the entity's financial performance and in other functions. The quality of system-generated information affects management's ability to make appropriate decisions in managing and controlling the entity's activities and to prepare reliable financial reports.

Source: *CICA Handbook,* section 5141, Appendix B.

CICA Handbook, section 5141 also requires the auditor to understand how the information system is used to facilitate communications within the organization. In particular, the auditor is interested in aspects of communications that relate to the implementation of internal control, as described in the following box. Internal control involves those activities, policies and procedures that help ensure that actions are taken to address threats that may prevent the business from achieving its strategy. Control activities occur within IT or manual systems, have various objectives and are applied at various organizational and functional levels; thus, effective communications between employees are essential for internal control to work properly.

Business processes and information systems in small businesses are likely to be less formal than in larger organizations, but are just as important. If management is highly involved

---

COMMUNICATION AND INTERNAL CONTROL

Communication involves providing an understanding of individual roles and responsibilities pertaining to internal control over financial reporting. It includes the extent to which personnel understand how their activities in the financial reporting information system relate to the work of others and the means of reporting exceptions to an appropriate higher level within the entity. Open communication channels help ensure that exceptions are reported and acted on.

Communication takes such forms as policy manuals, accounting and financial reporting manuals, and memoranda. Communication also can be made electronically, orally and through the actions of management.

Source: *CICA Handbook*, section 5141, Appendix B.

---

in the business processes, there may be no need for extensive written descriptions of company policies or accounting procedures. Communication may be easier, too, as management tends to be more accessible to other employees than is the case in a larger, more hierarchical organizational structure.

There are many business models that have evolved on the wide-open Internet. In addition to **business to business (B2B), business to consumer (B2C)** and **consumer to consumer (C2C)** (discussed in Appendix 7A), some of the newer models include **business to employee (B2E)**—typically a system enabling intercompany (intragroup) e-mails over the Internet to be directed to the correct department. These internal uses of Internet technology are referred to as **Intranets**. Other models include **business to government (B2G)**—(electronic submission of corporate tax returns and regulatory filings), and **customer to government (C2G)** (electronic submission of individual tax returns). It is evident that the rapid evolution of the Internet and IT have affected all aspects of the business world and management.

What auditors are mainly concerned with, however, is the security of IT processing, especially as it affects the accuracy and reliability of the accounting function. It is useful to look at IT in terms of the following elements: IT business processes, IT applications, and IT infrastructure. IT business processes relate to operations of the business in which IT is used. IT applications are the application software used by the IT. And IT infrastructure reflects all the technical resources necessary for the operation of the IT system, for example, hardware, operating system software and communications facilities to support internal and external networks. The IT control system controls how these elements operate together to achieve their objectives while reducing risk to a tolerable level. The IT control system is part of the internal control system.

When the automation of transactions becomes more complex, auditing firms need to employ IT audit specialists who understand computer technology and are aware of basic audit purposes. These "IT specialists" are members of the audit team and are called upon when the need for their skills arises, just as statistical sampling specialists or industry specialists are available when their expertise is needed. All auditors should have enough familiarity with computer processing and controls to enable them to complete the audit of simple systems and to work with IT specialists.

Some of the topics in IT can be quite technical and have a pervasive effect on client business practices, including accounting. In this text, we provide an introduction and overview of the major issues. Your IT audit course will cover these topics in more depth. Truly specialized expertise will require experience and even further study. As with all things to do with IT, much of the technology is in a constant state of flux. Rapid and radical technological changes can be risk factors to a business in many different ways. They can expose the organization to control risks such as unauthorized access to their proprietary or confidential information, as shown in the following box.

SCRAP YARD RECEIVING CIBC CUSTOMERS' PRIVATE DATA

HOST: Beverly Thomson

GUESTS: David Akin, CTV News; Wade Peer, Junkyard Owner

THOMSON: It's one of the worst security-breach scenarios imaginable. Your personal banking information, information you think is being kept confidential, is mistakenly sent to the wrong person. And that's exactly what happened to hundreds of CIBC customers. Instead of being sent to bank offices, their financial records were accidentally faxed to a junkyard man in West Virginia. And the faxes kept on coming, despite pleas from the frustrated yard owner to stop. CTV's David Akin has this exclusive.

[Taped segment begins]

DAVID AKIN (CTV News): The first faxes came through in 2001, confidential documents never intended to be seen outside a CIBC branch. And yet, they have ended up here, at Wade Peer's scrap yard in rural West Virginia.

WADE PEER (Junkyard Owner): I feel that CIBC's customers should know. I think that had that been my information I would be highly upset. I'd be livid.

AKIN: Here is why. Many faxes that Peer received contain some of the most sensitive data a bank has about its customers: names, phone numbers, social insurance numbers, bank account numbers, and even signatures. Peer needed his fax machine to talk to customers of his auto-accessories wholesale business. But a flood of faxes from the CIBC overwhelmed the phone system, Peer says, and he had to shut the accessories business down.

PEER: We couldn't even use them. We couldn't get calls in, we couldn't get calls out.

AKIN: But he didn't close down the fax number. And even as recently as this week the faxes sent by CIBC continue to arrive at this West Virginia scrap yard.

PEER: Cooksville, Edmonton, Calgary, Burlington, Port Hope, Toronto.

AKIN: Both he and the bank used similar toll-free 1-877 lines for their faxes. But neither he nor the bank can say how they got mixed up. Frustrated by the bank's response, Peer filed a lawsuit last spring. He wants $3-million US for the damage he says CIBC did to his business. The bank denies his allegations.

AKIN: The CIBC said it thought the problem of misdirected faxes was resolved in 2002. And in a statement issued to CTV News it said it takes the confidentiality of its customers' personal information very seriously. And that it was a disturbing revelation to learn that the faxes continue. It went on to say that "we are undertaking a full review of this matter."

[Taped segment ends]

THOMSON: . . . And wow. I mean, Wade Peer is an honest guy . . . who has not done anything sinister with this. What happens if it falls into the wrong hands?

AKIN: Well, you hit on it. I mean, by lucky chance this went to a responsible guy. He shredded a lot of the documents he first got. He knew exactly what he had at first. But when he started to get in this contest with the bank, he has kept many of the documents. They're locked up in a filing cabinet you saw in that piece. Experts say this is exactly the sort of information that online fraud artists, identity thieves, could use to go to a bank and get a debit card, get a new PIN number, and away they go.

THOMSON: False ID.

AKIN: I think it's important to point out, so far as we know, no CIBC customer has come to any harm or lost any money as a result of this.

THOMSON: And David, just very quickly, is it normal business practice to be faxing these kinds of pieces of information?

AKIN: The banks need your signature on these documents. So they have a central fax unit in Toronto, that most banks do, that the transaction will happen electronically. And this is just the backup document to authenticate it. So it's routine for banks to do this but, presumably, they're triple-checking fax numbers. And I'm sure all the banks this morning are triple-checking their fax numbers to make sure that the documents are going to where they're supposed to be going.

Source: "Scrap Yard Receiving CIBC Customers' Private Data," Canada AM—CTV Television, Transcript, Toronto: November 26, 2004. p. 1. CTV Television Inc.

Technological change also increases the risk that auditors will not detect critical business risks and/or control weaknesses, as noted in the *CICA Handbook* recommendation following. This is another reason to include IT specialists who are up-to-date on the latest developments on the audit team in audits where the client's business faces risks from rapid technological change.

> The auditor should obtain an understanding of how the entity has responded to risks arising from IT. The use of IT affects the way that control activities are implemented. The auditor considers whether the entity has responded adequately to the risks arising from IT by establishing effective general IT controls and application controls. From the auditor's perspective, controls over IT systems are effective when they maintain the integrity of information and the security of the data such systems process.
>
> Source: *CICA Handbook*, paragraph 5141.093.

Elements of an IT-Based Information System

If an accounting system is fully manual, much of the transaction processing can be readily followed and typically is supported by paper documents—approvals, vouchers, invoices and records of accountability, such as perpetual inventory records. Often many of the aspects of a IT-based systems are designed along similar lines to a manual system, so similar "documents" may exist in a computer system. However, in many cases these documents are available only in electronic, machine-readable form. Further, the basic records (ledgers and journals) of an IT-based accounting system frequently are electronic data files that cannot be read or changed without a computer, and may not be permanently retained.

An IT-based system includes the following elements:

1. *Hardware.* The physical equipment or devices that constitute a computer. These may include the central processing unit, optical reader, tape drives, disk devices, printers, terminals and other devices.

2. *Software.*

   (*a*) System programs. Programs that perform generalized functions for more than one application. These programs, sometimes referred to as supervisory programs, typically include "operating systems," which control, schedule and maximize efficient use of the hardware; "data management systems," which perform standardized data-handling functions for one or more application programs; and "utility" programs that can perform basic computer operations, such as sorting records. System programs generally are developed by the hardware supplier or by software development companies. Examples of system programs include the many versions of UNIX, LINUX, MAC OS and Windows.

   (*b*) Application (user) programs. Sets of computer instructions that perform data processing tasks. These programs usually are written within the organization or purchased from an outside supplier.

3. *Documentation.* A description of the system and its controls in relation to input, data processing, output, report processing, logic and operator instructions.

4. *Personnel.* Persons who manage, design, program, operate or control data processing systems.

5. *Data.* Transactions and related information entered, stored and processed by the system.

6. *Control Procedures.* Procedures designed to ensure the proper recording of transactions and to prevent or detect errors and irregularities, and for monitoring control effectiveness.

According to auditing standards, the establishment and maintenance of internal controls is an important responsibility of management. The policies and procedures included as elements of an information system are part of that responsibility. The audit team's responsibility is to make an assessment of the control risk in the system. Management can meet its responsibility and assist auditors in the following ways: (1) by ensuring that documentation of the system is complete and up to date, (2) by maintaining a system of transaction processing that includes an audit trail, and (3) by making IT resources and knowledgeable personnel available to the auditors to help them understand and audit the system. The next section describes control components in detail.

REVIEW CHECKPOINTS

7.1   What are the basic components and functions of an information system?

7.2   How do information system functions relate to assertions?

7.3   How does the information system facilitate communications within an organization? Why are these communications important?

7.4   What are the elements of an IT-based information system? What special risks arise when IT is used in an information system?

7.5   What are the main purposes of control procedures in an information system?

INTERNAL CONTROL COMPONENTS

LEARNING OBJECTIVE

2 Describe the basic components of internal control: the control environment; management's risk assessment process; information systems and communication; control activities; and monitoring.

Internal control consists of the following components:

(*a*) the control environment

(*b*) management's risk assessment process

(*c*) the information system, including the related business processes, relevant to financial reporting, and communication

(*d*) control activities

(*e*) monitoring of controls

All the internal control components are now explained briefly in the following text.

The five components come from the **COSO** (**Committee of Sponsoring Organizations of the Treadway Commission**) control framework discussed in previous chapters, and provide a useful way for auditors to consider how different aspects of an entity's internal control may affect the financial statements. Control components (*a*), (*b*), (*c*) and (*e*) can be referred to as **management controls** and operate at the company level. Company level controls permeate the company and can have a big impact on whether its financial reporting and disclosures objectives are met. Component (*d*), the control activities, are controls over processes, applications and transactions that are more closely related to accounting information; we will refer to these audit relevant controls as **accounting controls**.

The auditor is primarily interested in the accounting controls that help a company to safeguard its assets and prepare financial statements in conformity with generally accepted accounting principles. However, management is also interested in internal controls to assess adherence to management policy, promote operational efficiencies and address strategic risks. To meet these objectives, management controls are implemented as well.

As noted in previous chapters, the regulations in SOX 404 for internal control reporting and in PCAOB Auditing Standard No. 2, and the similar standards being introduced in Canada for audits of control reports require the assessment at company level and the control activity levels.[1] The following box provides a review on the first year's experience of implementing these new standards in the United States.

---

[1] CICA exposure draft, *An Audit of Internal Control over Financial Reporting Performed in Conjunction with an Audit of Financial Statements* and the Canadian Securities Administrators proposed Multilateral Instrument 52-111, *Reporting on Internal Control over Financial Reporting* plus MI-52-109, *Certification of Disclosure in Issuers' Annual and Interim Filings.*

POLICY STATEMENT REGARDING IMPLEMENTATION OF PCAOB AUDITING STANDARD NO. 2, AN AUDIT OF INTERNAL CONTROL OVER FINANCIAL REPORTING PERFORMED IN CONJUNCTION WITH AN AUDIT OF FINANCIAL STATEMENTS

This Policy Statement discusses some of the issues raised during the first year of auditors' implementation of the PCAOB's Auditing Standard No. 2, which implements Sections 103 and 404 of the Sarbanes-Oxley Act of 2002 (the "Act") by establishing a process for auditing public companies' internal control over financial reporting in conjunction with an audit of financial statements.

Section 404 of the Act aims to strengthen the internal controls that underpin the accuracy and reliability of a company's published financial information. That section, along with the SEC's implementing rule, requires a public company to annually report its assessment of the effectiveness of its internal control over financial reporting. The section also requires such a company to provide its auditor's attestation to, and report on, the company's assessment. Auditing Standard No. 2 governs the auditor's responsibilities under Section 404. In the simplest terms, investors can have much more confidence in the reliability of a corporate financial statement if corporate management demonstrates that it maintains adequate internal control over the preparation of accurate financial statements.

There is evidence that the benefits of the internal control requirements are already being realized:

Seventy-nine percent of the 222 financial executives surveyed by Oversight Systems, Inc. reported that their companies have stronger internal controls after complying with Section 404. Seventy-four percent said that their companies benefited from compliance with Sarbanes-Oxley, and, of those, 33 percent said that compliance lessened the risk of financial fraud. (See Oversight Systems, Inc., *The 2004 Oversight Systems Financial Executive Report on Sarbanes-Oxley*, December 2004).

Section 404 has, however, proven to be an enormous challenge for those involved in its implementation. Companies have found the requirements costly and demanding, and many have questioned whether the benefits are worth the cost. We take these concerns seriously and are committed to learning from the first year's experience implementing Section 404. As part of this effort, on April 13, 2005, we participated in the Commission's Roundtable to hear directly from issuers, auditors, and investors on the front line of the Section 404 implementation process. Many participants at the Roundtable expressed their support for Section 404's purpose. One of the most valuable aspects of the Roundtable, however, has been the constructive criticism provided by many of those currently involved in the implementation process.

The cost of Section 404 compliance was the primary concern raised at the Roundtable:

One survey found that for 217 public companies with average revenues of $5 billion, first year Section 404 compliance cost, on average, $4.36 million and consumed an average of nearly 27,000 hours. (See Financial Executives International, *FEI Special Survey on SOX Section 404 Implementation*, March 2005).

Among other reasons, commenters suggested that costs were too high because companies and their auditors did not sufficiently focus their efforts on higher risk areas of internal control over financial reporting. In addition, commenters expressed the view that auditors did not use the work of others sufficiently or fully integrate the audit of internal control with the audit of the financial statements. Some Roundtable participants also stated that auditors are often less willing than they were previously to provide guidance to clients on accounting issues for fear of compromising independence or triggering a material weakness finding.

Source: PCAOB Release No. 2005-009 May 16, 2005

Control Environment

The control environment begins with the tone at the top of the organization, which is reflected in management's and directors' attitudes, awareness and actions concerning the company's internal controls. The control environment also includes the way that integrity and ethical values are communicated and enforced in the company because the effectiveness of controls cannot rise above the integrity and ethical values of the people who create, administer and monitor them. Management must be taking action to remove or reduce incentives and temptations that might motivate people in the organization to act unethically. Management must assess requisite skills and knowledge for particular jobs and ensure people in those positions are competent. Directors or others charged with governance of the organization should be independent from management, and experienced and knowledgeable enough to raise and pursue difficult questions with management, and internal and external auditors. They should also be responsible for the design and effective operation of whistle-blower procedures and be engaged in a process for assessing the effectiveness of the company's internal control.

Management's approach to taking and monitoring business risks, attitudes toward financial reporting (conservative or aggressive selection of accounting principles and use of accounting estimates) and controls are critical to the strength of the control environment. Management's reactions when control violations occur should be immediate and appropriate to set the right example for others. The organization should have in place clear policies relating to appropriate business practices, knowledge and experience of key personnel, and resources provided for carrying out duties. Policies should ensure that all personnel understand the entity's objectives, know how their individual actions interrelate and contribute to those objectives, and recognize how and for what they will be held accountable.

The control environment is characterized by management attitudes, structure (organization chart), effective communication of control objectives and supervision of personnel and activities, as noted previously. The following are elements of internal control environments:

- management's philosophy and operating style
- company organization structure
- functioning of the board of directors, particularly its audit committee,
- methods of assigning authority and responsibility
- management's monitoring methods, including internal auditing.
- personnel policies and practices
- external influences (e.g., examinations by bank regulatory agencies)
- control environment for computerized systems also includes the organizational and logical controls that control access to computers and computer files, and authorization of changes to program and data files

Generally, such environmental controls can be characterized as preventive controls in the sense that they are there to prevent misstatements from arising in the first place. Preventive controls are more cost effective than controls designed to detect or correct misstatements that have entered the system. This is one reason why auditors tend to focus the preliminary evaluation on environmental controls. Another reason is the pervasive impact environmental controls have on the accounting cycles affected.

Since management fraud in financial statements became an acceptable topic for discussion in the mid-1980s, "tone at the top" has become a buzzword for the necessary condition for good internal control. The "tone" is virtually identical to the control environment. A wide variety of activities characterize the control environment. For example, the organization structure indicates to the auditor who has the immediate responsibility to authorize payments in payroll processing. Some aspects of the control environment, however, are hard for auditors to understand and document, such as management's philosophy. The following box illustrates some criteria to consider in evaluating the human factor in the control environment.

Tone at the Top

All control rests ultimately on people assuming responsibility for their decisions and actions. Organizational values that people find acceptable encourage them to assume responsibility for the continuous improvement of their organization.

Shared ethical values influence all behaviour in an organization. Together with an understanding of mission and vision, they constitute the basic identity that will shape the way an individual, group, organization or board will operate, and they provide stability over time. Shared values contribute to control because they provide a guide for individual, group or team decision-making, action and policy.

The values and preferences of senior management and the board of directors greatly influence an organization's objectives and systems. These values and preferences address issues such as:

- good corporate citizenship
- commitment to truth and fair dealing
- commitment to quality and competence
- leadership by example
- compliance with laws, regulations, rules and organizational policy
- respect for the privacy of client, organization and employee information
- fair treatment of and respect for individuals
- fair relationships with competitors
- integrity of transactions and records
- a professional approach to financial reporting

Ethical values are part of an organization's culture and provide an unwritten code of conduct against which behaviour is measured. A formal, written code of conduct offers a means of consistent communication of the standards of ethical behaviour. People can be asked periodically to confirm their understanding and observance of the code.

Source: COCO, *Guidance on Control* (November 1995), pp. 14–15.

For completeness, we add the board of directors and the audit committee as critical elements of high-level internal controls. Among the board's key functions is monitoring that traditionally least-monitored group of employees, top management. However, in the post-Enron environment, the role of the board and audit committee in monitoring management and financial reporting has risen to unprecedented levels. The audit committee's role is to help the board (usually a subcommittee of the board members) by overseeing the financial reporting, external and internal auditing functions. Relative to the external audit function, the audit committee's prime role is to act as intermediary between management and the auditor, thus helping make the external audit function more independently. Recall that we explained the traditional responsibilities of the board and audit committee, as well as their expanded corporate governance responsibilities in the post-Enron environment, in Chapter 5.

Application to Small Entities

Small entities may implement the control environment elements differently than larger entities; for example, by relying on oral communications and personal relations to establish ethical standards, rather than more formal methods. Directors are less likely to be independent of management.

Management's Risk Assessment Process

As explained in Chapter 6, the risk assessment process enables management to identify risks relevant to misstatements occurring in the preparation of financial statements, estimates the risks' significance and likelihood, and decide how to manage them efficiently and effectively. Risks can arise or change due to changing circumstances, so the risk assessment is a continuous process. The operating environment, personnel changes, growth, new technologies, new business lines, structural changes in the organization, and new accounting pronouncements can affect the risk assessment.

Application to Small Entities

Even small entities are expected to have a basic risk assessment process, but it is likely to be informal. Management may be aware of risks related to financial reporting mainly through direct personal involvement with employees and outside parties.

Information System, Related Business Processes and Communication

The information system relevant to financial reporting objectives consists of the procedures and records established to initiate, record, process and report entity transactions (as well as events and conditions), and to maintain accountability for the related assets, liabilities and equity. An information system encompasses procedures, records and controls that:

(a) identify and record all valid transactions

(b) describe on a timely basis the transactions in sufficient detail to permit proper classification of transactions for financial reporting

(c) measure the value of transactions in a manner that permits recording their proper monetary value in the financial statements

(d) determine the period in which transactions occurred to permit recording of transactions in the proper accounting period

(e) present properly the transactions and related disclosures in the financial statements

The quality of system-generated information affects management's ability to make decisions in managing and controlling the entity's activities and to prepare reliable financial reports.

Communication is also important to information system control because it helps ensure that procedures are implemented correctly, and exceptions are reported and acted on appropriately. Good communications procedures help ensure that important tasks do not just "fall between the cracks" because no one was sure whose job it was to do them.

Application to Small Entities

In small entities, accounting procedures, records or controls may not be documented in writing, but will exist informally if the organization has a good risk assessment process and related internal controls. Communication also may be less formal and easier to achieve as fewer people are involved.

Control Activities

Control activities are the policies and procedures that help ensure that necessary actions are taken to address risks that threaten the achievement of the entity's financial reporting objectives. The two broad groupings of control activities are general controls and application controls. General control activities relevant to an audit include performance reviews (e.g., comparisons to budgets and prior years), and application controls include checks on accuracy, completeness and authorization of transaction information processing. Specific control procedures are designed to meet control objectives, which are related to the assertions underlying financial statements. Control procedures are described in more specific terms later in the chapter, after the control objectives have been covered.

Certain control activities may depend on the existence of appropriate higher level policies established by management or those charged with governance. For example, authorization controls may be delegated under established guidelines, such as investment criteria set by the board of directors; alternatively, nonroutine transactions such as major acquisitions or disposals of assets or business units may require specific high-level approval, including in some cases that of shareholders. This further illustrates the relationship between the control environment and the other company-level controls and the specific control activities that auditors may test and rely on for audit evidence purposes.

Application to Small Entities

The concepts underlying control activities in small entities are likely to be similar to those in larger entities, but the formality with which they operate varies. Further, small entities may find that certain types of control activities are not relevant because of controls applied by management. For example, management's retention of authority for approving credit sales, significant purchases, and draw-downs on lines of credit can provide strong control over those activities, lessening or removing the need for more detailed control activities. An appropriate segregation of duties often appears to present difficulties in small entities. Even companies that have only a few employees, however, may be able to assign their responsibilities to achieve appropriate segregation or, if that is not possible, to use management oversight of the incompatible activities to achieve control objectives.

Monitoring Controls

An important management responsibility is to establish and maintain internal control on an ongoing basis. Management's monitoring of controls includes considering whether they are operating as intended and that they are modified as appropriate for changes in conditions. Monitoring of controls may include activities such as management's review of whether bank reconciliations are being prepared on a timely basis, internal auditors' evaluation of sales personnel's compliance with the entity's policies on terms of sales contracts and a legal department's oversight of compliance with the entity's ethical or business practice policies.

Monitoring of controls is a process to assess the quality of internal control performance over time. It involves assessing the design and operation of controls on a timely basis and taking necessary corrective actions. Monitoring is done to ensure that controls continue to operate effectively. For example, if the timeliness and accuracy of bank reconciliations are not monitored, personnel are likely to stop preparing them. Monitoring of controls is accomplished through ongoing monitoring activities, separate evaluations, or a combination of the two.

Ongoing monitoring activities are built into the normal recurring activities of an entity and include regular management and supervisory activities. Managers of sales, purchasing, and production at divisional and corporate levels are in touch with operations and may question reports that differ significantly from their knowledge of operations.

In many entities, internal auditors or personnel performing similar functions contribute to the monitoring of an entity's controls through separate evaluations. They regularly provide information about the functioning of internal control, focusing considerable attention on evaluating the design and operation of internal control. They communicate information about strengths, weaknesses and recommendations for improving internal control.

Monitoring activities may include using information from communications from external parties that may indicate problems or highlight areas in need of improvement. Customers implicitly corroborate billing data by paying their invoices or complaining about their charges. In addition, regulators may communicate with the entity concerning matters that affect the functioning of internal control; for example, communications concerning examinations by bank regulatory agencies. Also, management may consider communications relating to internal control from external auditors in performing monitoring activities.

Application to Small Entities

Ongoing monitoring activities of small entities are more likely to be informal and performed as a part of the overall management of the entity's operations. Management's close involvement in operations often will identify significant variances from expectations and inaccuracies in financial data leading to corrective action to the control.

Accounting Controls and the Accounting System

An accounting system processes transactions, records them in journals and ledgers (either computerized or manual), and produces financial statements without necessarily guaranteeing their accuracy. Nevertheless, the accounting policies and procedures often contain important elements of control. The accounting instruction of "Prepare sales invoices only when shipment has been made," is a control so long as the people performing the work follow the instruction. The control part of this policy could be expressed: "Prepare sales invoices and record them only when a shipping document is matched."

All accounting systems, whether computerized or manual, consist of four essential functions—data preparation, data entry, transaction processing, and report production and distribution.

Data preparation is the analysis of transactions and their "capture" for accounting purposes. The "capture" amounts to creation of source documents, such as sales invoices, credit memos, cash receipts listings, purchase orders, receiving reports, negotiable cheques, and the like. These source documents provide the information for data entry. However, in some computerized accounting systems the paper source documents are not produced first. Transactions may be entered directly on a keyboard, or electronic equipment may capture the transaction information. For example, your long-distance telephone charges are initially captured by the telephone company's computers using your telephone number, the location called, and the duration of the call.

Data entry often consists of accounting personnel using a batch of source documents to enter transaction information on a keyboard into an accounting software program. This process may produce a "book of original entry," another name for a journal, such as the sales journal, purchases journal, cash receipts journal, cash disbursements journal, general journal, and others. In advanced paperless systems, electronic equipment may enter the accounting information automatically without producing an intermediate journal. For example, your long-distance telephone call is entered automatically into the telephone company's revenue and receivable accounts. Your monthly telephone bill is later produced from the accounting information.

Transaction processing usually refers to posting the journals to the general ledger accounts, using the debits and credits you learned in other accounting courses. The posting operation updates the account balances. When all data are entered and processed, the account balances are ready for placement in reports.

Report production and distribution is the object of the accounting system. The account balances are put into internal management reports and external financial statements. The internal reports are management's feedback for monitoring and control of operations. The external reports are the financial information for outside investors, creditors, and others.

The accounting system produces a trail of accounting operations, from transaction analyses to reports. Often, this is called the **audit trail**, which starts with the source documents and proceeds through to the financial reports. Auditors often follow this trail frontwards and backwards! They will follow it backwards from the financial reports to the source documents to determine whether everything in the financial reports is supported by appropriate source documents. They will follow it forward from source documents to reports to determine that everything that happened (transactions) got recorded in the accounts and reported in the financial statements.

Accounting controls are client procedures (both computerized and manual) imposed on the accounting system for the purpose of preventing, detecting and correcting errors and irregularities that might enter and flow through to the financial statements. For example, a control procedure related to the accounting policy previously cited above would be: "At the end of each day, the billing supervisor reviews all the sales invoices to see that the file copy has a bill of lading copy attached."

Minimum documentation requirements for a good control-oriented accounting system include a chart of accounts and some written definitions and instructions about measuring and classifying transactions. In most organizations such material is incorporated in computer systems documentation, computer program documentation, systems and proce-dures manuals, flowcharts of transaction processing and various paper forms. A company's internal auditors and systems staff often review and evaluate this documentation. Independent auditors may review and study their work instead of doing the same tasks over again.

Accounting manuals should contain statements of objectives, policies and procedures. Management should approve statements of specific accounting and control objectives and ensure that appropriate procedures are used to accomplish them. In general, the overriding objective of an accounting system is to produce financial statement assertions that are cor-rect. Therefore, the objective of accounting is to produce correct statements of existence or occurrence, completeness, valuation, rights and obligations, and presentation and disclosure. An accounting system cannot accomplish this objective without an integrated set of control procedures.

· ·

REVIEW
CHECKPOINTS

7.6   What are the components of internal control?

7.7   What is the auditor's main purpose in understanding the client's internal control?

7.8   What are management controls?

7.9   How can management meet its responsibility for establishing and maintaining an internal control system and assist the auditors at the same time?

7.10   What are some of the important characteristics of "tone at the top" and control environment?

7.11   Are environmental controls preventive or detective? Explain.

7.12   Distinguish among environmental controls, general controls and application controls.

7.13   Where can an auditor find a client's documentation of the accounting system?

7.14   How do managers monitor control effectiveness? Why are controls monitored?

7.15   What are the key functions of the accounting system?

7.16   What is the audit trail? Of what use is it in the audit?

· ·

Effect of Information Processing

The methods used to process accounting transactions will affect a company's organizational structure and will influence the procedures and techniques used to accomplish the objectives of internal control. Most entities make use of IT systems for financial reporting and opera-tional purposes. Even when IT is used extensively, there will also be manual elements to the systems. An entity's system of internal control is likely to contain manual and automated procedures, and the characteristics of these procedures will affect the auditor's risk assess-ment and design of further audit procedures. The mix of manual and automated controls will depend on the nature and complexity of IT used in the information system.

Controls in a manual system include procedures such as approvals, management reviews of reports and activities, reconciliations and follow-up of reconciling items. When an entity uses automated procedures to initiate, record, process and report transactions, its records will be in electronic format rather than paper documents. Controls in IT systems will typi-cally be a combination of automated controls (e.g., controls embedded in computer pro-grams) and manual controls. The manual controls may use information produced by IT or may be independent of IT. Manual controls can involve monitoring whether IT and auto-mated controls are functioning effectively, and handling exceptions. In order to understand internal control, the auditor has to understand the risks arising from the use of IT or man-ual systems and whether management has responded adequately by establishing effective controls. Some of the risks and benefits of manual versus IT procedures in internal control are noted in the following box.

Manual Vs. IT Controls: Risks and Benefits

.059   Generally, IT provides potential benefits of effectiveness and efficiency for an entity's internal control because it enables an entity to:

(a) consistently apply predefined business rules and perform complex calculations in processing large volumes of transactions or data;

(b) enhance the timeliness, availability, and accuracy of information;

(c) facilitate the additional analysis of information;

(d) enhance the ability to monitor the performance of the entity's activities and its policies and procedures;

(e) reduce the risk that controls will be circumvented; and

(f) enhance the ability to achieve effective segregation of duties by implementing security controls in applications, databases, and operating systems.

.060   IT also poses specific risks to an entity's internal control, including the following:

(a) reliance on systems or programs that are inaccurately processing data, processing inaccurate data, or both;

(b) unauthorized access to data that may result in destruction of data or improper changes to data, including the recording of unauthorized or nonexistent transactions, or inaccurate recording of transactions (particular risks may arise where multiple users access a common database);

(c) the possibility of IT personnel gaining access privileges beyond those necessary to perform their assigned duties thereby breaking down segregation of duties;

(d) unauthorized changes to data in master files;

(e) unauthorized changes to systems or programs;

(f) failure to make necessary changes to systems or programs;

(g) inappropriate manual intervention; and

(h) potential loss of data or inability to access data as required.

.061   Manual aspects of systems may be more suitable where judgment and discretion are required, such as for the following circumstances:

(a) for large, unusual or non-recurring transactions;

(b) in circumstances where errors are difficult to define, anticipate or predict;

(c) in changing circumstances that require a control response outside the scope of an existing automated control; and

(d) in monitoring the effectiveness of automated controls.

.062   Manual controls are performed by people, and therefore pose specific risks to the entity's internal control. Manual controls may be less reliable than automated controls because they can be more easily bypassed, ignored, or overridden and they are also more prone to simple errors and mistakes. Consistency of application of a manual control element cannot therefore be assumed. Manual systems may be less suitable for:

(a) high volume or recurring transactions, or in situations where errors that can be anticipated or predicted can be prevented or detected by control parameters that are automated; and

(b) control activities where the specific ways to perform the control can be adequately designed and automated.

Source: *CICA Handbook*, paragraphs 5141.059–.062.

Following are some of the characteristics that are important in understanding controls in IT systems:

- *Transaction trails.* Some computer systems are so designed that a complete transaction trail useful for audit purposes may exist only for a short time or only in computer-readable form. (A transaction trail is a chain of evidence provided through coding, cross-references, and documentation connecting account balances and other summary results with the original transaction documents and calculations.) As IT evolves, it may become feasible for online real-time accounting systems to be used in some organizations. If information from such systems is reported on a real-time basis to external users who require assurance, the demand may arise for continuous auditing. **Continuous auditing** refers to auditing real-time transaction processing systems, using techniques such as audit programming codes that continuously select and monitor the processing of data (e.g., embedded audit modules).[2] Appendix 9C, on the Online Learning Centre, discusses continuous auditing and other Internet-based topics in financial reporting and assurance, including XBRL.

- *Uniform processing of transactions.* Computer processing uniformly subjects like transactions to the same processing instructions. Consequently, computer processing virtually eliminates the occurrence of random errors normally associated with manual processing. Conversely, programming errors (or other similar systematic errors in either the computer hardware or software) will result in all like transactions being processed incorrectly when those transactions are processed under the same conditions. This uniformity of processing characteristics causes a subtle change in the nature of audit testing of controls. The stress in auditing computerized files will be to test a small number of unusual or exceptional transactions rather than a large number of similar transactions, as is the case in manual systems. Of course, the test transactions should also include examples of the most typical, common transactions. Use of such strategies implies auditors will also need to get assurance that the software tested has not been tampered with between tests. This assurance is obtained through justified reliance on control systems that are in place to prevent unauthorized changes and to document all changes to the software.

- *Segregation of functions.* Many internal control procedures once performed by different individuals in manual systems may be concentrated in computer systems. Therefore, individuals who have access to the computer may be in a position to perform incompatible functions. As a result, other control procedures may be required in computer systems to achieve the degree of control ordinarily accomplished by segregating functions in manual systems. These may include such techniques as use of password control procedures to prevent incompatible functions from being performed by individuals who have access to assets and access to records through an online terminal. The concentration of recordkeeping activities normally associated with computer centres requires a change in the approach to auditing that puts more emphasis on the evaluation of internal controls of the computer centre.

- *Potential for errors and irregularities.* The potential for individuals, including those performing control procedures, to gain unauthorized access or alter data without visible evidence, as well as to gain access (direct or indirect) to assets, may be greater in computerized accounting systems than in manual systems (partly due to the lack of segregation of duties noted above). Less human involvement in handling transactions processed by computers can reduce the potential for observing errors and irregularities. Errors or irregularities made in designing or changing application programs can remain undetected for long periods.

- *Potential for increased management supervision.* Computer systems offer management a wide variety of analytical tools that may be used to review and supervise the operations of the company. The availability of these additional controls may enhance the entire system of internal control and, therefore, reduce the control risk. For example, traditional comparisons of actual operating ratios with those budgeted, as well as reconciliation of accounts, frequently are available for management review on a more timely basis when such information is computerized. Additionally, some programmed applications provide computer operating statistics that may be used to monitor the actual processing of transactions.

- *Initiation or subsequent execution of transactions by computer.* Certain transactions may be initiated or executed automatically by a computer system. The authorization of these transactions or procedures may not be documented in the same way as those in a manual accounting system, and management's authorization of those transactions may be implicit in its acceptance of the design of the system.

---

[2] Z. Rezaee, R. Elam and A. Sharbatoghile, "Continuous Auditing: The Audit of the Future," *Managerial Auditing Journal* 16 (3), 2001, p. 150.

REVIEW
CHECKPOINTS

7.17   Explain the difference between manual controls and IT controls. Give an example of each.

7.18   In which situations are manual controls preferrable and in which are IT controls preferrable?

7.19   List six characteristics that are important to the auditor's understanding of IT controls.

UNDERSTANDING INFORMATION SYSTEMS' INTERNAL CONTROL AND RISKS

LEARNING OBJECTIVE

3 Understand how a company's control environment, information systems and its general and application control activities are related to the risk that its financial statements are misstated.

The auditor must understand the control environment, the information system, and the control procedures in order to assess whether a material misstatement exists in the financial statements. This knowledge-gathering work should be designed to provide an understanding of the control environment and the flow of transactions through the accounting system, including a general knowledge of (*a*) the organizational structure, (*b*) the methods used by the client to communicate responsibility and authority, and (*c*) the methods used by management to supervise the system, including the existence of an internal audit function, if any. Elements of the control environment and the information system are described in this section, and are raised again in Chapter 9 in the context of evaluating and testing controls.

The control framework used in this text includes company-level controls (the control environment, risk assessment process, information and communication, and monitoring) and control activities (general and application). The extent of work involves obtaining an understanding of control in the context of the business and its risks, assessing significant risks of financial statement misstatement, and performing tests of controls, if needed to further assess risks or provide audit evidence. Exhibit 7–1 puts these elements in perspective.

EXHIBIT   7–1   CONTROL FRAMEWORK FOR EVALUATION

Company-Level Controls			
Control environment	**Risk assessment**	**Information and communication**	**Monitoring**
• Management actions and attitudes show character, integrity and ethical values. • Management's operating style and philosophy are consistent with sound control of business. • Management assigns authority and responsibility appropriately. • Human resource policies foster a strong control environment. • Audit committee and board directors are actively involved and have significant influence in the organization.	• Management has established sound practices for identifying, evaluating and mitigating risks.	• Management gathers information from and communicates information to appropriate people on a timely basis. • Management has established an effective "whistle-blower" program relating to financial reporting.	• Management has established effective monitoring procedures. • Management independently evaluates the organization's internal control environment to assess its effectiveness.

Control Activities

General controls
Application controls

Source: Adapted from J.S. McNally, "Assessing Company-Level Controls," *Journal of Accountancy* 199 (6), June 2005, pp.65–68. Copyright © 2005 by the American Institute of Certified Public Accountants, Inc. Reprinted with permission.

The Organizational Structure

The auditors' understanding of the organizational structure of a company should include an understanding of the organization's IT function. This understanding should contribute to the overall assessment of risk of material misstatement. In reviewing the organization structure of a company's computer function, auditors should obtain and evaluate:

- a description of the company's IT resources, including details of computer equipment used, the use of an outside services centre, if any, and locations from which the computer resources can be accessed
- a description of the organizational structure of IT operations as it relates to personnel within the IT department, and the interaction with personnel in other departments

The description of IT resources should give auditors (1) an overview of computer operating activities, (2) knowledge of access to IT resources used to process accounting information, and (3) knowledge of company policies regarding access only by authorized personnel. Auditors should enquire about the division of responsibilities between systems and programming staff and operations personnel to assess the segregation of duties. They should understand the existence and organization of the control function and its assigned responsibilities. Auditors should identify the position the computer function has in the overall organization structure, as well as understand the interaction between user departments and the computer department. Such an understanding helps the auditor to decide how much reliance to put on system controls and the effect of such reliance on substantive procedures.

Methods Used to Communicate Responsibility and Authority

In connection with understanding the methods used by the client to communicate responsibility and authority, the auditor should obtain information about the existence of (*a*) accounting and other policy manuals, including computer operations and user manuals, and (*b*) formal job descriptions for IT personnel. Related user personnel job descriptions may be helpful. Auditors should gain an understanding of how the client's IT resources are managed and how priorities are determined. Auditors also should gain an understanding of the extent to which other departments within the company have a clear understanding of how they must comply with computer processing-related standards and procedures.

Methods Used by Management to Supervise the System

Auditors should learn the procedures management uses to supervise the information system, including:

- the existence of systems design and documentation standards and the extent to which they are used
- the existence and quality of procedures for system and program modification, systems acceptance approval and output modification (such as changes in reports or files)
- the procedures limiting access to authorized information, particularly with respect to sensitive information
- the availability of financial and other reports, such as budget/performance reviews for use by management
- the existence of an internal audit function and the degree of its involvement in reviewing computer-produced accounting records and related controls and its involvement in systems development control evaluation and testing

After the audit team gains an understanding of the control environment, it should seek to understand the accounting information system—the flow of transactions. Auditors should consider the methods employed by a client to process significant accounting information, including the use of such outside organizations as data-processing service centres. The client's methods influence the design of the accounting system and the nature of the internal control procedures. Detailed guidance in *CICA Handbook,* section 5141 is set out in the following box.

THE INFORMATION SYSTEM RELEVANT TO FINANCIAL REPORTING OBJECTIVES

.080   The information system relevant to financial reporting objectives, which includes the accounting system, consists of the procedures and records established to initiate, record, process and report entity transactions (as well as events and conditions) and to maintain accountability for the related assets, liabilities and equity.

.081   The auditor should obtain an understanding of the information system, including the related business processes, relevant to financial reporting, including:

(a) the classes of transactions in the entity's operations that are significant to the financial statements;

(b) the procedures, within both IT and manual systems, by which those transactions are initiated, recorded, processed and reported in the financial statements;

(c) the related accounting records, whether electronic or manual, supporting information, and specific accounts in the financial statements, in respect of initiating, recording, processing and reporting transactions;

(d) how the information system captures events and conditions, other than classes of transactions, that are significant to the financial statements; and

(e) the financial reporting process used to prepare the entity's financial statements, including significant accounting estimates and disclosures.

.082   In obtaining this understanding, the auditor considers the procedures used to transfer information from transaction processing systems to general ledger or financial reporting systems. The auditor also understands the entity's procedures to capture information relevant to financial reporting for events and conditions other than transactions, such as the depreciation and amortization of assets and changes in the recoverability of accounts receivables.

.083   An entity's information system typically includes the use of standard journal entries that are required on a recurring basis to record transactions such as sales, purchases and cash disbursements in the general ledger, or to record accounting estimates that are periodically made by management, such as changes in the estimate of uncollectible accounts receivable.

.084   An entity's financial reporting process also includes the use of non-standard journal entries to record non-recurring, unusual transactions or adjustments. Examples of such entries include consolidating adjustments and entries for a business combination or disposal or non-recurring estimates such as an asset impairment. In manual, paper-based general ledger systems, non-standard journal entries may be identified through inspection of ledgers, journals and supporting documentation. However, when automated procedures are used to maintain the general ledger and prepare financial statements, such entries may exist only in electronic form and may be more easily identified through the use of computer-assisted audit techniques.

.085   Preparation of the entity's financial statements includes procedures that are designed to ensure information required to be disclosed by the applicable financial reporting framework is accumulated, recorded, processed, summarized and appropriately reported in the financial statements.

.086   In obtaining an understanding, the auditor considers risks of material misstatement associated with inappropriate override of controls over journal entries and the controls surrounding non-standard journal entries. For example, automated processes and controls may reduce the risk of inadvertent error but do not overcome the risk that individuals may inappropriately override such automated processes, for example, by changing the amounts being automatically passed to the general ledger or financial reporting system. Furthermore, the auditor maintains an awareness that when IT is used to transfer information automatically, there may be little or no visible evidence of such intervention in the information systems.

.087   The auditor also understands how the incorrect processing of transactions is resolved, for example, whether there is an automated suspense file and how it is used by the entity to ensure that suspense items are cleared out on a timely basis, and how system overrides or bypasses to controls are processed and accounted for.

.088   The auditor obtains an understanding of the entity's information system relevant to financial reporting in a manner that is appropriate to the entity's circumstances. This includes obtaining an understanding of how transactions originate within the entity's business processes. An entity's business processes are the activities designed to:

(a) develop, purchase, produce, sell and distribute an entity's products and services;

(b) ensure compliance with laws and regulations; and

(c) record information, including accounting and financial reporting information.

Source: *CICA Handbook,* paragraphs 5141.080–.088.

R E V I E W
C H E C K P O I N T S

7.20   What kinds of knowledge does the auditor gather to understand internal control?

7.21   What are company-level controls?

7.22   What are the two main types of control activities that are used information systems?

7.23   What aspects of the accounting system are relevant to financial reporting objectives?

7.24   What misstatement risks might not be eliminated by automated control procedures? How does this possibility affect the audit?

Control Activities

Companies use numerous detailed accounting and control procedures designed to achieve their control objectives. As explained previously in this chapter, the auditor uses a control framework to understand and evaluate the client's internal control. Control policies and procedures make up the control activities component of the company's control framework. All detail control procedures are directed, one way or another, toward preventing, detecting and correcting the kinds of errors, irregularities, frauds and misstatements that can occur.

Control activities can be complicated. The following box provides an overview of control activities. For your study purposes, we have organized the control activities under the headings of general controls and application controls.

OVERVIEW OF CONTROL ACTIVITIES

General Controls	APPLICATION CONTROLS		
	Applications	**System Functions to be Controlled**	**Control Objectives**
• Capable personnel	Revenues/Receivables/Receipts		
• Segregation of responsibilities	—		
• Supervision	Purchases/Payables/Payments	Transaction input	
• Controlled access	—		Specific procedures to ensure:
• Periodic comparison	Production and Payroll	Transaction processing	• authorization • accuracy
• IT controls	—		• completeness • audit trail
• Error checking routines	Investment and Finance	Transactions, balances and disclosure output	• error correction
• Performance reviews	—		
	Other applications		

General Controls

While the "tone at the top" (control environment) is pervasive, the control procedures of capable personnel, segregation of responsibilities, controlled access and periodic comparison are always important in a company's internal controls. General controls like environmental controls are primarily preventive in nature and have a pervasive impact on the various accounting cycles. For these reasons, auditors tend to focus on environmental and general controls in the preliminary evaluation of internal controls. The following organizational features act as general controls:

Capable Personnel   The most important feature of control is the people who make the system work. A company's personnel problems sometimes create internal control problems. High turnover in accounting jobs means that inexperienced people are doing the accounting and control tasks, and they generally make more mistakes than experienced people. New accounting officers and managers (e.g., financial vice president, controller, chief accountant, plant accountant, or data processing manager) may not be familiar with company accounting and may make technical and judgemental errors. Sometimes accounting officers and employees are fired because they refuse to go along with improper accounting procedures desired by a higher level of management. In general, accounting personnel changes may be a warning signal.

Segregation of Responsibilities   An important characteristic of reliable internal control is the appropriate segregation of functional responsibilities. Sometimes this characteristic is called **division of duties**. Proper segregation of responsibilities is a necessary condition for making detailed clerical control procedures effective. Examples of duties that should be done by separate individuals include reporting, reviewing and approving reconciliations, and approval and control of documents.

Four kinds of functional responsibilities should be performed by different departments, or at least by different people on the company's accounting staff:

1. *Authorization to execute transactions*. This duty belongs to people who have authority and responsibility for initiating the recordkeeping for transactions. Authorization may be general, referring to a class of transactions (e.g., all purchases), or it may be specific (e.g., sale of a major asset).

2. *Recording of transactions*. This duty refers to the accounting and recordkeeping function (bookkeeping) which in most organizations is delegated to a computer system. (People who control the computer processing are the **recordkeepers**.)

3. *Custody of assets involved in the transactions*. This duty refers to the actual physical possession or effective physical control of property.

4. *Periodic reconciliation of existing assets to recorded amounts*. This duty refers to making comparisons at regular intervals and taking appropriate action with respect to any differences.

Incompatible responsibilities are combinations of responsibilities that place a person alone in a position to create and conceal errors, irregularities and misstatements in her normal job. Duties should be so divided that no one person can control two or more functional responsibilities. The first and fourth responsibilities are management functions, the second is an accounting function, and the third is a custodial (physical access) function. If different departments or persons are forced to deal with these different facets of transactions, then two benefits are obtained: (1) irregularities are made more difficult because they would require collusion of two or more persons, and most people hesitate to seek the help of others to conduct wrongful acts, and (2) innocent errors are more likely to be found and flagged for correction. The old saying is that "two heads are better than one." The flip side of this is that the more people assigned to control duties, the better the controls and the higher the cost of the controls. Any control system will reflect compromises of benefits versus the costs.

Segregation of duties is an important control consideration in the auditor's risk assessment. If the company fails to assign different people the responsibilities of authorizing transactions, recording transactions, and maintaining custody of assets, it provides the opportunities that allow a person to be in a position to both perpetrate and conceal errors or fraud in the normal course of his duties.

Supervision   Supervision is an important element of control. You can readily imagine a company having clerks and computers to carry out the accounting and control procedures. Equally important is management's supervision of the work. A supervisor could, for example, oversee the credit manager's performance or could periodically compare the sum of customers' balances to the accounts receivable control account total. Supervisors or department heads can correct errors found by the clerical staff and make or approve accounting decisions. Supervision is important as management's means of monitoring and maintaining a system of internal control.

Controlled Access   Physical access to assets and important records, documents and blank forms should be limited to authorized personnel. Such assets as inventory and securities should not be available to persons who have no need to handle them. Likewise, access to cost records and accounts receivable records should be denied to people who do not have a recordkeeping responsibility for them.

Some blank forms are very important for accounting and control, and their availability should be restricted. Someone not involved in accounting for sales should not be able to pick up blank sales invoices and blank shipping orders. A person should not be able to obtain blank cheques (including computer-paper blank cheques) unless she is involved in cash disbursement activities. Sometimes, access to blank forms is the equivalent of access to, or custody of, an important asset. For example, someone who has access to blank cheques has a measure of actual custody and access to cash. In computerized systems, controlled access is achieved through the use of physically secure hardware and software and the use of passwords to control electronic access.

The extent to which physical controls intended to prevent theft of assets are relevant to the reliability of financial statement preparation and the audit depends on circumstances, such as whether assets are highly susceptible to misappropriation. For example, these controls would ordinarily not be relevant when any inventory losses would be detected by the client's periodic physical inspection and thus recorded in the financial statements. However, if, for financial reporting purposes, management relies solely on perpetual inventory records, the physical security controls would be relevant to the audit. It is not possible in that case to obtain sufficient appropriate audit evidence without having assurance that controls operated effectively throughout the period being audited.

Periodic Comparison   Management has responsibility for the recorded accountability of assets and liabilities. Managers should provide for periodic comparison of the recorded amounts with independent evidence of existence and valuation. Internal auditors and other people on an accounting staff can perform periodic comparison on a regular basis. However, the people who perform these periodic comparisons should not also have responsibility for authorization of related transactions, accounting or recordkeeping, or custodial responsibility for the assets.

Periodic comparisons may include counts of cash on hand, reconciliation of bank statements, counts of securities, confirmation of accounts receivable, accounts payable, and other such comparison operations undertaken to determine whether accounting records—the recorded accountability—represent real assets and liabilities. A management that performs frequent periodic comparisons has more opportunities to detect errors in the records than a management that does not. The frequency, of course, is governed by the costs and benefits. One should not try to count, compare or confirm assets with great frequency (say, weekly) unless those assets are especially susceptible to loss or error or unless they are unusually valuable. In other words, if the inherent risk is high the control risk should be made commensuratively lower by strengthening controls.

Subsequent action to correct differences is also important. Periodic comparison and action to correct errors lowers the risk that material misstatements will remain in the accounts. Such comparisons are frequently assigned to internal auditors and other employees.[3]

IT Controls   General IT controls are policies and procedures that relate to many applications and support the effective functioning of application controls by helping to ensure the continued proper operation of information systems. These controls apply to mainframe, server, and end-user environments. General IT controls commonly include:

(*a*) controls over data centre and network operations

(*b*) system software acquisition, change and maintenance

(*c*) access security

(*d*) application system acquisition, development, and maintenance

Other general IT control activities include physical controls, such as:

(*e*) the physical security of assets, including adequate safeguards such as secured facilities over access to assets and records

(*f*) authorization for access to computer programs and data files

(*g*) periodic counting and comparison with amounts shown on control records (e.g., comparing the results of cash, security, and inventory counts with accounting records)

Separation of the duties performed by analysts, programmers and operators is another important general IT control. The general idea is that anyone who designs a processing system should not do the technical programming work, and anyone who performs either of these tasks should not be the computer operator when "live" data are being processed. Persons performing each function should not have access to each other's work, and only the computer operators should have access to the equipment. Computer systems are susceptible to manipulative handling, and the lack of separation of duties along the lines described should be considered a serious weakness in general control. The control group or similar monitoring by the user departments can be an important compensating factor for weaknesses arising from lack of segregation of duties in computerized systems. The following box gives an example of what can happen when incompatible functions are performed by the same individual.

PROGRAMMER AND OPERATOR COMBINED

A programmer employed by a large savings and loan association in the United States wrote a special subroutine that could be activated by a command from the computer console. The computation of interest on deposits and certificates was programmed to truncate calculations at the third decimal place. The special subroutine instructed the program to accumulate the truncated mills, and, when processing was complete, to credit the amount to the programmer-operator's savings account. Whenever this person was on duty for the interest calculation run, she could "make" several hundred dollars! She had to be on duty to manipulate the control figures "properly" so the error of overpaying interest on her account would not be detected by the control group. She was a programmer with computer operation duties.

---

[3] Wayne Alderman and James Deitrick have described how companies with active internal auditors have fewer financial statement adjustments recommended by independent auditors than companies without active internal auditors. See "Internal Audit Impact of Financial Information Reliability," *The Internal Auditor*, April 1981, pp. 43–56.

Error-Checking Routines   The numerous techniques used to check for errors in accounting data can be categorized as (1) input controls, (2) processing controls, and (3) output controls. The weakest point in computer systems is input—the point at which transaction data are transformed from hard-copy source documents into machine-readable cards, tape or disk, or when direct entry is made with a communication device such as a remote terminal. When undetected errors are entered originally, they may not be detected during processing, and, if detected, they are troublesome to correct. For this reason preventive controls at input tend to be the most cost effective. Processing control refers to error-condition check routines written into the computer program. Output control refers primarily to control over the distribution of reports, but feedback on errors and comparison of input totals to output totals also are part of this "last chance" control point. Error-checking routines are closely related to application controls, but because of significant risk posed by compounding errors if they are not corrected quickly and appropriately, they have a pervasive impact on the entire accounting system's integrity. The auditor should consider the overall effectiveness of error correction procedures as a key part of the control environment.

Performance Reviews   High-level review by management of how reported performance compares to expectations is an effective general control. Reported performance should be compared to budgets and prior years. This is also an important part of management's risk assessment process. The procedures should require that management follow up on any discrepancies, and if errors or other irregularities are uncovered to take appropriate action to implement corrections and solutions. Performance review procedures can be re-performed by auditors as part of their analytical procedures and can reveal important control weaknesses, risks, or actual errors or fraud.

Application Controls

Application controls help ensure that all recorded transactions really occurred, are authorized, and are completely and accurately entered and processed through the system. Application controls can be viewed in terms of whether they relate to input, processing, or output of the accounting system. The different accounting processes—reveues/receivables/receipts, purchases/payables/payments, production/payroll and investing/financing—will each have its own particular risks that can lead to errors or make the business susceptible to fraud or other illegal acts. Thus, specific control procedures are designed to address the risks and control objectives for each accounting process. These are explained in more detail in Chapters 11 through 14 where the accounting processes are covered.

Examples of application controls include:

(*a*) authorization checks prior to data input

(*b*) arithmetical checks of the accuracy of records

(*c*) maintenance and review of accounts and trial balances

(*d*) automated controls such as edit checks of input data and numerical sequence checks

(*e*) manual follow-up of exception reports

. . . .

REVIEW
CHECKPOINTS

7.25   What organizational features can act as general controls?

7.26   What risks are addressed by controlled access?

7.27   Give some examples of periodic comparisons a company can perform. How do they control the accuracy of its financial records?

7.28   List general controls related to IT.

7.29   Which duties should be segregated within the information system? Why?

. . . .

SIMPLE COMPUTER SYSTEMS: CHARACTERISTICS AND CONTROL CONSIDERATIONS

LEARNING OBJECTIVE

4 Highlight the characteristics and control risks in simple LAN-based computer systems.

This section describes two simple information systems and their controls as a basis for developing your understanding of the characteristics of information systems more generally, and the risks presented by IT use. One simple type of system is a **local area network (LAN)**. The second is a system using a stand-alone **personal computer (PC)**, as is often found in smaller businesses.

A Simple LAN-based Information System Example

In a simple LAN-based system where all processing occurs at a central processing facility, usually a server or personal computer (PC) acts as the central processor and several other PCs are connected to the network. Several LANs can be combined to a wide-area network (WAN). LANs using wireless connections are expected to become more common as wireless telecommunications technology becomes more reliable and secure.

Characteristics of a Simple LAN-based Information System

At most there are three or four people involved in the operations of a simple LAN system. The central processing facility may be set up as a batch system. **Batch processing** (also called **serial** or **sequential processing**) means that all records to be processed are collected in groups (batches) of like transactions. The computer operator (or the operating system) obtains the programs and master files from the computer library. Following the instructions in the run manual, all like transactions then are processed utilizing the same programs and the same master files. For example, all payroll records are run at one time, and the input is in the form of a magnetic disk containing employees' identification numbers and hours worked. The programs edit and validate the input and match good transactions against the employee master file for pay rate and deduction information. Programs will execute the processing to compute the payroll, print cheques, update year-to-date records, and summarize payroll information for management. After completion of the run, the programs and data files will be returned to storage (magnetic disk) and the output of cheques and reports will be distributed.

Batches may be collected at a central computer site or other locations. Input transactions may be entered via terminals and stored on magnetic tape or disks. Many smaller systems now provide the online processing capability that traditionally has been associated with advanced systems. Online has a variety of meanings but a meaning that is relevant for all systems is the following: Data processing is termed **online** (or direct access or random) where users can access data and programs directly to terminal devices such as personal computers or **personal digital assistants (PDAs)**. Regardless of the method, batch processing is characterized by grouping like transactions to be processed in batches, all using the same programs. The master files take the place of subsidiary and general ledgers in manual systems. The batches of transactions are similar to journals in a manual system. All transactions in a batch may be listed in printed output. However, the detail of transactions usually is not printed and the familiar journal is nonexistent. Instead, summary entries are prepared for updating general ledger master files.

Master files contain records with two general types of fields—**static fields**, such as employee number and pay rate, and **dynamic fields**, such as year-to-date gross pay and account balances. Most of the computer processing of accounting data involves changing these fields in the master file records. The dynamic fields are changed in **update** processing, as was described for batch processing of payroll. Update processing does not change the static fields. The static fields are changed by **file maintenance** processing, which will add or delete entire records (e.g., add new employee) or change fields (e.g., new pay rate). Auditors are concerned with authorization and controls over both types of changes.

General IT Controls

Control procedures in a computerized accounting system may be classified into two types—general controls and application controls. **General IT controls** relate to all or many computerized accounting activities—for example, controls over access to computer programs and data files. **Application controls** relate to individual computerized accounting applications—for example, programmed validation controls for verifying customers' account numbers and credit limits. The general controls are presented first because they usually are considered early in the audit.

Organization and Physical Access

The proper segregation of functional responsibilities—authority to authorize transactions, custody of assets, recordkeeping, and periodic reconciliation—is as important in computer systems as in manual systems. However, computer systems involve such functions as systems analysis, programming, data conversion, library functions and machine operations that are unique. Therefore, further separation of duties is recommended. These separate functions are explained in more detail in Chapter 9.

The physical security of computer equipment, and limited access to computer program files and data files, are as important as segregation of technical responsibilities. Access controls help prevent improper use or manipulation of data files, unauthorized or incorrect use of computer programs, and improper use of the computer equipment.

The librarian function or librarian software should control access to systems documentation and access to program and data files by using a checkout log (a record of entry and use) or password to record the use by authorized persons. Someone who possesses both documentation and data files will have enough information to alter data and programs for his own purposes.

Locked doors, security passes, passwords, and check-in logs (including logs produced by the computer) can be used to limit physical access to the computer system hardware. Having definite schedules for running computer applications is another way to detect unauthorized access because the computer system software can produce reports that can be compared to the planned schedule. Variations then can be investigated for unauthorized use of computer resources.

Weakness or absence of organizational and access controls decreases the overall integrity of the computer system. The audit team should be uncomfortable when such deficiencies exist and should weigh their impact when evaluating control risk. Some typical questions asked by auditors are shown in the following box. A full set of questions, of which these are a part, is one method that auditors use to review and document the organization and access control of a computer facility.

ORGANIZATION AND PHYSICAL ACCESS:
SELECTED QUESTIONNAIRE ITEMS

PRELIMINARY

Prepare or have the client prepare a "Computer Profile," which should include an organization chart, hardware and peripheral equipment, communication network, major application processes (batch or online), significant input and output files, software used and a layout of the data centre.

ORGANIZATION

Are the following functions performed by different individuals so that proper segregation of duties exists?

(a) Application programming, computer operation and control of data files?

(b) Application programming and control and reconciliation of input and output?

Are computer operators rotated periodically from shift to shift?

Are programmers and systems analysts rotated periodically from application to application?

DATA AND PROCEDURAL CONTROL

Is there a separate group within the computer department to perform control and balancing of input and output?

Are there written procedures for setting up input for processing?

Is there a formal procedure for distribution of output to user departments?

ACCESS CONTROL

Is access to the computer room restricted to authorized personnel?

Are operators restricted from access to program and application documentation?

Does access to online files require that specific passwords be entered to identify and validate the terminal user?

Online control issues:
  viruses
  hackers
  firewalls

Documentation and Systems Development

Documentation is the means of communicating the essential elements of the data processing system. The following purposes may be served by computer system documentation:

- provide for management review of proposed application systems
- provide explanatory material for users
- instruct new personnel by providing background on previous application systems and serve as a guideline for developing new applications
- provide the data necessary for answering enquiries about the operation of a computer application
- serve as one source of information for an evaluation of controls
- provide operating instructions
- simplify program revision by providing details of processing logic
- supply basic information for planning and implementing audit software or other auditing techniques[4]

Auditors review the documentation to gain an understanding of the system and to determine whether the documentation is adequate, and whether systems development and documentation standards have been established by the client. Unless written standards exist, it is difficult to determine whether the systems development controls and the documentation are adequate. The **systems development and documentation standards manual** prepared by management should contain standards that ensure (1) proper user involvement in the systems design and modification process, (2) review of the specifications of the system, (3) approval by user management and data processing management, and (4) controls and auditability. Examples of questionnaire items related to systems development documentation are shown in the following box.

---

[4] Gordon B. Davis, Donald L. Adams, and Carol A. Schaller, *Auditing and EDP*, 2nd ed. (New York: AICPA, 1983), p. 59.

DOCUMENTATION AND SYSTEMS DEVELOPMENT: SELECTED QUESTIONNAIRE ITEMS

DEVELOPMENT

Does a written priority plan exist for development of new systems and changes to old systems?

Does the design and development of a new system involve the users as well as computer personnel?

Is there a formal review and approval process at the end of each significant phase in developing a new system?

DOCUMENTATION

Do written standards exist for documentation of new systems and for changing documentation when existing systems are revised?

Does the following documentation exist for each application?
- system flowchart
- record layouts
- program edit routines
- program source listing
- operator instructions
- approval and change record

In many modern networked information systems, much of the operating system and application software is purchased "off-the-shelf" from software companies. For example, Windows-based operating systems are used in a majority of organizations, both in network servers and individual desktops. Systems documentation tends to be online, accessed over the Internet by the network technicians. Since the development of systems, and the documentation of the specific configurations set up in the organization may be ad hoc, it is important for auditors to focus on considering risks that can affect financial reporting. The general environmental control components provide a framework that is flexible and adaptable to the variety of computer operations structures that exist in organizations, even though the specific systems descriptions may differ.

The following material explains aspects that the auditor should consider when a client uses custom-built information systems for applications that are significant to the financial reports, and where IT-related control weaknesses are likely to create the risk of material misstatement of the financial statements.

The manual describing systems development standards would be reviewed by the auditors to evaluate the standards to determine whether they are adequate. They would then review the documentation to determine whether the standards are followed. This review actually accomplishes a test of controls audit of systems development standards (and controls), as well as providing an understanding of how a particular system works. This kind of work may require the knowledge and skills of a computer audit specialist.

Auditors are interested in the following elements of the documentation of accounting applications: application description, problem definition, programs description, acceptance testing records, computer operator instructions, user department manual, change and modification log, and listing of controls. For example, the **application description** usually contains system flowcharts, description of all inputs and outputs, record formats, lists of computer codes and control features. The application system flowcharts frequently can be adapted to audit working paper flowcharts where the flow of transactions can be followed and control points noted. Copies of record formats of significant master files frequently are obtained for use in computer-assisted audit techniques (**CAATs**) described later.

The **program description** should contain a program flowchart, a listing of the program source code (such as C++ or Java), and a record of all program changes. Auditors should review this documentation to determine whether programmed controls such as input validations exist.

The **acceptance testing records** may contain test data that can be used by auditors when performing their own tests of controls audit procedures. The users' manual should indicate manual procedures and controls in the user departments that submit transactions and receive the output. The log of changes and modifications is important to auditors because it should provide assurance that the application systems have been operating as described for the period under review and that all changes and modifications have been authorized.

The **controls documentation** is also very important. Here all the computer controls described in other sections are repeated along with manual controls that affect the application program. Careful review by auditors of this section should provide a complete overview of the entire control over the processing of transactions in a particular application and of how the general controls are carried out in the application.

Hardware

Modern computer equipment is very reliable. Machine malfunctions that can go undetected are relatively rare. You are not expected to be a computer systems engineer, but you should be familiar with some of the hardware controls so that you can converse knowledgeably with computer personnel.

The most important hardware control now incorporated in all computers is a **parity check.** The parity check ensures that the coding of data internal to the computer does not change when it is moved from one internal storage location to another. An additional hardware control commonly found is an **echo check**. It involves a magnetic read after each magnetic write "echoing" back to the sending location and comparing results. Many computers also contain dual circuitry to perform arithmetic operations twice. Auditors (and management) cannot do much about the absence of such controls but should be concerned primarily with operator procedures when such errors occur. In addition, many clients now rely on back-end database servers to do much of their processing. The server manages application tasks, handles storage and security, and provides scalability—linking up more PCs and expanding the firm's network. The front-end of the system handles the user interface such as PDAs and PCs. Servers increase the reliability of IT systems by building in redundancies in memory, disk drives, and power supply. Modern computers are largely self-diagnostic. Therefore, written procedures should exist for all computer malfunctions, and all malfunctions should be recorded along with their causes and resolutions.

Another significant area of auditor interest is **preventive maintenance**. Auditors should determine whether maintenance is scheduled and whether the schedule is followed and documented. Maintenance frequently is under contract with the computer vendor. In such cases, auditors should review the contract as well as the record of regular maintenance work. Other general evidence on hardware reliability may be obtained from a review of operating reports and downtime logs.

Data File and Program Control and Security

Controls over physical access to the computer hardware were described previously in this chapter in conjunction with organization controls. Equally important and sensitive is control over access, use and security of the data files and programs. Since magnetic storage media can be erased or written over, controls are necessary to ensure that the proper file is being used and that the files and programs are appropriately backed up. **Backup** involves a retention system for files, programs and documentation so that master files can be reconstructed in case of accidental loss and processing can continue at another site if the computer centre is lost to fire or flood. Thus, backup files must be stored offsite, away from the main computer.

Some of the more important security and retention control techniques and procedures are listed and explained next.

External Labels   These labels are paper labels on the outside of a file (diskettes, cartridges, portable disk packs or magnetic tapes). The label identifies the contents, such as "Accounts Receivable Master File," so the probability of using the file inappropriately (e.g., in the payroll run) is minimized.

Header and Trailer Labels   These labels are special internal records on magnetic tapes and disks. They are magnetic records on the tape or disk; instead of containing data, they hold label information similar to the external file label. Therefore, the header and trailer labels are sometimes called **internal labels**. Their function is to prevent use of the wrong file during processing. The header label will contain the name of the file and relevant identification codes. The trailer label gives a signal that the end of the file has been reached. Sometimes these trailer labels are designed to contain accumulated control totals to serve as a check on loss of data during operation; for example, the number of accounts and the total balance of an accounts receivable file.

File Security   Security is enhanced by many physical devices, such as storage in fireproof vaults, backup in remote locations and files sorted in computer-readable, printed or microfilm form. In the majority of cases, the exposure to risk of loss warrants insurance on program and data files.

File Retention   Retention practices are related closely to file security, but, in general, retention may provide the first line of defence against relatively minor loss, while security generally consists of all measures taken to safeguard files against total loss. In essence, the problem is how to reconstruct records and files once they have been damaged. One of the most popular methods is the **grandparent-parent-child** concept. This involves the retention of backup files, such as the current transaction file and the prior master file, from which the current master file can be reconstructed. Exhibit 7-2 illustrates the file retention plan. Particularly important files may be retained to the great-grandparent generation if this is considered necessary.

EXHIBIT   7-2   GRANDPARENT, PARENT AND CHILD IN MAGNETIC TAPE FILES

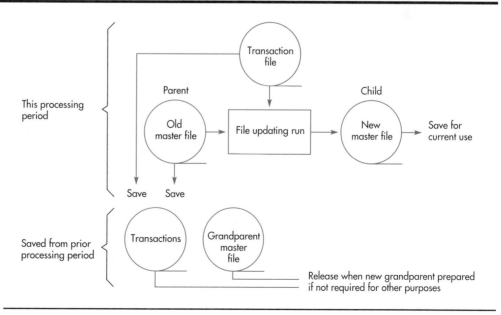

Disk files are more difficult to reconstruct than tape files because the process of updating old records with new information is "destructive." The old or superseded data on a record are removed (destroyed) when new data are entered in the same place on a disk. One means of reconstruction is to have a disk file "dumped" onto tape or cartridge periodically (each day or each week). This file copy, along with the related transaction file also retained, can serve as the parent to the current disk file (child).

IT Application Controls

Understanding the information system involves a review of the specific accounting processes and applications that generate financial information. The designation "application controls" comes from the fact that they are used in each "application"—sales and billing, purchasing, payroll and other specific accounting applications. IT application controls are organized under three categories—input controls, processing controls and output controls.

Input Control Procedures   Input controls are designed to provide reasonable assurance that data received for processing by the information system have been authorized properly and converted into machine-sensible form, and that data have not been lost, suppressed, added, duplicated or otherwise improperly changed. These controls also apply to correction and resubmission of data initially rejected as erroneous. The following control areas are particularly important:

- **Input authorized and approved.** Only properly authorized and approved input should be accepted for processing in the information system. Authorization may be a clerical (non-computer) procedure involving a person's signature or stamp on a transaction document. However, some authorizations can be general (e.g., a management policy of automatic approval for sales under $500), and some authorizations can be computer-controlled (e.g., automatic production of a purchase order when an inventory item reaches a predetermined reorder point). In many e-commerce applications, customers enter their own order information, and procedures to validate their entries and ensure they cannot repudiate their order improperly after it is shipped as key procedures in these applications.

- **Check digits.** Numbers often are used in computer systems in lieu of customer names, vendor names and so forth. One common type of number validation procedure is the calculation of a check digit. A check digit is an extra number, precisely calculated, that is tagged onto the end of a basic identification number, such as an employee number. The basic code with its check digit sometimes is called a **self-checking number**. An electronic device can be installed on a data input device or the calculation can be programmed. The device or the program calculates the correct check digit and compares it to the one on the input data. When the digits do not match, an error message is indicated on the device or printed out on an input error report. Check digits are used only on identification numbers (not quantity or value fields) to detect coding errors or keying errors such as the transposition of digits (e.g., coding 387 as 837).[5]

---

[5] One check digit algorithm is the "Modulus 11 Prime Number" method:

(a) Begin with a basic number: 814973.

(b) Multiply consecutive prime number weights of 19, 17, 13, 7, 5, 3 to each digit in the basic code number:

8	1	4	9	7	3	
×19	×17	×13	×7	×5	×3	
= 152	+17	+52	+63	+35	+9	= 328

Note: the sequence of weights is the same for all codes in given system.

(c) Add the result of the multiplication = 328.

(d) Determine the next higher multiple of 11, which is 330.

(e) Subtract the sum of the multiplication (330 − 328 = 2). This is the check digit.

(f) New account number: 8149732.

Now if this number is entered incorrectly, say it is keypunched as 8419732, the check digit will not equal 2 and an error will be indicated. See J. G. Burch, Jr., F. R. Strater, Jr., and G. Grudniski, *Information Systems: Theory and Practice*, fifth edition (New York: John Wiley & Sons, 1989), pp. 191–93.

Data Conversion   Conversion of data into machine-sensible form is a source of many errors. Control procedures include the following:

- **Record counts.** Counts of records are tallies of the number of transaction documents submitted for data conversion. The known number submitted can be compared to the count of records produced by the data-conversion device (e.g., the number of sales transactions or count of magnetic records coded). A count mismatch indicates a lost item or one converted twice. Record counts are used as batch control totals and also are used during processing and at the output stage—whenever the comparison of a known count can be made with a computer-generated count.

- **Batch financial totals**. These totals are used in the same way as record counts, except the batch total is the sum of some important quantity or amount (e.g., the total sales dollar in a batch of invoices). Batch totals are also useful during processing and at the output stage.

- **Batch hash totals.** These totals are similar to batch number totals, except the hash total is not meaningful for accounting records (e.g., the sum of all the invoice numbers on invoices submitted to the data input operator).

Edit or Validation Routines   Various computer-programmed editing or validation routines can be used to detect data conversion errors. Some of these are listed following:

- **Valid character tests.** These tests are used to check input data fields to see if they contain numbers when they are supposed to have numbers and alphabetic letters where they are supposed to have letters.

- **Valid sign tests.** Sign tests check data fields for appropriate plus or minus signs.

- **Missing data tests.** These edit tests check data fields to see if any are blank when they must contain data for the record entry to be correct.

- **Sequence tests.** These test the input data for numerical sequence of documents when sequence is important for processing, as in batch processing. This validation routine also can check for missing documents in a prenumbered series.

- **Limit or reasonableness tests.** These tests are computerized checks to see whether data values exceed or fall below some predetermined limit. For example, a payroll application may have a limit test to flag and reject any weekly payroll time record of 50 or more hours. The limit tests are a computerized version of scanning, the general audit procedure of reviewing data for indication of anything unusual that might turn out to be an error.

Error Correction and Resubmission   Errors should be subject to special controls. Usually the computer department itself is responsible only for correcting its own errors (data conversion errors, for example). Other kinds of errors, such as those due to improper coding, should be referred to and handled by the user departments. It is a good idea to have a control group log the contents of error reports in order to monitor the nature, disposition, and proper correction of rejected data. Unless properly supervised and monitored, the error-correction process itself can become a source of data input errors.

Processing Control Procedures   Processing controls are designed to provide reasonable assurance that data processing has been performed as intended without any omission or double-counting of transactions. Many of the processing controls are the same as the input controls, but they are used in the actual processing phases, rather than at the time input is checked. Other important controls are the following:

- **Run-to-run totals.** Movement of data from one department to another or one processing program to another should be controlled. One useful control is run-to-run totals. Run-to-run refers to sequential processing operations—runs—on the same data.

These totals may be batch record counts, financial totals and/or hash totals obtained at the end of one processing run. The totals are passed to the next run and compared to corresponding totals produced at the end of the second run.

- **Control total reports.** Control totals—record counts, financial totals, hash totals and run-to-run totals—should be produced during processing operations and printed out on a report. Someone (the control group, for example) should have the responsibility for comparing and/or reconciling them to input totals or totals from earlier processing runs. Loss or duplication of data thus may be detected. For example, the total of the balances in the accounts receivable master file from the last update run, plus the total of the credit sales from the current update transactions, should equal the total of the balances at the end of the current processing.

- **File and operator controls.** External and internal labels are means of assuring that the proper files are used in applications. The systems software should produce a log to identify instructions entered by the operator and to make a record of time and use statistics for application runs. These logs should be reviewed by supervisory personnel.

- **Limit and reasonableness tests.** These tests should be programmed to ensure that illogical conditions do not occur, for example, depreciating an asset below zero or calculating a negative inventory quantity. These conditions, and others considered important, should generate error reports for supervisory review. Other logic and validation checks, described previously under the heading of input edit checks, also can be used during processing.

Output Control Procedures   Output controls are the final check on the accuracy of the results of computer processing. These controls also should be designed to ensure that only authorized persons receive reports or have access to files produced by the system. Typical output control procedures are the following:

- **Control totals.** Control totals produced as output should be compared and/or reconciled to input and run-to-run control totals produced during processing. An independent control group should be responsible for the review of output control totals and investigation of differences.

- **Master file changes.** These changes should be reported in detail back to the user department from which the request for change originated because an error can be pervasive. For example, changing selling prices incorrectly can cause all sales to be priced wrong. Someone should compare computer-generated change reports to original source documents for assurance that the data are correct.

- **Output distribution.** Systems output should be distributed only to persons authorized to receive it. A distribution list should be maintained and used to deliver report copies. The number of copies produced should be restricted to the number needed.

IT Questionnaires

The brief sections following show some audit questionnaire items used to document input, processing and output control procedures.

Input Controls

Input controls are primarily preventive in nature, and with the increasing complexity of computer systems, auditors are placing increasing importance on the input controls. This follows from the **garbage in, garbage out** or **GIGO** philosophy. It is generally more cost-effective for a system to prevent misstatements rather than detect and correct misstatements once they have entered the system. The input controls procedures include the following:

- input authorization
- check digits
- record counts
- batch financial totals
- batch hash totals
- valid character tests
- valid sign tests
- missing data tests
- sequence tests
- limit/reasonableness tests
- error correction and resubmission

Some typical questionnaire items that may be asked during a review of input controls are shown in the next box. These questions should be asked about each significant accounting application.

INPUT CONTROL PROCEDURES: SELECTED QUESTIONNAIRE ITEMS

AUTHORIZATION OF TRANSACTIONS

Have procedures been established to ensure that only authorized transactions are accepted, such as (*a*) written approval on source documents, (*b*) general authorizations to process all of the user's transactions, and (*c*) use of identification numbers, security codes and passwords for remote terminal users?

COMPLETENESS OF INPUT

Are control totals established by the user prior to submitting data for processing? Does someone verify that input data are received on a timely basis from the user and physically controlled in the computer centre?

DATA CONVERSION

Have procedures been established to exercise proper control over processing rejected transactions, including (*a*) positive identification of rejected records, (*b*) review of the cause of rejection, (*c*) the correction of rejected records, (*d*) review and approval of the correction, and (*e*) prompt reentry of the correction at a point where it will be subjected to the same input controls as the original data?

Processing Controls

Processing controls are primarily oriented to detecting misstatements. Processing control procedures are as follows:

- run-to-run totals
- control total reports
- file logs
- limit/reasonableness tests

Some typical questionnaire items are shown in the following box.

PROCESSING CONTROL PROCEDURES: SELECTED QUESTIONNAIRE ITEMS

COMPLETENESS

Are programmed control procedures (run-to-run totals) included in each job step during the processing cycle?

Do application programs test the terminal identification or password, or both, for access authorization to that specific program?

Are control totals maintained on all files, and are these verified by the update or file maintenance application program each time a file is used in processing?

FILE CONTROL

Do application programs check for internal header and trailer labels?

Are disk or cartridge files subjected to adequate onsite and offsite backup support?

Are test data files documented, up to date and kept separate from live data files?

Output Controls

Output controls are primarily oriented to correcting misstatements already in the system. Output control procedures are as follows:

- control totals
- master file changes
- output distribution

Some typical questionnaire items are shown in the following box.

OUTPUT CONTROL PROCEDURES: SELECTED QUESTIONNAIRE ITEMS

Are input control totals reconciled to output totals?

Are input changes to master files compared item by item to output reports of these changes?

Do written distribution lists exist for all output reports from each application?

Are all output files appropriately identified with internal and external labels?

IT System Conversion Controls

Similar input, processing and output controls need to be in place whenever a system conversion occurs. A system conversion occurs when one system is replaced by a new one. All the information in the old system is transferred to the new system. There must be procedures in place to ensure the data are transferred completely and accurately.

An accurate cut-off between the two systems is essential. The conversion process and controls must be documented for the audit to assess if it was done properly without errors occurring. The auditor often performs audit procedures at the time of the conversion, even if it is not done at the year-end, because this can prevent errors from being made that will carryforward into the year-end balances. These procedures would involve verifying the cutoff and testing the accuracy and completeness of the data transferred.

REVIEW CHECKPOINTS

7.30   What are the characteristics of LAN-based information systems?

7.31   What general and application controls are used in LAN-based systems?

7.32   Application controls in information systems relate to input, processing and output. Which of these is mainly oriented to error detection? prevention? correction?

7.33   What is a self-checking number? Can you give an example of one of your own?

7.34   Describe five types of edit or validation controls and give an example of each for fields on a sales invoice form (e.g., customer name and number, dollar amount of the sale, shipping document number field).

7.35   What is the difference between an external label and an internal label in magnetic file media? What is the purpose of each?

7.36   What aspects of documentation, file security, and retention control procedures are unique to computer systems?

7.37   Describe the purposes of computer system documentation. Why should the auditor review the computer system documentation?

7.38   What does an auditor need to know about system conversion controls?

Control Risk Assessment in a Simple LAN Information System

Material weaknesses in manual and computer controls become a part of the independent auditor's assessment of control risk. Lack of input controls may permit data to be lost or double-counted, and poor processing control can permit accounting calculation, allocation and classification errors to occur. Poor output controls over distribution of reports and other output (negotiable cheques, for example) can be the source of misstatements that could make financial statements materially misleading.

Apparent weakness in any of the input, processing and output control procedures is a matter of concern. However, absence of a control at the input stage may be offset by other compensating controls at later stages. For example, if check digits are not calculated when the input is prepared, but transaction numbers are compared to master file numbers and non-matches are rejected and printed in an error report, the control is likely to be satisfactory and effective. Of course, it usually is more efficient to catch errors early, rather than later but control still can be considered effective for the accounting records and financial statements. Internal auditors, however, may be very interested in when controls are applied, since they are concerned about the efficiency of computer operations.

The purpose of the review of internal control is to gain an understanding of the flow of transaction processing and to determine strengths (controls) and weaknesses (lack of controls) that need to be considered in planning substantive audit procedures. In a computer environment the general control procedures must be reviewed if any application system contains important computer controls. Based on the audit documentation (working papers) of the computer controls and manual controls, the audit manager must determine whether processing is accurate and complete. The audit documentation may consist of questionnaires, such as those illustrated in this chapter, and flowcharts. The general control procedures and the controls in each application system may be subject to tests of controls auditing to determine whether the controls operate effectively. Generally, most auditors find it cost effective to follow a strategy of evaluating general and environmental controls before evaluating the more specific application controls. The reasoning for this is that the controls with a more pervasive impact and preventive in nature are the more important controls.

. . . .

REVIEW
CHECKPOINTS

7.39   How do control weaknesses affect the audit risk assessment?

7.40   What is a compensating control?

7.41   Why do auditors often evaluate environmental and general controls before application controls?

. . . .

A Simple PC-Based Information System Example

LEARNING OBJECTIVE

5 Highlight the characteristics and control risks in personal computer-based information systems.

The term **personal computer (PC)** is used to describe a family of computers that includes small business computers, laptops and intelligent terminals. These small computers can have any or all of the characteristics of advanced systems.

A simple information system is a PC used as stand-alone unit. However, given the ease with which any PC can be connected to the Internet (by modem, cable, wireless, etc.) even a simple system can be faced with the risks associated with e-commerce activities. Also, simple PC subsystems are often found even in larger organizations where users want more flexibility of access and software choices than the organization's main computing systems offer. In fact, important and relevant accounting functions and analyses are often done on PC workstations operating in a stand-alone mode. These informal systems may provide audit evidence that is produced under different (and often less rigorous) control conditions than information produced through the main system, therefore different evaluation may be needed if this kind of information is relied on for audit purposes.

Computer activity involving PCs should be included in the assessment of control risk. Since the control objectives do not change, the internal control questionnaires illustrated in this chapter may have to be tailored to the PC installation. The following explanations are designed to assist you in appreciating how the questionnaires, flowcharts, and audit techniques may have to be modified by directing attention to potential problems and controls normally affecting PCs.

Characteristics of a PC-Based Information System

PCs may be elements of a distributed system or a stand-alone system doing all the data processing for a business. The latter is considered here. The control environment, and not the computer technology, is the important aspect for auditors. Many small businesses use these resources:

- *Utility programs*. Purchased utility programs are used extensively to enter and change data.
- *Disks*. Magnetic disks and optical disks such as CD-ROMs are used extensively for accounting file storage.
- *Terminals*. Terminals and micro-minicomputers are used for transaction data entry, enquiry and other interactive functions.
- *Software packages*. Purchased software packages, rather than internally developed application software, are used extensively.
- *Documentation*. Available system, program, operation and user documentation may be limited or nonexistent.
- *Cartridge or magnetic tape backup*. Is used primarily as long-term backup file storage.

In a PC installation, the most significant control weakness is a lack of segregation of duties. This potential weakness may be compounded by the lack of control procedures in the operating system and application programs. Simply turning on the system may provide access to all the files and programs, with no record of use. The next box highlights these control problems.

CONTROL PROBLEMS IN PC ENVIRONMENTS

LACK OF SEGREGATION OF ACCOUNTING FUNCTIONS

People in user departments may initiate and authorize source documents, enter data, operate the computer, and distribute output reports.

LACK OF SEGREGATION OF COMPUTER FUNCTIONS

Small organizations may not separate the functions of programming and operating the computer. Programs and data are often resident on disk at all times and accessible by any operator.

LACK OF PHYSICAL COMPUTER SECURITY

The computer often is located in the user department instead of in a separate secure area. Ease of access and use is desired, and access to hardware, programs and data files may not be restricted.

LACK OF COMPUTER KNOWLEDGE

Individuals responsible for data processing sometimes have limited knowledge of computers, relying instead on packaged software and utility programs with convenient user manuals. Computer professionals may be assigned to monitor mainframe systems but not the PCs.

PC Control Considerations

Most control problems can be traced to the lack of segregation of duties and the lack of computerized control procedures. It follows that most of the auditors' control considerations and procedures are designed to overcome these deficiencies. Auditors should consider the entire control structure, including manual controls, and look for compensating control strengths that might offset apparent weaknesses. The various control considerations and techniques are explained following under headings similar to the general control procedures discussed previously—organizational, operation, processing, and systems development and modification.

Organizational Control Procedures
The environment in a PC installation is similar to the one-person bookkeeping department because the system analysis, design and programming functions are available using off-the-shelf software, with rudimentary client set-up and modification using one or two people. The main controls involve limiting the concentration of functions, to the extent possible, and establishing proper supervision. The implementation of the other control procedures explained following will help offset control weaknesses caused by lack of segregation of duties.

Operation Control Procedures

In PC installations, the most important controls are those over online data (accounting transactions) entry.

Restricting Access to Input Devices. Terminals may be physically locked and keys controlled. The utilization of various levels of passwords to access files, initiate changes and invoke programs should be strictly followed.

Standard Screens and Computer Prompting. The computer can be programmed to produce a standard screen format when a particular function is called. The operator must complete all blanks as prompted by the computer, thus ensuring that complete transactions are entered before they are processed.

Online Editing and Sight Verification. The input edit and validation controls discussed previously can be programmed to occur at time of input. In some installations the data on the screen are not released until the data have been sight-verified and the operator signals the computer to accept the entire screen.

Processing Control Procedures

The processing can be controlled by artificially creating the files equivalent to the grandparent-parent-child retention concept found in batch systems. The procedures that could ensure that the data processed are in balance, that an adequate audit trail is maintained and that recovery is possible include the following:

Transaction Logs. Transaction entry through the terminal should be captured automatically in a computerized log. The transaction logs (for each terminal or each class of terminals) should be summarized into the equivalent of batch totals (counts of transactions, financial totals or hash totals).

Control Totals. Master files should contain records that accumulate the number of records and financial totals. The update processing automatically should change these control records.

Balancing Input to Output. The summary of daily transactions and the master file control totals from the computer should be balanced to manual control totals maintained by the accounting department. If this external balancing is not feasible, techniques similar to the auditor's analytical procedures can be employed to test for reasonableness.

Audit Trail. The transaction logs and periodic dumps of master files should provide an audit trail and means for recovery. In addition, some PC installations have systems software that can provide a log of all files accessed and all jobs processed.

Systems Development and Modification

The control objectives and techniques in a PC installation are no different than on a larger system, even though the environment is different. Many application programs will be purchased from computer manufacturers or software vendors not completely familiar with control techniques. Purchased programs should be reviewed carefully and tested before acquisition and implementation. However, once the auditor becomes familiar with widely used off-the-shelf accounting software packages such as ACCPAC or MYOB, this knowledge can be used in the review of systems of other clients using the same software.

There are a variety of programming languages and application generators used in PC systems (C++, Java) and programming ability may develop within the user group. Most PCs have "menu-type" micro-instructions, which are simple to use without technical training. Further, the programming is in an interpretative language, which means it remains in the computer program library in source code form that is easy to change. Development standards and modification authorization become even more important than in larger systems. Since most programming will be done through terminals, special passwords should be required to access programs and only authorized personnel should be issued these passwords. The box that follows identifies key issues of general controls in small business systems.

INFORMATION SYSTEMS IN SMALL BUSINESSES

Three types of systems are encountered in small businesses: PCs, local area networks (LANs), and certain multi-user systems. Where PCs are used to process accounting records, the computers often "stand alone" and run a single software package purchased from a software vendor. Where computers are linked together, they form a LAN, again usually running packaged software. In fewer cases, the computers are linked together using a multi-user operating system, such as UNIX, and run custom software especially developed for the business, usually by an outside developer or consultant.

Access controls are important for all of these scenarios, as are backup procedures. The greater the number of users, the greater the opportunity for using access controls for enforcing division of duties. Program development controls are significant only for custom software.

As a minimum, a small business audit file should include a brief memo addressing each of these areas, identifying, for example, whether passwords are being used and how they are administered; whether and by whom programs are changed; and whether backups are made and stored off site. The more complex the system, the more fully the areas need to be addressed.

Source: G. Trites, *Audit of a Small Business* (CICA, 1994), pp. 46–47.

Control Risk Considerations in Small Business Environments

There is some controversy about the effect of computerization in small businesses and whether such computerization increases or decreases control risk. The International Federation of Accountants suggests that computerization in small businesses leads to increased control risk because of the increased risk of incompatible duties being performed. However, S. J. Gaston argues that adequate general controls can be achieved with "appropriate segregation of duties of only three or four employees" when combined with proper use of user identification and password capabilities.[6] Such general controls, when combined with "reasonably effective application controls," can result in a reduced level of control risk.[7]

. . . .

R E V I E W
C H E C K P O I N T S

7.42   Which important duties are generally not segregated in small business computer systems?

7.43   What control techniques can a company use to achieve control over the operation of a PC-based accounting system?

7.44   What control techniques can a company use to achieve control over the computer processing of accounting data in a PC system?

7.45   What are the major characteristics and control problems in PC installations?

. . . .

[6] S. J. Gaston, *Managing and Controlling Small Computer Systems Including LANS* (CICA, 1992), p. XIX.
[7] G. Trites, *Audit of a Small Business* (CICA, 1994) pp. 47–48.

SUMMARY

Even though information technology changes the accounting system and the control environment, it does not change basic auditing standards. Qualities of competence, independence, due care, planning, control risk assessment and sufficient competent evidence are not changed. However, the nuances and aspects of achieving them must be tailored to the IT world.

Chapter 7 covered an important component of the auditor's understanding of the client's business: the information systems that management has in place for running the business and meeting its information needs. This understanding is critical to assessing the possibility that the client's financial statements are misstated. This is because the financial statements result from its business processes and information systems and thus they are vulnerable to any control deficiencies and weaknesses that might exist.

Chapter 6 provided a description of businesses processes, how they are used to implement the business strategy and the role of information systems in the business processes. Chapter 7 continued the coverage of this topic by describing the elements of information systems and their relation to business processes. The idea of control risks that exist within information systems was introduced by a discussion of IT and manual procedures and controls, and consideration of their roles in addressing risks.

A conceptual framework consisting of company-level controls and specific control activities was described. Company-level controls are the responsibility of management, and include the control environment, management's risk assessment processes, information systems related to business processes and communications policies, and management's monitoring activities. Control activities consist of general and application controls. The chapter explained the function of the client's accounting system, and the role of control procedures within this framework and how these are evaluated and documented in the audit working papers.

The chapter also provided detailed descriptions of two simple computer installations: a LAN-based information system and a PC-based information system. These examples were used to illustrate in more concrete terms the hardware, software, people and organizational aspects of information systems that are relevant to producing financial information. General and application control procedures were described in the context of these simple systems, to illustrate the general characteristics of controls. (All aspects of controls will be explained in more detail in Chapter 9, where internal control concepts are integrated with the overall audit planning considerations concerning the design of tests of controls and other audit procedures to be performed.)

Chapter 7 also addressed issues that auditors need to consider to understand information systems in small businesses. Their characteristics and typical control problems were described. Simple information systems were described as being characterized by batch processing or PC processing while more advanced ones have sophisticated data communication, database integration, automatic transaction initiation or an unconventional audit trail. The issues introduced in advanced systems are becoming more widespread as most organizations make use of the Internet in various forms of e-commerce.

MULTIPLE-CHOICE QUESTIONS FOR PRACTICE AND REVIEW

7.46 In an IT-based information system, automated equipment controls or hardware controls are designed to:
a. Arrange data in a logical sequential manner for processing purposes.
b. Correct errors in the computer programs.
c. Monitor and detect errors in source documents.
d. Detect and control errors arising from use of equipment.

7.47 A good example of application (user) computer software is:
a. Payroll processing program.
b. Operating system program.
c. Data management system software.
d. Utility programs.

7.48 Which of the following statements most likely represents a disadvantage for a company that performs its accounting using PCs?

  a. It is usually difficult to detect arithmetic errors.

  b. Unauthorized persons find it easy to access the computer and alter the data files.

  c. Transactions are coded for account classifications before they are processed on the computer.

  d. Random errors in report printing are rare in packaged software systems.

7.49 A procedural control used in the management of a computer centre to minimize the possibility of data or program file destruction through operator error includes:

  a. Control figures.

  b. Crossfooting tests.

  c. Limit checks.

  d. External labels.

7.50 Which of the following is not a characteristic of a batch-processed computer system?

  a. The collection of like transactions that are sorted and processed sequentially against a master file.

  b. Keyboard input of transactions, followed by machine processing.

  c. The production of numerous printouts.

  d. The posting of a transaction, as it occurs, to several files, without intermediate printouts.

7.51 What is the computer process called when data processing is performed concurrently with a particular activity and the results are available soon enough to influence the particular course of action being taken or the decision being made?

  a. Batch processing.

  b. Real-time processing.

  c. Integrated data processing.

  d. Random access processing.

7.52 The client's computerized exception-reporting system helps an auditor to conduct a more efficient audit because it:

  a. Condenses data significantly.

  b. Highlights abnormal conditions.

  c. Decreases the tests of computer controls requirements.

  d. Is efficient computer input control.

7.53 Auditors often make use of computer programs that perform routine processing functions, such as sorting and merging. These programs are made available by software companies and are specifically referred to as:

  a. Compiler programs.

  b. Supervisory programs.

  c. Utility programs.

  d. User programs.

7.54 In the weekly computer run to prepare payroll cheques, a cheque was printed for an employee who had been terminated the previous week. Which of the following controls, if properly utilized, would have been most effective in preventing the error or ensuring its prompt detection?

  a. A control total for hours worked, prepared from time cards collected by the timekeeping department.

  b. Requiring the treasurer's office to account for the numbers of the prenumbered cheques issued to the computer department for the processing of the payroll.

  c. Use of the check digit for employee numbers.

  d. Use of a header label for the payroll input sheet.

Exercises and Problems

7.55 **Computer Internal Control Understanding.** Assume

LO.2 that, when conducting procedures to obtain an understanding of the control structure in the Denton Seed Company, you checked "No" to the following internal control questionnaire items (selected from those illustrated in the chapter):

  • Does access to online files require specific passwords to be entered to identify and validate the terminal user?

  • Are control totals established by the user prior to submitting data for processing? (Order entry application subsystem.)

  • Are input control totals reconciled to output control totals? (Order entry application subsystem.)

Required:

Describe the errors, irregularities or misstatements that could occur due to the weaknesses indicated by the lack of controls.

7.56 **Explain Computer Control Procedures.** At a meeting

LO.2 of the corporate audit committee attended by the general manager of the products division and you, representing the internal audit department, the following dialogue took place:

  Jiang (committee chair): Mr. Marks had suggested that the internal audit department conduct an audit of the computer activities of the products division.

  Smith (general manager): I don't know much about the technicalities of computers, but the division has some of the best computer people in the company.

  Jiang: Do you know whether the internal controls protecting the system are satisfactory?

  Smith: I suppose they are. No one has complained. What's so important about controls anyway, as long as the system works?

Jiang turns to you and asks you to explain computer control policies and procedures.

Required:

Address your response to the following points:

a. State the principal objective of achieving control over (1) input, (2) processing and (3) output.

b. Give at least three methods of achieving control over (1) source data, (2) processing and (3) output.

7.57   Testing Computer Processing. An experienced auditor
LO.3   remarked that it is only necessary to check the additions and extensions on one invoice generated by a computer-based system because if the computer program does one invoice correctly it will do them all correctly, so there is no point in testing a statistical sample of invoices.

Required:

a. Comment on whether or not you agree with this statement. Give your reasons.

b. Assume that a company had effective controls over program changes in prior years, but during the current year a new programmer was hired who was not qualified for the job and did not document changes to the programs that were made during the year. Would this fact have an impact on your response for (a)?

**7.58   Computer-Based Management Supervisory Con-
LO.1   trols.** Jabiru Inc.'s senior management recently obtained
LO.2   a new decision-support database system that allows the managers to generate standard reports and also customize enquiries that use data from all functional areas of their company. Before this system was in place, reports to senior managers were generated manually by the operations managers in the various departments, such as purchasing, marketing, inventory control, production, human resources and administration. The senior managers are much happier with the new system because now they can generate reports as soon as the period ends, they can draw the data directly from the company's computer databases, they can control the content and format of the reports and the operating managers have less opportunity to manipulate the information in the reports. For example, in the first two months of the new system, senior managers were able to identify a discrepancy in the production department that was resulting in significant shrinkage and were able to correct the control weakness quickly. The previous report, which had been designed and produced by the production manager, did not include the data needed to identify the shrinkage problem.

Required:

Comment how the new decision-support database system affects Jabiru's internal control.

**7.59   Back-Up Procedures, Impact on Internal Control
LO.3   Risk.** Whistler Corp. is a new audit client of your audit firm. Whistler backs up all its sales transaction detailed data for each month on a back-up tape. The tape is retained offsite for three months and then reused. This system is used because the company only has four tapes, which cost over $100 each, and offsite storage charges are on a per-tape basis. The Whistler information system manager considers this to be a cost-effective back-up procedure. Following the request of their former auditors, Whistler retains back-up tapes for December (the year-end) and the following January until the financial statement audit is completed. The audit is usually completed by the end of April.

Required:

Discuss the impact of this back-up procedure on Whistler's control risk. Suggest alternate feasible approaches that may improve internal control and explain fully how your recommendations improve control and reduce risk.

7.60   Control Risk Assessment. Consider the sales controls
LO.1   in these two different businesses.
LO.2
LO.3   **Avocet Inc.**

Avocet is a franchise fast food restaurant business. When customers order food, the counter person presses the appropriate buttons on the cash register. There is a button for each menu item. The point of sale (POS) system retrieves the current item prices from the price files, extends for quantities ordered and displays the sale total on the cash register screen. A sales entry is also generated in the daily sales register. The customer's payment is then entered and their food order is displayed on a screen in the food preparation area. The POS system generates a cash receipt entry for the cash register and also in the daily cash receipts register. Food preparation staff put together the order and place it in the pick-up area behind the front counter. When the food order is filled, the staff clears the order from the system; this generates an entry in the inventory system to remove the food and packaging items sold from the perpetual inventory listing.

A restaurant manager is on duty at all times. The manager circulates between the counter and food services areas, observing that cash received is placed in the register and spot-checking that food orders match with cash sales. If a customer receives an incorrect order, the manager can void the sale entry using a special key in the cash register and a secret password for the POS entries. A corrected order is then input by the usual method, if required. At the close of each day's business, the cash in the register is totalled and agreed to the cash, debit card and credit card slips collected in the register during the day. Differences of less than $10 are recorded in an account named "Cash over/under." Larger discrepancies will be investigated by scrutinizing the day's entries and interviewing all counter people using the register. The sales and cash information from the POS is then uploaded over a phone line to the franchise company head office, where it is consolidated with the reports from all the restaurants in the system. On a weekly basis, the food and packaging inventory on hand in the restaurant is counted and reconciled to the inventory system. The inventory usage is also compared to the sales records for reasonability.

Boblink Limited

Bobolink is a new-car dealership. Once a customer has decided to buy a car, the car salesperson fills out a purchase agreement form, including the description of the car, the serial number, and the name and address of the purchaser. The agreed sale price is entered, along with any extras such as options or extended warranties, any allowance for a used car traded in, additional dealer preparation fees, licensing fees, and various taxes. A second form is used outlining the car purchase financing. The financing can be cash, a bank loan prearranged by the customer, or a lease arranged by Bobolink's financing company. Both forms are reviewed by the customer, and if they are satisfactory, the customer signs. The salesperson then takes the signed forms to the dealership's general manager for review and approval. If payment is by cash, the cash is given to the general manager at this point. Any discrepancies in the payment or paperwork are corrected and must be agreed to by the customer. Once the sales documents are completed, the ownership papers and keys are handed over to the customer, who drives away with the car. The sales documents are faxed to the car manufacturer's sales head office for inventory and warranty purposes, and to the bank or leasing company, if applicable. The sales information is entered by the Bobolink bookkeeper to the financial system and the inventory system. The bookkeeper follows up on collection of the funds from the bank or leasing company, which usually takes two to three days. The sales information is also set up in the dealership management system for purposes of sales incentives and commissions, future service work and sales follow-up.

Required:

a. Compare and contrast the control risks in these two businesses.

b. Identify input, processing and output control procedures that exist in each business, including the control objective for each.

c. Comment on whether each business control system relies on prevention of errors, early detection of errors, or later detection and correction. Do you think the control method used by each business is the most effective and efficient system for its particular control risks? Can you recommend any more cost-effective control techniques?

7.61 **Control Risk Assessment, Online Input.** Federal tax
LO.3 department has introduced "e-filing." Registered tax professionals can submit taxpayers' annual income tax returns online over the Internet. The taxpayer's annual return information is automatically entered into the tax department's computer system. No paper forms or receipts need to be submitted, but the taxpayer must retain them because tax department auditors might ask to see them in the future. The tax return, and any refund due, are processed much more quickly than when paper forms are mailed in. A refund can be electronically deposited to the taxpayer's bank account, sometimes within one week.

Required:

Comment on the control strengths and weaknesses of the "e-file" system. In the case of weaknesses, provide recommendations on how they can be compensated for.

Kingston Case questions related to Chapter 7 are on the Online Learning Centre that accompanies this text.

CHAPTER

8

Audit Planning: Concepts and Tools

Chapter 8 covers the concepts and tools of audit fieldwork planning. These include the application of analytical procedures at the beginning of an audit, the materiality decisions, risk assessment using a conceptual audit risk model, the theory of evidence, general forms of audit evidence-gathering procedures, the preparation of audit programs, and the working papers that document the audit.

LEARNING OBJECTIVES

After completing this chapter, you will be able to:

1. Explain the purpose of preliminary analytical procedures and business risk analysis in the audit planning process.

2. Perform analytical procedures to identify potential misstatements in the accounts.

3. Explain how the planning materiality amount for the audit is determined.

4. Describe the conceptual audit risk model and its components.

5. Explain audit evidence in terms of its appropriateness and relative strength of persuasiveness.

6. Outline six general types of audit techniques for gathering evidence.

7. Describe the content and purpose of audit programs.

8. Review a set of audit working papers for proper form and content.

The Audit Planning Process

After the auditors finish the pre-engagement arrangements, understand the audit client's business and information systems, assess the business risks and risk of material misstatements, and obtain the draft financial statements, they use certain planning tools to guide and direct their audit work. These tools are classified as preliminary analytical procedures, materiality decisions, business and audit risk assessment, and audit programs. The usefulness of the first three is to help auditors design audit programs. As covered in Chapter 3, auditing standards recently introduced in the U.S. by the PCAOB include a requirement for auditors of a public company (SEC registrant) to report on the separate internal control statements that SOX 404 requires management to issue. The PCAOB Policy Statement states that auditors should integrate their audits of internal control with their audits of the financial statements so that the evidence gathered in either process will contribute to completion of both audits, a form of audit referred to as an integrated audit. Similar standards for internal control audits to be integrated with financial statement audits are being developed in Canada by CICA along the lines of the SOX requirements. At the time of writing, however, there is no regulatory requirement for auditors of Canadian public companies to report on internal control. CPAB would monitor the internal control audits for public companies.

Whether monitored by CPAB/PCAOB or not, auditors must exercise judgement in how they use control testing in the audit work that supports their opinion. For our study purposes, we will cover internal control auditing later in Chapter 9 where we will explain how auditors can select an audit approach that combines control testing with substantive audit testing of financial statement transactions and balances.

PRELIMINARY ANALYTICAL PROCEDURES

· · · · · · · · · · · ·

According to auditing standards, analytical procedures should be applied in the beginning planning stages of each audit for risk assessment[1] and as part of the overall evaluation at the end of the audit.[2] Analytical procedures are powerful techniques for identifying unusual changes and relations in financial statement data. The purpose of doing analysis at the beginning of the audit engagement is "attention directing"—to alert the audit team to problems (errors, fraud) that may exist in the account balances and disclosures and guide the design of further audit work. The auditor's understanding of the business risks is important in identifying what kinds of changes and relations are expected based on how the business performed during the audited period and what kinds might indicate the financial information is misstated. There are five general types of analytical procedures:

1. comparison of current-year account balances to balances for one or more comparable periods
2. comparison of the current-year account balances to anticipated results found in the company's budgets and forecasts
3. evaluation of the relationships of current-year account balances to other current-year balances for conformity with predictable patterns based on the company's experience
4. comparison of current-year account balances and financial relationships (e.g., ratios) with similar information for the industry in which the company operates
5. study of the relationships of current-year account balances with relevant nonfinancial information (e.g., physical production statistics)

Analytical procedures can take many forms, ranging from simple to complex. For the simpler and more easily applied procedures, auditors have begun to define a wide range of

---

[1] *CICA Handbook*, paragraph 5301.03. ISA 520 gives the same recommendations.
[2] Ibid., paragraph 5301.25.

early information-gathering activities as "analytical procedures," including: (*a*) review of adjustments proposed in prior years' audits; (*b*) conversations with client personnel; (*c*) reading and study of the minutes of the meetings of directors and committees of the board of directors (e.g., executive committee, finance committee, compensation committee, audit committee); (*d*) review of the corporate charter and bylaws or partnership agreement; (*e*) review of contracts, agreements and legal proceedings; (*f*) and many other activities that do not fit the strict definition of the five general types of analytical procedures. The following box outlines some of the key knowledge that auditors obtain from reading minutes.

WHAT'S IN THE MINUTES OF MEETINGS?

Boards of directors are supposed to monitor the client's business. The minutes of their meetings and the meetings of their committees (e.g., executive committee, finance committee, compensation committee, audit committee) contain information of vital interest to the independent auditors. Some examples:

- amount of dividends declared
- authorization of officers' salaries and bonuses
- authorization of stock options and other "perq" compensation
- acceptance of contracts, agreements, lawsuit settlements
- approval of major purchases of property and investments
- discussions of merger and divestiture progress. Authorization of financing by share issues, long-term debt and leases
- approval to pledge assets as security for debts
- discussion of negotiations on bank loans and payment waivers
- approval of accounting policies and accounting for estimates and unusual transactions
- authorizations for individuals to sign bank cheques

Auditors take notes or make copies of important parts of these minutes and compare them with information in the accounts and disclosures (e.g., compare the amount of dividends declared to the amount paid, compare officers' authorized salaries to amounts paid, compare agreements to pledge assets to proper disclosure in the notes to financial statements).

Because of the importance that the minutes have in determining what needs to be disclosed in order to obtain fair presentation, denial of access to the minutes of the board of directors meeting constitutes a major scope restriction by the client. Such denial is a common source of opinion reservation.

Other analytical procedures can be complex, including mathematical time series and regression calculations, comparisons of multi-year data, and trend and ratio analyses. In the sections that follow, two of the general analytical procedures are emphasized: (1) comparison of current year account balances to balances for one or more comparable periods, and (2) evaluation of the relationships of current-year account balances to other current-year balances for conformity with predictable patterns based on the company's experience.

Business Risk Approach to Auditing

Audit standards[3] introduce important developments in the areas of auditing planning, analytical procedures, materiality and risk assessment. These standards generally do not distinguish audit planning as a separate phase of the audit. Because of the importance of

---

[3] Ibid., sections 5150, 5301, 5142, 5141 and 5143, and ISA 300, 520, 320, 315 and 330.

EXHIBIT   8-1   AUDIT PLANNING—A PROCESS OF CONTINUOUS IMPROVEMENT

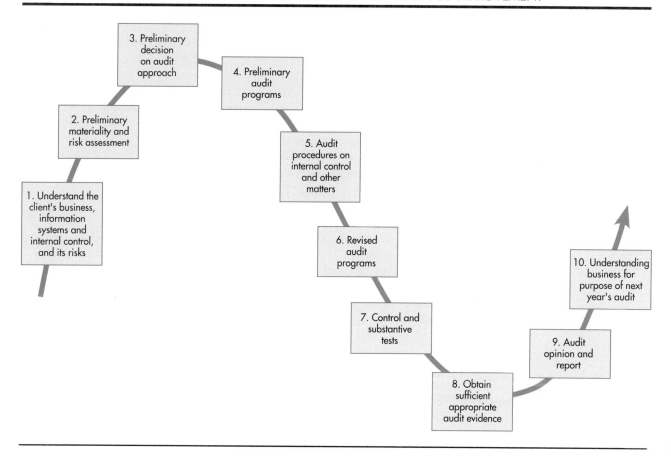

understanding the business, enquiries and analysis in obtaining audit evidence in complex modern organizations, the planning activities are highly integrated with the rest of the work the auditor does in performing the audit. As explained in Chapter 6, the auditor has to develop a deep knowledge base that may include strategic analysis, analysis of business processes, a continuous business risk assessment analysis and a detailed business performance analysis. The final set of audit procedures executed to complete the audit must take into account all this relevant knowledge that the audit team gains during the audit engagement, including the internal control evaluation that we will cover in more detail in the next chapter. Thus, we can see audit planning as a process of learning, feedback and continuous improvement. This process is illustrated in Exhibit 8-1.

REVIEW
CHECKPOINTS

8.1   What is the purpose of performing analytical procedures at the beginning of the audit engagement?

8.2   What is the role of the auditor's understanding of the business and its risks in performing analytical procedures?

8.3   What are five types of general analytical procedures?

8.4   What official documents and authorizations should an auditor read when performing preliminary analytical procedures?

8.5   What important information can be found in directors' minutes about officers' compensation? Business operations? Corporate finance? Accounting policies and control?

8.6   What is the role of business risk analysis in the audit planning process?

ANALYSIS OF MANAGEMENT'S DRAFT FINANCIAL STATEMENTS

. . . .

One of the first things the auditor receives during the audit engagement is management's draft financial statements. Depending on the client, these financial statements may be virtually complete and final (e.g., in a large company with many professionally qualified accountants on staff) or preliminary statements that still require adjustments for items such as bonuses and income taxes (e.g., in a small company with few in-house accountants). Auditors perform analytical procedures on these draft financial statements to look for relationships that do not make sense as these may indicate problems in the accounts that should be used to plan further audit work. Such analysis is of great importance in the business risk approach to auditing set out in the audit standards.

Attention Directing

In the planning stage, analytical procedures are used to identify potential problem areas so that subsequent audit work can be designed to reduce the risk of missing something important. The application demonstrated following can thus be described as attention directing—pointing out accounts that may contain misstatements. The insights derived from preliminary analytical procedures do not provide direct evidence about the numbers in the financial statements. They only help the audit team plan the audit program.

An Organized Approach

With an organized approach—a standard starting place—preliminary analytical procedures can provide considerable familiarity with the client's business. **Horizontal analysis** refers to changes of financial statement numbers and ratios across two or more years. **Vertical analysis** refers to financial statement amounts expressed each year as proportions of a base, such as sales for the income statement accounts and total assets for the balance sheet accounts. Many auditors start with comparative financial statements and calculate common-size statements (vertical analysis) and year-to-year change in balance sheet and income statement accounts (horizontal analysis). This is the start of describing the financial activities for the current year under audit. Exhibit 8-2 contains financial balances for the prior year (consider them audited) and the current year (consider them draft numbers not yet audited at this stage). Common-size statements (vertical) are shown in parallel columns, and the dollar amount and percentage change (horizontal) are shown in the last two columns. These analytical procedures generate basic analytical data that is the starting point for further evaluation and enquiry by the auditor.

Describe the Financial Activities

After generating these basic financial data, the next step is to describe the financial changes and relationships you can see in the data. According to the draft financial statements in Exhibit 8-2, the company increased the net income by increasing sales by 10 percent, reducing cost of goods sold as a proportion of sales and controlling other expenses. At least some of the sales growth appears to have been prompted by easier credit (larger accounts receivable) and more service (more equipment in use). The company also used much of its cash and borrowed more to purchase the equipment to make its payment on the long-term debt and to pay dividends.

Ask Relevant Questions

The next step is to ask: "What could be wrong?" and "What errors or fraud, as well as legitimate explanations, could account for these financial results?" For this explanation we will

EXHIBIT 8-2   ANYCOMPANY, INC.—PRELIMINARY ANALYTICAL PROCEDURES DATA

	Prior Year		Current Year		Change	
	Balance	Common Size	Balance	Common Size	Amount	Percent Change
Assets						
Cash	$ 600,000	14.78%	$ 200,000	4.12%	($ 400,000)	−66.67%
Accounts receivable	500,000	12.32	900,000	18.56	400,000	80.00
Allowance doubtful accounts	(40,000)	−0.99	(50,000)	−1.03	(10,000)	25.00
Inventory	1,500,000	36.95	1,600,000	32.99	100,000	6.67
Total current assets	2,560,000	63.05	2,650,000	54.63	90,000	3.52
Equipment	3,000,000	73.89	4,000,000	82.47	1,000,000	33.33
Accumulated amortization	(1,500,000)	−36.95	(1,800,000)	−37.11	(300,000)	20.00
Total assets	$4,060,000	100.00%	$4,850,000	100.00%	$ 790,000	19.46%
Liabilities and Equity						
Accounts payable	$ 500,000	12.32%	$ 400,000	8.25%	($ 100,000)	−20.00%
Bank loans, 11%	0	0.00	750,000	15.46	750,000	
Accrued interest	60,000	1.48	40,000	0.82	(20,000)	−33.33
Total current liabilities	560,000	13.79	1,190,000	24.53	630,000	112.50
Long-term debt, 10%	600,000	14.78	400,000	8.25	(200,000)	−33.33
Total liabilities	1,160,000	28.57	1,590,000	32.78	430,000	37.07
Share capital	2,000,000	49.26	2,000,000	41.24	0	0.00
Retained earnings	900,000	22.17	1,260,000	25.98	360,000	40.00
Total liabilities and equity	$4,060,000	100.00%	$4,850,000	100.00%	$ 790,000	19.46%
Income						
Sales (net)	$9,000,000	100.00%	$9,900,000	100.00%	$ 900,000	10.00%
Cost of goods sold	6,750,000	75.00	7,200,000	72.73	450,000	6.67
Gross margin	2,250,000	25.00	2,700,000	27.27	450,000	20.00
General expense	1,590,000	17.67	1,734,000	17.52	144,000	9.06
Amortization	300,000	3.33	300,000	3.03	0	0.00
Operating income	360,000	4.00	666,000	6.46	306,000	85.00
Interest expense	60,000	0.67	40,000	0.40	(20,000)	−33.33
Income taxes (40%)	120,000	1.33	256,000	2.59	136,000	113.33
Net income	$ 180,000	2.00%	$ 370,000	3.74%	$ 190,000	105.56%

limit our attention to the accounts receivable and inventory accounts. At this point some other ratios can help support the analysis. Exhibit 8-3 contains several familiar ratios. (Appendix 8A at the end of this chapter contains these ratios and their formulas.)

Question: Are the accounts receivable collectible? (Alternative: Is the allowance for doubtful accounts large enough?) Easier credit can lead to more bad debts. The company has a much larger amount of receivables (Exhibit 8-2), the days' sales in receivables has increased significantly (Exhibit 8-3), the receivables turnover has decreased (Exhibit 8-3), and the allowance for doubtful accounts is smaller in proportion to the receivables (Exhibit 8-3). If the prior-year allowance for bad debts at 8 percent of receivables was appropriate, and conditions have not become worse, perhaps the allowance should be closer to $72,000 than $50,000. The auditors should work carefully on the evidence related to accounts receivable valuation.

Question: Could the inventory be overstated? (Alternative: Could the cost of the goods sold be understated?) Overstatement of the ending inventory would cause the cost of goods sold to be understated. The percentage of cost of goods sold to sales shows a decrease (Exhibits 8-2 and 8-3). If the 75 percent of the prior year represents a more accurate cost of goods sold, then the income before taxes may be overstated by $225,000 (75 percent of $9.9 million minus $7.2 million unaudited cost of goods sold). The days' sales in inventory and the inventory turnover remained the same (Exhibit 8-3), but you might expect them to

EXHIBIT   8-3   ANYCOMPANY, INC.—SELECTED FINANCIAL RATIOS

	Prior Year	Current Year	Percent Change
Balance Sheet Ratios			
Current ratio	4.57	2.23	–51.29%
Days' sales in receivables	18.40	30.91	67.98
Doubtful accounts ratio	0.0800	0.0556	–30.56
Days' sales in inventory	80.00	80.00	0.00
Debt/equity ratio	0.40	0.49	21.93
Operations Ratios			
Receivables turnover	19.57	11.65	–40.47
Inventory turnover	4.50	4.50	0.00
Cost of goods sold/sales	75.00%	72.73%	–3.03
Gross margin percentage	25.00%	27.27%	9.09
Return on beginning equity	6.62%	12.76%	92.80
Financial Distress Ratios (Altman, 1968, Appendix 8A)			
Working capital/total assets	0.49	0.30	–38.89
Retained earnings/total assets	0.22	0.26	17.20
EBIT/total assets	0.09	0.14	54.87
Market value of equity/total debt	2.59	1.89	–27.04
Net sales/total assets	2.22	2.04	–7.92
Discriminant Z score	4.96	4.35	–12.32

change in light of the larger volume of sales. Careful work on the physical count and valuation of inventory appears to be needed.

Other questions can be asked and other relationships derived when industry statistics are available. Industry statistics can be obtained from such services as Statistics Canada, D & B, and Robert Morris Associates. These statistics include industry averages for important financial yardsticks, such as gross profit margin, return on sales, current ratio and debt/net worth. A comparison with client data may reveal out-of-line statistics, indicating a relatively strong feature of the company, a weak financial position or possibly an error or misstatement in the client's financial statements. However, care must be taken with industry statistics. A particular company may or may not be well represented by industry averages.

Comparing reported financial results with internal budgets and forecasts also can be useful. If the budget or forecast represents management's estimate of probable future outcomes, planning questions can arise for items that fall short of or exceed the budget. If a company expected to sell 10,000 units of a product but sold only 5,000 units, the auditors would want to plan a careful lower-of-cost-or-market study of the inventory of unsold units. If 15,000 were sold, an auditor would want to audit for sales validity. Budget comparisons can be tricky, however. Some companies use budgets and forecasts as goals, rather than as expressions of probable outcomes. Also, meeting the budget with little or no shortfall or excess can result from managers manipulating the numbers to "meet the budget." Auditors must be careful to know something about a company's business conditions from sources other than the internal records when analyzing comparisons with budgets and forecasts.

Cash Flow Analysis

If the client has not already prepared the cash flow statement, the auditors can use the comparative financial statements to prepare one. The analysis of changes in cash flows enable the auditors to see the crucial information of cash flow from operating, investment and financing activities. A cash flow deficit from operations may signal financial difficulty. Companies fail when they run out of cash (no surprise) and are unable to pay their debts when they become due.

You can use the information in Exhibit 8-2 to prepare a statement of cash flows as per *CICA Handbook*, paragraph 1540.01 if you want to practise a technique you learned in earlier accounting courses.

Analytical Procedures Requirements

Even though particular analytical procedures are not required by audit standards, the timing of required application is specified in two instances. Analytical procedures applicable in the circumstances are required (1) at the beginning of an audit—the planning stage application of analytical procedures discussed in this chapter—and (2) at the end of an audit when the partners in charge review the overall quality of the work and look for apparent problems.[4]

A recent study found that analytical procedures are most effective when used in an integrative fashion with other sources of information, especially when accompanied by a strong knowledge of the client's business. "Auditors must combine different types of knowledge (accounting, general business, industry and client-specific) and issues (operating, financing and investing) into a whole. This skill is needed whether analytical procedures are used for planning, substantive testing, or overall review purposes, but it appears to be most critical at overall review, where the auditor's goal is to examine the financial statements to determine whether they make sense taken as a whole."[5]

. . . .

REVIEW
CHECKPOINTS

8.7   What are management's draft financial statements?

8.8   What are the steps auditors can use to apply comparison and ratio analysis to management's financial statements?

8.9   What can the auditor learn from doing a vertical analysis?

8.10   What can the auditor learn from doing a horizontal analysis?

8.11   What are some of the ratios that can be used in preliminary analytical procedures?

8.12   How can computing the accounts receivable turnover ratio indicate potential misstatement in the accounts receivable balance?

8.13   How can computing the number of days of sales in inventory indicate potential misstatement in the inventory balance?

8.14   Is anything questionable about the relationship between retained earnings and income for the Anycompany data shown in Exhibit 8-2?

8.15   What is the operating cash flow for the current year for the Anycompany shown in Exhibit 8-2?

8.16   Why do preliminary analytical procedures not provide direct evidence about financial statement misstatements?

. . . .

Business Performance Analysis and Management's Financial Statements

The section expands on how the auditor applies her knowledge of the business in performing preliminary analyses. A key part of audit risk, the risk of material misstatement of the financial statements, is that the financial statements will not capture the underlying business reality in conformance with generally accepted accounting principles. Therefore, the auditor develops expectations about the contents of the financial statements by analyzing business performance. Business performance analysis ideally will use an integrated approach by considering financial performance measures and nonfinancial performance measures and the

---

[4] Ibid., section 5301.
[5] E. Hirst, L. Koonce, F. Philipps, "First, Know the Business," *CA Magazine*, August 1998, p. 41.

interrelationships between the two. The auditor considers whether the analysis of business performance is consistent with the performance portrayed in the financial statements. The auditor should also consider how performance measures are used, both externally (e.g., key performance indicators reported to analysts, creditors and shareholders) and internally (e.g., for personnel review and incentive programs). These uses can create pressures on the business that may increase the risk that managers are motivated to misstate the financial statements, as illustrated by the audit guidance in the following box.

POTENTIAL TROUBLE SPOTS

The fact that fraud is usually concealed can make it very difficult to detect. Nevertheless, when planning the audit, the auditor may identify events or conditions that indicate an incentive or pressure to commit fraud or provide an opportunity to commit fraud. Such events or conditions are referred to as "fraud risk factors." For example:

(a) the need to meet expectations of third parties to obtain additional equity financing may create pressure to commit fraud;

(b) the granting of significant bonuses if unrealistic profit targets are met may create an incentive to commit fraud; and

(c) an ineffective control environment may create an opportunity to commit fraud.

While fraud risk factors may not necessarily indicate the existence of fraud, they have often been present in circumstances where frauds have occurred. The presence of fraud risk factors may affect the auditor's assessment of the risks of material misstatement.

Source: *CICA Handbook*, paragraph 5135.049.

Financial Performance

Financial performance begins with a traditional financial analysis similar to that presented previously under the heading of analytical procedures. A financial analysis would include examining key sets of financial statement ratios (e.g., short-term liquidity ratios—see Appendix 8A for details), examining trends over time in those ratios and considering the interrelationships among the ratios for consistency. The auditor has expectations about what such a financial analysis should discover based on the previous audit analyses.

Financial performance analysis continues with a review of the significant accounting policy choices made by management and benchmarking those choices with significant competitors in the industry. Here the auditor is attempting to gain an understanding of the degree of conservatism of management's accounting policy selection. In particular, the auditor considers the revenue recognition policy in for-profit entities as this has been found to be a key area of abuse when apparently successful companies suddenly fail. See Exhibit 8-4 for examples. Should the accounting policies diverge significantly from industry norms, the auditor will re-perform the quantitative financial performance analysis after adjusting the financial statements to accounting policies common in the industry. The results are then compared with industry benchmarks. This analysis may suggest areas where the auditor has to do additional audit work to reduce audit risk to an appropriately low level or suggest that management modify its accounting policies and practices.

Part of the financial analysis in for-profit companies involves considering the quality of the earnings. **Quality of earnings** refers to the client's ability to replicate its earnings, both in terms of the amounts and the trends over relatively long periods. Exhibit 8-5 lists factors

EXHIBIT 8-4   ACCOUNTING "GIMMICKS" FOR EARNINGS MANIPULATION

- Recording revenue before it is earned
- Creating fictitious revenue
- Boosting profits with nonrecurring transactions
- Shifting current expenses to a later period
- Failing to record or disclose liabilities
- Shifting current income to a later period
- Shifting future expenses to an earlier period

thought to be indicative of high earnings quality. Indications of low-quality earnings may result in the auditor performing additional audit procedures to reduce risk to an appropriately low level or suggest changes to the financial statements prepared by management.

Canadian professional standards require the auditor to communicate with the audit committee, or those having oversight responsibility for the financial reporting process, on matters that have a significant effect on the qualitative aspects of accounting principles used in the entity's financial reporting. *CICA Handbook*, section 5751 suggests that, "Such communication is best accomplished through an open and frank discussion with the audit committee and management. The discussion would include items that have a significant effect on the understandability, relevance, reliability and comparability of the financial statements." Items that should be discussed include:

- impact on earnings of implementing changes in accounting policies
- effect of significant accounting policies in controversial or emerging areas, or those unique to an industry
- estimates, judgements, and uncertainties
- the existence of acceptable alternative policies and methods, the acceptability of the particular policy or method used by management, the financial statement amounts that are affected by the choice of principles, as well as information concerning accounting principles used by peer group companies
- unusual transactions
- timing of transactions that affect the recognition of revenues or avoid recognition of expenses

 In the United States, the AICPA's Statement of Auditing Standard (SAS) 61 also requires the auditor to discuss earnings quality with the audit committee. These standards were introduced as a result of the U.S. Blue Ribbon Committee on Improving the Effectiveness of Corporate Audit Committees, which recommended to standard setters and regulators that auditors be required to report to the audit committee their analysis of the auditee's earnings quality.

EXHIBIT 8-5   HIGH QUALITY EARNINGS

1. Earnings management practices that are not used by firms with high quality earnings:
   a. Using accounting accruals to smooth income increases over time.
   b. Structuring business transactions to ensure an outcome desired by management on accounting income for the period.
   c. Making management choices based primarily on short-term profitability.
2. High quality earnings have operating cash flows and income recognized closely together over time.
3. Indicators of high quality earnings include:
   a. Consistency of accounting accruals from year to year.
   b. Accounting policy changes reduce income.
   c. Short time lag between income recognition and the cash resulting transaction being received by the business.

Nonfinancial Performance

Through the key business process analysis discussed previously, the auditor has developed a deep understanding of the nonfinancial performance measures employed in various business processes. Nonfinancial performance analysis builds on that understanding by analyzing in greater depth the relationships among the resources the business has available, the process by which the business uses those resources and the ability of the firm to compete in the markets in which it sells products or services. Based on the business analysis, the auditor already has information about resources available to the entity and the business processes. The auditor locates information about how the firm is performing in the markets the firm competes in. Tools that the auditor can use in this analysis include: developing a "balanced scorecard" for the client and benchmarking the client firm with others in the industry. Exhibit 8-6 explains the concept of a **balanced scorecard** and your management accounting classes will provide more in-depth understanding. The scorecard reflects measures of resources (learning and growth), processes (internal business) and markets (customer related) in addition to relating all three to financial performance.

A key part of the nonfinancial performance analysis is determining whether the resources available to the firm combined with the relative efficiency and effectiveness of the business processes are consistent with the marketplace results. For example, a firm is competing in a technological industry with a high rate of change. The firm does not have up-to-date equipment or top engineers (both examples of resources). Its business processes are benchmarked as below industry average in performance. Therefore, the firm should have below-average market performance in terms of market share or customer satisfaction. This pattern would reflect a set of consistent results and increase the auditor's confidence in the assessment of business risk.

EXHIBIT   8-6   THE BALANCED SCORECARD

The balanced scorecard contains measures related to financial performance, customer relations, internal business processes, and measures related to learning and growth in the organization. **Financial** measures are those measures particularly relevant to the business unit (e.g., revenues per employee for a sales unit, or research and development expense for a pharmaceutical division). Measures related to **customers** include results of customer surveys, sales from repeat customers and customer profitability. **Internal business** process measures relate specifically to the operational processes of the business unit. For example, a petroleum distributor may measure investment in new product development and dealer quality. The final set of performance measures, those related to **learning and growth**, relate to employee capabilities, information systems capabilities and employee motivation and empowerment. The scorecard is a strategic management tool that should explicate the drivers of performance, as well as provide measures of performance.

Interrelationships Between Financial and Nonfinancial Performance

The auditor considers whether the financial results and the nonfinancial performance measures portray the same picture of the client's business. If the client's financial statements show increasing sales and increasing gross margins, there should be market share increases, resource advantages or process efficiencies found in the nonfinancial measures that support these financial results. Again, should discrepancies be found, additional substantive audit work may need to be carried out to reduce audit risk to an appropriately low level. This analysis also provides the auditor with the knowledge to consider going-concern issues and other areas of completing the audit as covered in Chapter 15.

The overall process of relating nonfinancial and financial performance can be illustrated with a simple model like the one shown in Exhibit 8-7. Here is a simple example of how this

---

EXHIBIT   8-7   RELATING NONFINANCIAL AND FINANCIAL PERFORMANCE

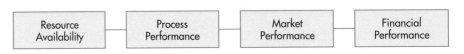

model can be applied. Consider a client company that has limited financial resources and therefore has not invested heavily in new production capability (Resource Availability). The company is producing its products with the same technology that the company founder employed ten years ago. An analysis of the nonfinancial performance measures is consistent with these limited resources, for example, measures of machine down time are increasing each year (Process Performance). The company's sales of the product remain as strong as in the last two years (Market Performance). The financial statements, however, show a lower percentage of repairs and maintenance expense to gross fixed assets than in previous years (Financial Performance). This would indicate an inconsistency that needs to be resolved before issuing an unqualified audit opinion. It would likely be resolved through additional substantive audit procedures examining repair expenses and additions to productive asset balances in detail.[6]

Business risk needs to be considered in determining the acceptable level of audit risk. Audit risks relate to accurate reporting on business risks. The higher the business risks the greater the need to report them accurately. As a consequence, the higher the client's business risk, the less chance the auditor can take that the financial statements do not adequately communicate the business risk to users and decision makers. As will be explained later, when the auditor cannot take a lot of risk of giving a clean opinion on financial statements that are misstated, the auditor sets audit risk at a low level.

R E V I E W
CHECKPOINTS

8.17   What are some examples of external and internal business performance measures? How can the external and internal performance measures used for a business motivate its management to misstate the financial statements?

8.18   What are some "gimmicks" that management can use to manipulate earnings?

8.19   What does earnings quality mean and what are some indicators of high-quality earnings?

8.20   What is the relationship between business risk and audit risk?

8.21   What are the three components of business performance analysis? Why does the auditor perform business performance analysis?

8.22   What are the activities carried out by the auditor in a financial performance analysis? When would the auditor design and carry out additional substantive audit procedures as a result of performance analysis?

8.23   What are the activities carried out by the auditor as part of nonfinancial performance analysis?

8.24   What is the auditor's objective when examining the relationship between the financial measures and nonfinancial performance measures?

PRELIMINARY ASSESSMENT OF PLANNING MATERIALITY

LEARNING OBJECTIVE
3 Explain how the planning materiality amount for the audit is determined.

Materiality is one of the first important judgements the auditor must make since it affects every other planning, examination and reporting decision. When planning a financial statement audit, auditors should think about "planning materiality" as the largest amount of uncorrected dollar misstatement that could exist in published financial statements, yet they would still fairly present the company's financial position and results of operations in conformity with GAAP.

---

[6] In some audits a much more sophisticated model might be built incorporating the nonfinancial and financial performance measures. See T. Bell et al., *Auditing Organizations Through a Strategic Systems Lens* (KPMG LLP, the U.S. member firm of KPMG International, a Swiss association. All rights reserved, 1997). See page 56 for an example.

Financial Statement Materiality

So what is materiality, and how can you deal with it? The concept of materiality pervades financial accounting and reporting in this context: Information is material and should be disclosed if it is likely to influence the economic decisions of financial statement users. The emphasis is on the users' point of view, not on accountants' or managers' points of view. Thus, material information is a synonym for important or significant information.[7]

Financial statement measurements and information in some footnote disclosures are not perfectly accurate. However, you should not leap to the unwarranted conclusion that financial reports are inherently imprecise and inaccurate. Some numbers are not perfectly accurate because mistakes exist in them, and some are not perfectly accurate because they are based on estimates. Everyone acknowledges that people make mistakes—billing a customer the wrong amount, using the wrong prices to compile an inventory, making a mathematical mistake in an amortization calculation. Furthermore, many financial measurements are based on estimates, for example, the estimated depreciable lives of fixed assets or the estimated amount of uncollectible accounts receivable. However, this imprecise nature of accounting should not be taken as licence to be sloppy about clerical accuracy or negligent in accounting judgements. The following box illustrates the auditor's approach for assessing management's estimates as an example of applying materiality to auditing accounting numbers that involve a high degree of management judgement.

AUDIT CONSIDERATIONS FOR ACCOUNTING ESTIMATES

An accounting estimate is an approximation of a financial statement number, and estimates are often included in financial statements. (See *CICA Handbook*, section 5305 or ISA 540.3.)

Examples include net realizable value of accounts receivable, market (lower than cost) of inventory, amortization expense, property and casualty insurance loss reserves, percentage-of-completion contract revenues, pension expense and warranty liabilities.

Management is responsible for making accounting estimates. Auditors are responsible for determining that all appropriate estimates have been made, that they are reasonable and that they are presented in conformity with GAAP and adequately disclosed.

Part of the audit process entails the auditors producing their own estimate and comparing it to management's estimate. Often, consideration of a range for an amount is involved. For example, management may estimate an allowance for doubtful accounts to be $50,000, and the auditors may estimate that the allowance could be $40,000 to $55,000. In this case management's estimate is within the auditors' range of reasonableness. However, the auditors should take note that the management estimate leans toward the conservative side (more than the auditors' $40,000 lower estimate, but not much less than the auditors' higher $55,000 estimate). If other estimates exhibit the same conservatism, and the effect is material, the auditors will need to evaluate the overall reasonableness of the effect of all estimates taken together.

If the auditors develop an estimate that differs (e.g., a range of $55,000 to $70,000 for the allowance that management estimated at $50,000), the preferred treatment is to consider the difference between management's estimate and the closest end of the auditors' range as an error (in this case, error = $5,000 = auditors' $55,000 minus management's $50,000). The remaining difference to the farthest end of the range ($15,000 = $70,000 − $55,000) is noted and reconsidered in combination with the findings on all management's estimates.

The best evidence of the reasonableness of estimates is the actual subsequent experience of the company with the financial amounts estimated at an earlier date. Keeping track of the accuracy of management's earlier estimates could provide the auditor with important information on the expected accuracy of future estimates.

---

[7] *CICA Handbook*, sections 5142 and ISA 320.

Auditors are limited by the nature of accounting. Some amount of inaccuracy is permitted in financial statements because (1) unimportant inaccuracies do not affect users' decisions and hence are not material, (2) the cost of finding and correcting small errors is too great, and (3) the time taken to find them would delay issuance of financial statements. As a leading accountant once said, summing up materiality: "If it doesn't really matter, don't bother with it."[8] Accounting numbers are not perfectly accurate, but accountants and auditors want to maintain that financial reports are materially accurate and do not contain material misstatements.

Materiality Judgement Criteria—Qualitative

Materiality assessment has both quantitative and qualitative aspects, which depend on the context of the client's specific circumstances. Recently, the qualitative aspects of materiality have seen renewed interest because of the perception in the post-Enron environment that the materiality concept has been "abused." Under new SEC regulations, auditors are no longer allowed to rely exclusively on the quantitative benchmarks. In particular, any quantitatively small misstatement that results from intentional misstatement, intentional violation of the law, or intentional earnings management is now considered material. Generally, an otherwise immaterial misstatement is now considered material if it:

- masks a change in earnings or other trends
- hides a failure to meet analysts' consensus expectations for the client
- changes a loss into net income or vice versa
- concerns a segment of the business that is considered significant
- affects the client's compliance with regulatory requirements
- involves concealment of an unlawful transaction
- has the effect of increasing management compensation—for example, by satisfying requirements for the award of bonuses or other forms of incentive compensation[9]

The next section covers some more traditional quantitative guidelines.

Materiality Judgement Criteria—Quantitative

Many accountants wish that definitive, quantitative materiality guides could be issued, but many also fear the rigidity of such guides. The CICA offers some guidance in *CICA Handbook*, section 5142 and the Assurance Guideline "Applying the Concept of Materiality" (AuG–41) on quantitative measures of materiality that might be appropriate when making a preliminary assessment of what is material to the financial statements. Some quantitative guidelines and common rules of thumb are as follows:

- 5 percent of income from continuing operations
- 5 percent of net income before bonus (for an owner-managed enterprise with a tax-minimization objective net income is consistently nominal)
- Industry-specific measures of materiality that have become generally accepted in practice can also be used. Examples include:
  (*a*) for a not-for-profit entity, ½ percent to 2 percent of total expenses or total revenues
  (*b*) in the mutual fund industry, ½ percent to 1 percent of net asset value
  (*c*) in the real estate industry when an entity owns income-producing properties, 1 percent of revenue

---

[8] Ernest L. Hicks, "Materiality," *Journal of Accounting Research*, Autumn 1964, p. 158.
[9] *SEC Staff Accounting Bulletin* (SAB) 99.

The selection of an alternate financial statement item or items for use in a quantitative determination of materiality is a matter for the auditor's professional judgement. Other bases that can be considered depending on circumstances include: gross revenues (for Internet-based companies) current assets, net working capital, total assets, total revenues, gross profit, total equity, and cash flows from operations.

The CICA suggests that if income is used it should be adjusted for abnormal or extraordinary items. Also, if income is negative or close to zero, or fluctuating significantly from year to year, a "normalized income based on some averaging could be used." But caution should be used in "normalizing" so that it is reasonable. If it is difficult to justify normalized income such as when income is negative or too small relative to other items, then using a different basis may be justified. The rules of thumb cannot simply just be applied mechanically as auditors must consider a number of factors in setting materiality. Some of the factors auditors often use in making materiality judgements are these:

Absolute Size

An amount of potential misstatement may be important regardless of any other considerations. Not many auditors use absolute size alone as a criterion because a given amount, say $50,000, may be appropriate in one case and too large or too small in another. Yet, some auditors have been known to say: "$1 million or some other large number is material, no matter what."

Relative Size

The relationship of potential misstatement to a relevant base number is often used. Potential misstatements in income statement accounts usually are related to net income either before or after taxes. Potential misstatements in balance sheet accounts may be related to a subtotal number, such as current assets or net working capital. A misstatement in segment information may be small in relation to the total business but important for analysis of the segment.

Nature of the Item or Issue

An illegal payment is important primarily because of its nature as well as because of its absolute or relative amount. Generally, potential errors in the more liquid assets (cash, receivables and inventory) are considered more important than potential errors in other accounts (such as capital assets and deferred charges). Other qualitative factors include whether a misstatement affects the trend of earnings, whether analysts' forecasts are met and whether a loan covenant is violated. Such qualitative factors can be very important as noted by former SEC Chairman Arthur Levitt: "Missing an earnings projection by a penny, for example, can result in a loss of millions in market capitalization."

Circumstances

Auditors generally place extra emphasis on lesser permitted misstatement in financial statements that will be widely used (publicly held companies) or used by important outsiders (bank loan officers). Auditors' liability is a relevant consideration. When management can exercise discretion over an accounting treatment, auditors tend to exercise more care and use a more stringent materiality criterion. Troublesome events, such as the string of corporate and audit failures that have characterized the post-Enron environment, have also caused auditors to try to be more accurate with measurement and disclosures. However, these matters relate as much to risks as they do to financial statement materiality.

Cumulative Effects

Auditors must evaluate the sum of known or potential misstatements. Considering five different $15,000 mistakes that all increase net income as immaterial is inappropriate when the net income-based materiality limit is $50,000.

The following box illustrates a materiality worksheet that considers these factors.

Client:_____   **Year end:**_____

Materiality assessment

1. Qualitative factors

		Comments
a)	Identify the specific users of the financial statements for this engagement.	
b)	Identify what expectations the users may have for the financial statements for this engagement.	
c)	Identify any possible situations or misstatements that would affect a user now or at some future point, regardless of the materiality level. (e.g., Consider environmental matters, policies, statutes, safety issues, etc.)	

2. Quantitative factors

a) Planning data

	This year actual (adjusted)	This year anticipated	Last year	2nd preceding year
Assets				
Liabilities				
Equity				
Sales/revenue				
Gross profit				
Expenses				
Income after tax				
Previous materiality				

b) Normalized after-tax income

	This year actual (adjusted)	This year anticipated	Last year	2nd preceding year
Estimated after-tax income	$			
Adjustment for non-recurring items or unadjusted errors brought forward				
Normalized after-tax income	$			

	Prepared	Reviewed	Index
Date & initials			

Materiality assesment

Client:_____   **Year end:**_____

3. Materiality considerations

a) Profit-oriented enterprises

Identify financial statement users	Measurement base	Factor applied*	Possible materiality	Comments
	Normalized after-tax income		$	
	Assets		$	
	Equity		$	
	Revenue		$	
	Gross profit		$	
	Other		$	

*Materiality guidelines
Normalized after-tax income   5–10%
Assets   ½–1%
Equity   ½–5%
Revenue   ½–1%
Gross profit   ½–5%

These materiality factors are provided as guidelines only, and should be used only as an aid in the development of your professional judgement. The materiality level should represent the largest amount of a misstatement or group of misstatements that would not, in your judgement, influence or change a decision based on the financial statements.

Often, normalized after-tax income is used as an initial reference point for businesses although it may not be sufficient for businesses with little or no income. Weighted averages are also used at times. Revenue is often used for NPOs. See AUG-41 for more guidance.

b) Not-for-profit enterprises

Identify financial statement users	Measurement base revenue/expenses	Factor applied*	Possible materiality	Comments
Governmental authorities				
Funding organizations				
Directors				
Other				

*Materiality factors
Total expenses or total revenues ½ to 2%

c) Other factors considered in determining materiality for this engagement

_____
_____
_____

Preliminary materiality assessment

Based on the anticipated financial statement amounts and on the other factors described above, preliminary materiality for this engagement is:

$_____   Misstatements below this threshold, if not corrected, will be accumulated on the Possible Adjustments Sheet unless such misstatements are deemed trial (below $ ____). Note: The auditor may designate an amount below which misstatements are deemed trivial and need not be accumulated because the auditor expects that the accumulation of such amounts clearly will not have a material effect on the financial statements. In so doing, the auditor considers the fact that the determination of materiality involves qualitative as well an quantitative considerations and that misstatements of a relatively small amount could nevertheless have a material effect on the financial statements. The summary of uncorrected misstatements included in or attached to the management representation letter need not include trivial misstatements.

Final materiality assessment

Based on the final adjusted financial statements and on other factors noted above, final materiality is:

$_____

	Prepared	Reviewed	Index
Date & initials			

Materiality assesment

Effect of Fraud-Related Considerations in Materiality Judgement

Under SOX, auditors need to add other fraud-related considerations in determining materiality. Under the PCAOB's definition there are two types of fraud: fraud for the company's benefit (and to the detriment of capital markets), and fraud against the company. Fraud for the company's benefit includes fraudulent financial reporting (e.g., inflating the company's earnings) whereas fraud against the company consists of actions misappropriating company assets, like employee theft. The key issue in determining financial reporting fraud is the intent of management. If the intent is to deceive the financial markets then it is considered fraud for the company. Any fraud for the company's benefit is material no matter how small. However, in frauds against the company, materiality is determined by the qualitative and quantitative guidelines discussed previously.

Similarly, when reviewing controls in place to prevent fraud or errors auditors need to consider how much could be stolen or misstated. If the risk of *any* theft or misstatement is more than remote, then this results in a "significant" deficiency. Significant deficiencies must be reported to audit committees. If the risk of *material* misstatement or theft is more than remote, then this is considered a "material" deficiency in internal controls. For public companies, the auditor would be required to issue an adverse opinion on the company's internal control over financial reporting if any material control deficiency is discovered.[10] Internal controls are covered in more detail in the next chapter.

Materiality Allocation Versus Nonallocation

To plan the audit of various accounts, some auditors assign part of the planning materiality to each account. The amount assigned to an account is called the tolerable misstatement for that account. The **tolerable misstatement** is the amount by which a particular account may be misstated (error not discovered by auditors!), yet still not cause the financial statements taken as a whole to be materially misleading. Thus, tolerable misstatement for each account is based on the overall financial statement materiality.

The extent to which tolerable misstatement is "based on" the overall materiality amount may vary from auditor to auditor. One method assigns tolerable misstatement amounts that add up to twice the overall materiality. The theory is that actual financial misstatements in accounts can be both overstatements and understatements, and the two directions will tend to balance out. Another is to assign tolerable misstatement in amounts such that the square root of the sum of the squared tolerable misstatements is equal to the overall materiality. The theory here is that the different misstatements behave like random errors in a calculation of statistical variance. Another method is to assign tolerable misstatement amounts that exactly add up to materiality. This method assumes that the worst case is that all the errors in the account balances have the same directional effect on income (i.e., overstatement of understatement, but not some of both). All these approaches are examples of materiality allocation. The simplest approach, however, is to not allocate but to use the same overall materiality level for the entire audit. This approach also results in the least testing and is implied by the *CICA Handbook*. This simplest approach is the one used in this text. Thus, tolerable misstatements will be set equal to overall materiality, and there is no difference between accounting and auditing materiality.[11]

Consider a materiality judgement for the current-year financial information of Anycompany, Inc., shown in Exhibit 8-2. The judgement involves directing attention to the most important financial decisions that may be related to the use of the financial statements. This centre of attention can be different for different audits. In some cases the centre of attention may be the current asset-liability position of a company in financial difficulty

---

[10] James Vorhies, "The New Importance of Materiality" *Journal of Accountancy*, May 2005, pp. 53–59.

[11] Depending on factors used in setting overall materiality, there may be secondary materiality levels (less than overall materiality) necessary to satisfy the requirements of certain specific users (for example, a bank that has negotiated loan covenants as part of the loan agreement). In these situations a secondary materiality level(s) may apply to some restricted accounts (e.g., current assets) but overall materiality to all the rest. See D. Leslie, *Materiality, The Concept and Its Application to Auditing* (CICA, 1985), Chapter 2.

seeking to renew its bank loans. Such a company may be experiencing operating losses, and the balance sheet, rather than the income statement, is of utmost importance. In other cases, the income statement and the net income number may be the most important because the company is growing and issuing shares to the public, so that decisions based on income performance are of greatest importance. The following boxed illustration shows a calculation of overall materiality based on an assumed effect of income misstatement on the share price. If the auditors decide the shares could be mispriced by 10 percent, and nobody would care, then the income before taxes and interest could be overstated (or understated) by as much as $71,000.

A POSSIBLE RELATIVE SIZE MATERIALITY DETERMINATION ILLUSTRATED

Suppose the auditors take the influence of **earnings per share (EPS)** on share price as an important consideration in determining materiality. For illustrative purposes, suppose the model for share price determination is a simple EPS multiple. (This is not to suggest that share prices actually are determined by such a simple method as multiplying the EPS in all cases. Analysts and investors use many other valuation models beyond the scope of this illustration.)

Assume that Anycompany, Inc., whose financial statements are in Exhibit 8–2, has 100,000 shares outstanding and its shares trade at a 14 price-earning multiple, thus indicating a share price of $51.80.

(Share price = EPS ($3.70 = $370,000/100,000) ×14 = $51.80.)

The auditors must make a judgement about how much investors could overpay for the shares, yet it would not make any difference to them, say 5 percent to 10 percent.

	Low (5%)	High (10%)
Indicated share price (14 × $3.70)	$ 51.80	$ 51.80
Price materiality judgement	2.59	5.18
Adjusted share price	49.21	46.62
Adjusted earnings per share (divide by 14 multiple)	3.52	3.33
Indicated net income (multiply by 100,000 shares)	352,000	333,000
Add pretax accounts that can be audited completely:		
Interest expense	40,000	40,000
Income tax expense (40%)	234,667	222,000
Indicated pretax income*	626,667	595,000
Unaudited pretax income	666,000	666,000
Indicated planning materiality based on pretax income	39,333	71,000

*Calculate the pretax income, which, when reduced by interest expense and 40 percent income taxes, produces the indicated net income (after-tax).

While the overall materiality assessment may frequently start with an expression of materiality for an income statement number, the materiality is audited in relation to one or more balance sheet accounts. The reason for this phenomenon is that income misstatements in the double-entry bookkeeping system leave a "dangling debit" or a "dangling credit" loose somewhere in the balance sheet accounts, and the audit challenge is to find it. If there is no dangling debit or credit, then the other side of the misstatement transaction has gone through the income statement, probably causing misstatement in two accounts (opposite directions), with no net effect on the net income bottom line. (For example, if fictitious credit sales were recorded, and the fictitious accounts receivable were written off as bad debt expense, both the revenue and expense would be overstated, but the income would not be misstated.)

Even though we will not use materiality allocation in this text, readers should remember the term "tolerable misstatement." Tolerable misstatement is the part of the overall materiality number assigned to an account. Since here we do not allocate overall materiality, tolerable misstatement is synonymous with overall materiality. The word "tolerable" is also frequently associated with the level of control deviations that is presumed to lead to material misstatements. "Tolerable" in this context is covered in more detail in Chapters 9 and 10.

REVIEW CHECKPOINTS

8.25   Why is the materiality decision one of the first decisions made in the audit?

8.26   What is material information in accounting and auditing? What is planning materiality in an audit context?

8.27   What limitations of accounting affect auditors?

8.28   What is involved in auditing an accounting estimate?

8.29   What do you think is the best objective evidence of the reasonableness of an accounting estimate? Use the allowance for doubtful accounts receivable as an example.

8.30   Why are qualitative criteria important in the auditor's materiality decision?

8.31   Do auditing standards require auditors to use a specific quantitative criterion to determine planning materiality?

8.32   How do fraud considerations relate to the auditor's materiality decision?

8.33   What are the advantages of using the same overall planning materiality level for the audit instead of assigning a part of the overall planning materiality to each account balance?

8.34   What benefits are claimed for auditors' preliminary assessment of materiality as a part of the audit planning? Is $500,000 a material amount of misstatement to leave uncorrected in financial statements?

AUDIT RISK ASSESSMENT

LEARNING OBJECTIVE

4 Describe the conceptual audit risk model and its components.

Audit risk is related to information risk (discussed in Chapter 1) associated with the financial statements. It is the risk that audited financial statements that are materially misstated will go out to users. Understanding the client's business and preliminary analytical procedures can help auditors identify problem areas and make an overall business risk assessment. However, to develop the audit program, these risks need to be assessed more specifically in audit-related terms. These are known as inherent risk, control risk, detection risk and audit risk. Since several adjectives are used to describe risks in the audit context, the term "risk" should always be used with a modifier (inherent, control, and so on) to specify the one you mean. Audit risk can be modelled conceptually as a function of inherent risk, control risk and detection risk. We discuss audit risk and this conceptual model in more detail after first considering each of the components.

Inherent Risk

Inherent risk is the probability that material misstatements have occurred, regardless of the existence of internal control, in transactions entering the accounting system used to develop financial statements, or that material misstatements have occurred in an account balance.[12] Put another way, inherent risk is the risk of material misstatements occurring in the first place. Inherent risk is a characteristic of the client's business, the major types of transactions and the effectiveness of its accountants. Auditors do not create or control inherent risk. They can only try to assess its magnitude.

---

[12] *CICA Handbook*, paragraph 5095.14(a); ISA 200.20.

An assessment of inherent risk can be based on a variety of information. Auditors may know that material misstatements were discovered during the last year's audit, so inherent risk will be considered higher than it would be if last year's audit had shown no material misstatements. Auditors may believe the client's accounting clerks tend to misunderstand GAAP and the company's own accounting policies, thus suggesting a significant probability of mistakes in transaction processing. The nature of the client's business may produce complicated transactions and calculations generally known to be subject to data processing and accounting treatment error. (For example, real estate, franchising and oil and gas transactions are frequently complicated and subject to accounting error. Some kinds of inventories are harder than others to count, value and keep accurately in perpetual records.) Some other accounts (e.g., cash and inventory) are more susceptible to embezzlement, theft or other loss than are other accounts (e.g., land or prepaid expenses). The important relationship you should understand is that audit care and attention should be greater where inherent risk is judged to be higher.

Auditor experience has shown that due to management optimism and bias, asset and income accounts tend to have a higher inherent risk of overstatement than understatement; and that liability accounts have a higher inherent risk of understatement than overstatement. Due to these predilections and biases, audit procedures that are more effective in detecting overstatements, such as vouching, are more widely used with asset and income accounts. At the same time, audit procedures that are more effective in detecting understatements, such as tracing subsequent payments, are more likely to be used with liability accounts. Thus, the inherent and relative risks determine the importance of various procedures for different accounts.

Control Risk

Control risk is the risk that the client's internal control will not prevent or detect a material misstatement. More specifically, control risk is the probability that the client's internal control policies and procedures will fail to detect or prevent material misstatements, provided any enter the accounting system in the first place.[13] Auditors do not create or control the control risk. They can only evaluate a company's control system and assess the probability of failure to detect material misstatements.

Various control frameworks are available to auditors for assessing controls at the company-level, as well as for auditing financial statement controls. These include COCO, COSO, and COBIT, which are all further described following. For public company audits, use of a control framewok is required by PCAOB Auditing Standard No. 2 and by proposed CICA standards. For other types of audit clients, frameworks are a useful tool to help improve audit quality.

Control, as defined by the CICA's Criteria of Control Committee (COCO), "comprises those elements of an organization (including its resources, systems, processes, culture, structure and tasks) that, taken together, support people in the achievement of the organizations objectives."[14] To effectively manage, management needs an integrated structure of control processes—processes for strategic control, management control and business process control. Strategic and management control processes encompass controls for that entity as a whole. These controls often entail the use of long-term and strategically relevant criteria by corporate managers to evaluate overall corporate performance of division and units, whereas business process controls include those controls at the process level. Management control systems are "all the systems that are used to maintain or alter the pattern in organizational activities."[15]

In the United States the *Committee of Sponsoring Organizations of the Treadway Commission, Internal Control—Integrated Framework* (COSO) also has a broader definition of internal control:

[13] Ibid, paragraph 5095.14(b), ISA 220.20.
[14] *Criteria of Control Committee: Guidance on Control*, 1995, paragraph 6.
[15] Robert Simons, "The Strategy of Control," *CA Magazine*, March 1992, p. 44.

a process, effected by an entity's board of directors, management and other personnel, designed to provide reasonable assurance regarding the achievement of objectives in the following categories:
• effectiveness and efficiency of operations
• reliability of financial reporting
• compliance with applicable laws and regulations

As can be seen from the previous discussion, management control systems are conceived much more broadly than are "internal control relevant to the audit." This phrase is defined as those policies and procedures established and maintained by management that affect control risk relating to specific financial statement assertions at the account balance or class of transactions level.[16] So, internal controls relevant to the audit would be a subset of this broader view of controls. Indeed, the *CICA Handbook* notes that there are many other controls present in companies that may not be relevant to the auditor.[17] As discussed in Chapter 7, auditors are mainly concerned with accounting controls and systems.

The COSO Report incorporates a set of "evaluation tools" that can be utilized as one approach in the evaluation of controls. The report presents five evaluation tools for each of the interrelated components of internal control. For each component, substantive issues or "points of focus" are presented as important topics relevant to the evaluation of that component of internal control. Points of focus for each tool can be added, deleted or modified to customize the tool for the specific entity under audit. Exhibit 8-8 outlines a sample of points of focus for the internal control components of control environment and risk assessment.

EXHIBIT   8-8   POINTS OF FOCUS SAMPLE

CONTROL ENVIRONMENT

Integrity and Ethical Values
Management must convey the message that integrity and ethical values cannot be compromised, and employees must receive and understand that message. Management must continually demonstrate, through words and actions, a commitment to high ethical standards.
• Existence and implementation of codes of conduct and other policies regarding acceptable business practices, conflicts of interest, or expected standards of ethical and moral behaviour.

Organizational Structure
The organizational structure should not be so simple that it cannot adequately monitor the enterprise's activities nor so complex that it inhibits the necessary flow of information. Executives should fully understand their control responsibilities and possess the requisite experience and levels of knowledge commensurate with their positions.
• Appropriateness of the entity's organizational structure, and its ability to provide the necessary information flow to manage its activities.

RISK ASSESSMENT

Risks
An entity's risk-assessment process should identify and consider the implications of relevant risks, at both the entity-level and the activity level. The risk assessment process should consider external and internal factors that could impact achievement of the objectives, should analyze risks, and provide a basis for managing them.
• Adequacy of mechanisms to identify risks arising from external sources.
• Identification of significant risks for each significant activity-level objective.

Managing Change
Economic, industry, and regulatory environments change and entities' activities evolve. Mechanisms are needed to identify and react to changing conditions.
• Existence of mechanisms to anticipate, identify and react to routine events or activities that affect achievement of entity or activity level objectives.
• Existence of mechanisms to anticipate, identify and reach to changes that can have a more dramatic and pervasive effect on the entity, and may demand the attention of top management.

Source: *Internal Control—Integrated Framework: Evaluation Tools*, Committee of Sponsoring Organizations of the Treadway Commission, September 1992.

---

[16] *CICA Handbook*, paragraph 5141.048 defines "controls relevant to an audit."
[17] Ibid., paragraph 5141.042 defines internal control more broadly.

The CICA's COCO guidance provides an alternate approach. Exhibit 8-9 outlines the criteria broken down into four categories: Purpose, Commitment, Capability, and Monitoring and Learning. These evaluation criteria and tools can serve as a starting point for developing a detailed assessment of the relevant management controls.

Guidance and a fundamental set of principles for internal control over information and the systems used to manage it are provided in *Control Objectives for Information and Related Technology* (COBIT), published by the IT Governance Institute (www.itgi.org). The COBIT Framework (see www.isaca.org/cobit) organizes IT activities into a process model made up of four domains: Plan and Organize, Acquire and Implement, Deliver and Support, and Monitor and Evaluate, as shown in Exhibit 8-10. COBIT also provides guidance on establishing control objectives by providing generic control statements that define what needs to be managed in various business processes.

EXHIBIT   8-9   THE CRITERIA OF CONTROL

Purpose
A1. Objectives should be established and communicated.
A2. The significant internal and external risks faced by an organization in the achievement of its objectives should be identified and assessed.
A3. Policies designed to support the achievement of an organization's objectives and the management of its risks should be established, communicated and practiced so that people understand what is expected of them and the scope of their freedom to act.
A4. Plans to guide efforts in achieving the organization's objectives should be established and communicated.
A5. Objectives and related plans should include measurable performance targets and indicators.

Commitment
B1. Shared ethical values, including integrity, should be established, communicated and practiced throughout the organization.
B2. Human resource policies and practices should be consistent with an organization's ethical values and with the achievement of its objectives.
B3. Authority, responsibility and accountability should be clearly defined and consistent with an organization's objectives so that decisions and actions are taken by the appropriate people.
B4. An atmosphere of mutual trust should be fostered to support the flow of information between people and their effective performance toward achieving the organization's objectives.

Capability
C1. People should have the necessary knowledge, skills and tools to support the achievement of the organization's objectives.
C2. Communication processes should support the organization's values and achievement of its objectives.
C3. Sufficient and relevant information should be identified and communicated in a timely manner to enable people to perform their assigned responsibilities.
C4. The decisions and actions of different parts of the organization should be coordinated.
C5. Control activities should be designed as an integral part of the organization, taking into consideration its objectives, the risks to their achievement, and the inter-relatedness of the control elements.

Monitoring and Learning
D1. External and internal environments should be monitored to obtain information that may signal a need to reevaluate the organization's objectives or control.
D2. Performance should be monitored against the targets and indicators identified in the organization's objectives and plans.
D3. The assumptions behind an organization's objectives should be periodically challenged.
D4. Information needs and related information systems should be reassessed as objectives change or reporting deficiencies are identified.
D5. Follow-up procedures should be established and performed to ensure appropriate change or action occurs.
D6. Management should periodically assess the effectiveness of control in its organization and communicate the results to those to whom it is accountable.

Source: CICA, Guidance on Control, 1995, p.9.

EXHIBIT 8-10 COBIT PROCESSES DEFINED WITHIN THE FOUR DOMAINS

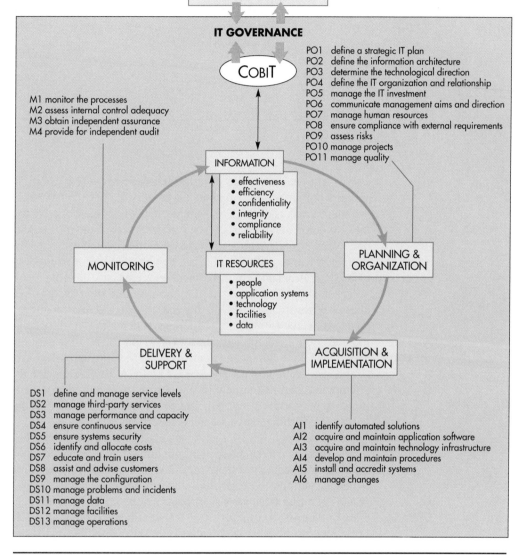

Source: *www.itgi.org.*

An auditor's assessment of control risk is based on the study and evaluation of the company's control system. Control risk assessment provides only an indirect assessment of the monetary amount of misstatement of financial statements. As a result, special labels such as **control testing** or **compliance testing** are given to the detailed procedures used in the control risk assessment. You will study this process in detail in Chapter 9.

Control effectiveness conclusions and risk assessments may be made on a preliminary basis for planning purposes. Auditors often carry over preconceived notions about control risk when they perform the audit on a client year after year. This carryover is known as **anchoring** the control risk assessment (starting with knowledge of last year's conclusions), and it represents (1) a useful continuity of experience with a particular client and (2) a potential pitfall if conditions change for the worse and the auditor fails to acknowledge the deterioration of control.

Control risk should not be assessed so low that auditors place complete reliance on controls and do not perform any other audit work. Many auditors conclude their control risk

EXHIBIT 8-11   INTERNAL CONTROL CONDITIONS AND CONCLUSIONS

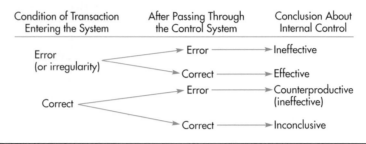

Source: Adapted from L. E. Graham, "Audit Risk-Part III," *CPA Journal*, October 1985, p. 39. Used with permission. Copyright © 1985, The CPA Journal.

assessment decisions with descriptive assessments (e.g., high, moderate, low), and some auditors put probability numbers on them (e.g., 1.0, 0.50, 0.30).

Inherent risk is difficult to evaluate, and sometimes its assessment can be combined with the evaluation of control risk. The problems arise from the fact that internal controls "work" only when errors, irregularities and other misstatements occur. Also, some controls are preventive in nature and so tend to reduce inherent risk. Exhibit 8-11 shows the combinations of original errors and control effectiveness, or lack thereof.

The newly introduced audit standards put increased emphasis on understanding a client's business and assessing the risk of material misstatement in planning the audit. The standards refer to a combined assessment of the "risk of material misstatement" that includes both inherent and control risks, but the auditor may make separate or combined assessments of inherent and control risk depending on preferred audit procedures and practical considerations. Audits governed by PCAOB would make a combined assessment and attempt to integrate their audits of controls, as required to issue a separate report on attesting to management's internal control assertions with their audits providing assurance on management's financial statements assertions.

The assessment of the risk of material misstatement may be expressed in quantitative terms, such as percentages, or in nonquantitative terms. The auditor assesses the risk of material misstatement at the assertion level as a basis for designing further audit procedures. When the auditor's assessment of the risk of material misstatement includes an expectation of the operating effectiveness of controls, the standards state that the auditor must perform tests of controls to support the risk assessment. Internal control is a complex and critical consideration in every audit; thus, control evaluation and testing are explained in more detail in Chapters 9 and 10.

Risk Alert notices are issued from time to time on the CICA website to highlight current risk areas that public accountants should take into account in their risk assessments and audit planning. An example of the table of contents of a *Risk Alert* is found in the following box.

RISK ALERT
DECEMBER 2005

Risk Alert provides an overview of current issues that may be of interest to public accountants who perform audit or review engagements. Risk Alert has been prepared and reviewed by Auditing and Assurance Staff. It has not been issued under the authority of the Auditing and Assurance Standards Board (AASB). Practitioners are expected to use professional judgement in determining whether to apply the material in this publication in an assurance engagement. Such determination includes being satisfied that the material is both relevant to the circumstances of the assurance engagement and appropriate.

TABLE OF CONTENTS

Source: http://www.cica.ca/multimedia/Download_Library/Standards/ASB/English/e_RA1205.pdf (accessed on February 19, 2006).

Detection Risk

Detection risk is the risk that any material misstatement that has not been corrected by the client's internal control will not be detected by the auditor.[18] In contrast to inherent risk and control risk, auditors are responsible for performing the evidence-gathering procedures that manage and control detection risk. These audit procedures represent the auditors' opportunity to detect material misstatements that can cause financial statements to be misleading.

In subsequent chapters you will study substantive procedures. These are the procedures used to provide a direct assessment of the monetary amount of misstatement in the client's proposed accounting. As a result, they are highly effective in detecting material misstatements in the financial statements and footnotes, and are therefore considered the most important audit procedures. The two categories of substantive procedures are (1) audit of the details of transactions and balances and (2) analytical procedures applied to produce circumstantial evidence about dollar amounts in the accounts. Detection risk is realized when procedures in these two categories fail to detect material misstatements.

Audit Risk

In an overall sense, **audit risk** is the probability that an auditor will fail to express a reservation that financial statements are materially misstated. The profession assumes audit risk can at best be controlled at a low level, not eliminated, even when audits are well planned and carefully performed. The risk is much greater in poorly planned and carelessly performed audits. The relationship between audit risk and business risk was explained in Appendix 1B on the Online Learning Centre. Planned audit risk may vary depending on client circumstances. Generally, the more risky the client or the more that users rely on the audited financial statements, the lower the planned audit risk. As the risk of being sued for material misstatement increases, the planned audit risk decreases to compensate for the increased risk associated with the engagement. Many accounting firms have developed internal guidelines for setting planned levels of audit risk.

The auditing profession has no hard standard for an acceptable level of overall audit risk, except that it should be "appropriately low" and involve the exercise of professional judgement. At one time, CICA guidance suggested that most auditors would strive to limit such

[18] Ibid., paragraph 5095.16, ISA 200.22.

risks to no more than 5 percent. However, auditors would be appalled to think that even 1 percent of their audits would be bad. For a large firm with 2,000 audit clients, 1 percent would mean 20 bad audits per year! But on the other hand, not all audits have material misstatements, so using 5 percent planned audit risk on every engagement may lead to a much lower level of bad audits. For example, if the risk of material misstatement is 5 percent, then with 5 percent audit risk the number of bad audits would be $0.05 \times 0.05 = 0.0025 = $ ¼ percent.

The concept of audit risk also applies to individual account balances and disclosures. Here the risk is that material misstatement is not discovered in an account (e.g., the inventory total) or in a disclosure (e.g., a pension plan footnote explanation). Audit risk is most often used in practice with regard to individual balances and disclosures. You should keep this context in mind when you study the risk model summary presented next. Audit risk of 0.05 at the account level, used by many CA firms, is presented as an illustrative audit risk.

In summary, audit risk is the same whether applied to financial statements as a whole or to individual account balances. Thus, for example, if audit risk is set at 0.05, it is used for all accounts as well as for financial statements as a whole.

Risk Model—A Summary

The foregoing concepts of audit risks can be expressed conceptually by using a model that assumes the elements of audit risk are independent. Thus, the risks are multiplied as follows:

Audit risk (AR) = Inherent risk (IR) 3 Control risk (CR) 3 Detection risk (DR)

An intuitive explanation for this formula can be given as follows. Audit risk is the probability that the audit fails to detect a material misstatement. This will occur only under the following circumstances: (1) there is a material misstatement to start with (probability of which is inherent risk), (2) the internal controls fail to detect and correct the material misstatement (probability of which is control risk), and (3) the audit procedures also fail to detect the material misstatement (probability of which is detection risk). The audit fails only if all three events occur and the probability of this happening is the product of the three risks as given above. Audit risk is thus the probability that the audit fails. Notice this also means that the probability that the audit succeeds is one minus the probability that it fails; therefore, if audit assurance is defined as the probability that the audit is successful, audit assurances equals 1 – audit risk. Thus, reducing acceptable (or planned) audit risk is equivalent to increasing acceptable (or planned) audit assurance.

Auditors want to perform an audit of a particular balance or disclosure well enough to hold the audit risk (AR) to a relatively low level (e.g., 0.05, which means that on average 5 percent of audit decisions when there is a material misstatement will be wrong). As such, AR is a quality criterion based on professional judgement. All the other risk assessments are estimates based on professional judgement and evidence.

For example, suppose an auditor thought a particular inventory balance was subject to great inherent risk of material misstatement (say, IR = 0.90) and that the client's internal control was not very effective (say, CR = 0.70). If he or she wanted to control audit risk at a low level (say, AR = 0.05), the other procedures would need to be designed so that detection risk (DR) did not exceed 0.08 (approximately). According to the model, this example would produce the following results:

$$AR = IR \times CR \times DR$$
$$0.05 = 0.90 \times 0.70 \times DR$$
Solving for DR: DR = 0.08

The practical problem here is knowing whether the audit has been planned and performed well enough to hold the detection risk as low as 0.08. Despite the simplicity of the risk model, it is only a conceptual tool. Auditors have few ways to calculate detection risk, so the model represents more of a way to think about audit risks than a way to calculate them. However, several accounting firms use this model to calculate risks and the related sample sizes.

The model produces some insights, including these:

1. Auditors cannot rely entirely on an estimate of zero inherent risk to the exclusion of other evidence-gathering procedures. Thus, you cannot have the condition:

   $$AR = IR\ (=0) \times CR \times DR = 0$$

2. Auditors cannot place complete reliance on internal control to the exclusion of other audit procedures. Thus, you cannot have the condition:

   $$AR = IR \times CR\ (=0) \times DR = 0$$

3. Audits would not seem to exhibit due audit care if the risk of failure to detect material misstatements were too high, for example:

   $$AR = IR\ (=0.80) \times CR\ (=0.80) \times DR\ (=0.50) = 0.32$$

4. Auditors can choose to rely almost exclusively on evidence produced by substantive procedures, even if they think inherent risk and control risk are high. For example, this combination is acceptable (provided AR = 0.05 is acceptable):

   $$AR = IR\ (=1.00) \times CR\ (=1.00) \times DR\ (=0.05) = 0.05$$

Despite the precision implied by the mathematical depiction of the audit risk model, in reality applying it is difficult and highly judgemental. The objective in an audit is to limit audit risk (AR) to a low level, as judged by the auditor. This is done by assessing inherent risk (IR) and control risk (CR) along a spectrum. Often in practice this assessment is reduced to three levels: high risk, moderate risk or low risk. The greater the inherent and control risks, the lower the detection risk needs to be, resulting in "more" procedures ("more" includes their nature and timing as well as their extent) that the auditor would need to carry out. At the end of the day, the objective is to limit audit risk (AR) to an appropriately low level, thus enabling the auditor to achieve high assurance that the financial statements are free of material misstatement. It is also important to remember that the model incorporates the concept of materiality in its definition and that materiality enters throughout the risk assessment process. Chapter 10 gives more details on the audit risk model.

Audit risk and materiality thus deal with the sufficiency of evidence, covered later in this chapter. Both audit risk and materiality will be planned at a pre-set level identified early in the engagement. These planned levels are the ones used throughout the audit unless situations discovered during performance of the audit indicate they should be adjusted. In other words, one planned level of materiality and a single acceptable level of audit risk is used throughout the audit for financial statements as a whole, as well as for individual accounts. Inherent risk, control risk and detection risk, however, will vary for each individual account, depending on the conditions for each account. Nonetheless, as long as the risk model is used so that the audit risk for each account balance and financial statement assertion is at or below the planned levels, the auditor knows that sufficient appropriate evidence has been obtained for each account and financial statement assertion to support the audit opinion.

Exhibit 8-12 shows the interrelationships among the auditing concepts discussed in this chapter, and how these concepts underlie the auditor's decision about what audit evidence is required. The materiality considerations are shown along the left side of the exhibit, the audit risk model components are in the centre, and the characteristics of potential audit evidence are on the right side. Notice that the evidence decision must take into account practical limitations—not all the evidence the auditor might want can be obtained at a reasonable cost or quickly enough to provide a timely audit report. Not all evidence has the same level of reliability. Trade-offs have to be made because of these limitations. The concepts of materiality and audit risk guide these trade-offs. This diagram shows the kind of complex analysis that is at the heart of professional judgement about the sufficiency and appropriateness of audit evidence.

EXHIBIT   8-12   INTERRELATIONSHIP OF AUDITING CONCEPTS—SUFFICIENCY AND
APPROPRIATENESS OF EVIDENCE

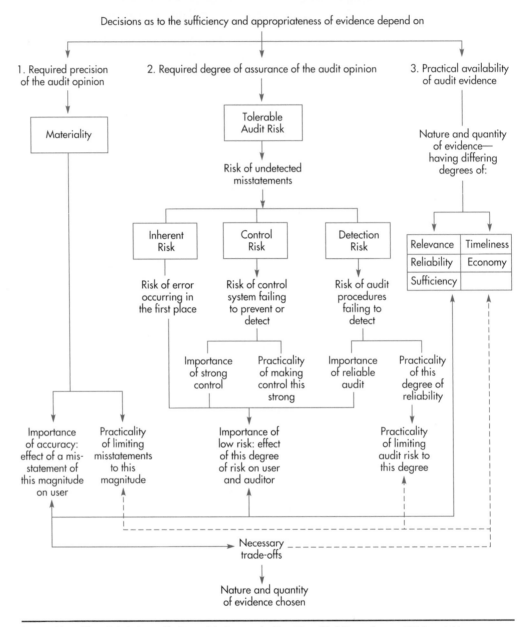

Source: Adapted from R. J. Anderson *The External Audit,* second edition (Copp Clark Pitman:Toronto, 1984), p. 144.

The materiality decision is based on the effect of misstatements on financial statement users. For example, the shareholders of a medium-sized private company may be relying on the audited income number for the purpose of calculating the hired managers' bonuses. They may be affected by a smaller misstatement than would be the case in a large public company where the audited income figure is less directly related to a user's financial decision. Understanding the business and its environment helps the auditor to identify financial statement users and assess what is significant to their decisions. Conceptually, the auditor decides on the materiality level independently of audit risk considerations.

Tolerable audit risk is determined by how much assurance the auditor requires. For example, if there is a high risk of the auditor being sued if the audit fails to uncover a material misstatement because venture capital investors are basing their financing conditions on the audited information, high assurance is required. High assurance is also desirable if the audited company is high profile and the auditor's reputation would be seriously damaged if the audit fails, such as a bank or trust company where many depositors are affected by the client company's financial strength and a lot of unfavourable news coverage about the audit failure can be expected. The tolerable audit risk is the inverse of audit assurance. If the auditor requires a high level of assurance then the tolerable audit risk is set low. The auditor is only willing to accept a small risk of missing a material misstatement.

Some auditors use quantitative measures to conceptualize audit risk, for example, a 1 percent probability of not detecting a material misstatement is "low," while a 5 percent probability is "high." To manage audit risk in a particular engagement, the risk is then broken down into inherent, control and detection components. The inherent and control risks come from the nature of the business and its risks.

The auditor's understanding of the business helps to assess inherent risk, and his understanding of the information systems and controls help to assess control risk. This understanding also helps to identify what kinds of evidence are available and at what cost, the third component of the evidence decision outlined in Exhibit 8-12. The practical considerations, and the trade-offs between the risk components and materiality guide trade-offs that lead to the decisions on what evidence to gather through control tests, analytical procedures and other tests of balances, and how much. These evidence decisions are the basis of the audit programs. The following section explains the fundamental evidence-gathering techniques that the auditor has available. These techniques are the basis of designing specific procedures to address the audit objectives set out in the program.

REVIEW CHECKPOINTS

8.35 What are the four risks included in the conceptual audit risk model? How are they related?

8.36 Give an example of one account with high inherent risk and one with low inherent risk.

8.37 What is the purpose of a control framework?

8.38 Describe two control frameworks that can help in the auditor's preliminary control risk assessment.

8.39 What is anchoring with regard to auditors' judgements about the quality or effectiveness of internal control?

8.40 What are some of the effects of bad economic times that produce risks that auditors should be alert to in clients' financial statements?

8.41 What is the difference between "audit risk in an overall sense" and "audit risk applied to individual account balances?"

8.42 How does the auditors decision on materiality relate to audit risk?

SUFFICIENT APPROPRIATE EVIDENCE IN AUDITING

LEARNING OBJECTIVE
5 Explain audit evidence in terms of its appropriateness and relative strength of persuasiveness.

After obtaining the financial statements, auditors proceed to the task of specifying procedures for gathering evidence about the assertions in them. However, before studying these procedures, you need to understand some features of evidence in auditing.

The third examination standard requires auditors to obtain sufficient appropriate evidential matter as a reasonable basis for an opinion on financial statements.[19] The accounting records (journals, ledgers, accounting policy manuals, computer files and the like) are evidence of the bookkeeping/accounting process but are not sufficient appropriate supporting

[19] Ibid., paragraph 5100.02, and 5300 or ISA 500.7.

evidence for the financial statements. Evidence corroborating these records must be obtained through auditors' direct personal knowledge, examination of documents and the enquiry of company personnel. The purpose of gathering and analyzing evidence is to support the decision on whether the financial statements are fairly presented and conform to GAAP.

The identification of audit evidence is a key critical thinking activity in the audit discipline. As discussed in Chapter 4, critical thinking is essential in forming an opinion on the fair presentation of the financial statements. The auditor requires evidence to judge rationally the financial statement assertions in the financial statements management has put forward for audit, and to provide logical support for the opinion expressed in the audit report.

Appropriateness of Evidence

Appropriateness of evidence relates to the qualitative aspects of evidence. To be considered appropriate, evidence must be relevant and reliable. To be relevant, audit evidence must assist the auditor in achieving the audit objectives. This means relevant evidence must relate to at least one of the assertions. If evidence does not relate to one of the management assertions, the evidence is not relevant to the auditor.

The reliability of audit evidence depends on its nature and source. The following hierarchy of evidential matter will help you understand the relative reliability and, when combined with relevance, the overall persuasive power or appropriateness of different kinds of evidence. The hierarchy starts with the strongest form of evidence and proceeds to the weakest.

1. An auditor's direct, personal knowledge, obtained through physical observation and his or her own mathematical computations, is generally considered the most reliable evidence.

2. Documentary evidence obtained directly from independent external sources (external evidence) is considered very reliable.

3. Documentary evidence that has originated outside the client's data processing system but that has been received and processed by the client (external-internal evidence) is generally considered reliable. However, the circumstances of internal control quality are important.

4. Internal evidence consisting of documents that are produced, circulated and finally stored within the client's information system is generally considered low in reliability. However, internal evidence is used extensively when it is produced under satisfactory conditions of internal control. Sometimes, internal evidence is the only kind available. Internal evidence is also generally easy to obtain and, therefore, tends to be less costly than other evidence.

5. Spoken and written representations given by the client's officers, directors, owners and employees are generally considered the least reliable evidence. Such representations should be corroborated with other types of evidence.

Auditors must be careful about the appropriateness of evidence. When specifying audit procedures for gathering evidence, the auditor's best initial approach is to seek the evidence of the highest reliability. If physical observation and mathematical calculation are not relevant to the account or are impossible or too costly, then move down the hierarchy to obtain the best evidence available. The evidence is best in the sense that it is the most appropriate or persuasive evidence under the circumstances. That is, it is the most reliable evidence that can be obtained in a cost-effective manner relative to a particular audit objective.

There may be situations, however, where no highly reliable source of evidence is available. Some examples are cash donations received by a charity, or e-commerce sales transactions that leave no paper trail. In these cases the auditor considers whether there may be two or more less reliable pieces of evidence that, when evaluated together, support the assertion. If these different pieces of evidence are found to be consistent with each other and are produced from two independent sources, this could raise the level of persuasiveness of the evidence to an appropriately high level. Examples would be observing employee procedures and testing controls over these, and reviewing summarized sales reports prepared for marketing purposes. Another example is obtaining reliable evidence for auditing related party transactions, as discussed in the following box.

RELATED PARTIES AND THE APPROPRIATENESS OF EVIDENCE

CICA Handbook, section 3840 contains extensive definitions and accounting standards concerning disclosure of balances and transactions that a company has with related parties. This note, however, deals only with the audit evidence aspect of related parties.

The Audit Guideline "Related Party Transactions and Economic Dependence" put the matter in perspective by stating: "The auditor should be aware that the substance of a particular transaction could be significantly different from its form and that financial statements should recognize the substance of particular transactions, rather than merely their legal form." Auditors are supposed to identify related party relationships and transactions and obtain evidence that the financial accounting and disclosure for them are proper.

The audit problem with related parties is that evidence obtained from them should not be considered highly reliable in terms of persuasiveness. The source of the evidence may be biased. Hence, auditors should obtain evidence of the purpose, nature and extent of related party transactions and their effect on financial statements; and the evidence should extend beyond enquiry of management.

Sufficiency of Evidence

Sufficiency is a question of how much appropriate evidence is enough. The auditing profession has no official standard, leaving the matter of sufficiency to auditors' professional judgement. Realistically, however, audit decisions must be based on enough evidence to stand the scrutiny of other auditors (supervisors and reviewers) and outsiders (such as critics, judges, or PCAB inspectors). The real test of sufficiency is whether you can persuade someone else that your evidential base is strong enough to reach the same conclusions you have reached. The fact that important evidence is difficult or costly to obtain is not an acceptable reason for failing to obtain it. If an auditor has not been able to obtain sufficient appropriate audit evidence about a material financial statement assertion, *CICA Handbook*, paragraph 5143.74 states that the auditor should express a qualified opinion or a denial of opinion, as further discussed in Chapter 3.

With these aspects of evidence in mind, you will be ready to study the general procedures for obtaining evidence that are covered next.

REVIEW
CHECKPOINTS

8.43   What is the relation between assertions and audit evidence?

8.44   What factors determine whether audit evidence is appropriate? What types of audit evidence are most reliable? least reliable?

8.45   How is an auditor's professional judgement applied in assessing the appropriateness of audit evidence?

8.46   How are external, external-internal and internal documentary evidence generally defined?

8.47   What's the problem with evidence obtained from related parties?

8.48   Distinguish between the appropriateness of audit evidence and the sufficiency of audit evidence.

8.49   What action is required if an auditor cannot obtain sufficient appropriate audit evidence?

EVIDENCE-GATHERING AUDIT PROCEDURES

· · · · · · · · · · · ·

LEARNING OBJECTIVE

6 Outline six general types of audit techniques for gathering evidence.

Auditors and the auditing standards set out six basic types of evidence, and identify six general techniques to gather it: (1) computation, (2) observation, (3) confirmation, (4) enquiry, (5) inspection, and (6) analysis. In practice, these techniques are usually subdivided into more specific procedures. One or more of these techniques may be used no matter what account balance, class of transactions, control procedure, or other information is under audit. Auditors arrange these specific procedures into an audit program, which is basically a list of procedures. Exhibit 8-13 shows the six types of evidence, the techniques most closely related to each and some examples of specific procedures that could be included in an audit program.

Computation

Computation, also referred to as recalculation or reperformance, consists of recalculating the calculations previously performed by a client. This produces compelling mathematical evidence. A client calculation is either right or wrong. Client calculations performed by computer programs can be recalculated using auditing software, with differences printed out for further audit investigation. Mathematical evidence can serve the objectives of both existence and valuation for financial statement amounts that exist principally as calculations—for example, depreciation, pension liabilities, actuarial reserves, statutory bad debt reserves and product guarantee liabilities. Recalculation, in combination with other procedures, also is used to provide evidence of valuation for all other financial data. Computation can provide the auditor with evidence that is highly reliable with respect to mathematical accuracy. However, the results of the computation are only as good as the components; the auditor must audit every significant component of the computation for this to provide strong, persuasive evidence.

EXHIBIT 8-1 3   AUDIT TECHNIQUES AND RELATED TYPES OF EVIDENCE

Audit Techniques	Types of Evidence	Examples of Specific Procedures
1. Computation	1. Auditor's calculations	1. Recompute amortization expense using declining balance method. Recompute Price × Quantity on invoices. Recompute sales tax as a % of total sale amount on invoices.
2. Observation	2. Physical observation	2. Observe data entry procedures. Observe petty cash control procedures. Observe physical inventory counting procedures.
3. Confirmation	3. Statements by independent partie	3. Obtain written confirmation of A/R balance and detail from customer. Obtain written confirmation of loan amount, interest, collateral, and payment dates from lender.
4. Enquiry	4. Statements by client personnel	4. Enquire about frequency of bank reconciliation procedures. Enquire about which employee totals cash receipts and deposits them to the bank.
5. Inspection	5a. Documents prepared by independent parties	5a. Read terms of lease agreement for lessee.
	5b. Documents prepared by the client	5b. Review inventory variance analysis report prepared by production department.
	5c. Physical inspection of tangible assets	5c. Auditor's test counts of physical inventory quantities on hand at year end. Auditor's observation of damaged inventory on hand.
6. Analysis	6. Data interrelationships	6. Analyze monthly gross margin by product line. Compare inventory turnover rate to previous year.

Observation

Observation consists of looking at the application of policy or procedures by others. It provides highly reliable evidence as to performance or conditions at a given point in time but does not necessarily reflect performance at other times or over long periods. The technique of observation is utilized whenever auditors view the client's physical facilities and personnel on an inspection tour, or watch personnel carry out accounting and control activities, or participate in a surprise petty cash count or payroll distribution. Physical observation can also produce a general awareness of events in the client's offices.

Confirmation

Confirmation consists of an enquiry, usually written, to verify accounting records. Confirmation by direct correspondence with independent parties is a procedure widely used in auditing. For example, confirmation is recommended for accounts receivable by section 5303 of the *CICA Handbook*. Confirmation can produce evidence of existence, and sometimes of ownership, valuation and cutoff. Most transactions involve outside parties and, theoretically, written correspondence could be conducted even on such items as individual paycheques. However, auditors limit their use of confirmation to major transactions and balances about which outside parties could be expected to provide information. A selection of confirmation applications includes:

- banks—account balances
- customers—receivables balances
- borrowers—note terms and balances
- agents—inventory or consignment or in warehouse
- lenders—note terms and balances
- policyholders—life insurance contracts
- vendors—accounts payable balances
- registrar—number of shares of stock outstanding
- legal counsel—litigation in progress
- trustees—securities held, terms of agreements
- lessors—lease terms

The important general points about confirmations are these:

- Confirmation letters should be printed on the client's letterhead, or a facsimile, and signed by a client officer.
- Auditors should be very careful that the recipient's address is reliable and not subject to alteration by the client in such a way as to misdirect the confirmation.
- The request should seek information the recipient can supply, like the amount of a balance or the amounts of specified invoices or notes.
- Confirmations should be controlled by the audit firm, not given to client personnel for mailing. Direct communication is required by auditing standards so there is no opportunity for the client to alter the confirmation responses.
- Responses should be returned directly to the audit firm, not to the client.

Confirmations of receivables and payables may take several forms. Two widely used forms are positive confirmation and negative confirmation. The positive confirmation requests a reply in all cases, whether the account balance is considered correct or incorrect. The negative confirmation requests a reply only if the account balance is considered incorrect. Auditors should try to obtain replies from all positive confirmations by sending second and third requests to no respondents. If there is no response to positive confirmations, or if the response to either positive or negative confirmations specifies an exception to the client's records, the auditors should investigate with other audit procedures, such as examining whether there is subsequent collection on the account or examination of internal evidence supporting the recording of the receivable. Cash and accounts receivable confirmations, as well as limitations, and issues arising from the use of faxes and e-mails in confirmation procedures, are explained more fully in Chapter 11.

Enquiry

Enquiry generally involves the collection of oral evidence from independent parties and client officials. Statements must be obtained in the written representation letter for all important enquiries (representation letters are covered in detail in Chapter 15). Auditors use enquiry procedures during the early office and plant tour and when conferences are conducted. Evidence gathered by formal and informal enquiry of persons working for the client generally cannot stand alone as convincing, and auditors must corroborate responses with other findings based on other procedures. Such corroboration may include making further enquiries from other appropriate sources within the entity. Consistent responses from different sources provide an increased degree of assurance. Sometimes, however, the auditor will encounter conflicting evidence in the form of a negative statement where someone volunteers adverse information, such as an admission of theft, irregularity or use of an accounting policy that is misleading. In these situations the auditor will have to use considerable judgement in reconciling the conflicting evidence or in deciding what additional evidence to gather. Skepticism and a critical attitude are important aspects of professional judgement.

Enquiries, interviews and other oral evidence are viewed as important within the profession because the client's explanations are an important way of obtaining an understanding of the business and the nature of specific transactions.[20] Management's explanations can be compared with that of other client employees, as well as that of industry experts and other sources of corroborating evidence. Oral evidence has always been viewed as critical evidence in public sector auditing.

The audit standards now tend to put more reliance on enquiry-type evidence as a means to a better understanding the client's strategy, and the risks and controls associated with it than previously. The CICA research report entitled *Audit Enquiry* identified ways of making audit enquiry a more reliable type of evidence. For example, to make the type of assessments required by the balanced scorecard as discussed in Exhibit 8-6, an auditor's primary source of information would be enquiries of the client's management, other employees and perhaps even others from outside the client organization such as regulators, former employees or suppliers. It is usually necessary to assess the reliability of the process used to make the client's accounting estimates. This frequently involves discussions with various members of the client's senior management. The CICA research report gives an illustration involving enquiry of senior management in customer service, manufacturing, quality controls, marketing and finance to assess the adequacy of an allowance for warranty claims.

To make the integration and synthesis of the whole range of estimates used in financial reporting feasible it may be necessary to create special environments for the audit team that facilitate sharing of enquiry evidence. "Debriefings following interviews and site visits should encourage perceptions and intuitive feelings to be brought out, and information challenged to help identify inconsistencies and gaps . . . and answer colleagues' questions about their findings and impressions . . . The objective, of course, is an integration of findings, capitalizing on the synergy that can come from focused group effort."[21]

Inspection

Inspection consists of looking at records and documents or at assets having physical substance. It encompasses procedures of varying degrees of thoroughness such as examining, perusing, reading, reviewing, scanning, scrutinizing and vouching.

[20] S. Smith, "A Matter of Evidence," *CA Magazine*, October 1994, pp. 57-58.
[21] CICA, *Audit Enquiry* (CICA, March 2000), p. 24.

Physical inspection of tangible assets provides reliable evidence of existence and may provide tentative evidence of condition, and hence valuation, but it does not provide reliable evidence regarding ownership. Physical inspection of formal documents having intrinsic value, such as securities certificates, can also provide reliable evidence about existence. Records and documents not having an intrinsic market value, such as invoices or purchase orders, have varying degrees of reliability for different assertions depending on their source.

Much auditing work involves gathering evidence by examining authoritative documents prepared by independent parties and by the client. Such documents can provide at least some evidence regarding all the assertions.

Documents Prepared by Independent Outside Parties

A great deal of documentary evidence is external-internal. Convincing documentation is that prepared or validated by other parties and sent to the client. The signatures, seals, engravings and other distinctive stylistic attributes of formal authoritative documents make such sources more reliable (less susceptible to alteration) than ordinary documents prepared by outsiders. Some examples of both types of documents are listed following:

Formal Authoritative Documents
1. Bank statements
2. Cancelled cheques
3. Insurance policies
4. Notes receivable
5. Securities certificates
6. Indenture agreements
7. Elaborate contracts
8. Title papers (e.g., autos)

Ordinary Documents
1. Vendor's invoices
2. Customers' purchase orders
3. Loan applications
4. Notes receivable (on unique forms and on standard bank forms)
5. Insurance policy applications
6. Simple contracts
7. Correspondence

Documents Prepared and Processed Within the Entity Under Audit

Documentation of this type is internal evidence. Some of these documents may be quite informal and not very authoritative or reliable. As a general proposition, the reliability of these documents depends on the quality of internal control under which they were produced and processed. Some of the most common of these documents are as follows:

Internal Documents
1. Sales invoice copies
2. Sales summary reports
3. Cost distribution reports
4. Loan approval memos
5. Budgets and performance reports
6. Documentation of transactions with subsidiary or affiliated companies
7. Shipping documents
8. Receiving reports
9. Requisition slips
10. Purchase orders
11. Credit memoranda
12. Transaction logs
13. Batch control logs (computer)

A Particular Inspection Procedure: Vouching—Examination of Documents

The important point about vouching in the examination of documents is the direction of the search for audit evidence. In **vouching**, an item of financial information is selected from an account (e.g., the posting of a sales invoice in a customer's master file record); then the auditor goes backward through the accounting and control system to find the source documentation that supports the item selected. The auditor finds the journal entry or data input list, the sales summary, the sales invoice copy and the shipping documents, and, finally, the customer's purchase order. Vouching of documents can help auditors decide whether all recorded data are adequately supported (the existence/occurrence assertion), but vouching does not provide evidence to show whether all events were recorded. (This latter problem is covered by tracing.)

A Particular Inspection Procedure: Tracing—Examination of Documents

In the examination of documents, **tracing** takes the opposite direction from vouching. When an auditor performs tracing, she selects sample items of basic source documents and proceeds forward through the accounting and control system (whether computer or manual) to find the final recording of the accounting transactions. For example, samples of payroll payments are traced to cost and expense accounts, sales invoices to the sales accounts, cash receipts to the accounts receivable subsidiary accounts and cash disbursements to the accounts payable subsidiary accounts.

Using tracing, an auditor can decide whether all events were recorded (the completeness assertion), and complement the evidence obtained by vouching. However, you must be alert to events that may not have been captured in the source documents and not entered into the accounting system. For example, the search for unrecorded liabilities for raw materials purchases must include examination of invoices received in the period following the fiscal year-end and examination of receiving reports dated near the year-end. (The "search for unrecorded liabilities" is explained in detail in Chapter 12.)

A Particular Inspection Procedure: Scanning

Scanning is the way auditors exercise their general alertness to unusual items and events in clients' documentation. A typical scanning directive in an audit program is "Scan the expense accounts for credit entries; vouch any to source documents."

In general, scanning is an "eyes-open" approach of looking for anything unusual. The scanning procedure usually does not produce direct evidence itself, but it can raise questions for which other evidence must be obtained. Scanning can be accomplished on computer records using computer audit software to select records to be analyzed online, or printed out for further audit investigation. Typical items discovered by the scanning effort include debits in revenue accounts, credits in expense accounts, unusually large accounts receivable write-offs, unusually large paycheques, unusually small sales volume in the month following the year-end and large cash deposits just prior to year-end. Scanning can contribute some evidence related to the existence of assets and the completeness of accounting records, including the proper cutoff of material transactions.

Scanning is valuable when sampling methods are applied in audit decisions. When a sample is the basis for selecting items for audit, the risk of choosing a sample that does not reflect the entire population of items always exists. Such an event may cause a decision error. Auditors subjectively reduce this detection risk by scanning items not selected in the sample. It can be feasible to scan the entire population being audited, e.g., all the sales invoice issued during the year.

Analysis

Auditors can obtain evidence about financial statement accounts by methods of study and comparison called **analysis**. *CICA Handbook,* section 5301, provides guidance on using analysis at three stages of the audit. First it is used in the planning (beginning) stage to identify risks and guide the design of the audit work. Second, in the field work stage substantive analytical procedures can be used for generating evidence that lowers the risk that the financial statement are materially misstated. Third, analysis is used at the end of the audit as an overall review and evaluation when forming a conclusion as to whether the financial statements as a whole are consistent with the auditor's understanding of the business. This conclusion is the basis of the opinion expressed in the audit report.

When auditors use analysis as a substantive procedure during the execution phase of the audit, it provides evidence related to assertions about specific account balances or classes of transactions. Analysis is the "other" category in the list of six auditing techniques. Analytical procedures are "everything else an auditor can think to do" that does not meet the definitions of computation, observation, confirmation, structured enquiry or inspection. The procedures themselves range from simple comparisons to application of complex mathematical estimation models. They can be used to obtain evidence on any of the management assertions, but the assertions for which they are most useful are completeness, valuation and presentation.[22]

---

[22] D.G. Smith, *Analytical Review* (CICA, 1983), Chapter 2.

Analytical procedures, or analysis, consists of:

(a) identifying the components of a financial statement item or account so that particular characteristics of these components can be considered in designing the nature, timing and extent of other audit procedures; and

(b) performing analytical procedures, which are techniques by which the auditor:
   (i) studies and uses meaningful relationships among elements of financial and non-financial information to form expectations about what amounts recorded in the accounts should be;
   (ii) compares such expectations with the recorded amounts to identify fluctuations and relationships that are not consistent with other relevant information or that deviate significantly from predicted amounts ; and
   (iii) uses the results of this comparison to help determine what, if any, other audit procedures are needed to obtain sufficient appropriate audit evidence that the recorded amounts are not materially misstated.[23]

The difference between part (a) above and "scanning" is that analysis relates to a higher level of aggregation—comparison of components of a financial statement—whereas scanning relates to the detail records about a particular component.

Analytical procedures can be classified into the five general types discussed in the first part of this chapter. When analysis is used to provide substantive evidence, auditors need to be careful to use independent, reliable information for comparison purposes. Thus, the sources of information used in analytical procedures need to be assessed for independence and objectivity. Quantitative information must be verified by the auditor if a high level of reliance is placed on the evidence provided by analysis. Examples of the types of independent information sources, and how their reliability can be verified are as follows:

Information Source	Evidence of Reliability of Information Source
Financial account information for comparable prior period(s)	Information agrees with audited financial statements, or information in prior year audit working papers (e.g., monthly results).
Company budgets and forecasts	Budgetting or forecasting process is reviewed by auditor and found to be based on realistic assumptions and methods, and targets are achievable under normal business conditions. Budget and forecast information is produced by the company's information systems under internal controls monitored by senior management; auditor has assessed these controls to be strong. Budgets and forecasts are used by board of directors for decision making.
Financial relationships among accounts in the current period	Account balances used in analysis should be agreed/referenced to audit working papers in current year file where they are verified substantively.
Industry statistics	Sources should be well known industry analysis services (e.g., Moody's or Standard and Poors), and reports used should be obtained by the auditors directly from those sources.
Nonfinancial information, such as physical production statistics	Nonfinancial information is prepared by the company's information systems under internal controls monitored by senior management; auditor has assessed these controls to be strong. The nonfinancial information is used by senior management and the board for decision making.

Because analytical procedures are loosely defined, it is tempting for auditors, and professors and students, to consider the evidence they produce to be "soft." Therefore, they may tend to concentrate more on computation, observation, confirmation, inspection of assets and vouching of documents that are perceived to produce "hard" evidence. However, analytical procedures can be very effective because they integrate evidence from a variety of information sources and often provide an independent way of providing evidence about

[23] CICA Handbook, section 5301.

whether the financial statement assertions hold true. Some examples of using analytical procedures to detect misstatements detected are given in the following box.

FINDING MISSTATEMENTS WITH ANALYTICAL PROCEDURES

Auditors noticed large quantities of rolled steel in the company's inventory. Several 30,000-kilogram rolls were entered in the inventory list. The false entries were detected because the auditor knew the company's fork-lift trucks had a 10,000-kilogram lifting capacity.

———

Auditors compared the total quantity of vegetable oils the company claimed to have inventoried in its tanks to the storage capacity reported in national export statistics. The company's "quantity on hand" amounted to 90 percent of the national supply and greatly exceeded its own tank capacity.

———

Last year's working papers showed that the company employees had failed to accrue wages payable at the year-end date. A search for the current accrual entry showed it had again been forgotten.

———

Auditors programmed a complex regression model to estimate the electric utility company's total revenue. They used empirical relations of fuel consumption, meteorological reports of weather conditions and population census data in the area. The regression model estimated revenue within close range of the reported revenue.

Auditing researchers Hylas and Ashton collected evidence on misstatements requiring financial statement adjustment in a large number of audits.[24] They were interested primarily in describing the audit procedures used to detect the misstatements. Their definition of analytical procedures was broad. It included data comparisons, predictions based on outside data, analyses of interrelationships among account balances, "reasonableness tests," "estimates," and cursory review of financial statements in the audit planning stage. They also had two procedure categories called expectations from prior years (which involves the carry over of analytical and detail knowledge about continuing audit clients) and discussions with client personnel.

They found that auditors gave credit for misstatement discovery to analytical procedures for 27.1 percent of all misstatements. They gave credit to "expectations" and "discussions" for another 18.5 percent. Altogether, the so-called soft procedures accounted for detection of 45.6 percent of the misstatements. All of these procedures typically are applied early in the audit, so you should not infer that other kinds of audit procedures would or would not have detected the same misstatements. The detection success of other procedures depends on the results of the early applied procedures because, as this study was designed, even a good physical observation procedure did not get credit for "discovery" of a misstatement that already had been discovered using analytical procedures.

Auditors must consider the value of analytical procedures, especially since they are usually less costly than more detailed, document-oriented procedures. Also, the "hard evidence" procedures have their own pitfalls. Auditors may not be competent to "see" things they are supposed to observe. Clients can manipulate confirmations by giving auditors the addresses of conspirators or by asking customers just to "sign it and send it back." The

---

[24] R.E. Hylas, and R.H. Ashton, "Audit Detection of Financial Statement Errors," *The Accounting Review*, October 1982, pp. 751–65.

following box illustrates problems that can arise in evaluating evidence obtained with "hard evidence" procedures. An audit program makes use of several different types of procedures, and analytical procedures deserve a prominent place.

POTHOLES IN THE AUDIT PROCEDURE ROAD

Computation:
An auditor calculated inventory valuations (quantities times price), thinking the measuring unit was gross (144 units each), when the client had actually recorded counts in dozens (12 units each), thus causing the inventory valuation to be 12 times the proper measure.

Inspection of Assets:
While inspecting the fertilizer tank assets in ranch country, the auditor was fooled when the manager was able to move them to other locations and place new numbers on them. The auditor "inspected" the same tanks many times.

Confirmation:
The insurance company executive gave the auditor a false address for a marketable securities confirmation, intercepted the confirmation, then returned it with no exceptions noted. The company falsified $20 million in assets.

Enquiry:
Seeking evidence of the collectibility of accounts receivable, the auditors "audited by conversation" and took the credit manager's word about the collection probabilities on the over-90-day past-due accounts. They sought no other evidence.

Inspection by Examination of Documents:
The auditors did not notice that the bank statement had been crudely altered. (Can you find the alteration in the bank statement in Exhibit 17–3 in Chapter 17?)

Inspection by the Scanning Procedure:
The auditors extracted a computer list of all the bank's loans over $1,000. They neglected to perform a similar scan for loans with negative balances, a condition that should not occur. The bank had data processing problems that caused many loan balances to be negative, although the trial balance balanced!

R E V I E W
C H E C K P O I N T S

8.50   List six types of evidence and the audit techniques used to gather them.

8.51   What are the strengths and limitations of computation-based audit evidence?

8.52   What are the strengths and limitations of observation-based audit evidence?

8.53   Why must the entire confirmation process be controlled by the audit firm?

8.54   What can auditors do to improve the effectiveness of confirmation requests?

8.55   Differentiate between authoritative and ordinary externally produced documents.

8.56   What is meant by vouching? tracing? and scanning?

8.57   What does analysis consist of?

8.58   What are three points in an audit engagement when analysis is used?

8.59   What sources of information are useful for performing analysis?

8.60   If analysis is used to provide substantive audit evidence, what steps must be taken regarding the source information used in the analysis?

8.61   Is analysis very effective for discovering errors and irregularities?

Effectiveness of Audit Procedures

Audits are supposed to be designed to provide reasonable assurance of detecting misstatements that are material to the financial statements.[25] When misstatements exist, and auditors do a good job of detecting them, adjustments will be made to management's unaudited financial statements before an audit report is issued. How often does this happen? Auditing researchers Wright and Ashton obtained information on 186 audits performed by KPMG Peat Marwick during 1984–85.[26] The reported frequency of audit adjustments is shown in Exhibit 8-14.

EXHIBIT   8-14   FREQUENCY OF AUDIT ADJUSTMENTS (sample of audits from one audit firm)

Number of Audit Adjustments*	Number of Audits	Percent of Audits
Zero or 1	22	12%
2–5	30	16
6–10	45	24
More than 10	89	48
Total	186	100%

*Total number of adjustments detected regardless of size or nature.

What kinds of misstatements did the auditors find? Wright and Ashton reported the data for 23 accounts. A selection of them is shown in Exhibit 8-15. The misstatements consisted of both understatements and overstatements. (However, you should remember that these are not "good" or "bad" descriptions. Overstatement of assets and understatement of liabilities both cause shareholders' equity to be overstated.) Since they come from respondents in one public accounting firm, these data may not be generalizable to all audits. In this case, however, the overstatements/understatements look mixed in the current assets, understatements

EXHIBIT   8-15   SUMMARY OF MISSTATEMENTS (selected accounts)

Account	Number of Misstatements	
	Overstatement	Understatement
Cash	6	10
Securities	21	17
Accounts receivable	48	22
Inventory	24	32
Property, plant	14	23
Other noncurrent	11	24
Accounts payable	21	25
Accrued liabilities	17	40
Other current liabilities	10	13
Long-term liabilities	12	24
Revenue	32	30
Cost of goods sold	38	45
Selling expense	11	16
Gen and admin. expense	39	52

Note: The effect of adjustments on income was that 43 percent of the adjustments reduced the reported income, while 28 percent increased the reported income. The other 29 percent of the adjustments were reclassifications that neither reduced nor increased income.

[25] See CICA Handbook, paragraph 5095.02.

[26] Data for Exhibit 8-14 and the other, related exhibits come from Wright, Arnold and Robert H. Ashton, "Identifying Audit Adjustments with Attention-Directing Procedures," The Accounting Review, October 1989, pp. 710–28.

EXHIBIT   8-16   INITIAL EVENTS THAT IDENTIFIED ADJUSTMENTS

Initial Event	Number of Adjustments	Percent
Tests of details: examination of transaction amounts and descriptions, account balance details, workups to support account balances, data on various reconciliations	104	28.7%
*Expectations from the prior year	78	21.5
*Analytical procedures: comparison of current unaudited balances with balances of prior years, predictions of current balances based on exogenous data, analyses of interrelationships	56	15.5
*Client enquiry	48	13.3
Test of detail: checks for mathematical accuracy	35	9.7
General audit procedures	8	2.2

*These were the three "attention-directing procedures" that accounted for 50.3 percent of the identified adjustments.

are in the majority in the noncurrent assets, understatements appear to be in the majority in the liabilities and understatements appear to be in the majority in the expense accounts.

As you can see, discovery of misstatements in management's unaudited financial statements is not unusual. How do the auditors do it? What procedures do they find effective? Wright and Ashton compiled data on seven "initial events" that identified misstatements in financial statements. They were called "initial events" instead of "audit procedures" because they were the first work that identified misstatements, and all of them did not correspond exactly with specific procedures auditors would list in an audit program. Exhibit 8-16 shows the initial events that indicated misstatements that required adjustment. The so-called "soft" information from expectations based on prior-year experience, analytical procedures and client enquiry accounted for an overall 50 percent of the discovered misstatements. (These data are consistent with the earlier Hylas-Ashton study. See footnote 25.)

Nevertheless, detail audit procedures also were effective. Wright and Ashton note that the "ordering effect" (the fact that the attention-directing procedures come first) biases the results against showing that detail procedures might have detected the misstatements if they had not already been detected. They note further that (1) few adjustments were initially signalled by confirmations or inventory observation and (2) simple methods of comparison and client enquiry detected many misstatements.

This research finding is consistent with the emphasis in current auditing standards on understanding the client's business, its environment and its business risks by using analysis at the early stages of the audit.

REVIEW CHECKPOINTS

8.62   Is there any pattern in auditors' experience in finding overstatements and understatements in accounts?

8.63   List several types of audit work (initial events, audit procedures) in their order of apparent effectiveness for identifying financial statement misstatements. Where would you put accounts receivable confirmation and inventory observation on the list?

PLANNING MEMORANDUM

Auditors usually prepare a planning memorandum summarizing the preliminary analytical review and the materiality and risk assessment with specific directions about the effect on the audit. The audit team discussions of the work done to understand the client's business and risks are also very relevant in developing the decisions included in the planning document. This planning memo also usually documents information about (1) investigation or review of the prospective or continuing client relationship, (2) needs for special technical or industry expertise, (3) staff assignment and timing schedules, (4) the assessed level of control risk, (5) significant industry or company risks, (6) computer system control environment, (7) utilization of the company's internal auditors, (8) identification of unusual accounting principles problems, and (9) schedules of work periods, meeting dates with client personnel and completion dates. The memo summarizes all the important overall planning information.

All the planning becomes a basis for preparing the audit programs; these are discussed in the next section. They list specific audit objectives and procedures that auditors use to guide the work of inherent and control risk assessment and to obtain sufficient competent evidence that serves as a basis for the audit report.

AUDIT PROGRAMS

. . . .

LEARNING OBJECTIVE
7 Describe the content and purpose of audit programs.

Audit programs set out the nature, timing and extent of the planned audit procedures. The "nature" of audit procedures refers to which of the general types of evidence techniques they will use. The "timing" refers to when they will be performed, whether before year end (interim date), at, or after the client's year end. Timing may have other aspects such as surprise procedures (unannounced to client personnel) or the need observe periodic client procedures, such as rotating inventory counts during the year. The "extent" usually refers to the sample sizes of data examined, such as the number of customer accounts receivable to confirm, or the number of inventory types to count

Auditors use two general types of audit programs, one we will call **internal control program** and the other the **balance audit program**. The internal control program lists the specific procedures for obtaining an understanding of the client's business and management's control system, and for assessing the inherent risk and the control risk related to the financial account balances. The balance audit program lists the substantive procedures for gathering direct evidence on the assertions (i.e., existence, completeness, valuation, ownership (or rights and obligations), presentation and disclosure) about dollar amounts in the account balances.

These audit programs combine all the considerations of audit planning discussed up to this point, including:

- understanding the client's business, its environment and risks, its information systems and its internal control
- assertions and objectives contained in the client's financial statements
- preliminary analytical procedures for identifying specific risk areas in the unaudited financial statements
- preliminary materiality decisions
- preliminary risk assessments
- persuasive strengths of evidence
- audit procedures for obtaining evidence

In actual field situations these audit programs are very lengthy. Special program documents may contain separate listings of procedures and questionnaires on the company's internal control environment, internal control procedures and management controls. The audit programs contain numerous detailed specifications of procedures the auditors intend to perform as the work progresses. The following box summarizes elements of audit programs for illustrative purposes, to put in perspective the sequence of topics you have read about thus far. The technical parts of internal control risk assessment programs are explained more fully in Chapter 9.

UNDERSTAND THE BUSINESS RISK, INHERENT RISK, CONTROL RISK

- Communicate with predecessor auditors.
- Study prior-year audit working papers, professional audit and accounting guides and industry publications concerning the company and its industry.
- Interview management with regard to business and accounting policies.
- Evaluate the competence and independence of the company's internal auditors.
- Determine the need for specialists on the engagement.
- Determine the extent of significant computer applications in the company's accounting system.
- Obtain the financial statements and make decisions about the planning materiality appropriate in the circumstances.
- Perform preliminary analytical procedures to identify risk areas in the financial statement accounts.
- Assess the inherent risk in general and with respect to particular accounts.

- Obtain an understanding of the company's internal control through interviews, observations and tests of controls (more on this topic in Chapter 9).
- Perform detail test of control procedures, if necessary (more on this topic in Chapters 9 and 10, and Appendix 10B on the Online Learning Centre for more advanced issues).
- Assess the control risk (more on this topic in Chapters 9 and 10, and Appendix 10B for more advanced issues).
- Use the control risk assessment to design the nature, timing and extent of substantive audit procedures (more on this topic in Chapters 9 and 10, and Appendix 10B for more advanced issues).

The balance audit program consists of several programs, each applicable to a particular account. Auditors first subdivide the financial statements into accounting processes or cycles (as explained in Chapter 6), then turn attention to the accounts in each cycle. The procedures in these audit programs are designed to obtain evidence about the existence or occurrence, completeness, valuation, ownership or rights and obligations, and presentation and disclosure assertions implicit in each account title and balance. The following box contains a partial program in the revenue process with brief specifications of procedures for auditing accounts receivable. The procedures contain many of the elements of the general techniques that were explained in the previous section (e.g., confirmation, computation, enquiry, inspection and the assertions toward which they are directed). Audit programs are presented in more detail in Chapter 10.

BALANCE AUDIT PROGRAM IN REVENUE, RECEIVABLES, RECEIPTS PROCESS

ACCOUNTS RECEIVABLE

- Prepare and send confirmations on a sample of customers' accounts receivable. Analyze the returns.

- Obtain an aged trial balance of the receivables. Calculate and analyze the age status of the accounts and the allowance for uncollectible accounts.
- Interview the credit manager concerning the past-due accounts. Obtain credit reports and financial statements for independent analysis of overdue accounts.
- Vouch receivables balances to cash payments received after the confirmation date.
- Read loan agreements and make note of any pledge of receivables, sales with recourse or other restrictions or contingencies related to the receivables.
- Read sales contracts for evidence of customers' rights of return or price allowance terms.
- Obtain written representations from the client concerning pledges for collateral, related party receivables, collectibility and other matters related to accounts receivable.

REVIEW CHECKPOINTS

8.64   What information is summarized in the audit planning memorandum? How does it relate to the preparation of audit programs?

8.65   What are the two kinds of audit programs and what is the purpose of each?

8.66   What is meant by the terms nature, timing and extent of audit procedures?

AUDIT WORKING PAPERS

LEARNING OBJECTIVE

8 Review a setup of audit working papers for proper form and content.

An audit is not complete without preparation of proper working paper documentation. Working papers are the auditors' record of compliance with generally accepted auditing standards. They should contain support for the decisions regarding procedures necessary in the circumstances and all other important decisions made during the audit. Even though the auditor is the legal owner of the working papers, professional ethics requires that those papers not be transferred without consent of the client because of the confidential information recorded in them. Detailed auditing standards concerning working paper documentation are in *CICA Handbook*, section 5145 and ISA 230. The following box outlines the impact of destroying audit working papers on the value of the audit and the reputation of the audit firm. This shows why documentation is considered important by audit firms and the auditing standard setters.

SHREDDED REPUTATION

Accounting researchers investigated the impact of the Enron audit failure on other Arthur Andersen clients. On the three days following Andersen's admission that a large number of Enron audit documents had been shredded, the researchers found that Andersen's other clients experienced a significant reduction in share prices, indicating investors downgraded the quality of the audits performed by Andersen.

The ability of investors to assess whether a firm's financial statements reflect its actual business performance rests on the reputation of its independent auditor. The auditor's reputation is directly related to the perceived and actual levels of quality reflected by the auditor's report. If auditor quality is jeopardized, the audit report provides a lower level of assurance to financial statement users that the financial statements reflect the firm's business reality, and a higher probablilty that its earnings and book values have been overstated with out being flagged by its auditor.

The events that led to the destruction of Andersen's reputation are reviewed below:

Andersen was the fifth largest auditing firm in the world, employing 85,000 people in 84 countries. For 2001, Andersen reported U.S. revenues of $9.3 billion.

On February 5, 2001, Andersen personnel from the Houston and Chicago offices discussed concerns about Enron's accounting. Yet, at the February 12, 2001, Enron Audit Committee meeting, Andersen stated that the 2000 Enron financial statements would receive an audit report containing an unqualified opinion and that Andersen had specifically reviewed the related-party transactions and did not find any impropriety with respect to the accounting for these related-party transactions.

After Enron's October 16, 2002, third-quarter earnings announcement, Andersen's independence from Enron began to be questioned because the audit firm had provided significant non-audit services to Enron in addition to its fees associated with the Enron audit. Andersen received $47.5 million in fees from Enron. Of this amount, $34.2 million, or 72%, was audit related and tax work. Total fees for other services totaled $13.3 million. Also, Enron had outsourced some internal audit functions to Andersen. Andersen's Houston office came under fire.

On November 8, Andersen received a subpoena from the SEC for documents related to Enron.

Perhaps the defining moment in the Enron collapse, with respect to Andersen, occurred on January 10, 2002. On this date, Andersen notified the SEC and the Department of Justice that Andersen personnel involved with the Enron engagement had disposed of a significant but undetermined number of electronic and paper documents as well as correspondence related to the Enron engagement.

In early March 2002, the Justice Department began pressuring Andersen with respect to its involvement with Enron and the eventual document shredding. Following a week of intense negotiations between Andersen and the Justice Department with respect to a possible criminal indictment for obstructing justice, a criminal indictment against Andersen was unsealed on March 15, 2002. On May 2, 2002, a jury trial began in Houston. On May 7, 2002, Andersen agreed to pay $217 million to settle civil litigation over its audits of the Baptist Foundation of Arizona (the second largest settlement in history by any of the Big 5 audit firms). Finally, on June 15, 2002, the federal jury convicted Andersen of a single count of obstructing justice. Andersen was barred from conducting and reporting on the audits of SEC-registered companies after August 2002.

The Enron audit was the fourth major audit failure affecting Andersen since 1999. In May 2001, Andersen paid $110 million (without accepting or denying blame) to settle Sunbeam's shareholders' lawsuit. In June 2001, Andersen agreed to pay a $7 million fine to the SEC in the Waste Management case. Andersen had already agreed to pay part of a $220 million suit to settle a class action case related to Waste Management, which had overstated income by approximately $1 billion.

Clearly, Andersen's reputation was negatively affected by the events described here. No financial services firm has ever survived a criminal conviction.

Source: Excerpted from P. Chaney and K. Philipich. "Shredded Reputation: The Cost of Audit Failure," *Journal of Accounting Research* 40 (4), pp. 1221–1245, © 2002, Blackwell Publishing.

Working papers can be classified into three categories: (1) permanent file papers, (2) audit administrative papers, and (3) audit evidence papers. The last two categories are often called the **current file** because they relate to the audit of one year.

Permanent File Papers

The **permanent file** contains information of continuing interest over many years' audits of the same client. This file can be used year after year, whereas each year's current audit evidence papers are filed away after they have served their purpose. Documents of permanent interest and applicability include (1) copies or excerpts of the corporate charter and bylaws or partnership agreements; (2) copies or excerpts of continuing contracts, such as leases, bond indentures, royalty agreements, management bonus contracts, etc.; (3) a history of the company, its products and its markets; (4) excerpts of minutes of shareholders' and directors' meetings on matters of lasting interest; and (5) continuing schedules of accounts whose balances are carried forward for several years, such as share capital, retained earnings, partnership capital and the like. Copies of prior years' financial statements and audit reports may also be included. The permanent file is a ready source of information for new auditors on the engagement who must familiarize themselves with the client.

Audit Administrative Papers

Administrative papers contain the documentation of the early planning phases of the audit. They usually include the engagement letter, staff assignment notes, conclusions related to understanding the client's business, results of preliminary analytical procedures, initial assessments of audit risks and initial assessments of audit materiality. Many accounting firms follow the practice of summarizing these data in an engagement planning memorandum.

Audit planning and administration also includes work on the preliminary assessment of control risk and preparation of a written audit program. In general, the following items are usually among the administrative working papers in each year's current file:

1. engagement letter
2. staff assignments
3. client organization chart
4. memoranda of conferences with management
5. memoranda of conferences with the directors' audit committee
6. preliminary analytical review notes
7. initial risk assessment notes
8. initial materiality assessment notes
9. engagement planning memorandum
10. audit engagement time budget
11. internal control questionnaire and control analyses
12. management controls questionnaire
13. computer controls questionnaire
14. internal control system flowcharts
15. audit program
16. a working trial balance of general ledger accounts
17. working paper record of preliminary adjusting and reclassifying entries
18. memoranda of review notes and unfinished procedures (all cleared by the end of the field work)

Audit Evidence Papers

The current-year audit evidence working papers contain the specific assertions under audit, the record of the procedures performed, the evidence obtained and the decisions made in the course of the audit (see Exhibit 8-17 following). These papers communicate the quality of the audit, so they must be clear, concise, complete, neat, well indexed and informative. Each separate working paper (or multiple pages that go together) must be complete in the sense that it can be removed from the working paper file and considered on its own, with proper cross-reference available to show how the paper co-ordinates with other working papers. Working papers may be on paper (handwritten, typed or printed from computer files) or

EXHIBIT 8-17   CURRENT WORKING PAPER FILE

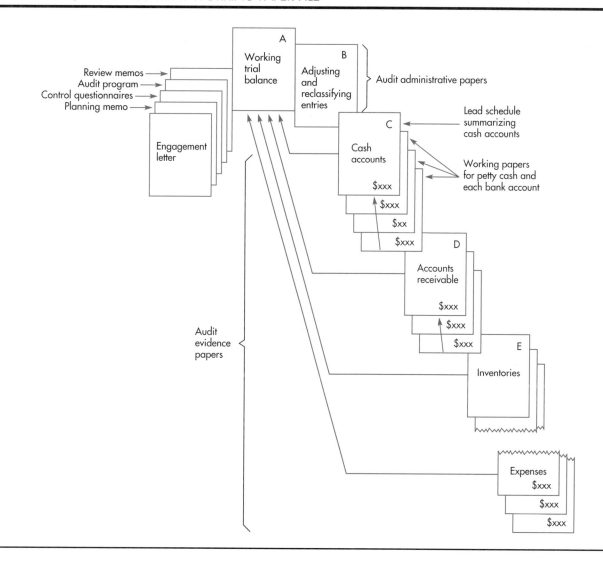

stored electronically, and evidence may be recorded in the form of magnetic tape or disks, or film, or photographs; or other media.

The most important facet of the current audit evidence papers is the requirement that they show the auditors' decision problems and conclusions. The papers must record the management assertions that were audited (book values or qualitative disclosures), the evidence gathered about them and the final decisions. Auditing standards[27] recommend that the working papers show (1) evidence that the work was adequately planned and supervised; (2) a description of audit evidence obtained include memoranda, check lists, questionnaires, flowcharts, audit programs, schedules, correspondence and extracts of legal documents; (3) evidence of the evaluation and disposition of misstatements; and (4) copies of letters or notes concerning audit matters reported to the client.[28] Common sense also dictates that the working papers be sufficient to show that the financial statements conform to GAAP and that the disclosures are adequate. The working papers also should explain how exceptions and unusual accounting questions were resolved or treated. (Notice in Exhibit 8-18 the auditor's confirmation of the disputed account payable liability.) Taken altogether, these features should demonstrate that all the auditing standards were observed.

[27] *CICA Handbook*, section 5145.
[28] Ibid., paragraph 5145.05 or ISA 230.11.

EXHIBIT 8-18   ILLUSTRATIVE WORKING PAPER

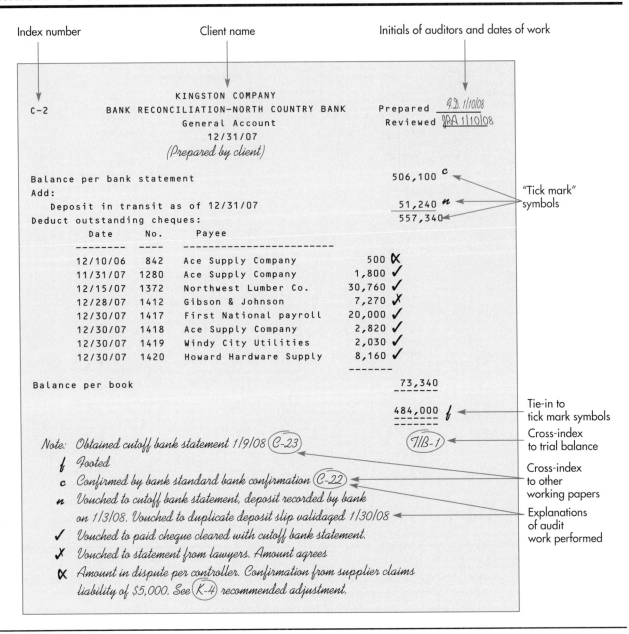

Index number   Client name   Initials of auditors and dates of work

KINGSTON COMPANY
BANK RECONCILIATION—NORTH COUNTRY BANK
C-2   General Account   Prepared ___ 9.D. 1/10/08
                      12/31/07   Reviewed ___ JRA 1/10/08
                (Prepared by client)

Balance per bank statement   506,100 *c*   "Tick mark"
Add: symbols
    Deposit in transit as of 12/31/07   51,240 *n*
Deduct outstanding cheques: 557,340
      Date   No.   Payee
    --------   ----   ----------------------
    12/10/06   842   Ace Supply Company   500 ⋉
    11/31/07   1280   Ace Supply Company   1,800 ✓
    12/15/07   1372   Northwest Lumber Co.   30,760 ✓
    12/28/07   1412   Gibson & Johnson   7,270 ✗
    12/30/07   1417   First National payroll 20,000 ✓
    12/30/07   1418   Ace Supply Company   2,820 ✓
    12/30/07   1419   Windy City Utilities   2,030 ✓
    12/30/07   1420   Howard Hardware Supply 8,160 ✓

Balance per book   73,340

                                                      484,000 *f*   Tie-in to
                                                                            tick mark symbols

Note: Obtained cutoff bank statement 1/9/08 (C-23)   (T/B-1)   Cross-index
                                                                            to trial balance
  f Footed
                                                                            Cross-index
  c Confirmed by bank standard bank confirmation (C-22)   to other
                                                                            working papers
  n Vouched to cutoff bank statement, deposit recorded by bank
       on 1/3/08. Vouched to duplicate deposit slip validaged 1/30/08   Explanations
                                                                            of audit
  ✓   Vouched to paid cheque cleared with cutoff bank statement.   work performed
  ✗   Vouched to statement from lawyers. Amount agrees
  ⋉   Amount in dispute per controller. Confirmation from supplier claims
       liability of $5,000. See (K-4) recommended adjustment.

Working Paper Arrangement and Indexing

Every auditing organization has a different method of arranging and indexing working
papers. In general, however, the papers are grouped in order behind the trial balance according to balance sheet and income statement captions. Usually, the current assets appear first,
followed by fixed assets, other assets, liabilities, equities, revenue and expense accounts.
A typical arrangement is shown in Exhibit 8-17.

Several working paper preparation techniques are quite important for the quality of the
finished product. The points that follow are illustrated in Exhibit 8-18.

- Indexing. Each paper is given an index number, like a book page number, so it can be
  found, removed, and replaced without loss. For example, an index number can consist
  of a section letter (e.g., "C") and a page number within that section (e.g., C-"2"). This

allows for each section to be given to different audit teams and for easy expansion within a given section without affecting other sections.

- Cross-indexing. Numbers or memoranda related to other papers carry the index of other paper(s) so that the connections can be followed.
- Heading. Each paper is titled with the name of the company, the period under audit date, and a descriptive title of the contents of the working paper.
- Signatures and initials. The auditor who performs the work and the supervisor who reviews it must sign the papers so that personnel can be identified.
- Dates of audit work. The dates of performance and review are recorded on the working papers so that reviewers of the papers can tell when the work was performed.
- Tick marks and explanations. "Tick marks" are the auditor's shorthand for abbreviating comments about work performed. Tick marks always must be accompanied by a full explanation of the auditing work.

Audit Working Paper Software

Specialized working paper software is becoming very common in public practice. Electronic working papers can boost productivity by automating many documentation tasks (for example, automatically carrying over adjustments to related working paper documents and the financial statements). Good electronic working paper software integrates the audit information and allows easy access, review and changes to the format, content or order of the files. Because most client data are already in electronic form, it is logical to integrate this data with electronic working paper files. In addition, the use of electronic working papers with laptop computers eliminates the need for voluminous file boxes and briefcases, and allows for electronic communication and sharing of information among staff and continuous monitoring and review of everyone's work even from a distance by a supervisor. The entire audit process can be re-engineered to be more efficient (for example, through use of standard templates and electronic questionnaires).

Audit working paper software can also facilitate analysis. Links can be established to other databases, or even websites so that data or information from these sources can be cross referenced or transferred to the working papers. Thus, audit staff work and various other sources of information can be integrated to support the auditor's opinion.

Some problems are associated with computer-generated working papers, however, including costs of hardware, software, training and the continuous upgrading with advances in technology. Also, some copies of original source documents such as important contracts still need to be kept in hard copy form. An example of a working paper software program used in public practice is CaseWare.

R E V I E W
C H E C K P O I N T S

8.67   Why do audit firms and audit standards require auditors to prepare and retain specific documentation of their audit work?

8.68   What information would you expect to find in a permanent audit file and how would auditors use this information?

8.69   What audit administration working papers are included in the current audit evidence working paper files?

8.70   What is considered the most important content of the current audit working papers?

8.71   What is the purpose of indexing and cross-referencing audit working papers?

8.72   What techniques can auditors use to improve the quality of working paper documentation?

8.73   How can software be used to prepare audit working papers?

SUMMARY

. . . .

The several topics under the heading of "audit planning" started in Chapter 6 with pre-engagement activities, understanding the client's business and industry, obtaining management's draft financial statements and organizing the accounts into cycles for efficient audit work. Chapter 6 also introduced the basic concepts of management assertions and audit objectives. The concepts are part of the theoretical foundation for performing audits. Chapter 7 expanded on the client's information systems, technology and internal controls and the need for the auditor to understand these. All this knowledge of the client comes together to help the auditor to identify significant risks of misstatements and plan how to do the audit.

Chapter 8 continued the series of audit planning topics by explaining several technical tools of planning. These tools are part of the nitty-gritty of audit work. They start with preliminary analytical procedures applied to the client's unaudited financial statements. The analytical process includes getting the financial data, calculating common-size and comparative financial statements, calculating ratios, describing the company's financial activities and asking relevant questions. This analysis enables auditors to look for problem areas and signs of potential misstatement in the financial statements. Detecting signs of problems enables the auditors to plan procedures for the audit program to follow up and to determine whether misstatements, errors, irregularities or frauds have affected the fair presentation of the financial balances.

The technical planning tools include auditors' determination of materiality with relation to the financial statements taken as a whole. Materiality in this sense is defined as the largest amount of uncorrected dollar misstatement that could exist in published financial statements, yet the statements would still fairly present the company's financial position and results of operations in conformity with GAAP. A method of calculating materiality based on judgements about acceptable misstatement was presented to connect income misstatement to earnings-per-share misstatements and an effect on share prices.

Risk assessment is the common language of auditing. The auditor's assessment of business risk was reviewed and related to the conceptual model of audit risk. The audit risk model was explained, and its elements of inherent risk, control risk, detection risk and audit risk were defined. Implications of the risk model were explored in relation to limits on the risks permitted in practical applications. The risk and materiality concepts are important because together they determine the sufficiency of audit evidence to support the audit opinion. The chapter then presented the underlying theory of evidence and its persuasiveness. The fundamental auditing concept of sufficient, appropriate audit evidence and the techniques used to gather it were also explained. Next, the general procedures for obtaining evidence were outlined. This explanation of procedures was enriched with additional notes about the ways in which procedures can be misapplied. Analytical procedures were introduced, and their power was illustrated with some empirical research findings based on actual audit results. The chapter provided a brief preview of audit programs. Programs were categorized as "internal control programs" and "balance audit programs." The illustrations were not complete programs for conducting any particular audit, but they showed the general nature and content of audit programs. We closed this chapter with some basic pointers about the form, content and purpose of audit working papers.

Now the stage is set to pursue a more detailed explanation of the auditor's review and understanding of the client's information systems and the evaluation and testing of internal control. Chapter 9 explains this part of the process of auditing.

MULTIPLE-CHOICE QUESTIONS FOR PRACTICE AND REVIEW

8.74   Analytical procedures are generally used to produce evidence from:
  a. Confirmations mailed directly to the auditors by client customers.
  b. Physical observation of inventories.
  c. Relationships among current financial balances and prior balances, forecasts and nonfinancial data.
  d. Detailed examination of external, external-internal and internal documents.

8.75   Auditors perform analytical procedures in the planning stage of an audit for the purpose of:
  a. Deciding the matters to cover in an engagement letter.
  b. Identifying unusual conditions that deserve more auditing effort.
  c. Determining which of the financial statement assertions are the most important for the client's financial statements.
  d. Determining the nature, timing and extent of audit procedures for auditing the inventory.

8.76   Which of the following match-ups of types of analytical procedures and sources of information makes the most sense?

	Type of Analytical Procedure	Source of Information
a.	Comparison of current account balances with prior-periods statistics	Physical production
b.	Comparison of current account balances with expected balances	Company's budgets and forecasts
c.	Evaluation of current account balances with relation to predictable historical patterns	Published industry ratios
d.	Evaluation of current account balances in relation to nonfinancial information	Company's own comparative financial statements

8.77   Analytical procedures can be used in which of the following ways?
  a. As a means of overall review at the end of an audit.
  b. As "attention directing" methods when planning an audit at the beginning.
  c. As substantive audit procedures to obtain evidence during an audit.
  d. All of the above.

8.78   Analytical procedures used when planning an audit should concentrate on:
  a. Weaknesses in the company's internal control procedures.
  b. Predictability of account balances based on individual transactions.

  c. Five major management assertions in financial statements.
  d. Accounts and relationships that may represent specific potential problems and risks in the financial statements.

8.79   When a company that has $5 million current assets and $3 million current liabilities pays $1 million of its accounts payable, its current ratio will:
  a. Increase.
  b. Decrease.
  c. Remain unchanged.

8.80   When a company that has $3 million current assets and $5 million current liabilities pays $1 million of its accounts payable, its current ratio will:
  a. Increase.
  b. Decrease.
  c. Remain unchanged.

8.81   When a company that has $5 million current assets and $5 million current liabilities pays $1 million of its accounts payable, its current ratio will:
  a. Increase.
  b. Decrease.
  c. Remain unchanged.

8.82   When a company that sells its products for a (gross) profit increases its sales by 15 percent and its cost of goods sold by 7 percent, the cost of goods sold ratio will:
  a. Increase.
  b. Decrease.
  c. Remain unchanged.

8.83   Which of the following is not a benefit claimed for the practice of determining materiality in the initial planning stage of starting an audit?
  a. Being able to fine-tune the audit work for effectiveness and efficiency.
  b. Avoiding the problem of doing more work than necessary (overauditing).
  c. Being able to decide early what kind of audit opinion to give.
  d. Avoiding the problem of doing too little work (underauditing).

8.84   Auditors are not responsible for accounting estimates with respect to:
  a. Making the estimates.
  b. Determining the reasonableness of estimates.
  c. Determining that estimates are presented in conformity with GAAP.
  d. Determining that estimates are adequately disclosed in the financial statements.

8.85   Tolerable misstatement in the context of audit planning means:
  a. Amounts that should be disclosed if they are likely to influence the economic decisions of financial statement users.

b. The largest amount of uncorrected dollar misstatement that could exist in published financial statements, yet they would still fairly present the company's financial position and results of operations in conformity with GAAP.

c. Part of the overall materiality amount for the financial statements assigned to a particular account.

d. A dollar amount assigned to an account as required by auditing standards.

8.86 The risk that the auditors' own work will lead to the decision that material misstatements do not exist in the financial statements, when in fact such misstatements do exist, is:

a. Audit risk.

b. Inherent risk.

c. Control risk.

d. Detection risk.

8.87 Auditors are responsible for the quality of the work related to management and control of:

a. Inherent risk.

b. Relative risk.

c. Control risk.

d. Detection risk.

8.88 The auditors assessed a combined inherent risk and control risk at .67 and said they wanted to achieve a .15 risk of failing to detect misstatements in an account with a material balance. What audit risk are auditors planning to accept for this audit?

a. .20.

b. .10.

c. .75.

d. .05.

8.89 An audit program contains:

a. Specifications of audit standards relevant to the financial statements being audited.

b. Specifications of procedures the auditors believe appropriate for the financial statements under audit.

c. Documentation of the assertions under audit, the evidence obtained and the conclusions reached.

d. Reconciliation of the account balances in the financial statements with the account balances in the client's general ledger.

8.90 When auditing the existence assertion for an asset, auditors proceed from the:

a. Financial statement numbers back to the potentially unrecorded items.

b. Potentially unrecorded items forward to the financial statement numbers.

c. General ledger back to the supporting original transaction documents.

d. Supporting original transaction documents to the general ledger.

8.91 The objective in an auditor's review of credit ratings of a client's customers is to obtain evidence related to management's assertion about:

a. Compliance.

b. Existence.

c. Ownership.

d. Valuation.

8.92 Jones, PA, is planning the audit of Rhonda's Company. Rhonda verbally asserts to Jones that all the expenses for the year have been recorded in the accounts. Rhonda's representation in this regard:

a. Is sufficient evidence for Jones to conclude that the completeness assertion is supported for the expenses.

b. Can enable Jones to minimize his work on the assessment of control risk for the completeness of expenses.

c. Should be disregarded because it is not in writing.

d. Is not considered a sufficient basis for Jones to conclude that all expenses have been recorded.

8.93 The evidence considered most competent by auditors is best described as:

a. Internal documents, such as sales invoice copies produced under conditions of strong internal control.

b. Written representations made by the president of the company.

c. Documentary evidence obtained directly from independent external sources.

d. Direct personal knowledge obtained through physical observation and mathematical recalculation.

8.94 Confirmations of accounts receivable provide evidence primarily about these two assertions:

a. Completeness and valuation.

b. Valuation and ownership.

c. Ownership and existence.

d. Existence and completeness.

8.95 When planning an audit, which of the following is not a factor that affects auditors' decisions about the quantity, type and content of audit working papers?

a. The auditors' need to document compliance with generally accepted auditing standards.

b. The existence of new sales contracts important for the client's business.

c. The auditors' judgement about their independence with regard to the client.

d. The auditors' judgements about materiality.

8.96 An audit working paper that shows the detailed evidence and procedures regarding the balance in the accumulated depreciation account for the year under audit will be found in the:

a. Current file evidence working papers.

b. Permanent file working papers.

c. Administrative working papers in the current file.

d. Planning memorandum in the current file.

8.97 An auditor's permanent file working papers would most likely contain:

a. Internal control analysis for the current year.

b. The latest engagement letter.

c. Memoranda of conference with management.

d. Excerpts of the corporate charter and by-laws.

EXERCISES AND PROBLEMS

• •

8.98 **Analytical Review Ratio Relationships.** The following
LO.1 situations represent errors and irregularities that could
LO.2 occur in financial statements. Your requirement is to
state how the ratio in question would compare (greater,
equal or less) to what the ratio "should have been" had
the error or irregularity not occurred.

a. The company recorded fictitious sales with credits to
sales revenue accounts and debits to accounts receivable. Inventory was reduced and cost of goods sold
was increased for the profitable "sales." Is the current
ratio greater than, equal to or less than what it should
have been?

b. The company recorded cash disbursements paying
trade accounts payable but held the cheques past the
year-end date—meaning that the "disbursements"
should not have been shown as credits to cash and
debits to accounts payable. Is the current ratio
greater than, equal to or less than what it should have
been? Consider cases in which the current ratio
before the improper "disbursement" recording would
have been (1) greater than 1:1, (2) equal to 1:1, and
(3) less than 1:1.

c. The company uses a periodic inventory system for
determining the balance sheet amount of inventory at
year-end. Very near the year-end, merchandise was
received, placed in the stockroom, and counted, but
the purchase transaction was neither recorded nor
paid until the next month. What was the effect on
inventory, cost of goods sold, gross profit and net
income? How were these ratios affected, compared
to what they would have been without the error: current ratio, return on beginning equity, gross margin
ratio, cost of goods sold ratio, inventory turnover and
receivables turnover?

d. The company is loathe to write off customer accounts
receivable, even though the financial vice president
makes entirely adequate provision for uncollectible
amounts in the allowance for bad debts. The gross
receivables and the allowance both contain amounts
that should have been written off long ago. How are
these ratios affected compared to what they would be
if the old receivables were properly written off: current ratio, days' sales in receivables, doubtful account
ratio, receivables turnover, return on beginning
equity, working capital/total assets?

e. Since last year, the company has reorganized its lines
of business and placed more emphasis on its traditional products while selling off some marginal businesses merged by the previous go-go management.
Total assets are 10 percent less than they were last
year, but working capital has increased. Retained
earnings remained the same because the disposals
created no gains, and the net income after taxes is
still near zero, the same as last year. Earnings before
interest and taxes remained the same, a small positive EBIT. The total market value of the company's

equity has not increased, but that is better than the
declines of the past several years. Proceeds from the
disposals have been used to retire long-term debt.
Net sales have decreased 5 percent because the sales
decrease resulting from the disposals has not been
overcome by increased sales of the traditional products. Is the discriminant Z score of the current year
higher or lower than that of the prior year?

8.99 **Auditing an Accounting Estimate.** Suppose management
LO.1 estimated the lower-of-cost-or-market valuation of
LO.2 some obsolete inventory at $99,000, and wrote it down
from $120,000, recognizing a loss of $21,000. The auditors obtained the following information: The inventory in question could be sold for an amount between
$78,000 and $92,000. The costs of advertising and
shipping could range from $5,000 to $7,000.

Required:

a. Would you propose an audit adjustment to the management estimate? Write the appropriate accounting
entry.

b. If management's estimate of inventory market (lower
than cost) had been $80,000, would you propose an
audit adjustment? Write the appropriate accounting
entry.

8.100 **Calculate a Planning Materiality Amount.** The audi-
LO.3 tors were planning the work on the financial statements
of the Mary Short Cosmetics Company. The unaudited
financial statements showed $515,000 net income after
providing an allowance of 35 percent for income taxes.
The company had no debt and no interest expense. Mary
Short's shares are traded over the counter, and investors
have generally assigned a price-earnings multiple of 16
to the shares. Press releases by the company have enabled analysts to estimate the income for the year at
about 515,000, which was forecast by the company at
the beginning of the year. There are 750,000 shares outstanding, and the last quoted price for them was $11.

The auditors have decided that a 6 percent mispricing error in the shares would not cause investors to
change their buying and selling decisions.

Required:

Calculate the "planning materiality" the auditors could
allow, based on the income before income taxes.

8.101 **Audit Risk Model.** Audit risks for particular accounts
LO.4 and disclosures can be conceptualized in this model: Audit risk (AR) = Inherent risk (IR) × Internal control risk
(CR) × Detection risk (DR). Use this model as a framework for considering the following situations and deciding
whether the auditor's conclusion is appropriate.

1. Ohlsen, PA, has participated in the audit of Limberg
Cheese Company for five years, first as an assistant
accountant and the last two years as the senior
accountant. He has never seen an accounting

adjustment recommended. He believes the inherent risk must be zero.

2. Jones, PA, has just (November 30) completed an exhaustive study and evaluation of the internal control system of Lang's Derfer Foods, Inc. (fiscal year ending December 31). She believes the control risk must be zero because no material errors could possibly slip through the many error-checking procedures and review layers used by Lang's.

3. Fields, PA, is lazy and does not like audit jobs in Toronto, anyway. On the audit of Hogtown Manufacturing Company, he decided to use detail procedures to audit the year-end balances very thoroughly to the extent that his risk of failing to detect material errors and irregularities should be 0.02 or less. He gave no thought to inherent risk and conducted only a very limited review of Hogtown's internal control system.

4. Shad, PA, is nearing the end of a "dirty" audit of Allnight Protection Company. Allnight's accounting personnel all resigned during the year and were replaced by inexperienced people. The controller resigned last month in disgust. The journals and ledgers were a mess because the one computer specialist was hospitalized for three months during the year. Shad thought thankfully, "I've been able to do this audit in less time than last year when everything was operating smoothly."

8.102 General Audit Procedures and Financial Statement
LO.5 **Assertions.** The six general audit procedures produce
LO.6 evidence about the principal management assertions in financial statements. However, some procedures are useful for producing evidence about certain assertions, while other procedures are useful for producing evidence about other assertions. The assertion being audited may influence the auditors' choice of procedures.

Required:
Prepare a two-column table with the six general procedures listed on the right. Opposite each one, write the management assertions most usefully audited by using each procedure.

8.103 Financial Assertions and Audit Objectives. You were
LO.6 engaged to audit the financial statements of Karachi Company for the year ended December 31, 20x1.

On June 1, 20x1 Karachi initiated a product warranty program to help it stay competitive with other companies in its industry. The warranty covers parts, labour and shipping to repair any defect within one year of purchase.

During 20x1 Karachi paid $50,000 in warranty costs on product sales of $4,000,000 (approximately 80,000 units). Based on this, management estimates its warranty liability at December 31 is $80,000.

Required:
What are the audit objectives for the audit of the estimated warranty liability?

Approach:
Develop specific assertions related to warranty liability based on the five general assertions.

8.104 Appropriateness of Evidence and Related Parties.
LO.6 Johnson & Company, PAs, audited the Guaranteed Trust Company. M. Johnson had the assignment of evaluating the collectibility of real estate loans. Johnson was working on two particular loans: (1) a $4 million loan secured by the Smith Street Apartments and (2) a $5.5 million construction loan on the Baker Street Apartments now being built. The appraisals performed by the Guaranteed Appraisal Partners, Inc., showed values in excess of the loan amounts. Upon enquiry, Mr. Bumpus, the trust company vice president for loan acquisition, stated: "I know the Smith Street loan is good because I myself own 40 percent of the partnership that owns the property and is obligated on the loan."

Johnson then wrote in the working papers: (1) the Smith Street loan appears collectible; Mr. Bumpus personally attested to knowledge of the collectibility as a major owner in the partnership obligated on the loan, (2) the Baker Street loan is assumed to be collectible because it is new and construction is still in progress, (3) the appraised values all exceed the loan amounts.

Required:
a. Do you perceive any problems with related party involvement in the evidence used by M. Johnson? Explain.
b. Do you perceive any problems with M. Johnson's reasoning or the appropriateness of evidence used in that reasoning?

8.105 Relative Appropriateness of Evidence. The third gen-
LO.6 erally accepted standard of audit fieldwork requires that auditors obtain sufficient appropriate evidential matter to afford a reasonable basis for an opinion regarding the financial statements under examination. In considering what constitutes sufficient appropriate evidential matter, a distinction should be made between underlying accounting data and all corroborating information available to the auditor.

Required:
What presumptions can be made about:
a. The relative appropriateness of evidence obtained from external and internal sources.
b. The role of internal control with respect to internal evidence produced by a client's data processing system.
c. The relative persuasiveness of auditor observation and recalculation evidence compared to the external, external-internal and internal documentary evidence.

(AICPA adapted)

8.106 Relative Appropriateness of Evidence.
LO.6 1. Classify the following evidential items by type (direct knowledge, external and so on), and rank them in order of appropriateness:
a. Amounts shown on monthly statements from creditors.

b. Amounts shown on "paid on account" in the accounts payable register.

c. Amount of "discounts lost expense" computed by the auditor from unaudited supporting documents.

d. Amounts shown in letters received directly from creditors.

2. Classify the following evidential items by type (direct knowledge, external and so on), and rank them in order of appropriateness.

a. Amounts shown on a letter received directly from an independent bond trustee.

b. Amounts obtained from minutes of board of directors' meetings.

c. Auditors' computation of bond interest and amortization expense when remaining term and status of bond are audited.

d. Amounts shown on cancelled cheques.

8.107 Audit Procedures. Auditors frequently refer to the
LO.6 terms *standards* and *procedures*. Standards deal with measures of the quality of performance. Standards specifically refer to the generally accepted auditing standards expressed in the Statements on Auditing Standards. Procedures specifically refer to the methods or techniques used by auditors in the conduct of the examination. Procedures are also expressed in the Statements on Auditing Standards.

Required:

List seven different types of procedures auditors can use during an audit of financial statements and give an example of each.

8.108 Confirmation Procedure. A PA accumulates various
LO.7 kinds of evidence on which to base the opinion on financial statements. Among this evidence are confirmations from third parties.

Required:

a. What is an audit confirmation?

b. What characteristics of the confirmation process and the recipient are important if a PA is to consider the confirmation evidence competent?

8.109 Audit Procedure Terminology. Identify the types of
LO.6 procedures(s) employed in each situation described below (vouching, tracing, recalculation, observation and so on):

1. An auditor uses audit software to select vendors' accounts payable with debit balances and compares amounts and computation to cash disbursements and vendor credit memos.

2. An auditor examines property insurance policies and checks insurance expense for the year. The auditor then reviews the expense in light of changes and ending balances in capital asset accounts.

3. An auditor uses audit software to test perpetual inventory records for items that have not been used in production for three months or more. The client states that the items are obsolete and have already been written down. The auditor checks journal entries to support the client's statements.

4. An auditor tests cash remittance advices to see that allowance and discounts are appropriate and that receipts are posted to the correct customer accounts in the right amounts and reviews the documents supporting unusual discounts and allowances.

5. An auditor watches the client take a physical inventory. A letter is also received from a public warehouser stating the amounts of the client's inventory stored in the warehouse. The company's cost flow assumption, FIFO, is then tested by the auditor's computer software program.

8.110 Audit Working Papers. The preparation of working pa-
LO.8 pers is an integral part of a PA's audit of financial statements. On a recurring engagement, PAs review their audit programs and working papers from their prior audit while planning the current audit to determine usefulness for the current-year work.

Required:

a. (1) What are the purposes or functions of audit working papers? (2) What records may be included in audit working papers?

b. What factors affect the PA's judgement of the type and content of the working papers for a particular engagement?

c. To comply with generally accepted auditing standards, a PA includes certain evidence in his or her working papers; for example, "evidence that the audit was planned and work of assistants was supervised and reviewed." What other evidence should a PA include in audit working papers to comply with generally accepted auditing standards?

d. How can a PA make the most effective use of the preceding year's audit programs in a recurring audit?

(AICPA adapted)

8.111 Potential Audit Procedure Failures. For each of the
LO.6 general audit procedures of (*a*) recalculation, (*b*) physical observations, (*c*) confirmation (accounts receivable, securities or other assets), (*d*) verbal enquiry, (*e*) examination of internal documents, and (*f*) scanning, discuss one way the procedure could be misapplied or the auditors could be misled in such a way as to render the work (audit evidence) misleading or irrelevant. Give examples different from the examples in Chapter 8.

8.112 Working Paper Review. The schedule in Exhibit
LO.8 8.112–1 was prepared by the controller of World Manufacturing, Inc., for use by the independent auditors during their examination of World's financial statements. All procedures performed by the audit assistant were noted in the bottom "Legend" section, and it was initialled properly, dated and indexed, and then submitted to a senior member of the audit staff for review. Internal control was reviewed and is considered to be satisfactory.

Required:

a. What information essential to the audit of marketable securities is missing from the schedule?

b. What essential audit procedures were not noted as having been performed by the audit assistant?

Approach:

Write specific assertions based on the five general assertions, then look to the working paper for documentation of evidence related to each one.

(AICPA adapted)

EXHIBIT 8.112-1 MARKETABLE SECURITIES (World Manufacturing, Inc., year ended December 31, 20X2)

Description of Security			Serial No.	Face Value of Bonds	General Ledger 1/1	Purchased in 20X2	Sold in 20X2	Cost	General Ledger 12/31	12/31 Market	Dividend and Interest		
											Pay Date(s)	Amt. Received	Accruals 12/31
Corp. Bonds	%	Yr. Due											
											1/15	300**b,d**	
A	6	09	21-7	10,000	9,400**a**				9,400	9,100	7/15	300**b,d**	275
D	4	03	73-0	30,000	27,500**a**				27,500	26,220	12/1	1,200**b,d**	100
G	9	06	16-4	5,000	4,000**a**				4,000	5,080	8/1	450**b,d**	188
R**c**	5	03	08/2	70,000	66,000**a**		57,000**b**	66,000			7/1	5,000**b,d**	5,000
S**c**	10	07	07-4	100,000		100,000**e**			100,000	101,250			5,000
					106,900	100,000	57,000	66,000	140,900	141,650		7,250	5,563
					a,f	**f**	**f**	**f**	**f,g**	**f**		**f**	**f**
Stocks													
											3/1	750**b,d**	
P 1,000 shs Common			1,044		75,00**a**				7,500	7,600	6/1	750**b,d**	
											9/1	750**b,d**	
											12/1	750**b,d**	250
											3/1	750**b,d**	
U 50 shs Common			8,530		9,700**a**				9,700	9,800	2/1	800**b,d**	
											8/1	800**b,d**	667
					17,200				17,200	17,400		4,600	917
					a,f				**f,g**	**f**		**f**	**f**

Legends and comments relative to above:

a = Beginning balances agreed to 20X1 working papers.
b = Traced to cash receipts.
c = Minutes examined (purchase and sales approved by the board of directors).
d = Agreed to general ledger entry to income account.
e = Confirmed by tracing to broker's advice.
f = Totals footed.
g = Agreed to general ledger.

DISCUSSION CASES

· ·

8.113 Planning, Inherent and Control Risk, Manufacturing Business. Darter Ltd. is a medium-sized business involved in manufacturing and assembling consumer electronic products such as DVD players, radios and satellite receivers. It is privately owned. Its minority shareholders requested that the annual financial statements be audited for the first time this year. Your firm is engaged to do the current year's audit. You are now reviewing Darter's preliminary general ledger trial balance in order to begin preparing the planning memorandum. Consider the following accounts that appear in this trial balance:

LO.2
LO.3

> Cash
> Inventory, finished goods
> Inventory, work-in-progress
> Inventory, unassembled components
> Inventory, spare parts
> Property, plant and equipment
> Deferred development costs
> Goodwill
> Accounts payable
> Warranty provision
> Bank loan, long term
> Share capital, common shares
> Retained earnings
> Revenue
> Cost of goods sold
> General and administration expense

Required:

a. Evaluate the inherent risk for each of the above accounts. Give the reasons that support your assessment and state any assumptions you need to make.

b. How will inherent risk level relate to the types of controls that Darter's management implements for each of these accounts? Consider costs and benefits of implementing effective controls.

c. For each account describe the procedures you would use to assess the control risk.

d. How would you expect the company's accounts to differ and how would your inherent risk assessment differ if the company's business was:

- an iron mine
- a piano manufacturer
- a bank
- a shipping line

8.114 Materiality. Your firm has done the audit of Rhea Fashions Inc. for many years. You are in charge of the fieldwork for the current year's audit. Rhea is a manufacturer of high fashion clothing. Its shares are publicly traded, but a majority of the common shares are held by the members of the family that started the business during the 1950s. During the current year, Rhea's business shrank substantially because of losing a major customer, a country-wide department store chain that went out of business. Rhea has not been able to replace the lost business. Since many of Rhea's long-time employees were happy to take an early retirement offer, Rhea management's strategy now is to continue to operate only a few unique clothing brands that represented about 50 percent of its sales volume in prior years. The materiality level used in the prior years was $80,000. The audit partner has determined that the appropriate materiality for the current year is $40,000.

LO.2
LO.3

Required:

a. Discuss the factors that the audit partner would have considered in deciding to reduce the materiality level.

b. What impact will the lower materiality level likely have on your audit procedures in the current year?

c. While reviewing the previous year's audit file, you note that last year's staff uncovered one error. Rhea had failed to accrue approximately $50,000 of customer volume discounts due to a calculation error in computing the customer's total sales. Since the error was less than materiality, no adjustment was made to the prior year's financial statements. Explain the impact this error had on the prior year's financial statements, the impact it will have on the current year's financial statements when it reverses and on your audit, given your new materiality level.

Kingston Case questions related to Chapter 8 are on the Online Learning Centre that accompanies this text.

APPENDIX 8A

SELECTED FINANCIAL RATIOS

. . . .

Balance Sheet Ratios	Formula*
Current ratio	$\dfrac{\text{Current assets}}{\text{Current liabilities}}$
Days' sales in receivables	$\dfrac{\text{Ending net receivables}}{\text{Credit sales}} \times 360$
Doubtful account ratio	$\dfrac{\text{Allowance for doubtful accounts}}{\text{Ending gross receivables}}$
Days' sales in inventory	$\dfrac{\text{Ending inventory}}{\text{Cost of goods sold}} \times 360$
Debt ratio	$\dfrac{\text{Current and long-term debt}}{\text{Shareholder equity}}$

Operations Ratios	
Receivables turnover	$\dfrac{\text{Credit sales}}{\text{Ending net receivables}}$
Inventory turnover	$\dfrac{\text{Cost of goods sold}}{\text{Ending inventory}}$
Cost of goods sold ratio	$\dfrac{\text{Cost of goods sold}}{\text{Net sales}}$
Gross margin ratio	$\dfrac{\text{Net sales} - \text{Cost of goods sold}}{\text{Net sales}}$
Return on beginning equity	$\dfrac{\text{Net income}}{\text{Shareholder equity (beginning)}}$

Financial Distress Ratios (Altman, 1968)	Formula*
(X_1) Working capital ÷ Total assets	$\dfrac{\text{Current assets} - \text{Current liabilities}}{\text{Total assets}}$
(X_2) Retained earnings ÷ Total assets	$\dfrac{\text{Retained earnings (ending)}}{\text{Total assets}}$
(X_3) Earnings before interest and taxes + Total assets	$\dfrac{\text{Net Income} + \text{Interest expense} + \text{Income tax expense}}{\text{Total assets}}$
(X_4) Market value of equity ÷ Total debt	$\dfrac{\text{Market value of common and preferred shares}}{\text{Current liabilities and long-term debt}}$
(X_5) Net sales ÷ Total assets	$\dfrac{\text{Net sales}}{\text{Total assets}}$
Discriminant Z score (Altman, 1968)	$1.2 \times X_1 + 1.4 \times X_2 + 3.3 \times X_3 + 0.6 \times X_4 + 1.0 \times X_5$

*These ratios are shown to be calculated using year-end, rather than year-average, numbers for such balances as accounts receivable and inventory. Other accounting and finance reference books may contain formulas using year-average numbers. As long as no dramatic changes have occurred during the year, the year-end numbers can have much audit relevance because they reflect the most current balance data. For comparative purposes, the ratios should be calculated on the same basis for all the years being compared. In the Anycompany example in Exhibits 8–2 and 8–3, the market value of the equity in the calculations is $3 million.

The discriminant Z score is an index of a company's "financial health." The higher the score, the more healthy the company. The lower the score, the closer financial failure approaches. The score that predicts financial failure is a matter of dispute. Research suggests that companies with scores above 3.0 never go bankrupt. Generally, companies with scores below 1.0 experience financial difficulty of some kind. The score can be a negative number. It should be stressed that these ratios are indicators only, and therefore need to be combined with in-depth analysis before any final conclusions can be reached.

CHAPTER

9

Internal Control Evaluation and Testing

Chapter 9 describes the activities involved in internal control evaluation, thus highlighting the role of control risk assessment and testing in planning the audit. Major themes from the earlier chapters in Part II—understanding the client's business and risks, as well as its information systems and controls that generate the financial statements—are carried forward into this chapter. In Chapter 9 these planning activities, concepts, and tools are used to identify and evaluate key controls that can detect or prevent material misstatements. Management assertions and their related audit objectives are applied to identify specific control risks in the client's information systems and processes, and indicate the objectives of the client's control procedures. These control objectives are thus used to assess the strengths and weaknesses in the client's internal control systems. The control strengths and weaknesses guide the auditor's plans on whether to test control procedures.

LEARNING OBJECTIVES

After completing this chapter, you will be able to:

1 Explain how the auditor's understanding of the client's business, information systems, technology, and controls plays a role in control evaluation and planning the audit.

2 Explain why the auditor evaluates a client's internal controls.

3 Distinguish between management's and the auditor's responsibility regarding a company's internal controls.

4 Define seven internal control objectives, relating them to the five management assertions in financial account balances.

5 Document accounting systems, identify controls and weaknesses, and write key control tests for an audit program.

6 Outline the auditor's responsibility when internal control evaluation work detects or indicates a high risk of fraudulent misstatement.

7 Explain reasonable assurance and cost-benefit in the context of control risk assessment and development of the audit approach.

*8 Compare and contrast these approaches to auditing information systems: auditing around the computer; auditing through the computer with computer-assisted audit techniques (CAATs); and auditing with the computer using generalized audit software (GAS).

*9 Apply the reasonable assurance concept and cost-benefit analysis to control risk assessment in a small business.

*Learning objectives marked with an asterisk (*) and their corresponding topics are considered advanced material.

Note: Appendices 9A, 9B, and 9C are located on the text Online Learning Centre.

INTERNAL CONTROL AND THE AUDIT PLAN

Internal control evaluation and control risk assessment are essential components of every financial statement audit and must be considered in planning the audit work. Generally accepted auditing standards emphasize internal control in the second examination standard: "The auditor should obtain an understanding of the entity and its environment, including internal control, sufficient to identify and assess the risks of material misstatement of the financial statements whether due to fraud or error, and sufficient to design and perform further audit procedures."[1] The CICA and IFAC describe the controls relevant to the audit.[2] The standards specify the extent of the auditors' work necessary to understand the client's controls related to significant risks[3] and to assess the risk of material misstatement.[4] When substantive audit procedures alone cannot provide sufficient appropriate audit evidence regarding significant risks of misstatement, the auditor may need to rely on the operating effectiveness of controls. When controls are relied on as a source of audit evidence, sufficient appropriate evidence should be obtained by testing these controls to corroborate the control assessment.

UNDERSTANDING THE ROLE OF SYSTEMS IN CONTROL EVALUATION

LEARNING OBJECTIVE

1 Explain how the auditor's understanding of the client's business, information systems, technology and controls plays a role in control evaluation and planning the audit.

When planning an audit of financial statements, auditors apply their knowledge of the client's business, risks, systems and controls to understand the impact of how a client produces financial information. The information systems and IT used in the client's significant accounting processes influence the nature, timing and extent of audit procedures. Significant accounting processes are those relating to accounting information that can materially affect the financial statements. Important matters to consider include the extent of IT use, complexity of IT operations, organizational structure of IT, availability of data, use of CAATs and the need for specialized skills. These issues are explained in detail in the following sections.

---

[1] *CICA Handbook,* paragraph 5100.02.
[2] Ibid., paragraphs 5141.047–.053 and ISA 315.
[3] Ibid., paragraph 5141.114.
[4] Ibid., paragraph 5141.101.

Extent of IT Use

The extent to which IT is used in each significant accounting process needs to be considered in planning the nature, timing and extent of audit procedures. When IT is used to process significant accounting applications, the audit team needs IT skills to understand the flow of these transactions. The nature, timing and extent of audit procedures may also be affected by the level of computer use. Historically, certain accounting applications like payroll, accounts receivable, accounts payable and inventory were the first business processes to be computerized. IT applications are now so pervasive that virtually every transaction is automated. In fact, the accounting applications are often a relatively small component of the enterprise's overall information system. The following box is an example of the types of integrated systems available to small and medium enterprises at the time of writing this text.

ERPs for Small- and Medium-Sized Business

Exact Software is a leading player in the European mid-market for enterprise resource planning systems and has recently been gaining momentum in North America. It entered the market with the purchase of a number of ERP systems, including Macola, JobBOSS, MAX and Alliance/ MFG. Headquartered in the Netherlands, it operates in more than 60 countries and has upwards of 180,000 customers and 2,000 employees worldwide, including about 450 across North America. The company has offices in both Montreal and Cambridge, Ont.

Exact took a different approach than many of its competitors with the release of e-Synergy a couple of years ago. This Web-based product runs on Microsoft Internet Explorer and includes customer relationship management, e-commerce and portals, as well as project, human resource, workflow, event and document/knowledge management. These are often called front-office applications, while financials, distribution and production are considered back office. What makes eSynergy so interesting is that it is a powerful CRM system in its own right and is tightly integrated with Exact's back-office systems. Since the front and back offices share one database (Microsoft SQL Server), you have no integration issues and all of your information is kept up to the second — in real time. When prospects respond to an e-mail and enter their personal information, the system updates the contact database. You can check for duplicates and add or merge the information. A workflow request is sent to the appropriate people for followup. When a customer places an order, the pricing used in the back-office system also appears on the website. The system offers a centralized view of all customers and their activities (workflow, etc.) from anywhere, anytime. Customers, suppliers and partners can also manage their accounts through secure portals.

Exact offers several choices for the back office, including Exact Globe Enterprise, which is just being introduced to North America. Globe has extensive functionality, including financials, distribution, light manufacturing, MRP and project management. Exact is targeted to small- and medium-sized businesses with $10 million to $50 million in revenue, as well as manufacturing and distribution companies and divisions of multinationals—a great potential market. The Globe product (including e-Synergy, general ledger, accounts receivable, accounts payable, distribution, order processing, inventory control and purchasing) costs $25,000, plus $1,500 per named user. For production, you'll pay another $25,000. You can also buy e-Synergy as a standalone system for $10,000, plus $1,500 per named user. The e-Synergy product does not make a lot of sense as a standalone solution unless your organization is focused on services and has no need for an ERP system. For manufacturers and distributors, the biggest advantage lies in the sharing of one database with the back-office system. But if you are looking for a tightly integrated back office or are currently using one of Exact's ERP systems, e-Synergy just might be your ticket.

Source: Adapted from Michael Burns, "Exact Ready for Takeoff," *CA Magazine*, August 2005, p. 18. Reproduced by permission from CA Magazine, published by the Canadian Institute of Chartered Accountants, Toronto, Canada.

Complexity of IT Operations

The complexity of the client's IT operations refers to factors such as the hardware configuration in place and the degree to which various systems share common files or are otherwise integrated. Another factor is the availability of transaction trails, as these may be available only in computer-readable form for short periods and possibly in a complex form. When assessing the complexity of computer processing, the auditor should consider his training and experience with information processing methods used by the client. If significant accounting applications are processed at outside service centres, it may be necessary to coordinate audit procedures with service auditors. (Refer to Chapter 16 for a discussion of service auditors.)

These factors affect the type and timing of audit evidence gathering activities, and need to be considered in audit planning.

Organizational Structure of IT

Clients can differ greatly in their approaches to organizing their information systems. The degree of centralization inherent in the organizational structure is the main factor that may vary. A highly centralized organizational structure generally will have all significant computer processing activities controlled and supervised at a central location. The control environment, the hardware and operating systems would be uniform throughout the company. Auditors may be able to obtain most of the necessary knowledge about information systems and processing by visiting the central location. At the other extreme, a highly decentralized organizational structure generally allows various departments, divisions, subsidiaries or geographical locations to develop, control and supervise information systems autonomously. In this situation the computer hardware and software usually will not be uniform throughout the company. Thus, auditors may need to visit many locations to obtain the necessary audit information.

The number of people in the company involved in operating the information systems and their levels of relevant IT knowledge are important audit considerations for assessing segregation of functions and control risk.

Availability of Data

Input data, system-generated files and other data required by the audit team may exist only for short periods or only in computer readable form. In some systems hard-copy input documents may not exist at all because information is entered directly. The data retention policies adopted by a client may require auditors to arrange for certain information to be retained for audit purposes. Also, auditors may need to plan to perform certain audit procedures at an interim date while the information is still available.

Certain information generated by the computer system for management's internal purposes may allow the auditors to perform analytical procedures. For example, the information system may report sales information by month, by product and by salesperson. These information details can be analyzed to determine whether the income statement amounts are reasonable and to identify risk areas in the business operations. These procedures can be included in the audit program and provide audit evidence if the reliability of the details can be verified.

Use of CAATs

Computer-assisted audit techniques (CAATs) may be used to increase the efficiency of certain audit procedures and also may provide auditors with opportunities to apply certain procedures to an entire population of accounts or transactions. There are two main categories of CAATs: (1) audit software and (2) test data. The use of these techniques requires advance planning and may require individuals with specialized IT skills as members of the audit team. These techniques are explained further later in this chapter.

Need for Specialized Skills

To determine the need for specialized IT skills, all aspects of a client's computer processing should be considered. In planning the engagement, the audit manager may conclude that certain specialized skills are needed to consider the effect of computer processing on the audit, to understand the flow of transactions or to design and perform audit procedures. For example, specialized skills relating to various methods of data processing, programming languages, software packages, or CAATs may be needed. Audit team members should possess sufficient IT knowledge to know when to call on specialists and to understand and supervise their work.

REVIEW
CHECKPOINTS

9.1   How does the extent to which information systems are computerized affect audit planning?

9.2   What impact does it have on the audit if the transaction trails in a client's system are only available in machine-readable form for a limited period?

9.3   How does the client's use of an outside service organization to process accounting information affect planned audit procedures?

9.4   List several aspects of the client's information systems and IT that indicate the need for an IT specialist on the audit team.

9.5   If a client has organized its information systems in a decentralized structure, what impact will this have on performing the audit?

9.6   What factors in the client's systems indicate audit work may need to be performed at an interim date?

REASONS FOR CONTROL EVALUATION

LEARNING OBJECTIVE

2 Explain why the auditor evaluates a client's internal controls.

Internal control is defined as:

> the process designed and effected by those charged with governance, management, and other personnel to provide reasonable assurance about the achievement of the entity's objectives with regard to reliability of financial reporting, effectiveness and efficiency of operations and compliance with applicable laws and regulations. It follows that internal control is designed and implemented to address identified business risks that threaten the achievement of any of these objectives.[5]

Control risk is the risk that internal control will fail to prevent or detect a material financial statement misstatement. In the business risk approach, the auditor's main goal is to assess the risk of the financial statements being misstated, and assessing inherent and control risks is a key step in performing this assessment. The standards do not give a specific definition of control risk, and allow for inherent and control risk assessments to be combined since they are closely related. For example, consider an item with high inherent risk, such as an inventory of Rolex watches in a jewelry business. The inherent risk is high because these items are easy to pick up and conceal, have a high dollar value and are easy to 'fence' (sell illegally). The auditor expects management to have a variety of strong controls in place to protect the business against these risks. If this were not the case, it is unlikely that the company could survive. So, the auditor will expect to observe the implementation of effective and continuous controls over the Rolex inventory in the business in management's risk assessment process. If this is not found, it would pose a significant risk and further procedures would be required to address the risk that the inventory is materially misstated.

---

[5] Ibid., paragraph 5141.042.

Control risk is a characteristic of the client's internal control. The auditors' task is to assess it; that is, to assign an evaluation to it. Many auditors conclude their internal control risk assessment decisions with descriptive assessments (e.g., high, moderate, low), and some auditors put probability numbers on them (e.g., 1.0, 0.50, 0.30).

The role of internal control evaluation in the audit is one of the more difficult topics in an audit course. Perhaps the easiest way to understand this role is to imagine two extreme types of audit situations, the "clean" audit and the "dirty" audit. In a **clean audit**, the accounting records are easy to verify and accurate. In a dirty audit, however, the accounting records may be incomplete, riddled with misstatements, and harder to verify. Most people find it intuitive that a clean audit should require less work than a dirty audit. The controls are most likely to be good in a clean audit because good controls, by definition of their objectives, should result in low risk of material misstatement. Conversely, a dirty audit is normally associated with poor or nonexistent controls. So, one reason auditors evaluate internal controls is because they are a good indicator of the accuracy of the accounting records and therefore reduce the amount of work needed to verify their accuracy more directly. Thus, evaluation of internal controls can create efficiencies in clean audits because it can result in reliance on controls, and thus less substantive work.

It is not just for efficiency purposes, however, that auditors rely on controls. There may be risks of misstatements that substantive procedures alone cannot remove. For example, one of the assertions, completeness, is virtually impossible to verify without some minimal reliance on controls. It is by relying on controls to some minimal extent that the auditors get sufficient assurance on whether items that they might not know about, such as accrued liabilities, get recorded. Since it is difficult for auditors to verify items that they might not know about, some level of control reliance is required to get enough assurance on the completeness assertion for these items. There are situations where controls are so bad, leading to such a dirty audit situation, that the client is not auditable. An example of such an extreme situation is given in the following box. This box illustrates that control risks are so great that the auditor cannot develop compensating audit procedures to reduce the risk of material misstatement to an acceptable level. This extreme case is a fairly rare occurrence. In many cases, if controls are weak, more substantive procedures can be performed to provide sufficient evidence about whether the financial statements contain a material error.

Understanding the Auditability of the Accounts
Bad Books Block Audit for Municipal Government

This story illustrates how there can be situations where the accounts are not auditable because of lack of controls.

Officials of a municipal government kept such poor financial records for four non-profit corporations they controlled that the PA appointed to audit the corporations reported to the municipal Council that the audits could not be done. The four corporations were conduits for more than $630 million in low-interest financing that the municipal government provides to local businesses. A public inquiry was called to investigate and report on the situation. The PA declared to the inquiry that the four corporations records were beyond horrid, in fact he found there were virtually no records at all.

Among the inquiry's findings were: (1) no records were kept of purchase and redemption of certificates of deposit for hundreds of thousands of dollars, (2) there may be certificates of deposit that the municipal officials do not know exist, (3) bank statements were not kept, (4) chequing accounts were not reconciled.

The former treasurer of the corporations reported to the inquiry that the corporations used a very simple bookkeeping system. Money went in and went out. The system wasn't sophisticated because it wasn't needed.

The primary reason for assessing control risk and evaluating a company's internal control is to give the auditors a basis for planning the audit and determining the nature, timing and extent of audit procedures in the account balance audit program. Note that this means the auditor's primary concern with regard to internal controls is the impact controls have on safeguarding the company's assets and the accuracy of the accounting records (accounting controls). This is the basis on which the auditors have prepared a preliminary audit program and have ideas about the work they want to do, including the extreme possibility of concluding that the client may not be auditable. This preliminary program might be last year's audit program or an off-the-shelf "standard program" that will need to be modified on the basis of client-specific preliminary analytical review findings, materiality and risk assessments. Exhibit 9-1 outlines the process.

In business risk based audits, as explained in Chapters 6 and 7, the auditor begins the preliminary risk evaluation by understanding the general controls associated with the overall

EXHIBIT   9-1   ROLE OF INTERNAL CONTROL IN ASSESSING RISK OF MATERIAL MISSTATEMENT

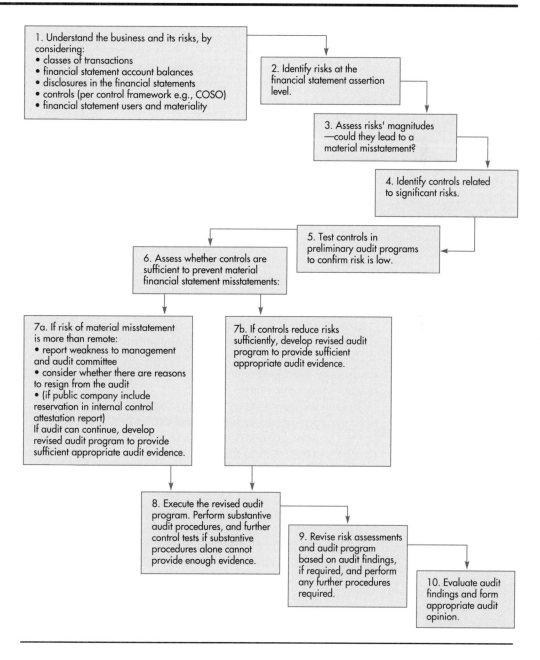

control environment, management's risk assessment process, the processes and related information systems and communication and the monitoring procedures in place. A framework such as the COSO one presented in Chapter 6 can be used, or the auditor may choose another accepted framework to guide this evaluation. The auditor will use this to identify any significant risks, then evaluate whether effective controls are in place to address them. The auditor also evaluates control activities—the more specific procedures that are used to control processes, applications and transactions.

Examining the business processes and related accounting cycles provides a structure for the auditor to consider how to design audit procedures to test controls and financial statement transactions and balances. Tests of controls are performed if it would be less costly to obtain the audit evidence this way, or if there is a need to rely on control to get sufficient appropriate audit evidence about one or more assertions. Often, auditors will try to design dual purpose tests, these are tests of controls that also provide substantive evidence. For example, a control test that involves vouching that all payments have been properly authorized could be extended to trace each payment to the cash records and the general ledger, to provide evidence that the correct amount was captured in the accounting system.

REVIEW CHECKPOINTS

9.7   Why does the auditor evaluate the client's internal controls?

9.8   Why does an inventory of Rolex watches have a high inherent risk and why does the auditor expect management to have strong controls over this inventory?

9.9   What are two ways auditors use to describe their control risk assessments?

9.10   What is the impact on audit work in a "clean" audit as compared to a "dirty" audit?

9.11   Why can it be efficient for the auditor to rely on internal controls?

9.12   If internal controls are weak, in what situations could an audit still be done and in what situations would it not be possible to do an audit?

How Control Risk Assessment Affects the Audit Program

The auditor's control risk assessment will affect the procedures to be included in the audit program. As explained in Chapter 8, an audit program is a list of specific audit procedures designed to produce evidence about the assertions in financial statements. Each procedure should have identifiable characteristics of nature, timing and extent, as well as a direct association with one or more financial statement assertions. The nature of procedures refers to the six general techniques: computation, confirmation, enquiry, inspection, observation and analysis. The timing of procedures is a matter of when they are performed: at "interim" before the balance sheet date or at "year-end" shortly before and after the balance sheet date. The extent of procedures refers to the amount of work done when the procedures are performed.

Exhibit 9-2 shows part of an audit program; it lists five procedures for auditing two of the accounts receivable assertions. These procedures are part of an account balance audit program. The existence and completeness subheadings and the columns in the exhibit help you to see the connections to financial statement assertions and to the nature, timing and extent of the procedures.

The procedures presented in Exhibit 9-2 reflect auditor decisions about the timing and extent of work that suggest the auditor has assessed control risk to be low, specifically:

- confirmation of a sample of customer accounts receivable before year-end, instead of confirmation of all accounts as of December 31
- vouching the last 5 days' recorded sales to bills of lading for cutoff evidence, instead of vouching the last 15 days' sales
- tracing the last 5 days' shipments to recorded sales invoices for cutoff evidence, instead of tracing the last 15 days' shipments

EXHIBIT 9-2   ACCOUNTS RECEIVABLE BALANCE-AUDIT PROGRAM (PARTIAL ILLUSTRATION)

Assertions/Procedures	Nature	Timing	Extent
Existence/Cutoff: Accounts receivable are authentic obligations owed to the company and represent sales made before December 31.			
1. Obtain a trial balance of customers' accounts. Select 75 for positive confirmation.	Confirmation	November 1 (interim date)	Limited sample
2. Obtain a year-end trial balance of customer accounts. Compare to the November 1 trial balance and investigate significant changes by vouching large increases to sales invoices and bills of lading.	Analytical procedures Document vouching	December 31 (year-end)	All customer accounts
3. Select all the sales invoices recorded in the last five days of the year, and vouch to bills of lading for December shipping date.	Document vouching	December 31 (year-end)	Last five days' sales
Completeness/Cutoff: Accounts receivable include all amounts owed to the company at December 31.			
4. Send positive confirmations to customers with zero balances.	Confirmation	December 31 (year-end)	All zero balance accounts
5. Select all the bills of lading dated in the last five days of the year, and trace to sales invoices recorded in December.	Document tracing	December 31 (year-end)	Last five days' shipments

You should assume the auditors think the preceding program is an efficient one. A different program would be more appropriate if the risk of financial statement misstatement were higher because of control weaknesses. It would probably take more time and cost more, too. For example, it would require the auditor to: (1) confirm all the customer accounts as of December 31; (2) omit the analytical comparison of the December accounts receivable trial balance because the confirmation was done as of December 31; (3) select all the sales invoices recorded in the last 15 days for vouching to December bills of lading; (4) send positive confirmations to customers with small balances and zero balances; and (5) select all bills of lading dated in the last 15 days for tracing to December sales invoices. (Note that in this higher risk situation, more substantive evidence is needed to provide assurance about whether or not there is a material financial statement misstatement.)

The preliminary audit program presented in Exhibit 9-2, therefore, depends on a low control risk related to the company's internal control structure. The audit task is to assess the inherent and internal control risks that there is a material misstatement (error or irregularity) in the accounts receivable total due to the improper or omitted recording of sales and customer invoices. If the risks are too high, some procedures may need to be changed to provide for greater extent (larger samples) and better timing (confirmation moved to December 31). Likewise, if the risk of omitted sales is not high, the confirmation of zero-balance receivables might be omitted, or negative confirmations might be used instead of positive confirmations. In general, a good system of internal control should result in less audit work than a bad system of internal control. Thus, it is possible to obtain audit efficiencies from good internal controls: less testing and spreading the audit work out over more convenient times.

REVIEW CHECKPOINTS

9.13 How does the auditor's control risk assessment affect the preliminary audit program?

9.14 What audit planning activities are performed to lead up to the control risk evaluation?

9.15 Give two reasons why controls would be tested.

9.16 In what situation(s) would controls not be tested?

Communicating Internal Control Weaknesses

A responsibility that arises from the auditor's internal control evaluation is the requirement to make the audit committee or equivalent aware of all significant weaknesses in internal control. *CICA Handbook*, paragraph 5141.121 requires the auditor to report weaknesses to an appropriate level of management; this is usually at least one level above the level of the managers responsible for the controls found to be deficient. In addition, *CICA Handbook,* section 5750, "Communication with Management of Matters Identified During the Financial Statement Audit," and *CICA Handbook,* section 5751 "Communications with Those Having Oversight Responsibility for the Financial Reporting Process," require the communication of (1) nontrivial misstatements, (2) fraud, and (3) consequential illegal or possibly illegal acts. Neither section requires communication in writing; however, auditors usually summarize and communicate any serious control weaknesses uncovered during the normal performance of the audit to management in a **management letter**.[6] We will call the contents of management letters **reportable matters** and define these as items the auditor believes should be communicated to the client in writing.

As of the time of writing this text, we know that auditors are not obligated to provide assurance for reportable matters and significant weaknesses to outside users. When they do communicate these matters to management, a copy of the letter, or a memorandum of the oral report if reported orally, should be placed in the working papers. Also, because the potential for misinterpretation is great, section 5750 recommends that even if no reportable conditions are found in the audit, a carefully worded report should be prepared stating that no specific matters were noted during the audit, as shown in the box below.

EXAMPLE OF MANAGEMENT LETTER COMMUNICATION WHEN THERE ARE NO REPORTABLE CONDITIONS

The objective of my audit was to obtain reasonable assurance that the financial statements were free of material misstatement and was not designed for the purpose of identifying matters to communicate. Accordingly my audit would not usually identify all such matters that may be of interest to you and it is inappropriate to conclude that no matters exist.

During the course of my audit of _____ for the year ended _____ I did not identify any of the following matters: misstatements, other than trivial errors; fraud; misstatements that may cause future financial statements to be materially misstated; illegal or possibly illegal acts, other than ones considered inconsequential; or significant weaknesses in internal control.

This communication is prepared solely for the information of management and is not intended for any other purpose. I accept no responsibility to a third party who relies on this communication.

Source: CICA *Handbook*, section 5750.18.

New requirements for public companies' management to issue reports on their internal controls and for their auditors to issue opinions on these will expand public company auditors' responsibilities to communicate the results of their internal control evaluation work. These new requirements were covered in Chapter 3,

For some financial institution regulators, auditors also have a "well-being" reporting requirement that includes reporting on significant internal control weaknesses, as described in CICA Guideline AuG–17. The matters that need to be reported are shown in the box following.

---

[6] For example, see S. Smith's article, "More Than a Drop in the Bucket," in *CA Magazine*, February 1993, pp. 50–52.

EXAMPLES OF REPORTABLE CONDITIONS IN FEDERAL INSTITUTIONS LEGISLATION

- significant weaknesses in internal control, or transactions or events that create risks potentially jeopardizing the institution's ability to continue as a going concern
- going concern uncertainties that require disclosure or change in accounting basis
- reservations in the auditor's opinion
- indicators of lack of good faith by management
- contraventions of legislated capital requirements

Source: CICA Guideline AuG–17, *Transactions or Conditions Reportable Under the Well-Being Reporting Requirement in Federal Institutions Legislation.*

R E V I E W
C H E C K P O I N T S

9.17   What is a reportable condition regarding internal control?

9.18   What are the auditor's reporting responsibilities when a material internal control weakness is found during the audit?

MANAGEMENT VERSUS AUDITOR RESPONSIBILITY FOR CONTROL

LEARNING OBJECTIVE

3 Distinguish between management's and auditors' responsibility regarding a company's internal controls.

A company's management must deal with rapidly shifting economic and competitive conditions and changes in customer demand, and it must respond to these changes to ensure survival and growth. Management puts internal controls in place to keep the company on course toward achieving its goals, and to help anticipate changes that can affect their plans. In this dynamic and risky environment, internal controls help management to improve operating efficiency, minimize risks of asset loss, enhance the reliability of financial statements and monitor compliance with laws and regulations. This broad concept of internal control is exemplified by the definition set out by COSO in the following box.

COSO INTERNAL CONTROL DEFINITION

Internal control is broadly defined as a process, effected by an entity's board of directors, management and other personnel, designed to provide reasonable assurance regarding the achievement of objectives in the following categories:

- Effectiveness and efficiency of operations.
- Reliability of financial reporting.
- Compliance with applicable laws and regulations.

The first category addresses an entity's basic business objectives, including performance and profitability goals and safeguarding of resources. The second relates to the preparation of reliable published financial statements, including interim and condensed financial statements and selected financial data derived from such statements, such as earnings releases, reported publicly. The third deals with complying with those laws and regulations to which the entity is subject. These distinct but overlapping categories address different needs and allow a directed focus to meet the separate needs.

> Internal control systems operate at different levels of effectiveness. Internal control can be judged effective in each of the three categories, respectively, if the board of directors and management have reasonable assurance that they understand the extent to which the entity's operations objectives are being achieved, published financial statements are being prepared reliably, and applicable laws and regulations are being complied with.
>
> While internal control is a process, its effectiveness is a state or condition of the process at one or more points in time. In small and mid-size companies controls may be less formal and less structured than in large companies, yet a small company can still have effective internal control.
>
> Source: "COSO Definition of Internal Control," Executive Summary of the COSO Internal Control Integrated Framework, Committee of Sponsoring Organizations of the Treadway Commission, 1992, page 3.

Management must balance the costs of controls with the benefit of risk reduction. At some point, the costs will exceed the benefits because it is not possible to reduce risks to zero. Managers need to decide what level of risk is acceptable. If they understate the risks in an attempt to cut costs, or through ignorance or poor analysis, this becomes a source of control risk.

External auditors are not responsible for designing effective internal control for audit clients. They are responsible for evaluating existing internal controls and assessing the risk of a material misstatement related to them. They use this assessment to determine the audit work required to support their opinion and develop appropriate audit programs. PAs may be involved in designing internal control systems as consulting engagements for nonaudit clients. Such design work must be separate and apart from an audit engagement because it could impair the PA's objectivity in assessing those controls for audit purposes. This is a threat to auditor independence.

External auditors' communications of reportable conditions and material weaknesses are intended to help management carry out its responsibilities for internal control monitoring and change. However, external auditors' observations and recommendations are usually limited to external financial reporting matters. External auditors' basis for knowing about reportable conditions and material weaknesses comes from their familiarity with the types of errors, frauds and misstatements that can occur in any account balance or class of transactions. Clearly, hundreds of innocent errors and not-so-innocent fraud schemes are possible. (Many of these are discussed in Chapter 17, on Fraud Awareness Auditing.) Instead of trying to learn hundreds of possible errors and frauds, it is better to start with seven general categories. Exhibit 9-3 shows these seven categories, with some examples. The external auditors' task of control risk assessment involves finding out what the company does to

EXHIBIT 9-3 GENERAL CATEGORIES AND EXAMPLES OF MISSTATEMENTS

1. Invalid transactions are recorded: Fictitious sales are recorded and charged to nonexistent customers.
2. Valid transactions are omitted from the accounts: Shipments to customers never get recorded.
3. Unauthorized transactions are executed and recorded: A customer's order is not approved for credit, yet the goods are shipped, billed and charged to the customer without requiring payment in advance.
4. Transaction amounts are inaccurate: A customer is billed and the sale is recorded in the wrong amount because the quantity shipped and the quantity billed are not the same and the unit price is for a different product.
5. Transactions are classified in the wrong accounts: Sales to a subsidiary company are recorded as sales to outsiders instead of intercompany sales, or the amount is charged to the wrong customer account receivable record.
6. Transaction accounting is incomplete: Sales are posted in total to the accounts receivable control account, but some are not posted to individual customer account records.
7. Transactions are recorded in the wrong period: Shipments made in January (next year) are backdated and recorded as sales and charges to customers in December; shipments in December are recorded as sales and charges to customers in January.

prevent, detect and correct these potential errors and irregularities. You will encounter the flip side of these when you study control objectives later in the next section.

R E V I E W
C H E C K P O I N T S

9.19   List the responsibilities of management regarding their company's internal control.

9.20   Why does management have to trade off between costs and benefits of internal controls?

9.21   How does management's cost-benefit trade-off decision affect control risk?

9.22   What are auditors' responsibilities in relation to a client's internal controls?

9.23   Why is being involved in designing internal controls considered a risk to auditor independence?

9.24   How do external auditors help managers meet their responsibilities for internal control?

9.25   Define control risk and list seven general categories of misstatements that controls are intended to prevent, detect, or correct.

CONTROL OBJECTIVES AND PROCEDURES

LEARNING OBJECTIVE

4 Define seven internal control objectives, relating them to the five management assertions in financial account balances.

The objective of control procedures is to process transactions correctly. Correctly processed transactions produce accurate account balances, which in turn help produce reliable assertions in the financial statements. These connections are shown in Exhibit 9-4. The exhibit gives an example of two revenue transaction streams, sales invoicing and cash receipts, and links these to the control objectives that the internal control system must meet. These control objectives are then linked to the impact of these transaction streams on the resulting Accounts Receivable account balance. Correct processing of sales invoices increases this balance and correct processing of cash receipts reduces it. If all the control objectives are met, the final account balance should be reliable, and all the assertions it contains should hold true.

Control Objectives

Note that each of the control objectives is the flip side of each of the seven errors and irregularities shown in Exhibit 9-3. Exhibit 9-4 summarizes each of the seven objectives, with a

EXHIBIT   9–4   CONTROL OBJECTIVES AND FINANCIAL STATEMENT ASSERTIONS

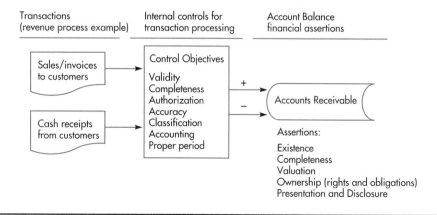

general statement of the objective and a specific example for the revenue transaction process. The explanations that follow tell you some more about these objectives and give some examples of client procedures designed to accomplish them.

Validity refers to ensuring that recorded transactions are ones that should have been recorded, i.e., they really "exist." The client's procedure can be to require matching of shipping documents with sales invoices before a sale is recorded. This procedure is supposed to prevent the recording of undocumented (possibly fictitious) sales.

Completeness refers to ensuring that valid transactions are not omitted entirely from the accounting records. If sales are represented by shipments, then every shipment should be matched with a sales invoice. Transaction documents (e.g., shipping documents) are often prenumbered. Accounting for the numerical sequence of prenumbered shipping documents is a control procedure designed to achieve the completeness objective.

Authorization refers to ensuring that transactions are approved before they are recorded, i.e., they are "owned" by the company. Credit approval for a sale transaction is an example. Management must establish criteria for recognizing transactions in the accounting system and for supervisory approval of transactions. A control system should allow only authorized transactions to be processed and should stop any unauthorized transactions from entering the accounting records.

Sometimes, you may need to ponder the nature of authorization for certain transactions. For example, what "authorization" is needed to record a cash receipt? Usually none—companies are happy to accept payments—but a sales manager may need to approve a good customer taking a discount after the discount period has elapsed. Even so, if the auditor finds unauthorized transactions of any kind have been processed this is a source of risk that the auditor needs to understand. For example, recording unauthorized cash receipts may be part of a fraud cover-up or an illegal money laundering scheme.

Authorization may be delegated to a fairly low level of management for routine transactions. For example, (1) all shipments amounting to more than $1,000 in value require credit approval, (2) all sales can be recorded in the accounting department upon receipt of a copy of a shipping document and (3) the receptionist's listing of payments received on account when the mail is opened may be sufficient authorization to accept and record cash receipts. Some authorizations have to come from a high level of the company's governance structure, such as the board of directors. For example, significant nonroutine transactions like sales of major assets and acquisition of another business, or responsibility for signing the company name to a loan agreement usually will be authorized specifically in the minutes of a board of directors' meeting.

Accuracy refers to ensuring that dollar amounts are calculated correctly. A manual or computer check that the quantity invoiced equals the quantity shipped and the correct list price is used, with correct multiplication and addition of the total, is a control procedure for accuracy.

Classification refers to ensuring that transactions are recorded in the right accounts, charged or credited to the right customers (including classification of sales to subsidiaries and affiliates, as mentioned in Exhibit 9-5), entered in the correct segment product line or inventory description, and so forth. Classification errors between balance sheet and income statement accounts present the greatest risk of misstatement because they will change the net income. For example, before its bankruptcy WorldCom misstated its income by misclassifying operating expenses as assets, concealing its poor financial performance from financial statement users.

Accounting is a general category concerned with ensuring that the accounting process for a transaction is performed completely and in conformity with GAAP. For example, a clerk can balance the total of individual customers' receivables with the control account to determine whether all charges and credits to the control account also have been entered in individual customers' accounts. Another example is a bank reconciliation done by a person who is independent of cash recording. Balancing and reconciliation procedures like these can meet more than one control objective. Control over accounting, in general, is a useful category if you cannot identify a control problem in one of the other categories.

EXHIBIT   9-5   INTERNAL CONTROL OBJECTIVES

Objectives	General	Specific Example (revenue process)
Validity	Recorded transactions are valid and documented.	Recorded sales are supported by invoices, shipping documents and customer orders.
Completeness	All valid transactions are recorded, and none are omitted.	All shipping documents are prenumbered and matched with sales invoices daily.
Authorization	Transactions are authorized according to company policy.	Credit sales over $1,000 are given prior approval by the credit manager.
Accuracy	Transaction dollar amounts are properly calculated.	Sales invoices contain correct quantities and are mathematically correct.
Classification	Transactions are properly classified in the accounts.	Sales to subsidiaries and affiliates are classified as intercompany transactions.
Accounting	Transaction accounting is complete.	All sales on credit are charged to customers' individual accounts.
Proper period	Transactions are recorded in the proper period.	Sales of the current period are charged to customers in the current period, and sales of the next period are charged in the next period.

Proper period refers to ensuring that the accounting for transactions is in the period in which they occur. This control objective relates to the cutoff aspect of the existence and completeness assertions. Procedurally, the client's accountants must be alert to the dates of transactions in relation to month-, quarter-, and year-end. Proper period accounting (cutoff) is a pervasive problem. You will see it mentioned in relation to all kinds of transactions— sales, purchases, inventories, expense accruals, income accruals and others. The risk of errors occurring in cutoff is high because they are complex and nonroutine events. Cutoff errors are also risky because they can be used to manipulate income, for example, by using accruals to record sales too early or expenses too late.

Control Objectives and Assertions

The control objectives are closely connected to management's assertions in financial statements. For example, the accuracy control objectives can be viewed as reflecting the principal assertions existence and completeness in that mechanical errors will result in either overstating or understating balances. However, thinking of the control objective in terms of assessing accuracy is more helpful in designing appropriate tests, for example, tests for errors of billing at too low or high a price or for a smaller or larger quantity than shipped. Accuracy errors can also affect the valuation assertion, for example, if price lists in U.S. dollars are used when the financial statement information should be in Canadian dollars.

Exhibit 9-6 shows how the control objectives are related to with the five assertions. The Xs in the exhibit show the primary relevance of control objectives to assertions. To interpret Exhibit 9-6, link the achievement of control objectives with the probability that an assertion may be materially misstated. For example, if a company has strong control over the validity of recorded sales and cash receipts transactions, if it has an effective system of credit authorization and if it ensures that sales transactions are correctly recorded in the proper period, then the control risk related to the existence/occurrence assertions for accounts receivable and sales balances may be assessed to be low.

However, an auditor may find that some, but not all, of the control objectives for a particular account balance (i.e., set of assertions) are achieved. For example, the situation cited above may coexist with failure to achieve control over the completeness of recording sales transactions and accounts receivable amounts. In such a case, the preliminary audit program

EXHIBIT   9-6   HOW CONTROL OBJECTIVES RELATE TO FINANCIAL STATEMENT ASSERTIONS

Control Objectives	*Financial Statement Assertions*				
	Existence, Occurrence	Completeness	Valuation	Ownership (rights and obligations)	Presentation and Disclosure
Validity	X			X	
Completeness		X		X	
Authorization	X		X	X	
Accuracy			X		
Classification					X
Accounting					X
Proper Period	X	X			

may be changed to require more work related to the completeness of accounts receivable (the assertion for which control risk is high) and be unchanged for the work on the existence of accounts receivable (the assertion for which control risk is low).

The final evaluation of a company's internal control is the assessment of the control risk (CR) related to each assertion. Control risk is the CR element in the audit risk model: $AR = IR \times CR \times DR$ (as explained in Chapter 8). This assessment is an auditor's expression of the effectiveness of the control system for preventing, detecting and correcting specific errors and irregularities in management's financial statement assertions.

REVIEW CHECKPOINTS

9.26   Why do control procedures affect financial statement assertions?

9.27   List the control objectives and the misstatement risk that each one relates to.

9.28   Why can some authorization procedures be performed by low-level managers? What kinds of authorizations need to come from the board of directors?

9.29   What are the risks related to cutoff procedures?

9.30   Match the seven control objectives to the five financial statement assertions

9.31   Can control risk be high for one assertion and low for another assertion for the same account balance? Explain.

9.32   How does the auditors control risk assessment relate to audit risk?

PHASES OF A CONTROL EVALUATION

LEARNING OBJECTIVE

5 Document accounting systems, identify key controls and weaknesses and write key control tests for an audit program.

The following sections describe the process of control evaluation in three phases:

- understanding control
- evaluating control risk
- testing controls

A major goal in audits is to be efficient. This means performing the work in minimum time and cost while still doing high-quality work to obtain sufficient, appropriate evidence. The allocation of work times between control evaluation and "substantive audit work" (e.g., the procedures in Exhibit 9-2) is a cost-benefit trade-off. Generally, the more auditors know about good controls, the less substantive year-end work they need to do. However, auditors do not necessarily need to evaluate or test the entire internal control structure. They need to understand it well enough to assess whether there are any significant risks of material misstatement so they can plan the other audit work.

If there are significant risks and certain controls are essential to prevent or detect these risks, those would be key controls. It is necessary to evaluate the key controls by testing their effectiveness during the audit period in order to ensure that material misstatements are unlikely to exist in the financial statements. For many nonkey controls auditors may only obtain a minimum understanding, and then rely primarily on substantive audit work on the financial statement balance or transactions. In some cases the risk of misstatement in a particular financial statement account is very low, they can perform very little substantive work. Some examples of transaction processing risks and the importance of controls in the audit are provided in the following box.

EXAMPLES	CONTROL IMPORTANCE (KEY VS. NONKEY)
The business processes a high volume of cash sales transactions through retail stores (e.g. Canadian Tire). There is a significant risk that not all sales will be recorded.	Controls over sales completeness will be considered key controls because a material misstatement could occur and there is no other reliable substantive procedure that auditors can use to verify that all sales have been recorded. If these are absent it would present a material risk of misstatement.
The inventory controller performs a monthly variance analysis to ensure production costs are staying within budget. There is a risk that avoidable cost overruns will occur if timely action is not taken when variances from budget occur.	Because the auditor plans to obtain evidence at year-end by extensive inventory valuation testing, controls over monthly production costs would be considered nonkey.
The company's petty cash fund of $200 is kept in a locked box by the receptionist, who must present valid signed receipts for all expenditures to the controller when the fund runs low. The controller authorizes the payables manager to issue a cheque to "cash" to replenish the fund back up to $200. There is a risk that petty cash funds will be misappropriated.	The controls here—reconciliation, supervision and segregation—are nonkey because the auditor plans to scrutinize the petty cash expenditure records for the whole year and expects the total value of these transactions to be immaterial. Thus there is no need to evaluate these controls. If a material amount of expenditures is found to have been processed through petty cash, this may suggest a fraud and this possibility will need to be investigated substantively. In either case, these controls will not relevant to the audit work planned.

This concept of a trade-off between costs of evaluating internal control and costs of substantive audit tests is simplified in the graph in Exhibit 9-7. The graph shows that if the auditor decides to obtain a high level of assurance from relying on controls, the costs of control evaluation and testing will be high, but should be offset by lower costs for substantive testing as less substantive evidence is required. On the other hand, if the auditor decides not to obtain a high level of assurance from testing controls, costs of control evaluation will be lower, but substantive testing will cost more because more work will need to be done to verify that the accounts are not misstated. An efficient audit program will try to use the combination of control evaluation and substantive work with the lowest total cost for each significant account balance and transaction stream.

The three phases of control evaluation work are described as if they are separate and distinct programs that are completed before any substantive audit work is started. In practice, work on the phases is overlapping. The distinction between the understanding phase and the control risk assessment phase is made to help you to comprehend the purpose of this part of

EXHIBIT 9-7   AUDIT COST TRADE-OFF

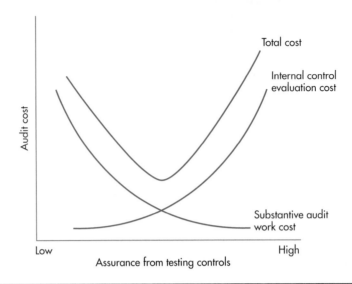

the audit work. However, most auditors in practice do the two together, since the purpose of understanding the controls is to assess control risk. The understanding and assessment can both involve control testing. For example, auditors may learn more about the existence and operating effectiveness of controls when they start to actually try to test them. The control evaluation phases can also overlap with substantive work. For example, account balance audit work may done at an interim date (before the company's fiscal year-end), at the same time some of the control evaluation work is being done. However, the three phases described here are a simple way to explain the analytical thinking that auditors follow to decide on the best approach for collecting sufficient appropriate audit evidence to support their opinion.

R E V I E W
CHECKPOINTS

9.33   Why is there a cost-benefit trade-off involved in evaluating internal controls for planning the audit?

9.34   What is a key control? Give a specific example.

9.35   What is a nonkey control? Give a specific example.

9.36   Why do key controls always need to be evaluated in an audit?

PHASE 1: UNDERSTANDING THE INTERNAL CONTROL

Nature and Timing of Phase 1 Work

The Phase 1 obtaining-an-understanding work is done early in the engagement. Understanding controls is a key component of understanding the business and risk of misstatement that we covered in Chapters 6 and 7. Now in Phase 1 we apply this understanding to identify significant risks in account balances, transaction streams and disclosures. These risks will indicate key controls that the client should have in place to minimize them. Phase 1 gives auditors an overall acquaintance with the control environment, the flow of transactions through the accounting system, and the effectiveness of some control procedures. It should produce general knowledge of the control environment along these lines:

- managers' and directors' attitudes and actions regarding control
- the client's organizational chart and personnel assignments
- the segregation of functional responsibilities
- methods used to communicate responsibility and authority
- methods used to monitor and supervise the accounting system and the control procedures and to control access to assets and documents
- the work assignments of internal auditors, if any

It should also produce general knowledge of the flow of transactions through the accounting system as follows:

- the various classes of significant accounting transactions
- the types of material errors and irregularities that could occur
- methods by which each significant class of transaction is:
  - authorized and initiated
  - documented and recorded
  - processed in the accounting system
  - placed in financial reports and disclosures

Auditors obtain an understanding of the internal controls through several sources of information. These sources include (1) previous experience with the company as found in last year's audit, (2) responses to enquiries directed to client personnel, (3) inspection of documents and records, and (4) observation of activities and operations made in a "walk-through" of one or a few transactions. Such "walk-through" tests of one transaction have traditionally been used to verify the accuracy of the auditor's narrative or flowchart description of the system.

Documentation of the Control Elements

Working paper documentation should include records showing the audit team's understanding of the internal controls. The understanding can be summarized in the form of questionnaires, narratives, and flowcharts.

The decision on how much reliance to place on controls and how much to place on substantive work should also be documented by a memorandum explaining the underlying reasons, i.e., to increase effectiveness and efficiency. This is helpful for future reference in next year's audit.

Internal Control Questionnaire and Narrative

The most efficient means of gathering evidence about internal control is to conduct a formal interview with knowledgeable managers, using a checklist type such as the **internal control questionnaire** illustrated in Exhibit 9-8. This questionnaire is organized under headings that identify the questions related to the control environment general controls, and the questions related to each of the seven control objectives. If you are assigned to create a questionnaire, using these seven categories helps to ensure the questionnaire will cover all the assertions.

Internal control questionnaires are designed to help the audit team obtain evidence about the control environment and about the accounting and control procedures that are considered good error-checking routines. Answers to the questions, however, should not be taken as final and definitive evidence about how well control actually functions. Evidence obtained through the interview-questionnaire process is hearsay evidence because its source is generally an individual who, while knowledgeable, may not be the person who actually performs the control work. This person may give answers that reflect what he or she believes the system should be, rather than what it really is. The person may be unaware of informal ways in which duties have been changed or may be innocently ignorant of the system details. Nevertheless, interviews and questionnaires are useful as a starting point. If a manager admits to a weak control, it is important to document and follow up in subsequent audit work.

A strong point about questionnaires is that an auditor is less likely to forget to cover some important point. Questions usually are worded so that a "no" answer points out some weakness or control deficiency, thus making analysis easier.

EXHIBIT 9-8   INTERNAL CONTROL QUESTIONNAIRE—SALES TRANSACTION PROCESSING

Client _____   Audit Date _____

Client Personnel Interviewed _____

Auditor _____   Date Completed _____

Reviewed by _____   Date Reviewed _____

Question	NA	Yes	No	Remarks
Environment and General Controls Related to Sales Transaction Processing				
1. Is the credit department independent of the marketing department?				
2. Are nonroutine sales of the following types controlled by the same procedures described below? Sales to employees, COD sales, disposals of property, cash sales and scrap sales.				
Assertion-based Control Evaluation				
Validity Objective				
3. Is access to sales invoice blanks restricted?				
4. Are prenumbered bills of lading or other shipping documents prepared or completed in the shipping department?				
Completeness Objective				
5. Are sales invoice blanks prenumbered?				
6. Is the sequence checked for missing invoices?				
7. Is the shipping document numerical sequence checked for missing bills of lading numbers?				
Authorization Objective				
8. Are all credit sales approved by the credit department prior to shipment?				
9. Are sales prices and terms based on approved standards?				
10. Are returned sales credits and other credits supported by documentation as to receipt, condition, and quantity and approved by a responsible officer?				
Accuracy Objective				
11. Are shipped quantities compared to invoice quantities?				
12. Are sales invoices checked for error in quantities, prices, extensions and footing, freight allowances and checked with customer's orders?				
13. Is there an overall check on arithmetic accuracy of period sales data by a statistical or product-line analysis?				
14. Are periodic sales data reported directly to general ledger accounting independent of accounts receivable accounting?				
Classification Objective				
15. Does the accounting manual contain instructions for classifying sales?				
Accounting Objective				
16. Are summary journal entries approved before posting?				
Proper Period Objective				
17. Does the accounting manual contain instructions to date sales invoices on the shipment date?				

One way to tailor these enquiry procedures to a particular company is to write a narrative description of each important control subsystem. Such a narrative would simply describe all the environmental elements, the accounting system and the control procedures. The narrative description may be efficient in audits of small businesses or simple systems within larger organizations.

Accounting and Control System Flowcharts

Another method for documenting auditors' understanding of accounting and control systems is to construct a flowchart. Many control-conscious companies will have their own flowcharts, usually prepared by internal auditors, and the external auditors can use them instead of constructing their own. Flowcharting is used widely by auditors. The advantages of flow-charts can be summarized by an old cliché: "A picture is worth a thousand words." Flowcharts can enhance auditors' evaluations, and annual updating of a chart is relatively easy—simply add or delete symbols and lines.

Construction of a flowchart takes time because an auditor must learn about the operating personnel involved in the system and gather samples of relevant documents. Thus, the information for the flowchart, like the narrative description, involves a lot of legwork and observation. When the flowchart is complete, however, the result is an easily evaluated, informative description of the system. Flowcharting software, is available that may save time or produce more readable output.

Exhibit 9-9 contains a few simple flowchart symbols. For any flowcharting application, the chart must be understandable to an audit supervisor. She should not need to consult a lengthy index of symbols to decipher a flowchart. A flowchart should be drawn with a template and ruler or with computer software. A messy chart is hard to read. The starting point

EXHIBIT   9-9   STANDARD FLOWCHART SYMBOLS

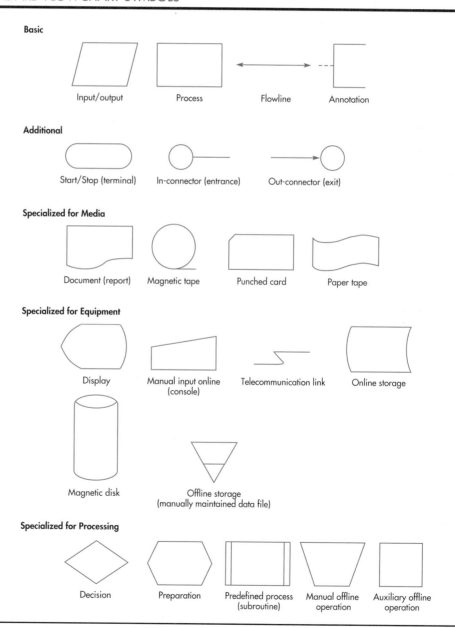

in the system should, if possible, be placed at the upper left-hand corner. The flow of procedures and documents should be from left to right and from top to bottom, as much as is possible. Narrative explanations should be written on the face of the chart as annotations or be written in a readily available reference key.

The flowchart should communicate all relevant information and evidence about segregation of responsibilities, authorization and accounting and control procedures in an understandable, visual form. Exhibit 9-10 contains a flowchart representation of the beginning stages of a sales and delivery processing system. This is a partial flowchart. The outconnectors shown by the circled A and B indicate continuation on other flowcharts. Ultimately, the flowchart ends showing entries in accounting journals and ledgers.

In Exhibit 9-10 you can see some characteristics of flowchart construction and some characteristics of this accounting system.[7] One general rule is to minimize the number of flow lines that cross each other.

By reading down the columns headed for each department, you can see that transaction initiation authority (both credit approval and sales invoice preparation) and custody of assets are separated. Notice that all documents have an intermediate or final resting place in a file. (Some of these files are in the flowcharts connected to A and B.) This flowchart feature gives auditors information about where to find audit evidence later.

EXHIBIT 9-10   CREDIT APPROVAL AND SALES PROCESSING, SHIPMENT AND DELIVERY

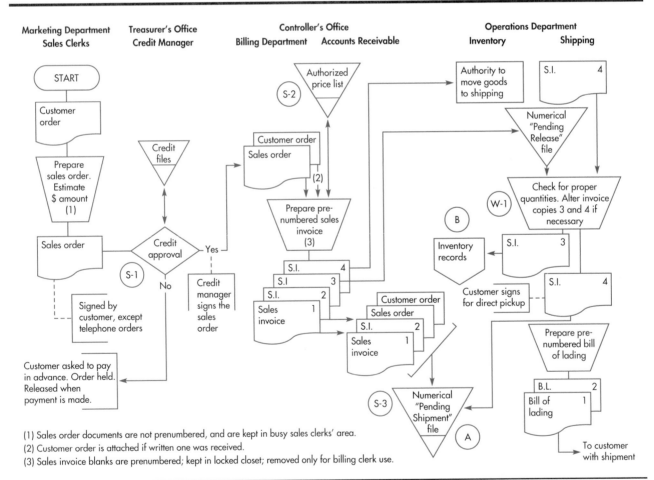

(1) Sales order documents are not prenumbered, and are kept in busy sales clerks' area.
(2) Customer order is attached if written one was received.
(3) Sales invoice blanks are prenumbered; kept in locked closet; removed only for billing clerk use.

---

[7] Accounting firms have various methods for constructing flowcharts. The illustrations in this book take the approach of describing an accounting subsystem completely. Some accounting firms use more efficient methods to flowchart only the documents, information flows, and controls considered important for the audit.

Technology has helped to automate the flowcharting process. Workflow charting software now available allows businesses to describe their processes, integrate various processes and automate routine management activities. An advertisement for one such product being marketed at the time of writing is in the following box, which illustrates a software tool available to chart business processes and integrate information systems. As new regulations like SOX expand the requirements for companies to document their controls, tools like these will be developed to help businesses to comply.

Regardless of the method used to develop the flowchart, an important way of verifying the accuracy of the flowchart is to perform a "walk through" test of the documents and procedures to verify that they are processed in the manner described in the flowchart. An understanding of the flow of transactions through the accounting system is required to support the design of substantive audit procedures. Gaining the understanding of the flow of transactions for each significant accounting application begins with referring to the client's description of the accounting processes. Descriptions could include user's manuals and instructions, file descriptions, system flowcharts and narrative descriptions.

The audit team may find that internal audit personnel or other client personnel already have prepared documentation relating to the flow of transactions. This documentation may be adequate for purposes of understanding the accounting system. Early in the audit planning, the internal auditors and other client personnel should be consulted to determine whether they have documentation that can be useful.

This section concludes with a brief overview of how internal controls affect audit strategy.[8]

1. All audit engagements involve some minimal reliance on internal controls, even if only on environmental controls affecting all cycles (for example, reconciliation of general ledger to subsidiary ledgers). Note: Under section 5141 and GAAS, section 5100, auditors are required to understand internal controls in order to assess the risk of material misstatement for all audits.

2. Internal control is documented through narratives, questionnaires and flowcharts. These are corroborated through "walk-through" tests or tracing of a representative transaction.

3. In reaching a preliminary evaluation of internal control, the auditor must consider:
   (a) possible errors that may arise
   (b) the controls that exist to prevent or detect those errors
   This requires application of professional judgment after obtaining the knowledge in point 2 above.

4. The review, preliminary evaluation and documentation must be applied to specific internal controls within an individual accounting process. The specific controls activities, not the entire system as a whole, are tested for reliability. Only the specific controls on which auditors intend to rely need to be tested.

5. If the auditor wishes to rely on internal controls as a component of audit evidence, tests of control need to be planned and executed. The decision to test the controls is a function of:
   (a) the evaluation of the design of the system
   (b) the cost-benefit tradeoffs of compliance testing, assuming the design is adequate

In summary, if the auditor decides not to test internal controls then there is no reduction in the extent of substantive audit procedures. This is referred to as the substantive audit approach. If, on a preliminary basis, the auditor does decide to test internal controls, and the tests confirm that the controls are operating effectively, then the auditor may reduce the extent of substantive audit procedures. Finally, in the case where the auditor cannot obtain sufficient appropriate audit evidence on the basis of substantive tests alone, testing controls and finding them to be effective can increase the evidence sufficiency to an acceptable level to support the audit opinion. These last two approaches are referred to as the combined audit approach, and also would be consistent with the integrated audit approach called for by the new internal control audits and reports required by SOX 404 and PCAOB regulations in the U.S. and proposed CICA standards as discussed previously.

---

[8] Adapted from J.M. Sylph, "How Internal Controls Affect Audit Strategy," *CA Magazine*, January 1983, pp. 47–51.

R E V I E W
C H E C K P O I N T S

9.37   What does the auditor need to understand about the client's control environment?

9.38   What does the auditor need to understand about the flow of transactions in the client's information systems?

9.39   What source of information can auditors used to gain knowledge about the client's internal controls?

9.40   What internal control documentation needs to be included in the audit files?

9.41   Why is audit file documentation required for the auditor's decision on whether to rely on controls in the audit planning?

9.42   What is an internal control questionnaire used for?

9.43   What is an internal control system narrative and what is it used for in an audit?

9.44   What is the purpose of an internal control systems flowchart? How does it differ from a narrative?

9.45   Why do some clients have documentation of their internal control system?

9.46   What is a walk-through and why is this procedure used in an audit?

9.47   What role can internal auditors play in internal control system documentation?

9.48   What is a substantive audit approach and how does it differ from a combined audit approach?

PHASE 2: ASSESSING THE CONTROL RISK

After Phase 1—obtaining an understanding of the internal control and making a preliminary decision on an audit approach—the audit team assesses the control risk. Control risk assessment involves:

- identifying specific control objectives based on the types of misstatements that may be present in significant accounting applications

- identifying the points in the flow of transactions where specific types of misstatements could occur

- identifying specific control procedures designed to prevent or detect misstatements

- identifying the control procedures that must function to prevent or detect misstatements

- evaluating the design of control procedures to determine whether it suggests the client has strong control procedures in place and whether it may be cost effective to test these controls as part of the audit

A useful assessment technique is to analyze control strengths and weaknesses. **Strengths** are specific features of effective control procedures that would prevent, detect or correct material misstatements. **Weaknesses** are the lack of controls in particular areas that would allow material errors to get by undetected.

The auditors' findings and preliminary conclusions on control strengths and weaknesses should be written up for the working paper files. Strengths and weaknesses can be documented in a working paper called a **bridge working paper**, so called because it connects (bridges) the control evaluation to subsequent audit procedures. The major strengths and weaknesses apparent in the flowchart (Exhibit 9-10) can be summarized as shown in the bridge working paper in Exhibit 9-11. On the flowchart the strengths are indicated by S-, and the weakness by W-. In Exhibit 9-11 the "audit program" column contains test of controls procedures for auditing the control strengths and suggestions about substantive account balance audit procedures related to the weaknesses (the last column in Exhibit 9-11).

EXHIBIT 9-11 BRIDGE WORKING PAPER

Index _____   By _____ Date _____
                         Reviewed _____ Date _____

KINGSTON COMPANY
Credit Approval, Sales Processing, Shipment and Delivery Control
December 31, 20X2

	Strength/Weakness	Audit Implication	Audit Program
S-1	Credit approval on sales order.	Credit authorization reduces risk of bad debt loss and helps check on validity of customer identification.	Select a sample of recorded sales invoices, and look for credit manager signature on attached sales order.
S-2	Unit prices are taken from an authorized list.	Prices are in accordance with company policy, minimizing customer disputes.	Using the S-1 sample of sales invoices, vouch prices used thereon to the price lists.
S-3	Sales are not recorded until goods are shipped.	Cutoff will be proper and sales will not be recorded too early.	Using the S-1 sample of sales invoices, compare the recording date to the shipment date on attached bill of lading or copy 4. (Also, scan the "pending shipment" file for old invoices that might represent unrecorded shipments.)
W-1	Shipping personnel have transaction alteration (initiation) authority to change the quantities on invoices, as well as custody of the goods.	Dishonest shipping personnel can alone let accomplices receive large quantities and alter the invoice to charge them for small quantities. If this happened, sales and accounts receivable would be understated, and inventory could be overstated.	The physical count of inventory will need to be observed carefully (extensive work) to detect material overstatement.

S = Strength
W = Weakness

Auditors do not need to test control weaknesses just to prove they are weak places. Doing so would be inefficient. However, auditors do always need to take control weaknesses into account in assessing the risk of material misstatements in the financial statements.

In terms of control risk assessment, at this stage the control risk related to the inventory balance might be set very high (e.g., 0.8 or 0.9 in probability terms). The three control strengths, however, relate to good control over sales validity and accounts receivable accuracy. The auditors probably will want to rely on these controls to reduce audit work on the accounts receivable balance. Tests of these control procedures ought to be performed to obtain evidence about whether the apparent strengths actually are performed well. The "audit program" segment of Exhibit 9-11 for each of the strengths describes specific control tests of the relevant control procedure. Testing controls (Phase 3) consists of tests designed to produce evidence of how well the controls worked in practice. If they pass the auditor's criteria (the required degree of compliance), control risk can be assessed low. If they fail the test, assess a high control risk and revise the audit plan to take the control weakness into account. Control tests only provide indirect evidence of the monetary accuracy of financial statement balances, because not all monetary misstatements are caused by control weaknesses. Substantive testing provides more direct evidence about monetary accuracy.

REVIEW CHECKPOINTS

9.49 What steps are involved in a control risk assessment?

9.50 What is a control strength? What is a control weakness? How do control strengths relate to control testing?

9.51   What is the purpose of a bridge working paper and what information does it contain?

9.52   Why is it not necessary to test control weaknesses? What action does the auditor need to take when control evaluation work indicates a control weakness?

9.53   What are the implications for the audit program if tests of key controls indicate they are operating effectively for the whole period being audited? What are the implications if a key control is tested and a high degree of noncompliance is found?

. . . .

Assessing the Control Risk in Complex IT and E-Commerce Environments

In a business with complex IT use and e-commerce activities challenges arise in maintaining the integrity of control systems in a rapidly changing environment, and in ensuring access to relevant records for management and audit purposes. In some circumstances (for example, when e-commerce systems are highly automated, when transaction volumes are high, or when electronic evidence comprising the audit trail is not retained), the auditor may determine that controls are critical to reducing financial reporting risks. In these situations it may not be possible to reduce audit risk to an acceptably low level by using only substantive procedures. It will be necessary to assess and test effectiveness of key controls. The auditor should assess whether controls are adequate to ensure that the requirements are met relevant to the financial statement assertions, information's authorization, authenticity, confidentiality, integrity, nonrepudiation and availability.

The following aspects of internal control are particularly relevant when the client engages in e-commerce:

- security
- transaction integrity
- process alignment

These aspects are explained in the following paragraphs.

Security

External parties' ability to access the client's information system using a public network such as the Internet creates security risks. The security infrastructure and related controls include an information security policy, an information security risk assessment process, and security procedures. These include both physical measures and logical and other technical safeguards, such as user identities, passwords, firewalls, encryption including both authorization and safeguarding of decryption keys. The control environment is important to ensure systems are updated to address risk posed by new technologies. Security concerns and controls can be broken down into the components shown in the following box.

SEVEN CORNERSTONES OF BASIC SECURITY

Security concerns	Controls
1. Network security	• network segmentation, intrusion detection software, all network devices at current patch level
2. Database security	• control administrator access accounts, update access restrictions
3. Operating system security	• upgrade Windows O/S to eliminate NetBIOS, penetration audits
4. External security	• firewalls, modem and wireless access, monitor trading partner access accounts

5. Application security	• rule of least access for users, review transaction routing, application triggers for unusual items, purge old users
6. Physical security	• annual physical security audit, surprise intrusion tests
7. Business continuance and disaster preparedness security	• server, applications, firewall and ISP redundancy, business continuance plan stored off-site at key employees' homes

Source: Adapted from Gordon E. Smith, "Information Security: Is Your Auditing Up to the Task?" *The Journal of Corporate Accounting and Finance* 15 (4), May/June 2004, p. 13.

In addition to internal risks, information security breaches in e-commerce applications can lead to authorized access to private information, for example customer credit card numbers, social insurance numbers, etc. Privacy laws require all businesses to have control over privacy of information in place, and weaknesses can result in legal action against a company, as well as action by private individuals whose information was improperly given out. The auditor needs to consider privacy controls over data, since a weakness could mean a material misstatement of the financial statements exists in the form of an undisclosed contingent liability.

Transaction Integrity

Risks related to the recording and processing of e-commerce transactions include the completeness, accuracy, timeliness and authorization of information in the entity's financial records. Control activities relating to transaction integrity in an e-commerce environment are often designed to, for example:

(a) validate input

(b) prevent duplication or omission of transactions

(c) ensure the terms of trade have been agreed before an order is processed, usually payment is obtained when an order is placed

(d) distinguish between customer browsing and orders placed, ensure a party to a transaction cannot later deny having agreed to specified terms (nonrepudiation), and ensure transactions are with approved parties when appropriate

(e) prevent incomplete processing by rejecting the order if all steps are not completed and recorded (for example, for a B2C transaction: order accepted, payment received, goods delivered and accounting system updated)

(f) ensure the proper distribution of transaction details across multiple systems in a network (for example, when data are collected centrally and communicated to various resource managers to execute the transaction)

(g) ensure records are properly retained, backed up and secured

Weaknesses in IT and e-commerce controls can increase the company's vulnerability to fraudulent activities by both inside employees and outside customers, suppliers or strangers, as described in the following box.

FRAUD RISKS IN E-COMMERCE

Possible fraudulent activities include the following:

• unauthorized movement of money, such as payments to fictitious suppliers located in jurisdictions where recovery of money will be difficult

- misrepresentations of company tenders
- corruption of electronic ordering or invoicing systems
- duplication of payments
- denying an order was placed
- denying an order was received
- denying receipt of goods
- denying that payment was received
- falsely declaring that a payment was made

Source: Jagdish Pathak, "A Conceptual Risk Framework for Internal Auditing in E-commerce," *Managerial Auditing Journal* 19 (4), 2004, p. 560.

Process Alignment

Process alignment refers to the way various IT systems are integrated to operate, in effect, as one system. Transactions generated on the business website should be processed properly by the entity's internal systems, such as the accounting system, customer relationship management systems and inventory management systems (often known as "back office" systems). Many websites are not automatically integrated with internal systems, increasing the risk of inconsistent recording and other errors.

Identifying specific control objectives is the same in both manual and IT-based data processing procedures. However, the points in the flow of transactions where misstatements could occur may be different. For example, when IT is used, these points (see Exhibit 9-12) are places where misstatements could occur:

Input

1. Activities related to source data preparation are performed, causing the flow of transactions to include authorization and initial execution.
2. Noncomputerized procedures are applied to source data, such as a manual summarization of accounting data (preparation of batch totals).
3. Source data are converted into computer-readable form.
4. Input files are identified for use in processing.

Processing

5. Information is transferred from one computer program to another.
6. Computer-readable files are used to supply additional information relating to individual transactions (e.g., customer credit reports).
7. Transactions are initiated by the computer.

Output

8. Output files are created or master files are updated.
9. Master files are changed (records added, deleted or modified) outside the normal flow of transactions within each cycle through file maintenance procedures.
10. Output reports or files are produced.
11. Errors identified by control procedures are corrected.

Once the audit team has identified the points in the transaction flow where misstatements might occur, specific control objectives can be related to such points. For example, one possible misstatement might involve invoicing customers with incorrect prices because the wrong price list file has been used. One way to state a control objective relating to this type of misstatement is: "Appropriate price information should be used during the invoicing process." The controls associated with prevention, detection and correction of misstatements can be grouped into three broad categories: input, processing and output controls. Input controls are the ones associated with preventing misstatements relating to the points

EXHIBIT 9-12   COMPUTER ACCOUNTING: POINTS OF VULNERABILITY TO MISSTATEMENT ERRORS

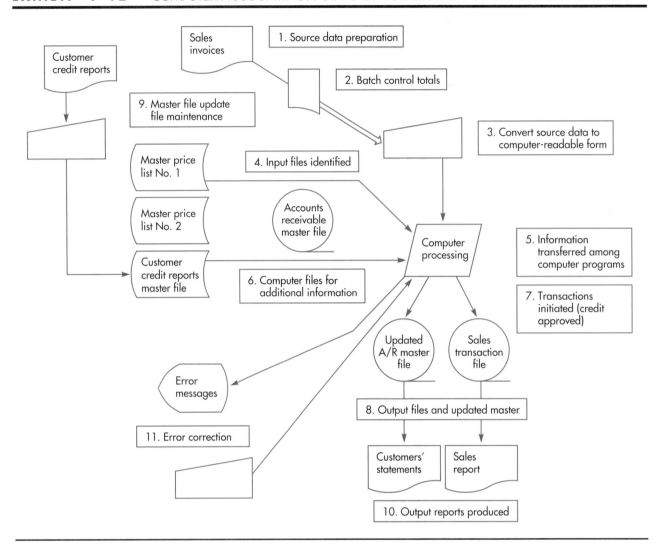

numbered 1 through 4 above. Processing controls are primarily designed to detect misstatements related to points 5 through 8 above. Output controls are primarily designed to correct misstatements related to points 9 through 11 above.

Control procedures should be considered in terms of specific control objectives. For example, for the objective of using appropriate price information, one control procedure might be "The invoicing program should use the most up-to-date price list file and the price list file date should appear on the invoicing summary management report. The accounts receivable manager should review the invoicing summary report and verify that the correct price list has been used to calculate the invoice amounts prior to releasing the invoices for printing and mailing to customers."

Manual control procedures may have characteristics that differ from computerized procedures that are designed to accomplish the same control objectives. For example, in a manual system, credit approval usually is indicated by an authorized person putting their signature on a source document, such as a customer's order or invoice. In a computerized system, however, approval can be accomplished by the authorized person using an approved password that releases a credit sale transaction by assigning a special code to it. The password provides access to programs that permit initiating a specific type of transaction or changing master files. In such a case, although the control objective is identical in the manual and computerized systems, the methods used to achieve the objective and the visible evidence of complying with authorized procedures differ and different audit approaches may be required.

The information gathered about the client's control environment, the accounting system and the control procedures should enable the auditor to reach one of the following three conclusions about control risk. The control risk conclusion determines the approach that will be followed in planning the audit.

- Control risk may be assessed low, and it seems efficient to test controls. The auditor believes the control procedures designed to prevent or detect misstatements can be audited for compliance in a cost-effective manner. In this case the auditor plans an audit approach that combines control reliance and substantive testing.

or

- Control risk may be assessed low, but audit inefficiencies would occur if controls were tested. Control policies and procedures appear to be good, but testing controls is not cost effective because substantive procedures can provide sufficient appropriate evidence and are cheaper than a combined approach. In this case the auditors would concentrate attention on the substantive audit procedures.

or

- Control risk may be assessed high. Control policies and procedures do not appear to be sufficient to prevent or detect material misstatements. In this case the auditors will concentrate on substantive audit procedures. The auditor also has additional responsibilities to report the control weaknesses to management and the audit committee (and further responsibilities in the case of public company audits, as discussed in Chapter 3).

According to GAAS, the auditor is required to make the control evaluation for the different classes of transactions and account balances at the assertion level. Therefore, it may be possible to identify specific control procedures that provide a low risk assessment with regard to some but not all assertions. In such situations the auditors may achieve some audit objectives through a combination of tests of controls and substantive auditing, while other audit objectives may be achieved through substantive procedures alone.

To summarize the control evaluation up to this point, Phases 1 and 2 can be described as dealing with the evaluation of the design of the system assuming it operates properly. Now we move on to Phase 3 where we test the actual operation of the system.

REVIEW CHECKPOINTS

9.54 What challenges arise for management and the auditor when a client company uses complex IT and/or is involved in e-commerce?

9.55 What is information security risk? What are the components of information risk?

9.56 Give examples of controls related to information security concerns.

9.57 Why are a client's privacy controls relevant to the audit?

9.58 What risks and controls relate to recording and processing transactions?

9.59 List fraud risks that exist in e-commerce activities.

9.60 What risk arise if IT processes are not aligned properly?

9.61 Identify the three main components in the flow of transactions.

9.62 Categorize the 11 points of vulnerability to misstatement errors in terms of manual input, computer processing and error correction activities in a computerized information system.

9.63 Why are the control objectives the same whether manual and computerized controls procedures are used?

9.64 Why might manual control procedures differ from computerized control procedures even if both are directed at the same control objective?

9.65   Describe one manual and one computerized control procedure designed to prevent a credit sale being processed without proper authorization by the credit manager.

9.66   What are the three different conclusions about control risk that an auditor can reach based on internal control evaluation? What are the implications of each for the audit approach selected?

. . . .

Phase 3: Testing Controls
. . . .

In the third phase of an internal control evaluation, auditors will have identified specific controls on which risk could be assessed very low (e.g., the strengths shown in Exhibit 9-11). To reach a final conclusion that control risk is low, auditors must determine (1) the required degree of company compliance with the control policies and procedures and (2) the actual degree of control compliance. The required degree of compliance is the auditors' decision criterion for assessing whether controls perform well. Knowing that compliance cannot realistically be expected to be perfect auditors might decide, for example, that evidence of using shipping documents to validate sales invoice recordings 96 percent of the time is sufficient to assess a low control risk for the audit of accounts receivable (controls relating to the existence assertion in receivables and sales).

Auditors can perform control tests to determine how well the company's control procedures actually worked during the period under audit. A control test has two parts. Part 1 is an identification of the data population from which a sample of items will be selected for audit. Part 2 is a description of the action taken to produce relevant evidence. In general, the action is to determine whether the selected items correspond to a standard (e.g., mathematical accuracy), and/or to determine whether the selected items agree with information in another data population. The control tests in Exhibit 9-11 show this two-part design.

One other important aspect of these audit procedures is known as the direction of the test. The procedures described in Exhibit 9-11 provide evidence about control over the validity of sales transactions. However, they do not provide evidence about control over completeness of recording all shipments. Another data population—the shipping documents—can be sampled to provide evidence about completeness. The direction of the test idea is illustrated in Exhibit 9-13. For example, if the completeness control is found to be strong, the auditors could omit the year-end procedure of confirming customers' zero-balance accounts receivable to search for unrecorded assets (understatements).

Some control tests involve reperformance—the auditors perform again the arithmetic calculations and the comparisons the company people were supposed to have performed. Some accountants, however, believe mere inspection is enough—the auditors just look to see whether the documents were marked with an initial, signature or stamp to indicate that they

EXHIBIT   9-13   DIRECTION OF CONTROL TESTING

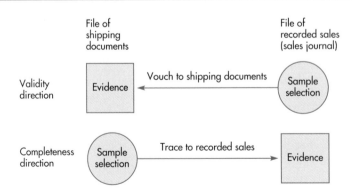

had been checked (some refer to this as "pure" tests of controls). They maintain that reperformance is not necessary.[9] A compromise is to perform both procedures (dual-purpose tests) on at least some of the tested transactions.

Some control tests depend on documentary evidence, like a sales entry supported by a shipping document. Documentary evidence in the form of signatures, initials, checklists, reconciliation working papers and the like provides better evidence than procedures that leave no documentary traces. Some control elements, such as segregation of employees' duties, may leave no documents behind. In this case, the best kind of procedures—reperformance of control operations—cannot be done, and the second procedure—observation—must be used. This procedure amounts to an auditor's unobtrusive eyewitness observation of employees at their jobs performing control operations.

Control tests, when performed, should be applied to samples of transactions and control procedures executed throughout the whole period being audited. The reason for this requirement is that, in the case of audited general purpose financial statements, the conclusions about whether controls operated effectively will apply to the whole period under audit.

Audit procedures regarding the integrity of information in the accounting system relating to e-commerce transactions are largely concerned with evaluating the reliability of the systems in use for capturing and processing such information. In a sophisticated system, the originating action (for example, receipt of a customer order over the Internet) will automatically initiate all other steps in processing the transaction. Therefore, in contrast to audit procedures for traditional business activities, which ordinarily focus separately on control processes relating to each stage of transaction capture and processing, audit procedures for sophisticated e-commerce often focus on automated controls that relate to the integrity of transactions as they are captured and then immediately and automatically processed.

R E V I E W
CHECKPOINTS

9.67   What do the terms "required degree of control compliance" and "actual degree of control compliance" mean?

9.68   How does the degree of control reliance relate to the auditor's control risk assessment?

9.69   What is a control test? Why do auditors perform control tests? What audit evidence is produced by control tests?

9.70   What two parts are important in writing out a control test for an audit program?

9.71   How does the direction of a control test relate to control objectives?

9.72   What is the difference between inspection and reperformance in control testing?

9.73   What is a dual purpose test?

9.74   How are control procedures that leave no documentary evidence tested?

9.75   Why are controls tested for the whole period being audited?

AUDITOR'S RESPONSIBILITY TO DETECT AND COMMUNICATE MATERIAL CONTROL WEAKNESSES AND MISSTATEMENTS

LEARNING OBJECTIVE

6 Outline the auditor's responsibility when internal control evaluation work detects or indicates a high risk of fraudulent misstatement.

After the auditor's evaluation of internal controls, the auditor is in a strong position to assess the likelihood of material misstatements. This is a good point to review auditor responsibilities for detecting and communicating misstatements as per the guidance in *CICA Handbook*, section 5135 or ISA 240.

Financial misstatements can arise from error, fraud or other misstatements. A **financial error** is defined as an unintentional misstatement, whereas **fraud** is defined as intentional

---

[9] When you go to work for an audit organization, one preference will prevail, but many auditors believe good evidence requires reperformance, where feasible, at least for part of the controls testing.

misstatements. Intent is not something that the auditor can observe, and so the standards provide the following guidance:

> Intent is often difficult to determine, particularly in matters involving accounting estimates and the application of accounting principles. For example, unreasonable accounting estimates may be unintentional or may be the result of an intentional attempt to misstate the financial statements. Although an audit is not designed to determine intent, the auditor has a responsibility to plan and perform the audit to obtain reasonable assurance about whether the financial statements are free of material misstatement, whether the misstatement is intentional or not.[10]

Because of this responsibility the audit needs to be performed with professional skepticism, meaning the auditor:

1. Should be aware of factors that increase the risk of misstatement and take these into account in performing the audit.
2. Should take appropriate action if there is evidence that contradicts the assumption of management's integrity.

Note that many risk factors relate to poor internal controls. If there are enough "red flags" present, the auditor will assess a higher inherent risk, and if control risk is also high, these higher assessments will cause the auditor to:

1. obtain more reliable evidence
2. expand the extent of audit procedures performed
3. apply audit procedures closer to or as of the balance sheet date
4. require more extensive supervision of assistants and/or assistants with more experience and training

In essence, if the auditor suspects that the financial statements are misstated, she or he should perform procedures to confirm or dispel that suspicion.

The auditor should inform the appropriate level of management whenever he or she obtains evidence of a nontrivial misstatement, and of weaknesses in internal control that could allow a material misstatement to occur. The audit committee or board of directors should be informed of all significant misstatements and all misstatements that appear to be intentional and fraud-related. Generally, the auditor is less likely to detect material misstatements arising from fraud because of the deliberate concealment involved. (Procedures for fraud detection are discussed in more detail later in Chapter 17 and in various examples, which we call "casettes" in this text.)

The auditor should consider obtaining legal advice if he or she has doubts about communicating misstatements to third parties, particularly if the auditor resigned, or was removed, or was unable to report on the financial statements.

REVIEW CHECKPOINTS

9.76 What is the financial statement auditor's responsibility for detecting and communicating misstatements?

9.77 What is professional scepticism? How does professional scepticism help financial statement auditors meet their responsibilities?

9.78 How does control risk relate to the risk of material misstatement?

9.79 What action should an auditor take if he suspects the financial statements are materially misstated?

9.80 What findings are auditors required to communicate to management? To the audit committee or board of directors?

[10] *CICA Handbook*, paragraph 5135.007.

Control Evaluation and Cost-Benefit

Internal controls are subject to cost-benefit considerations. Controls possibly could be made perfect, or nearly so, but at great expense. A fence could be erected; locks could be installed; lighting could be used at night; television monitors could be put in place; guards could be hired. Each of these successive safeguards costs money, as does extensive supervision of clerical personnel in an office. At some point the cost of protecting the inventory from theft (or of supervisors catching every clerical error) exceeds the benefit of control. Hence, control systems generally do not provide absolute assurance that the objectives of internal control are satisfied. Reasonable assurance is thought to be enough, in recognition that the cost of an entity's internal controls should not exceed the benefits that are expected to be received.

Notwithstanding the common sense of the concept of reasonable assurance, auditors must be careful to determine whether a system contains any internal control weakness. Business managers can make estimates of benefits they expect to get from controls and weigh them against the costs. Managers are perfectly free to make their own judgements about how much control is necessary and how much business risk they are willing to accept. However, auditors should be aware that the "cost-benefit" and "reasonable assurance" concepts can sometimes be used loosely by management to tolerate control deficiencies.

In discussion so far in this chapter we have learned that the primary purpose of evaluating internal control is to guide the design of the final audit plan. For this reason, audit documentation of the auditor's understanding of the internal control and the control risk assessment is required. These audit working papers can include internal control questionnaires, narrative descriptions, flowcharts, descriptions of controls, compliance criteria, and the evidence produced by control tests. For study purposes, we tend to discuss control tests and substantive tests of balances as if these are easily distinguishable. It is important to realize that the six general audit techniques described in Chapter 8 can be used in both tests of controls and substantive procedures.

Now that you have studied control tests and their relation to substantive tests of account balances, it may be helpful for you to think about the purposes of audit procedures instead of whether they are tests of controls and substantive procedures. As discussed earlier, a single procedure may produce both control and substantive evidence and serve both purposes, hence the name dual-purpose tests.[11] For example, a selection of recorded sales entries could be used (1) to vouch sales to supporting shipping documents and (2) to calculate the correct dollar amount of sales. The first part of the test provides information about control compliance. The second is dollar-value information that may help measure the amount of misstatement in the general ledger balance of sales. Another example is the confirmation of accounts receivable procedure. This procedure mainly has a substantive purpose but when confirmation replies tell about significant or systematic errors, the evidence is relevant to control evaluation as well as to measuring the dollar-value of misstatements. Since dual-purpose tests provide both compliance and substantive evidence, they can lower the cost of obtaining audit evidence.

The auditor's goal at the planning stage is to select the most cost-effective set of evidence gathering procedures to provide support for the audit opinion. An approach that integrates all aspects of the client's business and systems into the overall design of the audit will be most effective. The choice of control reliance and substantive evidence can be made to maximize efficiency and minimize auditing costs. Many audit procedures can be designed to serve dual purposes and yield evidence both about controls and about financial statement assertions. This allows the auditor to select an audit approach that uses a combination of control reliance and substantive evidence as the basis for a cost-effective overall audit plan.

---

[11] Ibid., paragraph 5143.33.

REVIEW CHECKPOINTS

9.81   Why do internal controls provide reasonable, but not absolute, assurance that control objectives are met?

9.82   How can management's cost-benefit judgements lead to internal control deficiencies?

9.83   Explain how using dual-purpose tests can lower audit costs.

9.84   What does it mean to say an overall audit plan is cost-effective? How do auditors develop a cost-effective overall audit plan?

EVALUATION APPROACHES FOR INFORMATION SYSTEMS

LEARNING OBJECTIVE

8 Compare and contrast these approaches to auditing information systems: auditing around the computer; auditing through the computer with computer assisted audit techniques (CAATs); and auditing with the computer using generalized audit software (GAS).

When businesses started using computers, two terms were coined to describe the nature of auditing work on computer systems. The first term, "auditing around the computer," came to mean that auditors were attempting to isolate the computer—to treat it like a "black box"—and to find audit assurance by vouching data from output to source documents and by tracing from source documents to output. As long as the computer was used as a speedy calculator, this method generally was considered adequate. In fact, it may be satisfactory today in a case where the information system provides all the physical documentation the auditor needs to collect sufficient appropriate audit evidence. Auditing around the computer is not always adequate, however. The audit team needs sufficient IT expertise to determine the appropriate approach whenever the client's information systems involve IT-based processing.

Nothing is inherently wrong with auditing around the computer if auditors are satisfied with the controls and the information system provides enough visible evidence, such as the input source data, the machine-produced error listings, visible control points (e.g., use of batch totals) and detailed printed output. Exhibit 9-14 shows an example of auditing around the computer. The auditors select a sample of source documents for a tracing procedure to test the controls over recording transactions, such as sales. The client's computer system processes the transactions, but the auditor treats it like a "black box," interested only in the correspondence of the input (customer's order, quantity shipped and amount invoiced) to the output (debit to accounts receivable, credit to sales revenue). In this case it was not necessary to test the actual processing that happens in the computer because sufficient evidence for the test can be obtained without it.

EXHIBIT   9–14   EXAMPLE OF AUDITING AROUND THE COMPUTER

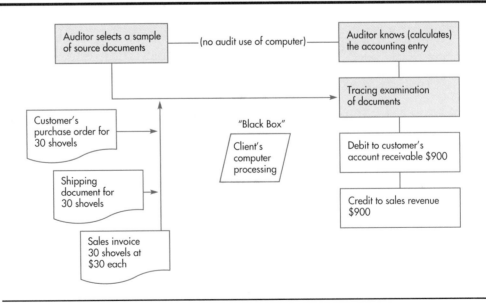

The second term that has evolved is "auditing through the computer." It refers to the auditor's actual evaluation of the hardware and software to determine the reliability of operations that cannot be viewed by the human eye. Auditing through has become more common in practice because IT-based information systems often have significant built-in control procedures. Thus, ignoring a computer system and the controls built into it would mean the auditors are ignoring important features of internal control.

The term "auditing through the computer" can also be referred to as using computer-assisted audit techniques (CAATs). CAATs refers to audit techniques such as:

- tests of general IT controls—for example, the use of test data to test access procedures to the programs and data
- compliance tests of IT application controls—for example, the use of test data or an imbedded audit program (continuous auditing) to test the functioning of programmed control procedures
- tests of details of transactions and balances—for example, the use of auditor-created or auditor-tested software to verify all (or a sample) of the transaction processing in a system
- analytical review procedures—for example, the use of audit software to identify unusual fluctuations in amounts or in the volume of transactions

A third approach can be referred to as "auditing with the computer." This approach involves using general audit software (GAS) to perform various audit tests and analytical procedures, and to prepare audit file documentation. Though some of the GAS techniques might also be viewed as types of CAATs, for study purposes we will discuss them separately.

. . . .

R E V I E W
CHECKPOINTS

9.85   When would it be appropriate for the financial statement auditor to audit around the computer, i.e. treat the computer systems like a black box?

9.86   What are CAATs? What does auditing through the computer using CAATs refer to?

9.87   What is GAS used for?

. . . .

Computer-Assisted Audit Techniques (CAATs)

In the simple information systems described in Chapter 7, adequate evidence of control performance frequently exists in the printed output and logs (thus, auditing around the computer is possible). However, external auditors sometimes must use the computer as an audit tool to test the controls within the application programs of even simple systems. (Internal auditors more frequently utilize these techniques.) Thus, a consideration of the use of the computer as an "auditor's assistant" in testing controls is explained following.

Two Approaches for Using the Computer in Control Testing

Auditors can use two approaches to audit through the computer to test controls: (1) audit the programmed processing controls with simulated data and (2) audit the programmed controls with live data reprocessed with an audit program. The auditing of programmed control procedures with simulated data generally is referred to as test data, while the reprocessing of live data to test program controls is called parallel simulation.

Test Data
The basic concept of test data is that once a computer is programmed to handle transactions in a certain logical way, it will faithfully handle every transaction exactly the same way. This is sometime called the uniformity principle. Therefore, the audit team need only prepare a limited number of simulated transactions (some with "errors" and some without) to determine whether each control operates as described in the program documentation.

Test data is a sample of one of each possible combination of data fields that may be processed through the real system. Simulated test data will most likely be on a disk. Test data also may be entered into an online system through computer terminals. The purpose of using test data is to determine whether controls operate as described in questionnaire responses and program flowcharts. Test transactions may consist of abstractions from real transactions and of simulated transactions generated by the auditors' imagination.[12] The auditors must prepare a worksheet listing each transaction and the predicted output based on the program documentation. Then these test transactions must be converted to the normal machine-sensed input form, and arrangements must be made to process the transactions with the actual program used for real transactions.

Auditors must be very familiar with the nature of the business and the logic of the programs to anticipate all data combinations that might exist as transaction input or that might be generated by processing. They must be able to assign degrees of audit importance to each kind of error-checking control method. Further, they must ensure that the test data do not get commingled with real transactions and change the actual master files.

Consider an example of processing sales transactions. Assume that the objective of the test is to check the controls over accuracy of input data. The problem is to assemble a set of transactions that includes important error conditions in order to determine whether the input and processing controls can detect them.

For example, the audit team can create hypothetical transactions with the following conditions:

1. no customer code number
2. invalid customer code number (wrong check digit)
3. bill of lading document number not entered
4. sales amount greater than $25,000
5. sales amount equal to zero
6. sales amount less than zero

These six conditions generate many possible combinations of transactions. The auditors know that transactions having no customer number or no bill of lading document number (missing data test), an invalid customer code number (self-checking number test), a sales amount greater than $25,000 (limit test), a sales amount equal to zero (missing data test) or a sales amount less than zero (sign test) should produce error messages. Transactions with valid conditions should not. The auditors arrange to run these simulated transactions on the client's system and to find out whether the controls operate.

Test data are processed at a single point in time with the client program that is supposed to have been used during the period under audit. After the analysis of test output, the auditor still must make an inference about processing throughout the entire period. In order to do so, he or she must be satisfied by a review of documentation that any program changes have been authorized and correctly made. Some auditors occasionally perform test data procedures on an irregular, surprise basis during the year. As real-time financial reporting on the Internet becomes more common, continuous auditing techniques will become more important—these are discussed in Appendix 9C which you will find on the Online Learning Centre.

Exhibit 9-15 shows the schema of testing controls with test data. (You should compare it to Exhibit 9-14, the example of auditing around the computer.) The auditors create source document input that can contain accurate as well as erroneous conditions, in this case a shipment of fewer units than the customer ordered. The auditors know the desired outcome—an error message that the quantity shipped and the quantity billed do not match, perhaps with an accounting entry to charge the customer for the shipped quantity. If this result does not appear from the processing of the test data, the auditors can conclude that the processing control over accurate sales recording contains a deficiency (weakness). The auditors are

---

[12] This is a simplification. IT-based information systems may have multiple controls that create thousands of error combinations and possible test transactions. Computerized test data generators are available to help auditors overcome the magnitude of the test data creation task.

EXHIBIT   9-15   EXAMPLE OF AUDITING CONTROLS WITH TEST DATA (through the computer)

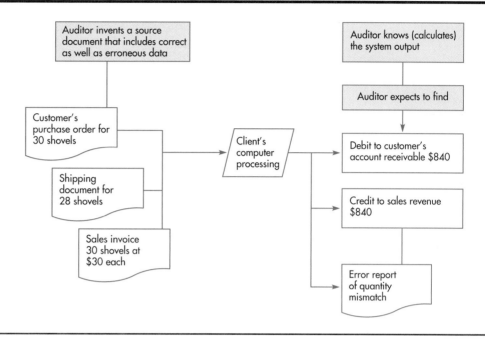

testing the control procedures embedded in the computer program, and they are using the actual processing program for the test. When using test data, the auditor can focus on unusual transactions or error conditions rather than a large number of similar transactions. The reasoning is that if the program handles one transaction correctly, then it will handle other similar transactions the same way. However, test data provides a control test only at a specific point in time. In order to rely on the program controls for a period of time, the auditor will also need to obtain assurance that general controls such as controls over program changes are in place and operating over the same period.

Parallel Simulation

In parallel simulation the audit team prepares a computer program (utilizing generalized audit software described later in this chapter) designed to process client data properly. The result of the auditors' processing of real client data is compared with the result of the real data processed by the actual client program. The concept of this method is illustrated in Exhibit 9-16.

To test the controls contained in computer programs, auditors have the options of (1) using the client's real programs, (2) having client personnel write special programs, or (3) writing their own special programs to collect evidence that the controls work. The first option would be used in the test data technique described in the previous section. The second option requires close supervision and testing to ensure that the client's personnel have prepared the audit program correctly. The third option is parallel simulation, and it requires significant programming expertise of the audit staff or close liaison with expert independent programmers.

However, with generalized audit software (GAS) the parallel simulation option is more feasible. The generalized audit software programs consist of numerous prepackaged subroutines that can perform most tasks needed in auditing and business applications. The auditor's programming task consists of writing simple instructions that call up one or more of the subroutines. Thus, there is no need to write complete, complex programs, and the expertise to use the generalized software can be acquired with a short course of training. (You will get a closer look at these generalized audit software programs and their capabilities later in this chapter.)

Using the generalized audit program capabilities, an auditor can construct a system of data processing that will accept the same input as the real program, use the same files, and attempt to produce the same results. This simulated system will contain all the controls the

EXHIBIT   9-16   SYSTEM CONCEPT OF PARALLEL SIMULATION

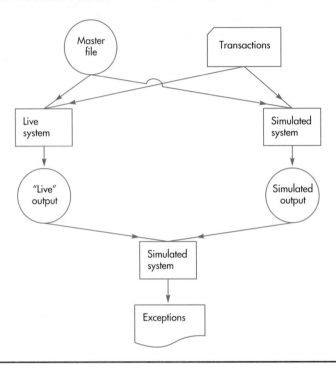

auditor believes appropriate, and, in this respect, the thought process is quite similar to the logic that goes into preparing test data. The simulated-system output then is compared to the real-system output for correspondence or difference, and at this point the audit evidence is similar to the evidence obtained by using test data with the real program: conclusions can be reached about the error-detection capabilities of the real system.

Another way to create a parallel system is to conduct a thorough technical audit of the controls in the client's actual program, then keep a copy of it secure in the auditors' files. Actual client data later can be processed using this audited copy of the client's program (e.g., at times later in the year under audit or in the following year audit). The goal is to determine whether output from the program the client actually used in processing data produces satisfactory accounting output when compared to the output from the auditors' controlled copy of the program. This approach is often called **controlled reprocessing**, and it is a version of parallel simulation.

The first audit application of parallel simulation may be very costly, although it probably will be more efficient than auditing without the computer or utilizing test data. Real economies are realized, however, in subsequent audits of the same client.

For the results of the parallel simulation to be valid and relevant to the audit, the audit team must take care to determine that the real transactions selected for processing are "representative." Thus, some exercise in random selection and identification of important transactions may be required in conjunction with parallel processing. The example of a parallel simulation in the following box is based on the sales–accounts receivable system described in the Kingston Company case study that accompanies this book.

PARALLEL SIMULATION

A parallel simulation of Kingston Company's sales invoice and accounts receivable processing system revealed that invoices that showed no bill of lading or shipment reference were processed and charged to customers with a corresponding credit to sales. Further audit of the exceptions showed that the real-data processing program did not contain a missing-data test and did not provide error messages for lack of shipping references. This finding led to (1) a more extensive test of the sales invoice population with comparison to shipping documents and (2) a more extensive audit of accounts receivable for customers who were charged with such sales.

As the example shows, the ultimate goal of using CAATs to test controls is to reach a conclusion about the actual operation of IT-based controls in an information system. This conclusion allows the audit team to assess the control risk and determine the nature, timing and extent of substantive audit procedures for auditing the related account balances. This control risk assessment decision determines whether subsequent audit work may be performed using machine-readable files that are produced in the system. The data processing control over such files is important since their content is utilized later in computer-assisted work using generalized audit software.

REVIEW
CHECKPOINTS

9.88   What is the difference between auditing "through the computer" and auditing "with the computer"?

9.89   What is the difference between the two approaches used to audit through the computer with computer-assisted audit techniques, "test data" and "parallel simulation"?

9.90   What types of control evidence can be provided by using CAATs?

9.91   What role do CAATs play in the overall audit plan?

9.92   Why does the test data approach only provide evidence that the control operated at a point in time?

9.93   Why is it important that data selected for parallel simulation tests is representative? How can the audit team determine that the data are representative?

Generalized Audit Software

Generalized audit software (GAS) programs are a set of functions that may be used to read, compute and operate on machine-readable records. Audit software provides access to audit evidence that otherwise would be unavailable or too costly to be feasible. This part of the chapter builds on the IT concepts and terminology introduced in Chapter 7, and the controls tests covered in this chapter. GAS includes tools used to test controls, and also for gathering substantive evidence about transaction details and account balances.

You need to know about GAS because it is used on most audits where the client's accounting records are stored in computer files or databases. The following material does not attempt to prepare you to use any particular generalized audit software package. There are many different packages in use. Instead, this section provides you with an understanding of what GAS can accomplish and, most important, where an IT specialist auditor needs to be involved.

Features of GAS

The audit challenges in assessing control risk in a computer environment are to gain access to machine-readable detail records, to select samples of items for manual or computer audit procedures, to perform calculations and analyses of entire data files and to produce audit working papers of the work performed. GAS packages were first developed by CA firms in the mid-1960s for specific application to audit engagements and have been improved and adapted with the changes in technology. The essential advantages of a generalized audit software package are:

- Original programming is not required.
- Designing tests is easy. Many GAS packages are PC based and menu-driven so they operate much like commonly used spreadsheet programs
- For special-purpose analysis of data files, GAS is more efficient than special programs written from scratch because of the little time required for writing the instructions to call up the appropriate functions of the generalized audit software package
- The same software can be used on various clients' computer systems. Control and specific tailoring are achieved through the auditors' own ability to program and operate the system.

Audit Procedures Performed by Generalized Audit Software

Computer accounting applications capture and generate voluminous amounts of data that usually are available only on machine-readable records. GAS can be used to access the data and organize it into a format useful to the audit team. Audit software can be used to perform the following basic audit techniques.[13]

1. *Computation.* Verification of calculations can be done by the computer with more speed and accuracy than by hand. The audit software can be used to test the accuracy of client computations and to perform analytical procedures to evaluate the reasonableness of account balances. Examples of this use are to (a) recalculate depreciation expense, (b) recalculate extensions on inventory items, (c) compute file totals, and (d) compare budgeted, standard and prior-year data with current-year data.

2. *Confirmation.* Auditors can program statistical or judgemental criteria for selecting customers' accounts receivable, loans and other receivables for confirmation. The GAS can be used to print the confirmations and get them ready for mailing. It can do everything except carry them to the post office!

3a. *Inspection.* GAS can compare audit evidence from other sources to company records efficiently. The audit evidence must be converted to machine-readable form and then can be compared to the company records on computer files. Examples are (a) comparing inventory test counts with perpetual records, (b) comparing adjusted balances on confirmed accounts receivable to the book balances, and (c) comparing vendor statement amounts to the company's record of accounts payable.

3b. *Inspection.* Auditors can use GAS to examine records to determine quality, completeness, consistency and correctness. This is the computer version of scanning the records for exceptions to the auditors' criteria. For example, GAS can scan (a) accounts receivable balances for amounts over the credit limit, (b) inventory quantities for negative or unreasonably large balances, (c) payroll files for terminated employees, and (d) loan files for loans with negative balances.

4a. *Analysis.* Comparing data on separate files can be accomplished by GAS to determine whether compatible information is in agreement. Differences can be printed out for investigation and reconciliation. Examples are comparing (a) payroll details with personnel records, (b) current and prior inventory to details of purchases and sales, (c) paid vouchers to check disbursements, and (d) current and prior-year fixed asset records to identify dispositions.

4b. *Analysis.* GAS can summarize and sort data in a variety of ways. Examples are (a) preparing general ledger trial balances, (b) sorting inventory items by location to facilitate observations, and (c) summarizing inventory turnover statistics for obsolescence analysis.

With enhanced PC processing capabilities, GAS has been further expanded to include expert system modules that incorporate the knowledge of human experts in various

[13] CICA, *Application of Computer-Assisted Audit Techniques Using Microcomputers* (Toronto: CICA, 1994), p. 16.

domains. Thus, audit expert systems have been developed to provide advice on various technical issues such as internal control evaluation, risk analysis, materiality assessment and management fraud.

Using Generalized Audit Software

For the most part, the widely used GAS packages are very similar. Regardless of the particular GAS used, five distinct phases are involved in developing a GAS application: (1) define audit objectives, (2) plan the application, (3) design the application, (4) test the application, and (5) process the application and evaluate the results.

1. **Define the Audit Objective**

   The first step in applying GAS is to determine specific audit objectives. GAS should be viewed as a special tool providing auditors with a means to accomplish their objectives, not as an objective in itself.

   For example, the general audit objectives might be to audit management's assertions that the accounts receivable balance represents detail accounts which exist, are complete and are valued correctly. Based on these general objectives, specific procedures may include footing the accounts subsidiary ledger master file, selecting a sample of accounts for confirmation, preparing an aged trial balance and investigating accounts with overdue balances.

2. **Feasibility and Planning**

   Feasibility should be considered in three ways: (1) Is the use of audit software technically feasible? (2) Are alternative ways to accomplish the audit task available? (3) Which of the alternatives is the most practical and economical? If the use of GAS is technically feasible, other considerations as listed in the following box must be weighed.

FEASIBILITY CONSIDERATIONS

Cost-effectiveness of hardware and software.

Technical complexity including access to client data.

Availability of qualified audit software staff.

Other issues including client concern about data security.

Source: *Application of Computer-Assisted Audit Techniques Using Microcomputers* (Toronto: CICA, 1994), p. 20.

Audit software may be the most practical way to achieve the audit objective, but it is seldom the only way. Audit resources (qualified people and their time) must be allocated carefully to achieve efficient and effective results. Using GAS requires considerable investment in time and effort and may be efficient only when repeated use is anticipated on return engagements. Obviously the data must be available. The desired files, especially detailed transaction files, often are retained only for a short time. The availability of data files and the degree of client co-operation normally would be determined during the general and application controls review. Client co-operation in turn could be affected by such issues as client concerns over the security of confidential or sensitive data, including the risk of auditors introducing computer viruses into client computers.

After determining the feasibility of using GAS, the audit manager should determine specifically how it will be used, establish control procedures for all subsequent steps and arrange the logistics with the data centre. Specific planning steps are listed in the following box.

GAS PLANNING STEPS

Set GAS application objectives clearly limited to audit objectives.

Determine content and accessibility of the client's files.

Determine hardware and software needs.

Define transactions to test procedures and output requirements.

Identify client personnel to provide technical assistance.

Prepare application budgets and timetables.

Execute application.

Evaluate the test results.

The planning phase is also the time to define the workpapers that will document the GAS application. The audit manager, not the IT-specialist, should determine what computer output representing the GAS application should be retained in the workpapers. The computer output may be in the form of computer-readable workpapers, such as audit files on disk.

3. Application Design

Developing a GAS application is much like the client's procedures for developing a new application system. Most GAS packages have an extensive repertoire of powerful instructions to facilitate processing data files and preparing audit output. Application design involves selecting the sequence of instructions to implement the required test. However, a complete description of the application phase is beyond the scope of this book. It should be undertaken only by specially trained audit staff. The documentation of the application design phase may include the GAS application system flowchart, logic descriptions, detailed report layouts, list of control points and procedures, record formats and a test plan. Frequently, the auditor must obtain a computer dump of a few records of each client file to ensure that the design is based on accurate information.

4. Testing

The logic of the application design must be tested with sample client data or simulated data until the auditor is confident that the GAS application works as desired. Testing is very similar to the test data approach used in CAATs as described earlier in this chapter. The client's files should not be used for testing; the auditor should obtain a copy for testing purposes. The test plan should be extensive enough to test each logic path and anticipate all variations of client data. Along with the application design, the tests and results should all be documented.

5. Processing and Evaluation

The foregoing phases are usually accomplished during interim work—before the year-end. Thus, everything is tested and ready for processing of the year-end balances. The processing phase involves (1) verifying that the status of the client file has not changed, (2) obtaining a copy of the client file, (3) processing the GAS application against the copy of the client's file(s), and (4) reviewing results, updating working papers, and retaining audit files. The audit team should carefully monitor and control the actual processing and the output. Control procedures established during the design phase should be followed. Planned totals should be compared to results and the totals logged on control working papers. The audit manager should review the output for reasonableness and clarity. Finally, the documentation workpapers of the application must be completed and filed. Special care must be taken to leave adequate documentation for subsequent use on a repeat engagement. (In a sense this documentation is the "audit trail of the audit.") The working papers frequently will contain a list of suggested modifications for next year's audit.

In summary, following the feasibility and planning phase, a GAS application should be designed to achieve specific audit objectives. The reliability of general application computer controls, the availability of client files, access to the computer and technical assistance and estimated costs and the availability of GAS-trained audit staff must be evaluated. If IT specialists are involved, the non-IT auditor should be actively involved in the definition of audit objectives and the application plan. Results of testing should be reviewed by the audit manager. The whole GAS process needs to be run under control of the audit team, including copying client files and printing out audit results.

Planning and testing are the most critical tasks in the development of a GAS application. If planning is not adequate, the audit objectives may not be achieved. Problems are likely to occur in subsequent phases and require excessive time and effort to correct. Testing must be adequate or the probability of success is low. Once processing is commenced after year-end, it is extremely difficult to correct errors and deficiencies.

Many larger companies have internal auditors skilled in using GAS. Independent (external) auditors may utilize the internal auditors to develop and run the GAS application under supervision and review of the external audit manager.

Generalized Audit Software Limitations

Notwithstanding the powers of the computer, several good auditing procedures are outside its reach. The computer can compare auditor-made counts to the computer records but it cannot observe and count physical things (inventory, for example).

The computer cannot examine external and internal documentation; thus, it cannot vouch accounting output to sources of basic evidence. An exception would exist in an advanced computer system that stored the basic source documents on magnetic or optical media. The auditor would have to test the controls over creation of the files but then would have no choice but to treat the file as a basic "document" source. When manual vouching is involved, computer-assisted selection of sample items is a great efficiency. Probably the biggest problem auditors encounter in using CAATs is obtaining the data in a format that can be used on their computers. Issues that must be addressed in advance include compatibility of the client's with the auditor's system, data structures in the client's system and availability of client staff to download the data for use by the auditor.[14] Finally, the computer cannot conduct an enquiry in the limited sense that the enquiry procedure refers to questionnaires and conversations.

Using the Personal Computer as an Audit Tool

The PC is widely used in audit practice. You have probably already learned to use a PC to prepare accounting schedules with spreadsheet software and to use word processing software to prepare your written class assignments. The audit PC software makes use of these same PC software tools to prepare auditing working papers, audit programs and audit memos. There also are several GAS programs that have been designed for use on PCs; some common ones are Caseware, ACL and IDEA. These are used internationally and are relatively easy to use since little or no programming is required.[15]

The PC is also used regularly in small and large public accounting firms to perform such clerical steps as preparing the working trial balance, posting adjusting entries, grouping accounts that represent one line item on the financial statement into lead schedules, computing comparative financial statements and common ratios for analytical review, preparing supporting workpaper schedules and producing draft financial statements. Audit firms also

---

[14] G. Trites, *Audit of a Small Business* (Toronto: CICA, 1994), pp. 50–51.
[15] Ibid., p. 50.

EXHIBIT   9-17   PHASES FOR THE USE OF THE PERSONAL COMPUTER AS AN AUDIT TOOL

Applications	Goals and Objectives	Software Available
Stage 1: Automating the Audit Process		
Trial balance and working papers.	Overall audit efficiency.	Automated workpapers vendor supplied, developed by PA firms and others.
Adjusting and updating financial data.	Automation of time-consuming activities.	
Time and budget data.	Improved control.	Vendor supplied.
Audit program, memo and report generation.	Efficient and more readable.	Word processing.
Stage 2: Basic Auditing Functions		
Spreadsheet analysis working papers.	Efficiency in common working papers.	Vendor supplied, firm-developed uses.
Analytical review.	Improved overall analysis.	Part of automated workpaper packages.
Sampling planning, selection and evaluation.	Evidence collection and evaluation efficiency.	Statistical, firm developed.
Stage 3: Advanced Auditing Functions		
Analytical procedures for specific accounts.	Improved auditor analysis.	Firm developed.
Access to client files on larger computers.	Ability to download directly into automated workpaper software.	Vendor supplied or firm developed.
Access to firm and public databases.	Provide auditor with reference information.	PC as a terminal, tele-communication.
GAS functions.	Mainframe GAS workpapers downloaded to PC.	Firm developed.
Modelling and decision support systems.	Improved auditor decisions.	Firm-developed decision support systems.
Continuous auditing.	Use the techniques outlined later in Appendix 9C.	Embedded Audit Modules.

Source: Adapted from Clinton E. White, "The Microcomputer as an Audit Tool," *Journal of Accountancy*, December 1983, page 117. Copyright © 1983 by the American Institute of Certified Public Accountants, Inc. Reprinted with permission.

are using the PC to assess control risk, perform sophisticated analytical functions on individual accounts, access public and firm databases for analysis of unusual accounting and auditing problems and utilize decision support software in making complex evaluations. Exhibit 9-17 illustrates the different stages a typical public accounting firm or internal audit department may go through in the use of the PC as an audit tool.

The trend in auditing is towards using highly integrated PC-based processes to control and document the audit from the engagement letter to the audit report. The preliminary audit program will be generated automatically following answers to internal control questionnaires and other programmed audit risk evaluators. The accounting data for the trial balance will be entered into the PC workpapers automatically, and all lead schedules and supporting workpapers will be generated. Related analytical procedure workpapers will be produced using not only client data but also related industry data downloaded from the Internet and audit firm intranets, with suggestions made to update the preliminary audit program. Virtually every element of this integrated PC audit is currently in use or being developed. The integration and the degree of sophistication will develop further uses of the PC as an audit tool. In particular, the availability of audit software enables the auditor to

- simulate all or part of the process by which the data supporting management's assertions were compiled
- extract information for substantive tests and tests of controls, based on the client's data supporting the subject matter of the engagement
- prepare information directly relevant to high inherent and control risk items (e.g., approvals of limits for high risk customers)[16]

[16] CICA, *Application of Computer-Assisted Audit Techniques Using Microcomputers* (Toronto: CICA, 1994), p. 17.

9.94   What are some advantages of using GAS?

9.95   What are five audit procedures that can be performed with GAS?

9.96   What are some limitations of using GAS?

INFORMATION SYSTEMS AND CONTROLS IN A SMALL BUSINESS

LEARNING OBJECTIVE

9 Apply the reasonable assurance concept and cost-benefit analysis to control risk assessment in a small business.

This section provides a discussion of information systems and controls in a small business. As a exercise in critical thinking, it illustrates how you can adapt your understanding of internal control and control risk assessment to apply to various types of entities. In the discussion below, the characteristics of a small business are analyzed. The issues involved in auditing small businesses are framed in terms of the reasonable assurance concept and the cost-benefit trade-offs faced in this type of audit client.

The explanations of internal control characteristics given in this chapter contain an underlying thread of bureaucratic organization theory and a large-business orientation. A company must be large and employ several people (about 10 or more) to have a theoretically appropriate segregation of functional responsibilities and its accompanying high degree of specialization of work. Supervision requires people. The paperwork and computer control necessary in most large systems is extensive. Large organization control theory and practice also suggests that people performing in accounting and control roles do not engage in frequent personal interaction across functional responsibility boundaries. None of these theoretical dimensions fit small business very well.

Auditors should be careful to recognize the bureaucratic, large-business orientation of internal control theory. When the business under audit is small, some allowances must be made for size, the number of people employed and the control attitude expressed by important managers and owners. One should also keep in mind that the extensive downsizing that took place in the nineties has had a generally adverse impact on the general control environment with the consequence that critical elements of the control environment may have been undermined even in large businesses. Cost-cutting in the staffing of accounting and internal control functions and weakening of internal control is one potential source of the corporate accounting scandals of the early 2000s. The Sarbannes Oxley legislation in the U.S. and similar measures in other countries are intended to strengthen internal control structures in public companies.

The key person in internal control in a small business is the owner-manager. Because the business is small, it does not exhibit the complexity that creates demand for elaborate internal control. A diligent owner-manager may be able to oversee and supervise all the important authorization, recordkeeping and custodial functions. He or she also may be able to ensure satisfactory data processing accuracy. Thus, an auditor evaluating control risk will study the extent of the owner-manager's involvement in the operation of the accounting and control system and evaluate the owner-manager's competence and integrity. This latter task emphasizes the importance of the "competent personnel" quality characteristic of internal control. Internal control questionnaires designed specifically for small businesses contain more items related to the owner-manager and other key personnel than do large-business questionnaires. The reason for this is that although small businesses may lack key elements of formal control such as segregation of duties, management involvement can compensate for lack of more formal controls.

As a small business begins to grow from, say, 4 people to 10 or 15, the transition to more formalized internal control tends to lag behind. The owner-manager may become overburdened with control duties and may tacitly delegate these to others. The intermediate-size stage represents a turning point where both owner-manager and auditor need to be very careful. At this point such measures as limited specialization and surety bonding of employees may help make the transition, and an auditor may offer many suggestions to the owner-manager as an added service.

In practice, most auditors rely primarily on substantive evidence with small business environments. This is probably due to cost-benefit considerations.

The minimum documentation for such situations is an internal control memorandum with a narrative description of the control system and the results of internal control evaluation. The description should include weaknesses, implications and recommendations.

However, as a result of acquisition of PC or computer services by even the smallest business, information in electronic format has become the norm. It is now standard for auditors to make effective use of PCs in small business audits. Some of the opportunities for using a PC in a small business audit relate to trial balance and financial statement software, preparation of audit programs, planning and administration, and computer-assisted audit techniques (most often using PC-based GAS). Common applications of GAS in small businesses include accounts receivable, confirmation and aging, footing and extending inventory files, and selecting inventory items for price testing. PC-based GAS that can be used to check an entire file with little additional effort is a major advantage because it allows the auditor to obtain a higher degree of audit assurance, at little additional cost.

REVIEW CHECKPOINTS

9.97 What aspects of good internal control are more likely to exist in large organizations than small ones? Why?

9.98 What are the two main features of internal control in a small business?

9.99 How does the cost of implementing controls affect large businesses differently than small ones?

9.100 What impact does the owner-manager role and lack of complexity have on the internal control requirements of a small business?

9.101 What control risks are related to rapid growth in a small business?

9.102 What cost-effectiveness considerations tend to be important in planning small business audits?

9.103 How are PCs used in small business audits?

SUMMARY

This chapter explained the theory and practice of auditors' involvement with a client's "internal control." The purposes of auditor involvement are to assess the control risk in order to plan the substantive audit program and to report control deficiencies to management and the audit committee or board of directors. The control understanding was explained in terms of understanding the client's business and its information systems. The distinction between management's and the auditor's responsibilities with respect to internal control was explained.

Elements of the accounting system were described in conjunction with control procedures designed to prevent, detect, and correct misstatements that occur in transactions. These misstatements were systematized in a set of seven categories of errors and irregularities that can occur. A reverse expression of them yielded the seven control objectives a company wishes to achieve. These control objectives were related to management's assertions found in financial statements.

Control procedures were organized under the headings of general controls (i.e., capable personnel, segregation of responsibilities, controlled access, periodic comparison, and error-checking routines, etc.), and applications controls procedures for addressing to the control objectives as they relate to input, processing and output of data in each accounting process. The explanations of these controls integrated computerized accounting systems with control practice.

Documentation of a control system was explained with reference to control questionnaires, flowcharts and narratives. Questionnaires and flowcharts were demonstrated. The understanding and the documentation were taken one step further to the test of controls decisions and the cost reduction reasons for doing work to obtain a low control risk assessment. The assessed control risk was connected to the control risk component in the audit risk model (covered in Chapter 8). Control evidence was linked to audit programs with a bridge working paper presentation.

The chapter discussed the auditor's responsibilities when control work reveals a fraudulent misstatement or a high risk of one occurring. It presented the cost-benefit and reasonable assurance considerations that affect the auditors choice of audit approach with respect to relying on controls and the extent to which substantive work will be used in forming the audit opinion. The chapter reviewed three approaches to auditing IT-based information systems and controls. The chapter finished with an analysis of how control theory and evaluations apply to small businesses. The discussion of control risk evaluation provided some basis for the theory and practice of audit sampling, which is covered next in Chapter 10.

The chapter includes three appendices on emerging issues in IT that affect auditing. Appendix 9A reviews the rapidly evolving world of e-commerce and the Internet economy and its foreseeable impact on the audit. These changes have been taking place so rapidly that authoritative guidance is challenged in keeping up with technological advances. Although the specific controls organizations use and the specific tests auditors will perform are likely to change with technology, the basic need to develop sufficient appropriate evidence to support the audit opinion will continue. The major change here is that evidence will increasingly take an electronic form and there will be more reliance on software controls. There could be as much reliance on controls outside as there is inside a client's organization. Both sets of controls may be necessary to provide sufficient assurance for management assertions. Specialized assurance engagements that are evolving to meet this need are discussed in Chapter 16. Appendix 9B describes the IT specialist designations that auditors can obtain. Appendix 9C discusses aspects of auditing Internet-based financial information including the XBRL reporting technology and continuous auditing techniques. All three appendices can be found on the text Online Learning Centre.

MULTIPLE-CHOICE QUESTIONS FOR PRACTICE AND REVIEW

9.104 The primary purpose for obtaining an understanding of an audit client's internal control structure is to:
 a. Provide a basis for making constructive suggestions in a management letter.
 b. Determine the nature, timing and extent of tests to be performed in the audit.
 c. Obtain sufficient appropriate evidential matter to afford a reasonable basis for an opinion on the financial statements under examination.
 d. Provide information for a communication of internal control structure-related matters to management.

9.105 What does management's internal control objectives include?
 a. Reducing the amount of testing done by the auditors.
 b. Allowing the auditor to assess control risk.
 c. Preventing and detecting fraud.
 d. Implementing policies and procedures such that control risk is assessed as being low.

9.106 Which of the following can an auditor observe as a general control procedure used by companies?
 a. Segregation of functional responsibilities.

 b. Management philosophy and operating style.
 c. Open lines of communication to the audit committee of the board of directors.
 d. External influences such as federal bank examiner audits.

9.107 A client's control procedure is:
 a. An action taken by auditors to obtain evidence.
 b. An action taken by client personnel for the purpose of preventing, detecting and correcting errors and irregularities in transactions.
 c. A method for recording, summarizing and reporting financial information.
 d. The functioning of the board of directors in support of its audit committee.

9.108 The control objective intended to reduce the probability that fictitious transactions get recorded in the accounts is:
 a. Completeness.
 b. Authorization.
 c. Proper period.
 d. Validity.

9.109 The control objective intended to reduce the probability that a credit sale transaction will get debited to cash instead of accounts receivable is:
  a. Validity.
  b. Classification.
  c. Accuracy.
  d. Completeness.

9.110 Which of the following employees normally would be assigned the operating responsibility for designing a computerized accounting system, including documentation of application systems?
  a. Computer programmer.
  b. Data processing manager.
  c. Systems analyst.
  d. Internal auditor.

9.111 When erroneous data are detected by computer program controls, such data may be excluded from processing and printed on an error report. The error report should most probably be reviewed and followed up by the:
  a. Control group.
  b. Systems analyst.
  c. Supervisor of computer operations.
  d. Computer programmer.

9.112 Totals of amounts in computer-record data fields that are not usually added but are used only for data processing control purposes are called:
  a. Record totals.
  b. Hash totals.
  c. Processing data totals.
  d. Field totals.

9.113 In updating a computerized accounts receivable file, which one of the following would be used as a batch control to verify the accuracy of the posting of cash receipts remittances?
  a. The sum of the cash deposits plus the discounts less the sales returns.
  b. The sum of the cash deposits.
  c. The sum of the cash deposits less the discounts taken by customers.
  d. The sum of the cash deposits plus the discounts taken by customers.

9.114 In most audits of large companies, internal control risk assessment contributes to audit efficiency, which means:
  a. The cost of year-end audit work will exceed the cost of control evaluation work.
  b. Auditors will be able to reduce the cost of year-end audit work by an amount more than the control evaluation costs.
  c. The cost of control evaluation work will exceed the cost of year-end audit work.
  d. Auditors will be able to reduce the cost of year-end audit work by an amount less than the control evaluation costs.

9.115 Which of the following is a device designed to help the audit team obtain evidence about the control environment and about the accounting and control procedures of an audit client:
  a. A narrative memorandum describing the control system.
  b. An internal control questionnaire.
  c. A flowchart of the documents and procedures used by the company.
  d. A well-indexed file of working papers.

9.116 A bridge working paper shows the connection between:
  a. Control evaluation findings and subsequent audit procedures.
  b. Control objectives and accounting system procedures.
  c. Control objectives and company control procedures.
  d. Financial statement assertions and test of control procedures.

9.117 Control tests are required for:
  a. Obtaining evidence about the financial statement assertions.
  b. Accomplishing control over the validity of recorded transactions.
  c. Analytical review of financial statement balances.
  d. Obtaining evidence about the operating effectiveness of client control procedures.

EXERCISES AND PROBLEMS

*Note: Problems 9.118, 9.121, 9.124 and 9.125 build on the same fact situations first presented in Chapter 7 problems.

*9.118 Computer Internal Control Questionnaire Evaluation. Assume that, when conducting procedures to obtain an understanding of the control structure in the Denton Seed Company, you checked "No" to the following internal control questionnaire items (selected from those illustrated in the chapter):
  • Does access to online files require specific passwords to be entered to identify and validate the terminal user?
  • Are control totals established by the user prior to submitting data for processing? (Order entry application subsystem.)
  • Are input control totals reconciled to output control totals? (Order entry application subsystem.)

Required:
Explain the impact these control weaknesses would have on the audit approach selected and on the design of the audit programs.

9.119 Tests of Controls, Computer-Based Sales System.
LO.5
LO.8
Garganey Corp. manufactures automobile dashboards and interior components for Big Motors Inc. (BMI). BMI requires that all its suppliers be connected to its

computerized procurement and manufacturing system. BMI's production planning system generates components requirements lists, which are then transferred electronically to various suppliers' computers for them to bid on. Garganey's production system calculates the cost of manufacturing the components at the required times, including materials, labour, overtime charges, overhead and profit. Garganey makes a bid on the order and if its bid is accepted by BMI, BMI's production schedule for that component is downloaded to Garganey's production system so that the required parts will be manufactured and delivered to BMI's plants at the times they are required in the BMI assembly lines. When the components are completed, Garganey's system generates a shipping instructions document, which is signed by the trucking company that picks up the components and delivers them to BMI. When the components arrive at BMI, they are inspected and, if approved, payment for the order is automatically transferred from BMI's bank account to Garganey's bank account. Any adjustments for quantities short-shipped are deducted from the amount BMI transfers and an adjustment memo is communicated electronically to Garganey's sales system.

Required:

Develop an internal control audit program that will generate evidence about the effectiveness of Garganey's internal controls. Using the tests of controls procedures described in the chapter as a starting point, adapt the procedures to be suitable for the computerized sales system used by Garganey.

9.120 Audit Approach, Computer Service Organization.
LO.5 Eider Equipment Leasing Limited is in the financing
LO.8 lease business. It uses a service organization to compute lease payment schedules. Eider's customers sign standard equipment leases ranging from 3 to 15 years. The details of the leases are summarized and sent to the service organization for generating the schedules. Hard copy reports from the service organization are delivered to Eider monthly and used by its bookkeeper to generate entries in the company's general ledger system, which is run on a popular accounting software package.

Required:

a. Design two or more appropriate audit approaches for verifying leasing revenues at this client.
b. List factors that would indicate which approach will be most efficient and effective.

*9.121 Management Controls, Impact on Audit. Jabiru Inc.'s
LO.1 senior management recently obtained a new decision-
LO.3 support database system that allows the managers to
LO.7 generate standard reports and also customize enquiries that use data from all functional areas of their company. Before this system was in place, reports to senior managers were generated manually by the operations managers in the various departments, such as purchasing, marketing, inventory control, production, human resources and administration. The senior managers are much happier with the new system because now they

can generate reports as soon as the period ends, they can draw the data directly from the company's computer databases, they can control the content and format of the reports and the operating managers have less opportunity to manipulate the information in the reports. For example, in the first two months of the new system, senior managers were able to identify a discrepancy in the production department that was resulting in significant shrinkage and were able to correct the control weakness quickly. The previous report, which had been designed and produced by the production manager, did not include the data needed to identify the shrinkage problem.

Required:

Comment on the potential audit planning implications of the new decision-support database system.

9.122 Online Sales, Audit Procedures. Online retailers, such
LO.1 as Amazon.com or Grocerygateway.com, make use of
LO.2 online customer order forms to allow customers to input
LO.5 all the required sale, delivery and payment data.

Required:

a. Identify control procedures that can be used in an online sales order system.
b. How would the revenue control objectives be audited in an online retail sales business?

9.123 Flowchart Control Points. Each number of the flow-
LO.5 chart in Exhibit 9.123–1 locates a control point in the labour processing system.

Required:

a. Make a list of the control points, and for each point, describe the type or kind of internal control procedure that ought to be specified.
b. Assume that Exhibit 9.123-1 is the system description in the client company's prior year's audit file. During the current year, the company converted to a magnetic security card system. Each employee is issued a security card with a magnetic stripe containing his or her identity code. At the start of the shift the employee swipes his or her security card to enter the factory floor. Using an internal clock, the scanner generates a start time entry in the system's attendance detail records file. The employee then reports to the floor supervisor to be assigned to a job for his or her shift. The supervisor uses a terminal that displays a real-time list of checked-in employees, and enters the job number assignment beside the employee's name. The job costing system automatically creates an open daily job transaction entry. At the end of the shift the employee swipes his or her card to exit the factory floor and the total shift time is entered to the open job transaction. The daily job transaction entry is then closed and a labour charge entry for the employee's shift is generated in the job costing system and in the payroll file.

You have been assigned to assess controls for the current year audit. Update Exhibit 9.123-1 to reflect the new employee attendance and job costing systems described above. Identify control points in the

EXHIBIT   9.123-1

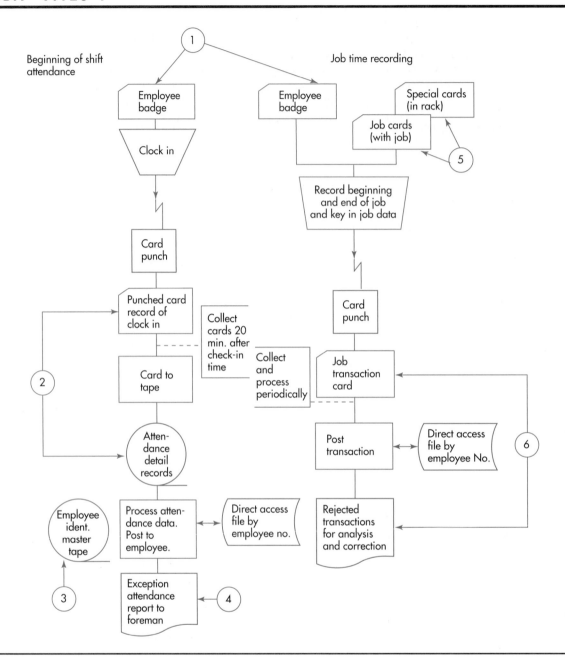

new systems, and indicate control procedures that should be used to prevent errors in payroll and job costing.

*9.124 Back-Up Procedures, Availability of Data for Audit tests. Whistler Corp. is a new audit client of your audit firm. Whistler backs up all its sales transaction detailed data for each month on a back-up tape. The tape is retained offsite for three months and then reused. This system is used because the company only has four tapes, which cost over $100 each, and offsite storage charges are on a per-tape basis. The Whistler information system manager considers this to be a cost-

LO.1
LO.5
LO.8

effective back-up procedure. Following the request of their former auditors, Whistler retains back-up tapes for December (the year-end) and the following January until the financial statement audit is completed. The audit is usually completed by the end of April.

Required:

Discuss the impact of this back-up procedure on your audit approach. Consider any limitations it may impose on audit tests or analytical procedures, or the possibility of your firm using a combined audit approach. Suggest alternate feasible approaches that may improve your audit scope.

*9.125 Control Testing Costs and Benefits. The following are
LO.1 narrative descriptions of sales systems for these two
LO.2 different businesses.
LO.5
LO.7 **Avocet Inc.**
Avocet is a franchise fast food restaurant business.
When customers order food, the counter person presses
the appropriate buttons on the cash register. There is a
button for each menu item. The point of sale (POS) system retrieves the current item prices from the price files,
extends for quantities ordered and displays the sale total on the cash register screen. A sales entry is also generated in the daily sales register. The customer's payment is then entered and their food order is displayed on
a screen in the food preparation area. The POS system
generates a cash receipt entry for the cash register and
also in the daily cash receipts register. Food preparation
staff put together the order and place it in the pick-up
area behind the front counter. When the food order is
filled, the staff clears the order from the system; this
generates an entry in the inventory system to remove
the food and packaging items sold from the perpetual
inventory listing.

A restaurant manager is on duty at all times. The
manager circulates between the counter and food
services areas, observing that cash received is placed in
the register and spot-checking that food orders match
with cash sales. If a customer receives an incorrect order, the manager can void the sale entry using a special
key in the cash register and a secret password for the
POS entries. A corrected order is then input by the usual
method, if required. At the close of each day's business,
the cash in the register is totalled and agreed to the cash,
debit card and credit card slips collected in the register
during the day. Differences of less than $10 are recorded
in an account named "Cash over/under." Larger discrepancies will be investigated by scrutinizing the day's
entries and interviewing all counter people using the
register. The sales and cash information from the POS is
then uploaded over a phone line to the franchise company head office, where it is consolidated with the reports from all the restaurants in the system. On a weekly
basis, the food and packaging inventory on hand in the
restaurant is counted and reconciled to the inventory
system. The inventory usage is also compared to the
sales records for reasonability.

Boblink Limited
Bobolink is a new-car dealership. Once a customer has
decided to buy a car, the car salesperson fills out a purchase agreement form, including the description of the
car, the serial number, and the name and address of the
purchaser. The agreed sale price is entered, along with
any extras such as options or extended warranties, any allowance for a used car traded in, additional dealer preparation fees, licensing fees, and various taxes. A second
form is used outlining the car purchase financing. The financing can be cash, a bank loan prearranged by the customer, or a lease arranged by Bobolink's financing company. Both forms are reviewed by the customer, and if
they are satisfactory, the customer signs. The salesperson
then takes the signed forms to the dealership's general

manager for review and approval. If payment is by cash,
the cash is given to the general manager at this point. Any
discrepancies in the payment or paperwork are corrected
and must be agreed to by the customer. Once the sales
documents are completed, the ownership papers and keys
are handed over to the customer, who drives away with
the car. The sales documents are faxed to the car manufacturer's sales head office for inventory and warranty
purposes, and to the bank or leasing company, if applicable. The sales information is entered by the Bobolink
bookkeeper to the financial system and the inventory system. The bookkeeper follows up on collection of the
funds from the bank or leasing company, which usually
takes two to three days. The sales information is also set
up in the dealership management system for purposes of
sales incentives and commissions, future service work
and sales follow-up.

Required:
a. Identify control strengths and weaknesses in the two
sales systems in relation to the seven control objectives described in the chapter.
b. Assume you are required to test controls in both
these audits. Write controls tests that address all the
control objectives. Also indicate which financial
statement assertion(s) each control test addresses.
c. Assume that it is your responsibility to decide
whether to rely on controls in these two audits.
Evaluate the cost-benefit trade-off of testing controls
in both clients and recommend an audit approach for
each, giving your reasons.

9.126 Controls, Irregularities. The SB Construction Com-
LO.2 pany has two divisions. The president, Su, manages the
roofing division. Su has delegated authority and responsibility for management of the modular manufacturing division to Jon Gee. The company has a competent accounting staff and a full-time internal auditor.
Unlike Su, however, Gee and his secretary handle all
the bids for manufacturing jobs, purchase all the materials without competitive bids, control the physical inventory of materials, contract for shipping, supervise
the construction work, bill the customers, approve all
bid changes and collect the payment from customers.
With Su's tacit approval, Gee has asked the internal auditor not to interfere with his busy schedule.

Required:
Discuss the internal control in this fact situation and
identify irregularities that could occur.

9.127 Costs and Benefits of Control. The following ques-
LO.1 tions and cases deal with the subject of cost-benefit
LO.3 analysis of internal control. Some important concepts in
LO.7 cost-benefit analysis are:
LO.9 1. Measurable benefit. Benefits or cost savings may be
measured directly or may be based on estimates of
expected value. An expected loss is an estimate of
the amount of a probable loss multiplied by the frequency or probability of the loss-causing event. A
measurable benefit can arise from the reduction of an
expected loss.

2. Qualitative benefit. Some gains or cost savings may not be measurable, such as company public image, reputation for regulatory compliance, customer satisfaction and employee morale.
3. Measurable costs. Controls may have direct costs such as wages and equipment expenses.
4. Qualitative cost factors. Some costs may be indirect, such as lower employee morale created by overcontrolled work restrictions.
5. Marginal analysis. Each successive control feature may have marginal cost and benefit effects on the control problem.

Case A

Porterhouse Company has numerous bank accounts. Why might management hesitate to spend $20,000 (half of a clerical salary) to assign someone the responsibility of reconciling each account every month for the purpose of catching the banks' accounting errors? Do other good reasons exist to justify spending $20,000 each year to reconcile bank accounts monthly?

Case B

Harper Hoe Company keeps a large inventory of hardware products in a warehouse. Last year, $500,000 was lost to thieves who broke in through windows and doors. Josh Harper figures that installing steel doors with special locks and burglar bars on the windows at a cost of $25,000 would eliminate 90 percent of the loss. Hiring armed guards to patrol the building 16 hours a day at a current annual cost of $75,000 would eliminate all the loss, according to officials of the Holmes Security Agency. Should Josh arrange for one, both or neither of the control measures?

Case C

The Merry Mound Cafeteria formerly collected from each customer as he or she reached the end of the food line. A cashier, seated at a cash register, rang up the amount (displayed on a digital screen) and collected money. Management changed the system, and now a clerk at the end of the line operates an adding machine and gives each customer a paper tape. The adding machine accumulates a running total internally. The customer presents the tape at the cash register on the way out and pays.

The cafeteria manager justified the direct cost of $10,000 annually for the additional salary and $500 for the new adding machine by pointing out that he could serve 4 more people each weekday (Monday through Friday) and 10 more people on Saturday and Sunday. The food line now moves faster and customers are more satisfied. (The average meal tab is $6, and total costs of food and service are considered fixed.) "Besides," he said, "my internal control is better." Evaluate the manager's assertions.

Case D

Assume, in the Merry Mound situation cited above, that the better control of separating cash custody from the end-of-food-line recording function was not cost beneficial, even after taking all measurable benefits into consideration. As an auditor, you believe the cash collection system deficiency is a material weakness in internal control, and you have written it as such in your letter concerning reportable conditions, which you delivered to Merry Mound's central administration. The local manager insists on inserting his own opinion on the cost-benefit analysis in the preface to the document that contains your report. Should you, in your report, express any opinion or evaluation on the manager's statement?

9.128 Cash Receipts Control. Sally's Craft Corner was
LO.4 opened in 1993 by Sally Moore, a fashion designer em-
LO.5 ployed by Bundy's Department Store. Sally is employed full-time at Bundy's and travels frequently to shows and marts in Vancouver, Montreal and Toronto. She enjoys crafts, wanted a business of her own and saw an opportunity in Vancouver. The Corner now sells regularly to about 300 customers, but business only began to pick up in 2000. The staff presently includes two salespeople and four office personnel, and Sally herself helps out on weekends.

Sales have grown, as has the Corner's reputation for quality crafts. The history is as follows:

	Sales	Discounts and Allowances	Net Sales
1996	$164,950	$5,000	$159,950
1997	185,750	5,500	180,250
1998	176,100	5,200	170,900
1999	183,800	5,700	178,100
2000	239,500	9,500	230,000
2001	294,700	14,800	279,900
2002	372,300	$22,300	350,000

With an expanding business and a need for inventory, the Corner is now cash poor. Prices are getting higher every month, and Sally is a little worried. The net cash flow is only about $400 per month after allowance of a 3 percent discount for timely payments on account. So she has engaged you as auditor and also asks for recommendations you might have about the cash flow situation. The Corner has never been audited.

During your review of internal control, you have learned the following about the four office personnel:

Janet Bundy is the receptionist and also helps customers. She is the daughter of the Bundy Department Store owner and a longtime friend of Sally. Janet helped Sally start the Corner. They run around together when Sally is in town. She opens all the mail, answers most of it herself, but turns over payments on account to Sue Kenmore.

Sue Kenmore graduated from high school and started working as a bookkeeper-secretary at the Corner in 2000. She wants to go to university but cannot afford it right now. She is very quiet in the office, but you have noticed she has some fun with her friends in her new BMW. In the office she gets the mailed-in payments on account from Janet, takes payments over the counter in the store, checks the calculations of discounts allowed, enters the cash collections in the cash receipts journal, prepares a weekly bank deposit (and mails it) and prepares a list (remittance list) of the payments on account. The list shows amounts received from each customer, discount allowed and amount to be credited to customers' account. She is also responsible for approving the discounts and credits for merchandise returned.

Ken Murphy has been the bookkeeper-clerk since 1996. He also handles other duties. Among them, he receives the remittance list from Sue, posts the customers' accounts in the subsidiary ledger, and gives the remittance list to David Roberts. Ken also prepares and mails customers' monthly statements. Ken is rather dull, interested mostly in hunting on weekends, but is a steady worker. He always comes to work in a beat-up pickup truck—an eyesore in the parking lot.

David Roberts is the bookkeeping supervisor. He started work in 1997 after giving up his small practice as a PA. He posts the general ledger (using the remittance list as a basis for cash received entries) and prepares monthly financial statements. He also approves and makes all other ledger entries and reconciles the monthly bank statement. He reconciles the customer subsidiary records to the accounts receivable control each month. David is very happy not to have to contend with the pressures he experienced in his practice as a PA.

Required:
a. Draw a simple flow chart of the cash collection and bookkeeping procedures.
b. Identify any reportable conditions or material weakness in internal control. Explain any reasons why you might suspect that errors or irregularities may have occurred.
c. Recommend corrective measures you believe necessary and efficient in this business.

9.129 Client's Control Procedures and Audit Programs. To
LO.4 test a client's internal control procedures, auditors de-
LO.5 sign a test of controls audit program. This audit program is a list of control tests to be performed, and each is directly related to an important client control procedure. Auditors perform the tests to obtain evidence about the operating effectiveness of the client's control procedures.

The controls listed below relate to a system for processing sales transactions. Each numbered item indicates an error or irregularity that could occur and specifies a control procedure that could prevent or detect it.

Required:
a. Identify the control objective satisfied by the client's control procedure.
b. Write the test of controls audit program by specifying an effective control test to produce evidence about the client's performance of the control procedure. [Hint: A control test is a two-part statement consisting of (1) identification of a data population from which a sample can be drawn and (2) expression of an action to take.]
1. The company wants to avoid selling goods on credit to bad credit risks. Poor credit control

could create problems with estimating the allowance for bad debts and a potential error by overstating the realizable value of accounts receivable. Therefore, the control procedure is: Each customer order is to be reviewed and approved for 30-day credit by the credit department supervisor. The supervisor then notes the decision on the customer order, which eventually is attached to copy 2 of the sales invoice and filed by date in the accounts receivable department. The company used sales invoices numbered 20,001 through 30,000 during the period under review.

2. The company considers sales transactions complete when shipment is made. The control procedures are: Shipping department personnel prepare prenumbered shipping documents in duplicate (sending one copy to the customer and filing the other copy in numerical order in the shipping department file). The shipping clerk marks up copy 3 of the invoice indicating the quantity shipped, the date and the shipping document number and sends it to the billing department where it is taken as authorization to complete the sales recording. Copy 3 is then filed in a daily batch in the billing department file. These procedures are designed to prevent the recording of sales (1) for which no shipment is made, or (2) before the date of shipment.

3. The company wants to control unit pricing and mathematical errors that could result in overcharging or undercharging customers, thus producing the errors of overstatement or understatement of sales revenue and accounts receivable. The accounting procedures are: Billing clerks use a catalogue list price to price the shipment on invoice copies 1, 2, and 3. They compute the dollar amount of the invoice. Copy 1 is sent to the customer. Copy 2 is used to record the sale and later is filed in the accounts receivable department by date. Copy 3 is filed in the billing department by date.

4. The company needs to classify sales to subsidiaries apart from other sales so the consolidated financial statement eliminations will be accurate. That is, the company wants to avoid the error of understating the elimination of intercompany profit and, therefore, overstating net income and inventory. The control procedure is: A billing supervisor reviews each invoice copy 2 to see whether the billing clerk imprinted sales to the company's four subsidiaries with a big red "9" (the code for intercompany sales). The supervisor does not initial or sign the invoices.

9.130 Controls Tests and Errors/Irregularities. The four
LO.4 questions below are taken from an internal control ques-
LO.5 tionnaire. For each question, state (a) one control test you could use to find out whether the control technique was really used, and (b) what error or irregularity could

occur if the question were answered "no," or if you found the control was not effective.

1. Are blank (sales) invoices available only to authorized personnel?
2. Are (sales) invoices checked for the accuracy of quantities billed? Prices used? Mathematical calculations?
3. Are the duties of the accounts receivable bookkeeper separate from any cash functions?
4. Are customer accounts regularly balanced with the control account?

9.131 Control Objectives and Procedures Associations. Exhibit 9.131–1 contains an arrangement of examples of transaction errors (lettered *a–g*) and a set of client control procedures and devices (numbered 1–15). You should photocopy the Exhibit 9.131–1 page or obtain a full-size copy from your instructor for the following requirements.

LO.4

Required:
a. Opposite the examples of transaction errors lettered a–g, write the name of the control objective clients wish to achieve to prevent, detect or correct the error.
b. Opposite each numbered control procedure, place an X in the column that identifies the error(s) the procedure is likely to control by prevention, detection or correction.

9.132 Control Objectives and Assertion Associations. Exhibit 9.131–1 contains an arrangement of examples of transaction errors (lettered *a–g*) and a set of client control procedures and devices (numbered 1–15).

LO.4

Required:
For each error/control objective, identify the financial statement assertion most benefitted by the control.

9.133 Client Control Procedures and Auditor's Control Tests. Exhibit 9.131–1 contains an arrangement of examples of transaction errors (lettered *a–g*) and a set of client control procedures and devices (numbered 1–15).

LO.5

Required:
For each client control procedure numbered 1–15, write an auditor's control test that could produce evidence on the question of whether the client's control procedure has been installed and is operating effectively.

9.134 Key Control, Control Test Evaluation. The auditor learns that the client has a control procedure in place that addresses the validity of sales and existence of accounts receivable. When a truck driver picks up goods from the warehouse, the warehouse employee has the driver sign a "shipper's receipt" showing the quantities and item numbers shipped, and the customer information. The shipper's receipts are filed in date order in the warehouse office. A copy of the signed shipper's receipt

LO.2
LO.5

EXHIBIT 9.131-1

a.	Sales recorded, goods not shipped
b.	Goods shipped, sales not recorded
c.	Goods shipped to a bad credit risk customer
d.	Sales billed at the wrong price or wrong quantity
e.	Product line A sales recorded as Product line B
f.	Failure to post charges to customers for sales
g.	January sales recorded in December

Control Procedures

1. Sales order approved for credit
2. Prenumbered shipping doc prepared, sequence checked
3. Shipping document quantity compared to sales invoice
4. Prenumbered sales invoices, sequence checked
5. Sales invoice checked to sales order
6. Invoiced prices compared to approved price list
7. General ledger code checked for sales product lines
8. Sales dollar batch totals compared to sales journal
9. Periodic sales total compared to same period accounts receivable postings
10. Accountants have instructions to date sales on the date of shipment
11. Sales entry date compared to shipping document date
12. Accounts receivable subsidiary totalled and reconciled to accounts receivable control account
13. Intercompany accounts reconciled with subsidiary company records
14. Credit files updated for customer payment history
15. Overdue customer accounts investigated for collection

is sent to the accounting office where it is used to record the reduction in inventory and issue a sales invoice. The invoice number is noted on the shipper's receipt and it is filed by invoice number in the accounting area. Since the client has a large number of customers, the auditor decides this is a key control that will be tested.

Required:

a. Why would the auditor decide this is a key control?

b. What will the auditor achieve by testing this control?

c. Design a control test the auditor could perform for this control procedure. Describe the two parts of the test in detail.

d. Assume the auditor performs a control test and finds the control procedure operated properly 95 percent of the time. How does this evidence affect the auditor's control risk assessment? What if the control operated 60 percent of the time? What if it operated 99 percent of the time?

9.135 Obtaining a "Sufficient" Understanding of Internal Control. The 12 partners of a regional-sized PA firm met in special session to discuss audit engagement efficiency. Jones spoke up, saying:

"We all certainly appreciate the firmwide policies set up by Martin and Smith, especially in connection with the audits of the large clients that have come our way recently. Their experience with a large national firm has helped build up our practice. But I think the standard policy of conducting reviews and tests of internal control on all audits is raising our costs too much. We can't charge our smaller clients fees for all the time the staff

spends on this work. I would like to propose that we give engagement partners discretion to decide whether to do a lot of work on assessing control risk. I may be an old mossback, but I think I can finish a competent audit without it."

Discussion on the subject continued but ended when Martin said, with some emotion: "But we can't disregard generally accepted auditing standards like Jones proposes!"

What do you think of Jones's proposal and Martin's view of the issue? Discuss.

9.136 Starting the "Logical Approach." One of the things you can do in a "logical approach" to the evaluation of internal control is to imagine what types of errors or irregularities could occur with regard to each significant class of transactions. Assume a company has the significant classes of transactions listed below. For each one, identify one or more errors or irregularities that could occur and specify the accounts that would be affected if proper controls were not specified or were not followed satisfactorily.

1. Credit sales transactions.
2. Raw materials purchase transactions.
3. Payroll transactions.
4. Equipment acquisition transactions.
5. Cash receipts transactions.
6. Leasing transactions.
7. Dividend transactions.
8. Investment transactions (short term).

Kingston Case questions related to Chapter 9 are on the Online Learning Centre that accompanies this text.

CHAPTER

10

Audit Sampling

In this chapter, we review the general topic of audit sampling, which relies heavily on the concepts of materiality and risk—audit risk, inherent risk, control risk and detection risk. Audit sampling is not an audit procedure in the same class as the procedures explained in previous chapters. Instead, it is a method of organizing the application of audit procedures, as well as a method of organizing the auditor's decision-making process.

LEARNING OBJECTIVES

After completing this chapter, you will be able to:

1. Explain the role of professional judgement in audit sampling decisions.

2. Distinguish audit sampling work from non-sampling work.

3. Compare and contrast statistical and non-statistical sampling.

4. Differentiate between sampling and non-sampling risk.

5. Develop a simple audit program for a test of a client's internal control procedures.

    a. Specify objectives, deviation conditions, populations and sampling units.
    b. Demonstrate some basic audit sampling calculations.
    c. Evaluate evidence from control testing.

6. Develop a simple audit program for an account balance, considering the influence of risk and tolerable misstatement.

    a. Specify objectives and a population of data.
    b. Determine sample size and select sample units.
    c. Evaluate monetary error evidence from a balance audit sample.

Note: Appendix 10B is located on the text Online Learning Centre.

INTRODUCTION TO AUDIT SAMPLING

. . . .

LEARNING OBJECTIVE

1 Explain the role of professional judgement in audit sampling decisions.

Audit sampling is the application of an audit procedure to less than 100 percent of the items within an account balance population or class of transactions for the purpose of evaluating some characteristic of the balance or class.[1] Testing is synonymous with sampling.[2] You have already seen the sampling idea incorporated in the explanation of a control test, which was defined as a two-part statement consisting of (1) an identification of the data population from which a sample of items will be selected for audit and (2) an expression of an action taken to produce relevant evidence.

To understand the definition of audit sampling, you must keep the following definitions in mind: **Audit procedure** refers to actions described as general audit techniques in Chapter 8 (computation, observation, confirmation, enquiry, inspection and analysis). An **account balance** refers to a control account made up of many constituent items; for example, an accounts receivable control account representing the sum of customers' accounts, an inventory control account representing the sum of various goods in inventory, a sales account representing the sum of many sales invoices or a long-term debt account representing the sum of several issues of outstanding bonds. A **class of transactions** refers to a group of transactions having common characteristics, such as cash receipts or cash disbursements, but which are not simply added together and presented as an account balance in financial statements.

Other definitions: A **population** is the set of all the elements that constitute an account balance or class of transactions. Each of the elements is a **population unit**; and when an auditor selects a sample, each element selected is called a sampling unit. A **sampling unit** can be a customer's account, an inventory item, a debt issue, a cash receipt, a cancelled cheque, and so forth. A **sample** is a set of sampling units.

How Risk and Materiality Are Used in Audit Sampling

Materiality and risk are key concepts in statistical sampling and auditing. This is illustrated in *CICA Handbook,* paragraph 5300.17:

> The determination of an appropriate sample on a representative basis may be made using either statistical or non-statistical methods. Whether statistical or non-statistical methods are used, their common purpose is to enable the auditor to reach a conclusion about an entire set of data by examining only a part of it. Statistical sampling methods allow the auditor to express in mathematical terms the uncertainty he or she is willing to accept and the conclusions of his or her test. The use of statistical methods does not eliminate the need for the auditor to exercise judgment. For example, the auditor has to determine the degree of audit risk he or she is willing to accept and make a judgement as to materiality.

The following box elaborates how the auditor's professional judgement is applied when deciding how much audit work is required and how the audit finding will be interpreted.

PROFESSIONAL JUDGEMENT AND THE EXTENT OF AUDIT TESTING

Handbook, 5142.08 states: "Decisions concerning materiality and audit risk are the most significant made in the course of an audit because they form the basis for determining the extent of the auditing procedures to be undertaken." Hence, professional judgement concerning these concepts is critical to audit practice.

In order to better understand why this is so, it's useful to imagine what the audit would be like if it were a purely scientific endeavour in which the management assertions were treated as hypotheses which had to be either supported (verified) or contradicted by the evidence. Perhaps a good analogy, but one not to be taken too literally, is to think of auditor opinions

---

[1] ISA 530.3.
[2] *Terminology for Accountants,* 4th Ed., CICA, Toronto, 1992.

as being similar to the opinion polls one frequently encounters in the media.

An opinion poll in *The Toronto Star* reported that a mayoral candidate M.L. led candidate B.H. with 51 percent and 46 percent support, respectively, of decided voters. This poll was the result of surveying 400 Toronto residents. A sample of this size is considered accurate to within 5 percentage points, 19 times out of 20. In other words, due to the uncertainties associated with the representatives of the sample of 400, the best the statistician can conclude about M.L.'s prospects is that there is a 95 percent confidence level that his actual support is in the range 51% ± 5% = 46% to 56%. The width of this band around the best point estimate (the 51%) is frequently referred to as **sampling precision**, which is related to materiality, and the confidence level is related to the amount of audit assurance.

Conceptually, an auditor can make a similar statement about financial statements. For example, after audit testing the auditor may conclude that a client's net income number is 200,000 ± 10,000, 19 times out of 20. It would be possible for the auditor to make this kind of statement if the appropriate statistical samples were drawn from all the various accounting components making up net income. In this statistical sampling framework, materiality is compared to the degree of accuracy or precision of the sample (i.e., the ± 10,000 for the client or ± 5 percent of the *Star* poll); and audit assurance is related to the statistical confidence (the 19 times out of 20 statement, which means the same as 95 percent = 19/20). Thus, if a purely statistical interpretation were to be put on the auditor's report, "presents fairly in all material respects" means that the difference between the audit estimate (the audit value or AV) based on audit testing and the reported amount (the book value or BV) is less than material. The level of audit assurance is assumed to be captured by the words *in our opinion* in the auditor's report.

The standard audit report can therefore be interpreted to mean there is a high level of assurance that there are no material misstatements in the financial statements. Conversely, we can look at the complement of assurance, which is audit risk, discussed in paragraph 5095.08, and interpret the standard audit report to mean there is a low level of risk that there are material misstatements in the financial statements after the audit.

In terms of a statistical sampling framework, the auditor's decision on the form of this report will be based on doing a sufficient amount of testing so that the auditor will be able to construct a confidence interval around his or her best estimate AV such that if BV is included in this interval *and* this interval is smaller than materiality, the auditor will have achieved the planned level of assurance from his or her testing. An equivalent but perhaps more intuitive approach can be developed which constructs an interval of possible errors around BV and if this precision is smaller than materiality, then the auditor has achieved the stated confidence that there is no material error. For example, assume the auditor has done enough testing at a client with a reported net income of $198,000 to conclude that the auditor has 95 percent confidence (assurance) that GAAP income is in the interval 198,000 ± 10,000. Assume materiality is set at 8 percent of reported income so that materiality equals .08 × 198,000 = 15,840. Since the achieved precision of 10,000 is less than materiality of 15,840, the auditor can conclude with at least 95 percent assurance that there is no material error in the reported net income of $198,000.

In order that the auditor can reach such a conclusion, he or she will have to plan the testing so that achieved precision is no larger than materiality. Note that if BV – AV is greater than materiality, then the auditor has not obtained the 95 percent assurance from testing and will either have to do more audit work or insist on an adjustment.

Sampling and the Extent of Auditing

Three aspects of auditing procedures are important—their nature, timing and extent. Nature refers to the six general techniques (computation, observation, confirmation, enquiry, inspection and analysis). Timing is a matter of when procedures are performed. More will be said about timing later in this chapter. Audit sampling is concerned primarily with matters of extent—the amount of work done when the procedures are performed. In the context of auditing standards, nature and timing relate most closely to the appropriateness of evidential matter, while extent relates most closely to the sufficiency (sample size) of evidential matter. The concept of testing is important to auditors because it is uneconomical to test client files exhaustively in many situations. It is common for client files on inventory and accounts receivable to contain thousands of accounting records.

Testing is a means of gaining assurance that the amount of errors in large files is not material. The formal theory supporting the concept of testing is statistical sampling. However, courts approved the concept of testing long before statistical theories were introduced to auditing. The majority of testing in auditing was once done on a judgemental basis. But as accounting populations increased in size auditors became aware that statistical sample sizes could be much smaller than intuition would suggest. For this reason statistical sampling became increasingly popular in the 1970s and 1980s. Both judgemental and statistical testing methods are equally acceptable by auditing standards. The reason for the focus on statistics here is that there is a theory underlying statistics that formalizes the reasoning used in pure judgemental testing. Brief summaries of the two types of audit programs introduced in Chapter 8 are set out following. Note that both these types of audit program can be performed on a statistical or nonstatistical basis.

TWO KINDS OF AUDIT PROGRAMS: TWO PURPOSES FOR AUDIT SAMPLING

Internal Control Program	Balance-Audit Program
Purpose Obtain evidence about client's control objective compliance	**Purpose** Obtain evidence about client's financial statement assertions
Validity Completeness Authorization Accuracy Classification Accounting Proper period	Existence (Occurrence) Completeness Valuation Ownership (Rights and obligations) Presentation and disclosure
Sample Usually from a class of transactions (population), such as:	**Sample** Usually from items in an asset or liability balance (population), such as:
Cash receipts Cash disbursements Purchases (inventory additions) Inventory issues Sales on credit Expense details Welfare payments (eligibility)	Accounts receivable Loans receivable Inventory Small tool fixed assets Depositors' savings accounts Accounts payable Unexpired magazine subscriptions

REVIEW CHECKPOINTS

10.1 Define the following terms: audit sampling, population, population unit and sample.

10.2 What role does professional judgement play in audit decisions regarding materiality, risk and sampling?

10.3 How does audit assurance relate to audit risk?

10.4 How does sampling relate to forming an audit opinion on financial statements?

Inclusions and Exclusions Related to Audit Sampling

LEARNING OBJECTIVE
2 Distinguish audit sampling work from non-sampling work.

Look again at the audit sampling definition, specifically the following section: "for the purpose of evaluating some characteristics of the balance or class." The meaning of this section is: an application of audit procedures is considered audit sampling if and only if the auditors' objective is to reach a conclusion about the entire account balance or transaction class (the population) on the basis of the evidence obtained from the audit of a sample drawn from the balance or class. If the entire population is audited, or if the purpose is only to gain general familiarity, the work is not considered to be audit sampling.

Perhaps the distinction between audit sampling and other methods can be seen more clearly in terms of the following work that is not considered audit sampling:

- Complete (100 percent) audit of all the elements in a balance or class, by definition, does not involve sampling.
- Analytical procedures, in the nature of overall comparisons, ratio calculations and the like, are normally not applied on a sample basis.
- A **walk-through**—following one or a few transactions through the accounting and control systems in order to obtain a general understanding of the client's systems—is not audit sampling because the objective is not to reach a conclusion about a balance or class.
- Several procedures do not lend themselves to sampling methods; for example, enquiry of employees, obtaining written representations, obtaining enquiry responses in the form of answers on an internal control questionnaire, scanning accounting records for unusual items and observation of personnel and procedures.[3]

Several procedures are typically used in audit sampling applications. They are recalculation, physical observation of tangible assets, confirmation and document examination. These procedures most often are applied to the audit of details of transactions and balances.

· ·

REVIEW CHECKPOINTS

10.5   Give examples of auditing procedures that are not sampling applications.

10.6   List audit procedures that are likely to be applied on a sample basis.

· ·

Why Auditors Sample

LEARNING OBJECTIVE
3 Compare and contrast statistical and nonstatistical sampling.

Auditors use audit sampling when (1) the nature and materiality of the balance or class does not demand a 100 percent audit, (2) a decision must be made about the balance or class, and (3) the time and cost to audit 100 percent of the population would be too great. So, auditors use sampling because they need to perform efficient audits on a timely basis and cannot do so by auditing 100 percent. The two sampling designs used by auditors are statistical sampling and nonstatistical sampling. Exhibit 10–1 provides an overview of the different choices auditors can make about the extent of their testing.

Statistical Sampling

Auditors define **statistical sampling** as audit sampling that uses the laws of probability for selecting and evaluating a sample from a population for the purpose of reaching a conclusion about the population. The essential points of this definition are that (1) a statistical sample is selected at random, and (2) statistical calculations are used to measure and express the results. Both conditions are necessary for a method to be considered statistical sampling rather than nonstatistical sampling.

A **random sample** is a set of sampling units so chosen that each population item has an equal likelihood of being selected in the sample. You can use a random sample in a

---

[3] "Audit Sampling," *Audit and Accounting Guide* (AICPA, 1983), pp. 1–3.

E X H I B I T   1 0 – 1   EXTENT OF AUDIT TESTING

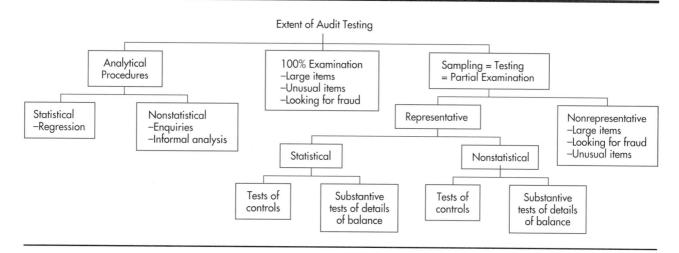

"nonstatistical sampling" design. However, you cannot use statistical calculations with a nonrandom sample. The mathematical laws of probability are not applicable for nonrandom samples, and basing such calculations on a nonrandom sample would be wrong.

A statistical calculation of sample size is not necessary for a method to be considered statistical sampling. You can use any sample size you feel appropriate in the circumstances. However, a preliminary estimate of sample size can be calculated using statistical models. A sampling method is statistical by virtue of random selection of the sample coupled with statistical calculation of the results.

Nonstatistical Sampling

A good definition of **nonstatistical (judgemental) sampling** is audit sampling in which auditors do not use statistical calculations to express the results. The sample selection

WHEN TO USE STATISTICAL SAMPLING

- Random numbers can be associated with population items.
- Objective results that can be defended mathematically are desired.
- Auditor has insufficient knowledge about the population to justify a basis for a nonstatistical sample.
- A representative (random) sample is required.
- Staff are adequately trained in statistical auditing.

ADVANTAGES OF STATISTICAL SAMPLING

- Requires a precise and definite approach to the audit problem.
- Incorporates evaluation that calculates a direct relation between the sample results and the entire population under audit.
- Requires auditors to specify, and even quantify, particular judgements on risk and materiality.
- Does not eliminate or reduce auditors' professional judgement.
- Allows more objective control of audit risks.
- Results in better planning and documentation when properly implemented (but can be more time-consuming and costly because of the greater formalism required).

technique can be random sampling or some other selection technique not based on mathematical randomness. Auditors are fond of saying that nonstatistical sampling involves "consideration of sampling risk in evaluating an audit sample without using statistical theory to measure that risk." "Consideration" in this context means "giving sampling risk some thoughtful attention" without direct knowledge or measurement of its magnitude. Be careful not to confuse sampling and nonsampling risk with statistical and nonstatistical sampling. They are not related, as further explained in the next learning objective.

10.7   Give three reasons why auditors may choose to use sampling.

10.8   What three choices are available to the auditor for deciding on the extent of audit procedures.

10.9   Are testing, partial examination and sampling the same thing? Explain your response.

10.10   Distinguish between statistical and nonstatistical sampling.

10.11   Differentiate between representative and nonrepresentative testing. What client factors determine which is most appropriate in planning audit procedures?

10.12   What is the difference between a statistical representative test and a nonstatistical representative test?

10.13   Why is it that a nonrepresentative test cannot be done statistically?

Sampling and Nonsampling Risk

LEARNING OBJECTIVE
4 Differentiate between sampling and nonsampling risk.

When auditors perform procedures on a sample basis and obtain sufficient evidence, a conclusion about the population characteristic can still be wrong. For example, suppose an auditor selected 100 sales invoices for audit and found no errors or irregularities in any of them. The conclusion that a significant incidence of errors and irregularities does not exist in the entire population of sales invoices from which the sample was drawn might be wrong. How, you ask? Simple: The sample might not reflect the actual condition of the population. No matter how randomly or carefully the sample was selected, it might not be a good representation of the extent of errors and irregularities actually in the population.

Sampling risk is defined as the probability that an auditor's conclusion based on a sample might be different from the conclusion based on an audit of the entire population. You could audit a sample of sales invoices and decide, based on the sample, that the population of sales invoices contained few errors and irregularities. However, suppose some auditors with more time could audit all the sales invoices and find a large number of errors and irregularities. In such a case, your sample-based decision would have been proved wrong. Apparently, your sample did not represent the population very well. Sampling risk expresses the probability of making a wrong decision based on sample evidence, and it exists in both statistical and nonstatistical sampling methods. You cannot escape it in audit sampling. With statistical sampling, you can measure it, and you can control it by auditing sufficiently large samples. With nonstatistical sampling, you can "consider" it without measuring it. However, considering sampling risk without measuring it requires experience and expertise. Other special aspects of sampling risk are discussed later in the sections on auditing control compliance and account balances.

There are two types of sampling risk: alpha and beta risk. **Alpha risk** is also frequently referred to as **Type I error risk** while **beta risk** is frequently referred to as **Type II error risk**. These can be defined various general ways and they apply to *all* statistical procedures. Alpha risk is the risk that the auditor concludes that the population is worse in terms of errors than it really is. Beta risk is the risk that the auditor concludes the population is better than it really is. Now, which risk covers the situation of the auditor failing to detect a material misstatement? If you said beta risk you are correct. Beta risk covers the situation where the auditor concludes the population is better (i.e., immaterial misstatements) than it actually is (i.e., material misstatements). Alpha and beta risk are the generic terms. As you will see auditors have developed more specific risk terms for various types of testing, but they are either an alpha or a beta type risk. Keep this basic classification in mind as it will help you better follow the subsequent terminology.

WHEN TO USE NONSTATISTICAL SAMPLING

- Association of population items with random numbers is difficult and expensive.
- Strictly defensible results based on mathematics are not necessary.
- Auditor has sufficient knowledge about the population to justify a basis for a nonstatistical sample with expectation of a reasonable conclusion about the population.
- A representative (random) sample is not required; for example, because an efficient nonstatistical sample of large items leaves an immaterial amount unaudited.
- The population is known to be diverse, with some segments especially error-prone.

ADVANTAGES OF NONSTATISTICAL SAMPLING

- Permits a less rigidly defined approach to unique problems that might not fit into a statistical method.
- Permits the auditors to reapply evaluation judgements based on factors in addition to the sample evidence.
- Permits auditors to be vague and less than definite about, and omit quantification of, particular judgements on risk and materiality.
- Permits auditors to assert standards of subjective judgement. (Thus, the alternative name is "judgement sampling.")

EXAMPLES OF NONSAMPLING RISK

Performing inappropriate procedures: Auditors based the evaluation of inventory obsolescence on forecasted sales without adequately evaluating the reasonability of the forecast assumptions.

Failure to consider test results appropriately: Auditor did not adequately investigate discrepancies in inventory counts and pricing, failing to note misstatements.

Neglecting the importance of analytical review: Auditor might have discovered client's failure to eliminate intercompany profits if year-to-year product mix, gross profit and recorded eliminations had been analyzed.

Failure to maintain control over audit procedures: Auditors' lax attitude permitted client employees to tamper with records selected for confirmation.

Lack of professional scepticism: Auditors accepted client's unsupported verbal representations instead of gathering independent evidence to support management's assertions.

Nonsampling risk is all risk other than sampling risk. You need to refer to the audit risk (AR) model (Chapter 8) to understand the breadth of this definition:

$$\text{Risk Model: } AR = IR \times CR \times DR$$

Nonsampling risk can arise from:

- Misjudging the inherent risk (IR). An auditor who mistakenly believes that few material errors or irregularities occur in the first place will tend to do less work and, therefore, may fail to detect problems.
- Misjudging the control risk (CR). An auditor who is too optimistic about the ability of controls to prevent, detect and correct errors and irregularities will tend to do less work, with the same results as misjudging the inherent risk.
- Poor choice of procedures and mistakes in execution—related to detection risk (DR). Auditors can select procedures inappropriate for the objective (e.g., confirming recorded accounts receivable when the objective is to find unrecorded accounts receivable), can fail to recognize errors or irregularities when vouching supporting documents or can sign off as having performed procedures when the work actually was not done.

Nonsampling risk also represents the possibility of making a wrong decision. It exists both in statistical and in nonstatistical sampling. The problem is that nonsampling risk cannot be measured. Auditors control it—and believe it is reduced to a negligible level—through adequate planning and supervision of audit engagements and personnel, by having policies and procedures for quality control of their auditing practices and by having internal monitoring and external peer review of their own quality control systems.

One other distinction is important: External critics (judges, juries, peer reviewers) have few grounds for criticizing auditors who fall victim to sampling risk, provided that an audit sampling application is planned and executed reasonably well. Auditors are more open to criticism and fault-finding when erroneous audit decisions result from nonsampling risk. These various risks in auditing are summarized in Exhibit 10–2.

Sampling Methods and Applications

Audit sampling is concerned with the amount of work performed and the sufficiency of audit evidence obtained. Audit sampling terminology contains many new concepts and definitions. The ones presented previously, however, are general and apply to all phases of audit sampling. You need to know them so you can "speak the language."

Auditors design audit samples to (1) evaluate control-effectiveness for the purpose of assessing control risk and (2) audit account balances for the purpose of getting direct evidence about financial statement assertions. The next major sections of this chapter explain

EXHIBIT 10-2

Summary of Risks in Audit Testing
(as categorized by type of test)

Risk	Tests of Controls	Substantive Tests of Balance
Audit risk AR	CR component of AR	RIA or APR component of AR
Sampling risk	Risk of selecting a nonrepresentative sample in tests of controls	Risk of selecting a nonrepresentative sample in substantive test
Alpha risk	Controlled indirectly via tests of controls	Controlled indirectly via substantive tests
Beta risk	Controlled directly via value for CR	Controlled directly via values for RIA and APR
Nonsampling risk	All other risks associated with testing of controls	All other risks associated with substantive testing

RIA: Risk of incorrect acceptance APR: Analytical procedures risk CR: Control risk.

these two designs. Each of the sections is organized in terms of (1) planning, (2) performing and (3) evaluating audit sampling.

This chapter is presented in general terms, avoiding the mathematics of sampling, along the same lines as the *CICA Handbook,* section 5300 and Auditing Guideline "Applying the Concept of Materiality," ISA 530 and the AICPA audit and accounting guide entitled "Auditing Sampling."

**REVIEW
CHECKPOINTS**

10.14   What is nonsampling risk? Give some examples.

10.15   Define sampling risk.

10.16   Does sampling risk always exist in both statistical and nonstatistical sampling? Explain your response.

10.17   Can sampling risk be avoided? Explain.

10.18   Can nonsampling risk be avoided? Explain.

10.19   Which type of risks are auditors most likely to be sued successfully for—sampling risk or nonsampling risk?

10.20   What two types of audit programs are ordinarily used as written plans for audit procedures?

10.21   What are control tests? What purpose do they serve?

TEST OF CONTROLS FOR ASSESSING CONTROL RISK

LEARNING OBJECTIVE

5 Develop a simple audit program for a test of a client's internal control procedures.

Auditors must assess the control risk to determine the nature, timing and extent of other audit procedures. Final evaluations of internal control are based on evidence obtained in the review and testing phases of an evaluation. Auditors' assessments of control risk are hard to describe because they always depend entirely on the circumstances in each specific situation. The judgements are usually very specific. For example, an auditor might learn that a company's validity control procedure to prevent recording of fictitious sales is to require the bookkeeper to match a shipping order with each sales invoice before recording a sale. Now suppose the control test of selecting recorded sales invoices and vouching them to shipping orders shows a number of mistakes (invoices without supporting shipping orders)—poor control, as performed. Sales might be overstated. One way to take this control deficiency into account is to perform more extensive work on accounts receivable using confirmation and enquiries and analytical review related to collectibility. (If sales are overstated, one result could be overstatement of receivables—the debit side of the accounting entry.) This illustrates that control testing provides indirect evidence of the monetary accuracy of the accounts. In this case, the shipping order might have been misplaced, so that the recorded sales invoice might still be correct. Hence, failure to have a matching shipping order only increases the probability of a monetary misstatement but does not guarantee that there is a misstatement. Only further substantive work such as direct confirmation with the customer would provide convincing evidence of a misstatement.

The previous example related a specific control (the validity-related control procedure of matching sales invoices with shipping orders) to a specific set of other audit procedures directed toward a possible problem (overstatement of sales and receivables). In a more general sense, auditors reach judgements about control risk along the lines shown in Exhibit 10–3. Some situations may call for a nonquantitative expression, and auditors sometimes need a quantitative expression. The quantitative ranges overlap to communicate the idea that auditors really cannot put exact numbers on these kinds of evaluations.

Audit sampling as a method and plan for conducting control is a structured, formal approach embodied in seven steps. The seven-step framework helps auditors plan, perform

EXHIBIT   10-3   AUDITOR'S ASSESSMENT OF CONTROL RISK

| | *Judgement Expression of Control Risk* | |
Evaluation of Internal Control	Nonquantitative	Quantitative
Excellent control, both as specified and in compliance.	Low (1)	10%–30%
Good control, but lacks something in specification or compliance.	Moderate (2)	20%–70%
Deficient control, either in specification or compliance or both.	High (3)	60%–95%
Little or no control.	Maximum	100%

If combining inherent and control risk evaluation is easier, then "low," "moderate," and "high" mean:
1. Low combined inherent and control risk.
2. Moderate combined inherent and control risk.
3. High combined inherent and control risk.

and evaluate control test results. It also helps auditors accomplish an eighth step—careful documentation of the work—by showing each of the seven areas to be described in the working papers. The first seven steps are as follows:

1. Specify the audit objectives.
2. Define the deviation conditions.
3. Define the population.
4. Determine the sample size.
5. Select the sample.
6. Perform the control tests.
7. Evaluate the evidence.

Plan the Procedures

LEARNING OBJECTIVE

5a Specify objectives, deviation conditions, populations and sampling units.

The first three steps are planning steps that represent the **problem-recognition** phase of the sampling method. When a client describes the control system, the implicit assertion is: "These controls work; people comply with the control procedures and achieve the control objectives." The auditors' question (problem) is: "Is it so? Are the validity (and other) control objectives achieved satisfactorily?"

Test of controls audit work is always directed towards producing evidence of the client's performance of its own control procedures. Thus, auditors' procedures should produce evidence about the client's achievement of the seven control objectives.

1. Specify the Audit Objectives
Take a control procedure under the validity objective as an example—namely, the client's procedure of requiring a shipping order to be matched with a sales invoice before a valid sale is recorded. The specific objective of an auditor's test of controls audit procedure would be: Determine whether recorded sales invoices are supported by matched shipping orders. The audit procedure itself would be: Select a sample of recorded sales invoices and vouch them to supporting shipping orders.

The client's matching of sales invoices to shipping orders in the example is a **key control**—it is important. Auditors should identify and audit only the key controls. Incidental controls that are not important will not be relied on to reduce control risk and need not be audited for compliance. Auditing them for compliance just wastes time if they really do not have much impact on the control risk assessment.

2. Define the Deviation Conditions
The terms **deviation**, **error**, **occurrence** and **exception** are synonyms in test of controls sampling. They all refer to a departure from a prescribed internal control procedure in a particular case: for example, an invoice is recorded with no supporting shipping order (bill of

lading). Defining the deviation conditions at the outset is important, so the auditors doing the work will know a deviation when they see one. As an assistant accountant, you would prefer to be instructed: "Select a sample of recorded sales invoices, vouch them to supporting shipping orders and document cases where the shipping order is missing," instead of "Check recorded sales invoices for any mistakes." The latter instruction does not clearly define the deviation conditions and can increase nonsampling risk.

The example is oversimplified. However, this vouching procedure for compliance evidence can be used to obtain evidence about several control objectives at the same time. The invoice can be compared to the shipping order for evidence of actual shipment (validity), reviewed for credit approval (authorization), prices compared to the price list (authorization and accuracy), quantity billed compared to quantity shipped (accuracy), recalculated (arithmetic accuracy), compared for correspondence of shipment date and record date (proper period), and traced to postings in the general ledger and subsidiary accounts (accounting). Exhibit 10–4 shows these deviation conditions laid out in a working paper designed to record the control testing results for a sample of sales invoices.

Time for some more terminology: Test of controls audit sampling is also called **attribute sampling**. Attribute sampling is audit sampling in which auditors look for the presence or absence of a control condition. In response to the audit question: "For each sales invoice in the sample, can a matched shipping order be found?" the answer can be only yes or no. With this definition, auditors can count the number of deviations and use the count when evaluating the evidence. Attribute sample can also be useful in balance auditing; an example is shown in the box on page 382.

EXHIBIT 10–4 TEST OF CONTROLS AUDIT DOCUMENTATION

Index _M 10.3_   By _J C_ Date _11-11-20X2_
Review _G.D._ Date _11-15-20X2_

KINGSTON COMPANY
Test of Controls Over Recorded Sales
December 31, 20X2

Invoice number	Date	Amount	Bill of lading	Credit approved	Approved prices	Quantities match	Arithmetic accurate	Dates match	Posted to customer
35000	Mar. 30	$ 3,000							
35050	Mar. 31	$ 800			X				
35100	Apr. 2	$ 1,200					Y		
35150	Apr. 3	$ 1,500			Y				
35200	Apr. 5	$ 400							
35250	Apr. 6	$ 300	X			X	Y	X	
32100	Jan. 3	$ 1,000							
32150	Jan. 4	$ 200							
34850	Mar. 25	Missing	X	X	X	X	X	X	
34900	Mar. 26	$ 100			Y				
34950	Mar. 27	$ 200							
Sample = 200		$98,000							
Uncorrected deviations			4	9	5	6	3	7	0

X = Uncorrected deviation.
Y = Deviation occurred but was detected and corrected later.

3. Define the Population

The specification of control test (compliance) audit objectives and the definition of deviation conditions usually define the population, which is the set of all elements in the balance or class of transactions. In the example the population consists of all the recorded sales invoices, and each invoice is a population unit. In **classical attribute sampling**, a sampling unit is the same thing as a population unit.[4]

Population definition is important because audit conclusions can be made only about the population from which the sample was selected. For example, evidence from a sample of recorded sales invoices (the population for our illustrative procedure) cannot be used for a conclusion about completeness. Controls related to the completeness objective (in this case, control over failure to record an invoice for goods shipped) can only be audited by sampling from a population representing goods shipped (the shipping order file) and not by sampling from the population of recorded invoices.

A complicating factor in population definition is the timing of the audit work. Control tests ideally should be applied to transactions executed throughout the period under audit because auditors want to reach a conclusion about control risk during the entire period. However, auditors often perform control tests at an **interim date**—a date some weeks or months before the client's year-end date—and at that time the entire population (say, recorded sales invoices for the year) will not be available for audit. Nothing is wrong with doing the work at an interim date, but auditors still cannot ignore the remaining period between the interim date and the year-end. Strategies for considering control in the period after the interim date are explained later.

Another complicating factor in population definition is the need to determine the correspondence of the **physical representation of the population** to the population itself. The physical representation of the population is the auditor's frame of reference for selecting a sample. It can be a journal listing of recorded sales invoices, a file drawer full of invoice copies, a computer file of invoices, or another physical representation. The sample actually will be selected from the physical representation, so it must be complete and correspond with the actual population. The physical representation of the recorded sales invoice as a list in a journal is fairly easy to visualize. However, an auditor should make sure that periodic listings (e.g., monthly sales journals) are added correctly and posted to the general ledger sales accounts. Now, a selection of individual sales invoices from the sales journal is known to be from the complete population of recorded sales invoices. You should be careful, however. Some physical frames may not be so easy to assess for complete correspondence to a population of interest.

A BALANCE-AUDIT APPLICATION OF ATTRIBUTE SAMPLING

Attribute control test samples usually are drawn from a class of transactions in order to obtain evidence about compliance with control objectives. Attribute samples also can be used sometimes for balance-audit purposes. This example suggests an attribute sample to obtain evidence about an ownership (rights) financial statement assertion.

Question: A lessor is in the business of leasing autos, large trucks, tractors and trailers. Is it necessary for the auditors to examine the titles to all the equipment?

Answer: It is not necessary, unless some extraordinary situation or circumstance is brought to light, for the auditors to examine titles to all the equipment. Random test verification of title certificates or proper registration of vehicles should be made.

Source: AICPA Technical Practice Aids, 8330.02.

---

[4] Dollar-unit sampling, however, defines a different sampling unit. Dollar-unit sampling (DUS) is explained in detail in Appendix 10B on the Online Learning Centre.

Perform the Procedures

LEARNING OBJECTIVE

5b Demonstrate some basic audit sampling calculations.

The next three performance steps represent the **evidence-collection** phase of the sampling method. These steps are performed to obtain the evidence.

4. Determine the Sample Size

Sample size—the number of population units to audit—should be determined thoughtfully. Some auditors operate on the "magic number theory" (e.g., select 30, because that's what we have always used on this audit). Be careful, however, because a magic number may or may not satisfy the need for enough evidence. A magic number may also be too large. Auditors must consider four influences on sample size: sampling risk, tolerable deviation rate, expected population deviation rate and population size.

Sampling Risk.   Previously, sampling risk was defined as the probability that an auditor's conclusion based on a sample might be different from the conclusion based on an audit of the entire population. In other words, when using evidence from a sample, an auditor might reach a wrong conclusion and decide that (1) control risk is very low when, in fact, it is not, or (2) control risk is very high when, in fact, it is not so bad. The more you know about a population (from a larger sample), the less likely you are to reach a wrong conclusion. Thus, the larger the sample, the lower the sampling risk of making either of the two decision errors. More will be said about these risks in the section on evaluation.

In terms of our example, the important sampling risk is the probability that the sample will reveal few or no recorded sales invoices without supporting shipping orders when, in fact, the population contains many such deviations. This result leads to the erroneous conclusion that the control worked well. The probability of finding few or no deviations when many exist is reduced by auditing a larger sample. Thus, sample size varies inversely with the amount of sampling risk an auditor is willing to take.

Tolerable Deviation Rate.   Auditors should have an idea about the correspondence of rates of deviation in the population with control risk assessments. Perfect control compliance is not necessary, so the question is: What rate of deviation in the population signals control risk of 10 percent? 20 percent? 30 percent? and so forth, up to 100 percent? Suppose an auditor believes that $90,000 of sales invoices could be exposed to control deviations without causing a minimum material misstatement in the sales and accounts receivable balances. If the total gross sales is $8.5 million, this judgement implies a **tolerable deviation rate** of about 1 percent ($90,000/$8.5 million). Since this 1 percent rate marks the minimum material misstatement, it indicates a low control risk (say, 0.05), and it justifies a great deal of reliance on internal control in the audit of the sales and accounts receivable balances.

However, there can be more than one tolerable deviation rate. Each successively higher rate is associated with a higher control risk. Continuing with our example, higher tolerable deviation rates could be associated with higher control risks as follows:[5]

Deviation Rate	Control Risk
1%	0.05
2	0.10
4	0.20
6	0.30
8	0.40
10	0.50
12	0.60
14	0.70
16	0.80
18	0.90
20	1.00

[5] Accounting firms have different policies for associating tolerable deviation rates with control risk categories. Some start with a minimum rate of 1 percent, and others start with higher rates.

Since sample size varies inversely with the tolerable deviation rate, the auditor who wants to assess control risk at 0.05 (tolerable rate = 1 percent) will need to audit a larger sample of sales transactions than another auditor who is willing to assess control risk at 0.40 (tolerable rate = 8 percent). The desired control risk level and its tolerable rate is a matter of auditor choice.

The tolerable rate is not a fixed rate until the auditor decides what control risk assessment suits the audit plan. Then it becomes a decision criterion involved in the sampling application. Some auditors express the tolerable rate as a number (necessary for statistical calculation of sample size), while others do not put a number on it. Appendix 10B on the text Online Learning Centre contains more explanation about the determination of various tolerable rates.

Expected Population Deviation Rate.   Auditors usually know or suspect some control performance conditions. Sometimes they have last year's audit experience with the client; sometimes they have information from a predecessor auditor. They have information about the client's personnel, the working conditions and the general control-environment. This knowledge contributes to an **expectation about the population deviation rate**, which is an estimate of the ratio of the number of expected deviations to population size. Suppose the auditors discovered 1 percent deviation in last year's audit. The expected population deviation rate could then be 1 percent. Auditors can also stipulate a zero expected deviation rate, which will produce a minimum sample size for audit.

The expected rate is important in a common-sense perspective. If auditors had reason to expect more deviations than they could tolerate, there would be no reason to perform any test of controls. Thus, the expected rate must be less than the tolerable rate. Also, the closer the expected rate is to the tolerable rate, the larger the sample will need to be to reach a conclusion that deviations do not exceed the tolerable rate. Consequently, the sample size varies directly with the expected deviation rate (especially in terms of larger samples when the expected rate nears the tolerable rate). Some auditors will express the expected rate as a number (necessary for statistical calculations of sample size), while others will not put a number on it.

The simplified approach we use will not put a number on the expected population deviation (effectively expected rate is zero). Appendix 10B on the text Online Learning Centre explains how to work with nonzero expected population deviation rates.

Population Size.   Common sense probably tells you that samples should be larger for bigger populations (a direct relationship). Strictly speaking, your common sense is accurate. As a practical matter, however, an appropriate sample size for a population of 100,000 units may be only 2 or 3 sampling units larger than an appropriate sample size for a 10,000-unit population. Not much difference! But also note that by using the same calculation for the 10,000 population as you would for the 100,000 population your sample size for the 10,000 population is slightly bigger, i.e., more conservative. The general principle is that if you use the simplified formulas for very large populations, you end up using simpler formulas and obtain slightly conservative results. Many practising auditors find this trade-off worthwhile.

The preceding discussion of sample size determinants is intended to give you a general understanding of the four influences on sample size. These influences are applicable to both statistical and nonstatistical sampling. A summary is presented in Exhibit 10–5. Next, we consider the simplified way of calculating sample sizes.

Brief Overview of Basic Formulas Used in Statistical Auditing

We introduce some basic formulas used to provide an overview of the most fundamental mechanics of statistical auditing. There are two key points at which the formulas and tables are used in statistical sampling: (1) sample size planning and (2) sample evaluation. We use an approach in which the same formula and table can be applied to both tests of controls and

E X H I B I T   1 0 – 5   SAMPLE SIZE RELATIONSHIPS: TEST OF CONTROLS AUDITING

Sample Size Influence	*Predetermined Sample Size Will Be*		
	High Rate or Large Population	Low Rate or Small Population	Sample Size Relationship
1. Acceptable sampling risk	Smaller	Larger	Inverse
2. Tolerable deviation rate	Smaller	Larger	Inverse
3. Expected population deviation rate	Larger**	Smaller	Direct
4. Population	Larger*	Smaller*	Direct

*Effect on sample size is quite small for population of 1,000 or more.
**Effect of this is explained in Appendix 10B on the Online Learning Centre. Many auditors do not quantify the expected rate. This results in the simplified approach described in this section.

substantive tests of balances. The approach is called dollar-unit sampling (DUS) and this is the most common approach in practice. The reasons DUS is so common are that it is effective, efficient and the easiest to use of all approaches. We begin by illustrating its use in sample size planning for tests of control.

For planning audit sample sizes, the equation $n = R/P$ summarizes the key factors that affect the sufficiency of audit evidence. This equation shows the relationship between the confidence level (as reflected by the R value) and materiality (as reflected by P), and the extent of audit testing (as reflected in sample size n). That is, the amount of audit work is directly proportional to the confidence level and inversely proportional to the materiality level used.

For both tests of controls and substantive tests, solve for n in the formula: $R = nP$. So that $n = R/P$, where $R = {}_{CL}R_K$ is a confidence level factor which is unique for each combination of confidence level (CL) and acceptable number of errors (K) from the table of values for R given in Appendix 10A, and P is materiality, or something based on materiality, that is represented as a rate or proportion. P is also referred to as UEL, which stands for upper error limit. The auditor must use professional judgement in specifying K, CL and P.

P is the amount, in terms of a rate, that the auditor considers material for the population being tested. It has to be set considering additive effect of errors in other accounting populations representing other balances or transaction streams. Planned P as used in this stage of sampling might be an amount lower than materiality so that the auditor can reduce alpha risk. Firm practice varies: firms can (indirectly) control alpha risk through using the *planned* K value, through the *planned* P value, or through a combination of the two. The most common strategy appears to be to use K = 0 and to use a *planned* P in the range of half to full materiality. We discuss these options in the online Appendix 10B. Here we simplify the calculations by assuming that P is set equal to materiality or tolerable deviation rate. This results in the smallest sample size possible for the stated confidence level and precision. This smallest sample size is used by many firms as a guide to minimum sample sizes (i.e., sufficient sample sizes) for all representative sampling whether statistical or nonstatistical.

In this formula CL = 1– beta risk, where beta risk is the risk that the test will fail to detect a material misstatement when it exists. In other words, beta risk is the same as the risk of incorrect acceptance (RIA). Alpha risk is the risk of concluding there is a material misstatement when in fact the misstatements are immaterial. In other words, alpha risk is the risk of incorrect rejection. Beta risk is the more serious risk in testing as it relates directly to the audit risk model and its components, depending on whether we are talking about tests of controls or substantive tests. Beta risk relates to audit effectiveness because the auditor concludes, based on his or her evidence, that there is no material misstatement. Alpha risk, on the other hand, relates to audit efficiency because the auditor will end up doing unnecessary work to clear up his or her mistake. The auditor is aware of this unnecessary work by the end of the audit. The K value implicitly controls the alpha risk. The higher the K value used in sample size planning, the lower the alpha risk and the larger the sample size.

To illustrate the calculations using the table of R values in Appendix 10A, let us assume the auditor wants a confidence level of 95 percent, uses K = 0 to make the sample planning as simple as possible (this results in the smallest sample size for the planned confidence level), and sets P so that it equals the tolerable deviation rate, which we assume here is 0.05, so that P = 0.05. Using our formula n = R/P and the table you should get the following results: n= 3.0/0.05 = 60 so that your planned sample size, given these objectives, is 60.

A Note on Testing of Controls for Audits of Internal Control Statements

Section 404 of the *Sarbanes-Oxley Act* introduced the requirement for management to prepare internal control statements and have them audited. This requirement led to PCAOB's Auditing Standard No. 2.

What does testing of controls mean in this new context? There are several critical differences to be aware of relative to the discussion of the rest of this chapter. First, internal control statements focus on company-level control objectives such as "tone at the top," corporate codes of conduct and corporate governance in general. Second, the focus is on the design of internal control at a specific point in time. Third, auditors need to evaluate an authoritative framework for evaluating this design. For example, the PCAOB requires that the following be considered as part of the framework for suitable internal control criteria for purposes of reporting on internal control: control environment, risk assessment, control activities, information and communication and monitoring.

The rest of this chapter stresses testing of detailed control activities. The other components of PCAOB's framework are broader, company-level controls as summarized in the following box.

COMPANY-LEVEL CONTROL OBJECTIVES

Control Environment
- Through its attitudes and actions, management demonstrates character, integrity and ethical values.
- Management's philosophy and operating style are consistent with a sound control environment.
- Management assigns authority and responsibility.
- Human resource policies and procedures are consistent with and reinforce the control environment.
- The audit committee and overall board of directors are actively involved and have significant influence over the organization.

Risk Assessment
- Management has established practices for identifying, evaluating and appropriately mitigating risks.

Information and Communication
- Management gathers information from and disseminates information to the appropriate people on a timely basis.
- Management has established an effective "whistleblower" program as it relates to financial reporting.

Monitoring
- Management has established effective ongoing monitoring activities.
- Management performs separate evaluations of the organization's internal control environment to confirm its effectiveness.

Source: J. Stephen McNally, *Journal of Accountancy*, June 2005, p. 66.

In order to effectively assess the broader corporate controls auditors will need to be more creative (more critical thinking as discussed in Chapter 4 will be needed!). For example, auditors may need to conduct surveys of employees or conduct tests of how effectively management responds to allegations of improprieties. Generally, auditors will need to rely less on detailed testing and more on observations and analytic type procedures such as interviews of board members. Auditors will need to gauge employee awareness and comfort level with company-level controls. As you can imagine trying to assess "comfort levels" and "tone at the top" will require auditors to evaluate character and ethical values of key people. Thus the critical thinking on these issues and its documentation will become more important than ever.[6]

5. Select the Sample

Auditing standards express two requirements for samples: (1) Sampling units must be selected from the population to which an audit conclusion will apply, ideally from transactions executed throughout the period under audit, and (2) a sample must be representative of the population from which it is drawn. In this context a **representative sample** is one that mirrors the characteristics of the population. Auditors, however, cannot guarantee representativeness. After all, that is what sampling risk is all about—the probability that the sample might not mirror the population well enough.

Auditors can try to attain representativeness by selecting random samples. A sample is considered **random** if each unit in the population has an equal probability of being included in the sample.

Intentional or accidental exclusion of a segment of a population can render a sample nonrepresentative. A popular way to select random samples is to associate each population unit with a unique number (easily done if the population units are prenumbered documents), then obtain a selection of random numbers to identify the sample units. You can use a printed random number table (one is provided in Appendix 10A) or a computerized random number generator to obtain a list of random numbers. This method is known as **unrestricted random selection**.

Another popular method is called **systematic random selection**. You need to know the population size and have a predetermined sample size to use it. The process is (1) obtain a random starting place in the physical representation (list of sales invoices recorded in a sales journal, for example) and select that unit, then (2) count through the file and select every kth unit, where k = Population size divided by Sample size. For example, if 10,000 invoices, numbered from 32071 to 42070, were issued, and you want a sample of 200, first use a random number table to get a starting place, say at invoice #35000, then select every kth = 10,000 divided by 200 = 50th invoice. So the next would be #35050, then #35100 . . . , then #42050, then #32100, #32150, and so on. (At the end of the list, you cycle back through the invoices #32071 through #34950.) Most systematic samples are selected using five or more random starts in the population.

Sample selection is the first step where a distinction between statistical and nonstatistical audit sampling is crucial. For statistical sampling evaluation, the sample must be random.

In nonstatistical plans, auditors sometimes use sample selection methods whose randomness and representativeness cannot be evaluated easily. **Haphazard selection** refers to any unsystematic way of selecting sample units; for example, closing your eyes and dipping into a file drawer of sales invoices to pick items. The problem is that you may pick only the crumpled ones that stick out, and they may be different from most of the other invoices in the drawer. Also, you cannot describe your method so someone else can **replicate** it—reperform your selection procedure and get the same sample units. Some auditors describe haphazard sampling as a method of choosing items without any special reason for including or excluding items, thus obtaining a representative sample. However, haphazard selection should be considered only as a last resort because it is hard to document and impossible to replicate.

Another method is **block sampling**, which is the practice of choosing segments of contiguous transactions; for example, choosing the sales invoices processed on randomly

---

[6] See J. Stephen McNally, "Assessing Company-Level Controls," *Journal of Accountancy*, June 2005, pp. 65–68.

chosen days, say February 3, July 17, and September 29. Implicitly, the block sampling auditor has defined the population unit as a business day (260 to 365 of them in a year) and has selected three—not much of a sample. Block sampling is undesirable because it is hard to get a representative sample of blocks efficiently. When you have enough blocks, you have a huge number of invoices to audit for compliance.

6. Perform the Control Tests

Now you are ready to obtain the evidence. An **internal control program** consists of procedures designed to produce evidence about the effectiveness of a client's internal control performance. The control tests listed in the following box can be performed to determine how well the control procedures were followed on the transactions affecting accounts receivable. After each action, the parenthetical note tells you the control objective the auditor is testing.

TEST OF CONTROLS AUDITING

1. Select a sample of recorded sales invoices and:
   a. Determine whether a bill of lading is attached (evidence of validity),
   b. Determine whether credit was approved (evidence of authorization),
   c. Determine whether product prices on the invoice agree with the approved price list (evidence of authorization and accuracy),
   d. Compare the quantity billed to the quantity shipped (evidence of accuracy),
   e. Recalculate the invoice arithmetic (evidence of accuracy),
   f. Compare the shipment date with the invoice record date (evidence of proper period),
   g. Trace the invoice to posting in the general ledger control account and in the correct customer's account (evidence of accounting), and
   h. Note the type of product shipped and determine proper classification in the right product-line revenue account (evidence of classification).

2. Select a sample of shipping orders and:
   a. Trace them to recorded sales invoices (evidence of completeness).
   b. The procedures in 1b, 1c, 1d, 1e, 1f and 1h also could be performed on the sales invoices produced by this sample. However, the work need not be duplicated.

3. Select a sample of recorded cash receipts and:
   a. Trace them to deposits in the bank statement (evidence of validity),
   b. Vouch discounts taken by customers to proper approval or policy (evidence of authorization),
   c. Recalculate the cash summarized for a daily report or posting (evidence of accuracy),
   d. Trace the deposit to the right cash account (evidence of classification),
   e. Compare the date of receipt to the recording date (evidence of proper period), and
   f. Trace the receipts to postings in the correct customers' accounts (evidence of accounting).

4. Select a sample of daily cash reports or another source of original cash records and:
   a. Trace to the cash receipts journal (evidence of completeness).
   b. The procedures in 3b, 3c, 3d, 3e and 3f also could be performed on this cash receipts sample. However, the work need not be duplicated.

5. Scan the accounts receivable for postings from sources other than the sales and cash receipts journals (e.g., general journal adjusting entries, credit memos). Vouch a sample of such entries to supporting documents (evidence of validity, authorization, accuracy and classification).

This program describes the **nature** of the control testing procedures. Each is a specific application of one of the general control testing techniques.

R E V I E W
CHECKPOINTS

10.22 Why can poor controls over the existence of sales result in an overstated accounts receivable balance at year end?

10.23 In control testing, why is it necessary to define a compliance deviation in advance? Give seven examples of compliance deviations.

10.24 Which judgements must an auditor make when deciding on a sample size?

10.25 Describe the influence of each judgement on sample size.

10.26 Name and describe four sample selection methods.

7. Evaluate the Evidence

LEARNING OBJECTIVE

5c Evaluate evidence from control testing.

The final step represents the **evidence-evaluation** phase of the sampling method. First, you recognized the problem as the task of determining whether each specified key control procedure worked satisfactorily. Then you gathered relevant compliance evidence. Now you need to evaluate the evidence and make justifiable decisions about the control risk.

Test of controls audit sampling is undertaken to provide evidence of whether a client's internal control procedures are being followed satisfactorily. Compliance evidence, therefore, is very important for the conclusion about control risk. When auditors evaluate sample-based compliance evidence, they run the sampling risks of making one of two decision errors: assessing the control risk too low or assessing the control risk too high. These two decision errors are related to the idea of sampling risk presented earlier.

The **risk of assessing the control risk too low** is the probability that the compliance evidence in the sample indicates low control risk when the actual (but unknown) degree of compliance does not justify such a low control-risk assessment. Assessing the control risk too low can lead to auditors' failure to do additional work that should be done and threatens the effectiveness of the audit. This is also referred to as beta risk for tests of controls. The **risk of assessing the control risk too high** is the probability that the compliance evidence in the sample indicates high control risk when the actual (but unknown) degree of compliance would justify a lower control-risk assessment. This is also referred to as the alpha risk for tests of controls. Assessing the control risk too high tends to trigger more audit work than was planned originally and threatens the efficiency of the audit.

Audit efficiency is certainly important, but audit effectiveness is considered more important. For this reason, auditing standards require auditors to allow for only a low level of risk of assessing the control risk too low, especially when this decision error could cause an auditor to do significantly less work on the related account balances. These risks and decisions are illustrated in Exhibit 10–6. Keeping these risks in mind, the evaluation of evidence consists of calculating the sample deviation rate, comparing it to the tolerable rate and following up all the deviations discovered.

> ## SUPERSEDED TERMINOLOGY: OVERRELIANCE AND UNDERRELIANCE
>
> Several years ago, professional terminology was changed from reference to "reliance on control" to "assessment of control risk." However, old habits die hard, and you will probably still encounter these uses of control terminology:
>
> **Overreliance** is the result of realizing the risk of assessing control risk too low. When auditors think control risk is low, when in fact it is higher, they will *overrely* on internal control and restrict other audit procedures when they actually should perform more work. Overreliance is the same as beta risk of tests of controls.
>
> **Underreliance** is the result of realizing the risk of assessing control risk too high. When auditors think control risk is high, when in fact it is lower, they will *underrely* on internal control and perform more audit work when less work would suffice. Underreliance risk is the same as alpha risk of tests of controls.

EXHIBIT　10-6　THE TEST OF CONTROLS AUDIT SAMPLING DECISION MATRIX

	Sample Population Deviation Rate	
Actual State of Internal Controls (actual population deviation rate)	Less than Tolerable Rate	Greater than Tolerable Rate
The deviation rate is less than the tolerable rate, so the control is performed satisfactorily.	Correct decision.	Control risk too high decision error. (Alpha risk for tests of controls.)
The deviation rate is greater than the tolerable rate, so the control is not performed satisfactorily.	Control risk too low decision error. (Beta risk for tests of controls.)	Correct decision.

Calculate the Sample Deviation Rate

The first piece of hard evidence is the sample deviation rate. Suppose an auditor selected 200 recorded sales invoices and vouched them to shipping orders (bills of lading), finding four without shipping orders. The sample deviation rate is 4/200 = 2 percent. This is the best single-point estimate of the actual, but unknown, deviation rate in the population. However, you cannot say that the deviation rate in the population is exactly 2 percent. Chances are the sample is not exactly representative; the actual but unknown population deviation rate could be lower or higher.

Judge the Deviation Rate in Relation to the Tolerable Rate and the Risk of Assessing the Control Risk Too Low

Suppose the auditor in the example believed the tolerable rate was 8 percent to justify a control risk assessment of CR = 0.40. In a nonstatistical sampling application, this auditor is supposed to think about the sample deviation rate (2 percent) in relation to the tolerable rate (8 percent), and about the risk (of assessing control risk too low) that the actual, but unknown, deviation rate in the population exceeds 8 percent. The decision in a nonstatistical evaluation depends on the auditor's experience and expertise. In our example a nonstatistical auditor might conclude that the population deviation rate probably does not exceed 8 percent because the sample deviation rate of 2 percent is so much lower.

In a statistical sample evaluation, an auditor does things that are more explainable in a text (which also helps explain why statistical sampling has become more popular with the profession). The auditor establishes decision criteria by (1) assigning a number to the risk of assessing the control risk too low, say 10 percent, and (2) assigning a number to the tolerable rate, say 8 percent. Then a statistical table is used to calculate a sampling error-adjusted upper limit, which is the sample deviation rate adjusted upward to allow for the idea that the actual population rate could be higher. In this example the adjusted limit (call it **UEL** for **"upper error limit"**) can be calculated to be 4 percent. This finding can be interpreted to mean: "The probability is 10 percent that the actual but unknown population deviation rate is greater than 4 percent." The decision criterion was: "The actual but unknown population deviation rate needs to be 8 percent or lower, with 10 percent risk of assessing the control risk too low." So the decision criterion is satisfied, and the control risk assessment (0.40) associated with the 8 percent tolerable rate can be justified.[7]

Sample Evaluation

Sample evaluation essentially involves solving for P in the formula R = nP so that P = R/n. When P is solved this way, it is referred to as the achieved P or as the achieved upper error

---

[7] Changing the example to suppose 11 deviations were found creates a problem for the nonstatistical sampler. He or she must think harder about the evidence (a 5.5 percent sample rate) in relation to the tolerable rate (8 percent) and acceptable risk. The statistical sampler can measure the UEL at 8.3 percent, which is greater than the 8 percent tolerable rate at 10 percent risk of overreliance. The control fails the decision criterion test. Appendix 10B on the text Online Learning Centre contains more information about making these calculations using statistical tables and formulas.

limit (UEL). This achieved UEL or achieved P is calculated after the sample has been taken and the results of the sample are known. This means that the number of errors (k) detected by the sample is already known, the confidence level (CL = 1 – beta risk) is known, and the sample size taken is already known as well. Thus we can solve for achieved UEL = achieved P = R/n, where R = $_{CL}R_k$ and CL is the specified confidence level, and k is the number of errors *found* in the sample (not the number expected as in sample size planning).

To illustrate sample evaluation for a test of controls, assume that two errors or deviations were found in a sample of 100 and you wish to calculate the achieved P at 95 percent confidence level (CL): then solve for P in the formula R = nP so that P = R/n = upper error limit = UEL. Plugging in the appropriate values from the table in Appendix 10A gives us: achieved P = R/n = upper error limit = UEL = 6.30/100 = 0.063. This is the maximum error at the specified confidence level. You compare this to what is material or tolerable. The basic rule is: if achieved P or upper error limit is greater than material or tolerable, then reject the population: otherwise accept it. In the case of tests of controls, rejection of the populaton is equivalent to assessing control risk as high, that is, there is no reliance on controls.

Achieved P can be interpreted as the maximum error rate for the specified confidence level. There are additional complications for substantive testing but the formulas already given are all one really needs to know to get a conceptual understanding.

The reason for this simplicity is that we use the easiest approach to statistical sampling in auditing. It is called **dollar-unit sampling** or **DUS** for short. These formulas are so simple and so effective that they are now the most widely used in audit practice.

Another reason DUS is widely used is that to take an appropriate sample one does not require knowledge of the recorded amount of the population in advance, as is required for other statistical approaches. This characteristic of DUS makes it particularly appropriate for continuous audits involving continuous online real-time reporting of sales and purchases as may be demanded in electronic commerce audits. This is further explained in Appendix 10B on the text Online Learning Centre.

Follow Up All the Deviations

All the evaluation described so far has been mostly quantitative in nature, involving counts of deviations, deviation rates and tolerable rate and risk judgement criteria. Qualitative evaluation is also necessary in the form of following up all the deviations to determine their nature and cause. A single deviation can be the tip of the iceberg—the telltale sign of a more pervasive deficiency. Auditors are obligated by the standard of due audit care to investigate known deviations so that nothing important will be overlooked.

The qualitative evaluation is sometimes called **error analysis** because each deviation from a prescribed control procedure is investigated to determine its nature, cause and probable effect on financial statements. The analysis is essentially judgemental and involves auditors' determination of whether the deviation is (1) a pervasive error in principle made systematically on all like transactions or just a mistake on the particular transaction; (2) a deliberate or intentional control breakdown, rather than unintentional; (3) a result of misunderstanding of instructions or careless inattention to control duties; or (4) directly or remotely related to a money amount measurement in the financial statements. You can see that different qualitative perceptions of the seriousness of a deviation would result from error analysis findings.

When the decision criteria are not satisfied and the preliminary conclusion is that the control risk is high, the auditors need to decide what to do next. The deviation follow-up can give auditors the obligation to do more account balance audit work by changing the nature, timing and extent of other audit procedures. If you suspect the sampling results overstate the actual population deviation rate (i.e., alpha risk is occurring), you can enlarge the sample and perform the control tests on more sample units in hopes of deciding that the control risk is actually lower. However, when faced with the preliminary "nonreliance" decision, you should never manipulate the quantitative evaluation by raising the tolerable rate or the risk of assessing the control risk too low. Supposedly, these two decision criteria were carefully determined in the planning stage, so now only new information would be a good basis for easing them.

Timing of Test of Controls Audit Procedures

Earlier in the chapter, you learned that auditors can perform the control testing at an interim date—a date some weeks or months before the client's year-end date. When control testing is timed early, an audit manager must decide what to do about the remaining period (e.g., the period October through December after doing test of controls auditing in September for a December 31 year-end audit).

The decision turns on several factors: (1) The results of the work at interim might, for example, indicate poor control performance and high control risk; (2) enquiries made after interim may show that a particular control procedure has been abandoned or improved; (3) the length of the remaining period may be short enough to forego additional work or long enough to suggest a need for continuing the test of controls audit; (4) the dollar amounts affected by the control procedure may have been much larger or much smaller than before; (5) evidence obtained about control as a byproduct of performing substantive procedures covering the remaining period may show enough about control performance that separate work on the control procedure performance may not be necessary; or (6) work performed by the company's internal auditors may be relied on with respect to the remaining period.

Depending on the circumstances indicated by these, an auditor can decide to (1) continue the test of controls audit work because knowledge of the state of control performance is necessary to justify restriction of other audit work or (2) stop further test of controls audit work because (*a*) compliance evidence derived from other procedures provides sufficient evidence or (*b*) information shows the control has failed, control risk is high, and other work will not be restricted. Whatever the final judgement, considerations of audit effectiveness and efficiency should always be uppermost in the auditor's mind.

R E V I E W
CHECKPOINTS

10.27 Why should auditors be more concerned in test of controls auditing with the risk of assessing the control risk too low than with the risk of assessing the control risk too high?

10.28 What important decision must be made when test of controls auditing is performed and control risk is evaluated at an interim date several weeks or months before the client's fiscal year-to-date?

SUBSTANTIVE PROCEDURES FOR AUDITING ACCOUNT BALANCES

LEARNING OBJECTIVE

6 Develop a simple audit program for an account balance, considering the influence of risk and tolerable misstatement.

When audit sampling is used for auditing the assertions in account balances, the main feature of interest is the monetary amount of the population units, not the presence or absence of control deviations, as is the case with attribute sampling. Test of controls auditing is a part of the evaluation of internal control. **Substantive tests of details auditing** is the performance of procedures to obtain direct evidence about the dollar amounts and disclosures in the financial statements.

Substantive-purpose procedures include (1) analytical procedures and (2) test (audit) of details of transactions and balances. Analytical procedures involve overall comparisons of account balances with prior balances, financial relationships, nonfinancial information, budgeted or forecasted balances and balances derived from estimates calculated by auditors (refer to the discussion of analytical procedures in Chapter 8). Analytical procedures are usually not applied on a sample basis. So, substantive procedures for auditing details are the normal procedures used in account balance audit sampling.

Risk Model Expansion

Up to now you have worked with a conceptual risk model that had a single term for **detection risk (DR)**. The detection risk is actually a combination of two risks: **Analytical procedures risk (APR)** is the probability that analytical procedures will fail to detect material errors, and the **risk of incorrect acceptance (RIA)** is the probability that test-of-detail procedures will fail to detect material errors. The two types of procedures are considered independent, so detection risk is DR = APR $\times$ RIA, and the expanded risk model is:

$$AR = IR \times CR \times APR \times RIA$$

This model is still a conceptual tool. It can now be used to help you understand some elements of sampling for auditing the details of account balances. First, recognize that auditors exercise professional judgement in assessing the inherent risk (IR), control risk (CR), analytical procedures risk (APR), and audit risk (AR). If these four risks are given, you can then manipulate the model to express the RIA:

$$RIA = \frac{AR}{IR \times CR \times APR}$$

With AR, IR, and APR held constant, RIA varies inversely with CR; that is, the higher the planned CR, the lower the planned RIA, and vice versa.

More About Sampling Risk

Substantive-purpose procedures are performed to produce the evidence necessary to enable an auditor to decide whether an account balance is or is not fairly presented in conformity with GAAP. Thus, auditors run the sampling risks of making one of two decision errors. The RIA represents the decision to accept a balance as being materially accurate when, in fact (unknown to the auditor), the balance is materially misstated. This is the beta risk for a substantive test. The other decision error risk is the **risk of incorrect rejection**, and represents the decision that a balance is materially misstated when, in fact, it is not. This is the alpha risk for a substantive test. These sampling risk relationships are shown in Exhibit 10–7.

Incorrect Acceptance (Beta Risk)
The risk of incorrect acceptance is considered the more important of the two decision error risks. When an auditor decides an account book balance is materially accurate (hence, needs no adjustment or change), the audit work on that account is considered finished, the decision is documented in the working papers, and the audit team proceeds to work on other accounts. When the account is, in fact, materially misstated, an unqualified opinion on the financial statements may well be unwarranted. Incorrect acceptance damages the effectiveness of the audit.

EXHIBIT 10-7   THE ACCOUNT BALANCE AUDIT SAMPLING DECISION MATRIX

Audit Decision Alternatives (based on sample evidence)	Unknown Actual Account Balance is	
	Materially* accurate.	Materially* misstated.
The book value of the account is materially accurate.	Correct decision.	Incorrect acceptance.
The book value of the account is materially misstated.	Incorrect rejection.	Correct decision.

*Materially in this context refers to the "material misstatement" assigned to the account balance.

Incorrect Rejection (Alpha Risk)

When an auditor decides an account book balance is materially misstated, some more audit work on that account is performed to determine the amount of an adjustment to recommend. The risk is that the book balance really is a materially accurate representation of the (unknown) actual value. At this point the event of incorrect rejection is about to be realized, and the audit manager may be inclined to recommend an adjustment that is not needed.

Incorrect rejection is not considered to be as serious an error as incorrect acceptance. When auditors first begin to think a balance may contain a material misstatement, efforts will be made to determine why the misstatement occurred and to estimate the amount. Thus, more evidence will be sought by the audit team or provided by the client. The data will be reviewed for a source of systematic error. The amounts of discovered errors will be analyzed carefully. Client personnel may be assigned to do a complete analysis to determine a more accurate account balance.

If the initial decision was, in fact, a decision error of incorrect rejection, this other work should allow the auditors to determine whether the recorded amount is really misstated or the sample was not representative. Hence, incorrect rejection is not considered as serious as incorrect acceptance because steps will be taken to determine the amount of error and the erroneous decision has a chance to be reversed. Incorrect rejection thus affects the efficiency of an audit by causing unnecessary work.

Materiality and Tolerable Misstatement

Determining a threshold for the materiality of misstatements in financial statements is a tough problem under any circumstances. Audit sampling for substantive audits of particular account balances adds another wrinkle. Auditors must also decide on an amount of material misstatement, which is a judgement of the amount of monetary misstatement that may exist in an account balance or class of transactions and cause the financial statements to be materially misstated. Audit risk (AR in the risk model), therefore, is the risk that all the audit work on an account balance will not result in discovery of material misstatement. This concept is further discussed in the online Appendix 10B.

Sampling Steps for Account Balance Audit

Audit sampling for the audit of account balances is structured much like the steps you studied in connection with test of controls audit sampling. As the steps are explained, an example related to auditing receivables is used. Remember, the example used with regard to test of controls sampling was the audit of a control procedure designed to prevent the recording of sales invoices without shipping orders. Now we move on to the next stage of work that can produce independent evidence of sales overstatement resulting from a breakdown of the control or from other causes. The seven-step framework explained in the next sections helps auditors plan, perform and evaluate account balance detail audit work. It also helps auditors accomplish an eighth step—careful documentation of the work—by showing each of the seven areas to be described in the working papers. The first seven steps are as follows:

1. Specify the audit objectives.
2. Define the population.
3. Choose an audit sampling method.
4. Determine the sample size.
5. Select the sample.
6. Perform the substantive-purpose procedures.
7. Evaluate the evidence.

Plan the Procedures

LEARNING OBJECTIVE

6a Specify objectives and a
population of data.

The three planning steps represent the problem-recognition phase of the sampling method. When a client presents the financial statements, the assertions include (for example): "The trade accounts receivable exist (existence) and are *bona fide* obligations owed to the company" (ownership); "All the accounts receivable are recorded" (completeness); "They are stated at net realizable value" (valuation); and "They are properly classified as current assets, presented and disclosed in conformity with GAAP" (presentation). Each assertion represents a hypothesis (problem) to be tested; for example, "The trade accounts receivable exist as *bona fide* obligations owed to the company." A test of this hypothesis is the objective. The set of recorded accounts receivable is the population of data.

1. Specify the Audit Objectives

When performing accounts receivable confirmations on a sample basis, the specific objective is to decide whether the client's assertions about existence, rights (ownership) and valuation are materially accurate. In this context, the auditing is viewed as **hypothesis testing**—the auditors hypothesize that the book value is materially accurate about existence, ownership and valuation. The evidence will enable them to accept or reject the hypothesis. The audit objective is to determine the monetary misstatement found by comparing the recorded balances to the balances determined from the evidence.

2. Define the Population

Auditors need to be sure the definition of the population matches the objectives. Defining the population as the recorded accounts receivable balances suits the objective of obtaining evidence about existence, ownership and valuation. This definition also suits the related objective of obtaining evidence about sales overstatement. In the case of accounts receivable, each customer's account balance is a population unit. However, if the objectives were to obtain evidence about completeness and sales understatement, the recorded accounts receivable would be the wrong population.

Ordinarily, the sampling unit is the same as the population unit. Sometimes, however, it is easier to define the sampling unit as a smaller part of a population unit. For example, if the client's accounting system keeps track of individual invoices charged to customers, an auditor may want to audit a sample of invoices by confirming them with customers instead of working with each customer's balance.

Since a sample will be drawn from a physical representation of the population (e.g., a printed trial balance or computer file of customers' accounts), the auditors must determine whether it is complete. Re-adding the trial balance and reconciling it to the control account total will accomplish the job.

Auditing standards require auditors to use their judgement to determine whether any population units should be removed from the population and audited separately (not sampled) because taking sampling risk (risk of incorrect acceptance or incorrect rejection) with respect to them is not justified. Suppose, for example, the accounts receivable amounted to $400,000, but six of the customers had balances of $10,000 or more, for a sum of $100,000. The next-largest account balance is less than $10,000. If we assume materiality level is $10,000 the six accounts are considered **individually significant items** because each of them exceeds the material misstatement amount, and they should be removed from the population and audited completely.

In the jargon of audit sampling related to account balances, subdividing the population is known as **stratification**. The total population is subdivided into subpopulations by account balance size. For example, a small number of accounts totalling $75,000 may be identified as the first (large balance) stratum when four strata are defined. Three more strata may be defined, each containing a total of approximately $75,000 of the recorded balances, but each made up of a successively larger number of customer accounts whose average balance is successively smaller. Stratification can be used to increase audit efficiency (smaller total sample size). A stratification example appears in the next box.

STRATIFICATION EXAMPLE—SELECTING SAMPLE SIZES

The stratification below subdivides the population into a first stratum of six individually significant accounts and four other strata, which each have approximately one-fourth ($75,000) of the remaining dollar balance. You can see the typical situation in which the accounts of smaller value are more numerous.

The example also shows one kind of allocation of a sample size of 90 to the last four strata. Such a stratification is referred to as *stratified sampling*. When each stratum gets one-fourth of the sample size, the sample is skewed toward the higher-value accounts: The second stratum has 23 in the sample out of 80 in the stratum, and the fifth stratum has 23 out of 910 in the stratum.

Stratum	Book Value	Number	Amount	Sample
1	Over $10,000	6	$100,000	6
2	$625–$9,999	80	75,068	23
3	$344–$624	168	75,008	22
4	$165–$343	342	75,412	22
5	$1–$164	910	74,512	23
		1,506	$400,000	96

This kind of stratification takes care of the normal situation in which the variability of the account balances and errors in them tend to be larger in the high-value accounts than in the low-value accounts. As a consequence, the sample includes a larger proportion of the high-value accounts (23/80) and a smaller proportion of the low-value accounts (23/910). In addition to size or variability, stratification can be based on other qualitative characteristics the auditor considers important, such as transactions stratified by individual, location, date, product and so forth.

3. Choose an Audit Sampling Method

You already have been introduced to statistical and nonstatistical sampling methods. At this point, an auditor must decide which to use. If he or she chooses statistical sampling, another choice needs to be made. In statistical sampling, classical variables sampling methods that utilize normal distribution theory are available. However, DUS, which uses attribute sampling theory, is used more widely in practice. Some of the technical characteristics of the statistical methods are explained more fully in the online Appendix 10B.

The calculation examples shown later in this chapter use the DUS method. This calculation is relatively simple and illustrates the important points.

Perform the Procedures

LEARNING OBJECTIVE

6b Determine sample size and select sample units.

The next three steps represent the evidence-collection phase of the sampling method. These steps are performed to get the evidence.

Figuring sample size for account balance auditing requires consideration of several influences. The main reason for figuring a sample size in advance is to help guard against under-auditing (not obtaining enough evidence) and overauditing (obtaining more evidence than needed). Another important reason is to control the cost of the audit. An arbitrary sample size could be used to perform the accounts receivable confirmation procedures; but if it turned out to be too small, sending and processing more confirmations might be impossible before the audit report deadline. Alternative procedures then could become costly and time-consuming. A predetermined sample size is not as important in other situations where the auditors can increase the sample simply by choosing more items available for audit in the client's office.

4. Determine the Sample Size

Whether using statistical or nonstatistical sampling methods, auditors first need to establish decision criteria for the risk of incorrect acceptance (beta risk for substantive testing), the risk of incorrect rejection (alpha risk for substantive testing) and the material misstatement. Also, auditors may want to estimate the expected dollar amount of misstatement. These decision criteria should be determined before any evidence is obtained from a sample.

a. Risk of Incorrect Acceptance (RIA).   This risk is assessed in terms of the audit risk model, which can be your guide. An acceptable risk of incorrect acceptance depends on the assessments of inherent risk, control risk and analytical procedures risk. The risk of incorrect acceptance varies inversely with the combined product of the other risks. The larger the combined product of the other risks, the smaller the allowable risk of incorrect acceptance.

Suppose, for example, two different auditors independently assess the client's control risk and their own analytical procedures and arrive at the following conclusions. Assume both auditors believe an acceptable level of audit risk—AR—is 0.05:

Auditor A believes the inherent risk is high (IR = 1.0), the control risk is moderate (CR = 0.50), and analytical procedures will not be performed (APR = 1.0). Audit procedures need to be so planned that the risk of incorrect acceptance will be about 10 percent.

$$RIA = AR/(IR \times CR \times APR) = 0.05/(1.0 \times 0.50 \times 1.0) = 0.10$$

Auditor B believes the inherent risk is high (IR = 1.0), the control risk is very low (CR = 0.20), and analytical procedures will not be performed (APR = 1.0). Audit procedures need to be so planned that the risk of incorrect acceptance will be about 25 percent.

$$RIA = AR/(IR \times CR \times APR) = 0.05/(1.0 \times 0.20 \times 1.0) = 0.25$$

Use the model with caution. The lesson you should learn from these examples is that auditor A's account balance sampling work must provide less risk than that of auditor B. Since sample size varies inversely with the risk of incorrect acceptance, auditor A's sample will be larger. In fact, when the control risk is lower, as in auditor B's evaluation, the acceptable RIA is higher. Thus, auditor B's sample of customers' accounts receivable can be smaller than auditor A's sample.

b. Risk of Incorrect Rejection.   Like the risk of incorrect acceptance, the risk of incorrect rejection exists both in statistical and nonstatistical sampling applications. It can be controlled, usually by auditing a larger sample. So, sample size varies inversely with the risk of incorrect rejection. DUS deals with incorrect rejection (alpha risk) by increasing sample size above the minimum associated with using k = 0 in sample planning. The simplified approach to sample planning we use here, sets k = 0 so that the sample size is the smallest possible for the stated confidence level and materiality.

c. Material Misstatement.   The material misstatement—usually the same as the overall materiality of misstatements—also must be considered in nonstatistical as well as statistical sampling applications. In statistical sampling, material misstatement must be expressed as a dollar amount or as a proportion of the total recorded amount. The sample size varies inversely with the amount of misstatement considered material. The greater the materiality, the smaller the sample size needed.

d. Expected Dollar Misstatement.   Auditors may want to estimate an **expected dollar misstatement** amount. The estimate may be based on last year's audit findings or on other knowledge of the accounting system. Expectations of dollar misstatement have the effect of increasing the sample size. The more dollar misstatement expected, the larger the sample size should be. Sample sizes should be larger when more dollar misstatement is expected. So, sample size varies directly with the amount of expected dollar misstatement.

e. Variability Within the Population.   Auditors using nonstatistical sampling must take into account the degree of dispersion among unit values in a population. The typical skewness of some accounting populations needs to be taken into account. **Skewness** is the concentration of a large proportion of the dollar amount in an account in a small number of the population items. In our illustration, $100,000 (25 percent) of the total accounts receivable is in six customers' accounts while the remaining $300,000 is in 1,500 customers' accounts.

As a general rule, auditors should be careful about populations whose unit values range widely, say from $1 to $10,000. Obtaining a representative sample in such a case, as you might imagine, would take a larger sample than if the range of the unit values were only from $1 to $500. Sample size should vary directly with the magnitude of the variability of population unit values. Populations with high variability should be stratified, as previously shown in the stratification example.

Auditors using classical statistical sampling methods must obtain an estimate of the population **standard deviation**, which is a measure of the population variability. When using DUS, the variability is taken into account with the expected dollar misstatement, and no separate estimate of a standard deviation needs to be made. This is because in dollar-unit sampling the unit of selection is each recorded dollar, rather than the account balance. Thus there is no variability in the population of recorded dollars, each dollar having the same value, as viewed by DUS. See the online Appendix 10B for more details.

The sample sizes for DUS can be calculated similar to the way they are calculated for tests of controls. We can apply the same sample planning formula for substantive tests using DUS as long as we convert all monetary amounts to a rate or percentage. Thus, for example, if you have an accounts receivable population with an account balance of $10,000,000, you determine materiality to be $300,000, and you wish to plan a sample size for confirming receivables with 95 percent confidence level, then first convert materiality as a rate by simply calculating its proportion of the recorded value: $P = 300,000/10,000,000 = 0.03$. Now you can apply the formula as before to calculate the sample size: $n = R/P = 3.0/0.03 = 100$.

As you can see the calculation of sample sizes under DUS are very similar for both tests of controls and tests of balances. The calculations for both are summarized in Exhibit 10–8.

You are now also in a position to prove to yourself the efficiency effects of relying on internal controls using the audit risk model. In the above receivables example assume you desired 95 percent confidence because you planned audit risk at 0.05, and you assessed inherent and control risk at the maximum of 1.0. Hence, you had to get all your assurance

EXHIBIT   10-8

Sufficiency of Audit Evidence:
Summary of Simplified Calculations of Sample Size

Key Concepts	Tests of Controls	Substantive Tests of Balance
Basic Formula	$R = nP$	$R = nP$
Assessment of materiality or tolerable error rate	P = Tolerable error rate	P = materiality as a proportion of the recorded balance
Assessment of beta risk = $1 -$ confidence level = $1 - CL$	Beta risk is based on CR from Audit risk model	Beta risk is RIA of audit risk model
R value	From table use $K = 0$ and desired confidence level	From table use $K = 0$ and desired confidence level
Extent of testing = sample size	$n = \frac{{}_{CL}R_K}{P}$	$n = \frac{{}_{CL}R_K}{P}$

CR = control risk n = sample size RIA = risk of incorrect acceptance from the substantive test using a detective risk (DR) of 0.05. The detective risk is the same as beta risk or the risk of incorrect acceptance. Now assume that you assessed control risk below maximum at 0.50 (instead of at maximum at 1.0), then using the risk model you can prove to yourself that DR is revised to 0.10. That is, you accept more risk (get less assurance) from your substantive testing. This is reflected by the reduced sample size: n = R/P = 2.31/0.03 = 77 (always round up to ensure sample is large enough). You have thus been able to reduce your substantive testing by 23 (100 - 77) as a result of your increased reliance on internal controls. This is a simple example, but it illustrates the basic principle of internal control reliance using the audit risk model.

These influences are summarized in Exhibit 10–9.

EXHIBIT   10-9   SAMPLE SIZE RELATIONSHIPS: AUDIT OF ACCOUNT BALANCES USING DUS

	Predetermined Sample Size Will Be		
Sample Size Influence	High Rate or Large Amount	Low Rate or Small Amount	Sample Size Relation
1. Risk of incorrect acceptance	Smaller	Larger	Inverse
2. Risk of incorrect rejection*	Smaller	Larger	Inverse
3. Tolerable misstatement	Smaller	Larger	Inverse
4. Expected misstatement*	Larger	Smaller	Direct

*These effects are discussed in the online Appendix 10B. They are ignored under the simplified approach used here and many practitioners treat these effects as insignificant.

ACCOUNT BALANCE AUDITING

1. Confirm a sample of the receivables, investigate exceptions and follow up nonrespondents by vouching sales charges and cash receipts to supporting documents (evidence of existence, rights and valuation).

2. Obtain an aged trial balance of the receivables. Audit the aging accuracy on a sample basis. Calculate and analyse the age status of the accounts and the allowance for uncollectible accounts in light of current economic conditions and the company's collection experience (evidence of valuation).

3. Discuss past-due accounts with the credit manager. Obtain credit reports and financial statements for independent analysis of large overdue accounts (evidence of valuation).

4. Vouch receivables balances to cash received after the cutoff date (evidence of existence, rights and valuation).

5. Distinguish names of trade customers from others (officers, directors, employees, affiliates) and determine that the two classifications are reported separately (evidence of presentation and disclosure).

6. Read loan agreements and note any pledge of receivables, sales with recourse or other restrictions or contingencies related to the receivables (evidence of presentation and disclosure).

7. Read sales contracts for evidence of customers' rights of return or price allowance terms (evidence of presentation and disclosure).

8. Obtain written representations from the client concerning pledges for collateral, related party receivables, collectibility and other matters relating to accounts receivable (detail assertions in writing).

> This program describes the nature of the procedures. Each is a specific application of one of the seven general procedures. However, this list does not include a procedure dealing explicitly with the completeness assertion. You can obtain completeness evidence with the dual-purpose nature of the completeness procedures done in the test of controls audit work (see test of controls procedures 2 and 4). The list also excludes analytical procedures based on interrelationships with budget, forecast, industry or historical data. More specific situational facts would need to be known to be specific about analytical procedures work.

5. Select the Sample

As was the case with test of controls audit samples, account balance samples must be representative. The same selection methods as discussed for tests of controls can be used for DUS in substantive testing. You can use unrestricted random selection and systematic selection to obtain the random samples necessary for statistical applications. The online Appendix 10B outlines unique features of DUS selection in more detail. Haphazard and block selection methods have the same drawbacks as they have in test of controls audit samples.

6. Perform the Substantive-Purpose Procedures

The basic assertions in a presentation of accounts receivable are that they exist, they are complete (no receivables are unrecorded), the company has the right to collect the money, they are valued properly at net realizable value and they are presented and disclosed properly in conformity with GAAP. A **substantive-purpose audit program** consists of account balance–related procedures designed to produce evidence about these assertions. The substantive-purpose procedures listed in the preceding box can be performed to obtain the evidence related to each assertion (shown in parentheses).

The confirmation procedures should be performed for all the sampling units. The other procedures should be performed as necessary to complete the evidence relating to existence, ownership and valuation. The important thing is to audit all the sample units. You cannot simply discard one that is hard to audit in favour of adding to the sample a customer whose balance is easy to audit. This action might bias the sample. Sometimes, however, you will be unable to audit a sample unit. Suppose a customer did not respond to the confirmation requests, sales invoices supporting the balance could not be found and no payment was received after the confirmation date. Auditing standards contain the following guidance:

- If considering the entire balance to be misstated will not alter your evaluation conclusion, then you do not need to work on it anymore. Your evaluation conclusion may be to accept the book value, as long as the account is not big enough to change the conclusion. Your evaluation conclusion already may be to reject the book value, so that considering another account misstated just reinforces the decision.

- If considering the entire balance to be misstated would change an acceptance decision to a rejection decision, you need to do something about it. Since the example seems to describe a dead end, you may need to select more accounts (expand the sample), perform the procedures on them (other than confirmation) and re-evaluate the results.

- If control risk related to the balance was assessed to be low, you should consider whether this finding contradicts the low control risk assessment.

REVIEW CHECKPOINTS

10.29 Write the expanded risk model. What risk is implied for "test of detail risk" when IR = 1.0, CR = 0.40, APR = 0.60, AR = 0.048, tolerable misstatement = $10,000 and the estimated standard deviation in the population = $25?

10.30 Explain why control risk is inversely related to the risk of incorrect acceptance.

10.31 Why does the alpha risk affect audit efficiency and the beta risk affect audit effectiveness?

10.32 When auditing account balances, why is an incorrect acceptance decision considered more serious than an incorrect rejection decision?

10.33 What should be the relationship between tolerable misstatement in the audit of an account balance and the amount of monetary misstatement considered material to the overall financial statements?

10.34 What general set of audit objectives can you use as a frame of reference to be specific about the particular objectives for the audit of an account balance?

10.35 What audit purpose is served by stratifying an account balance population and by selecting some units from the population for 100 percent audit verification?

· ·

7. Evaluate the Evidence

LEARNING OBJECTIVE

6c Evaluate monetary error evidence from a balance audit sample.

The final step represents the evidence evaluation and decision-making phase of the sampling method. Your decisions about existence, ownership and valuation need to be justifiable by sufficient, competent quantitative and qualitative evidence. You should be concerned first with the quantitative evaluation of the evidence. Qualitative follow-up is also important and is discussed later.

Quantitative evaluation of substantive tests of balances using DUS is the same as that for tests of controls, for example, if achieved P is greater than or equal to materiality then reject; otherwise accept the population total recorded amount. The complications arise from possible variability of the misstatements when calculating achieved P. The online Appendix 10B outlines how to deal with these complications. Exhibit 10–10 summarizes these statistical evaluations.

Auditing standards are not written with a particular approach, such as DUS, in mind. Instead they deal with general features of quantitative evaluation that are already captured by formulas using a particular approach. So we review these general considerations here. The reconciliation to particular calculations with DUS is given in the online Appendix 10B.

The basic steps in quantitative evaluation are these:

- Figure the total amount of actual monetary error found in the sample. This amount is the **known misstatement**.

- Project the known misstatement to the population. The projected amount is the **likely misstatement**.

EXHIBIT   10–10

Evaluating Sample Results (n is known and R is known based on detected errors K and confidence level planned)

Key Concepts	Tests of Control	Substantive Tests of Balance
Basic Formula	$R = nP$	$R = nP$
Solve for achieved P	$P = \frac{R}{n}$	$P = \frac{R}{n}$
Basic Decision Rule	If achieved P≥ tolerable error rate, then reject; otherwise, accept reliance on control.	If achieved P≥ materiality, then reject; otherwise, accept the recorded total for the population.
Consequence of Decision		
If Accept	Can rely on controls to extent planned at stated confidence level.	Can accept clients recorded amount at stated confidence level.
If Reject	Need to rely on controls less than expected.	Need to sample more or insist on an adjustment (adjust to most likely value as indicated by sample mean extrapolated to the population).

• Compare the likely misstatement (also called the **projected misstatement**) to the material misstatement for the account and consider: the risk of incorrect acceptance that likely misstatement is calculated to be less than material misstatement even though the actual misstatement in the population is greater; or the risk of incorrect rejection that likely misstatement is calculated to be greater than material misstatement, even though the actual misstatement in the population is smaller.

Amount of Known Misstatement

Now you need some illustrative numbers. Hypothetical audit evidence from the sample for the previous stratification example is shown in the box following. Recall that in this example total accounts receivable is $400,000, and $100,000 of the total is in six large balances, which are to be audited separately. The remainder is in 1,500 customer accounts whose balances range from $1 to $9,999. Suppose the audit team selected 90 of these accounts and applied the confirmation or vouching procedures to each of them. The evidence showed $136 of actual misstatement representing net overstatement of the recorded amounts. This amount is the known misstatement for this sample of 90 customer accounts.

Project the Known Misstatement to the Population

To make a decision about the population, you must project the known misstatement in the sample to the population. The key requirement for projecting the known misstatement to the population is that the sample must be representative. If the sample is not representative, a projection produces a nonsense number. Take an extreme example: Remember that all of the

---

STRATIFICATION EXAMPLE—HYPOTHETICAL SAMPLE DATA

Assume the following differences were detected in the 90 audited items

Sample Item	Stratum	Audited Amount	Recorded Amount	Difference* (Recorded – Audited)
1	2	$691	$691	$0
*		*	*	*
*		*	*	*
*		*	*	*
6	2	372	508	136
*		*	*	*
*		*	*	*
*		*	*	*
23	2	136	141	5
*		*	*	*
*		*	*	*
*		*	*	*
50	4	62	62	0
*		*	*	*
*		*	*	*
*		*	*	*
90	5	135	130	(5)
Totals		$18,884	$19,020	$136
Averages:				
Audited amount		$209.82		
Recorded amount			$211.33	
Difference				$1.51

*A positive difference is an account overstatement, and a negative difference is an account understatement.

six largest accounts ($100,000 in total) were audited. Suppose one of them contained a $600 disputed amount. Investigation showed the customer was right, management agreed, so the $600 is the amount of known misstatement. If an auditor takes this group of six accounts as being representative of the population, projecting the $100 average misstatement ($600/6) to 1,506 accounts ($100 × 1,506) would project a total misstatement of $150,600, compared to the recorded accounts receivable total of $400,000. This projection is neither reasonable nor appropriate. The six large accounts are not representative of the entire population of 1,506 accounts. Nothing is wrong with the calculation method. The nonrepresentative "sample" is the culprit in this absurd result.

A projection based on a sample applies only to the population from which the sample was drawn. Consider the sample of 90 accounts from the population of 1,500. The average difference is $1.51 (overstatement of the recorded amount), so the projected likely misstatement (PLM) is $2,267 (overstatement), provided the sample is representative. This projection method is called the average difference method, expressed in equation form as:

Projected likely misstatement (under the average difference method) =
((Dollar amount of misstatement in the sample)/(Number of sampling units)) ×
(Number of population units)

In this example if the population had not been stratified the calculation is:

Projected likely misstatement (under the average difference method) =
($136/90) × 1,500 = $2,267 (overstatement)

When the population is stratified, each stratum is more homogeneous according to account size than the population as a whole, and the known misstatement in each can be projected. Combining them into a single projection is shown in the stratification calculation example shown in the box following. It results in a much smaller PLM.

How can you tell whether a sample is representative? You cannot guarantee representativeness, but you can try to attain it by selecting a random sample and by carefully subdividing (stratifying) the population according to an important characteristic, such as the size of individual customers' balances. You can also inspect the sample to see whether it shows the characteristics of the population. In the example, for instance, the average recorded

STRATIFICATION EXAMPLE:

Stratification Calculation of Projected Likely Misstatement by Average Difference Method

Stratification of a population is said to be more efficient because you can usually calculate a smaller projected likely misstatement with the same sample size than would have been used in an unstratified sample (as illustrated in this chapter), or you can usually calculate the same projected likely misstatement with a smaller stratified sample. The example below illustrates a typical situation of finding larger misstatements in the larger accounts, resulting in a projected likely misstatement smaller than the $2,267 illustrated in the chapter for an unstratified sample. The calculation of projected likely misstatements (PLM), using the difference method, is applied separately to each stratum. Then, the amounts are added to get the whole sample result.

Stratum	Number	Amount	Sample	Misstatement*	PLM
1	80	75,068	23	$141	$490
2	168	75,008	22	0	0
3	342	75,412	22	0	0
4	910	74,512	23	−5	−198
	1,506	$400,000	96	$136	$292

*A positive misstatement indicates overstatement of the book value, and a negative misstatement indicates understatement.

amount of the population is $200 ($300,000 divided by 1,500); the average in the illustrative unstratified sample is $211.33 (a little high). You also can look to see whether the sample contains a range of recorded amounts similar to the population that ranged from $1 to $9,999. With statistics you can calculate the standard deviation of the sample recorded amounts and compare it to the standard deviation of the population.

The DUS projection method automatically takes into account the stratification of the population. You can project using the dollar-unit sampling method, expressed in equation form as follows:

Projected likely misstatement (dollar-unit method) = (Sum of the proportionate amount of misstatements or taintings of all dollar units in error in the sample) $\times$ (Recorded amount in the population)

Taintings are covered in more detail in the online Appendix 10B. In the example here:

Projected likely misstatement (dollar-unit method) =
$300,000 $\times$ (1/90) $\times$ ((136/508) + (5/141) − (5/130)) = $883 (overstatement)

The difference in the two projected likely misstatements illustrates the importance of having representative sampling. Auditors also need to be very careful about the adequacy of the sample size. You can see that small samples which produce large or small dollar differences can distort both the average difference and the average dollar-unit ratio, thus distorting the projected likely misstatement. One way to exercise care is to take the sampling risks into account.

Consider Sampling Risks

The risks of making wrong decisions (incorrect acceptance or incorrect rejection) exist in both nonstatistical and statistical sampling. The smaller the sample, the greater both risks. Common sense tells you that the less you know about a population because of a small sample, the more risk you run of making a wrong decision.

The problem is to consider the risk that the projected likely misstatement ($883 overstatement for the sample of 90 accounts in the example using the DUS method) could have been obtained even though the actual total misstatement in the population is greater than the material misstatement ($10,000 in the example). Auditing guidance suggests you can use your experience and professional judgement to consider the risk. If the projected likely misstatement is considerably less than tolerable misstatement, chances are good that the total actual misstatement in the population is not greater than tolerable misstatement. However, when projected likely misstatement is close to tolerable misstatement (say, $9,000, compared to $10,000), the chance is not so good, and the risk of incorrect acceptance may exceed the acceptable risk (RIA) that an auditor initially established as a decision criterion.

A similar situation exists with respect to the risk of incorrect rejection. Suppose the sample results had produced a projected likely misstatement of $15,000 overstatement. Now the question is: "What is the risk that this result was obtained even though the actual misstatement in the population is $10,000 or less?" Again, the judgement depends on the size of the sample and the kinds and distribution of misstatements discovered.

Auditors take the rejection decision as a serious matter and conduct enough additional investigation to determine the amount and adjustment required. Hence, the risk of incorrect rejection is mitigated by additional work necessary to determine the amount and nature of an adjustment. In the example, if the sample of 90 customers' accounts had shown total misstatement of $900 (yielding the $15,000 projected misstatement using the average difference method), most auditors would consider the evidence insufficient to propose a significant adjustment. (Incidentally, however, correction of the $900 should not by itself be a sufficient action to satisfy the auditors.)

When using nonstatistical sampling, auditors use their experience and expertise to take risks into account. Statistical samplers can add statistical calculations to these considerations of sampling risk.

Qualitative Evaluation

The numbers are not enough. Auditors are required to follow up each monetary difference to determine whether it arose from (a) misunderstanding of accounting principles, (b) simple mistakes or carelessness, (c) an intentional irregularity, or (d) management override of an internal control procedure. Auditors also need to relate the differences to their effect on other amounts in the financial statements. For example, overstatements in accounts receivable may indicate overstatement of sales revenue.

Likewise, you should not overlook the information that can be obtained in account balance auditing about the performance of internal control procedures—the dual-purpose characteristic of auditing procedures. Deviations (or absence of deviations) discovered when performing substantive procedures can help confirm or contradict an auditor's previous conclusion about control risk. If many more monetary differences arise than expected, the control risk conclusion may need to be revised, and more account balance auditing work may need to be done.

Knowledge of the source, nature and amount of monetary differences is very important. Such knowledge is required to explain the situation to management and to direct additional work to areas where adjustments are needed. The audit work is not complete until the qualitative evaluation and follow-up is done.

Evaluate the Amount of Misstatement

CICA Handbook, section 5142 and the CICA Auditing Guideline AUG-41, require the aggregation of known misstatement ("identified misstatement" in the Guideline) and projected likely misstatement ("likely aggregate misstatement" in the Guideline). The aggregation is the sum of (a) known misstatement in the population units identified for 100 percent audit (in the example, the six accounts totalling $100,000, with $600 overstatement discovered), and (b) the projected likely misstatement for the population sampled (in the example, the $883 overstatement projected using the DUS method). The theory underlying (b) is that the projected likely misstatement is the best single estimate of the amount that would be determined if all the accounts in the sampled population had been audited. You can see the importance of sample representativeness in this regard. This aggregation ($883 overstatement in the example) should be judged in combination with other misstatements found in the audit of other account balances to determine whether the financial statements taken as a whole need to be adjusted and, if so, in what amount.

The evaluation of amounts is not over yet, however. One thing that cannot be said about the projected likely misstatement is that it is the exact amount that would be found if all the units in the population were audited. The actual amount might be more or less, and the problem arises from **sampling error**—the amount by which a projected likely misstatement amount could differ from an actual (unknown) total as a result of the sample not being exactly representative. Of course, auditors are most concerned with the possibility that the actual total misstatement might be considerably more than the projected likely misstatement.

This sampling phenomenon gives rise to the concept of **possible misstatement** (the third kind, in addition to known and likely misstatement), which is interpreted in auditing standards as the further misstatement remaining undetected in the units not selected in the sample. Nonstatistical auditors resort to experience and professional judgement in considering additional possible misstatement. Statistical auditors, however, can utilize some statistical calculations to measure possible misstatement.

In Appendix 10B on the text Online Learning Centre, the basic example shows how to calculate a possible misstatement. For the illustration here the possible misstatement is in the amount of $6,331. For now treat this as a given. Thus, the aggregation of known, projected and possible misstatement is $600 + $884 + $6,331 = $7,814. This total suggests that the misstatement in the account does not exceed the amount considered material ($10,000). If the possible misstatement were higher, say $9,000, the total would be $10,483, and the evidence would suggest that the misstatement in the account exceeds $10,000.

Timing of Substantive Audit Procedures

Account balances can be audited, at least in part, at an interim date. When this work is done before the company's year-end date, auditors must extend the interim-date audit conclusion to the balance sheet date. The process of **extending the audit conclusion** amounts to nothing more (and nothing less) than performing substantive-purpose audit procedures on the transactions in the remaining period and on the year-end balance to produce sufficient competent evidence for a decision about the year-end balance.

Substantive procedures must be performed to obtain evidence about the balance after the interim date. You cannot audit a balance (say, accounts receivable) as of September 30, then without further work accept the December 31 balance. Internal control must be well designed and performed adequately. If the company's internal control over transactions that produce the balance under audit is not particularly strong, you should time the substantive detail work at year-end instead of at interim.

If rapidly changing business conditions might predispose managers to misstate the accounts (try to slip one by the auditors), the work should be timed at year-end. In most cases careful scanning of transactions and analytical review comparisons should be performed on transactions that occur after the interim date.

As an example, accounts receivable confirmation can be done at an interim date. Subsequently, efforts must be made to ascertain whether controls continued to be reliable. You must scan the transactions of the remaining period, audit any new large balances and update work on collectibility, especially with analysis of cash received after the year-end.

Audit work is performed at interim for two reasons: (1) to spread the accounting firms' workload so that not all the work on clients is crammed into December and January and (2) to make the work efficient and enable companies to report audited financial results soon after the year-end. Some well-organized companies with well-planned audits report their audited figures as early as five or six days after their fiscal year-ends.

BALANCE-AUDIT SAMPLING FAILURE

The company owned surgical instruments that were loaned and leased to customers. The auditors decided to audit the existence of the assets by confirming them with the customers who were supposed to be holding and using them. From the population of 880 instruments, the auditors selected eight for confirmation, using a sampling method that purported to produce a representative selection.

Two confirmations were never returned, and the auditors did not follow up on them. One returned confirmation said the customer did not have the instrument in question, and the auditors were never able to find it. Nevertheless, the auditors concluded that the $3.5 million recorded amount of the surgical instrument assets was materially accurate.

Judges who heard complaints on the quality of the audit work concluded that it was not performed in accordance with generally accepted auditing standards (GAAS) because the auditors did not gather sufficient evidence concerning the existence and valuation of the surgical instruments. GAAS requires auditors to project the sample findings to the population. The auditors did not do so. They never calculated (non-statistical) the fact that $1,368,750 of the asset amount could not be confirmed or found to exist. The sample of eight was woefully inadequate both in sample size and in the proportionately large number of exceptions reported. There was a wholly insufficient statistical basis for concluding that the account was fairly stated under generally accepted accounting principles.

Source: U.S. Securities and Exchange Commission, *Administrative Proceeding File No. 3-6579* (Initial Decision, June 1990).

REVIEW
CHECKPOINTS

10.36 What kind of evidence evaluation consideration should an auditor give to the dollar amount of a population unit that cannot be audited?

10.37 What are the three basic steps in quantitative evaluation of monetary amount evidence when auditing an account balance?

10.38 The projected likely misstatement may be calculated, yet further misstatement may remain undetected in the population. How can auditors take the further misstatement under consideration when completing the quantitative evaluation of monetary evidence? How is this done by formula?

10.39 What additional considerations are in order when auditors plan to audit account balances at an interim date several weeks or months before the client's fiscal year-end date?

Summary

Audit sampling was explained in this chapter as an organized method to make decisions. Two kinds of decisions were shown—assessment of control risk and the decision about whether financial statement assertions in an account balance are fairly presented. The method is organized by two kinds of audit programs to guide the work on these two decisions—the internal control program and the balance-audit program. The audit sampling itself can be attribute sampling for test of controls and balance-audit (variables) sampling for auditing the assertions in an account balance.

Audit sampling is a method of organizing the application of audit procedures and a disciplined approach to decision problems. Both types of sampling were explained in basic terms of planning the audit procedures, performing the audit procedures and evaluating the evidence produced by the audit procedures. The latter process was reinforced with some differences and DUS projections of misstatement amounts. The mechanics were illustrated in the last section.

Risk in audit decisions was explained in the context of nonsampling and sampling risk, with sampling risk further subdivided into two types of decision errors: (1) assessing control risk too low and incorrect acceptance of a balance and (2) assessing control risk too high and incorrect rejection of an account balance. The first pair damages the effectiveness of audits, and the second pair damages the efficiency of audits.

Audit programs for test of controls procedures and balance-audit procedures were illustrated. Separate sections explained the application of procedures at an interim date. Thus, the chapter covered the nature, timing and extent of audit procedures. One of the goals of this chapter was to enable students to be able to understand these procedural programs in the context of audit sampling.

Multiple-choice Questions for Practice and Review

10.40 In an audit sampling application, an auditor:

 a. Performs procedures on all the items in a balance and makes a conclusion about the whole balance.

 b. Performs procedures on less than 100 percent of the items in a balance and formulates a conclusion about the whole balance.

 c. Performs procedures on less than 100 percent of the items in a class of transactions for the purpose of becoming familiar with the client's accounting system.

 d. Performs analytical procedures on the client's unaudited financial statements when planning the audit.

10.41 Auditors consider statistical sampling to be characterized by the following:

 a. Representative sample selection and nonmathematical consideration of the results.

 b. Carefully biased sample selection and statistical calculation of the results.

c. Representative sample selection and statistical calculation of the results.

d. Carefully biased sample selection and nonmathematical consideration of the results.

10.42 In audit sampling applications, sampling risk is:

a. Characteristic of statistical sampling applications but not of nonstatistical applications.

b. The probability that the auditor will fail to recognize erroneous accounting in the client's documentation.

c. The probability that accounting errors will arise in transactions and enter the accounting system.

d. The probability that an auditor's conclusion based on a sample might be different from the conclusion based on an audit of the entire population.

10.43 When auditing the client's performance of control to accomplish the completeness objective related to ensuring that all sales are recorded, auditors should draw sample items from:

a. The sales journal list of recorded sales invoices.

b. The file of shipping documents.

c. The file of customer order copies.

d. The file of receiving reports for inventory additions.

10.44 Nelson Williams was considering the sample size needed for a selection of sales invoices for the test of controls audit of the LoHo Company's internal controls. He presented the following information for two alternative cases:

	Case A	Case B
Acceptable risk of underreliance	High	Low
Acceptable risk of overreliance	High	Low
Tolerable deviation rate	High	Low
Expected population deviation rate	Low	High

Nelson should expect the sample size for Case A to be:

a. Smaller than the sample size for Case B.

b. Larger than the sample size for Case B.

c. The same as the sample size for Case B.

d. Not determinable relative to the Case B sample size.

10.45 Nelson next considered the sample size needed for a selection of customers' accounts receivable for the substantive audit of the total accounts receivable. He presented the following information for two alternative cases:

	Case X	Case Y
Acceptable risk of incorrect acceptance	Low	High
Acceptable risk of incorrect rejection	Low	High
Tolerable dollar misstatement in the account	Small	Large
Expected dollar misstatement in the account	Large	Small
Estimate of population variability	Large	Small

Nelson should expect the sample size for Case X to be:

a. Smaller than the sample size for Case Y.

b. Larger than the sample size for Case Y.

c. The same as the sample size for Case Y.

d. Not determinable relative to the Case Y sample size.

10.46 Which of the following should be considered an audit procedure for obtaining evidence?

a. An audit sampling application in accounts receivable selection.

b. The accounts receivable exist and are valued properly.

c. Sending a written confirmation on a customer's account balance.

d. Nonstatistical consideration of the amount of difference reported by a customer on a confirmation response.

10.47 When calculating the total amount of misstatement relevant to the analysis of an account balance, an auditor should add to the misstatement discovered in individually significant items the following:

a. The projected likely misstatement and the additional possible misstatement estimate.

b. The known misstatement in the sampled items.

c. The known misstatement in the sampled items, the projected likely misstatement and the additional possible misstatement estimate.

d. The additional possible misstatement estimate.

10.48 Eddie audited the LoHo Company's inventory on a sample basis. She audited 120 items from an inventory compilation list and discovered net overstatement of $480. The audited items had a book (recorded) value of $48,000. There were 1,200 inventory items listed, and the total inventory book amount was $490,000. Which of these calculations is (are) correct:

a. Known misstatement of $48,000 using the average difference method.

b. Projected likely misstatement of $480 using the sample stratification method.

c. Projected likely misstatement of $49,000 using the taintings method.

d. Projected likely misstatement of $4,800 using the average difference method.

10.49 Steve Katchy audited the client's accounts receivable, but he could not get any good information about customer 102's balance. The customer responded to the confirmation saying, "Our system does not provide detail for such a response." The sales invoice and shipping document papers have been lost, and the customer has not yet paid. Steve should:

a. Get another customer's account to consider in the sample.

b. Treat customer 102's account as being entirely wrong (overstated), if doing so will not affect his audit conclusion about the receivables taken altogether.

c. Require adjustment of the receivables to write off customer 102's balance.

d. Treat customer 102's account as accurate because there is no evidence saying it is fictitious.

10.50 The risk of incorrect acceptance in balance-audit sampling and the risk of assessing control risk too low in test of controls sampling both relate to:
  a. Effectiveness of an audit.
  b. Efficiency of an audit.
  c. Control risk assessment decisions.
  d. Evidence about assertions in financial statements.

10.51 An advantage of statistical sampling is that it helps an auditor:
  a. Eliminate nonsampling risk.
  b. Reapply evaluation judgements based on factors in addition to the sample evidence.
  c. Be precise and definite in the approach to an audit problem.
  d. Omit quantification of risk and materiality judgements.

10.52 To determine the sample size for a balance-audit sampling application, an auditor should consider the tolerable misstatement, the risk of incorrect acceptance, the risk of incorrect rejection, the population size and the:
  a. Expected monetary misstatement in the account.
  b. Overall materiality for the financial statements taken as a whole.
  c. Risk of assessing control risk too low.
  d. Risk of assessing control risk too high.

EXERCISES AND PROBLEMS

10.53 **Sampling and Nonsampling Audit Work.** The accounting firm of Mason & Jarr performed the work described in each separate case below. The two partners are worried about properly applying standards regarding audit sampling. They have asked your advice.

Required:

Write a report addressed to them, stating whether they did or did not observe the essential elements of audit sampling standards in each case:
  a. Mason selected three purchase orders for raw materials from the LIZ Corporation files. He started at this beginning point in the accounting process and traced each one through the accounting system. He saw the receiving reports, purchasing agent's approvals, receiving clerks' approvals, the vendors' invoices (now stamped paid), the entry in the cash disbursement records and the cancelled cheques. This work gave him a firsthand familiarity with the cash disbursement system, and he felt confident about understanding related questions in the internal control questionnaire completed later.
  b. Jarr observed the inventory taking at SER Corporation. She had an inventory list of the different inventory descriptions with the quantities taken from the perpetual inventory records. She selected the 200 items with the largest quantities and counted them after the client's shop foreman had completed his count. She decided not to check out the count accuracy on the other 800 items. The shop foreman miscounted in 16 cases. Jarr concluded the rate of miscount was 8 percent, so as many as 80 of the 1,000 items might be counted wrong. She asked the foreman to recount everything.
  c. CSR Corporation issued seven series of short-term commercial paper notes near the fiscal year-end to finance seasonal operations. Jarr confirmed the obligations under each series with the independent trustee for the holders, studied all seven indenture agreements and traced the proceeds of each issue to the cash receipts records.
  d. At the completion of the EH&R Corporation audit, Mason obtained written representations, as required by auditing standards, from the president, the chief financial officer and the controller. He did not ask the chief accountant at headquarters or the plant controllers in the three divisions for written representations.

10.54 **Test of Controls Audit Procedure Objectives and Control Deviations.** This exercise asks you to specify control test objectives and define deviations in connection with planning the test of controls audit of Kingston Company's internal controls.

Required:
  a. For each control cited below, state the objective of an auditor's test of controls audit procedure.
  b. For each control cited below, state the definition of a deviation from the control.
    1. The credit department supervisor reviews each customer's order and approves credit by making a notation on the order.
    2. The billing department must receive written notice from the shipping department of actual shipment to a customer before a sale is recorded. The sales record date is supposed to be the shipment date.
    3. Billing clerks carefully look up the correct catalogue list prices for goods shipped and calculate and recheck the amounts billed on invoices for the quantities of goods shipped.
    4. Billing clerks review invoices for intercompany sales and mark each one with the code "9," so that they will be posted to intercompany sales accounts.

10.55 **Timing of Test of Controls Audit Procedures.** Auditor Magann was auditing the authorization control over cash disbursements. She selected cash disbursement entries made throughout the year and vouched them to paid invoices and cancelled cheques bearing the initials and signatures of people authorized to approve the disbursements. She performed the work on September 30, when the company had issued cheques numbered from 43921 to 52920. Since 9,000 cheques had been issued in nine months, she reasoned that 3,000 more could be issued in the three months before the December 31 year-end. About 12,000 cheques had been issued last year. She wanted to take one sample of 100 disbursements for the entire year, so she selected 100 random numbers in the sequence 43921 to 55920. She audited the 80 cheques in the sample that were issued before September 30, and she held the other 20 randomly selected cheque numbers for later use. She found no deviations in the sample of 80—a finding that would, in the circumstances, cause her to assign a low (20 percent) control risk to the probability that the system would permit improper charges to be hidden away in expense and purchase/inventory accounts.

Required:
Take the role of Magann and write a memo to the audit manager (dated October 1) describing the audit team's options with respect to evaluating control performance for the remaining period, October through December.

10.56 Evaluation of Quantitative Test of Controls Evidence. Assume you audited control compliance in the Kingston Company for the deviations related to a random selection of sales transactions, as shown in Exhibit 10.56–1. For different sample sizes, the number of deviations was as follows:

LO.5

Required:
For each deviation and each sample, calculate the rate of deviation in the sample (sample deviation rate).

10.57 Stratification Calculation of Projected Likely Misstatement Using the Ratio Method. The stratification calculation example in the chapter shows the results of

LO.6

calculating the projected likely misstatement using the difference method. Assume the results shown in Exhibit 10.57–1 were obtained from a stratified sample.

Required:
Apply the ratio calculation method to each stratum to calculate the projected likely misstatement (PLM). What is PLM for the entire sample?

10.58 Determining Risk of Incorrect Acceptance. In the dialogue between the Kingston auditors, Fred said: "Our analytical procedures related to receivables didn't show much. The total is down, consistent with the sales decline, so the turnover is up a little. If any misstatement is in the receivables total, it may be too small to be obvious in the ratios." Then Jack said: "That's good news if the problems are immaterial. Too bad we can't say analytical procedures reduce our audit risk. What about internal control?" Fred responded: "I'd say it's about a 50–50 proposition. Sometimes control seemed to work well, sometimes it didn't. I noticed a few new people doing the invoice processing last week when we were here for a conference. Incidentally, I lump the inherent risk problems and internal control risk problems together when I think about internal control risk. Anyway, firm policy is to plan a sample for a low overall audit risk for the receivables."

LO.6

Required:
Based on this dialogue information, use the expanded risk model to determine a test of detail risk. Relate this risk to sample size determination.

EXHIBIT 10.56–1

	Sample Sizes									
	30	60	80	90	120	160	220	240	260	300
Missing sales invoice	0	0	0	0	0	0	0	0	0	0
Missing bill of lading	0	0	0	0	0	1	2	2	3	3
No credit approval	0	3	6	8	10	14	17	23	26	31
Wrong prices used	0	0	0	0	2	4	8	9	9	12
Wrong quantity billed	1	2	4	4	4	5	5	5	5	5
Wrong invoice arithmetic	0	0	0	0	1	2	2	2	2	3
Wrong invoice date	0	0	0	0	0	2	2	2	2	2
Posted to wrong account	0	0	0	0	0	0	0	0	0	0

EXHIBIT 10.57–1

Stratum	Population Size	Recorded Amount	Sample	Sample Results	
				Recorded Amount	Misstatement Amount*
1	6	$100,000	6	$100,000	$ −600
2	80	75,068	23	21,700	−274
3	168	75,008	22	9,476	−66
4	342	75,412	22	4,692	−88
5	910	74,512	23	1,973	23
	1,506	$400,000	96	$137,841	$−1,005

*A negative misstatement indicates overstatement of the book value, and a positive misstatement indicates understatement.

DISCUSSION CASES

· ·

10.59 Application to Accounts Receivable. Toni Tickmark
LO.6 has been assigned to plan the audit of the Cajuzzi Corporation, and is currently planning the circularization
(confirmation) of accounts receivable. Cajuzzi sells a
number of products in the personal health care field but
its mainstay is a portable whirlpool unit for use in bath-
tubs called the "Ecstasizer." Offering the same thera-
peutic muscle-relaxing benefits as built-in units costing
up to four times more, the Ecstasizer has been an outstanding success and is largely responsible for the
14 percent jump in sales this year.

Cajuzzi has five major categories of customers:
wholesalers, department store chains, drug stores, hardware stores and sporting goods stores. Because the
health care industry is highly competitive and a number
of "clones" are appearing on the market, Cajuzzi has an
aggressive sales strategy coupled with fairly liberal
credit policies. Viewing onsite store displays as its primary advertising media, Cajuzzi actually gives each
customer a display unit for demonstration purposes.
These costs are charged to promotion expense. It is the
stated objective of the company to have every store in
the country displaying its products.

New customers are extended credit using a very liberal credit policy and terms are net 30. Cajuzzi will not
stop shipments unless balances are more than 120 days
old. Customers' credit status is returned to normal as
soon as the overdue balances are paid. Cajuzzi is loathe
to write off any account unless the customer is actually
insolvent or has given intent not to pay.

In Exhibit 10.59–1, Schedule A contains a five-year
summary of key financial data, and Schedule B has a
summary of accounts receivable at the year-end circularization date (06/30/X4).

This is the second year that Toni's firm has been the
auditor of Cajuzzi, and her first year on the engagement. Last year's working papers showed that the 50
largest accounts were circularized, which was coverage of 20 percent ($2,600,000). Overstatement of ac-
counts receivable of $190,000 was discovered, but no
adjustment was proposed as the error was deemed
immaterial.

EXHIBIT 10.59–1

SCHEDULE A
Cajuzzi—Five-Year Financial Summary
(in $000s)

	20X0	20X1	20X2	20X3	20X4
Sales	84,000	85,000	83,000	86,000	98,000
A/R (6/30)	11,000	12,500	12,000	13,000	18,000
Allowance for doubtful accounts	1,260	1,275	1,245	1,290	1,470
Pre-tax income	3,300	2,400	3,200	3,900	5,000
Total assets	25,000	25,000	26,000	26,000	29,000

SCHEDULE B
Cajuzzi—Accounts Receivable Summary
June 30, 20X4

Range	Number of Customers	Total $
$100,000–$500,000	6	$ 1,800,000
75,000–99,999	20	1,700,000
50,000–74,999	35	2,000,000
25,000–49,999	30	1,100,000
15,000–24,999	100	1,900,000
10,000–14,999	120	1,400,000
Less than 10,000	16,220	8,100,000
	16,531	$18,000,000

Cajuzzi—Aged Trial Balance at 06/30/X4

0–30 days	31–60 days	61–90 days	91–120 days	More than 120 days
$8,350,000	$5,740,000	$2,105,000	$1,350,000	$455,000

(ICAO adapted)

Required:

a. Critique last year's approach to the circularization of receivables and the subsequent disposition of errors discovered.

b. What is meant by random (representative) selection, and why is it the most fundamental principle of sampling theory? Under what conditions is nonrandom selection appropriate?

c. What is meant by the terms *sampling error* and *non-sampling error?* What steps can the auditor take to control these?

d. Design a sampling plan for the circularization of receivables for Cajuzzi at 06/30/X4.

Cajuzzi's product line includes the following:
- Bathtub whirlpool units.
- Exercise equipment (rowers, bikes and mini-gyms).
- Heating pads, massage units and footbaths.
- Air purifiers and ionizers.
- "Healthware" cooking utensils.
- Skin care products and vitamin supplements.
- Track suits, footwear and sportswear.

10.60 Statistical Confirmation of Receivables. You are about to commence the audit of Delta Ltd. (See Exhibit 10.60–1.) This is the first time you have worked in the field without direct supervision by a senior, and you are of course anxious to do a good job. The senior has preceded you in visiting the client and has left you an audit file containing the following:

LO.6

- An internal control questionnaire indicating no serious deficiencies in internal control over accounts receivable.
- An aged accounts receivable listing prepared by the client.
- A confirmation control schedule.
- Returned confirmations.

The confirmation control shows the following information:
- Number of accounts in the receivables subledger at December 31 = 65.
- Number of positive confirms mailed = 15.
- Number of negative confirms mailed = 30.

The client year-end, December 31, was selected as the circulation date. Trade terms are 2/10, net/30. Confirmation results are as follows:

1. Eight positive confirms returned indicating full agreement.

2. One positive confirm returned indicating the balance was correct but this is the outstanding balance as at November 30, 20X2, not December 31, 20X2.

3. One positive confirm returned stating the balance was correct but should also reflect a credit memo issued January 5, 20X3.

4. One positive confirm returned stating the company uses an open invoice system and is unable to respond.

5. One positive confirm responding that the amount shown is incorrect because it does not reflect the 2 percent cash discount taken January 3, 20X3.

6. One positive and three negative confirms returned by the post office marked "No Such Address."

7. One positive confirm stating that the balance was correct but that the company refuses to pay because of defective product quality.

8. One positive confirm not returned, even after two follow-up requests.

9. Two negative confirms returned with no notations made by customers.

10. One negative confirm returned stating the customer owed more than the balance shown.

11. One negative confirm returned stating that the balance was correct but asking for an extension of credit terms.

12. One negative confirm returned stating "sue us."

The *first* page of the aged trial balance supplied by the client for Delta as at December 31 is shown in Exhibit 10.60–1.

Notes made by the senior indicate the following additional information:
- Abbey is an employee of Delta.
- The $700 Babbitt account represents a consignment shipment.
- The $500 October balance of Cabal has been formalized by a note receivable.
- The Cadenza balance represents a deposit. No shipments have been made to them yet.

Another note in the working paper file indicates that the client asked you not to send confirmation requests to Dacron Ltd. because they are worried about jeopardizing the ongoing collection efforts for the $3,000 past-due balance. Also, you were requested not to circularize Cadaver because Delta is extremely happy to have such a large account and wants to avoid bothering them in any way.

Required:

Analyze the evidence already obtained and describe any further procedures required to complete the audit of accounts receivable.

(ICAO adapted)

10.61 Projected Likely Misstatement. When Marge Simpson, PA, audited the Candle Company inventory, a random sample of inventory types was chosen for physical observation and price testing. The sample size was 80 different types of candle and candle-making inventory. The entire inventory contained 1,740 types, and the amount in the inventory control account was $166,000. Simpson had already decided that a misstatement of as much as $6,000 in the account would not be material. The audit work revealed the following eight errors in the sample of 80.

LO.6

Book Value	Audit Value	Error Amount
$600.00	$622.00	$(22.00)
15.50	14.50	(1.00)
65.25	31.50	(33.75)
83.44	53.45	(29.99)
16.78	15.63	(1.15)
78.33	12.50	(65.83)
13.33	14.22	$(.89)
93.87	39.87	(54.00)
$966.50	$803.67	$(162.83)

EXHIBIT   10.60-1

Account	Balance	Dec	Nov	Oct	Prior
	(CR)				
Aardwark Enterprises	$4,200	$2,100	$2,100		
Abacus Inc.	900				$900
Abalone Co.	5,500	1,000	3,200	$1,200	
Abbey, Fred	<600>	<600>			
Abstract Enterprises	1,100	500	400		200
Babbitt Inc.	700	700			
Bacchus Co.	6,000	2,000	4,000		
Cabal Ltd.	1,000			500	500
Cacao Enterprises	<900>				<900>
Cadaver Inc.	30,000	30,000			
Cadenza Co.	<1,200>	<1,200>			
Dacron Ltd.	3,100	100		3,000	
Subtotal (first page)	$49,800	$34,600	$9,700	$4,700	$700

The negative difference indicates overstatement of the recorded amount.

Required:

Calculate the projected likely misstatement using the difference method. Discuss the decision choice of accepting or rejecting the $166,000 book value (recorded amount) without adjustment.

10.62 Exercises in Applying the Basic Formula and Using
LO.5 the R Value Table in Appendix 10A. The following (Exhibit 10.62–1) are auditor judgement and audit sampling results for six populations. Assume large population sizes.

Required:

a. For each population, did the auditor select a smaller sample size than is indicated by using the tables for determining sample size (assume K=0 in sample size planning)? Explain the effect of selecting either a larger or smaller size than those determined in the tables.

b. Calculate the sample deviation rate and the achieved P or upper error limit for each population.

c. For which of the six populations should the sample results be considered unacceptable? What options are available to the auditor?

d. Why is analysis of the deviations necessary even when the populations are considered acceptable?

e. For the following terms, identify which is an audit decision, a nonstatistical estimate made by the auditor, a sample result, and a statistical conclusion about the population:
   1. Estimated population deviation rate
   2. Tolerable deviation rate
   3. Acceptable risk of overreliance on internal control
   4. Actual sample size
   5. Actual number of deviations in the sample
   6. Sample deviation rate
   7. Achieved P or upper error limit

EXHIBIT   10.62-1

	1	2	3	4	5	6
Tolerable deviation rate or error rate as a percentage (equals materiality for the test)	6	3	8	5	20	15
Acceptable risk of overreliance on internal control in percentage = Beta Risk = 1 − Confidence Level	5	5	10	5	10	10
Actual sample size	100	100	60	100	20	60
Actual number of deviations (errors) in the sample	2	0	1	4	1	8

APPENDIX 10A

STATISTICAL SAMPLING TABLES

. . . .

R VALUE TABLE

75% R	Confidence Levels 80% R	85% R	90% R	K Value: Number of sample errors	95% R	Confidence Levels 97.5% R	99% R
1.39	1.61	1.90	2.31	0	3.00	3.69	4.51
2.70	3.00	3.38	3.89	1	4.75	5.58	6.64
3.93	4.28	4.73	5.33	2	6.30	7.23	8.41
5.11	5.52	6.02	6.69	3	7.76	8.77	10.05
6.28	6.73	7.27	8.00	4	9.16	10.25	11.61
7.43	7.91	8.50	9.28	5	10.52	11.67	13.11
8.56	9.08	9.71	10.54	6	11.85	13.06	14.58
9.69	10.24	10.90	11.78	7	13.15	14.43	16.00
10.81	11.38	12.08	13.00	8	14.44	15.77	17.41
11.92	12.52	13.25	14.21	9	15.71	17.09	18.79
13.03	13.66	14.42	15.41	10	16.97	18.40	20.15

TABLE OF RANDOM DIGITS

32942	95416	42339	59045	26693	49057	87496	20624	14819
07410	99859	83828	21409	29094	65114	36701	25762	12827
59981	68155	45673	76210	58219	45738	29550	24736	09574
46251	25437	69654	99716	11563	08803	86027	51867	12116
65558	51904	93123	27887	53138	21488	09095	78777	71240
99187	19258	86421	16401	19397	83297	40111	49326	81686
35641	00301	16096	34775	21562	97983	45040	19200	16383
14031	00936	81518	48440	02218	04756	19506	60695	88494
60677	15076	92554	26042	23472	69869	62877	19584	39576
66314	05212	67859	89356	20056	30648	87349	20389	53805
20416	87410	75646	64176	82752	63606	37011	57346	69512
28701	56992	70423	62415	40807	98086	58850	28968	45297
74579	33844	33426	07570	00728	07079	19322	56325	84819
62615	52342	82968	75540	80045	53069	20665	21282	07768
93945	06293	22879	08161	01442	75071	21427	94842	26210
75689	76131	96837	67450	44511	50424	82848	41975	71663
02921	16919	35424	93209	52133	87327	95897	65171	20376
14295	34969	14216	03191	61647	30296	66667	10101	63203
05303	91109	82403	40312	62191	67023	90073	83205	71344
57071	90357	12901	08899	91039	67251	28701	03846	94589

Continued

78471	57741	13599	84390	32146	00871	09354	22745	65806
89242	79337	59293	47481	07740	43345	25716	70020	54005
14955	59592	97035	80430	87220	06392	79028	57123	52872
42446	41880	37415	47472	04513	49494	08860	08038	43624
18534	22346	54556	17558	73689	14894	05030	19561	56517
39284	33737	42512	86411	23753	29690	26096	81361	93099
33922	37329	89911	55876	28379	81031	22058	21487	54613
78355	54013	50774	30666	61205	42574	47773	36027	27174
08845	99145	94316	88974	29828	97069	90327	61842	29604
01769	71825	55957	98271	02784	66731	40311	88495	18821
17639	38284	59478	90409	21997	56199	30068	82800	69692
05851	58653	99949	63505	40409	85551	90729	64938	52403
42396	40112	11469	03476	03328	84238	26570	51790	42122
13318	14192	98167	75631	74141	22369	36757	89117	54998
60571	54786	26281	01855	30706	66578	32019	65884	58485
09531	81853	59334	70929	03544	18510	89541	13555	21168
72865	16829	86542	00396	20363	13010	69645	49608	54738
56324	31093	77924	28622	83543	28912	15059	80192	83964
78192	21626	91399	07235	07104	73652	64425	85149	75409
64666	34767	97298	92708	01994	53188	78476	07804	62404
82201	75694	02808	65983	74373	66693	13094	74183	73020
15360	73776	40914	85190	54278	99054	62944	47351	89098
68142	67957	70896	37983	20487	95350	16371	03426	13895
19138	31200	30616	14639	44406	44236	57360	81644	94761
28155	03521	36415	78452	92359	81091	56513	88321	97910
87971	29031	51780	27376	81056	86155	55488	50590	74514
58147	68841	53625	02059	75223	16783	19272	61994	71090
18875	52809	70594	41649	32935	26430	82096	01605	65846
75109	56474	74111	31966	29969	70093	98901	84550	25769
35983	03742	76822	12073	59463	84420	15868	99505	11426

Source: The Rand Corporation, *A Million Random Digits with 100,000 Normal Deviates* (Glencoe: Free Press, 1955), p. 102.

PRELUDE TO PART III

. . . .

PERFORMING THE AUDIT

Overview: Linking Audit Planning to Performance

You are about to begin Part III of the text, which illustrates how the audit activities, concepts and tools presented in Part II are applied in practice to perform audits, using simplified business situations as examples.

Recall that the auditor's understanding of the client's business; its environment, risks, systems, and controls were discussed in Chapters 6 to 9. This work is the basis for developing an appropriate *overall strategy* for the audit. This strategy should reflect the audit team's preliminary decisions on the *scope* of the audit. As covered in Chapter 3, the scope defines the entity to be audited and the financial information of that entity that is the subject of the audit opinion. The overall strategy also sets out the audit's timing and the approach to be used to gather sufficient, appropriate evidence. As discussed in *CICA Handbook*, section 5150, the overall strategy addresses the following:

- planning materiality
- identifying material financial statement components
- identifying high risk audit areas
- determining the audit evidence required to assess internal control effectiveness (if the auditor is required to provide an assurance report on management assertions about internal control effectiveness this additional responsibility is included here)
- determining the control framework or criteria used to assess control risk
- identifying the nature and volume of transactions
- discovering any changes in the industry, legal and regulatory environment, GAAP, and the company's management or operations that can affect financial reports

The aspects of the overall strategy that involve client resources and cooperation are communicated to client management and the audit committee. This helps make the necessary arrangements for gaining access to the necessary records and client personnel required for interim and final audit work. The audit firm's internal resource needs are also specified in the overall strategy. For example, how many audit staff are required on the team and what experience levels do they need? Are specialists required for IT or tax issues? Are external specialists required for valuation assistance? Will other offices of the audit firm be involved for multilocation businesses or will other auditors' work be relied on for major subsidiaries audited by another audit firm?

Overall strategy development also sets out frequency and timing of audit team meetings, timing, and experience levels required for working paper reviews. The assessment of the client's internal controls involves assessing management's controls both at the company level and the application level (transactions, balances and disclosures, and the assertions of each). Details of this assessment are covered in Chapter 9, and this prelude provides a questionnaire that guides the auditor in this assessment for the overall strategy development stage of the audit.

The overall strategy is the basis for developing the **detailed audit plan** and specific programs used to perform the audit. To help develop these audit programs, consider that a business is composed of several separate processes and related accounting cycles. However, this process view is also a useful view for the organization's own management and system development purposes; thus, it is likely to be an effective approach in most audit engagements. The separate processes we will examine in Part III are as follows:

- the revenues, receivables and receipts process (Chapter 11)
- the purchases, payables, and payments process (Chapter 12)

- the production and payroll process (Chapter 13)
- the finance and investment process (Chapter 14)

Even though one organization may view its processes somewhat differently from another, generally these processes are key functions that will need to be managed in every organization. Consideration is given to cost-effectiveness and efficiency in specifying the nature, extent and timing of audit procedures that will be used to assess the inherent and control risk that could lead to material misstatements, the planned further audit procedures that will be done in response to these risks to reduce them to an acceptably low level and issue an audit opinion. The detailed audit plan also covers decisions about managing the investment team—how will less-experienced staff be directed, especially with regard to exercising professional scepticism, how will their work be supervised and reviewed, and what time budgets will be required?

Finally, the evidence obtained from performing the audit procedures and other events the auditor discovers provide feedback into the audit planning process. These factors may show that the current or future overall strategy and audit plan should be modified if evidence gathered in the audit indicates changes are required to the scope, timing, or other aspects of the audit approach. Exhibit PIII-1 summarizes the development process for the overall strategy and the detailed audit plan.

Business Processes and Accounting Cycles: The Big Picture

To keep things as simple as possible, we focus on the business processes and their related accounting cycles individually to design and execute audit programs. In an actual organization, however, all these processes are interrelated. How the various processes relate to one another is shown in Exhibit PIII-2, which provides the "big picture" view of an organization.

The Balance Sheet Approach to Auditing

To help us keep the big picture in mind as we look at how audit work is performed, it may also be helpful to consider the full set of financial statements that the auditor's opinion covers, that is, the balance sheet, the income and retained earnings statement, the cash flow statement and the statement of shareholders' equity. All these statements are **articulated** (i.e., you cannot simply change one number in particular statement without flowing that change through all the other related accounts in the other statements). These articulation relationships are another way to see the interrelationships among the different processes.

This articulation is also the basis of what is known as the **balance sheet approach to auditing.** By focussing on balance sheet accounts and changes in them, we are also gaining assurance about the rest of the financial statement accounts that result from these balances and the changes in them. To summarize, the key relation is as follows:

Change in net assets $\pm$ Net contributions from owners = Net Income

When we have a high level of audit assurance about the change in net assets and shareholder transactions, we also have assurance that the net income amount is correct. This means all we have left to verify is that the allocations within the income statement are reasonable. This can be done by using analytical procedures rather than more costly vouching or confirmation. This reflects the fundamental control provided by the double-entry accounting system and the financial statement definitions set out in generally accepted accounting principles.[1] These are important strengths of the accounting and reporting framework that are a big help in pulling all the audit work together to complete the audit.

Organization of Chapters 11 to 15

To illustrate how the audit plan is performed in these processes, each of Chapters 11 to 14 is organized as follows:

- The chapter starts with an overview of the business risks and the transactions, balances and disclosures in that process.
- Then the significant risks of misstatement at the assertion level are analyzed.

---

[1] *CICA Handbook,* section 1000.

EXHIBIT PIII-1   RELATING AUDIT PLANNING TO AUDIT PERFORMANCE

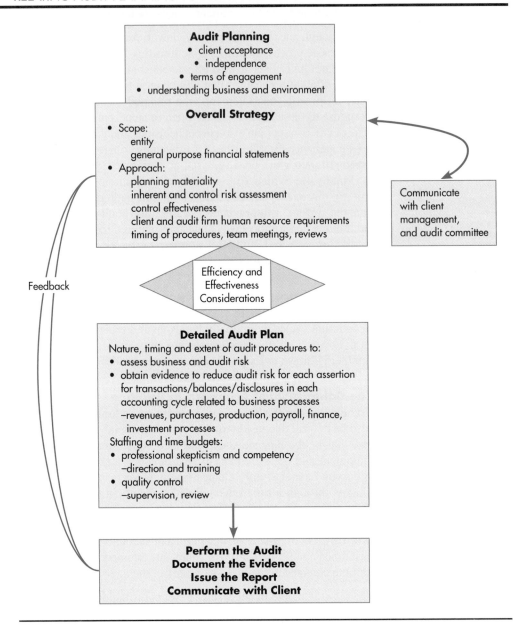

- Next, we describe a generic example of the process and the main accounts related to it.

- Next, we cover the key control assertions and risks, the types of control activities that would address those risks and procedures auditors can use to assess controls.

- This is followed by examples of controls tests that could used if the auditors decided in their overall strategy and plan that relying on effective controls would be cost-effective in reducing their risk of not detecting a material misstatement.

- Then each chapter gives several short cases ("casettes") that illustrate audit problems in that process and how audit procedures can be used to uncover them.

- As well, each of Chapters 11 to 14 gives an example of an audit program listing detailed audit procedures that are commonly used in each process/cycle.

- Finally, each chapter concludes with an overview of the balance sheet approach to analyzing related financial statement components, as the basis for developing analytical procedures to assess the overall presentation.

EXHIBIT   PIII-2   CAPTURING AN ORGANIZATION'S BUSINESS PROCESSES IN ITS FINANCIAL
STATEMENTS

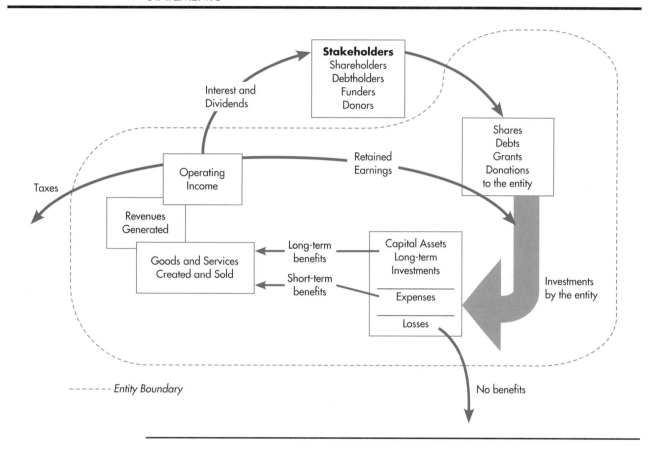

------- *Entity Boundary*

Part III concludes with Chapter 15, Completing the Audit, which covers several issues that the auditor must address in order to complete the audit and form an audit opinion. This includes audit procedures for the revenues and expenses, auditing estimates, and procedures for auditing the cash flow statement. Other issues that need to be addressed at the final stages include assessing errors and their materiality, financial statement adjustments, lawyers' letters, subsequent events, management representation letters, subsequent discovery of material facts and management letters. Finally, the standards for documenting the audit work in the final audit file are reviewed.

 Note that there are many references in Part III to details of generally accepted auditing standards issued in the *CICA Handbook* and in ISAs. Since this text is aimed at students who will most likely be auditing under Canadian or international GAAS, the text refers, for the most part, to the auditing and assurance recommendations set out only by CICA and IFAC. U.S. auditing standards are similar to their Canadian and international counterparts, and all three standard-setting groups are moving towards a high degree of harmonization of GAAS. However, U.S. pronouncements and standard setting are structured somewhat differently in response to unique U.S. legal, regulatory and political circumstances. This text refers to U.S. standards when they are likely to lead to similar developments in future Canadian or international GAAS. For those of you who wish to learn more about U.S. GAAS, refer to the PCAOB and AICPA websites for specific details.

Following is Exhibit PIII–3, an example of an Internal Control Questionnaire for company-level controls. Its points apply to all the processes and accounting cycles that will be covered later in Chapters 11–14.

EXHIBIT   PIII-3   INTERNAL CONTROL QUESTIONNAIRE FOR COMPANY-LEVEL CONTROLS AND CONTROL ACTIVITIES

This questionnaire is designed to assist the auditor in assessing the strength of internal control.

Internal control is divided into company-level controls and control activities. Company-level controls are: the overall control environment, management's risk assessment procedures, information systems and communication and monitoring. Control activities include general and application controls.

General controls are policies and procedures that apply to all information systems and business processes.

Application controls are those that are specific to each of the main operating processes and their related accounting cycles.

In this text we will provide separate detailed questionnaires for each process in the relevant chapters, after the nature of each business process and accounting cycle has been explained: revenues/receivables/receipts (Chapter 11); purchases/payables/payments (Chapter 12); production and payroll (Chapter 13); and finance and investment (Chapter 14).

COMPANY-LEVEL CONTROLS

CONTROL ENVIRONMENT

The control environment refers to management's overall attitude, awareness and actions concerning the importance of internal control to address the risks of the business and reduce inherent risks and the risk of a material misstatement. Consider the following aspects and evidence of strength.

"Tone at the Top"
- Do management actions and attitudes show character, integrity and ethical values?
- Are audit committee and board of directors (or others responsible for governance of the organization) competent, knowlegable, actively involved and influential in the organization?
- Does management have well-defined policies and objectives that communicate its commitment to integrity and ethical values?

Commitment to Competence
- Does management have sufficient experience to operate the business?
- Does management assign authority and responsibility appropriately?
- Does management provide accounting and key employees with the resources, training and information necessary to discharge their duties?
- Do management's hiring and promotion policies emphasize competence and trustworthiness?

Management's Operating Style and Philosophy
- Does management encourage a strong control environment?
- Does the organizational structure provide a framework for establishing key areas of authority, responsibility and reporting lines that promote strong internal control at all stages of planning, executing and reviewing the organization's activities for achieving its objectives?
- Do management actions remove or reduce incentives and opportunities for employees to act dishonestly?
- Is there a mandatory vacation policy for employees performing key control functions?
- Does management implement controls over information systems?
- Does management maintain appropriate physical safeguards over cash, investments, inventory and/or fixed assets?
- Does management establish adequate controls over accounting estimates and choice of accounting principles where applicable?

MANAGEMENT'S RISK ASSESSMENT PROCESS

For financial reporting purposes, management's risk assessment process should identify internal and external events and circumstances that can impair the organization's ability to initiate, record, process and report financial data that is consistent with the assertions management makes in its financial statements.

Consider the following aspects:

- Has management established policies and assigned responsibility to personnel for identifying, evaluating and mitigating risks?
- Does management have an ongoing process to identify risk and ensure exposure to such risks is minimized? Risks include:
  - changes in business and regulatory operating environment
  - new personnel
  - changes in information systems
  - rapid growth in operations
  - new technology
  - new business models, products or activities

Continued

– organizational restructuring
– foreign expansion
– new accounting standards
• Does management independently evaluate the organization's internal control environment to assess its effectiveness?

INFORMATION AND COMMUNICATIONS

High-quality management information is an essential component of internal control. Creating and communicating information is relevant to operating decisions and to financial reporting objectives. The auditor is concerned mainly with the financial reporting information system, consisting of the procedures and records established to initiate, record, process and report transactions, events and conditions and to maintain accountability for the related assets, liabilities and equity.

Consider the following aspects:

• Does management have documented policies and procedures to develop, operate and maintain information systems, related business processes and accounting cycles that produce reliable and timely financial information?
• Has management implemented an information system that is well designed to achieve the following financial reporting objectives:
– identify and record all valid transactions related to the organization in their proper reporting period;
– capture sufficient detail to permit proper classification, measurement and presentation of transactions in the financial statements and note disclosures in accordance with generally accepted accounting principles or other appropriate basis of accounting.
• Are appropriate lines of authority and reporting clearly established?
• Does management gather information from and communicate information to appropriate people on a timely basis?
• Is there a communication process available for people to report suspected improprieties? For example, has management established an effective whistle-blower program as it relates to financial reporting?
• Is there a disaster recovery plan in place to ensure minimum disruption should management information, accounting records or other important data be destroyed, damaged or stolen?

MONITORING

• Has management established effective monitoring procedures?
• Does management have a business plan which is monitored against actual results?
• Does management monitor compliance with internal control policies and procedures?
• Does management investigate variances and take proper and timely corrective action?

CONTROL ACTIVITIES

Control activities are the policies and procedures that ensure actions are taken to address risks that threaten the achievement of the entity's objectives.
Control activities are part of the information system, can be manual or IT-based, are directed toward the control objectives and are applied at various organizational and functional levels. This questionnaire divides control activities into general controls and application controls.

General controls

General controls are pervasive policies and procedures that tend to apply to most or all processes in the information system and most or all organizational levels.
• Are there policies and procedures in place to:
– prevent unauthorized access or changes to programs and data?
– ensure the security and privacy of data?
– control and maintain key systems?
– protect assets susceptible to misappropriation?
• Is the client's approach to IT planning and new systems development adequate to ensure new systems and systems changes protect the integrity of data and processing? In particular, note procedures that ensure the following: completeness, accuracy and authorization of data and processing; adequate management trails exist; and continuity of IT operations is protected by back-up procedures and a formal disaster plan.
• Are appropriate procedures in place for software and hardware upgrades and other system maintenance?
• Are day-to-day operations adequately controlled by IT support personnel to ensure data integrity?
• Are access controls adequate? Consider whether internal access is monitored across the information system such that appropriate personnel have access only to files they need to do their jobs and unauthorized access is prohibited.

Continued

• For IT systems and applications run over the Internet or other telecommunications systems, is external access security adequately protected by firewalls, virus protection software or other IT security features.

Application controls

Application controls relate to recording, processing and reporting information. They will be specific to the business processes and related accounting cycles that generate financial information. Recording includes identifying and capturing the relevant information for transactions or events. Processing includes calculation, measurement, valuation, and summarization, whether performed by IT-based or manual procedures. Reporting relates to the preparation of financial reports, electronic or printed, that management uses for measuring and reviewing the entity's financial performance and reporting to stakeholders.

For each accounting cycle, a separate detailed questionnaire should be completed, that assesses the following aspects of information processing.

• Are data integrity controls adequate? Identify and assess controls over data input to and processed in the accounting cycle that ensures data and processing are valid, complete and accurate. Consider functions such as edit and validation checks, programmed reasonability checks, dollar limits, sequence numbering, internal confirmation of transaction data transferred from database files to the application, reconciliation and other relevant control features.

• Are access and authorization controls adequate, e.g., are access points for data entry, enquiry (terminal, desktop, laptop, handheld device, etc.) set up to allow only designated functions to be performed and only authorized personnel to access data, processing and output?

Based on the application level assessment, the auditor will develop a detail plan setting out the planned approach, including decisions on whether to rely on controls as a component of audit evidence.

Refer to detailed Internal Control Questionnaires for each business process/accounting cycle provided in Chapters 11 to 14.

PART III
Audit Applications

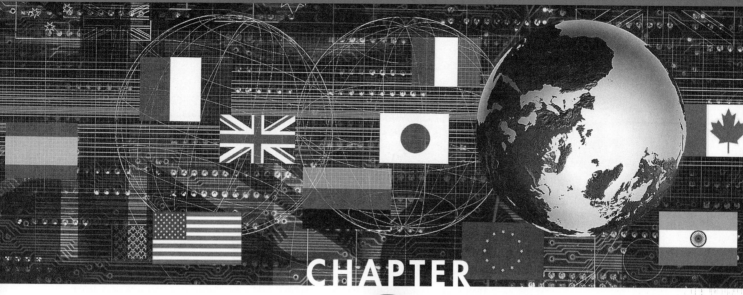

CHAPTER

11

Revenues, Receivables, and Receipts Process

This chapter offers a concise overview of the accounting cycle for the business processes related to placing customer orders and sales, delivering goods and services to customers, accounting for customer accounts receivable, collecting and depositing cash received from customers and reconciling bank statements. A series of short cases (casettes) demonstrates the application of audit procedures in situations where errors, irregularities and frauds might be discovered. The chapter ends with special technical notes on the existence assertion, using confirmations and auditing bank reconciliations.

LEARNING OBJECTIVES

After completing this chapter, you will be able to:

1 Describe the revenues, receivables and receipts process, including typical transactions, source documents, controls and account balances.

2 Outline control tests for auditing control over customer credit approval, delivery, accounts receivable, cash receipts and bank statements.

3 Design audit and investigative procedures for detecting common errors, irregularities and frauds in the revenues, receivables and receipts process.

4 Explain the importance of the existence assertion for the audit of cash and accounts receivable.

5 Identify considerations for using confirmations when auditing cash and accounts receivable.

6 Perform substantive audit procedures for the audit of bank statement reconciliations, explaining how auditors can search for lapping and kiting.

RISK ASSESSMENT FOR REVENUES, RECEIVABLES AND RECEIPTS

• • • • • • • • • • • •

Revenue creation is the main focus of the strategy and business processes of any organization because revenues provide the cash flows that are its lifeblood. The business's ability to generate revenues and use them to operate successfully are critical aspects that the auditor must understand to assess the business risk and the risk that the financial statements are misstated, as discussed in Chapter 6. Think of the business as a car: the revenue generating strategy is its engine and the cash flow is the gasoline that fuels it. In a for-profit business, costs that are incurred must generate enough sales revenue to provide profits to sustain operations and also provide investment returns to owners and creditors. A not-for-profit organization also must generate enough revenues to pay for the activities necessary to achieve its charitable or other purposes.

To assess risks in the revenue-generating processes, the auditor mainly considers revenue and cash receipts transactions, and accounts receivable balances. Important disclosures relating to revenues include revenue recognition policies, related party transactions, commitments and economic dependencies.

At the assertion level, risks related to the existence and ownership of revenues may arise if management chooses overly aggressive revenue recognition policies (e.g., Nortel), perhaps due to management incentives or pressure to meet performance targets. Ownership risks may exist where managers have the ability to transfer funds between related entities under their control (e.g., Enron, Hollinger). Completeness risks relate to recordkeeping and custodial controls over cash receipts; these must be strong enough to ensure that all revenues the business earns are received by the company and recorded in full. Fraudulent misappropriation of cash by employees is a key completeness risk in the revenue process. Because substantial flows of funds may be involved in the revenue processes of some businesses, **money laundering**—improperly processing monetary profits of crime to cover up their sources and convert them to "clean" cash—is also an ownership risk related to the revenue transactions (e.g., financial services, banking). Valuation and ownership risks can exist when substantial revenues are generated in foreign countries, due to currency exchange risks and potential restrictions on removing money from those countries. Disclosure risks include revenue recognition policy explanations, reporting the extent of barter transactions (e.g., in e-commerce), or disclosing contractual commitments to sell inventory at fixed prices. The foregoing are only some examples of risks that may exist in a particular business. You can see how an auditor's in-depth understanding of the client's business, the revenue-generating strategy that drives it, and the environment it operates in are critical to a comprehensive assessment of business risks and the possible financial misstatements that these risks can lead to.

This chapter uses simple examples to outline the business processes and the related accounting cycle for recording and controlling revenues, accounts receivable and cash receipts. It explains control activities that are important in these processes, how to evaluate and test the controls, and how to design and implement the substantive audit tests that provide evidence that the resulting financial statement components are fairly reported. The risk of nonexistent or incorrectly valued revenues or receivables can often be addressed by substantive testing such as confirmation and analytical procedures. Control tests in the revenue transaction processes may also be used to reduce the amount of substantive evidence required. Revenue completeness usually requires a reliance on controls and thus control testing; substantive testing alone may not provide sufficient evidence for the completeness assertion for revenues.

REVENUES, RECEIVABLES AND RECEIPTS PROCESS: TYPICAL ACTIVITIES

LEARNING OBJECTIVE

1 Describe the revenues, receivables and receipts process, including typical transactions, source documents, controls and account balances.

Exhibit 11–1 shows the activities and transactions involved in the revenues, receivables and receipts process. The basic activities are as follows: (1) receiving and processing customer orders, including credit granting; (2) delivering goods and services to customers; (3) billing customers and accounting for accounts receivable; (4) collecting and depositing cash received from customers; and (5) reconciling bank statements. As you follow the exhibit, you can track some of the elements of the control structure. Refer to Appendix 11A for examples of controls related to this system. In practice, you would have obtained a detailed organization chart as part of the audit planning. This chart identifies the specific client personnel who are responsible for the various functions in the process. These are the people you will work with to design and perform your audit work.

Sales and Accounts Receivable

Exhibit 11–2 presents an example of a system for processing customer sales orders. Company personnel receive the customer's purchase order and create a sales order, entering

EXHIBIT   11–1   REVENUES, RECEIVABLES AND RECEIPTS PROCESS EXAMPLE

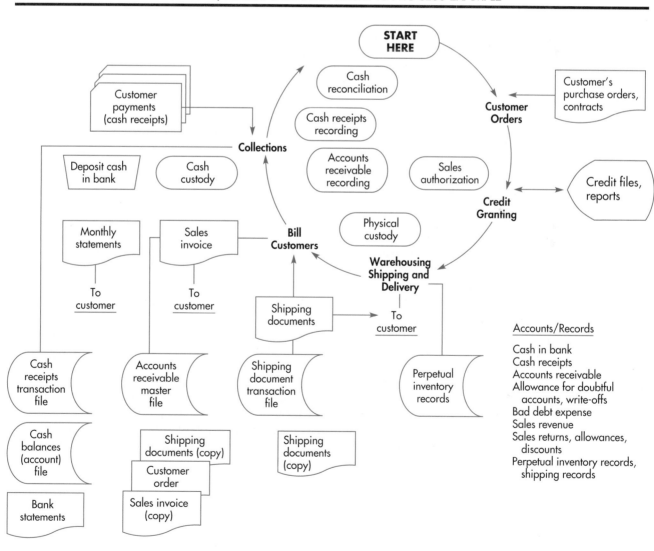

EXHIBIT 11-2   SALES AND ACCOUNTS RECEIVABLE: PROCESSING EXAMPLE

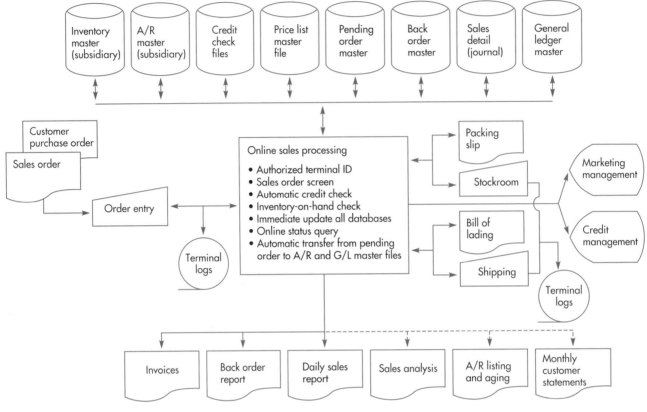

it in a computer terminal. The computer system then performs automatic authorization procedures—determining whether the customer is a regular or new customer, approving credit, and checking the availability of inventory to fill the order. (If inventory is short, a back order is entered.) When these authorizations are embedded in a computer system, access to the master files for additions, deletions and other changes must be limited to responsible persons. If these controls fail, orders might be processed for fictitious customers, credit might be approved for bad credit risks and packing slips might be created for goods that do not exist in the inventory.

When a customer order passes these authorizations, the system (1) creates a record in the pending order master file, (2) produces a packing slip that is transmitted to the stockroom and shipping department, and (3) updates the inventory master file to show the commitment (removal) of the inventory. At this stage the pending order and the packing slip should be numbered in a numerical sequence so that the system can determine later whether any transactions have not been completed (completeness objective of control). The packing slip is the stockkeeper's authorization to release inventory to the shipping department and the shipping department's authorization to release goods to a trucker or to the customer.

Another authorization in the system is the price list master file. It contains the product unit prices for billing customers. Persons who have power to alter this file have the power to authorize price changes and customer billings.

Custody

Physical custody of inventory starts with the stockroom or warehouse where inventory is kept. Custody is transferred to the shipping department upon the authorization of the packing slip that orders stockkeepers to release inventory to the shipping area. As long as the

---

PRICE FIXING

The company's computer programmer was paid off by a customer to cause the company to bill the customer at prices lower than list prices. The programmer wrote a subroutine that was invoked when the billing system detected the customer's regular code number. This subroutine instructed the customer billing system to reduce all unit prices 9.5 percent. The company relied on the computer billing system, and nobody ever rechecked the actual prices billed.

---

system works, custody is under proper control. However, if the stockkeepers or the shipping department personnel have the power to change the quantity shown on the packing slip, they can cause errors in the system by billing the customer for too small or too large a quantity. (This power combines custody with a recording function, a segregation-of-duties control weakness. A computer record or log of such changes is a control procedure that will create an electronic audit trail.)

Custody of accounts receivable records themselves implies the power to alter those records directly or to enter transactions to alter them (e.g., transfers, returns, allowance credits, write-offs). Personnel with this power have a combination of authorization and recording responsibility, another example of a control weakness due to a lack of segregation of incompatible duties.

Recording

When delivery or shipment is complete, the shipping personnel enter the completion of the transaction in the system. This event: (1) produces a bill of lading shipping document, which is evidence of an actual delivery/shipment; (2) removes the pending order from the inventory recording system; and (3) produces a sales invoice (prenumbered the same as the order and packing slip) that bills the customer for the quantity shipped, according to the bill of lading. Any personnel who have the power to enter or alter these transactions or to intercept the invoice that is supposed to be mailed to the customer have undesirable combinations of authorization, custody and recording responsibilities; they can authorize improper transaction changes and record them by making entries in systems under their control. This is a control weakness that provides an opportunity for employees to commit a fraud by misappropriating inventory and concealing it in the accounting records.

Periodic Reconciliation

The most frequent reconciliation is the comparison of the sum of customers' unpaid balances with the accounts receivable control account total. Usually, this reconciliation is done with an aged trial balance. An aged trial balance is a list of the customers and their balances, with the balances classified in columns headed for different age categories (e.g., current, 10–30 days past due, 31–60 days past due, 61–90 days past due and over 90 days past due). Internal auditors, or other employees who are independent of the inventory and receivables recording functions, can perform periodic comparison of the customers' obligations (according to the customers) with the recorded amount by sending confirmations to the customers. (Refer to the special note on using confirmations at the end of this chapter.)

Cash Receipts and Cash Balances

There are numerous ways to receive cash—over the counter, through the mail, by electronic funds transfer and by receipt in a lockbox. In a lockbox arrangement, a fiduciary (e.g., a bank) opens the box, lists the receipts, deposits the money and sends the remittance advices (stubs showing the amount received from each customer) to the company. Most companies need little authorization to accept a payment from a customer! However, authorization is important for approving customers' discounts and allowances taken. Receiving cash and approving discounts is yet another example of incompatible duties that provide an opportunity for employees to defraud the company. Exhibit 11–3 shows a manual system for processing cash receipts. You can see the "approval of discounts" noted in Exhibit 11–3.

Custody

Someone always gets the cash and cheques in hand and thus has custody of the physical cash for a time. Control over this custody can vary. Companies can rotate people through the custody responsibility so that one person does not have this custody all the time; they can have rotating teams of two or more people so that they would need to collude with one another to steal money; or they can make arrangements outside the company for actual cash custody (e.g., the lockbox arrangement). Since this initial custody cannot be avoided, it is always good control to prepare a list of the cash receipts as early in the process as possible, then separate the actual cash from the bookkeeping documents. The cash goes to the cashier or treasurer's office, where a bank deposit is prepared and the money is sent to the bank. The list goes to the accountants, who record the cash receipts. This list simply may be a stack of the remittance advices received with the customers' payments. (You yourself prepare a

EXHIBIT   11–3   CASH RECEIPTS PROCESSING EXAMPLE

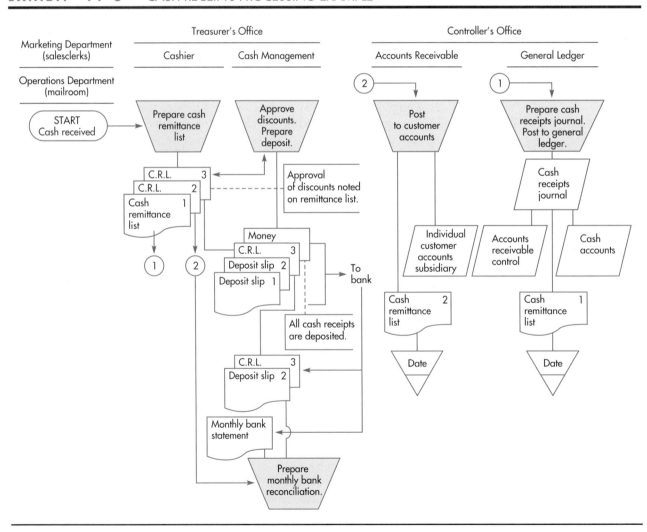

CAREFUL RECONCILIATION
(Refer to Exhibit 11–3)

Suppose the cashier who prepares the remittance list had stolen and converted Customer A's cheques for personal use. It might work for a short time until Customer A complained that the company had not given credit for payments. The cashier knows this. So, the cashier later puts Customer B's cheques in the bank deposit, but shows Customer A on the remittance list; thus, the accountants give Customer A credit. So far, so good for preventing Customer A's complaint, but now Customer B needs to be addressed. This "lapping" of customer payments to hide an embezzlement can be detected by a bank reconciliation comparison of the cheques deposited (Customer B) with the remittance credit recorded (Customer A). Sometimes the lapping is covered by issuing a credit slip for Customer B. This illustrates the importance of proper authorization and control of credit slips.

SHIPPING EMPLOYEE CAUGHT BY COMPUTER!

A customer paid off a shipping department employee to enter smaller quantities than actually shipped on the packing slip and bill of lading. This caused the customer's invoices to be understated. Unknown to the employee, a computer log recorded all the entries that altered the original packing slip record. An alert internal auditor noticed the pattern of "corrections" made by the shipping employee. A trap was laid by initiating fictitious orders for this customer, and the employee was observed making the alterations.

remittance advice each time you write the "amount enclosed" on the top part of your credit card or cellphone bill, tear it off, and enclose it with your cheque.)

Recording

The accountants who record cash receipts and credits to customer accounts should not handle the cash. They should use the remittance list to make entries to the cash and accounts receivable control accounts and to the customers' accounts receivable subsidiary account records. In fact, it is a good error-checking procedure to have control account and subsidiary account entries made by different people; then later the accounts receivable entries and balances can be compared (reconciled) to determine whether the proper source documents (remittance lists) were used to make error-free accounting entries. A further segregation would be to prevent the person who receives and lists cheques from having access to cash, bank accounts or receivables accounts. Some computerized accounting programs post the customers' accounts automatically by keying in the customer identification number.

Periodic Reconciliation

It is important that bank account reconciliations be prepared carefully. Deposit slips should be compared to the details on cash remittance lists, and the totals should be traced to the general ledger entries. Likewise, paid cheques should be traced to the cash disbursements listing (journal). This care is required to establish that all receipts recorded in the books were deposited and that credit was given to the right customer. The reconciliation should be done by someone other than the accountant, such as the office manager or administrative assistant. (Refer to the special note on auditing bank reconciliations at the end of this chapter.)

R E V I E W
CHECKPOINTS

11.1   What is the basic sequence of activities and accounting in the revenues, receivables and receipts process?

11.2   What purpose is served by prenumbering sales orders, shipping documents (packing slips and bills of lading) and sales invoices?

11.3   Why is controlled access to computer terminals and master files (such as credit files and price lists) important in a control environment?

11.4   Why is it a control weakness if the same employee can authorize inventory transfers and record accounts receivable entries?

11.5   Why should a list of cash remittance be made and sent to the accounting department? Is it easier to send the cash and cheques to the accountants so that they can enter accurately the credits to customers' accounts?

AUDIT EVIDENCE IN MANAGEMENT REPORTS AND DATA FILES

Management generates a variety of reports that can provide important audit evidence for revenues, accounts receivable and cash receipts. Some examples follow.

Pending Order Master File

This file contains sales transactions that were started in the system, but not yet completed, thus not recorded as sales and accounts receivable. Old orders may represent shipments that actually were made, but for some reason the shipping department did not enter the shipping information (or entered an incorrect code that did not match the pending order file). The pending orders can be reviewed for evidence of the completeness of recorded sales and accounts receivable.

Credit Check Files

The computer system may make automatic credit checks, but up-to-date maintenance of the credit information is very important. Credit checks on old or incomplete information are not good credit checks. A sample of the files can be tested for current status. Alternatively, the company's records on updating the files can be reviewed for evidence of updating operations.

Price List Master File

The computer system may produce customer invoices automatically; but if the master price list is wrong, the billings will be wrong. The computer file can be compared to an official price source for accuracy and authorization. (As a control, an employee should perform this comparison every time the prices are changed.)

PEAKS AND VALLEYS

During the year-end audit, the independent auditors reviewed the weekly sales volume reports classified by region. They noticed that sales volume was very high in Region 2 the last two weeks of March, June, September and December. The volume was unusually low in the first two weeks of April, July, October and January. In fact, the peaks far exceeded the volume in all the other six regions. Further investigation revealed that the manager in Region 2 was holding open the sales recording at the end of each quarterly reporting period in an attempt to make the quarterly reports look good.

Sales Detail (Sales Journal) File

This file should contain the detail sales entries, including the shipping references and dates. The file can be scanned for entries without shipping references (fictitious sales) and for matching recording dates with shipment dates (sales recorded before shipment). This file contains the population of debit entries to the accounts receivable.

Sales Analysis Reports

A variety of sales analyses can be produced, which the auditor can use them to perform analytical procedures. Sales classified by product lines is information for the business segment disclosures. Sales classified by sales employee or region can show unusually high or low volume that may bear further investigation if error is suspected.

Aged Accounts Receivable Trial Balance

The list of accounts receivable balance details is called the **accounts receivable subsidiary ledger**. The summary of the subsidiary ledger by invoice dates is called the **aged A/R trial balance**. If the general ledger control account total is larger than the sum in the aged trial balance, too bad! A receivable amount that cannot be identified with a customer cannot be collected! The trial balance is used as the population for selection of accounts for confirmation. (See the special note on the existence assertion and the special note on using confirmations at the end of this chapter.) The aging information is used in connection with assessing the allowance for doubtful accounts. (An aged trial balance is shown in Exhibit 11–8, on page 447.) The aged trial balance is used by the credit department for follow up of overdue and delinquent customer accounts.

Cash Receipts Journal

The cash receipts journal contains all the detail entries for cash deposits and credits to various accounts. It contains the population of credit entries that should be reflected in the credits to accounts receivable for customer payments. It also contains the adjusting and correcting entries that can result from the bank account reconciliation. These entries are important because they may signal the types of accounting errors or manipulations that happen in the cash receipts accounting.

REVIEW CHECKPOINTS

11.6 What accounting records and files could an auditor examine to find evidence of unrecorded sales? of inadequate credit checks? of incorrect product unit prices?

11.7 Suppose you selected a sample of customers' accounts receivable and wanted to find supporting evidence for the entries in the accounts. Where would you go to vouch the debit entries? What would you expect to find? Where would you go to vouch the credit entries? What would you expect to find?

CONTROL RISK ASSESSMENT

LEARNING OBJECTIVE
2 Outline control tests for auditing control over customer credit approval, delivery, accounts receivable, cash receipts and bank statements.

Control risk assessment is important because it governs the nature, timing and extent of substantive audit procedures that will be applied in the audit of account balances in the revenues, receivables and receipts processes. These account balances (listed in the lower right corner of Exhibit 11–1) include:

- cash in bank
- cash receipts
- accounts receivable
- allowance for doubtful accounts
- bad debt expense
- sales revenue
- sales returns, allowances and discounts
- perpetual inventory records, shipping records

General Control Considerations

Control procedures for proper segregation of responsibilities should be in place and operating. By referring to Exhibit 11–1, you can see that proper segregation involves authorization of sales and credit by persons who do not have custody, recording or reconciliation duties. Custody of inventory and cash is by those who do not directly authorize credit, record the accounting entries or reconcile the bank account. Recording (accounting) is performed by those who do not authorize sales or credit, handle the inventory or cash, or perform reconciliations. Periodic reconciliations should be performed by people who do not have authorization, custody or recording duties related to the same assets. Combinations of two or more of these responsibilities in one person, one office or one computerized system may open the door for errors, irregularities and frauds.

A common feature of cash management is to require that people who handle cash be insured under a fidelity bond. A **fidelity bond** is an insurance policy that covers most kinds of cash embezzlement losses. Fidelity bonds do not prevent or detect embezzlement, but the failure to carry the insurance exposes the company to complete loss when embezzlement occurs. Auditors may recommend fidelity bonding to companies that do not know about its coverage. However, a company can collect from the bonding agency only if it can prove its losses—another good reason for internal controls.

In addition, the control structure should provide for detail control checking procedures. For example: (1) policy should provide that no sales order should be entered without a customer order; (2) a credit-check code or manual signature should be recorded by an authorized means; (3) access to inventory and the shipping area should be restricted to authorized persons; (4) access to billing terminals and blank invoice forms should be restricted to authorized personnel; (5) accountants should be under orders to record sales and accounts receivable when all the supporting documentation of shipment is in order, and care should be taken to record sales and receivables as of the date the goods were shipped or services were provided and the cash receipts on the date the payments are received; (6) customer invoices should be compared with bills of lading and customer orders to determine that the customer is sent the goods ordered at the proper location for the proper prices, and that the quantity being billed is the same as the quantity shipped; (7) pending order files should be reviewed in a timely fashion to avoid failure to bill and record shipments; and (8) bank statements should be reconciled in detail monthly.

Information about the control structure often is gathered by completing an internal control questionnaire. Control risk assessment was introduced in Chapter 9. You should now refer to Exhibit 9–8 to review an internal control questionnaire for sales transaction control. A selection of other questionnaires for both general (manual) controls and computer controls over cash receipts and accounts receivable is found in Appendix 11A. You can study these questionnaires for details of desirable control policies and procedures. They are organized under headings that identify the important control objectives—environment, validity, completeness, authorization, accuracy, classification, accounting and proper period recording.

An illustration of improper period recording is in the Fictitious Revenue box following. It is an example of a widespread class of financial reporting problems commonly referred to as **revenue recognition problems**. More than half of the record number of 330 financial restatements filed with the SEC in 2002 involved revenue recognition. Most of these revenue recognition problems deal with the inappropriate (too early) timing of recording revenue.

Timing is a critical aspect of appropriate accounting for many issues. For example, most firms that buy in bulk, such as major retailers, receive discounts from suppliers if they meet sales targets. But how are these rebates accounted for? The prudent practice is to wait until the targets are met. However, companies such as now-bankrupt Kmart in the U.S. and Royal Ahold in the Netherlands, the world's third-largest food retailer, appear to have booked these payments before they were earned. Ahold may even have booked entire rebates as profit in the first-year of multi-year agreements, thereby overstating profits for 2001-02 by as much as $500 million. Its chief executive officer and chief financial officers both resigned in February 2002. Ahold has been referred to as "Europe's Enron." This illustrates that controls

---

FICTITIOUS REVENUE

A Mississauga computer peripheral equipment company was experiencing slow sales, so the sales manager entered some sales orders for customers who had not ordered anything. The invoices were marked "hold," while the delivery was to a warehouse owned by the company. The rationale was that these customers would buy the equipment eventually, so why not anticipate the orders! (However, it is a good idea not to send them the invoices until they actually make the orders, hence the "hold.") The "sales" and "receivables" were recorded in the accounts, and the financial statements contained overstated revenue and assets.

---

related to proper timing in the recording of transactions are becoming more important in the post-Enron environment.

Another way to obtain general information about internal controls is called a **walk-through**, or a **sample of one**. Here the auditors take a single example of a transaction and "walk it through" from its initiation to its recording in the accounting records. The revenue and collection cycle walk-through involves following a sale from the initial customer order through credit approval, billing, and delivery of goods, to the entry in the sales journal and subsidiary accounts receivable records, and finally to its subsequent collection and cash deposit. Sample documents are collected, and employees in each department are questioned about their specific duties. The purposes of a walk-through are to (1) verify or update the auditors' understanding of the client's sales/accounts receivable accounting system and control procedures and (2) learn whether the controls the client reported in the internal control questionnaire are actually in place. The walk-through, combined with enquiries, can contribute evidence about appropriate separation of duties, which might be a basis for assessing control risk to be low. However, a walk-through is too limited in scope to provide evidence of whether the client's control procedures were operating effectively during the period under audit. A larger sample of transactions for detail testing is necessary to provide actual control performance evidence.

Control Tests

An organization should have input, processing and output control procedures in place and operating to prevent, detect, and correct accounting errors. You studied the general control objectives in Chapter 9 (validity, completeness, authorization, accuracy, classification, accounting and proper period recording). Exhibit 11–4 puts these in the perspective of the revenue process with examples of specific objectives. You should study this exhibit carefully. It elevates control objectives from the abstract, expressing them in specific examples related to controlling sales accounting.

In particular, notice that the last general objective relates to recording sales in the proper period. As noted earlier in this chapter, such timing problems are becoming a bigger concern to the profession. One of the most important audit procedures in this cycle is the **sales cutoff test**. A cutoff test involves choosing a point in time, usually the balance sheet date, to establish a proper allocation of transactions or events between those that occur before and after that moment. This allocation is essential to properly determining revenues and expenses between periods. In sales cutoff tests, the auditors' concern is with proper timing of sales recognition so that all sales for the period are included and sales from other periods are excluded. This is particularly crucial at year-end with respect to shipment of goods. Recognition of sales is usually tied to passage of title to the buyer because that is when the risks and rewards of ownership of the goods switch from the seller to buyer. Thus, sales recognition is closely tied to shipment or delivery of the client's inventory. This is why

EXHIBIT   11-4   INTERNAL CONTROL OBJECTIVES: REVENUE CYCLE (SALES)

General Objectives	Examples of Specific Objectives
1. Recorded sales are *valid* and documented.	Customer purchase orders support invoices. Bills of lading or other shipping documentation exist for all invoices. Recorded sales in sales journal supported by invoices.
2. Valid sales transactions are *recorded* and none omitted.	Invoices, shipping documents and sales orders are prenumbered and the numerical sequence is checked. Overall comparisons of sales are made periodically by a statistical or product-line analysis.
3. Sales are *authorized* according to company policy.	Credit sales approved by credit department. Prices used in preparing invoices are from authorized price schedule.
4. Sales invoices are *accurately* prepared.	Invoice quantities compared to shipment and customer order quantities. Prices checked and mathematical accuracy independently checked after invoice prepared.
5. Sales transactions are properly *classified.*	Sales to subsidiaries and affiliates classified as intercompany sales and receivables. Sales returns and allowances properly classified.
6. Sales transaction *accounting* is proper.	Credit sales posted to customer's individual accounts. Sales journal posted to general ledger account. Sales recognized in accordance with generally accepted accounting principles.
7. Sales transactions are recorded in the *proper period.*	Sales invoices recorded on shipment date.

Exhibit 11–4, objective 7 example refers to shipment date. Since shipment of inventory is closely tied to the audit of inventory we will defer that discussion to the next chapter. This relationship also illustrates that the cycles are not completely independent of one another. The important thing to learn is that sales cutoff relating to proper recording of sales for the period is closely linked to inventory shipments that have been made to customers, and the shipping terms (**FOB shipping point** or **FOB destination**). The effect of these terms on cut-off tests is explained in Chapter 12.

Auditors can perform control tests to determine whether controls that are said to be in place and operating actually are being performed properly by company personnel. A control test consists of (1) identification of the data population from which a sample of items will be selected for audit and (2) an expression of the action that will be taken to produce relevant evidence. In general, the actions in control testing procedures involve vouching, tracing, observing, scanning and recalculating. Control tests can result in audit evidence that controls operated effectively and that control risk is low. Or they can indicate that controls were not effective, if personnel in the organization are not performing their control procedures well. In this latter case auditors will need to design substantive audit procedures to try to detect whether control failures have produced materially misleading account balances.

Tests of controls can be used to audit the accounting for transactions in two directions. This dual-direction testing involves samples selected to obtain evidence about control over completeness in one direction and control over validity in the other direction. The completeness direction determines whether all transactions that occurred were recorded (none omitted), and the validity direction determines whether recorded transactions actually occurred (were valid). An example of the first direction is the examination of a sample of shipping documents (from the file of all shipping documents) to determine whether invoices were prepared and recorded. An example of the second direction is the examination of a sample of sales invoices (from the file representing all recorded sales) to determine whether supporting shipping documents exist to verify the fact of an actual shipment. The content of each file is compared with the other. The example is illustrated in Exhibit 11–5. (The A-1-b and A-3-b codes correspond to the test of controls procedures in Exhibit 11–6).

Exhibit 11–6 contains a selection of control tests. Many of these control test procedures can be characterized as steps taken to verify the content and character of sample documents from one file with the content and character of documents in another file. These steps are

EXHIBIT   11–5   DUAL DIRECTION OF TEST AUDIT SAMPLES

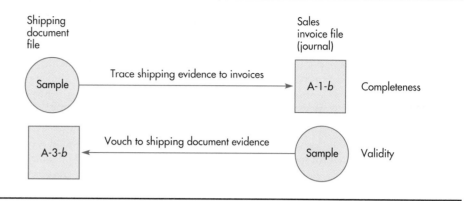

EXHIBIT   11–6   CONTROL TESTS FOR SALES, CASH RECEIPTS AND RECEIVABLES

	Control Objective
A. Sales	
1. Select a sample of shipping documents:	
a. Scan for missing numbers.	Completeness
b. Trace to related sales invoices.	Completeness
2. Scan sales invoices for missing numbers in the sequence.	Completeness
3. Select a sample of recorded sales invoices (sales journal):	
a. Perform recalculations to verify arithmetic accuracy.	Accuracy
b. Vouch to supporting shipping documents. Note dates and quantities.	Validity Accuracy Proper period
c. Vouch prices to approved price lists.	Authorization
d. Vouch credit approval.	Authorization
e. Trace posting to general ledger and proper customer account.	Accounting
4. Observe customer order handling and invoice preparation work.	Environment
B. Cash Receipts	
1. Select a sample of recorded cash receipts (cash receipts journal):	
a. Vouch to deposit slip and remittance list.	Validity
b. Trace to bank statement.	Validity
c. Trace posting to general ledger accounts.	Accounting
d. Trace posting to subsidiary accounts.	Accounting
2. Select a sample of remittance lists (or daily cash reports):	
a. Trace to cash receipts journal.	Completeness
b. Trace journal posting to general ledger.	Accounting
c. Trace to bank statement.	Accuracy
3. Observe the work habits of cashiers and their interactions with persons who keep cash records.	Environment
C. Accounts Receivable	
1. Trace sales invoices to accounts receivable posting (procedure A-3-e above).	Accounting
2. Trace cash receipts to accounts receivable posting (procedure B-1-d above).	Accounting
3. Select a sample of credit memos.	
a. Review for proper approval.	Authorization
b. Trace to posting in customers' accounts.	Accounting
4. Select a sample of customers' accounts:	
a. Vouch debits to supporting sales invoices.	Validity
b. Vouch credits to supporting cash receipts documents and approved credit memos.	Validity
5. Observe mailing of monthly customer statements.	Validity

designed to enable the audit team to obtain objective evidence about the effectiveness of controls and about the reliability of accounting records. These samples are usually attribute samples designed along the lines you studied in Chapter 10.

Exhibit 11–6 shows the control objectives tested by the audit procedures. Thus, the test of controls procedures produce evidence that helps auditors determine whether the specific control objectives listed in Exhibit 11–4 were achieved.

Notice that Exhibit 11–6 is very general in that it is not affected by whether manual or computerized procedures are used to record a transaction. In particular, the flowchart in Exhibit 11–2 can be related to sections A and C of Exhibit 11–6, and the flowchart in Exhibit 11–3 (manual processing) can be related to section B of Exhibit 11–6. Appendix 11A illustrates internal control questionnaires that would be used in deciding on the extent of testing related to controls in Exhibit 11–6. Appendix 11B illustrates substantive audit programs that would be affected by the control testing results illustrated in Exhibit 11–6.

Summary: Control Risk Assessment

The auditor must evaluate the evidence obtained from an understanding of the internal control structure and control tests. The initial process of obtaining an understanding of the control structure and the later process of obtaining evidence from actual test of controls are two of the phases of control risk assessment work (see Chapter 9).

If the control risk is assessed very low, the substantive audit procedures on the account balances can be limited in cost-saving ways. For example, the accounts receivable confirmations can be sent on a date prior to the year-end, and the sample size can be fairly small.

On the other hand, if tests of controls reveal weaknesses (such as posting sales without shipping documents, charging customers the wrong prices and recording credits to customers without supporting credit memos), the substantive procedures will need to be designed to lower the risk of failing to detect material error in the account balances. For example, the confirmation procedure may need to be scheduled on the year-end date with a large sample of customer accounts. Descriptions of major deficiencies, control weaknesses and inefficiencies may be incorporated in a management letter to the client.

- -

REVIEW
CHECKPOINTS

11.8   What account balances are included in the revenues, receivables and receipts process?

11.9   What specific control policies and procedures (in addition to separation of duties and responsibilities) should be in place and operating in a control structure governing revenue recognition and cash accounting?

11.10   What is a walk-through of a sales transaction? How can the walk-through work complement the use of an internal control questionnaire?

11.11   What are the two important characteristics of a control test? What actions are typically used to perform control tests?

11.12   What is dual direction test of controls sampling?

- -

CASETTES: SUBSTANTIVE AUDIT PROCEDURES

- - - - - - - - - - - -

LEARNING OBJECTIVE

3 Design audit and investigative procedures for detecting common errors, irregularities and frauds in the revenues, receivables and receipts process.

The audit procedures to gather evidence on account balances are called **substantive procedures**. Some amount of substantive audit procedures ought to follow the assessment of control risk. Auditors should not place total reliance on controls to the exclusion of other procedures. Substantive audit procedures differ from test of controls audit procedures in their basic purpose. Substantive procedures are designed to obtain direct evidence about the dollar amounts in account balances, while test of controls procedures are designed to obtain evidence about the company's performance of its own control procedures. Sometimes an

---

DUAL-PURPOSE NATURE OF ACCOUNTS RECEIVABLE CONFIRMATIONS

Accounts receivable confirmation is a substantive procedure designed to obtain evidence of the existence and gross amount (valuation) of customers' balances directly from the customer. If such confirmations show numerous exceptions, auditors will be concerned with the controls over the details of sales and cash receipts transactions even if previous control evaluations have seemed to show little control risk.

---

audit procedure can be used for both purposes simultaneously, which is then called a **dual-purpose procedure.**

The goal in performing substantive procedures is to detect evidence of errors, irregularities and frauds if any exist in the accounts as material overstatements or understatements of account balances. In the remainder of this part of the chapter, we will use a number of casettes (little cases) that contain specific examples of tests of controls and substantive audit procedures (recalculation, observation, confirmation, enquiry, vouching, tracing, scanning and analytical review). The case stories are used instead of listing schemes and detection procedures in the abstract. If you like lists of details, a selection of detail substantive procedures for cash and accounts receivable is found in Appendix 11B.

The casettes follow a standard format, which first tell about an error, irregularity or fraud situation. This is followed by an audit approach section that explains the audit objective (assertion), controls, test of controls and audit of balances (substantive procedures) that could be considered in an approach to the casette. The audit approach section presumes that the auditors do not know everything about the situation. (As a student of the casette, you have "inside information.") These are the parts of the case situation description for each casette:

Method: A cause of the misstatement (accidental error, intentional irregularity or fraud attempt), which usually is easier to make because of some kind of failure of controls.

Paper trail: A set of telltale signs of erroneous accounting, missing or altered documents, or a **dangling debit** (the false or erroneous debit that results from an overstatement of assets).

Amount: The dollar amount of overstated assets and revenue, or understated liabilities and expenses.

The audit approach section contains these parts:

Audit objective: A recognition of a financial statement assertion for which evidence needs to be obtained. The assertions are about existence of assets, liabilities, revenues and expenses; their valuation; their complete inclusion in the account balances; the rights and obligations inherent in them; and their proper presentation and disclosure in the financial statements. (These assertions were introduced in Chapter 6.)

Control: A recognition of the control procedures that should be used by an organization to prevent and detect errors and irregularities.

Test of controls: Ordinary and extended procedures designed to produce evidence about the effectiveness of the controls that should be in operation.

Audit of balances: Ordinary and extended substantive procedures designed to find signs of errors, irregularities and frauds in account balances and classes of transactions.

At the end of the chapter, some similar discussion cases are presented, in which you can write the audit approach to test your ability to design audit procedures for the detection of errors, irregularities and frauds.

CASETTE 11.1
THE CANNY CASHIER

Problem

Cash embezzlement caused overstated accounts receivable, overstated customer discounts expense and understated cash sales. Company failed to earn interest income on funds "borrowed."

Method

D. Bakel was the assistant controller of Sports Equipment, Inc. (SEI), an equipment retailer. SEI maintained accounts receivable for school districts in the region; otherwise, customers received credit by using their own credit cards.

Bakel's duties included being the company cashier, who received all the incoming mail payments on school accounts and the credit card account and all the cash and cheques taken over the counter. Bakel prepared the bank deposit (and delivered the deposit to the bank), listing all the cheques and currency, and also prepared a remittance worksheet (daily cash report) that showed amounts received, discounts allowed on school accounts and amounts to credit to the accounts receivable. Bakel also reconciled the bank statement. No one else reviewed the deposits or the bank statements except the independent auditors.

Bakel opened a bank account in the name of Sport Equipment Company (SEC), after properly incorporating the company in the Department of Corporate Affairs' office. Over-the-counter cash and cheques and school district payments were taken from the SEI receipts and deposited in the SEC account. (None of the customers noticed the difference between the rubber stamp endorsements for the two similarly named corporations, and neither did the bank.) SEC kept the money awhile, earning interest; then Bakel wrote SEC cheques to SEI to replace the "borrowed" funds, in the meantime taking new SEI receipts for deposit to SEC.

Bakel also stole payments made by the school districts, depositing them to SEC. Later, Bakel deposited SEC cheques in SEI, giving the schools credit, but approved an additional 2 percent discount in the process. Thus, the schools received proper credit later, and SEC paid in less by the amount of the extra discounts.

Paper Trail

SEI's bank deposits systematically showed fairly small currency deposits. Bakel was nervous about taking too many cheques, so cash was preferred. The deposit slips also listed the SEC cheques because bank tellers always compare the deposit slip listing to the cheques submitted. The remittance worksheet showed different details: Instead of showing SEC cheques, it showed receipts from school district and currency, but not many over-the-counter cheques from customers. The transactions became complicated enough that Bakel had to use the computer in the office to keep track of the school districts that needed to get credit. There were no vacations for this hard-working cashier because the discrepancies might be noticed by a substitute, and Bakel needed to give the districts credit later.

Amount

Over a six-year period, Bakel built up a $150,000 average balance in the Sport Equipment Company (SEC) account, which earned a total of $67,500 interest that should have been earned by Sports Equipment, Inc. (SEI). By approving the "extra" discounts, Bakel skimmed 2 percent of $1 million in annual sales, for a total of $120,000. Since SEI would have had net income before taxes of about $1.6 million over this six years (about 9 percent on the sales dollar), Bakel's embezzlement took about 12.5 percent of the income.

AUDIT APPROACH

Objective

Obtain evidence to determine whether the accounts receivable recorded on the books represent claims against real customers in the gross amounts recorded.

Control

Authorization related to cash receipts, custody of cash, recording cash transactions and bank statement reconciliation should be separate duties designed to prevent errors, irregularities and frauds. Some supervision and detail review of one or more of these duties should be performed as a next-level control designed to detect errors, irregularities and frauds if they have occurred. For example, the remittance worksheet should be prepared by someone else, or at least the discounts should be approved by the controller; the bank reconciliation should be prepared by someone else.

Bakel had all the duties. (While recording was not actually performed, Bakel provided the source docu-

ment—the remittance worksheet—the other accountant used to make the cash and accounts receivable entries.) According to the company president, the "control" was the diligence of "our" long-time, trusted, hard-working assistant controller. Note: An auditor who "thinks like a crook" to imagine ways Bakel could commit errors, irregularities or fraud could think of this scheme for cash theft and accounts receivable lapping.

Test of Controls

Since the "control" purports to be Bakel's honest and diligent performance of the accounting and control procedures that might have been performed by two or more people, the test of controls is an audit of cash receipts transactions as they relate to accounts receivable credit. The dual-direction samples and procedures are these:

Validity direction: Select a sample of customer accounts receivable, and vouch payment credits to remittance worksheets and bank deposits, including

Bank Deposit Slip		Cash Remittance Report				
		Name	Amount	Discount	AR	Sales
Jones	25	Jones	25	0	0	25
Smith	35	Smith	35	0	0	35
Hill Dist.	980	Hill Dist.	980	20	1,000	0
Sport Equip	1,563	Marlin Dist.	480	20	500	0
Currency	540	Waco Dist.	768	32	800	0
Deposit	3,143	Currency	855	0	0	855
		Totals	3,143	72	2,300	915

recalculation of discounts allowed in comparison to sales terms (2 percent), classification (customer name) identification and correspondence of receipt date to recording date.

Completeness direction: Select a sample of remittance worksheets (or bank deposits), vouch details to bank deposit slips (trace details to remittance worksheets if the sample is bank deposits) and trace forward to complete accounting posting in customer accounts receivable.

Audit of Balance

Since there is a control risk of incorrect accounting, perform the accounts receivable confirmation as of the year-end date. Confirm a sample of school district accounts, using positive confirmations.

Blank confirmations may be used. Since there is a control risk, the "sample" may be all the accounts, if the number is not too large.

As prompted by notice of an oddity (noted in the discovery summary following), use the Internet, telephone book, chamber of commerce directory and a visit to a local Ministry of Industry and Trade office to determine the location and identity of Sport Equipment Company.

Discovery Summary

The test of controls samples showed four cases of discrepancy, one of which looked like this:

The auditors sent positive confirmations on all 72 school district accounts. Three of the responses stated that the districts had paid the balances before the confirmation date. Follow-up procedures on their accounts receivable credit in the next period showed they had received credit in remittance reports, and the bank deposits had shown no cheques from the districts but had contained a cheque from Sports Equipment Company.

Investigation of SEC revealed the connection of Bakel, who was confronted and then confessed.

CASETTE 11.2
THE TAXMAN ALWAYS RINGS TWICE

Problem

Overstated receivables for property taxes in a school district because the tax assessor stole some taxpayers' payments.

Method

J. Shelstad was the tax assessor–collector in the Ridge School District, serving a large metropolitan area. The staff processed tax notices on a computer system and generated 450,000 tax notices each October. An office copy was printed and used to check off "paid" when payments were received. Payments were processed by computer and a master file of accounts receivable records (tax assessments, payments) was kept on the computer hard disk.

Shelstad was a good personnel manager, who often took over the front desk at lunchtime so the teller staff could enjoy lunch together. During these times, Shelstad took payments over the counter, gave the taxpayers a counter receipt, and pocketed some of the money, which was never entered in the computer system.

Shelstad resigned when he was elected to the Ridge school board. The district's assessor–collector office was eliminated upon the creation of a new regionwide tax agency.

Paper Trail

The computer records showed balances due from many taxpayers who had actually paid their taxes. The book of printed notices was not marked "paid" for many taxpayers who had received counter receipts. These records and the daily cash receipts reports (cash receipts journal) were available at the time the independent auditors performed the most recent annual audit in April. When Shelstad resigned in August, a power surge permanently destroyed the hard disk receivables file, and the cash receipts journals could not be found.

The new regional agency managers noticed that the total of delinquent taxes disclosed in the audited financial statements was much larger than the total turned over to the region's legal counsel for collection and foreclosure.

Amount

Shelstad had been the assessor–collector for 15 years. The "good personnel manager" pocketed 100–150 counter payments each year, in amounts of $500–$2,500, stealing about $200,000 a year for a total of approximately $2.5 million. The district had assessed about $800–$900 million per year, so the annual theft was less than 1 percent. Nevertheless, the taxpayers got mad.

AUDIT APPROACH

Objective

Obtain evidence to determine whether the receivables for taxes (delinquent taxes) represent genuine claims collectible from the taxpayers.

Control

The school district had a respectable system for establishing the initial amounts of taxes receivable. The professional staff of appraisers and the independent appraisal review board established the tax base for each property. The school board set the price (tax rate). The computer system authorization for billing was validated on these two inputs.

The cash receipts system was well designed, calling for preparation of a daily cash receipts report (cash receipts journal that served as a source input for computer entry). This report was always reviewed by the "boss," Shelstad.

Unfortunately, Shelstad had the opportunity and power to override the controls and become both cash handler and supervisor. Shelstad made the decisions about sending delinquent taxes to the region's legal counsel for collection, and the ones known to have been paid but stolen were withheld.

Test of Controls

The auditors performed dual-direction sampling to test the processing of cash receipts.

Validity direction: Select a sample of receivables from the computer hard disk, and vouch (1) charges to the appraisal record, recalculating the amount using the authorized tax rate and (2) payments, if any, to the cash receipts journal and bank deposits. (The auditors found no exceptions.)

Completeness direction: Select a sample of properties from the appraisal rolls, and determine that tax notices had been sent and tax receivables (charges) recorded in the computer file. Select a sample of cash receipts reports, vouch them to bank deposits of the same amount and date, and trace the payments forward to credits to taxpayers' accounts. Select a sample of bank deposits, and trace them to cash receipts reports of the same amount and date. In one of these latter two samples, compare the details on bank deposits to the details on the cash receipts reports to determine whether the same taxpayers appear on both documents. (The auditors found no exceptions.)

Audit of Balance

Confirm a sample of unpaid tax balances with taxpayers. Response rates may not be high, and follow-up procedures determining the ownership (region title files) may need to be performed, and new confirmations may need to be sent.

Determine that proper disclosure is made of the total of delinquent taxes and the total of delinquencies turned over to the region's legal counsel for collection proceedings.

Discovery Summary

Shelstad persuaded the auditors that the true "receivables" were the delinquencies turned over to the region's legal counsel. The confirmation sample and other work was based on this population. Thus, confirmations were not sent to fictitious balances that Shelstad knew had been paid, and the auditors never had the opportunity to receive "I paid" complaints from taxpayers.

The new managers of the regional tax district were not influenced by Shelstad. They questioned the discrepancy between the delinquent taxes in the audit report and the lower amount turned over for collection. Since the computer file was not usable, the managers had to use the printed book of tax notices, where paid accounts had been marked "paid." (Shelstad had not marked the stolen ones "paid" so the printed book would agree with the computer file.) Tax due notices were sent to the taxpayers with unpaid balances, and they began to show up bringing their counter receipts and loud complaints.

In a fit of audit overkill, the independent auditors had earlier photocopied the entire set of cash receipt reports (cash journal). They were thus able to determine that the counter receipts (all signed by Shelstad) had not been deposited or entered. Shelstad was prosecuted and sentenced to a jail term.

CASETTE 11.3
BILL OFTEN, BILL EARLY

Problem

Overstated sales and receivables, understated discounts expense and overstated net income resulted from recording sales too early and failure to account for customer discounts taken.

Method

McGossage Company experienced profit pressures for two years in a row. Actual profits were squeezed in a recessionary economy, but the company reported net income decreases that were not as severe as other companies in the industry.

Sales were recorded in the grocery products division for orders that had been prepared for shipment but not actually shipped until later. Employees backdated the shipping documents. Gross profit on these "sales" was about 30 percent. Customers took discounts on payments, but the company did not record them, leaving the debit balances in the customers' accounts receivable instead of charging them to discounts and allowances expense. Company accountants were instructed to wait 60 days before recording discounts taken.

The division vice president and general manager knew about these accounting practices, as did a significant number of the 2,500 employees in the division. The division managers were under orders from headquarters to achieve profit objectives they considered unrealistic.

Paper Trail

The customers' accounts receivable balances contained amounts due for discounts the customers already had taken. The cash receipts records showed payments received without credit for discounts. Discounts were entered monthly by a special journal entry.

The unshipped goods were on the shipping dock at year-end with papers showing earlier shipping dates.

Amount

As misstatements go, some of these were on the materiality borderline. Sales were overstated 0.3 percent and 0.5 percent in the prior and current year, respectively. Accounts receivable were overstated 4 percent and 8 percent. But the combined effect was to overstate the division's net income by 6 percent and 17 percent. Selected data were:

| | One Year Ago | | Current Year | |
	Reported	Actual	Reported	Actual
Sales	$330.0	$329.0	$350.0	$348.0
Discounts expense	1.7	1.8	1.8	2.0
Net income	6.7	6.3	5.4	4.6

AUDIT APPROACH

Objective

Obtain evidence to determine whether sales were recorded in the proper period and whether gross accounts receivable represented the amounts due from customers at year-end. Obtain evidence to determine whether discounts expense was recognized in the proper amount in the proper period.

Control

The accounting procedures manual should provide instructions to record sales on the date of shipment (or when title passes, if later). Management subverted this control procedure by having shipping employees date the shipping papers incorrectly.

Cash receipts procedures should provide for authorizing and recording discounts when they are taken by customers. Management overrode this control instruction by giving instructions to delay the recording.

Test of Controls

Questionnaires and enquiries should be used to determine the company's accounting policies. It is possible that employees and managers would lie to the auditors to conceal the policies. It is also possible that pointed questions about revenue recognition and discount recording policies would elicit answers to reveal the practices.

For detail procedures: Select a sample of cash receipts, examine them for authorization, recalculate the customer discounts, trace them to accounts receivable input for recording of the proper amount on the proper date. Select a sample of shipping documents and vouch them to customer orders, then trace them to invoices and to recording in the amounts receivable input with proper amounts on the proper date. These tests follow the tracing direction—starting with data that represent the beginning of transactions (cash receipts, shipping) and tracing them through the company's accounting process.

Audit of Balance

Confirm a sample of customer accounts. Use analytical relationships of past years' discount expense to a relevant base (sales, sales volume) to calculate an overall test of the discounts expense.

Discovery Summary

The managers lied to the auditors about their revenue and expense timing policies. The sample of shipping documents showed no dating discrepancies because the employees had inserted incorrect dates. The analytical procedures on discounts did not show the misstatement because the historical relationships were too erratic to show a deficient number (outlier). However, the sample of cash receipts transactions showed that discounts were not calculated and recorded at time of receipt. Additional enquiry led to discovery of the special journal entries and knowledge of the recording delay. Two customers in the sample of 65 confirmations responded with exceptions that turned out to be unrecorded discounts.

Two other customers in the confirmation sample complained that they did not owe for late invoices on December 31. Follow-up showed the shipments were goods noticed on the shipping dock. Auditors taking the physical inventory noticed the goods on the shipping dock during the December 31 inventory-taking. Inspection revealed the shipping documents dated December 26. When the auditors traced these shipments to the sales recording, they found them recorded "bill and hold" on December 29. (These procedures were performed and the results obtained by a successor audit firm in the third year!)

CASETTE 11.4
THANK GOODNESS IT'S FRIDAY

Problem

Overstated sales caused overstated net income, retained earnings, current assets, working capital and total assets. Overstated cash collections did not change the total current assets or total assets but they increased the amount of cash and decreased the amount of accounts receivable.

Method

Alpha Brewery Corporation generally has good control policies and procedures related to authorization of transactions for accounting entry, and the accounting manual has instructions for recording sales transactions in the proper accounting period. The company regularly closes the accounting process each Friday at 5 p.m. to prepare weekly management reports. The year-end date (cutoff date) is December 31, and, in 2000, December 31 was a Monday. However, the accounting was performed through Friday as usual, and the accounts were closed for the year on January 4.

Paper Trail

All the entries were properly dated after December 31, including the sales invoices, cash receipts and shipping documents. However, the trial balance from which the financial statements were prepared was dated December 31, 2000, even though the accounts were actually closed on January 4. Nobody noticed the slip of a few days because the Friday closing was normal.

Amount

Alpha recorded sales of $672,000 and gross profit of $268,800 over the January 1–4 period. Cash collections on customers' accounts came in the amount of $800,000.

AUDIT APPROACH

Objective

Obtain evidence to determine the existence, completeness and valuation of sales for the year ended December 31, 2000, and the cash and accounts receivable as of December 31, 2000.

Control

The company had in place the proper instructions to people to date transactions on the actual date on which they occurred and to enter sales and cost of goods sold on the day of shipment and to enter cash receipts on the day received in the company offices. An accounting supervisor should have checked the entries through Friday to make sure the dates corresponded with the actual events, and that the accounts for the year were closed with Monday's transactions.

Test of Controls

In this case the auditors need to be aware of the company's weekly routine closing and the possibility that the intervention of the December 31 date might cause a problem. Asking the question "Did you cut off the accounting on Monday night this week?" might elicit the "Oh, we forgot!" response. Otherwise, it is normal to sample transactions around the year-end date to determine whether they were recorded in the proper accounting period.

The procedure: Select transactions 7–10 days before and after the year-end date, and inspect the dates on supporting documentation for evidence of accounting in the proper period.

Audit of Balance

The audit for sales overstatement is partly accomplished by auditing the cash and accounts receivable at December 31 for overstatement (the dangling debit location). Confirm a sample of accounts receivable. If the accounts are too large, the auditors expect the debtors to say so, thus leading to detection of sales overstatement.

Cash overstatement is audited by auditing the bank reconciliation to see whether deposits in transit (the deposits sent late in December) actually cleared the bank early in January. Obviously, the January 4 cash collections could not reach the bank until at least Monday, January 7. That's too long for a December 31 deposit to be in transit to a local bank.

The completeness of sales recordings is audited by selecting a sample of sales transactions (and supporting shipping documents) in the early part of the next accounting period (January 2001). One way that sales of 2000 could be incomplete would be to postpone recording December shipments until January, and this procedure will detect them if the shipping documents are dated properly.

The completeness of cash collections (and accounts receivable credits) are audited by auditing the cash deposits early in January to see whether there is any sign of holding cash without entry until January.

In this case the existence objective is more significant for discovery of the problem than the com-

pleteness objective. After all, the January 1–4 sales, shipments, and cash collections did not "exist" in December 2000.

Discovery Summary

The test of controls sample from the days before and after December 31 quickly revealed the problem. Company accounting personnel were embarrassed, but there was no effort to misstate the financial statements. This was a simple error. The company readily made the following adjustment:

	Debit	Credit
Sales	$672,000	
Inventory	403,200	
Accounts receivable	800,000	
Accounts receivable		$672,000
Cost of goods sold		403,200
Cash		800,000

REVIEW CHECKPOINTS

11.13   What are the goals of dual-direction sampling in regard to an audit of the accounts receivable and cash collection system?

11.14   In Casette 11.1, name one bank reconciliation control procedure that could have revealed signs of embezzlement.

11.15   What feature(s) of a cash receipts internal control system would be expected to prevent the cash receipts journal and recorded cash sales from reflecting more than the amount shown on the daily deposit slip?

11.16   In Casette 11.2, what information could have been obtained from confirmations directed to the real population of delinquent accounts?

11.17   In Casette 11.3, what information might have been obtained from enquiries? from detail test of controls procedures? from observations? and from confirmations?

11.18   With reference to Casette 11.4, what contribution could an understanding of the business and the management reporting system have made to discovery of the open cash receipts journal cutoff error?

SPECIAL NOTE: THE EXISTENCE ASSERTION

LEARNING OBJECTIVE

4 Explain the importance of the existence assertion for the audit of cash and accounts receivable.

When considering assertions and obtaining evidence about accounts receivable and other assets, auditors must put emphasis on the existence and rights (ownership) assertions. (For liability accounts, the emphasis is on the completeness and obligations assertions, as will be explained in Chapter 12.) This emphasis on existence is rightly placed because companies and auditors sometimes have gotten into malpractice trouble by giving unqualified reports on financial statements that overstated assets and revenues and understated expenses. For example, credit sales recorded too early (fictitious sales?) result in overstated accounts receivable and overstated sales revenue; failure to amortize prepaid expense results in understated expenses and overstated prepaid expenses (current assets).

Discerning the population of assets to audit for existence and ownership is easy because the company has asserted their existence by putting them on the balance sheet. The audit procedures described in the following sections can be used to obtain evidence about the existence and ownership of accounts receivable and other assets.

Computation

Think about the assets that depend largely on calculations. They are amenable to auditors' recalculation procedures. Expired prepaid expenses are recalculated, using auditors' vouching of basic documents, such as loan agreements (prepaid interest), rent contracts (prepaid rent) and insurance policies (prepaid insurance). Goodwill and deferred expenses are recalculated by using original acquisition and payment document information and term (useful life) estimates. A bank reconciliation is a special kind of calculation, and the company's reconciliation can be audited. (See the special note on auditing a bank reconciliation later in this chapter.)

Inspection of Physical Assets

Inventories and fixed assets can be inspected and counted (more on inventory observation is in Chapter 12). Titles to autos, land and buildings can be vouched, sometimes using public records in a regional government office. Petty cash and undeposited receipts can be observed and counted, but the cash in the bank cannot. Securities held as investments can be inspected if held by the company.

Confirmation

Letters of confirmation can be sent to banks and customers, asking for a report of the balances owed the company. Likewise, if securities held as investments are in the custody of banks or brokerage houses, the custodians can be asked to report the names, numbers and quantity of the securities held for the company. In some cases inventories held in public warehouses or out on consignment can be confirmed with the other party. (Refer to the special note on confirmations later in this chapter.)

Enquiry

Enquiries to management usually do not provide very convincing evidence about existence and ownership. However, enquiries always should be made about the company's agreements to maintain compensating cash balances (these may not be classifiable as "cash" among the current assets), about pledge or sale of accounts receivable with recourse in connection with financings and about pledge of other assets as collateral for loans.

Inspection of Documents–Vouching

Evidence of ownership can be obtained by studying the title documents for assets. Examination of loan documents may yield evidence of the need to disclose assets pledged as loan collateral.

Inspection of Documents–Scanning

Assets are supposed to have debit balances. A computer can be used to scan large files of accounts receivable, inventory and fixed assets for uncharacteristic credit balances. Usually, such credit balances reflect errors in the recordkeeping—customer overpayments, failure to post purchases of inventory, depreciation of assets more than cost. The names of debtors can be scanned for officers, directors and related parties, amounts for which need to be reported separately or disclosed in the financial statements.

Analysis

A variety of analytical comparisons may be employed, depending on the circumstances and the nature of the business. Comparisons of asset and revenue balances with recent history may help detect overstatements. Such relationships as receivables turnover, gross margin ratio and sales/asset ratios can be compared to historical data and industry statistics for evidence of overall reasonableness. Account interrelationships also can be used in analytical review. For example, sales returns and allowances and sales commissions generally vary directly with dollar sales volume, bad debt expense usually varies directly with credit sales volume and freight expense varies with the physical sales volume. Accounts receivable write-offs should be compared with earlier estimates of doubtful accounts.

R E V I E W
CHECKPOINTS

11.19   Why is it important to place emphasis on the existence and ownership (rights) assertions when auditing cash and accounts receivable?

11.20   Which audit procedures are usually the most useful for auditing and existence and ownership (rights) assertions? Give some examples.

SPECIAL NOTE: USING CONFIRMATIONS

LEARNING OBJECTIVE
5 Identify considerations for using confirmations when auditing cash and accounts receivable.

The confirmation audit procedure was introduced in Chapter 8. This special note gives some details about using confirmations in the audit of cash and accounts receivable. The use of confirmations for cash balances and trade accounts receivable is considered a generally accepted audit procedure.[1] However, auditors may decide not to use them if suitable alternative procedures are available and applicable in particular circumstances. Auditors should document justifications for the decision not to use confirmations for trade accounts receivable in a particular audit. Justifications include (1) receivables are not material; (2) confirmations would be ineffective, based on prior years' experience or knowledge that responses could be unreliable; and (3) other substantive test of details procedures provide sufficient appropriate evidence and the auditor has assessed the combined level of inherent risk and control risk associated with the financial statement assertions being audited as low.

SIMPLE ANALYTICAL COMPARISON

The auditors prepared a schedule of the monthly credit sales totals for the current and prior years. They noticed several variations, but one, in November of the current year, stood out in particular. The current-year credit sales were almost twice as large as in any prior November. Further investigation showed that a computer error had caused the November credit sales to be recorded twice in the control accounts. The accounts receivable and sales revenue were materially overstated as a result.

A DECISION NOT TO USE ACCOUNTS RECEIVABLE CONFIRMATIONS

Sureparts Manufacturing Company sold all its production to three auto manufacturers and six aftermarket distributors. All nine of these customers typically paid their accounts in full by the 10th day of each following month. The auditors were able to vouch the cash receipts for the full amount of the accounts receivable in the bank statements and cash receipts records in the month following the Surepart year-end. Confirmation evidence was not considered necessary in these circumstances.

Confirmations of Cash and Loan Balances

The standard bank confirmation form is shown in Exhibit 11–7. This form is used to obtain bank confirmation of deposit and loan balances. (Other confirmation letters are used to obtain confirmation of contingent liabilities, endorsements, compensating balance agreements, lines of credit and other financial instruments and transactions. The standard form and illustrative letters are reproduced in the PA's professional engagement manuals.) A word of caution is in order: While financial institutions may note exceptions to the information typed in a confirmation and may confirm items omitted from it, the auditor should not put sole reliance on the form to satisfy the completeness assertion, insofar as cash and loan balances are concerned. Officers and employees of financial institutions

[1] *CICA Handbook*, section 5303 or ISA 505.

EXHIBIT 11-7   BANK CONFIRMATION

Bank Confirmation

Areas to be completed by client are marked §, while those to be completed by the financial institution are marked †

FINANCIAL INSTITUTION §
(Name, branch and full mailing address)

CONFIRMATION DATE §
(All information to be provided as of this date)
(See Bank Confirmation Completion Instructions)

CLIENT (LEGAL NAME) §

The financial institution is authorized to provide the details requested herein to the below-noted firm of accountants

§ _____
Client's authorized signature
Please supply copy of the most recent credit facility agreement (initial if required) § _____

1. LOANS AND OTHER DIRECT AND CONTINGENT LIABILITIES (If balances are nil, please state)

NATURE OF LIABILITY/ CONTINGENT LIABILITY †	INTEREST (Note rate per contract)		DUE DATE †	DATE OF CREDIT FACILITY AGREEMENT †	AMOUNT AND CURRENCY OUTSTANDING †
	RATE †	DATE PAID TO †			

ADDITIONAL CREDIT FACILITY AGREEMENT(S) _____
Note the date(s) of any credit facility agreement(s) not drawn upon and not referenced above † _____

2. DEPOSITS/OVERDRAFTS

TYPE OF ACCOUNT §	ACCOUNT NUMBER §	INTEREST RATE §	ISSUE DATE (If applicable) §	MATURITY DATE (If applicable) §	AMOUNT AND CURRENCY (Brackets if Overdraft) †

EXCEPTIONS AND COMMENTS (See Bank Confirmation Completion Instructions)†

STATEMENT OF PROCEDURES PERFORMED BY FINANCIAL INSTITUTION †
The above information was completed in accordance with the Bank Confirmation Completion Instructions.

_____   BRANCH CONTACT   _____
Authorized signature of financial institution   Name and telephone number

Please mail this form directly to our public accountant in the enclosed addressed envelope.

Name:
Address:

Telephone:
Fax:

Source: Developed by the Canadian Bankers Association and The Canadian Public Accounting Associations.

cannot be expected to search their information systems for balances and loans that may not be immediately evident as assets and liabilities of the client company. However, it is a good idea to send confirmations on accounts the company represents as closed during the year to get the bank to confirm zero balances. (If a nonzero balance is confirmed by a bank, the auditors have evidence that some asset accounting has been omitted in the company records.)

The auditor should also be alert for evidence of transactions with banks or bank accounts other than those for which there are general ledger accounts. For example, loan documents or cheques written on other banks may come to light during scanning or other document examination procedures. Enquiries of client management should be made to assess whether bank confirmations should be obtained from these banks and whether any financial statement impact exists.

Confirmation of Accounts and Notes Receivable

Confirmations provide evidence of existence and, to a limited extent, of valuation of accounts and notes receivable. The accounts and notes to be confirmed should be documented in the working papers with an aged trial balance. (An aged trial balance is shown in Exhibit 11–8, annotated to show the auditor's work.) Accounts for confirmation can be selected at random

EXHIBIT   11–8   AGED ACCOUNTS RECEIVABLE TRIAL BALANCE

```
D-2                          KINGSTON COMPANY              Prepared  AB
PG. 1 OF 15                 ACCOUNTS RECEIVABLE           Date  1-12-2013
                             December 31, 20X2            Reviewed  Terri Tough
                                                          Date
                                                             1-17-X3


                    ---------  -------- Aged --------    Jan. 2003 Collection
                               30-60    61-90  Over 90                    Past
                    Current    Days     Days   Days    Total   Current    Due
                    --------------------------------------------------------------
Able Hardware       12,337 X                           12,337 Xpc" 12,337
Baker Supply          712                                 712         712
Charley Company     1,486 X    420 X                    1,906 Xpc 1,486       420
Dogg General Store                            755         755

--------------------------------------------------------------
Welsch Windows                 531 X                      531 X NC           531
Zlat Stuff Place                              214         214               214

                    -------------------------------------------------
Balance per books   335,000  30,000  20,000  15,000  400,000  320,000  25,000
                                                         (J)
Billing errors      (11,000)         (1,000)         (12,000) (1)
                    -------------------------------------------------
Adjusted balance    324,000  30,000  19,000  15,000  388,000
                    =================================================
```

X Traced to accounts receivable subsidiary ledger.

pc Positive confirmation mailed Jan. 4. Replies D-2.3

NC Negative confirmation mailed Jan. 4. Replies D-2.4

u No reply to positive confirmation, vouched charges to invoices.

J Traced to general ledger control account.

(1) Billing error adjustment explained on working paper D-2.2

Note: See D-2.2 for analysis of doubtful accounts and our test
      of reasonableness

or in accordance with another plan consistent with the audit objectives. Statistical methods may be useful for determining the sample size. Generalized audit software to access computerized receivables files may be utilized to select and even to print the confirmations.

Two widely used confirmation forms are positive confirmations and negative confirmations. An example of a positive confirmation is shown in Exhibit 11–9. A variation of the positive confirmation is the blank form. A blank confirmation does not contain the balance; customers are asked to fill it in themselves. The blank positive confirmation may produce better evidence because the recipients need to get the information directly from their own records instead of just signing the form and returning it with no exceptions noted. (However, the effort involved may cause a lower response rate.)

The negative confirmation form for the same request shown in Exhibit 11–9 is in Exhibit 11–10. The positive form asks for a response. The negative form asks for a response only if something is wrong with the balance; thus, lack of response to negative confirmations is considered evidence of propriety.

The positive form is used when individual balances are relatively large or when accounts are in dispute. Positive confirmations may ask for information about either the account balance or specific invoices, depending on knowledge about how customers maintain their accounting records. The negative form is used mostly when inherent risk and control risk are considered low, when a large number of small balances is involved, and when the client's

EXHIBIT 11-9   POSITIVE CONFIRMATION LETTER

EXHIBIT 11-10 NEGATIVE CONFIRMATION LETTER

KINGSTON COMPANY
Kingston, Ontario

January 5, 20X3

Charley Company
Lake and Adams
Chicago, Illinois

Gentlemen:

Our auditors, Anderson, Olds & Watershed, are making their regular audit of our financial statements. Part of this audit includes direct verification of customer balances.

PLEASE EXAMINE THE DATA BELOW CAREFULLY AND COMPARE THEM TO YOUR RECORDS OF YOUR ACCOUNT WITH US. IF OUR INFORMATION IS NOT IN AGREEMENT WITH YOUR RECORDS, PLEASE STATE ANY DIFFERENCES ON THE REVERSE SIDE OF THIS PAGE, AND RETURN DIRECTLY TO OUR AUDITORS IN THE RETURN ENVELOPE PROVIDED. IF THE INFORMATION IS CORRECT, NO REPLY IS NECESSARY.

This is not a request for payment. Please do not send your remittance to our auditors.

Your prompt attention to this confirmation request will be appreciated.

Sandra Carboy
Sandra Carboy, Controller

As of December 31, 20X2, balance due to Kingston Company: $1,906
Date of Origination: November and December, 20X2
Type: Open trade account

---

customers can be expected to consider the confirmations properly. Sometimes, both forms are used: positive confirmations are sent on some customers' accounts and negative confirmations on others. *CICA Handbook*, paragraph 5303.13 states that negative confirmation would only be used when the auditor has no reason to believe the recipient will not disregard the request for confirmation, i.e., because the balance is material to the recipient. In any case, evidence from negative confirmation is considered less reliable than evidence from positive confirmations.

A special positive confirmation form that is increasingly being used for bill-and-hold transactions is illustrated in Exhibit 11–11. This form is in response to the growing problem of inappropriate accounting for bill-and-hold sales transactions mentioned previously in this chapter. While bill-and-hold sales transactions are not necessarily a GAAP violation, they are often associated with financial frauds and should be further investigated. The key issue is the substance as opposed to the form of the transaction. The CICA EIC–141 says all of the following conditions must be met for revenue recognition to be appropriate:

- The risks of ownership must have passed to the buyer.
- The customer must have a commitment to purchase, preferably in writing.
- A fixed delivery schedule must exist and must be reasonable for the seller.
- The seller must not retain any significant performance obligations.

E X H I B I T   1 1 – 1 1   CONFIRMATION REQUEST FOR A BILL-AND-HOLD TRANSACTION

[Client Letterhead]

[Date]

[Name and address of customer
employee with sufficient
authority to commit customer]

Dear [Name]:

Our auditors [PA firm name and address] are auditing our financial statements at [balance sheet date]. Please compare the following information with your records and report directly to our auditors whether that information is correct:

We sold you [product description] on [date] for [total sales price] under your purchase order [date and number].

[Product description] has been sold to you on our normal payment terms as described in our invoice [number and date] and those terms have not been modified. There are no written or oral amendments to the terms specified in the purchase order.

At your request we are holding [product description] at your risk on our premises, and title has passed to you.

You requested us to hold [product description] for you because [description of business reason for delayed shipment].

There are no written or oral amendments to the terms specified in the purchase order.

You are obligated to pay us [total sales price] by [payment due date].

Please use the enclosed preaddressed, postage-paid reply envelope. Because this response is needed for our auditors to complete their audit, we would appreciate a prompt response.

Very truly yours,

[Signature and title of authorized client representative]

If the above information is correct, please confirm. If your understanding of anything described above differs in any respect, please explain.

_____
_____
_____

Date: _____

Signed: _____

Source: AICPA

- The goods must be complete and ready for shipment and not subject to being used by the seller to fill other orders.
- The buyer must request the bill-and-hold transaction and substantiate a business purpose for it.

These points illustrate that auditors must have a good understanding of the client, his or her business and its products in order to identify the warning signs of revenue recognition misstatements and fraud. The bill-and-hold confirmation is an example of a confirmation request to verify the substance of a transaction from the customer's point of view. Note that the client's customer is being asked to put considerable effort into completing the response. This can lower the response rate.

Getting confirmations delivered to the intended recipient is a problem that requires auditors' careful attention. Auditors need to control the confirmations, including the addresses to which they are sent. Experience is full of cases where confirmations were mailed to company accomplices, who provided false responses. The auditors should consider carefully features of the reply, such as postmarks, fax responses, letterhead, e-mail, telephone or other characteristics, that may suggest false responses. Auditors should follow up electronic and telephone responses to determine their origin (e.g., returning the telephone call to a known number, looking up telephone numbers to determine addresses or using a criss-cross directory to determine the location of a respondent). Furthermore, the lack of response to a negative confirmation is no guarantee that the intended recipient received it unless the auditor carefully controlled the mailing.

The **response rate** for positive confirmations is the proportion of the number of confirmations returned to the number sent, generally after the audit team prompts recipients with second and third requests. Research studies have shown response rates ranging from 66 to 96 percent. Recipients seem to be able to detect account misstatements to varying degrees. Studies have shown **detection rates** (the ratio of the number of exceptions reported to auditors to the number of account errors intentionally reported to customers) ranging from 20 to 100 percent. Negative confirmations seem to have lower detection rates than positive confirmations. Also, studies show somewhat lower detection rates for misstatements favourable to recipients (i.e., an accounts receivable understatement). Overall, positive confirmations appear to be more effective than negative confirmations; but results depend on the type of recipients, the size of the account, and the type of account being confirmed. Effective confirmation practices depend on attention to these factors and on prior years' experience with confirmation results on a particular client's accounts.

Effective confirmation also depends on using a "bag of tricks" to boost the response rate. Often, auditors merely send out a cold, official-looking request in a metered mail envelope and expect customers to be happy to respond. However, the response rate can be increased by using (1) a postcard sent in advance, notifying that a confirmation is coming; (2) special delivery mail; (3) first-class stamp postage (not metered); and (4) an envelope imprinted "Confirmation Enclosed: Please Examine Carefully." These devices increase the cost of the confirmation procedure, but the benefit is a better response rate.[2]

The audit team should try to obtain replies to all positive confirmations by sending second and third requests to nonrespondents. If there is no response or if the response specifies an exception to the client's records, the auditors should carry out alternate substantive procedures to audit the account.

These alternative procedures include finding sales invoice copies, shipping documents and customer orders to verify the existence of sales transactions. They also include the finding of evidence of customers' payments in subsequent cash receipts and bank statements.

When random sampling is used, all selected accounts in the sample should be audited. It is improper to substitute an easy-to-audit customer account not in the sample for one that does not respond to a confirmation request.

Confirmation of receivables may be performed at a date other than the year-end. When confirmation is done at an interim date, the audit firm is able to spread work throughout the year and avoid the pressures of overtime that typically occur around December 31. Also, the audit can be completed sooner after the year-end date if confirmation has been done earlier. The primary consideration when considering confirmation of accounts before the balance sheet date is the client's internal control over transactions affecting receivables. When confirmation is performed at an interim date, the following additional procedures should be considered:

1. Obtain a summary of receivables transactions from the interim date to the year-end date.

2. Obtain a year-end trial balance of receivables, compare it to the interim trial balance and obtain evidence and explanations for large variations.

3. Consider the necessity for additional confirmations as of the balance sheet date if balances have increased materially or a material new customer balance has been added.

One final note about confirmations: Confirmations of accounts, loans and notes receivable may not produce sufficient evidence of ownership by the client (rights assertion). Debtors may not be aware that the auditor's client has sold their accounts, notes or loans receivable to financial institutions or to the public (collateralized securities). Auditors need

---

[2] CICA, *Confirmation of Accounts Receivable, An Audit Technique Study* (Toronto, 1980), Chapter 5. See also Paul Caster, "The Role of Confirmations as Audit Evidence," *Journal of Accountancy*, February 1992, pp. 73–76.

to perform additional enquiry and detail procedures to get evidence of the ownership of the receivables and of the appropriateness of disclosures related to financing transactions secured by receivables.

Summary: Confirmations

Confirmations of cash balances, loans, accounts receivable and notes receivable are required, unless auditors can justify substituting other procedures in the circumstances of a particular audit. The bank confirmation is a standard positive form. Confirmations for accounts and notes receivable can be in positive or negative form, and the positive form may be a blank confirmation.

Auditors must take care to control confirmations to ensure that responses are received from the real debtors and not from persons who can intercept the confirmations to give false responses. Responses by fax, e-mail, telephone or other means not written and signed by a recipient should be followed up to determine their genuine origins. Second and third requests should be sent to prompt responses to positive confirmations, and auditors should audit nonresponding customers by alternative procedures. Accounts in a sample should not be left unaudited (e.g., "They didn't respond"), and easy-to-audit accounts should not be substituted for hard-to-audit ones in a sample. Such "tricks" can be used to raise the apparent response rate but do not increase the persuasiveness of the audit evidence obtained.

Confirmations yield evidence about existence and gross valuation. However, the fact that a debtor admits to owing the debt does not mean the debtor can pay. Other procedures must be undertaken to audit the collectibility of the accounts. Nevertheless, confirmations can give some clues about collectibility when customers tell about balances in dispute. Confirmations of accounts, notes and loans receivable should not be used as the only evidence of the ownership (rights assertions) of these financial assets.

REVIEW
CHECKPOINTS

11.21 List the information a PA should solicit in a standard bank confirmation enquiry sent to an audit client's bank.

11.22 Distinguish between positive and negative confirmations. Under what conditions would you expect each type of confirmation to be appropriate?

11.23 Distinguish between confirmation response rate and confirmation detection rate.

11.24 What are some of the justifications for not using confirmations of accounts receivable on a particular audit?

11.25 What special care should be taken with regard to examining the sources of accounts receivable confirmation responses?

SPECIAL NOTE: AUDIT OF BANK RECONCILIATIONS WITH ATTENTION TO LAPPING AND KITING

LEARNING OBJECTIVE

6 Perform substantive audit procedures for the audit of bank statement reconciliations, explaining how auditors can search for lapping and kiting.

The company's bank reconciliation is the primary means of valuing cash in the financial statements. The amount of cash in the bank is almost always different from the amount in the books (financial statements), and the reconciliation purports to explain the difference. The normal procedure is to obtain the company-prepared bank reconciliation and audit it. Auditors should not perform the company's control function of preparing the reconciliation.

A client-prepared bank reconciliation is shown in Exhibit 11–12. The bank balance is confirmed and cross-referenced to the bank confirmation working paper (Exhibit 11–7). The reconciliation is recalculated, the outstanding cheques and deposits in transit totals are

EXHIBIT   11–12   BANK RECONCILIATION

```
                          KINGSTON COMPANY
C-2           BANK RECONCILIATION—NORTH COUNTRY BANK      Prepared   J.D. 1/10/X3
                          General Account                 Reviewed   JRA 1|10|20X3
                            12/31/20X2
                      (Prepared by client)

Balance per bank statement                            506,100  c
Add:
    Deposit in transit as of 12/31/X2                  51,240  n
Deduct outstanding checks:                             557,340
         Date     No.     Payee
       --------   ----   ------------------------
       12/10/X1    842   Ace Supply Company          500  ✗
       11/31/X2   1280   Ace Supply Company        1,800  ✓
       12/15/X2   1372   Northwest Lumber Co.      30,760  ✓
       12/28/X2   1412   Gibson & Johnson           7,270  ✗
       12/30/X2   1417   North Country payroll     20,000  ✓
       12/30/X2   1418   Ace Supply Company         2,820  ✓
       12/30/X2   1419   Windy City Utilities       2,030  ✓
       12/30/X2   1420   Howard Hardware Supply     8,160  ✓
                                                   -------
Balance per book                                    73,340
                                                   -------
                                                   484,000  f
                                                   -------
```

Note: Obtained cutoff bank statement 1/9/X3 (C-23) (T/B-1)
   f   Footed
   c   Confirmed by bank, standard bank confirmation (C-22)
   n   Vouched to cutoff bank statement, deposit recorded by bank
        on 1/3/X2. Vouched to duplicate deposit slip validaged 1/3/X3
   ✓   Vouched to paid check cleared with cutoff bank statement.
   ✗   Vouched to statement from attorneys.
   ✗   Amount in dispute per controller.

recalculated and the book balance is traced to the trial balance (which has been traced to the general ledger). The reconciling items should be vouched to determine whether outstanding cheques really were not paid and that deposits in transit actually were mailed before the reconciliation date. The auditor's information source for vouching the bank reconciliation items is a **cutoff bank statement,** which is a complete bank statement including all paid cheques and deposit slips. The client requests the bank to send this bank statement directly to the auditor. It is usually for a 10- to 20-day period following the reconciliation date. (It also can be the next regular monthly statement, received directly by the auditors.)

The vouching of outstanding cheques and deposits in transit is a matter of comparing cheques that cleared in the cutoff bank statement with the list of outstanding cheques for evidence that all cheques that were written prior to the reconciliation date were on the list of outstanding cheques. The deposits shown in transit should be recorded by the bank in the first business days of the cutoff period. If recorded later, the inference is that the deposit may have been made up from receipts of the period after the reconciliation date. For large outstanding cheques not clearing in the cutoff period, vouching may be extended to other documentation supporting the disbursement. These procedures are keyed and described by tick marks in Exhibit 11–12.

Accounts Receivable Lapping

When the business receives many payments from customers, a detailed audit would include comparison of the cheques listed on a sample of deposit slips (from the reconciliation month and other months) to the detail of customer credits listed on the day's posting to customer accounts receivable (daily remittance list or other record of detail postings). This procedure is a test for accounts receivable lapping. It is an attempt to find credits given to customers for whom no payments were received on the day in question. An example of this type of comparison is in the discovery summary section of Casette 11.1.

Cheque Kiting

Auditors also should be alert to the possibility of kiting. **Cheque kiting** is the practice of building up apparent balances in one or more bank accounts based on uncollected (float) cheques drawn against similar accounts in other banks. Kiting involves depositing money from one bank account to another, using a hot cheque. The depository bank does not know the cheque is on insufficient funds, but the deficiency is covered by another hot cheque from another bank account before the first cheque clears. Kiting is the deliberate floating of funds between two or more bank accounts. By this method a bank customer uses the time required for cheques to clear to obtain an unauthorized loan without any interest charge.

Professional money managers working for cash-conscious businesses try to have minimal unused balances in their accounts, and their efforts sometimes can look like cheque kites. Tight cash flows initiate kites, and intent to kite is the key for criminal charges. Kites evolve to involve numerous banks and numerous cheques. The more banks and broader geographical distance, the harder a perpetrator finds it to control a kite scheme.

Here is a simple illustration of how a kite scheme works:

Start with no money in Bank A and Bank B, and draw $5,000 cheques on each to "deposit" in the other:

	Bank A	Bank B	Total
Apparent balances	$5,000	$5,000	$10,000
Actual balances	0	0	0

Do it again with $8,000 cheques:

	Bank A	Bank B	Total
Apparent balances	$13,000	$13,000	$26,000
Actual balances	0	0	0

Make a $6,000 down payment on a Mercedes from Bank A:

	Bank A	Bank B	Total
Apparent balances	$7,000	$13,000	$20,000
Actual balances	(6,000)	0	(6,000)

At the same time that the first cheques for $5,000 clear, write some more, this time for $9,000 each:

	Bank A	Bank B	Total
Apparent balances	$11,000	$17,000	$28,000
Actual balances	(6,000)	0	(6,000)

Pay the balances ($28,000) to a travel agent and take a long trip (preferably to a country with no extradition treaty!):

	Bank A	Bank B	Total
Apparent balances	0	0	0
Actual balances	$(17,000)	$(17,000)	$(34,000)

These are some characteristic signs of cheque kiting schemes:

- frequent deposits and cheques in same accounts
- frequent deposits and cheques in round amounts
- frequent deposits with cheques written on the same (other) banks
- short time lag between deposits and withdrawals
- frequent ATM account balance enquiries
- many large deposits made on Thursday or Friday to take advantage of the weekend
- large periodic balances in individual accounts with no apparent business explanation
- low average balance compared to high level of deposits
- many cheques made payable to other banks
- bank willingness to pay against uncollected funds (bank has extended a line of credit on the company's bank account)
- cash withdrawals with deposit cheques drawn on another bank
- cheques drawn on foreign banks with lax banking laws and regulations

Auditors can detect the above signs of cheque kiting by reviewing bank account activity. The only trouble is that criminal cheque kiters often destroy the banking documents. If a company cannot or will not produce its bank statements, with all deposit slips and cancelled cheques, the auditors should be wary. Since cash is the key account and most operating transactions run through it, an inability to obtain sufficient evidence to audit cash will probably result in a pervasive limitation on the audit scope, and an inability to form an audit opinion on the financial statements.

If these cash transfers are recorded in the books, a company will show the negative balances that result from cheques drawn on insufficient funds. However, perpetrators may try to hide the kiting by not recording the deposits and cheques. Such manoeuvres may be detectable in a bank reconciliation audit. If auditors notice some sign of kiting, yet no uncleared items are on the reconciliation, a schedule of interbank transfers can be constructed from the cancelled cheques and the cleared deposits in the bank statements. This schedule shows each cheque amount, the name of the paying bank (with the book recording date and the cheque clearing date), and the name of the receiving bank (with the book deposit date and the bank clearing date). The purpose of this schedule is to see that both sides of the transfer transaction are recorded in the same period (and in the proper period).

Summary: Bank Reconciliations, Lapping and Kiting

The combination of all the procedures performed on the bank reconciliation provides evidence of existence, valuation and proper cutoff of the bank cash balances. Auditors use a cutoff bank statement to obtain independent evidence of the proper listing of outstanding cheques and deposits in transit on a bank reconciliation.

Notice that if the auditor performs the bank reconciliation, it is a substantive procedure because the auditor gets direct evidence on monetary misstatements. However, if the auditor tests to check if bank reconciliations are performed by the client on a regular basis, this is an indirect test of monetary misstatements and thus a test of controls.

Additional procedures can be performed to try to detect attempts at lapping accounts receivable collections and kiting cheques. For lapping these procedures, include auditing the details of customer payments listed in bank deposits in comparison to details of customer payment postings (remittance lists). For kiting these procedures, include being alert to the signs of kites and preparing a schedule of interbank transfers.

R E V I E W
CHECKPOINTS

11.26   What is a cutoff bank statement? How is it used by auditors?

11.27   What is lapping? What procedures can auditors employ for its detection?

11.28   What is cheque kiting? How might auditors detect kiting?

Analysis of Financial Statement Relationships

The audit of the revenues, receivables and receipts processes results in verifying that there is not a material misstatement in the balance of accounts receivable and the two transaction streams that run through it, revenues and cash receipts. In the balance sheet approach to auditing, we can analyze the accounts receivable balance changes and the financial statement items related to them by analyzing the continuity of the accounts receivable account over the period being audited. A **continuity schedule** is a working paper that shows the movements in the account balance and the other financial statement amounts that should tie in to these movements. The continuity schedule for the account receivable balance is shown following:

Audited Amount	Financial Statement Where Amount Is Reported
Opening balance of accounts receivable	Balance sheet (prior year comparative figures)
Add: Revenues from credit sales	Income statement (component of total revenues)
Deduct: Cash received against accounts receivable	Cash flow statement (direct method)
Deduct: Uncollectible accounts written off	Balance sheet (change in Allowance for Doubtful Accounts)*
Ending balance of accounts receivable	Balance sheet (current year figures)

*Note: The bad debt expense and the allowance for doubtful accounts balance can be analyzed using the same technique. Question 11.64 at the end of the chapter asks you to provide the continuity schedule for the allowance for doubtful accounts and to identify the related financial statement items that it will have to be agreed to in the audit file.

As these relationships illustrate, our procedures to audit the revenues, receivables and receipts process allow us to assess whether all components of this system of related amounts are reported accurately in the financial statements. These relationships also indicate analytical procedures that can detect material misstatements. For example, the ratios that measure collection period or number of days of sales in A/R exploit these relations and can indicate nonexistent sales revenues or receivables that are not likely to be collected.

Summary

• •

The revenue and collection cycle consists of customer order processing, credit checking, shipping goods, billing customers and accounting for accounts receivable, and collecting and accounting for cash receipts. Companies reduce control risk by having a suitable separation of authorization, custody, recording, and periodic reconciliation duties. Error-checking procedures of comparing customer orders and shipping documents are important for billing customers the right prices for the delivered quantities. Otherwise, many things could go wrong—ranging from making sales to fictitious customers or customers with bad credit to erroneous billings for the wrong quantities at the wrong prices at the wrong time.

Cash collection is a critical point for asset control. Many cases of embezzlement occur in this process. Casettes in this chapter told the stories of some of these cash embezzlement schemes, including the practice of lapping accounts receivable.

Three topics were given special technical notes in the chapter. The existence assertion is very important in the audit of cash and receivables assets because misleading financial statements often have contained overstated assets and revenue. The use of confirmations got a special section in this chapter because confirmation is frequently used to obtain evidence of asset existence from outside parties, such as customers who owe on accounts receivable. The audit of bank reconciliations was covered in the context of an audit opportunity to recalculate the amount of cash for the financial statements and to look for signs of accounts receivable lapping and cheque kiting.

Multiple-choice Questions for Practice and Review

• •

11.29 Which of the following would be the best protection for a company that wishes to prevent the lapping of trade accounts receivable?

a. Segregate duties so that the bookkeeper in charge of the general ledger has no access to incoming mail.

b. Segregate duties so that no employee has access to both cheques from customers and currency from daily cash receipts.

c. Have customers send payments directly to the company's depository bank.

d. Request that customer's payment cheques be made payable to the company and addressed to the treasurer.

11.30 Which of the following internal control procedures will most likely prevent the concealment of a cash shortage from the improper write-off of a trade account receivable?

a. Write-off must be approved by a responsible officer after review of credit department recommendations and supporting evidence.

b. Write-offs must be supported by an aging schedule showing that only receivables overdue several months have been written off.

c. Write-offs must be approved by the cashier who is in a position to know if the receivables have, in fact, been collected.

d. Write-offs must be authorized by company field sales employees who are in a position to determine the financial standing of the customers.

11.31 Auditors sometimes use comparisons of ratios as audit evidence. For example, an unexplained decrease in the ratio of gross profit to sales may suggest which of the following possibilities?

a. Unrecorded purchases.

b. Unrecorded sales.

c. Merchandise purchases being charged to selling and general expense.

d. Fictitious sales.

11.32 An auditor is auditing sales transactions. One step is to vouch a sample of debit entries from the accounts receivable subsidiary ledger back to the supporting sales invoices. What would the auditor intend to establish by this step?

a. Sales invoices represent bona fide sales.

b. All sales have been recorded.

c. All sales invoices have been properly posted to customer accounts.

d. Debit entries in the accounts receivable subsidiary ledger are properly supported by sales invoices.

11.33 To conceal defalcations involving receivables, the auditor would expect an experienced bookkeeper to charge which of the following accounts?

a. Miscellaneous income.

b. Petty cash.

c. Miscellaneous expense.

d. Sales returns.

11.34 Which of the following would the auditor consider to be an incompatible operation if the cashier receives remittances?

a. The cashier prepares the daily deposit.

b. The cashier makes the daily deposit at a local bank.

c. The cashier posts the receipts to the accounts receivable subsidiary ledger cards.

d. The cashier endorses the cheques.

11.35 The audit working papers often include a client-prepared, aged trial balance of accounts receivable as of the balance sheet date. The aging is best used by the auditor to:

a. Evaluate internal control over credit sales.

b. Test the accuracy of recorded charge sales.

c. Estimate credit losses.

d. Verify the existence of the recorded receivables.

11.36 Which of the following might be detected by an auditor's cutoff review and examination of sales journal entries for several days prior to the balance sheet date?

a. Lapping year-end accounts receivable.

b. Inflating sales for the year.

c. Kiting bank balances.

d. Misappropriating merchandise.

11.37 Confirmation of individual accounts receivable balances directly with debtors will, of itself, normally provide evidence concerning the:

a. Collectibility of the balances confirmed.

b. Ownership of the balances confirmed.

c. Existence of the balances confirmed.

d. Internal control over balances confirmed.

11.38 Which of the following is one of the better auditing techniques an auditor might use to detect kiting between intercompany banks?

a. Review composition of authenticated deposit slips.

b. Review subsequent bank statements.

c. Prepare a schedule of the bank transfers.

d. Prepare a year-end bank reconciliation.

11.39 The best reason for prenumbering in numerical sequence such documents as sales orders, shipping documents and sales invoices is:

a. Enables company personnel to determine the accuracy of each document.

b. Enables personnel to determine the proper period recording of sales revenue and receivables.

c. Enables personnel to check the numerical sequence for missing documents and unrecorded transactions.

d. Enables personnel to determine the validity of recorded transactions.

11.40 When a sample of customer accounts receivable are selected for the purpose of vouching debits therein for validity evidence, the auditors will vouch them to:

a. Sales invoices with shipping documents and customer sales invoices.

b. Records of accounts receivable write-offs.

c. Cash remittance lists and bank deposit slips.

d. Credit files and reports.

11.41 In the audit of cash and accounts receivable, the most important emphasis should be on the:

a. Completeness assertions.

b. Existence assertion.

c. Obligations assertion.

d. Presentation and disclosure assertion.

11.42 When accounts receivable are confirmed at an interim date, the auditors need not be concerned with:

a. Obtaining a summary of receivables transactions from the interim date to the year-end date.

b. Obtaining a year-end trial balance of receivables, comparing it to the interim trial balance and obtaining evidence and explanations for large variations.

c. Sending negative confirmations to all the customers as of the year-end date.

d. Considering the necessity for some additional confirmations as of the balance sheet date if balances have increased materially.

11.43 The negative request form of accounts receivable confirmation is useful particularly when the:

	Assessed level of control risk relating to receivables is:	Number of small balances is:	Proper consideration by the recipient is:
a.	Low	Many	Likely
b.	Low	Few	Unlikely
c.	High	Few	Likely
d.	High	Many	Likely

11.44 When an auditor selects a sample of shipping documents and takes the tracing direction of a test to find the related sales invoice copies, the evidence is relevant for deciding:

a. Shipments to customers were invoiced.

b. Shipments to customers were recorded as sales.

c. Recorded sales were shipped.

d. Invoiced sales were shipped.

(AICPA adapted)

Exercises and Problems

· ·

11.45 Cash Receipts: Control Objectives and Control Examples. Prepare a table similar to Exhibit 11–4 (internal control objectives) for cash receipts.

LO.2

11.46 Internal Control Questionnaire for Book Buy-Back Cash Fund. Taylor, a PA, has been engaged to audit the financial statements of University Books, Incorporated. University Books maintains a large, revolving cash fund exclusively for the purpose of buying used books from students for cash. The cash fund is active all year because the nearby university offers a large variety of courses with varying starting and completion dates throughout the year.

LO.2

Receipts are prepared for each purchase. Reimbursement vouchers periodically are submitted to replenish the fund.

Required:

Construct an internal control questionnaire to be used in evaluating the system of internal control over University Books' buying back books using the revolving cash fund. The internal control questionnaire should elicit a yes or no response to each question. Do not discuss the internal controls over books that are purchased.

(AICPA adapted)

11.47 Test of Controls Audit Procedures for Cash Receipts. You are the in-charge auditor examining the financial statements of the Gutzler Company for the year ended December 31. During late October you, with the help of Gutzler's controller, completed an internal control questionnaire and prepared the appropriate memoranda describing Gutzler's accounting procedures. Your comments relative to cash receipts are as follows:

LO.2

All cash receipts are sent directly to the accounts receivable clerk with no processing by the mail department. The accounts receivable clerk keeps the cash receipts journal, prepares the bank deposit slip in duplicate, posts from the deposit slip to the subsidiary accounts receivable ledger and mails the deposit to the bank.

The controller receives the validated deposit slips directly (unopened) from the bank. She also receives the monthly bank statement directly (unopened) from the bank and promptly reconciles it.

At the end of each month, the accounts receivable clerk notifies the general ledger clerk by journal voucher of the monthly totals of the cash receipts journal for posting to the general ledger.

Each month, with regard to the general ledger cash account, the general ledger clerk makes an entry to

record the total debits to cash from the cash receipts journal. In addition, the general ledger clerk, on occasion, makes debit entries in the general ledger cash account from sources other than the cash receipts journal—for example, funds borrowed from the bank. Certain standard auditing procedures listed below already have been performed by you in the audit of cash receipts:

All columns in the cash receipts have been totalled and cross-totalled.

Postings from the cash receipts journal have been traced to the general ledger.

Remittance advices and related correspondence have been traced to entries in the cash receipts journal.

Required:

Considering Gutzler's internal control over cash receipts and the standard auditing procedures already performed, list all other auditing procedures that should be performed to obtain sufficient audit evidence regarding cash receipts control and give the reasons for each procedure. Do not discuss the procedures for cash disbursements and cash balances. Also, do not discuss the extent to which any of the procedures are to be performed. Assume adequate controls exist to ensure that all sales transactions are recorded. Organize your answer sheet as follows:

Other Audit Procedures	Reason for Other Audit Procedures

(AICPA adapted)

11.48 Cash Receipts: Weaknesses and Recommendations. The Pottstown Art League operates a museum for the benefit and enjoyment of the community. During hours when the museum is open to the public, two volunteer clerks positioned at the entrance collect a $5 admission fee from each nonmember patron. Members of the Art League are permitted to enter free of charge on presentation of their membership cards.

LO.2

At the end of each day, one of the clerks delivers the proceeds to the treasurer. The treasurer counts the cash in the presence of the clerk and places it in a safe. Each Friday afternoon, the treasurer and one of the clerks deliver all cash held in the safe to the bank, and they receive an authenticated deposit slip that provides the basis for the weekly entry in the cash receipts journal.

The board of directors of the Pottstown Art League has identified a need to improve the system of internal control over cash admission fees. The board has determined that the cost of installing turnstiles or sales booths or otherwise altering the physical layout of the museum will greatly exceed any benefits that may be derived. However, the board has agreed that the sale of admission tickets must be an integral part of its improvement efforts.

Required:

The board of directors has requested your assistance. Prepare a report for presentation and discussion at their next board meeting that identifies the weaknesses in the existing system of cash admission fees and suggests recommendations.

(AICPA adapted)

11.49 Control Weaknesses: Shipping and Billing. Ajax,
LO.2 Inc., an audit client, recently installed a new computer system to process the shipping, billing and accounts receivable records more efficiently. During interim work, an assistant completed the review of the accounting system and the internal controls. The assistant determined the following information concerning the new computer systems and the processing and control of shipping notices and customer invoices.

The computer system documentation consists of the following items: program listings, error listings, logs and database dictionaries. The system and documentation are maintained by the IT administrator. To increase efficiency, batch totals and processing controls are not used in the system.

Ajax ships its products directly from two warehouses, which forward shipping notices to general accounting. There, the billing clerk enters the price of the item and accounts for the numerical sequence of the shipping notices. The billing clerk also manually prepares daily adding machine tapes of the units shipped and the sales amounts. The computer processing output consists of:

a. A three-copy invoice that is forwarded to the billing clerk.
b. A daily sales register showing the aggregate totals of units shipped and sales amounts that the billing clerk compares to the adding machine tapes.

The billing clerk mails two copies of each invoice to the customer and retains the third copy in an open invoice file that serves as a detail accounts receivable record.

Required:

a. Prepare a list of weaknesses in internal control (manual and computer), and for each weakness make one or more recommendations.
b. Suggest how Ajax's computer processing over shipping and billing could be improved through the use of remote terminals to enter shipping notices. Describe appropriate controls for such an on-line data entry system.

CASH: SUBSTANTIVE AUDIT PROCEDURES

11.50 Bank Reconciliation. The following client-prepared bank reconciliation is being examined by you during an audit of the financial statements of Cynthia Company:

CYNTHIA COMPANY
Bank Reconciliation
Village Bank Account 2
December 31, 20X0

Balance per bank (a):		$18,375.91
Deposits in transit (b):		
12/30	$1,471.10	
12/31	2,840.69	4,311.79
Subtotal		22,687.70
Outstanding cheques (c):		
837	6,000.00	
1941	671.80	
1966	320.00	
1984	1,855.42	
1985	3,621.22	
1987	2,576.89	
1991	4,420.88	(19,466.21)
Subtotal		3,221.49
NSF cheque Returned 12/29 (d):		200.00
Bank charges		5.50
Error cheque no. 1932		148.10
Customer note collected by the bank ($2,750 plus $275 interest (e):		(3,025.00)
Balance per books (f):		$550.09

Required:

Indicate one or more audit procedures that should be performed in gathering evidence in support of each of the items (*a*) through (*f*) above.

(AICPA adapted)

11.51 Sales Cutoff and Cutoff Bank Statement.
LO.2 a. You wish to test Houston Corporaton's sales cutoff at
LO.6 June 30. Describe the steps you should include in this test.
b. You obtain a July 10 bank statement directly from the bank. Explain how this cutoff bank statement should be used:
(1) In your review of the June 30 bank reconciliation.
(2) To obtain other audit information.

(AICPA adapted)

11.52 Bank Reconciliation—Cash Shortage. The Patrick
LO.6 Company had poor internal control over its cash transactions. Facts about its cash position at November 30 were the following:

The cash books showed a balance of $18,901.62, which included undeposited receipts. A credit of $100 on the bank statement did not appear on the books of the company. The balance according to the statement was $15,550.

When you received the cutoff bank statement on December 10, the following cancelled cheques were enclosed: No. 6500 for $116.25, No. 7126 for $150.00, No. 7815 for $253.25, No. 8621 for $190.71, No. 8623 for $206.80, and No. 8632 for $145.28. The only deposit was in the amount of $3,794.41 on December 7.

The cashier handles all incoming cash and makes the bank deposits personally. He also reconciles the monthly bank statement. His November 30 reconciliation is shown below.

Balance, per books, November 30		$18,901.62
Add: Outstanding cheques:		
8621	$190.71	
8623	206.80	
8632	145.28	442.79
		19,344.41
Less: Undeposited receipts		3,794.41
Balance per bank, November 30		15,550.00
Deduct: Unrecorded credit		100.00
True cash, November 30		$15,450.00

Required:

a. You suspect that the cashier has stolen some money. Prepare a schedule showing your estimate of the loss.

b. How did the cashier attempt to conceal the theft?

c. Based only on the information above, name two specific features of internal control that apparently were missing.

d. If the cashier's October 31 reconciliation is known to be in order and you start your audit on December 5, what specific auditing procedures could you perform to discover the theft?

(AICPA adapted)

RECEIVABLES AND REVENUES: SUBSTANTIVE AUDIT PROCEDURES

11.53 Alternative Accounts Receivable Procedures. Several
LO.1 accounts receivable confirmations have been returned
LO.3 with the notation "verification of vendors statements is no longer possible because our data processing system does not accumulate each vendor's invoices." What alternative auditing procedures could be used to audit these accounts receivable?

(AICPA adapted)

11.54 Receivables Audit Procedures. The ABC Appliance
LO.3 Company, a manufacturer of small electrical appliances,
LO.5 deals exclusively with 20 distributors situated throughout the country. At December 31 (the balance sheet date) receivables from these distributors aggregated $875,000. Total current assets were $1.3 million.

With respect to receivables, the auditors followed the procedures outline below in the course of the annual audit of financial statements:

1. Reviewed the system of internal control and found it to be exceptionally good.
2. Reconciled the subsidiary and control accounts at year-end.
3. Aged accounts. None were overdue.
4. Examined details sales and collection transactions for the months of February, July and November.
5. Received positive confirmations of year-end balances.

Required:
Criticize the completeness or incompleteness of the above program, giving reasons for your recommendations concerning the addition or omission of any procedures.

(AICPA adapted)

11.55 Rent Revenue. You were engaged to conduct an audit
LO.3 of the financial statements of Clayton Realty Corporation for the year ending January 31. The examination of the annual rent reconciliation is a vital portion of the audit.

The following rent reconciliation was prepared by the controller of Clayton Realty Corporation and was presented to you. You subjected it to various audit procedures:

CLAYTON REALTY CORPORATION
Rent Reconciliation
For the Year Ended January 31

Gross apartment rents (Schedule A)	$1,600,800*
Less vacancies (Schedule B)	20,000*
Net apartment rentals	1,580,300
Less unpaid rents (Schedule C)	7,800*
Total	1,572,500
Add prepaid rent collected (Schedule D)	500*
Total cash collected	$1,573,000*

Schedules A, B, C and D are available to you but have not been illustrated. You have conducted an assessment of the control risk and found it to be low. Cash receipts from rental operations are deposited in a special bank account.

Required:
What substantive audit procedures should you employ during the audit in order to substantiate the validity of each of the dollar amounts marked by an asterisk(*)?

(AICPA adapted)

DISCUSSION CASES

11.56 Accounts Receivable Audit Procedures. During the
LO.3 audit of the December 31, 20X5 financial statements, the auditor identifies cash amounts received subsequent to December 31, 20X5 and traces these amounts to the cash account in the general ledger and to the accounts receivable subledger balances at December 31, 20X5.

Required:

a. What kind of procedure is this? What evidence does it provide regarding which financial statement assertion?

b. What records or documents would the auditor need to look at to identify cash amounts received after the year-end?

11.57 Accounts Receivable Audit Procedures. The auditor is
LO.3 considering confirming zero-balance accounts from the
LO.5 client's accounts receivable subledger to provide evidence concerning the completeness assertion for

accounts receivable and sales.

Required:

a. What are the advantages and limitations of this procedure?

b. How would the decision to use this procedure relate to the auditor's control assessment? In particular, discuss the kinds of controls the client would be expected to have and the procedures the auditor could use to test them.

11.58 Business Risk, Evidence Analysis, Sales Detail.
LO.1 Rosella is the senior in charge of the current year audit
LO.5 of Harrier Limited, a company that designs and manu-
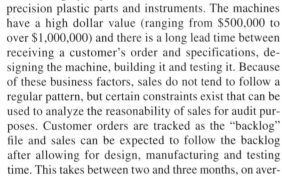
factures highly sophisticated machines used to make precision plastic parts and instruments. The machines have a high dollar value (ranging from $500,000 to over $1,000,000) and there is a long lead time between receiving a customer's order and specifications, designing the machine, building it and testing it. Because of these business factors, sales do not tend to follow a regular pattern, but certain constraints exist that can be used to analyze the reasonability of sales for audit purposes. Customer orders are tracked as the "backlog" file and sales can be expected to follow the backlog after allowing for design, manufacturing and testing time. This takes between two and three months, on average. Another factor is the physical limitation of the factory and equipment: there are 12 job stations where machines can be built, so a maximum of 12 machines can be in the work-in-process inventory at any one time.

Harrier's shares are privately held by its founder and president, and several outside investors, but it issued bonds to the public several years ago and is subject to debt covenants that require it to maintain a working capital ratio of 1.5 to 1.0 and a debt to equity ratio of 0.5 to 1.0 at each year end. In addition, no dividends or management bonuses can be paid out unless the net income before taxes is at least $1,000,000. The draft statements for the current year meet all covenants and show a net income before taxes of $1,300,000.

In reviewing the monthly sales for the current year, Rosella notices several anomalies. First, 15 machines were shipped in December, the last month of the current year, while in December of the prior year only six were shipped. The average monthly shipment volume is between five and six machines. Also, the average gross profit on sales in prior years, and in most months, is approximately 40 percent. The gross profit on the December sales is 75 percent. The annual sales were $66 million, with $15 million of this occurring in December. The annual gross profit is $33 million, with $11 million of this occurring in December. While scrutinizing the cash records for the first month of the new year to look for unaccrued liabilities, Rosella notices some large amounts paid for travel expenses for employees and for shipments of "spare parts" to customers. Enquiries of the employees reveals that they are engineers and technicians who were required to spend two or three weeks in various cities where the December machine sales were shipped in order to "work out the bugs" and add some parts to these machines.

Required:

a. What are the main business risks in Harrier Limited? What are the risks of financial statement misstatements that Rosella should be aware of?

b. Discuss the audit evidence collecting procedures used by Rosella. What types of procedures were used and what assertions do they provide evidence about?

c. Analyze the different pieces of information Rosella obtained and generate reasonable explanations for the sales anomalies noted. What additional enquiries would you recommend that Rosella make to form an opinion on the operating results reported in Harrier's draft financial statements? What is your conclusion on the draft sales and gross profits amounts, based on your analysis of the facts given?

d. Harrier's revenue recognition policy is to recognize revenue when the machines are shipped and title passes to customers. This point occurs when the machines are loaded on the truck at Harrier's factory. Given this policy, what adjustment (if any) would be required in Harrier's current financial statements given the conclusion you reached in part c) above?

11.59 Continuity Schedule for Allowance for Doubtful
LO.1 **Accounts.**
LO.5
Required:

a. Complete the following continuity schedule indicating how the movements in the allowance for doubtful accounts tie into other amounts in the financial statements.

b. Prepare an audit program listing the procedures that can be used to audit the accounts in this system. Demonstrate how your audit program addresses all the relevant assertions.

Audited Amount	Financial Statement Where Amount Is Reported
Opening balance of allowance for doubtful accounts	
Add:	
Deduct:	
Ending balance of allowance for doubtful accounts	

11.60 Negative Confirmations. The auditor of a stock bro-
LO.3 kerage company, Roller Securities Inc., sends out nega-
LO.5 tive confirmations of account details for a sample of
about 50 percent of the stock brokerage's customers, selected at random. Historically, between 2 and 5 percent
of the confirmations have been returned, and the majority of the discrepancies reported have been understate-

ments. Investigation of the discrepancies rarely indicates an error on Roller Securities Inc.'s part. Usually
the discrepancy is explained by transactions that are in
progress or pending over the year-end, by late payments
on the customer's part, or other mistakes in the customer's own records.

Required:

a. Describe the inherent risks and the internal control
risks that exist for customer accounts at Roller
Securities Inc.

b. Discuss the advantages and disadvantages of using
negative confirmations to provide audit evidence
about the assertions underlying Roller Securities
Inc.'s customer account balances. Comment on the
persuasiveness of the evidence the negative confirmations provide; do you think it can be sufficient to
support the auditor's opinion?

11.61 Controls Debit Card Fraud.
LO.1 Read the following article on debit card theft
LO.3 and answer the questions that follow.

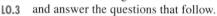

THE STING

The first sign of trouble was the kind of minor glitch
that's all too easy to ignore: My wife tried to pay for
a pair of shoes with her debit card while we were on
vacation. It didn't work. She tried again. Still no go.
She borrowed mine, and moved on.

A short time later, Marian tried her debit card
again. A message popped up on the screen, informing
her that the card had been cancelled. I went on-line at
our bank account. There wasn't much in it, but that's
typical for a Toronto family with two kids, a mortgage
and a renovation tab. Then I noticed something odd—
the bank had withdrawn $720 from our account to
cover an "empty envelope deposit."

I didn't remember depositing $720. And why was
the bank taking the money away from us? We called
Toronto-Dominion. The news wasn't good. Bank
staff believed that our account had been invaded.
After their security software noticed a series of suspicious transactions involving my wife's debit card,
they had cancelled it and left us a message on our
home number.

We began combing through our account, and
quickly found a series of payments and withdrawals
that clearly weren't ours. They came to more than
$1,200. Toronto-Dominion representatives told us
that we would be paid back. That was a relief, but it
was creepy to realize that someone had been able to
breach our defences with such apparent ease.

My wife and I had long been aware of how easy it
is to defraud a credit card. Ours had been raided several times, once to the tune of nearly $20,000. But we

had always thought our debit card, which requires a
PIN, was a virtual Fort Knox. We were wrong.

Debit-card fraud, the newest form of bank robbery,
is on the rise in Toronto, I discovered. The banks don't
like to talk about it, but Industry Canada figures show
that in big cities like Toronto, a hotbed of card fraud,
about 6 percent of bank accounts are raided.

Norman Inkster, a former RCMP commissioner
who now runs his own security firm, said the true
extent of debit-card fraud is unknown, since many
thefts are reported to the banks, but not to police.

"Let's just say there's a lot of it," Mr. Inkster said.

Detective Ken Reimer of the Toronto Police fraud
squad can confirm that personally. Just three weeks
ago, several hundred dollars was drained from his
own account. "That just shows you how much of it
there really is," he said. "It's ridiculous."

The Toronto-Dominion security representative we
dealt with gave us a quick primer on how it happens.
Somewhere in our travels, he told us, the electronic
information on my wife's card had probably been
"skimmed." It could have been done by a clerk at a corner store or a gas station, who swiped our card through
a small electronic machine called a card reader. (If a
clerk tells you he needs to swipe your card again
because the first try didn't work out, he may be running it for the second time through a reader, which
then allows a duplicate to be made.)

After that, all he needed was the PIN, which he
could get by watching us key it in, or by replaying the
store's security tape.

The Toronto Police fraud squad now devotes a large percentage of its energies to debit-card fraud, which is growing at an exceptional rate. In 2003, reported debit-card fraud was estimated at $40 million across Canada. By the next year, it had risen 50 percent, to $60 million. (Although there are no figures for 2005, everyone in the field says it has risen significantly.)

One of Det. Reimer and Det. Sgt. White's biggest busts was Project Bam, a cooperative effort with other police agencies that resulted in more than 50 arrests in 2003. It exposed a network of criminals who had raked in more than $10 million.

The criminals had used a series of techniques. In some cases, they attached card readers over the slots of bank machines. The card readers looked like part of the official machine, but fed the electronic data on the cards into a memory chip. To get the PINs, they installed tiny spy cameras next to the machines or above them, enclosed in plastic hoods that had been spray-painted to match the bank colours. Another common technique is known as the Lebanese Loop (named after a Lebanese crime syndicate that invented it). The fraudsters install a plastic slot with a loop of tape inside it on bank machines. When a customer puts in his cards, the tape catches it. Then a gang member comes to the aid of the customer as he tries to retrieve his card, and suggests that he punch in his PIN to get the card back. When the customer leaves, the gang member retrieves the card and uses it.

Detective Sergeant John White, another member of the squad, says most of their investigations begin with information provided by banks, which have sophisticated software that makes it relatively easy to spot fraudulent transactions by highlighting deviations from customers' typical patterns. "They have excellent security systems," Det. Sgt. White says.

Toronto-Dominion's system had certainly been more vigilant than my wife and I were, shutting off her card after spotting three or four oddities—including the fact that the card was being used in Toronto while we were in Halifax.

Bank data play a key role in investigations. By sorting and matching data, banks can find locations where a number of fraud victims shopped or made withdrawals—this is known as a "point of common purchase," and is the likely location of a card-skimmer. (Gas stations, I was told, were particularly notorious.) In most cases, unfortunately, the guilty party is long gone. One common modus operandi for debit-card fraudsters is for a gang member to get hired at a store under a false name, collect card data for a few weeks, then quit. The card information is then used to manufacture new cards and to milk bank accounts.

According to Det. Sgt. White, banks often know where your card was skimmed, but refuse to divulge the names of businesses because of the potential consequences. "They're afraid of what might happen when people find out that someone at their local store or gas station was the culprit," Det. Sgt. White says. "Some people would probably head over with a baseball bat."

Det. Reimer says a large number of electronic frauds are executed with extremely low-tech methods. Criminals dig through garbage to find credit-card statements or banking documents. PINs are gleaned by looking over people's shoulders. (In some cases, store employees fasten portable keypads to the counter so shoppers can't shelter them next to their chest.)

Det. Reimer says there are three cardinal rules in the fight against electronic theft: First, hide the keypad when you punch in your PIN. Second, check your bank and credit account on-line, as often as possible. (He now checks his every day.) Third, shred all financial documents.

"Don't just use a regular shredder," he says. "You need a crosscut shredder. There are guys out there who will tape it all back together."

My wife and I will be shopping for our crosscut shredder this weekend.

Source: Peter Cheney, "The Sting," *globeandmail.com*, September 10, 2005, pp. M1 and M6. Reprinted wih permission from the Globe and Mail.

Required:

a. What business processes in what business entities were used to perpetrate the debit card frauds described in the article?

b. What control weaknesses existed in these businesses that allowed these frauds to occur? Describe the weaknesses in terms of control objectives and explain how the weaknesses were exploited by the fraudsters.

c. Design control activities (policies and procedures) that could be implemented in these businesses to prevent and/or detect these types of frauds. Explain in detail how the control activities would be implemented and applied effectively.

d. Discuss the costs and benefits of the control activities you designed in part c). Do you think the benefits of these controls would exceed the costs? Why or why not?

Kingston Case questions related to Chapter 11 are on the Online Learning Centre that accompanies this text.

APPENDIX 11A

INTERNAL CONTROL QUESTIONNAIRES

. . . .

EXHIBIT   11A–1   INTERNAL CONTROL QUESTIONNAIRES
REVENUES, RECEIVABLES AND RECEIPTS PROCESS

OVERALL COMPANY-LEVEL CONTROL AND CONTROL ACTIVITIES ASSESSMENT
(Refer to responses recorded for questions in Exhibit PIII-3 on pages 420–422.)

Are company-level and general control activities adequate as they apply to the revenues, receivables and receipts components of the information system?

- Consider the impact of any weakness in company-level and general control activities on planned audit approach and procedures.
- Assess the potential for weaknesses to result in a material misstatement of the financial information generated from this accounting cycle. If a significant risk of misstatement is assessed, perform procedures to determine extent of any misstatement.

Consider adequacy of the following general controls in place in the revenue, receivables and receipts process to:

— prevent unauthorized access or changes to programs and data?

— ensure the security and privacy of data?

— control and maintain key systems?

— protect assets susceptible to misappropriation?

— ensure completeness, accuracy and authorization of data and processing

— ensure adequate management trails exist

CASH RECEIPTS PROCESSING APPLICATION
Environment and general control relevant to this application:
1. Are receipts deposited daily, intact and without delay?
2. Does someone other than the cashier or accounts receivable bookkeeper take the deposits to the bank?
3. Are the duties of the cashier entirely separate from recordkeeping for notes and accounts receivable? From general ledger recordkeeping? Is the cashier denied access to receivables records or monthly statements?
4. Are employees with access to cash covered by fidelity insurance against embezzlement losses (also called "fidelity bonding" of employees)?

Assertion-Based Control Evaluation
Validity objective:
5. Is a bank reconciliation performed monthly by someone who does not have cash custody or recordkeeping responsibility?
6. Are the cash receipts journal entries compared to the remittance lists and deposit slips regularly?

Completeness objective:
7. Does the person who opens the mail make a list of cash received (a remittance list)?
8. Are currency receipts controlled by mechanical devices? Are machine totals checked by the internal auditor?
9. Are prenumbered sales invoice or receipts books used? Is the numerical sequence checked for missing documents?

Authorization objective:
10. Does a responsible person approve discounts taken by customers with payments on account?

Accuracy objective:
11. Is a duplicate deposit slip retained by the internal auditor or someone other than the employee making up the deposit?
12. Is the remittance list compared to the deposit by someone other than the cashier?

Classification objective:
13. Does the accounting manual contain instructions for classifying cash receipts credits?

Accounting objective:
14. Does someone reconcile the accounts receivable subsidiary to the control account regularly (to determine whether all entries were made to customers' accounts)?

Proper period objective:
15. Does the accounting manual contain instructions for dating cash receipts entries the same day as the date of receipt?

SALES APPLICATION
Environment and general control evaluation relevant to this application:
1. Is the credit department independent of the marketing department?
2. Are non-routine sales controlled by the same procedures described below? For example, sales to employees, COD sales, disposals of property, cash sales and scrap sales.

Continued

EXHIBIT 11A-1 CONTINUED

Assertion-Based Control Evaluation
Validity objective:
3. Is access to sales invoice blanks restricted?
4. Are prenumbered bills of lading or other shipping documents prepared or completed in the shipping department?
Completeness objective:
5. Are sales invoice blanks prenumbered?
6. Is the sequence checked for missing invoices?
7. Is the shipping document numerical sequence checked for missing bills of lading numbers?
Authorization objective:
8. Are all credit sales approved by the credit department prior to shipment?
9. Are sales prices and terms based on approved standards?
10. Are returned sales credits and other credits supported by documentation as to receipt, condition, and quantity and approved by a responsible officer?
Accuracy objective:
11. Are shipped quantities compared to invoice quantities?
12. Are sales invoices checked for error in quantities, prices, extensions and footing, freight allowances and checked with customers' orders?
13. Is there an overall check on arithmetic accuracy of period sales data by a statistical or product-line analysis?
14. Are periodic sales data reported directly to general ledger accounting independent of accounts receivable accounting?
Classification objective:
15. Does the accounting manual contain instructions for classifying sales?
Accounting objective:
16. Are summary journal entries approved before posting?
Proper period objective:
17. Does the accounting manual contain instructions to date sales invoices on the shipment date?

ACCOUNTS RECEIVABLE APPLICATION

Environment and general controls relevant to this application:
1. Are customers' subsidiary records maintained by someone who has no access to cash?
2. Is the cashier denied access to the customers' records and monthly statements?
3. Are delinquent accounts listed periodically for review by someone other than the credit manager?
4. Are written-off accounts kept in a memo ledger or credit report file for periodic access?
5. Is the credit department separated from the sales department?
6. Are notes receivable in the custody of someone other than the cashier or accounts receivable recordkeeper?
7. Is custody of negotiable collateral in the hands of someone not responsible for handling cash or keeping records?
Assertion-Based Control Evaluation
Validity objective:
8. Are customers' statements mailed monthly by the accounts receivable department?
9. Are direct confirmations of accounts and notes obtained periodically by the internal auditor?
10. Are differences reported by customers routed to someone outside the accounts receivable department for investigation?
11. Are returned goods checked against receiving reports?
Completeness objective:
(Refer to completeness questions in the sales and cash receipts questionnaires.)
12. Are credit memo documents prenumbered and the sequence checked for missing documents?
Authorization objective:
13. Is customer credit approved before orders are shipped?
14. Are write-offs, returns and discounts allowed after discount date subject to approval by a responsible officer?
15. Are large loans or advances to related parties approved by the directors?
Accuracy objective:
16. Do the internal auditors confirm customer accounts periodically to determine accuracy?
Classification objective:
17. Are receivables from officers, directors and affiliates identified separately in the accounts receivable records?
Accounting objective:
18. Does someone reconcile the accounts receivable subsidiary to the control account regularly?
Proper period objective:
(Refer to proper period objective questions in the sales and cash receipts questionnaires.)

EXHIBIT   11A–2   EXAMPLES OF SALES AND ACCOUNTS RECEIVABLE CONTROLS RELATING TO EXHIBIT 11–1

- Each terminal performs only designated functions. For example, the terminal at the shipping dock cannot be used to enter initial sales information or to access the payroll database.
- An identification number and password (issued on an individual person basis) is required to enter the sales and each command that a subsequent action has been completed. Unauthorized entry attempts are logged and immediately investigated. Further, certain passwords have "ready only" (cannot change any data) authorization. For example, the credit manager can determine the outstanding balance of any account or view on-line "reports" summarizing overdue accounts receivable, but cannot enter credit memos to change the balances.
- All input information is immediately logged to provide restart processing should any terminal become inoperative during the processing.
- A transaction code calls up on the terminals a full screen "form" that appears to the operator in the same format as the original paper documents. Each clerk must enter the information correctly or the computer will not accept the transaction. This is called **online input validation** and utilizes validation checks, such as missing data, check digit and limit tests.
- All documents prepared by the computer are numbered, and the number is stored as part of the sales record in the accounts receivable database.
- A daily search of the pending order database is made by the computer, and sales orders outstanding more than seven days are listed on the terminal in marketing management.

APPENDIX 11B

SUBSTANTIVE AUDIT PROGRAMS

. . . .

EXHIBIT 11B-1   AUDIT PROGRAM FOR CASH: SELECTED SUBSTANTIVE PROCEDURES

1. Obtain confirmations from banks (standard bank confirmation).
2. Obtain reconciliations of all bank accounts.
   a. Trace the bank balance on the reconciliation to the bank confirmation.
   b. Trace the reconciled book balance to the general ledger.
   c. Recalculate the arithmetic on client-prepared bank reconciliations.
3. Review the bank confirmation for loans and collateral.
4. Ask the client to request cutoff bank statements to be mailed directly to the audit firm.
   a. Trace deposits in transit on the reconciliation to bank deposits early in the next period.
   b. Trace outstanding cheques on the reconciliation to cheques cleared in the next period.
5. Prepare a schedule of interbank transfers for a period of 10 business days before and after the year-end date. Document dates of book entry transfer and correspondence with bank entries and reconciliation items, if any.
6. Count cash funds in the presence of a client representative. Obtain a receipt for return of the funds.
7. Obtain written client representations concerning compensating balance agreements.

EXHIBIT 11B-2   AUDIT PROGRAM FOR ACCOUNTS AND NOTES RECEIVABLE AND REVENUE: SELECTED SUBSTANTIVE PROCEDURES

A. Accounts and Notes Receivable.
   1. Obtain an aged trial balance of individual customer accounts. Recalculate the total and trace to the general ledger control account.
   2. Send confirmations to all accounts over $X. Select a random sample of all remaining accounts for confirmation.
      a. Investigate differences reported by customers.
      b. Perform alternative procedures on accounts that do not respond to positive confirmation requests.
         (1) Vouch cash receipts after the confirmation date for subsequent payment.
         (2) Vouch sales invoices and shipping documents.
   3. Evaluate the adequacy of the allowance for doubtful accounts.
      a. Vouch a sample of *current* amounts in the aged trial balance to sales invoices to determine whether amounts aged current should be aged past due.
      b. Compare the current-year write-off experience to the prior-year allowance.
      c. Vouch cash receipts after the balance sheet date for collections on past-due accounts.
      d. Obtain financial statements or credit reports and discuss with the credit manager collections on large past-due accounts.
      e. Calculate an allowance estimate using prior relations of write-offs and sales, taking under consideration current economic events.
   4. Review the bank confirmations, loan agreements and minutes of the board for indications of pledged, discounted or assigned receivables.
   5. Inspect or obtain confirmation of notes receivable.
   6. Recalculate interest income and trace to the income account.
   7. Obtain written client representations regarding pledge, discount or assignment of receivables, and about receivables from officers, directors, affiliates or other related parties.
   8. Review the adequacy of control over recording of all charges to customers (completeness), audited in the sales transaction test of controls audit program.
B. Revenue
   1. Select a sample of recorded sales invoices and vouch to underlying shipping documents.
   2. Select a sample of shipping documents and trace to sales invoices.
   3. Obtain production records of physical quantities sold and calculate an estimate of sales dollars based on average sale prices.
   4. Compare revenue dollars and physical quantities with prior-year data and industry economic statistics.
   5. Select a sample of sales invoices prepared a few days before and after the balance sheet date and vouch to supporting documents for evidence of proper cutoff.

CHAPTER
12

Purchases, Payables, and Payments Process

This chapter summarizes the accounting cycle for business processes related to the acquisition of goods (inventory) and services (expenses), the acquisition of property, plant, and equipment (fixed assets) and the expenditure of cash (cash disbursements) to pay for purchases and acquisitions. A series of casettes demonstrates the application of audit procedures in situations where errors, irregularities and frauds might be discovered. The chapter concludes with special notes on inventory observation and accounts payable completeness.

LEARNING OBJECTIVES

After completing this chapter, you will be able to:

1. Describe the purchases, payables and payments process, including typical transactions, source documents, controls and account balances.

2. Outline control tests for auditing control over purchase of inventory, services, and fixed assets and disbursement of cash.

3. Design audit and investigative procedures for detecting common errors, irregularities and

frauds in the purchases, payables and payments process.

4. Explain the importance of the completion assertion for the audit of accounts payable liabilities and procedures used to search for unrecorded liabilities.

5. Identify audit considerations for observing the physical inventory count.

Note: Appendix 12B and 12C are located on the text Online Learning Centre.

Risk Assessment for Purchases, Payables and Payments

LEARNING OBJECTIVE

❶ Describe the purchases, payables and payments process, including typical transactions, source documents, controls and account balances.

Purchases of goods and services are a major cash outflow component in most organizations. For this reason they will be subject to a fairly high level of management planning and control. Purchases of goods may result in the organization acquiring assets, for example, inventory, fixed assets such as property, plant and equipment, or intangibles such as copyrights and customer lists. Some purchases of goods are expensed, such as supplies. Purchases of services are mainly expensed. Costs of purchasing goods and services may be deferred in some cases, if they relate to producing inventory (see Chapter 13) or internally developed assets such as buildings and new products (deferred development costs).

To assess risks in the purchasing-related processes, the auditor mainly considers purchasing and cash payment transaction streams, and accounts payable balances. Important disclosures relating to purchases include asset capitalization policies, inventory cost flow assumption policies, contractual commitments and related party transactions.

The auditor's understanding of the client's business and environment will point to specific business risks and the related financial misstatement risks that can arise from the client's purchasing, payables and payments activities.

Some examples of the risks that may exist at the assertion level are as follows. Risks related to the existence of purchased assets and services include improper capitalization of costs to increase reported profits (e.g., WorldCom). Ownership risks may exist where managers have the ability to transfer funds between related entities under their control (e.g., Enron, Hollinger) or in an owner-managed business some personal expenses of the owner may be run through the company to avoid income taxes. Completeness risks relate mainly to the possibility of unrecorded liabilities, for example, goods or services that were received but not yet paid for at the year-end. Frauds relating to purchases and payables can arise from collusion between suppliers and employees, for example, via kickback schemes; this affects the ownership assertion for those purchases and the control objective of authorization. Valuation risks can exist when purchases are denominated in foreign currency, and if inventory values decline because of market conditions, obsolescence or improper storage. Disclosure risks include inadequate capitalization policy notes or disclosing contractual commitments to make future purchases at fixed prices.

This chapter outlines simple examples of the business process for purchasing services, inventory and fixed assets and the related accounting cycle and control activities. The main risk in this process is incomplete recognition of expenses and liabilities. Control tests in the purchasing processes are used to address existence, completeness and valuation assertions, and some substantive evidence for completeness can be obtained from examining payments subsequent to year-end. Physical inspection of inventory and fixed assets supports the existence, completeness and valuation. Further evidence from inspection of documents and confirmation may be required to assess the ownership assertion.

Purchases, Payables and Payments Process: Typical Activities

Exhibit 12–1 on page 472 shows the activities and transactions involved in the purchases, payables and payments process. The exhibit also lists the accounts and records typically found in this process.

The basic activities are (1) purchasing goods and services and (2) paying the bills. As you follow the exhibit, you can track the elements of the control structure described in the following sections.

Authorization

Purchases are requested (requisitioned) by people who know the needs of the organization. A purchasing department seeks the best prices and quality and issues a purchase order to a selected supplier. Obtaining competitive bids is a good practice because it tends to produce the best prices and involves several legitimate suppliers in the process.

This also can reduce the risk of frauds that involve collusion between suppliers and purchasing department employees, such as inflating purchases to increase sales commissions to the supplier who then kicks back some of these commissions to the purchasing employee.

Cash disbursements are authorized by an accounts payable department matching purchase orders, supplier invoices and internal receiving reports to show a valid obligation to pay. Accounts payable obligations usually are recorded when the purchaser receives the goods or services ordered.

Cheques are signed by a person authorized by the management or the board of directors. A company may have a policy to require two signatures on cheques over a certain amount (e.g., $1,000). Invoices should be marked "paid" or otherwise stamped to show that they have been processed completely so that they cannot be paid a second time.

Custody

A receiving department inspects the goods received for quantity and quality (producing a receiving report), then puts them in the hands of other responsible persons (e.g., inventory warehousing, fixed asset installation). Services are not received in this manner, but they are accepted by responsible persons. Cash custody rests largely in the hands of the person or persons authorized to sign cheques.

Another aspect of custody involves access to blank documents, such as purchase orders, receiving reports and blank cheques or access to a computerized purchase authorization program. If unauthorized persons can perform these functions, they can forge a false purchase order to a fictitious supplier, forge a false receiving report, send a false invoice from a fictitious supplier and prepare a company cheque to the fictitious supplier, thereby accomplishing an embezzlement.

Recording

When the purchase order, supplier's invoice and receiving report are matched, accountants enter the accounts payable, with debits to proper inventory, fixed asset and expense accounts, and with a credit to accounts payable. When cheques are prepared, entries are made to debit the accounts payable and credit cash.

Periodic Reconciliation

A periodic comparison or reconciliation of existing assets to recorded amounts is not shown in Exhibit 12–1, but it occurs in several ways, including physical inventory-taking to compare inventory on hand to perpetual inventory records, bank account reconciliation to compare book cash balances to bank cash balances, inspection of fixed assets to compare to detail fixed asset records, preparation of an accounts payable trial balance to compare the detail of accounts payable to the control account and internal audit confirmation of accounts payable to compare suppliers' reports and monthly statements to recorded liabilities.

TOO MUCH TROUBLE

A trucking company self-insured claims of damage to goods in transit, processed claims vouchers and paid customers from its own bank accounts. Several persons were authorized to sign cheques. One person thought it "too much trouble" to stamp the vouchers PAID and said: "That's textbook stuff anyway." Numerous claims were recycled to other cheque signers, and $80,000 in claims were paid in duplicate before the problem was discovered.

EXHIBIT 12-1 PURCHASES, PAYABLES, AND PAYMENTS PROCESS EXAMPLE

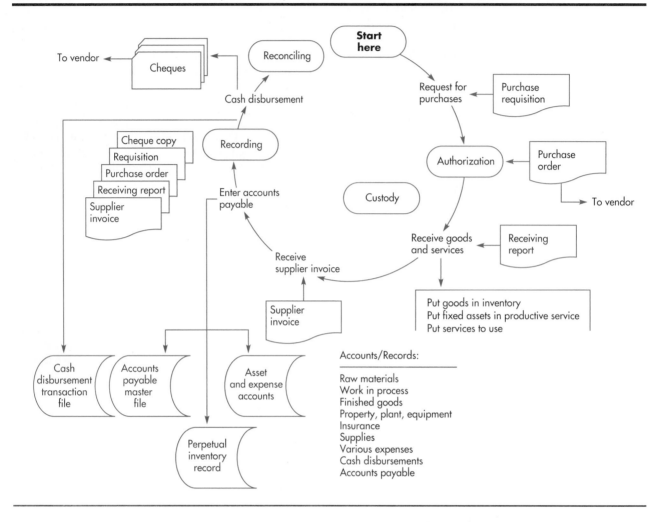

AUDIT EVIDENCE IN MANAGEMENT REPORTS

. . . .

Computer processing of purchasing and payment transactions makes it possible for management to generate reports for control purposes. These reports also can provide important audit evidence.

Exhibit 12–2 shows how various management control reports can be useful as audit evidence. These reports are further discussed following.

Open Purchase Orders

Purchase orders are open from the time they are issued until the goods and services are received. They are held in an open purchase order file. Generally, no liability exists to be recorded until the transactions are complete. However, auditors may find evidence of losses on purchase commitments in this file if market prices have fallen below the purchase price shown in purchase orders.

Unmatched Receiving Reports

Normally, liabilities should be recorded on the date the goods and services are received and accepted by the receiving department or by another responsible person. Sometimes, however, supplier invoices arrive later. In the meantime, the accounts payable department holds the

EXHIBIT 12-2   MANAGEMENT CONTROL REPORTS USEFUL FOR AUDIT EVIDENCE

Management Report	Control Purpose	Potential Audit Evidence
Open purchase orders	Completeness of accounts payable	Purchase commitments, valuation of inventory
Unmatched receiving reports	Validity of purchases recorded	Unaccrued liabilities for purchases
Unmatched supplier invoices	Validity of purchases recorded	Unaccrued liabilities for purchases
Accounts payable trial balance	Proper accounting Cash flow management	Existence and completeness of payables
Purchases journal	Completeness and validity of inventory, purchases, expenses	Analysis of inventory changes and expense reasonability
Inventory reports	Completeness, validity and valuation of inventory	Analysis of inventory balances, valuation, selection of samples for test counts and valuation tests
Fixed asset reports	Completeness, validity and valuation of fixed assets, accumulated depreciation and depreciation expense	Analysis of changes in fixed asset balances Selection of sample additions for vouching Recalculation of depreciation expense
Cash disbursements report	Expenditure reviews by management for validity, authorization	Selection of sample for testing existence, authorization and proper cutoff of payments

receiving reports unmatched with invoices, awaiting enough information to record an accounting entry. Auditors can inspect the unmatched receiving report file report to determine whether the company has material unrecorded liabilities on the financial statement date.

Unmatched Supplier Invoices

Sometimes, supplier invoices arrive in the accounts payable department before the receiving processing is complete. Such invoices are held unmatched with receiving reports, awaiting information that the goods and services were actually received and accepted. Auditors can inspect the unmatched invoice file and compare it to the unmatched receiving report file to determine whether liabilities are unrecorded. Systems failures and human coding errors can cause unmatched invoices and related unmatched receiving reports to sit around unnoticed when all the information for recording a liability is actually at hand.

Accounts Payable Trial Balance

This trial balance is a list of payable amounts by supplier, and the sum should agree with the accounts payable control account in the general ledger. (Some organizations keep records by individual invoices instead of supplier names, so the trial balance is a list of unpaid invoices. The sum still should agree with the control account balance.) The best kind

---

CLASSIFY THE DEBITS CORRECTLY

Invoices for expensive repairs were not clearly identified, so the accounts payable accountants entered the debits that should have been repairs and maintenance expense as capitalized fixed assets. This initially understated expenses and overstated income by $125,000 one year, although the incorrectly capitalized expenses were written off as depreciation in later years.

THINKING AHEAD

Lone Moon Brewing purchased bulk aluminum sheets and manufactured its own cans. To ensure a source of raw materials supply, the company entered into a long-term purchase agreement for 3 million kilos of aluminum sheeting at 80 cents per kilo. At the end of this year, 1.5 million kilos have been purchased and used, but the market price had fallen to 64 cents per kilo. Lone Moon was on the hook for a $240,000 (1.5 million kilos × 16 cents) purchase commitment in excess of current market prices.

of trial balance for audit purposes is one that contains the names of all the suppliers with whom the organization has done business, even if their balances are zero. The audit "search for unrecorded liabilities" should emphasize the small and zero balances, especially for regular suppliers, because these may be the places where liabilities are unrecorded.

All paid and unpaid accounts payable should be accompanied by supporting documents—purchase requisition (if any), purchase order (if any) supplier invoice, receiving report (if any), and cheque copy (or notation of cheque number, date and amount), as shown in Exhibit 12–1. In a computerized accounts payable system, similar records should be available to be extracted for audit verification purposes.

Purchases Journal

A listing of all purchases (the purchases journal) may or may not be printed. It may exist only in a computer transaction file. In either event it provides raw material for (1) computer-audit analysis or purchasing patterns, which may exhibit characteristics of errors and irregularities, and (2) sample selection of transactions for control tests of supporting documents for validity, authorization, accuracy, classification, accounting and proper period recording. (A company may have already performed analyses of purchases, and auditors can use these for analytical evidence, provided the analyses are produced under reliable control conditions.)

Inventory Reports (Trial Balance)

Companies can produce a wide variety of inventory reports useful for analytical evidence. One is an item-by-item trial balance that should agree with a control account (if balances are kept in dollars). Auditors can use such a trial balance (1) to scan for unusual conditions (e.g., negative item balances, overstocking and valuation problems) and (2) as a population for sample selection for a physical inventory observation (audit procedures to obtain evidence about the existence of inventory shown in the account). The scanning and sample selection may be computer-audit applications on a computer-based inventory report file.

Fixed Asset Reports

These reports are similar to inventory reports because they show the details of fixed assets in control accounts. They can be used for scanning and sample selection, much like inventory reports. The information for depreciation calculation (cost, useful life, method, salvage) can be used for the audit of depreciation on a sample basis or by computer applications to recalculate all the depreciation.

Cash Disbursements Report

The cash disbursements process will produce a cash disbursements journal—sometimes printed, sometimes maintained only on a computer file. This journal should contain the date, cheque number, payee, amount, account debited for each cash disbursement and a cross-reference to the voucher number (usually the same as the cheque number). This journal is a population of cash disbursement transactions available for sample selection for control tests of supporting documents for validity, authorization, accuracy, classification, accounting and proper period recording of payments.

THE SIGN OF THE CREDIT BALANCE

Auto Parts & Repair, Inc., kept perpetual inventory records and fixed assets records on a computer system. Because of the size of the files (8,000 parts in various locations and 1,500 asset records), the company never printed reports for visual inspection. Auditors ran a computer-audit "sign test" on inventory balances and fixed asset net book balances. The test called for a printed report for all balances less than zero. The auditors discovered 320 negative inventory balances caused by failure to record purchases and 125 negative net asset balances caused by depreciating assets more than their cost.

R E V I E W
C H E C K P O I N T S

12.1   What is a purchase requisition?

12.2   How can the situation where the same supporting documents are used for a duplicate payment be prevented?

12.3   Where could an auditor look to find evidence of losses on purchase commitments? Unrecorded liabilities to suppliers?

12.4   List the main supporting source documents used in a purchases, payables and payments process.

12.5   List the management reports that can be used for audit evidence. What information in them can be useful to auditors?

CONTROL RISK ASSESSMENT

LEARNING OBJECTIVE

2 Outline control tests for auditing control over purchase of inventory, services, and fixed assets and disbursements of cash.

Control risk assessment is important because it governs the nature, timing and extent of substantive audit procedures that will be applied in the audit of account balances in the purchases, payables and payments process. These account balances include:

- inventory
- fixed assets, intangible assets
- depreciation expense
- accumulated depreciation
- accounts and notes payable
- cash
- various expenses:
  - administrative: supplies, legal fees, audit fees, taxes, insurance
  - selling: commissions, travel, delivery, advertising
  - manufacturing: maintenance, freight in, utilities

General Control Considerations

Control procedures for proper segregation of responsibilities should be in place and operating. By referring to Exhibit 12–1, you can see that proper segregation involves authorization (requisitioning, purchase ordering) by persons who do not have custody, recording or reconciliation duties. Custody of inventory fixed assets and of cash is in persons who do not directly authorize purchases or cash payments, record the accounting entries or reconcile

---

PURCHASE ORDER SPLITTING

The school district authorized its purchasing agent to buy supplies in amounts of $1,000 or less without getting competitive bids for the best price. The purchasing agent wanted to favour local businesses instead of large chain stores, so she broke up the year's $350,000 supplies order into numerous $900–$950 orders, paying about 12 percent more to local stores than would have been paid to the large chains. In return, the purchasing agent received very generous discounts and gifts from these local businesses.

---

physical assets and cash to recorded amounts. Recording (accounting) is performed by persons who do not authorize transactions or have custody of assets or perform reconciliations. Periodic reconciliations should be performed by people who do not have authorization, custody or recording duties related to the same assets. Combinations of two or more of these responsibilities in one person, one office or one computerized system may open the door for errors, irregularities and frauds.

In addition, internal controls should provide for detail control-checking procedures. For example: (1) Purchase requisitions and purchase orders should be approved by authorized personnel. (Computer-produced purchase orders should come from a system whose master file specifications for reordering and supplier identification can only be changed by authorized persons.) (2) Inventory warehouses and fixed asset locations should be under adequate physical security (storerooms, fences, locks and the like). (3) Accountants should be under orders to record accounts payable only when all the supporting documentation is in order; care should be taken to record purchases and payables as of the date goods and services were received, and to record cash disbursements on the date the cheque leaves the control of the organization. (4) Supplier invoices should be compared to purchase orders and receiving reports to determine that the supplier is charging the approved price and that the quantity being billed is the same as the quantity received. The example of the box on the following page shows the consequences of weak management controls in a government department when authorization controls for contract payments are inadequate.

Information about the control structure often is gathered initially by completing an internal control questionnaire. Examples of questionnaires are provided in Appendix 12A. These questionnaires can be studied for details of desirable control policies and procedures. They are organized under headings that identify the important control objectives—environment, validity, completeness, authorization, accuracy, classification, accounting and proper period recording.

Control Tests

An organization should have detail control procedures in place and operating to prevent, detect and correct accounting errors. You studied the general control objectives in Chapter 9 (validity, completeness, authorization, accuracy, classification, accounting and proper period recording). Exhibit 12–3 following puts these in the perspective of a purchasing activity with examples of specific objectives. You should study this exhibit carefully. It expresses the general control objectives in specific examples related to purchasing.

Proper timing is very important in the recording of the purchase transaction. Assurance for this is provided through **purchase cutoff tests** as indicated in objective seven of Exhibit 12–3. In a perpetual inventory system, the inventory records are kept up-to-date continuously. In a periodic system, the inventory level is known only at the time of the count

WHERE TAX DOLLARS GO

The Auditor General of Canada had some harsh words for the federal government in an 83-page report released just days before an expected election call. The report criticized the way the government's departments and services spend money and was particularly critical of the Human Resources department (HRDC), pointing out its sloppy paperwork, careless spending and vague job creation figures.

HRDC was at the centre of a scandal starting in January 2000 when an internal audit found massive mismanagement in its $1-billion jobs grants program. The AG's report confirms that finding and condemns poor accountability between the department and its programs, and within HRDC itself. The audit cites breaches of authority, improper payment practices, and limited monitoring of recipient projects' finances and activities. It also found an inadequate process to decide which projects should get money, including examples of some that were not eligible for funding but received it anyway.

The jobs program administered by the HRDC was designed to create long-term jobs in areas of high unemployment by giving money to companies to hire workers. But HRDC counted some jobs twice, making it impossible to determine how successful a project really was.

Auditor General Sheila Fraser said in a 2002 speech:

"Our audit of HRDC grants and contributions showed what happens when there is no longer a balance between the insistence on performance and controls, and more emphasis is placed on one of these components.

"Management's priorities were to implement strategic initiatives and improve service. We found that it had not placed enough emphasis on maintaining vital control while it reduced red tape and improved service.

"This audit also pointed out the importance of internal audit as a fundamental tool for management. Internal audits at HRDC had previously identified many of the problems, but management took little action in response.

"Our recent investigation of the contracts awarded to Groupaction (in the federal government's advertising and sponsorship program) is another high-profile example of failure to comply with the basic rules of contract management. As a result, it is impossible to say whether taxpayers received value for the money spent."

Here are some of the major findings reported by Auditor General in 2004:

Senior government officials running the federal government's advertising and sponsorship contracts in Quebec, as well as five Crown corporations—the RCMP, Via Rail, Canada Post, the Business Development Bank of Canada and the Old Port of Montreal—wasted money and showed disregard for rules, mishandling millions of dollars since 1995.

More than $100 million was paid to various communications agencies in the form of fees and commissions. In most cases the agencies did little more than hand over the cheques.

The sponsorship program was designed to generate commissions for private companies, while hiding the source of the funding, rather than providing any benefit for Canadians, Fraser said.

"I think this is such a blatant misuse of public funds that it is shocking. I am actually appalled by what we've found."

"I am deeply disturbed that such practices were allowed to happen in the first place. I don't think anybody can take this lightly."

Sources: CBC News, *Auditor General Delivers Stinging Rebuke to Ottawa*, October 22, 2000, www.cbc.ca/stories/2000/10/17/auditor001014 (accessed October 2005); Notes for an address by Sheila Fraser, FCA, Auditor General of Canada, to Canada Mortgage and Housing, June 11, 2002, Ottawa, Ontario, www.oag-bvg.gc.ca/domino/other.nsf/html/02sp06_e.html (accessed October 2005); CBC News, *Auditor General's Report 2004*, October 22, 2000, www.cbc.ca/news/background/auditorgeneral/report2004.html (accessed October 2005).

date of the physical inventory. Even in perpetual systems, however, there should be an annual inventory count to reconcile records with actual inventory. The inventory count procedures are described in more detail later in this chapter. Thus, for both the periodic and perpetual inventory systems, the inventory cutoff test date is the date on which the physical inventory is taken and accounting records adjusted to accurately distinguish between sales and purchases before the cutoff date and those that occurred subsequently.

EXHIBIT 12–3   INTERNAL CONTROL OBJECTIVES (PURCHASES)

General Objectives	Examples of Specific Objectives
1. Recorded purchases are *valid* and documented.	Purchases of inventory (or fixed assets) supported by supplier invoices, receiving reports, purchase orders and requisitions (or approved capital budget).
2. Valid purchase transactions are *recorded* and none omitted.	Requisitions, purchase orders and receiving reports are prenumbered and numerical sequence is checked. Overall comparisons of purchases are made periodically by statistical or product-line analysis.
3. Purchases are *authorized* according to company policy.	All purchase orders are supported by requisitions from proper persons (or approved capital budgets). Purchase made from approved suppliers or only after bids are received and evaluated.
4. Purchase orders are *accurately* prepared.	Completed purchase order quantities and descriptions independently compared to requisitions and suppliers' catalogues.
5. Purchase transactions are properly *classified*.	Purchases from subsidiaries and affiliates classified as intercompany purchases and payables. Purchase returns and allowances properly classified. Purchases for repairs and maintenance segregated from purchases of fixed assets.
6. Purchase transaction *accounting* is complete and proper.	Account distribution for invoices are appropriate and reviewed independent of preparation. Freight-in included as part of purchase and added to inventory (or fixed-assets) costs.
7. Purchase transactions are recorded in the *proper period*.	Perpetual inventory and fixed asset records updated as of date goods are received or title of ownership is transferred.

The cutoff date is a date chosen by the auditor to carry out the cutoff procedures, such as the physical inventory count date. The better the internal controls the easier it is to use a cut-off date further removed from the balance sheet date. A **cutoff error** is a failure to assign a transaction to the proper period. For example, the shipping terms FOB destination and FOB shipping point indicate the date on which legal title to the inventory is transferred to the purchaser—when goods are received, in the case of FOB destination, and when goods leave the seller's premises, in the case of FOB shipping point. The delivery time can thus have a major impact on proper recording of purchases, payables, inventory, sales and receivables. The appropriate accounting depends on the shipping terms and whether the client is the buyer or seller in the transaction. These are major considerations in cutoff procedures-related inventory. Note that, to the extent the client's control system can detect and correct cutoff errors, the auditor is justified in performing fewer cutoff procedures.

Auditors can perform tests to determine whether controls that are said to be in place and operating actually are being performed properly by company personnel. A **control test** consists of (1) identification of the data population from which a sample of items will be selected for audit and (2) an expression of the action that will be taken to produce relevant evidence. In general, the actions involve vouching, tracing, observing, scanning and recalculating. These procedures are part of an audit program for obtaining evidence useful in a final control risk assessment. If personnel in the organization are not performing their control procedures well, auditors need to design substantive audit procedures to try to detect whether control failures have produced materially misleading account balances.

Exhibit 12–4 following contains a selection of tests for controls over purchase, cash disbursement and accounts payable transactions. The samples are usually attribute samples designed along the lines studied in Chapter 10. On the right the exhibit shows the control objectives tested by the audit procedures on the left.

Control Tests for Inventory Records

Many organizations have material investments in inventories. In some engagements auditors need to determine whether they can rely on the accuracy of perpetual inventory records.

EXHIBIT 12–4   CONTROL TESTS FOR PURCHASES, CASH DISBURSEMENTS AND ACCOUNTS PAYABLE

	Control Objective
Consider the control environment	
1. Observe whether purchasing department personnel understand and implement control activities assigned to them.	All control objectives
A. Purchases	
1. Select a sample of receiving reports:	
a. Vouch to related purchase orders, and note missing receiving reports (missing numbers).	Authorization Completeness
b. Trace to inventory record posting of additions.	Completeness
B. Cash Disbursements and Other Expenses:	
1. Select a sample of cash disbursement cheque numbers):	
a. Scan for missing documents (missing numbers).	Completeness
b. Vouch supporting documentation for evidence of accurate mathematics, correct classification, proper approval and proper date of entry.	Accuracy Classification Authorization Proper period
c. Trace disbursement debits to general and subsidiary ledger accounts.	Accounting
2. Select a sample of recorded expenses from various accounts and vouch them to (a) cancelled cheques, and (b) supporting documentation.	Validity Classification
C. Accounts Payable	
1. Select a sample of open accounts payable and vouch to supporting documents of purchase (purchase orders, suppliers' invoices).	Validity
2. Trace debits arising from accounts payable transactions for proper classification.	Classification
3. Select a sample of accounts payable entries recorded after the balance sheet date and vouch to supporting documents for evidence of proper cutoff—evidence that a liability should have been recorded as of the balance sheet date.	Proper period

For example if inventory is to be physically counted at a date other than year end, the controls need to be relied on to verify inventory changes in the "roll-forward" period (the period between the physical count and the year end). Tests of controls over accuracy involve tests of the additions (purchases) to the inventory detail balances and tests of the reductions (issues) of the item balances.

Exhibit 12–5 pictures the dual direction of test audit samples. The samples from the source documents (receiving reports, issue slips) meet the completeness direction require-

EXHIBIT 12–5   DUAL DIRECTION OF TEST AUDIT SAMPLES

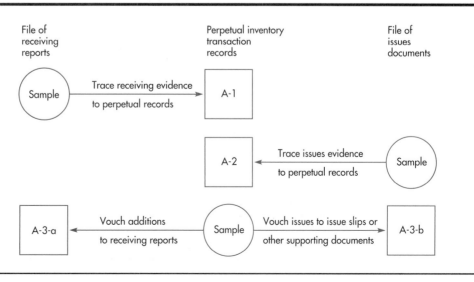

ment to determine whether everything received was recorded as an addition, and whether everything issued was recorded as a reduction of the balance. The sample from the perpetual inventory transaction records meets the validity direction requirement for determining whether everything recorded as an addition or reduction is supported by receiving reports and issue documents. (The symbols A-1, A-2, A-3-a, and A-3-b are cross-references to the procedures in Exhibit 12–6.)

Exhibit 12–6 is similar to Exhibit 12–4 in that it contains a selection of tests for controls over perpetual inventory records. As before, the samples are usually attribute samples designed along the lines studied in Chapter 10. Exhibit 12–6 shows the control objectives tested in the right-side column.

Summary: Control Risk Assessment

The audit manager or senior accountant in charge of the audit should evaluate the evidence obtained from an understanding of the internal controls and from the control tests procedures. If the control risk is assessed very low, the substantive audit procedures on the account balances can be limited in cost-saving ways. For example, the inventory observation test-counts can be performed on a date prior to the year-end, and the sample size can be fairly small. On the other hand, if tests of controls reveal weaknesses, the substantive procedures will need to be designed to lower the risk of failing to detect material error in the account balances. For example, the inventory observation may need to be scheduled on the year-end date with the audit team making a large number of test counts. Descriptions of major deficiencies, control weaknesses and inefficiencies may be incorporated in a management letter to the client.

EXHIBIT   12-6   CONTROL TESTS FOR INVENTORY RECORDS

	Control Objective
Consider the control environment	
1. Observe whether inventory department personnel understand and implement control activities assigned to them.	All control objectives
A. Inventory Receipts and Issues	
1. Select a sample of receiving reports:	
a. Trace to perpetual inventory record entry of receipt.	Authorization Completeness
2. Select a sample of sales invoices, bills of lading or other shipping documents, or produce requisitions:	
a. Trace to perpetual inventory record entry of issue.	Authorization Completeness
3. Select a sample of inventory item perpetual records:	
a. Vouch additions to receiving reports.	Validity
b. Vouch issues to invoices, bills of lading or other shipping documents, or production requisitions.	Validity
B. Cost of Sales	
1. With the sample of issues in A-2 above:	
a. Review the accounting summary of quantities and prices for mathematical accuracy.	Accuracy
b. Trace posting of amounts of general ledger.	Completeness
2. Obtain a sample of cost of goods sold entries in the general ledger and vouch to supporting summaries of finished goods issues.	Validity
3. Review (recalculate) the appropriateness of standard costs, if used, to price inventory issues and cost of goods sold. Review the disposition of variances from standard costs.	Accuracy

. . . .

R E V I E W
CHECKPOINTS

12.6   What are the primary functions that should be segregated in the purchases, payables and payments process?

12.7   What control would be expected to prevent an employee's embezzling cash through creation of fictitious supplier invoices?

12.8   How could an auditor determine whether the purchasing agent had practised purchase order splitting?

12.9   Describe the two general characteristics of a control test.

12.10 How is the information from the shipping department, receiving department and warehouse used to update perpetual inventory records?

12.11 In fixed asset management and accounting, which functional responsibilities should be delegated to separate departments or management levels?

. . . .

CASETTES: SUBSTANTIVE AUDIT PROCEDURES

. . . .

LEARNING OBJECTIVE

3 Design audit and investigative procedures for detecting common errors, irregularities and frauds in the purchases, payables and payments process.

The audit of account balances consists of procedural efforts to detect errors, irregularities and frauds that may exist in the balances, thus making them misleading in financial statements. If such misstatements exist, they are characterized by the following features:

Method: A cause of the misstatement (accidental error, intentional irregularity or fraud attempt), which usually is easier to make because of some kind of failure of controls.

Paper trail: A set of telltale signs of erroneous accounting, missing or altered documents or a dangling debit.

Amount: The dollar amount of overstated assets and revenue, or understated liabilities and expenses.

The casettes discuss an error, irregularity or fraud situation in terms of the method, the paper trail and the amount. The first part gives you the "inside story" that auditors seldom know before they perform the audit work. The next part is an audit approach section, which tells about the audit objective (assertion), controls, test of controls and test of balances (substantive procedures) that could be considered in an approach to the situation. The audit approach section presumes that the auditors do not know everything about the situation. The audit approach contains these parts:

Audit objective: A recognition of a financial statement assertion for which evidence needs to be obtained. The assertions are about existence of assets, liabilities, revenues and expenses; their valuation; their complete inclusion in the account balances; the rights and obligations inherent in them; and their proper presentation and disclosure in the financial statements. (These assertions were introduced in Chapter 6.)

Control: A recognition of the control procedures that should be used by an organization to prevent and detect errors and irregularities.

Test of controls: Ordinary and extended procedures designed to produce evidence about the effectiveness of the controls that should be in operation.

Audit of balance: Ordinary and extended substantive procedures designed to find signs of errors, irregularities and frauds in account balances and classes of transactions.

At the end of the chapter, some similar discussion cases are presented, in which you can write the audit approach to test your ability to design audit procedures for the detection of errors, irregularities and frauds.

CASETTE 12.1
PRINTING (COPYING) MONEY

Problem

Improper expenditures for copy services charged to motion picture production costs.

Method

Argus Productions, Inc., a motion picture and commercial production company, assigned M. Welby the authority and responsibility for obtaining copies of scripts used in production. Established procedures permitted Welby to arrange for outside script copying services, receive the copies and approve the bills for payment. In effect, Welby was the "purchasing department" and the "receiving department" for this particular service. To a certain extent, Welby was also the "accounting department" by virtue of approving bills for payment and coding them for assignment to projects. Welby did not make the actual accounting entries or sign the cheques.

 M. Welby set up a fictitious company under the registered name of Quickprint Company with himself as the incorporator and shareholder, complete with a post office box number, letterhead stationery, and nicely printed invoices but no printing equipment. Legitimate copy services were "subcontracted" by Quickprint with real printing businesses, which billed Quickprint. Welby then wrote Quickprint invoices billing Argus, usually at the legitimate shop's rate, but for a few extra copies each time. Welby also submitted Quickprint bills to Argus for fictitious copying jobs on scripts for movies and commercials that never went into production. As the owner of Quickprint, Welby endorsed Argus's cheques with a rubber stamp and deposited the money in the business bank account, paid the legitimate printing bills, and took the rest for personal use.

Paper Trail

Argus's production cost files contained all the Quickprint bills, sorted under the names of the movie and commercial production projects. Welby even created files for proposed films that never went into full production, and thus should not have had script copying costs. There were no copying service bills from any shop other than Quickprint Company.

Amount

M. Welby conducted this fraud for five years, stealing $475,000 in false and inflated billings. (Argus's net income was overstated a modest amount because copying costs were capitalized as part of production costs, then amortized over a 2–3 year period.)

AUDIT APPROACH

Objective

Obtain evidence of the valid existence (occurrence) and valuation of copying charges capitalized as film production cost.

Control

Management should assign the authority to request copies and the purchasing authority to different responsible employees. The accounting, including coding cost assignments to projects, also should be performed by other persons. Managerial review of production results could result in notice of excess costs.

 The request for the quantity (number) of copies of a script should come from a person involved in production who knows the number needed. This person should sign off for the receipt (or approve the bill) for this requested number of copies, thus acting as the "receiving department." This procedure could prevent waste (excess cost), especially if the requesting person were also held responsible for the profitability of the project.

 Actual purchasing always is performed by a company agent, and in this case, the agent was M. Welby. Purchasing agents generally have latitude to seek the best service at the best price, with or without bids from competitors. Requirements to obtain bids is usually a good idea, but much legitimate purchasing is done with sole-source suppliers without bid.

 Someone in the accounting department should be responsible for coding invoices for charges to author-

ized projects, thus making it possible to detect costs charged to projects not actually in production.

 Someone with managerial responsibility should review project costs and the purchasing practices. However, this is an expensive use of executive time. It was not spent in the Argus case. Too bad.

Test of Controls

In gaining an understanding of the control structure, auditors could learn of the trust and responsibility vested in M. Welby. Since the embezzlement was about $95,000 per year, the total copying cost under Welby's control must have been around $1 million or more. (It might attract unwanted attention to inflate a cost more than 10 percent.)

 Controls were very weak, especially in the combination of duties performed by Welby and in the lack of managerial review. For all practical purposes there were no controls to test, other than to see whether Welby had approved the copying cost invoices and coded them to active projects to test for proper classification, one of the control objectives. This test may have uncovered Welby's payments to Quickprint for copying scripts for movies that never went into production.

 Procedures: Select a sample of movie project files, and vouch costs charged to them to supporting source documents (validity of capitalized costs). Select a sample of payments, and trace them to the project cost records (completeness and proper classification of capitalized costs).

Audit of Balance

Substantive procedures are directed to obtaining evidence about the existence of film projects, completeness of the costs charged to them, valuation of the capitalized project costs, rights in copyright and ownership, and proper disclosure of amortization methods. The most important procedures are the same as the test of controls procedures; thus, when performed at the year-end date on the capitalized cost balances, they are dual-purpose audit procedures.

Either of the procedures previously described as test of controls procedures should show evidence of projects that had never gone into production. (Auditors should be careful to obtain a list of actual projects before they begin the procedures.) Chances are good that the discovery of bad project codes with copying cost will reveal a pattern of Quickprint bills.

Knowing that controls over copying costs are weak, auditors could be tipped off to the possibility of a Welby-Quickprint connection. Efforts to locate Quickprint should be taken (Internet, telephone book, chamber of commerce, other directories). Enquiry with the provincial ministry of Consumer and Commercial Relations for names of the Quickprint

incorporators should reveal Welby's connection. The audit findings can then be turned over to a trained investigator to arrange an interview and confrontation with M. Welby.

Discovery Summary

In this case internal auditors performed a review of project costs at the request of the manager of production, who was worried about profitability. They performed the procedures previously described, noticed the dummy projects and the Quickprint bills, investigated the ownership of Quickprint, and discovered Welby's association. They had first tried to locate Quickprint's shop but could not find it in telephone, chamber of commerce or other city directories. They were careful not to direct any mail to the post office box for fear of alerting the then-unknown parties involved. A sly internal auditor already had used a ruse at the post office and learned that Welby rented the box, but they did not know whether anyone else was involved. Alerted, the internal auditors gathered all the Quickprint bills and determined the total charged for nonexistent projects in the presence of witnesses. Welby was interviewed by Argus managers and readily confessed.

CASETTE 12.2
REAL CASH PAID TO PHONY DOCTORS

Problem

Cash disbursement fraud. Fictitious medical and dental benefit claims were paid by the company, which self-insured up to $50,000 per employee for health and dental costs not covered by the provincial plan. The expense account that included legitimate and false charges was "employee medical benefits."

Method

As manager of the claims payment department, Martha Lee was considered one of Beta Magnetic's best employees. She never missed a day of work in 10 years, and her department had one of the company's best efficiency ratings. Controls were considered good, including the verification by a claims processor that (1) the patient was a Beta employee, (2) medical treatments were covered in the plan, (3) the charges were within approved guidelines and not covered by the provincial plan, (4) the cumulative claims for the employee did not exceed $50,000 (if over $50,000, a claim was submitted to an insurance company), and (5) the calculation for payment was correct. After verification processing, claims were sent to the claims payment department to pay the doctor directly. No payments ever went directly to employees. Martha Lee prepared false claims on real employees, forging the signature of various claims processors, adding her own review approval, naming bogus doctors who would be paid by the payment department. The payments were mailed to various post office box addresses and to her husband's business address.

Nobody ever verified claims information with the employee. The employees received no reports of medical benefits paid on their behalf. While the department had performance reports by claims processors, these reports did not show claim-by-claim details. No one verified the credentials of the doctors.

Paper Trail

The falsified claim forms were in Beta's files, containing all the fictitious data on employee names, processor signatures, doctors' bills and phony doctors and addresses. The cancelled cheques were returned by the bank and were kept in Beta's files, containing "endorsements" by the doctors. Martha Lee and her husband were somewhat clever: They deposited the cheques in various banks in accounts opened in the names and identification of the "doctors."

Martha Lee did not stumble on the paper trail. She drew the attention of an auditor who saw her take her 24 claims-processing employees out to an annual staff appreciation luncheon in a fleet of stretch limousines.

Amount

Over the last seven years, Martha Lee and her husband stole $3.5 million, and until the last, no one noticed anything unusual about the total amount of claims paid.

AUDIT APPROACH

Objective

Obtain evidence to determine whether employee medical benefits "existed" in the sense of being valid claims paid to valid doctors.

Control

The controls are good as far as they go. The claims processors used internal data in their work—employee files for identification, treatment descriptions submitted by doctors and dentists with comparisons to plan provisions and mathematical calculations. This work amounted to all the approval necessary for the claims payment department to prepare a cheque.

There were no controls that connected the claims data with outside sources, such as employee acknowledgment or doctor investigation.

Test of Controls

The processing and control work in the claims processing department can be audited for deviations from controls.

Procedure: Select a sample of paid claims and reperform the claims processing procedures to verify the employee status, coverage of treatment, proper guideline charges, cumulative amount less than $50,000 and accurate calculation. However, this procedure would not help answer the question: "Does Martha Lee steal the money to pay for the limousines?"

"Thinking like a crook" points out the holes in the controls. Nobody tried to verify data with external sources. However, an auditor must be careful in an investigation not to create suspicions about a manager's integrity that may turn out to be untrue, for example by letting rumours start by interviewing employees to find out whether they actually had the medical claim paid on their behalf. If money is being taken, the company cheque must be intercepted in some manner.

Audit of Balance

The balance under audit is the sum of the charges in the employee medical benefits expense account, and the objective relates to the valid existence of the payments.

Procedure: The first procedure can be: Obtain a list of doctors and dentists paid by the company and look them up in the provincial medical and dental association directories. Look up their addresses and determine whether they are valid business addresses. You might try comparing claims processors' signatures on various forms but this is hard to do and requires training. An extended procedure would be: Compare the doctors' addresses to addresses known to be associated with Martha Lee and other claims-processing employees.

Discovery Summary

The comparison of doctors to the association directories showed eight "doctors" who were not licensed in the current period. Five of these eight had post office box addresses, and discreet enquiries and surveillance showed them rented to Martha Lee. The other three had the same mailing address as her husband's business. Further investigation, involving the Crown attorney and police, was necessary to obtain personal financial records and reconstruct the thefts from prior years.

CASETTE 12.3
RECEIVING THE MISSING OIL

Problem

Fuel oil supplies inventory and fuel expense inflated because of short shipments.

Method

Johnson Chemical started a new contract with Madden Oil Distributors to supply fuel oil for the plant generators on a cost-plus contract. Madden delivered the oil weekly in a 20,000-litre-tank truck and pumped it into Johnson's storage tanks. Johnson's receiving employees were supposed to observe the pumping and record the quantity on a receiving report, which was then forwarded to the accounts payable department, where it was held pending arrival of Madden's invoice. The quantities received then were compared to the quantities billed by Madden before the invoice was approved for payment and a cheque prepared for signature by the controller. Since it was a cost-plus contract, Madden's billing price was not checked against any standard price.

The receiving employees were rather easily fooled by Madden's driver. He mixed sludge with the oil; the receiving employees did not take samples to check for quality. He called out the storage tank content falsely (e.g., 4,000 litres on hand when 8,000 were actually in the tank); the receiving employees did not check the gauge themselves; and the tank truck was not weighed at entry and exit to determine the amount delivered. During the winter months, when fuel oil use was high, Madden ran in extra trucks more than once a week, but pumped nothing when the receiving employees were not looking. Quantities "received" and paid during the first year of the contract were (in litres):

Jan.	124,000	May	72,000	Sept.	84,000
Feb.	112,000	June	56,000	Oct.	92,000
Mar.	92,000	July	60,000	Nov.	132,000
Apr.	76,000	Aug.	56,000	Dec.	144,000

Paper Trail

The Johnson receiving reports all agreed with the quantities billed by Madden. Each invoice had a receiving report attached in the Johnson accounts payable files. Even though Madden had many trucks, the same driver always came to the Johnson plant, as evidenced by his signature on the receiving report (along with the Johnson company receiving employees' initials). Madden charged $.45 per litre, making the charges for the 1,100,000 litre a total of $495,000 for the year. Last year, Johnson paid a total of $360,000 for 900,000 litres, but nobody made a complete comparison with last year's quantity and cost.

Amount

During the first year, Madden shorted Johnson on quantity by 160,000 litres (loss = 160,000 × $.45 = $72,000) and charged 5 cents per gallon more than competitors (loss = 940,000 litres × $0.05 = $47,000) for a total overcharge of $119,000, not to mention the inferior sludge mix occasionally delivered.

AUDIT APPROACH

Objective

Obtain evidence to determine whether all fuel oil billed and paid was actually received in the quality expected at a fair price.

Control

Receiving employees should be provided the tools and techniques they need to do a good job. Scales at the plant entrance could be used to weigh the trucks in and out and determine the amount of fuel oil delivered. (The weight per gallon is a well-known measure.) They could observe the quality of the oil by taking samples for simple chemical analysis.

Instructions should be given to teach the receiving employees the importance of their job so they can be conscientious. They should have been instructed and supervised to read the storage tank gauges themselves instead of relying on Madden's driver.

Lacking these tools and instructions, they were easy marks for the wily driver.

Test of Controls

The control procedure supposedly in place was the receiving report on the oil delivered. A procedure to (1) take a sample of Madden's bills, and (2a) compare quantities billed to quantities received, and (2b) compare the price billed to the contract would probably not have shown anything unusual (unless the auditor became suspicious of the same driver always delivering to Johnson).

The information from the "understanding the control structure" phase would need to be much more detailed to alert the auditors to the poor receiving practices.

Procedure: Make enquiries with the receiving employees to learn about their practices and work habits.

Audit of Balance

The balances in question are the fuel oil supply inventory and the fuel expense.

The inventory is easily audited by reading the tank storage gauge for the quantity. The price is found in Madden's invoices. However, a lower-of-cost-or-market test requires knowledge of market prices of the oil. Since Johnson Chemical apparently has no documentation of competing prices, the auditor will need to make a few telephone calls to other oil distributors to get the prices. Presumably, the auditors would learn that the price is approximately $.40 per litre.

The expense balance can be audited like a cost-of-goods-sold number. With knowledge of the beginning fuel inventory, the quantity "purchased," and the quantity in the ending inventory, the fuel oil expense quantity can be calculated. This expense quantity can be priced at Madden's price per gallon.

Analytical procedures applied to the expense should reveal the larger quantities used and the unusual pattern of deliveries, leading to suspicions of Madden and the driver.

Discovery Summary

Knowing the higher expense of the current year and the evidence of a lower market price, the auditors obtained the fuel oil delivery records from the prior year. They are shown following, and the numbers in parentheses are the additional gallons delivered in the current year:

Having found a consistent pattern of greater "use" in the current year, with no operational explanation, the auditors took to the field. With the co-operation of the receiving employees, the auditors read the storage tank measure before the Madden driver arrived. They hid in an adjoining building and watched (and filmed) the driver call out an incorrect reading, pump the oil, sign the receiving report and depart. Then they took samples. These observations were repeated for three weeks. They saw short deliveries, tested inferior products and built a case against Madden and the driver.

Audit of Balance

The balance in question are the fuel oil supply inventory and the fuel expense.

Jan.	112,000 (12,000)	May	52,000 (20,000)	Sept.	60,000 (24,000)
Feb.	96,000 (16,000)	June	44,000 (12,000)	Oct.	80,000 (12,000)
Mar.	80,000 (12,000)	July	40,000 (20,000)	Nov.	112,000 (20,000)
Apr.	68,000 (8,000)	Aug.	36,000 (20,000)	Dec.	120,000 (24,000)

CASETTE 12.4
Go for the Gold

Problem

Fixed assets in the form of mining properties were overstated through a series of "flip" transactions involving related parties.

Method

In 1999 Alta Gold Company was a public "shell" corporation that was purchased for $1,000 by the Blues brothers.

Operating under the corporate names of Diamond King and Pacific Gold, the brothers purchased numerous mining claims in auctions conducted by the Ministry of Natural Resources. They invested a total of $40,000 in 300 claims. Diamond King sold limited partnership interests in its 175 Northwest Territories diamond claims to local investors, raising $20 million to begin mining production. Pacific Gold then traded its 125 British Columbia gold mining claims for all the Diamond King assets and partnership interests, valuing the diamond claims at $20 million. (Diamond King valued the gold claims received at $20 million as the fair value in the exchange.) The brothers then put $3 million obtained from dividends into Alta Gold and, with the aid of a bank loan, purchased half of the Diamond King gold claims for $18 million. The Blues brothers then obtained another bank loan of $38 million to merge the remainder of Diamond King's assets and all of Pacific Gold's mining claims by purchase. They paid off the limited partners. At the end of 1989, Alta Gold had cash of $16 million and mining assets valued at $58 million, with liabilities on bank loans of $53 million.

Paper Trail

Alta Gold had in its files the partnership offering documents, receipts and other papers showing partners' investment of $20 million in the Diamond King limited partnerships. The company also had Pacific Gold and Diamond King contracts for the exchange of mining claims. The $20 million value of the exchange was justified in light of the limited partners' investments.

Appraisals in the files showed one appraiser's report that there was no basis for valuing the exchange of Diamond King claims, other than the price limited partner investors had been willing to pay. The second appraiser reported a probable value of $20 million for the exchange based on proved production elsewhere, but no geological data on the actual claims had been obtained. The $18 million paid by Alta to Diamond King also had similar appraisal reports.

Amount

The transactions occurred over a period of 10 months. The Blues brothers had $37 million cash in Diamond King and Pacific Gold, as well as the $16 million in Alta (all of which was the gullible bank's money, but the bank had loaned to Alta with the mining claims and production as security). The mining claims that had cost $40,000 were now in Alta's balance sheet at $58 million, the $37 million was about to flee, and the bank was about to be left holding the bag containing 300 mining claim papers.

AUDIT APPROACH

Objective

Obtain evidence of the existence, valuation and rights (ownership) in the mining claim assets.

Control

Alta Gold, Pacific Gold and Diamond King had no control structure. All transactions were engineered by the Blues brothers, including the hiring of friendly appraisers. The only control that might have been effective was at the bank in the loan-granting process, but the bank failed.

Test of Controls

An effective control could have been the engagement of competent, independent appraisers. Since the auditors will need to use (or try to use) the appraisers' reports, the procedures involve investigating the reputation, engagement terms and independence of the appraisers. The auditors can use local business references, local financial institutions that keep lists of approved appraisers, membership directories of the professional appraisal associations and interviews with the appraisers themselves.

Audit of Balances

The procedures for auditing the asset values include analyses of each of the transactions through all their complications, including obtaining knowledge of the owners and managers of the several companies and the identities of the limited partner investors. If the Blues brothers have not disclosed their connection with the other companies (and perhaps with the limited partners), the auditors will need to enquire at the Ministry of Consumer and Commercial Relations offices where Pacific Gold and Diamond King are incorporated and try to discover the identities of the players in this flip game. Numerous complicated premerger transactions in small corporations and shells often signal manipulated valuations.

Loan applications and supporting papers should be examined to determine the representations made by Alta in connection with obtaining the bank loans. These papers may reveal some contradictory or exaggerated information.

Ownership of the mining claims might be confirmed with the Resources Ministry auctioneers or be found in the local deed records (spread all over the Northwest Territories and British Columbia).

Discovery Summary

The inexperienced audit staff was unable to unravel the Byzantine exchanges, and they never questioned the relationship of Alta to Diamond King and Pacific Gold. They never discovered the Blues brothers' involvement in the other side of the exchange, purchase and merger transactions. They accepted the appraisers' reports because they had never worked with appraisers before and thought all appraisers were competent and independent. The bank lost $37 million. The Blues brothers changed their names.

CASETTE 12.5
RETREAD TIRES

Problem

Inventory and income overstated by substitution of retread tires valued for inventory at new tire prices.

Method

Ritter Tire Wholesale Company had a high-volume truck and passenger car tire business in Hamilton, Ontario (area population 500,000). J. Lock, the chief accountant, was a longtime trusted employee who had supervisory responsibility over the purchasing agent as well as general accounting duties. Lock had worked several years as a purchasing agent before moving into the accounting job. In the course of normal operations, Lock often prepared purchase orders, but the manufacturers were directed to deliver the tires to a warehouse in Milton (a town of 30,000 population 30 kilometres north of Hamilton). Ritter Tire received the manufacturers' invoices, which Lock approved for payment. Lock and an accomplice (brother-in-law) sold the tires from the Milton warehouse and pocketed the money. At night, Lock moved cheaper retreaded tires into the Ritter warehouse so the space would not seem to be empty. As chief accountant, Lock could override controls (e.g., approving invoices for payment without a receiving report), and T. Ritter (president) never knew the difference because the cheques presented for signature were not accompanied by the supporting documents.

Paper Trail

Ritter Tire's files were well organized. Each cheque copy had supporting documents attached (invoice, receiving report, purchase order), except the misdirected tire purchases had no receiving reports. These purchase orders were all signed by Lock, and the shipping destination on them directed delivery to the Milton address. There were no purchase requisition documents because "requisitions" were in the form of verbal requests from salespersons.

There was no paper evidence of the retreaded tires because Lock simply bought them elsewhere and moved them in at night when nobody else was around.

Amount

Lock carried out the scheme for three years, diverting tires that cost Ritter $2.5 million, which Lock sold for $2.9 million. (Lock's cost of retread tires was approximately $500,000.)

AUDIT APPROACH

Objective

Obtain evidence of the existence and valuation of the inventory. (President Ritter engaged external auditors for the first time in the third year of Lock's scheme after experiencing a severe cash squeeze.)

Control

Competent personnel should perform the purchasing function. Lock and the other purchasing agents were competent and experienced. They prepared purchase orders authorizing the purchase of tires. (The manufacturers required them for shipments.)

A receiving department prepared a receiving report after counting and inspecting each shipment by filling in the "quantity column" on a copy of the purchase order. (A common form of receiving report is a "blind" purchase order that has all the purchase information except the quantity, which is left blank for the receiving department to fill in after an independent inspection and count.) Receiving personnel made notes if the tires showed blemishes or damage.

As chief accountant, Lock received the invoices from the manufacturers and approved them for payment after comparing the quantities with the receiving report and the prices with the purchase order. The cheques for payment were produced automatically on the computerized accounting system when Lock entered the invoice payable in the system. The computer software did not void transactions for lack of a receiving report reference because many other expenses legitimately had no receiving reports.

The key weakness in the control structure was the fact that no one else on the accounting staff had the opportunity to notice missing receiving reports for invoices that should have had them, and Ritter never had the supporting documents when cheques were signed. Lock was a trusted employee.

Test of Controls

Because the control procedures for cross-checking the supporting documents were said to have been placed in operation, the external auditors can test the controls.

Procedure: Select a sample of purchases (manufacturers' invoices payable entered in the microcomputer), and (1) study the related purchase order for (a) valid manufacturer name and address; (b) date; (c) delivery address; (d) unit price, with reference to catalogues or price lists; (e) correct arithmetic; and (f) approval signature. Then (2) compare purchase order information to the manufacturers' invoice; and (3) compare the purchase order and invoice to the receiving report for (a) date, (b) quantity and condition, (c) approval signature, and (d) location.

Audit of Balance

Ritter Tire did not maintain perpetual inventory records, so the inventory was a "periodic system" whereby the financial statement inventory figure was derived from the annual physical inventory count and costing compilation. The basic audit procedure was to observe the count by taking a sample of locations on the warehouse floor, recounting the employees' count, controlling the count sheets, and inspecting the tires for quality and condition (related to proper valuation). The auditors kept their own copy of all the count sheets with their test count notes and notes identifying tires as "new" or "retread." (They took many test counts in the physical inventory sample as a result of the test of controls work, described following.)

Discovery Summary

Forty manufacturers' invoices were selected at random for the test of controls procedure. The auditors were good. They had reviewed the business operations, and Ritter had said nothing about having operations or a warehouse in Milton, although a manufacturer might have been instructed to "drop ship" tires to a customer there. The auditors noticed three missing receiving reports, all of them with purchase orders signed by Lock and requesting delivery to the same Milton address. They asked Lock about the missing receiving reports, and got this response: "It happens sometimes. I'll find them for you tomorrow." When Lock produced the receiving reports, the auditors noticed these were in a current numerical sequence (dated much earlier), filled out with the same pen and signed with an illegible scrawl not matching any of the other receiving reports they had seen.

The auditors knew the difference between new and retread tires when they saw them, and confirmed their observations with employees taking the physical inventory count. When Lock priced the inventory, new tire prices were used, and the auditors knew the difference.

Ritter took the circumstantial evidence to a trained investigator who interviewed the manufacturers and obtained information about the Milton location. The case against Lock led to criminal theft charges and conviction.

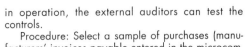

CASETTE 12.6
AMORTIZE "THE DRUM" SLOWLY

Problem

Net asset values (unamortized cost of films) was overstated by taking too little amortization expense.

Method

Candid Production Company was a major producer of theatrical movies. The company usually had 15–20 films in release at theatres across the nation and in foreign countries. Movies also produced revenue from video/DVD licences and product sales (T-shirts, toys and the like).

Movie production costs are capitalized as assets, then amortized to expense as revenue is received from theatre and video/DVD sales and from other sources of revenue. The amortization depends on the total revenue forecast and the current-year revenue amount. As the success or failure of a movie unfolds at the box office, revenue estimates are revised. (The accounting amortization is similar to depletion of a mineral resource, which depends upon estimates of recoverable minerals and current production.)

Candid Production was not too candid. For example, its recent film of *Bang the Drum Slowly* was forecast to produce $50 million total revenue over six years, although the early box office returns showed only $10 million in the first eight months in the theatres. (Revenue will decline rapidly after initial openings, and video/DVD and other revenues depend on the box office success of a film.)

Accounting "control" with respect to film cost amortization resides in the preparation and revision of revenue forecasts. In this case they were overly optimistic, showing the expense recognition and overstating assets and income.

Paper Trail

Revenue forecasts are based on many factors, including facts and assumptions about number of theatres, ticket prices, receipt-sharing agreements, domestic and foreign reviews and moviegoer tastes. Several publications track the box office records of movies. You can see them in newspaper entertainment sections and in industry trade publications. Of course, the production companies themselves are the major source of the information. However, company records also show the revenue realized from each movie.

Revenue forecasts can be checked against actual experience, and the company's history of forecasting accuracy can be determined by comparing actual to forecast over many films and many years.

Amount

Over a four-year period, Candid Productions postponed recognition of a $20 million amortization expense, thus inflating assets and income.

AUDIT APPROACH

Objective

Obtain evidence to determine whether revenue forecasts provide a sufficient basis for calculating film cost amortization and net asset value of films.

Control

Revenue forecasts need to be prepared in a controlled process that documents the facts and underlying assumptions built into the forecast. Forecasts should break down the revenue estimate by years, and the accounting system should produce comparable actual revenue data so that forecast accuracy can be assessed after the fact. Forecast revisions should be prepared in as much detail and documentation as original forecasts.

Test of Controls

The general procedures and methods used by personnel responsible for revenue forecasts should be studied (enquiries and review of documentation), including their sources of information both internal and external. Procedures for review of mechanical aspects (arithmetic) should be tested: Select a sample of finished forecasts and recalculate the final estimate.

Specific procedures for forecast revision also should be studied in the same manner. A review of the accuracy of forecasts of other movies with hindsight on actual revenues helps in a circumstantial way, but past accuracy on different film experiences may not directly influence the forecasts on a new, unique product.

Audit of Balance

The audit of amortization expense concentrates on the content of the forecast itself. The preparation of forecasts used in the amortization calculation should be studied to distinguish underlying reasonable expectations from "hypothetical assumptions." A hypothetical assumption is a statement of a condition that is not necessarily expected to occur, but nonetheless is used to prepare an estimate. For example, a hypothetical assumption is like an "if-then" statement: "If *Bang the Drum Slowly* sells 15 million tickets in the first 12 months of release, then domestic revenue and product sales will be $40 million, and foreign revenue can eventually reach $10 million." Auditors need to assess the reasonableness of the basic 15 million ticket assumption. It helps to have some early actual data from the film's release in hand before the financial statements need to be finished and distributed. For actual data, industry publications ought to be reviewed, with special attention paid to competing films and critics' reviews (yes, movie reviews!).

Discovery Summary

The auditors were not sceptical enough about optimistic revenue forecasts, and they did not weigh unfavourable actual/forecast history comparisons heavily enough. Apparently, they let themselves be convinced by exuberant company executives that the movies were comparable with *Gone with the Wind*! The audit of forecasts and estimates used in accounting determinations is very difficult, especially when company personnel have incentives to hype the numbers, seemingly with conviction about the artistic and commercial merit of their productions. The postponed amortization expense finally came home to roost in big write-offs when the company management changed.

R E V I E W
C H E C K P O I N T S

12.12   Give some examples of receiving departments.

12.13   Casettes 12.1, 12.2 and 12.5 all included fictitious people, businesses and locations. Where can an auditor obtain information that can reveal whether people, businesses and locations are real or not?

12.14   How can analysis be used for discovery of excess costs (see Casette 12.3) and understated expenses (see Casette 12.6)?

12.15   What impact can related party transactions have in some cases of asset valuation?

12.16   How can it help an auditor to know the physical characteristics of inventoried assets?

12.17   Why is professional scepticism important for auditors? Give two case examples.

12.18   What evidence could the verbal enquiry audit procedure produce in Casettes 12.1, 12.3, 12.4 and 12.5?

SPECIAL NOTE: THE COMPLETENESS ASSERTION

. . . .

LEARNING OBJECTIVE

4 Explain the importance of the completion assertion for the audit of accounts payable liabilities and procedures used to search for unrecorded liabilities.

When considering assertions and obtaining evidence about accounts payable and other liabilities, auditors must put emphasis on the completeness assertion. (For asset accounts the emphasis is on the existence and ownership assertions.) This emphasis on completeness is rightly placed because companies typically are less concerned about timely recording of expenses and liabilities than they are about timely recording of revenues and assets. Of course, generally accepted accounting principles require timely accrual of liabilities and their associated expenses.

Evidence is much more difficult to obtain to verify the completeness assertion than the existence assertion. Auditors cannot rely entirely on a management assertion of completeness, even in combination with a favourable assessment of control risk. Substantive procedures, tests of details or analytical procedures ought to be performed. The **search for unrecorded liabilities** is a set of procedures designed to yield audit evidence of liabilities that were not recorded in the reporting period. Such a search should normally be performed up to the audit report date in the period following the client's balance sheet date.

The following is a list of procedures useful in the search for unrecorded liabilities. The audit objective is to search all the places where evidence of them might exist. If these procedures reveal none, the auditors can conclude that all material liabilities were recorded.

1. Scan the open purchase order file at year-end for indications of material purchase commitments at fixed prices. Obtain current prices and determine whether any adjustments for loss and liability for purchase commitments are needed.

2. List the unmatched supplier invoices and determine when the goods were received, looking to the unmatched receiving report file and receiving reports prepared after the year-end. Determine which invoices, if any, should be recorded.

3. Trace the unmatched receiving reports to accounts payable entries, and determine whether ones recorded in the next accounting period need to be adjusted to report them in the current accounting period under audit.

4. Select a sample of cash disbursements from the accounting period following the balance sheet date. Vouch them to supporting documents (invoice, receiving report) to determine whether the related liabilities were recorded in the proper accounting period. Select the sample from the post-year-end cut-off bank statement obtained to audit the cash balance (see Chapter 11).

5. Trace the liabilities reported by financial institutions to the accounts. (See the bank confirmation in Exhibit 11–7, Chapter 11. However, a bank really is not expected to search all its files to report all client liabilities to auditors, so the bank confirmation is not the best source of evidence of unrecorded debts.)

6. Study Canada Revenue Agency notices of assessment for evidence of income or other taxes in dispute, and decide whether actual or estimated liabilities need to be recorded.

7. Confirm accounts payable with suppliers, especially regular suppliers showing small or zero balances in the year-end accounts payable. These are the ones most likely to be understated. (Suppliers' monthly statements controlled by the auditors also may be used for this procedure.) Be sure to verify the suppliers' addresses so that confirmations will not be misdirected—perhaps to conspirators in a scheme to understate liabilities.

8. Study the accounts payable trial balance for indications of dates showing fewer payables than usual recorded near the year-end. (A financial officer may be stashing supplier invoices in a desk drawer instead of recording them.)

9. Review the lawyers' responses to requests for information about pending or threatened litigation, and about unasserted claims and assessments (see Chapter 15). The

lawyers' information may signal the need for contingent liability accruals or disclosures. *CICA Handbook,* paragraph 6560.07 recommends that such an enquiry letter be prepared by the client and sent by the auditor.

10. Use a checklist of accrued expenses to determine whether the company has been conscientious about expense and liability accruals, including accruals for wages, interest, utilities, sales and excise taxes, payroll taxes, income taxes, real property taxes, rent, sales commissions, royalties and warranty and guarantee expense.

11. When auditing the details of sales revenue, pay attention to the terms of sales to determine whether any amounts should be deferred as unearned revenue. (Enquiries directed to management about terms of sales, such as enquiries about customers' rights of cancellation or return, can be used to obtain initial information.)

12. Prepare or obtain a schedule of casualty insurance on fixed assets, and determine the adequacy of insurance in relation to asset market values. Inadequate insurance and self-insurance should be disclosed in the notes to the financial statements.

13. Confirm life insurance policies with insurance companies to ask whether the company has any loans against the cash value of the insurance. In this confirmation, request the names of the beneficiaries of the policies. If the insurance is for the benefit of a party other than the company, the beneficiaries may be creditors on unrecorded loans. Make enquiries about the business purpose of making insurance proceeds payable to other parties.

14. Review the terms of debt due within one year but classified long-term because the company plans to refinance it on a long-term basis. Holders of the debt or financial institutions must have shown (preferably in writing) a willingness to refinance the debt before it can be classified long-term. Classification cannot be based solely on management's expressed intent to seek long-term financing.

15. Apply analytical procedures appropriate in the circumstances. In general, accounts payable volume and period-end balances should increase when the company experiences increases in physical production volume or engages in inventory stockpiling. Some liabilities may be functionally related to other activities, for example, sales taxes are functionally related to sales dollar totals, payroll taxes to payroll totals, excise taxes to sales dollars or volume and income taxes to income.

R E V I E W
C H E C K P O I N T S

12.19   Describe the purpose and give examples of audit procedures in the search for unrecorded liabilities.

12.20   Explain the difference in approach between confirmation of accounts receivable and confirmation of accounts payable.

12.21   In substantive auditing, why is the emphasis on the completeness assertion for liabilities instead of on the existence assertion as in the audit of assets?

Special Note: Physical Inventory Observation

LEARNING OBJECTIVE

5 Identify audit considerations for observing the physical inventory count.

In an audit engagement, the audit procedures for inventory and related cost of sales accounts frequently are extensive. A 96-page joint CICA–AICPA auditing technique study entitled *Audit of Inventories* published by the CICA in 1986 describes many facets of inherent risk and control risk, and of the process of obtaining evidence about inventory financial statement assertions. The significance of inventories is acknowledged in the following quotation:

Generally, inventories reflect the characteristics of a business more than any other asset. Significant to manufacturing, wholesale, and retail organizations, inventories frequently are also material to the financial statements of service organizations. It has been estimated that, for some types of businesses, inventories constitute 20 to 25 percent of total assets and represent the largest current asset.[1]

A material error or irregularity in inventory has a pervasive effect on financial statements. Errors in inventory cause misstatements in current assets, working capital, total assets, cost of sales, gross margin and net income. While analytical procedures can help indicate inventory presentation problems, the auditors' best opportunity to detect inventory errors and irregularities is during the physical observation of the client's inventory count taken by company personnel. (Auditors observe the inventory-taking and make test counts, but they seldom actually count the entire inventory.) Auditing standards express the requirement for inventory observation in paragraph 6030.04: "Usually, the checking of the quantities is accomplished most conveniently by observing and noting the counts made by the client's staff, but actual test counts are often undertaken by the auditors, before, during or after the client's physical stocktaking." ISA 501.5 expresses a similar requirement.

In many audits, obtaining evidence about an inventory's existence and valuation requires specialist knowledge. *CICA Handbook,* paragraph 5049 states that an auditor "should use a specialist when his or her subject matter expertise is insufficient to appropriately understand and assess significant aspects of an assurance engagement." Often auditors will use specialists employed by the client to provide tests and reports for this purpose. A client will likely have employees with expertise required in its business, e.g., assessing the stage of assembly of highly technical equipment, testing the purity of refined minerals, calculating the quantity of raw material in containers or stockpiles based on measures of volume and density, or identifying a chemical or pharmaceutical substance. In other cases, a specialist may be employed directly by the auditor to provide this evidence (this could be an employee of the audit firm or an independent specialist). In considering the need to use a specialist, the auditor first needs to consider whether alternative sources of sufficient appropriate evidence are available and cost-effective. For example, an outside specialist's report prepared for the client for another purpose may be relevant and reliable for the auditor's purposes.

The remainder of this special note gives details about auditors' observation of physical inventory-taking. The first task is to review the client's inventory-taking instructions. The instructions should include the following:

- names of client personnel responsible for the count
- dates and times of inventory taking
- names of client personnel who will participate in the inventory taking
- instructions for recording accurate descriptions of inventory items, for count and double-count, and for measuring or translating physical quantities (such as counting by measures of litres, barrels, meters, dozens)
- instructions for making notes of obsolete or worn items
- instructions for the use of tags, punched cards, count sheets or other media devices and for their collection and control
- plans for shutting down plant operations or for taking inventory after store closing hours, and plans for having goods in proper places (such as on store shelves instead of on the floor, or in a warehouse rather than in transit to a job)
- plans for counting or controlling movement of goods in receiving and shipping areas if those operations are not shut down during the count
- instructions for computer compilation of the count media (such as tags, punch cards) into final inventory listings or summaries
- instructions for pricing the inventory items
- instructions for review and approval of the inventory count; notations of obsolescence or other matters by supervisory personnel

[1] Carty, J., "Ask the Right Questions about Inventory," *World Accounting Report,* January 1984, p. 20.

These instructions characterize a well-planned counting operation. As the plan is carried out, the independent auditors should be present to hear the count instructions being given to the client's count teams and to observe the instructions being followed.

Many physical inventories are counted at the year-end when the auditor is present to observe. The auditors can perform dual-direction testing by (1) selecting inventory items from a perpetual inventory master file, going to the location and obtaining a test count, which produces evidence for the existence assertion; and (2) selecting inventory from locations on the warehouse floor, obtaining a test count and tracing the count to the final inventory compilation, which produces evidence for the completeness assertion. If the company does not have perpetual records and a file to test for existence, the auditors must be careful to obtain a record of all the counts and use it for the existence-direction tests.

However, the following other situations frequently occur.

Physical Inventory Not on Year-End Date

Clients sometimes count the inventory on a date other than the balance sheet date, either before or after. When the auditors are present to make their physical observation, they follow the procedures outlined above for observation of the physical count. However, with a period intervening between the count date and the year-end, additional roll forward or rollback auditing procedures must be performed on purchase, inventory addition and issue transactions during that period. The inventory on the count date is reconciled to the year-end inventory by appropriate addition or subtraction of the intervening receiving and issue transactions.

Cyclical Inventory Counting

Some companies count inventory on a cyclical basis or use a statistical counting plan but never take a complete count on a single date. In these circumstances the auditors must understand management's counting plan and evaluate its appropriateness. In this type of situation the auditors should attend and perform tests whenever the value of inventory to be counted is material. Businesses that count inventory in this manner purport to have accurate perpetual records and carry out the counting as a means of testing the records and maintaining their accuracy.

The auditors must be present during some counting operations to evaluate the counting plans and their execution. The procedures for an annual count enumerated previously are utilized, test counts are made and the audit team is responsible for a conclusion concerning the accuracy (control) of perpetual records.

Auditors Not Present at Client's Inventory Count

This situation can arise on a first audit when the audit firm is appointed after the beginning inventory already has been counted. The auditors must review the client's plan for the already completed count as before. Some test counts of current inventory should be made and traced to current records to make a conclusion about the reliability of perpetual records. If the actual count was recent, intervening transaction activity may be reconciled back to the beginning inventory.

However, the reconciliation of more than a few months' transactions to unobserved beginning inventories may be very difficult. The auditors may employ procedures utilizing such interrelationships as sales activity, physical volume, price variation, standard costs and gross profit margins for the decision about beginning inventory reasonableness. Nevertheless, much care must be exercised in "backing into" the audit of a previous inventory. If the auditors cannot satisfy themselves as to the beginning inventory balance, then a reservation in the auditor's report is normally called for.[2]

Inventories Located Off the Client's Premises

The auditors must determine where and in what dollar amounts inventories are located off the client's premises, in the custody of consignees or in public warehouses. If amounts are

---

[2] *CICA Handbook*, paragraph 6030.11.

material and if control is not exceptionally strong, the audit team may wish to visit these locations and conduct on-site test counts. However, if amounts are not material and/or if related evidence is adequate (such as periodic reports, cash receipts, receivables records, shipping records) and if control risk is low, then direct confirmation with the custodian may be considered sufficient appropriate evidence of the existence of quantities.[3]

INVENTORY COUNT AND MEASUREMENT CHALLENGES

Examples	Challenges
Lumber.	Problem identifying quality or grade.
Piles of sugar, coal, scrap steel.	Geometric computations, aerial photos.
Items weighed on scales.	Check scales for accuracy.
Bulk materials (oil, grain, liquids in storage tanks).	Climb the tanks. Dip measuring rods. Sample for assay or chemical analysis.
Diamonds, jewellery.	Identification and quality determination problems. Ask a specialist.
Pulp wood.	Quantity measurement estimation. Aerial photos.
Livestock.	Movement not controllable. Count critter's legs and divide by four (two for chickens).

Source: Adapted from CICA, Audit of Inventories, *Auditing Procedure Study* (1986), p. 28.

Inventory Existence and Completeness

The physical observation procedures are designed to audit for existence and completeness (physical quantities) and valuation (recalculation of appropriate FIFO, specific item or other pricing at cost and lower-of-cost-or-market write-down of obsolete or worn inventory). After the observation is complete, auditors should have sufficient appropriate evidence of the following physical quantities and valuations:

- Goods in the perpetual records but not owned were excluded from the inventory compilation.
- Goods on hand were counted and included in the inventory compilation.
- Goods consigned-out or stored in outside warehouses (goods owned but not on hand) were included in the inventory compilation.
- Goods in transit (goods actually purchased and recorded but not yet received) were added to the inventory count and included in the inventory compilation.
- Goods on hand already sold (but not yet delivered) were not counted and were excluded from the inventory compilation.
- Goods consigned-in (goods on hand but not owned) were excluded from the inventory compilation.

REVIEW CHECKPOINTS

12.22 In the review of a client's inventory-taking instructions, what characteristics are the auditors looking for?

12.23 Explain dual-direction sampling in the context of inventory test counts.

12.24 What procedures are employed to audit inventory when the physical inventory is taken on a cyclical basis or on a statistical plan, but never a complete count on a single date?

[3] *Ibid.*, paragraph 6030.07.

Analysis of Financial Statement Relationships

The audit of the purchases, payables and payments processes results in verifying the balance of accounts payables/accrued liabilities and the two transaction streams that run through it—purchases/expenses and cash payments. In the balance sheet approach to auditing, we can analyze balance changes and the financial statement items related to them by preparing a continuity schedule. The accrued legal fees balance is shown following as an example for the purchases, payables and payments process:

Audited Amount	Financial Statement Where Amount Is Reported
Opening balance of accrued liability for legal fees	Balance sheet (component of accrued liabilities in prior year comparative figures)
Add: New legal services expensed during the year*	Income statement expense (e.g., legal services acquired)
Deduct: Cash paid against payables	Cash flow statement (direct method)
Ending balance of accounts payable	Balance sheet (component of accrued liabilities in current year figures)

*Note: The relationship between inventory purchases and balance sheet amounts will be analyzed in Chapter 13.

As these relationships illustrate, our procedures to audit the purchases, payables and payments process allow us to assess whether all components of this system of related amounts are reported accurately in the financial statements. These relationships also indicate analytical procedures that can detect material misstatements. For example, the ratios that measure inventory turnover or expense-to-revenue ratios exploit these relationships and can indicate nonexistent inventory or misstatement in expense accounts and liability.

SUMMARY

The purchases, payables and payments process consists of purchase requisitioning, purchase ordering, receiving goods and services, recording suppliers' invoices and accounting for accounts payable and making disbursements of cash. Companies reduce control risk by having a suitable separation of authorization, custody, recording and periodic reconciliation duties. Error-checking procedures of comparing purchase orders and receiving reports to supplier invoices are important for recording proper amounts of accounts payable liabilities. Supervisory control is provided by having a separation of duties between preparing cash disbursement cheques and actually signing them. Otherwise, many things could go wrong, ranging from processing false or fictitious purchase orders to failing to record liabilities for goods and services received.

Cash disbursement is a critical point for asset control. Many cases of embezzlement occur in this process. Illustrative cases in the chapter told of some embezzlement schemes, mostly involving payment of fictitious charges to dummy companies set up by employees.

Two topics had special technical notes in the chapter. The completeness assertion is very important in the audit of liabilities because misleading financial statements often have contained unrecorded liabilities and expenses. The search for unrecorded liabilities is an important set of audit procedures. The physical inventory observation audit work received a special section because actual contact with inventories (and fixed assets, for that matter) provides auditors with direct eyewitness evidence of important tangible assets.

MULTIPLE-CHOICE QUESTIONS FOR PRACTICE AND REVIEW

12.25 When verifying debits to the perpetual inventory records of a nonmanufacturing company, an auditor would be most interested in examining a sample of purchase:

a. Approvals.

b. Requisitions.

c. Invoices.

d. Orders.

12.26 Which of the following is an internal control weakness for a company whose inventory of supplies consists of a large number of individual items?

a. Supplies of relatively little value are expensed when purchased.

b. The cycle basis is used for physical counts.

c. The warehouse manager is responsible for maintenance of perpetual inventory records.

d. Perpetual inventory records are maintained only for items of significant value.

12.27 An effective internal control procedure that protects against the preparation of improper or inaccurate cash disbursements would be to require that all cheques be:

a. Signed by an officer after necessary supporting evidence has been examined.

b. Reviewed by a senior officer before mailing.

c. Sequentially numbered and accounted for by internal auditors.

d. Perforated or otherwise effectively cancelled when they are returned with the bank statement.

12.28 A client's purchasing system ends with the recording of a liability and its eventual payment. Which of the following best describes the auditor's primary concern with respect to liabilities resulting from the purchasing system?

a. Accounts payable are not materially understated.

b. Authority to incur liabilities is restricted to one designated person.

c. Acquisition of materials is not made from one supplier or one group of suppliers.

d. Commitments for all purchases are made only after established competitive bidding procedures are followed.

12.29 Which of the following is an internal control procedure that would prevent a paid supplier invoice from being presented for payment a second time?

a. Invoices should be prepared by individuals who are responsible for signing disbursement cheques.

b. Disbursement cheques should be approved by a least two responsible management officials.

c. The date on a supplier invoice should be within a few days of the date it is presented for payment.

d. The official signing of the cheque should compare the cheque with the supplier invoice details and should stamp "paid" on the invoice.

12.30 Which of the following procedures would best detect the theft of valuable items from an inventory that consists of hundreds of different items selling for $1 to $10 and a few items selling for hundreds of dollars?

a. Maintain a perpetual inventory of only the more valuable items with frequent periodic verification of the validity of the perpetual inventory record.

b. Have an independent PA firm prepare an internal control report on the effectiveness of the administrative and accounting controls over inventory.

c. Have separate warehouse space for the more valuable items with frequent periodic physical counts and comparison to perpetual inventory records.

12.31 Budd, the purchasing agent of Lake Hardware Wholesalers, has a relative who owns a retail hardware store. Budd arranged for hardware to be delivered by manufacturers to the retail store on a COD basis, thereby enabling his relative to buy at Lake's wholesale prices. Budd was probably able to accomplish this because of Lake's poor internal control over:

a. Disbursement cheques.

b. Cash receipts.

c. Perpetual inventory records.

d. Purchase orders.

12.32 Which of the following is the best audit procedure for determining the existence of unrecorded liabilities?

a. Examine confirmation requests by creditors whose accounts appear on a subsidiary trial balance of accounts payable.

b. Examine a sample of cash disbursements in the period subsequent to the year-end.

c. Examine a sample of invoices a few days prior to and subsequent to the year-end to ascertain whether they have been properly recorded.

d. Examine unusual relationships between monthly accounts payable and recorded purchases.

12.33 When evaluating inventory controls with respect to segregation of duties, a PA would be least likely to:

a. Inspect documents.

b. Make enquiries.

c. Observe procedures.

d. Consider policy and procedure manuals.

12.34 An auditor will usually trace the details of the test counts made during the observation of the physical inventory taking to a final inventory compilation. This audit procedure is undertaken to provide evidence that items physically present and observed by the auditor at the time of the physical inventory count are:

a. Owned by the client.

b. Not obsolete.

c. Physically present at the time of the preparation of the final inventory schedule.

d. Included in the final inventory schedule.

12.35 Which of the following procedures is least likely to be performed before the balance sheet date?
  a. Observation of inventory.
  b. Review of internal control over cash disbursements.
  c. Search for unrecorded liabilities.
  d. Confirmation of receivables.

12.36 The physical count of inventory of a retailer was higher than shown by the perpetual records. Which of the following could explain the difference?
  a. Inventory items had been counted but the tags placed on the items had not been taken off the items and added to the inventory accumulation sheets.
  b. Credit memos for several items returned by customers had not been recorded.
  c. No journal entry had been made on the retailer's books for several items returned to its suppliers.
  d. An item purchased "FOB shipping point" had not arrived at the date of the inventory count and was not reflected in the perpetual records.

12.37 From the auditor's point of view, inventory counts are more acceptable prior to the year-end when:
  a. Internal control is weak.
  b. Accurate perpetual inventory records are maintained.

  c. Inventory is slow moving.
  d. Significant amounts of inventory are held on a consignment basis.

12.38 To determine whether accounts payable are complete, an auditor performs a test to verify that all merchandise received is recorded. The population for this test consists of all:
  a. Suppliers' invoices.
  b. Purchase orders.
  c. Receiving reports.
  d. Cancelled cheques.

12.39 Which of the following internal control procedures most likely addresses the completeness assertion for inventory?
  a. The work in process account is periodically reconciled with subsidiary inventory records.
  b. Employees responsible for the custody of finished goods do not perform the receiving function.
  c. Receiving reports are prenumbered and the numbering sequence is checked periodically.
  d. There is a separation of duties between the payroll department and inventory accounting personnel.

(AICPA adapted)

Exercises and Problems

12.40 Liabilities: Authorization Control. The essential characteristic of the liabilities control system is to separate the authorization and approval to initiate a transaction from the responsibility for recordkeeping. What would constitute the authorization for accounts payable recording? What documentary evidence could auditors examine as evidence of this authorization?
LO.1
LO.2

12.41 Cash Disbursements: Completeness Control. The use of prenumbered documents is an important feature for control to ensure that all valid transactions are recorded and none are omitted. How could auditors gather evidence that the control for completeness of cash disbursements was being used properly by a company?
LO.1
LO.2

12.42 Automated Transactions: Authorization Control. Two "automatic transactions" can be produced in a computerized accounting system: (1) cheque printing and signature and (2) purchase order at a preprogrammed stock reorder point. Assume management is uncomfortable with the computer creating transactions. How could management delay these transactions until they were "viewed" and authorized?
LO.1
LO.2

12.43 Liabilities: Insurance Coverage. Why should auditors be concerned with the adequacy of casualty insurance coverage of a client's physical property?
LO.1

12.44 Inventory: Enquiry-based Evidence. What evidence regarding inventories and cost of sales can the auditor typically obtain from enquiry?
LO.3

12.45 Specific Assertions: Fixed Assets. Auditors plan their audit procedures to gather evidence about management's assertions in the financial statements. In addition to the broad assertions, such as existence and completeness, specific assertions are made for each major account area. List 9 or 10 examples of such specific assertions for the fixed assets and related accounts.
LO.3

12.46 Repair and Maintenance Auditing. Why should the Repairs and Maintenance expense account be audited at the same time as the fixed asset accounts?
LO.3

12.47 Fixed Assets: Audit Procedures. Audit procedures may be classified as:
LO.3
  Inspection of physical assets,
  Computation,
  Confirmation,
  Inspection of documents (vouching and tracing),
  Enquiry,
  Scanning,
  Analysis.

Required:
Describe how each procedure may be used to gather evidence on fixed assets and which broad financial statement assertion(s) (existence, completeness, ownership (rights), valuation (allocation), and presentation and disclosure) is being addressed by the use of the procedure.

CONTROL TESTS

12.48 Payable Internal Control Questionnaire Items: Con-
LO.1 **trol Objectives, Test of Controls Procedures and**
LO.2 **Possible Errors or Irregularities.** Listed below is a selection of items from the internal control questionnaire
on payables shown in Appendix 12A.

1. Are invoices, receiving reports and purchase orders
   reviewed by the cheque signer?
2. Are cheques dated in the cheque register with the
   date of the cheque?
3. Are quantity and quality of goods received determined at time of receipt by receiving personnel independent of the purchasing department?
4. Are suppliers' invoices matched against purchase
   orders and receiving reports before a liability is
   recorded?

Required:

For each one:

a. Identify the control objective to which it applies.
b. Specify one test of controls audit procedure an auditor could use to determine whether the control was
   operating effectively.
c. Using your business experience, your logic or your
   imagination, or all three, give an example of an error
   or irregularity that could occur if the control was
   absent or ineffective.

12.49 Purchasing Control Procedures. Long, PA, has been
LO.1 engaged to examine and report on the financial state-
LO.2 ments of Maylou Corporation. During the review phase
of the study of Maylou's system of internal control over
purchases, Long was given the following document
flowchart for purchases (see Exhibit 12.55–1).

Required:

Identify the procedures relating to purchase requisitions
and purchase orders that Long would expect to find if
Maylou's system of internal control over purchases is
effective. For example, purchase orders are prepared
only after giving proper consideration to the time to order and quantity to order. Do not comment on the effectiveness of the flow of documents as presented in the
flowchart or on separation of duties.

(AICPA adapted)

12.50 Control Tests for Cash Disbursements. The Runge
LO.1 Controls Corporation manufactures and markets electri-
LO.2 cal control systems: temperature controls, machine controls, burglar alarms and the like. Electrical and semi-
conductor parts are acquired from outside vendors, and
systems are assembled in Runge's plant. The company
incurs other administrative and operating expenditures.
Liabilities for goods and services purchased are entered
in a vouchers payable journal, at which time the debits
are classified to the asset and expense accounts to which
they apply. The company has specified control procedures for approving vendor invoices for payment, for
signing cheques, for keeping records and for reconciling
the chequing accounts. The procedures appear to be
well specified and placed in operation. You are the senior auditor on the engagement, and you need to specify
a program (list) of control tests to audit the effectiveness
of the controls over cash disbursements.

Required:

Using the seven general internal control objectives, specify two or more control tests to audit the effectiveness of
typical control procedures. (Hint: From one sample of
recorded cash disbursements, you can specify control
tests related to several objectives. See Exhibit 12–3 for
examples of control test procedures over cash disbursements.) Organize your list according to the example
shown below for the "completeness" objective.

Completeness Objective	Test of Controls Program
All valid cash disbursements are recorded and none are omitted.	Determine the numerical sequence of cheques issued during the period and scan the sequence for missing numbers. (Scan the accounts payable records for amounts that appear to be too long outstanding indicating liabilities for which payment may have been made but not recorded properly.)

(AICPA adapted)

EXHIBIT   12.49–1   MAYLOU CORPORATION—DOCUMENT FLOWCHART FOR PURCHASES

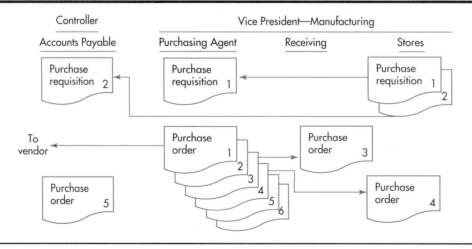

LIABILITIES: SUBSTANTIVE PROCEDURES

12.51 Unrecorded Liabilities Procedures. You were in the
L0.3 final stages of your audit of the financial statements of
L0.4 Ozine Corporation for the year ended December 31,
20X2, when you were consulted by the corporation's
president. The president believes there is no point to
your examining the 20X3 accounts payable records and
testing data in support of 20X3 entries. He stated: (1)
bills pertaining to 20X2 that were received too late to be
included in the December accounts payable were
recorded as of the year-end by the corporation by journal entry; (2) the internal auditor made tests after the
year-end; and (3) he would furnish you with a letter
certifying that there were no unrecorded liabilities.

Required:

a. Should your procedures for unrecorded liabilities be
   affected by the fact that the client made a journal
   entry to record 20X2 bills that were received later?
   Explain.
b. Should your test for unrecorded liabilities be
   affected by the fact that a letter is obtained in which
   a responsible management official certifies that to
   the best of his knowledge all liabilities have been
   recorded? Explain.
c. Should your test for unrecorded liabilities be eliminated or reduced because of the internal audit work?
   Explain.
d. What sources, in addition to the 20X3 voucher register, should you consider to locate possible
   unrecorded liabilities?

(AICPA adapted)

12.52 Accounts Payable Confirmations. Clark and his part-
L0.3 ner, Kent, both PAs, are planning their audit program for
the audit of accounts payable on the LeClair Corporation's annual audit. Saturday afternoon they reviewed
the thick file of last year's working papers, and both of
them remembered all too well the six days they spent
last year on accounts payable.

Last year, Clark had suggested that they mail confirmations to 100 of LeClair's suppliers. The company
regularly purchases from about 1,000 suppliers and
these account payable balances fluctuate widely, depending on the volume of purchase and the terms
LeClair's purchasing agent is able to negotiate. Clark's
sample of 100 was designed to include accounts with
large balances. In fact, the 100 accounts confirmed last
year covered 80 percent of the total accounts payable.

Both Clark and Kent spent many hours tracking
down minor differences reported in confirmation responses. Nonresponding accounts were investigated by
comparing LeClair's balance with monthly statements
received from suppliers.

Required:

a. Identify the accounts payable audit objectives that
   the auditors must consider in determining the audit
   procedures to be performed.

b. Identify situations when the auditors should use
   accounts payable confirmations, and discuss whether
   they are required to use them.
c. Discuss why the use of large dollar balances as the
   basis for selecting accounts payable for confirmation
   may not be the most efficient approach, and indicate
   a more efficient sample selection procedure that
   could be followed when choosing accounts payable
   for confirmation.

*INVENTORY AND FIXED ASSETS: SUBSTANTIVE
PROCEDURES*

**12.53 Inventory Count Observation: Planning and Sub-
L0.3 stantive Audit Procedures.** Cindy Li is the partner in
L0.4 charge of the audit of Blue Distributing Corporation, a
wholesaler that owns one warehouse containing 80 percent of its inventory. Cindy is reviewing the working papers that were prepared to support the firm's opinion on
Blue's financial statements. Cindy wants to be certain
essential audit procedures are well documented in the
working papers.

Required:

a. What evidence should Cindy expect to find that the
   audit observation of the client's physical count of
   inventory was well planned and that assistants were
   properly supervised?
b. What substantive audit procedures should Cindy find
   in the working papers that document management's
   assertions about existence and completeness of
   inventory quantities at the end of the year? (Refer to
   Appendix 12B for procedures.)

(AICPA adapted)

12.54 Sales/Inventory Cutoff. Your client took a complete
L0.3 physical inventory count under your observation as of
L0.5 December 15 and adjusted the inventory control account
(perpetual inventory method) to agree with the physical
inventory. Based on the count adjustments as of December 15 and after review of the transactions recorded
from December 16 to December 31, you are almost
ready to accept the inventory balance as fairly stated.

However, your review of the sales cutoff as of December 15 and December 31 disclosed the following
items not previously considered:

Cost	Sales Price	Shipped	Date Billed	Credited to Inventory Control
$28,400	$36,900	12/14	12/16	12/16
39,100	50,200	12/10	12/19	12/10
18,900	21,300	1/2	12/31	12/31

Required:

What adjusting journal entries, if any, would you make
for each of these items? Explain why each adjustment is
necessary.

(AICPA adapted)

12.55 Statistical Sampling Used to Estimate Inventory.

LO.3 ACE Corporation does not conduct a complete annual
LO.5 physical count of purchased parts and supplies in its principal warehouse but, instead, uses statistical sampling to estimate the year-end inventory. Ace maintains a perpetual inventory record of parts and supplies. Management believes that statistical sampling is highly effective in determining inventory values and is sufficiently reliable that a physical count of each item of inventory is unnecessary.

Required:

a. List at least 10 normal audit procedures that should be performed to verify physical quantities whenever a client conducts a periodic physical count of all or part of its inventory (see Appendix 12B for procedures).

b. Identify the audit procedures you should use that change or are in addition to normal required audit procedures (in addition to those listed in your solution to part [a]) when a client utilizes statistical sampling to determine inventory value and does not conduct a 100 percent annual physical count of inventory items.

(AICPA adapted)

12.56 Inventory Procedures Using Generalized Audit Soft-

LO.3 **ware.** You are conducting an audit of the financial state-
LO.5 ments of a wholesale cosmetics distributor with an inventory consisting of thousands of individual items. The distributor keeps its inventory in its own distribution centre and in two public warehouses. A perpetual inventory computer database is maintained on a computer disk. The database is updated at the end of each business day. Each individual record of the perpetual inventory database contains the following data:

    item number
    location of item
    description of item
    quantity on hand
    cost per item
    date of last purchase
    date of last sale
    quantity sold during year

You are planning to observe the distributor's physical count of inventories as of a given date. You will have available a computer tape, provided by the client, of the above items taken from their database as of the date of the physical count. Your firm has a generalized audit software package that will run on the client's computer.

Required:

List the basic inventory auditing procedures and, for each, describe how the use of the general-purpose audit software package and the perpetual inventory database might be helpful to the auditor in performing such au-

diting procedures. (See Appendix 12B for substantive audit procedures for inventory.)

Organize your answer as follows:

Organize your answer as follows:

Basic inventory auditing procedures	How general purpose audit software package and tape of the inventory tape file data might be helpful

(AICPA adapted)

12.57 Manufacturing Equipment and Accumulated

LO.3 **Depreciation.** In connection with a recurring examination of the financial statements of the Louis Manufacturing Company for the year ended December 31, you have been assigned the audit of the fixed assets accounts (Manufacturing Equipment, Manufacturing Equipment—Accumulated Depreciation, and Repairs to Manufacturing Equipment). Your review of Louis's policies and procedures has disclosed the following pertinent information:

1. The Manufacturing Equipment account includes the net invoice price plus related freight and installation costs for all of the equipment in Louis's manufacturing plant.

2. The Manufacturing Equipment—Accumulated Depreciation accounts are supported by a subsidiary ledger, which shows the cost and accumulated depreciation for each piece of equipment.

3. An annual budget for capital expenditures of $1,000 or more is prepared by the executive committee and approved by the board of directors. Capital expenditures over $1,000 that are not included in this budget must be approved by the board of directors, and variations of 20 percent or more must be explained to the board. Approval by the supervisor of production is required for capital expenditures under $1,000.

4. Company employees handle installation, removal, repair and rebuilding of the machinery. Work orders are prepared for these activities and are subject to the same budgetary control as other expenditures. Work orders are not required for external expenditures.

Required:

a. Prepare a list of the major specific objectives (assertions) for your audit of the Manufacturing Equipment, Manufacturing Equipment—Accumulated Depreciation, and Repairs of Manufacturing Equipment accounts. Do not include in this listing the auditing procedures designed to accomplish these objectives.

b. Prepare the portion of your audit program applicable to the review of current-year additions to the Manufacturing Equipment account. (You will find Appendix 12B helpful, although it does not specifically mention manufacturing equipment.)

(AICPA adapted)

DISCUSSION CASES

· ·

12.58 Peacock Company: Incomplete Flowchart of Inventory and Purchasing Control Procedures. Peacock Company is a wholesaler of soft goods. The inventory is composed of approximately 3,500 different items. The company employs a computerized batch processing system to maintain its perpetual inventory records. The system is run each weekend so that inventory reports are available on Monday morning for management use. The system has been functioning satisfactorily for the past 10 years, providing the company with accurate records and timely reports.

The preparation of purchase orders has been automatic as a part of the inventory system to ensure that the company will maintain enough inventory to meet customer demand. When an item of inventory falls below a predetermined level, a record of the inventory items is written. This record is used in conjunction with the vendor file to prepare the purchase orders.

Exception reports are prepared during the update of the inventory and the preparation of the purchase orders. These reports list any errors or exceptions identified during the processing. In addition, the system provides for management approval of all purchase orders exceeding a specified amount. Any exceptions or items requiring management approval are handled by supplemental runs on Monday morning and are combined with the weekend results.

A system flowchart of Peacock Company's inventory and purchase order procedure is in Exhibit 12.58–1.

Required:

a. The illustrated system flowchart (Exhibit 12.58–1) of Peacock Company's inventory and purchase order

EXHIBIT 12.58–1   PEACOCK COMPANY—INVENTORY AND PURCHASE ORDER PROCEDURE

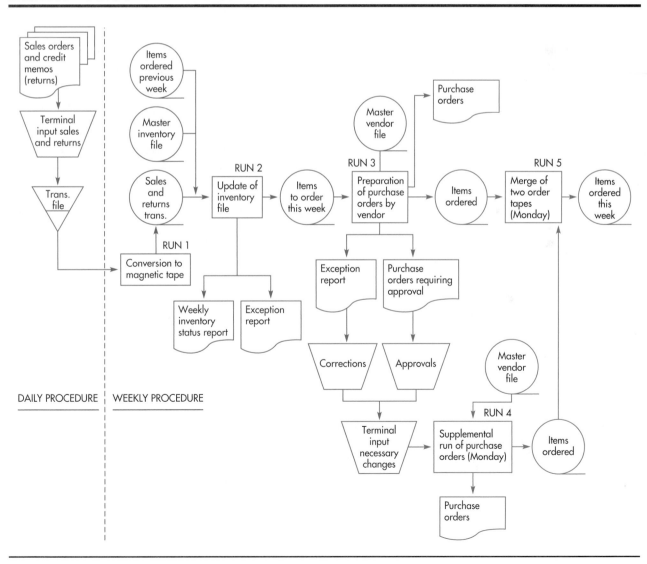

system was prepared but several steps that are important to the successful operations of the system are omitted from the chart. Describe the steps that have been omitted and indicate where the omissions have occurred. The flowchart does not need to be redrawn.

b. In order for Peacock's inventory/purchase order system to function properly, control procedures should be included in the system. Describe the type of control procedures Peacock Company should use in its system to ensure proper functioning, and indicate where these procedures would be placed in the system.

(CMA adapted)

12.59 Inventory Evidence and Long-Term Purchase Contracts. During the audit of Mason Company, Inc., for the calendar year 20X2, you noticed that the company produces aluminum cans at the rate of about 40 million units annually. On the plant tour, you noticed a large stockpile of raw aluminum in storage. Your inventory observation and pricing procedures showed this stockpile to be the raw materials inventory of 400 tons valued at $240,000 (LIFO cost). Enquiry with the production chief yielded the information that 400 tons was about a four-month supply of raw materials.

L0.3
L0.4

Suppose you learn that Mason had executed a firm long-term purchase contract with All Purpose Aluminum Company to purchase raw materials on the following schedule:

Quantity

Delivery Date	Quantity (tons)	Total Price
January 30, 20X3	500	$300,000
June 30, 20X3	700	420,000
December 30, 20X3	1,000	500,000

Because of recent economic conditions, principally a decline in the demand for raw aluminum and a consequent oversupply, the price stood at 40 cents per pound as of January 15, 20X3. Commodities experts predict that this low price will prevail for 12 to 15 months or until there is a general economic recovery.

Required:

a. Describe the procedures you would employ to gather evidence about this contract (including its initial discovery).

b. What facts recited in the problems are ones that you would have to discover for yourself in an audit?

c. Discuss the effect this contract has on the financial statements.

12.60 Deake Corporation: Property Accounting System. Deake Corporation is a medium-sized, diversified manufacturing company. Recently, Jack Richards was promoted to manager of the property accounting section. Richards is having difficulty responding to some of the requests from individuals in other departments for information about the company's fixed assets. Some of the requests are:

L0.1

1. The controller has requested schedules of individual fixed assets to support the balances in the general ledger. Richards has furnished the necessary information, but it was late. The manner in which the records are organized makes it difficult to obtain information easily.

2. The maintenance manager wishes to verify the existence of a punch press he thinks was repaired twice. He has asked Richards to confirm the asset number and location of the press.

3. The insurance department wants data on the cost and book values of assets to include in its review of current insurance coverage.

4. The tax department has requested data that can be used to calculate depreciation for tax purposes.

5. The company's internal auditors have spent a significant amount of time in the property accounting section recently, attempting to audit the annual depreciation expense.

The property account records consist of a set of manual books. These records show the date the asset was acquired, the account number for the asset, the dollar amount capitalized and the estimated useful life of the asset for depreciation purposes.

After many frustrations, Richards has realized that his records are inadequate and that he cannot supply data when requested. He has decided to discuss his problem with the controller, Jim Castle.

Richards: Jim, something has got to give. My people are working overtime and can't keep up. You worked in property accounting before you became controller. You know I can't tell the tax, insurance and maintenance people everything they need to know from my records. Also, that internal auditing team is living in my area and that slows down the work pace. The requests of these people are reasonable, and we should be able to answer these questions and provide the needed data. I think we need a computerized property accounting system. I would like to talk to the information systems people to see if they can help me.

Castle: Jack, I think you have a good idea, but be sure you are personally involved in the design of any system so you get all the information you need.

Required:

a. Identify and justify four major objectives Deake Corporation's computerized property accounting system should possess to provide the data necessary to respond to requests for information by company personnel.

b. Identify the data that should be included in the computer record for each asset included in the property account.

(CMA adapted)

12.61 Grover Manufacturing—Purchasing Defalcation. On January 11 at the beginning of your annual audit of the Grover Manufacturing Company's financial statements for the year just ended December 31, the com-

L0.3

pany president confides to you that an employee is living on a scale in excess of that which his salary would support.

The employee has been a buyer in the purchasing department for six years and has charge of purchasing all general materials and supplies. He is authorized to sign purchase orders for amounts up to $2,000. Purchase orders in excess of $2,000 require the countersignature of the general purchasing agent.

The president understands that the usual audit of financial statements is not designed to disclose immaterial fraud or conflicts of interest, although such events may be discovered. The president authorizes you, however, to expand your regular audit procedures and to apply additional audit procedures to determine whether there is any evidence that the buyer has been misappropriating company funds or has been engaged in activities that are a conflict of interest.

Required:

List the audit procedures that you would apply to the company records and documents in an attempt to:

1. Discover evidence within the purchasing department of defalcations being committed by the buyer. Give the purpose of each audit procedure.
2. Provide leads about possible collusion between the buyer and suppliers. Give the purpose of each audit procedure.

12.62 J. J. Barnicke Ltd. - Missing Millions and a Widow with a Lavish Lifestyle.[4]

Elizabeth (Liz) Lake lives in a million-dollar mansion in Don Mills. She spends time with her three children at a 1,134-square-metre waterfront "cottage" in central Ontario. The slim, attractive widow also gets about $ 22,600 a month—or $270,000 a year—to maintain those properties and cover living expenses.

And prominent realtor Joe Barnicke says it's all possible with money her late husband stole from him, his firm J.J. Barnicke Ltd.—and a family trust fund. Liz Lake, who is in her mid-30s, has kept that lifestyle for almost two years since her husband jumped in front of a train at York Mills subway station. Jim Lake committed suicide on the morning of March 18, 1996, less than an hour after Barnicke confronted him at the firm's downtown office about a lot of missing money. Lake, the firm's star chief financial officer, excused himself and never returned.

Barnicke and his company immediately filed a lawsuit in court against Liz Lake and her husband's estate to recover what was left of $19.8 million Lake allegedly swiped over a decade. But Barnicke, the firm's 74-year-old chairman, has found it isn't easy trying to get any of the alleged stolen money back. The courts are slow and Liz Lake is fighting him all the way for the mansion, country estate, cars, boats, snowmobiles and life insurance proceeds. Barnicke won't talk publicly about the case but acquaintances say he's bitter and disillusioned over Liz Lake's continuing monthly "allowances" and

the lengthy court proceedings. In the battle over the estate, Barnicke figures there's now only about $4 million to $5 million left—including life insurance proceeds—after all the spending.

No wonder. One of Lake's own accounting reports filed with the court reveals the couple spent almost $7 million after tax in the three years before his death. Expenses ranged from:

• $ 20,949.16 for booze,
• $ 110,577.25 for a BMW,
• $ 45,148.24 for his wife's clothes,
• $ 256,952.96 for vacations,
• $ 287,540.89 for gifts, and
• $ 720,550.38 for custom-made cottage furniture.

Lake fuelled that spending by jacking up his pay through misappropriation of Barnicke funds, documents filed in court show. After a brief probe, Barnicke and top-flight forensic accountants Lindquist Avey McDonald Baskerville Inc. said a paper trail revealed that the likeable Lake moved money from the company's operating funds and the chairman's personal accounts to a payroll system. He then transferred the money into personal bank accounts at the Bank of Nova Scotia.

Lake ran the payroll system, from which he was paid. Investigators found a copy of Lake's T4 form to Revenue Canada in his briefcase showing a gross income of $2,468,938.63 for 1995. But Lake's annual salary never exceeded $110,000, Barnicke said in the claim. Barnicke's lawsuit also alleges Lake, who was 36 when he died, had improperly moved $1.5 million from a trust fund for Barnicke's three children to his own account. Barnicke said his signature on the transfer requests were forgeries.

Liz Lake, who is the estate's litigation guardian, denies her husband stole the money. If her husband did, it's Barnicke's own fault and he should suffer the losses, her statement of defence said. If the company had shown a minimal amount of diligence, it could have stopped any alleged losses and Lake might still be alive, she added. "The plaintiffs (Barnicke) by their gross negligence caused or contributed to the death of her husband and the father of her three children," the statement of defence said. "She and her children have been and will continue to be subjected to embarrassment, humiliation and loss of reputation in the community." She noted that senior Barnicke executives visited the mansion on numerous occasions.

"Like other senior officers of J.J. Barnicke Limited, Mr. Lake openly lived an affluent lifestyle, which could only have been afforded by someone earning substantially in excess" of $100,000, Mrs. Lake alleges in the court documents. Barnicke has said Lake told co-workers he inherited the money.

She insists that all money received from the company was earned, "and was accurately recorded in J.J. Barnicke Ltd.'s books and records." Those books and records were kept at the company offices and in fact Lake paid taxes on the full amount. As well, Elizabeth

---

[4] Tony Van Alphen, *The Toronto Star*, December 14, 1997, p. A1; Scott Burnside, *The Toronto Sun*, June 23, 1996, p. 45.

Lake points out, the Barnicke books were made available to accountants Ernst & Young "at least annually" and that all her husband's earnings were deposited in their joint account at the Bank of Nova Scotia. (The bank is also named in the company's civil suit.)

Joe Barnicke, the blustery patriarch of the company, scoffs at the suggestion they are responsible for any financial loss. "He stole the money," he told *The Toronto Sun* this week. "He stole the money. That's all we can say."

Meanwhile, Barnicke's lawyer, Chris Osborne, said the cost of paying the mortgage, hydro and other upkeep of the luxurious properties for Liz Lake is "bleeding" the estate of hundreds of thousands of dollars. But moments before Osborne could ask the Ontario Court, general division, to stop it by selling most of the property, Liz Lake surprised everyone. Her lawyer indicated she wished to change counsel again and needed more time for preparation. She is now dealing with her third legal firm in the case.

Reports finally appeared on the public record in connection with the receiver's requests for further direction on the propriety of some of Lake's spending and other matters. Personal documents and other information in the reports suggest Liz and Jim Lake didn't hold back in the last years of his life. Lake collected annual paycheques ranging from $2.2 million to $4.3 million in gross income from 1990 to 1995. Lake's own printout of "inflows" and "outflows" covering July, 1993 to February, 1996, disclosed that income from work, interest and revenue on property sales totalled about $7 million. But the outflows or expenses left them with only $35,000. Furthermore, (the receiver) said at one point the couple regularly rang up credit card charges of more than $43,000 a month. The Lakes had "very lavish spending habits," the receiver noted.

There was the 558-square-metre Don Mills mansion, with five bedrooms, triple car garage and circular driveway near the exclusive Donalda Club at Don Mills and York Mills Rds. There was the cottage with six bedrooms and boathouse containing three slips at the northeast end of Balsam Lake. There were three autos, including a Cadillac and the BMW. There was a fleet of six boats featuring a 10-metre SeaRay luxury cruiser. There were five snowmobiles. There were country clubs, big parties and skiing weekends. Lake bought a 7-metre wooden antique boat for $7,500 and then spent $131,000 restoring it, the receiver said.

Annual carrying costs for the house and cottage including mortgages and taxes are a whopping $124,000 and $150,000 respectively. In 18 months, the receiver has disbursed more than $1 million from the estate, he said. The receiver's own costs have topped $200,000. Liz Lake has spent more than $800,000, including mortgage payments and her monthly stipend. Her lawyers' costs alone have accounted for $300,000 of that amount.

Required:

a. Comment on the apparent control weaknesses at J.J. Barnicke suggested by the events in the above story.

What general recommendations for the company's internal controls can you derive from this situation?

b. Assume the role of the judge. Which party's arguments do you think are more convincing? What additional evidence could each party provide to you that would strengthen their case?

c. What audit procedures might have been used to uncover the transfer of company funds to Mr. Lake's bank account?

12.63 Repairs Expense, Error Adjustment. You are the auditor of Bittern Inc. Bittern's long-standing policy is to capitalize all repairs and maintenance payments that exceed $10,000, without assessing the nature of the expenditure. Many of Bittern's buildings and equipment are aging and repairs are becoming frequent and more expensive. You have concerns that a material amount of building repairs and maintenance expense is being capitalized, and undertake a detailed examination of all the building asset additions during the current year. Your analysis indicates that approximately $400,000 of repairs expense has been capitalized as buildings in the current year. Materiality for the audit is $500,000. In the prior years audit, the staff noted approximately $100,000 of repairs expenses had been capitalized, but no adjustment was recorded. The estimated useful life of Bittern's buildings is 25 years, and the average remaining useful life of their buildings is approximately 8 years.

Required:

a. Describe the impact of the above error on the current year financial statements and the impact it will have on future periods' financial statements when the error reverses, if it is not adjusted.

b. Describe the impact the unadjusted error from the prior year will have on the current year's financial statements.

c. State whether you would require Bittern to adjust for this error, and support your conclusion. If you require an adjustment, provide the required journal entry.

d. What recommendation would you include in the management letter relating to the situation above?

12.64 Mining Properties, Using Work of Specialists. White Ice Mines Inc. is a mining company. During 20X4 White Ice acquired a diamond mine located in the far north for $800 million from Albatross Inc. The purchase price is based on the mine's inventory of extracted diamonds, with an appraised value of $300 million, plus diamond reserves estimated in the range of $600 million to over $2 billion. White Ice raised $100 million of the funds to acquire the mine by issuing public shares on the Canadian Adventure Exchange, with the remainder being lent by a consortium of three major Canadian banks. Shortly after the IPO, a shareholder resolution was passed to require White Ice to appoint new auditors from one of the large, national auditing firms. The previous auditor was a small firm that also was the auditor for Albatross for many years. The new auditor of White

Ice is examining the existence, valuation and ownership assertions for its mining assets for the year ended December 31, 20X4. White Ice informs the auditor that its mining specialists provided the appraisals that were used in the prospectus for their Initial Public Offering of shares, and to satisfy the due diligence enquiries of the three banks. The new auditor has determined that it will be necessary to rely on an independent specialist to provide a valuation report to support the audit opinion.

Required:
a. Refer to *CICA Handbook*, section 5049 (Use of Specialists in Assurance Engagements) and develop an audit program for verifying White Ice's diamond mine investment.
b. White Ice's management is concerned that using another specialist will drive up the audit cost. The managers (some of whom previously worked for a company called Bre-X) suggest it would be more efficient for the auditor to rely on the specialist reports already generated for the IPO and the bank financing. As the new auditor, how would you respond to this suggestion? You may want to refer to *CICA Handbook*, section 6010 on Audit of Related Party Transactions for guidance.

12.65 Inventory Count, Measurement. Consider the following examples of inventories in various businesses:

LO.3
LO.5

1. Pharmaceuticals in a drug company,
2. Fine chemical compounds in a biotechnology company,
3. Software in an information technology development company,
4. New condominium office units in a commercial real estate developer,
5. Fine art works in an interior design business.

Required:
For each item indicate the challenges auditors would face in trying to count and measure the inventory, and suggest an approach to obtain sufficient audit evidence.

12.66 Audit Issues in Internet Business. TheShoppingMall.com (TSM) is an Internet business that provides a web site with links to a variety of online shopping websites with which TSM has established "marketing partnerships." TSM also provides advertising, promotions and discount coupons for its partner shopping sites. TSM was incorporated under the laws of Canada in early 1999. The original financing to start TSM came from its president, Mr. Fogg, and several outside venture capital investors. Mr. Fogg's plan is to issue common shares to the public after the business model has proven itself. The proceeds from this share issue will be used to repay the debt financing provided by Mr. Fogg and the venture capitalists. It is now late 2002 and the financial results are being prepared for the year ended November 30, 2002. Mr. Fogg believes that early 2003 will be the right time to issue public shares.

LO.3

The preliminary financial statements for the year ended November 30, 2002 include the following items:

TSM contracted with three partners for $103.5 million to develop all their online shopping systems, including customer relation management and payment processing. The partners are name-brand product manufacturers that want to start direct online retailing. TSM has never completed this type of system before, but expects to complete it by the end of 2004. TSM recorded $36.5 million of the $103.5 as revenues, deferring the rest to be reported when the work was completed.

TSM also provides an online auction service where individuals and businesses can list items for sale and interested purchasers can bid on them. TSM provides the auction service, arranges delivery and processes payments for a fee of 8 percent of the selling price. TSM recognized the full selling price of these auction items as revenue and the net 92 percent paid to the seller as "product costs."

TSM provided an online travel agency, selling airline tickets and hotel rooms and car rentals. It recorded as revenue the entire fee paid by a customer for an airline ticket or hotel room. The amount TSM paid the airline or hotel chain that supplied the ticket or room was classified as "product costs." TSM reported that it earned $152 million in revenues, and its product costs came to $134 million, leaving $18 million of "gross profits." TSM's other costs—like advertising and salaries—netted out to a loss of $102 million. While a traditional travel agency, which has a fixed commission, would show only the commission as revenue, Mr. Fogg believes it is appropriate to use the gross bookings amounts as revenue, because, unlike a traditional travel agency, TSM purchased the hotel room outright, so it assumed the full risk of ownership and could control the profit made on each sale.

To build awareness for its site, TSM purchased $1 million of advertising on several other companies' retailing websites. In exchange for advertising on these sites, TSM sold advertising worth $1million for these other companies on TSM's site. Mr. Fogg believes this bartering was an astute business move that "…saves us tons of cash and generates revenues at the same time."

TSM used promotions to bring people to its website. For example, customers who bought a pizza from a national pizza chain, received a coupon for $10 off their next TSM purchase. TSM accounted for these costs as marketing expenses rather than recording them as a cost of goods sold. Mr. Fogg stated, "The gross profits line is very sensitive, so it is preferable to show these expenses below the gross profit line." Other expenses that TSM includes in "marketing expenses" are costs of warehousing, packaging and shipping goods to customers.

Mr. Fogg and several top TSM executives have received options to purchase common shares of at a fixed price of $1 per share.

Mr. Fogg realized the TSM financial statements must provide some disclosure of the accounting policies chosen. TSM's note on revenue recognition states, "Revenue is recognized when earned."

Required:

TSM plans to issue its Initial Public Offering of shares in early 2004. It will require a set of audited financial statements. Assume the role of TSM's auditor. What is your position on the accounting matters listed above?

12.67 On The Road Inc. (OTR) is a tour company owned by

LO.3 Joy Kerouak. OTR offers organized tours three weeks to six-month-long, targetted to early retirees 55 years old and over. OTR is in its third year of operations. Joy is not actively involved in the business and has hired a team of skilled managers to run the business. OTR is a private Canadian corporation, with Joy owning 100 percent of its common shares. The managers receive a bonus of 30 percent of monthly pretax profits.

OTR's tours are guided road trips across North America. Tour groups travel in brightly painted camper vans and visit sites of historic events of the 1950s and 1960s. The packages are sold online and through travel agents, under the following terms:

- A deposit of 40 percent is required upon booking, which is refundable until 14 days before the start of the tour and is nonrefundable after that point.
- The remaining 60 percent is due 14 days before the start of the tour. This is nonrefundable.
- If for some reason OTR is unable to offer the tour, 100 percent is refunded to the customer.

Online sales are paid by credit card. Travel agent sales are the same as those terms previously listed, except the agents receive payments from customers and forwards these to OTR within seven days. Travel agents receive a commission of 10 percent of the tour selling price, which they deduct prior to forwarding the payments to OTR. During OTR's three years of operating, about half the tours have been sold through travel agents and the other half online, but the online portion has been increasing each year.

Economic conditions in the travel industry have been declining recently, and bankruptcies of travel agents are increasing. If travel agents that sell OTR tours go bankrupt, OTR would probably lose any customer payments the travel agents had not yet forwarded. Over its three year history, the company's bad debts from travel agents have been about 5 percent of sales. To date, only one tour has had to be cancelled by

OTR due to Hurricane Katrina flooding New Orleans. This refund made up about 2 percent of the total 2005 revenues of OTR.

The main assets of OTR are a fleet of 50 camper vans that were purchased when the business started up. Since these are high-quality VW vans in classic designs, management chose to depreciate the cost of the camper vans over 9.4 years. However, this winter management informed Joy that at least 35 of the vans are in poor condition and will need to be replaced at a cost of $40,000 each before the spring tour season begins. Joy has contacted her banker, Nik Beat, to arrange to borrow the cost of replacing the camper vans. Currently, OTR is debt-free. Mr. Beat requested audited financial statements prepared in accordance with generally accepted accounting principles for the first three years of OTR's operations. Since to date OTR has mainly prepared its financial statements for the purpose of computing the managers' monthly bonuses, Joy is not sure if these statements will meet Mr. Beat's requirements. Joy has hired you to advise her on accounting issues and on how to obtain the audit that her banker is requesting.

Required:

Assume the role of an advisor to Joy and answer the following questions:

a. Identify the main users of OTR's financial statements and the kinds of decisions/evaluations that each user will make based on these financial statements.

b. What are the main objectives of OTR's management that may affect the accounting choices it makes in preparing OTR's financial statements?

c. Describe four or more possible revenue and expense recognition points for OTR's tour business, indicating the most appropriate method in your judgement. Provide the reasons that support your judgement.

d. Outline the key issues that would need to be addressed by a prospective auditor in order to decide whether to accept the engagement.

e. Prepare a report to Joy describing in detail a preliminary audit plan for OTR. Include explanations for each component you include in the preliminary plan that will help Joy understand the audit objectives and procedures.

Additional questions and Kingston Case questions related to Chapter 12 are on the Online Learning Centre that accompanies this text.

APPENDIX 12A

INTERNAL CONTROL QUESTIONNAIRES

. . . .

EXHIBIT   12A–1   INTERNAL CONTROL QUESTIONNAIRE
PURCHASES, PAYABLES AND PAYMENTS PROCESS

OVERALL COMPANY-LEVEL CONTROL AND CONTROL ACTIVITIES ASSESSMENT
(Refer to responses recorded for questions in Exhibit PIII-3 on pages 420–422)

Are company-level and general control activities adequate as they apply to the purchases, payables and payments components of the information system?

- Consider the impact of any weakness in company-level and general control activities on planned audit approach and procedures.
- Assess the potential for weaknesses to result in a material misstatement of the financial information generated from this accounting cycle. If a significant risk of misstatement is assess, perform procedures to determine extent of any misstatement.

Consider adequacy of the following general controls in place in the purchases, payables and payments process to:
— prevent unauthorized access or changes to programs and data
— ensure the security and privacy of data
— control and maintain key systems
— protect assets susceptible to misappropriation
— ensure completeness, accuracy and authorization of data and processing
— ensure adequate management trails exist

PURCHASING AND ACCOUNTS PAYABLE APPLICATION

Environment and general controls relevant to this application:
1. Is the purchasing department independent of the accounting department, receiving department and shipping department?
2. Are receiving report copies transmitted to inventory custodians? To purchasing? To the accounting department?

Assertion-Based Control Evaluation:

Validity objective:
3. Are suppliers' invoices matched against purchase orders and receiving reports before a liability is recorded?

Completeness objective:
4. Are the purchase order forms prenumbered and is the numerical sequence checked for missing documents?
5. Are receiving report forms prenumbered and is the numerical sequence checked for missing documents?
6. Is the accounts payable department notified of goods returned to vendors?
7. Are suppliers' invoices listed immediately upon receipt?
8. Are unmatched receiving reports reviewed frequently and investigated for proper recording?

Authorization objective:
9. Are competitive bids received and reviewed for certain items?
10. Are all purchases made only on the basis of approved purchase requisitions?
11. Are purchases made for employees authorized through the regular purchases procedures?
12. Are purchase prices approved by a responsible purchasing officer?
13. Are all purchases, whether for inventory or expense, routed through the purchasing department for approval?
14. Are shipping documents authorized and prepared for goods returned to vendors?
15. Are invoices approved for payment by a responsible officer?

Accuracy objective:
16. Are quantity and quality of goods received determined at the time of receipt by receiving personnel independent of the purchasing department?
17. Are suppliers' monthly statements reconciled with individual accounts payable accounts?
18. In the accounts payable department, are invoices checked against purchase orders and receiving reports for quantities, prices and terms?

Classification objective:
19. Does the chart of accounts and accounting manual give instructions for classifying debit entries when purchases are recorded?
20. Are account distributions recorded on supplier invoices and independently verified prior to being entered in the accounts payable system?

Accounting objective:
21. Is the accounts payable detail ledger balanced periodically with the general ledger control account?

Proper period objective:
22. Does the accounting manual give instructions to date purchase/payable entries on the date of receipt of goods?

Continued

EXHIBIT   12A-1   CONTINUED

CASH DISBURSEMENTS PROCESSING APPLICATION

Environment and general controls relevant to this application:
1. Are persons with cash custody or cheque-signing authority denied access to accounting journals, ledgers and bank reconciliations?
2. Is access to blank cheques denied to unauthorized persons?
3. Are all disbursements except petty cash made by cheque?
4. Are cheque signers prohibited from drawing cheques to cash?
5. Is signing blank cheques prohibited?
6. Are voided cheques mutilated and retained for inspection?

Assertion-Based Control Evaluation:
Validity objectives:
7. Are invoices, receiving reports and purchase orders reviewed by the cheque signer?
8. Are the supporting documents stamped "paid" (to prevent duplicate payment) before being returned to accounts payable for filing?
9. Are cheques mailed directly by the signer and not returned to accounts payable department for mailing?

Completeness objective:
10. Are blank cheques prenumbered and is the numerical sequence checked for missing documents?

Authorization objective:
11. Do cheques require two signatures? Is there dual control over machine signature plates?

Accuracy objective:
12. Are bank accounts reconciled by personnel independent of cash custody or recordkeeping?

Classification objective:
13. Do the chart of accounts and accounting manual give instructions for determining debit classifications of disbursements not charged to accounts payable?
14. Is the distribution of charges double-checked periodically by an official? Is the budget used to check on gross misclassification errors?
15. Are special disbursements (e.g., payroll and dividends) made from separate bank accounts?

Accounting objective:
16. Is the bank reconciliation reviewed by an accounting official with no conflicting cash receipts, cash disbursements or recordkeeping responsibilities?
17. Do internal auditors periodically conduct a surprise audit of bank reconciliations?

Proper period objective:
18. Are cheques dated in the cash disbursements journal with the date of the cheque?

EXHIBIT   12A-2   EXAMPLES OF PURCHASES AND PAYABLES CONTROLS RELATING TO EXHIBIT 12-1

- Each terminal performs only designated functions. For example, the receiving clerk's terminal cannot accept a purchase order entry.
- An identification number and password (used on an individual basis) is required to enter the nonautomatic purchase orders, vendors' invoices and the receiving report information. Further, certain passwords have "read only" authorization. These are issued to personnel authorized to determine the status of various records, such as an open voucher, but not authorized to enter data.
- All input immediately is logged to provide restart processing should any terminal become inoperative during the processing.
- The transaction codes call up a full-screen "form" on the terminals that appears to the operators in the same format as the original paper documents. Each clerk must enter the information correctly (online input validation) or the computer will not accept the data.
- All printed documents are computer numbered and the number is stored as part of the record. Further, all records in the open databases have the vendor's number as the primary search and matching field key. Of course, status searches could be made by another field. For example, the inventory number can be the search key to determine the status of a purchase of an item in short supply.
- A daily search of the open databases is made. Purchases outstanding for more than 10 days and the missing "document" records are printed out on a report for investigation of the delay.
- The cheque signature is printed, using a signature plate that is installed on the computer printer only when cheques are printed. A designated person in the treasurer's office maintains custody of this signature plate and must take it to the computer room to be installed when cheques are printed. This person also has the combination to the separate document storage room where the blank cheque stock is kept and is present at all cheque printing runs. The printed cheques are taken immediately from the computer room for mailing.

EXHIBIT   12A–3   INVENTORY TRANSACTION PROCESSING APPLICATION

Environment and general controls relevant to this application:
1. Are perpetual inventory records kept for raw materials? Supplies? Work in process? Finished goods?
2. Are perpetual records subsidiary to general ledger control accounts?
3. Do the perpetual records show quantities only? Quantities and prices?
4. Are inventory records maintained by someone other than the inventory stores custodian?
5. Is merchandise or materials on consignment-in (not the property of the company) physically segregated from goods owned by the company?

Assertion-Based Control Evaluation:
Validity objective:
6. Are additions to inventory quantity records made only on receipt of a receiving report copy?
7. Do inventory custodians notify the records department of additions to inventory?

Completeness objective:
8. Are reductions of inventory record quantities made only on receipt of inventory issuance documents?
9. Do inventory custodians notify inventory records of reductions of inventory?

Authorization objective:
  Refer to question 6 above (additions).
  Refer to question 8 above (reductions).

Accuracy objective:
10. If standard costs have been used for inventory pricing, have they been reviewed for current applicability?

Classification objective:
11. Are periodic counts of physical inventory made to correct errors in the individual perpetual records?

Accounting objective:
12. Is there a periodic review for overstocked, slow-moving or obsolete inventory? Have any adjustments been made during the year?
13. Are perpetual inventory records kept in dollars periodically reconciled to general ledger control accounts?

Proper period objective:
14. Does the accounting manual give instructions to record inventory additions on the date of the receiving report?
15. Does the accounting manual give instructions to record inventory issues on the issuance date?

EXHIBIT   12A–4   FIXED ASSET AND RELATED TRANSACTIONS PROCESSING APPLICATION

Environment and general controls relevant to this application:
1. Are detailed property records maintained for the various fixed assets?

Assertion-Based Control Evaluation:
Validity objective:
2. Is the accounting department notified of actions of disposal, dismantling or idling of a productive asset? For terminating a lease or rental?
3. Are fixed assets inspected periodically and physically counted?

Completeness objective:
4. Is casualty insurance carried? Is the coverage analyzed periodically? When was the last analysis?
5. Are property tax assessments periodically analyzed? When was the last analysis?

Authorization objective:
6. Are capital expenditure and leasing proposals prepared for review and approval by the board of directors or by responsible officers?
7. When actual expenditures exceed authorized amounts, is the excess approved?

Accuracy objective:
8. Is there a uniform policy for assigning depreciation rates, useful lives and salvage values?
9. Are depreciation calculations checked by internal auditors or other officials?

Classification objective:
10. Does the accounting manual contain policies for capitalization of assets and for expensing repair and maintenance?
11. Are subsidiary fixed assets records periodically reconciled to the general ledger accounts?
12. Are memorandum records of leased assets maintained?

Proper period objective:
13. Does the accounting manual give instructions for recording fixed asset additions on a proper date of acquisition?

CHAPTER

13

Production and Payroll Process

This chapter offers an overview of the production and payroll process. In this process, materials, labour and overhead are converted into finished goods and services. Our coverage separates this process into two distinct parts: Part I, which covers the production process including inventory valuation, amortization and cost of goods sold; and Part II, which covers the payroll process including labour cost accounting. A few casettes demonstrate the application of audit procedures in situations where errors, irregularities and frauds might be discovered.

LEARNING OBJECTIVES

After completing this chapter, you will be able to:

① Describe the production process, including typical transactions, source documents, controls and account balances.

② Outline control tests for auditing control over conversion of materials and labour in the production process.

③ Design audit and investigative procedures for detecting common errors, irregularities and frauds in the production process.

④ Describe the payroll process, including typical transactions, source documents, controls and account balances.

⑤ Outline control tests for auditing control over the payroll process.

⑥ Design audit and investigative procedures for detecting common errors, irregularities and frauds in the payroll process.

Note: Appendix 13B is located on the text Online Learning Centre.

RISK ASSESSMENT FOR THE PRODUCTION AND PAYROLL PROCESS

This chapter reviews typical activites in the production and payroll process. Risk considerations are explained following for each part of the process.

Production Process

In a manufacturing business the main function of the accounting cycle related to the production process is to allocate various material, labour and overhead costs to inventory. Other types of business produce different types of assets for sale or internal use, such as buildings, roads, software, trees, metals, pharmaceuticals, etc. They will have similar production accounting cycles to capture relevant costs and allocate them to asset accounts.

Production accounting produces important information for internal management decisions, such as setting selling prices, product-line profitability, whether to produce components internally or contract out, and production volume decisions. Considerable flexibility and judgement is needed to produce relevant information for these decisions. The reported balance sheet value of inventory or other produced assets also results from this process. The flexibility and judgement in these costing processes is a main source of risk of misstatement that the auditor has to assess. The inherent risk in this process also tends to be high because the information is complex and the transaction volumes involved can be large. In this text we focus mainly on manufacturing businesses. Other types of production businesses have the same basic accounting requirements but the specific activities and costs may differ.

The transactions streams in the production process are allocations from various material and overhead purchases, using accounts that were discussed in Chapter 12. Allocations are also made for labour costs, one type of payroll expenditure; these are discussed later in this chapter. The main balances are finished inventory and work-in-process. **Cost of goods sold** expense is a calculated amount that is determined from the changes in inventory, the purchases and other allocated costs, and adjustments arising from reconciling booked amounts to amounts determined from a physical count of the inventory. The main disclosure is the inventory valuation policy, including lower of cost and market policy.

The audit risks for inventory can be viewed as having two components: physical quantities and valuation (or pricing). Since the production process will tend to be the business's main activity, management will tend to have strong controls over existence and completeness as related to inventory quantities. Physical counts and reconciliation to booked quantities are very effective control procedures that auditors test substantively. Cut-off errors are a risk that can affect both existence and completeness assertions in inventory and related accounts receivable balance. The risks of misstatement for the valuation assertion require testing pricing controls and transactions to obtain sufficient audit assurance. Ownership risks are related to transfer of title to the inventory, since this may occur at a different time than the physical transfer. Enquiries and examination of documents and inventory movements subsequent to year-end provide assurance regarding the ownership assertion. Analytical procedures, often using detailed management reports, are an important procedure to test existence, completeness and valuation assertions simultaneously. Presentation risks include disclosure of inventory pledged as collateral.

Payroll Process

Payroll comprises payments to hourly wage workers and salaried employees. Hourly wages and salaries for employees involved in production may be transferred to the cost of inventory (or self-constructed assets, etc.), as explained previously. If not, they are expensed in the current period. Payments to employees are the main transaction stream. The main balances related to the payroll process are relatively small year-end accrual balances for payroll liabilities. The main risk related to payroll relates to the ownership assertion: because the process involves small cash payments to individuals it is vulnerable to employee fraud. Risk assessment involves ensuring payroll processing duties are well segregated. Substantive evidence is available from reconciling to government income tax reports.

PART I: PRODUCTION PROCESS: TYPICAL ACTIVITIES

· · · · · · · · · · · ·

LEARNING OBJECTIVE

① Describe the production process, including typical transactions, source documents, controls and account balances.

Exhibit 13–1 following shows the activities and accounting involved in a production process. The basic activities start with production planning, including inventory planning and management. Production planning can range from use of a sophisticated computerized long-range plan with just-in-time (JIT) inventory management to a simple ad hoc method ("Hey, Joe, we got an order today. Go make 10 units!"). Most businesses try to estimate or forecast sales levels and seasonal timing, and they try to plan facilities and production schedules to meet customer demand. As shown in Exhibit 13–1, the production cycle interacts with the purchasing process (Chapter 12) and the payroll process (later in this chapter) for the acquisition of fixed assets, materials, supplies, overhead and labour.

The physical output of a production process is inventory (starting with raw materials, proceeding to work-in-process, thence to finished goods). Most matters of auditing inventory and physical inventory-taking were explained in Chapter 12. In Chapter 11, Exhibit 11–1 showed the connection of inventory to the revenue process in terms of orders and deliveries.

Most of the transactions in a production cycle are cost accounting allocations, unit cost determinations and standard cost calculations. These are internal transactions produced entirely within the company's accounting system. Exhibit 13–1 shows the elements of depreciation cost calculation, cost of goods sold determination and job cost analysis as examples of these transactions.

It may help to think of the audit of inventory as consisting of two phases: the verification of the physical units and the testing of the unit costs. Physically observing the inventory count is the main procedure in verifying the physical units, including any equivalent units calculations for work-in-process (Chapter 12). The unit costing of inventory (also referred to as price tests) was also partly covered in Chapter 12, at least for purchased inventory such as the inventory of retailers. Chapter 13 continues the cost testing procedures for produced or manufactured inventory, where the cost allocations and computations are much more complex (as you may have noticed in your management accounting courses). For production processes the following formula is used:

$$\text{Unit Cost of Production} = \frac{\text{(Production Costs)}}{\text{(Equivalent Units of Production)}}$$

Once the unit costs of production are known, the total inventory production costs for reporting purposes is unit cost times number of units. The total inventory production cost must be allocated between cost of sales (on the income statement) and inventory (on the balance sheet). This allocation of costs between inventory and cost of goods sold will need to include proper allocation of any cost variances. This is necessary because a budget system is a control system and for external reporting purposes we need to disclose the actual costs, not the standard or budgeted costs. This allocation is crucial because it will affect lower cost or market tests in the valuation of inventory. The box on page 513 gives an example of how errors can arise in allocating standard overhead costs to inventory.

Note that these internal cost allocations are the basis of valuation of manufactured inventory, manufactured cost of goods sold, and any self-constructed property, plant and equipment assets. Therefore, analyzing the appropriateness of such cost allocations is a critical part of the audit of the valuation assertion of inventory and long-lived assets.

As you follow Exhibit 13–1, you can track the following elements of the control structure.

Authorization

The overall production authorization starts with production planning, which usually is based on a sales forecast. Production planning interacts with inventory planning to produce production orders. These production orders specify the materials and labour required and the timing for the start and end of production. Managers in the sales/marketing department and production department usually sign off their approval on plans and production orders. Since

EXHIBIT   13–1   PRODUCTION PROCESS

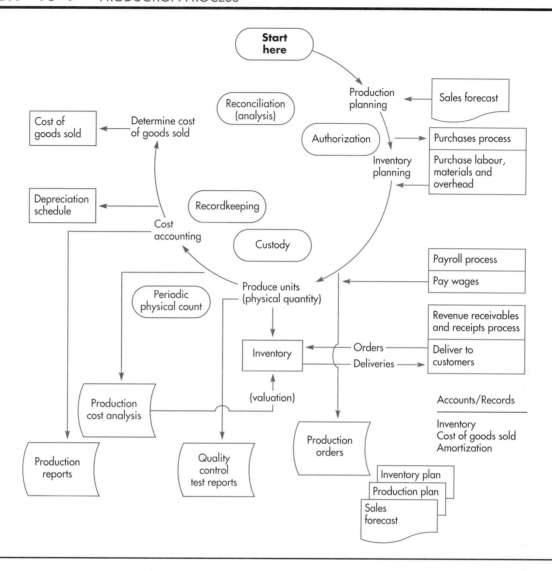

sales volume and inventory requirements change with economic conditions and company success or failure, these plans and approvals are dynamic. They are amended according to changing needs.

Authorization also can include plans and approvals for subcontracting work to other companies. The process of taking bids and executing contracts can be a part of the planning-authorization system.

The production order usually includes a **bill of materials** (a specification of the materials authorized for the production). This bill of materials is the source of authorization for the preparation of materials requisitions, and these requisitions are the authorization for the inventory custodian to release raw materials and supplies to the production personnel. These documents are the inventory recordkeepers' authorizations to update the raw materials inventory files to record the reductions of the raw materials inventory.

Later, when production is complete, the production reports, along with the physical units and the quality control test reports, are the authorizations for the finished goods inventory custodian to place the units in the finished goods inventory. These same documents are the inventory recordkeepers' authorization to update the inventory record files to record the additions to the finished goods inventory.

OVERHEAD ALLOCATION

The cost accounting department at Pointed Publications, Inc., routinely allocated overhead to book printing runs at the standard rate of 40 percent of materials and labour cost. The debit was initially to the finished books inventory, while the credit went to an "overhead allocated" account that was offset against other entries in the cost of goods sold calculation, which included all the actual overhead incurred. During the year 10 million books were produced and $40 million of overhead was allocated to them. The auditors noticed that actual overhead expenditures were $32 million, and 3 million books remained in the ending inventory.

The finding resulted in the conclusion that the inventory was overstated by $2.4 million, and the cost of goods sold was understated by $2.4 million.

	Company Accounting (Using overhead rate)	Proper Accounting (Using actual overhead)
Books produced	10 million	10 million
Labour and material cost	$100 million	$100 million
Overhead allocated	$ 40 million	$32 million
Cost per book	$ 14.00	$13.20
Cost of goods sold		
Labour and materials cost	$100 million	$100 million
Overhead allocated to books	40 million	
Overhead incurred	32 million	32 million
Overhead credited to cost	(40 million)	
Ending inventory	(42 million)	(39.6 million)
Total cost of goods sold	$ 90 million	$ 92.4 million

Custody

Supervisors and workers, skilled and unskilled, have physical custody of materials, equipment and labour while the production work is performed. They can requisition materials from the raw materials inventory, assign people to jobs and control the pace of work. In a sense they have custody of a moving inventory. The **work-in-process** (an inventory category) is literally "moving" and changing form in the process of being transformed from raw materials into finished goods.

Control over this custody is more difficult than control over a closed warehouse full of raw materials or finished goods. Control can be exercised by holding supervisors and workers accountable for the use of materials specified in the production orders, for the timely completion of production, and for the quality of the finished goods. This accountability can be achieved with good cost accounting, cost analysis and quality control testing.

Recordkeeping (Cost Accounting)

When production is completed, production orders and the related records of material and labour used are forwarded to the cost accounting department. Since these accounting documents may come from the production personnel, the effective separation of the recordkeeping function depends upon its receiving independent notices from other places, especially notifications of materials issued from the inventory custodian and the labour costs assigned by the payroll department.

The cost accounting department produces analyses of cost-per-unit, standard cost and variances. Cost accounting also may determine the allocation of overhead to production in general, to production orders and to finished units. Depending on the design of the company's accounting system, these costs are used in inventory valuation and ultimately in determination of the cost of goods sold. Often the cost accounting department also is responsible for calculating the depreciation of production assets and the amortization of intangibles.

Periodic Reconciliation

The function of periodic reconciliation generally refers to comparison of actual assets and liabilities to the amounts recorded in the company accounts (e.g., comparing the physical count of inventory to the perpetual inventory records, comparing vendors' monthly statements to the recorded accounts payable). Exhibit 13–1 shows the periodic reconciliation of physical inventory to recorded amounts. The features and audit considerations of this reconciliation were covered in Chapter 12. The work-in-process inventory also can be observed, although the "count" of partially completed units is subjective. It can be costed at the labour, materials and overhead assigned to its stage of completion.

Most other periodic reconciliations in the production cycle take the form of analyses of internal information. After all, with the exception of the physical inventory, no external transactions or physical units are unique to production and cost accounting. These analyses include costing the production orders, comparing the cost to prior experience or to standard costs, and determining **lower-of-cost-or-market (LCM)** valuations. In a sense the LCM calculations are a reconciliation of product cost to the external market price of product units.

REVIEW CHECKPOINTS

13.1   What are the functions normally associated with the production process?

13.2   Why is an understanding of the production process, including the related data processing and cost accounting, important to auditors evaluating the control structure as part of their assessment of control risk?

13.3   Describe a walk-through of a production transaction from production orders to entry in the finished goods perpetual inventory records. What document copies would be collected? What controls noted? What duties separated?

13.4   Describe how the separation of (1) authorization of production transactions, (2) recording of these transactions, and (3) physical custody of inventories can be specified among the production, inventory and cost accounting departments.

13.5   What features of the cost accounting system would be expected to prevent the omission of recording materials used in production?

AUDIT EVIDENCE IN MANAGEMENT REPORTS AND FILES

Most production accounting systems produce timely reports that managers need to supervise and control production. These reports can be used by auditors as supporting evidence for assertions about work-in-process and finished goods inventories and about cost of goods sold.

Sales Forecast

Management's sales forecast provides the basis for several aspects of business planning, notably the planning of production and inventory levels. If the auditors want to use the forecast for substantive audit decisions, some work to obtain assurance about its reasonableness needs to be performed. This work is not an examination or compilation of a forecast as contemplated by the assurance services standards. All the auditors need to accomplish is to learn about the assumptions built into the forecast for the purpose of ascertaining their reasonableness. In addition, some work on the mechanical accuracy of the forecast should be performed to avoid an embarrassing reliance on faulty calculations.

Forecasts can be used in connection with the auditor's knowledge of management's plans for the year under audit, most of which will have already passed when the audit work begins. This will help the auditor to understand the nature and volume of production orders and the level of materials inventory. Forecasts for the following year can be used in connection with valuing the inventory at lower-of-cost-or-market (e.g., by indicating slow-moving and potentially obsolete inventory). If a writedown from cost to market value is required, this

THE SALY FORECAST

The auditors were reviewing the inventory items that had not been issued for 30 days or more, to assess whether any items need to be written down because their market values are lower than cost. The production manager showed them the SALY forecast that indicated continuing need for the materials in products that were expected to have reasonable demand. The auditors agreed that the forecasts supported the prediction of future sales of products at prices that would cover the cost of the slow-moving material items.

Unfortunately, they neglected to ask the meaning of SALY in the designation of the forecast. They did not learn that it means "Same As Last Year." It is not a forecast at all. The products did not sell at the prices expected, and the company experienced losses the following year that should have been charged to cost of goods sold earlier.

increases the amount of cost of goods sold that is shown in the financial statements. Special care must be taken when using forecasts in connection with inventory valuation because an overly optimistic forecast can lead to a failure to write down inventory, accelerate the depreciation of production assets and account for more cost of goods sold.

Production Plans and Reports

Based on the sales forecast, management should develop a plan for the amount and timing of production. The production plan provides general information to the auditors, but the production orders and inventory plan associated with the production plan are even more important. The production orders carry the information about requirements for raw materials, labour and overhead, including the requisitions for purchase and use of materials and labour. These documents are the initial authorizations for control of the inventory and production.

Production reports record the completion of production quantities. When coupled with the related cost accounting reports, they are the company's record of the cost of goods placed in the finished goods inventory. In most cases auditors will audit the cost reports in connection with determining the cost valuation of inventory and cost of goods sold.

Amortization Schedule

The cost accounting department may be charged with preparing a schedule of the amortization (depreciation) of production assets. In many companies such a schedule is long and complicated, involving large dollar amounts of asset cost and calculated amortization expense. An abbreviated illustration of a production asset and amortization schedule is in the following table.

| | Production Assets and Amortization | | | | | | | |
| | Asset Cost (000s) | | | | Accumulated Amortization (000s) | | | |
Description	Beginning Balance	Additions	Disposals	Ending Balance	Beginning Balance	Additions	Disposals	Ending Balance
Land	10,000			10,000				
Bldg 1	30,000			30,000	6,857	857		7,714
Bldg 2		42,000		42,000		800		800
Computer A	5,000		5,000	0	3,750	208	3,958	0
Computer B		3,500		3,500		583		583
Press	1,500			1,500	300	150		450
Auto 1	15		15	0	15		15	0
Auto 2		22		22		2		2
Total	46,515	45,522	5,015	87,022	10,922	2,600	3,973	9,549

The amortization schedule is audited by recalculating the amortization expense, using the company's methods, estimates of useful life and estimates of residual value. (Problem 13.51 at the end of the chapter requires some work on the schedule presented here.) The asset acquisition and disposition information in the schedule gives the auditors points of departure for auditing the asset additions and disposals. When the schedule covers hundreds of assets and numerous additions and disposals, auditors can (*a*) use computer auditing methods to recalculate the amortization expense and (*b*) use sampling to choose additions and disposals for test of controls and substantive audit. The beginning balances of assets and accumulated amortization should be traced to the prior year's audit working papers. This schedule can be made into an audit working paper and placed in the auditor's files for future reference.

REVIEW CHECKPOINTS

13.6 When auditors want to use a client's sales forecast for general familiarity with the production process or for evaluation of slow-moving inventory, what kind of work should be done on the forecast?

13.7 If the actual sales for the year are substantially lower than the sales forecasted at the beginning of the year, what potential valuation problems may arise in the production cycle accounts?

13.8 What production documentation supports the valuation of manufactured finished goods inventory?

13.9 What items in a client's production asset and amortization schedule can auditors use for designing audit procedures? Describe these audit procedures.

CONTROL RISK ASSESSMENT

LEARNING OBJECTIVE

2 Outline control tests for auditing control over conversion of materials and labour in the production process.

Control risk assessment is important because it governs the nature, timing and extent of substantive audit procedures that will be applied in the audit of account balances in the production cycle. These account balances include:

– Inventory:
  • Raw materials
  • Work-in-process
  • Finished goods
– Cost of goods sold
– Amortization:
  • Amortization expense
  • Accumulated amortization

Several aspects of the audit of purchased inventories and physical quantities are covered in Chapter 12. With respect to inventory valuation, this chapter points out the cost accounting function and its role in determining the cost valuation of manufactured finished goods.

General Control Considerations

Control procedures for proper segregation of responsibilities should be in place and operating. By referring to Exhibit 13–1, you can see that proper segregation involves authorization (production planning and inventory planning) by persons who do not have custody, recording, or cost accounting and reconciliation duties. Custody of inventories (raw materials, work-in-process and finished goods) is in the hands of persons who do not authorize the amount or timing of production or the purchase of materials and labour, or perform the cost accounting recordkeeping or prepare cost analyses (reconciliations). Cost accounting (a recording function) is performed by persons who do not authorize production or have custody of assets in the process of production. However, you usually will find that the cost accountants prepare various analyses and reconciliations directly related to production activities. Combinations of two or more of the duties of authorization, custody, or cost accounting in one person, one office or one computerized system may open the door for errors, irregularities and frauds.

In addition, the control structure should provide for detail control-checking procedures. For example: (1) production orders should contain a list of materials and their quantities, and they should be approved by a production planner/scheduler; (2) materials requisitions should be compared in the cost accounting department with the list of materials on the production order, and the materials requisitions should be approved by the production operator and the materials inventory stockkeeper; (3) labour time records on jobs should be signed by production supervisors, and the cost accounting department should reconcile these cost amounts with the labour report from the payroll department; (4) production reports of finished units should be signed by the production supervisor and finished goods inventory custodian and forwarded to cost accounting. These control operations track the raw materials and labour from start to finish in the production process. With each internal transaction, the responsibility and accountability for assets are passed from one person or location to another.

Complex systems to manage production and materials flow are found in many companies. These information systems tend to be highly customized because production processes vary considerably for different products and factories. Even within the same company, different information systems may be used to manage different products or different locations. Some components of the production process and accounting may be done manually, and other components may be entirely automated. Paper source documents and authorization signatures may not exist for automated functions. Even though the information system and technology may be complex, the basic management and control functions of ensuring the flow of labour and materials to production and controlling waste should be in place. The feasibility of auditing through or around the computerized components of the production information system will need to be considered (refer to Chapter 9).

Internal Control Questionnaire

Information about the production process control structure often is gathered initially by completing an internal control questionnaire (ICQ). An example of an ICQ is in Exhibit 13A–1 in Appendix 13A. This questionnaire can be studied for details of desirable control policies and procedures. It is organized with headings that identify the important control objectives—environment, validity, completeness, authorization, accuracy, classification, accounting and proper period recording. The ICQ lists control activities that would be found in the manual components of a production cost accounting system. If components are computerized and have no paper trail, the auditor will need to assess whether each control objective is met by considering the application controls or other verification procedures the client has in place, for example, input/output checks. Problem 13.48 asks you to describe the errors and irregularities that can occur if certain ICQ items are not specified by a company.

Production Management—JIT

Just in time (JIT) manufacturing and supply chain management systems have expanded in many companies with the availability of EDI and other information technologies. Auditors need to be familiar with the components and functions of these systems and their implications for auditing. Appendix 13B provides further details on JIT manufacturing and supply chain management and is located on the text Online Learning Centre.

Control Tests

An organization should have control activities in place and operating to prevent, detect and correct accounting errors. You studied the general control objectives in Chapter 9 (validity, completeness, authorization, accuracy, classification, accounting and proper period recording). Exhibit 13–2 puts these in the perspective of production activity with examples of specific objectives. You should study this exhibit carefully. It expresses the general control objectives in specific examples related to production.

Auditors can perform control tests to determine whether controls that are said to be in place and operating actually are being performed properly by company personnel. Recall that a control test consists of (1) identification of the data population from which a sample of items will be selected for audit and (2) an expression of the action that will be taken to produce relevant evidence, such as vouching, tracing, observing, scanning and recalculating.

Exhibit 13–3 contains a selection of control tests for auditing controls over the accumulation of costs for work-in-process inventory. This is the stage of "inventory" while it is in the production process. Upon completion, the accumulated costs become the cost valuation of the finished goods inventory. The illustrative procedures presume the existence of production cost reports that are updated as production takes place, labour reports that assign labour cost to the job, materials used and materials requisitions charging raw materials to the production order and overhead allocation calculations. Some or all of these documents may be in the form of computer records. The samples are usually attribute samples designed along the lines studied in Chapter 10. On the right, Exhibit 13–3 shows the control objectives tested by the audit procedures.

Dual Direction of the Test of Controls Procedures

The test of controls procedures in Exhibit 13–3 are designed to test the production accounting in two directions. One is the completeness direction, in which the control performance of audit interest is the recording of all the production that was ordered to be

EXHIBIT 13-2   CONTROL OBJECTIVES (PRODUCTION PROCESS)

General Objectives	Examples of Specific Control Activities
1. Recorded production transactions are *valid* and documented.	Cost accounting separated from production, payroll and inventory control. Material use reports compared to raw material stores issue slips. Labour use reports compared to job time tickets.
2. Valid production transactions are *recorded* and none omitted.	All documents prenumbered and numerical sequence reviewed.
3. Production transactions are *authorized*.	Material use and labour use prepared by foreman and approved by production supervisor.
4. Production job cost transactions computations contain *accurate* figures.	Job cost sheet entries reviewed by person independent of preparation. Costs of inventory used and labour used reviewed periodically.
5. Labour and materials are *classified* correctly as direct or indirect.	Production supervisor required to account for all material and labour used as direct or indirect.
6. Production *accounting* is complete.	Open job cost sheets periodically reconciled to the work-in-process inventory accounts.
7. Production transactions are recorded in the *proper period*.	Production reports of material and labour used prepared weekly and transmitted to cost accounting. Job cost sheets posted weekly and summary journal entries of work-in-process and work completed prepared monthly.

EXHIBIT   13-3   CONTROL TESTS FOR WORK-IN-PROCESS INVENTORY

	Control Objective
1. Reconcile the open production cost reports to the work-in-process inventory control account.	Completeness
2. Select a sample of open and closed production cost reports:	
a. Recalculate all costs entered.	Accuracy
b. Vouch labour costs to labour reports.	Validity
c. Compare labour reports to summary of payroll.	Accounting
d. Vouch material costs to issue slips and materials-used reports.	Validity
e. Vouch overhead charges to overhead analysis schedules.	Accuracy
f. Trace selected overhead amounts from analysis schedules to cost allocations and to invoices or accounts payable vouchers.	Validity
3. Select a sample of issue slips from the raw materials stores file:	
a. Determine if a matching requisition is available for every issue slip.	Completeness
b. Trace materials-used reports into production cost reports.	Completeness
4. Select a sample of clock timecards from the payroll file. Trace to job time tickets, labour reports and production cost reports.	Completeness
5. Select a sample of production orders:	
a. Determine whether production order was authorized.	Authorization
b. Match to bill of materials and labour hour needs.	Completeness
c. Trace bill of materials to material requisitions, material issue slips, materials-used reports and production cost reports.	Completeness
d. Trace labour hour needs to labour reports and production cost reports.	Completeness

started. Exhibit 13–4 shows that the sample for this direction is taken from the population of production orders found in the production planning department. The procedures trace the cost accumulation forward into the production cost reports in the cost accounting department. The procedures keyed in the boxes (5-*a*, *b*, *c*, *d*) are cross-references to the procedures in Exhibit 13–3. A potential finding with these procedures is the cancellation of some production because of technical or quality problems, which should result in writing off or scrapping some partially completed production units.

The other direction is the validity direction of the test. The control performance of interest is the proper recording of work-in-process and finished goods in the general ledger. Exhibit 13–5 shows that the sample for this test is from the production reports (quantity and cost) recorded in the inventory accounts. This sample yields references to production cost reports filed in the cost accounting department. From these basic records the recorded costs can be recalculated, vouched to labour reports, compared to the payroll and vouched to records of material used and overhead incurred. The procedures keyed in the boxes (2-*a*, *b*, *c*, *d*, *e*, *f*) are cross-references to the procedures in Exhibit 13–3. A potential finding with these procedures is improper valuation of the recorded inventory cost.

Summary: Control Risk Assessment

The audit manager or senior accountant in charge of the audit should evaluate the evidence obtained from an understanding of the internal control structure and from the test of controls audit procedures. If the control risk is assessed very low, the substantive audit procedures on the account balances can be limited in cost-saving ways. For example, the inventory valuation substantive tests can be limited in scope (i.e., smaller sample size), and overall analytical procedures can be used with more confidence in being able to detect material misstatements not otherwise evident in the accounting details.

On the other hand, if tests of controls reveal weaknesses, amortization calculation errors and cost accumulation errors, the substantive procedures will need to be designed to lower the risk of failing to detect material error in the inventory and cost of goods sold account balances. For example, the amortization cost may need to be completely recalculated and

EXHIBIT 13-4   TEST OF PRODUCTION COST CONTROLS: COMPLETENESS DIRECTION

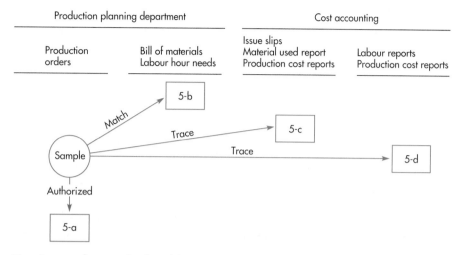

Note: 5-a etc., refer to tests listed in Exhibit 13-3.

reviewed again by the auditors. A large number of inventoried production reports may need to be selected for valuation calculations. Cost overruns will need to be investigated with reference to contract terms to determine whether they should be carried as assets (e.g., inventory or unbilled receivables) or written off. Descriptions of major deficiencies, control weaknesses and inefficiencies may be incorporated in a management letter to the client.

Computerized components of the production information system may range from simple batch systems, which automate the data processing, to transaction-driven integrated systems, which capture the production progress directly from automated devices on the production line. Computer audit techniques, such as test data, frequently are employed to audit controls in such systems, and generalized audit software may be employed to match data on different files. (Refer to Chapter 9 for these subjects.)

EXHIBIT 13-5   TEST OF PRODUCTION COST CONTROLS: VALIDITY DIRECTION

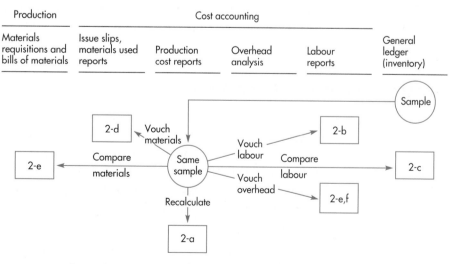

Note: 2-a etc., refer to tests listed in Exhibit 13-3.

IMPROPER PRODUCTION LOSS DEFERRALS

According to the SEC, Litton Corporation incurred cost overruns on its shipbuilding contracts and postponed writing off a $128 million cost overrun by classifying it as an asset for financial reporting purposes. If it had been written off timelier, the net income of $1 million for the year would have become a substantial loss. Litton wrote off the $128 million later.

****

According to the SEC, International Systems & Controls Corporation (ISC) recorded and reported cost overruns on fixed price contracts, claims for price escalation, and kickback arrangements with suppliers as unbilled receivables. Additional uncollectible contract costs, which indicated losses on fixed price contracts, were buried in other unrelated contracts. ISC used the unbilled receivables account as a dumping ground for improper and questionable payments on the contracts. It tried to show them as legitimate reimbursable contract costs in order to avoid (*a*) writing them off as expense and (*b*) showing the true nature of the items. ISC used the unbilled receivables account to record cost overruns on fixed price contracts, misrepresenting them as an escalation payment due from the owner, but the contract did not provide for any such payment.

Source: Kellog, I., *How to Find Negligence and Misrepresentation in Financial Statements* (New York: Shepard's/ McGraw-Hill, 1983), pp. 208–9, 302–3.

REVIEW CHECKPOINTS

13.10   What are the primary functions that should be segregated in the production process?

13.11   How does the production order document or record provide a control over the quantity of materials used in production?

13.12   Where might an auditor find accounting records of cost overruns on contracts? of improper charges? of improperly capitalized inventory?

13.13   Evaluate the following statement made by an auditing student: "I do not understand cost accounting; therefore, I want to get a job with an auditing firm where I will only have to know financial accounting."

13.14   From what population of documents or records would an auditor sample to determine whether all authorized production was completed and placed in inventory or written off as scrap? to determine whether finished goods inventory was actually produced and properly costed?

CASETTES: SUBSTANTIVE AUDIT PROCEDURES

LEARNING OBJECTIVE

3 Design audit and investigative procedures for detecting common errors, irregularities and frauds in the production process.

The audit of account balances consists of procedural efforts to detect errors, irregularities and frauds that may exist in the balances, thus making them misleading in financial statements. If such misstatements exist, they are characterized by the following features:

Method: A cause of the misstatement (accidental error, intentional irregularity or fraud attempt), which is usually made easier by some kind of failure of controls.

Paper trail: A set of telltale signs of erroneous accounting, missing or altered documents or a "dangling debit" (the false or erroneous debit that results from an overstatement of assets).

Amount: The dollar amount of overstated assets and revenue, or understated liabilities and expenses.

Each audit program for the audit of an account balance contains an audit approach that may enable auditors to detect misstatements in account balances. Each application of procedures contains these elements:

Audit objective: A recognition of a financial statement assertion for which evidence needs to be obtained. The assertions are about existence of assets, liabilities, revenue and expenses; their valuation; their complete inclusion in the account balances; the rights and obligations inherent in them; and their proper presentation and disclosure in the financial statements. (These assertions were introduced in Chapter 6.)

Control: A recognition of the control procedures that should be used by an organization to prevent and detect errors and irregularities.

Test of controls: Ordinary and extended procedures designed to produce evidence about the effectiveness of the controls that should be in operation.

Audit of balance: Ordinary and extended substantive procedures designed to find signs of errors, irregularities and frauds in account balances and classes of transactions.

The next portion of this chapter consists of two casettes that first set the stage with a story about an error, irregularity or fraud—its method, paper trail (if any) and amount. This part of the casette gives you the "inside story," which auditors seldom know before they perform the audit work. The second part of the casette, under the heading of the audit approach, tells a structured story about the audit objective, desirable controls, test of control procedures, audit of balance procedures and discovery summary. The audit approach segment illustrates how audit procedures can be applied and the discoveries they may enable auditors to make. At the end of the chapter, some similar discussion cases are presented, and you can write the audit approach to test your ability to design audit procedures for the detection of errors, irregularities and frauds.

CASETTE 13.1
UNBUNDLED BEFORE ITS TIME

Problem

Production "sold" as finished goods before actual unit completion caused understated inventory, overstated cost of goods sold, overstated revenue and overstated income.

Method

Western Corporation assembled and sold computer systems. A systems production order consisted of hardware and peripheral equipment specifications and software specifications with associated performance criteria. Customer contracts always required assembly to specifications, installation, hardware testing, software installation and software testing, after which the customer could accept the finished installation and pay the agreed price for the entire package. Completion of an order usually took three to eight months.

For internal accounting purposes, Western "unbundled" the hardware and software components of the customer orders. Production orders were split between the two components. Standard production processing and cost accounting were performed as if the two components were independent orders. When the hardware was installed and tested (with or without customer acceptance), Western recorded part of the contract price as sales revenue and the related cost of goods sold. The amount "due from customers" was carried in an asset account entitled "unbilled contract revenue." No billing statement was sent to the customer at this time.

When the software component was completed, installed, tested and accepted, the remainder of the contract price was recorded as revenue, and the cost of the software was recorded as cost of goods sold. A billing statement was sent to the customer. The "unbilled contract revenue," which now matched the customer's obligation, was moved to accounts receivable.

During the time either or both of the order components were in process (prior to installation at the customer's location), accumulated costs were carried in a work-in-process inventory account.

Paper Trail

Customer orders and contracts contained all the terms relating to technical specifications, acceptance testing and the timing of the customer's obligation to pay. Copies of the technical specification sections of the contracts were attached to the separate hardware and software production orders prepared and authorized in the production planning department. During production, installation and testing, each of these production orders served as the basis for the production cost accumulation and the subsidiary record of the work-in-process inventory. At the end the production report along with the accumulated costs became the production cost report and the supporting documentation for the cost of goods sold entry.

Amount

Western Corporation routinely recorded the hardware component of contracts too soon, recognizing revenue and cost of goods sold that should have been postponed until later when the customer accepted the entire system. In the last three years, the resulting income overstatement amounted to 12 percent, 15 percent and 19 percent of the reported operating income before taxes.

AUDIT APPROACH

Objective

Obtain evidence of the actual occurrence of cost of goods sold transactions, thereby yielding evidence of the completeness of recorded inventory.

Control

The major control lies in the production planning department approval of orders that identify a total unit of production (in this case, the hardware and software components combined). Nothing is wrong with approving separate orders for efficiency of production, but they should be cross-referenced so that both production personnel and the cost accounting department can see them as separate components of the same order unit.

Test of Controls

While the company conducted a large business, it had relatively few production orders (200–250 charged to cost of goods sold during each year). A sample of completed production orders should be taken and vouched to the underlying customer orders and contracts. The purpose of this procedure includes determining the validity of the production orders in relation to customer orders and determining whether the cost of goods sold was recorded in the proper period. (Procedures to audit the accuracy and completeness of the cost accumulation also are carried out on this sample.)

Even though the auditors can read the customer contracts, enquiries should be made about the company's standard procedures for the timing of revenue and cost of goods sold recognition to determine what is actually being done in practice.

Audit of Balances

The sample of completed production orders taken for the test of controls also can be used in a "dual pur-

pose test" to audit the details of the cost of goods sold balance. In connection with the balance audit, the primary points of interest are the validity and completeness of the dollar amounts accumulated as cost of the contracts and the proper cutoff for recording the cost.

The existence of the "unbilled contract revenue" asset account in the general ledger should raise a red flag. Such an account always means that management has made an estimate of a revenue amount that has not been determined according to contract and has not yet been billed to the customer in accordance with contract terms. Even though the revenue is "unbilled," the related cost of goods sold still should be in the cost of goods sold account. While accounting theory and practice permit recognizing unbilled revenue in certain cases (e.g., percentage of completion for construction contracts), the accounting has been known to harbour abuses in some cases.

Discovery Summary

When the company decided to issue shares to the public, a new audit firm was engaged. These auditors performed the dual-purpose procedures outlined previously, made the suggested enquiries and investigated the "unbilled contract revenue" account. They learned about management's unbundling policy and insisted that the policy be changed to recognize revenue only when all the terms of the contract were met. (The investigation yielded the information about prior years' overstatements of revenue, cost of goods sold and income.) Part of the reason for insisting on the change of policy was the finding that Western did not have a very good record of quality control and customer acceptance of software installation. Customer acceptance was frequently delayed several months while systems engineers debugged software. On several occasions Western solved the problems by purchasing complete software packages from other developers.

CASETTE 13.2
WHEN IN DOUBT, DEFER!

Problem

SaCom Corporation deferred costs under the heading of work-in-process, military contract claims and R&D test equipment, thus overstating assets, understating cost of goods sold and overstating income. Disclosure of the auditor's fees was manipulated and understated.

Method

SaCom manufactured electronic and other equipment for private customers and government military defence contracts. Near the end of the year, the company used a journal entry to remove $170,000 from cost of goods sold and to defer it as tooling, leasehold improvements and contract award and acquisition costs.

The company capitalized certain expenditures as R&D test equipment ($140,000) and as claims for reimbursement on defence contracts ($378,000).

In connection with a public offering of securities, the auditors billed SaCom $125,000 for professional fees. The underwriters objected. The auditors agreed to forgive $70,000 of the fees, and SaCom agreed to pay higher fees for work the following year (150 percent of standard billing rates). SaCom disclosed audit fees in the registration statement in the amount of $55,000. This amount was paid from the proceeds of the offering.

Paper Trail

The $170,000 deferred costs consisted primarily of labour costs. The company altered the labour time records in an effort to provide substantiating documentation. The auditors knew about the alterations. The cost was removed from jobs that were left with too little labour cost in light of the work performed on them.

The R&D test equipment cost already had been charged to cost of goods sold with no notice of deferral when originally recorded. Deferral was accomplished with an adjusting journal entry. The company did not have documentation for the adjusting entry, except for an estimate of labour cost (44 percent of all labour cost in a subsidiary was capitalized during the period).

The claim for reimbursement on defence contracts did not have documentation specifically identifying the costs as being related to the contract. (Auditors know that defence department auditors insist on documentation and justification before approving such a claim.)

The audit fee arrangement was known to the audit firm, and it was recorded in an internal memorandum.

Amount

SaCom reported net income of about $542,000 for the year, an overstatement of approximately 50 percent.

AUDIT APPROACH

Objective

Obtain evidence of the validity of production costs deferred as tooling, leasehold improvements, contract award and acquisition costs, R&D test equipment and claims for reimbursement on defence contracts.

Control

The major control lies in the procedures for documenting the validity of cost deferral journal entries.

Test of Controls

The test of controls procedure is to select a sample of journal entries, suspect ones in this case, and vouch them to supporting documentation. Experience has shown that nonstandard adjusting journal entries are the source of accounting errors and irregularities more often than standard repetitive accounting for systematic transactions. This phenomenon makes the population of adjusting journal entries a ripe field for control and substantive testing.

Audit of Balances

The account balances created by the deferral journal entries can be audited in a "dual-purpose procedure" by auditing the supporting documentation. These balances were created entirely by the journal entries, and their "existence" as legitimate assets, deferrals and reimbursement claims depends on the believability of the supporting explanations. In connection with the defence contract claim, auditors can review it with knowledge of the contract and the extent of documentation required by government contract auditors. (As a separate matter, the auditors could "search for unrecorded liabilities," but they already know about the deferred accounting fees, anyway.)

Discovery Summary

By performing the procedures outlined previously, the manager and senior and staff accountants on the engagement discovered all the questionable and improper accounting. However, the partners in the firm insisted on rendering unqualified opinions on the SaCom financial statements without adjustment. One partner owned 300 shares of the company's stock in the name of a relative (without the consent or knowledge of the relative). Another audit partner later arranged a bank loan to the company to get $125,000 to pay past-due audit fees. This partner and another, and both their wives, guaranteed the loan. (When the bank later disclosed the guarantee in a bank confirmation obtained in the course of a subsequent SaCom audit, the confirmation was removed from the audit working paper file and destroyed.)

The securities market regulator investigated, and, among other things, barred the audit firm for a period (about six months) from accepting new audit clients and also barred the partners involved in supervising various portions of the audit work from involvement with new audit clients for various periods of time. In addition the partners had violated several rules of professional conduct and were therefore subject to disciplinary action by their provincial institute (see Chapter 4 for discussion of Rules of Professional Conduct).

- -

REVIEW CHECKPOINTS

13.15 In a production situation similar to the Casette 13.1, what substantive audit work should be done on a sample of completed production orders (cost reports) recorded as cost of goods sold?

13.16 What red flag is raised when a company has an unbilled contract revenue account in its general ledger?

13.17   Why should auditors always select the client's adjusting journal entries for detail audit?

13.18   Is there anything wrong with auditors helping clients obtain bank loans to pay their accounting firm's fees?

. . . .

PART II: PAYROLL PROCESS: TYPICAL ACTIVITIES

. . . .

LEARNING OBJECTIVE

4 Describe the payroll process, including typical transactions, source documents, controls and account balances.

Every company has a payroll. It may include manufacturing labour, research scientists, administrative personnel or all of these. Subsidiary operations, partnerships and joint ventures may call it **management fees** charged by a parent company or general partner. Payroll can take different forms. Personnel management and the payroll accounting cycle not only includes transactions that affect the wage and salary accounts, but also the transactions that affect pension benefits, deferred compensation contracts, compensatory stock option plans, employee benefits (such as health insurance), payroll taxes and related liabilities for these costs. It is very important that auditors verify the payroll systems compliance with local, provincial and federal laws regarding deductions, overtime rules (e.g., after 8 hours in a day or 40 in a week), minimum hours, etc. Very large liabilities can arise from failures to comply. Many companies find it cost-effective to use an outside payroll service organization to process and distribute payroll directly to employees' bank accounts because income taxes, rates and calculations change frequently and service organizations are better able to keep up to date with these changes.

Exhibit 13–6 following shows a payroll process. It starts with hiring (and firing) people and determining their wage rates and deductions, then proceeds to attendance and work (timekeeping) and ends with payment followed by preparation of governmental (tax) and internal reports. One of these internal reports is a report of labour cost to the cost accounting department, which is how the payroll cycle is linked with cost accounting in the production cycle. Five functional responsibilities should be performed by separate people or departments. They are as follows:

- Personnel and Labour Relations—hiring and firing
- Supervision—approval of work time
- Timekeeping and Cost Accounting—payroll preparation and cost accounting
- Payroll Accounting—cheque preparation and related payroll reports
- Payroll Distribution—actual custody of cheques and distribution to employees

The elements that follow are part of the payroll control structure.

Authorization

A personnel or labour relations department that is independent of the other functions should have transaction initiation authority to add new employees to the payroll, to delete terminated employees, to obtain authorizations for deductions (such as insurance, saving bonds, withholding tax exemptions), and to transmit authority for pay rate changes to the payroll department.

Authorization also takes place in the supervision function. All pay base data (hours, job number, absences, time off allowed for emergencies and the like) should be approved by an employee's immediate supervisor.

Authorization is also a feature of the timekeeping and cost accounting function. Data on which pay is based (such as hours, piece-rate volume, incentives) should be accumulated independent of other functions.

Custody

The main feature of custody in the payroll cycle is the possession of the paycheques, cash or electronic transfer codes used to pay people. (**Electronic transfer codes** refer to the practice by some organizations of transferring pay directly into employees' bank accounts.)

E X H I B I T   1 3 – 6   PAYROLL PROCESS

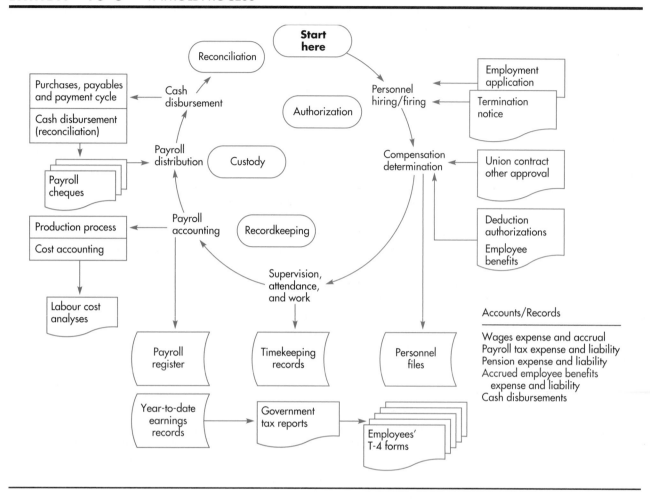

A payroll distribution function should control the delivery of pay to employees so that unclaimed cheques, cash or incomplete electronic transfers are not returned to persons involved in any of the other functions.

There are elements of custody of important documents in the supervision function and in the timekeeping function. Supervisors usually have access to time cards or time sheets that provide the basis for payment to hourly workers. Likewise, the timekeeping devices (e.g., time clocks, supervisory approval of time cards or time sheets, electronic punch-in systems) have a type of custody of employees' time-base for payroll calculations.

Approval of Fictitious Overtime

A supervisor at Austin Stoneworks discovered that she could approve overtime hours even though an employee had not worked 40 regular-time hours. She made a deal with several employees to alter their work time cards and split the extra payments. Over a 12-year period, the supervisor and her accomplices embezzled $107,000 in excess payments.

The employees' time cards were not reviewed after being approved by the supervisor. The company's payroll computer program did not have a valid data combination test that paid overtime only after 40 regular-time hours were paid.

Recordkeeping

The **payroll accounting** function should prepare individual paycheques, pay envelopes or electronic transfers using rate and deduction information supplied by the personnel function and base data supplied by the timekeeping-supervision functions. Persons in charge of the authorization and custody functions should not also prepare the payroll. They might be tempted to pay fictitious employees.

Payroll accounting maintains individual year-to-date earnings records and prepares the provincial and federal tax reports (income tax and Canada or Quebec Pension Plan with-holding, employment insurance reports and annual T-4 forms). The payroll tax returns (e.g., the federal T-4 summary that reports taxes withheld, employment insurance returns) and the annual T-4 summary to employees are useful records for audit recalculation and overall testing (analytical) procedures. They should correspond to company records. When an outside payroll processing service is used, it usually will provide the detailed journal entries to record each payroll as well as the year-end T-4 forms and summaries.

Periodic Reconciliation

The payroll bank account can be reconciled like any other bank account and the transactions also can be reconciled to recorded wage cost and expense. Some companies send to each supervisor a copy of the payroll register showing the employees paid under the supervisor's authority and responsibility. The supervisor gets a chance to reapprove the payroll after it is completed. This provides an opportunity to notice whether any persons not approved have been paid and charged to the supervisor's accountability.

The payroll report sent to cost accounting can be reconciled to the labour records used to charge labour cost to production. The cost accounting function should determine whether the labour paid is the same as the labour cost used in the cost accounting calculations.

Employees on Fixed Salary

The functional duties and responsibilities described previously relate primarily to non-salaried (hourly) employees. For salaried employees, the system is simplified by not having to collect timekeeping data. In nonmanufacturing businesses, the cost accounting operations may be very simple or nonexistent.

NOT ENOUGH CONTROL, NO FEEDBACK, BYE-BYE MONEY

Homer had been in payroll accounting for a long time. He knew it was not uncommon to pay a terminated employee severance benefits and partial pay after termination. Homer received the termination notices and the data for the final paycheques. But Homer also knew how to keep the terminated employee on the payroll for another week, pay a full week's compensation, change the electronic transfer code, and take the money for himself. The only things he could not change were the personnel department's copy of the termination notices, the payroll register, and the individual employee pay records used for withholding tax.

Fortunately for Homer, nobody reconciled the cost accounting labour charges to the payroll. The supervisors did not get a copy of the payroll register for postpayment approval, so they did not have any opportunity to notice the extra week. Nobody ever reviewed the payroll with reference to the termination notices. Former employees never complained about more pay and withholding reported on their T-4s than they actually received.

Homer and his wife, Marge, retired comfortably to a villa in Spain on a nest egg that had grown to $450,000. After Homer retired, the company experienced an unexpected decrease in labour costs and higher profits.

R E V I E W
CHECKPOINTS

13.19 What functional responsibilities are associated with the payroll process?

13.20 Describe a walk-through of the payroll transaction flow from hiring authorization to payroll cheque disbursement. What document copies would be collected? What controls noted?

13.21 In a payroll system, which duties should be separated?

13.22 What features of a payroll system can be expected to prevent or detect payment of a fictitious employee? Omission of payment to an employee?

AUDIT EVIDENCE IN MANAGEMENT REPORTS AND FILES

Payroll systems produce numerous reports. Some are internal reports and bookkeeping records. Others are government tax reports.

Personnel Files

The personnel and labour relations department keeps individual employee files. The contents usually include an employment application, a background investigation report, a notice of hiring, a job classification with pay rate authorization and authorizations for deductions (e.g., health insurance, life insurance, retirement contribution, union dues, T-4 form for income tax exemptions). When employees retire, quit or are otherwise terminated, appropriate notices of termination are filed. These files contain the raw data for important pension and post-retirement benefit accounting involving an employee's age, tenure with the company, wage record and other information used in actuarial calculations.

A personnel file should establish the reality of a person's existence and employment. The background investigation report (prior employment, references, social insurance number validity check, credentials investigation, perhaps a private investigator's report) is important for employees in such sensitive positions as accounting, finance and asset custody. One of the primary system controls is capable personnel. Experience is rich with errors, irregularities and frauds perpetrated by people who falsify their credentials (identification, education, prior experience, criminal record and the like). An additional protection from this risk is to obtain a fidelity bond for employees through an insurance company.

Timekeeping Records

Employees paid by the hour or on various incentive systems require records of time, production, piecework or other measures of the basis for their pay. (Salaried employees do not require such detail records.) Timekeeping or similar records are collected in a variety of ways. The old-fashioned time clock is still used. It accepts an employee's time card and

WHERE DID HE COME FROM?

The controller defrauded the company for several million dollars. As it turned out, he was no controller at all. He didn't know a debit from a credit. The fraudster had been fired from five previous jobs where money had turned up missing. He was discovered one evening when the president showed up unexpectedly at the company and found a stranger in the office with the controller. The stranger was doing all of the accounting for the bogus controller.

Source: "Auditing for Fraud," training course © 2006 Association of Certified Fraud Examiners.

imprints the time when work started and ended. More sophisticated systems perform the same function without the paper time card. Production employees may clock in for various jobs or production processes in the system for assigning labour cost to various stages of production. These records are part of the cost accounting for production labour.

Timekeeping records should be approved by supervisors. This approval is a sign that employees actually worked the hours (or produced the output) reported to the payroll department. The payroll department should find a supervisor's signature or initials on the documents used as the basis for periodic pay. In computer systems this approval may be automatic by virtue of the supervisory passwords used to input data into a computerized payroll system.

Payroll Register

The payroll register is a special journal. It typically contains a record for each employee showing the gross regular pay, gross overtime pay, income tax withheld, Employment Insurance (EI) and Canada Pension Plan (CPP) or Quebec Pension Plan (QPP) withheld, other deductions and net pay. The net pay amount usually is transferred from the general bank account to a special imprest payroll bank account. The journal entry for the transfer of net payroll, for example, is:

Payroll Bank Account	. . . .	.25,774
General Bank Account	. . . .	.25,774

When a payroll processing service is used, a cheque for the net payroll is usually issued to the payroll organization for it to distribute to employees' bank accounts; a separate payroll bank account is not required.

The payroll amounts are accumulated to create the payroll posting to the general ledger, like this example:

Wages clearing account	. . . .	.40,265
Employee income taxes payable	. . . .	.7,982
Employee Canada Pension plan	. . . .	.3,080
Employment Insurance premium payable	. . . .	.2,100
Life insurance premium payable	. . . .	.1,329
Payroll bank account	. . . .	.25,774

The payroll register is the primary original record for payroll accounting. It contains the implicit assertions that the employees are real company personnel (existence assertion), that they worked the time or production for which they were paid (rights/ownership assertion), that the amount of the pay is calculated properly (valuation assertion), and that all the employees were paid (completeness assertion). The presentation and disclosure assertion depends on the labour cost analysis explained following.

Payroll department records also contain the cancelled cheques (or a similar electronic-deposit record). The cheques will contain the employees' endorsements on the back.

Labour Cost Analysis

The cost accounting department can receive its information in more than one way. Some companies have systems that independently report time and production work data from the production floor directly to the cost accounting department. Other companies let their cost accounting department receive labour cost data from the payroll department. When the data is received independently, it can be reconciled in quantity (time) or amount (dollars) with a report from the payroll department. This is a type of reconciliation to make sure the cost accounting department is using actual payroll data and that the payroll department is paying only for work performed.

The cost accounting department (or a similar accounting function) is responsible for the "cost distribution." This is the most important part of the presentation and disclosure assertion with respect to payroll. The cost distribution is an assignment of payroll to the accounts where it belongs for internal and external reporting. Using its input data, the cost accounting department may make a distribution entry like this:

```
Production job A . . . . . . . . . . . . . . . . . . . . . . . . . . . .14,364
Production job B . . . . . . . . . . . . . . . . . . . . . . . . . . . .3,999
Production process A . . . . . . . . . . . . . . . . . . . . . . . .10,338
Selling expense . . . . . . . . . . . . . . . . . . . . . . . . . . . .8,961
General and administrative expense  . . . . . . . . . . . . . .2,603
           Wages clearing account  . . . . . . . . . . . . . . . . . . . . . . . . . . .40,265
```

Payroll data flows from the hiring process, through the timekeeping function, into the payroll department, thence to the cost accounting department and finally to the accounting entries that record the payroll for inventory cost determination and financial statement presentation. The same data are used for various governmental and tax reports.

Governmental and Tax Reports

Payroll systems have complications introduced by the provincial and federal income and pension plan laws. Several reports are produced. These can be used by auditors in tests of controls and substantive tests of the balances produced by accumulating numerous payroll transactions.

Year-to-Date Earnings Records

The year-to-date (YTD) earnings records are the cumulative subsidiary records of each employee's gross pay, deductions and net pay. Each time a periodic payroll is produced, the YTD earnings records are updated for the new information. The YTD earnings records are a subsidiary ledger of the wages and salaries cost and expense in the financial statements. Theoretically, like any subsidiary and control account relationship, their sum (e.g., the gross pay amounts) should be equal to the costs and expenses in the financial statements. The trouble with this reconciliation idea is that there are usually many payroll cost/expense accounts in a company's chart of accounts. The production wages may be scattered about in several different accounts, such as inventory (work-in-process and finished goods), selling, general, and administrative expenses.

However, these YTD records provide the data for periodic governmental and tax forms. They usually can be reconciled to the tax reports.

Companies in financial difficulty have been known to try to postpone payment of employee taxes, EI, and CPP or QPP withheld. However, the consequences can be serious. The Canada Revenue Agency can and will padlock the business and seize the assets for non-payment. After all, the withheld taxes belong to the employee's accounts with the government, and the employers are obligated to pay over the amounts withheld from employees along with a matching share for the Canada Pension Plan.

Employee T-4 Reports

The T-4 slip is the annual report of gross salaries and wages and the income, pension plan and employment insurance withheld. Copies are filed with the Canada (or Quebec) Pension

BEWARE THE "CLEARING ACCOUNT"

"Clearing accounts" are temporary storage places for transactions awaiting final accounting. Like the wages clearing account illustrated in the entries above, all clearing accounts should have zero balances after the accounting is completed.

A balance in a clearing account means that some amounts have not been classified properly in the accounting records. If the wages clearing account has a debit balance, some labour cost has not been properly classified in the expense accounts or cost accounting classifications. If the wages clearing account has a credit balance, the cost accountant has assigned more labour cost to expense accounts and cost accounting classifications than the amount actually paid.

Plan and the Canada Revenue Agency, and copies are sent to employees for use in preparing their income tax returns. The T-4 contains the annual YTD accumulations for each employee. They also contain each employee's address and social insurance number. In certain procedures (described later), auditors can use the name, address, social insurance number, and dollar amounts to obtain evidence about the existence of employees. The T-4 can be reconciled to the payroll tax reports.

R E V I E W
C H E C K P O I N T S

13.23   What important information can be found in employees' personnel files?

13.24   What is important about background checks using the employment applications submitted by prospective employees?

13.25   What payroll documentation supports the validity and accuracy of payroll ransactions?

13.26   Which government tax returns can be reconciled in total with employees' year-to-date earnings records? reconciled in total, but not in detail?

13.27   What is the purpose of examining endorsements on the back of payroll cheques?

CONTROL RISK ASSESSMENT

LEARNING OBJECTIVE
5 Outline control tests for auditing control over the payroll process.

The major risks in the payroll process are as follows:

- paying fictitious "employees" (invalid transactions, employees do not exist)
- overpaying for time or production (inaccurate transactions, improper valuation)
- incorrect accounting for costs and expenses (incorrect classification, improper or inconsistent presentation and disclosure)

The assessment of payroll system control risk takes on added importance because the transactions in this cycle are numerous during the year yet result in small amounts in balance sheet accounts at year-end. Therefore, in many audit engagements the review of controls and test of controls and transaction details using dual-purpose tests can provide most of the evidence. Thus, the substantive audit procedures devoted to auditing the payroll-related account balances can be limited.

General Control Considerations

Control procedures for proper segregation of responsibilities should be in place and operating. By referring to Exhibit 13–6, you can see that proper segregation involves authorization (personnel department hiring and firing, pay rate and deduction authorizations) by persons who do not have payroll preparation, paycheque distribution or reconciliation duties. Payroll distribution (custody) is in the hands of persons who neither authorize employees' pay rates or time, nor prepare the payroll cheques. Recordkeeping is performed by payroll and cost accounting personnel who do not make authorizations or distribute pay. Combinations of two or more of the duties of authorization, payroll preparation and record-keeping, and payroll distribution in one person, one office or one computerized system may open the door for errors, irregularities and frauds.

In addition, the control structure should provide for detail control-checking procedures. For example: (1) periodic comparison of the payroll register to the personnel department files to check hiring authorizations and terminated employees not deleted, (2) periodic rechecking of wage rate and deduction authorizations, (3) reconciliation of time and production paid to cost accounting calculations, (4) reconciliation of YTD earnings records with tax returns, and (5) payroll bank account reconciliation.

Computer-Based Payroll

Complex computer systems to gather payroll data, calculate payroll amounts, print cheques and transfer electronic deposits may be found in many companies. Even though the technology is complex, the basic management and control functions of ensuring a flow of data to the payroll department should be in place. Various paper records and approval signatures may not exist. They may all be imbedded in computerized payroll systems. Aspects that auditors need to consider when auditing computerized systems are covered in more detail in Chapters 7 and 9.

Internal Control Questionnaire

Information about the payroll cycle control structure often is gathered initially by completing an ICQ. An example is found in Appendix 13A, Exhibit 13A–2 with details of desirable control policies and procedures for the control environment and the important control objectives—validity, completeness, authorization, accuracy, classification, accounting and proper period recording.

Control Tests

An organization should have detail control procedures in place and operating to prevent, detect and correct accounting errors. You studied the general control objectives in Chapter 9 (validity, completeness, authorization, accuracy, classification, accounting and proper period recording). Exhibit 13–7 puts these in the perspective of the payroll functions with examples of specific objectives.

Auditors can perform control tests to determine whether controls that are said to be in place and operating actually are being performed properly by company personnel.

Exhibit 13–8 contains a selection of procedures for testing controls over payroll. Most of the illustrative procedures involve manual records, and B-5 refers to computerized systems. The samples are usually attribute samples designed along the lines you studied in Chapter 10. The right-hand column of Exhibit 13–8 shows the control objectives tested by the audit procedures.

EXHIBIT 1 3 - 7   CONTROL OBJECTIVES (PAYROLL PROCESS)

General Objectives	Examples of Specific Control Activities
1. Recorded payroll transactions are *valid* and documented.	Payroll accounting separated from personnel and timekeeping. Time cards approved by supervisor. Payroll files compared to personnel files periodically.
2. Valid payroll transactions are *recorded* and none are omitted.	Employees' complaints about paycheques investigated and resolved (written records maintained and reviewed by internal auditors).
3. Payroll names, rates, hours and deductions are *authorized*.	Names of new hires or terminations reported immediately in writing to payroll by the personnel department. Authorization for deductions kept on file. Rate authorized by union contract, agreement or written policy and approved by personnel officer.
4. Payroll computations contain *accurate* gross pay, deductions and net pay.	Payroll computations checked by person independent of preparation. Totals of payroll register reconciled to totals of payroll distribution by cost accounting.
5. Payroll transactions are *classified* correctly as direct or indirect labour or other expenses.	Employee classification reviewed periodically. Overall charges to indirect labour compared to direct labour and total product costs periodically.
6. Payroll transaction *accounting* is complete.	Details of employee withholding reconciled periodically to liability control accounts and tax returns. Employee tax expense and liabilities prepared in conjunction with payroll.
7. Payroll costs and expenses are recorded in the *proper period*.	Month-end accruals reviewed by internal auditors. Payroll computed, paid and booked in timely manner.

COVERT SURVEILLANCE

This sounds like spy work, and it indeed has certain elements of it.

Auditors can test controls over employees' clocking into work shifts by making personal observations of the process—observing whether anybody clocks in with two time cards or with two or more electronic entries, or leaves the premises after clocking in.

The auditors need to be careful not to make themselves obvious. Standing around in a manufacturing plant at 6 a.m. in the standard blue pinstripe suit uniform is as good as printing "Beware of Auditor" on your forehead. People then will be on their best behaviour, and you will observe nothing unusual.

Find an unobtrusive observation post. Stay out of sight. Use a video camera. Get a knowledgeable office employee to accompany you to interpret various activities. Perform an observation that has a chance of producing evidence of improper behaviour.

EXHIBIT 13-8   CONTROL TESTS FOR PAYROLL

	Control Objective
A. Personnel Files and Compensation Documents	
1. Select a sample of personnel files:	
a. Review personnel files for complete information on employment date, authority to add to payroll, job classification, wage rate and authorized deductions.	Authorization Classification Authorization
b. Trace pay rate to union contracts or other rate authorization. Trace salaries to directors' minutes for authorization.	Authorization
c. Trace pay rate and deduction information to payroll department files used in payroll preparation.	Completeness
2. Obtain copies of pension plans, stock options, profit sharing and bonus plans. Review and extract relevant portions that relate to payroll deductions, fringe benefit expenses, accrued liabilities and financial statement disclosure.	Validity Completeness
3. Trace management compensation schemes to minutes to verify board of directors approval.	Authorization Accuracy
B. Payroll	Accounting
1. Select a sample of payroll register entries:	
a. Vouch employee identification, pay rate and deductions to personnel files or other authorizations.	Authorization
b. Vouch hours worked to time clock records and supervisor's approval.	Validity Authorization
c. Recalculate gross pay, deductions, net pay.	Accuracy
d. Recalculate a selection of periodic payrolls.	Accuracy
e. Vouch to cancelled payroll cheque. Examine employees' endorsement or payroll distribution report details.	Accuracy Validity
2. Select a sample of time clock entries. Note supervisor's approval and trace to periodic payroll registers.	Authorization Completeness
3. Vouch a sample of periodic payroll totals to payroll bank account transfer vouchers and vouch payroll bank account deposit slip for cash transfer.	Accounting
4. Trace a sample of employees' payroll entries to individual payroll records maintained for tax reporting purposes. Reconcile total of employees' payroll records with payrolls paid for the year.	Completeness Accuracy
5. Review computer-printed error messages for evidence of the use of check digits, valid codes, limit tests and other input, processing and output application controls. Investigate correction and resolution of errors.	
6. Trace payroll information to management reports and to general ledger account postings.	Accounting
7. Obtain control of a periodic payroll and conduct a surprise distribution of paycheques.	Validity
C. Cost Distribution Reports	
1. Select a sample of cost accounting analyses of payroll:	
a. Reconcile periodic totals with payroll payments for the same periods.	Completeness
b. Vouch to time records.	Validity
2. Trace cost accounting labour cost distributions to management reports and postings in general ledger and subsidiary account(s).	Accounting Classification
3. Select a sample of labour cost items in (a) ledger accounts and/or (b) management reports. Vouch to supporting cost accounting analyses.	Validity

Dual Direction of Control Tests

The control tests in Exhibit 13–8 are designed to test the payroll accounting in two directions. One is the completeness direction, in which the control performance of audit interest is the matching of personnel file content to payroll department files and the payroll register. Exhibit 13–9 shows that the sample for this direction is taken from the population of personnel files. The procedures trace the personnel department authorizations to the payroll department files (procedure A-1–c).

The other direction is the validity direction of the test. The control performance of interest is the preparation of the payroll register. Exhibit 13–9 shows that the sample for this test is from the completed payroll registers. The individual payroll calculations are vouched to the personnel files (procedure B-1–a).

Generalized audit software can be used extensively to test controls in the payroll process. Files can be matched (e.g., personnel master file and payroll master file), and unmatched records and differences in common fields can be printed out. Statistical samples of files can be selected and printed for vouching to union contracts or to other authorizations. Statistical samples can be selected for recalculation, using the generalized software or printed out as working papers for tracing and vouching, using the procedures in Exhibit 13–8.

In both manual and computer systems, the test of controls and transaction details is highly important because the evidence bears on the reliability of internal management reports and analyses. In turn, reliance on these reports and analyses, along with other analytical relationships, constitutes a major portion of the substantive audit of payroll, compensation costs and labour costs assigned to inventory and costs of goods sold.

The test of controls procedures are designed to produce evidence of the following:

- adequacy of personnel files, especially the authorizations of pay rate and deductions used in calculating pay

- accuracy of the periodic payrolls recorded in accounts and in employees' cumulative wage records. The procedures tend to centre on the periodic payroll registers

- accuracy of cost accounting distributions and management reports (The cost accounting for labour costs must be reasonably accurate because good management reports contribute to cost control. The auditor who wishes to rely on the cost accounting system must determine whether it contains and transmits accurate information.)

EXHIBIT   13–9   DUAL DIRECTION TEST OF PAYROLL CONTROLS

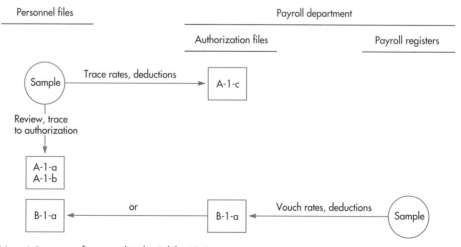

Note: A-1-a, etc., refer to tests listed in Exhibit 13–8.

OVERT SURVEILLANCE

SURPRISE PAYROLL DISTRIBUTION

Auditors may perform a surprise observation of a payroll distribution in connection with tests for overstatement. Such an observation involves taking control of paycheques and accompanying a company representative as the distribution takes place. The auditor is careful to see that each employee is identified and that only one cheque is given to each individual. Unclaimed cheques are controlled, and in this manner the auditor hopes to detect any fictitious persons on the payroll. Auditors need to be extremely careful to notice any duplication of employee identification or instance of one person attempting to pick up two or more cheques.

Computerized payroll and cost accounting systems are encountered frequently. Their complexity, however, ranges from an application of simply writing payroll cheques to an integrated system that prepares management reports and cost analyses based on payroll and cost distribution inputs. Payroll accounting is frequently contracted out to specialized service organizations.

Summary: Control Risk Assessment

The audit manager or senior accountant in charge of the audit should evaluate the evidence obtained from an understanding of the internal control structure and from the test of controls audit procedures. If the control risk is assessed very low, the substantive audit procedures on the account balances can be limited in cost-saving ways. For example, the auditors may decide it is appropriate to place considerable reliance on management reports generated by the payroll system.

On the other hand, if tests of controls reveal weaknesses, improper segregation of duties, inaccurate cost reports, inaccurate tax returns or lax personnel policies, then substantive procedures will need to be designed to lower the risk of failing to detect material error in the financial statements. The problem in payroll is that the irregularities of paying fictitious employees and overpaying for fraudulent time records do not normally misstate the financial statements as long as the improper payments are expensed. (The losses are expensed, as they should be!) The only misstatement is failing to distinguish and disclose "payroll fraud losses" from legitimate wages expense and cost of goods sold, but such losses are usually immaterial in a single year's financial statements, anyway. Nevertheless, auditors habitually perform procedures designed to find payroll fraud. It is more of a service to clients than a crucial part of the effort to detect material misstatements in financial statements.

REVIEW CHECKPOINTS

13.28 What are the most common errors and irregularities in the payroll process? Which control characteristics are auditors looking for to prevent or detect these errors?

13.29 Why is it unwise for an auditor to stand by the plant gate and time clock at starting time to observe employees checking in for work shifts?

13.30 How can an auditor determine whether the amount of labour cost charged to production was actually paid to employees?

13.31 Why might an auditor conduct a surprise observation of a payroll distribution? What should be observed?

13.32 Assume the processing of payroll is computerized. Describe a control test that can be performed using generalized audit software.

CASETTES: SUBSTANTIVE AUDIT PROCEDURES

. . . .

LEARNING OBJECTIVE

6 Design audit and investigative procedures for detecting common errors, irregularities and frauds in the payroll process.

The audit of account balances consists of procedural efforts to detect errors, irregularities and frauds that may exist in the balances, thus making them misleading in financial statements. If such misstatements exist, they are characterized by the following features:

Method: A cause of the misstatement (accidental error, intentional irregularities, or fraud attempt), which usually is made easier by some kind of failure of controls.

Paper trail: A set of telltale signs of erroneous accounting, missing or altered documents or a "dangling debit" (the false or erroneous debit that results from an overstatement of assets).

Amount: The dollar amount of overstated assets and revenue, or understated liabilities and expenses.

Each audit program for the audit of an account balance or class of transactions like payroll contains an audit approach that may enable auditors to detect errors, irregularities and frauds. Each application of procedures contains these elements:

Audit objective: A recognition of a financial statement assertion for which evidence needs to be obtained. The assertions are about existence of assets, liabilities, revenue and expenses; their valuation, their complete inclusion in the account balances; the rights and obligations inherent in them; and their proper presentation and disclosure in the financial statements. (These assertions were introduced in Chapter 9.)

Control: A recognition of the control procedures that should be used by an organization to prevent and detect errors and irregularities.

Test of controls: Ordinary and extended procedures designed to produce evidence about the effectiveness of the controls that should be in operation.

Audit of balance: Ordinary and extended substantive procedures designed to find signs of errors, irregularities and frauds in account balances and classes of transactions.

The next portion of this chapter consists of two casettes that first set the stage with a story about an error, irregularity or fraud—its method, paper trail (if any) and amount. This part of the casette gives you the "inside story," which auditors seldom know before they perform the audit work. The second part of the casette, under the heading of the audit approach, tells a structured story about the audit objective, desirable controls, test of control procedures, audit of balance procedures and discovery summary. The audit approach segment illustrates the manner in which audit procedures can be applied and the discoveries they may enable auditors to make. At the end of the chapter, some similar discussion cases are presented, and you can write the audit approach to test your ability to design audit procedures for the detection of errors, irregularities and frauds.

CASETTE 13.3
TIME CARD FORGERIES

Problem

False claims for work time caused the overpayment of wages.

Method

A temporary personnel agency assigned Nurse Jane to work at Municipal Hospital. She claimed payroll hours on agency time cards, which showed approval signatures of a county nursing shift supervisor. The shift supervisor had been terminated by the county several months prior to the periods covered by the time cards in question. Nurse Jane worked one or two days per week but submitted time cards for a full 40-hour work week.

The personnel agency paid Nurse Jane, then billed Municipal Hospital for the wages and benefits. Supporting documents were submitted with the personnel agency's bills.

Paper Trail

Each hospital work station keeps ward shift logs, which are sign-in sheets showing nurses on duty at all times. Nurses sign in and sign out when going on and off duty.

Municipal Hospital maintains personnel records showing, among other things, the period of employment of its own nurses, supervisors and other employees.

Amount

Nurse Jane's wages and benefits were billed to the hospital at $22 per hour. False time cards overcharging about 24 extra hours per week cost the hospital $528 per week. Nurse Jane was assigned to Municipal Hospital for 15 weeks during the year, so she caused overcharges of about $7,900. However, she told three of her crooked friends about the procedure, and they overcharged the hospital another $24,000.

AUDIT APPROACH

Audit Objective

Obtain evidence to determine whether wages were paid to valid employees for actual time worked at the authorized pay rate.

Control

Control procedures should include a hiring authorization putting employees on the payroll. When temporary employees are used, this authorization includes contracts for nursing time, conditions of employment and terms including the contract reimbursement rate. Control records of attendance and work should be kept (ward shift log). Supervisors should approve time cards or other records used by the payroll department to prepare paycheques.

In this case the contract with the personnel agency provided that approved time cards had to be submitted as supporting documentation for the agency billings.

Test of Controls

Although the procedures and documents for control were in place, the controls did not operate because nobody at the hospital ever compared the ward shift logs to time cards, and nobody examined the supervisory approval signatures for their validity. The scam was easy in the temporary personnel agency situation because the nurses submitted their own time cards to the agency for payment. The same scam might be operated by the hospital's own employees if they, too, could write their time cards and submit them to the payroll department.

Auditors should make enquiries (e.g., internal control questionnaire) about the error-checking procedures performed by hospital accounting personnel. Test of control audit procedures are designed to determine whether control procedures are followed properly by the organization. Since the comparison and checking procedures were not performed, there is nothing to test.

However, the substantive tests described following are identical to the procedures that could be called "tests of controls," but in this case they are performed to determine whether nurses were paid improperly (a substantive purpose).

Audit of Balances

Select a sample of agency billings and their supporting documentation (time cards). Vouch rates billed by the agency to the contract for agreement to proper rate. Vouch time claimed to hospital work attendance records (ward shift logs). Obtain handwriting examples of supervisors' signatures and compare them to the approval signatures on time cards. Use personnel records to determine whether supervisors were actually employed by the hospital at the time they approved the time cards. Use available work attendance records to determine whether supervisors were actually on duty at the time they approved the time cards.

Discovery Summary

The auditors quickly found that Nurse Jane (and others) had not signed in on ward shift logs for days they claimed to have worked. Further investigation showed that the supervisors who supposedly signed the time cards were not even employed by the hospital at the time their signatures were used for approvals. Handwriting comparison showed that the signatures were not written by the supervisors.

The agency was informed and refunded the $31,900 overpayment proved by the auditors. The auditors continued to comb the records for more![1]

CASETTE 13.4
THE WELL-PADDED PAYROLL

Problem

Embezzlement with fictitious people on the payroll.

Method

Maybelle had responsibility for preparing personnel files for new hires, approval of wages, verification of time cards and distribution of payroll cheques. She "hired" fictitious employees, faked their records and ordered cheques through the payroll system. She deposited some cheques in several personal bank accounts and cashed others, endorsing all of them with the names of the fictitious employees and her own.

[1] Adapted from vignette published in *Internal Auditor*, April 1990.

Paper Trail

Payroll creates a large paper trail with individual earnings records, T-4 tax forms, payroll deductions for taxes, insurance and pension plans and payroll tax reports. She mailed all the T-4 forms to the same post office box.

Amount

Maybelle stole $160,000 by creating some "ghosts," usually 3 to 5 out of 112 people on the payroll, and paying them an average of $256 per week for three years. Sometimes the ghosts quit and were later replaced by others. But she stole "only" about 2 percent of the payroll funds during the period.

AUDIT APPROACH

Objective

Obtain evidence of the existence and validity of payroll transactions.

Control

Different people should be responsible for hiring (preparing personnel files), approving wages, and distributing payroll cheques. "Thinking like a crook" leads an auditor to see that Maybelle could put people on the payroll and obtain their cheques.

Test of Controls

Audit for transaction authorization and validity. Random sampling may not work because of the small number of ghosts. Look for the obvious. Select several weeks' cheque blocks, account for numerical sequence (to see whether any cheques have been removed), and examine cancelled cheques for two endorsements.

Audit of Balances

There may be no "balance" to audit other than the accumulated total of payroll transactions, and the total may not appear out of line with history because the fraud is small in relation to total payroll and has been going on for years.

Conduct a surprise payroll distribution; follow up by examining prior cancelled cheques for the missing employees. Scan personnel files for common addresses.

Discovery Summary

Both the surprise distribution and the scan for common addresses provided the names of 2–3 exceptions. Both led to prior cancelled cheques (which Maybelle had not removed and the bank reconciler had not noticed) that carried Maybelle's own name as endorser. Confronted, she confessed.

REVIEW CHECKPOINTS

13.33 Why are control documents and control procedures used if company personnel do not use them to prevent, detect and correct payroll errors, irregularities and frauds?

13.34 How can an auditor find out whether payroll control documents and control procedures were followed by client personnel?

13.35 Give some examples of payroll control omissions that would make it easy to "think like a crook" and see opportunities for errors, irregularities and frauds.

13.36 What difference is there, if any, between tests of controls and tests (audit) of balances in the payroll area?

Analysis of Financial Statement Relationships

The audit of the production and payroll processes results in verifying the balances of inventory, various payroll liabilities, cost of goods sold and wages/salary expense. In the balance sheet approach to auditing, we can analyze balance changes and the financial statement items related to them by preparing a continuity schedule. The finished goods inventory balance is used as an example for the production process:

Audited Amount	Financial Statement Where Amount Is Reported
Opening balance of finished goods inventory	Balance sheet (prior year comparative figures)
Add: Purchases of materials during the year Labour costs allocated Overhead costs allocated	Cash flow statement (direct method)

Continued

Deduct:	Balance sheet
Costs allocated to inventory work-in-process	(current year balance of work-in-process inventory)
Deduct:	
Cost of goods sold	Income statement expense
Ending balance of finished goods inventory	Balance sheet
	(current year figures)

Analytical procedures that use these relations include inventory turnover ratios and gross margin analysis. Misstatements in the existence, completeness and valuation assertions for inventory may result in unexplained fluctuations in these relations.

SUMMARY

The production and payroll process consists of two parts that are closely related. Production involves production planning; inventory planning; acquisition of labour, materials and overhead (purchases, payables and payment process); custody of assets while work is in process and when finished products are stored in inventory; and cost accounting. Payroll is a part of every business and an important part of every production cycle. Management and control of labour costs are important. The payroll process consists of hiring, rate authorization, attendance and work supervision, payroll processing and paycheque distribution.

Production and payroll information systems produce many internal documents, reports and files that are sources of audit information. These processes are characterized by having mostly internal documentation as evidence and by having relatively little external documentary evidence. Aside from the physical inventory in the production process, the accounts in the production and payroll process are intangible. They cannot be observed, inspected, touched or counted in any meaningful way. Most audit procedures for this cycle are analytical procedures and dual-purpose procedures that test both the company's control procedures and the existence, valuation and completeness assertions made by accumulating the results of numerous labour and overhead transactions.

Companies reduce control risk by having a suitable separation of authorization, custody, recording and periodic reconciliation duties. Error-checking procedures of analyzing production orders and finished production cost reports are important for proper determination of inventory values and proper valuation of cost of goods sold. Without these procedures, many things could go wrong, ranging from overvaluing the inventory to understating costs of production by deferring costs that should be expensed.

Cost accounting is a central feature of the production process. Illustrative casettes in this chapter told the stories of financial reporting manipulations and of the audit procedures that detected them.

Payroll accounting is a critical operation for expenditure control. Many cases of embezzlement occur during this process. Illustrative casettes in the chapter told the stories of some fictitious employees and false-time embezzlements and thefts.

MULTIPLE-CHOICE QUESTIONS FOR PRACTICE AND REVIEW

13.37 When an auditor tests a company's cost accounting system, the auditor's procedures are designed primarily to determine that:

a. Quantities on hand have been computed based on acceptable cost accounting techniques that reasonably approximate actual quantities on hand.

b. Physical inventories are in substantial agreement with book inventories.

c. The system is in accordance with generally accepted accounting principles and is functioning as planned.

d. Costs have been properly assigned to finished goods, work-in-process and cost of goods sold.

13.38 The auditor tests the quantity of materials charged to work-in-process by vouching these quantities to:
   a. Cost ledgers.
   b. Perpetual inventory records.
   c. Receiving reports.
   d. Material requisition.

13.39 Effective internal control over the payroll function should include procedures that segregate the duties of making salary payments to employees and:
   a. Controlling unemployment insurance claims.
   b. Maintaining employee personnel records.
   c. Approving employee fringe benefits.
   d. Hiring new employees.

13.40 Which of the following is the best way for an auditor to determine that every name on a company's payroll is that of a bona fide employee presently on the job?
   a. Examine personnel records for accuracy and completeness.
   b. Examine employees' names listed on payroll tax returns for agreement with payroll accounting records.
   c. Make a surprise observation of the company's regular distribution of paycheques.
   d. Control the mailing of annual T-4 tax forms to employee addresses in their personnel files.

13.41 It would be appropriate for the payroll accounting department to be responsible for which of the following functions?
   a. Approval of employee time records.
   b. Maintenance of records of employment, discharges and pay increases.
   c. Preparation of periodic governmental reports as to employees' earnings and withholding taxes.
   d. Temporary retention of unclaimed employee paycheques.

13.42 One of the auditor's objectives in observing the actual distribution of payroll cheques is to determine that every name on the payroll is that of a bona fide employee. The payroll observation is an auditing procedure that is generally performed for which of the following reasons?
   a. The professional standards that are generally accepted require the auditor to perform the payroll observation.
   b. The various phases of payroll work are not sufficiently segregated to afford effective internal control.
   c. The independent auditor uses personal judgement and decides to observe the payroll distribution on a particular audit.
   d. The standards that are generally accepted by the profession are interpreted to mean that payroll observation is expected on an audit unless circumstances dictate otherwise.

13.43 During the year, a bookkeeper perpetrated a theft by preparing erroneous T-4 forms. The bookkeeper's employment insurance (EI) withheld was overstated by $500 and the EI withheld from all other employees was understated. Which of the following is an audit procedure that would detect such a fraud?
   a. Multiplication of the applicable rate by the individual gross taxable earnings.
   b. Utilizing Form T-4 and withholding charts to determine whether deductions authorized per pay period agree with amounts deducted per pay period.
   c. Recalculating the totals in the payroll register followed by tracing postings to the general ledger.
   d. Vouching cancelled cheques to federal tax report.

13.44 A common audit procedure in the audit of payroll transactions involves vouching selected items from the payroll journal to employee time cards that have been approved by supervisory personnel. This procedure is designed to provide evidence in support of the audit proposition that:
   a. Only bona fide employees worked and their pay was properly computed.
   b. Jobs on which employees worked and their pay was properly computed.
   c. Internal controls relating to payroll disbursements are operating effectively.
   d. All employees worked the number of hours for which their pay was computed.

13.45 To minimize the opportunities for fraud, unclaimed cash payroll should be:
   a. Deposited in a safe deposit box.
   b. Held by the payroll custodian.
   c. Deposited in a special bank account.
   d. Held by the controller.

13.46 An effective client internal control procedure to prevent lack of agreement between the cost accounting for labour cost is and the payroll paid is:
   a. Reconciliation of totals on production job time tickets with job reports by the employees responsible for the specific jobs.
   b. Verification of agreement of production job time tickets with employee clock cards by a payroll department employee.
   c. Preparation of payroll transaction journal entries by an employee who reports to the personnel department director.
   d. Custody of pay rate authorization forms by the supervisor of the payroll department.

(AICPA adapted)

13.47 In a computerized payroll system, an auditor would be least likely to use test data to test controls related to:
   a. Missing employee numbers.
   b. Proper signature approval of overtime by supervisors.
   c. Time tickets with invalid job numbers.
   d. Agreement of hours per clock card with hours on time tickets.

EXERCISES AND PROBLEMS

. . . .

PRODUCTION PROCESS

13.48 ICQ Items: Possible Error or Irregularity Due to
LO.1   **Weakness.** Refer to the internal control questionnaire
LO.2   (Appendix 13A, Exhibit 13A–1) and assume the answer
to each question is no. Prepare a table matching questions to errors or irregularities that could occur because of the absence of the control. Your column headings should be:

Question	Possible Error or Irregularity Due to Weakness

13.49 Control Tests Related to Controls and Objectives.
LO.1   Each of the following test of control audit procedures
LO.2   may be performed during the audit of the controls in the production and conversion cycle. For each procedure: (*a*) identify the internal control procedure (strength) being tested, and (*b*) identify the internal control objective(s) being addressed.

1. Balance and reconcile detail production cost sheets to the work-in-process inventory control account.
2. Scan closed production cost sheets for missing numbers in the sequence.
3. Vouch a sample of open and closed production cost sheet entries to (*a*) labour reports and (*b*) issue slips and materials-used reports.
4. Locate the material issue forms. Are they prenumbered? kept in a secure location? available to unauthorized persons?
5. Select several summary journal entries in the work-in-process inventory: (*a*) vouch to weekly labour and material reports and to production cost sheets, and (*b*) trace to control account.
6. Select a sample of the material issue slips in the production department file. Examine for:
   a. Issue date/materials-used report date.
   b. Production order number.
   c. Supervisor's signature or initials.
   d. Name and number of material.
   e. Raw material stores clerk's signature or initials.
   f. Matching material requisition in raw material stores file. Note date of requisition.
7. Determine by enquiry and inspection if cost clerks review dates on report of units completed for accounting in the proper period.

13.50 Control over Departmental Labour Cost in a Job-
LO.1   **Cost System.** The Brown Printing Company accounts
LO.2   for the services it performs on a job-cost basis. Most
 jobs take a week or less to complete and involve two or more of Brown's five operating departments. Actual costs are accumulated by job. To ensure timely billing, however, the company prepares sales invoices based on cost estimates.

Recently, several printing jobs have incurred losses. To avoid future losses, management has decided to focus on cost control at the department level. Since labour is a major element of cost, management has proposed the development of a department labour cost report. This report will originate in the payroll department as part of the biweekly payroll and then go to an accounting clerk for comparison to total labour cost estimates by department. If the actual total department labour costs in a payroll are not much more than the estimated total departmental labour cost during that period, the accounting clerk will send the report to the department foreman. If the accounting clerk concludes that a significant variance exists, the report will be sent to the assistant controller. The assistant controller will investigate the cause when time is available, and recommend corrective action to the production manager.

Required:
Evaluate the proposal:
a. Give at least three common aspects of control with which the department labour cost report proposal complies. Give an example from the case to support each aspect cited.
b. Give at least three common aspects of control with which the departmental labour cost report proposal does not comply. Give an example from the case to support each aspect cited.

(CIA adapted)

13.51 Audit the Fixed Asset and Amortization Schedule.
LO.1   Bart's Company has prepared the fixed asset and amor-
LO.2   tization schedule shown in Exhibit 13.51–1. The following information is available:

- The land was purchased eight years ago when Building 1 was erected. The location was then remote but now is bordered by a major freeway. The appraised value is $35 million.
- Building 1 has an estimated useful life of 35 years and no residual value.
- Building 2 was built by a local contractor this year. It also has an estimated useful life of 35 years and no residual value. The company occupied it on May 1 this year.
- The Computer A system was purchased January 1 six years ago, when the estimated useful life was eight years with no residual value. It was sold on May 1 for $500,000.
- The Computer B system was placed in operation as soon as the Computer A system was sold. It is estimated to be in use for six years with no residual value at the end.
- The company estimated the useful life of the press at 20 years with no residual value.
- Auto 1 was sold during the year for $1,000.
- Auto 2 was purchased on July 1. The company expects to use it five years and then sell it for $2,000.
- All amortization is calculated on the straight-line method using months of service.

EXHIBIT 13.51–1

	Asset Cost (000s)				Accumulated Amortization (000s)			
					Fixed Assets and Amortization			
Description	Beginning Balance	Added	Sold	Ending Balance	Beginning Balance	Added	Sold	Ending Balance
Land	10,000			10,000				
Bldg. 1	30,000			30,000	6,857	857		7,714
Bldg. 2		42,000		42,000		800		800
Computer A	5,000		5,000	0	3,750	208	3,958	0
Computer B		3,500		3,500		583		583
Press	1,500			1,500	300	150		450
Auto 1	15		15	0	15		15	0
Auto 2		22		22		2		2
Total	46,515	45,522	5,015	87,022	10,922	2,600	3,973	9,549

Required:

a. Audit the amortization calculations. Are there any errors? Put the errors in the form of an adjusting journal entry, assuming 90 percent of the amortization on the buildings and the press has been charged to cost of goods sold and 10 percent is still capitalized in the inventory, and the other amortization expense is classified as general and administrative expense.

b. List two audit procedures for auditing the fixed asset additions.

c. What will an auditor expect to find in the "gain and loss on sale of assets" account? What amount of cash flow from investing activities will be in the statement of cash flows?

PAYROLL PROCESS

13.52 ICQ Items: Errors That Could Occur from Control
LO.4   **Weaknesses.** Refer to the internal control questionnaire
LO.5   on a payroll system (Exhibit 13A–2 in Appendix 13A) and assume the answer to each question is no. Prepare a table matching the questions to errors or irregularities that could occur because of the absence of the control. Your column headings should be:

Question Number	Possible Error or Irregularity Due to Weakness

13.53 ICQ Items: Control Objectives, Control Tests and
LO.4   **Possible Errors or Irregularities.** Listed below is a se-
LO.5   lection of items from the payroll processing internal
LO.6   control questionnaire in Exhibit 13A–2.

1. Are names of terminated employees reporting in writing to the payroll department?
2. Are authorizations for deductions, signed by the employees, on file?
3. Is there a timekeeping department (function) independent of the payroll department?
4. Are timekeeping and cost accounting records (such as hours, dollars) reconciled with payroll department calculations of wage and salaries?

Required:

For each question above:

a. Identify the control objective to which the question applies.

b. Specify one test of controls audit procedure an auditor could use to determine whether the control was operating effectively (see Exhibit 13–8 for procedures).

c. Using your business experience, your logic and/or your imagination, give an example of an error or irregularity that could occur if the control were absent or ineffective.

13.54 Control Tests, Evaluation of Possible Diversion of
LO.4   **Payroll Funds.** The Generous Loan Company has 100
LO.5   branch loan offices. Each office has a manager and four
LO.6   or five subordinates who are employed by the manager. Branch managers prepare the weekly payroll, including their own salaries, and pay employees from cash on hand. Employees sign the payroll sheet signifying receipt of their salary. Hours worked by hourly personnel are inserted in the payroll register sheet from time cards prepared by the employees and approved by the manager.

The weekly payroll register sheets are sent to the head office along with other accounting statements and reports. The head office compiles employee earnings records and prepares all federal and provincial salary reports from the weekly payroll sheets.

Salaries are established by head office job-evaluation schedules. Salary adjustments, promotions, and transfers of full-time employees are approved by a head office salary committee based on the recommendations of branch managers and area supervisors. Branch managers advise the salary committee of new full-time employees and terminated employees. Part-time and temporary employees are hired without advising the salary committee.

Required:

a. Prepare a payroll audit program to be used in the head office to audit the branch office payrolls of the Generous Loan Company. See Exhibit 13–8 for sample audit procedures.

b. Based on your review of the payroll system, how might funds for payroll be diverted?

(AICPA adapted)

13.55 Major Risks in Payroll Process. Prepare a schedule of the major risks in the payroll process. Identify the control objectives and the financial statement assertions related to each. Lay out a three-column schedule like this:

LO.4
LO.5

Payroll Process Risk	Control Objective	Assertion

13.56 Payroll Authorization in a Computer System. Two accountants were discussing control procedures and test of control auditing for payroll systems. The senior accountant in charge of the engagement said: "It is impossible to determine who authorizes transactions when the payroll account is computerized."

LO.4
LO.5

Required:
Evaluate the senior accountant's statement about control in a computerized payroll system. List the points in the flow of payroll information where authorization takes place.

13.57 Payroll Processed by a Service Organization. Assume that you are the audit senior conducting a review of the payroll system of a new client. In the process of interviewing the payroll department manager, she makes the following statement: "We don't need many controls since our payroll is done outside the company by Automated Data Processing, a service organization."

LO.5

Required:
Evaluate the payroll department manager's statement and describe how a service organization affects an auditors' review of controls. You may want to refer to Chapter 9.

Discussion Cases

13.58 Croyden Factory, Inc.: Evaluation of Flowchart for Payroll Control Weaknesses. A PA's audit working papers contain a narrative description of a segment of the Croyden Factory, Inc., payroll system and an accompanying flowchart (Exhibit 13.58–1 on page 545) as follows:

NARRATIVE:
The internal control system, with respect to the personnel department, is well functioning and is not included in the accompanying flowchart.

At the beginning of each workweek, payroll clerk No. 1 reviews the payroll department files to determine the employment status of factory employees. Clerk No. 1 then prepares clock time cards and distributes them as each individual arrives at work. This payroll clerk, who also is responsible for custody of the cheque signature stamp machine, verifies the identity of each payee before delivering signed cheques to the supervisor.

At the end of each workweek, the supervisor distributes payroll cheques for the preceding workweek. Concurrent with this activity, the supervisor reviews the current week's employee timecards, notes the regular and overtime hours worked on a summary form, and initials the clock time cards. The supervisor then delivers all time cards and unclaimed payroll cheques to payroll clerk No. 2.

Required:
a. Based on the narrative and accompanying flowchart (Exhibit 13.58–1), what are the weaknesses in the system of internal control?
b. Based on the narrative and accompanying flowchart, what enquiries should be made with respect to clarifying the existence of possible additional weaknesses in the system of internal control?

Note: Do not discuss the internal control system of the personnel department.

(AICPA adapted)

13.59 Vane Corporation: Control Weaknesses in Computerized Payroll System. The Vane Corporation is a manufacturing concern that has been in business for the past 18 years. During this period, the company has grown from a very small family owned operation to a medium-sized manufacturing concern with several departments. Despite this growth, a substantial number of the procedures employed by Vane have been in effect since the business was started. Just recently, Vane has computerized its payroll function.

LO.5

The payroll function operates in the following manner. Each worker picks up a weekly time card on Monday morning and writes in his or her name and identification number. These blank cards are kept near the factory entrance. The workers write on the time card the times of their daily arrival and departure. On the following Monday, the factory supervisor collect the completed time cards for the previous week and send them to data processing.

In data processing the time cards are entered into the computerized payroll system. The system updates the payroll records and prints out the paycheques. The cheques are written on the regular chequing account and imprinted by a signature plate with the treasurer's signature. The cheques are sent to the factory supervisors who distribute them to the workers or hold them for absent workers to pick up later.

The supervisors notify data processing of new employees and terminations. Any changes in hourly pay rate or any other changes affecting payroll usually are communicated to data processing by the supervisors.

EXHIBIT   13.58-1   CROYDEN, INC., FACTORY PAYROLL SYSTEM

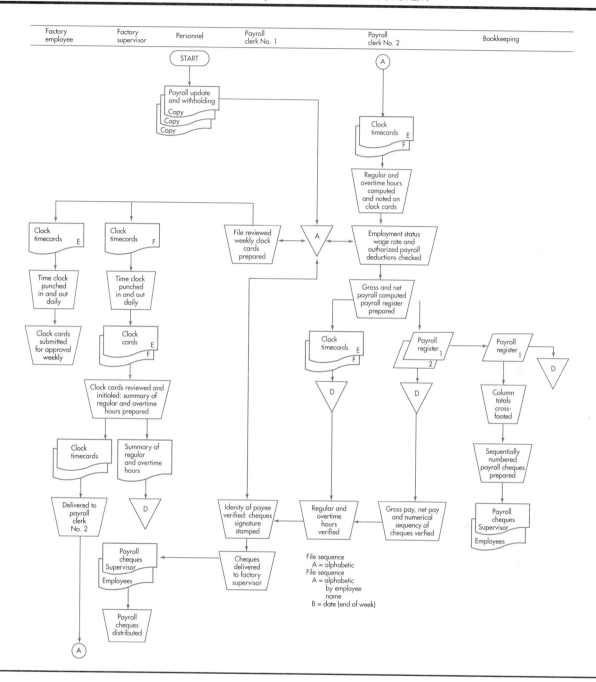

The workers also complete a job time ticket for each individual job they work on each day. The job time tickets are collected daily and sent to cost accounting, where they are used to prepare a cost distribution analysis.

Further analysis of the payroll function reveals the following:

1. A worker's gross wages never exceed $300 per week.
2. Raises never exceed 55 cents per hour for the factory workers.

3. No more than 20 hours of overtime are allowed each week.
4. The factory employs 150 workers in 10 departments.

The payroll function had not been operating smoothly for some time but even more problems have surfaced since the payroll was computerized. The factory supervisors have indicated that they would like a weekly report indicating worker tardiness, absenteeism, and idle time, so that they can determine the amount of productive time lost and the reason for the lost time.

The following errors and inconsistencies have been encountered the past few pay periods:

1. A worker's paycheque was not processed properly because he had transposed two numbers in his identification number when he filled out his time card.
2. A worker was issued a cheque for $1,531.80 when it should have been $153.18.
3. One worker's paycheque was not written, and this error was not detected until the paycheques for that department were distributed by the supervisor.
4. Some of the payroll register records were accidentally erased from the system when a data processing clerk tried to reorganize and rename the files in the hard drive of the computer used to process the payroll. Data processing attempted to re-establish the destroyed portion from original source documents and other records.
5. One worker received a paycheque for an amount considerably larger than he should have. Further investigation revealed that 84 had been keyed instead of 48 for hours worked.
6. Several paycheques that were issued to employees were not included in the totals used to post the payroll journal entry to the general ledger accounts. This was not detected for several pay periods.
7. In processing nonroutine changes, a data processing clerk included a pay rate increase for one of his friends in the factory. By chance, this was discovered by another employee.

Required:
Identify the control weaknesses in Vane's payroll procedures and in the computer processing as it is now conducted. Recommend the necessary changes to correct the system. Arrange your answer in the following columnar format:

Control Weaknesses	Recommendations
1.	1.

13.60 **Payroll Test of Controls.** The diagram in Exhibit
LO.4 13.60–1 describes several payroll test of control proce-
LO.5 dures. It shows the direction of the tests, leading from samples of clock cards, payrolls and cumulative year-to-date earnings records to blank squares.

Required:
For each blank square in Exhibit 13.60–1, write a payroll test of controls procedure and describe the evidence it can produce. (Hint: Refer to Exhibit 13–8.)

13.61 **Cost Accounting Test of Controls.** The diagram in Ex-
LO.1 hibit 13.61–1 on page 547 describes several cost ac-
LO.2 counting test of control procedures. It shows the direction of the tests, leading from samples of cost accounting analyses, management reports and the general ledger to blank squares.

Required:
For each blank square in Exhibit 13.61–1, write a cost accounting test of controls procedure and describe the evidence it can produce. (Hint: Refer to Exhibit 13–8.)

E X H I B I T   1 3 . 6 0 – 1   DIAGRAM OF PAYROLL TEST OF CONTROLS

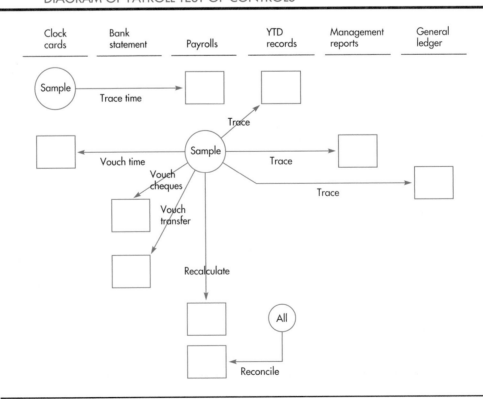

EXHIBIT 13.61-1   DIAGRAM OF COST ACCOUNTING TEST OF CONTROLS

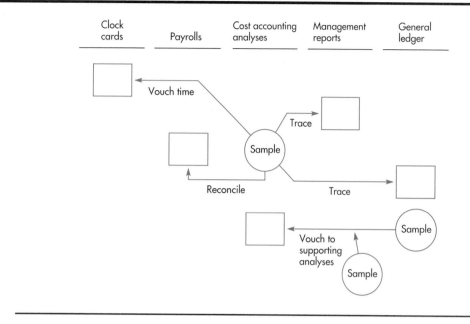

13.62 Inventory Costing Errors, Standard Manufacturing

LO.3 **Costs.** Thermox Inc. is a manufacturer of heating elements and devices. One of its main raw material components is steel tubing. During the current year, Thermox's new raw material buyer began purchasing steel tubing from a U.S. supplier. The buyer found this supplier's prices to be considerably lower than the previous Canadian suppliers that Thermox had been buying from.

Thermox's cost accounting department uses standard manufacturing costs to determine its inventory cost and cost of goods sold. In her audit of the reasonability of the standard costs, the audit senior is vouching the raw materials components listing to supplier invoices and supporting documents. She notes several steel tubing purchases in March that were invoiced in U.S. dollars (a U.S. dollar at this time was worth about $1.50 Canadian). However, the U.S. dollar amount, not the converted Canadian dollar amount, is used in the standard costing formula. Steel tubing comprises 70 percent of Thermox's standard manufacturing cost of a heating element. The audit senior extends her vouching and discovers that all steel tubing purchases from March to the December year-end were from the same U.S. supplier, and were invoiced in U.S. dollars.

As further investigation, the audit senior examines the U.S. suppliers monthly statements of account and discovers that Thermox's accounts payable department has been paying the U.S. steel tubing invoices in Canadian dollars. This resulted in Thermox short-paying the U.S. supplier by about 50 percent. Because of this related error, no significant cost variances appeared for raw materials, which would have alerted Thermox management to the problem.

Required:

a. What impact will this error have on Thermox's year-end inventory balance and its cost of sales if standard costs are used and no variances are adjusted? What impact will this error have on accounts payable? State any assumptions you make.

b. What records will the audit senior need to examine and what tests and analyses will she need to perform to assess the magnitude of the error in inventory, cost of goods sold and accounts payable?

c. What control deficiency would allow this type of error to occur, and what kind of control procedure(s) could be implemented to prevent this type of error?

13.63 Work-In-Process Inventory, Tests of Control. As-

LO.2 sume an auditor finds the following errors while performing tests of controls for work-in-process inventory in a custom machinery manufacturing business. For each finding, state which control objective is affected, what control deficiency is indicated and what further investigation (if any) should be undertaken by the auditor.

a. Budgeted labour hours are 30 percent lower than actual labour costs and production cost reports.

b. Of 20 time clock entries examined for July 14, three do not appear on the daily labour report or production cost report for that day.

c. Weekly labour cost reports do not agree with the weekly payroll summary.

d. The open production report used to cost work-in-process inventory contains costs of materials for which no matching amount and description is found on the material used reports and no material issue slip is on file in the material storage department.

13.64 Auditor Independence. Review the SaCom case given
LO.3 in the chapter (Casette 13.2). Discuss the auditor inde-

pendence issues present in this case and how these issues may have contributed to the audit deficiencies that
occurred. Discuss whether the security market regulator's penalties were appropriate in the circumstances, in
your view.

13.65 Audit of Inventory. During his examination of the in-
LO.3 ventories and related accounts of Consumer Electronics,
manufacturer and distributor of small appliances, a PA
encountered the following:

a. During the inventory observation, the PA noticed
several trucks loaded with finished goods parked at
the shipping dock. He noted that the contents of the
trucks were excluded from the physical inventory.

b. The finished goods inventory at the company's plant
included several products for which there was a high
volume of goods on hand, with many of the cartons
being old and covered with dust. In response to the
PA's questions, the plant manager stated that there
was no problem as "all of these goods will eventually
be sold although some price incentives may be
necessary."

c. While reviewing the complex calculations used to
develop the unit production costs of items in finished
goods, the PA noted that the costs of the company's
electrical engineering department, which had been
treated as period expenses in previous years, were
included as part of manufacturing overhead in the
current year.

d. The company installed a new computerized perpetual inventory system during the year. The PA noted
that numerous year-end quantities as per the perpetual records differed from the actual physical inventory counts. In part because of these problems, the
company took a complete physical inventory at
year-end.

Required:

Describe the additional audit procedures (if any) that
the PA should perform to obtain sufficient appropriate
evidence in each of the preceding situations.

(CGA-Canada adapted)

13.66 Audit Estate Inventory. Desai Developments Limited
LO.3 (DDL) is in the business of buying undeveloped land in

the regions outside of Calgary and holding it until development permits have been obtained and market conditions are favourable for development. DDL began operations 12 years ago as a developer of residential
subdivisions. Once a property is ready for development,
DDL contracts with various construction companies to
build the houses. DDL handles all the promotions and
sales of the houses once they are completed.

Due to recent changes in environmental laws and
zoning restrictions, some of the sites DDL originally
purchased for subdivision developments can no longer
be used for this purpose. However, golf courses are still
permissible on these sites because they preserve

wetlands and forests. As a result of these changes in its
industry, DDL is undertaking a new business model that
involves developing and operating golf courses. DDL
will also sell off the outer edges of the golf course properties as building lots for large homes. Large "estate lot"
homes are still permitted because they have a low
impact on the environment.

The president of DDL, Mira Desai, owns 51 percent
of the DDL common shares. The remaining common
shares are held by various relatives of Ms. Desai. DDL
also has financed its operation by bank mortgages on the
land. Mira Desai now wants to issue preferred shares in
DDL to public investors, using the proceeds to pay back
the bank mortgages and fund the golf course developments. The plan is for the preferred shares to be non-
voting, paying a 6 percent noncumulative dividend per
year plus a life-long membership in one of the golf
courses. She has found a securities firm to sell the preferred shares to the public, but DDL will need to provide prospective investors with DDL's 20X5 financial
statements prepared in accordance with generally accepted accounting principles, and projected financial
information for the new golf course development
business.

Mira Desai has asked for your advice in preparing
GAAP financial statements and the projected financial
information. She is considering engaging your audit
firm as its auditor for the 20X5 financial statements. Up
until now DDL has only prepared unaudited financial
statements primarily for tax purposes, and has always
used accounting methods that result in paying the minimum amount of tax. In discussions with Mira Desai,
and from reviewing DDL's most recent annual financial
statements (for the year ended December 31, 20X5),
you learn the following:

1. DDL currently owns four properties that have been
   approved for golf course development. DDL has
   finalized the golf course development plans and will
   start development in the spring of 20X6. DDL owns
   five other properties that may be suitable for future
   golf course developments.

2. DDL owns another eight properties that can still be
   developed into residential subdivisions. Recently
   DDL received an offer from another property development company, Atim Corp., to purchase all eight
   of these properties for $50 million. The mortgages
   on these eight properties are $45 million. Mira
   Desai is interested in exiting from the subdivision
   development activities as it would allow DDL to
   focus on the golf course business. She is considering
   making a counter-offer in which DDL would form a
   50:50 joint venture with Atim Corp: DDL would
   contribute the properties to this joint venture entity
   and Atim would contribute the cash and management skills needed to construct and sell the subdivision homes.

3. DDL has capitalized the purchase price of the land,
   legal fees relating to the purchase, and land transfer
   taxes. All other costs related to the properties, such

as property taxes, interest, earth-moving costs, and fees for architectural and landscaping plans have all been expensed to maximize tax deductions.

4. DDL's net income from the subdivision business has varied widely over the years, with profits arising in years when housing developments are completed and sold, and losses arising in other years. Revenue is recognized when each house is sold. The average subdivision development takes about 18 months to complete from the time construction begins. It is expected that a golf course development will take about two years to complete because of the extensive landscaping and planting required.

5. The golf course development costs can be partly financed by selling off the estate lots around the golf course site to the construction companies that will build the custom houses. As part of its agreement with these construction companies, DDL will handle the sales promotions and marketing of the houses as they become ready for occupancy for a 10 percent commission on selling prices.

6. To date, DDL has completed five housing subdivision developments. The first development, completed about 10 years ago, has recently been in the news because many of the home owners have noticed methane and other noxious gases seeping into their basements. Environmental assessments of the properties have determined that the subdivision was built on a site that was used as a landfill site in the 1950s. The landfill site was never properly sealed off prior to redevelopment and is now releasing gases that are dangerous to people. Environmental consultants estimate it will cost up to $2 million to remediate the properties so the houses will be safe for people to live in. The current owners of these homes have started legal action against DDL. DDL's lawyers

believe that the company that sold DDL the land had fraudulently withheld relevant information about the prior use of the land, so that DDL will not be liable for the remediation costs.

7. DDL received a government loan of $6 million in early 20X5, under a government program aimed at helping developers cope with the impact of the change in environmental regulations on their business plans. The entire loan is forgivable if DDL produces a commercially viable golf course by the end of 2007. Half of the government loan amount was recorded as revenue in 20X5 since in DDL management's view, the golf course development is 50 percent complete.

8. Late in 20X5, DLL rented earth-moving equipment to start the golf course development work. The equipment lease agreement has a 10-year term and required a $200,000 payment at the start of the term, with payments of $200,000 thereafter at the start of each of the next nine years. The equipment could have been purchased for $1,265,650 in cash and has an expected useful life of 10 years. The relevant borrowing rate for assessing this lease is 12 percent per year.

Required:

a. Prepare a report outlining the considerations your firm would have to make before accepting the audit of DDL.

b. Prepare a detailed and complete audit plan that addresses the accounting and other information items noted previously, under the assumption that your firm accepts DDL as an audit client. Also, suggest any other information that you would want to obtain for planning the audit.

Kingston Case questions related to Chapter 13 are on the Online Learning Centre that accompanies this text.

APPENDIX 13A

INTERNAL CONTROL QUESTIONNAIRES

. . . .

EXHIBIT 13A-1 PRODUCTION AND COST ACCOUNTING APPLICATION

Environment and general controls relevant to this application:

1. Is access to blank production order forms denied to unauthorized persons?
2. Is access to blank bills of materials and labour needs forms denied to unauthorized persons?
3. Is access to blank material requisitions forms denied to unauthorized persons?

Assertion-Based Control Evaluations

Validity objective:

4. Are material requisitions and job time tickets reviewed by the production supervisor after the supervisor prepares them?
5. Are the weekly direct labour and materials-used reports reviewed by the production supervisor after preparation by the supervisor?

Completeness objective:

6. Are production orders prenumbered and the numerical sequence checked for missing documents?
7. Are bills of materials and labour needs forms prenumbered and the numerical sequence checked for missing documents?
8. Are material requisitions and job time tickets prenumbered and the numerical sequence checked for missing documents?
9. Are inventory issue slips prenumbered and the numerical sequence checked for missing documents?

Authorization objective:

10. Are production orders prepared by authorized persons?
11. Are bills of materials and labour needs prepared by authorized persons?

Accuracy objective:

12. Are differences between inventory issue slips and materials-used reports recorded and reported to the cost accounting supervisor?
13. Are differences between job time tickets and the labour report recorded and reported to the cost accounting supervisor?
14. Are standard costs used? If so, are they reviewed and revised periodically?
15. Are differences between reports of units completed and products-received reports recorded and reported to the cost accounting supervisor?

Classification objective:

16. Does the accounting manual give instructions for proper classification of cost accounting transactions?

Accounting objective:

17. Are summary entries reviewed and approved by the cost accounting supervisor?

Proper period objective:

18. Does the accounting manual give instructions to date cost entries on the date of use? Does an accounting supervisor review monthly, quarterly and year-end cost accruals?

EXHIBIT 13A-2   PAYROLL APPLICATION

Environment and general controls relevant to this application:

1. Are all employees paid by cheque or direct deposit to their bank accounts?
2. If a special payroll bank account is used is the payroll bank account reconciled by someone who does not prepare, sign or deliver paycheques?
3. Are payroll cheques signed by persons who neither prepare cheques nor keep cash funds or accounting records?
4. If an outside payroll processing service is used is the list of employees paid by the service reviewed by the employees' supervisor or someone else who cannot add or make changes to the employee payroll list submitted to the processing service?
5. Are payroll department personnel rotated in their duties? required to take vacations? bonded?
6. Is there a timekeeping department (function) independent of the payroll department?

Assertion-Based Control Evaluations:
Validity objective:

7. Are names of terminated employees reported in writing to the payroll department?
8. Is the payroll compared to personnel files periodically?
9. Are cheques distributed by someone other than the employee's immediate supervisor?
10. Are unclaimed wages deposited in a special bank account or otherwise controlled by a responsible officer?
11. Do internal auditors conduct occasional surprise distributions of paycheques?

Completeness objective:

12. Are names of newly hired employees reported in writing to the payroll department?
13. Are blank payroll cheques prenumbered and the numerical sequence checked for missing documents?

Authorization objective:

14. Are all wage rates determined by contract or approved by a personnel officer?
15. Are authorizations for deductions, signed by the employees, on file?
16. Are time cards or piecework reports prepared by the employee approved by his or her supervisor?
17. Is a time clock or other electromechanical or computer system used?
18. Is the payroll register sheet signed by the employee preparing it and approved prior to payment?

Accuracy objective:

19. Are timekeeping and cost accounting records (such as hours, dollars) reconciled with payroll department calculations of hours and wages?
20. Are payrolls audited periodically by internal auditors?

Classification objective:

21. Do payroll accounting personnel have instructions for classifying payroll debit entries?
Accounting objective:
22. Are payroll records reconciled with tax reports?

Proper period objective:

23. Are monthly, quarterly and annual wage accruals reviewed by an accounting officer?

CHAPTER

14

Finance and Investment Process

In essence, the finance and investment process is the manner in which a company plans for capital requirements and raises the money by borrowing, selling shares and entering into acquisitions and joint ventures. Dividend, interest and income tax payments are part of the related accounting cycle. This cycle also includes the accounting for investments in marketable securities, joint ventures and partnerships and subsidiaries. The finance portion of the process deals with acquiring money to fund the company's activities. The investment portion deals with investing money in revenue-generating assets and other long-term investments.

LEARNING OBJECTIVES

After completing this chapter, you will be able to:

1. Describe the finance and investment process, risk assessment, and typical transactions, source documents, controls and account balances.

2. Outline control tests for auditing control over debt, owner's equity and investment transactions.

3. Design audit and investigative procedures for detecting common errors, irregularities and frauds in the finance and investment process.

Note: Appendices 14B and 14C are located on the text Online Learning Centre.

RISK ASSESSMENT FOR FINANCE AND INVESTMENT PROCESS

The finance and investment process involves the client company's legal structure, how it raises capital from shareholders and creditors, its intercorporate investments and related parties. These components tend to be specific to each entity. Understanding these important aspects of the corporate structure and their implications for financial statement misstatement risks requires the imput of the most experienced audit team members. The corporate governance controls introduced in Chapter 5 are relevant to this risk assessment and are discussed in more detail in this chapter.

The balances in the process includes financial instruments such as long-term investments and debt, share capital and contributed surplus. Transactions include dividends and interest. Disclosure requirements are extensive and include: accounting policies for intercorporate investments; valuation bases of financial instruments; continuity of financial instrument balances and share capital; detailed terms, interest rates and repayment dates of debt; and details of any contingent liabilities.

Many recently introduced accounting standards apply to accounts in the finance and investment process, including measurement and recognition of financial instruments and derivatives at fair values, comprehensive income reporting and consolidation of variable interest entreprises. The issue of risks in public companies as compared to companies "without public accountability" are relevant. In particular, the latter group in Canada have the option to use **differential reporting**, which means they can use simpler accounting principles such as cost basis for financial assets or taxes payable basis for income taxes.

At the assertion level, the main risks are completeness of debt, valuation of financial instruments, disclosures of risks relating to financial instruments and derivatives, and presentation and disclosure of intercorporate investments. Controls in the finance and investment process involves the highest level of management, and auditors usually use substantive procedures to assess presentation and verify changes and balances. Since these parts of the financial statements are long term (financing/investing) or permanent (shares issued), it is important to obtain and include in audit documentation copies of all legal documents relating to loans, partnerships, leases, joint venture investments (JVs) and other long-term legal arrangements the client enters. These legal documents must be retained in permanent audit files so auditors can check that the contracts are properly accounted for and disclosed in future years' audits. The same goes for **articles of incorporation** (which set out authorized classes of shares, their features, shareholder rights, etc.) and records of issuing shares approved by board of directors in the minutes.

It is also important for auditors to document management's procedures and rationales for accounting estimates and the audit procedures used to verify them, both to help future auditors assess the methods and to see whether they are applied consistently when there is no reason to change them. Note that changing economic and business conditions are risk factors that may indicate that estimation methods should be changed if the old method is no longer appropriate for the new circumstances.

FINANCE AND INVESTMENT PROCESS: TYPICAL ACTIVITIES

LEARNING OBJECTIVE

1 Describe the finance and investment process, risk assessment, and typical transactions, source documents, controls and account balances.

The finance and investment process relates to a large number of accounts and records, ranging across tangible and intangible assets, liabilities, deferred credits, shareholders' equity, gains and losses, expenses and related taxes such as income tax, goods and services tax (GST) and provincial sales tax (PST). The major accounts and records are listed in Exhibit 14–1 following. These include some of the more complicated topics in accounting—equity method accounting for investments, consolidation accounting, goodwill, income taxes and financial instruments, to name a few. It is not the purpose of this chapter to explain the accounting for these balances and transactions. Rather, we will concentrate

EXHIBIT 14–1   FINANCE AND INVESTMENT PROCESS

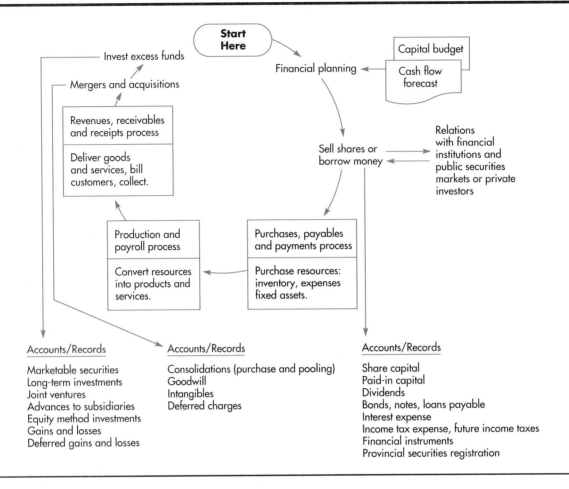

on a few important aspects of auditing them. Exhibit 14–1 shows a skeleton outline of the finance and investment process. Its major functions are financial planning and raising capital; interacting with the processes of purchases, payables and payments; production and payroll; and revenues, receivables and receipts processes; and entering into mergers, acquisitions and other investments.

Good Corporate Governance: A Key Control for the Finance and Investment Process

According to *CICA's Guidance for Directors on Governance Processes for Control*,[1] the responsibilities of boards of directors are determined by the legal and administrative framework within which organizations function. In this guidance, the view of board responsibilities is founded on the principle that the directors are stewards of the organization. As such, they have a responsibility to oversee the conduct of the business and to monitor management, endeavouring to ensure that all major issues affecting the business and affairs of the organization are given proper consideration.

The guidance identifies the contributions of the board of directors to internal control as follows.

Approving and monitoring mission, vision and strategy deals with the board's role in endeavouring to see that the organization has the right approach to add to shareholder and/or stakeholder value, and improve its chances of viability and success.

[1] CICA, Toronto, Canada, 1996.

Approving and monitoring the organization's ethical values deals with the board's role as guardian of the organization's values, as its conscience.

Monitoring management control deals with the board's overview of the systems whereby the chief executive officer and senior management exercise their power and influence over the rest of the organization.

Evaluating senior management deals with the board's evaluation of the competence and integrity of the chief executive officer and other members of senior management, as it is primarily through them that the board exercises its power and influence.

Overseeing external communications deals with the board's responsibility with respect to the organization's communications information to and from external parties.

Assessing the board's effectiveness deals with how the board assesses how well it discharges its roles and responsibilities as part of the organization's overall control.

It should be evident that this is a comprehensive, idealized role of the board which might not be fully realized in practice. Nevertheless, the guideline represents an authoritative source on good corporate governance practices with respect to control of management activities. This control is especially important in the finance and investment process. For this reason these elements of board control, especially the last four, can provide a useful benchmark in auditor evaluation of internal controls in this cycle.

Debt and Shareholder Equity Capital

Transactions in debt and shareholder equity capital are typically few in number but large in monetary amount. They are handled by the highest levels of management. The control-related duties and responsibilities reflect this high-level attention.

Authorization

Financial planning starts with the chief financial officer's (CFO's) cash flow forecast. This forecast informs the board of directors and management of the business plans, the prospects for cash inflows and the needs for cash outflows. The cash flow forecast usually is integrated with the capital budget, which contains the plans for asset purchases and business acquisitions. A capital budget approved by the board of directors constitutes the authorization for major asset acquisitions and investments.

Sales of share capital and debt financing transactions usually are authorized by the board of directors. All the directors must sign registration documents for public securities offerings. However, authority normally is delegated to the CFO to complete such transactions as periodic renewals of notes payable and other ordinary types of financing transactions without specific board approval of each transaction. Auditors should expect to find the authorizing signatures of the chief executive officer (CEO), CFO, chair of the board of directors and perhaps other high-ranking officers on financing documents.

Many financing transactions are **off the balance sheet**. Companies can enter into obligations and commitments that are not required to be recorded in the accounts. Examples of such authorizations include leases, endorsements on discounted notes or on other companies' obligations, letters of credit, guarantees, repurchase or remarketing agreements, commitments to purchase at fixed prices, commitments to sell at fixed prices and certain kinds of stock options. These are among the business and financing options available to companies. Many of these were discussed in previous chapters as factors the auditor considers to assess risk of material misstatement related to the disclosure assertion.

Custody

In large companies custody of share certificate books is not a significant management problem. Large companies employ banks and trust companies to serve as registrars and transfer agents. A **registrar** keeps the shareholder list and, from time to time, determines the shareholders eligible to receive dividends (shareholders of record on a dividend record date) and those entitled to vote at the annual meeting. A **transfer agent** handles the exchange of shares, cancelling the shares surrendered by sellers and issuing new certificates to buyers. It is not unusual to find the same bank or trust company providing both services.

Small companies often keep their own shareholder records. A **share certificate book** looks like a chequebook. It has perforated stubs for recording the number of shares, the owner's name and other identification, and the date of issue. Actual unissued share certificates are attached to the stubs, like unused cheques in a chequebook. The missing certificates are the ones outstanding in the possession of owners. Custody of the share certificate book is important because the unissued certificates are like money or collateral. If improperly removed, share certificates can be sold to buyers who think they are genuinely issued or can be used as collateral with unsuspecting lenders.

Lenders have custody of **debt instruments** (e.g., leases, bonds, notes and loans payable). A CFO may have copies, but they are merely convenience records. However, when a company repurchases its debt instruments, these become the custody of trustees or company officials, usually the CFO. Until they are cancelled and destroyed, it is possible to misuse them by improperly reselling them to unsuspecting investors.

Recordkeeping

Records of notes, loans and bonds payable are maintained by the accounting department and the CFO or controller. The recordkeeping procedures should be similar to those used to account for vendor accounts payable: payment notices from lenders are compared to the accounting records, due dates are monitored, interest payments are set up for payment on due dates and accruals for unpaid interest are made on financial reporting dates. If the company has only a few debt instruments outstanding, no subsidiary records of these are needed. All the information is in the general ledger accounts. (Companies with a large number of bonds, loans, and notes may keep control and subsidiary accounts, as is done for accounts receivable.) When all or part of the notes become due within the next year, the CFO and controller have the necessary information for properly classifying current and long-term amounts.

Another class of credit balances is treated here under the heading of Recordkeeping, for which the functions of authorization, custody and reconciliation are not easy to describe. They are the **calculated liabilities and credits**—lease obligations, future income taxes, pension and post-retirement benefit liabilities and foreign currency translation gains and losses, to name a few. These are accounting creations, calculated according to accounting rules and using basic data from company plans and operations. Management usually enjoys considerable discretion in structuring leases, tax strategies, pension plan and employee benefit terms, foreign holdings and the like. These accounting calculations often involve significant accounting estimates made by management. Company accountants should try to capture the economic reality of these calculated liabilities by following generally accepted accounting principles and by paying careful attention to how these estimates may affect decisions of financial statement users.

Periodic Reconciliation

A responsible person should periodically inspect the share certificate book to determine whether the only missing certificates are those known to be outstanding in the possession of *bona fide* owners. If necessary, company officials can confirm the ownership of shares with the holders of record. Reports with similar information content can be obtained from registrars and transfer agents to verify that the company's record of the number of shares outstanding agrees with the registrar's number. (Without this reconciliation, counterfeit shares handled by the transfer agent and recorded by the registrar might go unnoticed.)

Ownership of bonds can be handled by a trustee having duties and responsibilities similar to those of registrars and transfer agents. Confirmations and reports from bond trustees can be used to reconcile the trustee's records to the company's records.

Investments and Intangibles

A company may have many investments or only a few, and may have a large variety or a limited set of types of investments. Intangible assets may be in the form of purchased assets (e.g., patents, trademarks) or in the form of accounting allocations (e.g., goodwill, deferred charges). The sections following are phrased in the context of a manufacturing or service company for which investments and intangibles are fairly incidental in the business. Financial institutions (banks, trust companies), investment companies, mutual funds, insurance companies and the like have more elaborate systems for managing their investments and intangibles.

Authorization

All investment policies should be approved by the board of directors or its investment committee. It is not unusual to find board or executive committee approval required for major individual investment transactions. However, auditors should expect to find a great deal of variation across companies as to the nature and amount of transactions that must have specific high-level approval. The board of directors always is closely involved in major acquisitions, mergers and share buy-back plans.

THE LITTLE LEASE THAT COULD

The Quick-Fly commuter airline was struggling. According to its existing debt covenants, it could not incur any more long-term liabilities. The company needed a new airplane to expand its services, so it "rented" one. The CFO pointed out that the deal for the $12 million airplane was a noncancellable operating lease because (1) Quick-Fly does not automatically own the plane at the end of the lease; (2) the purchase option of $1,500,000 is no bargain; (3) the lease term of 133 months is 74 percent, not 75 percent, of the estimated 15-year economic life; and (4) the present value of the lease payments of $154,330 per month, discounted at the company's latest borrowing rate of 14 percent, is $10.4 million, which is less than the 90 percent of fair value (0.90 × $12 million = $10.8 million) criterion in the *CICA Handbook* in paragraph 3065.06.

The CFO did not record a long-term lease obligation (liability). Do you agree with this accounting conclusion?

Custody

Custody of investments and intangibles depends on the nature of the assets. Some investments, such as shares and bonds, are represented by negotiable certificates. The actual certificates may be kept in a brokerage account in a "house name" (the brokerage company), and, in this case, custody rests with the company official who is authorized to order the buy, sell and delivery transactions. They also may be in the actual possession of the owner (client company). If they are kept by the company, they should be in a safe or a bank safe-deposit box. Only high-ranking officers (e.g., CFO, CEO, president, chair of board) should have combinations and keys.

Other kinds of investments do not have formal negotiable certificates, and custody may take the form of management responsibility instead of actual physical handling. Examples are joint ventures and partnerships in which the client company is a partner. Venture and partnership agreements are evidence of these investments, but they usually are merely filed with other important documents. Misuse of them is seldom a problem because they are not readily negotiable. Real custody rests with management's supervision and monitoring of the venture or partnership operations.

AUTHORIZATION: HERE TODAY, GONE TOMORROW

The treasurer of Travum County had many responsibilities as a chief financial officer. She invested several million dollars of county funds with a California-based investment money manager. Soon thereafter, news stories of the money manager's expensive personal lifestyle and questionable handling of client's funds began to circulate, indicating that clients could lose much of their investments. At the same time, news stories about the treasurer's own credit-card spending habits were published locally, indicating that she had obtained a personal credit card by using the county's name.

Although no county funds were lost and no improper credit-card bills were paid, the county commissioners temporarily suspended the treasurer's authority to choose investment vehicles for county funds.

Having custody of most intangibles is like trying to keep Jell-O in your pocket—good in theory but messy in practice. However, patents, trademarks, copyrights and similar legal intangible rights may be evidenced in legal documents and contracts. These seldom are negotiable, and are usually kept in ordinary company files. Company managers may be assigned responsibility to protect exclusive rights granted by various intangibles.

Accounts like goodwill, deferred charges, and pension obligations are intangible accounts created by accountants' estimates and calculations. They have no physical substance, but you can view them as being in the custody of the accountants who are responsible for calculating them.

Recordkeeping

The procedures for purchase of share and bond investments involve authorization by the board of directors or other responsible officials. Because a higher level of approval is required than for routine purchases discussed in Chapter 12, the cheque for the investment is signed by a high-ranking finance officer, such as the CFO or treasurer. If the company has few investments, no subsidiary records are maintained and all information is kept in the general ledger accounts. If the company has many investments, a control account and subsidiary ledger may be maintained.

The recordkeeping for many kinds of investments and intangibles can be complicated. Complications arise not so much from the original recording of transactions as from the maintenance of the accounts over time. This is the place where complex accounting standards for equity method accounting, consolidations, goodwill, intangibles amortization and valuation, deferred charges, future income taxes, pension and postretirement benefit liabilities and various financial instruments enter the picture. High-level accountants who prepare financial statements get involved with the accounting rules and management estimates required to account for such investments and intangibles. Management plans and estimates of future events and interpretations of the accounting standards often influence the accounting for these balances. These decisions are risk areas for overstatement of assets, understatement of liabilities and understatement of expenses because managers can exercise considerable discretion and auditors seldom have hard evidence that can confirm or refute these management assessments.

Periodic Reconciliation

The most significant reconciliation opportunity in the investments and intangibles accounts is the inspection and count of negotiable securities certificates. This reconciliation is similar to a physical inventory in that it consists of an inspection of certificates on hand, along with comparison to the information recorded in the accounts. (When securities are held by a brokerage firm, the "inspection" is accomplished with a written confirmation.)

A securities count is not a mere handling of pieces of paper. A securities "inventory count" should include a record of the name of the company represented by the certificate, the interest rate for bonds, the dividend rate for preferred shares, the due date for bonds, the serial numbers on the certificates, the face value of bonds, the number or face amount of bonds and shares and notes on the name of the owner shown on the face of the certificate or on the endorsements on the back (should be the client company). Companies should perform this reconciliation reasonably often not waiting for an annual visit by the independent auditors. A securities count in a financial institution that holds thousands of shares in multimillion-dollar asset accounts is a major undertaking.

When auditors perform the securities inspection and count, the same kind of information should be recorded in the audit working papers. An example of these elements in an audit working paper is in Problem 8.115 at the end of Chapter 8. You can see several elements of evidence in the information: existence is established by handling the securities, ownership is established by viewing the client name as owner, valuation evidence is added by finding the cost and market value (see the example in Problem 8.115). If a security certificate is not available for inspection, it may be pledged as collateral for a loan and in the hands of a creditor. It can be confirmed or inspected, if the extended procedure of visiting the creditor is necessary. The pledge as collateral may be important for a disclosure note. A securities count and reconciliation is important for management and auditors because companies have been known to try to substitute others' securities for missing ones. If securities have been sold and replaced without any accounting entries, the serial numbers will show that the certificates recorded in the accounts is not the same as the ones on hand.

REVIEW CHECKPOINTS

14.1 When a management carefully crafts a lease agreement to barely fail the tests for lease capitalization and liability recognition, do you believe that auditors should insist on capitalization anyway?

14.2 What would constitute the authorization for loans payable? What documentation might auditors examine as evidence of this authorization?

14.3 Give five examples of off-balance-sheet information. Why should auditors be concerned with such items?

14.4 What features of a client's share capital are of importance in the audit?

14.5 What information about share capital could be confirmed with outside parties? How could this information be corroborated by the auditors?

14.6 What procedures can auditors employ in the audit of investment securities to obtain the names of the issuers, the number of shares held, certificate numbers, maturity value and interest and dividend rates?

14.7 Describe the procedures and documentation of a controlled count of client's investment securities.

14.8 What information should be included in a working paper for the audit of investment securities?

CONTROL RISK ASSESSMENT

LEARNING OBJECTIVE

2 Outline control tests for auditing control over debt, owner equity and investment transactions.

In the finance and investment process, auditors look for control procedures, such as authorization, custody, recordkeeping and periodic reconciliation. They especially look for information about the level of management involved in these functions. Tests of controls generally amount to enquiries and observations related to these features. Samples of transactions to test for control performance are not normally a part of the control risk assessment work as they can be in the other operations processes covered in Chapters 11 to 13. Because finance and investment transactions are usually individually material, each transaction is audited in detail. Reliance on control does not normally reduce the extent of substantive audit work on finance and investment cycle accounts. However, lack of control can lead to performance of significant extended procedures because the risk of material misstatement from improper financing and investing transactions is high.

General Control Considerations

Control procedures for suitable handling of responsibilities should be in place and operating. By referring to the discussion accompanying Exhibit 14–1, you can tell that these responsibilities are basically in the hands of senior management officials. You can also tell that different companies may have widely differing policies and procedures.

Note that the idea of segregation of incompatible duties does not really apply in the financing and investing functions. It is hard to have a strict segregation of functional responsibilities when the principal officers of a company authorize, execute and control finance and investment activities. Subsequently, it is not realistic to maintain that a CEO can authorize investments but cannot have access to shareholder records, securities certificates and the like. Real segregation of duties can be found in middle management and lower ranks, but it is hard to create and enforce in upper-level management.

In light of this problem of control, a company should have compensating control procedures. A compensating control is a control feature used when a standard control procedure (such as strict segregation of function responsibilities) is not specified by the company. In the areas of finance and investment, the compensating control feature is the involvement of two or more persons in each kind of important functional responsibility.

If involvement by multiple persons is not specified, then oversight or review can be substituted. For example, the board of directors can authorize purchase of securities or creation of a partnership. The CFO or CEO can carry out the transactions, have custody of certificates and agreements, manage the partnership or the portfolio of securities, oversee the recordkeeping and make the decisions about valuations and accounting (authorizing the journal entries). These are rather normal management activities, and they combine several responsibilities. The compensating control can exist in the form of periodic reports to the board of directors, oversight by the investment committee of the board and internal audit involvement in making a periodic reconciliation of securities certificates in a portfolio with the amounts and descriptions recorded in the accounts.

Control over Accounting Estimates

An accounting estimate is the amount included in financial statements to approximate the effect of past business transactions or events on the present status of an asset or liability. The use of accounting estimates in financial reporting is common. Examples include such items as allowance for doubtful receivables, loss provisions and valuation of stock options using a mathematical model. Accounting estimates can have a significant or pervasive effect on reported results, either individually or when considered in the aggregate.[2]

Accounting estimates often are included in basic financial statements because (1) the measurement of some amount of valuation is uncertain, perhaps depending upon the outcome of future events, or (2) relevant data cannot be accumulated on a timely, cost-effective basis. Some examples of accounting estimates in the finance and investment process are shown in the box on page 560.

A client's management is responsible for making estimates and should have a process and control structure designed to reduce the likelihood of material misstatements in them. Specific relevant aspects of such a control structure include:

---

[2] *CICA Handbook*, paragraph 5305.02 and ISA 540.4.

- management communication of the need for proper accounting estimates
- accumulation of relevant, sufficient and reliable data for estimates
- preparation of estimates by qualified personnel
- adequate review and approval by appropriate levels of authority
- comparison of prior estimates with subsequent results to assess the reliability of the estimation outcomes
- consideration by management of whether particular accounting estimates are consistent with the company's operational plans

Auditors' test of controls over the production of estimates amounts to enquiries and observations related to the features listed immediately preceding. Such enquiries are: Who prepares estimates? When are they prepared? What data are used? Who reviews and approves the estimates? Have you compared prior estimates with subsequent actual events? Observations include study of data documentation, study of comparisons of prior estimates with subsequent actual experience and study of intercompany correspondence concerning estimates and operational plans.

The audit of an estimate starts with the test of controls, much of which has a bearing on the substantive quality of the estimation process and of the estimate itself. Further substantive audit procedures include recalculating the mathematical estimate, developing an auditor's own independent estimate based on reasonable alternative assumptions and comparing the estimate to subsequent events to the extent they are known before the end of the field work.

FINANCE AND INVESTMENT CYCLE ESTIMATES

Financial instruments: Valuation of securities, classification into trading versus investment portfolios, probability of a correlated hedge, sales of securities with puts and calls.

Accruals: Compensation in stock option plans, actuarial assumptions in pension costs.

Leases: Initial direct costs, executory costs, residual values, capitalization interest rate.

Rates: Imputed interest rates on receivables and payables.

Other: Losses and net realizable value on segment disposal and business restructuring, fair values in nonmonetary exchanges.

Control Risk Assessment for Notes and Loans Payable

From the preceding discussion, you can tell that test of controls audit procedures take a variety of forms—enquiries, observations, study of documentation, comparison with related data, such as tax returns, and detail audit of some transactions. The detail audit of transactions, however, is a small part of the test of controls because of the nature of the finance and investment transactions, their number (few), and their amount (large). However, some companies have numerous debt financing transactions, and in such cases a more detailed approach to control risk assessment can be used, including the selection of a sample of transactions for control risk assessment evidence.

An internal control questionnaire for notes and loans payable is found in Exhibit 14–2. It illustrates typical questions about the control objectives. These enquiries give auditors insights into the client's specifications for review and approval of major financing transactions, the system of accounting for them and the provision for error-checking review procedures.

Auditors can select a sample of notes payable transactions for detail test of controls, provided that the population of notes is large enough to justify sample-based auditing.

EXHIBIT   14-2   INTERNAL CONTROL QUESTIONNAIRE: NOTES AND LOANS PAYABLE APPLICATION

Environment and general controls relevant to this application:
1. Are records kept by someone who cannot sign notes or cheques?
Assertion-Based Control Evaluation
Validity objective:
2. Are paid notes cancelled, stamped "paid" and filed?
Completeness objective:
3. Is all borrowing authorization by the directors checked to determine whether all notes payable are recorded?
Authorization objective:
4. Are direct borrowings on notes payable authorized by the directors? by the treasurer or by the chief financial officer?
5. Are two or more authorized signatures required on notes?
Accuracy objective:
6. Are bank due notices compared with records of unpaid liabilities?
Classification objective:
7. Is sufficient information available in the accounts to enable financial statement preparers to classify current and long-term debt properly?
Accounting objective:
8. Is the subsidiary ledger of notes payable periodically reconciled with the general ledger control account(s)?
Proper period objective:
9. Are interest payments and accruals monitored for due dates and financial statement dates?

Exhibit 14–3 lists a selection of such procedures, with notation of the relevant control objectives shown on the right.

Control Risk Assessment for Derivatives

Guidance for the audit of derivative financial instruments is in *CICA Handbook* AuG-39, IAPS 1012 (International) and SAS No.92 (AICPA).

According to SAS No. 92 key control procedures for derivatives include:

1. monitoring by control staff that is fully independent of derivatives activities
2. derivatives personnel to obtain, prior to exceeding limits, at least oral approval from members of senior management who are independent of derivatives activities
3. senior management to properly address limit excesses and divergences from approved derivatives strategies
4. the accurate transmittal of derivatives positions to the risk measurement systems

EXHIBIT   14-3   CONTROL TESTS FOR NOTES AND LOANS PAYABLE

	Control Objective
1. Read directors' and finance committee's minutes for authorization of financing transactions Authorization (such as short-term notes payable, bond offerings).	
2. Select a sample of paid notes:	
a. Recalculate interest expense for the period under audit.	Accuracy
b. Trace interest expense to the general ledger account. Completeness	
c. Vouch payment to cancelled cheques.	Validity
3. Select a sample of notes payable:	
a. Vouch to authorization by directors or finance committee. Authorization	
b. Vouch cash receipt to bank statement.	Validity

5. the performance of appropriate reconciliations to ensure data integrity across a full range of derivatives

6. derivatives traders, risk managers, and senior management to define constraints, monitor activities and justify identified excesses

7. senior management, an independent group, or an individual that management designates to perform a regular review of the identifying controls and financial results of the derivatives activities to determine whether controls are being effectively implemented in the entity's business objectives and strategies are being achieved

8. a review of limits in the context of changes and strategy, risk tolerance of the entity, and market conditions

When applicable, auditors would design tests of the preceding controls to determine the extent of substantive tests for derivatives. Key substantive procedures for derivatives include the following: confirmations with issuers, brokers, or counterparties; physical inspection of the derivatives contract; inspection of underlying agreements and other forms of supporting documentation in paper or electronic form; review of minutes of the board of directors' meetings; and the need to obtain quoted prices from broker-dealers or from derivatives exchanges. For more background in the unique risks represented by derivatives activities of clients, see Appendix 14B on the text Online Learning Centre, where Sample Letter 2 illustrates the important substantive procedure of a confirmation request detailing outstanding derivative instruments for a client.

Summary: Control Risk Assessment

The audit manager or senior accountant in charge of the audit should evaluate the evidence obtained from an understanding of the internal control structure and from test of controls audit procedures. These procedures can take many forms because management systems for finance and investment accounts can be quite varied among clients. The involvement of senior officials in a relatively small number of high-dollar transactions makes control risk

AN ESTIMATED VALUATION BASED ON FUTURE DEVELOPMENT

Gulf & Western Industries (G&W) sold 450,000 shares of Pan American stock from its investment portfolio to Resorts International (Resorts). Resorts paid $8 million plus 250,000 shares of its unregistered common stock. G&W recorded the sale proceeds as $14,167,500, valuing the unregistered Resorts shares at $6,167,500, which was approximately 67 percent of the market price of Resorts shares at the time ($36.82 per share). G&W reported a gain of $3,365,000 on the sale.

Four years later, Resorts shares fell to $2.63. G&W sold its 250,000 shares back to Resorts in exchange for 1,100 acres of undeveloped land on Grand Bahamas Island. For its records, Resorts got a broker-dealer's opinion that its 250,000 shares were worth $460,000. For property tax assessment purposes, the Bahamian government valued the undeveloped land at $525,000.

G&W valued the land on its books at $6,167,500, which was the previous valuation of the Resorts shares. The justification was an appraisal of $6,300,000 based on the estimated value of the 1,100 acres when ultimately developed (i.e., built into an operating resort and residential community). However, G&W also reported a loss of $5,527,000 in its tax return (effectively valuing the land at $640,500). The SEC accused G&W of failing to report a loss of $5.7 million in its financial statements. Do you think the loss should have appeared in the G&W income statement?

Source: Kellog, I., *How to Find Negligence and Misrepresentation in Financial Statements* (New York: Shepard's/ McGraw Hill, 1983), p. 279.

assessment a process tailored specifically to the company's situation. Some companies enter into complicated financing and investment transactions, while others keep to the simple transactions.

However, some control considerations can be generalized. Control over management's production of accounting estimates is characterized by some common features. In some cases, such as a company with numerous notes payable transactions, samples of transactions for detail testing can be used to produce evidence about compliance with control policies and procedures.

In general, substantive audit procedures on finance and investment accounts are not limited in extent. It is very common for auditors to perform substantive audit procedures on 100 percent of these transactions and balances. The number of transactions is usually not large, nor is the audit cost high for complete coverage. Nevertheless, control deficiencies and unusual or complicated transactions can cause auditors to adjust the nature and timing of audit procedures. Complicated financial instruments, pension plans, exotic equity securities, related party transactions and nonmonetary exchanges of investment assets call for procedures designed to find evidence of errors, irregularities and frauds in the finance and investment accounts. The next section deals with some of the finance and investment process assertions, and it has some cases for your review.

REVIEW CHECKPOINTS

14.9   What is a compensating control? Give some examples for finance and investment accounts.

14.10 What are some of the specific relevant aspects of management's control over the production of accounting estimates? What are some enquiries auditors can make?

14.11 When a company has produced an estimate of an investment valuation based on a nonmonetary exchange, what source of comparative information can an auditor use?

14.12 If a company does not monitor notes and loans payable for due dates and interest payment dates in relation to financial statement dates, what misstatements can appear in the financial statements?

14.13 Generally, how much emphasis is placed on adequate internal control in the audit of long-term debt? of share capital? of contributed surplus? and of retained earnings?

ASSERTIONS, SUBSTANTIVE PROCEDURES, AND CASETTES FOR FINANCE AND INVESTMENT ACCOUNTS

Owners' Equity

Management makes assertions about the existence, completeness, rights and obligations, valuation and presentation and disclosure of owners' equity. Typical specific assertions include:

1. The number of shares shown as issued is in fact issued.
2. No other shares (including options, warrants and the like) have been issued and not recorded or reflected in the accounts and disclosures.
3. The accounting is proper for options, warrants and other share issue plans, and related disclosures are adequate.
4. The valuation of shares issued for noncash consideration is proper, in conformity with accounting principles.
5. All owners' equity transactions have been authorized by the board of directors.

An illustrative program of substantive audit procedures for owners' equity is in Exhibit 14A–1 in Appendix 14A. Some key substantive procedures are discussed following.

Documentation   Owners' equity transactions usually are well documented in minutes of the meetings of the board of directors, in proxy statements and in securities offering registration statements. Transactions can be vouched to these documents, and the cash proceeds can be traced to the bank accounts.

Confirmation   Share capital may be subject to confirmation when independent registrars and transfer agents are employed. Such agents are responsible for knowing the number of shares authorized and issued and for keeping lists of shareholders' names. The basic information about share capital—such as number of shares, classes of shares, preferred dividend rates, conversion terms, dividend payments, shares held in the company name, expiration dates and terms of warrants and share dividends and splits—can be confirmed with the independent agents. Many of these items can be corroborated by the auditors' own inspection and reading of share certificates, charter authorizations, directors' minutes and registration statements. However, when there are no independent agents, most audit evidence is gathered by **vouching** share record documents (such as certificate book stubs). When circumstances call for extended procedures, information on outstanding shares may be confirmed directly with the holders.

Long-term Liabilities and Related Accounts

The primary audit concern with the verification of long-term liabilities is that all liabilities are recorded and that the interest expense is properly paid or accrued. Therefore, the assertion of completeness is paramount. Alertness to the possibility of unrecorded liabilities during the performance of procedures in other areas frequently will uncover liabilities that have not been recorded. For example, when fixed assets are acquired during the year under audit, auditors should enquire about the source of funds for financing the new asset.

Management makes assertions about existence, completeness, rights and obligations, valuation and presentation and disclosure. Typical specific assertions relating to long-term liabilities include:

1. All material long-term liabilities are recorded.
2. Liabilities are properly classified according to their current or long-term status. The current portion of long-term debt is properly valued and classified.
3. New long-term liabilities and debt extinguishments are properly authorized.
4. Terms, conditions and restrictions relating to noncurrent debt are adequately disclosed.
5. Disclosures of maturities for the next five years and the capital and operating lease disclosures are accurate and adequate.
6. All important contingencies are either accrued in the accounts or disclosed in footnotes.

An illustrative program of substantive audit procedures for notes and loans payable and long-term debt is in Appendix 14A, Exhibit 14A–2. Some key audit procedures are following:

Confirmation   When auditing long-term liabilities, auditors usually obtain independent written confirmations for notes, loans and bonds payable. In the case of loans payable to banks, the standard bank confirmation may be used. The amount and terms of bonds payable, mortgages payable and other formal debt instruments can be confirmed by requests to holders or a trustee. The confirmation request should include questions not only of amount, interest rate and due date but also about collateral, restrictive covenants and other items of agreement between lender and borrower. Confirmation requests should be sent to lenders with whom the company has done business in the recent past, even if no liability balance is shown at the confirmation date. Such extra coverage is a part of the search for unrecorded liabilities. (Refer to Chapter 12 for more on the "search for unrecorded liabilities.")

Off-Balance Sheet Financing

Confirmation and enquiry procedures may be used to obtain responses on a class of items loosely termed **off-balance sheet information**. Within this category are terms of loan agreements, leases, endorsements, guarantees and insurance policies (whether issued by a client insurance company or owned by the client). Among these items is the difficult-to-define set of "commitments and contingencies" that often pose evidence-gathering problems. Some common types of commitments are shown in Exhibit 14–4.

Footnote disclosure should be considered for the types of commitments shown in Exhibit 14–4. Some of them can be estimated and valued and, thus, can be recorded in the accounts and shown in the financial statements themselves (such as losses on fixed price purchase commitments and losses on fixed price sales commitments).

Analytical relationships interest expense generally is related item by item to interest-bearing liabilities. Based on the evidence of long-term liability transactions (including those that have been retired during the year), the related interest expense amounts can be recalculated. The amount of debt, the interest rate and the time period are used to determine whether the interest expense and accrued interest are properly recorded. By comparing the audit results to the recorded interest expense and accrued interest accounts, auditors may be able to detect (1) greater expense than their calculations show, indicating some interest paid on debt unknown to them, possibly an unrecorded liability; (2) lesser expense than their calculations show, indicating misclassification, failure to accrue interest or an interest payment default; or (3) interest expense equal to their calculations. The first two possibilities raise questions for further study, and the third shows a correct correlation between debt and debt-related expense.

Deferred Credits—Calculated Balances

Several types of deferred credits depend on calculations for their existence and valuation. Examples include: (1) deferred profit on installment sales involving the gross margin and the sale amount; (2) future income taxes and investment credits involving tax-book timing differences, tax rates and amortization methods; and (3) deferred contract revenue involving contract provisions for prepayment, percentage-of-completion revenue recognition methods or other terms unique to a contract. All of these features are incorporated in calculations that auditors can check for accuracy.

Investments and Intangibles

Companies can have a wide variety of investments and relationships with affiliates. Investment accounting may be on the cost method, equity method without consolidation or full consolidation, depending on the size and influence represented by the investment. Purchase method consolidations usually create problems of accounting for the fair value of acquired assets and the related goodwill. Specific assertions typical of a variety of investment account balances are these:

1. Investment securities are on hand or are held in safekeeping by a trustee (existence).

2. Investment cost does not exceed market value (valuation).

3. Significant influence investments are accounted for by the equity method (valuation).

EXHIBIT   14–4   OFF-BALANCE-SHEET COMMITMENTS

Type of Commitment	Typical Procedures and Sources of Evidence
1. Repurchase or remarketing agreements.	1. Vouching of contracts, confirmation by customer, enquiry of client management.
2. Commitments to purchase at fixed prices.	2. Vouching of open purchase orders, enquiry of purchasing personnel, confirmation by supplier.
3. Commitments to sell at fixed prices.	3. Vouching of sales contracts, enquiry of sales personnel, confirmation by customer.
4. Loan commitments.	4. Vouching of open commitment file, enquiry of loan officers.
5. Lease commitments.	5. Vouching of lease agreement, confirmation with lessor or lessee.

4. Purchased goodwill is properly valued (valuation).

5. Capitalized intangible costs relate to intangibles acquired in exchange transactions (valuation).

6. Research and development costs are properly classified (presentation).

7. Amortization is properly calculated (valuation).

8. Investment income has been received and recorded (completeness).

9. Investments are adequately classified and described in the balance sheet (presentation).

An illustrative program of substantive audit procedures for investments, intangibles and related accounts is shown in Appendix 14A, Exhibit 14A–3.

Unlike the current assets accounts, which are characterized by numerous small transactions, the noncurrent investment accounts usually consist of a few large entries. This difference has internal control and substantive audit procedure implications. The impact on the auditors' consideration of the control environment is concentration on the authorization of transactions, since each individual transaction is likely to be material in itself and the authorization will give significant information about the proper classification and accounting method. The controls usually are not reviewed, tested or evaluated at an interim date but are considered along with the year-end procedures when the transactions and their authorizations are audited.

The following box shows a few of the trouble spots in audits of investments and intangibles.

TROUBLE SPOTS IN AUDITS OF INVESTMENTS AND INTANGIBLES

- Valuation of investments at cost or market and classification as held-to-maturity or financial assets held for trading or available for sale.
- Determination of significant influence relationship for equity method investments.
- Proper determination of goodwill in consolidations.
- Capitalization and continuing valuation of intangibles.
- Realistic distinctions of research, feasibility and production milestones for capitalization of development costs.
- Adequate disclosure of restrictions, pledges or liens related to investment assets.

Confirmation   The practice of obtaining independent written confirmation from outside parties is fairly limited in the area of investments, intangibles and related income and expense accounts. Securities held by trustees or brokers should be confirmed, and the confirmation request should seek the same descriptive information as that obtained in a physical count by the auditor (described previously in this chapter).

Enquiries About Intangibles   Company counsel can be queried about knowledge of any lawsuits or defects relating to patents, copyrights, trademarks or trade names. This confirmation can be sought by a specific request in the enquiry letter to the law firm. (Chapter 15 contains more information regarding the enquiry letter to the law firm.)

Income from Intangibles   Royalty income from patent licences received may be confirmed. However, such income amounts are usually audited by examining licence agreements, and vouching the licensee's reports and related cash payment.

Inspection   Investment property may be inspected in a manner similar to the physical inspection of fixed assets. The principal goal is to determine actual existence and condition of the property. Official documents of patents, copyrights and trademark rights can be inspected to see that they are, in fact, in the name of the client.

Documentation Vouching   Investment costs should be vouched to brokers' reports, monthly statements or other documentary evidence of cost. At the same time, the amounts of sales are traced to gain or loss accounts, and the amounts of sales prices and proceeds are vouched to the brokers' statements. Auditors should determine what method of cost-out assignment was used (i.e., FIFO, specific certificate or average cost) and whether it is consistent with prior years' transactions. The cost of real and personal property likewise can be vouched to invoices or other documents of purchase, and title documents (such as on land, buildings) may be inspected.

Market valuation of securities may be required. Starting in 2006, most companies will need to record financial assets and liabilities at their fair values at year end. Auditor will need to obtain evidence regarding market values or recent sales of investments to verify these fair values.

Vouching may be extensive in the areas of research and development (R&D), and deferred development costs. The principal evidence problem is to determine whether costs are properly classified as assets or as R&D expense. Recorded amounts generally are selected on a sample basis, and the purchase orders, receiving reports, payroll records, authorization notices and management reports are compared to them. Some R&D costs may resemble non-R&D costs (such as supplies, payroll costs), so auditors must be very careful in the vouching to be alert for costs that appear to relate to other operations.

External Documentation   By consulting quoted market values of securities, auditors can calculate market values. If quoted market values are not available, financial statements related to investments must be obtained and analyzed for evidence of basic value. If such financial statements are unaudited, evidence indicated by them is considered to be extremely weak.

Income amounts can be verified by consulting published dividend records for quotations of dividends actually declared and paid during a period (e.g., Moody's, and Standard & Poor's dividend records). Since auditors know the holding period of securities, dividend income can be calculated and compared to the amount in the account. Any difference could indicate a cutoff error, misclassification, defalcation or failure to record a dividend receivable. In a similar manner, application of interest rates to bond or note investments produces a calculated interest income figure (making allowance for amortization of premium or discount if applicable).

Equity Method Investments

When equity method accounting is used for investments, auditors need to obtain financial statements of the investee company. These should be audited statements. Inability to obtain financial statements from a closely held investee may indicate that the client investor does not have the significant controlling influence required by *CICA Handbook,* section 3051. When available, these statements are used as the basis for recalculating the amount of the client's share of income to recognize in the accounts. In addition, these statements may be used to audit the disclosure of investees' assets, liabilities and income presented in footnotes (a disclosure recommended when investments accounted for by the equity method are material).

Amortization Recalculation   Amortization of intangibles should be recalculated. Amortization expense owes its existence to a calculation, and recalculation based on audited costs and rates is sufficient audit evidence.[3]

Merger and acquisition transactions should be reviewed in terms of the appraisals, judgements and allocations used to assign portions of the purchase price to tangible assets, intangible assets, liabilities and goodwill. In the final analysis, nothing really substitutes for the inspection of transaction documentation, but verbal enquiries may help auditors to understand the circumstances of a merger.

---

[3] Under *CICA Handbook,* section 3061, the official terminology is now "capital assets" and "amortization" although "depreciation" still receives common use when reference is to amortization of tangible (fixed) assets.

Questions about lawsuits challenging patents, copyrights or trade names may produce early knowledge of problem areas for further investigation. Likewise, discussions and questions about research and development successes and failures may alert the audit team to problems of valuation of intangible assets and related amortization expense. Responses to questions about licensing of patents can be used in the audit of related royalty revenue accounts.

Enquiries About Management Intentions   Enquiries should deal with the nature of investments and the reasons for holding them. Management's expressed intention that a marketable security investment be considered a long-term investment may be the only available evidence for classifying it as long term and not as a current asset. The classification will affect the accounting treatment of market values and the unrealized gains and losses on investments.

REVIEW CHECKPOINTS

14.14   What are some of the typical assertions found in owners' equity descriptions and account balances?

14.15   How can confirmations be used in auditing shareholder capital accounts? in auditing notes, loans and bonds payable?

14.16   What are some of the typical assertions found in long-term liability accounts?

14.17   What procedures do auditors employ to obtain evidence of the cost of investments? of investment gains and losses? of investment income?

14.18   Why are auditors interested in substantial investment losses occurring early in the period following year-end?

14.19   What is the concept of "substance versus form" in relation to financing and investment transactions and balances? (Refer to the off-balance-sheet and consolidation casettes in the chapter.)

14.20   What are some of the trouble spots for auditors in the audits of investments and intangibles?

CASETTES

LEARNING OBJECTIVE

3 Design audit and investigative procedures for detecting common errors, irregularities and frauds in the finance and investment process.

This part of the chapter covers the audit of various account balances and gains and losses. It is presented in three sections—owners' equity, long-term liabilities and related accounts, and investments and intangibles. As in previous chapters, some casettes illustrating errors, irregularities and frauds are used to describe useful audit approaches. In addition, this chapter gives some assertions and procedures related to accounts in the process.

The cases begin with a description containing these elements:

Method: A cause of the misstatement (mistaken estimate or judgement, accidental error, intentional irregularity or fraud attempt), which usually is made easier by some kind of failure of controls.

Paper trail: A set of telltale signs of erroneous accounting, missing or altered documents or a "dangling debit" (the false or erroneous debit that results from an overstatement of assets).

Amount: The dollar amount of overstated assets and revenue, or understated liabilities and expenses.

Each audit program for the audit of an account balance contains an Audit Approach that may enable auditors to detect misstatements in account balances. Each application of procedures contains these elements:

Audit objective: A recognition of a financial statement assertion for which evidence needs to be obtained. The assertions are about the existence of assets, liabilities, revenue and expenses; their valuation; their complete inclusion in the account balances; the rights and obligations inherent in them; and their proper presentation and disclosure in the financial statements. (These assertions were introduced in Chapter 6.)

Control: A recognition of the control procedures that should be used by an organization to prevent and detect errors and irregularities.

Test of controls: Ordinary and extended procedures designed to produce evidence about the effectiveness of the controls that should be in operation.

Audit of balance: Ordinary and extended substantive procedures designed to find signs of mistaken accounting estimates, errors, irregularities and frauds in account balances and classes of transactions.

The cases first set the stage with a story about an accounting estimate, error, irregularity or fraud—its method, paper trail (if any) and amount. This part of the casette gives you the "inside story," which auditors seldom know before they perform the audit work. The second part of the casette, under the heading of Audit Approach, tells a structured story about the audit objective, desirable controls, test of control procedures, audit of balance procedures and discovery summary. The Audit Approach segment illustrates how audit procedures can be applied and the discoveries they may enable auditors to make. At the end of the chapter, some similar discussion cases are presented, and you can write the Audit Approach to test your ability to design audit procedures for the detection of mistaken accounting estimates, errors, irregularities and frauds.

CASETTE 14.1
UNREGISTERED SALE OF SECURITIES

Problem

The Bliss Solar Heating Company (Bliss) sold investment contracts in the form of limited partnership interests to the public. These "securities" sales should have been under a public registration filing with the Provincial Securities Regulator, but they were not.

Method

Bliss salespeople contacted potential investors and sold many of them limited partnership interests. The setup deal called for these limited partnerships to purchase solar hot water heating systems for residential and commercial use from Bliss. All the partnerships entered into arrangements to lease the equipment to Nationwide Corporation, which then rented the equipment to end users. The limited partnerships were, in effect, financing conduits for obtaining investors' money to pay for Bliss's equipment. The investors depended on Nationwide's business success and ability to pay under the lease terms for their return of capital and profit.

Paper Trail

Bliss published false and misleading financial statements, which used a non-GAAP revenue recognition method and failed to disclose cost of goods sold. Bliss overstated Nationwide's record of equipment installation and failed to disclose that Nationwide had little cash flow from end users (resulting from rent-free periods and other inducements). Bliss knew—and failed to disclose to prospective investors—the fact that numerous previous investors had filed petitions with the federal tax court to contest the disallowance by the Canada Revenue Agency of all their tax credits and benefits claimed in connection with their investments in Bliss's tax-sheltered equipment lease partnerships.

Amount

Not known, but all the money put up by the limited partnership investors was at risk largely not disclosed to the investors.

AUDIT APPROACH

Audit Objective

Obtain evidence to determine whether capital fund-raising methods comply with provincial securities laws and whether financial statements and other disclosures are misleading.

Control

Management should employ experts—lawyers, underwriters and accountants—who can determine whether securities and investment contract sales require registration.

Test of Controls

Auditors should learn the business backgrounds and securities-industry expertise of the senior managers. Study the minutes of the board of directors for authorization of the fund-raising method. Obtain and study opinions rendered by lawyers and underwriters about the legality of the fund-raising methods. Enquire about management's interaction with the Provincial Securities Regulator in any presale clearance. (The Provincial Securities Regulator will give advice about the necessity for registration.)

Audit of Balances

Auditors should study the offering documents and literature used in the sale of securities to determine whether financial information is being used properly. In this case the close relationship with Nationwide and the experience of earlier partnerships give reasons for extended procedures to obtain evidence about the representations concerning Nationwide's business success (in this case, lack of success).

Discovery Summary

The auditors gave unqualified reports on Bliss's materially misstated financial statements. They apparently did not question the legality of the sales of the limited partnership interests as a means of raising capital. They apparently did not perform procedures to verify representations made in offering literature respecting Bliss or Nationwide finances. Two partners in the audit firm were enjoined from violations of the securities laws. They resigned from practice before the Provincial Securities Regulator and were ordered not to perform any assurance services for companies making filings with the Provincial Securities Regulator. They later were expelled from the ICAO for failure to co-operate with the Disciplinary Committee in its investigation of alleged professional ethics violations.

CASETTE 14.2
TAX LOSS CARRYFORWARDS

Problem

Aetna Life & Casualty Insurance Company had losses in its taxable income operations in 2001 and 2002. Confident that future taxable income would absorb the loss, the company booked and reported a future income tax asset for the tax loss carryforward. The Provincial Securities Regulator maintained that the company understated its tax expense and overstated its assets. Utilization of the loss carryforward was not "more likely than not to be realized," as required by *CICA Handbook,* paragraph 3465.24.

Method

Aetna forecasted several more years of taxable losses (aside from its nontaxable income from tax-exempt investments), then forecasted years of taxable income, eventually offsetting the losses and obtaining the benefit of the tax law allowing losses to be carried forward to offset against future taxable income. The company maintained there was no reasonable doubt that the forecasts would be achieved.

Paper Trail

The amounts of tax loss were clearly evident in the accounts. Aetna made no attempt to hide the facts. The size of the portfolio of taxable investments and all sources of taxable income and deductions were well known to the company accountants, management and independent auditors.

Amount

At first, the carryforward tax benefit was $25 million, soon growing to over $200 million, then forecast to become an estimated $1 billion before it was forecast to reverse by being absorbed by future taxable income. In 2003, the first full year affected, Aetna's net income was 35 percent lower than 2001, instead of 6 percent lower with the carryforward benefit recognized.

AUDIT APPROACH

Audit Objective

Obtain evidence to determine whether realization of the benefits of the tax loss carryforward are "more likely than not."

Control

The relevant control in this case concerns the assumptions and mathematics involved in preparing the forecasts used to justify the argument for recording the tax loss carryforward benefit. These forecasts are the basis for an accounting estimate of "more likely than not."

Test of Controls

Auditors should make enquiries and determine: Who prepared the forecasts? When were they prepared? What data were used? Who reviewed and approved the forecast? Is there any way to test the accuracy of the forecast with actual experience?

Audit of Balances

Aside from audit of the assumptions underlying the forecast and recalculations of the compilation, the test of balances amounted to careful consideration of whether the forecast, or any forecast, could meet the test required by accounting standards. The decision was a judgement of whether the test of "more likely than not to be realized" was met.

The auditors should obtain information about other situations in which recognition of tax loss carryforward benefits were allowed in financial statements. Other companies have booked and reported such benefits when gains from sales of property were realized before the financial statement was issued and when the loss was from discontinuing a business line, leaving other businesses with long profit histories and prospects in operation.

Discovery Summary

The Provincial Securities Regulator was tipped off to Aetna's accounting recognition of the tax loss carry-

forward benefit by a story in *Financial Post* magazine, which described the accounting treatment. In its defence Aetna and its auditors argued on the basis of the forecasts. The Provincial Securities Regulator countered that the forecasts did not provide assurance beyond any reasonable doubt that future taxable income would be sufficient to offset the loss carryforward and would be earned during the carryforward period prescribed by the tax laws, as prescribed by paragraph 3465.28 of the *CICA Handbook*. For this reason, the Provincial Securities Regulator concluded that the "virtually certain realization" was not established. The Provincial Securities Regulator won the argument. Aetna revised its previously issued quarterly financial statements, and the company abandoned the attempt to report the tax benefit.

CASETTE 14.3
OFF-BALANCE-SHEET INVENTORY FINANCING

Problem

Verity Distillery Company used the "product repurchase" ploy to convert its inventory to cash, failing to disclose the obligation to repurchase it later. Related party transactions were not disclosed.

Method

Verity's president incorporated the Veritas Corporation, making himself and two other Verity officers the sole shareholders. The president arranged to sell $40 million of Verity's inventory of whiskey in the aging process to Veritas, showing no gain or loss on the transaction. The officers negotiated a 36-month loan with a major bank to get the money Veritas used for the purchase, pledging the inventory as collateral. Verity pledged to repurchase the inventory for $54.4 million, which amounted to the original $40 million plus 12 percent interest for three years.

Paper Trail

The contract of sale was in the files, specifying the name of the purchasing company, the $40 million amount and the cash consideration. Nothing mentioned the relationship between Veritas and the officers. Nothing mentioned the repurchase obligation. However, the sale amount was unusually large.

Amount

The $40 million amount was 40 percent of the normal inventory. Verity's cash balance was increased 50 percent. While the current asset total was not changed, the inventory ratios (e.g., inventory turnover, day's sales in inventory) were materially altered. Long-term liabilities were understated by not recording the liability. The ploy was actually a secured loan with inventory pledged as collateral, but this reality was neither recorded nor disclosed. The total effect would be to keep debt off the books, to avoid recording interest expense and later to record inventory at a higher cost. Subsequent sale of the whiskey at market prices would not affect the ultimate income results, but the unrecorded interest expense would be buried in the cost of goods sold. The net income in the first year when the "sale" was made was not changed, but the normal relationship of gross margin to sales was distorted by the zero-profit transaction.

	Before Transaction	Recorded Transaction	Should Have Recorded
Assets	$530	$530	$570
Liabilities	390	390	430
Shareholder Equity	140	140	140
Debt/Equity ratio	2.79	2.79	3.07

AUDIT APPROACH

Audit Objective

Obtain evidence to determine whether all liabilities are recorded. Be alert to undisclosed related party transactions.

Control

The relevant control in this case would rest with the integrity and accounting knowledge of the senior officials who arranged the transaction. Authorization in the board minutes might detail the arrangements; but, if they wanted to hide it from the auditors, they also would suppress the telltale information in the board minutes.

Test of Controls

Enquiries should be made about large and unusual financing transactions. This may not elicit a response because the event is a sales transaction, according to Verity. Other audit work on controls in the revenues, receivables and receipts process may turn up the large sale. Fortunately, this one sticks out as a large one.

Audit of Balances

Analytical procedures to compare monthly or seasonal sales probably will identify the sale as large and unusual. This identification should lead to an examination of the sales contract. Auditors should discuss the business purpose of the transaction with knowledgeable officials. If being this close to discovery does not bring out an admission of the loan and repurchase arrangement, the auditors nevertheless should investigate further. Even if the "customer" name is not a giveaway, a quick enquiry at the corporate search branch of the provincial ministry of consumer and commercial relations for corporation records (online in some databases) will show the names of the officers, and the auditors will know the related party nature of the deal. A request for the financial statements of Veritas should be made.

Discovery Summary

The auditors found the related party relationship between the officers and Veritas. Confronted, the president admitted the attempt to make the cash position and the debt/equity ratio look better than they were. The financial statements were adjusted to reflect the "should have recorded" set of figures shown previously.

CASETTE 14.4
A CONSOLIDATION BY ANY OTHER NAME

Problem

Digilog, Inc., formed another company named DBS International (DBSI), controlled it and did not consolidate its financial position and results of operations in the Digilog financial statements. Digilog income was overstated, and assets and liabilities were understated.

Method

Digilog, Inc. formed DBSI as a separate corporation to market Digilog's computer equipment. DBSI was formed separately to avoid the adverse impact of reporting expected startup losses in Digilog's financial statements. Instead of owning shares in DBSI, Digilog financed the company with loans convertible at will into 90 percent of DBSI's stock. (Otherwise, the share ownership was not in Digilog's name.) Since Digilog did not control DBSI (control defined as 50 percent or more ownership), DBSI was not consolidated, and the initial losses were not reported in Digilog's financial statements. See *Handbook,* paragraph 1590.08 for the usual presumptions concerning the level of ownership leading to control.

Paper Trail

Formation of DBSI was not a secret. It was authorized. Incorporation papers were available. Loan documents showing the terms of Digilog's loans to DBSI were in the files.

Amount

Several hundred thousand dollars of losses in the first two years of DBSI operations were not consolidated. Ultimately, the venture became profitable and was absorbed into Digilog.

AUDIT APPROACH

Audit Objective

Obtain evidence to determine whether proper accounting methods (cost, equity, consolidation) were used for investments.

Control

The relevant control in this case would rest with the integrity and accounting knowledge of the senior officials who arranged the transaction. Proper

documentation of authorization and financing and operating transactions between the two corporations should be in the companies' files.

Test of Controls

Enquiries should be made about large and unusual financing transactions. Minutes of the board of directors' meetings should be studied to find related authorizations. These authorizations and supporting papers signal the accounting issues and the interpretations of generally accepted accounting principles required in the circumstances.

Audit of Balances

The central issue in this case was the interpretation of accounting standards regarding required consolidation. Existence, completeness, valuation and ownership were not problematic audit issues. Unless these are extenuating factors as per *CICA Handbook*, paragraph 1590.08, accounting standards require consolidation of over-50 percent owned subsidiaries, and prohibits consolidation of subsidiaries owned less than 50 percent. Digilog's purpose in financing DBSI with loans instead of direct share ownership

was to skirt the 50 percent "ownership" criterion, thus keeping the DBSI losses out of the Digilog consolidated financial statements. The "test of the balance" (decision of whether to require consolidation) amounted to an interpretation of the substance versus form of "ownership" through convertible notes instead of direct shareholding.

Discovery Summary

Digilog, with concurrence of its independent audit firm, adopted the narrow interpretation of "ownership." Since Digilog did not "own" DBSI stock, DBSI was not "controlled," and its assets, liabilities and results of operations were not consolidated. The regulator disagreed and took action on the position that the convertible feature of the loans and the business purpose of the DBSI formation were enough to attribute control to Digilog. The company was enjoined from violating certain reporting and antifraud provisions of the provincial securities act and was required to amend its financial statements for the years in question (consolidating DBSI). The regulator also took action against the audit firm partner in charge of the Digilog audit.

OTHER ASPECTS OF CLEVER ACCOUNTING AND FRAUD

The types of clever accounting and fraud that must be considered are those affecting the fair presentation of material equity accounts, investments and intangibles. Improper accounting presentations are engineered more frequently by senior officials than by middle management or lower ranks. Top management personnel who deal with the transactions involved in investments, long-term debt and shareholders' equity are not subject to the same kind of control as lower-level employees, and they generally are able to override detail procedural controls.

Long-Term Liabilities and Owners' Equity

The kinds of clever accounting and fraud connected with liability and owners' equity accounts differ significantly from those associated with asset and revenue accounts. Few employees are tempted to steal a liability, although fictitious liabilities may be created as a means of misdirecting cash payments into the hands of an officer. Auditors should be alert for such fictions in the same sense that they are alert to the possibility of having fictitious accounts receivable.

Although there are opportunities for employee fraud against the company, the area of liabilities and owners' equity also opens up possibilities for company fraud against outsiders. This class of fraud is most often accomplished through material misrepresentations or omissions in financial statements and related disclosures.

Officers and employees can use share or bond instruments improperly. Unissued shares or bonds and treasury stock may be used as collateral for personal loans. Even though the company may not be damaged or suffer loss by this action (unless the employee defaults and the securities are seized), the practice is unauthorized and is contrary to company interests. Similarly, employees may gain access to shareholder lists and unissued coupons and cause improper payments of dividends and interest on securities that are not outstanding.

Proper custodial control of securities (either by physical means, such as limited access vaults, or by control of an independent disbursing agent) prevents most such occurrences.

An auditing procedure of reconciling authorized dividend and interest payments (calculated using declared dividend rates, coupon interest rates and known quantities of outstanding securities) to actual payments detects unauthorized payments. If the company did not perform this checking procedure, auditors should include it among their own analytical recalculation procedures. Many liability, equity and off-balance-sheet transactions are outside the reach of normal internal control procedures, which can operate effectively over ordinary transactions (such as purchases and sales) processed by clerks and machines. Auditors generally are justified in performing extensive substantive auditing of long-term liability, equity and other high-level managed transactions and agreements because control depends in large part on the integrity and accounting knowledge of management.

Income tax evasion and fraud result from actions taken by managers. Evasion and fraud may be accomplished (1) by simple omission of income, (2) by unlawful deductions (such as contributions to political campaigns, capital cost allowance on nonexistent assets or capital cost allowance in excess of cost), or (3) by contriving sham transactions for the sole purpose of avoiding taxation. Auditors should be able to detect errors of the first two categories if the actual income and expense data have been sufficiently audited in the financial statements. The last category—**contrived sham transactions**—is harder to detect because a dishonest management can skilfully disguise them. Some of the fraud awareness procedures outlined in Chapter 17 may be useful and effective.

Financial statements may be materially misstated by reason of omission or understatement of liabilities and by failure to disclose technical defaults on loan agreement restrictions. These restrictions or test covenants can be very important to the viability of the client because if they are violated, creditors can force the client into bankruptcy. Hence, auditor knowledge of these restrictions and comparison with the client's current financial condition is important for pinpointing audit risk areas and for properly assessing the going concern assumption. The procedures you have learned to discover unrecorded liabilities through a search for unrecorded liabilities may be used to discover such omissions and understatements (Chapter 12). If auditors discover that loan agreement terms have been violated, they should bring the information to the client's attention and insist on proper disclosure in notes to the financial statements. In both situations (liability understatement and loan default disclosure), management's actions, reactions and willingness to adjust the financial figures and to make adverse disclosures are important insights for auditors' subjective evaluation of managerial integrity. An accumulation of inputs relevant to managerial integrity can have an important bearing on the auditors' perceptions of relative risk for the audit engagement taken as a whole.

Misstatements in the financial statements can arise from error or fraud. According to *CICA Handbook,* section 5135, the term "error" refers to an *unintentional* misstatement in financial statements, including the omission of an amount or a disclosure, or an incorrect accounting estimate arising from oversight or misinterpretation of facts. The term "fraud" refers to an *intentional* act by one or more individuals to intentionally misstate the financial statements to deceive users and obtain an unjust or illegal advantage. Although fraud is a broad legal concept, the auditor is only concerned with fraud that causes a material misstatement in the financial statements. Auditors do not make legal determinations of whether fraud has actually occurred.

Intent is difficult to prove, but if the auditor identifies a possible bias on the part of management in making accounting estimates, the auditor should consider whether the circumstances indicate a risk of material misstatement due to fraud.[4] For example, is it possible that the cumulative effect of bias in management's accounting estimates is designed to smooth earnings over two or more accounting periods, or to achieve a designated earnings level in order to deceive financial statement users? The audit needs to be performed with professional skepticism, meaning the auditor:

(*a*) should be aware of factors that increase the risk of misstatement, and

(*b*) should be sensitized to evidence that contradicts the assumption of management's good faith.

[4] *CICA Handbook,* paragraph 5135.081.

If there are enough "red flags" present, the auditor will assess a higher inherent risk and for a given control risk these higher assessments will cause the auditor to:

(*a*) obtain more reliable evidence

(*b*) expand the extent of audit procedures performed

(*c*) apply audit procedures closer to or as of the balance sheet date

(*d*) require more extensive supervision of assistants and/or assistants with more experience and training

In essence, if the auditor suspects that the financial statements are misstated, he should perform procedures to confirm or dispel that suspicion.

Generally, the auditor is less likely to detect material misstatements arising from fraud because of the deliberate concealment involved.

The auditor should inform the appropriate level of management whenever she obtains evidence of a nontrivial misstatement or fraud; and the audit committee or board of directors should be informed of all significant misstatements or fraud.[5]

A company, its individual managers and the auditors can violate securities regulations if they are not careful. Chapter 5 covers the general framework of regulation by provincial securities commissions. Auditors must know the provisions of the securities laws to the extent that they can identify situations that constitute obvious fraud, and so that they can identify transactions that may be subject to the law. Having once recognized or raised questions about a securities transaction, auditors should not act as their own lawyer. The facts should be submitted to competent legal counsel for an opinion. Even though auditors are not expected to be legal experts, they have the duty to recognize obvious instances of impropriety and to pursue investigations with the aid of legal experts.

Similarly, auditors should assist clients in observing securities commission rules and regulations on matters of timely disclosure. In general, the timely disclosure rules are phrased in terms of management's duties, and they do not require auditors to carry out any specific procedures or to make any specific disclosures. The regulations' purpose is to require management to disseminate to the public any material information, whether favourable or unfavourable, so that investors can incorporate it in their decision making. Various rule provisions require announcements and disclosures very soon after information becomes known. Often, relevant situations arise during the year when the independent auditors are not present, so, of course, they cannot be held responsible or liable. However, in other situations, auditors may learn of the information inadvertently or the auditors' advice may be sought by the client. In such cases auditors should advise their clients, consistent with the requirements of law and regulations.

Presently, pressures are on the auditors to discover more information about off-balance-sheet contingencies and commitments and to discover the facts of management involvement with other parties to transactions. Auditors' knowledge of contingencies and commitments that are not evidenced in accounting records depends in large part on information the management and its legal counsel will reveal. Nevertheless, certain investigative procedures are available (see Chapter 17). The current pressures on auditors to discover more information is a part of the public pressure on auditors to take more responsibility for fraud detection.

Investments and Intangibles

Theft, diversion and unauthorized use of investment securities can occur in several ways. If safekeeping controls are weak, securities simply may be stolen, in which case the theft becomes a police problem rather than an auditing problem. Somewhat more frequent are diversions, such as using securities as collateral during the year, returning them for a count, then giving them back to the creditor without disclosure to the auditor. If safekeeping

---

[5] *Ibid.*, section 5135.

methods require entry signatures (as at a safe deposit vault), auditors may be able to detect the in-and-out movement. The best chance of discovery is that the creditor will confirm the collateral arrangement. In a similar manner, securities may be removed by an officer and sold, then repurchased before the auditors' count. The auditors' record of the certificate numbers should reveal this change, since the returned certificates (and their serial numbers) will not be the same as the ones removed. The rapid growth in use of derivative securities as investments and hedges has created new and rather unique problems for auditors, not the least of which is lack of familiarity with these financial instruments. Appendix 14B (on the text Online Learning Centre) provides an overview of the recent global problems in this area.

Cash receipts from interest, royalties on patent licences, dividends and sales proceeds may be stolen. The accounting records may or may not be manipulated to cover the theft. In general, this kind of defalcation should be prevented by cash receipts control; however, since these receipts usually are irregular and infrequent, the cash control system may not be as effective as it is for regular receipts on trade accounts. If the income accounts are not manipulated to hide stolen receipts, auditors will find less income in the account than the amount indicated by their audit calculations based on other records, such as licence agreements or published dividend records. If sales of securities are not recorded, auditors will notice that securities are missing when they try to inspect or confirm them. If the income accounts have been manipulated to hide stolen receipts, vouching of cash receipts will detect the theft, or vouching may reveal some offsetting debit buried in some other account.

Accounting values may be manipulated in a number of ways, involving purchase of assets at inflated prices, leases with affiliates, acquisitions of patents for shares given to an inventor or promoter, sales to affiliates and fallacious decisions about amortization. Business history has recorded several cases of non-arm's-length transactions with promoters, officers, directors and controlled companies (even "dummy" companies) designed to drain the company's resources and fool the auditors.

In one case a company sold assets to a dummy purchaser set up by a director to bolster sagging income with a gain. The auditors did not know that the purchaser was a shell. All the documents of sale looked in order, and cash sales proceeds had been deposited. The auditors were not informed of a secret agreement by the seller to repurchase the assets at a later time. This situation illustrates a devious manipulation. All transactions with persons closely associated with the company (related parties) should be audited carefully with reference to market values, particularly when a nonmonetary transaction is involved (such as shares exchanged for patent rights). Sales and lease-back and straight lease transactions with insiders likewise should be audited carefully.

REVIEW CHECKPOINTS

14.21 What is the single most significant control consideration in connection with clever accounting and fraud in finance and investment accounts?

14.22 Which is more likely to exist in the finance and investment cycle accounts: (1) fraud against the company or (2) fraud by the company in financial or tax reporting? Explain.

14.23 What should an auditor do when violation of securities laws is suspected?

14.24 What is the danger for auditors when company officials engage in undisclosed related party transactions?

Analysis of Financial Statement Relationships

The audit of the finance and investment process results in verifying that there is not a material misstatement in the balance of long-term investments and liabilities (financial instruments) and share capital, or in the transaction streams that are related to them, dividends and interest. As an example, the continuity of the share capital account is shown following.

Audited Amount	Financial Statement Where Amount Is Reported
Opening balance of share capital	Balance sheet (prior year comparative figures)
Add: Proceeds of shares issued during the year	Statement of Shareholders' Equity and Cash flow statement (financing activity)
Deduct: Reductions for shares redeemed during the year	Statement of Shareholders' Equity and Cash flow statement (financing activity)
Ending balance of share capital	Balance sheet (current year figures)

SUMMARY

The finance and investment process contains a wide variety of accounts—share capital, dividends, long-term debt, interest expense, tax expenses and future income taxes, financial instruments, derivatives, equity method investments, related gains and losses, consolidated subsidiaries, goodwill and other intangibles. These accounts involve some of the most technically complex accounting standards. They create most of the difficult judgements for financial reporting.

Transactions in these accounts generally are controlled by senior officials. Therefore, internal control is centred on the integrity and accounting knowledge of these officials. The procedural controls over details of transactions are not very effective because senior managers can override them and order their own desired accounting presentations. As a consequence, auditors' work on the assessment of control risk is directed toward the senior managers, the board of directors and their authorizations and design of finance and investment deals.

Fraud and clever accounting in the finance and investment cycle get directed most often to producing misleading financial statements. While theft and embezzlement can occur, the accounts in this cycle frequently have been the ones subject to manipulation and spurious valuation for the purpose of reporting financial position and results of operations better than the reality of companies' situations. Off-balance-sheet financing and investment transactions with related parties are explained as ripe areas for fraudulent financial reporting.

This chapter ends the book's coverage of audit applications for various processes and their related accounts. Chapter 15 contains several topics involved in putting the finishing touches on an audit.

MULTIPLE-CHOICE QUESTIONS FOR PRACTICE AND REVIEW

14.25 Jones was engaged to examine the financial statements of Gamma Corporation for the year ended June 30, 20X3. Having completed an examination of the investment securities, which of the following is the best method of verifying the accuracy of recorded dividend income?

   a. Tracing recorded dividend income to cash receipts records and validated deposit slips.

   b. Utilizing analytical review techniques and statistical sampling.

   c. Comparing recorded dividends with amounts appearing on federal tax returns.

   d. Comparing recorded dividends with a standard financial reporting service's record of dividends.

14.26 When a large amount of negotiable securities is held by the client, planning by the auditor is necessary to guard against:

   a. Unauthorized negotiation of the securities before they are counted.

b. Unrecorded sales of securities after they are counted.

c. Substitution of securities already counted for other securities which should be on hand but are not.

d. Substitution of authentic securities with counterfeit securities.

14.27 Which of the following is the most important consideration of an auditor when examining the shareholders' equity section of a client's balance sheet?

a. Changes in the share capital account are verified by an independent share transfer agent.

b. Stock dividends and stock splits during the year under audit were approved by the shareholders.

c. Stock dividends are capitalized at par or stated value on the dividend declaration date.

d. Entries in the share capital account can be traced to resolutions in the minutes of the board of directors' meetings.

14.28 If the auditor discovers that the carrying amount of a client's available for sale financial assets is greater than its market value at the balance sheet date, the auditor should insist that:

a. The approximate market value of the investments be shown in parentheses on the face of the balance sheet.

b. The investments be classified as long term for balance sheet purposes with full disclosure in the footnotes.

c. The decline in value be recognized in the financial statements.

d. The liability section of the balance sheet separately shows a charge equal to the amount of the loss.

14.29 The primary reason for preparing a reconciliation between interest-bearing obligations outstanding during the year and interest expense in the financial statements, is to:

a. Evaluate internal control over securities.

b. Determine the validity of prepaid interest expense.

c. Ascertain the reasonableness of imputed interest.

d. Detect unrecorded liabilities.

14.30 The auditor should insist that a representative of the client be present during the inspection and count of securities in order to:

a. Lend authority to the auditor's directives.

b. Detect forged securities.

c. Co-ordinate the return of all securities to proper locations.

d. Acknowledge the receipt of securities returned.

14.31 When independent share transfer agents are not employed and the corporation issues its own shares and maintains share records, cancelled share certificates should:

a. Be defaced to prevent reissuance and attached to their corresponding stubs.

b. Not be defaced, but segregated from other share certificates and retained in a cancelled certificates file.

c. Be destroyed to prevent fraudulent reissuance.

d. Be defaced and sent to the federal finance minister.

14.32 When a client company does not maintain its own share capital records, the auditor should obtain written confirmation from the transfer agent and registrar concerning:

a. Restrictions on the payment of dividends.

b. The number of shares issued and outstanding.

c. Guarantees of preferred share liquidation value.

d. The number of shares subject to agreements to repurchase.

(AICPA adapted)

14.33 All corporate share capital transactions should ultimately be traced to the:

a. Minutes of the board of directors.

b. Cash receipts journal.

c. Cash disbursements journal.

d. Numbered share certificates.

14.34 A corporate balance sheet indicates that one of the corporate assets is a patent. An auditor will most likely obtain evidence of this patent by obtaining a written representation from:

a. A patent lawyer.

b. A regional patent office.

c. The patent inventor.

d. The patent owner.

14.35 An audit program for the examination of the retained earnings account should include a step that requires verification of the:

a. Market value used to charge retained earnings to account for a two-for-one share split.

b. Approval of the adjustment to the beginning balance as a result of a write-down of an account receivables.

c. Authorization for both cash and share dividends.

d. Gain or loss resulting from disposition of available for sale financial assets.

EXERCISES AND PROBLEMS

· ·

INVESTMENTS AND INTANGIBLES

14.36 ICQ for Equity Investments. Cassandra Corporation,
LO.1 a manufacturing company, periodically invests large
LO.2 sums in marketable equity securities. The investment policy is established by the investment committee of the board of directors. The treasurer is responsible for carrying out the investment committee's directives. All securities are held by Cassandra's brokerage company.

Your internal control questionnaire with respect to Cassandra's investments in equity securities contains the following three questions:

1. Is investment policy established by the investment committee of the board of directors?
2. Is the treasurer solely responsible for carrying out the investment committee's directive?
3. Are all securities stored in a bank safe-deposit vault?

Required:

a. What is the purpose of the above three questions?
b. What additional questions should your internal control questionnaires include with respect to the company's investment in marketable equity securities? (Hint: Prepare questions to cover the control objectives—validity, completeness, authorization, accuracy, classification, accounting and proper period.)

(AICPA adapted)

14.37 Noncurrent Investment Securities. You are engaged
LO.3 in the audit of the financial statements of Bass Corporation for the year ended December 31, and you are about to begin an audit of the noncurrent investment securities. Bass's records indicate that the company owns various bearer bonds, as well as 25 percent of the outstanding common shares of Commercial Industrial, Inc. You are satisfied with evidence that supports the presumption of significant influence over Commercial Industrial, Inc. The various securities are at two locations as follows:

1. Recently acquired securities are in the company's safe in the custody of the treasurer.
2. All other securities are in the company's bank safe deposit box. All securities in Bass's portfolio are actively traded in a broad market.

Required:

a. Assuming that the system of internal control over securities is satisfactory, what are the objectives (specific assertions) for the audit of the noncurrent securities?
b. What audit procedures should you undertake with respect to the audit of Bass's investment securities?

(AICPA adapted)

14.38 Securities Examination and Count. You are in charge
LO.3 of the audit of the financial statements of the Demot Corporation for the year ended December 31. The corporation has had the policy of investing its surplus funds in marketable securities. Its share and bond certificates are kept in a safe-deposit box in a local bank. Only the president and the treasurer of the corporation have access to the box.

You were unable to obtain access to the safe-deposit box on December 31 because neither the president nor the treasurer was available. Arrangements were made for your assistant to accompany the treasurer to the bank on January 11 to examine the securities. Your assistant has never examined securities that were being kept in a safe-deposit box and requires instructions. Your assistant should be able to inspect all securities on hand in an hour.

Required:

a. List the instructions that you would give to your assistant regarding the examination of the share and bond certificates kept in the safe-deposit box. Include in your instructions the details of the securities to be examined and the reasons for examining these details.
b. After returning from the bank, your assistant reports that the treasurer had entered the box on January 4 to remove an old photograph of the corporation's original building. The photograph was loaned to the local chamber of commerce for display purposes. List the additional audit procedures that are required because of the treasurer's action.

(AICPA adapted)

14.39 Securities Procedures. You were engaged to examine
LO.3 the financial statements of Ronlyn Corporation for the year ended June 30. On May 1 the corporation borrowed $500,000 from the Second National Bank to finance plant expansion. However, due to unexpected difficulties in acquiring the building site, the plant expansion had not begun as planned. To make use of the borrowed funds, management decided to invest in shares and bonds; on May 16 the $500,000 was invested in securities.

Required:

In your audit of investments, how would you:
a. Audit the recorded dividend or interest income?
b. Determine market value?
c. Establish the authority for security purchases?

(AICPA adapted)

14.40 Research and Development. The Hertle Engineering
LO.3 Company depends on innovation of new product development to maintain its position in the market for drilling tool equipment. The company conducts an extensive research and development program for this purpose, and has charged all research and development costs to current operations in accordance with *CICA Handbook* requirements.

The company began a project called Project Able in January 20X1 with the goal of patenting a revolutionary drilling bit design. Work continued until October 20X2 when the company applied for a patent. Costs were charged to the research and development expense account in both years, except for the cost of a computer program that engineers plan to use in Project Baker, scheduled to start in December 20X2. The computer program was purchased from Computeering, Inc., in January 20X1 for $45,000.

Required:

a. Give an audit program for the audit of research and development costs on Project Able. Assume that you are auditing the company for the first time at December 31, 20X2.
b. What evidence would you require for the audit of the computer program that has been capitalized as an

intangible asset? As of December 31, 20X2, this account has a balance of $40,000 (cost less $5,000 amortized as a part of Project Able).

(AICPA adapted)

14.41 Intangibles. Sorenson Manufacturing Corporation was
LO.1 incorporated on January 3, 20X1. The corporation's fi-
LO.3 nancial statements for its first year's operations were not examined by a PA. You have been engaged to audit the financial statements for the year ended December 31, 20X2, and your examination is substantially completed.

A partial trial balance of the company's accounts is given in Exhibit 14.41–1:

The following information relates to accounts which may yet require adjustment:

1. Patents for Sorenson's manufacturing process were purchased January 2, 20X2, at a cost of $68,000. An additional $17,000 was spent in December 20X2 to improve machinery covered by the patents and charged to the patents account. The patents had a remaining legal term of 17 years.

2. The balance in the goodwill account includes $24,000 paid December 30, 20X1, for an advertising program, which it is estimated will assist in increasing Sorenson's sales over a period of four years following the disbursement.

3. The leasehold improvement account includes (*a*) the $15,000 cost of improvements, with a total estimated useful life of 12 years, which Sorenson, as tenant, made to leased premises in January 20X1; (*b*) movable assembly line equipment costing $8,500, which was installed in the leased premises in December 20X2; and (*c*) real estate taxes of $2,500 paid by

Sorenson which, under the terms of the lease, should have been paid by the landlord. Sorenson paid its rent in full during 20X2. A 10-year nonrenewable lease was signed January 3, 20X1, for the leased building that Sorenson used in manufacturing operations. No amortization of the leasehold improvements has been recorded.

Required:

Prepare adjusting entries as necessary.

(AICPA adapted)

LONG-TERM LIABILITIES AND COMMITMENTS

14.42 Long-Term Note. You were engaged to examine the fi-
LO.3 nancial statements of Ronlyn Corporation for the year ended June 30. On May 1 the corporation borrowed $500,000 from the Second National Bank to finance plant expansion. The long-term note agreement provided for the annual payment of principal and interest over five years. The existing plant was pledged as security for the loan.

Due to unexpected difficulties in acquiring the building site, the plant expansion had not begun as planned. To make use of the borrowed funds, management decided to invest in shares and bonds, and on May 16 the $500,000 was invested in securities.

Required:

a. What are the audit objectives in the examining of long-term debt?

b. Prepare an audit program for the examination of the long-term note agreement between Ronlyn and Second National Bank.

(AICPA adapted)

14.43 Long-Term Financing Agreement. You have been en-
LO.3 gaged to audit the financial statements of Broadwall Corporation for the year ended December 31, 20X2. During the year, Broadwall obtained a long-term loan from a local bank pursuant to a financing agreement, which provided that:

1. Loan was to be secured by the company's inventory and accounts receivable.
2. Company was to maintain a debt-to-equity ratio not to exceed 2:1.
3. Company was not to pay dividends without permission from the bank.
4. Monthly installment payments were to commence July 1, 20X2.

In addition, during the year the company also borrowed, on a short-term basis, from the president of the company, substantial amounts just prior to the year-end.

Required:

a. For the purposes of your audit of the financial statements of Broadwall Corporation, what procedures should you employ in examining the described loans? Do not discuss internal control.

b. What financial statement disclosures should you expect to find with respect to the loan from the president?

EXHIBIT 14.41–1

SORENSON MANUFACTURING CORPORATION
Partial Trial Balance at
December 31, 20X2

	Trial Balance	
	Debit	Credit
Cash	$11,000	
Accounts receivable	42,500	
Allowance for doubtful accounts		$ 500
Inventories	38,500	
Machinery	75,000	
Equipment	29,000	
Accumulated amortization		10,000
Patents	85,000	
Leasehold improvements	26,000	
Prepaid expenses	10,500	
Goodwill	24,000	

14.44 Bond Indenture Covenants. The following covenants
LO.3 are extracted from the indenture of a bond issue. The indenture provides that failure to comply with its terms in any respect automatically advances the due date of the loan to the date of noncompliance (the regular date is 20 years hence). Give any audit steps or reporting requirements you believe should be taken or recognized in connection with each of the following:
1. "The debtor company shall endeavour to maintain a working capital ratio of 2:1 at all times, and, in any fiscal year following a failure to maintain said ratio, the company shall restrict compensation of officers to a total of $500,000. Officers for this purpose shall include chairman of the board of directors, president, all vice presidents, secretary and treasurer."
2. "The debtor company shall keep all property which is security for this debt insured against loss by fire to the extent of 100 percent of its actual value. Policies of insurance comprising this protection shall be filed with the trustee."
3. "The debtor company shall pay all taxes legally assessed against property which is security for this debt within the time provided by law for payment without penalty and shall deposit receipted tax bills or equally acceptable evidence of payment of same with the trustee."
4. "A sinking fund shall be deposited with the trustee by semiannual payments of $300,000, from which the trustee shall, in his discretion, purchase bonds of this issue."

(AICPA adapted)

14.45 Shareholders' Equity. You are a PA engaged in an
LO.1 examination of the financial statements of Pate Corpora-
LO.3 tion for the year ended December 31. The financial statements and records of Pate Corporation have not been audited by a PA in prior years.

The shareholders' equity section of Pate Corporation's balance sheet at December 31 follows:

Shareholders' equity:

Share capital—10,000 no par value shares authorized; 5,000 shares issued and outstanding	$ 50,000
Contributed capital	32,580
Retained earnings	47,320
Total shareholders' equity	$129,900

Pate Corporation was founded in 1992. The corporation has 10 shareholders and serves as its own registrar and transfer agent. There are no capital share subscription contracts in effect.

Required:

a. Prepare the detailed audit program for the examination of the three accounts composing the shareholders' equity section of Pate Corporation's balance sheet. Organize the audit program under broad financial statement assertions. (Do not include in the audit program the audit of the results of the current year's operations.)

b. After every other figure on the balance sheet has been audited, it may appear that the retained earnings figure is a balancing figure and requires no further audit work. Why don't auditors audit retained earnings as they do the other figures on the balance sheet? Discuss.

(AICPA adapted)

DISCUSSION CASES

• •

14.46 Intercompany and Interpersonal Investment Rela-
LO.3 **tions.** You have been engaged to audit the financial

statements of Hardy Hardware Distributors, Inc., as of December 31. In your review of the corporate nonfinancial records, you have found that Hardy Hardware owns 15 percent of the outstanding voting common shares of Hardy Products Corporation. Upon further investigation, you learn that Hardy Products Corporation manufactures a line of hardware goods, 90 percent of which is sold to Hardy Hardware.

Mr. James L. Hardy, president of Hardy Hardware, has supplied you with objective evidence that he personally owns 30 percent of the Hardy Products voting shares and that the remaining 70 percent is owned by Mr. John L. Hardy, his brother and president of Hardy Products. James L. Hardy also owns 20 percent of the voting common shares of Hardy Hardware Distributors. Another 20 percent is held by an estate of which James and John are beneficiaries, and the remaining 60 percent is publicly held.

Hardy Hardware consistently has reported operating profits greater than the industry average. Hardy Products Corporation, however, has a net return on sales of only 1 percent. The Hardy Products investment always has been reported at cost, and no dividends have been paid by the company. During the course of your conversations with the Hardy brothers, you learn that you were appointed as auditor because the brothers had a heated disagreement with the former auditor over the issues of accounting for the Hardy Products investment and the prices at which goods have been sold to Hardy Hardware.

For Discussion

a. Identify the issues in this situation as they relate to (1) conflicts of interest and (2) controlling influences among individuals and corporations.

b. Should the investment in Hardy Products Corporation be accounted for on the equity method?

c. What evidence should the auditor seek with regard to

the prices paid by Hardy Hardware for products purchased from Hardy Products Corporation?

    d. What information would you consider necessary for adequate disclosure in the financial statements of Hardy Hardware Distributors?

INSTRUCTIONS FOR DISCUSSION CASES 14.46–14.47

These cases are designed like the ones in the chapter. They give the problem, the method, the paper trail and the amount. Your assignment is to write the Audit Approach portion of the case, organized around these sections:

Objectives: Express the objective in terms of the facts supposedly asserted in financial records, accounts and statements. (Refer to discussion of assertions in Chapter 6.)

Control: Write a brief explanation of control considerations, especially the kinds of manipulations that may arise from the situation described in the case.

Test of controls: Write some procedures for getting evidence about existing controls, especially procedures that could discover management manipulations. If there are no controls to test, then there are no procedures to perform; go then to the next section. A "procedure" should instruct someone about the source(s) of evidence to tap and the work to do.

Audit of balance: Write some procedures for getting evidence about the existence, completeness, valuation, ownership or disclosure assertions identified in your objective section above.

Discovery summary: Write a short statement about the discovery you expect to accomplish with your procedures.

14.47 Related Party Transaction "Goodwill."

LO.3

HIDE THE LOSS UNDER THE GOODWILL

Problem: A contrived amount of goodwill was used to overstate assets and disguise a loss on discontinued operations.

Method: Gulwest Industries, a public company, decided to discontinue its unprofitable line of business of manufacturing sporting ammunition. Gulwest had capitalized the start-up cost of the business, and, with its discontinuance, the $7 million deferred cost should have been written off.

Instead, Gulwest formed a new corporation named Amron and transferred the sporting ammunition assets (including the $7 million deferred cost) to it in exchange for all the Amron shares. In the Gulwest accounts the Amron investment was carried at $12.4 million, which was the book value of the assets transferred (including the $7 million deferred cost).

In an agreement with a different public company (Big Industrial), Gulwest and Big created another company (BigShot Ammunition). Gulwest transferred all the Amron assets to BigShot in exchange for (1) common and preferred shares of Big, valued at $2 million, and (2) a note from BigShot in the amount of $3.4 million. Big Industrial thus acquired 100 percent of the shares of BigShot. Gulwest management reasoned that it had "given" Amron shares valued at $12.4 million to receive shares and notes valued at $5.4 million, so the difference must be goodwill. Thus, the Gulwest accounts carried amounts for Big Industrial shares ($2 million), BigShot note receivable ($3.4 million), and goodwill ($7 million).

Paper trail: Gulwest directors included in the minutes an analysis of the sporting ammunition business's lack of profitability. The minutes showed approval of a plan to dispose of the business, but they did not use the words "discontinue the business." The minutes also showed approval of the creation of Amron, the deal with Big Industrial along with the formation of BigShot, and the acceptance of Big's shares and Bigshot's note in connection with the final exchange and merger.

Amount: As explained above, Gulwest avoided reporting a write-off of $7 million by overstating the value of the assets given in exchange for the Big Industrial shares and the BigShot Ammunition note.

14.48 Related Party Transaction Valuation. Follow the in-
LO.3 structions preceding Discussion Case 14.47. Write the audit approach section of the case.

IN PLANE VIEW

Problem: Whiz Corporation overstated the value of shares given in exchange for an airplane and, thereby, understated its loss on disposition of the shares. Income was overstated.

Method: Whiz owned 160,000 Wing Company shares, carried on the books as an investment in the amount of $6,250,000. Whiz bought a used airplane from Wing, giving in exchange (1) $480,000 cash and (2) the 160,000 Wing shares. Even though the quoted market value of the Wing shares was $2,520,000, Whiz valued the airplane received at $3,750,000, indicating a share valuation of $3,270,000. Thus, Whiz recognized a loss on disposition of the Wing shares in the amount of $2,980,000.

Whiz justified the airplane valuation with another transaction. On the same day it was purchased, Whiz sold the airplane to the Mexican subsidiary of one of its subsidiary companies (two layers down; but Whiz owned 100 percent of the first subsidiary, which in turn owned 100 percent of the Mexican subsidiary). The Mexican subsidiary paid Whiz with US$25,000 cash and a promissory note for US$3,725,000 (market rate of interest).

Paper trail: The transaction was within the authority of the chief executive officer, and company policy did not require a separate approval by the board of directors. A contract of sale and correspondence with Wing detailing the terms of the transaction were in the files. Likewise, a contract of sale to the Mexican subsidiary, along with a copy of the deposit slip, and a memorandum of the promissory note was on file. The note itself was kept in the company vault. None of the Wing papers cited a specific price for the airplane.

Amount: Whiz overvalued the Wing shares and justified it with a related party transaction with its own subsidiary company. The loss on the disposition of the Wing shares was understated by $750,000.

14.49 Audit of Long-Term Debt In Note 12 of its December
LO.3 2001 consolidated financial statements, Bell Canada reports long-term debt outstanding totalling $9,075 million. This amount is made up of 35 separate debentures, with maturity dates ranging from 2001 to 2054, in amounts ranging from $125 to $700 million, with inter-

est rates ranging from 2.7 percent to 11.45 percent. The income statement for the year reports interest expense on this long-term debt of $725 million.[6]

Required:

List the assertions relating to Bell Canada's long-term debt and interest expense. Describe the audit procedures that you would perform to verify the debt and interest expense for 2001.

14.50 Long-Term Debt Working Paper Review. The long-term debt working paper in Exhibit 14.50–1 was prepared by client personnel and audited by AA, an audit staff assistant, during the calendar year 20X2 audit of Canadian Widgets, Inc., a continuing audit client. You are the engagement supervisor, and your assignment is to review this working paper thoroughly.

Required:

Identify and prepare a list explaining the deficiencies that should be discovered in the supervisory review of the long-term debt working paper.

(AICPA adapted)

14.51 **Audit of Pension Expense.** Clark, PA, has been en-
LO.3 gaged to perform the audit of Kent Ltd.'s financial statements for the current year. Clark is about to commence auditing Kent's employee pension expense. Her preliminary enquiries concerning Kent's pension plan lead her to believe that some of the actuarial computations and assumptions are so complex that they are beyond the competence ordinarily required of an auditor. Clark is considering engaging Lane, an actuary, to assist with this portion of the audit.

EXHIBIT 14.50-1

CANADIAN WIDGETS, INC.
Working Papers December 31, 20X2

Index	K1	
	Initials	Date
Prepared by	AA	3/22/X2
Approved by		

Lender	Interest Rate	Payment Terms	Collateral	Balance 12/31/X1	20X2 Borrowings	20X2 Reductions	Balance 12/31/X2	Interest paid to	Accrued Interest Payable 12/31/X2	Comments
⊕ First Commercial Bank	12%	Interest only on 25th of month, principal due in full 1/1/X6, no prepayment penalty	Inventories	$ 50,000 ✓	$300,000 1/31/X2	A $100,000 6/30/X2	⊕ $ 250,000 CX	12/25/X2	$2,500 NR	Dividend of $80,000 paid 9/2/X2 (W/P N-3) violates a provision of the debt agreement, which thereby permits lender to demand immediate payment; lender has refused to waive this violation.
⊕ Lender's Capital Corp.	Prime plus 1%	Interest only on last day of month, principal due in full 3/5/X4	2nd Mortgage on Park St. Building	100,000 ✓	50,000	A —	200,000 C	12/31/02	—	
⊕ Gigantic Building & Loan Assoc.	12%	$5,000 principal plus interest due on 5th of month, due in full 12/31/X13	1st Mortgage on Park St. Building	720,00 ✓	—	60,000 ⊖	660,000 C	12/5/02	5,642 R	Prime rate was 8% to 9% during the year.
⊕ J. Lott, majority shareholder	0%	Due in full 12/13/X5	Unsecured	300,000 ✓	—	100,000 N	200,000 C	—	—	Reclassification entry for current portion proposed (See RJE-3)
				$1,170,000 F	$350,000 F	$260,000 F	$1,310,000 T/B F		$8,142 T/B F	Borrowed additional $100,000 from J. Lott on 1/7/X3.

Tick-mark legend
F   Readded, foots correctly.
C   Confirmed without exception, W/P K-2.
CX Confirmed with exception, W/P K-3.
NR Does not recompute correctly.
A   Agreed to loan agreement, validated bank deposit ticket, and board of directors authorization, W/P W-7.
⊖   Agreed to cancelled cheques and lender's monthly statements.
N   Agreed to cash disbursements journal and cancelled cheques dated 12/31/X2, clearing 1/8/X3.
T/B Traced to working trial balance.
✓   Agreed to 12/31/01 working papers.
⊕   Agreed interest rate, term, and collateral to copy of note and loan agreement.
⊕   Agreed to cancelled cheques and board of director's authorization, W/P W-7.

Interest costs for long-term debt

Interest expense for year	$ 281,333 T/B
Average loan balance outstanding	$1,406,667 R

Five year maturities (for disclosure purposes)

Year end		
	12/31/X3	$ 60,000
	12/31/X4	260,000
	12/31/X5	260,000
	12/31/X6	310,000
	12/31/X7	60,000
	Thereafter	360,000
		$1,310,000 F

Overall Conclusions
Long-term debt, accrued interest payable, and interest expense are correct and complete at 12/31/X2.

---

[6] Bell Canada, 2001 Consolidated Financial Statements.

Required:

a. What are Clark's responsibilities with respect to the findings of Lane, if she wishes to rely on those findings?

b. Distinguish between the circumstances where it is and is not appropriate for Clark to refer to Lane in the auditor's report.

(CGA-Canada adapted)

14.52 Board of Directors, Control Role. What is the role of
LO.2 the company's board of directors in controlling management's activities? Why is this particularly important in the financing and investing cycle? How does the board exercise this control and how can the auditor evaluate the board's effectiveness?

14.53 Derivative Instruments, Controls and Audit Proce-
LO.2 **dures.** Barrick Gold Corporation, a Canadian public
LO.3 corporation, has operations in six main countries. Barrick produces and sells gold, its primary product, as well as byproducts such as silver and copper. These activities expose Barrick to a variety of market risks, such as changes in commodity prices, foreign-currency exchange rates and interest rates. Barrick has a risk-management program that seeks to reduce the potentially adverse effects that volatility in these markets may have on its operating results. It uses derivative instruments to mitigate significant unanticipated earnings and cash flow fluctuations that may arise from volatility in commodity prices. These instruments include spot deferred sales contracts, options contracts, interest-rate swaps and foreign-currency forward exchange contracts. Barrick's derivatives activities are subject to the management, direction, and control of its finance committee as part of its oversight of Barrick's investment activities and treasury function. The finance committee, comprised of five members of Barrick's board of directors, including its CEO, approves corporate policy on risk-management objectives, provides guidance on derivative instrument use, reviews internal procedures relating to internal control and valuation of derivative instruments, monitors derivatives activities and reports to the board. Implementation of these policies is delegated to Barrick's treasury function.[7]

Required:

a. Identify the control risks in Barrick's derivatives activities and the key controls indicated in the above description. Provide a brief description of specific control procedures that likely are used by Barrick's treasury function to implement the risk-management policies.

b. Describe audit procedures that could be used to test these controls, and substantive tests for derivatives activities at Barrick.

14.54 Audit of Finance Transactions: Internet Business. City Search Inc. (CSI) is a search technology company providing local search engine services in the Greater Toronto Area (GTA). CSI combines online search capability with a print directory (City Pages) focusing specifically on GTA websites. Consumers use the search engine and print directory to locate local businesses that offer the products and services they want to buy. Businesses use the search engine and print directory to attract potential customers to their places of business through paid advertisements. CSI began operations in March 20X3 and launched its first sales campaign for print and online search advertisements in June 20X3. Since that time, over 600,000 copies of the City Pages have been distributed to businesses and residences.

The original financing to start CSI came from several wealthy investors who purchased common shares. Additional common shares were issued to the public in late 20X4. These shares initially sold for $2.40, but during 20X5, the share price fell to less than $1.00. The decline in price is mainly because two of the original investors sold large blocks of shares for whatever they could get as the business was not proving to be as successful as they expected. In early 20X5, the CSI board of directors hired a new president, Bill Dorado, to aggressively promote the CSI directory as a superior directory for local shopping and entertainment searches, and to find innovative ways to increase revenues and CSI's share price.

Businesses that are clients of CSI pay an advertising fee for print and online directory listings that include the business name, address, phone number, type of products/services offered, and website link. CSI will also create a website for clients for a one-time fee. This fee varies depending on the number of pages, links, and type of content the client wants in the website. CSI clients also can purchase banner advertising that pops up when users browse through the online directory. Clients sign a contract for the ad frequency they require, and are billed monthly. Clients can also purchase additional advertising features, such as moving graphics, audio, and a special patented "bull's eye target" (BT) feature, which concentrates the client's ads in directory locations they choose. For example, a home decorating service can sign up for BT service that will cause their ads to be shown whenever users are searching for home products businesses.

In February 20X6, CSI entered into an agreement with Flogg Investments Inc. (FII) in which FII agreed to sell newly issued common shares of the company for total gross proceeds of up to $8 million. The proceeds raised from the new common shares will be used by CSI to support its growth initiatives and for working capital and general corporate purposes, including repayment of loans from shareholders that amounted to approximately $4 million as of December 31, 20X5.

Your firm has recently accepted to audit CSI's 20X5 financial statements. The previous auditor that reported on the 20X3 and 20X4 financial statements has resigned. In communicating with the predecessor auditor,

---

[7] Barrick Gold Corporation, 2001 Consolidated Financial Statements.

you find out that the predecessor resigned due to a change in circumstances that lead to the predecessor's firm partners not being independent of CSI. To date, CSI has provided the audit partner of your firm, who is in charge of the audit, with preliminary financial statements (prior to audit) for its most recent year end, December 31, 20X5. You are assigned to plan the audit. From reviewing these preliminary financial statements and talking to Bill Dorado you have learned the following:

1. CSI recognizes revenue on a straight-line basis as each service is provided over the terms of its individual client contracts. The contracts range in length from three months to four years, with the majority lasting for two years. Revenues from contracts ranging from one to four years are deferred and amortized as each service is provided. Upfront direct costs associated with these revenues, including the production costs and selling commissions, are deferred and amortized over the life of each client contract on a straight-line basis. Adjustments are made to deferred revenue and deferred production costs for cancellations at the time the cancellation is made. Cancellations are permitted if clients relocate outside the GTA or close their business. CSI management estimates the future value of contracts in progress and compares this value to deferred production costs to ensure these costs are fully recoverable.

2. CSI's revenue is generated mainly through the sale of advertising to local businesses, many of which are small- and medium-sized enterprises (up to 50 employees). In the ordinary course of operations, CSI may extend credit to these advertisers for advertising purchases on a case-by-case basis, a practice that is common in the industry. CSI management evaluates the collectibility of its trade receivables from its clients based upon a combination of factors, including aging of receivables, on a periodic basis and records a general allowance for doubtful accounts and bad debt expense. When management becomes aware of a client's inability to meet its financial obligations to CSI (such as in the case of bankruptcy or significant deterioration in the client's financial position and payment experience), a specific bad debt provision is recorded to reduce the client's related trade receivable to its estimated net realizable value.

3. CSI is a registered member of three barter networks serving the GTA marketplace. CSI sells its services and purchases goods and services through these networks. The full market value of a contract sale settled through a barter network is recorded in accounts receivable and deferred revenue at the time of the sale. Revenues are recognized in income on a straight-line basis over the term of the contract. Receivables are reduced when a good or service purchased through a barter network has been received. The president believes this bartering arrangement was an astute business move that "saves us tons of cash and increases revenues at the same time."

4. CSI has signed contracts with two partners that are well-known, local retail chains. These retail chains want to start direct online retailing, and have paid CSI $13.5 million to develop all their online shopping systems including customer relation management and payment processing. CSI has never completed this type of system before, but has the technical expertise from developing its own systems. CSI expects the contract to be completed by the end of 20X6. CSI recorded $6.5 million of the $13.5 million as revenues in 20X5, deferring the rest to be reported when the work is completed.

5. The president and several top CSI executives have received options to purchase common shares at a fixed price of $1 per share. None of the options have been exercised yet

6. The BT technology was patented by CSI in early 20X4. In late 20X4 the BT patent was sold for $7 million to LivePatents Inc., which is owned by one of the original CSI investors, who is also a board member of CSI. CSI repurchased the patent in early 20X5 for $10 million, by paying $7 million in cash and issuing a loan payable to LivePatents Inc. for the remainder. The patent is shown on CSI balance sheet at its cost of $10 million, and is being amortized over 17 years.

7. Internal search engine development costs are recorded at cost. The company provides for amortization of these costs at the following annual rates:
   • Directory, research and design costs—30 percent declining-balance basis
   • Internal directory design costs—30 percent declining-balance basis

Required:
Prepare a detailed and complete audit plan that addresses the accounting and other information items noted in this case. Also, suggest any other information that you would want to obtain for planning the audit.

Kingston Case questions related to Chapter 14 are on the Online Learning Centre that accompanies this text.

APPENDIX 14A

SUBSTANTIVE AUDIT PROGRAMS

· ·

EXHIBIT   14A-1   AUDIT PROGRAM FOR OWNERS' EQUITY
_____

1. Obtain an analysis of owners' equity transactions. Trace additions and reductions to the general ledger.
   a. Vouch additions to directors' minutes and cash receipts.
   b. Vouch reductions to directors' minutes and other supporting documents.
2. Read the directors' minutes for owners' equity authorization. Trace to entries in the accounts. Determine whether related disclosures are adequate.
3. Confirm outstanding common and preferred shares with share registrar agent.
4. Vouch stock option and profit-sharing plan disclosures to contracts and plan documents.
5. Vouch treasury stock transactions to cash receipts and cash disbursement records and to directors' authorization. Inspect treasury stock certificates.
6. When the company keeps its own share records:
   a. Inspect the share record stubs for certificate numbers and number of shares.
   b. Inspect the unissued certificates.
   c. Obtain written client representations about the number of shares issued and outstanding.

_____

EXHIBIT   14A-2   AUDIT PROGRAM FOR NOTES AND LOANS PAYABLE AND LONG-TERM DEBT
_____

1. Obtain a schedule of notes payable and other long-term debt (including capitalized lease obligations) showing beginning balances, new notes, repayment and ending balances. Trace to general ledger accounts.
2. Confirm liabilities with creditor: amount, interest rate, due date, collateral and other terms. Some of these confirmations may be standard bank confirmations.
3. Review the standard bank confirmation for evidence of assets pledged as collateral and for unrecorded obligations.
4. Read loan agreements for terms and conditions that need to be disclosed and for pledge of assets as collateral.
5. Recalculate the current portion of long-term debt and trace to the trial balance, classified as a current liability.
6. Study lease agreements for indications of need to capitalize leases. Recalculate the capital and operating lease amounts for required disclosures.
7. Recalculate interest expense on debts and trace to the interest expense and accrued interest accounts.
8. Obtain written representations from management concerning notes payable, collateral agreements and restrictive covenants.

_____

EXHIBIT   14A-3   AUDIT PROGRAM FOR INVESTMENTS AND RELATED ACCOUNTS
_____

A. Investments and related accounts.
   1. Obtain a schedule of all investments, including purchase and disposition information for the period. Reconcile with investment accounts in the general ledger.
   2. Inspect or confirm with a trustee or broker the name, number, identification, interest rate and face amount (if applicable) of securities held as investments.
   3. Vouch the cost of recorded investments to brokers' reports, contracts, cancelled cheques and other supporting documentation.

Continued

EXHIBIT 14A–3 CONTINUED

4. Vouch recorded sales to brokers' reports and bank deposit slips, and recalculate gain or loss on disposition.
5. Recalculate interest income and look up dividend income in a dividend reporting service (such as Moody's or Standard & Poor's annual dividend record).
6. Obtain market values of investments and determine whether any write-down or write-off is necessary. Scan transactions soon after the client's year-end to see if any investments were sold at a loss. Recalculate the unrealized gains and losses required for marketable equity securities disclosures.
7. Read loan agreements and minutes of the board, and enquire of management about pledge of investments as security for loans.
8. Obtain audited financial statements of joint ventures, investee companies (equity method of accounting), subsidiary companies and other entities in which an investment interest is held. Evaluate indications of significant controlling influence. Determine proper balance sheet classification. Determine appropriate consolidation policy in conformity with accounting principles.
9. Obtain written representations from the client concerning pledge of investment assets as collateral.

B. Intangibles and related expenses.
1. Review merger documents for proper calculation of purchased goodwill.
2. Enquire of management about legal status of patents, leases, copyrights and other intangibles.
3. Review documentation of new patents, copyrights, leaseholds and franchise agreements.
4. Vouch recorded costs of intangibles to supporting documentation and cancelled cheque(s).
5. Select a sample of recorded R&D expenses. Vouch to supporting documents for evidence of proper classification.
6. Recalculate amortization of copyrights, patents and other intangibles.

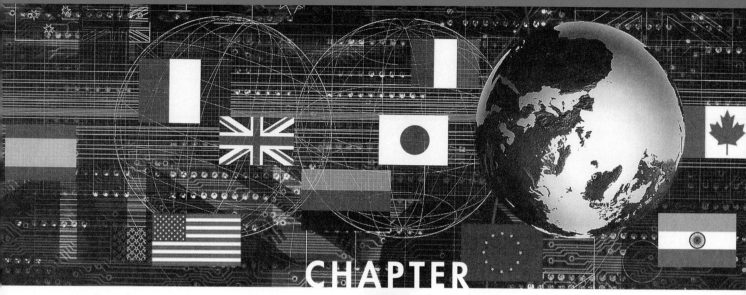

CHAPTER

15

Completing the Audit

In this chapter, we will complete the field work, tying up the loose ends of the audit. The following principal items are covered:

- completing the audit of revenues and expenses
- considering contingencies and obtaining letters from the client's lawyers
- obtaining written client representations
- considering events subsequent to the balance sheet date and events subsequent to the audit report date
- wrapping up the final audit

LEARNING OBJECTIVES

After completing this chapter, you will be able to:

1 Describe the related balance sheet account group where the audit of major revenue and expense accounts are normally associated.

2 Outline the analytical procedures to be performed at the final stage of a financial statement audit, including analysis of the revenue and expense accounts.

3 Explain the use of lawyers' letters in the completion of the audit.

4 Explain why written client representations are obtained, including items entered without regard to materiality.

5 Given a set of facts and circumstances, classify a subsequent event by type and proper treatment in the financial statements.

6* Analyze the decisions and actions auditors must consider upon discovering (after the issuance of the audit report) facts that may have existed at the date of the audit report.

7* Analyze the decisions and actions auditors must consider upon concluding (after the audit report date) that one or more auditing procedures were omitted.

8 Explain the final steps for adjusting entries, second-partner reviews and management letters.

Note: Those learning objectives marked with an asterisk (*) and their corresponding topics are considered advanced material.

INTRODUCTION

This chapter covers the completion of the financial statement audit. It reviews the issues, techniques, procedures and documents that are normally considered in effectively and efficiently completing an audit. At the completion of the audit, the auditor must provide an opinion that is properly supported by the audit evidence and reflected in the audit files. The audit of the flow accounts that are reported in the income statement, the cash flow statement and the statement of retained earnings cannot be completed until year-end when all the transactions for the period have also been completed. As a result, some year-end audit procedures relate to revenue and expense accounts. This part of the year-end audit is covered in the first half of the chapter.

Furthermore, some audit procedures relate to the year-end amounts on the balance sheet. The audit of these amounts has already been covered in previous chapters relating to the different accounting processes. However, there are procedures unique to the year-end such as audit for subsequent events, contingencies, commitments or contractual obligations, overall evaluation of audit results, proper presentation and disclosure issues that need to be considered after the balances have been audited but before signing off on the audit file. These and related issues are covered in the second half of this chapter.

AUDIT OF REVENUES AND EXPENSES

LEARNING OBJECTIVE

1 Describe the related balance sheet account group where the audit of major revenue and expense accounts are normally associated.

As the field work nears its end, the major revenue and expense accounts will have been audited in connection with related balance sheet accounts. Now auditors need to consider other revenue and expense accounts. The broad financial statement assertions are the bases for specific assertions and audit objectives for these accounts. Typical specific assertions for the revenue and expense accounts are as follows:

1. Revenue accounts represent all the valid transactions recorded correctly in the proper account, amount and period.

2. The accounting for consignments and goods sold with rights of return is in conformity with accounting principles.

3. Expense accounts represent all the valid expense transactions recorded correctly in the proper account, amount and period.

4. Revenues; expenses; cost of goods sold; and extraordinary, unusual or infrequent transactions are adequately classified and disclosed.

Exhibit 15–1 is an audit program for revenues and expenses.

EXHIBIT   15-1   AUDIT PROGRAM FOR REVENUES AND EXPENSES

REVENUES

1. Obtain client's monthly analyses of sales, cost of goods sold and gross profit by product line, department, division or location.
   a. Trace amounts to the general ledger.
   b. Compare the analyses to prior years and seek explanations for significant variations.
   c. Determine one or more standard markup percentages and calculate expected gross profits. Enquire for explanations of significant variations compared to actual results.
2. Co-ordinate procedures for audit of revenue with evidence obtained in other audit programs:

Sales and sales returns.	Sales control.	Gain, loss on asset disposals.	Fixed assets.
	Cash receipts control.		Investments.
	Accounts receivable.	Rental revenue.	Accounts receivable.
Lease revenue.	Capital assets.		Investments.
	Accounts receivable.	Royalty and licence revenue.	Accounts receivable.
Franchise revenue.	Accounts receivable.		Investments.
	Intangibles.	Long-term sales commitments.	Accounts receivable.
Dividends and interest.	Accounts receivable.		Inventory.
	Investments.		

3. Scan the revenue accounts for large or unusual items and for debit entries. Vouch any such items to supporting documentation.
4. Obtain written client representation about terms of sales; rights of return; consignments; and unusual or infrequent transactions.

EXPENSES

5. Obtain schedules of expense accounts comparing the current year with one or more prior years.
   a. Trace amounts to the general ledger.
   b. Compare the current expenses to prior years and seek explanations for significant variations.
   c. Be alert to notice significant variations that could indicate failure to defer or accrue expenses.
6. Compare the current expenses to the company budget, if any. Enquire and investigate explanations for significant variances.
7. Co-ordinate procedures for audit of expenses with evidence obtained in other audit programs:

Purchases, cost of goods sold.	Acquisition control.	Bad debt expense.	Accounts receivable.
	Cash disbursement control.	Depreciation expense.	Fixed assets.
	Inventory.	Property taxes, insurance.	Prepaids and accruals.
Inventory valuation losses.	Inventory.		Fixed assets.
Warranty and guarantee expense.	Inventory.	Lease and rental expense.	Fixed assets.
	Prepaids and accruals.	Repairs and maintenance.	Fixed assets.
	Accounts payable.	Interest expense.	Long-term liabilities.
Royalty and licence expense.	Inventory.	Pension and retirement benefits.	Liabilities.
Marketing and product R&D.	Investments.		Payroll control.
	Intangibles.	Payroll and compensation.	Payroll control.
Investment value losses.	Investments.	Sales commissions.	Payroll control.
Rental property expenses.	Investments.		
Amortization of intangibles.	Intangibles.		

8. Prepare analyses of sensitive expense accounts, such as legal and professional fees, travel and entertainment, repairs and maintenance, taxes, and others unique to the company. Vouch significant items therein to supporting invoices, contracts, reimbursement forms, tax notices and the like for proper support and documentation.
9. Scan the expense accounts for large or unusual items and for credit entries. Vouch items to supporting documentation.
10. Obtain written client representations about long-term purchase commitments; contingencies; and unusual or infrequent transactions.

Revenue

The following types of revenue and related topics already will have been audited, either in whole or in part, prior to the completion stage of the engagement:

Revenue and Related Topics	Related Account Groups
Sales and sales returns	Receivables
Lease revenue	Capital assets and receivables
Franchise revenue	Receivables, intangibles
Dividends and interest	Receivables, investments
Gain, loss on asset disposals	Fixed assets, receivables and investments
Rental revenue	Receivables and investments
Royalty and licence revenue	Receivables and investments
Long-term sales commitments	Revenue and receivables
Product line reporting	Revenue and receivables
Accounting policy disclosure	Revenue and receivables

To the extent that these revenue items have already been audited, the working papers should show cross reference indexing to the revenue account in the trial balance. The accounts that have not been audited completely will be evident. Auditors should ascertain by reference to the trial balance that they have a list of all the revenue and gain or loss accounts and their amounts.

Expenses

Although many major expense items will have been audited in connection with other account groupings, numerous minor expenses may still remain unaudited. As a brief review, the following major expenses may have been audited in whole or in part as the audit nears its end:

Expenses	Related Account Groups
Purchases, cost of goods sold	Inventories
Inventory valuation losses	Inventories
Warranty and guarantee expense	Inventories and liabilities
Royalty and licence expense	Inventories
Marketing and product R&D	Investments and intangibles
Investment value losses	Investments and intangibles
Rental property expenses	Investments and intangibles
Amortization of intangibles	Investments and intangibles
Bad debt expense	Receivables
Amortization expense	Capital assets
Property taxes, insurance	Capital assets and liabilities
Lease and rental expense	Capital assets
Repairs and maintenance	Capital assets and liabilities
Legal and professional fees	Liabilities and equity
Interest expense	Liabilities
Pension and retirement benefits	Liabilities, equity and payroll
Payroll and compensation costs	Payroll
Sales commissions	Payroll

As with the revenue accounts mentioned in the previous section, if audit work is complete for expense accounts, the working papers should show cross-reference indexing from the working papers to the trial balance. Some of the expenses may not have been audited completely (such as property tax expense), and some finishing-touch vouching of supporting documents may be required.

Several minor expenses, such as office supplies, telephone, utilities and similar accounts, are not audited until late in the engagement. Generally, the dollar amounts in these accounts are not material (taken individually), and the relative risk is small that they may be misstated in such a way as to create misleading financial statements. Auditors usually audit these kinds of accounts with substantive **analytical procedures.** These procedures include making a list of the expenses with comparative balances from one or more prior periods. The dollar amounts are then reviewed for unusual changes (or lack of unusual changes if reasons for change are known). This analysis of comparative balances may be enough to decide whether the amounts are fairly presented.

On the other hand, questions may be raised and additional evidence sought. In this case auditors may vouch some expenses to supporting documents (invoices and cancelled cheques). Some documentary vouching evidence already may be available about these minor expenses. If the auditors performed detail tests of controls procedure on a sample of expenditure transactions in the acquisition and expenditure cycle audit program, a few expense transactions were selected for testing the client's compliance with control objectives (validity, completeness, authorization, accuracy, classification, accounting and proper period). This evidence should be used.

Analytical comparisons to budgets, internal reports and forecasts may also be made. Variations from budget already may have been subject to management explanation, or the auditors may need to investigate variations.

All miscellaneous or other expense accounts and clearing accounts with debit balances should be analyzed by listing each important item on a working paper and vouching it to supporting documents. Miscellaneous and other expenses may include abandonments of property, items not deductible for tax purposes and payments that should be classified in other expense accounts. Clearing accounts should be analyzed and items therein classified according to their nature or source so that all clearing account balances are removed and accounted for properly.

Advertising, travel and entertainment expense and contributions are accounts that typically are analyzed in detail. These accounts are particularly sensitive to management policy violations and income tax consequences. Travel, entertainment and contributions must be documented carefully if they are to stand the Canada Revenue Agency auditor's examination. Questionable items may have an impact on the income tax expense and liability. Travel and entertainment sometimes harbour abuses of company policy respecting expense allowances. Minor embezzlements or cheating can be detected by careful auditors. However, a detailed audit of expense account payments may be of greater interest to the efficiency-minded internal auditor than to the independent auditor. As far as independent auditors are concerned, even if employees did overstate their reimbursable expenses, the actual paid-out amount still is fairly presented as a financial fact. If there is evidence of expense account cheating, independent auditors may present the data to management.

Analytical Procedures

LEARNING OBJECTIVE

2 Outline the analytical procedures to be performed at the final stage of a financial statement audit, including analysis of the revenue and expense accounts.

According to the CICA study *Analytical Review*,[1] analytical procedures can be used at these points during the audit: (1) at the planning stage, (2) during the overall evaluation of the financial statements at the end of the audit, and (3) as a substantive test procedure. The use of analytical procedures as part of the overall evaluation at the end of the audit is the most common use of analytical review in practice. This overall verification "can be an effective means of obtaining assurance as to the reasonableness of reported results. There is a broad spectrum of overall verification procedures, many particular to a specific industry, which provides a range of assurance from virtually 100 percent assurance to reasonable approximation."[2] Paragraph 5301.01 requires use of analytical procedures to assist in evaluating the overall financial statement presentation upon substantial completion of the audit.

Analytical procedures can be used to compare the revenue accounts and amounts to prior-year data and to multiple-year trends to ascertain whether any unusual fluctuations are present. Comparisons also should be made to budgets, monthly internal reports and forecasts to ascertain whether events have occurred that require explanation or analysis by management. These explanations would then be subjected to audit. For example, a sales dollar increase may be explained as a consequence of a price increase that can be corroborated by reference to price lists used in the test of controls audit of sales transactions.

Auditors also should ascertain whether account classifications, aggregations and summarizations are consistent with those of the prior year. This information will have a bearing on the consistency issue in financial reporting.

All miscellaneous or other revenue accounts and all clearing accounts with credit balances should be analyzed. Account analysis in this context refers to the identification of each important item and amount in the account, followed by document vouching and enquiry to determine whether amounts should be classified elsewhere. All clearing accounts should be eliminated and the amounts classified as revenue, deferred revenue, liabilities, deposits or contra-assets.

---

[1] D.G. Smith, *Analytical Review* (CICA, 1983).

[2] Ibid., p. 3.

Miscellaneous revenue and other suspense accounts can harbour many accounting errors. Proceeds from sale of assets, insurance premium refunds, insurance proceeds and other receipts simply may be credited to such an account. Often, such items reveal unrecorded asset disposals, expiration of insurance recorded as prepaid or other asset losses covered by insurance. Recall that Exhibit 15–1 lists common analytical procedures for revenue and expense accounts.

Unusual Transactions

Significant audit evidence and reporting problems can arise if transactions are created by management to manufacture earnings artificially. Frequently, such transactions are run through a complicated structure of subsidiaries, affiliates and related parties. Generally, the amounts of revenue are large. The transactions themselves may not be concealed, but certain guarantees may have been made by management and not revealed to the auditors. The timing of the transactions may be arranged carefully to provide the most favourable income result.

These unusual transactions contain a wide variety of characteristics and are difficult to classify for useful generalization. Controversies have arisen in the past over revenue recognized on bundled sales of hardware, software and technology services and on the construction percentage-of-completion method, over sales of assets at inflated prices to management-controlled dummy corporations, over sales of real estate to independent parties with whom the seller later associates for development of the property (making guarantees on indemnification for losses) and over disclosure of revenues by source. These revenue issues pose a combination of evidence-gathering problems and reporting-disclosure problems. Three illustrations of such problems are given in the text box titled "Unusual Revenue Transactions."

UNUSUAL REVENUE TRANSACTIONS

MERGER

National Fried Chicken, Inc., a large fast-food franchiser, began negotiations in August to purchase Provincial Hot Dog Company, a smaller convenience food chain. At August 1, 20X6, Provincial's net worth was $7 million, and National proposed to pay $8 million cash for all the outstanding shares. In June 20X7, the merger was consummated and National paid $8 million, even though Provincial's net worth had dropped to $6 million. Consistent with prior years, Provincial lost $1 million in the 10 months ended June 1; as in the past, the company showed a net profit of $1.5 million for June and July. At June 1, 20X7, the fair value of Provincial's net assets was $6 million, and National accounted for the acquisition as a purchase, recording $2 million goodwill. National proposed to show in consolidated financial statements the $1.5 million of post-acquisition income.

Audit Resolution. The auditors discovered that the purchase price was basically set at 16 times expected earnings and that management had carefully chosen the consummation date in order to maximize goodwill (and reportable net income in fiscal 20X7). The auditors required that $1 million of goodwill be treated as prepaid expenses which expired in the year ended July 31, 20X7, so that bottom-line income would be $500,000.

REAL ESTATE DEAL

In August, a company sold three real estate properties to BMC for $5,399,000 and recognized profit of $550,000. The agreement that covered the sale committed the company to use its best efforts to obtain permanent financing and to pay underwriting costs for BMC. The agreement provided BMC with an absolute guarantee against loss from ownership and a commitment by the company to complete construction of the properties.

According to the provincial securities commission accountant, the terms of this agreement made the recognition of profit improper because the company had not shifted the risk of loss to BMC.

REAL ESTATE DEVELOPMENT, STRINGS ATTACHED

In December 20X6, Black Company sold one half of a tract of undeveloped land to Red Company in an arm's-length transaction. The portion sold had a book value of $1.5 million, and Red Company paid $2.5 million in cash. Red Company planned to build and sell apartment houses on the acquired land. In January 20X7, Black and Red announced a new joint venture to develop the entire tract. The two companies formed a partnership, each contributing its one half of the total tract of land. They agreed to share equally in future capital requirements and profits or losses.

Audit Resolution. The $1 million profit from the sale was not recognized as income in Black's 20X6 financial statements but, instead, was classified as a deferred credit. Black's investment in the joint venture was valued at $1.5 million. Black's continued involvement in development of the property and the uncertainty of future costs and losses were cited as reasons.

REVIEW CHECKPOINTS

15.1   Certain revenue and expense accounts usually are audited in conjunction with related balance sheet accounts. For the following revenue and expense accounts, list the most likely related balance sheet accounts: lease revenue, franchise revenue, royalty and licence revenue, amortization expense, repairs and maintenance expense and interest expense.

15.2   Why are many of the revenue and expense accounts only audited by analytical procedures and not by other procedures?

15.3   Why can usual revenue transactions cause significant audit evidence and reporting problems?

15.4   What procedures can be used to obtain information about the material accuracy of balances in minor expense accounts?

A SEQUENCE OF AUDIT EVENTS

LEARNING OBJECTIVE
3 Explain the use of lawyers' letters upon completion on an audit.

Based on the material presented on the organization of the audit, you could easily visualize some audit work being done at an interim period sometime before a balance sheet date followed by completion of the work on the magic balance sheet date. True, much audit work is done months before the balance sheet date, with auditors working for a time, leaving the client's offices, and then returning for the year-end work. Actually, auditors may not even do any work on the balance sheet date itself, but they always perform evidence-gathering after that date—sometimes as much as several months afterwards.

Interim and Final Audit Work in Independent Auditing

In the "interim" audit work period, the auditor evaluates internal control with questionnaires, flowcharts and/or written narratives; identifies strengths and deficiencies; and completes the test of controls part of the audit. Some test of controls procedures usually are performed at interim, and tentative judgements about control risk for certain transaction cycles are made early. Also, auditors can apply audit procedures for substantive audit of balances as of an interim date; in this way a significant amount of recalculating, vouching, tracing, observing and confirming can be performed early. (Refer to Chapter 8 for a more complete discussion.)

When the audit team returns after year-end and receives the final unaudited financial statements (or trial balance) prepared by the client personnel, they can start where they left off at interim and complete the work on control risk assessment and audit of balances.

However, the procedures of obtaining the lawyer's letter and the written client representations are deferred until the end of field work. These written representations are dated at the end of the field work (audit report date) because the auditors are responsible until that date for determining whether important events that occurred after the balance sheet date are properly entered in the accounts or disclosed in the financial statement notes.

Contingencies and Lawyer's Letters

One of the most important confirmations is the response known as the lawyer's representation letter. Some difficulties had arisen over lawyers' willingness to respond to auditors' requests for information about contingencies, litigation, claims and assessments. Lawyers themselves have faced legal liability for failure to respond properly.

CICA Handbook, section 6560, "Communications With Law Firms," requires auditors to make certain enquiries designed to elicit information on claims and possible claims as part of the auditor's examination of financial statements. Exhibit 15–2 is an example of an enquiry letter, in which the auditor would request the client to send to all lawyers who had performed work for the client during the period under audit. The client must make this request because it informs the lawyer that his client is waiving the privilege of communications between the lawyer and his client, and gives the lawyer permission to give information to the auditors.

As implied by the client's letter to the lawyers in Exhibit 15–2, questions about contingencies, litigations, claims and assessments should be directed not only to legal counsel but also to management because an auditor has the right to expect to be informed by management about all material contingent liabilities. Audit procedures useful in this regard include the following:

- Enquire and discuss with management the policies and procedures for identifying, evaluating and accounting for litigation, claims and assessments.
- Obtain from management a description and evaluation of litigation, claims and assessments.
- Examine documents in the client's possession concerning litigation, claims and assessments, including correspondence and invoices from lawyers.
- Obtain assurance from management that it has disclosed all material unasserted claims that the lawyer has advised them are probable of litigation.
- Read minutes of meetings of shareholders, directors and appropriate committees. Read contracts, loan agreements, leases and correspondence from taxing or other governmental agencies.
- Obtain information concerning guarantees from bank confirmations.

The enquiry letter serves as a major means of learning about material contingencies. Even so, a devious or forgetful management or a careless lawyer may fail to tell the auditor of some important factor or development. Auditors have to be alert and sensitive to all possible contingencies so that they can ask the right questions at the right time.

If management or its lawyers fail to provide adequate information about lawsuit contingencies, the auditor should consider whether this represents a scope limitation on the audit. A serious audit scope limitation requires a qualification in the audit report or a disclaimer of opinion.

Auditors have a natural conservative tendency to look out for adverse contingencies. However, potentially favourable events also should be investigated and disclosed (such as

EXHIBIT   15-2   SAMPLE ENQUIRY LETTER¹

Version 1—when there are claims or possible claims to be listed
(On client letterhead)

(To law firm)

(Date)

Dear Sir(s):

In connection with the preparation and audit of our financial statements for the fiscal period ended (date), (which include the accounts of the following entities)², we have made the following evaluations of claims and possible claims with respect to which your firm's advice or representation has been sought:

Description (name of entity, name of other party, nature, amount claimed and current status)	Evaluation (indicate likelihood of loss (or gain) and estimated amount of ultimate loss (or gain), if any; or indicate that likelihood is not determinable or amount is not reasonably estimable)

Would you please advise us, as of (effective date of response), on the following points:

    (a) Are the claims and possible claims properly described?

    (b) Do you consider that our evaluations are reasonable?

    (c) Are you aware of any claims not listed above which are outstanding? If so, please include in your response letter the names of the parties and the amount claimed.

This enquiry is made in accordance with the Joint Policy Statement of January 1978 approved by The Canadian Bar Association and the Auditing Standards Committee of the Canadian Institute of Chartered Accountants.

Please address your reply, marked "Privileged and Confidential," to this company and send a signed copy of the reply directly to our auditor, (name and address of auditor).

Yours truly,

c.c. (name of auditor)

---

¹The letter should be appropriately modified if the client advises that certain matters have been excluded in accordance with paragraph 12 of the Joint Policy Statement.

²Delete if inapplicable. If applicable, refer to paragraph 11 re signing of the enquiry letter.

Source: *CICA Handbook*, section 6560.A, Schedule A.

---

the contingency of litigation for damages wherein the client is the plaintiff). In an effort to assist management in observing the law and to provide adequate disclosure of information in financial statements, the auditor should be alert to all types of contingencies. The following box illustrates the kinds of wording lawyers provide. It shows the challenges auditors face in using these responses to audit contingency disclosures.

INTERPRETING THE LAWYERS' LETTERS

Lawyers take great care making responses to clients' requests for information to be transmitted to auditors. This care causes problems of interpretation for auditors. The difficulty arises over lawyers' desire to preserve lawyer-client confidentiality yet co-operate with auditors and the financial reporting process that seeks full disclosure.

The Canadian Bar Association policy statement¹ observes: It is in the public interest that the confidentiality of lawyer-client communications be maintained. Accordingly, the law firm will not indicate in the response letter any possible claims which are omitted from the enquiry letter.

Consequently, lawyers' responses to auditors may contain vague and ambiguous wording. Auditors need to determine whether a contingency is "likely, unlikely or not determinable."² Although there are no comparable Canadian guidelines, in the United

States the following lawyer responses can be properly interpreted to mean "remote," even though the word is not used:

- We are of the opinion that this action will not result in any liability to the company.
- It is our opinion that the possible liability to the company in this proceeding is nominal in amount.
- We believe the company will be able to defend this action successfully. We believe that the plaintiff's case against this company is without merit.
- Based on the facts known to us, after a full investigation, it is our opinion that no liability will be established against the company in these suits.

However, auditors should view the following response phrases as unclear—providing no information—about the probable, reasonably possible or remote likelihood of an unfavourable outcome for a litigation contingency:[3]

- We believe the plaintiff will have serious problems establishing the company's liability; nevertheless, if the plaintiff is successful, the damage award may be substantial.
- It is our opinion the company will be able to assert meritorious defences. ["Meritorious," in lawyer language, apparently means "the judge will not summarily throw out the defences."]
- We believe the lawsuit can be settled for less than the damages claimed.
- We are unable to express an opinion on the merits of the litigation, but the company believes there is absolutely no merit.
- In our opinion the company has a substantial chance of prevailing. ["Substantial chance," "reasonable opportunity," and similar phrases indicate uncertainty of success in a defence.]

[1] *CICA Handbook*, paragraph 6560A.14.
[2] Paragraph 3290.15.
[3] Adapted from AU 9337.

Client Representations

LEARNING OBJECTIVE

④ Explain why written client representations are obtained, including items entered without regard to materiality.

Management makes numerous responses to auditors' enquiries during the course of an audit. Many of these responses are very important. To the extent that additional evidence is obtainable through other procedures, auditors should corroborate client representations.

In addition, auditors should obtain written client representations on matters of audit importance.[3] The written representations take the form of a letter on the client's letterhead, addressed to the auditor, signed by responsible officers (normally the chief executive officer, chief financial officer, and other appropriate managers) and dated as of the date of the auditor's report. Thus, the letter, referred to as the "client's rep letter" in practice, covers events and representations running beyond the balance sheet date up to the end of all important field work. These written representations, however, are not substitutes for corroborating evidence obtainable by applying other auditing procedures.

In most cases the written client representations are merely more assertions, like the ones already in the financial statements (perhaps more detailed, in some cases). In this context they are not evidence for auditors. They are not good defences against criticisms for failing to perform audit procedures independently. ("Management told us in writing that the inventory costing method was FIFO and adequate allowance for obsolescence was provided" is

[3] *CICA Handbook*, paragraph 5370.16, ISA 580.3.

not a good excuse for failing to get the evidence from the records and other sources!) However, in some cases the written management representations are the only available evidence about important matters of management intent. For example: (1) "We will discontinue the parachute manufacturing business, wind down the operations and sell the remaining assets" (i.e., accounting for discontinued operations); and (2) "We will exercise our option to refinance the maturing debt on a long-term basis" (i.e., classifying maturing debt as long-term).

One of the major purposes of the management representation letter is to impress upon the management its primary responsibility for the financial statements. These representations also may establish an auditor's defences if a question of management integrity arises later. If the management lies to the auditors, the management representation letter captures the lies in writing. Auditors draft the management representation letter to be prepared on the client's letterhead paper for signature by company representatives. This draft is reviewed with senior client personnel, then finalized.

The management representation letter generally deals only with material matters. Notwithstanding, auditing standards provide that the following representations must appear in the letter without limitation based on materiality (5370.17):

1. management's acknowledgment of its responsibility for the fair presentation of the financial statements in accordance with generally accepted accounting principles

2. management's belief that the financial statements are presented fairly in accordance with generally accepted accounting principles, or in accordance with the disclosed basis of accounting described in the notes to the financial statements as applicable

3. when differential reporting options have been used to present the financial statements, management's acknowledgment that the entity meets the criteria, that owners have been appropriately informed and that the owners' written unanimous consent has been given

4. when the audit engagement results in the auditor reporting on the financial statements in accordance with auditor's report on financial statements prepared using a basis of accounting other than generally accepted accounting principles, management's confirmation of compliance with section 5600

5. knowledge of any known or probable instances of non-compliance with legislative or regulatory requirements, including financial reporting requirements

6. knowledge of any illegal or possibly illegal acts

7. acknowledgment of its responsibility for the design and implementation of internal control to prevent and detect fraud and error

8. results of management's assessment of the risk that the financial statements may be materially misstated as a result of fraud[4]

9. knowledge of fraud or suspected fraud affecting the entity involving management, employees who have significant roles in internal control; or others, where the fraud could have a nontrivial effect on the financial statements

10. knowledge of any allegations of fraud or suspected fraud affecting the entity's financial statements communicated by employees, former employees, analysts, regulators or others

Other matters that should be included, based on materiality are as follows:

- completeness of records provided to the auditors
- completeness of information about related parties and transactions
- the reasonableness of significant assumptions underlying fair value measurements and disclosures in the financial statements
- plans or intentions that may affect the carrying value or classification of assets or liabilities

[4] See *CICA Handbook*, paragraph 5135.090(b).

- measurement and disclosure of transactions with related parties
- all areas of measurement uncertainty known to management and that are required to be disclosed
- claims and possible claims, whether or not they have been discussed with the entity's law firm
- other liabilities and contingent gains or losses, including those associated with guarantees
- satisfactory title to assets, liens or encumbrances on assets, and assets pledged as collateral
- compliance with aspects of contractual agreements that may affect the financial statements
- information concerning subsequent events
- management's representations for which the auditor neither reasonably expects nor is able to obtain sufficient direct or indirect corroborating evidence

Several other representations are suggested for matters that may be relevant in certain businesses or industries, e.g., environmental liabilities, derivative financial instruments, the appropriateness of accounting policies for complex areas of accounting and areas involving management's judgement and estimates, such as revenue recognition, fair value measurements, transfers of receivables, hedging relationships and consolidation of variable interest entities.

The representation letter is also used to provide management with a summary of the uncorrected financial statement misstatements found by the auditor during the audit, and obtain management's representation of its belief that the effects of these are immaterial to the financial statements—a summary of such items is included in or attached to the letter.

Management representations are also required for auditor's involved with prospectuses[5] and for review engagements.[6] Exhibit 15–3 shows an example of a representation letter for illustration.

EXHIBIT 15-3   **EXAMPLE OF A CANADIAN MANAGEMENT REPRESENTATION LETTER**

[Client company letterhead]

[Date]

To: [the Auditor]

Dear Sir/Madam:

We are providing this letter in connection with your audits of the [consolidated] financial statements of [name of entity] as of December 31, 20X4 and 20X3, and for the years then ended, for the purpose of expressing an opinion as to whether the [consolidated] financial statements present fairly, in all material respects, the financial position, results of operations, and cash flows of [name of entity] in accordance with Canadian generally accepted accounting principles.

We acknowledge that we are responsible for the fair presentation of the [consolidated] financial statements in accordance with Canadian generally accepted accounting principles and for the design and implementation of internal control to prevent and detect fraud and error. We have assessed the risk that the [consolidated] financial statements may be materially misstated as a result of fraud, and have determined such risk to be low. Further, we acknowledge that your examination was planned and conducted in accordance with Canadian generally accepted auditing standards so as to enable you to express an opinion on the [consolidated] financial statements. We understand that while your work includes an examination of the accounting system, internal control and related data to the extent you considered necessary in the circumstances, it is not designed to identify, nor can it necessarily be expected to disclose, fraud, shortages, errors and other irregularities, should any exist.

Certain representations in this letter are described as being limited to matters that are material. An item is considered material, regardless of its monetary value, if it is probable that its omission from or misstatement in the [consolidated] financial statements would influence the decision of a reasonable person relying on the [consolidated] financial statements.

We confirm, to the best of our knowledge and belief, as of [date of the auditor's report], the following representations made to you during your audit.

Financial statements

1. The [consolidated] financial statements referred to above present fairly, in all material respects, the financial position of the company as at December 31, 20X4 and 20X3, and the results of its

---

[5] *Ibid.*, section 7110.
[6] *Ibid.*, paragraphs 8200.25–41.

EXHIBIT   15–3   Continued

operations and its cash flows for the years then ended, in accordance with Canadian generally accepted accounting principles.

2. We confirm that the entity is a non-publicly accountable enterprise and is a qualifying enterprise for the application of differential reporting. We have provided appropriate information to all owners, including those not otherwise entitled to vote, regarding the selection of differential reporting options and obtained their unanimous consent, in writing, to the application of each differential reporting option as disclosed in [note number] to the [consolidated] financial statements. The owners' consent has not been withdrawn.

Completeness of information

3. We have made available to you all financial records and related data and all minutes of the meetings of shareholders, directors and committees of directors.

4. There are no material transactions that have not been properly recorded in the accounting records underlying the [consolidated] financial statements.

5. We are unaware of any known or probable instances of non-compliance with the requirements of regulatory or governmental authorities, including their financial reporting requirements.

6. We are unaware of any violations or possible violations of laws or regulations the effects of which should be considered for disclosure in the [consolidated] financial statements or as the basis of recording a contingent loss.

7. We have identified to you all known related parties and related party transactions, including guarantees, non-monetary transactions and transactions for no consideration.

Fraud and error

8. We have no knowledge of fraud or suspected fraud affecting the entity involving management; employees who have significant roles in internal control; or others, where the fraud could have a non-trivial effect on the [consolidated] financial statements.

9. We have no knowledge of any allegations of fraud or suspected fraud affecting the entity's financial statements communicated by employees, former employees, analysts, regulators or others.

10. We believe that the effects of the uncorrected financial statement misstatements summarized in the accompanying schedule are immaterial, both individually and in the aggregate, to the [consolidated] financial statements taken as a whole.

Recognition, measurement and disclosure

11. We believe that the significant assumptions used in arriving at the fair values of financial instruments as measured and disclosed in the [consolidated] financial statements are reasonable and appropriate in the circumstances.

12. We have no plans or intentions that may materially affect the carrying value or classification of assets and liabilities reflected in the [consolidated] financial statements.

13. All related party transactions have been appropriately measured and disclosed in the [consolidated] financial statements.

14. The nature of all material measurement uncertainties has been appropriately disclosed in the [consolidated] financial statements, including all estimates where it is reasonably possible that the estimate will change in the near term and the effect of the change could be material to the [consolidated] financial statements.

15. We have informed you of all outstanding and possible claims, whether or not they have been discussed with legal counsel.

16. All liabilities and contingencies, including those associated with guarantees, whether written or oral, have been disclosed to you and are appropriately reflected in the [consolidated] financial statements.

17. The company has satisfactory title to all assets, and there are no liens or encumbrances on the company's assets.

18. We have disclosed to you, and the company has complied with, all aspects of contractual agreements that could have a material effect on the [consolidated] financial statements in the event of non-compliance, including all covenants, conditions or other requirements of all outstanding debt.

19. There have been no events subsequent to the balance sheet date up to the date hereof that would require recognition or disclosure in the [consolidated] financial statements. Further, there have been no events subsequent to the date of the comparative financial statements that would require adjustment of those financial statements and the related notes.

Yours very truly,

....
[Name of Chief Executive Officer or equivalent and title]

....
[Name of Chief Financial Officer or equivalent and title]

Source: *CICA Handbook*, section 5370, Appendix.

ROOM FOR IMPROVEMENT IN LITIGATION CONTINGENCY DISCLOSURES

American research on 126 lawsuits lost by public companies examined the disclosures about the suits in prior years' financial statements. The contingencies involved material, uninsured losses. Subsequent failure in the defence indicates the contingencies to have been "reasonably possible," calling for FASB 5 (comparable to Section 3290) disclosure. For the 126 cases, wide disclosure diversity existed. As indicated in the table below, the majority of cases carried satisfactory disclosure while the lawsuits were in progress, but a significant minority did not.

	Number	Percent
Satisfactory disclosure:		
Disclosure conceded the possibility of liability	60	47.6%
Disclosure included an estimate of the related liability	5	4.0
Disclosure along with booked liability	7	5.6
Total	72	57.2%
Unsatisfactory disclosure:		
No mention of the litigation	45	35.7%
Litigation mentioned but with a strong disclaimer of liability	9	7.1
Total	54	42.8%

Among the types of lawsuits covered in the 126 cases, the ones dealing with securities law violations had the highest frequency of satisfactory disclosure (8 out of 11, or 73 percent). The ones dealing with fraud or misrepresentation had the lowest frequency of satisfactory disclosure (2 out of 8, or 25 percent).

Speculations about the reasons company officials and lawyers have difficulty providing auditors with appropriate information include:

- High level of emotion surrounding the lawsuits.
- Fear that financial statement disclosure will be construed as an admission of guilt.
- The legal framework for evaluating litigation outcomes varies significantly from the framework used by auditors.
- More appropriate channels exist for disclosure of litigation information [e.g., business press].
- FASB 5 disclosure requirements are viewed as only a guide and, therefore, need not be taken literally.

Source: "Disclosure of Litigation Contingencies Faulted," *Journal of Accountancy*, July 1990, pp. 15–16.

Audit of Related Party Transactions

Two questions typically asked in a representation letter are whether the client has identified all its related parties to the auditor, and whether it has been involved in any related party transactions (see Representations 7 and 13 in Exhibit 15–3). Auditors have a responsibility to obtain reasonable assurance that related parties have been identified and that there is appropriate disclosure with such parties in the financial statements.[7] Related party transactions are particularly important in Canada because of the high degree of concentration of corporate ownership. The problem with related party transactions is that since they are not arm's length they may not reflect the normal terms of trade that occur with most transactions with external parties. *CICA Handbook*, section 3840 provides the measurement and

---

[7] *Ibid.*, section 6010 or ISA 550.

disclosure standards for related party transactions of profit-oriented enterprises. The major problem for the auditor is identifying related party transactions. The most important procedure is to enquire of management (as in Exhibit 15–3). Other important procedures include reading the minutes of meetings of shareholders, directors, executive and audit committees, as well as acquiring a general knowledge of the client's business.[8]

Auditors should watch for unusual transactions in the course of the audit. According to paragraph 6010.21:

> Example of circumstances that might indicate the existence of undisclosed related parties include
>
> (*a*) abnormal terms of trade, such as unusual prices, interest rates, guarantees and repayment terms;
>
> (*b*) transactions which are unusual as to nature or size, particularly those that:
>
> > (i)   have been recognized at or near the balance sheet date;
> >
> > (ii) have been made with unfamiliar enterprises; and
>
> (*c*) transactions whose substance appear to differ from their form;
>
> (*d*) transactions that lack an apparent business reason.

Also, "related parties exist when one party has the ability to exercise directly or indirectly, control, joint control or significant influence over the other. Two or more parties are related when they are subject to common control, joint control or common significant influence. Related parties include management and immediate family members."[9]

As noted previously, an auditor's knowledge of the business can help identify transactions between related parties. Procedures that can be used to identify the existence of related party transactions include:[10]

(*a*) review of prior year working papers for related party transactions;

(*b*) review the entity's procedures for identification of related parties; and

(*c*) obtaining written representation from management concerning identification and adequacy of related party disclosures.

Having identified related party transactions the auditor can perform the following substantive procedures:

(*a*) confirm the terms and amounts of the transactions with the related parties;

(*b*) inspect evidence in possession of the related party; and

(*c*) confirm or discuss information with persons associated with the transactions, such as banks, lawyers, guarantors and agents.

Paragraph 6010.29 also requires that audit committees be informed of unusual related party transactions or related party transactions that involve significant management judgements.

The box on the next page illustrates how related party transactions can be used to significantly alter the financial statements. The illustration is based on an actual Canadian company trading on NASDAQ and the TSE.

Summary of Audit Correspondence

Many types of formal correspondence have been mentioned in this text. Since you are learning the final procedures to complete the audit, this is a good place to summarize these various correspondence items. Exhibit 15–4 is a summary of audit correspondence. The management letter will be covered later in this chapter.

---

[8] *Ibid.*, sections 6010 and 5141.

[9] *Ibid.*, paragraph 3840.03.

[10] *Ibid.*, section 6010; ISA 550.

EXHIBIT   15–4   AUDIT CORRESPONDENCE

Type	From	To	Time
Engagement letter (acceptance)	Auditor (client)	Client (auditor)	Before engagement
Independence letter	Auditor	Client	Before engagement
Internal control weaknesses	Auditor	Client	Interim or after audit
Confirmations (replies)	Client (third parties)	Third parties (auditor)	Throughout the audit
Lawyer's letter (reply)	Client Lawyer	Lawyer (auditor)	Near end of audit
Client representation letter	Client	Auditor	End of field work
Management letter	Auditor	Client	After audit
Communication with client audit committee	Auditor	Directors	Before, during and after audit report

REVIEW
CHECKPOINTS

15.5   What is the purpose of a client representation letter? What representations would you request management to make in a client representation letter with respect to receivables? to inventories? to minutes of meetings? to subsequent events?

15.6   Why are written client representations and lawyers' letters obtained near the end of the audit field work and dated on or near the audit report date?

15.7   In addition to the lawyer's letter, what other procedures can be used to gather evidence regarding contingencies?

15.8   The following was included in a letter auditors received from the client's lawyers, in response to a letter sent to them similar to Exhibit 15–2: "Several agreements and contracts to which the company is a party are not covered by this response since we have not advised or been consulted in their regard." How might the auditor's report be affected by such a statement in a letter from the client's lawyer regarding a pending lawsuit against a client? Explain.

15.9   Why might companies and auditors experience difficulty making appropriate disclosures about litigation contingencies?

TURNING EXPENSES INTO REVENUES

CB is a major biotechnology company in Canada that did not like the effect expensing R&D had on its earnings. So, CB proceeded to create a related entity, CC, to which it made a capital contribution of $100 million. After a series of share exchanges involving shares of both companies, the net effect on CB's financial statements was to debit retained earnings and credit cash for $100 million. An agreement was then reached in which CC paid CB a fee in exchange for a technology licence. CC used the $100 million it had received from CB to repay CB for CB's R&D costs. CB accounted for the amounts received from CC as revenue.

In the words of CB's Chairman of the Board, "This initiative will enable us to leverage our investment in R&D and pursue the ongoing development of exciting new products, without unduly affecting the company's baseline earnings."

EVENTS SUBSEQUENT TO THE BALANCE SHEET DATE

LEARNING OBJECTIVE

5 Given a set of facts and circumstances, classify a subsequent event by type and proper treatment in the financial statements.

Certain material events that occur subsequent to the balance sheet date, but before the end of field work (thus, before issuance of the audit report), require disclosure in the financial statements and related notes.[11] Auditors (and management) are responsible for gathering evidence on these subsequent events and evaluating the proposed disclosure. Material subsequent events have been classified into two types, which are disclosed differently. The first type (**Type I**) requires adjustment of the dollar amounts in the financial statements and appropriate disclosure (financial statement notes), while the second (**Type II**) requires note disclosure and sometimes *pro forma* financial statements.

Type I: Adjustment of Dollar Amounts Required

This type of subsequent event provides new information regarding a financial condition that existed at the date of the balance sheet. The subsequent event information affects the numbers and requires adjustment of amounts in the financial statements for the period under audit.

The following are examples of Type I subsequent events:

- a loss on uncollectible trade accounts receivable as a result of the bankruptcy of a major customer (The customer's deteriorating financial condition existed prior to the balance sheet date.)
- the settlement of litigation for an amount different than estimated (assuming the litigation had taken place prior to the balance sheet date)

Type II: No Adjustment of Financial Statements, but Disclosure Required

The second type of subsequent event involves occurrences that had both their cause and their manifestation arising after the balance sheet date. Recall that the auditor's responsibility for adequate disclosure runs to the date marking the end of the field work. Consequently, even for events that occurred after the balance sheet date and that are not of the first type requiring financial statement adjustment, auditors must consider their importance and may insist that disclosure be made. Type II events that occur after the balance sheet date may be of such magnitude that disclosure is necessary to keep the financial statements from being misleading as of the report date. Disclosure normally is in a narrative note. Occasionally, however, an event may be so significant that the best disclosure is *pro forma* financial data. *Pro forma* **financial data** is the presentation of the financial statements "as if" the event had occurred on the date of the balance sheet. Such *pro forma* data are given in a note disclosure. For example, in addition to historical financial statements, *pro forma* financial data may be the best way to show the effect of a business purchase or other merger or the sale of a major portion of assets.

Examples of Type II subsequent events are as follows:

- loss on an uncollectible trade receivable resulting from a customer's fire or flood loss subsequent to the balance sheet date (as contrasted with a customer's slow decline into bankruptcy cited as a Type I event previously)
- issue of bonds payable or share capital
- settlement of litigation when the event giving rise to the claim took place subsequent to the balance sheet date
- loss of plant or inventories as a result of fire or flood

---

[11] ISA 560 and *CICA Handbook*, section 5405.

The aspect of retroactive recognition of the effect of stock dividends and splits is an exception that may be explained briefly with an example. The problem is one of timing and one of informative communication to financial statement users. When the financial statements reach the users, the stock dividend or split will have been completed, and to report financial data as if they had not occurred might be considered misleading.

Double-Dating in the Audit Report

Double-dating refers to dating the audit report as of the end of field work along with an additional later date attached to disclosure of a significant Type II subsequent event. Sometimes, after completion of field work but before issuance of the report, a significant event comes to the audit team's attention. For example, imagine that in the illustration given in the following box, field work had been completed on February 1 and the audit report was to be so dated. However, before the report was typed and delivered, the auditors learned of the two-for-one stock split. In this case the report would be dated "February 1 except as to footnote X which is dated February 15" (where footnote X is the disclosure of the stock split). The accounting treatment would be the same as described in the following illustration.

SUBSEQUENT EVENT STOCK SPLIT

The company approved on February 15 a two-for-one stock split to be effective on that date. The fiscal year-end was the previous December 31, and the financial statements as of December 31 showed 50 million shares authorized, 10 million shares issued and outstanding, and earnings per share of $3.

Audit Resolution. Note disclosure was made of the split and of the relevant dates. The equity section of the balance sheet showed 100 million shares authorized, 20 million shares issued and outstanding. The income statement reported earnings per share of $1.50. Earnings per share of prior years were adjusted accordingly. The note disclosed comparative earnings per share on the predividend shares. The audit report was dated February 1, with a double-date of February 15 for the note disclosure.

The purpose of double-dating is twofold: (1) to provide a means of inserting important information in the financial statement footnote disclosures learned after field work is complete and (2) to inform users that the auditor takes full responsibility for discovering subsequent events only up to the end of field work (February 1 in the example) and for the specifically identified later event (the stock split disclosed in the note in the example, which occurred on February 15). However, responsibility is not taken for other events that may have occurred after the end of field work.

Double-dating is used to cut off the subsequent event procedural responsibility at the earlier date.

Audit Program for the Subsequent Period

Some audit procedures performed in the period subsequent to the balance sheet date may be part of the audit program for determining cutoff and proper valuation of balances as of the balance sheet date (Part A in Exhibit 15–5). However, the procedures specifically designed for gathering evidence about the two types of subsequent events are different and separate from the rest of the audit program (Part B in Exhibit 15–5).

R E V I E W
C H E C K P O I N T S

15.10   What are the two types of subsequent events? In which way(s) are they treated differently in the financial statements?

15.11   What treatment is given stock dividends and splits that occur after the balance sheet date but before the audit report is issued? Explain.

15.12   What is the purpose of double-dating an audit report?

15.13   Generally, what additional actions should auditors take in the period between the audit report date and the effective date of a prospectus registration statement?

EXHIBIT   15–5   AUDITING PROCEDURES FOR THE PERIOD SUBSEQUENT TO THE BALANCE SHEET DATE

A. Procedures performed in connection with other audit programs.
  1. Use a cutoff bank statement to:
      a. Examine cheques paid after year-end that are, or should have been, listed on the bank reconciliation.
      b. Examine bank posting of deposits in transit listed on the bank reconciliation.
  2. Vouch collections on accounts receivable in the month following year-end for evidence of existence and collectibility of the year-end balances.
  3. Trace cash disbursements of the month after year-end to accounts payable for evidence of any liabilities unrecorded at year-end.
  4. Vouch write-downs of fixed assets after year-end evidence that such valuation problems existed at the year-end date.
  5. Vouch sales of investment securities, write-downs or write-offs in the months after the audit date for evidence of valuation at the year-end date.
  6. Vouch and trace sales transactions in the month after year-end for evidence of proper sales and cost of sales cutoff.

B. Auditing procedures for subsequent events.
  1. Read the latest available interim financial statements, compare them with the financial statements being reported on and make any other comparisons considered appropriate in the circumstances.
  2. Enquire of officers and other executives having responsibility for financial and accounting matters about whether the interim statements have been prepared on the same basis as that used for the statements under examination.
  3. Enquire of and discuss with officers and other executives having responsibility for financial and accounting matters (limited where appropriate to major locations):
      a. Whether any substantial contingent liabilities or commitments existed at the date of the balance sheet being reported on or at the date of enquiry.
      b. Whether there was any significant change in the share capital, long-term debt or working capital to the date of enquiry.
      c. The current status of items in the financial statements being reported on that were accounted for on the basis of tentative, preliminary or inconclusive data.
      d. Whether any unusual adjustments have been made during the period from the balance sheet date to the date of enquiry.
  4. Read the available minutes of meetings of shareholders, directors and appropriate committees; enquire about matters dealt with at meetings for which minutes are not available.
  5. Request that the client send a letter to legal counsel enquiring about outstanding claims, possible claims and management's evaluation, with the reply to be sent directly to the auditor.
  6. Obtain a letter of representation, dated as of the date of the auditor's report, from appropriate officials, generally the chief executive officer and chief financial officer, about whether any events occurred subsequent to the date of the financial statements that, in the officer's opinion, would require adjustment or disclosure in these statements.
  7. Make such additional enquiries or perform such procedures as considered necessary and appropriate to dispose of questions that arise in carrying out the foregoing procedures, enquiries and discussions.

RESPONSIBILITIES AFTER THE AUDIT REPORT HAS BEEN ISSUED

LEARNING OBJECTIVE

6 Analyze the decisions and actions auditors must consider upon discovering (after the issuance of the audit report) facts that may have existed at the date of the audit report.

The next two topics do not deal with responsibilities or concerns during the audit, but with responsibilities after the audit is completed and the report has been issued. They are covered here because they are related to subsequent event responsibilities. The topics are (1) subsequent discovery of facts existing at the date of the audit report and (2) consideration of the omission of audit procedures discovered after the report date. The most important thing to remember is that auditors have an active, procedural responsibility for discovering Type I and Type II subsequent events and for their proper disclosure, but they are not required to perform procedures after the audit report date. However, auditors have responsibilities once they become aware of the facts or omitted procedures because they are associated with financial statements that they have given an audit opinion on.

Subsequent Discovery of Facts Existing at the Date of the Auditor's Report

Auditing standards actually deal with two subsequent things: (*a*) events that occur after the balance sheet date and (*b*) knowledge gained after the audit report date of events that occurred or conditions that existed on or before the audit report date. The subsequent event or subsequently acquired knowledge may arise (1) before the end of audit field work, (2) after the end of field work but before issuance of the report, or (3) after the audit report is issued. Exhibit 15–6 shows a time continuum of these combinations with a key to the auditing standards sections that deal with them.

Auditors are under no obligation to continue performing any auditing procedures past the report date (except when engaged on an SEC registration statement). However, when they happen to learn of facts that are important, they have the obligation to (1) determine whether the information is reliable and (2) determine whether the facts existed at the date of the report. When both of these conditions are affirmed and the auditors believe persons are relying on the report, steps should be taken to withdraw the first report, issue a new report and inform persons currently relying on the financial statements. These measures are facilitated by the client's co-operation. However, the auditors' duty to notify the public that an earlier report should not be relied on is not relieved by client objections.[12]

A sequence of decisions is explained in Exhibit 15–7. Basically, the decisions relate to the importance and impact of the information, the co-operation of the client in taking necessary action and the actions to be taken.

EXHIBIT   15–6   SUBSEQUENT EVENTS AND SUBSEQUENT DISCOVERY

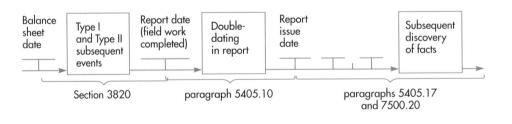

---

[12] The discussion here is cast in terms of subsequent discovery of facts while the auditor remains engaged by the client. However, the responsibilities to determine whether the subsequent information is reliable and whether the facts existed at the date of the already-issued report remain in force even when the auditor has resigned from the engagement or has been fired by the client.

EXHIBIT   15–7   SUBSEQUENT DISCOVERY OF FACTS EXISTING AT THE DATE OF THE
AUDITOR'S REPORT

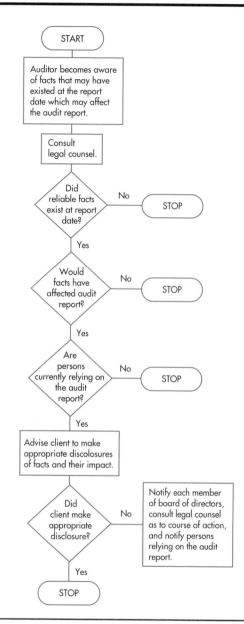

Source: "Omitted Audit Procedures," *CPA Journal*, March 1984, p. 38. Reprinted from *The CPA Journal*, March 1984, copyright © 1984 with permission from the New York State Society of Certified Public Accountants.

Consideration of Omitted Procedures After the Report Date

LEARNING OBJECTIVE

Analyze the decisions and actions auditors must consider upon concluding (after the audit report date) that one or more auditing procedures were omitted.

Although auditors have no responsibility to continue to review their work after the audit report has been issued, the report and working papers may be subjected to postissuance review by an outside peer review or practice inspection or by the firm's internal inspection program. A **peer review** is a quality assurance review by another auditing firm of an audit firm's quality control policies and procedures and the compliance thereof. **Practice inspection** is to ensure that all members in public practice maintain appropriate levels of professional standards. Practice inspection is primarily educational in focus, to help practitioners improve their professional standards where necessary.[13]

[13] *Practice Inspection Program*, ICAO, November 1992.

CICA Handbook, section 5405, "Date of Auditor's Report," provides guidance for such subsequent discovery of material misstatement situations. A possible sequence of decisions is presented in Exhibit 15–8. Because of legal implications of some of the actions proposed, consultation with the firm's legal counsel is advised. The relevance of the omitted procedure (and the evidence the auditors failed to obtain) should be measured against the auditors' present ability to support the previously expressed opinion. It may be that, after a review of the working papers and discussions with audit staff personnel, other procedures may be shown to have produced the evidence needed. In such circumstances the omitted procedure is not considered to impair the report.

However, if the other procedures did not produce sufficient appropriate evidence, and therefore the previously expressed opinion cannot be supported, further action is necessary. As with subsequent discovery of facts, the next step is to determine whether the auditors'

EXHIBIT   15–8   CONSIDERATION OF OMITTED PROCEDURES AFTER THE REPORT DATE

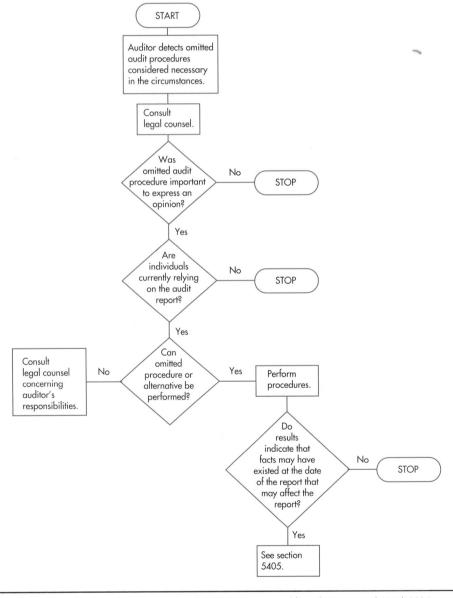

report is still being relied on. If reliance is still possible, the omitted procedure (or alternative procedures) should be undertaken promptly to provide a basis for the audit opinion. If such work reveals facts that existed at the date of the original report, then the actions related to subsequent discovery of facts (Exhibit 15–7) must be taken.

REVIEW
CHECKPOINTS

15.14   What is the difference between a subsequent event and a subsequent discovery of fact existing at the report date? Describe the auditors' responsibility for each.

15.15   If, subsequent to issuance of a report, the audit partner discovers information that existed at the report date and materially affects the financial statements, what actions should the partner take if the client consents to disclose the information? What action should be taken if the client (including the board of directors) refuses to make disclosure?

15.16   What are the steps an auditor should take if, after the report has been issued, someone discovers that an important audit procedure was omitted?

FINAL WRAP-UP

LEARNING OBJECTIVE
⑧ Explain the final steps for adjusting entries, second-partner reviews and management letters.

Several items must be completed before an audit can be considered finished. The client must approve of the proposed adjusting entries and the financial statement notes, and the audit work must be reviewed.

Communications with Audit Committees (or Equivalent)

The auditor should review with management in advance the information to be covered with the audit committee. On certain matters (e.g., company operations), management should report to the audit committee and the auditor then comments; on other matters, such as audit findings, the auditor should report to the audit committee and management then comments. Both should be present in meetings with the audit committee to discuss the reports, which may be written or oral. When the auditor communicates in writing, the report should indicate that it is intended solely for use by the audit committee.

In some instances the auditor may identify matters to discuss with the audit committee without the presence of management.

The auditor should keep notes of audit committee discussions at which the auditor is present. These notes should be compared to the minutes of the audit committee. Any inconsistencies should be resolved with the audit committee or board of directors.

The auditor should communicate all matters affecting approval of the annual financial statements to the board of directors prior to such approval. Normally, the auditor should work within the audit committee's regular cycle of meetings.

The audit committee's expectations need to be clarified and put in writing. The most important matters arising from the audit of financial statements that the auditor should communicate to the audit committee include:

1. auditor's responsibility under GAAS
2. the planning of the current audit
3. deficiencies in internal controls
4. illegal acts
5. fraud
6. significant accounting principles and policies
7. management judgements and accounting estimates
8. misstatements

9. other information in annual reports (e.g., narrative information)

10. disagreements with management

11. consultation with other accountants by management

12. major issues that influence the audit appointment

13. difficulties encountered in performing the audit (e.g., unreasonable delays in obtaining information from management)

14. effects of new developments in accounting standards, or legislative or regulatory requirements, on the client's financial reporting

15. use of specialists

16. audit and non-audit services that the auditor is providing to the client

17. a summary of the audit approach

These responsibilities are covered in *CICA Handbook,* section 5751. In addition, the *Sarbanes-Oxley Act* is further increasing audit committee responsibilities with respect to the external auditor.

The Act provides for significant corporate governance reforms regarding audit committees and their relationship to the auditor, making the audit committee responsible for the appointment, compensation and oversight of the external auditor. This should fundamentally change the auditor/client relationship. Further, the auditor reports directly to the audit committee, not to management, reinforcing the position that the auditor's duties run to the shareholders, rather than management. Each member of the audit committee must be independent, and the audit committee must have the authority to hire independent counsel and other advisers. In addition, each publicly traded client must provide appropriate funding, as determined by the audit committee, for compensating the auditor and any advisers retained by the audit committee. The audit committee also must establish procedures for handling complaints regarding accounting or auditing manners and for the confidential submission by employees of clients regarding questionable accounting or auditing matters. In light of these new increasingly important audit committee responsibilities, the audit committee must forge an effective working relationship between itself and the auditor… The full scope of the Act is not yet apparent as the Act mandates the completion of several studies which may result in additional legislation or rulemaking, and the new Accountability Boards may yet introduce additional rules over time.[14]

The auditor also has a responsibility to communicate (or determine that management has communicated) matters of concern to the audit committee.[15] If the auditor considers the audit committee's action seriously inappropriate, the auditor may need to communicate directly with the board of directors, and in some cases has an obligation to report to outside regulatory authorities. For example, the "well-being reporting requirement" under federal financial institutions legislation described in AUG–17 may require the auditor to report to the Superintendent of Financial Institutions "any significant weaknesses in internal control which have the potential to jeopardize the financial institution's ability to continue as a going concern." Since there is the issue of client confidentiality, the auditor should seek legal advice concerning the best manner of reporting to outside authorities.

Client Approval of Adjusting Entries and Financial Statement Disclosure

The financial statements, including the adjustments to the draft financial statements, are the responsibility of management. The adjusting entries shown in Exhibit 15–9 are labelled "proposed" to indicate this responsibility of management.

Many of the adjusting entries will be approved by management as they are prepared during the work on an area; others will await the final wrap-up to be approved. A formal list of all approved adjusting entries should be given to the client so that formal entries can be made in the accounting records to bring them into balance with the financial statements.

---

[14] www.cpa2biz.com
[15] *CICA Handbook,* section 5220.

Similarly, approval of all disclosure in notes must be obtained from the client. Any additional notes considered necessary usually are drafted as proposed notes by auditors performing the audit procedures. They must be considered carefully by the audit manager and partner before being presented to the client management for acceptance as the company's disclosures.

Exhibit 15–9 is a summary worksheet ("scoresheet") showing the end-of-audit consideration of proposed adjusting journal entries. Auditors can prepare this summary to see how the proposed adjustments affect the financial statements. This review helps auditors decide which adjustments must be made to support an unqualified audit report and which adjustments may be passed. A passed adjustment is a proposed adjustment on which the auditors decide not to insist because it does not have a material effect on the financial position and results of operations.

In the exhibit the illustrative proposed adjustments are (1) recording cheques written and mailed but not recorded in the books; (2) reversing recorded sales for goods shipped after the balance sheet date, and reversing the 60 percent cost of goods sold; (3) writing off obsolete and damaged inventory; (4) recording the amounts found in the search for unrecorded liabilities; (5) correcting an amortization calculation error; (6) reclassifying the current portion of long-term debt from the long-term classification; and (7) recording a tax refund asset for overpaid income taxes (could be a debit to tax liability if all the taxes for the year had not already been paid). Some summary effects on income, current assets, current liabilities and working capital are appended to the bottom of the exhibit. These help auditors to assess

EXHIBIT 15–9   PROPOSED ADJUSTING JOURNAL ENTRIES (Illustrative Scoresheet Working Paper)

	Income Statement		Balance Sheet	
	Debit	Credit	Debit	Credit
(1) Unrecorded cash disbursements:				
Accounts payable			$42,000	
Cash				$42,000
(2) Improper sales cutoff:				
Sales	$13,000			
Inventory			7,800	
Cost of goods sold (60%)		$7,800		
Accounts receivable				13,000
(3) Inventory write-off:				
Cost of goods sold	21,000			
Inventory				21,000
(4) Unrecorded liabilities:				
Utilities expense	700			
Commissions expense	3,000			
Wages	2,500			
Accounts payable				700
Accrued expenses payable				5,500
(5) Amortization calculation error:				
Accumulated amortization			17,000	
Amortization expense		17,000		
(6) Reclassify current portion of long-term debt:				
Notes payable			50,000	
Current portion of debt				50,000
(7) Income tax @ 40%:				
Income tax refund receivable			6,160	
Income tax expense		6,160		
	$40,200	$30,960	$122,960	$132,200
Net income change		($9,240)		
Current assets change				($62,040)
Current liabilities change				$14,200
Working capital change				($76,240)

the potential impact of the adjustments on financial statement users, e.g., lenders who are monitoring working capital ratios limits in debt covenants.

OVERALL EVALUATION OF AUDIT TESTS

The important thing about the audit tests is that they are the basis for deciding if the amount of unadjusted error is material at the end of the audit. The adjusted errors by definition have been corrected, so the real issue at the end of the audit is whether the uncorrected errors are material in amount. A minimal way to estimate this is on the basis of known uncorrected errors as in Exhibit 15–9. We refer to this as "minimal" because it is based on known errors, not most likely or possible errors (with which the client may disagree). We cover adjustments based on most likely and possible errors in Appendix 10A because they are less common in practice.

The principle of audit decision-making based on known unadjusted errors is to aggregate these in various ways to see if they total to a material amount. For example, say materiality is based on net income and is assessed to be 10 percent of recorded net income. Then the auditor will need to aggregate all errors affecting net income. This can be done on the basis of either (1) changes in net assets (assets-liabilities), or equivalently, (2) revenues less expenses. Both approaches should yield the same number. Note that, due to the nature of the double-entry system, in both cases understatements in liabilities/expenses must be *added* to over- or understatements of assets/revenues, while overstatements in liabilities/expenses must be subtracted from over- or understatements of assets/revenues.

Perhaps this is better explained by example than in words. Refer to Exhibit 15–9. The way to compute net effect of unadjusted (uncorrected) known errors on net income in this illustration is as follows:

Errors in net income = Errors in changes in net assets =

Errors in changes in assets minus errors in changes in liabilities =

$42,000_{(A)} + 13,000_{(A)} + 21,000_{(A)} - 7,800_{(A)} - 17,000_{(A)} - 6,160_{(A)} - (+ 42,000_{(L)} - 700_{(L)} - 5,500_{(L)} + 50,000_{(L)} - 50,000_{(L)}) = 9,240 =$

Errors in revenues minus errors in expenses =

$13,000_{(R)} - (6,160_{(E)} + 7,800_{(E)} - 21,000_{(E)} - 700_{(E)} - 3,000_{(E)} - 2,500_{(E)} + 17,000_{(E)}) = 9,240 =$

Total net errors in net income (overstatement, i.e., to eliminate all error the adjusting entry must reduce client's proposed net income by 9,240). This 9,240 is then compared to predetermined overall materiality. If 9,240 is less than material, then the auditor concludes that she does not need to make any more adjustments.

To reiterate, the previous analysis is based on known uncorrected errors only and is therefore perfectly appropriate whenever the auditor tests 100 percent of the transactions. This 100 percent testing is likely for cash, capital assets, noncurrent liabilities and owner's equity. It is less likely for inventory, receivables and payables, which can represent large populations of individual items, thus the auditor may wish to use sampling theory concepts for adjusting these accounts by most likely and possible error. We cover adjustments and decision making based on these sampling situations in Appendix 10A. Another complication in audit evaluation is measurements involving management estimates. Auditors are supposed to keep track of the differences between (1) management estimates and (2) the closest reasonable estimates supported by the audit evidence. They are also supposed to evaluate (1) the differences taken altogether for indications of a systematic bias and (2) the combination of differences with other likely errors in the financial statements found by other audit procedures.

One final point on overall evaluation: how does materiality relate to assertions? Materiality is defined as the amount of errors *from all sources* that would affect a user decision. Thus, materiality can be viewed as the minimum error that financial statement users find unacceptable from all assertions that have been violated. In other words, it is presumed users do not care which assertion is violated, only that aggregate violations from all sources are less than material. Again, review Exhibit 15–9 and note the assertions affected by the errors—they include completeness, valuation, existence and presentation assertions.

Working Paper and Report Review

In a typical audit team, the on-site audit supervisor makes a final review to ensure that all accounts on the trial balance have a **working paper reference index** (an indication that the audit work has been finished for that account) and that all procedures in the audit program are "signed off" with a date and initials.

The working papers of the audit staff are reviewed by the audit supervisor, and sometimes by the audit manager, soon after being completed. This review is to ensure that all tick-mark notations are clear, that all procedures performed are adequately documented and that all necessary procedures were performed with due professional care.

The review by the audit manager and engagement partner will focus more on the overall scope of the audit. The audit manager and engagement partner are very involved with the planning of the audit, and they perform some of the field work on difficult areas. However, they are usually not involved in preparing the detailed working papers. Even though the working papers are reviewed by the on-site audit supervisor, the review by the partner who is going to sign the audit report is essential. To-do lists are prepared during these reviews citing omissions or deficiencies that must be cleared before the final work is completed.

Audit firms vary in their treatment of the to-do lists. Some firms prefer to destroy the lists after the work is performed and documented in the working papers. After all, they want to "clean up" the working papers, and the to-do lists were merely notes directing the staff to tie a neat ribbon around any loose ends or difficult issues. Other firms prefer to keep the lists as signed off and cross-referenced for the work performed. They believe that the lists are "working papers" that show evidence of careful review and completion of the audit. Sometimes, retained to-do lists backfire on auditors by showing questions raised but not resolved.

The working papers and financial statements, including footnotes, are given a final review on large engagements by a partner not responsible for client relations. This **second-partner review** ensures that the quality of audit work and reporting is in keeping with the quality standards of the audit firm.

The final audit time reports must be prepared and the working papers prepared for storage. At the completion of the field work, performance evaluation reports of the staff auditors usually are prepared by the audit supervisor.

Management Letter

During the audit work (especially the evaluation of the control structure and assessment of the control risk), matters are noted that can be made as recommendations to the client. When field work is completed, and in some cases after the audit report is delivered, these items are evaluated and written in a letter (commonly referred to as the **management letter**) to be sent to the client. One firm calls this communication a letter of client advisory comments and characterizes it as a voluntary and constructive dimension of an audit designed to provide clients with an important value-added service.

The management letter is not required by professional standards and should not be confused with the communication of matters identified during the financial statement audit, which is now required by auditing standards (*CICA Handbook,* section 5751, discussed in Chapter 9) or with significant weaknesses in internal control, which must be reported to the audit committee under *CICA Handbook,* section 5220 and ISA 260.11. Management letters are a service provided as a by-product of the audit. The management letter is an excellent opportunity to develop a rapport with the client and to increase client satisfaction. A brief management letter is shown in Exhibit 15–10.[16]

---

[16] W. A. Wallace, "More Effective Management Letters," *CPA Journal,* December 1983, pp. 18–28.

EXHIBIT 15-10 MANAGEMENT LETTER

Anderson, Olds & Watershed
Public Accountants
Toronto, Ontario
April 1, 20X2

Mr. Larry Lancaster, Chairman
Kingston Company
Kingston, Ontario

Dear Mr. Lancaster:

During our audit of the Kingston Company financial statements for the year ended December 31, 20X2, we observed certain matters we believe should be brought to your attention. Our audit work was not designed to be a study of the overall efficiency and economy of the management and operation of Kingston Company, but ordinary audit procedures nevertheless enabled us to notice some actions that could enhance the profitability of the Company.

Summary

When we audited the physical inventory and compared the quantities actually on hand to the quantities shown in the perpetual inventory records, we noted several shortages. Follow-up with your warehouse personnel revealed that the "shortages" were usually in the assembly department, where numerous items of custom lawn maintenance equipment were being assembled for customers prior to delivery. The removal of the inventory from the records was routinely entered when the assembled equipment was delivered. These procedures eventually maintained the records accurately, but the delay in posting the inventory records has resulted in lost sales and some customer dissatisfaction with the custom-assembly service.

The Problem

The warehouse personnel remove parts according to the specification of custom-assembly work orders, moving the parts to the assembly area. If another customer orders these parts soon thereafter, the inventory records show them on hand, and the new customer is told that the order can be filled. Shortly thereafter, warehouse personnel find that the parts are actually not on hand, and the customer is disappointed when informed of a delay. Sales department personnel confirmed that several (20–25 during the last six months) withdrew their orders and bought the parts from a competitor. They estimated that approximately $25,000 was lost in sales during the last six months, amounting to about $9,000 in lost profits.

Custom-Assembly Losses

The inventory "shortages," noticed by warehouse personnel when they try to fill new orders, cause another difficulty. People spend extra time looking around for the parts, and usually their enquiries reach the assembly area, where workers leave their jobs unfinished while trying to help locate the "missing" parts. This helpfulness causes assembly jobs to be delayed, customers get dissatisfied, and, in one case, a customer refused to pay because of late delivery. This one case resulted in lost profits of $10,000 because the equipment had to be disassembled and returned to the inventory.

Recommendation

We discussed the following recommendation with Mr. James Worthy in the warehouse, and he agrees that it can be a practical solution. We recommend that you design a form for "Work in Progress," which will be used to make accounting and inventory entries to remove parts from the main inventory as soon as they are transferred to the assembly area. At that stage, the cost would be classified as "work in progress," which will be entered in cost of goods sold as soon as the assembly is completed and the goods are delivered. Judging from our limited knowledge of the extent of the problem during the year under audit, we estimate that you might produce $20,000–$30,000 additional profit per year, while development and use of the form should cost about $3,000.

Very truly yours,

Anderson, Olds & Watershed

REVIEW
CHECKPOINTS

15.17   Why are auditors' drafts of adjusting entries and note disclosures always labelled "proposed" near the end of the audit? Should the auditors just write them in final form and give them to the client?

15.18   What are review to-do lists? Cite several items that such lists might contain. Why must such lists be cleared before the field work is considered completed?

15.19   What is a good reason for keeping the to-do list in the audit working paper files?

15.20   Describe a second-partner review. What is its purpose?

15.21 What is a management letter? Is a management letter required by generally accepted auditing standards?

15.22 Why would PA firm personnel be able to provide a management letter at the end of an audit?

15.23 How can well-prepared management letters lead to higher client satisfaction with audit engagements? Should a PA promote other services that could be provided to the client in the management letter?

SUMMARY

This chapter covered several aspects of completing an audit. As the work draws to a close, several income and expense accounts may remain to be audited. Analytical comparisons of their balances with prior years and current expectations accomplish this auditing in most cases. Large and significant revenues and expenses usually have already been audited in connection with the audit of other accounts in the cycles. At this late stage in the audit, it is always a good idea to step back and review large and unusual revenue and gain transactions recorded near the end of the year. These often have been the vehicles for income statement manipulation. Some examples were given in the chapter.

Two of the most important topics for the audit completion work involve the client's written representation letter and the lawyer's letter. These submissions to the auditors are virtually required for an unqualified audit report. Without them, the audit scope is considered limited. Several requirements for the client representation letter were specified in the chapter. A special insert described particular problems interpreting lawyers' letters. Information from lawyers is especially important for getting evidence about litigation contingencies and their disclosure according to *CICA Handbook,* section 3290. Some descriptive research on *CICA Handbook,* section 3290 disclosure experience in the U.S. was provided to emphasize the difficulties faced by managers and auditors.

Subsequent events topics were explained in considerable detail, including (1) procedural responsibility for events following the balance sheet date; (2) the double-dating alternative for reporting on events that occurred between the end of field work and the delivery of the report; (3) auditors' discovery, after a report was delivered, of facts that existed at the balance sheet date; and (4) auditors' finding, after a report was delivered, that one or more audit procedures they thought were performed were not actually performed.

This chapter closed this text's adventures in auditing with explanation of proposed adjusting journal entries and disclosure notes, working paper review and the management letter. All that remains is the audit report itself, which was explained in Chapter 3 because it is the final objective and focal point of the whole financial statement audit engagement. The next chapter will discuss other types of engagements that are common in public practice.

MULTIPLE-CHOICE QUESTIONS FOR PRACTICE AND REVIEW

15.24 When auditing the year-end balance of interest-bearing notes payable, the auditors are most likely to audit at the same time the company's:
a. Interest income.
b. Interest expense.
c. Amortization of goodwill.
d. Royalty revenue.

15.25 The main purpose of a written client representation letter is to:

a. Shift responsibility for financial statements from the management to the auditor.
b. Provide a substitute source of evidence for detail procedures auditors would otherwise perform.
c. Provide management a place to make assertions about the quantity and valuation of the physical inventory.
d. Impress upon management its ultimate responsibility for the financial statements and disclosures.

15.26 Which one of these procedures or sources is not used to obtain evidence about contingencies?

a. Scan expense accounts for credit entries.

b. Obtain a representation letter from the client's lawyer.

c. Read the minutes of the board of directors' meetings.

d. Examine terms of sale in sales contracts.

15.27 A Type I subsequent event involves subsequent information about a condition that existed at the balance sheet date. Subsequent knowledge of which of the following would cause the company to adjust its December 31 financial statements?

a. Sale of an issue of new shares for $500,000 on January 30.

b. Settlement of a damage lawsuit for a customer's injury sustained February 15 for $10,000.

c. Settlement of litigation in February for $100,000 that had been estimated at $12,000 in the December 31 financial statements.

d. Storm damage of $1 million to the company's buildings on March 1.

15.28 A. Griffin audited the financial statements of Dodger Magnificat Corporation for the year ended December 31, 20X2. She completed the audit field work on January 30, and later learned of a stock split voted by the board of directors on February 5. The financial statements were changed to reflect the split, and she now needs to dual-date the audit report before sending it to the company. Which of the following is the proper form?

a. December 31, 20X2, except as to Note X, which is dated January 30, 20X3.

b. January 30, 20X3, except as to Note X, which is dated February 5, 20X3.

c. December 31, 20X2, except as to Note X, which is dated February 5, 20X3.

d. February 5, 20X3, except for completion of field work, for which the date is January 30, 20X3.

15.29 In connection with a company's filing a registration statement under most provincial securities acts, auditors have a responsibility to perform procedures to find subsequent events until:

a. The year-end balance sheet date.

b. The audit report date.

c. The date the registration statement and audit report are delivered to the provincial securities commission.

d. The "effective date" of the registration statement, when the securities can be offered for sale.

15.30 The auditing standards regarding "subsequent discovery of facts that existed at the balance sheet date" refers to knowledge obtained after:

a. The date the audit report was delivered to the client.

b. The audit report date.

c. The company's year-end balance sheet date.

d. The date interim audit work was complete.

15.31 Which of the following is not required by Canadian auditing standards?

a. Client representation letter.

b. Lawyer's letter.

c. Management letter.

d. Engagement letter.

15.32 Which of these persons generally do not participate in writing the management letter (client advisory comments)?

a. Client's outside lawyers.

b. Client's accounting and production managers.

c. Audit firm's audit team on the engagement.

d. Audit firm's IT specialists and tax experts.

EXERCISES AND PROBLEMS

15.33 Client Representation Letter. In connection with your audit, you request that management furnish you with a letter containing certain representations. For example:

LO.4

(1) The client has satisfactory title to all assets;

(2) No contingent or unrecorded liabilities exist except as disclosed in the letter;

(3) No shares of the company's stock are reserved for options, warrants or other rights; and

(4) The company is not obligated to repurchase any of its outstanding shares under any circumstances.

Required:

a. Explain why you believe a letter of representation should be furnished to you.

b. In what way, if any, do these client representations affect your audit procedures and responsibilities?

(AICPA adapted)

15.34 Engagement and Client Representation Letters. The two major written understandings between a PA and client, in connection with an audit of financial statements, are the engagement letter and the client representation letter.

LO.4

Required:

a. (1) What are the objectives of the engagement letter?

(2) Who should prepare and sign the engagement letter?

(3) When should the engagement letter be sent?

(4) Why should the engagement letter be renewed periodically?

b. (1) What are the objectives of the client representation letter?

(2) Who should sign the client representation letter?

(3) When should the client representation letter be obtained?

(4) Why should the client representation letter be prepared for each examination?

c. A PA's responsibilities for providing accounting services sometimes involve an association with unaudited financial statements. Discuss the need in this circumstance for:

(1) An engagement letter.

(2) Client representation letter.

(AICPA adapted)

15.35 Client Representations Letter Omissions. During the
LO.4 audit of the annual financial statements of Amis Manufacturing, Inc., the company's president, Vance Molar, and Wayne Dweebins, the engagement partner, reviewed matters that were supposed to be included in a written representation letter. Upon receipt of the following representation letter, Dweebins contacted Molar to state that it was incomplete.

To John & Wayne, PAs:

In connection with your examination of the balance sheet of Amis Manufacturing, Inc., as of December 31, 20X2, and the related statements of income, retained earnings and cash flows for the year then ended, for the purpose of expressing an opinion on whether the financial statements present fairly the financial position, results of operations and cash flows of Amis Manufacturing, Inc., in conformity with generally accepted accounting principles, we confirm, to the best of our knowledge and belief, the following representations made to you during your audit. There were no:

Plans or intentions that may materially affect the carrying value or classification of assets or liabilities.

Communications from regulatory agencies concerning noncompliance with, or deficiencies in, financial reporting practices.

Agreements to repurchase assets previously sold.

Violations or possible violations of laws or regulations whose effects should be considered for disclosure in the financial statements or as a basis for recording a loss contingency.

Unasserted claims or assessments that our lawyer has advised are probable of assertion that must be disclosed in accordance with Canadian GAAP.

Capital stock purchase options or agreements or capital stock reserved for options, warrants, conversions or other requirements.

Compensating balance or other arrangements involving restrictions on cash balances.

Vance Molar, President
Amis Manufacturing, Inc.
March 14, 20X3

Required:

Identify the other matters that Molar's representation letter should specifically confirm.

(AICPA adapted)

15.36 Subsequent Events and Contingent Liabilities.
LO.5 Crankwell, Inc., is preparing its annual financial statements and annual report to shareholders. Management wants to be sure that all of the necessary and proper disclosures are incorporated into the financial statements and the annual report. Two classes of items that have an important bearing on the financial statements are subsequent events and contingent liabilities. The financial statements could be materially inaccurate or misleading if proper disclosure of these items is not made.

Required:

a. With respect to subsequent events:

(1) Define subsequent events.

(2) Identify the two types of subsequent events and explain the appropriate financial statement presentation of each type.

b. With respect to contingent liabilities:

(1) Identify the essential elements of a contingent liability.

(2) Explain how a contingent liability should be disclosed in the financial statements.

c. Explain how a subsequent event may relate to a contingent liability. Give an example to support your answer.

(CMA adapted)

15.37 Subsequent Events Procedures. You are in the process
LO.5 of "winding up" the field work on Top Stove Corporation, a company engaged in the manufacture and sale of kerosene space heating stoves. To date there has been every indication that the financial statements of the client present fairly the position of the company at December 31 and the results of its operations for the year then ended. Top Stove had total assets at December 31 of $4 million and a net profit for the year (after deducting federal and provincial income taxes) of $285,000. The principal records of the company are a general ledger, cash receipts record, voucher register, sales register, cheque register and general journal. Financial statements are prepared monthly. Your field work will be completed on February 20, and you plan to deliver the report to the client by March 12.

Required:

a. Write a brief statement about the purpose and period to be covered in a review of subsequent events.

b. Outline the program you would follow to determine what transactions involving material amounts, if any, have occurred since the balance sheet date.

(AICPA adapted)

15.38 Subsequent Events—Cases. The following events oc-
LO.5 curred in independent cases, but in each instance the event happened after the close of the fiscal year under

audit but before all members of the audit team had left the office of the client. State in each case what disclosure, if any, you would expect in the financial statements (and notes thereto). The balance sheet date in each instance is December 31.

1. On December 31, commodities handled by the company had been traded in the open market in which the company procures its supplies at $1.40 per pound. This price had prevailed for two weeks, following an official market report that predicted vastly enlarged supplies; however, no purchases were made at $1.40. The price throughout the preceding year had been about $2, which is the level experienced over several years. On January 18 the price returned to $2, following public disclosure of an error in the official calculations of the prior December—correction of which destroyed the expectations of excessive supplies. Inventory at December 31 had been valued on a lower-of-cost-or-market basis.

2. On February 1 the board of directors adopted a resolution accepting the offer of an investment banker to guarantee the marketing of $100 million of preferred shares.

3. On January 22 one of the three major plants of the client burned down, resulting in a loss of $50 million, which was covered to the extent of $40 million by insurance.

4. The client in this case is an investment company of the open-end type. In January a wholly new management came into control. By February 20 the new management had sold 90 percent of the investments carried at December 31 and had purchased others of a substantially more speculative character.

5. This company has a wholly owned but not consolidated subsidiary producing oil in a foreign country. A serious rebellion began in that country on January 18 and continued beyond the completion of your audit work. The press in this country has carried extensive coverage of the progress of the fighting.

6. The client, Comtois Corp. sells property management software systems. Shortly before its December 31, 20X1 year-end Comtois' president finalized a large sale to a ministry of the provincial government. The contract has been completed and all the terms agreed to by the assistant deputy minister. However, the minister herself is the only one authorized to sign the contract because of the large dollar amount involved. As of the last day of audit fieldwork, March 3, 20X2, Comtois has not yet received the signed contract because the minister has not yet been available to sign it. The president wants to recognize the revenue in Comtois' 20X1 fiscal year anyway, so that the sales people and managers involved can be paid a bonus this year based on their profitable effort. The client's stated accounting policy for revenue recognition on these types of sales, established five years earlier, is to recognize revenue when the sales contract is signed.

7. During its fiscal year ending December 31, 20X1 Noriker Inc. issued common shares to its vice-president of marketing. At the date of issuing these shares, the company also provided the vice-president with a non-interest bearing loan of $50,000 to use to purchase the shares. While reviewing the minutes of all the Noriker board of directors meetings during the audit fieldwork, Noriker's auditor notes that in a meeting on February 12, 20X2 the Noriker board agreed to forgive this loan to the vice-president, effective on that day.

(AICPA adapted)

15.39 Subsequent Events—Cases. In connection with your
LO.5 examination of the financial statements of Olars Manufacturing Corporation for the year ended December 31, your post-balance sheet audit procedures disclosed the following items:

1. January 3: The provincial government approved a plan for the construction of an expressway. The plan will result in the appropriation of a portion of the land area owned by Olars Manufacturing Corporation. Construction will begin late next year. No estimate of the condemnation award is available.

2. January 4: The funds for a $25,000 loan to the corporation made by Mr. Olars on July 15 were obtained by him with a loan on his personal life insurance policy. The loan was recorded in the account loan payable to officers. Mr. Olars's source of the funds was not disclosed in the company records. The corporation pays the premiums on the life insurance policy, and Mrs. Olars, wife of the president, is the owner and beneficiary of the policy.

3. January 7: The mineral content of a shipment of ore en route on December 31 was determined to be 72 percent. The shipment was recorded at year-end at an estimated content of 50 percent by a debit to raw material inventory and a credit to accounts payable in the amount of $20,600. The final liability to the vendor is based on the actual mineral content of the shipment.

4. January 15: A series of personal disagreements have arisen between Mr. Olars, the president, and Mr. Tweedy, his brother-in-law, the treasurer. Mr. Tweedy resigned, effective immediately, under an agreement whereby the corporation would purchase his 10 percent share ownership at book value as of December 31. Payment is to be made in two equal amounts in cash on April 1 and October 1. In December the treasurer had obtained a divorce from Mr. Olars's sister.

5. January 31: As a result of reduced sales, production was curtailed in mid-January and some workers were laid off. On February 5 all the remaining workers went on strike. To date the strike is unsettled.

6. February 10: A contract was signed whereby Mammoth Enterprises purchased from Olars Manufacturing corporation all of the latter's capital assets (including rights to receive the proceeds of any property condemnation), inventories and the right to conduct business under the name "Olars Manufacturing Division." The effective date of the

transfer will be March 1. The sale price was $500,000, subject to adjustment following the taking of a physical inventory. Important factors contributing to the decision to enter into the contract were the policy of the board of directors of Mammoth Industries to diversify the firm's activities and the report of a survey conducted by an independent market appraisal firm, which revealed a declining market for Olars's products.

Required:

Assume that the above items came to your attention prior to completion of your audit work on February 15. For each of the above items:

a. Give the audit procedures, if any, that would have brought the item to your attention. Indicate other sources of information that may have revealed the item.

b. Discuss the disclosure that you would recommend for the item, listing all details that should be disclosed. Indicate those items or details, if any, that should not be disclosed. Give your reasons for recommending or not recommending disclosure of the items or details.

(AICPA adapted)

15.40 Warranty Provision Audit Issues. Breton Inc. manu-
LO.8 factures industrial lighting fixtures. It has two main product lines, interior and exterior fixtures. The fixtures are sold with a one-year warranty on parts and labour. During 20X0 Breton's engineering group undertook a five-year review of its warranty claims history and costs and established that an appropriate accounting policy for warranty costs is to accrue 3 percent of annual sales for exterior fixtures and 2 percent of annual sales for interior fixtures. PA, Breton's auditor, has used this engineering analysis for the past two year's audits as the basis for evaluating Breton's provision for estimated warranty cost at year-end. During 20X3 Breton's competition increased dramatically as imported light fixtures from China entered the market, selling for prices 40 to 50 percent lower than Breton's prices. To maintain its customer base, Breton's senior management decided to go for a strategy of promoting the higher quality of Breton's products, and to expand Breton warranty coverage to two years to support these quality claims. However, to keep costs in line, no changes were made to the materials used or the production methods. PA is now assessing the 20X3 year-end provision for estimated warranty costs. On enquiring of the CFO, PA learns that there is no plan to change the approach that has been used to develop the estimate. It will be the same approach as in prior years. Breton sales people receive commissions of 1 percent of gross sales. Breton's senior managers, including the CFO, receive bonuses only if the company's pre-tax profit exceeds $300,000.

Required:

a. Discuss the implications of the changes in Breton's competitive environment and business strategy for the audit of its warranty liability estimate.

b. If you were the CFO, what arguments would you make to support your position that the method used to estimate warranty liability not be changed in the current year?

c. What actions do you recommend PA take in this case?

15.41 Fixed Asset Dispositions, Accounting Errors. During
LO.8 the current year, Karabakh Limited sold off all the heating and air conditioning equipment installed in one of its buildings. This equipment was no longer required because the building was converted from an assembly plant to a warehouse. It was sold to a neighbouring business, which paid $400,000 cash. The equipment was about 10 years old, originally cost $1 million, and was approximately 80 percent depreciated. Karabakh's bookkeeper recorded the sale as follows:

dr Cash   400,000

    cr Sales revenue   400,000

Required:

a. What impact does the error have on Karabakh's financial statements? Outline which accounts will be affected and the dollar amounts of these effects.

b. Assume this transaction is material to Karabakh's financial statements. What procedures would allow the Karabakh auditor to find this bookkeeping error?

c. Provide a draft adjusting journal entry to correct the entry.

15.42 Franchising Revenues. You are an auditor with ZZ, a
LO.1 PA firm. Your firm has just accepted a new engagement to audit the annual financial statements of Chestnut Limited, a medium-sized restaurant business. Chestnut operates a chain of specialty fast food restaurants. Most of the restaurants are franchised, and Chestnut receives franchise fees that are based on the franchisee store's net sales revenues.

Chestnut receives 4 percent of net sales as a base franchise fee, 1 percent as an advertising fee, and 0.5 percent as an administration fee for processing franchisee accounting information and issuing reports in standard format. Franchisee sales information is uploaded daily to Chestnut's central accounting system, where it is input into the franchise reporting system to generate daily, monthly and year-end management reports.

Required:

Design an audit plan for franchise revenues at Chestnut. State any assumptions you make.

15.43 Lawyer's Letter Responses. Omega Corporation is in-
LO.3 volved in a lawsuit brought by a competitor for patent infringement. The competitor is asking $14 million actual damages for lost profits and unspecified punitive damages. The lawsuit has been in progress for 15 months, and Omega has worked closely with its outside counsel preparing its defence. Omega recently requested its outside lawyers with the firm of Wolfe & Goodwin to provide information to the auditors.

The managing partner of Wolfe & Goodwin asked four different lawyers who have worked on the case to prepare a concise response to the auditors. They returned these:

1. The action involves unique characteristics wherein authoritative legal precedents bearing directly on the plaintiff's claims do not seem to exist. We believe the plaintiff will have serious problems establishing Omega's liability; nevertheless, if the plaintiff is successful, the damage award may be substantial.

2. In our opinion, Omega will be able to defend this action successfully, and, if not, the possible liability to Omega in this proceeding is nominal in amount.

3. We believe the plaintiff's case against Omega is without merit.

4. In our opinion Omega will be able to assert meritorious defences and has a reasonable chance of sustaining an adequate defence, with a possible outcome of settling the case for less than the damages claimed.

Required:

a. Interpret each of the four responses separately. Decide whether each is (1) adequate to conclude that the likelihood of an adverse outcome is "remote," requiring no disclosure in financial statements, or (2) too vague to serve as adequate information for a decision, requiring more information from the lawyers or from management.

b. What kind of response do you think the auditors would get if they asked the plaintiff's counsel about the likely outcome of the lawsuit? Discuss.

15.44 Revenue, Audit Procedures. While performing ana-
LO.1 lytical procedures as part of her audit of the revenue
LO.2 and expense accounts at Galloway Inc., PA notes that Galloway's sales revenues in the current year have increased by 20 percent over the prior year. Galloway manufactures and sells business forms, and has seen declining sales over the past few years as its customers have been changing many of their business processes to paperless, online methods. In fact, in the prior year's audit there was considerable concern about Galloway's ability to meet its long-term debt covenants which require at least a 2:1 current ratio and pre-tax earnings that are at least 10 times long-term debt interest charges. In order for Galloway to meet these debt covenant restrictions, no bonuses could be paid to management in the prior year. When PA discussed the current year sales figures with the sales manager, he informed her that Galloway had increased its prices by 50 percent in the third quarter of the current year, to offset the lower sales volumes. Management had determined that Galloway's remaining customers were restricted to using paper-based documentation for various business reasons and thus would accept higher prices. During this interview, the chief accountant was passing by and, overhearing the topic, pointed out to PA that: "Note that accounts receivable balance is also much higher than last year, which is totally consistent with the

higher sales. This should tie together your analysis, so your audit work on sales and AR must now be complete. We are looking forward to having our boardroom back when you auditors finally finish the job and leave!"

Required:

Discuss the nature and the persuasiveness of the audit evidence PA is gathering in the above scenario. What additional evidence would you recommend she obtain to support her conclusion on the sales revenue figure?

15.45 Revenues, General Journal Entries. Town & Country
LO.1 Cable Inc. (TCC) is a cable television provider servicing customers in small towns and rural areas. Its shares are privately held, but it issued a 20-year bond eight years ago to the public. The bond contains restrictive covenants, which include requirements for TCC to maintain a current ratio of at least 2:1 at each fiscal year-end, and a ratio of operating cash flow to current liabilities of at least 1.0. If the covenants are violated, the bond holders have the right to demand repayment, raise the interest rate, and/or liquidate the company. In recent years TCC has seen very little growth from new customer installations as most people are now choosing a satellite television service instead of cable. At the same time, TCC's existing installed customer base has been shrinking as many existing customers have switched to satellite because it offers more channels and more reliable service. As a result of these changes in its operating environment, TCC has been close to violating its restrictive covenants in the past two years.

PA is the senior on the current-year audit. While scrutinizing a 300-page print-out of the general journal entries for the year for material entries and seeing nothing but small adjustments for payroll and purchasing discounts PA is about to sign off on the procedure. Then she notices ten journal entries in a row in the middle of November that debit account #22000 (current accrued liabilities) and credit account #54400 (other operating income). The entries are all for different immaterial amounts, but all are to the same two accounts, and all have the same explanatory note: 'To adjust accrued liabilities as per instructions memo of Nov 2. On further investigation, PA finds 40 more entries to these accounts with the same explanatory comment. The entries are all for different, immaterial amounts but in total add up to a large, material amount. The accountant who made these general journal entries is no longer employed by TCC, and no one else in the accounting department knows anything about the "memo of Nov 2."

Required:

a. What are some possible explanations for the PA findings described above? How can the PA determine whether these entries result in a misstatement to the financial statements?

b. If these entries do result in financial statements that are materially misstated, what other procedures in the audit may have revealed these entries?

15.46 Lawyer's Letters. Auditors are required to obtain representation letters from the client's lawyer to elicit information on claims and possible claims that may affect the financial statements.

LO.3

Required:

a. Discuss the audit evidence provided by a lawyer's letter. Explain which assertions and which financial statement amounts the lawyer's letter relates to. What other audit evidence is available for these assertions, if any?

b. What other evidence may be available to an auditor that can corroborate the completeness of the claims the client has listed in the lawyer's letter?

c. What should be the effective date of the lawyer's letter? Why?

15.47 Subsequent Events, Pro Forma Disclosures. Assume that you are the financial statement auditor in the following independent cases, and you are completing your fieldwork in February 20X2. For each of these subsequent events, indicate if you would require the client company to adjust its December 20X1 year-end financial statements, disclose the event in the 20X1 financial statements, and/or provide pro forma financial information in the 20X1 financial statements. Give reasons to support your responses. State any assumptions you make.

LO.5

a. During January 20X2, the company's management decided to sell rental real estate properties that accounted for approximately 40 percent of its total revenues in 20X1.

b. The company's main factory was closed for six weeks in January and February of 20X2 due to ice storm damage. The factory resumed full operations in late February.

c. One of the company's factories was destroyed by a fire in January. The plant was old and will not be replaced as its production can be taken up by excess capacity in other newer plants that the company owns.

d. In late February, the company's board of directors agreed to settle an outstanding claim by paying $15 million to former employees. The employees suffered health problems from being exposed to asbestos that the company used in its operations during the years of their employment. A contingent liability was disclosed but not accrued as of December 31, 20X1 because of the uncertainty surrounding the outcome of the lawsuit.

e. For the past four years, the company has made 90 percent of its revenues and profits from sales of specialty cable to computer manufacturers. Early in 20X2, it has become apparent that there is massive overcapacity in this industry, and demand for the company's cable has fallen to almost zero. Demand is not expected to recover for several years, and may never recover if alternate technologies are developed in the meantime that make the company's product unnecessary.

15.48 Stock Splits, Audit Report Date. Orlov Inc. approves a two-for-one stock split on February 7, 20X2. Orlov's auditor completed its fieldwork on January 31, 20X2.

LO.6

a. Why is this subsequent event adjusted in the December 31, 20X1 financial statements? What would be the impact on users of not making this adjustment?

b. Orlov has requested that the auditor date its audit report on February 7, 20X2 instead of double-dating it for January 31, 20X2 and February 7, 20X2. What additional procedures would the auditor need to provide an audit opinion as of February 7, 20X2 instead of January 31, 20X2?

15.49 Errors, Adjustments. For the following findings, indicate the income statement and balance sheet accounts that are affected, whether these accounts are over- or understated, and provide an adjusting entry to correct the error, if required. Assume a December 31 year-end.

LO.8

Required:

a. Outstanding cheques totaling $44,000 were deducted from the cash balance on December 23, but deliberately not mailed out to avoid a bank overdraft over the holidays. The cheques were in payment of various raw material supplier accounts.

b. Sales of $79,000 were recorded on goods that were shipped after year-end and included in the year-end inventory count. The cost of these goods is $53,000.

c. A lawyer's bill for services rendered in November was not paid or accrued.

d. The allowance for bad debts has a credit balance of $80,000. The accounts receivable balance is $150,000 and a reasonable estimate is that all but $10,000 of this will be collected.

e. As of December 31 the company has recognized $250,000 of revenue on a $750,000 contract to construct a bridge. The construction work has not yet started, but $40,000 of building materials for the job were received and expensed as contract costs.

15.50 Management Representation Letters. Refer to the example of a Canadian management representation letter illustrated in Exhibit 15–3.

LO.4

a. What assumptions about the audit engagement underly this illustration of a management representation letter?

b. Which of the representations in the example letter need to be provided regardless of their materiality?

c. If an event subsequent to the date of the balance sheet has been disclosed in the financial statements, what modification would be made to the example letter?

d. If management has received a communication regarding an allegation of fraud or suspected fraud, what modification would be made to the example letter?

e. If the engagement results in the auditor reporting in accordance with section 5600, what modification would be made to the example letter?

15.51   Professional Judgement. Professional judgement is
LO.8   critical to auditors and the quality of audits.

Required:
a. Explain professional judgement in the context of an
    audit, giving three examples of situations in the
    audit process that require professional judgement.
b. The generally accepted auditing standards from
    CICA Handbook, section 5100, include specific
    standards intended to enhance the quality and value
    of audits. Explain each of the standards in section
    5100, emphasizing how each one can help junior
    auditors develop their professional judgement.

15.52   Business Processes, Financial Statement Articula-
LO.8   **tion.** For each of the items included in the entity's busi-
    ness processes in Exhibit III–2, identify which financial
    statement it will appear on and list all the other finan-
    cial statement items to which it is related.

15.53   "Take it to the Web" (XBRL). XBRL is an Internet-
    based technology for presenting financial data on web-
    pages and exchanging it over the Internet with other
    users' systems.
a. Starting with the website XBRL.org, research the
    underlying structure of XBRL and briefly explain how
    it works. Other XBRL references: KOSDAC.com,
    ubmatrix.com.
b. For the financial statement items you identified in
    the question 15.52 above, describe how each data
    item could be defined/tagged in XBRL to appear in
    the financial statements.
c. If the financial data item has been audited, can
    XBRL allow the auditor's assurance be communi-
    cated to users at the same time as the data? How?

Kingston Case questions related to Chapter 15 are on the Online Learning Centre that accompanies this text.

APPENDIX 15A

SAMPLE AUDIT WORKING PAPERS

This appendix provides a sample index containing a comprehensive list of the various working papers used to document audit work.

The requirements for documenting the audit and preparing the final audit file are set out in *CICA Handbook*, section 5145. The documentation should provide a complete record of the support for the auditor's opinion in a form that is useful for future audit planning, for peer reviews or quality control reviews, for practice inspection by the professional institute that regulates the auditor and audit firm, and as legal evidence should the audit become the subject of a legal action.

This index is from a professional engagement manual developed and maintained by one of the provincial accounting institutes as a guide for auditors in practice. Many of the working papers listed are based on checklists that are also available in the professional engagement manual. Not all of these working papers and checklists listed are required on every engagement, this depends on the client circumstances and the audit approach the PA has decided to use. Some larger audit firms will have developed their own working paper documenting systems and checklists, but many smaller audit firms can benefit from the support provided by professional engagement manuals that the institutes publish, to maintain the high quality of their audits and other assurance engagements.

SAMPLE INDEX FOR THE YEAR-END AUDIT FILE

Client _____

Year-end _____

FINANCIAL STATEMENTS AND AUDIT REPORT
1.1   Financial statements

INCOME TAX RETURNS
2.1   Federal tax returns
2.2   Provincial tax returns

COMPLETION DOCUMENTS
3.1   Completion checklist
3.2   Client discussion notes
3.3   Matters for discussion
3.4   Client/Management letter
3.5   Client's letter of representation
3.6   Extracts from minutes
3.7   Legal correspondence

ENGAGEMENT ACCEPTANCE
4.1   Engagement acceptance checklist
4.2   Client retention checklist
4.3   Engagement letter
4.4   First audit engagement checklist

PLANNING DOCUMENTS
5.1   Planning the audit engagement
5.1S Team planning meeting—worksheet
5.2   Knowledge of business checklist
5.3   Organization chart
5.4   Materiality worksheet
5.5   Time and expense budget and actual

5.6   Letter from predecessor auditor
5.7   Inherent risk questionnaire
5.7A Risk assessment worksheet
5.8   Inherent risk by significant financial statement assertions
5.8S Identification of possible fraud risk factors
5.9   Control environment questionnaire
5.10 Audit strategy memorandum
5.10S Auditor's response to identified fraud risk factors
5.11 Environmental contingencies

GENERAL WORK
6.1   Notes to financial statements
6.2   Working papers supporting statement of cash flows
6.3   Trial balance
6.4   Adjusting and reclassifying journal entries
6.5   Grouping schedules
6.6   Elimination entries
6.8   Schedule of unadjusted differences

INTERNAL SYSTEMS OF CONTROL
7.1   Summary of significant accounting systems
7.2   Internal control evaluation questionnaires (I.C.E.Q.)
7.3   Weakness investigation worksheet

FINANCIAL STATEMENT AREAS

Assets
A.   Cash
B.   Temporary investments
C.   Accounts receivable, trade and other
D.   Inventory
E.   Current loans and advances receivable
L.   Prepaid and other current assets
M.   Long-term loans and advances receivable
N.   Long-term investments
U.   Property, plant and equipment
W.   Goodwill and intangibles
Y.   Other long-term assets

Liabilities
AA.   Notes payable and bank debt
BB.   Accounts payable and accrued liabilities
FF.   Income taxes
GG.   Current loans and advances payable
HH.   Other current liabilities
KK.   Long-term debt
LL.   Long-term loans and advances payable
NN.   Other long-term liabilities
OO.   Contingencies, commitments, and subsequent events

Equity
UU.   Equity
VV.   Related party transactions

Income statement
10.0   Earnings
10.1   Earnings program
10.2   Financial ratios
10.3   Analytical review
20   Sales or gross income
30   Cost of sales
40   Operating expenses
41   Stock-based compensation expense
70   Other income or expenses
80   Provision for income taxes

Substantive tests of transactions
100.1   Revenues, receivables and receipts
100.2   Purchases, payables and payments
100.3   Production/Inventory costing
100.4   Payroll
100.7   General journal
100.8   Trial balance, adjusting journal entries and working papers

Source: Adapted from *Professional Engagement Manual*, CICA, 2004.

PART IV
Other Professional Services

CHAPTER
16

Other Public Accounting Services and Reports

This chapter covers several other areas of public accounting than audited historical financial statements practised by PAs. Specifically, the following areas are explained:

- unaudited financial statements: review and compilation
- review of interim financial information
- special reports—other comprehensive bases of accounting
- internal control reporting (including audit report reservations on internal control)
- forecasts, projections, prospectuses and MD&A
- financial statements to be used outside of Canada
- assurance engagement concepts
- the association framework

These areas of accounting involve assurance standards, auditing standards, and accounting and review service standards that were introduced in Chapter 2.

4* Contrast an audit report on supplementary current value financial statements with a standard report on historical cost financial statements.

5* Describe the various reports on internal control and their connection with public reporting and reporting to a client's audit committee.

6* Define the various financial presentations and levels of service involved in association with financial forecasts, projections, prospectuses and MD&A.

7* Describe the umbrella standards for assurance engagements. (Appendix 16A)

8* Identify assurance engagements unique to e-business. (Appendix 16A)

9* Explain the concept of environmental audits.

10 Describe the association framework.

Note: Those learning objectives marked with an asterisk (*) and their corresponding topics are considered advanced material. Also, Appendix 16A is located on the text Online Learning Centre.

INTRODUCTION

Public accountants offer numerous assurance services on information other than the standard historical cost financial statements. These services grow from consumer demand for association by an objective expert. Naturally, business, government and the public want the credibility that goes along with PAs' association. However, PAs need to be careful in their reports on such information that they will not suggest the addition of more credibility than is warranted. As you study the topics in this chapter, you will see the standards for PA association and the care with which reports are worded.

UNAUDITED FINANCIAL STATEMENTS

LEARNING OBJECTIVE

1 Prepare reports for review and compilation of unaudited financial statements, given specific facts.

Many PA firms conduct practice in accounting and review services for small-business clients. These engagements include bookkeeping, financial statement preparation and financial statement review to help small businesses prepare financial communications. Until the late 1970s, auditing standards concentrated on one level of assurance based on a full audit and appeared to deny small clients the full benefit of PAs' services.

The investigations by the Adams Committee in Canada and in the U.S. Congress during 1977–78 highlighted the problem by focusing attention on the idea that auditing standards handicapped the business of small public accounting firms and their services to small-business clients. The argument has become known as the "Big GAAS–Little GAAS" question. Big GAAS was portrayed as the villain in the play, with the proposition that existing standards were enacted under the influence of large PA firms whose practice is centred on big business. Even though this proposition is not true, the fact is that small PA firms want to give, and small businesses want to receive, some level of assurance as a result of accountants' work even though an audit in accordance with GAAS is not performed.

A separate part of the *CICA Handbook*, the 8000 sections, and International Standard on Review Engagements (ISRE) 2400 have been set aside to deal with review engagements. *CICA Handbook*, section 9200 and International Standard on Related Services (ISRS) 4410 deal with compilation engagements.

Review Services

The review services explained in this section apply specifically to accountants' work on unaudited financial statements. In a review services engagement, an accountant performs some procedures to achieve a moderate level of assurance. This level is not the same as that obtained by performing an audit in accordance with GAAS. According to *CICA Handbook,* paragraph 8100.05:

> Reviews are distinguishable from audits in that the scope of a review is less than that of an audit and therefore the level of assurance provided is lower. A review consists primarily of enquiry, analytical procedures and discussions related to information supplied to the public accountant by the enterprise with the limited objective of assessing whether the information is being reported on appropriate criteria. In this section, the word *plausible* is used in the sense of appearing to be worthy of belief based on the information obtained by the public account-ant in connection with the review.

Paragraph 8100.15 identifies standards applicable to a review engagement. They are stated as follows:

Standards Applicable to Review Engagements
General standard
The review should be performed and the review engagement report prepared by a per-son or persons having adequate technical training and proficiency in conducting reviews, with due care and with an objective state of mind.
Review standards
(*i*)   The work should be adequately planned and properly executed. If assistants are employed, they should be properly supervised.
(*ii*) The public accountant should possess or acquire sufficient knowledge of the busi-ness carried on by the enterprise so that intelligent enquiry and assessment of information obtained can be made.
(*iii*) The public accountant should perform a review with the limited objective of assess-ing whether the information being reported on is plausible in the circumstances within the framework of appropriate criteria. Such a review should consist of:
   (*a*) enquiry, analytical procedures and discussion; and
   (*b*) additional or more extensive procedures when the public accountant's knowl-edge of the business carried on by the enterprise and the results of the enquiry, and analytical procedures and discussion cause him or her to doubt the plausibility of such information.
Reporting standards
(*i*) The review engagement report should indicate the scope of the review. The nature of the review engagement should be made evident and be clearly distinguished from an audit.
(*ii*) The report should indicate, based on the review:
   (*a*) whether anything has come to the public accountant's attention that causes him or her to believe that the information being reported on is not, in all material respects, in accordance with appropriate criteria; or
   (*b*) that no assurance can be provided.
The report should provide an explanation of the nature of any reservations contained therein and, if readily determinable, the effect.

A similar set of standards is given in ISRE 2400.

These standards suggest that auditors need special training and experience in conducting reviews, especially with respect to working within a plausibility framework. As can be seen by the second review standard, obtaining knowledge of the business is a critical part of the review engagement. Such knowledge is critical to determining whether the information obtained during the course of the engagement is plausible. Sufficient knowledge of the busi-ness (and industry) is required to make intelligent enquiries and a reasonable assessment of responses and other information obtained. However, the knowledge of business required for review engagements is normally less detailed than that required in an audit.

The review standards indicate that review work on unaudited financial statements con-sists primarily of enquiry and analytical procedures. The information gained thereby is sim-ilar to audit evidence; but the recommended limitation on procedures (see following) does not suggest performance of typical auditing procedures of assessing control risk, conducting physical observation of tangible assets, sending confirmations or examining documentary details of transactions.

- Obtain knowledge of the client's business. Know the accounting principles of the client's industry. Understand the client's organization and operations.
- Enquire about the accounting system and bookkeeping procedures.
- Perform analytical procedures to identify relationships and individual items that appear to be unusual.
- Enquire about actions taken at meetings of shareholders, directors and other important executive committees.
- Read (study) the financial statements for indications that they conform with generally accepted accounting principles.
- Obtain reports from other accountants who audit or review significant components, subsidiaries or other investees.
- Enquire of officers and directors about the following: conformity with generally accepted accounting principles, consistent application of accounting principles, changes in the client's business or accounting practices, matters about which questions have arisen as a result of applying other procedures (listed above), events subsequent to the date of the financial statements.
- Perform any other procedures considered necessary if the financial statements appear to be incorrect, incomplete or otherwise unsatisfactory.
- Prepare working papers showing the matters covered by the enquiry and analytical review procedures, especially the resolution of unusual problems and questions.
- Obtain a written representation letter from the owner, manager or chief executive officer and from the chief financial officer.

Many firms will perform more detailed procedures such as bank reconciliations and bank confirmations to corroborate information obtained by enquiry. However, there is no requirement to perform such more detailed procedures under current review standards. Reviews have traditionally been supposed to provide negative assurance, or (in the words of the new assurance framework, to be discussed later in this chapter) a moderate level of assurance that indicates the financial information is "plausible" (paragraph 5025.12) or "moderate."[1] The reason the term negative assurance has been traditionally used is because of the "nothing has come to my attention . . ." wording that is used in the review report (see Exhibit 16–1).

A review service does not provide a basis for expressing an opinion on financial statements. Each page of the financial statements should be conspicuously marked as being unaudited. The standards indicate that a report on a review services engagement should include the following:

- statement on the scope of the review engagement and that a review service was performed in accordance with generally accepted standards for review engagement
- statement that a review consists primarily of enquiries of company personnel and analytical procedures applied to financial data
- statement that a review service does not constitute an audit, and that an opinion on financial statements is not expressed (This is a disclaimer of any audit opinion.)
- statement that the accountant is not aware of any material modifications that should be made; or, if aware, a disclosure of departure(s) from generally accepted accounting principles (This is a negative assurance.)

When other independent accountants are involved in audit or review of parts of the business, the principal reviewer cannot divide responsibility by referring to the other accountants in the review report, unless the disclosure helps explain the reason for a reservation. You can follow the spirit of the auditing standards to write the form and content of the reference to the work and reports of other auditors.[2] An example of a review report is given in Exhibit 16–1.

---

[1] *CICA Handbook*, paragraph 5025.12 or ISRE 2400.9.
[2] *CICA Handbook*, paragraphs 6930.22–23.

EXHIBIT   16-1   PUBLIC ACCOUNTANT'S REPORT

To (person engaging the public accountant)

I have reviewed the balance sheet of Client Limited as at ...., 20... and the statements of income, retained earnings and changes in cash flow for the year then ended. My review was made in accordance with Canadian generally accepted standards for review engagements and accordingly consisted primarily of enquiry, analytical procedures and discussion related to information supplied to me by the company.

A review does not constitute an audit and consequently I do not express an audit opinion on these financial statements.

Based on my review, nothing has come to my attention that causes me to believe that these financial statements are not, in all material respects, in accordance with Canadian generally accepted accounting principles.

City

Date

(signed) . . . .

CHARTERED ACCOUNTANT

Source: *CICA Handbook,* paragraph 8200.42.

Compilation Services

Compilation is a synonym for an older term—write-up work. Both terms refer to an accountant helping a client "write up" the financial information in the form of financial statements. A compilation service is accounting work in which an accountant performs few, if any, procedures, and it is substantially less than a review service. The description of a compilation of financial statements, according to *Handbook,* paragraph 9200.03 is

> one in which a public accountant receives information from a client and arranges it into the form of a financial statements. The public accountant is concerned that the assembly of information is arithmetically correct, however the public accountant does not attempt to verify the accuracy or completeness of the information provided. Unlike an audit or review engagement in which the public accountant does sufficient work to issue a communication that provides assurance regarding the financial statements, no expression of assurance is contemplated in a compilation engagement.

A similar description is given in ISRS 4410.3.

Since no assurance credibility is provided by compilation engagements, the public accountant is limited in what action she or he can take. However, the public accountant also has a responsibility to not be associated with misleading information.

> When the public accountant is aware that there are matters which the public accountant believes would cause the financial statements to be false or misleading, she or he should request additional or revised information in order to complete the statements. If the client does not provide the information requested or agree with the statements, the public accountant should not release the statements and should withdraw from the engagement.[3]

Financial statements may be compiled on a basis other than GAAP if in the auditor's judgment this other basis is appropriate for the circumstances of the engagement. This appropriate non-GAAP basis is referred to as **another appropriate disclosed basis of accounting** or **AADBA** in the literature. The best way to disclose AADBA statement is through the statement's title (e.g., "Statements Based on Income Tax Accounting") or in a note discussing the statements. The reasons for the compilation are also best achieved through notes to the statements or via the title.

In a compilation service, an accountant should understand the client's business, read (study) the financial statements looking for obvious clerical or accounting principle errors, and follow up on information that is incorrect, incomplete or otherwise unsatisfactory. Each page of the financial statements should be marked **unaudited—see Notice to Reader.** The report can be issued by an accountant who is not independent, provided the lack of

---

[3] *CICA Handbook,* paragraph 9200.18, also see ISRS 4410.14.

EXHIBIT 16–2   NOTICE TO READER

I have compiled the balance sheet of Client Limited as at December 31, 20X1, and the statements of income, retained earnings and cash flows for the (period) then ended from information provided by management (the proprietor). I have not audited, reviewed or otherwise attempted to verify the accuracy or completeness of such information. Readers are cautioned that these statements may not be appropriate for their purposes.

I am not independent with respect to Client Limited.

City   (printed or signed) . . . .

Date   CHARTERED ACCOUNTANT

Source: *CICA Handbook*, paragraph 9200.24.

independence is disclosed, as required by some professional bodies such as the ICAO, which requires disclosure in the Notice to Reader (see Exhibit 16–2). The report should contain the following (see Exhibit 16–2):

- statement that the public accountant compiled the statement from information provided by management (or proprietor)
- statement that the public accountant has not audited, reviewed or otherwise attempted to verify the accuracy or completeness of such information
- caution to readers that the statement may not be appropriate for their purposes
- no expression of any form of opinion or negative assurance

Exhibit 16–2 illustrates that two kinds of reports on compiled financial statements can be given: (1) a report stating that the accountant is not independent (as in Exhibit 16–2); or (2) a report by an independent public accountant on financial statements prepared using an appropriate basis of accounting such as GAAP. In the second case, the basis of accounting may be an "appropriate disclosed basis of accounting other than GAAP," just like other kinds of accounting services, and reports can cover financial statements presented on such other bases of accounting. (Other appropriate bases of accounting are discussed later in this chapter.)

Although compilation engagements do not provide any attest assurance or credibility, they can be viewed as providing accounting credibility. A public accountant's compilation of the statements as opposed to a nonprofessional's must add some kind of credibility, otherwise there would be no reason to pay the extra cost of a PA to do the compilation.

Note that the Notice to Reader is not a proper place to make non-GAAP AADBA disclosures because the Notice to Reader does not mention GAAP or any other basis of accounting.

Exhibit 16–3 summarizes the major differences between audit, review and compilation engagements.

EXHIBIT 16–3   AUDIT VERSUS MAJOR NONAUDIT ENGAGEMENTS SUMMARY

Compilation	Review	Audit
Prepared for internal use of restricted users	Plausibility, consistency	Conformity with GAAP, GAAS
IC not evaluated	IC not evaluated	Evaluate IC
No independent corroborating evidence	Some evidence	Independent corroborating evidence
Compilation, bookkeeping	Enquiry-based review, discussions, reasonableness	Substantive and compliance testing
Accounting credibility	Negative assurance	Positive assurance, audit credibility
Notice to reader	Public accountant's report or review engagement report	Auditor's report
IC = Internal control		

OTHER REVIEW AND COMPILATION TOPICS

There are several other aspects of review and compilation engagements and reports that differ from audit standards. The following topics point out some of the different problems in dealing with unaudited financial statements.

Prescribed Forms

Industry trade associations, banks, government agencies and regulatory agencies often use prescribed forms (standard reprinted documents) to specify the content and measurement of accounting information required for special purposes. Such forms may not request disclosures required by GAAP or may specify measurements that do not conform to GAAP.

When such forms are compiled (not when reviewed) by an accountant, the compilation report does not need to call attention to the GAAP departures or to GAAP disclosure deficiencies.

There's nothing in either section 9200 or in the Guideline, "Compilation Engagements—Financial Statement Disclosures,"[4] requiring public accountants to disclose known departures from GAAP in either the compiled statements or the Notice to Reader. Moreover, in the latter the accountant specifically states that no attempt has been made to determine whether the statements contain GAAP departures. The reason for this is that disclosure of known departures could be confusing or even misleading. If such disclosures were required, readers might assume the accountant is responsible for disclosing *all* GAAP departures in the statements and that the only departures are the disclosed departures. Such a responsibility is beyond the scope of a compilation engagement.

How then does the auditor deal with situations of known departures from GAAP or other AADBA? Well, for one thing the Notice to Reader contains a caution to readers that the financial statements may not be appropriate for their purposes. For another, compiled statements may not be appropriate for general purposes and, hence, are restricted in their use depending on the purpose of the engagement. For example, compiled statements are frequently prepared for management, and they are aware of the limitations. Moreover, "when the accountant is aware that the statements may be misleading for some users or purposes, then the public accountant may need to include appropriate disclosures (in the statements, themselves, not the Notice to Reader) to prevent them from being misleading. Of course, if management will not allow the disclosures considered necessary, he or she has clearly no alternative but to withhold the statements and withdraw from the engagement."[5] Despite this responsibility, keep in mind that with the limited amount of work involved in compilations there is no assurance that the PA can determine whether the financial statements achieve the specified intended purpose.

Personal Financial Plans

Personal financial planning has become a big source of business for PA firms. Most personal financial plan documentation includes personal financial statements. Ordinarily, an accountant associated with such statements would need to give the standard compilation report (disclaimer), which seems rather awkward in a personal financial planning engagement when the client is the only one using the statements. In Canada a PA who wishes to meet the requirements as a certified financial planner under the Financial Planning Standards Council of Canada must satisfy that body's Rules of Conduct in disclosing any potential conflicts of interest to his or her clients. Although there is no distinction for compilation of personal financial information in Canada, U.S. standards exempt such personal financial statements from the reporting requirement. However, the following report must be given, with each page of the financial report marked "See accountant's report":

---

[4] AUG–5.
[5] R.J. Johnston, *CA Magazine*, May 1988, p. 53.

The accompanying Statement of Financial Condition of Edward Beliveau, as of December 31, 2002, was prepared solely to help you develop your personal financial plan. Accordingly, it may be incomplete or contain other departures from generally accepted accounting principles and should not be used to obtain credit or for any purposes other than developing your financial plan. We have not audited, reviewed, or compiled the statements.

A Note on GAAP Departures and Review Engagement Reports

An accountants' report of known GAAP departures must be treated carefully in review reports.

As in audit reports, the accountant can and should add an explanatory paragraph pointing out known departures from GAAP, including omitted disclosures. The knowledge of GAAP departures means that the accountant must make exception to the departure in the negative assurance sentence, like this: "Except for the failure, as described in the preceding paragraph, to (describe the departure), based on my review nothing has come to my attention . . ."

A separate paragraph describing the departure in more detail would be inserted as the next to last paragraph in the Review Engagement Report. See Exhibit 16–4 for the complete report.

The range of review reports possible is similar to that for audit reports, and they arise for similar reasons. Exhibit 16–5 illustrates an adverse report resulting from a GAAP departure, and Exhibit 16–6 illustrates a denial of assurance report as a result of a newer scope limitation.

REVIEW CHECKPOINTS

16.1   Explain what led to the creation of Review and Compilation Standards.

16.2   What considerations should a successor accountant make in accepting a new engagement?

16.3   How should a public accountant disclose misleading statements detected during a compilation engagement?

16.4   What is the difference between a review services engagement and a compilation service engagement regarding historical financial statements? Compare both of these to an audit engagement.

EXHIBIT   16-4   QUALIFICATION RESULTING FROM A DEPARTURE FROM GENERALLY ACCEPTED ACCOUNTING PRINCIPLES WHEN THE EFFECTS ARE NOT READILY DETERMINABLE

REVIEW ENGAGEMENT REPORT

To (person engaging the public accountant)

I have reviewed the balance sheet of Client Limited as at ......, 20... and the statements of income, retained earnings and cash flows for the year then ended. My review was made in accordance with Canadian generally accepted standards for review engagements and accordingly consisted primarily of enquiry, analytical procedures and discussion related to information supplied to me by the company.

A review does not constitute an audit and consequently I do not express an audit opinion on these financial statements.

Note .... indicates that the investments in companies subject to significant influence have not been accounted for on the equity basis. The effects of this departure from generally accepted accounting principles on the unaudited financial statements have not been determined.

Except for the failure, as described in the preceding paragraph, to account for the investments on an equity basis, based on my review, nothing has come to my attention that causes me to believe that these financial statements are not, in all material respects, in accordance with Canadian generally accepted accounting principles

City

Date

(signed) . . . .

CHARTERED ACCOUNTANT

Source: *CICA Handbook*, section 8200, Appendix B, Example C.

EXHIBIT   16–5   ADVERSE REPORT RESULTING FROM A DEPARTURE FROM GENERALLY ACCEPTED ACCOUNTING PRINCIPLES

REVIEW ENGAGEMENT REPORT

To (person engaging the public accountant)

I have reviewed the balance sheet of Client Limited as at ......, 20... and the statements of income, retained earnings and cash flows for the year then ended. My review was made in accordance with Canadian generally accepted standards for review engagements and accordingly consisted primarily of enquiry, analytical procedures and discussion related to information supplied to me by the company.

A review does not constitute an audit and consequently I do not express an audit opinion on these financial statements.

Note .... indicates that commencing this year the company ceased to consolidate the financial statements of its subsidiary companies because management considers consolidation to be inappropriate when there are substantial non-controlling interests. Under Canadian generally accepted accounting principles, the existence of such noncontrolling interests is not an acceptable reason for not consolidating the financial statements of subsidiary companies with those of the reporting enterprise. Had consolidated financial statements been prepared, virtually every account in, and the information provided by way of notes to, the accompanying financial statements would have been materially different. The effects of this departure from generally accepted accounting principles on the accompanying financial statements have not been determined.

My review indicates that, because the investment in subsidiary companies is not accounted for on a consolidated basis, as described in the preceding paragraph, these financial statements are not in accordance with Canadian generally accepted accounting principles.

City

Date

(signed) ....

CHARTERED ACCOUNTANT

Source: *CICA Handbook*, section 8200, Appendix B, Example D.

EXHIBIT   16–6   DENIAL OF ASSURANCE

REVIEW ENGAGEMENT REPORT

To (person engaging the public accountant)

I have reviewed the balance sheet of Client Limited as at ......, 20... and the statements of income, retained earnings and cash flows for the year then ended. My review was made in accordance with Canadian generally accepted standards for review engagements and accordingly consisted primarily of enquiry, analytical procedures and discussion related to information supplied to me by the company, except as explained below.

A review does not constitute an audit and consequently I do not express an audit opinion on these financial statements.

My review indicated serious deficiencies in the accounting records of the company. As a consequence, I was unable to complete my review. Had I been able to complete my review, I might have determined adjustments to be necessary to these financial statements.

Because of my inability to complete a review, as described in the preceding paragraph, I am unable to express any assurance as to whether these financial statements are, in all material respects, in accordance with Canadian generally accepted accounting principles.

City

Date

(signed) ....

CHARTERED ACCOUNTANT

Source: *CICA Handbook*, section 8200, Appendix B, Example F.

INTERIM FINANCIAL INFORMATION

LEARNING OBJECTIVE
2 Write a report on a review of interim financial information.

Accounting principles do not require interim financial information as a basic and necessary element of financial statements conforming to GAAP. When interim information is presented, however, it should conform to the accounting Recommendation in the *CICA Handbook*.[6] Examples of situations where audited interim financial statements might be prepared are buy/sell situations for a business, or to fulfill financial reports required by

[6] *CICA Handbook*, section 1751.

regulatory authorities, particularly those Canadian companies whose securities are traded in U.S. capital markets and therefore must comply with SEC requirements. On occasion, regulators such as the SEC may insist that the interim financial information be audited, but at the present time interim statements are not normally audited.

A common type of review engagement is the review of interim financial statements or information.

A review of interim financial information differs considerably from an audit. According to section 7050, a key objective of a review of interim financial statements is to assess whether accounting principles have been applied on a basis consistent with the annual report as well as to the corresponding interim financial statements of the previous year. In particular the auditor is concerned that interim financial statements are not misleading relative to the annualized report. The interim review requires neither a complete assessment of internal control risk each quarter nor the gathering of sufficient, appropriate evidential matter on which to base an opinion on interim financial statements. The nature, timing and extent of review procedures explained below presume that the reviewer has a knowledge base of the company from the audit of the most recent annual financial statements. Note that the presumption of an existing audit knowledge base from the annual audit means there can be significantly more information guiding the review of interim statements than for a review without such a knowledge base. For this reason some observers feel that a review with an audit knowledge base provides more assurance than a review without an audit knowledge base. One significant difference, for example, is that the public accountant has more familiarity with the system of internal controls when there is an existing audit knowledge base.

Nature of Review Procedures

Review procedures consist mainly of enquiry and analytical procedures. Paragraph 8200.23 and ISRE 2400.20 suggest checklists that includes the following:

- Enquire about the accounting system.
- Obtain an understanding of the system. Determine whether there have been any significant changes in the system used to produce interim information.
- Perform analytical procedures to identify relationships and individual items that appear to be unusual.
- Read the minutes of shareholder, board of director and board committee meetings to identify actions or events that may affect interim financial information.
- Read (study) the interim financial information and determine whether it conforms with generally accepted accounting principles.
- Obtain reports from other accountants who perform limited reviews of significant components, subsidiaries or other investees.
- Enquire of officers and executives about the following: conformity with generally accepted accounting principles, consistent application of accounting principles, changes in the client's business or accounting practices, matters about which questions have arisen as a result of applying other procedures (listed above), events subsequent to the date of the interim information.
- Obtain written representations from management about interim information matters.

Timing of Review Procedures

Review procedures should be performed at or near the date of the interim information. Starting the engagement prior to the cutoff date will give auditors a chance to deal with problems and questions without undue deadline pressures.

Extent of Review Procedures

The accountant needs to acquire a sufficient knowledge of the client's business, just as if the engagement were a regular audit. Knowledge of strengths and deficiencies in the internal control system and of problem accounting areas obtained during the most recent audit is very useful in judging the extent of review procedures. Basically, the extent of review procedures depends on the accountant's professional judgement about problem areas in the system of internal control, the severity of unique accounting principles problems and the errors that have occurred in the past. With knowledge of these areas, the accountant can direct and fine-tune the review procedures in the interest of improving the quality of the interim information.

Reporting on a Review of Interim Information

An accountant may report on interim information presented separately from audited financial statements, provided that a review has been satisfactorily completed. The basic content of the report is as follows:[7]

- a statement that a review was made in accordance with standards established for review engagements
- an identification of the interim information reviewed
- a description of the review procedures
- a statement that a review is not an audit
- a denial of opinion on the interim information
- negative assurance about material conformity with the disclosed basis of accounting
- each page should be marked "unaudited"

An example report on reviewed interim information presented in a quarterly report (not within an annual report) is shown in Exhibit 16–7.

When the interim information is presented in a note to audited annual financial statements as supplemental information and when it is presented voluntarily under GAAP and the client has requested a review, the auditors give the standard audit report without mentioning the reviewed interim information, unless there is a reason to take exception. Under this exception basis of reporting, interim information is mentioned in a modified standard audit report only if it departs from section 1750 principles, or if management indicates the auditor performed procedures without also saying the auditor expresses no opinion or if management fails to label interim information in the note to annual audited financial statements as "unaudited."

EXHIBIT   16–7   REPORT ON INTERIM INFORMATION IN A COMPANY'S QUARTERLY REPORT (SECTION 7050.61)

The Shareholders, XYZ Inc.:

At the request of the Board of Directors and Stockholders, we have made a review of the unaudited condensed balance sheets of Analog Devices, Inc., at April 28, 20X6, and April 29, 20X5, the related unaudited consolidated statements of income for the three- and six-month periods ended April 28, 20X5, and April 29, 20X5, and the unaudited consolidated statements of cash flows for the six-month periods ending April 28, 20X6, and April 29, 20X5, in accordance with standards established by the CICA.

A review of interim financial information consists principally of obtaining an understanding of the system for the preparation of the interim financial information, applying analytical review procedures to financial data and making inquiries to persons responsible for financial and accounting matters. It is substantially less in scope than an examination in accordance with generally accepted auditing standards, the objective of which is the expression of an opinion regarding the financial statements taken as a whole. Accordingly, we do not express such an opinion.

Based on our review, nothing has come to our attention that causes us to believe that the accompanying financial statements are not in all material respects in accordance with generally accepted accounting principles.

Public Accountants
Montreal, Quebec
May 16, 20X6

---

[7] Ibid., paragraph 8200.04.

Additional Interim Information Communication

During the difficult economic times of the 1980s, especially in financial institutions, auditors were criticized in the United States for taking no action when they became aware of material problems with interim financial information. The auditors responded that they were not required to take any action because they were not engaged to perform an interim review and issue a report.

Several regulatory agencies were distressed that some companies issued misleading interim information—sometimes their auditors knew about it—but nothing was done to inform the public or the regulators. Suggestions were conveyed to the AICPA Auditing Standards Board, and it responded with SAS 100, "Communication of Matters about Interim Financial Information Filed or to Be Filed with Specified Regulatory Agencies—An Amendment to SAS No. 36, Review of Interim Financial Information."

This AICPA standard requires that auditors do something when they learn that interim information filed or to be filed with certain specified agencies is probably materially misstated as a result of a departure from GAAP. The required action is to (*a*) discuss the matter with management as soon as possible, (*b*) inform the company's audit committee if management does not take appropriate and timely action, and (*c*) if the audit committee does not respond appropriately, decide whether to resign from the interim review engagement or resign as the company's auditor. However, auditing standards do not require resignation or direct communication to the "specified agencies." The auditing standard appears to be a compromise between regulators who probably wanted direct reporting and auditors who wanted to handle difficult problems within the affected companies. Again, this requirement only affects Canadian companies falling within the jurisdiction of the SEC.

REVIEW CHECKPOINTS

16.5   Must interim financial information required to be presented for annual financial statements be in conformity with GAAP?

16.6   In what respects is a review of the interim financial information similar to a review of the unaudited annual financial statements of a nonpublic company?

16.7   When interim information is presented in a note to annual financial statements, under what circumstances would an audit report on the annual financial statements be modified with respect to the interim financial information?

SPECIAL REPORTS AND AADBA

LEARNING OBJECTIVE

3 Give examples of another appropriate disclosed basis of accounting (AADBA), distinguishing them from GAAP.

For a long time, a small war has been waged over the Big GAAP–Little GAAP controversy. Many accountants have been dismayed by the complexity of generally accepted accounting principles and have openly questioned their relevance to small businesses with uncomplicated operations. They believe that business managers and users of the financial statements care little about accounting for such things as pension obligations, capitalized leases, deferred taxes and similar complicated topics. They characterize such topics as "standards overload" that may be necessary for big business but are largely superfluous for small business.

For a while, the little GAAP advocates lobbied for formal GAAP exemptions for small businesses. However, resistance was encountered in the counterargument that there was a danger of creating second-class GAAP for small business while reserving real GAAP for big companies. Bankers and other users of financial statements were not nearly as eager to have little GAAP financial statements as some accountants wanted them to be. Anyway, many small businesses aspire to be large businesses, and their managers may not want to be stigmatized by little GAAP beginnings. Another reason to distinguish different bases of accounting is that in some industries, notably banks and other financial institutions, there is no GAAP for the industry other than that specified by regulation. For example, in April 1989 in response to the November 1988 CICA Exposure Draft "Banks," the Superintendent of Financial Institutions stated that "until a great deal more work is done my office will not accept the inclusion of banks within the scope of the *CICA Handbook.*"[8]

In addition, there may be legislative reporting requirements that differ from the *CICA Handbook;* for example, public sector reporting requirements to Parliament may deviate from those reflected in generally accepted public sector accounting principles. Also, some users of financial statements—limited groups of specified users—may have special information needs that necessitate reports deviating from GAAP: for example, financial statements in conformity with contractual requirements or buy/sell agreements. For all of these reasons, reports may be prepared on a basis other than GAAP using another appropriate basis of accounting (AADBA).

The authoritative literature on AADBA is seen in section 5600 of the *CICA Handbook.* In addition, section 1300 allows differential reporting options for nonpublic (usually smaller) companies as long as the reporting options used are appropriately disclosed and there in unanimous consent by the owners. Section 1100 allows considerable flexibility in measurement and disclosure requirements.

Studies in the United States have shown that AADBA financial statements can be less expensive to produce and easier to interpret than full GAAP statements. Surveys report that 50 percent of AADBA financial statements for small businesses are on the "tax basis of accounting," and 49 percent are on the "cash basis." However, these studies also show that AADBA is only appropriate when it meets user needs.

Another Appropriate Disclosed Basis of Accounting

Companies that are not subject to securities regulations and filing requirements can choose to present financial information in accordance with a comprehensive basis of accounting other than GAAP. A comprehensive basis in this context refers to a coherent accounting treatment in which substantially all the important financial measurements are governed by criteria other than GAAP. Examples include (1) treatment applied by financial institutions to statements conforming to the accounting rules of the Office of the Superintendent of Financial Institutions (OFSI) that are not in accordance with GAAP as discussed in AUG–40, para 8, (2) tax basis accounting, (3) cash basis accounting, and (4) some other fairly well-defined methods, such as constant-dollar, price-level-adjusted financial statements.

AADBA financial statements should not use the titles normally associated with GAAP statements, such as "balance sheet," "statement of financial position," "statement of operations," "income statement," and "statement of cash flows."[9] Even the titles are said to suggest GAAP financial statements. Instead, AADBA statements should use titles like the ones shown in the following box.

AADBA statements can be audited, reviewed or compiled like any other financial statements. All the general and field work auditing standards and the standards for review and compilation apply, just as they apply for GAAP financial statements. The reporting standards regarding consistency, adequate disclosure and report responsibility (fourth reporting standard) also apply to AADBA statements. Disclosure requirements are not reduced by AADBA. However, the first reporting standard, which requires the audit report statement on whether the financial statements are presented in conformity with GAAP, is handled differently.

---

[8] *Audit of the Allowance for Credit Losses*, CICA, 1993, p. 3.
[9] The only exception would be if AADBA were the only available alternatives, such as with the banking industry in Canada. See "GAAP vs. AADBA" by D. Cockburn, *CA Magazine*, January 1992, pp. 35–37.

SOME NON-GAAP FINANCIAL STATEMENT TITLES USED IN PRACTICE

Statement of Assets and Liabilities—Regulatory Basis

Statement of Assets and Liabilities—Cash Basis

Statement of Admitted Assets, Liabilities and Surplus—Statutory Basis Required by the Insurance Superintendent of the Province

Statement of Assets, Liabilities and Capital—Income Tax Basis

Statement of Income—Regulatory Basis

Statement of Revenue and Expenses—Income Tax Basis

Statement of Revenue Collected and Expenses Paid—Cash Basis

Statement of Changes in Partners' Capital Accounts—Income Tax Basis

When a non-GAAP accounting method is used, the first reporting standard is satisfied by a sentence in the report that presents the AADBA basis of accounting; and the opinion sentence refers to the AADBA instead of to GAAP. Disclosures in the financial statements should (1) contain an explanation of the AADBA, and (2) describe in general how the AADBA differs from GAAP, but (3) the differences do not have to be quantified—that is, the AADBA does not need to be reconciled to GAAP with dollar amounts. For all practical purposes, the GAAP criteria are replaced by criteria applicable to the AADBA.[10] An example of a special report on cash basis statements is in Exhibit 16–8.

EXHIBIT 16-8   SPECIAL REPORT ON NON-GAAP COMPREHENSIVE BASIS

Independent Auditors' Report

To Trust North Bank Association (Trustee)
and the Unit Holders of the Mega Offshore Trust:

We have audited the accompanying statements of assets, liabilities, and trust corpus—cash basis, of the Mega Offshore Trust as of December 31, 20X2 and 20X1, and the related statements of changes in trust corpus—cash basis, for each of the three years in the period ended December 31, 20X2. These financial statements are the responsibility of the Company's management. Our responsibility is to express an opinion on these financial statements based on our audits.

(Standard scope paragraph here)

As described in Note 2, these financial statements were prepared on the cash receipts and disbursements basis of accounting, which is a comprehensive basis of accounting other than generally accepted accounting principles.

In our opinion, the financial statements referred to above present fairly, in all material respects, the assets, liabilities and trust corpus arising from cash transactions of the Mega Offshore Trust as of December 31, 20X2 and 20X1, and the related changes in trust corpus arising from cash transactions for each of the three years in the period ended December 31, 20X2, on the basis of accounting described in Note 2.

/s/ Auditor signature
March 18, 20X3

Note 2 describes a cash basis of accounting and concludes:

This basis for reporting royalty income is considered to be the most meaningful because distributions to the Unit holders for a month are based on net cash receipts for such month. However, it will differ from the basis used for financial statements prepared in accordance with generally accepted accounting principles because, under such accounting principles, royalty income for a month would be based on net proceeds for such month without regard to when calculated or received.

---

[10] *CICA Handbook*, paragraph 5600.17.

GAAP, Other Than Historical Cost

You should be aware that GAAP sometimes is not historical cost. The prime examples are market value accounting for the assets in defined benefit pension plans, investment companies (e.g., venture capital companies, small business investment companies, mutual funds), and personal financial statements (e.g., individual or family). In these cases current value accounting is GAAP. The audit report on such financial statements gives an opinion that they are "in conformity with generally accepted accounting principles." No mention is made of an AADBA, because the current value accounting is GAAP and not an AADBA. Indeed, if such financial statements are prepared using the normal historical cost accounting, they contain departures from GAAP, and a qualified audit opinion would be given.

Another informally recognized basis of accounting that has no formal body of rules is "liquidation basis accounting." Some mention is made of this basis in the literature, but you will not find much official guidance. In fact there is some controversy as to whether the liquidation basis of accounting is GAAP or AADBA when the going concern assumption is no longer appropriate. One of the authors found that there is a split opinion on this within the CICA (as of December 1999). Nevertheless, auditors sometimes give reports on liquidation basis financial statements without referring to them as an AADBA. An excerpt is in the box following. (Be aware, however, that this type of opinion is not illustrated in any standard. It was invented in practice.)

OPINION PARAGRAPH ON LIQUIDATION BASIS STATEMENTS

In our opinion, the financial statements referred to above present fairly, in all material respects, the financial position of Canada Liquidating Corporation at December 31, 20X2, and the excess of revenues over costs and expenses and its cash flows for the year then ended, in conformity with generally accepted accounting principles for a company in liquidation.

REVIEW CHECKPOINTS

16.8 Why does AADBA exist? Can AADBA financial statements be audited?

16.9 Why do you think standard setters have not created little GAAP by exempting small businesses from compliance with many complicated accounting standards?

16.10 What should auditors do about the fourth reporting standard when financial statements are presented on a comprehensive basis of accounting other than GAAP?

Current Value Financial Statements

LEARNING OBJECTIVE
4 Contrast an audit report on supplementary current value financial statements with a standard report on historical cost financial statements.

Accounting theorists have long favoured various measurements in current value accounting, including discounted present value of cash flows, entry values (replacement cost, current cost), and exit values (disposal value, current cash equivalent) for all types of companies and industries. Measurement by anything other than historical cost received little notice from the practising profession until the mid-1970s, when five things happened: (1) inflation accelerated in Canada and worldwide; (2) critics voiced loud discontent with historical-cost measurement; (3) British, Australian, Dutch and other accountants started promoting accounting measurement alternatives; (4) the SEC issued Accounting Series Release No. 190 requiring disclosure of certain replacement cost information; and (5) the CICA moved into the phase of considering new measurement bases, including some kinds of current value accounting, which culminated in the *CICA Handbook,* section 4510 recommending the presentation of supplementary information on both a current cost and price level adjusted basis. (This section was dropped in the early 1990s.)

Interest on the part of accountants in current value and inflation-adjusted financial statements virtually disappeared with the decline in the inflation rate after 1985. However, as the number of failures among banks and trust companies, brokerages and financial services companies surged after 1984, regulators began to beat the drum for "mark to market" (current value) accounting for loans and securities held by financial institutions. In 1992 the FASB made some rules requiring disclosure of market values for financial institution assets. Many regulators also require disclosure of current market values on a supplemental basis.

In the past the real estate and the hotel/motel industries have been particularly interested in reporting the current value of real estate assets. One of the earliest disclosures of current asset values was by the Rouse Company, owners of several major mall developments. Excerpts from the balance sheet and the audit report are shown in Exhibit 16–9. You can see that the audit report contains an unqualified opinion on the historical cost financial statements. It also contains an explanatory paragraph, complete with cautions about the realization of the current values, and a special report opinion on the current value information.

Auditors can accept engagements to audit and report on current value financial statements as long as (1) the company's measurement and disclosure criteria are reasonable and (2) the measurements and disclosures are reasonably reliable. However, auditing standards do not acknowledge general current financial statements to be a stand-alone AADBA. They regard the current value information as supplementary to the GAAP financial statements. (In this regard general current-value financial statements are different from current value as GAAP for defined benefit plans, investment companies and personal financial statements, and also different from a stand-alone AADBA, such as cash-basis accounting.)

Audits of Public Sector and Not–for-Profit Financial Statements

Most public sector and not-for-profit organizations have their own accounting standards that need to be followed. There are the public sector accounting standards of the CICA and *CICA Handbook,* sections 4400–4460 for not-for-profit organizations. The *CICA Handbook* considers that fair presentation follows from its recommendations for the specified organizations. However, some public sector organizations are required under legislation to use other accounting policies. If the auditor feels such requirements are misleading and in conflict with the *CICA Handbook* recommendations, then the auditor is required to issue an opinion reservation. Under PS 5200.04 the auditor must issue an opinion on fairness of presentation in accordance with GAAP or disclosed basis of accounting "appropriate to public sector or not-for-profit organizations."

R E V I E W
CHECKPOINTS

16.11   What are some examples of AADBA and of entities for which current value is GAAP? of current value financial statements that are supplementary to historical financial statements?

16.12   Insofar as the opinion paragraph in an audit report is concerned, what difference does the client's use of an AADBA make? What difference if the client is one for whom current value is GAAP? What difference if a real estate or manufacturing company presents supplementary current value information?

EXHIBIT   16-9   REPORT ON CURRENT VALUE FINANCIAL STATEMENTS

THE ROUSE COMPANY AND SUBSIDIARIES
Consolidated Cost Basis and Current Value Basis Balance Sheets
December 31, 1991 and 1990
(in thousands)

	1991		1990	
	Current Value Basis (note 1)	Cost Basis	Current Value Basis (note 1)	Cost Basis
Assets				
Property (notes 4, 5, 8 and 14):				
Operating properties:				
Current value	$3,638,801		$3,825,882	
Property and deferred costs of projects			$2,482,292	$2,424,003
Less accumulated depreciation and amortization		331,312		287,365
	3,638,801	2,150,980	3,825,882	2,136,638
Development operations:				
Construction and development in progress	59,513	54,290	56,186	49,890
Pre-construction costs, net	14,734	14,734	17,196	17,196
	74,247	69,024	73,382	67,086
Property held for development and sale	192,195	158,472	166,616	125,387
Other property, net (note 14)	18,878	9,004	20,234	9,727
Other assets	87,843	87,843	78,338	78,338
Accounts and notes receivable (note 6)	75,547	75,547	85,153	85,153
Investments in marketable securities . . .	27,505	27,505	41,758	41,578
Cash and cash equivalents	59,077	59,077	70,790	70,790
Total	$4,174,093	$2,637,452	$4,362,153	$2,614,877

Independent Auditors' Report

The Board of Directors and Shareholders,
The Rouse Company:

We have audited the accompanying consolidated cost basis balance sheets of The Rouse Company and subsidiaries as of December 31, 1991 and 1990, and the related consolidated cost basis statements of operations, common stock, and other shareholders' equity and cash flows for each of the years in the three-year period ended December 31, 1991. We have also audited the supplemental consolidated current value basis balance sheets of The Rouse Company and subsidiaries as of December 31, 1991 and 1990, and the related supplemental consolidated current value basis statements of changes in revaluation equity for each of the years in the three-year period ended December 31, 1991. These financial statements are the responsibility of the Company's management. Our responsibility is to express an opinion on these financial statements based on our audits.

We conducted our audits in accordance with generally accepted auditing standards. Those standards require that we plan and perform the audit to obtain reasonable assurance about whether the financial statements are free of material misstatement. An audit includes examining, on a test basis, evidence supporting the amounts and disclosures in the financial statements. An audit also includes assessing the accounting principles used and significant estimates made by management, as well as evaluating the overall financial statement presentation. We believe that our audits provide a reasonable basis for our opinion.

In our opinion, the aforementioned consolidated cost basis financial statements present fairly, in all material respects, the financial position of The Rouse Company and subsidiaries at December 3, 1991 and 1990, and the results of their operations and their cash flows for each of the years in the three-year period ended December 31, 1991, in conformity with generally accepted accounting principles.

As more fully described in note 1 to the consolidated financial statements, the supplemental consolidated current value basis financial statements referred to above have been prepared by management to present relevant financial information about The Rouse Company and its subsidiaries which is not provided by the cost basis financial statements and are not intended to be a presentation in conformity with generally accepted accounting principles. In addition, as more fully described in note 1, the supplemental consolidated current value basis financial statements do not purport to present the net realizable, liquidation or market value of the Company as a whole. Furthermore, amounts ultimately realized by the Company from the disposal of properties may vary from the current values presented.

In our opinion, the aforementioned supplemental consolidated current value basis financial statements present fairly, in all material respects, the information set forth therein on the basis of accounting described in note 1 to the consolidated financial statements.

KPMG Peat Marwick
February 19, 1992

Source: KPMG Peat Marwick, 1992.

Special Reports—Additional Topics

Auditors may perform a variety of services acting in the capacity of auditor (not as tax adviser or management consultant) that require a report, other than the standard unqualified audit report. Such services involve special reports issued in connection with:

- engagements to report on specified elements, accounts or items of a financial statement[11]
- engagements to report on compliance with contractual agreements or regulatory requirements[12]
- limited-scope engagements to perform procedures agreed on by the client[13]

Specified Elements, Accounts or Items

Auditors may be requested to render special reports on such things as rentals, royalties, profit participations or a provision for income taxes. The fourth CICA reporting standard does not apply because the specified element, account or item does not purport to be a financial statement of financial position or results of operations. The consistency disclosure via footnotes should be made in all cases.

Special engagements with limited objectives enable auditors to provide needed services to clients. Section 5805 gives the standards for these engagements. Examples include grant application data, reports relating to amount of sales used in computing rental, reports relating to royalties, reports on a profit participation and a report on the adequacy of a tax provision in financial statements. Exhibit 16–10 contains an illustrative report on a company's accounts receivable.

Compliance with Contractual Agreements or Regulatory Requirements

Clients may have restrictive covenants in loan agreements. Lenders may require a periodic report on whether the client has complied with such contractual agreements. Following a scope paragraph referring to the report on the audited financial statements, the auditor may give a negative assurance of the following type:

> In connection with our audit, nothing came to our attention that caused us to believe that the company failed to comply with the terms, covenants, provisions, or conditions of sections 32

EXHIBIT   16-10   EXAMPLE OF A REPORT ON A SCHEDULE OF ACCOUNTS RECEIVABLE

AUDITOR'S REPORT
ON SCHEDULE OF ACCOUNTS RECEIVABLE

To the Directors of Client Limited

I have audited the schedule of accounts receivable of Client Limited as at ...., 20... This financial information is the responsibility of the management of Client Limited. My responsibility is to express an opinion on this financial information based on my audit.

I conducted my audit in accordance with generally accepted auditing standards. Those standards require that I plan and perform an audit to obtain reasonable assurance whether the financial information is free of material misstatement. An audit includes examining, on a test basis, evidence supporting the amounts and disclosures in the financial information. An audit also includes assessing the accounting principles used and significant estimates made by management, as well as evaluating the overall presentation of the financial information.

In my opinion, this schedule presents fairly, in all material respects, the accounts receivable of Client Limited as at ...., 20... in accordance with generally accepted accounting principles.

City   (signed) ....
Date   CHARTERED ACCOUNTANT

Source: *CICA Handbook*, paragraph 5805.19.

[11] *CICA Handbook*, section 5805 or ISA 800.
[12] *CICA Handbook*, section 5815 or ISA 800.
[13] *CICA Handbook*, section 9100 or ISA 920.

through 46 of the indenture dated January 1, 1988, with North Country Bank. However, our audit examination was not directed primarily toward obtaining knowledge of such noncompliance.

A similar negative assurance may be given with regard to federal and provincial regulatory requirements. Examples include limitations on investments for mutual funds, and provincial insurance commissioner regulations about the nature of insurance company investments. When the auditor is engaged to provide an audit opinion as to a client's compliance with criteria established by provisions of agreements statutes or regulations, section 5815 provides the appropriate guidance. In this case positive assurance is provided and other than criteria and scope the auditor's report is similar to that for audits of financial statements. An example of an opinion on compliance given in a separate report is provided in Exhibit 16–11.

Regulatory agencies may seek to have auditors sign assertions in prescribed report language that go beyond acceptable professional reporting responsibilities and involve auditors in areas outside their function and responsibility. In such cases auditors should insert additional wording in the prescribed report language or write a completely revised report that reflects adequately their position and responsibility.

Applying Agreed-upon Procedures

In some cases clients may ask auditors to perform a specified set of procedures—the agreed-upon procedures—to examine a particular element, account or item in a financial statement. Such work should not be considered an audit because the specified set of agreed-upon procedures is usually not sufficient to be considered in accordance with generally accepted auditing standards. These special-purpose engagements have a limited scope, so the second and third GAAS examination standards (control risk assessment and sufficient competent evidence for an opinion) and the GAAS reporting standards do not apply.

For example, a client may request procedures on the long-term debt of a company it plans to acquire—not an audit of the company's complete financial statements. Section 9100, "Reports on the Results of Applying Specified Auditing Procedures," gives an example report on such an engagement. The scope paragraph, quoted in Exhibit 16–12, is clearly not a standard scope explanation describing an audit in accordance with generally accepted auditing standards:

The conclusions paragraph quoted earlier follows the recommendation in section 9100 by (1) denying an audit opinion on the accounts and items, (2) giving a negative assurance

---

EXHIBIT   16–11   EXAMPLE OF AN OPINION ON COMPLIANCE GIVEN IN A SEPARATE REPORT

AUDITOR'S REPORT
ON COMPLIANCE WITH AGREEMENT

To A Trust Company Limited

I have audited Client Limited's compliance as at December 31, 20X1 with the criteria established by (describe nature of provisions to be complied with) described in Sections ...... to ...... inclusive of (name of agreement) dated ...., 20... with (name of party to agreement) and the interpretation of such agreement as set out in note 1 attached. Compliance with the criteria established by the provisions of the agreement is the responsibility of the management of Client Limited. My responsibility is to express an opinion on this compliance based on my audit.

I conducted my audit in accordance with generally accepted auditing standards. Those standards require that I plan and perform an audit to obtain reasonable assurance whether Client Limited complied with the criteria established by the provisions of the agreement referred to above. Such an audit includes examining, on a test basis, evidence supporting compliance, evaluating the overall compliance with the agreement, and where applicable, assessing the accounting principles used and significant estimates made by management.

In my opinion, Client Limited is in compliance, in all material respects, with the criteria established by (the provisions to be complied with) described in Sections ...... to ...... of this agreement.

City   (signed) ....
Date   CHARTERED ACCOUNTANT

Source: *CICA Handbook*, paragraph 5815.11.

EXHIBIT 16-12   EXAMPLE OF A REPORT ON SPECIFIED AUDITING PROCEDURES CARRIED OUT ON
LONG-TERM DEBT

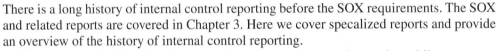

To A. Trustee Limited

As specifically agreed, I have performed the following procedures in connection with the above company's certificate dated ...., 20.... as to the amount of the company's Funded Obligations as at
........................., 20....:

(list the procedures)

As a result of applying the above procedures, I found no (the following) exceptions (list of exceptions).
However these procedures do not constitute an audit of the company's Funded Obligations and
therefore I express no opinion on the amount of Funded Obligations as at ...., 20.....
This letter is for use solely in connection with the closing on ...., 20.... of the issue of
.... securities of the company.

City   (signed) ....

Date   CHARTERED ACCOUNTANT

Source: *CICA Handbook*, paragraph 9100.13.

as to "no exceptions," (3) listing the procedures, and (4) stating that the report is for
restricted use only. You can see how the objectives of this kind of service are very limited
and how the report conclusions are also very limited.

REPORTING ON INTERNAL CONTROL

LEARNING OBJECTIVE

5 Describe the various reports on internal control and their connection with public reporting and reporting to a client's audit committee.

There is a long history of internal control reporting before the SOX requirements. The SOX
and related reports are covered in Chapter 3. Here we cover specalized reports and provide
an overview of the history of internal control reporting.

Managements and boards of directors have been encouraged to make public reports on
internal control, and auditors have been encouraged by the regulators such as Quebec's
inspector general of financial institutions to become associated with such reports. Many
annual reports of public companies contain a "report from management" that includes brief
commentary about internal control responsibilities. Apart from these brief reports, public
reports on internal control were not commonplace.

The topic of internal control reports has led a topsy-turvy life. In 1980 the SEC expressed
the belief that management's comments in its own report on controls were "other information" and that auditors had a responsibility to disclose any material deficiencies that management did not disclose. This event prompted the Auditing Standards Board in the U.S. to
issue an interpretation stating that auditors are responsible for seeing whether a management report contains a material misstatement of fact or fails to be complete insofar as
known material weaknesses in internal accounting control are concerned. In 1983 the SEC
expressed satisfaction with management's tendency toward volunteering reports on internal accounting control and decided not to require such reports. At the same time, the SEC
dropped its consideration of requiring some form of auditor association with management's
comments on control. At the time the SEC was in a "deregulation mode" and loath to enact
new requirements. In 1988 the SEC once again proposed a rule to require a management
report on companies' internal control. Nothing came of this proposal. However, by 1991,
with bank failures at an all-time high, Congress passed legislation requiring internal control reports by insured depository institutions. In 2002 with the passage of SOX and the creation of PCAOB with its standard setting powers, the PCAOB's Auditing Standard No. 2
requires audits of management's internal control statements of public companies (see
Chapter 3).

Meanwhile in Canada similar concerns about banks and trust and insurance companies prompted the CICA to issue the Auditing Guideline "Special Reports on Regulated Financial Institutions" in May 1992.[14] In 2005 the CICA issued an exposure draft on audits of management's internal control statement. This exposure or ballot draft is closely related to that of the PCAOB.

Regulated financial institutions such as banks, insurance and trust companies, pension funds, mutual funds and investment dealers often include special reporting responsibilities beyond those for financial statements to shareholders. The auditor must sometimes communicate in writing transactions or conditions that come to his attention (i.e., negative assurance is provided). This form of communication is referred to as a **derivative report**. At other times the auditor is required to carry out procedures relating to the matters specified in addition to those required by GAAS. The required communication that reports on such specified procedures is referred to as a **nonderivative report**.

Especially in the case of derivative reporting, the audit firm should take steps to inform all staff providing services to the financial institution to be sensitized to this reporting responsibility and to be observant concerning potentially relevant transactions or conditions.

When considering an appointment as auditor of a financial institution, the public accountant should obtain an understanding of any special reporting responsibilities and if necessary contact the regulator or obtain interpretation of the regulatory responsibility from legal counsel.

The extent of management involvement will vary with the nature of the special reporting responsibility to the regulator. As a minimum, however, management will need to have an understanding of (*a*) the reporting responsibility, (*b*) the information, including management representation, that the auditor will need, and (*c*) the process the auditor will follow in issuing a report. All understanding should be documented in writing.

Normally, the auditor would send a copy of the report to the board of directors and other members of management before sending the report to the regulator. In some cases the auditor may wish to seek legal advice and report solely to the regulator.

A derivative report is a by-product of the financial statement audit. The only additional audit procedures are (1) understanding and clarifying the derivative reporting responsibility, (2) making all relevant parties aware of it, and (3) reporting separately to the regulator.

The auditor looks for evidence that affects the viability of the financial institution. Unfortunately, the legislation governing auditor's responsibilities often uses such general and subjective terms as "sound financial practices," and "well-being," which are left to the auditor's judgement, and this may differ from the regulator's interpretation (for example, see AUG–17). This may lead to varying interpretations of the matters specified by legislation and to inconsistencies in the types of transactions or conditions identified and reported by auditors.

As a result there are three limitations on the usefulness of derivative reports:

- The auditor is not required to carry out procedures directed at providing positive assurance on the matters or reportable conditions specified in legislation.

- There may be no comprehensive and precise interpretation of the matters or reportable conditions.

- The financial statement audit may not be designed to address such matters.

In deciding on the types of matters or reportable conditions that should go into a derivative report, the auditor should consider not only the significance of individual transactions and conditions encountered, but also whether a combination of insignificant items should be included in the derivative report. The findings should be discussed with appropriate levels of management, including the audit committee.

The derivative report should be titled "Derivative Report by the Auditor." An illustration is given in Exhibit 16–13.

---

[14] AUG-13.

EXHIBIT 16–13   DERIVATIVE REPORT BY THE AUDITOR

To the Chief Executive Officer of X Financial Institution:

I have audited the financial statements of X Financial Institution as at December 31, 20X1 and for the year then ended, and reported thereon under date of February 19, 20X2.

Pursuant to the requirements of Section XXX of the Y Act (the Act), I am required to report to you any transactions or conditions encountered during the aforementioned audit that (describe matters specified in legislation). For the purposes of understanding the types of transactions or conditions that (describe matters specified in legislation), I have used the following interpretations developed from the following sources:

(Describe the interpretations used and the sources of such interpretations)

During the course of the aforementioned audit, based on the interpretations referred to above, I encountered no relevant transactions or conditions.

No procedures have been carried out in addition to those necessary to form an opinion on the financial statements.

This report has been prepared in accordance with the applicable Auditing and Related Services Guideline issued by the Canadian Institute of Chartered Accountants, and is to be used solely to satisfy the requirements of Section XXX of the Act and should not be referred to or used for any other purpose.

City   (signed) . . . .
Date   CHARTERED ACCOUNTANT

cc: Superintendent of Financial Institutions

Source: *CICA Handbook*, Auditing Guideline AuG-13, Example A.

A nonderivative reporting responsibility involves a reporting engagement separate from the audit of the financial statements. Unique features of such engagements are as follows:

- The auditor may be asked to provide an opinion without a specific assertion from management.
- The auditor may be required to report directly to the regulator.
- The matters are often subjective and thus open to different interpretations, and there may be no established criteria for evaluating the matters.

The Special Reports Recommendations can be applied to many of the nonderivative reporting responsibilities specified in legislation. For example, sections 5805, 5815, 8500, 8600, and 9100 can all be relevant for specific nonderivative reporting engagements. AUG–13 focuses on the following nonderivative reporting engagement matters:

- The methods of management concerning administration and safekeeping of property administered for others
- The methods of management adopted by the company to comply with laws relating to self-dealing and conflicts of interest
- The procedures adopted by management to safeguard the interests of creditors and members

Legislation may require an opinion on the adequacy of methods of management, the effectiveness of controls or the adequacy of procedures. However, to do the job the auditor needs to understand a regulator's expectations. The auditor requires reasonable and attainable standards and criteria to serve as benchmarks for evaluating the adequacy of matters to be reported on. Most legislation does not specify the criteria to be used. The auditor may need to consult with the regulator. An agreement reached on appropriate criteria should be put in writing.

It is also desirable to put in writing any other terms of the engagement with the regulator, such as form of opinion and the period to be covered.

If criteria cannot be established in consultation with the regulator, the auditor may agree to (1) industry standards, (2) authoritative literature, (3) other specialists, and (4) management's view on the matters to be reported on. In all cases it is important for the auditor to describe in his or her report the criteria used and the source of the criteria.

The general and applicable examination standards of section 5100 apply to nonderivative reports. The auditor should obtain an understanding of the policies and procedures established by the client to address the matters on which the auditor is to report. The auditor would also obtain sufficient evidence as to whether the policies and procedures existed and operated effectively throughout the period covered by the report; and evaluate the adequacy of policies and procedures against appropriate criteria.

The auditor should obtain a letter of representation from management concerning management's responsibility for the legislated matters and responsibility to inform the auditor of the status of policies and procedures that affect the legislated matters.

The auditor's report is addressed to the party specified in legislation and should be titled "Auditor's Report on [specify matters]." The report consists of an introductory paragraph, a scope paragraph, an opinion paragraph (that there is reasonable assurance that matters being reported on were adequate or effective) and a concluding paragraph stating that the report has been prepared in accordance with this guideline and is to be used solely to satisfy the legislative requirement. An example of a nonderivative report is given in Exhibit 16–14.

A reservation in a nonderivative report would be guided by the recommendations in section 5510, "Reservations in the Auditor's Report."

EXHIBIT 16–14   EXAMPLE OF A NONDERIVATIVE REPORT

Example of a nonderivative report when:

(i) legislation require the auditor to report to the regulator directly on the adequacy of the procedures adopted to safeguard the interests of creditors and members; and

(ii) the auditor has decided on appropriate criteria.

AUDITOR'S REPORT ON PROCEDURES TO SAFEGUARD THE INTERESTS OF CREDITORS AND MEMBERS

To the Superintendent of Financial Institutions:

Pursuant to the requirements of Section XXX of the Act Respecting X Financial Institutions (the Act), I have audited the procedures employed by XYZ Financial Institution (the Company) to safeguard the interests of its creditors and members for the year ended December 31, 20X7. These procedures are the responsibility of the Company's management. My responsibility is to express an opinion on these procedures based on my audit.

I conducted my audit in accordance with generally accepted auditing standards. Those standards require that I plan and perform an audit to obtain reasonable assurance whether the procedures adopted by the Company were adequate to safeguard the interests of its creditors and members based on appropriate criteria. Such an audit includes obtaining an understanding of the procedures employed by management to safeguard the interests of creditors and members, obtaining sufficient appropriate audit evidence to determine whether these procedures operated effectively throughout the year and evaluating the adequacy of the procedures against appropriate criteria. I used the following criteria developed from the sources noted:

(Describe the criteria used and the sources of such criteria)

Because of the inherent limitations of any procedures adopted by a financial institution to safeguard the interests of its creditors and members, only reasonable assurance can be obtained with respect to the adequacy of such procedures.

In my opinion, based on the above criteria, there is reasonable assurance that the procedures adopted by the Company for the year ended December 31, 20X7 were adequate to safeguard the interests of its creditors and members.

This report has been prepared in accordance with the applicable Auditing and Related Services Guideline issued by The Canadian Institute of Chartered Accountants, and is intended to be used solely to satisfy the requirements of Section XXX of the Act and should not be referred to or used for any other purpose.

City
Date

(signed) . . . .
CHARTERED ACCOUNTANT

cc: Senior company management

Source: *CICA Handbook*, Auditing Guideline AuG–13, Example B.

Public and Restricted Reports

Several different kinds of reports on internal control based on a special study of controls have evolved in practice:

- public reports on control in effect as of a specific date
- public reports on control in effect during a specified time period
- restricted use reports based on the control risk assessment work during an audit, not sufficient for expressing an opinion on control
- restricted use reports based on regulatory agencies' pre-established criteria
- restricted use reports based on a review without tests of controls or based on application of agreed-upon procedures

Some restricted use reports have been illustrated in Exhibits 16–13 and 16–14. Other restricted use internal control reports are covered in section 5970, "Opinions on Control Procedures in Service Organizations," and in section 5750. It is the public reports on internal controls for which we have little authoritative Canadian guidance currently. As an illustration of what we may expect, see Chapter 3 for the PCAOB required report for public companies (i.e., those traded on securities exchanges). Exhibit 16–15 illustrates the AICPA recommended report applying to privately held companies. In Exhibit 16–15 you can see that the last paragraph expresses positive assurance (opinion) on the controls. We will discuss general assurance engagements later in this chapter.

If reporting to a regulatory agency, reports modelled on this standard form may be acceptable. If not, a special report can be issued that, among other things, states the accountant's conclusions based on the agency's criteria and restricts use of the report to the agency (see Exhibit 16–14). Such reports most often are requested in connection with audits of financial institutions.

Other special-purpose reports on control systems can be issued, but their scope is generally limited. Such reports should (*a*) describe the scope of the engagement, (*b*) disclaim an opinion on the system as a whole, (*c*) state the accountant's findings, and (*d*) restrict the report to management or specified third parties.[15]

EXHIBIT 16–15   REPORTING ON INTERNAL ACCOUNTING CONTROL

To the Company, Directors, Stockholders,
Management, a Regulatory Agency, or Specified Others:

We have made a study and evaluation of the system of internal accounting control of Anycompany and subsidiaries in effect at December 31, 20X5. Our study and evaluation was conducted in accordance with standards established by the American Institute of Certified Public Accountants.

The management of Anycompany is responsible for establishing and maintaining a system of internal accounting control. In fulfilling this responsibility, estimates and judgements by management are required to assess the expected benefits and related costs of control procedures. The objectives of a system are to provide management with reasonable, but not absolute, assurance that assets are safeguarded against loss from unauthorized use or disposition, and that transactions are executed in accordance with management's authorization and recorded properly to permit the preparation of financial statements in accordance with generally accepted accounting principles.

Because of inherent limitations in any system of internal accounting control, errors or irregularities may occur and not be detected. Also, projection of any evaluation of the system to future periods is subject to the risk that procedures may become inadequate because of changes in conditions, or that the degree of compliance with the procedures may deteriorate.

In our opinion, the system of internal accounting control of Anycompany and subsidiaries in effect at December 31, 20X5, taken as a whole, was sufficient to meet the objectives stated above insofar as those objectives pertain to the prevention or detection of errors or irregularities in amounts that would be material in relation to the consolidated financial statements.

/s/ Auditor signature, PA
February 18, 20X6

---

[15] *CICA Handbook*, section 5220.

A problem with the public report noted in Exhibit 16–15 relates to which internal controls should be evaluated. For example, should only accounting controls be evaluated? What about accounting controls plus operational controls? Or accounting controls plus operational plus management controls? These questions relate to what should be the internal control objectives for publicly issued internal control reports. Other questions in regard to issuing public general-purpose internal control reports relate to the criteria to be used in evaluating controls. (For example, is effectiveness of management and operating controls too subjective to be measured and evaluated? Current standards focus on accounting controls.) Also, what procedures should the auditors perform in support of such a report, and how should they distinguish between review and examination of internal controls? Some feel these issues can be addressed in a broader attestation/assurance framework rather than in a specific internal control framework.

In May 1990 the CICA sponsored a conference on "criteria of control." The conclusion was that to report on internal control the CICA needed to develop systems criteria for internal control similar to GAAP in accounting. Only with such criteria would auditors be able to address Recommendation 49 of the Macdonald Commission Report (1988) to evaluate and report on the design and functioning of internal control systems of financial institutions. With this goal in mind, the CICA's board of governors established the Criteria of Control Committee in 1992. The initial focus of this committee is on financial reporting controls, but an attempt will also be made to develop generic control principles that would also be applicable to operations.

In November 1995 the Criteria of Control Committee of the CICA issued its first publication in the control and governance series, "Guidance on Criteria on Control," or "COCO," for short. The executive summary of the exposure draft provides a useful perspective on the committee's work efforts and is therefore reproduced here in full.

> The guidance describes and defines control and sets out criteria for its effectiveness. The guidance is applicable to all kinds of organizations, and to part of organizations.
>
> The guidance adopts a broad understanding of control. It involves the coordination of activities toward the achievement of objectives, and includes the identification and mitigation of known risks, the identification and exploitation of opportunities, and the capacity to respond and adapt to the unexpected. Thus, control can provide assurance regarding a broad range of objectives in three general categories: the effectiveness and efficiency of operations, the reliability of financial and management reporting, and compliance with applicable laws and regulations and internal policies.
>
> While people at all levels of an organization participate in control, the decisions and actions of senior management and the board of directors and their level of interest in control set the tone. Management is accountable for control, and therefore needs to assess its overall functioning.
>
> The guidance sets out a control framework, which is a way of looking at an organization so that important aspects of control and relationships between them are apparent. The guidance acknowledges that no one control framework will be perfectly suited to all organizations. It also gives examples of how the criteria can be reorganized into other frameworks, and how other management approaches such as total quality management can be compared to the control framework.
>
> The guidance sets out twenty-three control criteria, stated at a high level in order to be broadly applicable. They address areas such as the culture and values that support good control; objective-setting, risk assessment and planning; control activities that provide assurance that necessary actions are performed; and the monitoring of all aspects of performance to learn what improvements are required. Considerable judgement will be required in applying the criteria, for example, in interpreting them into actionable steps that can be integrated with other management activities; in identifying indicators or early-warning signs so that timely reporting about control can be integrated with reporting about other aspects of performance; and in deciding on the acceptability of risk remaining after control processes have been taken into account.

COCO is written in general, abstract terms in order to provide a flexible framework for future guidelines. The primary intended audience of the guidelines are "auditors who are asked to provide assurance on the reliability of assertions about effectiveness of controls." Control is defined as comprising "those elements of an organization (including its resources, systems, processes, culture, structure and taxes) that, taken together, support people in the achievement of the organization's objectives."

According to the guidance, key concepts in evaluating controls are as follows:

1. Control is effected by people throughout the organization, including the board of directors or its equivalent,[16] management and all other staff.

2. People who are accountable, as individuals or teams, for achieving objectives should also be accountable for the effectiveness of control that supports achievement of those objectives.

3. Organizations are constantly interacting and adapting.

4. Control can be expected to provide only reasonable assurance, not absolute assurance.

5. Effective control demands that a balance be maintained:
   i) Between autonomy and integration—Keeping this balance often involves shifting between centralization and decentralization and between imposing constraints to achieve consistency and granting freedom to act.
   ii) Between the statuus quo and adapting to change—Keeping this balance often involves shifting between demanding greater consistency to gain efficiency and granting greater flexibility to respond to change.

Perhaps the most important features of the guidelines are the 20 control criteria they identify. They are quite detailed but can be summarized by the following categories or components:

1. Purpose groups criteria, which provide a sense of the organization's direction. They address:
   • objectives (including mission, vision and strategy)
   • risks (and opportunities)
   • policies
   • planning
   • performance targets and indicators

2. Commitment groups criteria, which provide a sense of the organization's identity and values. They address:
   • ethical values, including integrity
   • human resource policies
   • authority, responsibility and accountability
   • mutual trust

3. Capability groups criteria, which provide a sense of the organization's competence. They address:
   • knowledge, skills and tools
   • communication processes
   • information
   • co-ordination
   • control activities

4. Monitoring and learning groups criteria, which provide a sense of the organization's evolution. They address:
   • monitoring internal and external environments
   • monitoring performance
   • challenging assumptions
   • reassessing information needs and information systems
   • follow-up procedures
   • assessing the effectiveness of control

---

[16] The governing body of a government or not-for-profit entity may be called by a different name. In a unit within an organization, the equivalent to the board of directors is the senior management or other leadership group.

The basic control framework consists of the definition of control and the criteria as summarized by the broad categories.

Reaction to the criteria appear to be favourable so far. They are consistent with the Canadian philosophy of developing guidelines that are not so detailed that they resemble a "cookbook" approach to evaluating controls. The committee deliberately crafted the criteria at a high level so that they could be applied to all systems at all organizations. There is considerable scope for experimentation and creativity, and auditors will have to use considerable professional judgement in applying the criteria to specific situations.

There is a comparable effort in the United States titled *Internal Control—An Integrated Framework* (commonly referred to as **COSO**). Although both COCO and COSO have the same objective of providing guidance about control and criteria for control, COCO builds on COSO by expanding the notion of what control is and taking a particularly people-oriented approach.

At the present time the guidance is not included in the *CICA Handbook*. The guidance therefore does not have the authority of *CICA Handbook* accounting or auditing recommendations. A member's decision to use the control guidance to assess internal controls will depend on whether he or she finds the guidance useful and relevant. In this sense the guidance is somewhat experimental.

A second project of the CICA Criteria of Control Committee is the Guidance for Directors—Governance processes for control issued in December 1995. This is the second in a series addressing various aspects of control systems. The purpose of the document is to set out guidance on governance processes to meet the responsibilities of board of directors to control.

It identifies six key areas of board control responsibilities:

1. establishing and monitoring the organization's ethical values

2. approval and monitoring of mission, vision and strategy

3. overseeing external communication

4. evaluating senior management

5. monitoring management control systems

6. assessing the board's effectiveness

The primary focus of the document and of Guidance on Criteria of Control is shown in Exhibit 16–16. This exhibit illustrates the evolving framework for evaluating management and operational controls as part of the internal control framework. To assist auditors in interpreting this guidance relative to other authoritative pronouncements, the Criteria of Control Committee prepared a degree of authoritativeness framework, which is presented in Exhibit 16–17. This exhibit makes clear that the control and governance series are not

EXHIBIT   16-16   CICA'S CRITERIA OF CONTROL GUIDANCE

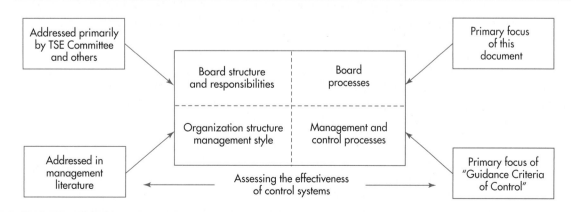

Source: CICA, *Criteria of Control Guidance.*

EXHIBIT   16-17   DEGREE OF AUTHORITATIVENESS FRAMEWORK

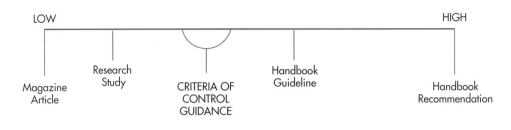

Source: CICA, *Criteria of Control Guidance.*

intended to become *CICA Handbook* recommendations at the current time. Instead, the intent seems to be to get client organizations to experiment with the framework until a more fine-tuned standard can be developed. The resulting framework will probably first be used for internal reporting with an eventual goal of developing sufficiently articulated and supported standards for external reporting purposes.

SOX of 2002 has greatly accelerated the evolution of internal control reporting because it requires public companies in the U.S. to publicly report on internal controls and to have these reports audited, just like the financial statements are currently. COCO may be used as suitable criteria in evaluating internal control, and may further evolve along with assurance engagements on internal control. This continuing evolution of criteria and dynamic change in the audit environment underscores the need for a broad framework like critical thinking to guide professional judgement.

Audit Report Reservations on Internal Control Statements

Chapter 3 introduced Audit Reports of Internal Control Statements. The official title of this ballot draft is *An Audit of Internal Control over Financial Reporting in Conjunction with an Audit of Financial Statements.* This CICA ballot draft had not been approved at time of writing and audits of internal control statements are optional. Not unlike the other internal control reports discussed here, the ballot draft reports are not restricted to limited classes of users.

Consistent with the CICA's objective of minimizing differences between Canadian and U.S. standards, this standard is similar to the U.S. Public Company Accounting Oversight Board's (PCAOB) Audit Standard No. 2.

Chapter 3 introduced the unqualified audit report for this standard. Here we briefly review the requirements for report reservations. It is important to understand that this standard requires two opinions on internal controls. One is an attest opinion on management's written assertion (the internal control statement), and the other opinion is a direct reporting opinion, meaning the opinion is directly on the state of controls. This two part opinion introduces complications to the report reservations possible. The most common complication occurs when management recognizes material weaknesses in its internal control via its statement and the auditor agrees. In this situation, the auditor issues an unqualified attest opinion (because the auditor believes the internal control statement is fairly stated) but an adverse direct reporting opinion (because the internal controls have material weaknesses). An example is available from the Ballot Draft and this is given in Exhibit 16–18.

Under this new standard a total of three audit opinions are required: the two audit opinions relating to internal controls and the traditional audit opinion on financial statements that we discussed in Chapter 3. A large number of report reservation combinations are thus possible. This explains the length and complexity of the standard. However, from the illustrations in the back of the standard, the CICA seems to expect most reservations to arise from scope restrictions on internal controls. The many possible reservations that can arise are summarized in Exhibit 16–19. For your reference the key paragraph numbers are listed in parentheses. You should at least be familiar with these paragraphs of this lengthy standard.

EXHIBIT   16-18   AN ADVERSE OPINION ON INTERNAL CONTROL OVER FINANCIAL REPORTING

Example B

Illustrative report expressing an unqualified opionion on management's assessment of the effectiveness of internal control over financial reporting and an adverse opinion on the effectiveness of internal control over financial reporting because of the existence of a material weakness.

AUDITOR'S REPORT

To the Shareholders of W Company Ltd.

I have audited the effectiveness of W Company Ltd.'s internal control over financial reporting as at December 31, 20X3, in accordance with [the suitable control criteria, for example, "criteria established in Internal Control — Integrated Framework issued by the Committee of Sponsoring Organizations of the Treadway Commission (COSO)"] and management's assessment thereof included in the accompanying [title of management's report] W Company Ltd.'s management is responsible for maintaining effective internal control over financial reporting and for its assessment of the effectiveness of internal control over financial reporting. My responsibility is to express an opinion on management's assessment and an opinion on the effectiveness of the company's internal control over financial reporting based on my audit.

A company's internal control over financial reporting is a process designed to provide reasonable assurance regarding the reliability of financial reporting and the preparation of financial statements for external purposes in accordance with generally accepted accounting principles. A company's internal control over financial reporting includes those policies and procedures that (1) pertain to the maintenance of records that, in reasonable detail, accurately and fairly reflect the transactions and dispositions of the assets of the company; (2) provide reasonable assurance that transactions are recorded as necessary to permit preparation of financial statements in accordance with generally accepted accounting principles, and that receipts and expenditures of the company are being made only in accordance with authorizations of management and directors of the company; and (3) provide reasonable assurance regarding prevention or timely detection of unauthorized acquisition, use or disposition of the company's assets that could have a material effect on the financial statements.

I conducted my audit of the effectiveness of W Company Ltd.'s internal control over financial reporting, and management's assessment thereof, in accordance with the standards established by the Canadian Institute of Chartered Accountants (CICA) for audits of internal control over financial reporting. Those standards require that I plan and perform the audit to obtain reasonable assurance about whether effective internal control over financial reporting was maintained in all material aspects. My audit included obtaining an understanding of internal control over financial reporting, evaluating management's assessment, testing and evaluating the design and operating effectiveness of internal control over financial reporting, and performing such other procedures as I considered necessary in the circumstances. I believe that my audit provides a reasonable basis for my opinion.

A material weakness is a control deficiency, or combination of control deficiencies, that result in more than a remote likelihood that a material misstatement of the annual or interim financial statements will not be prevented or detected. The following material weakness has been identified and included in management's assessment. [Description of the material weakness and its effect on the achievement of the objectives of the control criteria.] This material weakness was considered in determining the nature, timing and extent of audit tests applied in my audit of the company's 20X3 financial statements, which I audited in accordance with Canadian generally accepted auditing standards, and this material weakness does not affect my report dated [date of report, which should be the same as the date of this report on internal control over financial reporting] on those financial statements.

In my opinion, management's assessment that W Company Ltd. did not maintain effective internal control over financial reporting as at December 31, 20X3, is fairly stated, in all material respects, in accordance with [the suitable control criteria, for example, "criteria established in Internal Control — Integrated Framework issued by the Committee of Sponsoring Organizations of the Treadway Commission (COSO)"]. Also, in my opinion, because of the effect of the material weakness described above on the achievement of the objectives of the control criteria, W Company Ltd. has not maintained effective internal control over financial reporting as at December 31, 20X3, in accordance with [the suitable control criteria, for example, "criteria established in Internal Control — Integrated Framework issued by the Committee of Sponsoring Organizations of the Treadway Commission (COSO)"].

Because of its inherent limitations, internal control over financial reporting may not prevent or detect misstatements. Also, projections of any evaluation of effectiveness to future periods are subject to the risk that controls may become inadequate because of changes in conditions, or that the degree of compliance with the policies or procedures may deteriorate.

[City]   (signed).......................................
[Date]   CHARTERED ACCOUNTANT

Source: CICA Handbook, Ballot Draft on Audits of Internal Control over Financial Reporting.

In the U.S. some internal control statements leading to reservations in the audit report on internal control have already been published. Exhibit 16–20 is an example of an internal control statement that would result in the reservation illustrated in Exhibit 16–18. See **www.ge.com/ar2004/mariocofr.jsp** for an example of an actual report.

Special Reports: Service Organizations

Occasionally, some clients' transactions are handled by a **service organization**—another business that executes or records transactions, or both, on behalf of the client. Examples of service organizations include computer data processing service centres, trust departments of banks, insurers that maintain the accounting records for ceded insurance (reinsurance transactions), mortgage bankers and trust companies that service loans for owners, and transfer agents that handle the shareholder accounting for mutual and money market investment funds. An auditor may need information about the service organization's control over its mutual client's transactions. However, the auditor may not have access to do the work when the service organization is not an audit client. This situation is described in Exhibit 16–21.

EXHIBIT   16-19   SUMMARY OF MOST LIKELY REPORTING SCENARIOS—INTERNAL CONTROL (IC) OVER FINANCIAL REPORTING (CICA BALLOT DRAFT)

	Management's Report on IC	Attest Opinion	Direct Reporting Opinion	Attest Opinion
			Auditor's Report On:	
Internal Control Situation		Management's Assessment of IC	Effectiveness of IC	Financial Statements
No material weakness identified	Effective	Unqualified (paragraph .166)	Unqualified (paragraph .129)	Unqualified
Material weakness identified by management and by the author	Not Effective	Unqualified (paragraph .166)	Adverse (paragraph .175)	Unqualified[1]
Material weakness identified by the auditor, but not by management[2]	Effective	Adverse (paragraph .166 and .173)	Adverse (paragraph .173)	Unqualified[1]
Material weakness identified by the auditor, but not by management[2]	Effective	Adverse or qualified, depending on the circumstances (paragraph .140 and .173)	Adverse or qualified, depending on the circumstances (paragraph .140 and .173)	Adverse or qualified due to accounting deficiency
Auditor is not in a position to determine if there is a material weakness	Effective	Denial, qualification, or withdrawal depending on the circumstances (paragraph .178)	Denial, qualification, or withdrawal depending on the circumstances (paragraph .178)	Unqualified, or denial, or qualified due to audit deficiency based on scope limitations due to circumstances

[1]Presumes the auditor is able to perform sufficient procedures to conclude that the financial statements are fairly stated.

[2]In this situation, management and the auditor disagree on whether a control deficiency constitutes a material weakness.

EXHIBIT   16-20   MANAGEMENT'S ANNUAL REPORT ON INTERNAL CONTROL OVER FINANCIAL REPORTING (AS RESTATED)

The management of ABC is responsible for establishing and maintaining adequate internal control over financial reporting for the company. With the participation of the Chief Executive Officer and the Chief Financial Officer, our management conducted an evaluation of the effectiveness of our internal control over financial reporting as of December 31, 200X, based on the framework and criteria established in Internal Control — Integrated Framework, issued by the Committee of Sponsoring Organizations of the Treadway Commission.

In the company's Annual Report for the year ended December 31, 200X, filed on March 1, 200Y, management concluded that our internal control over financial reporting was effective as of December 31, 200X. Subsequently, management identified the following material weakness in internal control over financial reporting.

• (Describe material weakness.)

This material weakness has caused us to amend our Annual Report for the year ended December 31, 200X, in order to restate the financial statements for the years ended December 31, 200X, 200W and 200V and to restate financial information for the year ended December 31, 200U and each of the quarters in 200W and 200X.

Solely as a result of this material weakness, our management has revised its earlier assessment and has now concluded that our internal control over financial reporting was not effective as of December 31, 200X.

ABC Company's independent auditor, a registered public accounting firm, has issued an audit report on our management's revised assessment of our internal control over financial reporting as of December 31, 200X. This audit report follows.

Chairman of the Board and
Chief Executive Officer
May 5, 2005

Senior Vice President, Finance
and Chief Financial Officer

EXHIBIT   16-21   SERVICE ORGANIZATION AUDITS

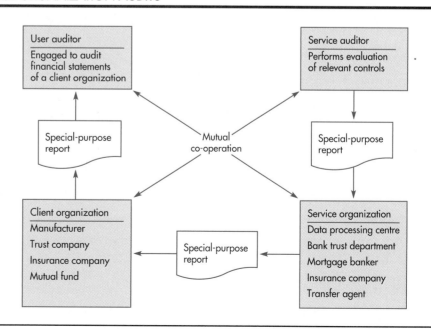

In such situations all the parties concerned—the user auditor and its client organization, and the service auditor and its client (the service organization)—co-operate to enable the user auditor to obtain enough information about controls that affect the audit client's transactions. Certain special-purpose reports on internal accounting control, described more fully in section 5900 and ISA 402.12, can be relied on by the user auditor in connection with the assessment of control risk of the client organization. The reports provide opinions about the service organization's controls as they are applied to the client organization's transactions. Ordinarily, service auditors' reports are not public reports on internal controls. They are used mainly by other auditors.

Section 5970 and ISA 402 describe the form of internal control report under several conditions. In particular, the opinion paragraph should express an opinion on whether the stated internal control objectives were achieved and the control procedures exist either at a point in time or throughout the period covered by the service auditor. Exhibit 16–22 is a report on control procedures at a specified point in time, while Exhibit 16–23 is a report on control procedures over a specified time period.

As noted in Chapter 9, service organization reports will play an increasingly important role in obtaining assurance on security controls in e-business, and validity of Internet transaction controls.

Other Communication on Control and Other Matters

Regulators, parliaments, and the public have been concerned about auditors' communication of internal control and other matters to high levels in public corporations, especially in banks and other financial institutions. In response, the CICA issued two recommendations that address auditors' responsibilities to (1) communicate internal control matters noted in an audit,[17] and (2) communicate certain matters to those having financial reporting oversight responsibility (usually, the audit committee).[18]

When performing an audit, auditors may notice **reportable matters.** These include significant deficiencies in the design or operation of the company's internal control structure, which could adversely affect the organization's ability to record, process, summarize and report

---

EXHIBIT   16-22   AUDITOR'S REPORT ON CONTROL PROCEDURES AT SPECIFIC POINT IN TIME

To Y Service Organization

I have audited the accompanying description of the stated internal control objectives of X system of Y Service Organization and the control procedures designed to achieve those objectives and have performed tests of the existence of those control procedures as at June 30, 20X1. My examination was made in accordance with Canadian generally accepted auditing standards, and accordingly included such tests and other procedures as I considered necessary in the circumstances.

In my opinion, the control procedures included in the accompanying description were suitably designed to provide reasonable, but not absolute, assurance that the stated internal control objectives of the system described therein were achieved and the control procedures existed as at June 30, 20X1.

As I tested the existence of the control procedures only as at June 30, 20X1, I do not express an opinion on whether the control procedures existed at any other time.

The description of stated internal control objectives of X system at Y Service Organization, and the control procedures designed to achieve those objectives is as of June 30, 20X1. Any projection of that description to the future is subject to the risk that, because of change, the description may no longer portray the control procedures in existence. The potential effectiveness of specific control procedures at Y Service Organization is subject to inherent limitations and, accordingly, errors or fraud may occur and not be detected. Furthermore, the projection of any conclusions, based on my findings, to future periods is subject to the risk that changes may alter the validity of such conclusions.

City   (signed) . . . .
July 15, 20X1   CHARTERED ACCOUNTANT

Source: *CICA Handbook*, paragraph 5970, Example A, Appendix A.

---

[17] *CICA Handbook*, section 5750.
[18] Ibid., section 5751.

EXHIBIT 16-23 AUDITOR'S REPORT ON CONTROL PROCEDURES OVER SPECIFIED TIME PERIOD

To B Service Organization

I have audited the accompanying description of the stated internal control objectives of A system of B Service Organization and the control procedures designed to achieve those objectives and have performed tests of the effectiveness of those control procedures for the period from January 1, 20X1 to June 30, 20X1. My examination was made in accordance with Canadian generally accepted auditing standards, and accordingly included such tests and other procedures as I considered necessary in the circumstances.

In my opinion, the control procedures included in the accompanying description were suitably designed to provide reasonable, but not absolute, assurance that the stated internal control objectives of the system described therein were achieved, and the control procedures operated effectively from January 1, 20X1 to June 30, 20X1.

The description of stated internal control objectives of A system at B Service Organization, and the control procedures designed to achieve those objectives is as of June 30, 20X1. Any projection of that description to the future is subject to the risk that, because of change, the description may no longer portray the control procedures in existence. The potential effectiveness of specific control procedures at B Service Organization is subject to inherent limitations and, accordingly, errors or fraud may occur and not be detected. Furthermore, my tests of the operating effectiveness of specific controls covers the period from January 1, 20X1 to June 30, 20X1. The projection of any conclusions, based on my findings, to future periods is subject to the risk that changes may alter the validity of such conclusions.

City   (signed) . . . .
July 15, 20X1   CHARTERED ACCOUNTANT

Source: *CICA Handbook*, paragraph 5970, Appendix A, Example B.

financial data in conformity with GAAP.[19] Auditing standards do not require auditors to search for reportable matters, but they do require auditors to report the ones that come to their attention.[20] The report, preferably in writing, is to be addressed to the management, or the board of directors or its audit committee. An illustration of such a report is in Exhibit 16–24.

Auditors often issue another type of report to management called a management letter (see Chapter 15). This letter may contain commentary and suggestions on a variety of matters in addition to internal control matters. Examples are operational and administrative efficiency, business strategy and profit-making possibilities. These management letters are not required by auditing standards. They are a type of management advice rendered as a part of an audit. (An illustration of a management letter is shown in Chapter 15, Exhibit 15–10, in connection with completing the audit.)

The concern about reporting control-related matters within a company has spilled over into a set of other important matters that auditors are required to report to companies' audit committees or others having oversight responsibility.[21] The purpose of these communications is to enhance the audit committees' ability to oversee the audit functions (external and

EXHIBIT 16-24 COMMUNICATION OF MATTERS IDENTIFIED DURING THE FINANCIAL STATEMENT AUDIT

During the course of my audit of . . . . for the year ended . . . . I identified matters which may be of interest to management. The objective of an audit is to obtain reasonable assurance whether the financial statements are free of material misstatement and it is not designed to identify matters that may be of interest to management in discharging its responsibilities. Accordingly an audit would not usually identify all such matters.

The matters identified were . . . .

This communication is prepared solely for the information of management and is not intended for any other purpose. I accept no responsibility to a third party who uses this communication.

Source: *CICA Handbook*, paragraph 5750.08.

[19] AUG–13, "Special Reports on Regulated Financial Institutions."
[20] *CICA Handbook*, section 5750.
[21] Ibid., section 5751.

internal) in a company. The auditors are responsible for informing the audit committee about these matters:

- independent auditors' responsibilities regarding financial statements and other information in documents that include the audited financial statements (e.g., the annual report to shareholders, filings with the regulatory agencies such as the OSC or Superintendent of Financial Institutions)
- management's significant accounting policies
- management judgements about accounting estimates used in the financial statements
- significant audit adjustments recommended by the auditors
- disagreements with management about accounting principles, accounting estimates, the scope of the audit, disclosures in the notes and the wording of the audit report
- the auditor's view on accounting matters on which management has consulted with other accountants
- major accounting and auditing issues discussed with management in connection with beginning or continuing an auditor-client relationship
- illegal acts
- difficulties with management encountered while performing the audit—delays in starting the audit or providing information, unreasonable time schedule, unavailability of client personnel and failure of client personnel to complete data schedules

Auditors also have responsibilities to communicate in a letter to the audit committee (or equivalent) on matters that bear on independence (covered in Chapter 15). *CICA Handbook* paragraph 5751.32 requires a letter on the following:

- confirmation of auditor's independence
- disclosure of relationships that might impair independence
- disclosure of total fees for audit and non-audit services for clients having public accountability (such as companies whose securities are traded on regulated exchanges, public sector companies, and not-for-profit organizations)

REVIEW CHECKPOINTS

16.13 Does the standard public report on internal control give the opinion known as "positive assurance"?

16.14 What reports on control and other matters are auditors required to give to a company's management, board of directors or audit committee?

16.15 What three types of engagements can produce an auditor's written report on internal control intended for external use? Describe the reports in general terms.

FORECASTS AND PROJECTIONS

LEARNING OBJECTIVE
6 Define the various financial presentations and levels of service involved in association with financial forecasts, projections, prospectuses and MD&A.

Accountants are associated with prospective financial information when a client requests them to help assemble or submit a report on a forecast or projection. Several provincial securities commissions have encouraged publication of forecasts. For example, the OSC has allowed forecasts since 1984. In September 1989 the CICA issued a new *CICA Handbook* pronouncement, section 4250, dealing with accounting issues involved with forecasts, or more generally, **future-oriented financial information (FOFI)**. At the same time, an auditing and related services guideline was issued covering the examination of a financial forecast or projection included in a prospectus or other public offering document. In February 1993 the CICA issued an auditing guideline for compilation of a financial forecast or projection, AUG–16. Similar guidance is also provided in International Standards on Assurance Engagements (ISAE) 3400.

When accountants have compiled, examined or helped prepare prospective financial statements, they should render a report on them. The characteristics of compilation and examination of prospective financial statements are explored later in this section.

Presentation Guides

Prospective financial statements can be completed in the same format as historical statements or less than complete, but in any event they must contain the following items (if applicable in the circumstances):

- *a.* sales or gross revenue
- *b.* gross profit or cost of sales
- *c.* unusual or infrequently occurring items
- *d.* provision for income taxes
- *e.* discontinued operations or extraordinary items
- *f.* income from continuing operations
- *g.* net income
- *h.* primary and fully diluted earnings per share
- *i.* significant changes in financial position
- *j.* statement that assumptions are based on current information, with a warning that the prospective results may not be achieved
- *k.* summary of significant assumptions
- *l.* summary of significant accounting policies

These items are what usually appear in historical financial statements for a future period, and so FOFI should be prepared in accordance with the accounting policies expected to be used in the future period.[22]

Any presentation omitting one or more of the items (*a*) through (*l*) in this list is considered a partial presentation, not a prospective financial statement. Partial and *pro forma* presentations are not covered by the standards and not recommended for public use.

With the minimum items listed, the nature of prospective financial statements can be one of the following:

1. **Financial forecast.** A forecast presents, to the best of the preparer's knowledge and belief, an entity's expected financial position, results of operations and changes in financial position (cash flow). A forecast is based on assumptions about expected conditions and expected courses of action.

2. **Financial projection.** A projection is similar to a forecast, with the important exception being that a projection depends on one or more **hypothetical assumption(s).** A hypothetical assumption expresses a condition and course of action the issuer expects could take place. A projection answers the questions: "What might happen if . . . ?" For example, a promoter trying to sell limited partnership interests in a new hotel project might present a cash flow projection based on the hypothetical assumption: "What will be the cash flow if annual hotel room occupancy averages 75 percent?" Financial projections may be multiple projections based on a range of hypothetical assumptions (e.g., hotel room occupancy of 50 percent, 75 percent and 90 percent). A preparer should reasonably expect the future results to fall within the range, however.

Reporting on Prospective Financial Statements

Accountants can report on forecasts and projections three ways. The primary objective of association with forecasts and projections is to lend credibility to them—similar to the assurance objective related to historical financial statements.

---

[22] Ibid., paragraph 4250.18.

1. **Examination of prospective financial statements.** An examination of a forecast or projection is a substantial task. For all practical purposes, it is the equivalent of an audit because the accountant is expected to:

- evaluate the preparation of the prospective financial statements
- evaluate the support underlying the assumptions
- evaluate the presentation for conformity with section 4250 presentation recommendations
- issue an examination report stating (*a*) whether the prospective financial statements are presented in conformity with CICA standards, (*b*) whether the assumptions provide a reasonable basis for the forecast or projection, and (*c*) a disclaimer as to achievability of the forecast

Exhibit 16–25 organizes the forecast/projection examination guidelines. You should compare them to the assurance and GAAS standards in Exhibit 2–1.

2. **Compilation of prospective financial statements.** A compilation involves considerably less work than an examination. Compilation procedures mainly facilitate the mechanical preparation of the forecast or projection presentation. Accountants are not expected to gather a significant amount of supporting evidence. However, they are expected to notice assumptions that are obviously inappropriate in the circumstances. These compilation procedures are similar to the ones specified for a compilation of unaudited historical financial statements.

3. **Application of agreed-upon procedures.** Clients can engage accountants for specified work on forecasts and projections by establishing the nature and scope of the work. In such arrangements (*a*) the users of the statements and accountant's report must take responsibility for the adequacy of the agreed-upon procedures for their purposes, (*b*) the report is to be restricted to these users, and (*c*) the prospective financial statements must contain a summary of significant assumptions. These engagements are the means of obtaining tailored services, so they can take a wide variety of specifications. The accountant's report is similarly tailored to the circumstances.

Reports on Prospective Financial Statements
Standard compilation and examination reports on forecasts are reproduced in Exhibits 16–26 and 16–27. The reports identify the financial statements and describe the accountants' work. The compilation report contains a disclaimer. It offers no conclusions or any other form of assurance. The examination report, in contrast, gives the accountants' conclusions about proper presentation and the reasonableness of the assumptions.

EXHIBIT   16-25   FORECAST/PROJECTION EXAMINATION GUIDELINES

1. The examination should be performed by a person or persons having adequate technical training and proficiency to examine prospective financial statements.
2. In all matters related to the examination of prospective financial statements, the accountant should be independent.
3. Due professional care should be exercised in the performance of the examination and the preparation of the report.
4. The work should be adequately planned and assistants, if any, should be properly supervised.
5. Sufficient appropriate evidence should be obtained to provide a reasonable basis for the examination report.
6. The examination report should be given an opinion that the prospective financial statements are presented in conformity with presentation guidelines and that the underlying assumptions provide a reasonable basis for the forecast.
7. The report should give a *caveat* that the prospective results may not be achieved.
8. The examination report should identify the prospective financial statements and state that the examination of them was made in accordance with standards established by the CICA.
9. The report should contain a statement that the accountant assumes no responsibility to update the report for events and circumstances occurring after the date of the report.

EXHIBIT   16-26   NOTICE TO READER ON THE COMPILATION OF A FINANCIAL FORECAST

To:......

I have compiled the financial forecast of .... consisting of a balance sheet as at (date) and statements of income, retained earnings and changes in financial position for the (period) then ending using assumptions with an effective date of ...., and other information provided by management. My engagement was performed in accordance with the applicable guidance on compilation of a financial forecast issued by the Canadian Institute of Chartered Accountants.

A compilation is limited to presenting, in the form of a financial forecast, information provided by management and does not include evaluating the support for the assumptions or other information underlying the forecast. Accordingly, I do not express an opinion or any other form of assurance on the financial forecast or assumptions. Further, since this financial forecast is based on assumptions regarding future events, actual results will vary from the information presented and the variations may be material. I have no responsibility to update this communication for events and circumstances occurring after the date of this communication.

City   (signed) ....
Date   CHARTERED ACCOUNTANT

Source: *CICA Handbook,* Auditing Guideline AUG-16, para. 21.

In an engagement to examine (audit) and report on a forecast or projection, accountants can give opinions that are unqualified (see Exhibit 16–27), qualified or adverse, or that are disclaimers resulting from scope limitations. The qualified or adverse opinions are given when the forecast or projection omits some information required to be presented by section 4250. The adverse opinion is given when the presentation fails to disclose significant assumptions and when significant assumptions are not reasonable. The disclaimer is given when necessary examination procedures are not performed.

An accountant should not write a report that may lead readers to believe that she attests to the achievability of the prospective results. You can see in Exhibit 16–27 that the accountant's report lends credibility and assurance to the forecast, but does not attest to achievability. Accountants must be independent to give the examination report, and this independence includes independence from all promoters using the forecast to organize or market a venture as well as independence from the entity being promoted.

An OSC study found that forecasts issued in 1990 and 1991 were inaccurate by a larger margin than in previous surveys. According to this study, 77 percent of established firms sur-

EXHIBIT   16-27   AUDITOR'S REPORT ON FINANCIAL FORECAST

To the Directors of ....

The accompanying financial forecast of .... consisting of a balance sheet as at (date) and the statements of income, retained earnings and changes in financial position for the (period(s)) then ending has been prepared by management using assumptions with an effective date of .... I have examined the support provided by management for the assumptions, and the preparation and presentation of this forecast. My examination was made in accordance with the applicable Auditing Guideline issued by the Canadian Institute of Chartered Accountants. I have no responsibility to update this report for events and circumstances occurring after the date of my report.

In my opinion:

• as at the date of this report, the assumptions developed by management are suitably supported and consistent with the plans of the Company, and provide a reasonable basis for the forecast;

• this forecast reflects such assumptions; and

• the financial forecast complies with the presentation and disclosure standards for forecasts established by the Canadian Institute of Chartered Accountants.

Since this forecast is based on assumptions regarding future events, actual results will vary from the information presented and the variations may be material. Accordingly, I express no opinion as to whether this forecast will be achieved.

City   (signed) ....
Date   CHARTERED ACCOUNTANT

Source: *CICA Handbook,* Auditing Guideline AUG-6, para. 43.

veyed overestimated their profit, compared with 71 percent in an earlier survey. Moreover, 62 percent overestimated profit by more than 20 percent, up from 51 percent who did so in the previous survey.

In a *Globe and Mail* article, portfolio manager John Saltz of Bolton Tremblay said that management is likely to be biased and optimistic. "I don't pay for stocks based on management's forecast of future earnings."

He also complained about the auditor's role. "The auditor says that the forecast is fine based on underlying assumptions but they don't comment on the underlying assumptions."

The OSC's acting head of corporate finance, Ram Ramachandran, said the audit requirement "may unconsciously add an element of respectability" and lead people to rely too much on the document. Auditors are working in a new area—forecasting—and "the process may not lend itself to crystal ball gazing. As a result, Ontario may ban forecasts altogether."[23]

A recent comprehensive study of financial statement user needs by the AICPA known commonly as the **Jenkins Report** found that "in general, users do not expect management to provide forecasted financial statements. They are concerned about the reliability of the information and believe that forecasting financial performance is a function of financial analysis rather than business reporting."[24] Instead, users prefer improved disclosure of risks, uncertainties and opportunities—key aspects on which to base forecasts. The Jenkins Report will probably have a major impact on reporting and ultimately auditing.

The business press and regulators have recently expressed concerns about fraudulent reporting that is designed to meet analysts' quarterly forecasts.[25] The May 2000 Exposure Draft by the Panel on Audit Effectiveness had this to say about fraudulent reporting:

> Frauds often start in one of the first three quarters of a company's fiscal year. Auditors have limited responsibilities for interim financial information (generally quarterly financial reports). Auditors are engaged to review that information, but it is not subjected to the same scrutiny as are the full year's audited financial statements. Furthermore matters potentially material to an interim financial report might not be material to the annual financial statements, and therefore may not receive scrutiny from auditors either in their limited quarterly reviews or the annual audit. Perpetrators may use this fact to their advantage in their efforts at concealment. In addition, manipulations of earnings in interim periods often are rationalized by management as being only temporary "borrowings" since there is plenty of time left in the year to correct the problem. The rationalization also may include a belief that the manipulations are intended to avoid earnings volatility and surprises and therefore are in the shareholders' best interests.[26]

Given this possible latitude with interim information, it is not surprising that if analysts' quarterly expectations are missed by even as little as a penny there can be a loss of millions of dollars in market capitalization. For this reason there has been renewed interest in how materiality is set by the auditor. Both quantitative, as well as qualitative factors, need to be considered. For example, will a misstatement allow the client to meet analysts' expectations, or will a misstatement convert a loss into a profit? Please review Chapter 8 for more discussion.

Prospectuses

Whenever a client wants to make a new public offering of its securities (e.g., stock, bonds) it needs to provide certain information for each new offering (the prospectus). The prospectus is supposed to give prospective investors enough information so that they can evaluate the merits of the proposed use of funds. Auditors' involvement with prospectuses can be quite extensive and these are covered in sections 7110, 7115, and 7200 and audit guidelines AUG–6,16, and 30.

If a prospectus is issued within a short period after the client's year-end, usually 90 days, the auditor's involvement with the prospectus can be quite minimal. Minimal involvement includes auditing the financial statements, reading the prospectus for any "material incon-

[23] "Ontario may ban firm's profit forecasts," *The Globe and Mail*, March 1, 1994, p. B3.

[24] AICPA Special Committee on Financial Reporting, "Improving Business Reporting: A Customer Focus—Making the Information Needs of Investors and Creditors" (Jenkins Report), AICPA, 1994, pp. 11–15.

[25] For example, see News Report, *Journal of Accountancy*, December 1999, p. 17.

[26] www.pobauditpanel.org on July 7, 2000, paragraph 3.25.

sistencies"[27] relative to the audited financial statements, and performing subsequent event review procedures.

If a prospectus is issued after a legislatively specified period after the balance sheet date, then the auditor will need to become more involved with interim financial statements and any other financial information (such as forecasts). In such situations the auditor may be asked to prepare a comfort letter to securities regulators.[28]

If after performing the required procedures outlined previously and listed in detail in paragraph 7110.07 the auditor finds no significant inconsistencies, the auditor consents to use his or her report in the prospectus. The recommended auditor's consent communication is given in Exhibit 16–28.

If more than one auditor is involved in the audit all auditors must issue a consent letter.

EXHIBIT   16-28   AUDITOR'S CONSENT

I have read the [short form] prospectus of X Limited (the Company) dated March 15, 20X5 relating to the issue and sale of [description of securities offered] of the Company. I have complied with Canadian generally accepted standards for an auditor's involvement with offering documents.

I consent to the [use/incorporation by reference] in the above-mentioned prospectus of my report to the [directors/shareholders] of the Company on the balance sheets of the Company as at December 31, 20X4 and 20X3, and the statements of earnings, retained earnings and cash flows for each of the years in the [three-/two-year] period ended December 31, 20X4. My report is dated February 15, 20X5 (except as to note . . . which is as of March 15, 20X5).

City   (signed) . . . .
Date   CHARTERED ACCOUNTANT

Source: *CICA Handbook*, section 7110.69.

CICA's MD&A Guidance

With the increasing interest in corporate governance, the profession is becoming more involved in broader corporate disclosures and their relationship to the financial statements. This interest is reflected in the CICA's initiative on providing guidance on **management's discussion and analysis (MD&A)** accompanying the financial statements in the client's annual report. The guidance is primarily geared to directors and management but is also useful to auditors in reviewing for consistency with the financial statements. No recommendations or standards have been issued yet, but a guidance document has been prepared as indicated in the following box.

CICA's MD&A Guidance

This Guidance breaks new ground by establishing six disclosure principles and a five-part framework for organizing and presenting Management's Discussion and Analysis (MD&A) disclosures, thus adding new dimensions to conventional MD&A reporting. Further, it reflects trends in the continuous disclosure requirements of Canadian securities jurisdictions and provides for updating of previous disclosures.

A significant feature of the Guidance is a series of questions audit committees and boards of directors might ask in reviewing the completeness and reliability of the MD&A—an important aspect of fulfilling their oversight and governance responsibilities. These questions should also assist management in determining the appropriateness of their MD&A disclosures and help officers of U.S. registered companies in making certifications specified under recent requirements.

Source: "CICA's MD&A Guidance," *CA Magazine*, January/February 2003, p. 30. Reproduced by permission from *CA Magazine*, published by the Canadian Institute of Chartered Accountants, Toronto, Canada.

[27] ISA 720.
[28] *CICA Handbook*, paragraph 7200.05.

The principles stress that MD&A is management's explanation of why past performance turned out the way it did, and what the future prospects are from management's perspective. The principles also state that MD&A should complement, as well as supplement, the financial statements and should be clearly worded. Future guidance for auditors will likely focus on what represents material inconsistencies between MD&A and the financial statements, and on how to detect such inconsistencies.

REVIEW CHECKPOINTS

16.16 How are prospective financial statements defined?

16.17 What are the similarities and differences between examination reports on forecasts and audit reports on historical financial statements? on compilation reports on forecasts? on compilation reports on historical financial statements?

16.18 What is the auditor's responsibility for information reported in MD&A in the audit of a public company?

FINANCIAL STATEMENTS FOR USE IN OTHER COUNTRIES

LEARNING OBJECTIVE

6 (Continued) Define the various financial presentations and levels of service involved in association with financial forecasts, projections, prospectuses and MD&A.

Auditors practising in Canada are increasingly often being asked to report on Canadian companies' financial statements that are intended for use in other countries, especially the United States. Such financial statements may be used by foreign investors or by foreign parent companies for consolidation in foreign financial statements. For many years, American auditors have obtained financial statements of foreign companies and of subsidiaries of U.S.-based multinational companies for consolidation in a U.S. parent company's financial statements. These foreign statements have been prepared on the basis of U.S. GAAP by foreign managements and auditors, even though the foreign company's statements may also be prepared on the basis of foreign GAAP in other countries for use in those countries.

With increasing globalization of corporate ownership, the shoe is on the other foot, and many U.S. companies are owned by foreign parents. Now, the U.S. company's financial statements must be prepared on the basis of accounting principles used in other countries.

In engagements requiring use of foreign standards, Canadian auditors are expected to follow the Canadian general and field work auditing standards, just as they would in any audit. However, some differences in accounting may arise, and these will change some of the audit objectives. For example, some South American countries permit or require general price-level adjusted measurements (because of high rates of inflation), and these management calculations, applied to the Canadian company's account balances, will need to be audited. Likewise, some countries do not permit recognition of deferred taxes, so no deferred tax account balances will exist for audit. Clearly, the auditors must know the accounting principles applied in the country for which the financial statements are intended. The starting place is in the International Accounting Standards established by the International Accounting Standards Committee.

In addition to knowing the foreign accounting principles, the Canadian auditor may be expected to apply foreign auditing standards and procedures. Some countries have codified their auditing standards in professional literature, like Canada, while others put their auditing standards in statutes and legal-like regulations. They may, in some cases, require more auditing of compliance with laws and regulations or other procedures than Canadian standards require. The audit report can take different forms, depending on the circumstances and the distribution of the foreign-GAAP financial statements:

A. Foreign-GAAP financial statements used only outside Canada. The options are as follows:
1. a Canadian-style report modified to refer to the GAAP of the other country (similar to an AADBA report)
2. the report form used by auditors in the other country

B. Foreign-GAAP financial statements that will have more than limited distribution in Canada. The options are as follows:
   1. the CICA standard report, qualified or adverse for departures from Canadian GAAP, with another separate paragraph expressing an opinion on the fair presentation in conformity with the foreign GAAP
   2. both (*a*) the report form used by auditors in the other country (A2 above) or a Canadian-style report modified to refer to the GAAP of the other country (A1 above), and (*b*) the qualified or adverse Canadian standard report with an additional paragraph expressing an opinion on the foreign GAAP (B1 above)
C. Two sets of financial statements, foreign GAAP and Canadian GAAP, both of which may be distributed in the foreign country and in Canada. Report on each one:
   1. report on the foreign-GAAP financial statements as in A1 above, with an additional paragraph notifying users that another report has been issued on Canadian GAAP financial statements
   2. report on Canadian-GAAP financial statements as normally done for Canadian financial statements, but add a paragraph notifying users that another report has been issued on foreign-GAAP financial statements

When a Canadian client must file with the U.S.'s SEC *and* when there is either a disclaimer due to uncertainty or an explanatory paragraph resulting from a change in accounting principle, a CICA Guideline on Canada–U.S. reporting conflicts[29] should be followed. This Guideline recommends that a Canadian GAAS audit report be issued along with comments that should be added as additional information for American readers.

· ·

R E V I E W
C H E C K P O I N T S

16.19   Why do you think a Canadian-style report on foreign-GAAP financial statements is similar to a report on AADBA financial statements?

16.20   What precautions should Canadian auditors take when reporting on foreign-GAAP financial statements that will be distributed in the United States?

· ·

THE ASSURANCE FRAMEWORK
· · · · · · · · · · · ·

LEARNING OBJECTIVE

7 Describe the umbrella standards for assurance engagements.

Many of the engagements discussed in the preceding sections fell under the new umbrella framework of the assurance engagements issued by the CICA in *CICA Handbook,* section 5025 in April 1997. This standard was introduced in Chapter 2 and compared to GAAS. You should begin by reviewing the discussion there.

The foundation of section 5025 is that of an accountability relationship: "An accountability relationship exists when one party (the "accountable party") is answerable to and/or responsible to another party (the "user") for a subject matter or voluntarily chooses to report to another party on a subject matter."[30]

An assurance engagement can take place only when there is an accountability relationship. Therefore, paragraph 5025.21 makes clear that the auditor needs to obtain evidence that such a relationship exists before taking on an assurance engagement. The usual form of this evidence is acknowledgment of the existence of the relationship by the accountable party, usually management. Failure to obtain such acknowledgment by the accountable party should be disclosed in the practitioner's report.

The existence of the accountability relationship is what distinguishes assurance engagements from other types of engagements such as tax planning and consulting work.[31] In our discussions in Appendix 16A (on the Online Learning Centre), and subsequent chapters, we

---

[29] AUG–21.
[30] *CICA Handbook,* paragraph 5025.04.
[31] Ibid., paragraph 5025.15.

will see that the distinctions between assurance and nonassurance engagements can be very fine indeed. Yet they are very important because assurance engagements with respect to financial statements are what distinguish the PA profession from other professional groups. Thus, the assurance standards delineate the unique responsibilities of auditors (or, more generally now, the assurers).

The type of communication provided by the practitioner or assurer depends on the nature of the assurance engagement. The CICA envisions two major categories of assurance engagements. **Attestation engagements** are those in which the practitioner's (attestation) conclusion will be on a written assertion prepared by the accountable party. The assertion is used to evaluate, using suitable criteria, the subject matter for which the accountable party is responsible. The party making the assertion is sometimes referred to as the asserter.

The other category of assurance engagement is a **direct reporting engagement**. "In a direct reporting engagement, the practitioners' conclusion will evaluate directly using suitable criteria, the subject matter for which the accountable party is responsible."[32] By this definition, the essential distinction between an assurance and a direct reporting engagement is that the assertions are written out by the asserter in an assurance engagement but may be only implied by the asserter in a direct reporting engagement. Despite this seemingly straightforward distinction, we will see that what exactly is meant by a written assertion is still considered by some to be a controversial matter in the current standard. We will discuss the ramifications of this in Appendix 16A, which covers outstanding issues that some feel should remain with the standard.

In order to operationalize the preceding concepts, it is necessary to clarify additional concepts and relate them to the preceding assurance framework. This is shown in paragraphs 5025.08–.13 as follows:

> The practitioner forms a conclusion concerning a subject matter by referring to suitable criteria. Criteria are benchmarks against which the subject matter and, in an attest engagement, mangement's written assertion on the subject matter, can be evaluated.
>
> In an assurance engagement, the practitioner reduces engagement risk to a level that is appropriate for the assurance provided in his or her report. The term engagement risk is the risk that the practitioner may express an inappropriate conclusion. The three components of engagement risk are inherent risk, control risk and detection risk.
>
> Practitioners should in theory be able to vary infinitely the level of assurance provided in assurance engagements. However, in order to help users understand the level of assurance being provided by the practitioner, the standards in this Section limit assurance to two distinct levels—a high level and a moderate level.
>
> In an audit engagement, the practitioner provides a high, though not absolute, level of assurance by designing procedures so that in the practitioner's professional judgment, the risk of an inappropriate conclusion is reduced to a low level through procedures such as inspection, observation, enquiry, confirmation, computation, analysis and discussion. Use of the term "high level of assurance" refers to the highest reasonable level of assurance a practitioner can provide concerning a subject matter. Absolute assurance is not attainable as a result of factors such as the use of judgment, the use of testing, the inherent limitations of control and the fact that much of the evidence available to the practitioner is persuasive rather than conclusive in nature. Assurance will also be influenced by the degree of precision associated with the subject matter itself.
>
> In a review engagement, the practitioner provides a moderate level of assurance by designing procedures so that, in the practitioner's professional judgment, the risk of an inappropriate conclusion is reduced to a moderate level through procedures which are normally limited to enquiry, analysis and discussion. Such risk is reduced to a moderate level when the evidence obtained enables the practitioner to conclude the subject matter is plausible in the circumstances.
>
> Both attest engagements and direct reporting engagements can be completed with either a high or a moderate level of assurance. The level of assurance appropriate for a particular engagement will depend on the needs of users and the nature of the subject matter.

With these concepts and definitions it is now possible to develop meaningful standards for assurance engagements. These have already been listed in Chapter 2 and compared to GAAS. As noted there, the assurance standards are subdivided into (*a*) general standards that

---

[32] Ibid., paragraph 5025.05.

relate to attributes of the practitioner and the need for the practitioner to use suitable criteria in evaluating a subject matter (for example, criteria for control discussed in this chapter); (*b*) performance standards relating to obtaining sufficient appropriate evidence to support the practitioner's conclusion and documenting the basis for the conclusion including the concepts of significance (materiality) and engagement risk as used in assurance engagements; and (*c*) reporting standards prescribing the minimum requirements of the practitioner's report, including those for reservations and the conditions for issuing a reservation in an assurance engagement report.

The truly novel aspects of these standards deal with suitability of criteria, significance, engagement risk and the increasing reliance on specialists contemplated by these standards. As we will see in Chapter 18, all of these concepts originated with public sector auditing standards. Given the varied nature of the engagements contemplated by this standard, it is expected that there could be far more reliance on specialists from other fields, and this creates responsibilities on the practitioner to understand the specialists' work to the extent necessary to fulfill the objectives of the engagement. There is an additional responsibility on the part of the specialist to understand the objectives of the engagement at least as to how they relate to the specialists' expertise.[33] Thus the standards contemplate use of multidisciplinary audit team members to a significantly greater extent than in financial statement audits.

The concept of significance as used in the standard appears to have been influenced by public sector standards (covered in Chapter 18), which use the same concept. Significance can be viewed as an extension of materiality to include broader classes of users whose decisions may be influenced by nonfinancial factors such as, for example, the effectiveness of health care.

Engagement risk is defined in paragraphs 5025.51 and .52 as:

> the risk that the practitioner will express an inappropriate conclusion in his or her report. This risk consists of (a) risks that are beyond the control of management and the practitioner (inherent risk), (b) the risks that are within control of management (control risk) and (c) risks that are within the control of the practitioner (detection risk). The extent to which the practitioner considers the relevant components of engagment risk will be affected by the nature of the subject matter and the level of assurance to be provided.

An interesting aspect of this definition of engagement risk and its components is that the risk is no longer limited to (*a*) risk of failing to detect significant misrepresentations or omissions, but also explicitly includes (*b*) the possibility that the practitioner may report significant items that in fact are not significant relative to the users. The traditional concept of audit risk is consistent with (*a*), but risk (*b*) has never before been explicitly considered in the audit risk model because it has been assumed that this risk is self-correcting. In other words, if the auditor concludes erroneously that there is a material misstatement it has been assumed that additional work will always point out the error to the auditor. The reason risk (*a*) has traditionally been considered the more serious risk is that when this risk occurs the auditor has no evidence to support the proposition of material misstatement when in fact that is the case. Since the auditor's job can be characterized as finding material misstatements, control of risk (*a*) is the reason the auditor was hired in the first place. By extending the risk definition to include risks of the (*b*) type, the standard has potentially changed the risk model for generalized assurance engagements in a significant way that is not completely consistent with the traditional concept of audit risk. The justification for this perhaps is that in the significantly changed environment of assurance engagements auditors need to be explicitly aware of what should be considered significant for various subject matters. A more complete discussion of this risk definition is provided in Appendix 16A.

Perhaps the most important change introduced by section 5025 is the concept of suitable criteria. Paragraph 5025.38 identifies five characteristics of suitable criteria: relevance, reliability, neutrality, understandability and completeness. Since these criteria are supposed to apply to all assurance engagements including financial statement audits, these criteria introduce a potentially revolutionary link to accounting theory in that new characteristics of accounting information may now be contemplated. Notably, financial statement concepts listed in *CICA Handbook,* section 1000 do not list completeness as a characteristic of financial

[33] Ibid., paragraph 5025.34.

statements. Currently, this does not create a problem in the standards because paragraph 5025.02 explicitly exempts existing *CICA Handbook Recommendations* from the assurance engagement standard. In the longer term, however, it appears that some reconciliation may be necessary. Perhaps the most notable aspect of this development is that assurance and accounting standards are for the first time being linked, albeit in a tentative way. Perhaps this indicates a closer co-ordination between accounting and auditing standard setting in the future—a development some consider long overdue in an increasingly complicated and interrelated business world. This also relates to the focus on accountability relations in assurance engagements, which also happens to be a primary objective of financial statements. In Chapter 18 we will see that suitable criteria and accountability relations are also central concepts in public sector auditing.

The introduction to the standard makes it clear that existing *CICA Handbook Recommendations* override the current standard, but that nevertheless the long-term objective of the standard is to provide guidelines where standards currently do not exist and to provide future guidance on more specific recommendations in assurance engagements. In the scope of paragraph 5025.01, the long-term overall objective is described as follows:

> These standards establish a framework for all assurance engagements performed by practitioners and for the on-going development of related standards. The standards apply to:
>
> *(a)* engagements in the private and public sectors;
>
> *(b)* attest engagements and direct reporting engagements;
>
> *(c)* engagements designed to provide a high (i.e., audit) level of assurance; and
>
> *(d)* engagements designed to provide a moderate (i.e., review) level of assurance
>
> The assurance standard appendix makes it clear that the standards apply only when the practitioner provides a conclusion on a subject matter. The following services are not considered to provide a conclusion on a subject matter:
>
> *(a)* specified auditing procedure engagements[34]
>
> *(b)* compilation engagements[35]
>
> *(c)* derivative reporting[36]
>
> *(d)* reports on the application of accounting principles, auditing standards, or review standards[37]

A good overview of the various services and the extent of the PA's involvement is provided as section 5020.B, which is reproduced in the following box.

The purpose of this . . . is to provide examples of information and the nature and extent of the public accountant's involvement with such information.

NOTE: In addition to the professional responsibilities outlined below, the public accountant would comply with the rules of professional conduct of his or her provincial Institute and would therefore, in all cases, exercise due professional skill and care in the work he or she carries out.

TYPE OF INFORMATION RESPONSIBILITIES	NATURE AND EXTENT OF INVOLVEMENT	NATURE AND EXTENT OF ASSOCIATION	PROFESSIONAL WORK	REPORTING
Information that is the subject matter of an assurance	Assurance engagement	The practitioner has associated himself or herself with the subject matter by virtue of the assurance engagement carried out (see paragraph 5020.04)	The practitioner discharges his or her responsibilities by complying with the Recommendations contained in STANDARDS FOR ASSURANCE ENGAGEMENTS, section 5025.	Reporting section of STANDARDS FOR ASSURANCE ENGAGEMENTS, section 5025.

Continued

---

[34] Ibid., paragraph 9100.

[35] Ibid., paragraph 9200.

[36] Ibid., section 5025.A and AUG-13.

[37] *CICA Handbook*, section 7600.

TYPE OF INFORMATION RESPONSIBILITIES	NATURE AND EXTENT OF INVOLVEMENT	NATURE AND EXTENT OF ASSOCIATION	PROFESSIONAL WORK	REPORTING
Financial statements REPORT	Audit	The auditor has associated himself or herself with the financial statements by virtue of the audit work carried out (see paragraph 5020.04)	The auditor discharges his or her responsibilities by complying with the Recommendations contained in GENERALLY ACCEPTED AUDITING STANDARDS, section 5100.	THE AUDITOR'S STANDARD, section 5400.
Financial statements	Review	The public accountant has associated himself of herself with the financial statements by virtue of the review carried out (see paragraph 5020.04).	The public accountant discharges his or her responsibilities by complying with the relevant Recommendations contained in GENERAL REVIEW STANDARDS, section 8100, or REVIEWS OF FINANCIAL STATEMENTS, section 8200.	GENERAL REVIEW STANDARDS, section 8100, or REVIEWS OF FINANCIAL STATEMENTS, section 8200.
Financial statements	Compilation	The public accountant has associated himself or herself with the financial statements by virtue of compiling the financial statements (see paragraph 5020.04).	The public accountant discharges his or her responsibilities by complying with the relevant Recommendations contained in COMPILATION ENGAGEMENTS, section 9200.	COMPILATION ENGAGEMENTS, section 9200
Financing document containing financial information extracted from the audited financial statements.	Consent to use of the auditor's name in the document in connection with the condensed financial information, by consenting to a statement in the document such as, "This condensed financial information has been extracted from the audited financial statements for the year ended December 31, 1986, previously reported on by our auditors ZYX & Co."	The auditor has associated himself or herself with the financial information by consenting to the use of his or her name in connection with that information (see paragraph 5020.04).	The auditor discharges his or her responsibilities by complying with paragraph 5020.13.	No reporting standard. See paragraph 5020.10.
Financing document containing financial information prepared by the client and not reported on by the auditor.	Consent to the inclusion of the auditor's name in the document by, for example, consenting to a factual statement in the document naming lawyers, auditors, etc.	The auditor does not associate himself or herself with the information contained in the document by merely consenting to the inclusion of his or her name in the document (see paragraphs 5020.04 and 5020.16).	The auditor discharges his or her responsibilities by complying with paragraph 5020.17.	No reporting standard. See paragraph 5020.10.
Financial statements	Typing or reproduction services.	The public accountant has associated himself or herself with the financial statements by virtue of the typing or reproduction services carried out (see paragraph 5020.04)	No professional responsibilities other than those discussed in the Note on the first page of this Appendix.	No reporting standard. See paragraph 5020.10.
Annual report or other public documents containing audited or reviewed information.	To determine whether the financial statements and the auditor's report thereon are accurately reproduced in the annual report. To read the other information in the annual report and consider whether any of this information is inconsistent with the financial statements on which the auditor has reported.	The auditor has already associated himself or herself with the financial statements in the annual report by virtue of the audit work carried out. The auditor has also associated himself or herself with the other information in the annual report by virtue of the work carried out under section 7500 (see paragraph 5020.04).	The auditor discharges his or her responsibilities by complying with the Recommendations contained in THE AUDITOR'S ASSOCIATION WITH ANNUAL REPORTS OR OTHER PUBLIC DOCUMENTS, section 7500.	No reporting standard. See paragraph 5020.10.

Continued

TYPE OF INFORMATION RESPONSIBILITIES	NATURE AND EXTENT OF INVOLVEMENT	NATURE AND EXTENT OF ASSOCIATION	PROFESSIONAL WORK	REPORTING
Tax return and financial statements as attachments to the tax returns.	Preparation of tax return (financial statements were prepared by the client).	The public accountant has associated himself or herself with the tax return by virtue of preparing it and providing related tax advice (see paragraph 5020.04). The public accountant has not associated himself or herself with the financial statements because he or she has not performed services in respect of the financial statements or consented to the use of his or her name in connection with the financial statements (see paragraph 5020.04).	No professional responsibilities other than those discussed in the Note on the first page of this Appendix.	No reporting standard. See paragraph 5020.10.

THE ASSOCIATION FRAMEWORK
• • • • • • • • • • • •

LEARNING OBJECTIVE
🔟 Describe the association framework.

The public accounting services covered in this chapter are part of the broadest concept of auditor involvement with information about business enterprises—that of association. Compilation and review engagements are forms of association. *Association* is a term generally used within the profession to indicate a public accountant's involvement with an enterprise or with information issued by that enterprise. General standards for association are covered in section 5020 of the *CICA Handbook*.

Association can arise in three ways:

1. The public accountant associates himself or herself by some action on his or her part with information issued by the enterprise.

2. When the enterprise indicates that the public accountant was involved with information issued by the enterprises without the public accountant's knowledge or consent.

3. A third party assumes the public accountant is involved with information issued by an enterprise.

A public accountant by paragraph 5020.04 associates herself or himself with information when she or he:

(*a*) performs services in respect of that information or

(*b*) consents to use his or her name in connection with that information

A public accountant's professional responsibilities when he or she is associated with information are the following:

1. compliance with applicable standards in the *CICA Handbook*

2. compliance with the rules of professional conduct of his or her provincial institute

3. appropriate communication of the extent of his or her involvement with the information

The PA should ensure that the information he or she is associated with is accurate, accurately reproduced and not misleading. If the client attempts to make inappropriate use of the PA's name, the PA should amend the information or get legal advice.

Exhibit 16–29 provides a framework illustrating the relationships of various types of engagements and *CICA Handbook* sections. As a result of the changes to public accounting

EXHIBIT 16-29 FRAMEWORK FOR ASSOCIATION

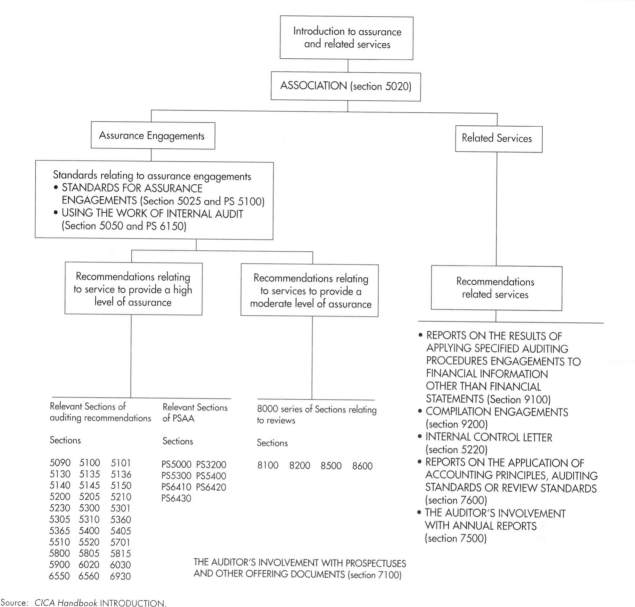

Source: *CICA Handbook* INTRODUCTION.

brought on by section 5025, the concept of association also had to be revised to incorporate the new assurance framework. The new association responsibilities are illustrated in section 5020.A (see the box on page 674).

Revising the concept of association has also necessitated changes to PAs' responses to various client actions with respect to PA communications. The decision tree summarizing PAs' responsibilities with information or subject matters that they are inappropriately associated with is reproduced for section 5020.A (see the box on page 675).

Exhibit 16–28 provides a fairly comprehensive association framework for all assurance engagements.

The CICA and provincial institutes are in the process of sorting out what is public accounting: specifically, should public accounting include or exclude compilations? This is an important issue for CGAs and other practitioners because if a provincial public

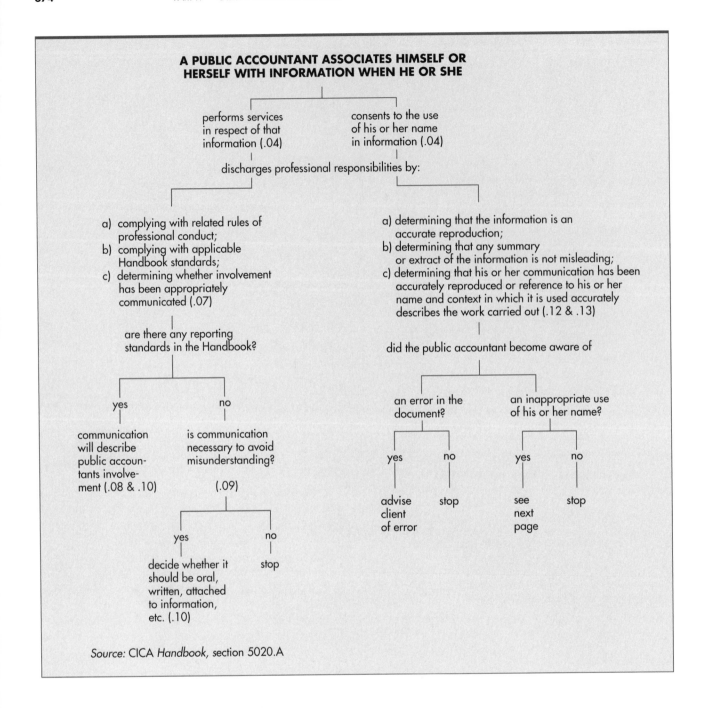

A PUBLIC ACCOUNTANT ASSOCIATES HIMSELF OR HERSELF WITH INFORMATION WHEN HE OR SHE

performs services in respect of that information (.04)

consents to the use of his or her name in information (.04)

discharges professional responsibilities by:

a) complying with related rules of professional conduct;
b) complying with applicable Handbook standards;
c) determining whether involvement has been appropriately communicated (.07)

a) determining that the information is an accurate reproduction;
b) determining that any summary or extract of the information is not misleading;
c) determining that his or her communication has been accurately reproduced or reference to his or her name and context in which it is used accurately describes the work carried out (.12 & .13)

are there any reporting standards in the Handbook?

did the public accountant become aware of

yes

no

communication will describe public accountants involvement (.08 & .10)

is communication necessary to avoid misunderstanding?

(.09)

an error in the document?

an inappropriate use of his or her name?

yes

no

yes

no

decide whether it should be oral, written, attached to information, etc. (.10)

stop

advise client of error

stop

see next page

stop

Source: CICA Handbook, section 5020.A

accountancy act excludes CGAs, then what CGAs can practise is determined by the definition of public accountancy. The trend appears to exclude compilation from the definition of public accountancy.

SUMMARY

Public accountants are highly regarded for assurance services. Many forms of services, in addition to audits of historical financial statements, have arisen or have been proposed. Managers of companies often develop innovative financial presentations, and they want to give the public some assurance about them, so they engage auditors. Regulators also

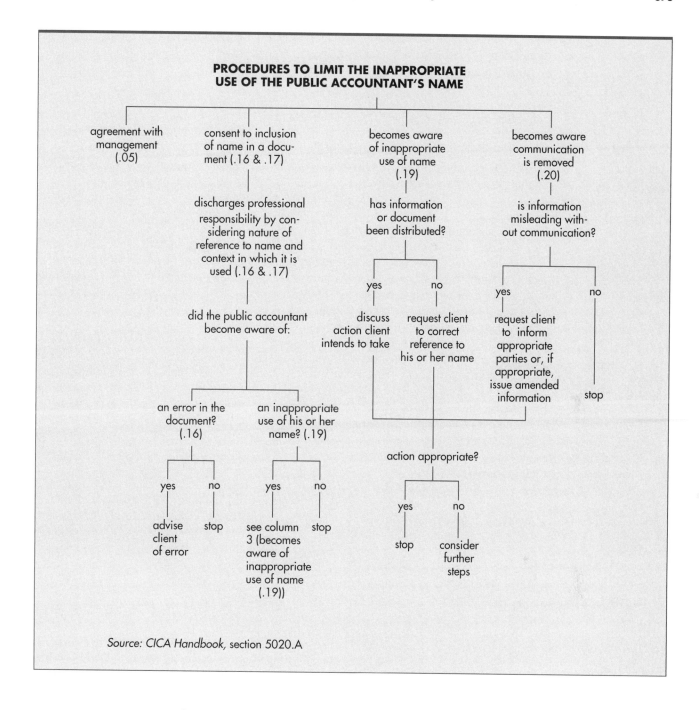

**PROCEDURES TO LIMIT THE INAPPROPRIATE
USE OF THE PUBLIC ACCOUNTANT'S NAME**

agreement with management (.05)

consent to inclusion of name in a document (.16 & .17)

becomes aware of inappropriate use of name (.19)

becomes aware communication is removed (.20)

discharges professional responsibility by considering nature of reference to name and context in which it is used (.16 & .17)

has information or document been distributed?

is information misleading without communication?

did the public accountant become aware of:

yes — discuss action client intends to take

no — request client to correct reference to his or her name

yes — request client to inform appropriate parties or, if appropriate, issue amended information

no — stop

an error in the document? (.16)

an inappropriate use of his or her name? (.19)

yes — advise client of error

no — stop

yes — see column 3 (becomes aware of inappropriate use of name (.19))

no — stop

action appropriate?

yes — stop

no — consider further steps

Source: CICA Handbook, section 5020.A

often become interested in PAs' communication of information and press for assurance involvement.

Guided by auditing, accounting, and review services' standards and the general concepts of assurance, PAs offer services and render reports in several areas. These standards were summarized in Exhibit 16–28.

Unaudited financial statements have been around for a long time. Work on them is known in public practice as review and compilation. The difference lies in the amount of work performed and the level of assurance given in an accountant's report. Review engagements involve less work than an audit, and the report gives a low level of negative assurance instead of an audit opinion. Compilation engagements involve merely writing up the financial statements, which is less work than a review, and the report gives no assurance in the form of an outright denial.

Another type of review is accountants' review of interim financial information (e.g., quarterly financial reports). This review is technically similar to a review of unaudited financial statements, and the report on free-standing interim financial statements gives the negative assurance.

Not everyone wants to produce financial statements fully in conformity with generally accepted accounting principles. Managers have the option to prepare their statements for public use on another appropriate disclosed basis of accounting (AADBA). Auditors can audit and report on such financial statements. This track gives managers an opportunity to avoid the complications of many of the GAAP rules. AADBA audits and reporting are in the auditing standards under the heading of "special reports." Other kinds of special audit reports can be given on parts of financial statements and on current value financial statements.

A special kind of engagement can result in a report on a company's internal control. This report is a positive assurance report on the internal control system. Regulators in some provinces, the SEC, and federal banking agencies have been interested in management reports and audit reports on internal control. This topic of reporting on internal control spills over into auditing standards designed to require auditors to report internally to managers and the board of directors in a company about internal control deficiencies and relations with management in connection with the annual audit.

Innovative managers and promoters frequently use forecasts and projections (known collectively as FOFI) to obtain investors and otherwise inform financial statement users about their estimates of future performance. Auditors can become involved with such presentations by examining or compiling forecasts and projections. In a report on an examination, which is similar to an audit, the accountant gives assurances about the reasonableness of the assumptions underlying the forecast or projection.

The next section in the chapter outlined auditors' responsibilities for reporting on financial statements prepared in accordance with the accounting principles generally accepted in other countries.

Next, the chapter covered the CICA's recent attempt to develop an umbrella framework for many of the PA services via the assurance engagement concept. The chapter concluded with a modified framework for all PA services resulting from introduction of the assurance engagement concept.

MULTIPLE-CHOICE QUESTIONS FOR PRACTICE AND REVIEW

16.21 Which of the following can be considered a prospective financial statement?
a. Balance sheet based on current values of assets and liabilities.
b. Interim-date balance sheet for the first quarter of the fiscal year.
c. Forecasted income statement based on assumptions about expected conditions and expected conditions and expected courses of action.
d. Forecasted valuation of securities held by a venture capital company.

16.22 Which of the following statements is correct?
a. An examination report on prospective financial statements gives the same assurance as an audit report on historical financial statements.
b. An examination report on prospective financial statements does not attest to the achievability of the forecast.

c. In a compilation report on prospective financial statements, an accountant attests to the reasonableness of the underlying forecast assumptions.
d. In reports on prospective financial statements, accountants undertake the obligation to update the reports for important subsequent events.

16.23 Under the Securities and Exchange Commission "safe harbour" rule regarding financial forecasts, persons connected with a company's forecast can be liable for monetary damages if:
a. The plaintiffs are able to prove that the persons connected with the forecast showed lack of good faith and lack of a reasonable basis for belief in the forecast.
b. The plaintiffs are able to prove that the persons connected with the forecast were merely negligent.
c. The persons connected with the forecast had good faith and a reasonable basis for belief in its presentation.

d. The persons connected with a forecast cannot sustain the burden of proof that they acted in good faith and with a reasonable basis for belief in the forecast.

16.24 In a current-value presentation of the balance sheet of a manufacturing company:

a. The basis of valuation must always be explained in notes to the financial statements.

b. The basis of valuation is well known as a "comprehensive basis of accounting other than GAAP."

c. An auditor can attest to the fair presentation of financial position in conformity with GAAP.

d. The company must follow the AICPA guides for presentation of a financial forecast.

16.25 Practice in connection with unaudited historical-cost financial statements is conducted by:

a. International accounting firms only.

b. Regional- and local-size PA firms.

c. Local-size PA firms only.

d. All PA firms.

16.26 The official CICA Recommendations for Compilation and Review services are applicable to practice with:

a. Audited financial statements of public companies.

b. Unaudited financial statements of some companies.

c. Unaudited financial statements of all companies.

d. Audited financial statements of nonpublic companies.

16.27 A review service engagement for an accountant's association with unaudited financial statements involves:

a. More work than a compilation, and more than an audit.

b. Less work than an audit, but more than a compilation.

c. Less work than a compilation, but more than an audit.

d. More work than an audit, but less than a compilation.

16.28 When an accountant is not independent, the following report can nevertheless be given:

a. Compilation report.

b. Standard unqualified audit report.

c. Examination report on a forecast.

d. Review report on unaudited financial statements.

16.29 An accountant is permitted to express "negative assurance" in which of the following types of reports.

a. Standard unqualified audit report on audited financial statements.

b. Compilation report on unaudited financial statements.

c. Review report on unaudited financial statements.

d. Adverse opinion report on audited financial statements.

16.30 When a company's financial statements in a review or compilation engagement contain a known material departure from GAAP, the accountant's report can:

a. Make no mention of the departure in a compilation report because it contains an explicit disclaimer of opinion.

b. Express the adverse conclusion: "The accompanying financial statements are not presented in conformity with generally accepted accounting principles."

c. Explain the departure as necessary to make the statements not misleading, then give the standard compilation report disclaimer.

d. Explain the departure as necessary to make the statements not misleading, then give the standard eview report negative assurance.

16.31 When interim financial information is presented in a note to annual financial statements, the standard audit report on the annual financial statements should:

a. Not mention the interim information unless there is an exception the auditor needs to include in the report.

b. Contain an audit opinion paragraph that specifically mentions the interim financial information if it is not in conformity with GAAP.

c. Contain an extra paragraph that gives negative assurance on the interim information, if it has been reviewed.

d. Contain an extra explanatory paragraph if the interim information note is labelled "unaudited."

16.32 According to auditing standards, financial statements presented on another comprehensive basis of accounting should not:

a. Contain a note describing the other basis of accounting.

b. Describe in general how the other basis of accounting differs from generally accepted accounting principles.

c. Be accompanied by an audit report that gives an unqualified opinion with reference to the other basis of accounting.

d. Contain a note with a quantified dollar reconciliation of the assets based on the other comprehensive basis of accounting with the assets based on generally accepted accounting principles.

16.33 For which of the following reports is an expression of negative assurance not permitted?

a. A review report on unaudited financial statements.

b. An audit report on financial statements prepared on a comprehensive basis of accounting other than GAAP.

c. A report based on applying selected procedures agreed upon by the client and the auditor.

d. A review report on interim financial information.

16.34 Which one of these events is an auditor not required to communicate to a company's audit committee or board of directors?

a. Management's significant accounting policies.

b. Management judgements about accounting estimates used in the financial statements.

c. Immaterial errors in processing transactions discovered by the auditors.

d. Disagreements with management about accounting principles.

EXERCISES AND PROBLEMS

. . . .

16.35 Review of Forecast Assumptions. You have been engaged
LO.6 by the Dodd Manufacturing Corporation to attest to the
reasonableness of the assumptions underlying its forecast
of revenues, costs and net income for the next calendar
year, 20X4. Four of the assumptions are shown following.

a. The company intends to sell certain real estate and
other facilities held by Division B at an aftertax
profit of $600,000; the proceeds of this sale will be
used to retire outstanding debt.

b. The company will call and retire all outstanding
9 percent subordinated debentures (callable at 108).
The debentures are expected to require the full call
premium given present market interest rates of 8 percent on similar debt. A rise in market interest rates to
9 percent would reduce the loss on bond retirement
from the projected $200,000 to $190,000.

c. Current labour contracts expire on September 1,
20X4, and the new contract is expected to result in a
wage increase of 5.5 percent. Given the forecasted
levels of production and sales, aftertax operating
earnings would be reduced approximately $50,000
for each percentage-point wage increase in excess of
the expected contract settlement.

d. The sales forecast for Division A assumes that the
new Portsmouth facility will be complete and operating at 40 percent of capacity on February 1, 20X4.
It is highly improbable that the facility will be operational before January of 20X4. Each month's delay
would reduce sales of Division A by approximately
$80,000 and operating earnings by $30,000.

Required:

For each assumption, state the evidence sources and
procedures you would use to determine the reasonableness.

16.36 Auditing a Current Value Balance Sheet. Your client,
LO.5 the Neighbourhood Paper Company (NPC), has a fiscal
year-end of December 31. NPC needs to borrow money
from a local bank and believes current value financial
statements that report the appreciated value of its assets
would be helpful. A loan is needed for working capital
purposes.

NPC owns two paper-recycling processors. Old paper
is chemically processed, reduced to a wet mass, and then
pressed out into thick, semifinished paper mats. The mats
are sold to customers who use them for packing material.
Recycling processors are fairly complex pieces of integrated machinery and are built on a customized basis by
a few specialized engineering companies.

NPC has owned one of the processors for five years.
It was appraised last year at $135,000 by a qualified en-
gineering appraiser. The second processor was purchased last month for $125,000—its appraised value—
and $10,000 was spent in bringing certain maintenance
up to date. Both processors have identical throughput
production capabilities.

The other major asset is a nine-acre plot of land NPC
bought four years ago when management thought the
plant would be moved. The land was purchased for
$195,000 and was appraised by a qualified appraiser at
$250,000 only 20 months after the purchase date. The
nine acres are located near a rapidly expanding industrial area.

Since the recycling processors were appraised/pur-
chased so recently, management does not want to bear
the expense of new appraisals this year. No plans have
been made to obtain a new appraisal on the land. NPC,
however, is a profitable operation. The unaudited income statement for the current year (historical-cost
basis) shows net income of $46,000.

Required:

a. What practice standards are applicable to the
engagement to review and report on the current value
balance sheet?

b. What primary auditing procedures should you apply
in addition to those necessary for the audit of the
historical-cost financial statements?

c. Will any additional disclosures in footnotes be
necessary?

d. Are there any evidential problems in the NPC situation that might prevent your rendering a report on the
current value balance sheet?

16.37 Compilation Presentation Alternatives. Jimmy C op-
LO.1 erates a large service station, garage, and truck stop on
Freeway 95 near Plainview. His brother, Bill, has recently joined as a partner, even though he still keeps a
small PA practice. One slow afternoon, they were discussing financial statements with Bert, the local PA who
operates the largest public practice in Plainview.

Jimmy: The business is growing, and sometimes I need
to show financial statements to parts suppliers and
to the loan officers at the bank.

Bert: That so.

Jimmy: Yea-boy, and they don't like the way I put 'em
together.

Bert: That so.

Bill: Heck, Jimmy, I know all about that. I can compile
a jim-dandy set of financial statements for us.

Jimmy: What does Jim Dan over at the café have to do
with it?

Bert: Never mind, Jimmy. Bill can't do compiled financial statements for you. He's not independent.

Jimmy: I know, Momma didn't let him outa the house
'til he was 24. The neighbours complained.

Bert: That so.

Bill: Shucks.

Jimmy: But Bert, those fellas are always asking me
about accounting policies, contingencies and stuff
like that. Said something about "footnotes." I
don't want to fool with all that small print.

Required:

Think about the financial disclosure problems of Jimmy and Bill's small business. What three kinds of compiled financial statements can be prepared for them and by whom?

16.38 Negative Assurance in Review Reports. One portion
LO.2 of the report on a review services engagement is the following: Based on my review, I am not aware of any material modifications that should be made to the accompanying financial statements in order for them to be in conformity with generally accepted accounting principles.

Required:

a. Is this paragraph a "negative assurance" given by the PA?

b. Why is "negative assurance" generally prohibited in audit reports?

c. What justification is there for permitting "negative assurance" in a review services report on unaudited financial statements and on interim financial information?

16.39 Reporting on a Forecast. Kingston Company proposed
LO.6 to sell to investors limited partnership interests in 40 new hardware store buildings. Kingston Company would be the general partner. The deal was structured to raise funds for business expansion by offering a real estate investment. As part of the offering material, Kingston management produced a forecast based on the assumption of $1.5 million gross annual revenue for each new location. The lease income to the partnership is to be a base rental fee plus 10 percent of gross revenue in excess of $1 million. Kingston's existing stores have gross revenues ranging from $800,000 to $1.75 million. Kingston also produced related balance sheets and statements of changes in financial position, all in conformity with AICPA forecast presentation guidelines.

Kingston engaged Anderson, Olds & Watershed to examine the forecast and submit a report. One of the assistant accountants on the engagement drafted the opinion paragraph of the report as follows:

> In our opinion, the accompanying forecast is presented in conformity with guidelines for presentation of a forecast established by the American Institute of Certified Public Accountants, and the underlying assumption of $1.5 million average revenue per store is sufficient to cover the fixed and variable expenses of store maintenance, taxes and insurance, which are the obligations of the limited partners. However, there will usually be differences between the forecasted and actual results because store revenues frequently do not materialize as expected, and the shortfall may be material. We have no responsibility to update this report for events and circumstances occurring after the date of this report.

Required:

Identify and explain the errors, if any, in this portion of the forecast examination report.

16.40 Review Standards, Knowledge of Business. Two PAs
LO.1 are discussing review engagements.

A: As I see it, in a review we are providing a lower level of assurance and so we don't need the same extent of knowledge of the client's business and industry as we do in an audit.

B: That seems to be what the profession's review standards imply. But, at the same time, performing a review requires us to develop a "plausibility framework" that involves using enquiries and analytical procedures to assess whether the information being reported on is plausible in the circumstances. I don't see how this can be done unless I have an in-depth understanding of the client's business and its industry. To me this seems logically inconsistent: knowledge of the business and industry is critical in doing a review effectively so how can I do a review with less knowledge than I need for an audit? And how do I know how much knowledge is "enough"?

A: I see your point. In some ways it seems knowledge of business is MORE critical in a review, not less, because in the audit you can rely on evidence. In a review you have to do it all by judgment.

B: And then, to make it even more confusing, there is also the "Strategic Systems Approach" to auditing that some auditors use, that seems to rely heavily on gathering knowledge of the business, its strategy and its industry environment, but less on gathering hard, transaction-based audit evidence. So how does an SSA audit differ from a review?

Required:

Discuss the differences between these types of engagements, the assurance levels provided, and the knowledge and procedures required. Are the standards consistent in your view? What factors do PAs need to consider in deciding how much knowledge is enough and what procedures are required in a particular assurance engagement?

16.41 Review Procedures, Bank Confirmations You have
LO.1 recently been hired as a junior accountant for a local PA firm. The firm's main practice involves reviews, compilations and tax return preparation for small to medium business clients. The firm's policy for all review engagements is to always obtain a bank confirmation and reperform the client's year-end bank reconciliation. You have recently been studying about review engagement standards for one of your professional accounting exams, and point out to your senior that these procedures are not actually required by the standards. This means your firm could save some money by skipping them. The senior agrees because, in her view, "Cash is a pretty low-risk account anyway. It's either right or wrong." but she notes that the firm's five partners are the ones who set the policy. "Maybe you should pull together a report on the advantages and disadvantages of this policy and present it to the partners — you might be able to make a big impression on them right away!"

Required:

a. Prepare the report suggested by your senior and include your conclusion on whether on not this policy is appropriate.

b. Why do you think the partners have this policy? How do you think they will respond to your report and your conclusion?

16.42 Compilations, Independence. PA has compiled the an-
LO.1 nual financial statements for her sister's pharmacy business since it started four years ago. The financial statements are attached to the pharmacy's corporate tax
return and are also provided to the company's banker to
support the company's operating credit line. The banker
has been satisfied with receiving tax-based financial
statements compiled by PA.

Required:
a. Draft the report that PA should attach to the pharmacy company's financial statements.
b. Assume that in the fifth year of the pharmacy's business, PA's sister decides to increase her bank credit
line to renovate the pharmacy store and stock an
expanded product line. To approve the higher credit
line, the banker now requires financial statements
prepared in accordance with GAAP. What actions
must PA take under these new circumstances? How
would these requirements differ if PA was not related
to the pharmacy's owner?

16.43 Communications with Predecessor Auditor. Assume
LO.7 the role of the predecessor auditor and state what you
would include in your communication with the successor auditor in the following independent situations.
a. You resigned from the audit because the client has
not paid your fees for the previous year's audit.
b. You resigned from the audit because of concerns
about management's integrity after discovering
many personal expenses of the senior managers had
been improperly charged to the company's account.
c. The client dismissed you as auditor over a disagreement about the amount of inventory that should be
written down for obsolescence.
d. The client dismissed you because your audit report
in the previous year was a Denial of Opinion, resulting from serious deficiencies in the company's
accounting records and internal controls
e. For each of the situations in a) to d) above assume
instead that you are the successor auditor and have
received the above communications from the predecessor auditor. What action would you take on
receiving the communication in each case?

16.44 Reviews, Interim Reports. PA is the auditor of Shire
LO.2 Corp., a public company, and has also been engaged to
review Shire's third quarter interim financial statements.
Shire's third quarter financial statements will be filed
with the securities regulator within 30 days of the quarter end, and will also be posted on Shire's corporate
website at that time.

Required:
a. Describe the procedures PA will use to review the
quarterly financial statements and the contents of
PA's review engagement report.

b. How might PA's work on the prior year-end audit
relate to and help with the review of the third quarter report? (Consider what difficulties PA might have
in conducting this review if PA did not also do the
audit.)

16.45 Special Reports. P. Nonius is the owner/manager of a
LO.3 company that owns several suburban shopping malls.
The retail store lease contracts require the store tenants
to pay a flat amount monthly, plus 1/2 percent of their
gross retail sales revenues quarterly. Nonius is concerned that some of the lessees are understating their
quarterly gross retail sales. Nonius has contacted you, a
PA, to enquire about getting some assurance on the
completeness of the retail sales reported by the tenants.
You have arranged to meet with Nonius next week to
discuss this engagement?

Required:
a. Prepare notes for your meeting with Nonius that
describe the assurance reporting options available
here (e.g., audit of the sales revenues, or applying
specified procedures, or other options) and outline
the features of each option to help Nonius decide on
the type of assurance that will meet the objective in
the most cost-effective way.
b. You are aware that Nonius is very cost conscious and
will be reluctant to incur the additional cost of getting assurance on the tenants' sales revenues. What
additional points could you raise in the meeting with
Nonius to show the value that can be provided to
Nonius's business by the assurance report itself, and
by other aspects of the assurance engagement?

16.46 Assurance Framework, Accountability Report. In a
LO.7 recent round of federal-provincial healthcare funding
negotiations, the federal government took the position
that any additional funding it provides to the provinces
needs to be targeted to specific healthcare programs,
such as homecare. As a condition of funding, the federal
government would require that the provincial governments provide reports on their "accountability" for
spending the funds on the programs specified by the
federal government. Consider the case of a hospital that
is accountable for implementing a homecare program,
where people who require medical care will be treated
in their home by hospital staff rather than being kept in
the hospital.

Required:
a. Consider what information, or "subject matters," the
hospital would include in a "homecare accountability" report. Give a brief list of general categories that
would be relevant in this report.
b. List the five characteristics of suitable criteria for an
assurance engagement provided in CICA Section
5025 and in the chapter, and explain how each would
be applied to the categories of information that you
generated in part a) above.
c. Briefly describe some procedures you would perform to provide a high level of assurance on the

subject matters reported. How would your procedures differ if you were providing only a moderate level of assurance?

16.47 Environmental Matters in a Financial Statement
LO.9 **Audit.** PA is the senior in charge of the November 30, 20X1 audit of Baint's Paints Inc., a manufacturer of various latex and oil-based paints. Baint's plant is located on the banks of the Nod River. It was originally constructed on this site in the 1930's because the river provided a ready supply of water for manufacturing the paint, for cleaning out the tanks the paint is made in, and for dumping various surplus liquids that are produced in the manufacturing process. With the passage of environmental legislation in the 1970s, Baint's was no longer permitted to use the river water to clean its manufacturing tanks and was required to have all surplus manufacturing liquid removed by tanker truck for disposal elsewhere because many of these liquids were toxic to the environment and wildlife. While this environmental regulation severely cut into Baint's profitability, it was able to reduce costs in other aspects of the operation and remain in business, though at a somewhat lower level of profitability. During her tour of the manufacturing operation, PA learns from Baint's production manager that the plant capacity is approximately 80,000 litres of paint per month and paint is manufactured from February to November. No paint is made in December and January because of the cold weather. These two months are used for plant maintenance and clean up. Baint's can sell all the paint it produces, and so production volumes are quite consistent from year to year. The wastage in the paint manufacturing process ranges between 5 and 6 percent of volume. The plant manager estimates that tank cleaning produces about 20,000 litres of waste water a month during production, and about 100,000 litres in December and January as all the pipes and pumping equipment is thoroughly flushed during the plant shutdown. Waste water and paints are stored in 500 litre drums until the disposal company takes them away. The disposal company returns the empty drums to Baint's plant for refilling.

During her analytical review of the revenue and expense accounts, PA notes that the processing costs are significant lower in the current year than in the prior years. The main component of processing costs contributing to the decline is the cost of waste disposal. Suspecting a possible error in recording these costs, PA finds out from the accounts payable clerk that the disposal company charges $100 per drum. Using this in her analysis she estimates that Baint's has not paid for dis-

posal of approximately 80 percent of the waste liquid it would have produced during the year. When she presents her analysis to the General Manager for further explanation, he reports that during the shutdown last year, he found a new disposal company that will take away the waste liquid for only $12 a drum, thus providing this substantial saving in the current year. While she is assessing the plausibility of all this analytical evidence, it occurs to PA that she has been working on the audit at the plant for two weeks now, arriving before light and leaving just at nightfall each day, and has never observed a disposal truck taking away the waste liquid drums.

Required:
a. Use the analytical information provided in the case to assess the approximate disposal costs and volumes. State any assumptions you make.
b. Does the General Manager's explanation make sense? What other possibilities might PA consider and what additional information might she try to obtain.
c. To what extent is PA responsible for assessing the environmental compliance of Baint's Paints? Consider the implications of possible financial misstatements, as well as of possible illegal acts by management.

16.48 Association. State whether PA is associated with the
LO.10 financial information in the following independent situations.
a. PA compiles financial statements and prepares the corporate tax return for Appaloosa Inc.
b. PA advised Brumby Inc. on a sinking-fund amortization policy for its real estate investments; Brumby is the audit client of a different public accountant.
c. Criollo Inc. provides its banker with internal financial statements that have not been compiled, reviewed or audited by PA, and informs the banker that PA is Criollo's independent accountant.
d. Fjord Company Ltd. is producing promotional material for its sales staff to use to get new customers. The promotional material includes a section titled "Fjord Company Facts" that lists company information such as the names of Fjord's CEO, CFP, COO, law firm, and accountant.
e. PA has performed an audit of Haflinger Inc. and has concluded that a denial of opinion is warranted because of severe internal control weaknesses and concerns about management's integrity.
f. PA prepares Hunter Inc.'s corporate tax return based solely on financial information produced by Hunter's accounting staff.

DISCUSSION CASES

· ·

16.49 Internal Control Reports. Do a class
LO.5 survey of internal control reports by auditors in 2006 at www.sec.gov. What is the most common criteria used to evaluate internal controls? Discuss.

16.50 Controls and Financial Statements. Should
LO.5 there be a relationship between audit reports on internal control statements and audit reports of financial statements? Discuss.

CHAPTER

17

Fraud Awareness Auditing

Fraud awareness auditing can be exciting with its aura of detectives investigating situations that people wish to keep hidden. However, fraud awareness auditing and examination are complex auditing activities that should not be pursued without proper training, experience and care.

LEARNING OBJECTIVES

After completing this chapter, you will be able to:

1 Differentiate among frauds, errors, irregularities and illegal acts that might occur in an organization.

2 Explain the auditing standards related to external, internal and governmental auditors' responsibilities to detect and report frauds, errors, irregularities and illegal acts.

3 Outline some of the conditions that lead to frauds.

4 Describe ways and means to prevent frauds.

5 Explain the audit and investigative procedures for detecting common employee fraud schemes.

6 Explain the audit and investigative procedures for detecting common fraudulent financial reporting.

7* Explain the use of extended audit procedures for detecting fraud.

8* Summarize how PAs can assist in prosecuting fraud perpetrators.

Note: Those learning objectives marked with an asterisk (*) and their corresponding topics are considered advanced topics.

INTRODUCTION

· · · · · · · · · · · ·

This chapter is not intended to make you a fraud examiner or fraud auditor. Instead, its purpose is to heighten your familiarity with the nature, signs, prevention, detection and reaction to fraud that can enable you to perform financial statement audits with awareness of fraud possibilities.

Users of audited financial statements generally believe that one of the main objectives of audits is fraud detection. External auditors know the issue is very complex, and they fear the general view that their work should ferret out all manner of major and minor fraud and misstatement in financial statements. This difference in viewpoints is one of the chronic "expectation gaps" between external auditors and users of published financial statements. However, in the post-Enron environment this expectation gap is increasingly being closed by meeting user needs.

Part of the gap arises from the ability and expertise needed to be a fraud examiner or fraud auditor. Most of the trained and experienced fraud examiners come from government agencies, such as Canada Revenue Agency, the Royal Canadian Mounted Police (RCMP), the Office of the Auditor General of Canada (OAG), provincial securities commissions (especially the OSC), the Minister of Justice and various police departments. Alumni of these agencies often practise as consultants and fraud examiners, but few of them enter public accounting to become financial statement auditors. So, what are most financial statement auditors to do? One option is to become more aware of fraud possibilities so that they can perform a limited set of procedures and determine when it is necessary to call upon people with greater fraud examination expertise. Financial statement auditors need to understand fraud and potential fraud situations, and they need to know how to ask the right kinds of questions during an audit. We know this is not impossible because there has always been the odd investigative job to be done by accountants. For example, one of the best known fraud auditors in Canada got started by doing an investigative audit of a former owner of the Toronto Maple Leafs hockey team.

DEFINITIONS RELATED TO FRAUD

· · · · · · · · · · · ·

LEARNING OBJECTIVE

1 Differentiate among frauds, errors, irregularities and illegal acts that might occur in an organization.

There are several kinds of fraud. Some are defined in laws, while others are matters of general understanding. Exhibit 17–1 shows some acts and devices often involved in financial frauds. Collectively, these are known as **white-collar crime**—the misdeeds done by people who wear ties to work and steal with a pencil or a computer terminal. In white-collar crime there are ink stains instead of bloodstains.

Fraud consists of knowingly making material misrepresentations of fact, with the intent of inducing someone to believe the falsehood and act upon it and, thus, suffer a loss or damage. This definition encompasses all the varieties by which people can lie, cheat, steal and dupe other people.

Employee fraud is the use of fraudulent means to take money or other property from an employer. It usually involves falsifications of some kind—false documents, lying, exceeding authority or violating an employer's policies. It consists of three phases: (1) the fraudulent act, (2) the conversion of the money or property to the fraudster's use, and (3) the cover-up.

Embezzlement is a type of fraud involving employees' or nonemployees' wrongfully taking money or property entrusted to their care, custody and control, often accompanied by false accounting entries and other forms of lying and cover-up.

Defalcation is another name for employee fraud and embezzlement. Technically, defalcation is the term used when somebody in charge of safekeeping the assets is doing the stealing.

EXHIBIT 17-1   AN ABUNDANCE OF FRAUDS

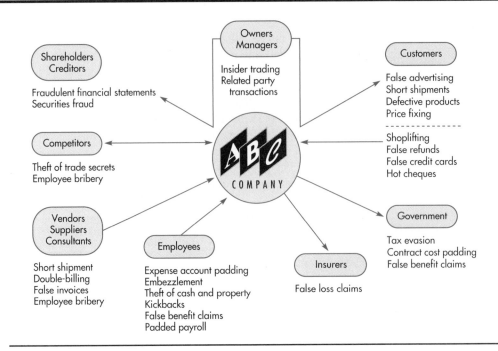

Management fraud is deliberate fraud committed by management that injures investors and creditors through exploitation of authority delegated to management. Weaknesses in corporate governance create opportunities for management fraud. The class of perpetrators is management; the class of victims is investors and creditors; and the instrument of perpetration is the corporation.[1] A special type of management fraud is fraudulent financial reporting. **Fraudulent financial reporting** was defined by the National Commission on Fraudulent Financial Reporting (1987) as intentional or reckless conduct, whether by act or omission, that results in materially misleading financial statements.

The *CICA Handbook,* section 5135, concept of fraud can be summarized as follows

Fraud and other irregularities refer to an intentional misstatement in financial statements, including an omission of amount or disclosure, or to a misstatement arising from theft of the entity's assets. Fraud also involves:

(*i*) the use of deception such as manipulation, falsification, or alteration of accounting records or documentation;

(*ii*) misrepresentation or intentional omission of events, transactions, or other significant information; or

(*iii*) intentional misapplication of accounting principles relating to amount, classification, or manner of presentation of disclosure.

The word *fraud* is used in this section, although in practice the auditor will normally be concerned with a suspected rather than a proven fraud. Final determination of whether fraud has occurred is a legal matter to be decided by a court of law.

Errors are unintentional misstatements or omissions of amounts or disclosures in financial statements. **Irregularities** are intentional misstatements or omissions in financial statements, including fraudulent financial reporting (management fraud) and misappropriations of assets (defalcations). **Direct-effect illegal acts** are violations of laws or government regulations by the company or its management or employees that produce direct and material effects on dollar amounts in financial statements.

---

[1] Elliott, R. K., and J. J. Willingham, *Management Fraud: Detection and Deterrence* (New York: Petrocelli Books, Inc., 1980), p. 4.

Fraud auditing has been defined in courses conducted by the Association of Certified Fraud Examiners as a proactive approach to detect financial frauds using accounting records and information, analytical relationships and an awareness of fraud perpetration and concealment schemes. A good overview of the nature and scale of the fraud problem in Canada is provided by KPMG's Annual Fraud Report. For example, the 2004 report included the findings listed in the box following.

KPMG 2004 SURVEY ON THE RISK OF MANIPULATION OF FINANCIAL STATEMENTS

In a survey sent to the directors of 75 of Canada's largest corporations, 84 percent said that they think it is likely they will hear of a public company in Canada that has been involved in financial statement manipulation in 2004, according to the *2004 Survey on the Risk of Manipulation of Financial Statements* published by KPMG Forensic.

A further 46 percent thought it possible that such manipulation could occur in the company of the Board on which they themselves sit.

"It's illuminating that our survey results show that this type of fraudulent behaviour carried out as a conspiracy by a group of senior people to deceive corporate directors, auditors, lenders and other stakeholders to line their own pockets, has come to be seen as commonplace," says James Hunter, President, KPMG Forensic.

Sixty-two percent of directors said that compensation models based on profitability encourage manipulation by CEOs and CFOs. However, directors also argued that the CEO and CFO both bear the greatest responsibility for protecting stakeholders against fraud.

Only 28 percent of respondents thought the Board of Directors are ultimately responsible for ensuring that financial statements have not been deliberately manipulated. However, 47 percent felt that it is the CEO who bears the greatest responsibility for protecting against such manipulations.

Source: www.kpmg.ca/en/services/advisory/forensic/manipulationSurvey2004.html. © 2006 KPMG LLP, the Canadian member firm of KPMG International, a Swiss cooperative. All rights reserved.

Characteristics of Fraudsters

White-collar criminals are not like typical bank robbers, who are often described as "young and dumb." Bank robbers and other strong-arm artists often make comical mistakes like writing the holdup note on the back of a probation identification card, leaving the getaway car keys on the convenience store counter, using a zucchini as a holdup weapon and timing the holdup to get stuck in rush-hour traffic. Then there's the classic story about the robber who ran into his own mother at the bank (she turned him in!).

Burglars and robbers average about $400–$500 for each hit. Employee frauds average $20,000, or up to $500,000 if a computer is used. Yet, employee frauds are not usually the intricate, well-disguised ploys you find in espionage novels. Who are these thieves wearing ties? What do they look like? Unfortunately, they "look like" most everybody else, including you and me. They have these characteristics:

- likely to be married
- not likely to be divorced
- probably not tattooed
- member of a church
- educated beyond high school

- no arrest record
- range in age from teens to over 60
- socially conforming
- employment tenure from 1 to 20 or more years
- usually act alone (70 percent of incidents)

White-collar criminals do not make themselves obvious, although there may be telltale signs, which will be described later as "red flags." Unfortunately, the largest frauds are committed by people who hold high executive positions, have long tenure with an organization and are respected and trusted employees. After all, these are the people who have access to the largest amounts of money and have the power to give orders and override controls.

The Art of Fraud Awareness Auditing

Fraud examination work combines the expertise of auditors and criminal investigators. Fraud examiners are fond of saying that their successes are the result of accidents, hunches or luck. Nothing can be further from the truth. Successes come from experience, application of logic and the ability to see things that are not obvious (as Sherlock Holmes noticed the dog that did not bark). Fraud awareness auditing, broadly speaking, involves familiarity with many elements: the human element, organizational behaviour, knowledge of common fraud schemes, evidence and its sources, standards of proof and sensitivity to red flags.[2]

Independent auditors of financial statements and fraud examiners approach their work differently. While there are many differences, these are some of the most important and obvious ones:

- Financial auditors follow a program/procedural approach designed to accomplish a fairly standard job, while fraud examiners float in a mindset of sensitivity to the unusual where nothing is standard.
- Financial auditors make note of errors and omissions, while fraud examiners focus as well on exceptions, oddities and patterns of conduct.
- Financial auditors assess control risk in general and specific terms to design other audit procedures, while fraud examiners habitually "think like a crook" to imagine ways that controls could be subverted for fraudulent purposes.
- Financial auditors work to a level of materiality (dollar size big enough to matter) that is usually much higher than the amounts that fraud examiners consider worth pursuing. Financial auditors use materiality as a measure of importance one year at a time,

---

WHO DOES IT?

Alex W. was a 47-year-old treasurer of a credit union. Over a seven-year period, he stole $160,000. He was a good husband and the father of six children, and he was a highly reputed official of the credit union. His misappropriations came as a stunning surprise to his associates. He owed significant amounts on his home, cars, university for two children, two side investments and five different credit cards. His monthly payments significantly exceeded his take-home pay.

Source: "Auditing for Internal Fraud," training course © 2006 Association of Certified Fraud Examiners.

---

[2] These and other aspects of the art of fraud auditing are more fully developed in G.J. Bologna and R.J. Lindquist, *Fraud Auditing and Forensic Accounting* (New York: John Wiley & Sons, 1987), pp. 27–42; W.S. Albrecht, M.B. Romney, D.J. Cherrington, I.R. Payne, and A.J. Roe, *How to Detect and Prevent Business Fraud* (New York: Prentice-Hall, 1982); R. White and W.G. Bishop, III, *The Role of the Internal Auditor in the Deterrence, Detection, and Reporting of Fraudulent Financial Reporting* (The Institute of Internal Auditors); and M.J. Barrett and R.N. Carolus, *Control and Internal Auditing* (The Institute of Internal Auditors).

> ## THE CASE OF THE EXTRA CHECKOUT
>
> The district grocery store manager could not understand why receipts and profitability had fallen and inventory was hard to manage at one of the largest stores in her area. She hired an investigator who covertly observed the checkout clerks and reported that no one had shown suspicious behaviour at any of the nine checkout counters. Nine? That store only has eight, she exclaimed! (The store manager had installed another checkout aisle, not connected to the cash receipts and inventory maintenance central computer, and was pocketing all the receipts from that register.)

whereas fraud examiners think in terms of cumulative materiality. (Theft of $20,000 per year may not loom large each year, but after a 15-year fraud career, $300,000 is a considerable loss.)

- Financial audits are based on theories of financial accounting and auditing logic, while fraud examination has a theory of behavioural motive, opportunity and integrity.

External and internal auditors get credit for finding about 10–20 percent of discovered frauds. Larger percentages are discovered by voluntary confessions, anonymous tips and other haphazard means. Fraud examiners have a higher success rate because they are called in for a specific purpose when fraud is known or highly suspected.

Some aspects of audit methodology make a big difference in the fraud discovery success experience. Financial auditors often utilize inductive reasoning—that is, they sample accounting data, derive audit findings and project ("induct") the finding to a conclusion about the population of data sampled. Fraud examiners often enjoy the expensive luxury of using deductive reasoning—that is, after being tipped off that a certain type of loss occurred or probably occurred, they can identify the suspects, make clinical observations (stakeouts), conduct interviews and interrogations, eliminate dead-end results and concentrate on running the fraudster to ground. They can conduct covert activities that usually are not in the financial auditors' tool kit. The "expensive luxury" of the deductive approach involves surveying a wide array of information and information sources, eliminating the extraneous and retaining the selection that proves the fraud.

REVIEW
CHECKPOINTS

17.1   What are the defining characteristics of white-collar crime, employee fraud, embezzlement, defalcation, management fraud, errors, irregularities and illegal acts?

17.2   What does a fraud perpetrator look like? And how does one act?

17.3   Compare and contrast the type of work performed by external auditors (auditing financial statements to render an audit report) and fraud examiners.

AUDITORS' AND INVESTIGATORS' RESPONSIBILITIES

LEARNING OBJECTIVE

2 Explain the auditing standards related to external, internal and governmental auditors' responsibilities to detect and report frauds, errors, irregularities and illegal acts.

Audit standards from several sources explain the responsibilities for errors, irregularities and illegal acts. The term **external auditors** refers to independent PAs who audit financial statements for the purpose of rendering an opinion; **internal auditors** and **certified internal auditors** are persons, who can be both independent and PAs, employed within organizations; **government auditors** are auditors whose work is governed by the public sector sections of the audit standards, whether they be audit employees of governments or public accounting firms engaged to perform government audits; and **fraud examiners** are those engaged specifically for fraud investigation work. Forensic or investigative accounting deals with the relationship and application of financial facts to legal problems, particularly in use of the findings at a trial. "The involvement of the forensic accountant is almost always on a reactive basis which distinguishes the forensic accountant from the fraud auditor, who more usually tends to be involved on an active basis with the aspects of prevention and detection in a corporate or regulatory environment.[3]

External Auditors' Responsibilities

The CICA auditing standards are rigorous. Relevant standards concern misstatements, section 5135; misstatements due to illegal acts by clients, section 5136; auditing accounting estimates, section 5305; communication with those having responsibility for financial reporting, sections 5135 and 5751; and communication of matters identified during the financial statement audit, section 5750. These have been covered in previous chapter.

Auditor's Responsibility to Consider Fraud and Error in an Audit of Financial Statements

CICA Handbook, section 5135 was revised in 2004 and again in 2006 in response to the post-Enron environment. This section requires the auditor to make enquiries of management about fraud and to consider fraud risk factors on every audit engagement. Examples of such factors are given later in this chapter.

> The auditor should document fraud risk factors identified as being present during the auditor's assessment process and document the auditor's response to any such factors. If during the performance of the audit, fraud risk factors are identified that cause the auditor to believe that additional audit procedures are necessary, the auditor should document the presence of such risk factors and the auditor's response to them.[4]

The auditor should assess inherent and control risks so that in conjunction with substantive tests the risk of material misstatement from fraud or error is appropriately low.[5] The auditor should also obtain written management representations about the extent of fraud. Findings should be communicated to management, the audit committee or equivalent and, in some circumstances, to outside agencies.

Section 5135 requires auditors to remove the traditional assumption on management's honesty.[6] Specifically, the auditor must now presume a risk of fraudulent revenue recognition but this presumption is "rebuttable." That is, if the auditors can convince themselves that the risk is appropriately low (the PCAOB suggests it should be "remote") then the presumption is considered rejected. This logic is similar to the burden of proof concept in critical thinking.

How does the auditor justify that the fraud risk is sufficiently low? Under section 5135, auditors are required to perform additional procedures regarding this rebuttable presumption. They are required to perform analytical procedures of revenues, make enquiries, scan for unusual entries especially at year-end, and they should have brainstorming sessions of the audit team to identify and share information on fraud risk factors during the audit. Auditors also need to identify biases in management accounting estimates, and be able to understand the business rationale of transactions. If the auditors cannot reject the rebuttable presumption, then they need to raise the matter with the audit committee (or equivalent) and take it from there.

The traditional role of the investigative or forensic auditor was to get involved when the risk of fraud was not sufficiently low (e.g., when there is predication or cause for concern because there are too many fraud risk factors, and the audit committee authorizes further investigation). Fraud auditors are increasingly used to proactively perform the initial risk assessments in planning the audit, however. Thus, for example, fraud auditors are increasingly used to screen clients and to be involved in the initial meetings with audit committees

---

[3] Bologna, G.J., and R.J. Lindquist, *Fraud Auditing and Forensic Accounting* (Wiley, 1987), p. 85.

[4] *CICA Handbook*, section 5135.049.

[5] *Ibid.*, paragraph 5135.39.

[6] For example, see D. Selley and E. Turner, "Detecting Fraud and Error," *CA Magazine*, August 2004, p. 38.

and management. There are several reasons for this trend. First, it acts as a fraud deterrent and makes the client aware of how seriously the profession takes its fraud detection responsibilities. Second, fraud examiners are specially trained in techniques that are more likely to detect when people are lying. Finally, fraud auditors are more familiar with legal requirements regarding documentation of frauds, such as witness statements, confessions, control of chain of custody of evidence and preparation of written reports for use as evidence in a court of law.

Illegal Acts by Clients

Section 5136 does not distinguish between the two kinds of illegal acts identified in U.S. SAS 54:

(1) Direct-effect illegal acts produce direct and material effects on financial statement amounts (e.g., violations of tax laws and government contracting regulations for cost and revenue recognition), and they come under the same responsibilities as errors and irregularities; and (2) Indirect-effect illegal acts is the term used to refer to violations of laws and regulations that are far removed from financial statement effects (e.g., violations relating to insider securities trading, occupational health and safety, food and drug administration, environmental protection and equal employment opportunity).

In the United States the far-removed illegal acts come under a responsibility for general awareness, particularly in matters of contingent liability disclosure, but not routine responsibility for detection and reporting.

Section 5136, on the other hand, requires auditors to consider the consequences of the illegal acts and the best way of disclosing such consequences. If failures to disclose would result in a material misstatement, then the auditor should attempt to reduce this risk to an appropriately low level. Section 5136 acknowledges that illegal acts may be difficult to detect because of (1) efforts made to conceal them, and (2) questions about whether an act is illegal, which are complex and may only be resolved by a court of law. For these reasons paragraph 5136.10 recommends that the engagement letter inform management of limitations in detecting illegal acts through the audit.

The auditor should use knowledge of the business and make enquiries of management to identify laws and regulations that could result in material misstatements if violated and not reported (paragraph 5136.11). In addition, auditors should enquire and obtain representations about awareness and disclosure of possibly illegal acts (paragraph 5136.21). Discovery of material possibly illegal acts should be communicated to the audit committee and other appropriate levels of management. Paragraph 5136.23 gives a list of circumstances that may indicate illegal acts.

From a critical-thinking perspective, the most important development regarding sections 5135 and 5136 was to drop the assumption that management is honest. This change took place in 2004. Now auditors must explicitly address the risks of fraud in revenue recognition. If risk is present the auditor must perform further procedures. Even without the presence of this risk, however, auditors must now document the reasons (i.e., from a critical thinking perspective the auditor must develop an informal argument that there is no risk). If sufficient risk of fraud is shown to exist, then a fraud auditor would be called in (with the approval of the client's directors, audit committee, or management).

Auditing Accounting Estimates

Section 5306 is related to fraudulent financial reporting because numerous fraud cases have involved manipulation of estimates. This area is difficult to manage because an accounting estimate is an approximation of a financial statement element, item or account made by an organization's management. (Examples include allowance for loan losses, net realizable value of inventory, percentage-of-completion revenue and fair value in nonmonetary exchanges.)

Management is responsible for making the accounting estimates, and auditors are responsible for evaluating their reasonableness in the context of the financial statements taken as a whole. Auditors are supposed to keep track of the differences between (1) management's estimates and (2) the closest reasonable estimates supported by the audit evidence. And they are supposed to evaluate (1) the differences taken altogether for indications of a systematic bias and (2) the combination of differences with other likely errors in the financial statements found by other audit procedures.

Communication with Audit Committees

CICA Handbook, section 5751 sets forth requirements intended to ensure that audit committees are informed about the scope and results of the independent audit. The auditing standards place great faith in audit committees and boards of directors, although their effectiveness has been questioned elsewhere.[7] Section 5751 requires external auditors to make oral or written communication on the following matters: (a) misstatements other than trivial errors; (b) fraud; (c) misstatements that may cause future financial statements to be materially misstated; (d) illegal or possibly illegal acts, other than ones considered inconsequential; and (e) significant weaknesses in internal control.

P.J. Cockburn[8] noted that there is some inconsistency in the *Handbook* regarding responsibility to detect material misstatements due to error and those due to fraud. Specifically, paragraph 5000.04 states: "The auditor seeks reasonable assurance whether the financial statements are free of material misstatement" without qualifying the sources of misstatement, whereas paragraph 5135.16 explains that an auditor is "less likely" (because of concealment) to detect misstatement arising from fraud than he or she would be to detect misstatement from error. In addition, section 5136 suggests that some illegal acts such as building code violations may have an even lower chance of being detected by an external auditor. These would appear to correspond to indirect-effect illegal acts.

AICPA Standard SAS 99 was issued in 2002 as a response to the post-Enron environment. Its distinguishing feature is that it is the first standard to require forensic procedures on all financial statement audit engagements. The AICPA views SAS 99 as the "cornerstone" of its comprehensive antifraud and corporate responsibility program. The goal of the program is to "rebuild the confidence of investors in our capital markets and reestablish audited financial statements as a clear picture window into corporate America." These words acknowledge the extensive harm done to the profession by Enron, Andersen and WorldCom.

SAS 99 significantly extends audit requirements in a number of ways. These can be summarized via the extensive documentation requirements supporting compliance with the major features of the standard. The standard requires auditors to document the following:

- the discussion among engagements personnel in planning the audit regarding the susceptibility of the entity's financial statements to material misstatement due to fraud, including how and when the discussion occurred, the audit team members who participated and the subjects discussed

- the procedures performed to obtain information necessary to identify and assess the risks of material misstatement due to fraud (Note this includes knowledge of client business risks and its effect on audit risk as per the international exposure draft on audit risk. This requirement also strongly suggests use of risk-based audit approaches as explained in Chapter 6.)

- specific risks of material misstatement due to fraud that were identified and a description of the auditor's response to those risks

- the reasons supporting that conclusion, if the auditor has not identified improper revenue recognition as a risk of material misstatement due to fraud in a particular circumstance

- the results of the procedures performed to further address the risk of management override of controls

---

[7] Wechsler reported the findings of the National Commission on Fraudulent Financial Reporting: that of the 120 fraudulent financial reporting cases brought by the SEC between 1981 and 1986, two-thirds involved companies that had audit committees. This caused Professor Briloff to remark: "Now I see that they are not functioning as they should." (D. Wechsler, "Giving the Watchdog Fangs," *Forbes*, November 13, 1989, p. 130.) However, these observations beg the question of the thousands of companies with and without audit committees that did not get involved in fraudulent financial reporting.

[8] D.J. Cockburn, "Closing the Gap," *CA Magazine*, November 1993, pp. 31–32.

- conditions and analytical relationships that caused the auditor to believe additional auditing procedures or other responses were required and any further responses the auditor concluded where appropriate to address such risks
- the nature of the communications about fraud made to management, the audit committee and others[9]

External auditors assess the risk of fraud by looking for warning signs. A study by American researchers provides more specific guidance on fraud warning signs. "The lack of awareness of the warning signs of fraud is a frequently cited cause of audit failure. If auditors better understood the signs and applied professional scepticism, they would decrease their risk of not detecting fraud. Knowing the most important warning signs should help auditors do a better job of assessing fraud risk." A survey of 130 auditors asked them to rank 30 commonly cited warning signals of fraud according to their relative importance. The auditors ranked client dishonesty as the most important factor. The survey revealed an interesting pattern. Auditors generally perceived "attitude" factors to be more important warning signs of fraud than "situational" factors.

The top 15 warning signs are listed in the following box.

AUDITORS' RANKING OF THE RELATIVE IMPORTANCE OF FRAUD WARNING SIGNS

Auditors' rankings	Fraud warning signs
1.	Managers have lied to the auditors or have been overly evasive in response to audit enquiries.
2.	The auditor's experience with management indicates a degree of dishonesty.
3.	Management places undue emphasis on meeting earnings projections or the quantitative targets.
4.	Management has engaged in frequent disputes with auditors, particularly about aggressive application of accounting principles that increases earnings.
5.	The client has engaged in opinion shopping.
6.	Management's attitude toward financial reporting is unduly aggressive.
7.	The client has a weak control environment.
8.	A substantial portion of management compensation depends on meeting quantified targets.
9.	Management displays significant disrespect for regulatory bodies.
10.	Management operating and financial decisions are dominated by a single person or a few persons acting in concert.
11.	Client managers display a hostile attitude toward the auditors.
12.	Management displays a propensity to take undue risks.
13.	There are frequent and significant difficult-to-audit transactions.
14.	Key managers are considered highly unreasonable.
15.	The client's organization is decentralized without adequate monitoring.

Source: V.B. Heiman-Hoffman, K.P. Morgan, and J.M. Patton, "The Warning Signs of Fraudulent Financial Reporting," *Journal of Accountancy*, October 1996, pp. 76–77.

[9] Michael Ramos, "Auditors' Responsibility for Fraud Detection," *Journal of Accountancy*, January 2003, pp. 29, 35–36.

Internal Auditors' Responsibilities

Traditional internal auditors' attitudes about fraud responsibilities cannot be usefully generalized. Some hesitate to get involved because they believe that a watchdog role will damage their image and effectiveness as internal consultants. Others have flocked to the fraud investigation education programs run by the Association of Certified Fraud Examiners because they want to add the fraud expertise dimension to their skills.

The Nature of Work section of the internal audit standards gives the basic charge to internal auditors for fraud awareness auditing: internal auditors review the reliability and integrity of financial and operating information; review the systems established to ensure compliance with policies, plans, procedures, laws and regulations; and review the means of safeguarding assets and verify the existence of assets. This charge has been expanded as follows: "The internal auditor should have sufficient knowledge to identify indicators of fraud but is not expected to have the expertise of a person whose primary responsibility is detecting and investigating fraud." However, SOX is changing expectations for internal auditors to take increased responsibility for detecting fraud.

Currently, the internal auditing standards appear to be carefully written to impose no positive obligation for fraud detection and investigation work in the ordinary course of assignments. However, internal auditors are encouraged to be aware of the various types of frauds, their signs (red flags) and the need to follow up on the notice of signs and control weaknesses to determine whether a suspicion is justified; then, alert management to call in the experts. The standards caution that internal auditors are not expected to guarantee that fraud will be detected in the normal course of most internal audit assignments.

Public Sector Auditing Standards

As will be explained in Chapter 18, public sector standards are applicable for audits conducted by government employees and public accounting firms engaged to perform audits on governmental organizations, programs, activities and functions. Consequently, the public sector standards control a significant portion of audits by public accountants. The basic governmental audit requirements are to know the applicable laws and regulations, design the audit to detect abuse or illegal acts and report to the proper level of authority.

Auditors are supposed to prepare a written report on their tests of compliance with applicable laws and regulations, including all material instances of noncompliance and all instances or indications of illegal acts that could result in criminal prosecution. (More discussion of compliance auditing and reports relating to laws and regulations is in Chapter 18.) Reports should be directed to the top official of an organization and, in some cases to an appropriate oversight body, including other government agencies and audit committees. Persons receiving the audit reports are responsible for reporting to law enforcement agencies.

The following box illustrates the dramatic impact that fraud can have in the public sector:

FORMER CHIEF MOUNTIE HIRED AFTER SUN EXPOSÉ BLITZ ON HEALTH-CARE FRAUD

Ontario Health Minister Jim Wilson contracted Inkster, now president of KPMG Investigation and Security, after widespread cheating was exposed by Sun columnist Christie Blatchford yesterday.

"The number of reported fraud cases quoted in (*The*) *Toronto Sun* are of great concern to me," Wilson said in a statement hand-delivered by aide Cynthia Janzen yesterday.

Blatchford revealed every single day, between 30 and 50 people show up at Ontario's hospitals and clinics seeking treatment with bogus health cards, and the government ignores it. In February, stolen health cards were presented for treatment 1,057 times, she wrote.

Despite promises to crack down on fraud in the 1995 throne speech and fall economic statement, Ontario's health ministry employs just one fraud investigator for every 1.6 million provincial residents. Wilson employs more political staff than enforcement officers in his $18-billion ministry, which has prosecuted only one case of fraud this year.

Janzen said Wilson was motivated after reading Blatchford's column. A 1993 internal governmental report found that fraud costs the health ministry $284 million a year. And, unfortunately, the Conservative government has failed in its promise to weed out health-care fraud, Tory and Liberal MPPs said.

"Basically, there is no enforcement," Tory MPP and Crown attorney Toni Skarica said in an interview.

"There are virtually no resources put into fraud investigations or prosecutions. As a result, we could get major frauds that undermine the economy," Skarica said.

Liberal critic Dominic Agostino said the province is losing "hundreds of millions a year" to illegitimate hucksters.

Source: Jeff Harder, "Former Chief Mountie Hired after Sun Exposé Blitz on Health Care Fraud," *The Toronto Sun,* May 31, 1997, p. 5. Sun Media Corporation.

Fraud Examiner Responsibilities

If you try to make an informal ranking of the strength of commitment to fraud matters, it appears that the external auditors come first, followed by the public sector auditors, then the internal auditors. However, this situation is rapidly changing under SOX with its increased reliance on internal controls to prevent fraudulent reporting and misappropriation of assets. Of course, fraud examiners have the strongest spirit of fraud detection and investigation. They differ significantly from other kinds of auditors. When they take an assignment, fraud is already known or strongly suspected. They do not fish around for fraud while performing "normal" work. In fact, the Association of Certified Fraud Examiners (ACFE) teaches that assignments are not begun without predication, which means a reason to believe fraud may have occurred.

Fraud examiners' attitudes and responsibilities differ from those of other auditors in two additional respects—internal control and materiality. Their interest in internal control policies and procedures lies not so much in evaluating their strengths, but in evaluating their

No Separation of Duties

An electronic data processing employee instructed the company's computer to pay his wife rent for land she had allegedly leased to the company by assigning her an alphanumeric code as a lessor and then ordering the payments. The control lesson: Never let a data entry clerk who processes payment claims also have access to the approved vendor master file for additions or deletions.

Source: G.J. Bologna and R.J. Lindquist, *Fraud Auditing and Forensic Accounting* (New York: John Wiley & Sons, 1987), p. 70–71.

MONEY, MONEY, MONEY CASE

Brian Molony, a 29-year-old assistant branch manager and lending officer of a large downtown Toronto bank, defrauded the bank of some $10.2 million over a 20-month period. He fabricated loans to real and fictitious customers and gambled away the proceeds at an Atlantic City casino. Molony was such a valued customer that the casino flew its corporate jet to Toronto to pick him up for weekend jaunts.

The defalcation came to light when Canadian law enforcement authorities arrested Molony for a traffic violation on his return from a trip to Atlantic City. A search of his person disclosed that he was carrying about $29,000 in currency. That information was passed on to the bank, which then conducted an audit and found the fictional loans and transfers of funds to the casino. The bank is suing the casino to recover at least part of its loss.

Molony used a *lapping scheme* to keep auditors off his trail—that is, he paid off earlier loans with subsequent loans so that no delinquencies would show. However, the fictional loan balances grew and grew. Molony's superior at the branch had approved the larger loans because "he had no reason to mistrust him." The branch manager was subsequently suspended along with the assistant branch manager for administration, a credit officer and an auditor.

Source: G.J. Bologna and R.J. Lindquist, *Fraud Auditing and Forensic Accounting*, 2nd ed. (New York: John Wiley & Sons, 1995), pp. 230–231. Reprinted by permission of John Wiley & Sons, Inc.

weaknesses. Fraud examiners "think like crooks" to imagine fraud schemes for getting around an organization's internal controls. They imagine scenarios of white-collar crime in situations where controls are not in place.

Fraud examiners have a different attitude about materiality. While other auditors may have a large dollar amount as a criterion for an error that is big enough to matter, fraud examiners have a much lower threshold. An oddity is an oddity regardless the amount of money involved, and small oddities ought not be passed by just because "$5,000 isn't material to the financial statements taken as a whole." External auditors comprehend materiality in relation to each year's financial statements, so that, for example, a $50,000 misstatement of income might not be big enough to matter. Fraud examiners think of materiality as a cumulative amount as discussed earlier.

REVIEW CHECKPOINTS

17.4   What are the CICA auditing standards requirements regarding (*a*) awareness of fraud, (*b*) procedural audit work, (*c*) professional skepticism, and (*d*) reporting? Do these standards differ for (1) errors, irregularities, and direct-effect illegal acts; and (2) indirect-effect illegal acts?

17.5   To what extent would internal auditors include fraud detection responsibility in their normal audit assignments?

17.6   How does the requirement for design of audit procedures differ in public sector audit work from external auditors' work on financial statement audits (not involving governmental auditing)? Consider both errors/irregularities and illegal acts aspects.

17.7   Why is the order of strength of commitment to fraud matters is (1) government auditors, (2) external auditors, (3) internal auditors?

17.8   Why might fraud examiners have attitudes about control systems and materiality different from those of other auditors?

Conditions That Make Fraud Possible, Even Easy

· · · · · · · · · · ·

LEARNING OBJECTIVE

3 Outline some of the conditions that lead to frauds.

When can fraud occur? Imagine the probability of fraud being a function of three factors— motive, opportunity and lack of integrity. When one or two of these factors weigh heavily in the direction of fraud, the probability increases. When three of them lean in the direction of fraud, it almost certainly will occur.[10] As Bologna and Lindquist put it: Some people are honest all the time, some people (fewer than the honest ones) are dishonest all the time, most people are honest some of the time, and some people are honest most of the time.[11]

Motive

A **motive** is some kind of pressure experienced by a person and believed unshareable with friends and confidants. *Psychotic* motivation is relatively rare; but is characterized by the "habitual criminal," who steals simply for the sake of stealing. *Egocentric* motivations drive people to steal to achieve more personal prestige. *Ideological* motivations are held by people who think that their cause is morally superior, and that they are justified in making someone else a victim. However, economic motives are far more common in business frauds than the other three.

The economic motive is simply a need for money, and at times it can be intertwined with egocentric and ideological motivations. Ordinarily honest people can fall into circumstances where there is a new or unexpected need for money, and the normal options for talking about it or going through legitimate channels seem to be closed. Consider these needs:

- Pay college or university tuition.
- Pay hospital bills for a parent with cancer.
- Pay gambling debts.
- Pay for drugs.
- Pay alimony and child support.
- Pay for high lifestyle (homes, cars, boats).
- Finance business or stock speculation losses.
- Report good financial results.

Probably the most important motive for external auditors to consider is compensation tied to accounting measures of performance. This creates incentives to manipulate the accounting measurements.

Opportunity

An **opportunity** is an open door for solving the unshareable problem in secret by violating a trust. The violation may be a circumvention of internal control policies and procedures, or it may be simply taking advantage of an absence or lapse of control in an organization. We have no police state where every person is shadowed by an armed guard. Everyone has some degree of trust conferred for a job, even if it is merely the trust not to shirk and procrastinate. The higher the position in an organization, the greater the degree of trust; and, hence, the greater the opportunity for larger frauds. Here are some examples:

- Nobody counts the inventory, so losses are not known.
- The petty cash box is often left unattended.
- Supervisors set a bad example by taking supplies home.

---

[10] For further references, see D.R. Cressey, "Management Fraud, Accounting Controls, and Criminological Theory," pp. 117–47, and Albrecht et al., "Auditor Involvement in the Detection of Fraud," pp. 207–61, both in R.K. Elliott and J.J. Willingham, *Management Fraud: Detection and Deterrence* (New York: Petrocelli Books, Inc., 1980).; J.K. Loebbecke, M.M. Eining, and J.J. Willingham, "Auditors' Experience with Material Irregularities: Frequency, Nature, and Detectability," *Auditing: A Journal of Practice and Theory*, Fall 1989, pp. 1–28.

[11] Bologna and Lindquist, *Fraud Auditing*, p. 8.

I Couldn't Tell Anyone

An unmarried young woman stole $300 from her employer to pay for an abortion. Coming from a family that strongly disdained premarital sex, she felt that her only alternative was to have the secret abortion. Once she realized how easy it was to steal, however, she took another $86,000 before being caught.

Source: W.S. Albrecht, "How CPAs Can Help Clients Prevent Employee Fraud," *Journal of Accountancy,* December 1988, p. 113.

- Upper management considered a written statement of ethics but decided not to publish one.
- Another employee was caught and fired, but not prosecuted.
- The finance vice president has investment authority without any review.
- Frequent emergency jobs leave a lot of excess material just lying around.

Probably the most important opportunity as far as external auditors are concerned is lack of controls at the highest levels (corporate governance) to prevent management from overriding accounting controls.

Lack of Integrity

Practically everyone, even the most violent criminals, knows the difference between right and wrong. Unimpeachable integrity is the ability to act in accordance with the highest moral and ethical values all the time. Thus, it is the lapses and occasional **lack of integrity** that permit motive and opportunity to take form as fraud. But people normally do not make deliberate decisions to "lack integrity today while I steal some money." They find a way to describe (rationalize) the act in words that make it acceptable for their self-image. Here are some of these rationalizations:

- I need it more than the other person (Robin Hood theory).
- I'm borrowing the money and will pay it back.
- Nobody will get hurt.
- The company is big enough to afford it.
- A successful image is the name of the game.
- Everybody is doing it.

It is noteworthy that lack of integrity appears to be the most important factor affecting the risk of management fraud. This is evident from the list in the box on page 691, which primarily reflects on management integrity. This perhaps should not be too surprising since given their authority, responsibilities and incentives, management's other factors of motive and

She Can Do Everything

Mrs. Lemon was the only bookkeeper for an electrical supply company. She wrote the cheques and reconciled the bank account. In the cash disbursements journal, she coded some cheques as inventory, but she wrote the cheques to herself, using her own true name. When the cheques were returned with the bank statement, she simply destroyed them. She stole $416,000 over five years. After being caught and sentenced to prison, she testified to having continuous guilt over doing something she knew was wrong.

Source: "Auditing for Internal Fraud" training course © 2006 Association of Certified Fraud Examiners.

THE MOST COMMON COMPUTER-RELATED CRIMES

Whereas computer hacking (pranksters breaking into computers) has received most of the recent media attention, the most prevalent computer crime is the fraudulent disbursement of funds, which is generally preceded by the submission of a spurious claim in the following forms:

- false vendor, supplier or contractor invoice
- false governmental benefit claim
- false fringe benefit claim
- false refund or credit claim
- false payroll claim
- false expense claim

Fraudulent disbursement of funds usually requires a data entry clerk in accounts payable, payroll or the benefits section, acting either alone or in collusion with an insider or outsider (depending on how tight the internal controls are). From an accountant's perspective, the claim is a false debit to an expense so that a corresponding credit can be posted to the cash account for the issuance of a cheque. Auditors assert that such disbursement frauds represent more than half of all frauds by lower-level employees.

At higher management levels, the typical fraud involves overstating profits by the fabrication of such data as sales, which are increased arbitrarily (sales booked before the sales transaction is completed), and the understatement of expenses, which are arbitrarily reduced or disguised as deferrals to the next accounting period. There are numerous variations on these two main themes: overstatement of sales, and understatement of expenses. One of the more common ploys to overstate profits is to arbitrarily increase the ending inventory of manufactured goods or merchandise held for sale. That ploy results in understating the cost of goods sold and thereby increasing the net profit.

The executive compensation system often provides the incentive to overstate profits. If bonus awards depend on profits, executives have an economic incentive to fudge the numbers. They may also be tempted to do so if they own a great many company shares, whose value depends on investors' perceptions of profitability. If profits are down, investors are unhappy and may rush to sell, thus causing a lowered share price and depressing the value of the executive's own shares.

Manipulations of this type often require line executives and personnel in accounting and data processing capacities to conspire together. Such conspiracies have become a recurring theme in business. The pressure on executives for high performance grows each year. We are therefore likely to see more such frauds in the future.

Source: G.J. Bologna and A.J. Lindquist, *Fraud Auditing and Forensic Accounting*, 2nd ed. (New York: John Wiley & Sons, 1995), pp. 176–179. Reprinted by permission of John Wiley & Sons, Inc.

opportunity are already largely present, and so management integrity is the only factor remaining that can prevent fraud at the top levels of the organization. This may be one of the reasons why the "tone at the top" is one of the most important aspects of good internal controls.

The importance of the three risk factors—motive, opportunity and lack of integrity—has also been acknowledged in ISA 240 and SAS 99. Both standards use these risk factors as a framework for linking various sources of these risks to audit procedures. In ISA 240 and SAS 99, motive is referred to as incentives or pressures, and lack of integrity is characterized as rationalization or attitude.

. . . .

REVIEW
CHECKPOINTS

17.9   What are some of the pressures that can cause honest people to contemplate theft? List some egocentric and ideological ones, as well as economic ones.

17.10 What kinds of conditions provide opportunities for employee fraud and financial statement fraud?

17.11 Give some examples of rationalizations that people have used to excuse fraud. Can you use them?

. . . .

FRAUD PREVENTION
. . . .

LEARNING OBJECTIVE

4 Describe ways and means to prevent frauds.

Accountants and auditors have often been exhorted to be the leaders in fraud prevention by employing their skills in designing tight control systems. This strategy is, at best, a short-run solution to a large and pervasive problem. Business activity is built on the trust that people at all levels will do their jobs properly. Control systems limit trust and, in the extreme, can strangle business in bureaucracy. Imagine street crime being "prevented" by enrolling half the population in the police force to control the other half! Managers and employees must have freedom to do business, which means giving them freedom to commit frauds as well.[12] Effective long-run prevention measures are complex and difficult, and involve the elimination of the causes of fraud by mitigating the effects of motive, opportunity and lack of integrity.

Managing People Pressures in the Workplace

From time to time, people will experience financial and other pressures. The pressures cannot be eliminated, but the facilities for sharing them can be created. Some companies have "ethics officers" to serve this purpose. Their job is to be available to talk over the ethical dilemmas faced in the workplace and help people adopt legitimate responses. However, the ethics officers are normally not psychological counsellors.

Many companies have "hot lines" for anonymous reporting of ethical problems. Reportedly, the best kind of hot-line arrangement is to have the responding party be an agency outside the organization. In the United States some organizations are in the business of being the recipients of hot-line calls, co-ordinating their activities with the management of the organization.

The most effective long-run prevention, however, lies in the practice of management by caring for people. Managers and supervisors at all levels can exhibit a genuine concern for the personal and professional needs of their subordinates and fellow managers, and subordinates can show the same concern for one another and their managers. The approach is idealistic and calls for the elimination of interpersonal competition, of climbing up over the bodies of colleagues and of office politics. Nevertheless, it is practised in many organizations in the form of staff meetings, personal counselling and "quality circles" (groups of employees from all levels who plan production, selling and administrative activities together). Some organizations have daycare centres, alcohol and drug counselling, financial counselling and other programs to help people share their problems with experts.

When external auditors are engaged in the audit of financial statements, they must obtain an understanding of the company's control structure. The control structure includes the control environment, which relates to the overall scheme of management activity in the company. Management that carefully considers the people pressures in the workplace, using some of the devices mentioned previously, has a good control environment and the beginnings of a good control structure.

[12] Cressey, "Management Fraud," p. 124.

Control Procedures and Employee Monitoring

Auditors would be aghast at an organization that had no control policies and procedures, and rightly so. Controls in the form of job descriptions and performance specifications are indeed needed to help people know the jobs they are supposed to accomplish. Almost all people need some structure for their working hours. An organization whose only control is "trustworthy employees" has no control.[13] Unfortunately, "getting caught" is an important consideration for many people when coping with their problems. Controls provide the opportunity to get caught.

Without going into much detail about controls at this point, let it be noted that procedures for recognizing and explaining red flags are important for nipping frauds in the bud before they get bigger. Controls that reveal the following kinds of symptoms are necessary:[14]

- missing documents
- second endorsements on cheques
- unusual endorsements
- unexplained adjustments to inventory balances
- unexplained adjustments to accounts receivable
- old items in bank reconciliations
- old outstanding cheques
- customer complaints
- unusual patterns in deposits in transit

The problem with control systems is that they are essentially negative restrictions on people. The challenge is to have a bare minimum of useful controls and to avoid picky rules that are "fun to beat." The challenge of "beating the system," which can lead to bigger and better things, is an invitation to fraudulent types of behaviour. (How many university students find ways to get into course registration before their scheduled times?)

Integrity by Example and Enforcement

The key to integrity in business is "accountability"—that is, each person must be willing to put his decisions and actions in the sunshine. There must be norms for these decisions and actions. Many organizations begin by publishing codes of conduct. Some of these codes are simple, while others are quite elaborate. Government agencies and defence contractors typically have the most elaborate rules for employee conduct. Sometimes they work, sometimes they do not. A code can be effective if the "tone at the top" supports it. When the chair of the board and the president make themselves visible examples of the code, then other people

---

DISHONESTY IS BAD POLICY

Now be honest. When fixing your car following an accident, your body shop includes extra repairs and puts them on the insurance company's tab. Do you say thanks and let the insurer pay?

---

[13] W.S. Albrecht, "How CPAs Can Help Clients Prevent Employee Fraud," *Journal of Accountancy*, December 1988, pp. 110–14.
[14] Ibid., pp. 113–14.

According to an ethics poll conducted recently for the **Canadian Coalition Against Insurance Fraud,** 25 percent of those surveyed said they'd go along with the mechanic's bill padding.

For the property and casualty insurers who make up the membership of the coalition, this ethical laxity adds up to an estimated $1.3-billion-a-year problem, including the cost of police and fire officials' investigations.

That's how much is lost on fraudulent claims relating to homes. Insurance fraud is second only to illegal drug sales as a source of criminal profit.

Put another way, fraud accounts for 10 percent to 15 percent of all claims paid out—money that ends up being covered by honest policyholders in the form of increased premiums.

The coalition is conducting a study to analyse the kinds of insurance fraud that are most frequently perpetrated, says executive director Mary Lou O'Reilly.

She says a link has been found between the ethical decisions people make in their everyday lives and opportunistic fraud.

"Fraud for the average Canadian is an opportunity to 'get back' some of what they feel is rightfully theirs when they have a legitimate claim."

Sometimes, for example, they inflate a claim to cover the deductible. "But these are not seasoned criminals," she says. "These are honest people who just don't recognize that fraud is a crime."

Or people who get clumsy when they veer from the straight and narrow. Insurers have dozens of anecdotes about people whose 12-inch televisions suddenly develop 29-inch screens once they're lost. Then there was the one about the policyholder with the damaged 20-foot boat that turned out to have been stored in an 18-foot garage.

The coalition has helped cut down on fraud through an alliance with Crime Stoppers, which are volunteer-run, privately funded, anonymous telephone-tip services operated in co-operation with local police forces.

Under the arrangement, a tip called in to Crime Stoppers about a possible fraud is relayed to the Insurance Crime Prevention Bureau and investigated. Police may also be called in.

If a claim is denied, Crime Stoppers receives 5 percent of the damage claim up to $1,500, which is then passed on to the tipster at the discretion of Crime Stoppers.

Source: Susan Yellin, "Dishonesty is Bad Policy," *The Financial Post*, May 23, 1997, p. 10. Sun Media Corp.

will believe it is real. Subordinates will tend to follow the boss's lead. This should help create a positive workplace environment that deters fraud.

Hiring and firing are important. Background checks on prospective employees are advisable. A new employee of questionable repute in some earlier organization will probably be worthy of suspicion in a new place. Organizations have been known to hire private investigators to make these background checks. Fraudsters should be fired and, in most cases, prosecuted. They have a low rate of recidivism (repeat offences) if they are prosecuted, but they have a high rate if not.[15] Prosecution delivers the message that management does not believe that "occasional dishonesty" is acceptable. Training employees is also important. If acceptable levels of behaviour and company standards are not communicated and taught, then do not expect employees to do what is required. Ask each employee to periodically confirm adherence to the company code of ethics.

[15] Ibid., p. 114.

HOW TO ENCOURAGE FRAUD

Practise autocratic management.
Orient management to low trust and power.
Manage by crisis.
Centralize authority in top management.
Measure performance on a short-term basis.
Make profits the only criterion for success.
Make rewards punitive, stingy and political.
Give feedback that is always critical and negative.
Create a highly hostile, competitive workplace.
Insist that everything be documented with a rule for everything.

Source: Adapted from G.J. Bologna and R.J. Lindquist, *Fraud Auditing and Forensic Accounting* (New York: John Wiley & Sons, 1987), pp. 47–49.

REGULATORS UNITE TO FIGHT TELEMARKETING SCAMS

Two Canadian securities commissions have joined regulators from 21 U.S. states and the U.S. Federal Trade Commission in an offensive on telemarketing scams that cost investors about $40 billion a year.

Securities regulators in Quebec and British Columbia are taking part in the campaign, "Project Field of Schemes," by publicizing some of the most significant cases of the past three months.

Frauds over the Internet are a new source of concern, an extension of the telemarketing campaigns that target old people.

"The Internet is like a huge classified ad section, with a money wanted column showing you where to invest, and it becomes a perfect medium for conveying investment offers," said Mark Griffin, president of the North American Securities Administrators Association.

The British Columbia Securities Commission supported the campaign because it knows all regulators deal with the same types of scams, often orchestrated by the same people.

"Frauds are similar wherever you go—and often the perpetrators have crossed jurisdictional boundaries so they can start fresh in a new place where they are not known," said Barbara Barry, communications manager at the BCSC.

"Basically, people and their greed are universal."

She noted a recent case involving a company called Goldman-Stanley consultants, which controlled four other firms. Its name was purposely similar to that of the well-known New York investment house and its stationery had a similar look.

"People who bought believed that Goldman-Stanley consultants were agents that were placing foreign exchange contract purchases for legitimate companies in other jurisdictions," Berry said.

Goldman-Stanley also used a storefront location to mimic a well-known Hong Kong investment firm in a successful attempt to solicit Asian clients.

Source: Ian Karleff, "Regulations Unite to Fight Telemarketing Scams," *The Financial Post,* July 3, 1997, p. 8. Sun Media Corp.

WHERE DID HE COME FROM?

The controller defrauded the company for several million dollars. As it turned out, he was no controller at all. He didn't know a debit from a credit. The fraudster had been fired from five previous jobs where money had turned up missing. He was discovered one evening when the president showed up unexpectedly at the company and found a stranger in the office with the controller. The stranger was doing all of the accounting for the bogus controller.

Source: "Auditing for Internal Fraud" training course © 2006 Association of Certified Fraud Examiners.

REVIEW CHECKPOINT

17.12 Make a two-column list with fraud-prevention management-style characteristics in one column and, opposite each of these, management-style characteristics that might lead to fraud.

FRAUD DETECTION

Since an organization cannot prevent all fraud, its auditors, accountants and security personnel must be acquainted with some detection techniques. Frauds consist of the fraud act itself, the conversion of assets to the fraudster's use and the cover-up. Catching people in the fraud act is difficult and unusual. The act of conversion is equally difficult to observe, since it typically takes place in secret away from the organization's offices (e.g., fencing stolen inventory). Many frauds are investigated by noticing signs and signals of fraud, then following the trail of missing, mutilated or false documents that are part of the accounting records cover-up.

This chapter has already mentioned signs and signals in terms of red flags, oddities and unusual events. Being able to notice signs takes some experience, but this text can give some starting places.

Red Flags

LEARNING OBJECTIVE

5 Explain the audit and investigative procedures for detecting common employee fraud schemes.

Employee Fraud.   Employee fraud usually, but not always, involves people below the top executive levels. Observation of persons' habits and lifestyle and changes in habits and lifestyle may reveal some red flags. Fraudsters in the past have exhibited these characteristics:

- Lose sleep.
- Take drugs.
- Can't relax.
- Can't look people in the eye.
- Go to confession (e.g., priest, psychiatrist).
- Work standing up.
- Drink too much.
- Become irritable easily.
- Get defensive, argumentative.
- Sweat excessively.
- Find excuses and scapegoats for mistakes.
- Work alone, work late.

High Style in the Mailroom

A female mailroom employee started wearing designer clothes (and making a big deal about it). She drove a new BMW to work. An observant manager, who had known her as an employee for seven years and knew she had no outside income, became suspicious. He asked the internal auditors to examine her responsibilities extra carefully. They discovered she had taken $97,000 over a two-year period.

Source: "Auditing for Internal Fraud" training course © 2006 Association of Certified Fraud Examiners.

Personality red flags[16] are problematic because (1) honest people sometimes show them and (2) they often are hidden from view. It is easier to notice changes, especially when a person changes her lifestyle or spends more money than the salary justifies—for example, on homes, furniture, jewellery, clothes, boats, autos, vacations and the like.

Often, telltale hints of the cover-up are visible. These generally appear in the accounting records. The key is to notice exceptions and oddities, such as transactions that are at odd times of the day, month or season; too many or too few; in the wrong branch location; and in amounts too high, too low, too consistent or too different. Exceptions and oddities can appear in these forms:

- missing documents
- cash shortages and overages
- excessive voids and credit memos
- customer complaints
- common names or addresses for refunds
- adjustments to receivables and payables
- general ledger that does not balance
- increased past due receivables
- inventory shortages
- increased scrap
- alterations on documents
- duplicate payments
- employees who cannot be found
- second endorsements on cheques
- documents being photocopied
- dormant accounts becoming active

Fraudulent Financial Reporting by Management

LEARNING OBJECTIVE

6 Explain the audit and investigative procedures for detecting common fraudulent financial reporting.

Fraud that affects financial statements and causes them to be materially misleading often arises from the perceived need to "get through a difficult period." The difficult period may be characterized by a cash shortage, increased competition, cost overruns and similar events. Managers usually view these conditions as temporary, believing they can be overcome by getting a new loan, selling shares or otherwise buying time to recover. In the meantime, falsified financial statements are used to "benefit the company." These conditions and circumstances have existed along with frauds in the past:

[16] Long lists of red flags can be found in Bologna and Lindquist, *Fraud Auditing*, pp. 49–56; Albrecht et. al., in *Management Fraud*, pp. 223–26; Statement on Auditing Standard 82; "Auditing for Fraud" courses of the Association of Certified Fraud Examiners; and courses offered by other organizations, such as the CICA and the Institute of Internal Auditors.

> ## BROKER VOWS TO REPAY HUGE CLIENT LOSSES
>
> A former investment-market whiz kid facing multi-million-dollar lawsuits and fraud charges has vowed to reimburse client's losses, his lawyer says.
>
> Mr. X faces 15 fraud charges totalling $22 million and lawsuits from more than 20 ex-clients claiming $10 million . . .
>
> Investors accused Mr. X, 33, of misrepresenting the value of their funds, negotiating without their knowledge and not repaying loans. His ex-employers and wife are also being sued.
>
> After retirees, a taxi owner, a dentist, accountants, a builder and an actress told First Marathon Securities Ltd. and Midland Walwyn Capital Inc of unusual losses, Mr. X was fired and his licence suspended. Charged Monday in one of Canada's largest brokerage frauds, he was freed on bail.
>
> Gone are the couple's Porsche, Jaguar and lavish parties, the couple's lawyer said. Their $1.3 million Forest Hill home and their Cobourg house are so heavily mortgaged "there might be no equity."
>
> Two Toronto retirees claimed US$582,121 was lost with Mr. X, court documents say.
>
> Eight clients in million dollar claims cite Mr. X for "deceit, fraud . . . negligence and breach of contract," said their lawyer, Neil Gross. "All of them have suffered devastating losses."
>
> *Source:* Ian Robertson, "Broker Vows to Repay Huge Client Losses," *The Toronto Sun,* June 12, 1997, p. 2. Sun Media Corp.

- unfavourable industry conditions
- excess capacity
- high debt
- profit squeeze
- strong foreign competition
- lack of working capital
- rapid expansion
- product obsolescence
- slow customer collections
- related party transactions

By both fraud and "creative accounting," companies have caused financial statements to be materially misleading by (1) overstating revenues and assets, (2) understating expenses and liabilities, and (3) giving disclosures that are misleading or that omit important information. Generally, fraudulent financial statements show financial performance and ratios that are better than current industry experience or better than the company's own history. Sometimes the performance meets exactly the targets announced by management months earlier.

Because of the double-entry bookkeeping system, fraudulent accounting entries always affect two accounts and two places in financial statements. Since many frauds involve improper recognition of assets, there is a theory of the "dangling debit," which is an asset amount that can be investigated and found to be false or questionable. Frauds may involve the omission of liabilities, but the matter of finding and investigating the "dangling credit" is normally very difficult. It "dangles" off the books. Misleading disclosures also present difficulty, mainly because they involve words and messages instead of numbers. Omissions may be hard to notice, and misleading inferences may be very subtle.

A client's far-removed illegal acts may cause financial statements to be misleading, and external auditors are advised to be aware of circumstances that might indicate them.

Following is a list of some signs and signals of the potential for illegal acts:

- unauthorized transactions
- government investigations
- regulatory reports of violations
- payments to consultants, affiliates, employees for unspecified services
- excessive sales commissions and agent's fees
- unusually large cash payments
- unexplained payments to government officials
- failure to file tax returns, to pay duties and fees

OVERSTATED REVENUE, RECEIVABLES AND DEFERRED COSTS

Cali Computer Systems, Inc., sold franchises enabling local entrepreneurs to open stores and sell Cali products. The company granted territorial franchises, in one instance recording revenue of $800,000 and in another $580,000. Unfortunately, the first of these "contracts" for a territorial franchise simply did not exist, and the second was not executed and Cali had not performed its obligations by the time it was recorded. In both cases the imaginary revenue was about 40 percent of reported revenues. These franchises were more in the nature of business hopes than completed transactions.

Cali was supposed to deliver computer software in connection with the contracts and had deferred $277,000 of software development cost in connection with the programs. However, this software did not work, and the contracts were fulfilled with software purchased from other suppliers.

Source: SEC Accounting and Auditing Enforcement Release 190, 1988.

BRIBERY AND CORRUPTION: A NEW GLOBAL SOCIAL CONCERN

An article[17] identifies corruption as a major challenge in the new global, high-tech economy. A long section of the article talks about Transparency International, a unique organization dedicated to fighting global corruption. This section is reproduced in full following.

Transparency International Encourages Governments to Fight Corruption

In 1993, Dr. Peter Eigen, former World Bank director, founded Transparency International (TI) in Berlin as a not-for-profit, nongovernmental organization, "to counter corruption . . . in international business transactions," according to its mission statement.

The small group, which has organized over 60 chapters throughout the world, says that it encourages governments to establish laws, policies and anti-corruption programs. TI is funded by multilateral groups (including the World Bank), national programs and private companies.

TI says that corruption is causing vast sums of money to be misallocated by public officials in dozens of countries. The group says that funds which were originally earmarked for new schools, hospitals and institutions to serve the most needy, are often channelled into projects of negligible social value by officials receiving kickbacks from commercial contractors.

[17] "The Global Explosion of Corruption—the Misuse of Public Power for Private Profit or Political Gain," *White Paper*, May/June 1997, a publication of the Association of Certified Fraud Examiners.

Corruption is also the enemy of progress, TI says. Corrupt leaders cling to power, opposing efforts to open government, curbing personal freedoms and abusing human rights, the group says. Also, the honest business person goes broke, the rules of a healthy economic system become twisted, and companies addicted to paying bribes become rotten, TI says.

The group says there are too many countries where corporations can pay bribes abroad and claim these as tax deductible expenses in their home countries. "We will do our best to get our house in order," said Ethiopian Prime Minister Meles Zenawi at an international conference a year ago, "but our Northern friends: please do not support the bribery by your exporters by giving them tax deductions for their bribes."

One of the most effective ways that TI has publicized the corruption problem is through its annual Corruption Perception Index based on the experience of multinational corporations. See the following box. This index is increasingly used to develop international efforts to fight worldwide corruption and bribery.

"The mounting support for anti-corruption action in the international organizations is a vital requirement in raising this issue to highest political levels in governments around the globe," said Eigen. "But these initiatives only have an impact if they are followed up at the national level and if organizations like TI constantly monitor the official agencies to see their bold rhetoric is matched by meaningful action."

Electronic trading and funds transfer systems (see Chapter 7) combined with offshore banking havens and new financial instruments have facilitated the laundering of criminal and illegal funds. It has been estimated that up to 25 percent of financial instruments and foreign currency trading involves some kind of illegal money laundering scheme. Cross border capital flows now amount to $1.25 trillion per day. The illegitimate amounts are so huge that they threaten world financial markets. The only way to deal with money laundering of this scale is through international efforts.

As part of an international fight against bribery sponsored by TI and the Organization for Economic Cooperation and Development (OECD), early in 1999 Canada made it illegal to pay foreign bribes. Modelled on the U.S.'s Foreign Corrupt Practices Act, Canada's

THE TRANSPARENCY INTERNATIONAL CORRUPTION PERCEPTION INDEX (CPI), 2004

Country rank	Selected countries	CPI score (out of 10)
1	Finland	9.7
11	UK	8.6
12	Canada	8.5
17	USA	7.5
22	France	7.1

Higher-risk countries (5.0 or less) in which Canadian companies are most likely to do business

42	Italy	4.8
47	South Korea	4.5
59	Brazil	3.9
64	Mexico	3.6
71	China	3.4
90	India	2.8
90	Russia	2.8
102	Philippines	2.6
108	Argentina	2.5
129	Pakistan	2.1
133	Indonesia	2.0

Source: www.transparency.org

WORTH A CLOSER LOOK

CONSIDER THE FOLLOWING AUDIT PROCEDURES WHEN THE COMBINED INHERENT AND CONTROL RISK IS ASSESSED AS "NOT LOW"

- Examine all relevant contracts and source documents thoroughly. Discuss them with management to assess whether they reflect the transaction's substance.
- When applicable, check documentation concerning the bidding process for major contracts in foreign countries, including the inclusion of unusually large agency fees or other amounts that do not appear to relate directly to the contract's substance.
- Review banking records for large and unusual transactions or cash transactions. Consider using analytical procedures such as data-mining techniques.
- If local auditors are involved (whether affiliates of the Canadian auditor or not), discuss the risk assessment with them and obtain their views of the likelihood of a bribe having been paid; also discuss the procedures they have carried out or might perform. Be aware, too, that the position of such auditors may be very sensitive in their local environment and that telephone and other communications may not be secure. It may be appropriate to visit the locations concerned.
- If payments are made through offshore companies or bank accounts, obtain information about the companies and financial institutions to assess their legitimacy.
- If inexplicably large payments are made to an agent, attempt to contact the agent to determine how the fees were disbursed. This will often be a fruitless exercise, but a refusal to answer on the agent's part significantly increases the likelihood that the Corruption of Foreign Public Officials Act has been breached. An agent should not be contacted without the client's permission.

Source: S. Chester and D. Selley, "Giving Kickbacks the Boot," *CA Magazine*, August 1999, Exhibit 2, p. 23. Reproduced by permission from *CA Magazine* published by the Canadian Institute of Chartered Accountants, Toronto, Canada.

Corruption of Foreign Public Officials Act makes foreign bribes illegal and a nondeductible business expense. Thus foreign bribes now fall under section 5136 "Misstatements—Illegal Acts." This makes auditors responsible for the detection of foreign bribes that can have a material effect on the financial statements. Auditors now need to assess the risk of such material misstatements by, for example, checking to see how much and the nature of business done in "high risk" countries in the corruption index. Other risk factors to consider include a past record of having to pay bribes and unnecessarily complex or unusual payment methods.[18]

Controls to compensate for these high inherent risks include a corporate code of conduct with specific policies and procedures designed to avoid violating the Act, and effective monitoring and communication of these procedures. If combined inherent and control risks are assessed as too high, then the auditor would consider additional procedures as listed in the preceding box.

In June 2000, Bill C-22 became law. It was passed as a measure to combat the international problem of money laundering—the conversion of funds from criminal activities to legitimate ones. Canada was among the last of the industrialized countries to pass such legislation.

PAs are affected because, unknowingly, they may be manipulated into recycling funds through complex transactions. Moreover, the PAs' association helps legitimize racketeers' criminal activities.

Under the new law, accountants need to be careful not to be considered accomplices under the concept of "willful blindness," which is very close to actual knowledge. This is said to occur

[18] S. Chester and D. Selley, "Giving Kickbacks the Boot," *CA Magazine*, August 1999, pp. 20–24.

when a person prefers to remain ignorant despite having well-founded suspicions that something is amiss. Accordingly, the refusal of the CA to investigate or ask relevant questions because he or she suspects the existence of an illegal or dishonest situation can be considered an act of complicity.[19]

The best way to avoid this risk is to be knowledgeable about the client and the client's business. The PA needs to be skeptical about unusual transactions that are inconsistent with industry standards and do not make economic sense. The PA should be especially cautious when asked to carry out transactions for third parties. In short, the same scepticism and responsibilities apply to money laundering activities as to fraud and other illegal acts involving deception.

REVIEW CHECKPOINTS

17.13 Is there anything odd about these situations? (1) Auditors performed a surprise payroll distribution, and J. Jones, S. Smith, and D. Douglas were absent from work. (2) A cheque to Larson Lectric Supply was endorsed with "Larson Lectric" above the signature of "Eloise Garfunkle." (3) Numerous cheques were issued dated January 1, May 22, July 1, September 4, October 9, and December 25, 2000.

17.14 What account could you audit to determine whether a company had recorded fictitious sales?

Internal Control

A 2004 study by the Association of Certified Fraud Examiners showed that 40 percent of all frauds are detected by tips from employees. This explains why SOX is requiring audit committees to encourage anonymous whistle-blowing by employees. Almost 30 percent of frauds were detected by internal audit, 18 percent were detected by other internal controls, 21 percent were detected by accident and 11 percent by external auditors.[20]

THE TRUSTED EMPLOYEE

A small business owner hired his best friend to work as his accountant. The friend was given full unlimited access to all aspects of the business and was completely responsible for the accounting. Five years later, the owner finally terminated the friend because the business was not profitable. Upon taking over the accounting, the owner's wife found that cash receipts from customers were twice the amounts formerly recorded by the accountant "friend." An investigation revealed that the friend had stolen $450,000 in cash sales receipts from the business, while the owner had never made more than $16,000 a year. (The friend had even used the stolen money to make loans to the owner and to keep the business going!)

NO LOCKS ON THE DOOR

Perini Corporation kept blank cheques in an unlocked storeroom, where every clerk and secretary had access. Also in the storeroom was the automatic cheque-signing machine. The prenumbered cheques were not logged and restricted to one person. The bookkeeper was very surprised to open the bank statement one month and find that $1.5 million in stolen cheques had been paid on the account.

Source: "Auditing for Internal Fraud" training course © 2006 Association of Certified Fraud Examiners.

---

[19]Eric Lavoie and Guylaine Leclerc, "Keeping Your Hands Clean," *CA Magazine*, October 2001, p. 36.
[20]J.T. Wells, "Small Business, Big Losses" *Journal of Accountancy*, December 2004, pp. 42–47.

WHEN YOUR IDENTITY IS STOLEN

Even your utility bills can be turned to fraudulent use.

A 22-year-old secretary realizes she's got an evil twin travelling around the country when Canada Revenue Agency begins demanding she cough up unpaid taxes. Her imposter—who'd apparently applied for and received a social insurance number under her name years earlier—has been moving from job to job without paying taxes.

The names of children who died years ago are used to set up phony businesses that collect GST refunds. An Etobicoke man, who is eventually jailed for tax fraud, collected the names from tombstones.

Another con man opens a number of accounts at Vancouver-area banks using someone else's SIN and birth certificate. He defrauds the banks of more than $170,000 by depositing phony cheques and withdrawing the money from ATMs.

Identity thieves take over someone else's identity to commit fraud—either by applying for a credit card or loan, opening a bank account or using social insurance numbers to hide from the taxman.

These are some of the stories on the growing list of Canadian cases involving identity theft as identified by privacy commissioner Ann Cavoukian.

The victim often doesn't find out what's happened until months later and by that time his or her credit report is such a mess it can take years to sort out.

Cavoukian has just released a report on some of the steps she believes need to be taken to stop the crime. Some of the less obvious ones include the following:

TIPS TO PREVENT IDENTITY THEFT

- Shred or tear up sensitive documents before throwing them away. These include phone and utility bills, pre-approved credit applications and anything that provides credit card number, bank account number, tax information, your driver's license number or your birth date.

- Install a locked mailbox.

- Obtain a copy of your credit report regularly to check for fraudulent accounts and false address changes. Contact Equifax Canada Inc at 1-800-465-7166.

- Don't leave a paper record behind after using bank machines.

- Avoid writing your credit card number or SIN on a cheque.

- Don't give your credit card number out over the phone unless you know the company you're dealing with well. It's especially important not to provide personal information over cordless or cellular phones.

Source: Valerie Lawton, *The Toronto Star,* July 6, 1997, B5. Reprinted with permission—Torstar Syndication Services.

Fraud awareness auditing involves perceptions of the controls installed (or not installed) by a company, plus "thinking like a crook" to imagine ways and means of stealing. When controls are absent, the ways and means may be obvious. Otherwise, it may take some scheming to figure out how to steal from an organization.

REVIEW
CHECKPOINTS

17.15   What could happen if a person could authorize medical insurance claims and enter them into the system for payment without supervisory review?

17.16   What could happen if the inventory warehouse manager also had responsibility for making the physical inventory observation and reconciling discrepancies to the perpetual inventory records?

SCHEMES AND DETECTION PROCEDURES
· · · · · · · · · · · ·

 The importance of internal control in preventing and detecting fraud cannot be underestimated. In designing a system of controls it's important to identify weaknesses or improper utilization of materials, people or equipment. A good first step is to investigate the

1. FOCUS ON FRAUD POSSIBILITIES

Hard as it is to accept, most preventive controls can be beaten by a motivated thief. And when thieves are inside the organization, they may be part of the control effort itself.

Ask yourself how management steps such as reengineering, downsizing, outsourcing, computerization and globalization affect the reliability of controls—as well as the attitudes of those who have access to the assets.

Other places to look are industry resources. Many industry organizations maintain data on fraud cases. Since banks, insurers and others all support fraud prevention, contact your industry association's security professionals for guidance.

Keep files of news reports of fraud. These articles often contain enough detail to allow you to understand how the deed was done. But be careful not to get caught up in the drama of the fraud: Put less emphasis on the thieves and their reasons for stealing, focusing instead on the modus operandi.

Typical questions you should ask:

- What jobs are likely to provide opportunities for fraud?
- What opportunities exist for employees, executives, vendors, contractors' agents, customers and others?
- How could they get around approval or transaction confirmation controls?
- What general ledger account and cost center could the fraud be charged to?
- How could the thief deceive the manager in charge of those cost centers when the month-end reports are reviewed?

2. KNOW THE SYMPTOMS

Here's a short list of some fraud symptoms:

- Multiple endorsements on commercial cheques,
- The use of common or repetitive names for refunds—such as Smith or Jones or a commercial name that is very similar to one in your industry but is spelled slightly differently,
- Line items in standard reconciliations that don't go away,
- Customer complaints about having paid invoices for which they are being dunned,
- Adjustments to either inventory records or customer accounts,
- The addresses of vendors that are the same as employee addresses,
- No proceeds from the disposition of used assets.

When one of these symptoms appears, use caution. Often there are reasonable explanations and they usually don't lead to a thief—just an error or an ill-designed process. So don't jump to conclusions. Instead, track down the cause for the symptom.

Be especially cautious when reacting to a person's suspicious lifestyle. While such signs should sound an alarm, by themselves they prove nothing, but certainly more investigation is warranted.

3. DESIGN CONTROLS AND AUDIT PROCEDURES

In developing procedures, be sure to include specific steps calculated to look for fraud symptoms. And while measuring fraud exposure, assess the reliability of such controls.

4. FOLLOW THROUGH ON ALL SYMPTOMS OBSERVED

Whoever finds a symptom of fraud—the external or internal auditor or a company manager—should resolve the situation before going on. Operate with an attitude of healthy professional skepticism. Beware of pressures to complete work within unreasonable deadlines. Be aware that the single symptom you are looking at may not be an isolated occurrence, it may be one of many.

If you believe the follow-up is beyond your capabilities, consider giving the problem to a professional investigator. There are legal liability dangers inherent in mishandling possible fraud cases."

Source: J. Hall, "How to Spot Fraud," *Journal of Accountancy*, October 1996.

THE REBATE SCAM

A construction company's project manager engineered a simple scam that earned him about $250,000 before he was unmasked. Here's how he did it—and how he was tripped up:

The project manager opened a bank account using a name very similar to the name of the construction project he was managing. He then approached three major suppliers and requested cash rebates in excess of normal industry practice. In exchange, he guaranteed each would be the sole source for their respective products. In addition, he promised they would be paid promptly for all materials delivered. He told them the rebates were due on the first of each month for all transactions of the proceeding month. The cheques were to be made payable to the name on the bogus bank account.

The suppliers agreed to the unusual terms in order to secure the business. None questioned the name on the cheques because it was close enough to the actual project name.

The arrangement worked smoothly for several months. Rebate cheques were delivered to the project manager each month and he deposited them into his account. After the cheques cleared, he withdrew most of the funds using cashier's cheques.

The scheme came to light when a supervisor in the construction company's accounts payable department questioned why prompt-payment discounts weren't being made to the three suppliers. She had just attended a fraud-awareness seminar and remembered that such an unusual arrangement might be a symptom of fraud. Rather than question either the project manager or the suppliers, she correctly referred the matter to the corporate audit department for investigation.

The auditors made simultaneous unannounced visits to all three suppliers. Two wouldn't talk, but the third explained the relationship and provided copies of the cancelled rebate cheques.

Lessons learned from the case:

- It's relatively easy to open unauthorized bank accounts because most banks have limited ability to verify the identity of the person opening an account.

- Scam artists know how to cash cheques—to any payee, in any amount.

- Schemes that involve relationships with suppliers are particularly hard to prevent and detect.

- When contracting with suppliers, try to secure the right to review any appropriate records. While this is fairly common in the contracting environment, it's also something to consider for other relationships in which purchase orders are used.

Source: J. Hall, "How to Spot Fraud," *Journal of Accountancy*, October 1996.

company's historical experience with losses and how to prevent the losses. A system of checks and balances should be designed to address these risks. To the extent possible every transaction should be authorized, initiated, approved, executed and recorded. No transaction should be handled by one person. Preprinted serial numbered documents such as purchase orders, sales and purchases invoices, receiving reports, cheques and debit or credit memos should be used. All policies and procedures should be documented, including procedures in the event of an internal control breakdown. Once implemented, the internal control system should be communicated orally and in writing to all employees. The policies should communicate firmly and clearly that fraud will not be tolerated and the consequences of fraud involvement. The internal control system should be evaluated periodically for cost effectiveness, and employee feedback should be encouraged and rewarded. The following box gives a basic system of controls to deter common types of fraud.

A SIMPLE INTERNAL CONTROLS CHECKLIST FOR COMPANIES

- Allow for a system of checks and balances. Every transaction should be authorized, initiated, approved, executed and recorded.
- Divide or segregate duties. Do not allow one person to handle all aspects of a transaction from beginning to end.
- Do not allow the same person to have custody of an asset (i.e. cash and inventory) and the responsibility to record transactions.
- Use serial numbers on debit or credit memos, sales and purchases invoices, cheques, tickets, purchase orders and receiving reports.
- Use a safe, and maintain adequate safekeeping of all assets. Make deposits on a daily basis, and if necessary, several times per day.
- Use a budget or forecast to detect whether goals are achieved. Investigate the differences—what happened and why.
- Incorporate hiring policies and practices, which include drug testing and background checks. Subscribe to an ethics hot line, such as the Association's *EthicsLine*, to provide a way for employees to report anonymously suspected infractions or violations within a company to an independent party.

SAFEGUARDING SMALL BUSINESSES

The minimum controls for a small organization are as follows:

- Deposit all cash receipts intact daily.
- Make all payments by serial-numbered cheques with the exception of small transactions by petty cash.
- Reconcile bank accounts monthly.
- Record all cash receipts immediately.
- Balance ledgers at regular intervals.
- Prepare comparative financial statements in sufficient detail every month to disclose significant variations in revenue and expense categories.

Source: D. A. Sebert, "Repeat After Me: Internal Controls, Internal Controls, Internal Controls . . ." *The White Paper*, Association of Certified Fraud Examiners, September/October 1998, p. 33.

SOME NEWER APPROACHES TO FRAUD DETECTION

The understanding of business approach to audits discussed in previous chapters has been promoted as a means to increase the auditor's effectiveness in detecting fraud. "The use of complex analytical procedures comprising a business knowledge acquisition framework, coupled with an assessment of other fraud risk factors, should improve the auditor's ability to detect and diagnose anomalies associated with management fraud. And, a comprehensive knowledge decision frame will serve to heighten the auditor's level of professional skepticism when appropriate, e.g., by enabling the auditor to develop his own hypotheses about unusual financial-statement trends and fluctuations without relying exclusively on management's explanations."[21]

Another recent development in the auditor's fraud detection arsenal is the use of Benford's Law to detect anomalies in the accounting records as indicated in the box following.

In this section of the chapter we will consider some casettes. They will follow a standard format in two major parts: (1) Case Situation, and (2) Audit Approach. Some problems at the end of the chapter will give the case situation, and you will be assigned to write the audit approach section. The first three casettes deal with employee fraud, and the last two deal with management fraud. With the first three casettes, you can practise Learning Objective 5. With the last two casettes, you can practise Learning Objective 6.

BENFORD'S LAW AND AUDITING

Do financial statements universally "favour" some numbers over others? The idea seems to defy logic. In a random string of numbers pulled from a company's books, each digit, 1–9, would seem to have one chance in nine of starting a given number. But according to a 60-year-old formula making its way into the accounting field, some numbers really *are* more "popular" than others. A disruption in the pattern may reveal an inefficient process, an honest mistake or outright fraud. Benford's Law is the newest tool in the auditor's arsenal.

According to Mark J. Nigrini, PhD, "Benford's Law gives us the expected patterns of the digits in a list of numbers . . . These patterns would appear in accounts payable invoices and accounts receivable numbers, for example." When patterns vary from those set down by Benford, there may be a problem. "Variations may reveal employees are listing expenses as $24 to avoid a $25 voucher limit. Or consider a manager who has a $3,000 signing authority. Benford's Law tells me that say, only 0.6 percent of all numbers should start with 29. If I get more than that, maybe a manager is approving too many $2,900 invoices right under his limit." . . . "Maybe managers are breaking down one project into several pieces to circumvent a higher level of oversight for some reason. Clients want to know when employees are going around their control systems." . . . Sometimes, said Nigrini, patterns change because of an error. "Invoices entered more than once will change the frequencies."

"At other times we see spikes—digit frequencies that violate Benford's Law—at $15 or $25," said Ernst & Young partner James Searing. "Even though these are low-dollar items, that might mean a client is writing a separate cheque for each express-mail delivery. That is a very expensive way to process invoices and write cheques." By advising the client to arrange for monthly billing for express mail, E&Y can make the audit a value-added service.

Benford's Law may also catch fraud, thanks to psychology, said Nigrini. "People just don't think 'Benford-like.' If someone is cutting a $400 cheque every week for nonexistent janitorial services, those cheques will skew the digit distribution. A thorough application of the law will find the fraud."

E&Y has developed proprietary software that applies Benford's Law to a client's data. "The more we use such analytical tools, the more we find," said Searing. "In the long term, advanced analytical tools, such as application of Benford's Law, will be part of the audit. They may very well help us reduce the overall risk of auditing, increase the reliability of the audit opinion and increase value to the client."

Source: "Numerology for Accountants," *Journal of Accountancy*, November 1998, p. 15. Copyright © 1998, 1999 from the *Journal of Accountancy* by the American Institute of Certified Public Accountants, Inc. Opinions of the authors are their own and do not reflect policies of the AICPA. Reprinted with permission.

---

[21] T. Bell, F. Marrs, I. Solomon and H. Thomas, *Auditing Organizations Through a Strategic-Systems Lens*, KPMG, 1997, p. 69.

CASETTE 17.1
CASE OF THE MISSING PETTY CASH

Problem

Petty cash embezzlement.

Method

The petty cash custodian (1) brought postage receipts from home and paid them from the fund, (2) persuaded the supervisor to sign blank authorization slips the custodian could use when the supervisor was away, and using these to pay for fictitious meals and minor supplies, (3) took cash to get through the weekend, replacing it the next week.

Paper Trail

Postage receipts were from a distant post office station the company did not use. The blank slips were dated on days the supervisor was absent. The fund was cash short during the weekend and for a few days the following week.

Amount

The fund was small ($100), but the custodian replenished it about every two working days, stealing about $20 each time. With about 260 working days per year and 130 reimbursements, the custodian was stealing about $2,600 per year. The custodian was looking forward to getting promoted to general cashier and bigger and better things!

AUDIT APPROACH

Objective

Obtain evidence of the existence and validity of petty cash transactions.

Control

A supervisor is assigned to approve petty cash disbursements by examining them for validity and signing an authorization slip.

Test of Controls

Audit for transaction authorization and validity. Select a sample of petty cash reimbursement cheque copies with receipts and authorization slips attached; study them for evidence of authorization and validity (vouching procedure). Notice the nature and content of the receipts. Obtain supervisor's vacation schedule and compare dates to authorization slip dates.

Audit of Balance

On Friday count the petty cash and receipts to see that they add up to $100. Then, count the fund again later in the afternoon. (Be sure the second count is a surprise and that the custodian and supervisor sign off on the count working paper so the auditor will not be accused of theft.)

Discovery Summary

Knowing the location of the nearby post office branch used by the company, the auditor noticed the pattern of many receipts from a distant branch, which was near the custodian's apartment. Several authorizations were dated during the supervisor's vacation, and he readily admitted signing the forms in blank so his own supervisor "wouldn't be bothered." The second count on the same day was a real surprise, and the fund was found $35 short.

CASETTE 17.2
THE LAUNDRY MONEY SKIM

Problem

Stolen cash receipts skimmed from collection.

   Albert owned and operated 40 coin laundries around town. As the business grew, he could no longer visit each one, empty the cash boxes, and deposit the receipts. Each location grossed about $140 to $160 per day, operating 365 days per year. (Gross income about $2 million per year.)

Method

Four part-time employees each visited 10 locations, collecting the cash boxes and delivering them to Albert's office, where he would count the coins and currency (from the change machine) and prepare a bank deposit. One of the employees skimmed $5 to $10 from each location visited each day.

Paper Trail

None, unfortunately. The first paper that gets produced is Albert's bank deposit, and the money is gone by then.

Amount

The daily theft does not seem like much, but at an average of $7.50 per day from each of 10 locations, it was about $27,000 per year. If all four of the employees had stolen the same amount, the loss could have been about $100,000 per year.

AUDIT APPROACH

Objective

Obtain evidence of the completeness of cash receipts—that is, that all the cash received is delivered to Albert for deposit.

Control

Controls over the part-time employees were nonexistent. There was no overt or covert surprise observation and no times when two people went to collect cash (thereby needing to agree, in collusion, to steal). There was no rotation of locations or other indications to the employees that Albert was concerned about control.

Test of Controls

With no controls there are no test of control procedures. Obviously, however, "thinking like a crook" leads to the conclusion that the employees could simply pocket money.

Audit of Balance

The "balance" in this case is the total revenue that should have been deposited, and auditing for completeness is always difficult. Albert marked a quantity of coins with an etching tool and marked some $1 and $5 bills with ink. Unknown to the employees, he put these in all the locations, carefully noting the coins and bills in each.

Discovery Summary

Sure enough, a pattern of missing money emerged. When confronted, the employee confessed.

CASETTE 17.3
THE WELL-PADDED PAYROLL

Problem

Embezzlement with fictitious people on the payroll.

Method

Maybelle had responsibility for preparing personnel files for new hires, approval of wages, verification of time cards and distribution of payroll cheques. She "hired" fictitious employees, faked their records and ordered cheques through the payroll system. She deposited some cheques in several personal bank accounts and cashed others, endorsing all of them with the names of the fictitious employees and her own.

Paper Trail

Payroll creates a large paper trail with individual earnings records, T4 tax forms, payroll deductions for taxes and insurance and payroll tax reports. Maybelle mailed all the T4 forms to the same post office box.

Amount

Maybelle stole $160,000 by creating some "ghosts," usually three to five out of 112 people on the payroll, and paying them an average of $256 per week for three years. Sometimes the ghosts quit and were later replaced by others. But she stole "only" about 2 percent of the payroll funds during the period.

AUDIT APPROACH

Objective

Obtain evidence of the existence and validity of payroll transactions.

Control

Different people should be responsible for hiring (preparing personnel files), approving wages and distributing payroll cheques. "Thinking like a crook" leads an auditor to see that Maybelle could put people on the payroll and obtain their cheques.

Test of Controls

Audit for transaction authorization and validity. Random sampling might not work because of the small number of ghosts. Look for the obvious. Select several weeks' cheque blocks, account for numerical sequence (to see whether any cheques have been removed), and examine cancelled cheques for two endorsements.

Audit of Balance

There may be no "balance" to audit, other than the accumulated total of payroll transactions, and the total may not appear out of line with history because the fraud is small in relation to total payroll and has been going on for years. Conduct a surprise payroll distribution, follow up by examining prior cancelled cheques for the missing employees. Scan personnel files for common addresses.

Discovery Summary

Both the surprise distribution and the scan for common addresses provided the names of two or three exceptions. Both led to prior cancelled cheques (which Maybelle had not removed and the bank reconciler had not noticed), which carried Maybelle's own name as endorser. Confronted, she confessed.

CASETTE 17.4
FALSE SALES, ACCOUNTS RECEIVABLE AND INVENTORY

Problem

Overstated sales and accounts receivable caused overstated net income, retained earnings, current assets, working capital and total assets.

Method

Q.T. Wilson was a turnaround specialist who took the challenge at Mini Marc Corporation, a manufacturer of computer peripheral equipment. He set high goals for sales and profits. To meet these goals, managers shipped bricks to distributors and recorded some as sales of equipment to retail distributors and some as inventory out on consignment. No real products left the plant. The theory was that actual sales would grow, and the bricks would be replaced later with real products. In the meantime, the distributors may have thought they were holding consignment inventory in the unopened cartons.

Paper Trail

All the paperwork was in order because the managers had falsified the sales and consignment invoices, but they did not have customer purchase orders for all the false sales. Shipping papers were in order, and several shipping employees knew the boxes did not contain disk drives.

Amount

Prior to the manipulation, annual sales were $135 million. During the two falsification years, sales were $185 million and $362 million. Net income went up from a loss of $20 million to $23 million (income), then to $31 million (income); and the gross margin percent went from 6 percent to 28 percent. The revenue and profit figures outpaced the industry performance. The accounts receivable collection period grew to 94 days, while it was 70 days elsewhere in the industry.

AUDIT APPROACH

Objective

Obtain evidence about the existence and valuation of sales, accounts receivable and inventory.

Control

Company accounting and control procedures required customer purchase orders or contracts evidencing real orders. A sales invoice was supposed to indicate the products and their prices, and shipping documents were supposed to indicate actual shipment. Sales were always charged to the customer's account receivable.

Test of Controls

There were no glaring control omissions such that "thinking like a crook" would have pointed to fraud possibilities. Sensitive auditors might have noticed the high tension created among employees by concentration on meeting profit goals. Normal selection of sales transactions with vouching to customer orders and shipping documents might turn up a missing customer order. Otherwise, the paperwork would seem to be in order. The problem lay in the managers' power to override controls and instruct

shipping people to send bricks. Most auditors do not ask the question: "Have you shipped anything, other than company products, this year?"

Audit of Balance

Confirmations of distributors' accounts receivable might have elicited exception responses. The problem was to have a large enough confirmation sample to pick up some of these distributors or to be sceptical enough to send a special sample of confirmations to distributors who took the "sales" near the end of the accounting period. Observation of inventory should include some inspection of goods not on the company's premises.

Discovery Summary

The overstatements were not detected. The confirmation sample was small and did not contain any of the false shipments. Tests of detail transactions did not turn up any missing customer orders. The inventory out on consignment was audited by obtaining a written confirmation from the holders, who apparently had not opened the boxes. The remarkable financial performance was attributed to good management.

CASETTE 17.5
OVERSTATE THE INVENTORY, UNDERSTATE THE COST OF GOODS SOLD

Problem

Overstated inventory caused understated cost of goods sold, overstated net income and retained earnings, and overstated current assets, working capital and total assets.

Method

A division manager at Doughboy Foods wanted to meet his profit goals and simply submitted overstated quantities in inventory reports. The manager (a) inserted fictitious count sheets in the independent auditors' working papers, (b) handed additional count sheets to the independent auditors after the count was completed saying "these got left out of your set," and (c) inserted false data into the computer system that produced a final inventory compilation (even though this ploy caused the computer-generated inventory not to match with the count sheets).

Paper Trail

In general, management reports should correspond to accounting records. The manager's inventory reports showed amounts larger than shown in the accounts. He fixed the problem by showing false inventory that was "not recorded on the books."

Amount

The food products inventory was overstated by $650,000. Through a two-year period, the false reports caused an income overstatement of 15 percent in the first year and would have caused a 39 percent overstatement the second year.

AUDIT APPROACH

Objective

Obtain evidence of the existence, completeness and valuation of inventory.

Control

Inventory counts should be taken under controlled conditions, but not under the control of managers who might benefit from manipulation. (However, if these managers are present, auditors should nevertheless be prepared to perform the audit work.) Inventory-takers should be trained and follow instructions for recording quantities and condition.

Test of Controls

Auditors should attend the inventory-taker training sessions and study the instructions for adequacy. Observation of the inventory-taking should be conducted by managers and by auditors to ensure compliance with the instructions.

Audit of Balance

For evidence of existence, select a sample of inventory items from the perpetual records and test-count them in the warehouse. For evidence of completeness, select a sample of inventory items in the warehouse, test-count them, and trace them to the final inventory compilation. For evidence of valuation, find the proper prices of inventory for one or both of the samples, calculate the total cost for the items, and compare to their amounts recorded in the books. Compare book inventory amounts to management reports. Control the working papers so that only members of the audit team have access. Analytical procedures gave some signals. The particular manager's division had the lowest inventory turnover rate (6.3) among all the company divisions (comparable turnover, about 11.1) and its inventory had consistently increased from year to year (227 percent over the two-year period).

Discovery Summary

In the second year, when the manager handed over the count sheets "that got left out of your set," the auditor thanked him, then went to the warehouse to check them out. Finding them inaccurate, she compared book inventories to his management reports and found an overstatement in the reports. This prompted further comparison of the computer-generated inventory with the count sheets and more evidence of overstated quantities on 22 of the 99 count sheets.

REVIEW
CHECKPOINTS

17.17 If the petty cash custodian were replaced and the frequency of fund reimbursement decreased from every two days to every four days, what might you suspect?

17.18 Give some examples of control omissions that would make it easy to "think like a crook" and see opportunities for fraud.

17.19 If sales and income were overstated by recording a false cash sale at the end of the year, what "dangling debit" might give the scheme away?

17.20 What three general descriptions can be given to manipulations that produce materially misleading financial statements?

DOCUMENTS, SOURCES AND "EXTENDED PROCEDURES"

. . . .

References are often made in the auditing literature to "extended procedures," but these are rarely defined and listed. Authorities are afraid that a list will limit the range of such procedures, so "extended procedures" are generally left undefined as an open-ended set to refer vaguely to "whatever is necessary in the circumstances." This section describes some of the extended procedures with the proviso that (1) some auditors may consider them ordinary and (2) other auditors may consider them unnecessary in any circumstances. Even so, they are useful detective procedures in either event.

Content of Common Documents

Auditing textbooks often advise beginner auditors to "examine cheques," and to "check the employees on a payroll." It helps to know something about these common documents and the information that can be seen on them.

Information on a Cheque
Exhibit 17–2 describes the information found on a typical cheque. Knowledge of the codes for Bank of Canada districts, offices, provinces and bank identification numbers could enable an auditor to spot a crude cheque forgery. Similarly, a forger's mistakes with the optical

EXHIBIT   17-2   HOW TO READ A CANCELLED CHEQUE AND ENDORSEMENT

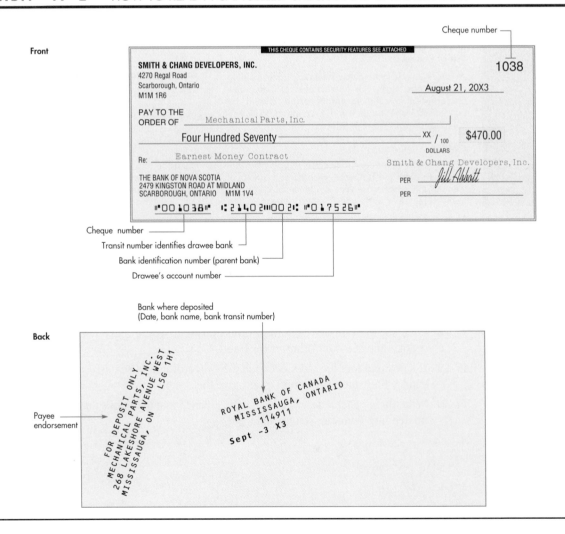

identification printing or the magnetic cheque number might supply a tipoff. If the amount of a cheque is altered after it has cleared the bank, the change would be noted by comparing the magnetic imprint of the amount paid to the amount written on the cheque face. The back of a cheque carries the endorsement(s) of the payees and holders in the due course; the date and the name and routing number of the bank where the cheque was deposited; and the date, identification of the Bank of Canada office, and its routing number for the federal reserve cheque clearing. (Sometimes there is no Bank of Canada clearing identification when local cheques are cleared locally without going through a Bank of Canada office.) Auditors can follow the path of a cancelled cheque by following the banks where it was deposited and cleared. This route may or may not correspond with the characteristics of the payee. (For example, ask why a cheque to a local business in Mississauga, Ontario, should be deposited in a small Missouri bank and cleared through the St. Louis federal reserve office.)

Information on a Bank Statement

Most of the information shown on the bank statement in Exhibit 17–3 is self-explanatory. However, auditors should not overlook the usefulness of some of the information: the bank's count and dollar amount of deposits and cheques can be compared to the detail data on the

EXHIBIT   17-3   SMALL BUSINESS BANK STATEMENT

```
                                                                    27
      North Country Bank
      MISSISSAUGA, ON                                          ACCOUNT
      P.O. BOX 908                         ---           604017-526-5
      KINGSTON, ON   K5G 2H3               ---     ---
                                           ---                    PAGE
                                              ---                    1


      CAULCO INC                                       SIN/TAX ID
      BLDG 1 OFFICE F                                  74-2076251
      5450 BEE CAVE RD
      MISSISSAUGA, ON                                 CYC MC FREQ
      L5G 1H2                                          01 01 M0000


        **   YOUR CHEQUING ACCOUNT     01-29-X3 THRU 02-29-X3 **

      TO YOUR PREVIOUS BALANCE OF - - - - - - - - -      7,559.06
      YOU ADDED          1 DEPOSITS FOR  - - - - - -      5,654.16
      YOU SUBTRACTED   26 WITHDRAWALS FOR - - - - -      10,838.29
      GIVING YOU A CURRENT BALANCE OF - - - - - - -       7,374.93

      NUMBER OF DAYS USED FOR AVERAGES  - - - - - -             31
      YOUR AVERAGE LEDGER BALANCE - - - - - - - - -       4,014.67
      YOUR LOW BALANCE OCCURRED ON 02-22 AND WAS  -       2,374.93

                       THANK YOU
      --------------------------------------------------------------
      --------------------------------------------------------------
                  DEPOSITS AND OTHER ADDITIONS

            DATE    AMOUNT
            0204    5654.16 ✓
      --------------------------------------------------------------
                  CHEQUES AND OTHER WITHDRAWALS

      CHEQUE DATE    AMOUNT CHEQUE DATE   AMOUNT CHEQUE DATE    AMOUNT
       2201  0211     57.83✓ 2214  0203   403.92✓2225  0217  ✓182.77
        **                   2215  0203   135.59✓  **
       2205  0222     16.72✓ 2216  0216     6.16✓2231  0205  ✓254.37
       2206  0203    533.28✓ 2217  0217   138.43✓2232  0210  ✓ 60.61
       2207  0203   1312.15✓ 2218  0217   131.92✓
        **                   2219  0217    82.97✓2234  0217  ✓ 64.69
       2209  0203    247.10✓ 2220  0217    87.49✓2235  0218  ✓279.97
       2210  0203    249.98✓ 2221  0217    85.68✓  **
       2211  0203    255.26✓ 2222  0217    84.69✓2238  0219  ✓ 90.00
       2212  0203    242.09✓  **
       2213  0203    384.91✓ 2224  0217   449.71✓
```

statement; the account holder's business identification number is on the statement, and this can be used in other databases (for individuals, this is a place to get a person's social insurance number); and the statement itself can be studied for alterations.

Valid Social Insurance Numbers

In Canada, **social insurance numbers** (**SIN**s) have become a universal identification number. They can be useful to auditors when checking the personnel files and the validity of people on the payroll. Here are some characteristics of SINs:[22]

- The SIN is a nine-digit number, the ninth digit is a check digit that is calculated using the first eight digits.

- There are two types of SIN, regular numbers and distinctive numbers. Regular numbers are issued to Canadian citizens, registered Native peoples and permanent residents. Distinctive numbers start with digit 9. They are issued to people who do not have status as above, e.g., foreign workers, visitors.

- If the first digit is not a nine, then it is used to indicate the province or territory where the number was issued.

- The middle seven digits are issued in generally ascending numerical order. This makes it feasible to apply Benford's Law to analyzing these digits.

- Working with Human Resources Development Canada, an auditor may be able to detect fictitious SINs.

REVIEW CHECKPOINTS

17.21   How could you tell whether the amount on a cheque had been raised after it was paid by a bank?

17.22   If a false social insurance number of a new employee is entered in the payroll system, and the employee receives a paycheque, what control in the system is not being used?

Sources of Information

A wide variety of records and information is available for various kinds of investigations ranging from personal background checks to business enquiries. Our concern here is with public records and ways to get them. A few of the hundreds of sources are described briefly following.

General Business Sources

City and county tax assessor–collectors keep files on real property by address and legal description, owner, taxable value, improvements and amount of taxes and delinquencies. Provincial (and some city) regulatory agencies have directories of liquor licences and various professionals (e.g., PAs, dentists, doctors, plumbers, electricians). Provincial building ministries and ministers of public housing may have a central index file of appraisers, real estate brokers and most components of the building industry. The industry and trade ministries have data on companies that apply for import and export licences. The federal Ministry of Transportation maintains files on the chain of ownership of all civil aircraft in Canada. Provincial securities commissions have extensive financial information on registered companies and their properties, principal officers, directors and owners. Local Better Business Bureaus keep information about criminal rackets, cons and their operators, and can provide information about the business reputation of local businesses. Standard & Poor's Register of Corporations, Directors and Executives lists about 37,000 public and private

---

[22] Caution: Human Resources Development Canada periodically adds numbers that have been issued and may use numbers assigned to one geographic area for another. If the validity of an SIN becomes important in an audit, check with Human Resources Development Canada to ascertain the current status of numbers issued. For further reference, see M. L. Levy, "Financial Fraud: Schemes and Indicia," *Journal of Accountancy*, August 1985, p. 85; E. J. Pankau, *Check it Out* (Houston: Cloak & Data Press, 1990), pp. 20–27.

companies and the names and titles of over 400,000 officials. The Internet and various on-line information sources are becoming increasingly important not only in investigative accounting, but also as part of gaining familiarity with a new client in a normal audit.[23]

Business and Asset Identification Sources

According to Pankau, each region and province has a system for registering businesses—corporations, joint ventures, sole proprietorships and partnerships. They keep files on registered "assumed names" (**DBA**, or **doing business as** names). Some businesses may be registered with a province and not a region, or with a region and not a province. All real corporations are chartered by a province or federal government, and each province's ministry of consumer and corporate affairs keeps corporate record information, such as the date of registration and the initial officers and owners. (Using these sources, you can find the assets or businesses "hidden" in the spouse's name.) Crooks often work through a labyrinth of business entities, and you can find all the registered ones in these sources. You can also find phony vendor companies created by real employees to bilk employers with false billings. Banks, finance companies and other creditors often file **Uniform Commercial Code (UCC)** records to record the interest of the creditor in assets used as collateral for a loan so that other parties cannot claim interest in the assets (e.g., boats, business equipment, appliances). UCCs are found in regional clerks' offices and in the province's office of the ministry of consumer and/or commercial affairs. (They are also online in some commercial databases.)[24] The two following boxes provide illustrations of procedures used in public sector auditing and by insurance fraud auditors, respectively.

QUOTA REPORTS FISHY?

HALIFAX—New recruits to the ranks of the federal fisheries enforcement program are to be given courses in accounting so they can net fishermen who have been cooking their books. And inspectors currently on the payroll of the Fisheries and Oceans Department will be given crash courses in audit procedures over the next several months that will teach them to focus on crooked practices in the fishing industry. A 1994 audit suggested that much of the fish caught on the country's coasts slips through the federal quota system as a result of misreporting of black market trading. The report by federal auditors was obtained by The Canadian Press news service under the *Access to Information Act*.

It is said the inspectors, who tend to concentrate on the mesh sizes of nets and the species and volumes of fish in a trawler's hold, should focus more on the records and catch reports maintained by fishermen. Authors of the report suggested the inspectors attend commercial-crime courses conducted by the RCMP. The audit pointed to some fishermen, provided with individual quotas, as possible villains who have taken advantage of procedural gaps in enforcement to cheat the quota system.

Over the last few years, individual quotas have replaced the shared quota system, which set overall limits on catches within designated fisheries. The new system reduced competition for the total allowable catches and extended the season for fishermen who survived devastation of the east coast cod fishery. It was eventually extended to the west coast and Lake Erie fisheries.

Despite its shortcomings, however, the bureaucrats who reviewed the process hailed the individual quota system as a stabilizing factor in the fragile fishing industry.

Source: The Bottom Line, September 1996, p. 6.

---

[23] Hundreds of sources and directories under the categories of business, finance, people, property and electronic databases are listed and described in the U.S. General Accounting Office publication *Investigators' Guide to Sources of Information* (GAO/OSI-88-1, March 1988, updated periodically).

Also, insider information is increasingly difficult to "keep under the lid" as investors form online investor forums to assist each other in passing on "hot tips." See J.A. Abbey, "Fools and Their Money," *Time*, June 17, 1996, pp. 51–54). Auditors may find these online services useful sources of information on risks and uncertainties facing their clients.

[24] These and other sources of business and personal information are described in Pankau, *Check It Out.*

Federal and Provincial Revenue Agencies

Ever wonder how revenue agents find tax evaders? One accountant described the following sources of tips for possible big audit findings: (1) police arrest records point to people who may have illicit unreported income; (2) real estate sales records may identify people who "forget" to put their sales in a tax return; (3) auto registrations of expensive cars point to people who have a lot of money to spend—maybe some unreported income; (4) comparison of provincial sales tax returns with income tax revenue amounts may reveal discrepancies (depending on which tax collector is feared the most); and (5) agents have used

---

FORENSICS ON FRONT LINES IN WAR ON INSURANCE FRAUDS

TORONTO—Forensic accountants play an increasingly important role in documenting, proving and reducing insurance fraud.

Insurance adjusters and lawyers have long used accountants to document clearly fraudulent claims. However, many insurance companies, concerned about huge losses to fraud—about $1.3 billion a year in property and casualty (P&C) claims alone—have recently set up their own fraud-busting Special Investigation Units (SIUs).

The SIUs, staffed mostly by ex commercial crime unit police officers, work proactively to reduce fraud by investigating all claims above a certain amount, as well as suspicious claims.

Once they have established the possibility of fraud, the SIUs (or insurance counsel, if the claim has already progressed to the litigation stage) turn to forensic accountants for the hard proof. "It's just starting to happen," said Ted Baskerville of Lindquist Avey MacDonald Baskerville. "Our role up to now has always been to deal with claims that are overstated—or appear to be—or with arson, or staged theft."

In suspected arson or staged theft cases, Lindquist Avey's forensic specialists determine the insured's possible financial motive by looking at details of ownership or management, historical financial results, past and future obligations, profitability and cash flow.

They prepare a general profile of the company, including its relationship with creditors, and try to answer the following: Do owners have financial needs they can't satisfy legitimately through the business? What do the owners withdraw from the company, or how do they benefit from it in other ways?

In cases of possible theft, it's important to look at other businesses owned by the insureds; maybe they're trying to run down one business for the benefit of another.

The growing use of electronic document storage systems can have unexpected benefits for the forensic sleuth.

According to Ken Gibson of Mintz & Partners in Toronto, "people sometimes don't realize what they have stored." Many systems automatically back up computer communications like e-mail.

Aspiring fraud perpetrators may destroy the e-mail record in their own computers, but forget, or don't know, that investigators can read the backup disk.

Gibson typically deals with commercial damage claims—theft for example, where inventory appears to be gone, but there's little evidence of a break-in.

In those sorts of cases, he said, investigators try to establish whether anything is in fact missing and, if so, whether it had any real value.

Often, a line of goods, such as video or electronic products, isn't selling, and then it allegedly disappears.

The forensic investigator looks at sales figures, dealings with suppliers and interviews employees or others involved.

Fraud by employees, leading to fidelity bond claims, is a growth industry, according to Ivor Gottschalk of Ernst & Young's Toronto-based forensic and litigation accounting group.

Often, an employee in a company's purchasing department orders an unnecessary or nonexistent material or service, and gets a kickback for the order.

Other types of fraud include setting up fake suppliers, fictitious employees on a payroll or phony accounts payable.

"People are getting more and more creative," said Gottschalk.

"We're seeing fraud on the other side, where there's actually fraud in collusion with customers. Companies will normally control their purchasing departments quite closely because they're aware that purchasing is very vulnerable to outside forces.

"But generally, you wouldn't think of your accounts receivable clerk as being in a position to benefit somebody outside the company, writing off invoices to customers, for example."

Many forensic accountants are members of the Association of Certified Fraud Examiners, based in the U.S., but with more than 900 Canadian members in nine chapters.

Source: Copyright 1996 by Derek Lundy. Reprinted with permission.

university-town newspaper rental ads to identify people who rent rooms, garage apartments, duplex halves and the like, but forget to report the income.

R E V I E W
C H E C K P O I N T

17.23 Where could you find information about real estate valuation, aircraft ownership, names of licensed doctors, assumed (fictitious) business names and liens on personal property?

Extended Procedures

LEARNING OBJECTIVE
7 Explain the use of extended audit procedures for detecting fraud.

The nature of extended procedures is limited only by an auditor's imagination and, sometimes, the willingness of management to co-operate in extraordinary audit activities. Next is a short series of extended procedures, with some brief explanations.[25]

Enquire, Ask Questions

Be careful not to discuss fraud possibilities with the managers who might be involved. It gives them a chance to cover up or run. Wells described **fraud audit questioning (FAQ)** as a nonaccusatory method of asking key questions of personnel during a regular audit to give them an opportunity to furnish information about possible misdeeds. Fraud possibilities are addressed in a direct manner, so the FAQ approach must have the support of management. Example questions are "Do you think fraud is a problem for business in general?", "Do you think this company has any particular problem with fraud?", "In your department, who is beyond suspicion?" and "Is there any information you would like to furnish regarding possible fraud within this organization?"[26]

Count the Petty Cash Twice in a Day

The second count is unexpected, and you might catch an embezzling custodian short.

Investigate Suppliers (vendors)

Check the Better Business Bureau for reputation, the telephone book for a listing and address and the provincial corporation records for owners and assumed names. You may find fictitious vendors being used to make false billings or companies related to purchasing department employees.

Investigate Customers

As with vendors, investigation may reveal companies set up by insiders, with billings at below-list prices so that the insiders can buy goods and resell them at a profit.

Examine Endorsements on Cancelled Cheques

Look for second endorsements, especially the names of employees. Most business payments are deposited with one endorsement. Be sure to include cheques payable to "cash" or to a bank for purchase of cashiers' cheques. The second endorsee indicates that the payee may not have received the benefit of the payment.

Add Up the Accounts Receivable Subsidiary

Cash payments on customer accounts have been stolen, with receipts given credit entry to the customer account, but no cash deposit and no entry have made to the control account.

---

[25] Further explanation of these and other procedures can be found in the books and articles cited in preceding footnotes and in these sources: *AICPA Technical Practice Aids* (TPA 8200.02); D. Churbuck, "Desktop Forgery," *Forbes*, November 27, 1989, pp. 246–254; O. Hilton, *Scientific Examination of Questioned Documents*, rev. ed. (New York: Elsevier North Holland, 1982); A.C. Levinston, "40 Years of Embezzlement Tracking," *Internal Auditor*, April 1991, pp. 51–55.

[26] Joseph T. Wells, "From the Chairman: Fraud Audit Questioning," *The White Paper*, National Association of Certified Fraud Examiners, May-June 1991), p. 2. This technique must be used with extreme care and practice.

Want to Fudge Your Tax Deductions?

Don't try to turn that $300 receipt into $800 with the stroke of a ballpoint pen. The U.S. IRS has ultraviolet scanners, ink chromatographers, densitometers and argon-ion lasers that can identify the brand of pen, the age of the paper and the source of the paper. Something printed on a laser printer is harder, but they're working on it.

Source: D. Churbuck, "Desktop Forgery," *Forbes*, November 27, 1989, p. 252.

Audit General Journal Entries

Experience has shown that the largest number of accounting errors requiring adjustment are found in nonroutine, nonsystematic journal entries. (Systematic accounting is the processing of large volumes of day-to-day ordinary transactions.)

Match Payroll to Life and Medical Insurance Deductions

Ghosts on the payroll seldom elect these insurance coverages. Doing so reduces the embezzler's take and complicates the cover-up.

Match Payroll to Social Insurance Numbers

Fictitious SINs may be chosen at random; if so, the fraudster will have made the mistake of using an unissued number or one that does not match with the birthdate. Sort the payroll SINs in numerical order and look for false, duplicate or unlikely (e.g., consecutive) numbers.

Match Payroll with Addresses

Look for multiple persons at the same address.

Retrieve Customers' Cheques

If an employee has diverted customer payments, the cancelled cheques showing endorsements and deposits to a bank where the company has no account are not available because they are returned to the issuing organization (customer). Ask the customer to give originals or copies, or to provide access for examination.

Use Marked Coins and Currency

Plant marked money in locations where cash collections should be gathered for turning over for deposit.

Measure Deposit Lag Time

Compare the dates of cash debit recording and deposit slip dates to dates credited by the bank. Someone who takes cash, then holds the deposit for the next cash receipts to make up the difference, causes a delay between the date of recording and the bank's date of deposit.

Document Examination

Look for erasures, alterations, copies where originals should be filed, telltale lines from a copier when a document has been pieced together, handwriting and other oddities. Professional document examination is a technical activity that requires special training (e.g., RCMP), but crude alterations may be observed, at least enough to bring them to specialists' attention.

Covert Surveillance

Observe activities while not being seen. External auditors might watch employees clocking onto a work shift, observing whether they use only one time card. Travelling hotel auditors may check in unannounced, use the restaurant and entertainment facilities and watch the employees skimming receipts and tickets. (Trailing people on streets and maintaining a "stakeout" should be left to trained investigators.)

Horizontal and Vertical Analyses

This is analytical review ratio analysis and is very similar to the preliminary analytical procedures explained in Chapter 8. **Horizontal analysis** refers to changes of financial statement numbers and ratios across several years. **Vertical analysis** refers to financial statement amounts expressed each year as proportions of a base, such as sales for the income statement accounts and total assets for the balance sheet accounts. Auditors look for relationships that do not make sense as indicators of potential large misstatement and fraud.

Net Worth Analysis

Net worth analysis is used when fraud has been discovered or strongly suspected, and the information to calculate a suspect's net worth can be obtained (e.g., asset and liability records, bank accounts). The method is to calculate the suspect's net worth (known assets less known liabilities) at the beginning and end of a period (months or years), then try to account for the difference as (1) known income less living expenses and (2) unidentified difference. The unidentified difference may be the best available approximation of the amount of a theft.

Expenditure Analysis

Experience analysis is similar to net worth analysis, except the data are the suspect's spending for all purposes compared to known income. If spending exceeds legitimate and explainable income, the difference may be the amount of a theft.

It should be noted that an analysis like this normally represents only indirect (circumstantial) evidence in a court of law and normally by itself it cannot prove the "guilt beyond a reasonable doubt" that is required in criminal cases.

Valuation Services

Forensic accounting and fraud auditing frequently involve quantification of economic losses resulting from illegal activities. This may require the specialized services of chartered business valuators.[27]

. . . .

R E V I E W   17.24   What is the difference between a normal procedure and an extended procedure?
C H E C K P O I N T S   17.25   What might be indicated by two endorsements on a cancelled cheque?

17.26   What three oddities might be found connected with ghosts on a padded payroll?

17.27   What can an auditor find using horizontal analysis, vertical analysis, net worth analysis and expenditure analysis?

. . . .

AFTER DISCOVERING A FRAUD
. . . .

Building a case against a fraudster is a task for trained investigators. Most internal and external auditors take roles as assistants to fraud examiners, who know how to conduct interviews and interrogations, perform surveillance, use informants and obtain usable confessions. In almost all cases, the postdiscovery activity proceeds with a special prosecutorial assignment with the co-operation or under the leadership of management. A Crown attorney and police officials may be involved. Prosecution of fraudsters is advisable because, if left unpunished, they often go on to steal again. This is no place for "normal" auditing, but auditors have been given some guidelines related to relevant communications.

---

[27] For example, see the CICA practice aid, *Investigative and Forensic Accounting Practice Issues* (1995).

CICA and Internal Audit Standards

Standards for external auditors contain materiality thresholds related to reporting auditors' knowledge of errors, irregularities and illegal acts. Immaterial errors are supposed to be reported to management at least one level above the people involved.[28] The idea is that small matters can be kept in the management family. However, errors material to the financial statements must be adjusted and handled by management persons responsible for the financial statements to the satisfaction of auditors, or else the audit report will be qualified.

Irregularities receive a slightly different treatment, but there is still a materiality standard in effect. The auditors should inform the audit committee of the board of directors of all irregularities, except ones that are "clearly inconsequential." Irregularities involving senior management are never "inconsequential." In the CICA audit standards, room is always left for auditors' discretion in determining whether something is minor enough not to matter and not to report. However, management and directors must deal with irregularities to the satisfaction of the auditors. If uncertainties persist about the irregularities and management's actions, the audit report should be qualified, explaining all the unsavoury reasons, or the auditors may withdraw from the engagement.

Clients' illegal acts also come under the "clearly inconsequential" materiality standard. Ones that amount to more than this should be reported to the organization's audit committee,

FRAUDULENT FINANCIAL REPORTING: 1987–1997 AN ANALYSIS OF U.S. PUBLIC COMPANIES

SUMMARY OF RESEARCH COMMISSIONED BY THE COMMITTEE OF SPONSORING ORGANIZATIONS (COSO) OF THE TREADWAY COMMISSION

- The companies committing fraud generally were small, and most were not listed on the New York or American Stock Exchanges.
- The frauds went to the very top of the organizations. In 72 percent of the cases, the CEO appeared to be associated with the fraud.
- The audit committees and boards of the fraud companies appeared to be weak. Most audit committees rarely met, and the companies' boards of directors were dominated by insiders and others with significant ties to the company.
- A significant portion of the companies was owned by the founders and board members.
- Severe consequences resulted when companies committed fraud, including bankruptcy, significant changes in ownership, and delisting by national exchanges.
- Cumulative amounts of fraud were relatively large for the many small companies involved, for example, resulting in an average financial misstatement of 25 percent of total assets.

The study results highlight the need for an effective control environment, or "tone at the top." The risk of fraud is much higher in small companies. A strong CEO, with significant share ownership in a small organization, needs an experienced, independent board to insure objectivity.

COSO's mission is to improve the quality of financial reporting through internal controls, governance, and ethics. This study validates the need for continued focus on all three areas. We believe the study will provide a platform for those responsible for financial reporting to improve their effectiveness.

Source: www.aicpa.org as of April 15, 1999.

[28] *CICA Handbook,* paragraph 5135.19.

and the financial statements should contain adequate disclosures about the organization's illegal acts.[29] External auditors always have the option to withdraw from the engagement if management and directors do not take action satisfactory in the circumstances.

Under the CICA audit standards, disclosures of irregularities and clients' illegal acts to outside agencies are limited. If the auditors are fired, the firm can cite these matters in the letter attached to the provincial securities commission, which may require explanation of an organization's change of auditors. A fired auditor can tell the successor auditor about the firm when the successor makes the enquiries required by professional ethics.

Auditors must respond when answering a subpoena issued by a court or other agency with authority, which will happen in a lawsuit or prosecution. When performing work under public sector audit standards, auditors are required to report irregularities and illegal acts to the client agency under the audit contract, which may be an agency or office different from the organization audited.

SIAS No. 3 requires internal auditors to inform management of suspected wrongdoing. They are expected to report fraud findings to management, the board of directors, or the audit committee of the board, being careful not to report to persons who might be involved in a fraud scheme. But, as the preceding box indicates, much can still be done to improve the financial fraud record of companies even in the highly regulated securities markets of North America.

Former SEC Chairman Arthur Levitt was critical of the profession for allowing **hocus-pocus accounting** that facilitates financial statement fraud. The following box summarizes the most common forms of hocus-pocus accounting.

HOCUS-POCUS ACCOUNTING

EXECUTIVE SUMMARY

- Public companies that fail to report quarterly earnings that meet or exceed analysts' expectations often experience a drop in their stock prices. This can lead to practices that sometimes include fraudulent overstatement of quarterly revenue.

- One of the most common schemes is the bill-and-hold sales transaction. While it's not necessarily a GAAP violation, it's often associated with financial frauds and calls for deeper investigation. The SEC says that all of the following conditions must be met for revenue recognition to be appropriate:
  - The risks of ownership must have passed to the buyer.
  - The customer must have a commitment to purchase, preferably in writing.
  - The buyer must request the bill-and-sale transaction and substantiate a business purpose for it.
  - A fixed delivery date must exist.
  - The seller must not retain any significant specific performance obligations.
  - The goods must be complete and ready for shipment and not subject to being used to fill other orders.

- Deals called sham transactions refer specifically to sales schemes that appear genuine but actually are rigged for the purpose of letting the seller recognize revenue. Other indicators that fraudulent financial reporting might exist include bogus shipping dates, revenue figures that always meet analysts' expectations and transactions with unusual payment terms.

- Auditors with a good understanding of the client, the business and its products are well prepared to see the warning signs of revenue-recognition fraud.

Source: D.R. Carmichael, "Hocus-Pocus Accounting," *Journal of Accountancy*, October 1999, p. 60.

---

[29] Ibid., paragraph 5136.04.

Consulting and Assisting

LEARNING OBJECTIVE

8* Summarize how PAs can assist in prosecuting fraud perpetrators.

While engaged in the audit work, auditors should know how to preserve the chain of custody of evidence. The chain of custody is the crucial link of the evidence to the suspect, called the "relevance" of evidence by lawyers and judges. If documents are lost, mutilated, coffee-soaked or compromised (so that a defence lawyer can argue that they were altered to frame the suspect), they can lose their effectiveness for the prosecution. Auditors should learn to mark the evidence, writing an identification of the location, condition, date, time and circumstances as soon as it appears to be a signal of fraud. This marking should be on a separate tag or page, the original document should be put in a protective envelope (plastic) for preservation, and audit work should proceed with copies of the documents instead of originals. A record should be made of the safekeeping and of all persons who use the original. Any eyewitness observations should be timely recorded in a memorandum or on tape (audio or video), with corroboration of colleagues, if possible. There are other features to the chain of custody relating to interviews, interrogations, confessions, documents obtained by subpoena and other matters, but these activities usually are not conducted by auditors.

Independent PAs often accept engagements for litigation support and expert witnessing. This work can be termed **forensic accounting**, which means the application of accounting and auditing skills to legal problems, both civil and criminal. Litigation support can take several forms, but it usually amounts to consulting in the capacity of helping lawyers document cases and determine damages. Expert witness work involves testifying to findings determined during litigation support and testifying about accounting principles and auditing standards applications. The CICA and the Institute of Internal Auditors conduct continuing education courses for auditors who want to become experts in these fields.

The CICA now offers a specialization certificate in investigative and forensic accounting (IFA).

FIRMS SHOULD TAKE FRAUD SERIOUSLY

Company managers are increasingly aware of fraud and have taken initiatives to address its costly consequences, but there is no reason for complacency.

KPMG Investigation and Security Inc. says 62 percent of respondents to its survey of 1,000 of the country's largest companies as ranked by FP reported that fraud had taken place in their organization in the past year, up from 52 percent in the 1996 survey. Better detection is responsible for some of the rise, KPMG says, but a large part is attributable to an actual increase in the incidence of fraud.

Those surveyed see a host of factors as key in allowing fraud to take place, such as poor hiring practices, management override of internal controls and collusion between employees and third parties. However, poor internal controls are viewed as the leading factor.

Internal fraud remains a huge problem. The survey indicates that based on dollar losses 55 percent of all scams are from inside companies. Management accounts for 17 percent of all fraud—usually phoney expense accounts. Employee fraud—38 percent—is predominantly cheque forgery or counterfeiting. What is equally disturbing is that almost half the respondents conduct business in such a way as to be vulnerable to money laundering.

The sad fact is many companies—25 percent of those surveyed—haven't taken even basic measures to shrink the possibility of fraud. These include devising a corporate code of conduct and checking new employees. With the incidence of fraud rising, this is hardly a responsible way to manage a company.

Source: Editorial, "Firms Should Take Fraud Seriously," *The Financial Post,* May 16, 1997, p. 14. Sun Media Corp.

FRAUD AUDITS AS ASSURANCE ENGAGEMENTS

An obvious question is whether investigations and audits of the types discussed in this chapter are assurance or consulting engagements. Much depends on the nature of the engagement and whether an accountability relationship exists. But if we view every employee, including management, as being accountable for resources entrusted to them by the company, many fraud audits would appear to be of the direct reporting type, with an implied assertion that defalcations are not occurring.

Currently, the only authoritative guidance on fraud audit reports is that developed by the Association of Certified Fraud Examiners in their *Fraud Examiners Manual*. Exhibit 17–4 illustrates a "clean" opinion on a fraud audit. Notice, however, that although the term *opinion* is used, suggesting high assurance for the assertion "there is no fraud," the wording of the opinion paragraph is more in the nature of the moderate-assurance, "nothing came to our attention" type that is used in review engagements. This is probably because there is no agreed-upon set of standardized procedures such as GAAS that can provide high assurance for this particular type of assertion.

The equivalent of an adverse opinion, on the other hand, which is given in Exhibit 17–5, provides much higher assurance for the assertion that a fraud did occur (especially if there is a signed confession satisfying all legal requirements, for example, that the confession was not coerced). But note that the high assurance is provided in part because of the way the opinion is worded. The opinion does not state that the fraud can be proven legally—that is, "beyond a reasonable doubt," as would be required in a criminal court. Instead the conclusion is a much milder one—"if proven in a court of law," the actions would be considered fraudulent. In other words, the fraud auditor is not claiming that there is fraud beyond a reasonable doubt, which is something only the courts can decide. Rather, the auditor is saying that he or she is providing high assurance that a fraud may have taken place. Thus, by properly wording the conclusion the auditor can provide high assurance for the conclusion, and the use of the word "opinion" would appear to be warranted in this case under section 5025.

EXHIBIT   17–4   FRAUD EXAMINATION OPINION (EVIDENCE DOES NOT SUPPORT ALLEGATION)

Investigation Appendix   **Engagement Contracts/Opinion Letters**

[Date]

[   ], Esq.
[Law Department]
[Company Name]
[Address]
[City, State, Zip Code]

RE: [Fraud Examination]

Dear Mr./Mrs. [   ]:

We have conducted a fraud examination concerning a possible misappropriation of assets of the [Company Name]. This examination was predicated upon information resulting from a routine audit of the company's books by the company's internal auditors.

Our examination was conducted in accordance with lawful fraud examination techniques, which include, but are not limited to: examination of books and records; voluntary interviews of appropriate personnel; and other such evidence-gathering procedures as necessary under the circumstances.

Because concealment and trickery are elements of fraud, no assurance can be given that fraud does not exist. However, based on the results of our examination, we have found no evidence to indicate a violation of criminal and/or civil fraud-related statutes in connection with this matter.

Very truly yours,

Source: *The Fraud Examiners Manual* © 2006 Association of Certified Fraud Examiners.

EXHIBIT 17–5   FRAUD EXAMINATION OPINION (EVIDENCE SUPPORTS ALLEGATION)

Investigation Appendix	Engagement Contracts/Opinion Letters

[Date]

[   ], Esq.
[Law Department]
[Company Name]
[Address]
[City, State, Zip Code]

RE: [Fraud Examination]

Dear Mr./Mrs. [   ]:

We have conducted a fraud examination concerning a possible misappropriation of assets of the [Company Name]. This examination was predicted upon information resulting from a routine audit of the company's books by the company's internal auditors.

Our examination was conducted in accordance with lawful fraud examination techniques, which include, but are not limited to: examination of books and records; voluntary interviews of appropriate witnesses/personnel; and other such evidence-gathering procedures as necessary under the circumstances.

During the pendency of this fraud examination, Mr. [   ] voluntarily furnished a signed statement indicating that he misappropriated $...................... to his personal benefit.

Based on the results of our examination and the confession of Mr. [ ], it is our opinion that his actions, if proven in a court of law, could constitute a violation of relevant criminal and/or civil fraud-related statutes.

Very truly yours,

Source: *The Fraud Examiners Manual* © 2006 Association of Certified Fraud Examiners.

There are two important lessons to be learned from these illustrative reports: one is that the level of assurance depends greatly on the ability to identify suitable criteria—for example, a signed confession; the other is that the level of assurance depends greatly on the specific phrasing of the conclusion. For example, if in Exhibit 17–5 the auditor had concluded that fraud had taken place, such an opinion would provide only low assurance because fraud is a legal matter that must be proven in the courts. In addition, because the fraud assertion has not yet been proven in the courts—and because fraud is a matter to be proven under criminal law—the auditor might even be accused of defamation! There is the related issue that even if the auditor *does* have high assurance that a fraud has been perpetrated, high audit assurance does not necessarily equate to the "beyond a reasonable doubt" burden of proof that is required by the Criminal Code. On the other hand, under civil law, if, for example, the client's company is expecting to recover only damages or trying to obtain sufficient cause to fire the employee, then the burden of proof is considerably lower. In civil law the burden of proof is "on balance of probabilities" and an opinion, such as in Exhibit 17–5, may very well satisfy this requirement. Thus, the amount of assurance depends on the circumstances, and the wording should properly reflect the circumstances.

For example, since fraud is a legal term and legal conditions must be met before the term is assigned to anyone, perhaps a better term to use in an assurance report is "irregularities," which is a term defined by the PA profession. An auditor can then reach a conclusion about the likelihood of irregularities occurring (including but not limited to fraud) without being encumbered with legal definitions and the responsibilities inherent in using specific legal terms such as fraud. As long as there is ambiguity between the level of assurance provided by the assurance engagement, and legal assurance required by terms such as "on balance of probabilities" and "proof beyond a reasonable doubt," it is likely in the auditor's best interest to use terminology that does not have a precise legal meaning but instead reflects the standards of the PA profession. Otherwise the auditors will need to be very careful when the legal terms are used in the report, or risk being caught in defamation suits.

We hope this section has illustrated some of the complexities of expanding assurance engagements into new areas not familiar to most PAs.

R E V I E W CHECKPOINTS

17.28   Why is prosecution of fraud perpetrators generally a good idea?

17.29   What are the CICA materiality guidelines for reporting errors, irregularities and illegal acts?

17.30   Why must care be taken with evidence of fraudulent activity?

SUMMARY

Fraud awareness auditing starts with knowledge of the types of errors, irregularities, illegal acts and frauds that can be perpetrated. External, internal and governmental auditors all have standards for care, attention, planning, detection and reporting of some kinds of errors, irregularities and illegal acts. Fraud examiners, on the other hand, have little in the way of standard programs or materiality guidelines to limit their attention to fraud possibilities. They float on a sea of observations of exceptions and oddities that may be the tip of a fraud iceberg.

Fraud may be contemplated when people have motives, usually financial needs, for stealing money or property. Motive, when combined with opportunity and a lapse of integrity, generally makes the probability of fraud or theft high. Opportunities arise when an organization's management has a lax attitude about setting an example for good behaviour and about maintenance of a supportive control environment. The fear of getting caught by control procedures deters some fraudsters. Otherwise, attentive management of personnel can ease the pressures people feel and, thus, reduce the incidence of fraud.

Auditors need to know about the red flags, those telltale signs and indications that have accompanied many frauds. When studying a business operation, auditors need to "think like a crook" to uncover ways to steal that can help in the planning of procedures designed to determine whether fraud occurred. Often, imaginative extended procedures can be employed to unearth evidence of fraudulent activity. However, technical and personal care must always be exercised because accusations of fraud are always taken very seriously. For this reason, after preliminary findings indicate fraud possibilities, auditors should enlist the co-operation of management and assist fraud examination professionals in bringing an investigation to a conclusion.

For information on the Association of Certified Fraud Examiners (CFEs), visit their website at **www.acfe.com**.

MULTIPLE-CHOICE QUESTIONS FOR PRACTICE AND REVIEW

17.31 One of the typical characteristics of management fraud is:

a.   Falsification of documents in order to steal money from an employer.

b.   Victimization of investors through the use of materially misleading financial statements.

c.   Illegal acts committed by management to evade laws and regulations.

d.   Conversion of stolen inventory to cash deposited in a falsified bank account.

17.32 CICA auditing standards do not require auditors of financial statements to:

a.   Understand the nature of errors and irregularities.

b.   Assess the risk of occurrence of errors and irregularities.

c.   Design audits to provide reasonable assurance of detecting errors and irregularities.

d.   Report all finding of errors and irregularities to police authorities.

17.33 Which of the following types of auditors have the highest expectations in their audit standards regarding the detection of fraud?
a. External auditors of financial statements.
b. Government auditors of financial statements, programs, activities and functions.
c. Internal auditors employed by companies.
d. Management advisory consultants engaged to design a company's information system.

17.34 Which two of the following characterize the work of fraud examiners and are different from the typical attitude of external auditors?
a. Analysis of control weaknesses for opportunities to commit fraud.
b. Analysis of control strengths as a basis for planning other audit procedures.
c. Determination of a materiality amount that represents a significant misstatement of the current-year financial statements.
d. Thinking of a materiality amount in cumulative terms—that is, as becoming large over a number of years.

17.35 When auditing with "fraud awareness," auditors should especially notice and follow up employee activities under which of these conditions?
a. The company always estimates the inventory but never takes a complete physical count.
b. The petty cash box is always locked in the desk of the custodian.
c. Management has published a company code of ethics and sends frequent communication newsletters about it.
d. The board of directors reviews and approves all investment transactions.

17.36 The best way to enact a broad fraud-prevention program is to:
a. Install airtight control systems of checks and supervision.
b. Name an "ethics officer" who is responsible for receiving and acting upon fraud tips.
c. Place dedicated "hot line" telephones on walls around the workplace with direct communication to the company ethics officer.
d. Practise management "of the people and for the people" to help them share personal and professional problems.

17.37 Which of the following gives the least indication of fraudulent activity?
a. Numerous cash refunds have been made to different people at the same post office box address.
b. Internal auditor cannot locate several credit memos to support reductions of customers' balances.
c. Bank reconciliation has no outstanding cheques or deposits older than 15 days.
d. Three people were absent the day the auditors handed out the paycheques and have not picked them up four weeks later.

17.38 Which of the following combinations is a good means of hiding employee fraud but a poor means of carrying out management (financial reporting) fraud?
a. Overstating sales revenue and overstating customer accounts receivable balances.
b. Overstating sales revenue and overstating bad debt expense.
c. Understating interest expense and understating accrued interest payable.
d. Omit the disclosure information about related party sales to the president's relatives at below-market prices.

17.39 Which of these arrangements of duties could most likely lead to an embezzlement or theft?
a. Inventory warehouse manager has responsibility for making the physical inventory observation and reconciling discrepancies to the perpetual inventory records.
b. Cashier prepared the bank deposit, endorsed the cheques with a company stamp, and took the cash and cheques to the bank for deposit (no other bookkeeping duties).
c. Accounts receivable clerk received a list of payments received by the cashier so that he could make entries in the customers' accounts receivable subsidiary accounts.
d. Financial vice president received cheques made out to suppliers and the supporting invoices, signed the cheques, and put them in the mail to the payees.

17.40 If sales and income were overstated by recording a false credit sale at the end of the year, where could you find the false "dangling debit?" In the:
a. Inventory?
b. Cost of goods sold?
c. Bad debt expense?
d. Accounts receivable?

17.41 Which of these is an invalid social insurance number?
a. 462 003 335.
b. 473 09 7787.
c. 506 98 5529.
d. 700 051 135.

17.42 Public records from which of these sources could be used to find the owner of an office building?
a. Ministry of Industry and Trade export/import licence files.
b. Transport Canada records.
c. City and county tax assessor-collector files.
d. Securities commission filings.

17.43 Experience has shown that the largest number of accounting errors requiring adjustment are found in:
a. Systematic processing of large volumes of day-to-day ordinary transactions.
b. Payroll fraudsters' mistakes in using unissued social insurance numbers.
c. Petty cash embezzlements.
d. Nonroutine, nonsystematic journal entries.

17.44 The type of financial analysis that expresses balance sheet accounts as percentages of total assets is known as:

a. Horizontal analysis.

b. Vertical analysis.

c. Net worth analysis.

d. Expenditure analysis.

EXERCISES AND PROBLEMS
. . . .

17.45 Give Examples of Errors, Irregularities and Frauds.

LO.1 This is an exercise concerning financial reporting misstatements, not employee theft. Give an example of an error, irregularity or fraud that would misstate financial statements to affect the accounts as follows, taken one case at a time. (Note: "overstate" means the account has a higher value than would be appropriate under GAAP, and "understate" means it has a lower value.)

a. Overstate an asset, state another asset.

b. Overstate an asset, overstate shareholder equity.

c. Overstate an asset, overstate revenue.

d. Overstate an asset, understate an expense.

e. Overstate a liability, overstate an expense.

f. Understate an asset, overstate an expense.

g. Understate a liability, understate an expense.

17.46 Overall Analysis of Accounting Estimates. Oak In-

LO.1 dustries, a manufacturer of radio and cable TV equipment and an operator of subscription TV systems, had a multitude of problems. Subscription services in a market area, for which $12 million cost had been deferred, were being terminated, and the customers were not paying on time ($4 million receivables in doubt). The chances are 50–50 that the business will survive another two years.

An electronic part turned out to have defects that needed correction. Warranty expenses are estimated to range from $2 million to $6 million. The inventory of this part ($10 million) is obsolete, but $1 million can be recovered in salvage; or, the parts in inventory can be rebuilt at a cost of $2 million (selling price of the inventory on hand would then be $8 million, with 20 percent of selling price required to market and ship the products, and the normal profit expected is 5 percent of the selling price). If the inventory were scrapped, the company would manufacture a replacement inventory at a cost of $6 million, excluding marketing and shipping costs and normal profit.

The company has defaulted on completion of a military contract, and the government is claiming a $2 million refund. Company lawyers think the dispute might be settled for as little as $1 million.

The auditors had previously determined that an overstatement of income before taxes of $7 million would be material to the financial statements. These items were the only ones left for audit decisions about possible adjustment. Management has presented the analysis below for the determination of loss recognition:

Write-off deferred subscription costs	$ 3,000,000
Provide allowance for bad debts	4,000,000
Provide for expected warranty expense	2,000,000
Lower of cost or market inventory write-down	2,000,000
Loss on government contract refund	—
Total write-offs and losses	$11,000,000

Required:

Prepare your own analysis of the amount of adjustment to the financial statements. Assume that none of these estimates have been recorded yet, and give the adjusting entry you would recommend. Give any supplementary explanations you believe necessary to support your recommendation.

17.47 Select Effective Extended Procedures. Given below

LO.7 are some "suspicions," and you have been requested to select some effective extended procedures designed to confirm or deny the suspicion.

Required:

Write the suggested procedures for each case in definite terms so that another person can know what to do.

a. The custodian of the petty cash fund may be removing cash on Friday afternoon to pay for his weekend activities.

b. A manager has noticed that eight new vendors have been added to the purchasing department approved list since the assistant purchasing agent was promoted to chief agent three weeks ago. She suspects that all or some of them may be phony companies set up by the new chief purchasing agent.

c. The payroll supervisor may be stealing unclaimed paycheques of people who quit work and don't pick up the last cheque.

d. Although no customers have complained, cash collections on accounts receivable are down, and the counter clerks may have stolen customers' payments.

e. The cashier may have "borrowed" money, covering it by holding each day's deposit until cash from the next day(s) collection is enough to make up the shortage from an earlier day, then sending the deposit to the bank.

17.48 Horizontal and Vertical Analysis. Horizontal analysis

LO.6 refers to changes of financial statement numbers and ratios across two or more years. Vertical analysis refers to financial statement amounts expressed each year as proportions of a base, such as sales for the income statement accounts, and total assets for the balance sheet accounts. Exhibit 17.48–1 contains the Retail Company's prior year (audited) and current year (unaudited) financial statements, along with amounts and percentages of change from year to year (horizontal analysis) and common-size percentages (vertical analysis). Exhibit 17.48–2 contains selected financial ratios based on these financial statements. Analysis of these data may enable auditors to discern relationships that raise questions about misleading financial statements.

Required:
Study the data in Exhibits 17.48–1 and 17.48–2. Write a memo identifying and explaining potential problem areas where misstatements in the current year financial statements might exist. Additional information about Retail Company is as follows:
- The new bank loan, obtained on July 1 of the current year, requires maintenance of a 2:1 current ratio.
- Principal of $100,000 plus interest on the 10 percent long-term note obtained several years ago in the original amount of $800,000 is due each January 1.

- The company has never paid dividends on its common shares and has no plans for a dividend.

17.49 **Expenditure Analysis.** Expenditure analysis is used
LO.5 when fraud has been discovered or strongly suspected, and the information to calculate a suspect's income and expenditures can be obtained (e.g., asset and liability records, bank accounts). Expenditure analysis consists of establishing the suspect's known expenditures for all purposes for the relevant period, subtracting all known sources of funds (e.g., wages, gifts, inheritances, bank balances and the like), and calling the difference the expenditures financed by unknown sources of income.

FORENSIC ACCOUNTING
CONSULTING ENGAGEMENT 1
You have been hired by the law firm of Gleckel and Morris. The lawyers have been retained by Blade Manufacturing Company in a case involving a suspected kickback by a purchasing employee, E. J. Cunningham.

EXHIBIT 17.48–1 RETAIL COMPANY

	Prior Year Audited		Current Year		Change	
	Balance	Common Size	Balance	Common Size	Amount	Percent
Assets:						
Cash	$ 600,000	14.78%	$ 484,000	9.69%	(116,000)	–19.33%
Accounts receivable	500,000	12.32	400,000	8.01	(100,000)	–20.00
Allowance doubt accts.	(40,000)	–0.99	(30,000)	–0.60	10,000	–25.00
Inventory	1,500,000	36.95	1,940,000	38.85	440,000	29.33
Total current assets	$2,560,000	63.05	2,794,000	55.95	234,000	9.14
Capital assets	3,000,000	73.89	4,000,000	80.10	1,000,000	33.33
Accum. depreciation	(1,500,000)	–36.95	(1,800,000)	–36.04	(300,000)	20.00
Total assets	$4,060,000	100.00%	$4,994,000	100.00%	934,000	23.00%
Liabilities and equity:						
Accounts payable	$ 450,000	11.08%	$ 600,000	12.01%	150,000	33.33%
Bank loans, 11%	0	0.00	750,000	15.02	750,000	NA
Accrued interest	50,000	1.23	40,000	0.80	(10,000)	–20.00
Accruals and other	60,000	1.48	10,000	0.20	(50,000)	–83.33
Total current liab.	560,000	13.79	1,400,000	28.03	840,000	150.00
Long–term debt, 10%	500,000	12.32	400,000	8.01	(100,000)	–20.00
Total liabilities	1,060,000	26.11	1,800,000	36.04	740,000	69.81
Share capital	2,000,000	49.26	2,000,000	40.05	0	0
Retained earnings	1,000,000	24.63	1,194,000	23.91	194,000	19.40
Total liabilities and equity	$4,060,000	100.00%	$4,994,000	100.00%	934,000	23.00%
Statement of operations:						
Sales (net)	$9,000,000	100.00%	$8,100,000	100.00%	(900,000)	–10.00%
Cost of goods sold	6,296,000	69.96	5,265,000	65.00	(1,031,000)	–16.38
Gross margin	2,704,000	30.04	2,835,000	35.00	131,000	4.84
General expense	2,044,000	22.71	2,005,000	24.75	(39,000)	–1.91
Amortization	300,000	3.33	300,000	3.70	0	0
Operating income	360,000	4.00	530,000	6.54	170,000	47.22
Interest expense	50,000	0.56	40,000	0.49	(10,000)	–20.00
Income taxes (40%)	124,000	1.38	196,000	2.42	72,000	58.06
Net income	$ 186,000	2.07%	$ 294,000	3.63%	108,000	58.06%

NA means not applicable.

EXHIBIT   17.48-2   RETAIL COMPANY

	Prior Year	Current Year	Percent Change
Balance sheet ratios:			
Current ratio	4.57	2.0	−56.34%
Days' sales in receivables	18.40	16.44	−10.63
Doubtful accounts ratio	0.08	0.075	−6.25
Days' sales in inventory	85.77	132.65	54.66
Debt/equity ratio	0.35	0.56	40.89
Operations ratios:			
Receivables turnover	19.57	21.89	11.89
Inventory turnover	4.20	2.71	−35.34
Cost of goods sold/sales	69.96%	65.00%	−7.08
Gross margin %	30.04%	35.00%	16.49
Return on equity	6.61%	9.80%	48.26

Cunningham is suspected of taking kickbacks from Mason Varner, a salesman for Tanco Metals. He has denied the charges, but Lanier Gleckel, the lawyer in charge of the case, is convinced the kickbacks have occurred.

Gleckel filed a civil action and subpoenaed Cunningham's books and records, including his last year's bank statements. The beginning bank balance January 1 was $3,463, and the ending bank balance December 31 was $2,050. Over the intervening 12 months, Cunningham's gross salary was $3,600 per month, with a net of $2,950. His wife doesn't work at a paying job. His house payments were $1,377 per month. In addition, he paid $2,361 per month on a new Mercedes 500 SEL and paid a total of $9,444 last year toward a new Nissan Maxima (including $5,000 down payment). He also purchased new state-of-the-art audio and video equipment for $18,763, with no down payment, and total payments on the equipment last year of $5,532. A reasonable estimate of his household expenses during the period is $900 per month ($400 for food, $200 for utilities and $300 for other items).

Required:
Using expenditure analysis, calculate the amount of income, if any, from "unknown sources."

17.50 Net Worth Analysis. Net worth analysis is used when
L0.5 fraud has been discovered or strongly suspected, and the information to calculate a suspect's net worth can be obtained (e.g., asset and liability records, bank accounts). The procedure is to calculate the person's change in net worth (excluding changes in market values of assets), and to identify the known sources of funds to finance the changes. Any difference between the change in net worth and the known sources of funds is called "funds from unknown sources," which may be ill-gotten gains.

FORENSIC ACCOUNTING
CONSULTING ENGAGEMENT 2
C. Nero has worked for Bonne Consulting Group (BCG) as the executive secretary for administration for nearly 10 years. His dedication has earned him a reputation as an outstanding employee and has resulted in increasing responsibilities. C. Nero is a suspect in fraud.

This is the hindsight story. During Nero's first five years of employment, BCG subcontracted all of its feasibility and marketing studies through Jackson & Company. This relationship was terminated because Jackson & Company merged with a larger, more expensive consulting group. At the time of termination, Nero and his supervisor were forced to select a new firm to conduct BCG's market research. However, Nero never informed the accounting department that the Jackson & Company account had been closed.

Since his supervisor allowed Nero to sign the payment voucher for services rendered, Nero was able to continue to process cheques made payable to Jackson's account. Nero was trusted to be the only signature authorizing payments less than $10,000. The accounting department continued to write the cheques and Nero would take responsibility for delivering them. Nero opened a bank account in a nearby city under the name of Jackson & Company, where he would make the deposit.

Required:
C. Nero's financial records (see Exhibit 17.50-1) have been obtained by subpoena. You have been hired to estimate the amount of loss by estimating Nero's "funds from unknown sources" that financed his comfortable lifestyle. Below is a summary of the data obtained from Nero's records.

EXHIBIT   17.50-1   NERO'S RECORDS

	Year One	Year Two	Year Three
Assets:			
Residence	$100,000	$100,000	$100,000
Shares and bonds	30,000	30,000	42,000
Automobiles	20,000	20,000	40,000
Certificate of deposit	50,000	50,000	50,000
Cash	6,000	12,000	14,000
Liabilities:			
Mortgage balance	90,000	50,000	—
Auto loan	10,000	—	—
Income:			
Salary		34,000	36,000
Other		6,000	6,000
Expenses:			
Scheduled mortgage payments		6,000	6,000
Auto loan payments		4,800	—
Other living expenses		20,000	22,000
Hint:			
Set up a working paper like this:			
	End Year 1	End Year 2	End Year 3

Assets (list)
Liabilities (list)
Net worth (difference)
Change in net worth
Add total expenses
= Change plus expenses
Subtract known income
= Funds from unknown sources

DISCUSSION CASE

. . . .

17.51 Famous Fraud Case Analysis: Enron. Given the
successful prosecution of CEOs in Worldcom, Tyco, and
Adelphia through 2006, do a Web search on one of these
cases and answer the following:

a. How was the fraud detected?
b. How was the fraud perpetrated? Was it a financial
statement fraud?

c. What was the weakness in internal control or corporate governance that allowed the fraud to occur?
d. Should a financial statement audit have detected this
fraud? Discuss.
e. Would an internal control audit have detected this
fraud? Discuss.

CHAPTER

18

Internal Auditing and Public Sector Auditing

This chapter introduces internal and public sector auditing in the context of comprehensive auditing. These forms of auditing differ substantially from financial statement auditing practised by independent PAs in public accounting firms. However, you will find that all forms of auditing share many similarities. The explanations and examples in this chapter should help you understand the working environment, objectives and procedures that characterize internal auditing and public sector auditing.

LEARNING OBJECTIVES

After completing this chapter, you will be able to:

1 Compare and contrast internal audits and public sector audits with independent financial statement audits.

2 Define internal auditing and public sector auditing.

3 Outline the independence problems of internal, external and public sector auditors.

4 Specify the expanded scope of auditing in both internal and public sector audit practice.

5* Summarize the internal control audit standards. (Appendix 18B)

6* Itemize the steps involved in preliminary survey, evaluation of administrative control, evidence-gathering field work and report preparation for internal and public sector audits. (Appendix 18B)

7* Explain how economy and efficiency are used to measure the results of internal and public sector audits. (Appendix 18B)

8* Explain the requirements for internal and public sector audit reports. (Appendix 18A)

9* Describe the new role of internal auditors and audit committees in the Canadian SOX environment. (Appendix 18A)

10* Summarize public sector audit standards. (Appendix 18C)

Note: Those learning objectives marked with an asterisk (*) and their corresponding topics are considered advanced material. Appendices 18A, 18B and 18C are located on the text Online Learning Centre.

INTERNAL, PUBLIC SECTOR AND EXTERNAL AUDITS

LEARNING OBJECTIVE

1 Compare and contrast internal audits and public sector audits with independent financial statement audits.

Internal auditing and public sector auditing are extensive subjects. This chapter explains some of the main features. Even though points of similarity and difference in comparison to external auditing would be useful, space does not permit presentation of a detailed comparison. Many such similarities and differences will be apparent, however, when you study this chapter after having studied Chapters 1 and 2.

Perhaps you have already noticed the reference to external auditing. Ordinarily, you can refer to public sector, internal, and independent auditors—the latter referring to PAs in public practice. Yet labels are potentially confusing. Many public sector and internal auditors are PAs, and take pride in their independence in mental attitude. For purposes of this chapter, therefore, external auditors will refer to PAs in public accounting firms, thereby distinguishing public practice from public sector and internal practice.

Internal Auditing

Internal auditing is practised by auditors employed by an organization, such as a bank, hospital, city government or industrial company. The **Institute of Internal Auditors (IIA)** is the international organization that governs the standards, continuing education and general rules of conduct for internal auditors as a profession. The IIA also sponsors research and development of practices and procedures designed to enhance the work of internal auditors wherever they are employed. For example, the IIA actively provides courses in numerous internal audit and investigation subjects and promotes its massive, multivolume *Systems Auditability and Control Guide* for dealing with computerized information systems.

The IIA also controls the **Certified Internal Auditor (CIA)** program. This certification is a mark of professional achievement that has gained widespread acceptance throughout the world. See **www.theiia.org** for information on becoming a CIA.

Public Sector Auditing

Public sector auditors are auditors employed by federal, provincial and municipal levels of government.

The Office of the Auditor General (OAG) is headed by the Auditor General of Canada. In one sense OAG auditors are the highest level of internal auditors for the federal government as a whole. Provincial (and other federal agencies and other local governmental units) use the *CICA Public Sector Standards* to guide their audits. These standards are published in separate *CICA Handbook* sections. We will use the acronym **PS** for public sector auditing standards developed by the CICA. Because of the wide adoption of the PSs, you will be introduced to them in this chapter.

Novatel, or the Chamber of Horrors

Provincial auditors' reports have always cited cases of waste, flagrant mismanagement and not-so-flagrant cover-ups as springboards for recommendations on better accounting and accountability systems. Typically, such disclosures give rise to a flurry of damning articles in the provincial press—not to speak of indignant reactions from the opposition. As horror tales go, however, few have been more politically charged, brought more coverage in the national media, or served as a greater catalyst for improvements to a government's accounting systems than that of Novatel Communications Ltd., as documented in a special 1992 report by Alberta auditor general Donald Salmon.

Novatel was a joint venture created in 1983 between government-owned Alberta Government Telephones (AGT) and energy giant Nova Corp. The company's cellular systems and subscriber equipment business were to serve as a mainstay for the province's high-technology industry—a safeguard for the day when the oil revenues ran dry. By the end of 1988, however, it had accumulated losses of $148.7 million. In 1990, it issued a forecast in which it predicted a second-half profit of $16.9 million—which it had to revise eight days later into a $4.1-million shortfall. Shortly thereafter plans to find a strategic partner were scuttled when the German company Robert Bosch GmbH backed off from an agreement to buy 50 percent of Novatel. The government ended up with the company on its own hands, and the drain continued. In May 1992, it finally sold off part of the business to Northern Telecom Ltd. and another part to Telexel Holding Ltd., admitting to a $566-million loss on the deal.

By this time, the need to determine exactly what went wrong over Novatel's nine-year history was painfully apparent to all. Conscious of the expense that a full public inquiry would entail, Alberta's Executive Council chose instead to ask Don Salmon to conduct a review. Although this decision was criticized by the opposition as a deliberate attempt on the government's part to avoid a full probe, Salmon promised that the report would speak for itself. And that it did. Issued in September 1992, two weeks after Premier Donald Getty announced his resignation, the 201-page document described in exacting detail the events that ultimately led to what Salmon calculated as a $614-million tab for Alberta's taxpayers. It showed how mismanagement, cronyism and lack of strategic direction ultimately turned the Conservative government's much-touted ticket to the future into an albatross of loss, and how this could have been prevented. More important, it offered broad recommendations designed to strengthen accountability systems in the province.

The recommendations were as follows:

1. The province should consider using the expertise of the public service commissioner to short-list suitable candidates for appointments to the boards of all provincial agencies and Crown corporations. The primary criterion should be "proven relevant expertise."

2. All provincial agencies and Crown-controlled organizations, including subsidiaries, should be required to prepare annual budgets as a basis for comparison with actual results.

3. The public accounts should include the financial statements of all provincial agencies and Crown-controlled organizations and their subsidiaries.

4. The public accounts committee should consider the reasons why actual results are significantly worse than budgeted results.

5. The definition of a Crown-controlled organization should be widened to include a 50 percent interest in, or equal control of, an organization.

Although Getty officially stepped down shortly after the report's release, Salmon says he nevertheless indicated that he "was pleased and accepted the recommendations."

But the story did not quite end there: In January 1993, after Ralph Klein had taken over as premier, the AG had a further opportunity to admonish the government when he released his 1991–92 report. That report was rife with additional horror stories, including the fact that the government had lost $80.8 million on Gainers Inc. since it took the meatpacking plant over from Peter Pocklington in 1989. The stories were so numerous, in fact, that they prompted *Calgary Herald* columnist Don Braid to quip: "Salmon could truly destroy the government if he ever decided to get annoyed about the dismal facts in his reports . . . [He] probably figures that the information in his reports is damning enough. If so, he's right."

Indeed, further developments tended to confirm Braid's assessment. In that same annual report, Salmon made eight main recommendations—five of which were the same as those put forward in the Novatel report. Klein, who was planning an election later in the year, hastened to accept virtually all of them. Salmon recalls: "So here for the first time we have a government that accepts all of our recommendations."

In Salmon's view, this link between the Novatel report and the ensuing acceptance of his recommendations is not a chance occurrence. He concludes in these terms: "In Alberta we were fortunate—we were given that special assignment on Novatel, which was much broader than our normal work. And because of the large loss in one organization we were able to then give some strong and broad recommendations. I think this has helped the government focus on financial accountability—and that, of course, is what we're interested in."

Source: M. Craig-Bourdin, "On Guard for Thee," *CA Magazine,* January/February 1994, pp. 30–31. Reproduced by permission from *CA Magazine*, published by the Canadian Institute of Chartered Accountants, Toronto, Canada.

The preceding box illustrates the unique influence that public sector auditors have in Canada.

Many provinces also have provincial auditors similar to the OAG. They answer to provincial legislatures and perform the same types of work described herein as OAG auditing. In another sense OAG and similar provincial agencies are really external auditors with respect to government agencies they audit because they are organizationally independent.

Many government agencies have their own internal auditors and auditor general. Well-managed local governments also have internal audit departments. For example, many federal agencies (Health Canada, the Canada Revenue Agency, Natural Resources Canada), provincial agencies (education, welfare, health), and local governments (cities, regions, townships) have internal audit staffs. In the private sector, certain huge industrial companies have revenues and assets as large as some governments, and the corporate internal auditors are in the same position relative to such a company as a whole as the auditor general is to the federal government. Both in matters of scale and the positions they occupy, governmental and internal auditors have much in common. The discussion in this chapter contrasts and compares their activities.

Interaction with External Auditors

External auditors often find themselves working with internal auditors on an independent audit of a company's financial statements. They also often take engagements to perform audits in accordance with the CICA standards.

Considering the Internal Audit Function in an Independent Audit of Financial Statements

External auditors consider the internal audit function in two contexts: (1) internal audit is part of a company's control environment and external auditors must understand how it operates in order to gain an understanding of the company's control structure (second GAAS examination standard) and (2) internal auditors may help the external auditors gather evidence about internal control and about balances in accounts (third GAAS examination standard). External auditors can make their audits more efficient by utilizing the work of a company's internal auditors and, thereby, avoiding duplication of effort. The increased stress on strong internal controls to prevent fraudulent financial reporting is increasing the prominence of internal auditors in corporate governance under SOX and Canadian equivalents.[1]

External auditors must obtain an understanding of a company's internal audit department and its program of work. This task is part of the understanding of the entire control structure. If a preliminary review of the internal audit function shows that the internal auditors have developed, monitored and made recommendations about internal controls, the external auditors will probably decide that it is efficient to use internal audit information to reduce their own work on the audit. When this decision is made, the external auditors are obligated to investigate the competence and objectivity of the internal auditors. These investigations become a part of the external auditors' work program.

Internal auditors' competence is investigated by obtaining evidence about their educational and experience qualifications, their certification (CIA) and continuing education status, the department's policies and procedures for work quality and for making personnel assignments, the supervision and review activities, and the quality of reports and working paper documentation. This evidence enables the external auditors to make an evaluation of internal auditors' performance.

Internal auditors' objectivity is investigated by learning about their organizational status and lines of communication in the company. The theory is that objectivity is enhanced when internal auditors are responsible to high levels of management and can report directly to the audit committee of the board of directors. Objectivity is questioned when internal auditors report to divisional management, line managers or other persons with a stake in the outcome of their findings. Objectivity is especially questioned when managers have some power over the pay or job tenure of the internal auditors. Likewise, objectivity is questioned when individual internal auditors have relatives in audit-sensitive areas or are scheduled to be promoted to positions in the activities under internal audit review.

Favourable conclusions about competence and objectivity enable external auditors to accept internal auditors' documentation and work on review, assessment and monitoring of a company's internal control procedures. This information, combined with other evidence obtained through the external auditors' own work, leads to an assessment of control risk that is used in the remainder of the external audit planning.

Competent, objective internal auditors may also have performed some external audit-like procedures to obtain evidence about the dollar balances in accounts (substantive procedures). For example, they often confirm accounts receivable and make observations during interim counts of physical inventory. By relying in part on this work, external auditors may be able to relax the nature, timing or extent of their own procedures in the same areas. Be careful to note, however, that this utilization of internal auditors' work may not be a complete substitute for the external auditors' own procedures and evidence related to accounting judgements and material financial statement balances.

The external auditors cannot share responsibility for audit decisions with the internal auditors and must supervise, review, evaluate and test the work performed by the internal auditors. This requirement applies both to the work of obtaining an understanding of the internal control structure and to the work of using internal auditors' evidence about financial statement balances.

Compliance Auditing Applicable to Governmental Entities and Other Recipients of Governmental Financial Assistance

When independent accountants in public practice take engagements governed by the OAG audit standards, they are supposed to conduct the work in accordance with PSs. In fact, failure to follow PSs in such engagements is an "act discreditable to the profession." Some parliamentary regulatory laws require auditors to test and report on an entity's compliance with

---

1 See "Control Panel," *CA Magazine*, January/February 2006, p. 37.

laws and regulations. This work is known as **compliance auditing**, which has a special relevance in government-standard audit engagements.

External auditors have responsibilities under the CICA's generally accepted auditing standards for detecting material errors, irregularities and certain illegal acts in connection with the independent audits of commercial and not-for-profit financial statements. These are detailed in Chapter 17 in this text. However, governmental entities and government fund recipients contend with many more laws and regulations, especially ones concerned with eligibility, procedure and payment of amounts under various entitlements and programs. Auditors must study the laws and regulations, ensuring management provides a list of all those applicable in the circumstances. Auditors can then determine whether to perform specific procedures to obtain evidence about compliance with the laws and regulations.

The public sector sometimes requires reports on compliance. The auditors can give positive assurance on areas tested with compliance procedures and negative assurance on those areas not tested. An example of part of a report on compliance test results is shown in the following box.

UNIVERSITY OF XYZ, PROVINCE OF XYZ

University Student Loan Program:

Finding: Of the 50 student records tested for a total dollar amount of $94,181, fifteen loan application forms were completed incorrectly ... These applications must be completed correctly to ensure that the students will not be overawarded. These errors resulted in 1 student being overawarded by a total amount of $1,387; 2 students being underawarded by a total of $631; and with no effect on the awarded amount for the remaining 12 students.

Recommendations: Management should ensure that the costs and estimates are calculated correctly. The loan applications should be reviewed.

University's response: The overaward resulted because one student's Student Aid Report was received late. The award was based on preliminary information from the Comprehensive Financial Aid Report. Underawards were the result of clerical errors. Management will monitor the completion of the loan applications more closely.

Certain public sector agencies also require reports on internal control. (Some aspects of such reports for nongovernmental entities were discussed in Chapter 16.) The reports on internal controls must describe the entity's control structure, report the scope of the auditors' work, and describe any reportable conditions and material control weaknesses. The requirements for such reports can be very detailed and go beyond the scope of this text.

REVIEW
CHECKPOINTS

18.1   What special professional certification is available for internal auditors and OAG auditors?

18.2   What must external auditors do to use the work of internal auditors in the audit of a company's financial statements?

18.3   Why do you think special attention is paid to compliance auditing for governmental-type audits when independent PAs may perform compliance procedures in all types of audits anyway?

DEFINITIONS AND OBJECTIVES

· · · · · · · · · · · · ·

LEARNING OBJECTIVE

2 Define internal auditing
and public sector audit-
ing.

The Institute of Internal Auditors (IIA) defined internal auditing and stated its objective as
follows:

> Internal auditing is an independent, objective assurance and consulting activity designed to
> add value and improve an organization's operations. It helps an organization accomplish its
> objectives by bringing a systematic, disciplined approach to evaluating and improving the
> effectiveness of risk management, control and governance processes.

Operational Auditing

Internal auditors perform audits of financial reports for internal use, much as external auditors audit financial statements distributed to outside users. Thus, much internal auditing
work is similar to the auditing described elsewhere in this text. However, some internal
auditing activity is known as **operational auditing**. Operational auditing (also known as
performance auditing and **management auditing**) refers to auditors' study of business
operations for the purpose of making recommendations about economic and efficient use of
resources, effective achievement of business objectives and compliance with company policies. The goal of operational auditing is to help managers discharge their management
responsibilities and improve profitability. Operational auditing, thus, is included in the definition of internal auditing given above. In a similar context, an operational or effectiveness
audit performed by independent PA firms is a distinct type of assurance service with the goal
of helping the client evaluate the use of its capabilities and resources to achieve its objectives. So, internal auditors consider operational auditing an integral part of internal auditing, and external auditors define it as a type of assurance service offered by public
accounting firms.

Independence

Internal auditors hold independence, and the objectivity thus obtained, as a goal. Although
internal auditors cannot be disassociated from their employers in the eyes of the public, they
seek operational and reporting independence. Operationally, internal auditors should be
independent when obtaining evidence in the sense of being free from direction or constraint
by the managers of the business unit under audit (e.g., program, division, subsidiary).
Independence and objectivity are enhanced when internal auditors have the authority and
responsibility to report to a high executive level and to the audit committee of the board of
directors. The goal here is a measure of practical independence from the control or direct
influence of operating managers whose functions, operations and results they may be assigned
to audit. Practical independence enables internal auditors to be objective in reporting findings
without having to fear for their jobs.

Public sector auditors, like external and internal auditors, hold independence as a goal.
PS 5000.04 and IFAC Public Sector Guidelines recommend that public sector auditors
should adhere to established rules of professional conduct. This relates to maintaining
integrity and objectivity as well as to the independence-damaging appearance of financial
and managerial involvement. As a public sector auditor, you must be aware that such personal factors as preconceived ideas about programs, political or social convictions and loyalty to a level of government may impair the integrity and objectivity that is the foundation
of real independence. Like internal auditors, public sector auditors must be alert to external
sources of independence impairment, such as interference by higher-level officials and
threats to job security.

Organizational separation from such influences is essential for independence so that auditors can report directly to top management without fear of job or compensation retribution. Auditors of governmental units are presumed independent when they are (1) free from sources of personal impairment, (2) free from sources of external impairment, (3) organizationally independent, (4) independent under provincial Rules of Professional Conduct, (5) elected or appointed and reporting to a legislative body of government, or (6) auditing in a level or branch of government other than the one to which they are normally assigned.

On any particular assignment, public sector auditors may perform services for the benefit of several interested parties—the management of the auditee, officials of the agency requiring the audit, officials of one or more agencies that fund the auditee's programs, members and committees of local governments, a provincial legislature, and/or the national Parliament and the public. All such parties should receive the audit report unless laws or regulations restrict public distribution (e.g., for reasons of national security). In fact, the annual reports of the OAG and provincial auditors to their respective legislatures are widely reported media events—which suggests that public sector auditors do not face the expectations gap of external auditors. In contrast, standard audit reports on financial statements given by independent external auditors are addressed to the client and distributed only by the client to whomever the client wishes (except in the case of securities commission-registered companies, where the law usually requires the reports to be filed for public inspection).

Scope of Service

The stated objective of internal auditing is phrased in terms of service to "the organization," not just to management or some narrow internal interest group. Internal auditors, exercising their objectivity, function for the benefit of the whole organization—whether it is represented by the board of directors, the chief executive officer, the chief financial officer or other executives. The services provided by internal auditors include (1) audits of financial reports and accounting control systems; (2) reviews of control systems that ensure compliance with company policies, plans and procedures and with laws and regulations; (3) appraisals of the economy and efficiency of operations; and (4) reviews of effectiveness in achieving program results in comparison to established objectives and goals. Internal auditors often make recommendations that result in additional profits or cost savings for their companies. In this capacity they function like management consultants.

The Office of the Auditor General of Canada shares with internal auditors these same elements of expanded-scope services. The OAG, however, emphasizes the accountability of public officials for the efficient, economical and effective use of public funds and other resources. The OAG defines and describes expanded scope governmental auditing in terms of the types of government audits that can be performed, which are as follows:

1. Financial Statement Audits (PS 5200)
   a. Financial statement audits determine (1) whether the financial statements of an audited entity present fairly the financial position, results of operations and cash flows or changes in financial position in conformity with generally accepted accounting principles and (2) whether the entity has complied with laws and regulations for transactions and events that may have a material effect on the financial statements.

2. Compliance Audits (PS 5300).
   Compliance audits are those in which audit mandates are required to do one or more of the following:
   a. Express an opinion on whether an entity complied with specified authorities or whether its transactions were carried out in compliance with specified authorities.

INTERNAL AUDITORS PRODUCE INTEREST INCOME

During an audit of the cash management operations at branch offices, internal auditors found that bank deposits were not made until several days after cash and cheques were received. Company policy was to complete the bookkeeping before making the deposit.

The auditors showed branch managers a cost-efficient way to capture the needed bookkeeping information that would permit release of the cash and cheques. Management agreed to implement the timely deposit of cheques and transfer to headquarters through an electronic funds transfer system from local banks to the headquarters bank, performing the bookkeeping afterward.

The change resulted in additional interest income in the first year in the amount of $150,000.

---

    b. Express an opinion on whether the transactions that have come to their notice in the cause of discharging their other audit responsibilities were carried out in compliance with specified authorities.

    c. Report instances of noncompliance with authorities observed in the course of discharging their audit responsibilities.

3. Value-for-Money (Performance) Audits (PS 5400)

    a. Economy and efficiency audits include determining (1) whether the entity is acquiring, protecting and using its resources (such as personnel, property and space) economically and efficiently; (2) the causes of inefficiencies or uneconomical practices; and (3) whether the entity has complied with laws and regulations concerning matters of economy and efficiency.

    b. Effectiveness or program audits include determining (1) the extent to which the desired results or benefits established by the legislature or other authorizing body are being achieved; (2) the effectiveness of organizations, programs, activities or functions; and (3) whether the agency has complied with laws and regulations applicable to the program.

The audit of a governmental organization, program, activity or function may involve one or more of these types of audits. The term "comprehensive audit" is used to describe engagements that include all three types of the audits described above. The OAG, however, and other public sector auditors do not require comprehensive audits. Most public sector engagements involve just one or two of the above three types of audits. The scope of the work is supposed to be determined according to the needs of the users of the audit results. However, the OAG recommends observance of PS standards in audits of governmental units by external auditors as well as by governmental auditors at federal, provincial and local levels.

· ·

R E V I E W
C H E C K P O I N T S

18.4   What is operational auditing, and why can it be called a type of consulting service?

18.5   How can internal auditors achieve practical independence?

18.6   What general auditing services do internal auditors provide?

18.7   What general auditing services do governmental auditors provide?

18.8   What factors should governmental auditors consider in determining whether they are independent?

· ·

INTERNAL AUDITING STANDARDS

· · · · · · · · · · · ·

3 Outline the independence problems of internal, external and public sector auditors.

The Standards for the Professional Practice of Internal Auditing are issued by the Institute of Internal Auditors (IIA).

The standards are classified into three major categories:

1. Attribute Standards (the 1000 series)
2. Performance Standards (the 2000 series)
3. Implementation Standards (the higher level series)

Attributes relate to the characteristics of individuals and internal auditing departments. Performance Standards describe internal audit activities and criteria for their quality. The Attribute and Performance Standards are more general in that they apply to all internal audit activities. The Implementation Standards apply to specific types of engagements such as performance or compliance audits.

The major categories of Attribute Standards are the following:

1. Purpose, Authority and Responsibility (1000)
2. Independence and Objectivity (1100)
3. Proficiency and Due Professional Care (1200)
4. Quality Assurance and Improvement (1300)

The major categories of Performance Standards are as follows:

1. Managing the Internal Audit Activity (2000)
2. Nature of Work: Evaluate and contribute to improving (2100)
    (i)   risk management
    (ii) control systems
    (iii) governance systems
3. Engagement Planning (2200)
4. Performing the Engagement (2300)
5. Communicating the Results (2400)

These categories are further subdivided into 35 different guiding standards. Members of the IIA are required to comply with these standards.

Students usually learn the CICA generally accepted auditing standards first, then study other assurance standards. The IIA standards include the spirit of all the general and field work standards of the CICA GAAS. On the assumption that GAAS are familiar, we will look only at the IIA standards that are significantly different.

Three of the implementation standards call for (1) review of compliance with policies, plans, procedures, laws and regulations; (2) review of economy, efficiency in the use of resources; and (3) review of the results of programs for effectiveness. These standards all go considerably beyond the requirements of GAAS and closely resemble those of two of three types of public sector audits.

The IIA performance standards include a requirement for monitoring progress to ascertain that appropriate action is taken on reported audit findings or to ascertain that management or the board of directors has taken the risk of not taking action on reported findings. GAAS have no comparable follow-up requirement because external audit reports do not make recommendations related to financial statements.

Six of the IIA standards deal with the quality assurance and improvement program of the internal audit department. Accountants in public practice have similar guidance, but this guidance is not in GAAS. Rather, it is in the form of quality control standards or studies as discussed in Chapter 2. However, observance of quality control guidance is considered essential for proper auditing practice in accordance with GAAS. The quality control standards are "incorporated by reference" in GAAS and enforced through practice inspections of provincial institutes, quality control reviews of accounting firms, and, increasingly in the post-Enron era, by accountability boards and regulators.

The IIA standards view internal auditing as a type of assurance engagement. In particular, they recognize the important distinction that internal audits are a form of three-party accountability whereas consulting and other internal audit services are viewed as two-party accountability. For internal auditors both types of accountabilities take place within the same organization, but they are viewed as applying to different people with different responsibilities. An individual's responsibilities determine what they are accountable for. Thus internal auditors use the same framework as in Exhibit 2-4 except that the practitioner is now the internal auditor and the other parties are all part of the same organization. Internal auditors thus provide internal assurance that, for example, the internal controls are reliable. Because internal auditors are auditing year round they are increasingly viewed as a key attribute of good corporate controls and good governance. For this reason their role has been greatly enhanced in the post-Enron, SOX environment. This is further discussed in Appendix 5A, and in Appendix 18A on the text Online Learning Centre, which reviews the key role internal auditors and audit committees play in the post-Enron environment. See **www.theüa.org** and **www.aicpa.org**.

Through the use of a consistent assurance concept, the IIA is bringing about greater convergence between core auditing activities as they relate to internal, external and public sector auditing. The importance of this distinction should be evident to you when you look at examples of audit reports and consulting engagement reports by auditors later in this chapter. The subject matter is frequently the same, but note that the type of accountability is different. This can be determined in the report by whether or not it is addressed to a third party—if it is, then we have an audit report; if not, then it is a consulting report as per the IIA standards. Fundamentally, three-party accountability is what distinguishes assurance engagements, and their practitioners, from all other professional engagements and their associated professional groups. It is within three-party accountability that internal auditing, external auditing and public sector auditing are really differentiated. For example, internal auditors do not provide assurance on financial statements whereas external and public sector auditors do.

The four GAAS reporting standards are comprehensive insofar as audit reports on financial statements are concerned, but the related IIA standard merely says, "Internal auditors should communicate the engagement results promptly." Since the details under this standard are similar to the public sector standards, further explanation is given in the discussion of the public sector standards in Appendix 18C on the text Online Learning Centre.

Our focus here is on the auditing standards rather than the consulting or other engagements. Here we spotlight the main differentiating aspects of internal and public sector auditing from traditional auditing. The main difference is the concept of VFM audits introduced in Chapter 1, and especially the economy, efficiency and effectiveness components of VFM audits.

ECONOMY, EFFICIENCY AND EFFECTIVENESS AUDITS

Economy and efficiency measures are fairly straightforward. Auditors can use these tools and techniques to evaluate them: financial and organizational analysis; computer-assisted data analysis and EDP testing; value analysis; productivity measurement and quantitative analysis; methods analysis using work study techniques; work measurement; and productivity–opportunity matrices. **Economy** is related to the price variance, while efficiency is related to the efficiency variance of standard variance analysis in managerial accounting for control. The products here, however, are usually services or activities instead of tangible goods, and thus it may not be possible to measure them as discrete units.

Effectiveness is more difficult to define and evaluate, but it may be helpful to view it as a type of "volume" or "capacity" variance where "volume(s)" are measured relative to some objective or objectives of the organization. The Canadian Comprehensive Auditing Foundation (CCAF-FCVI Inc.) prepared a report called *Effectiveness Reporting and Auditing in the Public Sector* to deal with the question of effectiveness. The report enumerated 12 different attributes of effectiveness that the auditor must examine in performing a value-for-money audit. The attributes are as follows:

1. *Management direction.* How well integrated are the organization's objectives and component programs with management decision making?

2. *Relevance.* Does the program still serve the originally intended purpose?

3. *Appropriateness.* Is the program's structure appropriate considering its purpose?

4. *Achievement of results.* Has the program realized its goals and objectives?

5. *Acceptance.* How well have constituents or customers received the service or output of the organization?

6. *Secondary impacts.* Has the organization caused any other intended or not-intended results?

7. *Costs and productivity.* How efficient has the organization been?

8. *Responsiveness.* Has the organization adapted well to changes in its environment?

9. *Financial results.* Has the organization accounted properly for revenues and expenses, and valued assets and liabilities properly?

10. *Working environment.* Is the work environment appropriate, given the organization's purpose, and does it promote initiative and achievement?

11. *Protection of assets.* Does the organization safeguard valuable assets?

12. *Monitoring and reporting.* Does the organization know where it stands with regard to key performance indicators?

Effectiveness can mean much more than the extent to which program objectives are being met and encompasses all the above characteristics.

When defining effectiveness, the client (Parliament or other legislative bodies) may have completely different perceptions than the stakeholder (the program recipient).

Audit mandates specify what is required of auditors and provide auditors with the authority to carry out their work and report. The amount of discretion an auditor has in establishing the objectives and scope of the VFM audit varies. Some VFM audit mandates embodied in legislation provide only general direction about objectives and scope. In such cases the auditor decides on audit objectives and scope for a particular VFM audit. Other legislated mandates, such as that for special examinations of federal Crown corporations, may be more specific in defining objectives and scope. In contractual mandates, audit objectives and scope are usually specified by the client. In such cases the auditor would assess the appropriateness of the audit objectives and scope before accepting the engagement.

VFM audit mandates also have different reporting requirements. Many mandates require direct reporting about the entity. For example, auditors may report deficiencies, or provide an opinion on whether there is reasonable assurance, based on specified criteria, that there are no significant deficiencies in the systems and practices examined. Auditors may be asked to attest to management assertions. When the mandate does not specify the reporting requirements, auditors would choose, often in consultation with their clients, how the results of the audit will be reported. The reporting requirements affect the nature and extent of work that must be performed in the audit.

Government audits require more work on compliance and reporting on internal control than external auditors normally do in an audit of financial statements of a private business. The reason is the public's concern for laws, regulations and control of expenditures. One-third of the Canadian economy and several $100 billion of federal funds used is represented by the public sector, so the stakes are high. We conclude with a summary of the differences between VFM audits (which have similar counterparts in internal audit via the performance or operational audit concepts) and traditional auditing.

· ·

R E V I E W
CHECKPOINTS

18.9   Identify the twelve attributes of effectiveness.

18.10 What is a comprehensive audit?

18.11 Explain the difference between compliance and VFM audits.

18.12 Compare and contrast economy, efficiency and effectiveness measures of performance. Which of these is the hardest to audit? Explain.

LEARNING OBJECTIVE

4 Specify the expanded scope of auditing in both internal and public sector audit practice.

Summary of the Differences Between Traditional Auditing and VFM Auditing

1. In traditional audits, the objective is to render an opinion on the financial statements, and scope restrictions can result in qualification. In VFM audits, the auditor's mandate may provide the auditor with the discretion to establish the audit objectives and scope.

    In most cases VFM audits have mandates established through legislation or contracts. These mandates specify what is required for the auditor.

2. In VFM audits the objectives and scope vary from one audit to another, depending on the function and characteristics of the organization being audited.

    According to PS 6410.07, an auditor always has to use his or her professional judgment when faced with a broad mandate and define it in specific terms with specific objectives. In the case where the mandate is specific, an auditor must still assess the objectives' appropriateness.

3. In VFM audits much of the audit focuses on matters that are not necessarily financial, such as human resource management.

4. There is no body of standards analogous to GAAP. Standards may be management-defined, legislative or defined by professions and associations.

5. The nature and sources of evidence may differ from those in financial statement auditing. PS 6410.25 states that sufficient appropriate evidence should be obtained to afford a reasonable basis to support the content of the auditor's report.

    Since a VFM audit can be required to report deficiencies rather than to form an overall opinion, the amount of evidence needed may be lower.

    The fact that a VFM audit can focus more on processes than results also influences the nature of the evidence.

6. A VFM audit will tend to use a multidisciplinary audit team with expertise in different areas (like economics, statistics, engineering). The make-up of the group will depend on the type of organization being audited and the needs of the mandate.

7. VFM audits may not relate to a standard time period, such as a year-end.

8. There is no standard audit report for VFM audits. The form of the report will depend on the mandate, and can take the form of a report on deficiencies, or an overall opinion or an attestation of management assertions. By contrast, an audit of the financial statements of an entity has a standard report prescribed by the *CICA Handbook*.

9. VFM audits use the concept of "significance" rather than materiality. Significance, broadly defined, will include the following considerations:

    a. Financial magnitude. Areas with larger dollar amounts will receive greater attention.

    b. Importance. Some programs, operations and activities are more important than others in the entity's strategy to achieve its objectives.

    c. Economic, social and environmental impact. A project or program with a small budget may have a significant impact on the population, or the environment.

    d. Previous VFM recommendations. The auditor may choose to emphasize deficient areas previously pointed out that appear not to have improved.

10. The concept of "audit risk" takes on unique meanings in a VFM audit. "Inherent risk" is the probability of lack of due regard to value-for-money. "Control risk" is the probability that a system, control or practice designed to ensure that VFM will fail. "Detection risk" is the risk that the auditor will fail to detect significant errors.

In summary, there are many differences between traditional financial statement and VFM audits. However, as noted in Chapter 16, the assurance engagement concept introduced in the *CICA Handbook*, section 5025 incorporates, with modifications, many of the concepts of VFM audits. This is understandable, since an objective of section 5025 is to provide an umbrella framework for *all* audits, including VFM audits.

SUMMARY

Internal auditing and governmental standards include the essence of the CICA GAAS and go much further by expressing standards for audits of economy, efficiency and effectiveness of program results. These come under the umbrella of the VFM auditing concept. In addition, the internal auditing standards contain many guides for the management of an internal audit department within a company.

All auditors hold independence as a primary goal, but internal auditors must look to an internal organization independence from the managers and executives whose areas they audit. Public sector auditors must be concerned about factual independence with regard to social, political and level-of-government influence.

Internal and public sector audit engagements are an application of the practical audit method—essentially a fact-finding approach. Auditors start the work with an understanding of the audit objectives involved in the assignment and carry them out through the major blocks of work—preliminary survey, study and evaluation of administrative control, application of audit procedures and reporting of the audit conclusions and recommendations. Auditors try to achieve objectivity by determining appropriate standards for economy, efficiency and effectiveness of program results, by measuring their evidence, and by comparing their measurements to the standards in order to reach objective conclusions.

Public sector auditing is complicated by the special context of audit assignments intended to accomplish accountability by agencies that handle federal funds—grants, subsidies, welfare programs and the like. The requirements of the public sector auditing standards impose on the audit function the responsibility for compliance audit work designed to determine agencies' observance of laws and regulations, of which there are many. Auditors must report not only on financial statements but also on internal control, violations of laws and regulations, fraud, abuse and illegal acts. These elements are all part of Ottawa's oversight of federal spending, facilitated by auditors.

Internal audit and public sector reports and similar reports on public accountants' consulting services are not standardized like the GAAS reports on audited financial statements. Auditors must be very careful that their reports communicate their conclusions and recommendations in a clear and concise manner. The variety of assignments and the challenge of reporting in such a free-form setting contribute to making governmental auditing, internal auditing and consulting services exciting fields for career opportunities.

A useful website for this chapter is **www.theiia.org**. The Institute of Internal Auditors site includes association news releases on ethics, professional standards and membership options.

MULTIPLE-CHOICE QUESTIONS FOR PRACTICE AND REVIEW

18.13 Which of the following is considered different and more limited in objectives than the others?
    a. Operational auditing.
    b. Performance auditing.
    c. Management auditing.
    d. Financial statement auditing.

18.14 A typical objective of an operational audit is for the auditor to:
    a. Determine whether the financial statements fairly present the company's operations.
    b. Evaluate the feasibility of attaining the company's operational objectives.
    c. Make recommendations for achieving company objectives.
    d. Report on the company's relative success in attaining profit maximization.

18.15 A government auditor assigned to audit the financial statements of the provincial highway department would not be considered independent if the auditor:
    a. also held a position as a project manager in the highway department.
    b. Was the provincial audit official elected in a general provincewide election with responsibility to report to the legislature.
    c. Normally works as a provincial auditor employed in the department of human services.
    d. Was appointed by the provincial minister with responsibility to report to the legislature.

18.16 Government auditing can extend beyond audits of financial statements to include audits of an agency's efficient and economical use of resources and:
    a. Constitutionality of laws and regulations governing the agency.
    b. Evaluation of the personal managerial skills shown by the agency's leaders.
    c. Correspondence of the agency's performance with public opinion regarding the social worth of its mission.
    d. Evaluations concerning the agency's achievements of the goals set by the legislature for the agency's activities.

18.17 Which of the following best describes how the detailed audit program of the external auditor who is engaged to audit the financial statements of a large publicly held company compares with the audit client's comprehensive internal audit program?
    a. The comprehensive internal audit program covers areas that would normally not be reviewed by the external auditor.
    b. The comprehensive internal audit program is more detailed although it covers fewer areas than would normally be covered by the external auditor.
    c. The comprehensive internal audit program is substantially identical to the audit program used by the external auditor because both review substantially identical areas.
    d. The comprehensive internal audit program is less detailed and covers fewer areas than would normally be reviewed by the external auditor.

18.18 Which of the following would you not expect to see in an auditor's report(s) on the financial statements of an independent government agency?
    a. A statement that the audit was conducted in accordance with generally accepted government audit standards.
    b. A report on the agency's compliance with applicable laws and regulations.
    c. Commentary by the agency's managers on the audit findings and recommendations.
    d. A report on the agency's internal control structure.

18.19 Public Sector Auditing Standards require auditors to determine and report several things about provincial and local governments that receive federal funds. Which of the following is not normally required to be reported?
    a. An opinion on the fair presentation of the financial statements in accordance with generally accepted accounting principles.
    b. A report on the government's internal control structure related to the federal funds.
    c. The government's performance in meeting goals set in enabling legislation.
    d. A report on the government's compliance with applicable laws and regulations.

18.20 In government and internal performance auditing, which of the following is the least important consideration when performing the field work?
    a. Determining the applicable generally accepted government accounting principles pronounced by the GASB.
    b. Defining problem areas or opportunities for improvement and defining program goals.
    c. Selection and performance of procedures designed to obtain evidence about operational problems and production output.
    d. Evaluation of evidence in terms of economy, efficiency and achievement of program goals.

18.21 Which of the following is the least important consideration for a government auditor who needs to be objective when auditing and reporting on an agency's achievement of program goals?
    a. Measure the actual output results of agency activities.
    b. Compare the agency's actual output results to quantitative goal standards.
    c. Perform a comprehensive review of administrative controls.
    d. Determine quantitative standards that describe goals the agency was supposed to achieve.

18.22 When an external auditor obtains an understanding of a client's internal control in connection with the annual audit of financial statements, the external auditor must obtain information and evaluate:

    a. The competence and objectivity of the internal auditors.

    b. The education, experience and certification of the internal auditors.

    c. The employment of internal auditors' relatives in management positions.

    d. The internal audit department and its program of work.

18.23 Compliance auditing in audits performed in accordance with public sector auditing standards is necessary for an auditor's:

    a. Report on the auditee's internal control, including reportable conditions and material weaknesses.

    b. Opinion on the auditee's observance, or lack thereof, of applicable laws and regulations.

    c. Opinion on the auditee's financial statements.

    d. Report of a supplementary schedule of federal assistance programs and amounts.

EXERCISES AND PROBLEMS

18.24 Identification of Audits and Auditors. Audits may be characterized as (*a*) financial statement audits, (*b*) compliance audits, (*c*) economy and efficiency audits, and (*d*) program results audits. The work can be done by independent (external) auditors, internal auditors or governmental auditors (including Canada Revenue Agency auditors and federal bank examiners). Below is a list of the purpose or products of various audit engagements.

    1. Determining the appropriateness of interest rates charged on federally guaranteed loans to students.

    2. Determining the fair presentation in conformity with GAAP of an advertising agency's financial statements.

    3. Study of Ministry of Natural Resources (MNR) policies and practices on grant-related income.

    4. Determination of costs of municipal garbage pickup services compared to comparable service sub-contracted to a private business.

    5. Audit of tax shelter partnership financing terms.

    6. Study of a private aircraft manufacturer's test pilot performance in reporting on the results of test flights.

    7. Periodic Superintendent of Financial Institution examination of a bank for solvency.

    8. Evaluation of the promptness of materials inspection in a manufacturer's receiving department.

    9. Report of how better care and disposal of vehicles confiscated by drug enforcement agents could save money and benefit law enforcement.

    10. Rendering a public report on the assumptions and compilation of a revenue forecast by a sports stadium/racetrack complex.

Required:

Prepare a three-column schedule showing (1) each of the engagements listed above; (2) the type of audit (financial statement, compliance, economy and efficiency, or program results); and (3) the kinds of auditors you would expect to be involved.

18.25 Organizing a Preliminary Survey. You are the director of internal auditing of a large municipal hospital. You receive monthly financial reports prepared by the accounting department, and your review of them has shown that total accounts receivable from patients has steadily and rapidly increased over the past eight months.

Other information in the reports shows the following conditions:

    a. The number of available hospital beds has not changed.

    b. The bed occupancy rate has not changed.

    c. Hospital billing rates have not changed significantly.

    d. The hospitalization insurance contracts have not changed since the last modification 12 months ago.

Your internal audit department audited the accounts receivable 10 months ago. The working paper file for that assignment contains financial information, a record of the preliminary survey, documentation of the study and evaluation of administrative and internal accounting controls, documentation of the evidence-gathering procedures used to produce evidence about the validity and collectibility of the accounts and a copy of your report which commented favourably on the controls and collectibility of the receivables.

However, the current increase in receivables has alerted you to a need for another audit so that things will not get out of hand. You remember news stories last year about the manager of the city water system who got into big trouble because his accounting department double-billed all the residential customers for three months.

Required:

You plan to perform a preliminary survey in order to get a handle on the problem, if indeed a problem exists. Write a memo to your senior auditor listing at least eight questions he should use to guide and direct the preliminary survey. (Hint: The questions used in the last preliminary survey were organized under these headings: (1) Who does the accounts receivable accounting? (2) What data processing procedures and policies are in effect? and (3) How is the accounts receivable accounting done? This time, you will add a fourth category: What financial or economic events have occurred in the last 10 months?)

(CIA adapted)

18.26 Study and Evaluation of Administrative Control.

LO.4 The study and evaluation of administrative controls in a governmental or internal audit is not easy. First, auditors must determine the controls subject to audit. Then, they must find a standard by which performance of the control can be evaluated. Next, they must specify procedures to obtain the evidence on which an evaluation can be based. Insofar as possible, the standards and related evidence must be quantified.

Students working on this case usually do not have the experience or theoretical background to figure out control standards and audit procedures, so the description below gives certain information that internal auditors would know about or be able to figure out on their own. Fulfilling the requirement thus amounts to taking some information from the scenario below and figuring out other things by using accountants' and auditors' common sense.

The Scenario: Ace Corporation ships building materials to more than a thousand wholesale and retail customers in a five-province region. The company's normal credit terms are net/30 days, and no cash discounts are offered. Fred Clark is the chief financial officer, and he is concerned about maintaining control over customer credit. In particular, he has stated two administrative control principles for this purpose.

1. Sales are to be billed to customers accurately and promptly. Fred knows that errors will occur but thinks company personnel ought to be able to hold quantity, unit price and arithmetic errors down to 3 percent of the sales invoices. He considers an invoice error of $1 or less not to matter. He believes that prompt billing is important since customers are expected to pay within 30 days. Fred is very strict in thinking that a bill should be sent to the customer one day after shipment. He believes that he has staffed the billing department well enough to be able to handle this workload. The relevant company records consist of an accounts receivable control account; a subsidiary ledger of customers' accounts in which charges are entered by billing (invoice) date and credits are entered by date of payment receipts; a sales journal that lists invoices in chronological order; and a file of shipping documents cross-referenced by the number on the related sales invoice copy kept on file in numerical order.

2. Accounts receivable are to be aged and followed up to ensure prompt collection. Fred has told the accounts receivable department to classify all the customer accounts in categories of (*a*) current, (*b*) 31–59 days overdue, (*c*) 60–90 days overdue, and (*d*) more than 90 days overdue. He wants this trial balance to be complete and to be transmitted to the credit department within five days of each month-end. In the credit department, prompt follow-up means sending a different (stronger) collection letter to each category, cutting off credit to customers over 60 days past due (putting them on cash basis), and giving the over-90-days accounts to an outside collection agency. These actions are supposed to be

taken within five days after receipt of the aged trial balance. The relevant company records, in addition to the ones listed above, consist of the aged trial balance, copies of the letters sent to customers, copies of notices of credit cutoff, copies of correspondence with the outside collection agent and reports of results—statistics of subsequent collections.

Required:

Take the role of a senior internal auditor. You are to write a memo to the internal audit staff to inform them about comparison standards for the study and evaluation of these two administrative control policies. You also need to specify two or three procedures for gathering evidence about performance of the controls. The body of your memo should be structured as follows:

1. Control: Sales are billed to customers accurately and promptly.
   a. Accuracy.
      (1) Policy standard . . .
      (2) Audit procedures . . .
   b. Promptness.
      (1) Policy standard . . .
      (2) Audit procedures . . .
2. Control: Accounts receivable are aged and followed up to ensure prompt collection.
   a. Accounts receivable aging.
      (1) Policy standard . . .
      (2) Audit procedures . . .
   b. Follow-up prompt collection.
      (1) Policy standard . . .
      (2) Audit procedures . . .

18.27 Analytical Review of Inventory. External auditors

LO.4 usually calculate inventory turnover (cost of goods sold for the year divided by average inventory) and use the ratio as a broad indication of inventory age, obsolescence or overstocking. External auditors are interested in evidence relating to the material accuracy of the financial statements taken as a whole. Internal auditors, on the other hand, calculate turnover by categories and classes of inventory in order to detect problem areas that might otherwise get overlooked. This kind of detailed analytical review might point to conditions of buying errors, obsolescence, overstocking and other matters that could be changed to save money.

The data shown in Exhibit 18.27–1 are turnover, cost of sales and inventory investment data for a series of four historical years and the current year. In each of the historical years, the external auditors did not recommend any adjustments to the inventory valuations.

Required:

Calculate the current year inventory turnover ratios. Interpret the ratio trends and point out what conditions might exist, and write a memo to the vice president for production explaining your findings and the further investigation that can be conducted.

18.28 PA Involvement in an Expanded-Scope Audit. A pub-

LO.4 lic accounting firm received an invitation to bid for the

EXHIBIT 18.27-1   INVENTORY DATA

Ending	Inventory Turnover				Current-year Inventory (000)	
	20X1	20X2	20X3	20X4	Beginning	
Total inventory	2.1	2.0	2.1	2.1	$3,000	$2,917
Materials and parts	4.0	4.1	4.3	4.5	1,365	620
Work in process	12.0	12.5	11.5	11.7	623	697
Finished products:						
Computer games	6.0	7.0	10.0	24.0	380	500
Floppy disk drives	8.0	7.2	7.7	8.5	64	300
Semiconductor parts	4.0	3.5	4.5	7.0	80	400
Electric typewriters	3.0	2.5	2.0	1.9	488	400

Additional Information

	Current Year (000)				
	Transfers	Sales	Cost of Goods Sold	Gross Profit	Compared to 20X4
Materials and parts	$3,970*	NA	NA	NA	
Work in process	7,988†	NA	NA	NA	
Computer games	2,320‡	$2,000	$2,200	$<200>	Sales volume declined 60%§
Floppy disk drives	2,236‡	3,000	2,000	1,000	Sales volume increased 35%
Semiconductor parts	2,720‡	4,000	2,400	1,600	Sales volume increased 40%
Electric typewriters	712‡	1,000	800	200	Sales volume declined 3%

NA means not available.
* Cost of materials transferred to Work in Process.
† Cost of materials, labour and overhead transferred to Finished Goods.
‡ Cost of goods transferred from Work in Process to Finished Product Inventories.
§ Selling prices also were reduced and the gross margin declined.

audit of a local food commodity distribution program funded by the Ministry of Agriculture. The audit is to be conducted in accordance with the public sector audit standards published by the CICA. The accountants have become familiar with the public sector standards and recognize that the public sector standards incorporate the CICA generally accepted auditing standards (GAAS).

The public accounting firm has been engaged to perform the audit of the program, and the audit is to encompass both financial and performance audits that constitute the expanded scope of a public sector audit.

Required:

a. The accountants should perform sufficient audit work to satisfy the financial and compliance element of public sector auditing standards. What is the objective of such audit work?

b. The accountants should be aware of general and specific kinds of uneconomical or inefficient practices in such a program. What are some examples?

c. What might be some standards and sources of standards for judging program results?

DISCUSSION CASES

. . . .

18.37 Internal Auditors and Fraud. Do you think
LO.1   the internal auditors' responsibility to detect fraud should be different from that of external auditors? Discuss.

18.38 Internal Auditors and Fraud. What is the
LO.1   *Income Tax Act's* position on fraud detection?

KEY TERMS

acceptance testing records contain computerized test data that can be used by auditors when performing their own audit procedures *(Chapter 7)*

accountability relationship a relationship in which at least one of the parties needs to be able to justify its actions or claims to another party in the relationship *(Chapter 1)*

accounting controls policies and procedures that prevent, detect, and correct misstatements by ensuring that accounting is complete, accurate, authorized, and supported *(Chapter 7)*

accounting deficiency review a review of audit file documentation to check if audit standards were adhered to in a situation where the auditor failed to detect an accounting deficiency in audited financial statements *(Chapter 3)*

Accounting Standards Oversight Council (AcSOC) *(Chapter 4)*

accounts receivable subsidiary ledger a detailed listing of outstanding accounts receivable balances by individual customer that adds up to the total balance in the general ledger accounts receivable "control" account; reconciliation of the subsidiary ledger and the control account is an important control procedure and a key audit test *(Chapter 11)*

adverse opinion states that financial statements are not in accordance with GAAP *(Chapter 2)*

aged A/R trial balance a list of all outstanding accounts receivable balances organized by how long they have been outstanding; used to manage collection and assess the accounting requirement to provide an allowance for possible uncollectible accounts *(Chapter 11)*

alpha risk the risk that the auditor will incorrectly reject an account balance that is not materially misstated; a type of sampling risk *(Chapter 10)*

analysis techniques for identifying unusual changes and relations in financial statement data that alert the audit team to problems (errors, fraud) that may exist in the account balances and disclosures to guide the design of further audit work; involves developing expectations and designing procedures to assess whether the data conform to expectations *(Chapter 8)*

analytical procedures specific methods and tests used to perform analysis on client account balances, such as: comparison of current-year account balances to balances for one or more comparable periods; comparison of the actual balances to budgets; evaluation of the relationships between different current-year account balances for conformity with predictable patterns and expectations; comparison of current-year account balances and financial relationships (e.g., ratios) with similar information for the client's industry; study of the relationships of current-year account balances with relevant nonfinancial information *(Chapter 8)*

analytical procedures risk (APR) *(Chapter 10)*

anchoring preconceived notions about control risk that auditors carry over when they perform an audit on a client year after year, a potential pitfall if conditions have changed *(Chapter 8)*

application control procedures individual computerized accounting applications, for example, programmed validation controls for verifying customers' account numbers and credit limits *(Chapter 7)*

application description computer application information, which includes system flowcharts, record formats, and control features *(Chapter 7)*

articles of incorporation a corporation's legal documents that set out its purpose, classes of shares that can be issued, etc. *(Chapter 14)*

articulated the way certain numbers in different financial statements are interconnected, for example: cash in balance sheet agrees to the cash flow statement; net income in the income statement agrees to the amount entered in the retained earnings statement *(Prelude to Part III)*

associated with financial statements any involvement of a public accountant with financial statements issued by a client *(Chapter 3)*

assurance verifying the truthfulness of an assertion by an accountable party with independent corroborating evidence *(Chapter 1)*

assurance engagement an engagement in which the auditor adds either reasonable (high) or moderate (negative) levels of assurance *(Chapter 1)*

attestation the lending of some credibility to financial or other information involving written assertions by professional auditors who serve as objective intermediaries *(Chapter 3)*

attestation engagement when a public accountant is hired to perform procedures and issue a report resulting from those procedures that affirms the validity of an assertion *(Chapter 3)*

attribute sampling in control testing this is the type of audit sampling in which auditors look for the presence or absence of a control condition *(Chapter 10)*

audit balance the account balance that the auditor believes is correct based on the audit evidence *(Chapter 10)*

Audit Guidelines (AuGs) the part of the *CICA Handbook* that provides procedural guidance on implementing GAAS *(Chapter 2)*

audit of internal control over financial reportings the engagement that results in an audit report on the effectiveness of a client's internal control over financial reporting *(Chapter 3)*

audit program a list of the audit procedures auditors need to perform to produce sufficient, competent evidence as the basis for good audit decisions *(Chapters 2 and 8)*

audit risk (account level) the probability that an auditor will fail to find a material misstatement that exists in an account balance *(Chapters 2 and 8)*

audit risk (global) (AR) the probability that an auditor will give an inappropriate opinion on financial statements *(Chapter 5)*

audit sampling testing less than 100 percent of a population (items in an account balance or class of transactions) to form a conclusion about some characteristic of the balance or class of transactions *(Chapter 10)*

audit societies the term coined by Michael Power for societies in which there is extensive examination by auditors of economic and other politically important activities *(Chapter 1)*

audit trail the series of accounting operations in a client's system that goes from transaction analyses to entry to output reports; in auditing work the trail starts with the source documents and proceeds through the information system processes to the final financial statement amounts *(Chapter 7)*

auditee the entity (company, proprietorship, organization, department, etc.) being audited; usually it refers to the entity whose financial statements are being audited *(Chapter 1)*

Auditing and Assurance Standards Board (AASB) *(Chapter 2)*

Auditing and Assurance Standards Oversight Council (AASOC) *(Chapter 4)*

auditing standards the subset of assurance standards dealing with "high" or "positive" levels of assurance in assurance engagements *(Chapter 2)*

backup retention system for computer files, programs, and documentation so that records can be recreated in case of accidental loss *(Chapter 7)*

balance sheet approach to auditing a view of the audit that takes into account the articulation of the financial statements in that the changes in each balance sheet account are made up of changes in the income statement and cash flow statement; using this articulation as the basis for identifying the transactions that need to be verified to prove the ending balance is correct *(Prelude to Part III)*

balanced scorecard a tool used to analyze business performance that measures resources (learning and growth), processes (internal business), and markets (customer relations), relating all three to financial performance; an approach that the auditor can use for benchmarking the client firm with others in its industry *(Chapter 8)*

batch processing when all records to be processed are collected in groups of like transactions; batch totals are used as a control procedure to ensure completeness and accuracy of data entry; see also **sequential processing** and **serial processing** *(Chapter 7)*

beta risk the risk that the auditor will incorrectly accept an account balance that is materially misstated; it can result in audit failure and so is considered to be a more serious problem for the audit than incorrect rejection; a type of sampling risk *(Chapter 10)*

block sampling the practice of choosing segments of contiguous transactions; undesirable because it is hard to get a representative sample of blocks efficiently *(Chapter 10)*

bridge working papers audit documentation that connects (bridges) the control evaluation to subsequent audit procedures by summarizing the major control strengths and weaknesses, listing test of controls procedures for auditing the control strengths, and suggesting substantive audit procedures related to the weaknesses *(Chapter 9)*

business risk the chance a company takes when it engages in any economic activity, such as taxes increasing or customers buying from competitors *(Chapter 1)*

business risk approach the requirement for the auditor to understand the client's business risks and strategy in order to assess the risks of material misstatement in the financial statements and design appropriate audit procedures in response to those risks *(Chapter 6)*

business to business (B2B) when commercial transactions are conducted over the Internet between business entities, such as a manufacturer and its suppliers *(Chapter 7)*

business to consumer (B2C) when commercial transactions are conducted over the Internet between business entities and their end customers, such as online book sales *(Chapter 7)*

business to employee (B2E) when administrative transactions are conducted over the Internet between a business and its employees, such as payroll and benefits *(Chapter 7)*

calculated liabilities and credits liability and deferred credit balances that arise from management calculations rather than directly from contracts or other legal instruments; examples are warranty provisions, capital lease obligations, and asset retirement obligations *(Chapter 14)*

Canadian Coalition Against Insurance Fraud (CCAIF) *(Chapter 17)*

Canadian Coalition for Good Governance (CCGG) group of the largest pension and mutual funds whose purpose is to monitor executives and boards of directors to comply with good corporate governance and financial reporting practices *(Chapter 1)*

Canadian Institute of Chartered Accountants (CICA) *(Chapter 1 and throughout text)*

Canadian Public Accountability Board (CPAB) board that oversees auditors of public companies in Canada, created by the CICA *(Chapter 1)*

Canadian Securities Administrators (CSA) *(Chapter 3)*

Certified General Accountants Association of Canada (CGAAC) *(Chapter 1)*

Certified Internal Auditors (CIA) persons who have met the Institute of Internal Auditors' criteria for professional CIA credentials *(Chapter 18)*

cheque kiting the practice of building up apparent balances in one or more bank accounts based on uncollected (float) cheques drawn against similar accounts in other banks *(Chapter 11)*

class of transactions groups of accounting entries that have the same source or purpose, for example credit sales, cash sales, and cash receipts are three different classes *(Chapter 10)*

classical attribute sampling when a sampling unit is the same thing as an invoice or population unit *(Chapter 10)*

clean audit an audit of a client where the accounting records are accurate and easy to verify and there are good controls *(Chapter 9)*

client the person or company who retains the auditor and pays the fee *(Chapter 1)*

commission a percentage fee charged for professional services for executing a transaction or performing some other business activity *(Chapter 4)*

compliance auditing when an audit engagement is being done for the sole purpose of reporting on compliance with laws, regulations, or rules *(Chapter 18)*

comprehensive governmental auditing auditing that goes beyond an audit of financial reports to include economy, efficiency, and effectiveness audits *(Chapter 1)*

computer-assisted audit techniques (CAATs) using information technology to perform extensive audit testing; a CAAT can check an entire file with little additional effort, enabling the auditor to obtain a high degree of audit assurance at little extra cost *(Chapter 7)*

conflict of interest reason for society's demand for audit services because financial decision makers usually obtain accounting information from companies that want to obtain loans or sell stock *(Chapter 1)*

consequentialism the moral theory that an action is right if it produces at least as much good (utility) as any other action. Also referred to as **utilitarianism** or **utility theory**. Note that economics and business are based on this theory *(Chapter 4)*

continuing professional education (CPE) *(Chapter 4)*

continuity schedule a working paper that shows the movements in an account balance from the beginning to the end of the period under audit, used to analyze the account balance changes and the other financial statement items related to them *(Chapter 11)*

continuous auditing auditing real-time transaction processing systems, using techniques such as audit programming codes that continuously select and monitor the processing of data; more recently can refer to auditing the continuous disclosures of public companies that are required by securities market regulations *(Chapter 7)*

contrived sham transactions fictitious transactions created for illegal purposes such as evading taxes *(Chapter 14)*

control documentation client's documentation of its control procedures, including computer and manual controls; a reference auditors use to understand and assess a client's internal control *(Chapter 7)*

control risk (CR) the risk that the client's internal control will not prevent or detect a material misstatement *(Chapters 2 and 8)*

control risk assessment the process the auditor uses to understand the client's internal control that will be sufficient to identify and assess the risks of material misstatement of the financial statements whether due to fraud or error, and to design and perform further audit procedures; required to comply with the second examination standard of generally accepted auditing standards *(Chapter 11)*

control testing (compliance testing) performing procedures to assess whether controls are operating effectively *(Chapter 8)*

controlled reprocessing using a secure copy of a thorough technical audit of the controls in a client's actual program, which can then be used to determine whether output from the client's program produces satisfactory accounting output from the auditors' copy *(Chapter 9)*

corporate governance the ways in which the suppliers of capital to corporations assure themselves of getting a return on their investment. More generally, under the corporate social responsibility view, corporate governance is the system set up to hold a corporation accountable to employees, communities, the environment, and similar broader social concerns, in addition to being accountable to the capital providers. *(Chapter 5)*

COSO (Committee of Sponsoring Organizations of the Treadway Commission) an organization that investigated corporate fraud and developed a control framework that has become the standard for the design of controls by companies and evaluation of controls by auditors; the COSO control framework is cited by the PCAOB in its auditing standards on internal control as an acceptable framework against which control design and effectiveness should be evaluated *(Chapters 7 and 16)*

cost of goods sold includes costs such as materials, labour, overheads, freight, etc., that are necessary to get goods to the stage when they can be sold; calculated as the beginning inventory plus costs added during the period less the ending inventory; offset against sales revenues it indicates the gross profit or gross margin on sales on which analytical expectations can be based *(Chapter 13)*

critical-thinking framework principles and concepts to help structure your thinking so that your conclusions will be better justified *(Chapter 4)*

current file the administrative and evidence audit working papers that relate to the audit work for the year being audited *(Chapter 8)*

customer to government when transactions between individuals or organizations and government are conducted over the Internet, such as electronic tax return filing *(Chapter 7)*

cutoff   accounting for all transactions that occurred during a period and neither postponing some recordings to the next period nor accelerating next period transactions into the current-year accounts *(Chapter 6)*

cutoff error   when transactions are recorded in the wrong period, either by postponing to the next period or accelerating next period transactions into the current period *(Chapter 12)*

cutoff test   an audit procedure that examines whether transactions are recorded in the proper period *(Chapter 11)*

dangling debit   a false or erroneous debit balance that exists because one or more accounts are misstated *(Chapter 11)*

data   unprocessed raw facts about transactions and relevant events that are entered, stored, and processed into a useful form by an information system *(Chapter 7)*

data entry   putting data into an information system for storage and processing *(Chapter 7)*

data preparation   getting data into a form that is ready to be entered into the information system *(Chapter 7)*

debt instrument   a legally documented obligation between a borrower and a lender, such as a bond payable, lease, mortgage payable *(Chapter 14)*

defalcation   when somebody in charge of safekeeping the assets is stealing them; another name for employee fraud and embezzlement *(Chapter 17)*

denial of opinion   auditor's declaration that no opinion is given on financial statements and the reasons why this is so, usually due to a scope limitation; also called a **disclaimer of opinion** *(Chapter 2)*

deontological (Kantian) ethics   the moral theory that an action is right if it is based on a sense of duty or obligation *(Chapter 4)*

derivative report   a report that results as a side-product of another engagement, such as an auditor providing a report on internal control deficiencies that were uncovered in the process of providing an audit report on the financial statements *(Chapter 16)*

detailed audit plan   an audit planning document outlining the nature timing and extent of audit procedures to assess risk of financial statement misstatement, obtain the necessary audit evidence for each assertion for all significant transactions/balances/disclosures, including staffing decisions and time budget *(Prelude to Part III)*

detection risk (DR)   the risk that the auditor's procedures will fail to find a material misstatement that exists in the accounts *(Chapter 8)*

differential reporting   a reporting option under current Canadian GAAP that allows private companies to use less complex accounting policies than other companies if there is unanimous shareholder approval; special wording is required in the audit report when differential reporting options are used *(Chapter 14)*

direct reporting engagement   a type of assurance engagement in which the assertions are implied and not written down in some form *(Chapters 1, 2, and 16)*

disclaimer of opinion   auditor's declaration that no opinion is given on financial statements and the reasons why this is so, usually due to a scope limitation; also called a **denial of opinion** *(Chapter 3)*

discreditable acts rules   the parts of the rules of professional conduct that prohibit members from discrediting the profession *(Chapter 4)*

division of duties   the organization of tasks and responsibilities in an organization so that the same person is not given incompatible functions that would make it easy for them to commit a fraud and cover it up; also called **segregation of duties** *(Chapter 7)*

doing business as (DBA)   *(Chapter 17)*

double-dating   putting two dates in an audit report; when a subsequent event is reported in the financial statements the auditor extends procedures related to that event to the second date noted in a double-dated audit report; the other procedures conducted in regular field work are not extended so the first date is the end of the regular field work *(Chapter 15)*

dual-purpose procedure   an audit procedure which is used simultaneously for testing controls over a transaction and to provide substantive audit evidence about its amount *(Chapter 11)*

dynamic fields   in a computer-based information system are items such as year-to-date gross pay and account balances that are changed in the master file records to reflect new information by update processing; an example is batch processing of payroll *(Chapter 7)*

earnings per share (EPS)   *(Chapter 7)*

echo check   in computerized information processing magnetic read after each magnetic write is echoed back to the sending location and results are compared *(Chapter 7)*

electronic transfer codes   used by companies to transfer pay amounts directly to employees' bank accounts *(Chapter 13)*

embezzlement   type of fraud involving employees' or non-employees' wrongfully taking money or property entrusted to their care, custody, and control; often accompanied by false accounting entries and other forms of lying and cover-up *(Chapter 17)*

emphasis of a matter   additional information in the auditor's report that enriches the information content by emphasizing a matter they believe readers should consider important or useful *(Chapter 3)*

employee fraud   the use of fraudulent means to take money or other property from an employer *(Chapter 17)*

engagement letter   sets forth terms of engagement, including an agreement about the fee when a new audit client is accepted *(Chapter 6)*

enterprise resource planning systems (ERPS) an information system in which inputs and outputs from many or all the business processes will be processed in an integrated manner, so the accounting component of the information system will be closely related to many other functional areas such as sales, inventory, human resources, cash management, etc. *(Chapters 6 and 7)*

entity's risk assessment process management's process for identifying business risks that could affect financial reporting objectives and for deciding on actions to address and minimize these risks; understanding this process helps auditors to assess the risk that the financial statements could be materially misstated *(Chapter 6)*

error synonym of deviation in test of controls sampling *(Chapter 10)*

error analysis qualitative evaluation of control risk *(Chapter 10)*

evidence all the influences on auditors' minds that ultimately guide their decisions *(Chapter 2)*

evidence-collection steps 4, 5 and 6 of the sampling method, which are performed to get the evidence *(Chapter 10)*

evidence evaluation the final step of the sampling method, to evaluate the evidence and make justifiable decisions about the control risk *(Chapter 10)*

exception synonym of deviation in test of controls sampling *(Chapter 10)*

expectation about the population deviation rate an estimate of the ratio of the number of expected deviations to population size *(Chapter 10)*

extending the audit conclusion performing substantive-purpose audit procedures on the transactions in the remaining period and on the year-end balance to produce sufficient competent evidence for a decision about the year-end balance *(Chapter 10)*

external auditor an auditor who is an outsider and independent of the entity being audited *(Chapters 1, 2, and 17)*

fidelity bond a type of insurance policy that covers theft of cash by employees *(Chapter 11)*

file maintenance the computer system process that makes changes to the static fields *(Chapter 7)*

financial error an unintentional misstatement of the financial statements; in contrast, fraud is defined as intentional misstatement *(Chapter 9)*

financial reporting broad-based process of providing statements of financial position (balance sheets), statements of results of operations (income statements), statements of results of changes in financial position (cash flow statements) and accompanying disclosure notes (footnotes) to outside decision makers who have no internal source of information like the management of the company has *(Chapter 1)*

FOB destination terms of sale indicating that title to goods sold transfers from seller to buyer when the goods reach the buyer's destination, can give rise to an amount of inventory-in-transit at year end that is owned by a client but not physically on hand at the client's premises *(Chapter 11)*

FOB shipping terms of sale indicating that title to goods sold transfers from seller to buyer when the goods are handed over from the seller to the shipping company that will ultimately deliver them to the buyer; can give rise to an amount of inventory-in-transit at year end that is owned by a client but not physically on hand at the client's premises *(Chapter 11)*

forensic accounting application of accounting and auditing skills to legal problems, both civil and criminal *(Chapter 1)*

fraud auditing a proactive approach to detect financial frauds using accounting records and information, analytical relationships, and an awareness of fraud perpetration and concealment efforts (ACFE) *(Chapter 1)*

fraudulent financial reporting intentional or reckless conduct, whether by act or omission, that results in materially misleading financial statements *(Chapter 17)*

garbage in, garbage out (GIGO) the view that the quality of the input to a computer system determines the quality of the output, making it more cost-effective to ensure input is accurate and complete than to try to find and correct errors later in the process *(Chapter 7)*

general control procedures relate to many or all of computerized and manual accounting activities, for example, controls over access to data files and division of duties *(Chapter 7)*

generally accepted accounting principles (GAAP) those accounting methods that have been established in a particular jurisdiction by formal recognition by a standard-setting body, or by authoritative support or precedent such as the accounting recommendations of the *CICA Handbook (Chapter 1)*

generally accepted auditing standards (GAAS) those auditing recommendations that have been established in a particular jurisdiction by formal recognition by a standard-setting body, or by authoritative support or precedent such as the auditing and assurance recommendations of the *CICA Handbook*; also refers to the general, examination and reporting standards included in *CICA Handbook*, section 5100; the minimum standards for performing an acceptable audit *(Chapter 1)*

grandparent-parent-child file backup approach that involves retention of the current transaction file and the prior master file, from which the current master file can be reconstructed *(Chapter 7)*

haphazard selection unsystematic way of selecting sample units *(Chapter 10)*

harmonization co-ordination of standards throughout the world *(Chapter 2)*

high assurance highest level of conclusion of an audit report, which states that the financial statements present fairly in all material respects; also known as **positive assurance** *(Chapter 3)*

hypothesis testing when auditors hypothesize that the book value is materially accurate regarding existence, ownership and valuation *(Chapter 10)*

hypothetical assumption expresses a condition and course of action that the issuer of a financial projection believes could take place *(Chapter 16)*

imperative a universal principle assumed by monistic moral theories *(Chapter 4)*

individually significant items items in account balances that exceed the material misstatement amount; in audit sampling these should be removed from the population and audited completely *(Chapter 10)*

information data that are selected, processed, and reported in a way that is relevant and useful for decision making or evaluation, the output of information systems *(Chapter 7)*

information risk the failure of financial statements to appropriately reflect the economic substance of business activities *(Chapter 1)*

information system infrastructure (physical and hardware components), software, people, procedures and data, used to create and communicate information about an organization, includes automated and manual components *(Chapter 7)*

information technology (IT) the hardware and software needed to process data *(Chapters 1 and 7)*

inherent risk (IR) the probability that material misstatements have occurred *(Chapters 2 and 8)*

initial public offering (IPO) a first time offering of a corporation's shares to the public *(Chapter 1)*

Institute of Internal Auditors (IIA) *(Chapter 18)*

Intranet internal communications network using Internet technology, such as an employee e-mail system *(Chapter 7)*

interim date a date before the end of the period under audit when some of the audit procedures might be performed, such as control evaluation and testing *(Chapters 2 and 10)*

Internal Audit Practice Statements (IAPSs) term used for the standards passed by the predecessor to the IFAC's International Auditing and Assurance Standards Board (IAASB). This predecessor to IAASB was the International Auditing Practices Committee (IAPC). The auditing standards passed by the IAASB are referred to as International Standards on Auditing (ISA) *(Chapter 2)*

internal auditing verification work performed by company employees who are trained in auditing procedures, mainly used for internal control purposes but external auditors can rely on internal audit work if certain criteria are met *(Chapter 1)*

internal control the system of policies and procedures needed to maintain adherence to a company's objectives; especially the accuracy of recordkeeping and safegarding of assets *(Chapter 1)*

internal control program an audit planning document listing the specific procedures for obtaining an understanding of the client's business and management's control system, and for assessing the inherent risk and the control risk related to the financial account balances. *(Chapters 8 and 10)*

internal control questionnaire (ICQ) checklist to gather evidence about the control environment *(Chapter 9)*

internal labels special internal records on magnetic tapes and disks which prevent use of the wrong file during processing *(Chapter 7)*

International Auditing Assurance and Standards Board (IAASB) the audit standard-setting body for International Standards on Auditing (ISAs) *(Chapter 1)*

International Federation of Accountants (IFAC) an organization dedicated to developing international auditing standards *(Chapter 1)*

international harmonization international convergence of national auditing standards with ISAs, including going concern, fraud, and the audit risk model *(Chapter 1)*

International Standards on Auditing (ISAs) the auditing standards of IFAC *(Chapters 1 and 2)*

joint and several liability a legal liability regime in which one party found to be liable can be required to pay the full amount of the damages even if there are other parties that are partially liable but they are bankrupt or otherwise unable to pay a proportionate share of the damages *(Chapter 5)*

just-in-time (JIT) an inventory production system where inventory holding is minimized by having raw materials and supplies delivered as close as possible to the time that they will be used in the production process *(Chapter 13)*

key control important control procedure; auditors should identify and audit only these controls *(Chapter 10)*

known misstatement the total amount of actual monetary error found in a sample *(Chapter 10)*

legal responsibilites auditor responsibilities imposed by the legal system *(Chapter 4)*

levels of assurance the amount of credibility provided by accountants and auditors *(Chapter 3)*

likely misstatement the projected amount of the known misstatement in the population of a sample *(Chapter 10)*

limited liability partnership (LLP) company whose partners' liability is limited to the capital they have invested in the business *(Chapters 1 and 5)*

local area network (LAN) an information system where all processing occurs at a central processing facility such as a server or desktop and several other personal computers are connected to the network *(Chapter 7)*

lower of cost or market (LCM) accounting valuation test that assesses whether the recorded cost of inventory exceeds its market value in which case the value needs to be written down to the lower market value *(Chapter 13)*

management auditing auditors' study of business operations for the purpose of making recommendations about economic and efficient use of resources, effective achievement of business objectives and compliance with company policies; see **operational auditing** *(Chapters 1 and 18)*

management controls aspects of internal control that operate at the company level including the control environment; the entity's risk assessment process; the information system, including the related business processes, relevant to financial reporting, and communication; monitoring of controls *(Chapter 7)*

management fraud deliberate fraud committed by management that injures investors and creditors through materially misleading financial statements *(Chapter 17)*

management letter communication sent to client in which recommendations are noted and evaluated *(Chapters 9 and 15)*

management's discussion and analysis (MD&A) a section of the annual report that includes management's analysis of past operating and financial results, can also include forward-looking information; the financial statement auditor reviews the information to ensure there is nothing that is inconsistent with the audited financial statements but the MD&A itself is not audited *(Chapter 16)*

materiality amount of misstatement that would likely affect a user's decision *(Chapters 1 and 8)*

mitigating factors elements of financial flexibility (saleability of assets, lines of credit, debt extension, dividend elimination) available as survival strategies in circumstances of going concern uncertainty which may reduce the financial difficulty problems *(Chapter 3)*

money laundering engaging in specific financial transactions in order to conceal the identity, source, and/or destination of money resulting from an illegal act, which may involve organized crime, tax evasion, or false accounting *(Chapter 11)*

monistic theories ethical theories that assume universal principles apply regardless of the specific facts of a situation *(Chapter 4)*

moral responsibilities auditor responsibilities to conform to broad social norms of behaviour *(Chapter 4)*

nature (of **audit procedures**) refers to the six general techniques of an account balance audit program: computation, confirmation, enquiry, inspection, observation, and analysis *(Chapter 10)*

negative assurance synonym for moderate assurance *(Chapter 3)*

no assurance an engagement in which the PA provides zero assurance credibility because there is no independent verification of the data provided by the client; a prime example involving financial information is a compilation engagement *(Chapter 3)*

nonstatistical (judgemental) sampling choosing items in a population for audit testing and evaluating the findings based on the auditor's own knowledge and experience rather than statistical methods *(Chapter 10)*

occurrence (as in **control failure**, also **deviation**, **error**, and **exception**) synonym of deviation in test of controls sampling *(Chapter 10)*

off the balance sheet refers to how certain obligations and commitments do not have to be reported on the balance sheet, such as purchase commitments and operating leases *(Chapter 14)*

online transferring information electronically over the Internet or other computerized telecommunications link *(Chapter 7)*

online input validation inputting information correctly or computer will not accept the transaction; uses validation checks, such as missing data, check digit and limit tests *(Chapter 1)*

operational auditing see **management auditing** *(Chapters 1 and 18)*

overall strategy audit planning decisions about the scope and approach to the audit outline the materiality, the risk assessment control evaluation, planned procedures and related decisions on staffing, supervision, and timing *(Prelude to Part III)*

overreliance the result of assessing control risk too low *(Chapter 10)*

parity check ensures that coding of data internal to the computer does not change when it is moved from one internal storage location to another *(Chapter 7)*

payroll accounting function of recordkeeping that prepares individual paycheques, pay envelopes, or electronic transfers *(Chapter 11 and 13)*

peer review study of a firm's quality control policies and procedures, followed by a report on a firm's quality of audit practice *(Chapters 2 and 15)*

performance auditing see **management auditing** and **operational auditing** *(Chapters 1 and 8)*

permanent file audit working papers that are of continuing interest from year to year, including the client company's articles of incorporation, shareholder agreements, major contracts, minutes *(Chapter 8)*

personal computer (PC) a self-contained computer that can be operated by a person without needing to connect to a mainframe or network or involvement of computer operating specialists *(Chapter 7)*

personal digital assistants (PDAs) hand-held devices that have some data processing functions and may also have wireless telecommunications capabilities *(Chapter 7)*

physical representation of the population the auditor's frame of reference for selecting a sample, for example, a journal listing of recorded sales invoices *(Chapter 10)*

population the set of all the elements that constitute an account balance or class of transactions *(Chapter 10)*

population unit each element of a population *(Chapter 10)*

positive assurance see **high assurance** *(Chapter 3)*

possible misstatement   the further misstatement remaining undetected in the units not selected in the sample *(Chapter 10)*

post-Enron world   the audit environment characterized by the failure of the Enron Corporation in December 2001 and its consequences since then *(Chapter 1)*

pre-audit risk management activities   procedures auditors perform before accepting an audit engagement to ensure the client and the engagement do not pose an unacceptably high risk of audit failure *(Chapter 6)*

predecessor   the auditor that held the engagement previously, before a new successor auditor took on the engagement *(Chapter 6)*

preventive maintenance   auditors should determine whether maintenance is scheduled and whether the schedule is followed and documented, and also review contract with computer vendor *(Chapter 7)*

primary beneficiaries   third parties for whose primary benefit the audit or other accounting service is performed *(Chapter 5)*

private placement   sale of securities to a small number of persons or institutional investors (usually not more than 35), who can demand and obtain sufficient information without the formality of registration *(Chapter 17)*

pro forma   the presentation of financial statements as if the event had occurred on the date of the balance sheet; for example, perhaps the best way to show the effect of a business purchase or other merger *(Chapter 15)*

problem-recognition   the first three steps of the sampling method *(Chapter 10)*

professional skepticism   an auditor's tendency to question management representations and look for corroborating evidence before accepting them *(Chapter 2)*

program description   description of computer programs, which includes program flowchart, a listing of the program source code (e.g., C++ or Java) and a record of all program changes *(Chapter 7)*

projected misstatement   the estimated amount of likely misstatement in a population based on extrapolating a misstatement discovered in a sample (known/identified misstatement) over the whole population *(Chapter 10)*

proportionate liability   a legal liability regime where a party found to be partly liable is only responsible for paying a part of the damages in proportion to their share of the blame *(Chapter 5)*

Provincial Institutes of Chartered Accountants (PICA) *(Chapter 4)*

prospectus   set of financial statements and disclosures distributed to all purchasers in an offering registered under Securities Law *(Chapter 1)*

Public Company Accounting Oversight Board (PCAOB) *(Chapter 1)*

purchase cutoff   recording purchase transactions in the proper period, including accruals of payments not due until the following period *(Chapter 12)*

qualified reports   audit reports that contain an opinion paragraph that does not give the positive assurance that everything in the financial statements is in conformity with GAAP *(Chapter 3)*

quality earnings   reported accounting earnings that are highly correlated with the underlying economic performance of the business and free of management bias or manipulation *(Chapter 7)*

random sample   a set of sampling units so chosen that each population item has an equal likelihood of being selected in the sample *(Chapter 10)*

recordkeeper   person responsible for collecting and recording transactions and other information about an entity's activities *(Chapter 7)*

replication   process of reperforming a selection procedure and getting the same sample units *(Chapter 10)*

report production and distribution   phase in information processing where the output of the information system is created in a summary form and delivered to interested parties *(Chapter 7)*

reportable matters   significant deficiencies   in the design or operation of the company's internal control structure, which could adversely affect its ability to report financial data in conformity with GAAP *(Chapters 9 and 16)*

representative sample   sample that mirrors the characteristics of the population being studied *(Chapter 10)*

response rate   the proportion of the number of confirmations for bill-and-hold transactions returned to the number sent *(Chapter 11)*

revenue recognition problems   techniques used by financial statement preparers to manipulate reported revenues resulting in low-quality earnings *(Chapter 11)*

risk model $AR = IR \times CR \times DR$ *(Chapter 8)*; $AR = IR \times CR \times APR \times RIA$ *(Chapter 10)*

risk of assessing the control risk too high   the probability that the compliance evidence in the sample indicates high control risk when the actual (but unknown) degree of compliance would justify a lower control-risk assessment *(Chapter 10)*

risk of incorrect acceptance (RIA)   the decision to accept a balance as being materially accurate when the balance is materially misstated *(Chapter 10)*

risk of incorrect rejection   the decision to accept a balance as being materially misstated when it is not *(Chapter 10)*

sales cutoff   recording sales transactions in the proper period *(Chapter 11)*

sample   a set of sampling units *(Chapter 7)*

sample of one   see **walk-through**

sampling error   the amount by which a projected likely misstatement amount could differ from an actual (unknown) total as a result of the sample not being exactly representative *(Chapter 10)*

sampling risk   the probability that an auditor's conclusion based on a sample might be different from the conclusion based on an audit of the entire population *(Chapter 10)*

sampling unit   unit used for testing a client's population, for example, a customer's account, an inventory item, a debt issue or a cash receipt *(Chapter 10)*

scanning   reviewing a report or listing for unusual or interesting items that should be investigated in further audit work *(Chapter 8)*

scope   the entity and its financial statements that will be covered by the audit engagement, the client documents and records to be examined to provide the necessary audit evidence *(Prelude to Part III)*

scope limitations   conditions where auditors are unable to obtain sufficient appropriate evidence *(Chapter 3)*

search for unrecorded liabilities   set of procedures designed to yield audit evidence of liabilities that were not recorded in the period following the audit client's balance sheet date *(Chapter 12)*

second audit partner   one who reviews the work of the audit team *(Chapter 4)*

second-partner review   review of working papers and financial statements by a partner not responsible for client relations; ensures that quality of audit work is in keeping with the standards of the audit firm *(Chapter 15)*

Securities and Exchange Commission (SEC)   *(Chapter 1)*

segregation of duties   see **division of duties** *(Chapter 7)*

self-checking number   a basic code number with its check digit *(Chapter 7)*

self-regulation   refers to a situation where a professional group is given the power to monitor and discipline its members by the government *(Chapters 1 and 4)*

sequential processing   See **batch processing** *(Chapter 7)*

serial processing   See **batch processing** *(Chapter 7)*

service organization   a business other than the client's that executes or records transactions on behalf of the client *(Chapter 16)*

Society of Management Accountants of Canada (SMAC) *(Chapter 1)*

standard deviation   a measure of population variability *(Chapter 10)*

static fields   items in an information system that are not normally changed, examples are employee number and pay rate *(Chapter 7)*

statistical sampling   audit sampling that uses the laws of probability for selecting and evaluating a sample from a population for the purpose of reaching a conclusion about the population *(Chapter 10)*

strategic systems approach to auditing (SSA audits)   an auditing approach that has a top-down focus, starting with an in-depth understanding of the auditee's business. This focus enables the auditor to understand the strategic objectives of the auditee, the risks the auditee faces in relation to these objectives, and the controls necessary for the business to respond to these risks. After obtaining an understanding of the business as a whole, the SSA auditor then proceeds to look at the details of the risky transactions in the context of the knowledge gained at the broader level. *(Chapter 6)*

stratification   subdividing the population in an audit sample by, for example, account balance size *(Chapter 10)*

strengths   specific features of good detail controls that would prevent, detect, or correct material misstatements *(Chapter 9)*

substantive tests of details auditing   the performance of procedures to obtain direct evidence about the dollar amounts and disclosures in the financial statements *(Chapter 10)*

substantive-purpose audit program   account balance-related procedures designed to produce evidence about the basic assertions in a presentation of accounts receivable *(Chapter 10)*

successor auditor   a new auditor who takes over the engagement from the predecessor *(Chapter 6)*

supply chain management   system for organizing all the entities and activites involved in supplying the requirements of a business operation *(Chapter 13)*

systematic random selection   using a predetermined population and sample size and random starting places *(Chapter 10)*

systems development and documentation standards manual   computer documentation containing standards that ensure (1) proper user involvement in the systems design and modification process, (2) review of the specifications of the system, (3) approval by user management and data processing management and (4) controls and auditability *(Chapter 7)*

three-party acountability   an accountability relationship in which there are three distinct parties (individuals): an asserter, an assurer, and a user of the asserted information *(Chapter 1)*

tolerable deviation rate   rate of deviation that can exist without causing a minimum material misstatement in the sales and accounts receivable balances *(Chapter 10)*

tort   legal action covering civil complaints other than breach of contract; normally initiated by users of financial statements *(Chapter 5)*

transaction processing   phase in the information system where transaction data are classified and combined to update financial records *(Chapter 7)*

Type 1 error risk   see **alpha risk** *(Chapter 10)*

Type 2 error risks   see **beta risk** *(Chapter 10)*

unaudited   note accountant places on each page of financial statements in performing write-up or compilation work *(Chapter 16)*

underreliance   the result of realizing the risk of assessing control risk too high *(Chapter 10)*

Uniform Commercial Code (UCC)   *(Chapter 17)*

unqualified reports   reports in which auditors are not calling attention to anything wrong with the audit work or financial statements *(Chapter 2)*

unrestricted random selection   using a printed random number table or computerized random number generator to obtain a list of random numbers *(Chapter 10)*

utilitarianism   the moral theory that an action is right if it produces at least as much good (utility) as any other action. It relies on the principle of utility; also referred to as **consequentialism**. *(Chapter 4)*

value-for-money (VFM) audit   audit concept from public sector that incorporates audits of economy, efficiency, and effectiveness *(Chapter 1)*

vertical analysis   analytical procedure of comparing all financial statement items to a common base, for example, total assets or total sales *(Chapter 7)*

vouching   obtaining audit evidence by examining supporting documents and checking that they compare in detail to the information recorded in the accounts *(Chapter 14)*

walk-through   following one or more transactions through the accounting and control systems to obtain a general understanding of the client's systems *(Chapter 10)*

weaknesses   the lack of controls in particular areas that would allow material errors to get by undetected *(Chapter 9)*

working paper reference index   table of contents listing all the index numbers used to identify section of the audit working paper files *(Chapter 15)*

work-in-progress   inventory in a manufacturing operation that is partly completed *(Chapter 13)*

year-end audit work   audit procedures performed shortly before and after the balance sheet date *(Chapter 4)*

INDEX